ST/ESA/STAT/SER.G/60 (Vol. I)

Department of Economic and Social Affairs
Statistics Division

2011
International Trade Statistics Yearbook

Volume I
Trade by Country

United Nations
New York, 2012

DEPARTMENT OF ECONOMIC AND SOCIAL AFFAIRS

The Department of Economic and Social Affairs of the United Nations Secretariat is a vital interface between global policies in the economic, social and environmental spheres and national action. The Department works in three main interlinked areas: (i) it compiles, generates and analyses a wide range of economic, social and environmental data and information on which States Members of the United Nations draw to review common problems and to take stock of policy options; (ii) it facilitates the negotiations of Member States in many intergovernmental bodies on joint courses of action to address ongoing or emerging global challenges; and (iii) it advises interested Governments on the ways and means of translating policy frameworks developed in United Nations conferences and summits into programmes at the country level and, through technical assistance, helps build national capacities.

NOTE

Symbols of United Nations documents are composed of capital letters combined with figures.

The designations employed and the presentation of material in this publication do not imply the expression of any opinion whatsoever on the part of the Secretariat of the United Nations concerning the legal status of any country, territory, city or area, or of its authorities, or concerning the delimitation of its frontiers or boundaries.

Where the designation "country or area" appears in this publication, it covers countries, territories, cities or areas. In previous issues of this publication, where the designation "country" appears in the headings of tables, it should be interpreted to cover countries, territories, cities or areas.

In some tables, the designation "developed" economies is intended for statistical convenience and does not necessarily express a judgement about the stage reached by a particular country or area in the development process.

ST/ESA/STAT/SER.G/60 (Vol. I)

UNITED NATIONS PUBLICATION
Sales No. E.13.XVII.2 H

ISBN 978-92-1-161561-6
eISBN 978-92-1-055599-9
ISSN 1010-447X

Enquiries should be directed to
Sales and Marketing Section
Outreach Division
Department of Public Information
United Nations
New York 10017
USA

E-mail: publications@un.org
Internet: http://unp.un.org

PREFACE

The *2011 International Trade Statistics Yearbook* (2011 ITSY) is the sixtieth edition of this yearbook. Its objective is to inform about the detailed merchandise imports and exports of individual countries (areas) by commodity and partner country (volume I), the world trade in individual commodities (3-digit SITC groups) (volume II) and total world trade - up to the year 2011. The two volumes are prepared at different points in time during 2011: *Volume I - Trade by Country* is made electronically available in June and *Volume II - Trade by Commodity* in December, as the preparation of the tables in Volume II requires additional country data which, normally, become available later in the year.

Beginning with the 2008 edition, the yearbook is published in a redesigned format in respect to the presentation of data for individual countries and commodities to provide a more analytical and condensed view of the international merchandise trade data. The detailed information about the trade of particular countries by commodity and partner (values and quantities) contained in the tables and graphs for individual countries in Volume I and commodities in Volume II are taken from the publicly available database UN Comtrade (http://comtrade.un.org/db/default.aspx). Users are advised to visit UN Comtrade for any additional and more current information as it is continuously updated.

The *International Trade Statistics Yearbook* is prepared by the International Merchandise Trade Statistics Section, Trade Statistics Branch of the Statistics Division, Department of Economic and Social Affairs of the United Nations Secretariat. Under the general supervision of the Chief of Branch, Ronald Jansen, the programme manager is Matthias Reister and the chief editor is Marjorie Imperial-Damaso, assisted by Melissa Paca. Bekuretsion Amdemariam has the leading role in the processing of the data for UN Comtrade. However, all staff of the section are involved in the generation of the data and the yearbook. Markie Muryawan, Salomon Cameo and Luis Gonzalez Morales developed the software which is maintained by Salomon Cameo. Nelnan Koumtingue made very substantial contributions to this redesigned yearbook as its first chief editor. Comments on the present yearbook are welcome. They may be sent to comtrade@un.org or to United Nations Statistics Division, International Merchandise Trade Statistics Section, New York, New York 10017, USA.

TABLE OF CONTENTS

Part 2 COUNTRY TRADE PROFILES

INTRODUCTION

The new yearbook

1. The *2011 International Trade Statistics Yearbook* (2011 ITSY) is being issued in two volumes which are prepared at different points in time during 2012.[1] Volume I is compiled early in 2012 to allow for an advanced release of an overview of international merchandise trade in 2011 and for a much earlier publication of the available 2011 country (area) data. Volume II contains the detailed tables showing international trade in main commodity groups and is finalized approximately six months after the completion of Volume I as the preparation of those tables requires additional country data which, normally, become available later in the year. Volume II contains also updated versions of the two world trade tables published in Volume I.

2. Detailed data for a total of 174 countries (or areas) are shown in Volume I with the 2011 data on imports and exports by commodity and trading partner provided for 92 countries (areas), representing approximately 79 percent of world trade of 2011. All tables of Volume I are made available electronically shortly after the completion of the manuscript. Beginning with the 2008 edition, Volume I is published in a redesigned format in respect to the presentation of data for individual countries with the aim to provide a more analytical and condensed view of a country's trade performance (country trade profile).

3. The detailed information about the trade of particular countries by commodity and partner (values and quantities) contained in the tables and graphs for individual countries in Volume I and commodities in Volume II are taken from the publicly available database UN Comtrade (http://comtrade.un.org/db/default.aspx). Users are advised to visit UN Comtrade for any additional and more current information as it is continuously updated.

Concepts and definitions of International Merchandise Trade Statistics

4. The statistics in this Yearbook have been compiled by national statistical authorities largely consistent with the United Nations recommended *International Merchandise Trade Statistics, Concepts and Definitions 2010* (IMTS 2010).[2] The main elements of the concepts and definitions are:

1. Coverage: As a general guideline, it is recommended that international merchandise trade statistics record all goods which add to or subtract from the stock of material resources of a country by entering (imports) or leaving (exports) its economic territory. The general guideline is subject to the clarifications provided in IMTS 2010, in

---

[1] The 2011 ITSY is the sixtieth edition of this yearbook.

[2] At its forty-first session, held from 23 to 26 February 2010, the Statistical Commission adopted the revised recommendations "International merchandise trade statistics: concepts and definitions 2010" (IMTS 2010) which provide very important amendments while retaining the existing conceptual framework contained in the previous recommendations. The publication is available under Statistical Papers, Series M No. 52, Rev.3 (United Nations publication, Sales No. E.10.XVII.13) and electronically at: http://unstats.un.org/unsd/pubs/gesgrid.asp?id=449.

particular, to the specific guidelines in chapter 1 concerning the inclusion or exclusion of certain categories of goods.

2. Time of recording: As a general guideline, it is recommended that goods be recorded at the time when they enter or leave the economic territory of a country.

3. Statistical territory: The statistical territory of a country is the territory with respect to which trade data are being compiled. The definition of the statistical territory may or may not coincide with the economic territory of a country or its customs territory, depending on the availability of data sources and other considerations. It follows that when the statistical territory of a country and its economic territory differ, international merchandise trade statistics do not provide a complete record of inward and outward flows of goods.

4. Trade systems: Depending on what parts of the economic territory are included in the statistical territory, the trade data-compilation system adopted by a country (its trade system) may be referred to as general or special.

(a) The general trade system is in use when the statistical territory coincides with the economic territory. Consequently, it is recommended that the statistical territory of a country applying the general trade system comprises all applicable territorial elements. In this case, imports include goods entering the free circulation area, premises for inward processing, industrial free zones, premises for customs warehousing or commercial free zones and exports include goods leaving those territorial elements;

(b) The special trade system is in use when the statistical territory comprises only a particular part of the economic territory, so that certain flows of goods which are in the scope of IMTS 2010 are not included in either import or export statistics of the compiling country. The strict definition of the special trade system is in use when the statistical territory comprises only the free circulation area, that is, the part within which goods "may be disposed of without customs restriction". Consequently, in such a case, imports include only goods entering the free circulation area of a compiling country and exports include only goods leaving the free circulation area of a compiling country.

(c) *The relaxed definition of the special trade system* is in use when (a) goods that enter a country for, or leave it after, inward processing, as well as (b) goods that enter or leave an industrial free zone, are also recorded and included in international merchandise trade statistics

5. Classification: It is recommended that countries use the *Harmonized Commodity Description and Coding System* (HS) for the collection, compilation and dissemination of international merchandise trade statistics as suggested by the Statistical Commission at its twenty-seventh session (22 February to 3 March 1993).[3] The Harmonized System was adopted by the Customs Co-operation Council in June 1983, and the International Convention on the Harmonized System (HS Convention) entered

[3] See Official Records of the Economic and Social Council, 1993, Supplement No. 6 (E/1993/26), para. 162 (d).

into force on 1 January 1988 (HS 1988).[4] In accordance with the preamble to the HS Convention, which recognized the importance of ensuring that the HS be kept up to date in the light of changes in technology or in patterns of international trade, the HS is regularly reviewed and revised. The fourth edition, HS 2007 which is a substantial revision from previous versions came into effect 1 January 2007.[5] The *Standard International Trade Classification (SITC)*[6] which was in the past used by countries in data compilation and reporting has been recognized for its continued use in analysis.[7]

6. Valuation: At its fifteenth session, in 1953, the Economic and Social Council, taking the view that trade statistics must reflect economic realities, recommended that the Governments of Member States of the United Nations, wherever possible, use transaction values in the compilation of their national statistics of external trade or, when national practices are based on other values, endeavor to provide supplementary statistical data based on transaction values (Economic and Social Council resolution 469 B (XV)). To promote the comparability of international merchandise trade statistics and taking into account the commercial and data reporting practices of the majority of countries, it is recommended that: (a) The statistical value of imported goods be a CIF-type value; (b) The statistical value of exported goods be an FOB-type value; however, countries are encouraged to compile FOB-type value of imported good as supplementary information. FOB-type values include the transaction value of the goods and the value of services performed to deliver goods to the border of the exporting country. CIF-type values include the transaction value of the goods, the value of services performed to deliver goods to the border of the exporting country and the value of the services performed to deliver the goods from the border of the exporting country to the border of the importing country.

7. Partner country: It is recommended that in the case of imports, the country of origin be recorded; and that in the case of exports, the country of last known destination be recorded. The country of origin of a good (for imports) is determined by rules of origin established by each country. The country of last known destination is the last country - as far as it is known at the time of exportation - to which goods are to be delivered, irrespective of where they have been initially dispatched to and whether or not, on their way to that last country, they are subject to any commercial transactions or other operations which change their legal status. Further, it is recommended that country of consignment be recorded for imports as the second partner country attribution, alongside country of origin; the compilation of export statistics on the country of consignment basis is only encouraged, depending on a country's needs and circumstances.

5. The pages containing the country profiles (part 2 of this publication) indicate the trade

---

[4] See Customs Co-operation Council, The Harmonized Commodity Description and Coding System, Brussels, 1989.

[5] See World Customs Organization, Harmonized Commodity Description and Coding System, Fourth Edition (2007), Brussels 2005.

[6] Standard International Trade Classification, Original, Statistical Papers, Series M No.10, Second Edition, 1951 (United Nations publication, Sales No. E.51.XVII.1); subsequent editions are published as United Nations publications under Series M No.34.

[7] See Official Records of the Economic and Social Council, 1999, Supplement No. 4 (E/1993/24), para. 24 (c).

system, valuation and partner attribution each country is following. For more detailed information on national practices in the compilation and dissemination of international merchandise trade data please go to http://unstats.un.org/unsd/tradereport/introduction_MM.asp.

Sources and Presentation

6. Sources: Figures on the total imports and exports of countries (or areas) presented in world table A are mainly taken from *International Financial Statistics* (IFS) published monthly by the International Monetary Fund (IMF) but also from other sources such as national publications and websites and the *United Nations Monthly Bulletin of Statistics Questionnaire* for the following countries: Andorra, Bermuda, Cayman Islands, Cuba, Gibraltar, Montenegro (beginning 2006), Niue, Occupied Palestinian Territory, Russian Federation (beginning 1994), Serbia and Montenegro (before 2006), Turkmenistan, Turks and Caicos, Tuvalu and Uzbekistan. Estimates for missing data are made in order to arrive to regional totals but are otherwise not shown. The estimation process is automated using quarterly year-on-year growth rates for the extrapolation of missing quarterly data (unless quarterly data can be estimated using available monthly data within the quarter). Regional totals containing estimated data are printed in bold. Estimates are reviewed and adjusted where necessary. Table A shows data as available by end of May 2012.

7. Figures presented in world table D are calculated using UN Comtrade data (see details below). Data for missing reporters are estimated either through the extrapolation of the data of the two adjacent years, or, if this is not possible, through the use of the data reported by the trading partners (so called mirror data). Mirror statistics is also used in case the partner distribution or confidential data make it necessary to adjust the reported data. All estimates are reviewed and adjusted where necessary. Table D uses data as available on UN Comtrade by end of May 2012.

8. The figures in the country tables and graphs of part 2 (country trade profiles) are obtained from data directly submitted by countries to the United Nations Statistics Division (UNSD) or received via international and regional partner organizations such as the Organization for Economic Co-operation and Development (OECD), the Food and Agriculture Organization of the United Nations (FAO), the International Trade Centre (ITC), the Caribbean Community (CARICOM) Secretariat, the Common Market of Eastern and Southern Africa (COMESA), the Economic Community of West African States (ECOWAS) and the UN regional commissions such as the Economic Commission for Latin America and the Caribbean (ECLAC) and the Economic and Social Commission for Western Asia (ESCWA). Data for the European Union (EU-27) is received from the Statistical Office of the European Union (Eurostat). All data published in the country profiles is available on UN Comtrade (http://comtrade.un.org/). Modifications to the received data are only made in the case the provided data is obviously incomplete (in particular in the case of unreported oil exports). Quantity information that is missing or does not comply with the World Customs Organization's recommendations for the quantity unit is estimated (and flagged on UN Comtrade accordingly). For data processed before June 2009 some quantity information that were identified as 'extreme' – meaning far outside a pre-defined 'normal' range were replaced on UN Comtrade with estimates. In this publication

some quantity information (in table 3 and 5) is not shown as deemed appropriate. The estimation of quantities is either based on the country's own data or uses so called standard unit values which are derived from the available information for all countries of the previous year. The country tables and graphs contain data as available on UN Comtrade by end of May 2012.

9. The totals of imports and exports presented in table A on the one hand and table D and the country profiles on the other hand are not necessarily identical as IFS and UN Comtrade are based on different data collection systems with different aims, procedures, timetable and sources for update and maintenance. Nevertheless, discrepancies are in general minor and usually do not affect the overall information provided in these tables. A systematic comparison of the figures from both sources (which includes the description of known and relevant conceptual differences) is available at http://unstats.un.org/unsd/trade/imts/annual%20totals.htm. Overall, the discrepancy in the world total or world aggregate of exports in table A and table D is around 0.5 percent or less for all years shown, which is minor, given the differences between the two sources.

10. Currency conversion: For data in this publication, conversion of values from national currencies into United States dollars is done by means of currency conversion factors based on official exchange rates. Values in currencies subject to fluctuation are converted into United States dollars using weighted average exchange rates specially calculated for this purpose. The weighted average exchange rate for a given currency for a given year is the component monthly factors, furnished by the International Monetary Fund in its IFS publication, weighted by the value of the relevant trade in each month; a monthly factor is the exchange rate (or the simple average rate) in effect during that month. These factors are applied to total imports and exports and to the trade in individual commodities with individual countries. The conversion factors applied to the data presented in table A are published quarterly in the *UN Monthly Bulletin of Statistics* (http://unstats.un.org/unsd/mbs/default.aspx) and are also available at: http://unstats.un.org/unsd/trade/imts/analyticaltradetables.htm. For data published on UN Comtrade the applied conversion factors are available in a country's metadata on UN Comtrade.

11. Classification: Essentially all countries follow the recommendation to report their detailed merchandise trade data according to the Harmonized Commodity Description and Coding System (HS) (see paragraph 5). In order to provide comparable time series data on UN Comtrade for all countries, the data reported in the latest HS classification is converted into earlier versions of the HS and to corresponding or earlier versions of the Standard International Trade Classification (SITC).[8] Beginning 2007 many countries (or areas) started to compile their trade data according to the 2007 edition of the HS classification[9] and following the past practices the United Nations Statistics Division (UNSD) developed and implemented the required conversion tables. The commodities in this publication are mostly presented according to the one-digit sections of SITC, Rev.3[10] as the SITC sections provide a limited set of economically

---

[8] Detailed information on the data conversions used for UN Comtrade can be found on the website of the United Nations Statistics Division at:
http://unstats.un.org/unsd/trade/conversions/HS%20Correlation%20and%20Conversion%20tables.htm.

[9] See World Customs Organization, Harmonized Commodity Description and Coding System, Fourth Edition (2007), Brussels 2005.

[10] Standard International Trade Classification, Revision 3, Statistical Papers, Series M No.34/Rev.3, (United Nations publication, Sales No. E.86.XVII.12). SITC, Revision 4 was accepted by the United Nations Statistical

meaningful main categories. In addition, data according to SITC, Rev.3 is available for long time series. In two tables commodities are presented in terms of four-digit headings of the HS, often according to the 2007 version of HS but in many cases also in earlier HS versions.[11] The HS headings provide a meaningful description of traded commodities at the detailed (but not too detailed) level and also allow the presentation of quantity information.

12. Period: Generally, data refer to calendar years; however, for those countries which report according to some other reference year, the data are presented in the year which covers the majority of the reference year used by the country. Concerning the data on UN Comtrade, the only country for which data is not available by calendar year is Nepal for which the data refers to the fiscal year from mid of July of the previous to mid of July of the current year.

13. Country nomenclature: The naming of countries (or areas) in this publication follows in general the *United Nations Standard Country or Area Codes for Statistical Use.*[12] The names and composition of countries as reporter are changing over time. Also, countries rarely follow the identical nomenclature in the recording of partner information. For example, where former geographical entities commonly referred to in national statistics have changed, countries may introduce the corresponding changes in their statistics at different times. In this publication, wherever possible, parts of the world have been designated by the names they currently bear and the trading partner attribution has been standardized. The following information is relevant for the data presented in this publication:

1. In this publication, the data published under the heading China exclude those for Taiwan Province. Figures representing the trade with Taiwan Province, which may have been reported by any reporting country or area, are included in the grouping Asia. For statistical purposes, the data for China do not include those for Hong Kong Special Administrative Region and Macao Special Administrative Region.

2. Beginning 1 January 1997, the overseas departments of France were included in the statistical territory of France for the purposes of international trade statistics. Values on this basis have been provided by France for 1996 also, and values are published on that basis in this publication.

3. Beginning 1 January 1999, Belgium and Luxembourg provide their international trade statistics separately.

4. Beginning 1 January 2000, Botswana, Lesotho, Namibia, South Africa and Swaziland provide their international trade statistics separately. For periods prior to 1

Commission at its thirty-seventh session in March 2006 (see Official Records of the Economic and Social Council, 2006, Supplement No. 4, (E/CN.3/2006/32), chapter III, para. 26 (b)). Yet it will require several years until a time series of data according to SITC, Revision 4 will be sufficiently long for publication.

[11] World Customs Organization, Harmonized Commodity Description and Coding System, Third Edition (2002) (HS 2002); World Customs Organization, Harmonized Commodity Description and Coding System, Second Edition (1996) (HS 1996); World Customs Organization, Harmonized Commodity Description and Coding System (1992) (HS 1992).

[12] Standard Country or Area Codes for Statistical Use, Series M No. 49, Rev.4, (United Nations publication, Sales No. M.98.XVII.9). The latest information is available online at: http://unstats.un.org/unsd/methods/m49/m49.htm.

January 2000, unless otherwise indicated, data are shown for the Southern African Customs Union.

5. On 4 February 2003, the official name of the Federal Republic of Yugoslavia has been changed to Serbia and Montenegro. Data provided for Yugoslavia prior to 1 January 1992 refer to the Socialist Federal Republic of Yugoslavia which was composed of six republics. Data referring to the years 1992 and later are attributed to Bosnia and Herzegovina, Croatia, Serbia and Montenegro, Slovenia and the Former Yugoslav Republic of Macedonia.

6. On 3 June 2006, Serbia and Montenegro formally dissolved into two independent countries: Montenegro and Serbia.

7. On 10 October 2010 the federation of the Netherlands Antilles was formally dissolved. The former Dutch Caribbean dependency ceased to exist with a change of the five islands' constitutional status. Under the new political structure, Curaçao and Sint Maarten (Dutch part) have become autonomous countries within the Kingdom of the Netherlands, joining Aruba, which gained the status in 1986. The islands of the remaining territorial grouping, alternately known as Bonaire, Sint Eustatius and Saba or the BES islands, are special municipalities and part of the country of the Netherlands and overseas territories of the European Union. For statistical purposes, the data for the Netherlands do not include the BES islands.

14. Regional groupings: This publication uses the regional groupings of the Millennium Development Goal (MDG) Indicator Database which are shown below (for their composition see table A and http://unstats.un.org/unsd/mdg/default.aspx). The category 'Other' applies only to the presentation of data by trading partner and consists of Antarctica, Bunkers, Free Zones, 'Special Categories' (confidential partner) and Areas nes.:

World
Developed Countries
- Asia-Pacific
- Europe
- North America

South-eastern Europe
Commonwealth of Independent States
- CIS Europe
- CIS Asia

Northern Africa
Sub-Saharan Africa
Latin America & the Caribbean
- Caribbean
- Latin America

Eastern Asia
Southern Asia
South-eastern Asia
Western Asia
Oceania
Other

15. Aggregations: All regional aggregations are calculated as the sum of their components. This also includes the regional and world totals presented in table A (in bold) which up to the 2007 edition of this yearbook and in the tables currently published in the *United Nations Monthly Bulletin of Statistics* are calculated by subtracting re-exports from the imports and exports.

16. Additional country groupings: The composition of the additional country groupings which are used in world table A is as follows:

ANCOM-Andean Common Market
Bolivia (Plurinational State of), Colombia, Ecuador and Peru

APEC-Asian-Pacific Economic Co-operation
Australia, Brunei Darussalam, Canada, Chile, China, Hong Kong Special Administrative Region of China, Indonesia, Japan, Malaysia, Mexico, New Zealand, Papua New Guinea, Peru, Philippines, Republic of Korea, Russian Federation, Singapore, Taiwan Province of China, Thailand, United States of America and Viet Nam

ASEAN-Association of South-East Asian Nations
Brunei Darussalam, Cambodia, Indonesia, Lao People's Democratic Republic, Malaysia, Myanmar, Philippines, Singapore, Thailand and Viet Nam

CACM-Central American Common Market
Costa Rica, El Salvador, Guatemala, Honduras and Nicaragua

CARICOM-Caribbean Community and Common Market
Antigua and Barbuda, Bahamas (member of the Community only), Barbados, Belize, Dominica, Grenada, Guyana, Haiti, Jamaica, Montserrat, Saint Kitts and Nevis, Saint Lucia, Saint Vincent and the Grenadines, Suriname, Trinidad and Tobago

COMESA-Common Market for Eastern and Southern Africa
Burundi, Comoros, Democratic Republic of the Congo, Djibouti, Egypt, Eritrea, Ethiopia, Kenya, Libya, Madagascar, Malawi, Mauritius, Rwanda, Seychelles, Sudan, Swaziland, Uganda, Zambia and Zimbabwe

ECOWAS - Economic Community of West African States
Benin, Burkina Faso, Cape Verde, Cote d'Ivoire, Gambia, Ghana, Guinea, Guinea-Bissau, Liberia, Mali, Niger, Nigeria, Senegal, Sierra Leone and Togo

EFTA - European Free Trade Association
Iceland, Liechtenstein, Norway and Switzerland

EMCCA – Economic and Monetary Community of Central Africa
Cameroon, Central African Republic, Chad, Congo, Equatorial Guinea and Gabon

EU-27 - European Union 27
Austria, Belgium, Bulgaria, Cyprus, Czech Republic, Denmark, Estonia, Finland, France, Germany, Greece, Hungary, Ireland, Italy, Latvia, Lithuania, Luxembourg, Malta, Netherlands, Poland, Portugal, Romania, Spain, Slovakia, Slovenia, Sweden and United Kingdom.

EU-25 - European Union 25
Austria, Belgium, Denmark, Finland, France, Germany, Greece, Ireland, Italy, Luxembourg, Netherlands, Portugal, Spain, Sweden and United Kingdom (EU15) plus Czech Republic, Estonia, Hungary, Latvia, Lithuania, Malta, Poland, Slovakia, Slovenia, and Cyprus

LAIA - Latin American Integration Association (formerly Latin American Free Trade Association)
Argentina, Bolivia (Plurinational State of), Brazil, Chile, Colombia, Cuba, Ecuador, Mexico, Paraguay, Peru, Uruguay and Venezuela (Bolivarian Republic of)

LDC - Least developed countries
Afghanistan, Angola, Bangladesh, Benin, Bhutan, Burkina Faso, Burundi, Cambodia, Central African Republic, Chad, Comoros, Democratic Republic of the Congo, Djibouti, Equatorial Guinea, Eritrea, Ethiopia, Gambia, Guinea, Guinea-Bissau, Haiti, Kiribati, Lao People's Democratic Republic, Lesotho, Liberia, Madagascar, Malawi, Mali, Mauritania, Mozambique, Myanmar, Nepal, Niger, Rwanda, Samoa, Sao Tome and Principe, Senegal, Sierra Leone, Solomon Islands, Somalia, Sudan, Timor-Leste, Togo, Tuvalu, Uganda, United Republic of Tanzania, Vanuatu, Yemen and Zambia

MERCOSUR-Mercado Comun Sud-Americano
Argentina, Brazil, Paraguay and Uruguay

NAFTA-Northern American Free Trade Area
Canada, Mexico and United States of America

OECD-Organization for Economic Cooperation and Development
Australia, Austria, Belgium, Canada, Chile, Czech Republic, Denmark, Estonia, Finland, France, Germany, Greece, Hungary, Iceland, Ireland, Israel, Italy, Japan, Luxembourg, Mexico, Netherlands, New Zealand, Norway, Poland, Portugal, Republic of Korea, Slovakia, Slovenia, Spain, Sweden, Switzerland, Turkey, United Kingdom and United States of America

OPEC-Organization of Petroleum Exporting Countries
Algeria, Angola, Ecuador, Iran (Islamic Republic of), Iraq, Kuwait, Libya, Nigeria, Qatar, Saudi Arabia, United Arab Emirates and Venezuela (Bolivarian Republic of).

Description of world trade tables of part 1 (Tables A and D)

17. Total imports and exports by regions and countries or areas in U.S. dollars (Table A): The total value of world trade reached U.S. dollar 17.9 trillion in 2011, measured in terms of exports valued FOB at the border of the exporting country. This is an increase of 19 percent compared with the previous year during which trade rose by 22 percent. Table A provides a breakdown of this figure by country (or area) and also shows imports and the trade balance. For example, the biggest exporter in 2011 with exports of U.S. dollar 1,899 billion was China, followed by the United States with U.S. dollar 1,480 billion and Germany with U.S. dollar 1,475 billion. The United States was the biggest importer with imports of U.S. dollar 2,265 billion in 2011 which resulted in a trade deficit of U.S. dollar 785 billion, while Germany and China recorded trade surpluses of U.S. dollar 220 billion and 157 billion respectively.

18. World exports by provenance and destination in U.S. dollars (Table D): This table provides a breakdown of the world exports by regions and countries according to their provenance and destination, for the total of trade but also detailed by individual SITC sections or groupings of sections (the same list as for Table 1 and 2 applies – see para. 22 below). For example, the table shows that in 2011 developed economies of Asia-Pacific, Europe and North America were the destination of 54% of world exports (U.S. dollar 9.7 trillion) and the origin of 52% of world exports (9.3 trillion).[13]

19. For the general note and footnotes, see the end of the tables. A slightly different version of Table A containing quarterly and monthly data is published on a monthly basis as table 34 in the *United Nations Monthly Bulletin of Statistics* (MBS).[14] Updated, although different versions

[13] These percentages or shares of world trade are measured based on the trade between countries (or areas) which includes the trade of the countries within one region.
[14] The difference between table A in this publication and table 34 in the MBS relates to the calculation of regional aggregations (see paragraph 15).

of Table D, are published as table 40, 41 and 42 in the July, September and November editions of the MBS.

Description of country tables and graphs of part 2

20. Part 2 contains detailed data (the country profile) for individual countries or areas. Given the economic importance of the European Union (EU), separate pages have been added for the external trade of the EU (with its 27 members) as a whole. These pages are given as a memorandum item after the country pages.

21. Not all countries have data up to 2011 and not all countries have data for imports and exports for all years. The publication of a country (or area) in part 2 requires that data for at least up to the year 2007 is available. Depending on the availability of data the following tables and graphs usually appear for each country or area:

22. Exports and Imports by SITC sections (Table 1 and Table 2): These tables show the structure of exports and imports in 2011 (or the latest available year) by SITC sections in terms of value, share of the total, growth in respect to the previous year and annual average growth for the last four years which is calculated as the geometric mean. The description of the SITC sections used in the tables is provided below:[15]

SITC sections	Description
0+1	Food, beverages and tobacco
2+4	Crude materials (excluding fuels), oils, fats
3	Mineral fuels, lubricants and related materials
5	Chemicals and related products, n.e.s
6	Manufactured goods classified chiefly by material
7	Machinery and transport equipment
8	Miscellaneous manufactured articles
9	Commodities and transactions not classified elsewhere in SITC

23. Top 10 export and import commodities (Table 3 and Table 5): These tables present the top 10 commodities in terms of 4-digit HS headings for exports and imports, respectively, using the aggregate of trade values for the last three reporting years as available. For countries which reported the last three years of data in HS 2007 the data in these tables is following HS 2007. For most other countries the data in these tables is presented in HS 2002 with data for some years converted from HS 2007 into HS 2002 as required (see paragraph 11). For a few countries the table contains data according to the HS 1996 or even HS 1992. For the convenience of users the last column shows the SITC group (3 digits) that corresponds to the HS heading. The SITC group is identified based on the correlation and conversion tables between HS and SITC, Rev 3. The conversion tables are available on the website of UNSD at http://unstats.un.org/unsd/trade/methodology%20imts.htm.

[15] For the purpose of presentation, the section 0 ("Food and live animals") and section 1 ("Beverages and tobacco") have been aggregated into 0+1 named "Food, beverages and tobacco" and section 2 ("Crude materials, inedible, except fuels") and section 4 ("Animal and vegetable soils, fats and waxes") have been aggregated into 2+4 named "Crude materials (excluding fuels), oils, fats".

24. For those commodities and those years, the tables contain trade values and unit values. Unit values are expressed in U.S. dollars (US$) per indicator of unit (kg, unit, Megawatt-hours (Mwh), pair, litre, carat etc.). The calculation of unit values on the heading level requires the availability of value and quantity information for all of the underlying detailed data (6-digit subheadings). In some cases the quantity information for some sub-headings was estimated (see paragraph 8) and the unit value for the heading appears in italics.

25. Exports by principal countries and SITC sections (Table 4): This table presents the top 10 partners for exports of the latest available year. For each country in the top 10, the table reports the value of exports to that country and the structure of those exports according to SITC sections. For the definition of SITC sections used in this table, see paragraph 22 above.

26. Total imports, exports and trade balance (Graph 1): This graph presents the evolution of imports, exports and trade balance over the last fifteen years.

27. Trade balance by MDG Regions (Graph 2): This graph presents the trade balance by regions according to the regions used in the Millennium Development Goal (MDG) Indicator Database (see paragraph 14 above) for the most recent year for which information on exports and imports is available.

28. Partner concentration of trade (Graph 3): This graph shows the partner concentration of imports and exports for the latest available year for the top 25 partners which usually account for a very large share of exports or imports in most countries. On the horizontal axis from the center to the right are the cumulative percent of exports and from the center to the left the cumulative percent of imports. On the vertical axis is the cumulative number of partners ranked by total value of exports and imports in a decreasing order.

29. Graph 3 shows as additional information the Herfindahl-Hirschman (HH) Index for imports and exports, which is a measure of concentration. In the case of exports (imports), the HH index is the sum of squares of the percentages of the partner's share of total exports (imports):

$$HH\ Index = \sum_{i=1}^{n} \left(\frac{X_i}{X} \right)^2$$

30. N is the number of trading partners for exports (imports) and X_i is the value of exports (imports) to partner country i and X is the total value of exports (imports). The lower the HH index, the lower the partner concentration, and vice versa. If there is only one trading partner the HH index would equal 1.[16]

[16] Users might wish to define a specific limit of the HH index to indicate low concentration and a limit to indicate high concentration. Yet, for its application in the measurement of partner concentration in international merchandise trade statistics no such boundaries are known to be established.

Abbreviations and Explanation of symbols

Names of some countries (or areas) or groups of countries (or areas) and of some commodities or groups of commodities have been abbreviated. Exact titles of countries or commodities can be found in various editions of the following publications referred to in the introduction (see paragraphs 11 and 13):

(i) Standard Country or Area Codes for Statistical Use
(ii) Standard International Trade Classification (SITC)
(iii) Harmonized Commodity Description and Coding System (HS)

In addition, the following abbreviations and symbols are used in this publication:

Not available	(na)
Not available	blank
Not available	...
Not applicable	–
Not applicable	.
Magnitude of less than half the unit used	0 or 0.0
Thousand	thsd
Million	mln
Billion	bln
Weight (kilograms)	kg
Megawatt-hours	Mwh
Average	Avg.
Not elsewhere specified	nes
U.S. dollar	US$
Imports	Imp
Exports	Exp
Balance	Bal
General trade system	G
Special trade system	S
Cost, insurance and freight	CIF
Free on board	FOB

Disclaimer

The tables, graphs and text contained in part 2 of this publication are provided only for illustration and despite all efforts might contain errors. When using this data users are advised to verify the latest information on UN Comtrade which is the source of this data.

UN Comtrade Subscription information

UN Comtrade is (with the exception of table A) the source of the data in this Volume I of the 2011 ITSY. UN Comtrade is available at http://comtrade.un.org/. All data can be viewed and up to 50,000 records per query can be downloaded for free. The use of additional features requires a subscription – for rates and subscription go to https://unp.un.org/comtrade.aspx.

Contact

This yearbook has been produced by the International Merchandise Trade Statistics Section of the United Nations Statistics Division/ Department of Economic and Social Affairs. For questions or comments please contact us at:

International Merchandise Trade Statistics Section
United Nations Statistics Division
2 United Nations Plaza, DC2-1540
New York, New York 10017
e-mail: comtrade@un.org

http://comtrade.un.org/ or
http://unstats.un.org/unsd/trade/imts/imts_default.htm

2011
INTERNATIONAL TRADE
STATISTICS YEARBOOK

VOLUME I
TRADE BY COUNTRY

PART 1 – WORLD TRADE TABLES

Total imports and exports by regions and countries or areas in U.S. dollars (Table A)

World exports by provenance and destination in U.S. dollars (Table D)

Total imports and exports by regions and countries or areas (Table A)

Imports CIF, exports FOB and balance: million U.S. dollars

Importations et exportations totales par régions et pays ou zones (Tableau A)

Importations CIF, exportations FOB, et balance : en millions de dollars E.-U.

Country or Area - Pays ou Zone	IMP EXP BAL	G/S	2000	2003	2004	2005	2006	2007	2008	2009	2010	2011
World	IMP		6530063	7615258	9295522	10576475	12154236	14030537	16217350	12466709	15127376	17952902
Monde	EXP		6359078	7453819	9071852	10346857	11965744	13821381	15973126	12367890	15056068	17939399
	BAL		-170985	-161439	-223670	-229618	-188492	-209156	-244224	-98819	-71308	-13503
Developed Countries[1,2]	IMP		4499480	5183510	6178343	6875887	7790604	8797278	9828832	7394064	8616342	10070802
Pays Developpés[1,2]	EXP		4129849	4786947	5640801	6147429	6940387	7953800	8876135	6876054	7986364	9274110
	BAL		-369631	-396563	-537543	-728458	-850217	-843478	-952697	-518010	-629979	-796691
Asia-Pacific	IMP		464933	490733	587170	666504	745314	815912	997567	741599	925899	1134888
Asie-Pacifique	EXP		556448	560075	672507	722502	792508	882279	999884	759534	1014427	1132041
	BAL		91516	69342	85337	55998	47194	66368	2317	17936	88527	-2847
Australia	IMP	G	71537	89089	109383	125283	139279	165364	200564	165470	201640	243713
Australie	EXP	G	63878	71551	86420	105833	123316	141122	187249	153884	212364	271692
	BAL		-7659	-17539	-22962	-19449	-15963	-24241	-13314	-11587	10724	27978
Japan	IMP	G	379490	383085	454593	514987	579603	619662	762629	550550	692435	854100
Japon	EXP	G	479274	471998	565742	594940	646755	714211	782052	580719	769773	822674
	BAL		99783	88914	111149	79953	67151	94549	19423	30169	77337	-31426
New Zealand	IMP	G	13906	18560	23194	26234	26431	30886	34374	25578	31824	37075
Nouvelle-Zélande	EXP	G	13297	16527	20344	21728	22437	26946	30582	24931	32289	37675
	BAL		-608	-2033	-2850	-4506	-3994	-3940	-3792	-647	466	600
Europe	IMP		2535270	3149222	3791023	4149165	4776249	5578936	6252075	4724530	5328580	6215889
Europe	EXP		2514496	3228985	3844674	4157876	4719628	5491589	6122374	4745294	5307794	6208841
	BAL		-20774	79763	53651	8711	-56620	-87347	-129701	20764	-20787	-7049
Andorra	IMP	S	1021	1513	1762	1796	1780	1917	1931	1589	1518	1596
Andorre	EXP	S	45	89	123	142	150	127	96	63	54	77
	BAL		-975	-1424	-1639	-1654	-1630	-1790	-1835	-1526	-1464	-1519
Austria	IMP	S	68986	91595	113344	119950	130945	156760	176174	136081	150326	180371
Autriche	EXP	S	64167	89257	111720	117722	130376	157317	173394	130791	144645	169673
	BAL		-4819	-2339	-1623	-2228	-570	557	-2780	-5290	-5681	-10698
Belgium	IMP	S	176992	234947	286504	319798	351575	412012	471567	353246	393505	461941
Belgique	EXP	S	187876	255598	307792	335738	366758	431118	477252	370514	409303	476351
	BAL		10884	20650	21288	15941	15184	19106	5685	17267	15798	14409
Croatia	IMP	G	7887	14209	16589	18560	21488	25830	30728	21203	20051	20415
Croatie	EXP	G	4432	6187	8024	8773	10376	12364	14112	10474	11806	12405
	BAL		-3455	-8022	-8565	-9788	-11112	-13465	-16617	-10729	-8244	-8009
Czech Republic	IMP	S	33934	53807	71635	76343	93453	118467	142172	105256	126600	151406
République tchèque	EXP	S	29057	48715	67198	77988	95165	122760	146406	113175	133020	162177
	BAL		-4877	-5092	-4438	1645	1712	4293	4234	7920	6420	10771
Denmark	IMP	S	44364	56227	66845	74265	85103	97324	109158	81926	84744	97763
Danemark	EXP	S	50390	65280	75568	83569	91703	101954	116069	92844	96773	112748
	BAL		6025	9052	8723	9303	6600	4631	6911	10917	12029	14985
Estonia	IMP	S	4237	6480	8334	10213	13472	15687	16058	10151	12282	17602
Estonie	EXP	S	3166	4539	5934	7676	9705	10948	12468	9058	11607	16793
	BAL		-1070	-1942	-2400	-2537	-3767	-4739	-3590	-1094	-675	-809
Faeroe Islands	IMP	G	532	738	628	743	790	1016	988	783	774	...
Iles Féroé	EXP	G	472	594	616	599	651	746	852	762	817	...
	BAL		-60	-144	-12	-144	-139	-270	-136	-22	44	...
Finland	IMP	G	33900	41601	50677	58474	69448	81756	92160	60822	68772	84013
Finlande	EXP	G	45482	52514	60916	65238	77287	90091	96890	62859	69491	78866
	BAL		11582	10913	10239	6764	7839	8335	4730	2037	719	-5146

Total imports and exports by regions and countries or areas (Table A)

Imports CIF, exports FOB and balance: million U.S. dollars *[cont.]*

Importations et exportations totales par régions et pays ou zones (Tableau A)

Importations CIF, exportations FOB et balance : en millions de dollars E.-U. *[suite]*

Country or Area - Pays ou Zone	IMP EXP BAL	G/S	2000	2003	2004	2005	2006	2007	2008	2009	2010	2011
France	IMP	S	310831	376261	447636	490611	546505	631447	715783	559678	605639	701059
France	EXP	S	298765	367271	422377	443619	490702	550458	608957	475795	515312	581188
	BAL		-12066	-8990	-25259	-46992	-55803	-80989	-106826	-83883	-90328	-119870
Germany	IMP	S	495450	604742	715903	780514	922376	1055997	1186681	926154	1056170	1255417
Allemagne	EXP	S	550222	751829	909513	977970	1122112	1323818	1451390	1120666	1261577	1475491
	BAL		54772	147087	193610	197456	199736	267822	264709	194512	205408	220074
Gibraltar	IMP		480	468	535	550	676	853	824	750	745	...
Gibraltar	EXP		126	147	199	199	242	304	281	266	259	...
	BAL		-354	-320	-336	-351	-434	-548	-543	-484	-486	...
Greece	IMP	S	29221	44375	51559	49817	59121	75100	77831	59293	50694	...
Grèce	EXP	S	10747	13195	14996	15511	20180	23472	25231	19868	20919	...
	BAL		-18474	-31180	-36564	-34306	-38940	-51628	-52600	-39425	-29774	...
Hungary	IMP	S	31955	47602	59636	65783	77206	94375	106380	78034	87612	100989
Hongrie	EXP	S	28016	42532	54893	62179	74217	93377	107466	84586	94759	110897
	BAL		-3939	-5070	-4744	-3604	-2989	-997	1085	6552	7147	9908
Iceland	IMP	G	2591	2788	3551	4554	5077	6354	5614	3604	3920	4709
Islande	EXP	G	1891	2385	2896	2944	3241	4509	5191	4057	4605	5396
	BAL		-700	-403	-654	-1610	-1836	-1845	-423	453	685	688
Ireland	IMP	G	51444	53315	61413	69177	83889	85624	82658	62595	60686	66717
Irlande	EXP	G	77097	92431	104204	109605	104639	122622	126144	117092	118260	128881
	BAL		25653	39117	42791	40428	20750	36998	43485	54498	57574	62165
Italy	IMP	S	238071	297405	355269	384837	440852	509937	563436	414725	486967	556859
Italie	EXP	S	239934	299468	353544	372962	416231	499933	544962	406685	446852	523009
	BAL		1863	2063	-1726	-11875	-24621	-10004	-18474	-8040	-40116	-33851
Latvia	IMP	S	3187	5242	7048	8592	11430	15182	15775	9346	11064	15063
Lettonie	EXP	S	1867	2893	3983	5108	5896	7892	9278	7174	8817	12012
	BAL		-1320	-2350	-3066	-3483	-5535	-7290	-6497	-2173	-2247	-3051
Lithuania	IMP	G	5219	9668	12386	15510	19413	24445	31295	18341	23385	31552
Lituanie	EXP	G	3548	6970	9307	11782	14153	17162	23770	16496	20726	28108
	BAL		-1671	-2698	-3079	-3729	-5259	-7283	-7525	-1845	-2658	-3444
Luxembourg	IMP	S	10718	13694	16829	17565	19434	22301	25514	18652	21738	25670
Luxembourg	EXP	S	7950	9980	12181	12699	14172	16144	17590	12786	14293	16718
	BAL		-2768	-3714	-4648	-4866	-5262	-6157	-7924	-5866	-7444	-8952
Malta	IMP	G	3400	3399	3824	3807	4073	4508	5399	4393	4959	6720
Malte	EXP	G	2443	2468	2628	2376	2705	2985	3077	2327	2994	5000
	BAL		-957	-931	-1196	-1432	-1368	-1523	-2322	-2066	-1966	-1720
Netherlands	IMP	S	198926	234014	284020	310600	358510	421084	495043	382268	440562	507703
Pays-Bas	EXP	S	213425	264849	318066	349844	399635	476787	541398	431839	492423	563133
	BAL		14499	30835	34046	39244	41125	55703	46355	49571	51861	55431
Norway	IMP	G	34351	39284	48062	55472	64272	80378	90293	69290	77252	90697
Norvège	EXP	G	60063	67103	81709	103738	122112	136371	172636	120884	131395	158229
	BAL		25712	27818	33646	48265	57840	55993	82343	51594	54144	67532
Poland	IMP	S	48970	68153	89096	100759	127260	162437	204873	149723	178149	206844
Pologne	EXP	S	31684	53699	74829	89214	110941	138756	168674	136786	159829	187151
	BAL		-17285	-14454	-14267	-11545	-16319	-23680	-36200	-12938	-18320	-19693
Portugal	IMP	S	38196	40853	49240	53398	65609	76371	94726	71729	75590	79734
Portugal	EXP	S	23280	30719	33035	32129	42894	50241	57565	44343	48742	58727
	BAL		-14916	-10134	-16205	-21269	-22716	-26129	-37161	-27386	-26848	-21007

Total imports and exports by regions and countries or areas (Table A)

Imports CIF, exports FOB and balance: million U.S. dollars *[cont.]*

Importations et exportations totales par régions et pays ou zones (Tableau A)

Importations CIF, exportations FOB et balance : en millions de dollars E.-U. *[suite]*

Country or Area - Pays ou Zone	IMP EXP BAL	G/ S	2000	2003	2004	2005	2006	2007	2008	2009	2010	2011
Slovakia	IMP	S	13413	23760	30469	36168	47250	62102	74034	56898	66110	78880
Slovaquie	EXP	S	11889	21966	27605	31997	41939	57766	70982	55553	64012	78496
	BAL		-1524	-1794	-2864	-4171	-5311	-4336	-3052	-1345	-2098	-384
Slovenia	IMP	S	10116	13853	17571	19626	23014	29481	34000	23852	26370	30844
Slovénie	EXP	S	8732	12767	15879	17896	20985	26553	28624	22294	24189	28517
	BAL		-1384	-1086	-1692	-1730	-2029	-2928	-5377	-1558	-2182	-2327
Spain	IMP	S	152901	208553	257672	287610	326046	382651	417049	290744	315548	362835
Espagne	EXP	S	113348	156024	182156	191021	213350	246752	277695	220848	246274	298458
	BAL		-39553	-52529	-75516	-96589	-112697	-135899	-139353	-69897	-69274	-64377
Sweden	IMP	G	73328	84199	100792	111219	126613	153463	168993	120262	148471	174755
Suède	EXP	G	87737	102407	123311	130147	147191	168979	183907	131042	158089	187267
	BAL		14409	18209	22519	18928	20578	15516	14914	10780	9619	12512
Switzerland	IMP	S	76104	95600	110324	119784	132030	153181	173683	147894	166910	196990
Suisse	EXP	S	74867	100744	117820	126099	141679	164809	191810	166847	185774	223507
	BAL		-1237	5144	7496	6314	9649	11627	18127	18953	18865	26517
United Kingdom	IMP	G	334546	380879	451870	483068	547540	620899	641255	485245	561470	637386
Royaume-Uni	EXP	G	281776	304367	341654	371393	428244	434473	468210	356520	410178	480347
	BAL		-52770	-76512	-110215	-111675	-119296	-186426	-173046	-128725	-151292	-157039
North America	IMP		**1499277**	**1543554**	**1800150**	**2060219**	**2269041**	**2402430**	**2579189**	**1927935**	**2361863**	**2720024**
Amérique du Nord	EXP		**1058904**	**997886**	**1123620**	**1267052**	**1428250**	**1579932**	**1753877**	**1371225**	**1664143**	**1933228**
	BAL		**-440373**	**-545668**	**-676530**	**-793167**	**-840791**	**-822498**	**-825312**	**-556710**	**-697719**	**-786796**
Bermuda	IMP	G	720	833	988	985	1094	1167	1160	1067	1050	...
Bermudes	EXP	G	...	52	73	49	27	27	24	29	32	...
	BAL		...	-781	-915	-936	-1067	-1140	-1136	-1038	-1018	...
Canada[3]	IMP	G	238811	239085	273084	323365	348958	379794	407165	320287	390527	452131
Canada[3]	EXP	G	276641	272699	304623	359411	389513	416432	452170	313981	386011	451736
	BAL		37830	33614	31538	36046	40555	36638	45005	-6306	-4515	-395
Greenland	IMP	G	363	465	546	593	618	678	871	680	779	495
Groenland	EXP	G	272	349	382	402	396	431	489	360	383	864
	BAL		-92	-117	-164	-190	-222	-247	-383	-320	-396	369
United States[4]	IMP	G	1259300	1303050	1525370	1735060	1918080	2020400	2169490	1605300	1968760	2265420
Etats-Unis[4]	EXP	G	781918	724771	818520	907158	1038270	1162980	1301110	1056750	1277580	1480410
	BAL		-477382	-578279	-706850	-827902	-879810	-857420	-868380	-548550	-691180	-785010
South-Eastern Europe	IMP		29538	51865	69728	**82986**	103593	140430	170949	114542	125101	154168
Europe du Sud-est	EXP		19549	31032	41415	**49008**	61183	76807	94028	73459	89772	115243
	BAL		-9989	-20833	-28314	**-33979**	-42410	-63624	-76920	-41083	-35329	-38926
Albania	IMP	G	1091	1864	2309	2618	3058	4188	5251	4550	4406	5165
Albanie	EXP	G	261	448	605	658	798	1078	1355	1091	1545	1957
	BAL		-829	-1416	-1704	-1960	-2261	-3110	-3896	-3459	-2861	-3208
Bosnia and Herzegovina	IMP	S	3083	4853	5991	7072	7345	9772	12282	8794	9204	11047
Bosnie-Herzégovine	EXP	S	1067	1409	1916	2400	3323	4166	5066	3939	4802	5850
	BAL		-2017	-3445	-4075	-4672	-4023	-5606	-7217	-4856	-4402	-5196
Bulgaria	IMP	S	6505	10887	14467	18162	23270	30086	37018	23552	25473	32114
Bulgarie	EXP	S	4809	7540	9931	11739	15101	18575	22485	16378	20571	27986
	BAL		-1696	-3346	-4536	-6423	-8168	-11511	-14532	-7175	-4902	-4128
Montenegro[5]	IMP	S	.	.	.	.	1874	3206	3644	2310	2186	2543
Monténégro[5]	EXP	S	.	.	.	.	791	827	659	403	437	632
	BAL		.	.	.	.	-1082	-2378	-2985	-1908	-1749	-1911

Total imports and exports by regions and countries or areas (Table A)

Imports CIF, exports FOB and balance: million U.S. dollars *[cont.]*

Importations et exportations totales par régions et pays ou zones (Tableau A)

Importations CIF, exportations FOB et balance : en millions de dollars E.-U. *[suite]*

Country or Area - Pays ou Zone	IMP EXP BAL	G/S	2000	2003	2004	2005	2006	2007	2008	2009	2010	2011
Romania	IMP	S	13055	24003	32664	40463	51106	69602	82965	54256	61885	76251
Roumanie	EXP	S	10367	17619	23485	27730	32336	40042	49539	40621	49357	62659
	BAL		-2688	-6384	-9179	-12733	-18770	-29560	-33426	-13635	-12528	-13592
Serbia[5]	IMP	S	.	.	.	.	13188	18400	22945	16047	16499	20069
Serbie[5]	EXP	S	.	.	.	.	6437	8817	11004	8338	9771	11780
	BAL		.	.	.	.	-6752	-9584	-11941	-7709	-6728	-8289
Serbia and Montenegro[5]	IMP	S	3711	7952	11366	...	.	.	.	.	.	.
Serbie et Monténégro[5]	EXP	S	1723	2650	3801	...	.	.	.	.	.	.
	BAL		-1988	-5302	-7565	...	.	.	.	.	.	.
TFYR Macedonia	IMP	S	2094	2306	2932	3228	3752	5177	6844	5032	5449	6979
L'ex-Ry de Macédoine	EXP	S	1323	1367	1676	2041	2398	3302	3920	2691	3291	4378
	BAL		-771	-939	-1256	-1187	-1355	-1875	-2923	-2341	-2159	-2601
CIS	IMP		**70777**	114705	**151075**	**188633**	**253241**	**352232**	**468958**	**303961**	**385312**	**517532**
CEI	EXP		**143256**	191629	**263552**	**336579**	**418435**	**497491**	**707334**	**440219**	**574677**	**765562**
	BAL		**72479**	76924	**112477**	**147945**	**165195**	**145259**	**238376**	**136258**	**189365**	**248030**
Asia	IMP		**13519**	21377	**28245**	**34788**	**45334**	**59477**	**72860**	**59216**	**56175**	**78492**
Asie	EXP		**17793**	24171	**34469**	**43806**	**58030**	**70649**	**138894**	**76194**	**98779**	**138082**
	BAL		**4274**	2794	**6224**	**9018**	**12696**	**11172**	**66034**	**16978**	**42604**	**59590**
Armenia	IMP	S	882	1280	1351	1768	2194	3282	4427	3303	3783	4196
Arménie	EXP	S	294	686	715	950	1004	1219	1057	698	1011	1316
	BAL		-588	-594	-636	-818	-1190	-2063	-3370	-2605	-2771	-2881
Azerbaijan	IMP	G	1172	2626	3516	4211	5267	5714	7170	6123	6599	...
Azerbaïdjan	EXP	G	1745	2590	3616	4347	6372	6058	47756	14701	21325	...
	BAL		573	-36	100	136	1106	345	40586	8578	14726	...
Georgia	IMP	G	709	1141	1846	2490	3678	5217	6066	4386	5097	6948
Géorgie	EXP	G	323	461	647	865	993	1240	1507	1140	1581	2188
	BAL		-387	-680	-1199	-1624	-2685	-3977	-4559	-3246	-3516	-4760
Kazakhstan	IMP	G	5040	9554	13818	17979	24120	33260	38452	28409	24024	38039
Kazakhstan	EXP	G	8812	13233	20603	28301	38762	48351	71971	43196	57244	88118
	BAL		3772	3679	6785	10322	14642	15091	33519	14787	33220	50079
Kyrgyzstan	IMP	S	558	722	947	1101	1718	2412	4072	3040	3228	4261
Kirghizistan	EXP	S	511	583	721	672	794	1134	1618	1442	1489	1979
	BAL		-47	-139	-226	-429	-924	-1278	-2455	-1599	-1739	-2282
Tajikistan	IMP	G	675	881	1191	1354	1723	2455	3270	2569	2658	3186
Tadjikistan	EXP	G	784	797	915	891	1399	1468	1406	1010	1206	1257
	BAL		109	-84	-276	-464	-324	-987	-1864	-1559	-1452	-1930
Turkmenistan	IMP	G	...	2512	...	...	...	...	...	...	...	...
Turkménistan	EXP	G	...	2632	...	...	...	...	...	...	...	...
	BAL		...	120	...	...	...	...	...	...	...	...
Uzbekistan	IMP	G	2697	2662	3392	3666	4380	4848	7076	9023	8386	9953
Ouzbékistan	EXP	G	2817	3189	4280	4749	5617	8029	10369	10735	11587	13254
	BAL		120	527	888	1083	1237	3181	3293	1712	3201	3301
Europe	IMP		57259	93328	122830	153845	207907	292755	396098	244745	329137	439040
Europe	EXP		125463	167458	229083	292772	360406	426842	568440	364025	475898	627480
	BAL		68205	74130	106253	138927	152499	134087	172342	119280	146761	188440
Belarus	IMP	G	8646	11558	16491	16708	22351	28693	39381	28569	34884	45636
Bélarus	EXP	G	7326	9946	13774	15979	19734	24275	32571	21304	25284	40409
	BAL		-1320	-1612	-2717	-729	-2618	-4418	-6811	-7265	-9601	-5227

Total imports and exports by regions and countries or areas (Table A)

Imports CIF, exports FOB and balance: million U.S. dollars *[cont.]*

Importations et exportations totales par régions et pays ou zones (Tableau A)

Importations CIF, exportations FOB et balance : en millions de dollars E.-U. *[suite]*

Country or Area - Pays ou Zone	IMP EXP BAL	G/S	2000	2003	2004	2005	2006	2007	2008	2009	2010	2011
Republic of Moldova	IMP	G	776	1403	1773	2293	2710	3690	4081	3278	3855	5192
République de Moldova	EXP	G	472	789	980	1091	1060	1340	1335	1283	1542	2222
	BAL		-305	-614	-793	-1202	-1650	-2350	-2746	-1995	-2314	-2970
Russian Federation	IMP	G	33880	57347	75569	98708	137807	199754	267101	167411	229655	305605
Fédération de Russie	EXP	G	103093	133656	181663	241473	301244	351930	467581	301656	397668	516481
	BAL		69213	76309	106093	142766	163437	152176	200480	134245	168013	210877
Ukraine	IMP	G	13956	23020	28997	36136	45039	60618	85535	45487	60742	82608
Ukraine	EXP	G	14573	23067	32666	34228	38368	49296	66954	39782	51405	68368
	BAL		617	47	3669	-1908	-6671	-11322	-18581	-5705	-9337	-14240
Northern Africa	IMP		**46953**	**52760**	**67990**	**80214**	**86800**	**112469**	**164473**	**146452**	**161412**	**184598**
Afrique du nord	EXP		**49876**	**60740**	**79004**	**109622**	**131233**	**153521**	**207537**	**134078**	**164232**	**200630**
	BAL		**2923**	**7980**	**11014**	**29408**	**44433**	**41051**	**43064**	**-12374**	**2820**	**16032**
Algeria	IMP	S	9169	12392	18166	20356	20985	27525	39578	39333	40228	46430
Algérie	EXP	S	22030	23206	31300	46000	52760	59761	79587	45240	57786	73320
	BAL		12861	10814	13133	25644	31775	32236	40010	5907	17558	26890
Egypt[6,7]	IMP	G	13963	10878	12831	19816	20722	27063	48775	44946	52923	58903
Egypte[6,7]	EXP	G	4675	6163	7683	10652	13694	16200	26246	23062	26438	30528
	BAL		-9288	-4715	-5149	-9163	-7028	-10863	-22528	-21884	-26485	-28376
Libya	IMP	G	3703	4312	6333	6058	6053	6753	9116	10037	10506	...
Libye	EXP	G	10137	14557	20403	31278	40333	47048	62031	37265	46016	...
	BAL		6434	10245	14069	25220	34280	40295	52915	27228	35510	...
Morocco	IMP	S	11534	14250	17822	20790	23980	32010	42366	32881	35524	44135
Maroc	EXP	S	7175	8778	9925	11190	12744	15340	20345	14054	17559	21218
	BAL		-4359	-5472	-7897	-9601	-11236	-16670	-22021	-18827	-17965	-22917
Tunisia	IMP	G	8567	10910	12818	13177	15043	19101	24622	19241	22218	23958
Tunisie	EXP	G	5850	8027	9685	10494	11694	15163	19319	14449	16427	17847
	BAL		-2717	-2883	-3133	-2683	-3349	-3938	-5303	-4791	-5791	-6111
Sub-Saharan Africa	IMP		**78693**	**105025**	**135405**	**165901**	**197707**	**244997**	**300662**	**251578**	**282894**	**331591**
Afrique subsaharienne	EXP		**93240**	**112815**	**150244**	**203289**	**232645**	**277375**	**362176**	**254873**	**328976**	**432433**
	BAL		**14547**	**7790**	**14839**	**37388**	**34937**	**32378**	**61514**	**3295**	**46082**	**100842**
Angola[3]	IMP	S	3040	5480	5832	8353	8778	13661	20982	22660	16574	...
Angola[3]	EXP	S	7703	9237	12975	23670	31084	43452	72179	40080	46492	65901
	BAL		4663	3757	7143	15317	22306	29791	51197	17420	29918	...
Benin	IMP	S	567	898	896	1018	1228	2037	2290	2110	2354	...
Bénin	EXP	S	392	541	564	574	741	1052	1285	1109	1240	...
	BAL		-174	-357	-332	-445	-487	-984	-1005	-1001	-1113	...
Botswana	IMP	G	2079	2467	3237	3172	3076	4077	5232	4771	5672	...
Botswana	EXP	G	2661	2809	3516	4455	4509	5170	5077	3514	4724	...
	BAL		581	342	279	1283	1434	1093	-155	-1257	-948	...
Burkina Faso	IMP	G	608	932	1273	1255	1323	1685	2008	1882	2157	...
Burkina Faso	EXP	G	213	320	480	467	588	623	693	893	1203	...
	BAL		-395	-612	-793	-788	-735	-1062	-1315	-989	-954	...
Burundi	IMP	S	148	157	176	267	431	319	402	402	509	752
Burundi	EXP	S	50	38	47	56	58	62	54	62	100	122
	BAL		-98	-119	-129	-211	-372	-257	-348	-340	-409	-630
Cameroon	IMP	S	1483	2176	2411	2725	3161	4218	5376	4322	4847	...
Cameroun	EXP	S	1823	2297	2481	2849	3587	3622	4279	3391	3896	...
	BAL		341	122	70	123	427	-596	-1097	-931	-952	...

Total imports and exports by regions and countries or areas (Table A)

Imports CIF, exports FOB and balance: million U.S. dollars *[cont.]*

Importations et exportations totales par régions et pays ou zones (Tableau A)

Importations CIF, exportations FOB et balance : en millions de dollars E.-U. *[suite]*

Country or Area - Pays ou Zone	IMP EXP BAL	G/S	2000	2003	2004	2005	2006	2007	2008	2009	2010	2011
Cape Verde	IMP	G	237	352	432	438	543	753	819	709	743	...
Cap-Vert	EXP	G	11	13	15	18	21	19	32	35	45	...
	BAL		-227	-339	-417	-420	-522	-734	-788	-674	-698	...
Cent. Afr. Rep.	IMP	S	118	119	152	175	203	251	298	300	341	...
Rép. centrafricaine	EXP	S	163	128	134	127	158	181	150	121	139	...
	BAL		45	9	-18	-48	-44	-70	-149	-179	-202	...
Chad	IMP	S	483	788	953	954	1346	1794	1906	2289	2507	...
Tchad	EXP	S	236	599	2192	3095	3342	3653	4345	2636	3411	...
	BAL		-248	-189	1239	2141	1995	1859	2439	347	903	...
Comoros	IMP	S	43	70	86	98	116	139	174	171	190	...
Comores	EXP	S	14	27	19	12	10	14	9	16	18	...
	BAL		-29	-43	-67	-86	-106	-125	-165	-155	-172	...
Congo	IMP	S	480	856	999	1344	2072	2605	3145	2984	2990	...
Congo	EXP	S	2482	2686	3435	4733	6092	5649	8288	6123	8192	...
	BAL		2003	1830	2437	3389	4020	3045	5144	3139	5202	...
Cote d'Ivoire	IMP	S	2485	3285	4724	5860	5825	6694	7863	6973	7844	...
Côte d'Ivoire	EXP	S	3611	5803	6955	7693	8477	8692	10301	10518	10532	...
	BAL		1127	2518	2231	1834	2652	1998	2438	3545	2688	...
Dem. Rep. of the Congo	IMP	S	697	1495	2051	2690	2892	3400	4300	3800	4500	...
Rép. dém. du Congo	EXP	S	824	1378	1917	2403	2705	3100	4400	3500	5400	...
	BAL		126	-117	-134	-288	-187	-300	100	-300	900	...
Djibouti	IMP	G	...	238	261	277	336	473	574	451	420	...
Djibouti	EXP	G	...	37	38	40	55	58	69	77	100	...
	BAL		...	-201	-223	-238	-281	-415	-505	-373	-320	...
Equatorial Guinea	IMP	G	451	909	1089	1310	2023	2369	3933	5205	5680	...
Guinée équatoriale	EXP	G	1097	2803	4588	7062	8218	10205	15995	9108	9964	...
	BAL		646	1895	3498	5753	6195	7836	12062	3903	4285	...
Ethiopia	IMP	G	1261	2686	2874	4095	5207	5805	8268	7644	...	...
Ethiopie	EXP	G	486	496	678	903	1043	1279	1606	1635	...	...
	BAL		-775	-2190	-2195	-3191	-4164	-4526	-6663	-6009	...	...
Gabon	IMP	S	996	1206	1344	1472	1726	2155	2607	2199	2492	...
Gabon	EXP	S	2605	3063	3719	5068	5454	6302	9566	5499	8374	...
	BAL		1610	1857	2375	3596	3728	4147	6959	3299	5882	...
Gambia	IMP	G	187	156	229	260	259	323	324	304	301	...
Gambie	EXP	G	15	8	10	8	11	13	14	15	15	...
	BAL		-172	-148	-219	-252	-248	-310	-310	-289	-286	...
Ghana	IMP	G	2974	3208	4072	5344	6748	8057	10243	8038	11038	...
Ghana	EXP	G	1317	...	...	2801	3725	4322	5625	...	...	...
	BAL		-1657	...	...	-2543	-3023	-3735	-4618	...	...	...
Guinea	IMP	S	612	640	780	820	956	1218	1366	1060	1100	...
Guinée	EXP	S	666	609	744	853	1033	1203	1342	1050	1450	...
	BAL		54	-31	-36	33	77	-15	-24	-10	350	...
Guinea-Bissau	IMP	G	59	66	96	119	111	111	159	...	...	...
Guinée-Bissau	EXP	G	62	65	75	90	74	106	131	119	118	...
	BAL		4	-1	-21	-29	-37	-5	-28	...	...	...
Kenya	IMP	G	3105	3725	4553	6149	7311	8989	11074	10207	12076	...
Kenya	EXP	G	1734	2411	2684	3293	3437	4080	4972	4463	5145	...
	BAL		-1372	-1314	-1869	-2856	-3874	-4910	-6102	-5743	-6931	...

Total imports and exports by regions and countries or areas (Table A)

Imports CIF, exports FOB and balance: million U.S. dollars *[cont.]*

Importations et exportations totales par régions et pays ou zones (Tableau A)

Importations CIF, exportations FOB et balance : en millions de dollars E.-U. *[suite]*

Country or Area - Pays ou Zone	IMP EXP BAL	G/S	2000	2003	2004	2005	2006	2007	2008	2009	2010	2011
Lesotho	IMP	G	809	1129	1450	1410	1496	1741	1995	1973	2206	...
Lesotho	EXP	G	221	481	714	650	689	770	883	723	801	...
	BAL		-589	-649	-736	-760	-807	-971	-1113	-1250	-1404	...
Liberia	IMP	S	...	170	337	310	467	499	813	552	650	...
Libéria	EXP	S	...	109	104	131	158	200	242	150	200	...
	BAL		...	-61	-233	-179	-309	-299	-571	-402	-450	...
Madagascar	IMP	S	999	1311	1616	1685	1810	2671	3800	3197	2507	...
Madagascar	EXP	S	828	863	946	835	993	1262	1304	1050	1087	...
	BAL		-171	-449	-670	-850	-817	-1408	-2496	-2147	-1420	...
Malawi	IMP	G	533	785	932	1163	1206	1380	1700	2096	...	...
Malawi	EXP	G	379	520	483	508	541	709	860	1080	1130	...
	BAL		-153	-265	-449	-655	-665	-671	-840	-1015	...	...
Mali	IMP	S	807	1270	1365	1544	1819	2183	3343	2646	2855	...
Mali	EXP	S	552	926	979	1092	1559	1567	2082	2055	2248	...
	BAL		-255	-345	-386	-453	-260	-616	-1261	-590	-607	...
Mauritania	IMP	S	354	387	1346	1344	1089	1428	1669	1337	1708	...
Mauritanie	EXP	S	343	321	435	556	1268	1356	1651	1407	1799	...
	BAL		-11	-66	-911	-787	180	-72	-18	70	91	...
Mauritius	IMP	G	2091	2364	2771	3157	3627	3894	4655	3734	4387	5159
Maurice	EXP	G	1551	1899	1993	2138	2329	2238	2386	1939	2262	2647
	BAL		-540	-465	-778	-1018	-1298	-1656	-2269	-1795	-2125	-2512
Mozambique	IMP	S	1158	1753	2035	2408	2869	3050	4008	3764	4550	...
Mozambique	EXP	S	364	1045	1504	1783	2381	2412	2653	2147	3200	...
	BAL		-794	-708	-531	-625	-488	-638	-1355	-1617	-1350	...
Namibia	IMP	G	1539	1999	2408	2567	2868	3528	4314	5066	5372	...
Namibie	EXP	G	1317	1269	1833	2067	2638	2924	3113	3379	4096	...
	BAL		-222	-730	-575	-500	-230	-604	-1201	-1687	-1276	...
Niger	IMP	S	390	630	757	934	955	1163	1659	1926	2212	...
Niger	EXP	S	284	353	439	490	507	664	902	888	907	...
	BAL		-107	-277	-318	-444	-448	-499	-757	-1038	-1305	...
Nigeria	IMP	G	8721	10853	14164	21314	26760	37576	42378	33906	37000	...
Nigéria	EXP	G	20975	19887	31148	55145	57444	65133	80615	53000	79000	...
	BAL		12254	9034	16984	33831	30684	27557	38237	19094	42000	...
Rwanda	IMP	G	211	258	285	432	547	736	1131	1227	1401	...
Rwanda	EXP	G	52	63	99	125	147	176	267	193	255	...
	BAL		-159	-195	-187	-307	-400	-559	-865	-1035	-1146	...
Sao Tome and Principe	IMP	S	30	41	41	50	71	79	114	103	125	...
Sao Tomé-et-Principe	EXP	S	3	7	5	7	8	7	11	8	11	...
	BAL		-27	-34	-36	-43	-63	-72	-103	-95	-114	...
Senegal	IMP	G	1513	2394	2853	3190	3444	4271	5706	4549	4442	5390
Sénégal	EXP	G	921	1263	1510	1576	1556	1652	2007	1906	2059	2432
	BAL		-592	-1131	-1344	-1614	-1888	-2618	-3699	-2643	-2383	-2958
Seychelles	IMP	G	343	412	497	675	758	861	1106	821	989	...
Seychelles	EXP	G	193	273	291	340	380	356	437	402	400	...
	BAL		-150	-139	-206	-335	-378	-506	-668	-419	-588	...
Sierra Leone	IMP	S	149	305	286	345	389	445	535	518	...	...
Sierra Leone	EXP	S	13	92	139	159	231	245	216	232	...	...
	BAL		-136	-214	-147	-186	-158	-199	-319	-285	...	...

Total imports and exports by regions and countries or areas (Table A)

Imports CIF, exports FOB and balance: million U.S. dollars *[cont.]*

Importations et exportations totales par régions et pays ou zones (Tableau A)

Importations CIF, exportations FOB et balance : en millions de dollars E.-U. *[suite]*

Country or Area - Pays ou Zone	IMP EXP BAL	G/S	2000	2003	2004	2005	2006	2007	2008	2009	2010	2011
South Africa[3,8]	IMP	G	26795	34204	47421	54848	67644	79873	94901	64439	80131	99726
Afrique du Sud[3,8]	EXP	G	29987	36503	46148	51640	58197	69787	84488	62627	81822	96922
	BAL		3192	2299	-1272	-3208	-9447	-10086	-10413	-1812	1691	-2804
Sudan	IMP	G	1553	2882	4075	6757	8074	8775	9352	9691	9960	...
Soudan	EXP	G	1807	2542	3778	4824	5657	8879	11671	7834	10500	...
	BAL		254	-340	-297	-1933	-2417	104	2319	-1857	540	...
Swaziland	IMP	G	1039	1534	1937	1897	1918	1853	...	1617	1710	...
Swaziland	EXP	G	903	1656	1962	1761	1779	1885	...	1479	1557	...
	BAL		-137	122	25	-136	-139	33	...	-138	-153	...
Togo	IMP	S	562	775	883	1054	1088	1243	1499	1409	1502	...
Togo	EXP	S	362	600	601	659	631	700	901	801	850	...
	BAL		-200	-176	-281	-396	-457	-543	-598	-607	-652	...
Uganda	IMP	G	1512	1375	1731	2049	2555	3497	4559	3787	4264	4590
Ouganda	EXP	G	469	564	758	1017	1188	2003	2717	2327	2164	2410
	BAL		-1043	-811	-974	-1033	-1367	-1494	-1841	-1461	-2100	-2180
United Rep. of Tanzania	IMP	G	1523	2125	2515	2661	4254	5337	7081	6296	7714	10801
Rép.-Unie de Tanzanie	EXP	G	663	1129	1336	1479	1655	2022	2674	2367	3524	4355
	BAL		-860	-996	-1179	-1182	-2598	-3315	-4407	-3929	-4190	-6446
Zambia	IMP	S	997	1576	2018	2567	2931	4014	5023	3791	...	...
Zambie	EXP	S	681	980	1576	1780	3828	4641	5186	4389	7207	...
	BAL		-316	-595	-442	-786	896	628	163	599	...	...
Zimbabwe	IMP	G	1861	1710	2204	2350	2300	2550	2950	2900	3700	...
Zimbabwe	EXP	G	1923	1670	1887	1850	2000	2400	2200	2269	2500	...
	BAL		62	-40	-317	-500	-300	-150	-750	-631	-1200	...
Latin America & The Caribbean	IMP		**376134**	**356535**	**434697**	**515039**	**614231**	**733210**	**896644**	**674628**	**864793**	**1023715**
Amérique latine et les Caraïbes	EXP		**354602**	**374871**	**461230**	**559147**	**668680**	**757873**	**886929**	**683163**	**875632**	**1077160**
	BAL		**-21532**	**18335**	**26533**	**44109**	**54449**	**24664**	**-9715**	**8535**	**10839**	**53445**
The Caribbean	IMP		**26914**	**27725**	**29935**	**37615**	**44022**	**50407**	**61307**	**48323**	**50635**	**56531**
Les Caraïbes	EXP		**11412**	**11676**	**13475**	**17534**	**23739**	**24782**	**30511**	**22384**	**32103**	**50135**
	BAL		**-15503**	**-16048**	**-16460**	**-20081**	**-20283**	**-25626**	**-30796**	**-25939**	**-18532**	**-6397**
Anguilla	IMP	S	99	80	105	133	143	248	272	169	157	...
Anguilla	EXP	S	4	4	6	7	13	9	11	23	12	...
	BAL		-95	-76	-100	-126	-130	-239	-260	-146	-145	...
Antigua and Barbuda	IMP	G	338	391	454	550	623	727	742	650	520	...
Antigua-et-Barbuda	EXP	G	23	46	57	124	153	174	198	181	48	...
	BAL		-316	-346	-397	-426	-470	-553	-544	-469	-472	...
Aruba	IMP	S	835	848	875	1028	1041	1114	1134	1090	1003	...
Aruba	EXP	S	173	83	80	102	109	98	100	136	124	...
	BAL		-662	-764	-796	-927	-932	-1016	-1034	-955	-878	...
Bahamas[9]	IMP	G	2074	1762	1905	2230	2401	2449	2354	2699	2863	...
Bahamas[9]	EXP	G	576	425	477	562	674	485	560	585	620	...
	BAL		-1498	-1337	-1428	-1668	-1726	-1965	-1794	-2114	-2243	...
Barbados	IMP	G	1156	1195	1413	1604	1586	1709	1879	1471	1562	1805
Barbade	EXP	G	272	250	278	359	385	419	445	369	429	465
	BAL		-884	-946	-1135	-1245	-1201	-1291	-1433	-1102	-1133	-1340
Cayman Islands	IMP	G	693	666	877	1191	1042	1032	1055	883	826	...
Îles Caïmanes	EXP	G	4	24	25	60	26	27	17	19	13	...
	BAL		-689	-642	-852	-1130	-1017	-1005	-1039	-864	-813	...

Total imports and exports by regions and countries or areas (Table A)

Imports CIF, exports FOB and balance: million U.S. dollars *[cont.]*

Importations et exportations totales par régions et pays ou zones (Tableau A)

Importations CIF, exportations FOB et balance : en millions de dollars E.-U. *[suite]*

Country or Area - Pays ou Zone	IMP EXP BAL	G/S	2000	2003	2004	2005	2006	2007	2008	2009	2010	2011
Cuba	IMP	S	3363	4613	5562	8130	10174	10889	14249	...	...	...
Cuba	EXP	S	1219	1672	2188	2159	2980	3998	3680	...	...	...
	BAL		-2144	-2941	-3374	-5972	-7194	-6892	-10570	...	...	...
Dominica	IMP	S	148	128	145	165	167	196	247	233	224	...
Dominique	EXP	S	54	41	41	41	42	38	40	36	35	...
	BAL		-95	-87	-104	-124	-124	-158	-207	-197	-189	...
Dominican Republic[3,10]	IMP	G	6416	5266	5368	7207	8745	11289	14020	9946	12885	14522
République dominicaine[3,10]	EXP	G	966	1041	1251	1398	1933	2635	2394	1690	2536	3651
	BAL		-5450	-4225	-4117	-5809	-6812	-8654	-11626	-8256	-10349	-10871
Grenada	IMP	S	246	254	253	334	331	365	377	293	317	...
Grenade	EXP	S	78	42	32	28	25	33	30	29	24	...
	BAL		-168	-213	-220	-306	-305	-332	-347	-264	-293	...
Haiti	IMP	G	1040	1187	1317	1449	1880	1681	2310	2121	3147	...
Haïti	EXP	G	313	346	394	470	480	522	475	576	579	...
	BAL		-727	-841	-923	-979	-1401	-1159	-1835	-1546	-2568	...
Jamaica	IMP	G	3302	3633	3772	4458	5314	6394	7734	4860	5201	6489
Jamaïque	EXP	G	1295	1177	1390	1499	1874	2070	2542	1319	1331	1603
	BAL		-2007	-2457	-2382	-2959	-3440	-4324	-5192	-3540	-3870	-4886
Montserrat	IMP	S	...	28	29	30	30	30	38	30	30	...
Montserrat	EXP	S	...	2	4	1	1	3	4	3	1	...
	BAL		...	-27	-24	-28	-29	-27	-34	-26	-29	...
Neth. Antilles	IMP	S	2862	2606	1723	1950	2209	2549	3079	2607	2800	...
Antilles néer.	EXP	S	2009	1161	521	608	695	676	1088	810	800	...
	BAL		-853	-1445	-1202	-1342	-1515	-1872	-1991	-1797	-2000	...
Saint Kitts-Nevis	IMP	S	196	200	182	210	250	272	325	302	228	...
Saint-Kitts-et-Nevis	EXP	S	29	51	37	30	35	32	43	43	45	...
	BAL		-167	-149	-145	-180	-214	-241	-282	-260	-183	...
Saint Lucia	IMP	S	355	403	437	479	592	635	657	539	601	...
Sainte-Lucie	EXP	S	47	85	125	89	98	107	145	163	228	...
	BAL		-308	-318	-312	-390	-494	-528	-512	-376	-373	...
Saint Vincent-Grenadines	IMP	S	148	200	225	241	269	327	373	334	345	...
St.Vincent-Grenadines	EXP	S	50	38	37	40	38	48	52	50	44	...
	BAL		-97	-162	-189	-201	-231	-279	-321	-284	-301	...
Trinidad and Tobago	IMP	S	3308	3892	4858	5694	6484	7662	9596	6953	6390	...
Trinité-et-Tobago	EXP	S	4274	5177	6518	9941	14159	13393	18663	9140	11156	...
	BAL		966	1285	1660	4247	7675	5731	9067	2187	4766	...
Turks and Caicos Islands	IMP	G	149	171	220	304	498	581	591	375	302	...
Îles Turques et Caïques	EXP	G	9	10	12	15	18	16	25	21	16	...
	BAL		-140	-161	-208	-289	-480	-564	-566	-355	-286	...
Latin America	IMP		**349220**	**328811**	**404761**	**477423**	**570209**	**682802**	**835336**	**626305**	**814158**	**967184**
Amérique latine	EXP		**343191**	**363194**	**447755**	**541613**	**644941**	**733092**	**856418**	**660779**	**843529**	**1027025**
	BAL		**-6030**	**34384**	**42993**	**64190**	**74732**	**50290**	**21081**	**34474**	**29371**	**59841**
Argentina	IMP	S	25154	13833	22445	28693	34158	44707	57413	39105	56443	73923
Argentine	EXP	S	26341	29566	34576	40351	46568	55779	70588	56065	68499	84269
	BAL		1187	15732	12131	11658	12410	11072	13174	16961	12056	10347
Belize	IMP	G	524	552	514	593	676	684	837	668	699	...
Belize	EXP	G	218	205	213	208	266	254	271	250	...	...
	BAL		-306	-347	-301	-385	-410	-430	-566	-418	...	...

Total imports and exports by regions and countries or areas (Table A)
Imports CIF, exports FOB and balance: million U.S. dollars *[cont.]*

Importations et exportations totales par régions et pays ou zones (Tableau A)
Importations CIF, exportations FOB et balance : en millions de dollars E.-U. *[suite]*

Country or Area - Pays ou Zone	IMP EXP BAL	G/S	2000	2003	2004	2005	2006	2007	2008	2009	2010	2011
Bolivia (Plurinational State of)	IMP	G	1830	1616	1844	2341	2814	3457	5081	4434	5182	7551
Bolivie (État plurinational de)	EXP	G	1230	1598	2146	2791	3875	4458	7058	4918	6179	8107
	BAL		-600	-18	302	450	1060	1001	1977	483	998	555
Brazil	IMP	G	58643	50881	66433	77628	95838	126645	182377	133673	191464	214131
Brésil	EXP	G	55119	73203	96678	118529	137807	160649	197942	152995	201915	258914
	BAL		-3524	22322	30244	40901	41969	34004	15565	19322	10451	44783
Chile	IMP	S	18507	19322	24794	32735	38406	47164	61903	42571	58956	73545
Chili	EXP	S	19210	21664	32520	41267	58680	67666	66456	54004	71028	80027
	BAL		703	2342	7727	8532	20274	20502	4553	11434	12073	6482
Colombia	IMP	G	11539	13889	16746	21204	26046	33164	39320	32898	40683	54675
Colombie	EXP	G	13043	13080	16224	21146	24388	29786	38265	32784	39710	56507
	BAL		1505	-809	-522	-59	-1658	-3378	-1055	-114	-973	1832
Costa Rica	IMP	S	6389	7663	8268	9812	11520	12952	15366	11460	13557	16218
Costa Rica	EXP	S	5850	6102	6301	7026	8216	9340	9575	8711	9343	10238
	BAL		-539	-1561	-1967	-2786	-3305	-3613	-5791	-2750	-4214	-5980
Ecuador	IMP	G	3721	6703	8226	10287	12114	13565	18852	15090	20591	24286
Equateur	EXP	G	4927	6223	7753	10100	12728	13852	18818	13863	17415	22345
	BAL		1206	-480	-473	-187	615	287	-34	-1227	-3176	-1941
El Salvador	IMP	S	4948	5754	6329	6834	7628	8677	9754	7255	8548	10118
El Salvador	EXP	S	2941	3128	3305	3387	3513	3977	4579	3797	4472	4979
	BAL		-2006	-2626	-3024	-3448	-4115	-4700	-5175	-3457	-4077	-5139
Guatemala	IMP	S	5171	6722	7812	8810	10157	11861	12835	10066	12051	14518
Guatemala	EXP	S	2711	2632	2939	3477	3665	4468	5412	3835	5907	7201
	BAL		-2460	-4090	-4873	-5333	-6492	-7393	-7423	-6232	-6145	-7317
Guyana	IMP	S	582	576	652	788	889	1059	1312	1161	1397	1763
Guyana	EXP	S	502	513	593	553	588	679	795	763	880	1116
	BAL		-80	-63	-59	-235	-301	-381	-518	-398	-517	-647
Honduras	IMP	S	2980	3448	4212	4853	5695	6762	8831	6133	7079	8953
Honduras	EXP	S	1297	1359	1640	1892	2054	2120	2883	2304	2712	3892
	BAL		-1682	-2089	-2572	-2960	-3641	-4642	-5948	-3829	-4367	-5060
Mexico[3,11]	IMP	G	174500	170490	197347	221414	256130	283264	310561	234385	301482	350856
Mexique[3,11]	EXP	G	166367	165396	189084	213891	250441	272055	291827	229683	298138	349569
	BAL		-8133	-5094	-8263	-7523	-5689	-11209	-18734	-4702	-3344	-1287
Nicaragua	IMP	G	1805	1879	2212	2595	3000	3579	4300	3438	4229	5180
Nicaragua	EXP	G	643	605	756	858	1027	1194	1473	1393	1845	2294
	BAL		-1163	-1275	-1457	-1737	-1973	-2385	-2827	-2045	-2384	-2886
Panama[12]	IMP	S	3379	3086	3594	4180	4831	6872	9050	7801	9145	...
Panama[12]	EXP	S	859	864	944	1018	1093	1164	1247	948	832	...
	BAL		-2519	-2222	-2651	-3162	-3738	-5709	-7803	-6853	-8313	...
Paraguay	IMP	S	2193	2228	3097	3790	6090	5859	9033	6940	10040	12317
Paraguay	EXP	S	869	1242	1627	1688	1906	2817	4463	3167	4534	5531
	BAL		-1324	-986	-1470	-2102	-4184	-3042	-4570	-3773	-5507	-6786
Peru[3]	IMP	S	7407	8244	9812	12084	14897	19580	28373	21006	28818	37112
Pérou[3]	EXP	S	6955	9091	12809	17368	23830	27882	31529	26885	35565	45321
	BAL		-452	846	2997	5284	8933	8301	3157	5879	6747	8209
Suriname	IMP	G	243	444	591	829	894	1111	1521	1356	1310	1610
Suriname	EXP	G	395	519	713	789	1123	1287	1668	1393	1851	2344
	BAL		152	75	122	-40	229	177	146	37	541	733

Total imports and exports by regions and countries or areas (Table A)

Imports CIF, exports FOB and balance: million U.S. dollars *[cont.]*

Importations et exportations totales par régions et pays ou zones (Tableau A)

Importations CIF, exportations FOB et balance : en millions de dollars E.-U. *[suite]*

Country or Area - Pays ou Zone	IMP EXP BAL	G/S	2000	2003	2004	2005	2006	2007	2008	2009	2010	2011
Uruguay	IMP	G	3466	2190	3114	3879	4757	5667	8943	6209	8619	10623
Uruguay	EXP	G	2295	2206	2931	3405	3953	4490	6421	5417	6707	7997
	BAL		-1171	16	-183	-474	-804	-1178	-2523	-792	-1912	-2626
Venezuela (Bolivarian Rep. of)	IMP	G	16213	9256	16679	24027	33615	46097	49602	40597	33815	38346
Venezuela (Rép. bolivarienne du)	EXP	G	31413	23990	33994	51859	59208	69165	95138	57595	65786	...
	BAL		15200	14734	17315	27832	25593	23068	45536	16998	31971	...
Eastern Asia	IMP		**743016**	**955806**	**1231411**	**1410160**	**1646432**	**1909526**	**2206817**	**1857507**	**2516769**	**3047875**
Asie Orientale	EXP		**779060**	**1003758**	**1293254**	**1538470**	**1840228**	**2185632**	**2473784**	**2089331**	**2714089**	**3199323**
	BAL		**36043**	**47952**	**61843**	**128311**	**193795**	**276106**	**266968**	**231824**	**197320**	**151449**
China	IMP	S	225024	412760	561229	660206	791797	956233	1131620	1004170	1396200	1742070
Chine	EXP	S	249203	438228	593326	761953	969380	1217815	1428660	1201790	1578270	1899180
	BAL		24179	25468	32097	101747	177583	261582	297040	197620	182070	157110
China, Hong Kong SAR	IMP	G	212805	231896	271074	299533	334681	367864	388505	347311	433111	483633
Chine, Hong Kong RAS	EXP	G	201860	223762	259260	289337	316816	344629	362675	318510	390143	428732
	BAL		-10945	-8134	-11814	-10196	-17865	-23235	-25830	-28801	-42968	-54901
China, Macao SAR	IMP	G	2255	2755	3478	3913	4565	5366	5365	4622	5513	7769
Chine, Macao RAS	EXP	G	2539	2581	2812	2476	2557	2543	1997	961	870	869
	BAL		284	-174	-666	-1438	-2008	-2823	-3368	-3661	-4643	-6899
Korea, Republic of	IMP	G	160481	178827	224463	261238	309383	356648	435275	322843	425212	524366
Corée, République de	EXP	G	172267	193817	253845	284419	325465	371554	422007	361614	466384	556602
	BAL		11786	14990	29382	23181	16082	14906	-13268	38771	41172	32236
Mongolia	IMP	G	615	801	1021	1184	1486	2117	3616	2131	3278	6527
Mongolie	EXP	G	536	616	870	1065	1543	1889	2539	1903	2899	4780
	BAL		-79	-185	-151	-119	57	-228	-1077	-229	-379	-1747
Southern Asia	IMP		94680	131184	175429	**235818**	**280684**	**342932**	**465570**	**379013**	**500772**	**632883**
Asie Méridionale	EXP		90988	116113	145525	**187186**	**233715**	**276988**	**351197**	**283324**	**367465**	**492702**
	BAL		-3693	-15071	-29904	**-48632**	**-46968**	**-65944**	**-114372**	**-95689**	**-133307**	**-140181**
Afghanistan	IMP	G	1176	2101	2177	...	...	...	...	...	...	...
Afghanistan	EXP	G	137	144	314	...	...	...	...	...	...	...
	BAL		-1039	-1957	-1863	...	...	...	...	...	...	...
Bangladesh	IMP	G	8358	9516	12611	12881	14964	17263	22473	20631	26071	...
Bangladesh	EXP	G	4787	5263	6615	7233	9103	10233	11777	12443	14195	...
	BAL		-3572	-4253	-5996	-5648	-5861	-7030	-10695	-8188	-11877	...
Bhutan	IMP	G	175	275	406	515	530	686	730	786	925	...
Bhoutan	EXP	G	103	163	222	320	488	658	587	578	631	...
	BAL		-72	-112	-184	-195	-42	-27	-143	-208	-294	...
India[13]	IMP	G	51563	72559	99757	142865	178485	229349	321026	257200	350192	447385
Inde[13]	EXP	G	42378	58964	76647	99618	121812	150160	194816	164912	219656	298010
	BAL		-9185	-13595	-23110	-43247	-56674	-79189	-126210	-92288	-130536	-149376
Iran (Islamic Rep. of)[14,15]	IMP	S	14347	24798	31976	40041	40772	44942	57401	50469	62670	...
Iran (Rép. islamique d')[14,15]	EXP	S	28345	33750	41697	56252	77012	88733	113668	78830	100900	...
	BAL		13998	8952	9721	16211	36240	43791	56267	28361	38230	...
Maldives	IMP	G	389	471	642	745	927	1096	1388	967	1091	...
Maldives	EXP	G	76	113	122	103	135	108	126	76	74	...
	BAL		-313	-358	-519	-641	-791	-989	-1262	-891	-1017	...
Nepal	IMP	G	1526	1755	1939	2282	2488	3139	3562	4398	5501	...
Népal	EXP	G	700	662	772	863	838	870	937	823	951	...
	BAL		-826	-1093	-1167	-1419	-1650	-2269	-2625	-3574	-4550	...

Total imports and exports by regions and countries or areas (Table A)

Imports CIF, exports FOB and balance: million U.S. dollars *[cont.]*

Importations et exportations totales par régions et pays ou zones (Tableau A)

Importations CIF, exportations FOB et balance : en millions de dollars E.-U. *[suite]*

Country or Area - Pays ou Zone	IMP EXP BAL	G/S	2000	2003	2004	2005	2006	2007	2008	2009	2010	2011
Pakistan	IMP	G	10864	13038	17949	25356	29828	32590	42326	31648	37783	...
Pakistan	EXP	G	9028	11930	13379	16050	16932	17837	20323	17523	21409	...
	BAL		-1836	-1107	-4570	-9306	-12896	-14753	-22003	-14125	-16373	...
Sri Lanka	IMP	G	6281	6672	7973	8833	10259	11301	13953	10049	13512	...
Sri Lanka	EXP	G	5433	5125	5757	6347	6886	7740	8137	7085	8307	...
	BAL		-848	-1547	-2216	-2487	-3373	-3560	-5816	-2965	-5205	...
South-eastern Asia	IMP		379501	**398695**	**500673**	**600573**	**688631**	**776921**	**947451**	**728375**	**954968**	**1151791**
Asie du Sud-est	EXP		431651	**453754**	**568191**	**653858**	**770881**	**865370**	**998343**	**813601**	**1051660**	**1239486**
	BAL		52149	**55059**	**67518**	**53286**	**82250**	**88449**	**50891**	**85227**	**96692**	**87695**
Brunei Darussalam	IMP	S	1107	1327	1422	1447	1679	2101	2572	2449	2460	...
Brunéi Darussalam	EXP	S	3907	4423	5060	6242	7634	7693	10319	7200	8908	...
	BAL		2801	3096	3638	4794	5956	5592	7747	4751	6448	...
Cambodia	IMP	S	1424	2560	3193	3927	4749	5300	6508	5876	7500	...
Cambodge	EXP	S	1123	2118	2798	3200	3800	4400	4708	4302	5030	...
	BAL		-302	-442	-395	-727	-949	-900	-1800	-1574	-2470	...
Indonesia	IMP	S	43075	41568	55009	75725	80650	93101	127538	93786	135323	176355
Indonésie	EXP	S	65404	64109	70767	86995	103528	118014	139606	119646	158074	201472
	BAL		22329	22541	15758	11270	22878	24913	12068	25860	22751	25117
Lao P.Dem.R.	IMP	S	535	462	713	882	1060	1067	1405	1461	2060	...
Rép. dém. populaire lao	EXP	S	330	335	363	553	882	923	1085	1053	1746	...
	BAL		-205	-127	-349	-329	-177	-144	-320	-408	-314	...
Malaysia	IMP	G	81963	81948	105298	114410	131085	146767	164410	123693	164734	187592
Malaisie	EXP	G	98230	99369	125745	140870	160571	176028	209668	157483	198800	228262
	BAL		16266	17421	20446	26459	29486	29261	45258	33790	34067	40671
Myanmar	IMP	G	2401	2092	2196	1927	2564	3277	4299	4393	4807	9109
Myanmar	EXP	G	1647	2485	2380	3813	4585	6313	6950	6731	8749	9330
	BAL		-755	392	184	1887	2021	3036	2651	2338	3941	221
Philippines	IMP	G	36887	39502	42345	46963	54077	57708	60492	45743	58229	...
Philippines	EXP	G	39794	36231	39680	39879	47413	50270	49205	38308	51432	...
	BAL		2907	-3271	-2664	-7084	-6665	-7438	-11287	-7435	-6797	...
Singapore	IMP	G	134546	127935	163851	200050	238711	263155	319781	245785	310791	365770
Singapour	EXP	G	137806	144183	198633	229652	271809	299270	338176	269832	351867	409503
	BAL		3259	16248	34782	29602	33098	36115	18396	24048	41076	43733
Thailand	IMP	S	61923	75824	94410	118158	128654	141294	179168	134734	185121	228848
Thaïlande	EXP	S	68963	80324	96248	110178	130795	153858	175897	151910	195371	226402
	BAL		7039	4499	1838	-7980	2142	12563	-3270	17176	10250	-2446
Viet Nam	IMP	G	15638	25256	31969	36761	45015	62682	80714	69949	83779	104041
Viet Nam	EXP	G	14447	20149	26485	32442	39826	48561	62685	57096	71658	94518
	BAL		-1191	-5107	-5484	-4319	-5188	-14121	-18029	-12853	-12121	-9523
Western Asia	IMP		**204345**	**255723**	**340513**	**410204**	**479804**	**605894**	**750082**	**600769**	**700376**	**816464**
Asie Occidentale	EXP		**261901**	**316405**	**422164**	**555013**	**659803**	**766522**	**1004954**	**710996**	**893104**	**1132258**
	BAL		**57556**	**60682**	**81651**	**144809**	**179998**	**160628**	**254872**	**110226**	**192728**	**315793**
Bahrain	IMP	G	4634	5657	7385	9393	10515	11488	10800	7300	9800	...
Bahreïn	EXP	G	6195	6632	7558	10242	12200	13634	17316	11874	15400	...
	BAL		1561	974	173	849	1685	2146	6516	4574	5600	...
Cyprus	IMP	G	3846	4288	5659	6282	6951	8687	10873	7882	8646	8722
Chypre	EXP	G	951	834	1081	1303	1153	1254	1755	1342	1507	1959
	BAL		-2895	-3455	-4577	-4979	-5798	-7433	-9118	-6540	-7139	-6763

Total imports and exports by regions and countries or areas (Table A)

Imports CIF, exports FOB and balance: million U.S. dollars *[cont.]*

Importations et exportations totales par régions et pays ou zones (Tableau A)

Importations CIF, exportations FOB et balance : en millions de dollars E.-U. *[suite]*

Country or Area - Pays ou Zone	IMP EXP BAL	G/ S	2000	2003	2004	2005	2006	2007	2008	2009	2010	2011
Israel[16]	IMP	S	37686	36303	42864	47142	50334	59039	67656	49278	61209	75472
Israël[16]	EXP	S	31404	31784	38618	42770	46789	54065	60825	47934	58392	64551
	BAL		-6282	-4519	-4245	-4371	-3544	-4973	-6831	-1344	-2817	-10921
Jordan	IMP	G	4597	5743	8128	10506	11447	13511	16764	14534	15085	18463
Jordanie	EXP	G	1899	3082	3922	4302	5175	5725	7788	6531	7023	7964
	BAL		-2698	-2662	-4206	-6204	-6272	-7786	-8976	-8002	-8062	-10499
Kuwait	IMP	S	7156	10992	12630	15534	17252	21388	24836	20340	21996	...
Koweït	EXP	S	19434	20678	28599	45189	56022	62871	87648	51979	66042	...
	BAL		12278	9685	15968	29655	38769	41483	62812	31638	44046	...
Lebanon	IMP	G	6230	7315	9609	9633	9647	12251	16754	16574	18460	...
Liban	EXP	G	715	1813	2199	2337	2814	3574	4454	4187	5021	...
	BAL		-5515	-5502	-7410	-7296	-6833	-8677	-12300	-12387	-13439	...
Occupied Palestinian Territory	IMP	S	2383	1800	2373	2668	2759	3141	3466	3593	...	4492
Territoire palestinien occupé	EXP	S	401	280	313	335	367	513	558	506	...	759
	BAL		-1982	-1521	-2061	-2332	-2392	-2628	-2908	-3087	...	-3733
Oman	IMP	G	5040	6572	8865	8827	10915	15978	22925	17865	19775	...
Oman	EXP	G	11319	11669	13341	18692	21585	24136	37719	28053	36601	...
	BAL		6279	5096	4476	9865	10670	8158	14795	10188	16827	...
Qatar	IMP	S	3252	4898	6005	10061	16440	23429	27900	24922	22000	...
Qatar	EXP	S	11594	13382	18684	25762	34052	42019	56593	41000	61500	...
	BAL		8342	8485	12680	15701	17611	18590	28693	16078	39500	...
Saudi Arabia	IMP	S	30197	36915	44744	59458	69800	90215	115133	95544	106865	111745
Arabie saoudite	EXP	S	77480	93245	125997	180736	211306	233300	313427	192296	251149	...
	BAL		47283	56331	81253	121278	141506	143086	198294	96752	144284	...
Syrian Arab Rep.	IMP	S	4055	5119	8411	10862	11488	14655	18150	15443	17562	...
République arabe syrienne	EXP	S	4674	5731	7485	9174	10919	11546	15304	10559	12304	...
	BAL		620	611	-926	-1688	-569	-3109	-2846	-4884	-5257	...
Turkey	IMP	S	54503	69340	97540	116774	139576	170063	201964	140928	185544	240834
Turquie	EXP	S	27775	47253	63167	73476	85535	107272	132027	102143	113883	134972
	BAL		-26728	-22087	-34373	-43298	-54041	-62791	-69937	-38785	-71661	-105862
United Arab Emirates	IMP	G	35009	52074	72082	84654	100057	132500	177000	150000	170000	...
Emirats arabes unis	EXP	G	49835	67135	90997	117287	145587	178630	239213	185000	235000	...
	BAL		14827	15061	18915	32633	45530	46130	62213	35000	65000	...
Yemen	IMP	S	2327	3680	3988	5401	6081	8513	10548	9206	9746	...
Yémen	EXP	S	3795	3732	4072	5604	6653	6299	7584	6256	8497	...
	BAL		1469	52	85	204	572	-2215	-2964	-2949	-1249	...
Oceania	IMP		**6945**	**9449**	**10258**	**11059**	**12508**	**14649**	**16913**	**15821**	**18636**	**21482**
Océanie	EXP		**5107**	**5755**	**6473**	**7255**	**8555**	**10003**	**10708**	**8793**	**10096**	**10492**
	BAL		**-1838**	**-3694**	**-3785**	**-3804**	**-3953**	**-4646**	**-6205**	**-7028**	**-8540**	**-10991**
American Samoa[17]	IMP	S	506	624	604	520	579	650	680	600	550	...
Samoa américaines[17]	EXP	S	346	460	446	374	439	450	570	470	480	...
	BAL		-160	-164	-158	-146	-141	-200	-110	-130	-70	...
Cook Islands	IMP	G	50	71	76	81	100	99	140	185	...	...
Iles Cook	EXP	G	9	9	7	5	3	5	4	3	...	...
	BAL		-41	-62	-69	-76	-96	-94	-136	-182	...	...
Fiji	IMP	G	857	1208	1444	1607	1804	1800	2264	1440	1800	...
Fidji	EXP	G	539	676	696	705	694	755	922	630	811	...
	BAL		-318	-531	-748	-903	-1110	-1046	-1342	-810	-990	...

Total imports and exports by regions and countries or areas (Table A)

Imports CIF, exports FOB and balance: million U.S. dollars *[cont.]*

Importations et exportations totales par régions et pays ou zones (Tableau A)

Importations CIF, exportations FOB et balance : en millions de dollars E.-U. *[suite]*

Country or Area - Pays ou Zone	IMP EXP BAL	G/S	2000	2003	2004	2005	2006	2007	2008	2009	2010	2011
French Polynesia	IMP	S	905	1585	1500	1723	1656	1863	2187	1732	1740	...
Polynésie française	EXP	S	200	156	199	217	235	197	273	167	175	...
	BAL		-705	-1429	-1301	-1506	-1420	-1667	-1914	-1565	-1565	...
Guam	IMP	G	...	...	...	...	501	688	649	635	698	708
Guam	EXP	G	...	43	53	52	53	91	105	51	46	43
	BAL		...	...	...	...	-448	-596	-544	-584	-652	-664
Kiribati	IMP	G	39	52	59	74	63	70	70	68	100	...
Kiribati	EXP	G	4	3	2	4	6	10	15	20	15	...
	BAL		-36	-49	-57	-70	-57	-60	-55	-48	-85	...
Marshall Islands	IMP	G	55	...	68	68	...	...	...	...	...	...
Iles Marshall	EXP	G	9	...	...	...	...	...	...	...	...	...
	BAL		-46	...	...	...	...	...	...	...	...	...
New Caledonia	IMP	S	922	1541	1636	1774	2117	2809	3233	2574	3313	...
Nouvelle-Calédonie	EXP	S	606	785	1033	1093	1352	2104	1300	1029	1272	...
	BAL		-317	-756	-603	-681	-766	-705	-1933	-1546	-2041	...
Niue	IMP	G	2	2	8	...	4	7	8	...	...	...
Nioué	EXP	G	0	0	0	0	1	3	0	...	...	...
	BAL		-2	-2	-8	...	-2	-4	-8	...	...	...
Palau	IMP	S	123	...	...	...	...	...	...	...	...	...
Palaos	EXP	S	...	...	...	...	...	...	...	...	...	...
	BAL		...	...	...	...	...	...	...	...	...	...
Papua New Guinea	IMP	G	1151	1368	1681	1728	2287	2945	3550	...	...	...
Papouasie-Nouvelle-Guinée	EXP	G	2068	2212	2555	3276	4167	4685	5719	4635	5414	...
	BAL		917	844	874	1548	1880	1740	2169	...	...	...
Samoa	IMP	S	106	128	155	187	219	227	249	204	278	319
Samoa	EXP	S	14	15	11	12	11	15	11	12	13	15
	BAL		-92	-113	-145	-175	-208	-212	-238	-193	-265	-304
Solomon Islands	IMP	S	98	94	121	185	217	287	329	270	300	...
Iles Salomon	EXP	S	65	74	97	103	121	165	210	163	221	...
	BAL		-33	-20	-24	-82	-95	-123	-119	-107	-79	...
Tonga	IMP	G	69	94	105	120	116	143	168	145	159	...
Tonga	EXP	G	9	18	15	10	10	9	9	8	8	...
	BAL		-60	-76	-90	-110	-107	-134	-158	-137	-151	...
Tuvalu	IMP	G	5	8	11	13	13	16	...	...	...	...
Tuvalu	EXP	G	0	0	0	0	0	0	...	...	...	...
	BAL		-5	-8	-11	-13	-13	-16	...	...	...	...
Vanuatu	IMP	G	87	106	128	149	217	231	314	294	285	312
Vanuatu	EXP	G	26	27	37	38	49	50	57	57	49	69
	BAL		-61	-79	-91	-111	-168	-180	-257	-238	-236	-243
Non Petrol. Export[18]	IMP		...	...	...	...	...	...	...	...	...	...
Pétrole N. Compris[18]	EXP		**102397**	**86061**	**79766**	**73931**	**68523**	**63510**	**58864**	**54558**	**50567**	**46868**
	BAL		...	...	...	...	...	...	...	...	...	...
Additional Country Groupings												
ANCOM[19]	IMP		24496	30452	36629	45917	55871	69767	91626	73428	95273	123624
ANCOM[19]	EXP		26154	29991	38932	51405	64821	75978	95671	78449	98869	132280
	BAL		1658	-461	2303	5488	8950	6212	4045	5021	3596	8656

Total imports and exports by regions and countries or areas (Table A)

Imports CIF, exports FOB and balance: million U.S. dollars *[cont.]*

Importations et exportations totales par régions et pays ou zones (Tableau A)

Importations CIF, exportations FOB et balance : en millions de dollars E.-U. *[suite]*

Country or Area - Pays ou Zone	IMP EXP BAL	G/S	2000	2003	2004	2005	2006	2007	2008	2009	2010	2011
APEC	IMP		3312671	3633938	4414655	5088704	5780574	6436015	7376474	**5701882**	**7355712**	**8787439**
CEAP	EXP		3116531	3338159	4065700	4686744	5455551	6219978	7070236	5634210	7231380	**8475788**
	BAL		-196140	-295780	-348955	-401960	-325023	-216037	-306238	**-67672**	**-124332**	**-311651**
ASEAN	IMP		379501	398474	500406	600251	688243	776452	946886	727868	954805	**1151738**
ANASE	EXP		431651	453725	568159	653824	770844	865330	998300	813562	1051636	**1239471**
	BAL		52149	55251	67754	53574	82601	88878	51414	85694	96832	**87733**
CACM	IMP		21293	25466	28833	32904	37999	43831	51085	38353	45464	54987
MCAC	EXP		13442	13825	14941	16640	18475	21098	23921	20040	24279	28604
	BAL		-7850	-11641	-13892	-16264	-19524	-22732	-27164	-18313	-21186	-26383
CARICOM	IMP		**13681**	14847	16747	19655	22386	25302	30301	23669	24834	**30035**
CARICOM	EXP		**8127**	8917	10911	14735	19942	19543	25930	14898	**17474**	**21622**
	BAL		**-5555**	-5930	-5836	-4919	-2443	-5760	-4372	-8771	**-7360**	**-8413**
COMESA	IMP		**34638**	**38165**	**47704**	**62685**	**69391**	**83882**	**119466**	**111518**	**127867**	**142938**
COMESA	EXP		**26753**	**36149**	**47253**	**63826**	**80188**	**96403**	**128107**	**93056**	**114580**	**143424**
	BAL		**-7885**	**-2016**	**-451**	**1141**	**10797**	**12522**	**8641**	**-18462**	**-13287**	**486**
ECOWAS	IMP		**20021**	25934	33147	43803	51915	68257	81005	**66812**	**75022**	**84899**
CEDEA	EXP		**29437**	**32681**	**45701**	71753	76755	86193	106389	**78300**	**105545**	**145898**
	BAL		**9417**	**6747**	**12554**	27950	24840	17936	25383	**11488**	**30523**	**60998**
EMCCA	IMP		4011	6053	6948	7980	10531	13391	17266	17299	18858	**20361**
CEMAC	EXP		8407	11576	16549	22935	26851	29613	42623	26877	33976	**44185**
	BAL		4396	5523	9601	14955	16320	16222	25357	9578	15119	**23824**
LAIA	IMP		326534	303265	376100	446213	535039	640059	785708	**589381**	**767013**	**906926**
ALAI	EXP		328987	348929	432529	524553	626365	712596	832185	**644569**	**829537**	**1021569**
	BAL		2452	45664	56429	78339	91326	72537	46476	**55188**	**62524**	**114644**
LDCs[19]	IMP		**41744**	**58891**	**71494**	**85060**	**99206**	**122075**	**158421**	**152093**	**166269**	**198649**
PMA[19]	EXP		**33188**	**43872**	**58338**	**80067**	**100101**	**125872**	**174259**	**124624**	**152749**	**201626**
	BAL		**-8556**	**-15018**	**-13156**	**-4992**	**896**	**3797**	**15837**	**-27469**	**-13519**	**2977**
MERCOSUR	IMP		89456	69132	95089	113990	140843	182879	257767	185926	266566	310994
MERCOSUR	EXP		84624	106217	135811	163973	190235	223735	279414	217644	281655	356712
	BAL		-4832	37084	40722	49983	49392	40856	21647	31718	15089	45718
NAFTA	IMP		1672611	1712625	1995801	2279839	2523168	2683458	2887216	2159972	2660769	3068407
ALENA	EXP		1224926	1162866	1312227	1480460	1678224	1851467	2045107	1600414	1961729	2281715
	BAL		-447685	-549759	-683575	-799379	-844944	-831991	-842109	-559558	-699039	-786692
OECD[19]	IMP		4922265	5621135	6720883	7503837	8522780	9637470	10816716	8125314	9583674	**11256581**
OCDE[19]	EXP		4533594	5227097	6192680	6773792	7672657	8784311	9797213	7633376	8948164	**10400033**
	BAL		-388671	-394039	-528203	-730046	-850123	-853159	-1019503	-491939	-635510	**-856548**
OPEC[19]	IMP		**137959**	**183699**	**247069**	**313153**	**369168**	**478686**	**608092**	**530258**	**571818**	**638977**
OPEP[19]	EXP		**298303**	**334448**	**459676**	**661079**	**797181**	**925648**	**1241660**	**817484**	**1047102**	**1366510**
	BAL		**160344**	**150749**	**212607**	**347926**	**428013**	**446962**	**633568**	**287226**	**475284**	**727534**
EU27	IMP		2435710	3033799	3662361	4012612	4631463	5417783	6078869	4565107	5153415	**6017095**
UE27	EXP		2388726	3077728	3667785	3956155	4489768	5232230	5811175	4500283	5044518	**5900716**
	BAL		-46985	43929	5424	-56457	-141695	-185553	-267694	-64825	-108898	**-116379**
Extra-EU27[20]	IMP		913310	1057673	1277865	1465103	1699468	1966873	2306624	1671715	1989022	2345994
Extra-UE27[20]	EXP		781270	984116	1185169	1307303	1458219	1702746	1930284	1527713	1785453	2130904
	BAL		-132040	-73557	-92696	-157800	-241250	-264127	-376340	-144003	-203568	-215089
EU25	IMP		2416151	2998910	3615230	3953987	4557087	5318095	5958887	4487299	5066058	**5908730**
UE25	EXP		2373550	3052569	3634369	3916686	4442331	5173613	5739151	4443284	4974590	**5810071**
	BAL		-42601	53660	19138	-37301	-114757	-144482	-219736	-44015	-91467	**-98659**

Total imports and exports by regions and countries or areas (Table A)

Imports CIF, exports FOB and balance: million U.S. dollars *[cont.]*

Importations et exportations totales par régions et pays ou zones (Tableau A)

Importations CIF, exportations FOB et balance : en millions de dollars E.-U. *[suite]*

Country or Area - Pays ou Zone	IMP EXP BAL	G/S	2000	2003	2004	2005	2006	2007	2008	2009	2010	2011
Extra-EU25[20]	IMP		916360	1063891	1283846	1456866	1702321	1967370	...	...	...	...
Extra-UE25[20]	EXP		788642	999614	1205511	1330464	1489696	1742459	...	...	...	...
	BAL		-127718	-64277	-78335	-126402	-212625	-224911	...	...	...	...
Memorandum Items												
World excluding intra-EU27 trade	IMP		**5007663**	**5639131**	**6911026**	**8028965**	**9222242**	**10579627**	**12445104**	**9573317**	**11962983**	**14281800**
Monde excl. le intra-UE27 com.	EXP		**4751623**	**5360206**	**6589236**	**7698005**	**8934194**	**10291897**	**12092234**	**9395320**	**11797003**	**14169587**
	BAL		**-256040**	**-278925**	**-321789**	**-330960**	**-288047**	**-287730**	**-352870**	**-177997**	**-165979**	**-112213**
World excluding intra-EU27 trade as percent of World	IMP		**77**	**74**	**74**	**76**	**76**	**75**	**77**	**77**	**79**	**80**
Monde excl. le intra-UE27 com. comme pour cent du Monde	EXP		**75**	**72**	**73**	**74**	**75**	**74**	**76**	**76**	**78**	**79**

Total imports and exports by regions and countries or areas (Table A)

Imports CIF, exports FOB and balance: million U.S. dollars

Importations et exportations totales par régions et pays ou zones (Tableau A)

Importations CIF, exportations FOB, et balance: en millions de dollars E.-U.

General note:

Table A is based on data as available at the end of May 2012. An updated version of this table will be published in Volume II of the 2011 ITSY which will be produced later this year. The totals of imports and exports presented in world trade table A and D are not necessarily identical as table A is mainly based on data of the IMF's International Financial Statistics (IFS) which is a different data collection system with different aims, procedures, timetable and sources for update and maintenance than UN Comtrade on which table D is based (see the introduction for details). Nevertheless, discrepancies between both tables are in general minor and usually do not affect the overall information provided. A systematic comparison of the figures from both sources (which includes the description of known and relevant conceptual differences) is available at http://unstats.un.org/unsd/trade/imts/annual%20totals.htm. Overall, the discrepancies in the world total or world aggregate of exports in table A and table D is around 0.5 percent or less for all years shown, which is minor, given the differences between the two sources. Column "G/S" indicates the trade system: G = General Trade System; S = Special Trade System. For further information on sources and presentation of table A as well as for a brief table description please see the introduction, paragraphs 6 -16 and paragraph 17.

Remarque générale:

Tableau A est basé sur les données telles que disponible en fin Mai 2012. Une version antérieure de ce tableau est publiée dans le volume I de l'annuaire 2011 ITSY qui a été produit plus tôt cette année. Les importations et exportations totales présentées dans les tableaux A et D ne sont pas nécessairement identiques du fait que le tableau A est basé principalement sur les données des Statistiques Financières Internationales (IFS) du FMI qui est un différent système de collecte des données avec des objectifs, des procédures, un calendrier et des sources de mise à jour et de maintenance différents de ceux de UN Comtrade sur lequel le tableau D est basé (voir l'introduction pour les détails). Toutefois, les écarts entre les deux tableaux sont en général mineurs et n'affectent pas substantiellement l'information fournie. Une comparaison systématique des données de ces deux sources (incluant une description des différences conceptuelles pertinentes connues) est disponible à http://unstats.un.org/unsd/trade/imts/annual%20totals.htm. En général, la différence entre les totaux des exportations mondiales présentés dans les tableaux A et D est inférieure à 0.5 pour cent pour chacune des années publiées, ce qui est mineur étant donné les différences entre les deux sources.
La colonne "G/S" indique le système commercial : G=Système du Commerce Général ; S= Système du Commerce Spécial. Pour plus d'information sur les sources et la présentation du tableau A ainsi qu'une brève description, veuillez vous référer aux paragraphes 6-16 et 17 de l'introduction.

1 This classification is intended for statistical convenience and does not, necessarily, express a judgement about the stage reached by a particular country in the development process.

2 Developed Economies of America, Europe, and the Asia-Pacific region.

3 Imports FOB.

4 Including the trade of the U.S. Virgin Islands and Puerto Rico but excluding shipments of merchandise between the United States and its other possessions (Guam and American Samoa). Data include imports and exports of non-monetary gold.

5 Beginning 2006, data for Serbia and Montenegro is reported separately.

6 Prior to 2008, special trade.

7 Imports exclude petroleum imported without stated value. Exports cover domestic exports.

8 Exports include gold.

9 Trade statistics exclude certain oil and chemical products.

10 Export and import values exclude trade in the processing zone.

11 Trade data include maquiladoras and exclude goods from customs-bonded warehouses. Total exports include revaluation and exports of silver.

12 Exports include petroleum products.

13 Excluding military goods, fissionable materials, bunkers, ships, and aircraft.

14 Year ending 20 March of the year stated.

1 Cette classification est utilisée pour plus de commodité dans la présentation des statistiques et n'implique pas nécessairement un jugement quant au stade de développement auquel est parvenu un pays donné.

2 Économies développées de l'Amérique, de l'Europe, et de la région Asie-Pacifique.

3 Importations FOB.

4 Y compris le commerce des Iles Vierges américaines et de Porto Rico mais non compris les échanges de marchandise, entre les Etats-Unis et leurs autres possessions (Guam et Samoa américaines). Les données comprennent les importations et exportations d'or non-monétaire.

5 Depuis début 2006, les données relatives à la Serbie et au Monténégro sont déclarées séparément.

6 Avant 2008, commerce special.

7 Non compris le pétrole brute dont la valeur des importations ne sont pas stipulée. Les exportations sont les exportations d'intérieur.

8 Les exportations comprennent l'or.

9 Les statistiques commerciales font exclusion de certains produits pétroliers et chimiques.

10 Les valeurs à l'exportation et à l'importation excluent le commerce de la zone de transformation.

11 Les statistiques du commerce extérieur comprennent maquiladoras et ne comprennent pas les marchandises provenant des entrepôts en douane. Les exportations comprennent la réévaluation et les données sur les exportations d'argent.

12 Exportations comprennent produits pétroliers.

13 À l'exclusion des marchandises militaires, des matières fissibles, des soutes, des bateaux, et de l'avion.

14 Année finissant le 20 mars de l'année indiquée.

15 Data include oil and gas.The value of oil exports and total exports are rough estimates based on information published in various petroleum industry journals.

16 Imports and exports net of returned goods. The figures also exclude Judea and Samaria and the Gaza area.

17 Year ending 30 September of the years stated.

18 Data refer to total exports less petroleum exports of Asia Middle East countries where petroleum, in this case, is the sum of SITC groups 333, 334 and 335.

19 The figures for the country groupings aim to always reflect the membership of the grouping of the latest year published.

20 Excluding intra-EU trade.

15 Les données comprennent le pétrole et le gaz. La valeur des exportations de pétrole et des exportations totales sont des évaluations grossières basées sur l'information publiée à divers journaux d'industrie de pétrole.

16 Importations et exportations nets, ne comprennant pas les marchandises retournées. Sont également exclues les données de la Judée et de Samaria et ainsi que la zone de Gaza.

17 Année finissant le 30 septembre de l'année indiquée.

18 Les données se rapportent aux exportations totales moins les exportations pétrolières de Moyen-Orient d'Asie. Dans ce cas, le pétrole est la somme des groupes CTCI 333, 334 et 335.

19 Les données pour les regroupements de pays visent à toujours refléter la composition des regroupements de la dernière année publiée.

20 Non compris le commerce d'intra-UE.

World exports by provenance and destination (Table D)

In million U.S. dollars f.o.b.

Exports to →			Developed economies 2/ Économies développées 2/							Commonwealth of Independent States Communauté d'Etats Indépendants	
				Asia-Pacific Asie-Pacifique		Europe		North America Amérique du Nord			
↓ Exports from	Year	World 1/ Monde 1/	Total	Total	Japan Japon	Total	Germany Allemagne	Total	U.S.A. É.-U.	Total	Europe
					Total trade (SITC, Rev. 3, 0-9)						
World 1/	2000	6337849	4374903	413661	337372	2549479	474942	1411764	1176012	77403	65291
	2008	15945284	9579892	811829	607481	6348828	1117795	2419235	1966146	516893	426699
	2009	12396195	7208261	608006	441582	4794316	860954	1805939	1449933	313402	243914
	2010	14979599	8385289	741900	539964	5433800	1000572	2209588	1776033	399747	324610
	2011	17925002	9661168	879921	639739	6264426	1131706	2516822	2016516	471790	391296
Developed Economies - Asia-Pacific 2/	2000	556339	283778	30765	14422	93424	21063	159589	150831	1004	824
	2008	998843	383873	80118	45307	139257	26140	164498	152014	20845	20007
	2009	759418	268557	57392	31762	96682	18166	114483	105249	4848	4332
	2010	1007411	331697	73639	41538	115968	22128	142089	131244	10412	9621
	2011	1106557	364518	85521	49933	128354	25928	150643	139864	15191	13801
Japan	2000	479276	243818	9835	.	83786	19997	150197	142480	793	624
	2008	781412	284386	19818	.	115044	23955	149524	138705	19335	18629
	2009	580719	196115	13675	.	79347	16653	103092	95303	4120	3700
	2010	769774	243061	17798	.	95563	20290	129700	120338	9161	8543
	2011	823292	262277	19743	.	105906	23505	136627	127679	13760	12536
Developed Economies - Europe 2/	2000	2511802	2110328	63263	45917	1790571	343434	256493	231909	31171	28093
	2008	6127335	4843605	114175	70352	4284615	803186	444815	396936	220236	203102
	2009	4734391	3718271	93458	57748	3277526	620933	347287	310350	135608	120770
	2010	5320428	4115414	107327	65738	3613107	706238	394980	351958	164061	148677
	2011	6221758	4690230	127434	77295	4113418	801484	449378	401176	211505	192340
France	2000	295345	239365	6445	4983	204528	44461	28392	25937	2392	1952
	2008	594505	447724	13701	8255	394488	86842	39534	35110	13803	12437
	2009	464113	342892	10405	6649	301736	68985	30751	27347	9372	8087
	2010	511651	371697	12364	7793	326578	82989	32755	29231	10476	9481
	2011	581542	422207	14954	9065	370762	96160	36490	32468	12971	11898
Germany	2000	549607	458641	15684	12137	382583	.	60374	56393	8923	8069
	2008	1466137	1134421	29702	18848	990263	.	114455	105211	65207	60585
	2009	1127840	865255	24702	15068	758245	.	82308	75017	40011	36127
	2010	1271096	946837	28739	17374	821272	.	96826	86847	48260	43828
	2011	1482202	1075668	34224	21400	927929	.	113515	103075	66060	60460
Developed Economies - North America 2/	2000	1057790	699131	86693	71335	193929	31336	418509	241624	3504	2715
	2008	1756128	1061625	104488	77038	341455	58895	615683	353789	15814	13047
	2009	1372383	795765	82057	58478	271555	46477	442153	236490	9350	7321
	2010	1664241	937669	96158	69520	303105	51730	538407	289466	10700	8799
	2011	1931184	1068988	110355	77042	345408	52660	613225	331752	14740	12252
United States	2000	780332	436300	79685	65252	179776	29242	176839	.	3325	2563
	2008	1299899	655762	91571	66573	302443	54672	261747	.	13823	11404
	2009	1056712	520933	72935	51178	242463	43221	205536	.	8200	6437
	2010	1277109	599501	85165	60543	265503	48041	248832	.	9164	7484
	2011	1479730	678910	97169	66160	300433	48779	281308	.	12823	10583
South-Eastern Europe	2000	19514	13491	50	37	12585	2634	857	764	994	854
	2008	93910	61376	228	148	59576	12661	1572	1431	5537	4791
	2009	73589	49989	193	138	48860	11465	935	849	3575	3001
	2010	89896	59318	263	216	57746	13489	1310	1135	4959	4263
	2011	115514	76555	354	275	74232	18567	1970	1624	6830	5863
Commonwealth of Independent States	2000	143026	80471	2958	2943	70243	11069	7269	5779	29063	24135
	2008	707367	406842	12100	11912	369479	37851	25264	22978	134424	101417
	2009	439954	236728	8029	7816	213639	22285	15060	12359	86826	62811
	2010	576963	311297	14053	13825	276620	29259	20625	16490	107630	80777
	2011	722174	376896	15605	15431	335586	30194	25705	21050	94985	74509
Russian Federation 4/	2000	103093	65496	2771	2764	57875	9232	4850	4648	13824	10807
	2008	467994	294155	10516	10429	268946	33187	14693	13753	69921	48410
	2009	301796	179803	7427	7263	162602	18708	9775	9286	46941	31192
	2010	400100	238827	12965	12833	212262	25103	13600	12467	59867	42283
	2011	473274	267846	14388	14317	237156	22960	16302	15733	26133	18543

For general note and footnotes see end of table

Exportations mondiales en provenance et de destination (Tableau D)

En millions de dollars E.-U. f.o.b.

← Exportations vers

South-Eastern Europe Europe du Sud-Est	Northern Africa Afrique septentrio-nale	Sub-Saharan Africa Afrique subsahari-enne	Latin America and the Caribbean Amérique latine et Caraïbes	Eastern Asia Asie orientale	Southern Asia Asie méridionale	South-eastern Asia Asie du Sud-Est	Western Asia Asie occidentale	Oceania Océanie	Other 3/ Autres 3/	Année	Exportations en provenance de ↓
			Commerce total (CTCI, Rev. 3, 0-9)								
27378	54323	74262	363648	698613	81045	355646	191177	6349	33101	2000	Monde 1/
150309	181425	289519	882348	2217465	391855	850236	705804	23038	156500	2008	
103043	160999	247932	678102	1895919	352252	697514	567525	25625	145623	2009	
115635	177998	291109	884133	2554518	441435	905542	649214	26109	148871	2010	
138301	196963	362235	1077458	3059037	526063	1069718	788126	31554	542589	2011	
153	1694	4909	22054	140231	6988	78409	13637	2260	1223	2000	Economies développées - Asie-Pacifique 2/
825	4754	13332	43350	327332	25887	126114	45169	4612	2750	2008	
370	3469	9377	34207	282693	23696	98367	27597	4508	1729	2009	
422	4118	12141	46359	393669	31535	135540	32799	6490	2228	2010	
611	3673	14397	47090	431114	34098	151960	34286	6943	2677	2011	
108	1196	3721	20779	124536	4751	68494	10619	460	0	2000	Japon
637	3867	9447	39201	271282	12612	103462	35785	1397	...	2008	
321	2671	6777	31349	225619	10138	80399	21776	1435	...	2009	
384	3160	8849	42346	306983	14261	112867	25991	2710	0	2010	
565	2365	10811	42231	322696	16701	123095	26202	2589	0	2011	
19331	29933	31303	57248	77496	21606	40231	83204	1256	8695	2000	Economies développées - Europe 2/
98564	86604	91370	131864	220389	76468	88127	236697	4730	28680	2008	
70335	77088	75570	99569	203317	64557	74919	188091	2577	24490	2009	
76005	82527	85557	127718	264931	74307	87825	216448	3182	22452	2010	
90598	84832	104765	151194	327708	86459	103773	259095	3130	108468	2011	
1282	9180	7741	7237	9366	2416	4752	10136	822	658	2000	France
5737	21731	15742	16170	23413	8453	13395	25340	1889	1109	2008	
4228	19013	13613	10903	19415	6204	12036	24120	1579	738	2009	
4676	20396	15016	13984	26338	7000	13568	25906	1610	983	2010	
5537	21799	17517	15314	33476	7288	14872	27591	1841	1129	2011	
4185	4001	5607	13858	21330	4087	9799	17506	132	1537	2000	Allemagne
21876	11916	17094	35613	77169	20088	22928	56766	332	2728	2008	
15782	10938	13115	26344	73359	18415	19196	43364	185	1876	2009	
16420	11127	15445	35536	100250	19628	23476	53170	532	415	2010	
19914	10320	18784	40939	124083	22059	27631	63769	309	12668	2011	
562	5660	6348	174598	88921	5584	48918	23864	393	308	2000	Economies développées - Amérique du Nord 2/
2304	11934	20722	301454	170313	26749	72629	71695	703	187	2008	
1349	10670	16563	247078	153234	24130	57509	55749	751	235	2009	
1408	12628	18984	312634	203268	27974	74625	63141	834	377	2010	
1799	12936	23226	378972	237416	32724	81447	77728	976	232	2011	
509	5028	5928	170376	83248	4635	47368	22928	378	307	2000	Etats-Unis
1929	10017	18613	287831	153590	22629	68156	66749	619	183	2008	
1153	9141	15135	237538	138015	20596	53844	51250	674	234	2009	
1137	11215	17076	300493	183656	24298	70437	59046	709	376	2010	
1437	11509	21102	364814	210382	28320	76434	72895	880	225	2011	
2212	358	156	159	218	139	76	1700	1	9	2000	Europe du Sud-Est
13096	1112	911	821	769	994	565	8320	84	326	2008	
10086	1176	596	449	913	701	520	5356	21	207	2009	
12160	1293	881	486	1382	840	564	7654	16	343	2010	
14648	1688	1145	650	1929	1094	315	9864	21	775	2011	
2635	1375	555	5984	9137	2996	1716	9070	4	19	2000	Communauté d'Etats Indépendants
15933	8766	2574	11577	44350	19389	7645	55750	8	108	2008	
7113	6516	1975	5286	35043	18335	6186	32216	77	3654	2009	
10184	7097	1902	7024	52158	18840	10643	42313	4	7871	2010	
11949	9001	3276	11517	76333	18848	11529	40883	12	66944	2011	
1822	746	344	4307	6980	1896	1120	6556	2	0	2000	Fédération de Russie 4/
10644	5103	1182	6669	31533	9403	4371	34987	7	20	2008	
4272	4295	969	3357	24551	9487	3608	20986	76	3451	2009	
6106	4407	695	4164	34400	10722	6729	26992	2	7187	2010	
5978	6186	1757	7565	52106	9194	7659	22444	9	66396	2011	

Voir la fin du tableau pour la remarque générale et les notes.

World exports by provenance and destination (Table D)

In million U.S. dollars f.o.b.

Exports to → / ↓ Exports from	Year	World 1/ Monde 1/	Developed economies 2/ Économies développées 2/ Total	Asia-Pacific Asie-Pacifique Total	Japan Japon	Europe Total	Germany Allemagne	North America Amérique du Nord Total	U.S.A. É.-U.	Commonwealth of Independent States Communauté d'Etats Indépendants Total	Europe
					Total trade (SITC, Rev. 3, 0-9) *[cont.]*						
Northern Africa	2000	50201	41077	490	424	35543	3933	5043	4216	101	81
	2008	206917	161152	2732	2105	127241	10717	31180	25653	707	589
	2009	135155	97437	723	546	79568	6340	17146	14541	489	460
	2010	163590	118332	989	521	95689	6684	21654	18445	592	525
	2011	201120	143729	1312	666	118686	9392	23731	18916	842	795
Sub-Saharan Africa	2000	94739	56996	2651	2078	32071	3097	22274	21301	194	191
	2008	345579	192070	13266	11161	92659	9764	86145	80670	950	885
	2009	242644	117734	6873	5894	65613	6108	45248	40103	683	611
	2010	321133	160615	10329	8197	81257	8339	69029	61755	896	805
	2011	439568	215317	13071	10769	110485	10381	91761	81430	1557	1073
South Africa	2000	26298	13520	1866	1355	9026	1900	2629	2409	33	32
	2008	73966	43419	9737	8120	25229	5749	8453	7987	391	378
	2009	53864	26845	4889	4096	16742	3513	5214	4860	243	215
	2010	71484	36166	7461	6425	21197	5529	7508	7061	385	354
	2011	92976	41167	8617	7663	23701	5488	8849	8357	383	361
Latin America and the Caribbean	2000	353078	265627	8570	7727	43899	6927	213158	206834	1330	1280
	2008	887302	535686	21562	18383	133993	21743	380132	364142	8965	8456
	2009	697282	412128	16613	14473	102060	14918	293455	262020	6110	5733
	2010	886245	506385	24097	21232	119573	17942	362716	327263	8128	7746
	2011	1101238	609129	30201	26102	152196	21694	426732	384438	9404	8785
Brazil	2000	55119	33697	2852	2481	16229	2520	14615	14049	522	487
	2008	197942	87551	7466	6134	49275	8843	30809	28936	5526	5239
	2009	152995	60565	4812	4281	37179	6250	18574	16679	3332	3137
	2010	197356	74437	7750	7123	45134	8080	21553	19240	4747	4510
	2011	256039	94812	10365	9473	55374	9039	29074	25943	5110	4673
Eastern Asia	2000	776206	410957	101770	90092	125355	27229	183831	173168	4994	3848
	2008	2483374	1066516	218059	177602	438765	87717	409692	377313	81155	55327
	2009	2101812	887825	184914	148327	356661	73769	346250	319800	47263	27767
	2010	2723194	1118738	230253	183712	447018	95697	441466	408128	68075	47620
	2011	3222798	1275650	280790	223926	496310	104404	498550	460387	85989	62116
China	2000	249203	142806	45499	41654	41976	9278	55331	52156	3183	2411
	2008	1430693	712184	140889	116132	296563	59209	274732	252844	64719	41075
	2009	1201647	598610	120642	97911	238921	49920	239047	221295	38973	21471
	2010	1577764	771088	151029	121044	313723	68047	306336	283780	53821	36052
	2011	1898388	896344	185915	148269	359795	76400	350633	325011	67227	46853
Southern Asia	2000	91744	55121	8446	7710	29168	3860	17507	16426	1851	1206
	2008	337887	118054	6823	4771	78910	9541	32321	30187	4946	2638
	2009	294576	103011	6160	4090	67578	9223	29273	27370	3748	2078
	2010	349813	121178	8346	5893	77344	10191	35489	33311	5159	3342
	2011	484988	163011	11380	8119	106786	13860	44846	41912	7241	4530
South-Eastern Asia	2000	426829	218830	69524	57855	65422	12035	83884	80872	606	556
	2008	984324	381999	149852	106111	121173	21572	110975	104391	5659	5254
	2009	811582	302743	112936	78325	101055	17861	88752	82366	3853	3333
	2010	1051311	376247	145345	103230	124335	23033	106567	100258	5073	4585
	2011	1228831	423694	173956	126271	137882	24407	111856	105004	6325	5720
Western Asia	2000	251583	136104	36649	35896	56361	8137	43094	42034	2575	1496
	2008	1006064	360789	84406	81340	159744	17669	116639	56352	17651	11182
	2009	724157	212551	35220	33049	111737	13131	65593	38141	11044	5691
	2010	815828	222898	27177	25126	120733	15575	74987	36315	14054	7842
	2011	1139572	247940	26071	22873	143757	18448	78112	28654	17177	9507
Oceania	2000	4996	2993	1832	937	907	189	255	252	15	11
	2008	10254	6304	4021	1251	1962	338	321	291	4	4
	2009	9252	5521	3437	935	1780	279	304	295	6	5
	2010	9546	5499	3924	1217	1306	266	269	265	7	7
	2011	9701	5510	3870	1035	1326	285	314	309	6	6

For general note and footnotes see end of table

Exportations mondiales en provenance et de destination (Tableau D)

En millions de dollars E.-U. f.o.b.

← Exportations vers

South-Eastern Europe Europe du Sud-Est	Northern Africa Afrique septentrio-nale	Sub-Saharan Africa Afrique subsahari-enne	Latin America and the Caribbean Amérique latine et Caraïbes	Eastern Asia Asie orientale	Southern Asia Asie méridionale	South-eastern Asia Asie du Sud-Est	Western Asia Asie occidentale	Oceania Océanie	Other 3/ Autres 3/	Année	Exportations en provence de ↓
			Commerce total (CTCI, Rev. 3, 0-9) *[suite]*								
92	1179	336	2058	315	793	277	3122	1	849	2000	Afrique septentrionale
636	7113	2993	6596	6471	6869	1679	10497	3	2201	2008	
488	6065	2429	3380	7393	4142	1114	10516	5	1698	2009	
524	6388	3415	4316	8835	5848	1434	12294	11	1600	2010	
502	6990	4248	5625	9519	9382	1805	16388	50	2042	2011	
64	418	12170	2545	8632	5258	1952	2117	40	4354	2000	Afrique subsaharienne
320	1702	48658	13982	57523	15174	4830	6602	75	3693	2008	
432	1734	45514	8973	41237	13399	4405	6349	439	1744	2009	
194	2169	52502	11976	55085	19749	7012	8790	185	1960	2010	
215	2643	67815	16970	77352	27296	9571	11488	222	9123	2011	
27	91	3903	572	1797	524	731	971	6	4122	2000	Afrique du sud
153	532	12006	1446	7754	2735	1995	2806	39	690	2008	
39	435	10092	782	8451	2588	1643	2134	71	540	2009	
53	445	11880	1559	12119	3522	2236	2629	36	454	2010	
86	529	14239	2163	17197	3831	2756	2992	21	7611	2011	
324	1359	1680	61878	8864	2275	2795	2808	18	4122	2000	Amérique latine et Caraïbes
1867	7246	11096	214944	64804	9032	15006	13494	66	5093	2008	
1480	5680	8375	156199	68902	10826	14634	11776	66	1106	2009	
1633	7746	8586	187602	102354	13637	18390	14731	54	16998	2010	
2229	11288	11867	230194	127193	14733	18716	19967	70	46448	2011	
129	506	888	13886	2603	621	926	1338	4	...	2000	Brésil
801	3145	7742	51912	23011	2872	6825	8537	22	0	2008	
573	3038	5938	35880	25752	5616	5305	6970	26	...	2009	
603	4182	5053	47682	37983	6603	6597	9440	28	...	2010	
836	5407	6814	57236	53552	6658	9346	11423	32	4814	2011	
688	3065	8358	25191	220123	13062	68294	18703	1258	1511	2000	Asie orientale
6629	19168	50439	116739	725750	81869	226831	97675	6721	3883	2008	
4656	19474	45454	91115	635234	76484	197847	81681	12724	2054	2009	
5648	22699	57312	137839	838588	104777	258845	98293	9322	3057	2010	
6812	21572	74963	173849	989874	129155	323563	125180	11637	4554	2011	
356	1410	3602	7125	62121	4510	17341	6683	65	2	2000	Chine
4934	14320	36784	71240	296081	52553	114326	62430	1121	...	2008	
3658	14135	33512	56558	245199	49778	106320	52703	2201	...	2009	
4371	15588	44235	91249	322611	68699	138203	64868	3032	...	2010	
5360	16636	56302	121082	394265	86063	170146	81714	3248	1	2011	
48	2666	2172	1906	13214	3400	3789	7538	32	8	2000	Asie méridionale
582	6672	14266	8082	82515	23370	22407	55345	177	1471	2008	
712	5456	12110	5939	64742	18071	20290	53181	74	7243	2009	
638	6268	16330	11228	78348	23123	25686	60640	177	1038	2010	
756	8978	21750	13957	113624	31542	35727	78784	108	9509	2011	
156	1009	4130	6783	75806	11389	98159	8581	996	386	2000	Asie du Sud-est
714	5456	16492	24439	215527	45418	251015	31975	4423	1205	2008	
499	4667	14521	19591	196547	39604	199516	25529	3554	957	2009	
687	5975	18598	27395	265499	53057	263290	29654	4776	1058	2010	
944	11023	19839	36708	313337	65224	308802	34502	7128	1307	2011	
1112	5608	2105	2934	55140	7538	10744	16833	9	10881	2000	Asie occidentale
8837	20898	16599	8480	300401	60356	32778	72579	1181	105516	2008	
5516	19003	15412	6289	205395	58225	21410	69474	666	99173	2009	
6133	19090	14858	9531	288872	67604	21080	62450	696	88562	2010	
7237	22338	14875	10684	352133	75365	21919	79956	982	288965	2011	
2	0	41	310	514	15	286	2	80	736	2000	Océanie
0	0	67	20	1321	280	609	6	255	1387	2008	
7	1	35	27	1268	83	797	10	163	1333	2009	
0	0	42	25	1527	144	607	7	362	1327	2010	
0	0	69	48	1506	144	592	7	275	1544	2011	

Voir la fin du tableau pour la remarque générale et les notes.

World exports by provenance and destination (Table D)

In million U.S. dollars f.o.b.

Exports to → / ↓ Exports from	Year	World 1/ Monde 1/	Developed economies 2/ Économies développées 2/ Total	Asia-Pacific Asie-Pacifique Total	Asia-Pacific: Japan Japon	Europe Total	Europe: Germany Allemagne	North America Amérique du Nord Total	North America: U.S.A. É.-U.	Commonwealth of Independent States Communauté d'Etats Indépendants Total	CIS: Europe
Food, beverages and tobacco (SITC, Rev. 3, 0 and 1)											
World 1/	2000	386759	271140	40604	36961	175040	32423	55496	44015	9865	8663
	2008	954477	610460	59146	48725	444255	74238	107060	81658	47110	39439
	2009	870750	553202	52998	43255	399853	67278	100351	75598	36224	30067
	2010	966919	588967	60244	48759	416483	70408	112240	84403	44285	37553
	2011	1170735	693733	73592	59574	489004	82375	131137	99492	52439	43930
Developed Economies - Asia-Pacific 2/	2000	19827	9700	4291	3295	2442	277	2967	2615	52	44
	2008	39723	17658	8124	5304	4637	589	4896	4258	700	605
	2009	35858	15294	6743	4194	4032	456	4518	3952	347	282
	2010	41755	16131	7646	4517	3938	434	4548	3953	698	597
	2011	49215	18119	8647	5131	4544	559	4927	4251	733	620
Japan	2000	2088	612	72	.	107	14	432	395	9	9
	2008	3867	920	76	.	163	29	681	634	50	50
	2009	3895	938	78	.	170	31	691	650	51	51
	2010	4615	957	81	.	193	34	683	640	81	80
	2011	4489	1028	95	.	205	32	728	682	38	38
Developed Economies - Europe 2/	2000	177876	151306	5141	4316	135733	26322	10432	8968	3783	3518
	2008	446228	375809	8749	6402	347825	60333	19235	15969	16094	15284
	2009	399827	338756	7705	5587	313991	54992	17060	14122	12405	11751
	2010	423570	351040	8306	5953	323675	56757	19058	15796	15669	14791
	2011	497381	407437	10155	7251	374697	65489	22585	18831	18544	17479
France	2000	31410	26548	981	902	23387	4572	2180	1853	351	335
	2008	65387	53274	1635	1379	48358	7641	3280	2569	1088	1046
	2009	55320	45343	1343	1148	41033	6763	2966	2370	759	726
	2010	58758	45877	1426	1190	41011	6755	3441	2776	902	852
	2011	69712	52464	1612	1338	46933	7838	3920	3156	985	915
Germany	2000	21712	18446	290	250	17384	.	772	696	643	595
	2008	66524	57796	962	741	55159	.	1676	1429	2817	2584
	2009	60755	52998	797	566	50644	.	1558	1330	2190	1997
	2010	62920	53953	774	524	51373	.	1806	1554	2757	2530
	2011	75568	63905	1165	813	60427	.	2313	1984	3271	2972
Developed Economies - North America 2/	2000	63390	38861	13367	12830	6717	914	18777	10624	986	886
	2008	123560	63317	16301	14956	11148	1337	35869	18333	2803	2614
	2009	104075	55669	13883	12502	9019	1096	32767	15561	1932	1781
	2010	118065	61082	14885	13367	9979	1297	36218	17305	1883	1679
	2011	141991	70139	18055	16172	11818	1488	40266	18995	2256	1995
United States	2000	47084	25762	11994	11534	5619	835	8149	.	955	858
	2008	91269	40311	13951	12842	8837	1178	17523	.	2303	2154
	2009	76576	36104	11936	10806	6975	941	17193	.	1685	1562
	2010	88113	39643	12717	11457	8054	1158	18872	.	1475	1306
	2011	107718	45934	15502	13890	9217	1312	21214	.	1614	1396
South-Eastern Europe	2000	1232	650	17	12	588	125	45	39	87	69
	2008	7155	3425	27	11	3278	382	120	101	285	262
	2009	7176	3971	19	5	3829	396	123	102	210	196
	2010	8679	4413	21	6	4278	450	113	91	328	296
	2011	10613	5544	54	35	5350	640	139	115	462	413
Commonwealth of Independent States	2000	3276	710	150	145	524	90	35	32	2130	1733
	2008	23051	2892	147	146	2637	344	107	94	12186	7374
	2009	21207	2249	298	293	1852	285	99	88	9634	5783
	2010	21665	2060	256	249	1688	260	116	104	11411	7516
	2011	28251	3870	263	253	3490	343	118	100	13284	8406
Russian Federation 4/	2000	1016	394	140	137	231	34	23	21	379	91
	2008	7426	854	125	124	676	123	53	45	3255	880
	2009	8340	807	228	224	531	126	48	43	2709	610
	2010	7304	895	215	211	615	97	65	59	2044	658
	2011	10084	1463	227	222	1183	109	53	44	2127	810

For general note and footnotes see end of table

Exportations mondiales en provenance et de destination (Tableau D)

En millions de dollars E.-U. f.o.b.

South-Eastern Europe Europe du Sud-Est	Northern Africa Afrique septentrio-nale	Sub-Saharan Africa Afrique subsahari-enne	Latin America and the Caribbean Amérique latine et Caraïbes	Eastern Asia Asie orientale	Southern Asia Asie méridionale	South-eastern Asia Asie du Sud-Est	Western Asia Asie occidentale	Oceania Océanie	Other 3/ Autres 3/	Année	← Exportations vers / Exportations en provence de ↓
Produits alimentaires, boisson et tabac (CTCI, Rev. 3, 0 et 1)											
2493	7289	8375	22274	23737	5196	16035	17832	783	1739	2000	Monde 1/
12056	21201	29584	57693	52653	18772	44617	55647	1868	2816	2008	
11167	17098	28335	49244	54309	19431	42973	53372	1804	3591	2009	
11613	21624	31224	56483	70664	22627	55090	59109	1980	3252	2010	
13460	28836	39428	70857	92263	26945	70175	75005	2288	5305	2011	
5	395	395	490	3381	857	3013	996	446	98	2000	Économies développées - Asie-Pacifique 2/
12	658	858	1315	7137	855	6654	2995	776	106	2008	
9	587	681	762	7216	1058	5420	2601	705	1179	2009	
14	827	870	988	9453	1561	7013	2977	824	399	2010	
12	1131	1138	1229	10882	1614	8553	3817	959	1027	2011	
0	0	18	23	1135	6	205	26	56	0	2000	Japon
0	21	54	29	2103	11	562	71	45	...	2008	
0	28	28	29	2219	8	474	76	43	...	2009	
0	39	29	37	2728	14	593	103	33	...	2010	
0	7	40	35	2484	11	738	71	36	...	2011	
1688	2958	3092	3113	2850	484	2052	5475	135	940	2000	Économies développées - Europe 2/
7953	7439	8487	5298	6464	1453	4305	11179	318	1429	2008	
7123	5794	7708	4334	6578	1283	4017	10440	295	1094	2009	
7081	7013	8798	5148	8846	1369	4980	12867	316	444	2010	
8182	9056	10531	6291	12198	1636	6276	16133	379	719	2011	
79	984	883	429	542	106	406	968	112	2	2000	France
269	3190	2224	494	1481	203	1241	1641	260	22	2008	
212	2371	1842	403	1547	105	1034	1451	240	12	2009	
243	3103	2206	611	2247	131	1345	1825	255	14	2010	
349	4625	2591	768	3331	215	1717	2341	301	25	2011	
193	367	112	203	255	126	188	974	1	204	2000	Allemagne
1106	632	546	301	604	392	377	1709	3	241	2008	
1076	442	658	251	564	430	376	1747	2	19	2009	
1026	507	746	333	733	300	426	2110	2	25	2010	
1264	520	884	416	1362	290	609	3008	3	37	2011	
73	1936	805	9298	5475	785	2248	2770	78	74	2000	Économies développées - Amérique du Nord 2/
200	3378	2899	24253	12361	2881	5823	5376	169	99	2008	
133	1926	2187	19393	11231	2169	4700	4434	228	72	2009	
121	2936	2584	21626	14634	2072	5677	5048	231	171	2010	
119	3369	3357	26722	19630	2385	7283	6470	159	104	2011	
71	1499	658	8266	4943	268	1952	2558	77	74	2000	Etats-Unis
157	2308	2314	21936	11154	1231	4825	4480	153	99	2008	
101	1323	1774	17355	9997	710	4034	3205	216	72	2009	
94	2355	2081	19367	12760	828	4981	4145	214	171	2010	
90	2856	2749	24284	17006	989	6381	5564	146	104	2011	
284	44	6	3	4	34	5	114	1	1	2000	Europe du Sud-Est
2059	157	162	7	41	247	24	720	0	27	2008	
2149	85	97	12	83	36	33	476	0	24	2009	
2597	126	52	6	182	91	122	749	0	14	2010	
2965	249	48	20	84	32	23	1132	0	54	2011	
27	17	15	7	160	31	2	163	...	14	2000	Communauté d'Etats Indépendants
138	1884	232	38	577	1708	64	3267	0	65	2008	
110	1804	378	92	1872	1711	350	2964	0	43	2009	
112	1863	297	91	2047	839	155	2659	0	132	2010	
178	2621	641	114	2239	1203	71	3852	0	177	2011	
6	6	0	1	155	7	1	67	...	0	2000	Fédération de Russie 4/
51	897	150	23	391	567	24	1204	0	9	2008	
63	1062	127	43	1566	408	94	1454	0	7	2009	
62	985	132	39	1914	124	51	985	...	73	2010	
107	1482	576	64	2089	137	19	1923	0	98	2011	

Voir la fin du tableau pour la remarque générale et les notes.

World exports by provenance and destination (Table D)

In million U.S. dollars f.o.b.

Exports to → / ↓ Exports from	Year	World 1/ Monde 1/	Developed economies 2/ Économies développées 2/ Total	Asia-Pacific Asie-Pacifique Total	Japan Japon	Europe Total	Germany Allemagne	North America Amérique du Nord Total	U.S.A. É.-U.	Commonwealth of Independent States Communauté d'Etats Indépendants Total	Europe
Food, beverages and tobacco (SITC, Rev. 3, 0 and 1) *[cont.]*											
Northern Africa	2000	2277	1661	281	279	1299	71	81	58	63	63
	2008	7098	3864	211	203	3462	178	190	139	445	439
	2009	7907	3700	155	148	3326	211	219	163	418	405
	2010	8497	3653	129	121	3295	222	229	171	459	451
	2011	9233	4318	148	140	3900	256	269	200	652	634
Sub-Saharan Africa	2000	10623	6487	527	454	5340	618	620	545	113	112
	2008	22619	12925	560	432	11067	1041	1298	1125	345	306
	2009	25388	13370	608	476	11267	1038	1495	1307	328	288
	2010	28181	14889	846	554	11984	1221	2059	1576	381	333
	2011	34951	18179	944	709	14655	1550	2580	2141	451	392
South Africa	2000	2168	1261	176	144	923	69	161	110	8	7
	2008	5202	2710	243	165	2193	221	274	168	133	131
	2009	5266	2543	226	152	2052	223	265	172	132	127
	2010	5977	2920	297	199	2294	247	329	203	186	181
	2011	6578	2861	291	182	2258	245	312	192	191	185
Latin America and the Caribbean	2000	47176	31343	2605	2313	13658	2245	15080	14395	1096	1082
	2008	126642	69745	5184	4542	36156	5413	28405	26586	7368	7055
	2009	119684	63785	4599	3996	31399	4788	27788	25909	5398	5164
	2010	139538	71248	5760	5137	34421	5192	31066	28700	6803	6560
	2011	177446	89374	7865	6845	43089	6740	38420	35536	7675	7366
Brazil	2000	10142	6609	710	514	4599	667	1300	1179	471	460
	2008	40330	18317	1949	1719	13386	2203	2982	2554	4654	4430
	2009	38904	15749	1333	1195	11532	1978	2885	2365	3109	2949
	2010	48051	18169	1823	1701	13047	2210	3299	2678	4258	4052
	2011	58415	23427	2890	2668	15964	2900	4573	3792	4410	4166
Eastern Asia	2000	21062	11179	7892	7697	1446	308	1841	1605	297	254
	2008	45487	21304	9774	8906	5275	1216	6255	5505	2148	1817
	2009	45815	20586	9766	8906	4892	1153	5928	5154	1764	1440
	2010	56783	24737	11703	10685	5903	1345	7131	6206	2221	1843
	2011	69278	28898	14052	12757	6717	1457	8129	7106	2728	2276
China	2000	13027	7217	4960	4877	1214	296	1044	910	189	162
	2008	34291	17718	7507	6888	4961	1188	5251	4637	1775	1492
	2009	34244	17055	7535	6950	4595	1126	4925	4298	1490	1209
	2010	43054	20634	9041	8313	5554	1309	6039	5282	1923	1585
	2011	52771	24192	10901	9947	6369	1425	6921	6077	2406	2010
Southern Asia	2000	8369	3495	830	756	1720	289	945	858	584	435
	2008	30624	6517	1065	841	4058	547	1393	1195	1644	1058
	2009	23697	5567	816	604	3434	425	1317	1140	1323	901
	2010	28176	6153	1081	861	3675	512	1397	1198	1532	1020
	2011	38577	8174	1439	1159	4905	719	1830	1564	2161	1401
South-Eastern Asia	2000	23695	12541	5245	4705	3056	465	4241	3874	168	159
	2008	59005	25594	8409	6620	8888	1404	8298	7480	1369	1262
	2009	55313	23495	7912	6288	7509	1172	8074	7240	885	793
	2010	64341	26341	9073	7032	7967	1316	9300	8439	985	885
	2011	78828	31198	11309	8771	9222	1488	10666	9626	1212	1071
Western Asia	2000	7475	2824	147	100	2321	624	356	328	508	307
	2008	22145	6641	392	259	5495	1327	755	661	1718	1360
	2009	23791	6122	306	167	5025	1171	791	690	1577	1277
	2010	26665	6584	311	159	5453	1293	820	680	1908	1575
	2011	33892	7792	406	217	6370	1522	1016	838	2277	1872
Oceania	2000	479	385	113	58	196	76	76	75	0	0
	2008	1141	770	202	104	330	124	237	212	4	4
	2009	1013	636	186	90	277	96	173	170	5	5
	2010	1003	639	227	119	226	107	186	183	6	6
	2011	1079	692	256	135	245	122	191	188	6	6

For general note and footnotes see end of table

En millions de dollars E.-U. f.o.b.

South-Eastern Europe Europe du Sud-Est	Northern Africa Afrique septentrio-nale	Sub-Saharar Africa Afrique subsahari-enne	Latin America and the Caribbean Amérique latine et Caraïbes	Eastern Asia Asie orientale	Southern Asia Asie méridionale	South-easter Asia Asie du Sud-Est	Western Asia Asie occidentale	Oceania Océanie	Other 3/ Autres 3/	⟵ Exportations vers Année	Exportations en provence de ↓
Produits alimentaires, boisson et tabac (CTCI, Rev. 3, 0 et 1) *[suite]*											
10	169	84	5	11	2	10	238	1	24	2000	Afrique septentrionale
47	648	509	51	31	53	34	1312	2	101	2008	
56	704	647	42	20	77	66	1952	2	224	2009	
44	854	984	55	34	116	76	2123	2	98	2010	
62	739	932	68	49	113	87	2103	2	109	2011	
23	204	2074	82	236	458	190	718	6	32	2000	Afrique subsaharienne
67	474	5202	315	433	926	674	1155	21	81	2008	
93	527	5761	1503	452	997	669	1517	95	77	2009	
90	647	6221	616	824	950	1050	1881	104	528	2010	
67	646	7311	1280	1123	1606	1556	2286	128	318	2011	
4	8	536	11	103	65	36	130	0	7	2000	Afrique du sud
7	22	1590	24	199	63	134	275	5	39	2008	
2	53	1643	22	198	97	202	325	9	41	2009	
5	44	1602	37	396	60	203	482	13	29	2010	
3	15	1745	437	602	78	195	436	6	8	2011	
167	811	566	8780	1541	396	736	1499	12	230	2000	Amérique latine et Caraïbes
640	3919	3841	23864	5491	2098	3353	6025	34	263	2008	
571	3217	3768	21057	6564	3815	4452	6832	27	198	2009	
633	4580	3910	25008	8514	4909	5691	8021	18	204	2010	
769	7450	5887	31588	12783	3693	7310	10249	24	645	2011	
85	185	264	1061	372	139	250	705	0	...	2000	Brésil
431	1667	2203	4171	2235	1055	1502	4087	9	...	2008	
339	1761	2533	3190	2733	3049	1824	4610	6	...	2009	
371	2837	2732	4412	3258	3737	2703	5569	5	...	2010	
526	4019	3803	5425	4744	2833	2913	6305	10	...	2011	
26	145	346	185	6265	195	2052	310	34	28	2000	Asie orientale
114	444	1042	1194	11448	571	5630	1369	201	21	2008	
89	488	1055	976	11597	906	6831	1356	151	15	2009	
87	545	1181	1527	14002	1043	9489	1778	160	12	2010	
113	635	1749	1868	17148	1188	12882	1852	205	11	2011	
26	142	295	145	3365	152	1242	247	5	...	2000	Chine
110	416	973	1094	6715	460	3928	1028	74	...	2008	
85	464	990	898	6680	779	4746	1005	52	...	2009	
84	512	1108	1415	8372	937	6700	1298	72	...	2010	
108	596	1603	1742	10657	985	8977	1419	87	...	2011	
11	217	182	104	414	821	623	1915	2	1	2000	Asie méridionale
58	550	1452	214	1886	4876	3432	9950	23	22	2008	
51	412	1053	167	1250	3706	2566	7511	4	87	2009	
42	627	1431	220	1792	4646	3180	8514	7	30	2010	
59	839	1871	302	2447	6707	4368	11596	10	43	2011	
36	127	650	150	3276	655	5000	976	46	70	2000	Asie du Sud-est
151	859	3873	1009	6515	1726	14002	3398	222	286	2008	
145	752	3844	782	7177	1920	13191	2678	218	227	2009	
145	743	3702	1022	8512	2636	16844	2833	248	329	2010	
170	979	4488	1169	11045	3348	20782	3732	335	371	2011	
143	266	151	58	102	478	71	2659	0	217	2000	Asie occidentale
617	791	1020	126	229	1375	412	8901	2	314	2008	
638	802	1153	117	220	1753	450	10612	2	344	2009	
646	862	1188	167	1771	2394	595	9659	3	889	2010	
763	1122	1468	200	2570	3420	771	11784	4	1723	2011	
0	...	8	0	21	0	33	0	23	10	2000	Océanie
0	0	7	8	41	2	207	0	100	1	2008	
0	0	2	7	47	1	229	0	79	6	2009	
0	...	5	8	54	1	217	1	69	3	2010	
0	...	6	6	66	1	215	0	83	3	2011	

Voir la fin du tableau pour la remarque générale et les notes.

World exports by provenance and destination (Table D)

In million U.S. dollars f.o.b.

Exports to →			Developed economies 2/ Économies développées 2/							Commonwealth of Independent States Communauté d'Etats Indépendants	
				Asia-Pacific Asie-Pacifique		Europe		North America Amérique du Nord			
↓ Exports from	Year	World 1/ Monde 1/	Total	Total	Japan Japon	Total	Germany Allemagne	Total	U.S.A. É.-U.	Total	Europe
Crude materials (excluding fuels), oils, fats (SITC, Rev. 3, 2 and 4)											
World 1/	2000	212927	134987	21280	19734	83823	15200	29884	23149	3298	2947
	2008	654155	323792	48154	44456	224338	40492	51301	38673	15039	12679
	2009	494234	217106	33313	30921	150240	27654	33553	24744	9437	7741
	2010	693909	298626	50859	47677	202534	37802	45233	33451	12196	10295
	2011	882251	359713	59855	55944	244735	44300	55124	41406	14811	12505
Developed Economies - Asia-Pacific 2/	2000	17277	6994	3049	2577	2422	328	1523	1155	175	174
	2008	60327	16078	9882	9206	3961	501	2234	1827	704	700
	2009	51381	10499	6737	6259	1910	414	1852	1446	350	341
	2010	81493	15590	11183	10549	2872	637	1535	1135	571	538
	2011	106149	19726	14251	13787	4014	864	1461	1007	223	194
Japan	2000	3369	747	30	.	437	96	280	268	5	4
	2008	10337	1553	48	.	961	247	544	524	36	33
	2009	9005	1069	42	.	543	129	484	469	31	25
	2010	10992	1554	44	.	824	162	686	667	57	49
	2011	12380	1817	42	.	1077	227	698	676	77	67
Developed Economies - Europe 2/	2000	60995	51423	1528	1331	47527	9912	2368	2049	810	783
	2008	169711	135318	2384	1931	127967	26100	4966	4255	3401	3203
	2009	122048	93542	1943	1551	88294	18263	3306	2869	2380	2244
	2010	158087	120311	2355	1862	113852	23581	4105	3470	2784	2636
	2011	192179	145946	2761	2196	138424	28473	4761	3998	3635	3453
France	2000	6036	5195	62	54	4960	957	173	159	43	39
	2008	15360	13401	69	53	13051	2480	280	256	197	184
	2009	10118	8362	55	41	8108	1690	199	178	125	120
	2010	13471	11107	66	50	10818	2019	223	201	157	150
	2011	17316	14428	91	72	14039	2945	298	274	211	204
Germany	2000	9272	7481	98	75	7114	.	269	236	175	169
	2008	29058	23534	215	143	21997	.	1323	1171	816	776
	2009	19413	15106	157	104	14291	.	658	601	582	556
	2010	25909	20697	205	138	19539	.	953	860	637	610
	2011	33158	26710	236	170	25373	.	1101	992	815	778
Developed Economies - North America 2/	2000	53039	35036	6987	6666	10335	1651	17714	12780	60	49
	2008	119056	55160	9528	8868	22106	3810	23527	14655	337	328
	2009	91171	36031	5971	5629	14914	2146	15146	9275	240	230
	2010	121242	49484	7877	7392	21808	2972	19799	12178	332	298
	2011	141927	53732	9243	8672	21236	2971	23252	14381	279	245
United States	2000	30471	15489	4053	3903	6505	965	4931	.	55	43
	2008	81110	28350	5142	4936	14390	2448	8818	.	274	266
	2009	65183	19652	3270	3099	10550	1459	5832	.	209	201
	2010	85505	26687	4215	3947	14854	1878	7618	.	296	264
	2011	97215	26529	4554	4247	13106	2209	8869	.	258	227
South-Eastern Europe	2000	1742	850	9	8	826	121	15	5	108	108
	2008	6244	2989	76	76	2819	361	93	76	66	62
	2009	4796	2364	92	92	2260	323	12	11	35	32
	2010	6901	3350	163	162	3172	459	15	15	51	43
	2011	9773	4977	185	185	4707	588	85	15	71	64
Commonwealth of Independent States	2000	9303	4919	598	597	4233	461	88	79	1650	1383
	2008	33323	11997	543	541	11339	686	115	97	7103	5308
	2009	21609	6532	377	375	6034	426	121	95	4228	2939
	2010	28429	9403	384	382	8761	643	259	246	4706	3341
	2011	38117	11752	530	524	10996	847	227	214	6131	4505
Russian Federation 4/	2000	4752	2850	588	587	2214	173	48	40	338	229
	2008	17537	6966	542	540	6329	310	95	81	1895	573
	2009	10009	3562	372	370	3110	219	80	69	1197	284
	2010	13274	5253	364	363	4687	352	202	191	1248	381
	2011	18017	6510	476	476	5856	436	179	168	1345	424

For general note and footnotes see end of table

Exportations mondiales en provenance et de destination (Tableau D)

En millions de dollars E.-U. f.o.b.

← Exportations vers

South-Eastern Europe Europe du Sud-Est	Northern Africa Afrique septentrionale	Sub-Saharan Africa Afrique subsaharienne	Latin America and the Caribbean Amérique latine et Caraïbes	Eastern Asia Asie orientale	Southern Asia Asie méridionale	South-eastern Asia Asie du Sud-Est	Western Asia Asie occidentale	Oceania Océanie	Other 3/ Autres 3/	Année	Exportations en provenance de ↓
			Matières brutes (sauf combustibles), huiles et graisses (CTCI, Rev. 3, 2 et 4)								
1141	2690	3043	10290	32742	6981	9124	6397	84	2152	2000	Monde 1/
5845	11872	10377	30110	169925	29772	28092	27956	203	1172	2008	
3726	8129	7965	19241	159898	26726	22090	18664	210	1041	2009	
5452	11126	10795	27685	231905	35461	31218	28200	218	1025	2010	
7127	13940	14054	35991	307450	44667	40743	36518	250	6985	2011	
56	116	351	117	6159	678	1505	377	29	721	2000	Économies développées - Asie-Pacifique 2/
58	30	701	236	35943	1776	2752	1605	65	381	2008	
13	23	547	182	34627	1444	2219	1320	69	89	2009	
11	47	727	251	56599	2567	3330	1643	92	63	2010	
16	25	298	260	73923	2593	3676	242	103	5064	2011	
1	3	41	33	1879	111	525	22	1	...	2000	Japon
0	10	138	43	7169	214	1100	73	1	...	2008	
2	9	136	41	6510	183	953	70	1	...	2009	
6	11	170	53	7490	230	1329	90	2	...	2010	
8	14	183	79	8344	249	1523	85	1	...	2011	
397	1136	626	613	2814	636	633	1535	11	360	2000	Économies développées - Europe 2/
2086	3705	1363	1608	11287	2743	1850	5890	27	433	2008	
1517	2874	1106	1328	10766	2597	1556	4099	22	262	2009	
2197	3636	1449	1540	14310	3316	1901	6375	24	243	2010	
2620	4010	1866	1856	17763	4216	2351	7506	24	386	2011	
16	118	62	61	280	115	29	109	7	0	2000	France
87	310	102	122	715	134	94	181	17	1	2008	
64	272	86	85	746	130	69	166	12	0	2009	
72	300	102	107	1032	171	129	281	10	3	2010	
104	376	117	112	1207	204	211	331	14	1	2011	
95	91	101	110	601	125	140	206	1	146	2000	Allemagne
275	265	286	290	1838	489	349	746	1	168	2008	
197	317	202	271	1572	348	306	511	2	0	2009	
270	247	297	287	1980	421	330	735	7	0	2010	
311	334	407	343	2397	605	382	851	0	1	2011	
26	190	314	5427	8312	522	1923	975	21	232	2000	Économies développées - Amérique du Nord 2/
101	1669	971	13152	34826	2034	5409	5272	41	84	2008	
81	1360	557	8843	33532	2472	4459	3411	23	162	2009	
138	1848	640	11512	43868	2792	5546	4843	35	205	2010	
220	2246	782	14635	52951	3572	6668	6673	48	122	2011	
21	165	250	5057	6440	360	1472	911	19	232	2000	États-Unis
76	1436	663	11475	28138	1560	4662	4367	25	84	2008	
44	1176	409	8068	26915	1912	3730	2888	18	162	2009	
35	1519	481	10328	35122	2024	4717	4070	20	205	2010	
40	1851	575	12963	41047	2648	5731	5406	45	122	2011	
231	122	2	8	102	6	3	310	0	0	2000	Europe du Sud-Est
1210	183	59	23	181	25	5	1500	0	3	2008	
712	159	112	8	255	93	7	1048	0	2	2009	
1100	177	141	12	381	81	6	1594	0	8	2010	
1532	180	223	11	495	150	7	2087	0	40	2011	
129	270	6	49	1264	180	65	771	0	0	2000	Communauté d'Etats Indépendants
702	1958	58	207	6849	1734	228	2485	1	0	2008	
369	797	29	30	5661	2312	112	1537	0	0	2009	
642	1020	71	80	8404	1431	155	2510	1	6	2010	
799	1310	174	240	12108	1968	174	3447	1	12	2011	
23	190	1	12	973	45	21	300	0	0	2000	Fédération de Russie 4/
164	1410	39	117	4979	358	183	1426	1	0	2008	
61	417	14	22	3703	384	85	565	0	0	2009	
65	508	27	50	4572	456	91	996	1	6	2010	
100	843	62	161	6873	540	106	1464	1	12	2011	

Voir la fin du tableau pour la remarque générale et les notes.

World exports by provenance and destination (Table D)

In million U.S. dollars f.o.b.

Exports to →			Developed economies 2/ Économies développées 2/								Commonwealth of Independent States Communauté d'Etats Indépendants	
				Asia-Pacific Asie-Pacifique		Europe		North America Amérique du Nord				
↓ Exports from	Year	World 1/ Monde 1/	Total	Total	Japan Japon	Total	Germany Allemagne	Total	U.S.A. É.-U.		Total	Europe
Crude materials (excluding fuels), oils, fats (SITC, Rev. 3, 2 and 4) *[cont.]*												
Northern Africa	2000	1414	946	61	24	773	42	111	102		12	12
	2008	6036	3526	422	45	2503	103	601	587		42	39
	2009	3721	1615	70	18	1203	72	342	329		9	9
	2010	4449	2083	132	25	1508	90	442	423		21	20
	2011	5263	2575	158	30	1881	112	536	513		37	35
Sub-Saharan Africa	2000	7463	4487	522	506	3428	537	537	477		15	15
	2008	27375	12625	1744	1667	9382	1520	1500	1055		407	396
	2009	22287	8718	958	919	6599	910	1161	784		209	200
	2010	30780	11711	1606	1522	8237	1333	1868	1260		374	358
	2011	40835	14294	2092	2016	10303	1246	1899	1573		363	354
South Africa	2000	2693	1932	411	400	1205	338	315	306		8	8
	2008	10737	5176	1419	1356	3321	991	436	404		110	110
	2009	8538	2970	724	705	1877	568	369	313		17	15
	2010	13231	4630	1209	1145	3018	825	404	385		94	94
	2011	18549	5765	1571	1526	3697	541	496	452		66	66
Latin America and the Caribbean	2000	25161	15222	2677	2602	7717	1255	4828	4006		149	149
	2008	104252	44729	9858	9547	25281	4497	9591	8157		555	514
	2009	80796	30263	7241	7019	16215	3056	6807	5572		377	338
	2010	121694	44837	12403	12015	23270	4858	9164	7443		747	693
	2011	160808	55484	14777	13993	29519	5195	11188	9024		809	703
Brazil	2000	9140	6169	900	881	4222	771	1047	980		12	12
	2008	42307	19543	2880	2740	14020	2414	2643	2031		219	181
	2009	35272	13204	1777	1730	9536	1314	1891	1264		99	75
	2010	54257	19555	3922	3790	13083	2666	2550	1810		321	295
	2011	75880	24734	5210	5003	16701	2443	2822	1961		347	269
Eastern Asia	2000	11347	4318	1979	1894	1470	229	869	814		91	88
	2008	25680	10189	3385	3122	4331	846	2474	2180		394	351
	2009	19019	6871	2529	2345	2736	578	1606	1401		225	193
	2010	25956	9486	3317	3121	3923	790	2246	1933		350	321
	2011	34190	12152	4351	4028	4915	1083	2886	2520		521	487
China	2000	4575	2767	1241	1205	1051	169	475	454		56	53
	2008	11914	6610	1941	1784	3015	549	1655	1476		229	191
	2009	8495	4472	1455	1356	1907	450	1111	974		133	107
	2010	11994	6162	1885	1773	2767	590	1510	1316		203	177
	2011	15546	7613	2285	2083	3381	795	1947	1737		323	296
Southern Asia	2000	2592	1254	296	277	665	105	292	279		92	72
	2008	17011	2714	639	586	1454	276	620	590		215	60
	2009	13865	2245	606	520	1207	211	433	401		105	37
	2010	19738	2767	471	416	1603	307	693	658		581	497
	2011	27040	3847	646	573	2240	440	961	913		790	663
South-Eastern Asia	2000	18177	7768	3106	2833	3214	376	1448	1324		71	69
	2008	71647	24065	8648	7995	9990	1382	5427	5074		1363	1326
	2009	53902	15732	6049	5559	7052	994	2631	2440		1093	1063
	2010	81802	25762	9881	9282	10924	1737	4956	4561		1397	1340
	2011	108710	31261	10007	9226	13571	2040	7684	7092		1605	1543
Western Asia	2000	2650	1083	115	110	885	111	83	73		61	47
	2008	10111	2371	218	165	2011	199	143	110		451	392
	2009	7400	1443	105	86	1206	152	132	114		187	116
	2010	10218	2125	109	92	1873	238	143	124		282	210
	2011	14428	2497	132	110	2191	281	175	147		345	259
Oceania	2000	1768	687	353	308	328	71	6	6		3	0
	2008	3381	2031	828	707	1193	211	11	10		0	0
	2009	2239	1250	634	549	610	108	6	5		0	0
	2010	3120	1718	977	858	733	158	8	7		1	1
	2011	2831	1469	722	602	739	161	9	9		0	...

For general note and footnotes see end of table

Exportations mondiales en provenance et de destination (Tableau D)

En millions de dollars E.-U. f.o.b.

← Exportations vers

South-Eastern Europe Europe du Sud-Est	Northern Africa Afrique septentrio-nale	Sub-Saharan Africa Afrique subsahari-enne	Latin America and the Caribbean Amérique latine et Caraïbes	Eastern Asia Asie orientale	Southern Asia Asie méridionale	South-eastern Asia Asie du Sud-Est	Western Asia Asie occidentale	Oceania Océanie	Other 3/ Autres 3/	Année	Exportations en provenance de ↓
Matières brutes (sauf combustibles), huiles et graisses (CTCI, Rev. 3, 2 et 4) *[suite]*											
35	45	13	89	63	63	32	106	0	9	2000	Afrique septentrionale
121	302	147	393	301	422	123	641	...	18	2008	
27	274	195	144	397	341	94	489	...	135	2009	
38	327	225	261	369	443	125	529	0	28	2010	
47	320	219	314	426	517	154	625	0	30	2011	
18	109	1004	116	754	328	374	229	1	27	2000	Afrique subsaharienne
62	217	3446	245	7106	1146	1381	713	10	19	2008	
47	162	2649	208	7583	904	1118	648	34	7	2009	
55	196	3557	623	10245	1188	1555	1188	6	82	2010	
71	281	4748	855	14900	1754	2035	1470	7	57	2011	
10	6	112	23	358	62	154	29	0	0	2000	Afrique du sud
38	9	364	117	3732	496	559	127	7	2	2008	
3	10	228	72	4390	291	459	95	1	2	2009	
13	15	323	84	6606	577	770	114	2	1	2010	
22	18	471	135	10180	715	958	217	2	0	2011	
145	361	222	3381	3244	1370	669	389	1	7	2000	Amérique latine et Caraïbes
1023	2196	830	12068	32778	4207	3343	2441	2	80	2008	
677	1177	548	7117	33752	3204	2111	1353	1	216	2009	
827	1807	761	10736	50703	4930	3182	2913	2	248	2010	
1137	2804	973	14117	70014	5720	4350	4518	2	880	2011	
41	196	50	682	1211	328	210	241	1	...	2000	Brésil
270	912	375	2197	14329	1013	1803	1645	2	0	2008	
105	691	141	1052	17163	756	1132	929	0	...	2009	
143	859	182	2229	26216	824	1628	2297	1	...	2010	
243	994	261	3148	38540	1283	2594	3733	0	...	2011	
7	33	46	98	5248	440	948	116	1	1	2000	Asie orientale
112	115	301	560	9546	1299	2383	773	6	0	2008	
53	100	234	443	7382	1042	2097	564	9	0	2009	
82	144	308	628	9311	1694	3159	788	4	0	2010	
123	216	397	956	11529	2257	4763	1271	4	0	2011	
6	18	23	42	1000	251	360	52	0	...	2000	Chine
102	85	136	300	2302	625	1014	505	4	...	2008	
48	70	111	235	1693	500	871	355	7	...	2009	
74	109	150	346	2324	851	1277	496	2	...	2010	
113	176	194	591	2740	1180	1800	814	2	...	2011	
6	31	40	56	495	216	223	179	0	0	2000	Asie méridionale
23	100	121	142	9886	1979	924	894	1	13	2008	
62	76	134	89	8268	1380	718	738	2	49	2009	
23	82	159	137	11516	2157	1150	1140	3	24	2010	
36	112	197	186	15716	2959	1594	1566	3	33	2011	
41	202	375	281	4017	2230	2377	794	15	4	2000	Asie du Sud-est
170	1207	2256	1366	18553	10733	9122	2758	42	9	2008	
69	985	1661	784	15389	9582	7069	1487	44	8	2009	
143	1685	2618	1831	22819	12970	10449	2069	48	12	2010	
239	2261	3988	2423	33311	16355	14180	3014	53	20	2011	
49	73	35	55	159	300	142	617	0	75	2000	Asie occidentale
178	190	122	104	1832	1416	331	2984	1	132	2008	
101	143	194	60	1658	1289	246	1968	0	111	2009	
196	155	138	64	2463	1766	315	2609	0	104	2010	
287	176	191	125	3400	2490	474	4099	2	341	2011	
1	...	8	1	112	10	229	...	4	714	2000	Océanie
0	0	2	6	838	257	240	0	7	0	2008	
0	...	1	4	628	67	283	0	5	0	2009	
0	...	0	10	915	127	345	0	4	0	2010	
...	...	0	13	913	115	316	1	4	0	2011	

Voir la fin du tableau pour la remarque générale et les notes.

World exports by provenance and destination (Table D)

In million U.S. dollars f.o.b.

Exports to → / ↓ Exports from	Year	World 1/ Monde 1/	Developed economies 2/ Économies développées 2/ Total	Asia-Pacific Asie-Pacifique Total	Asia-Pacific: Japan Japon	Europe Total	Europe: Germany Allemagne	North America Amérique du Nord Total	North America: U.S.A. É.-U.	Commonwealth of Independent States Communauté d'Etats Indépendants Total	CIS: Europe
					Mineral fuels and related materials (SITC. Rev. 3, 3)						
World 1/	2000	655551	441242	71801	66627	221459	29156	147982	137274	11180	9725
	2008	2774565	1626789	195012	165229	937284	92441	494493	399978	50252	40773
	2009	1736058	945211	101108	82740	569792	52840	274310	211150	31866	26000
	2010	2189424	1166248	119447	96212	700529	66749	346272	269451	37456	31734
	2011	2924755	1445799	138560	106730	886031	90957	421208	320970	30914	25830
Developed Economies - Asia-Pacific 2/	2000	15224	7843	5798	5119	901	85	1144	1143	7	7
	2008	80747	39343	31068	26325	6366	502	1909	1908	100	97
	2009	57092	24541	21285	18609	2691	123	564	543	40	39
	2010	74265	30482	25201	22064	4180	237	1102	1030	55	53
	2011	86922	27444	21598	17199	4818	304	1029	989	69	68
Japan	2000	1520	518	83	.	40	4	395	394	7	7
	2008	18776	4211	2349	.	1131	7	731	731	73	71
	2009	10530	2320	1285	.	649	9	386	365	40	39
	2010	13048	2884	1467	.	568	3	849	778	54	53
	2011	16303	3336	2269	.	332	5	734	694	69	68
Developed Economies - Europe 2/	2000	130040	117996	136	102	100926	20418	16933	13145	384	367
	2008	473761	406659	972	833	361394	60170	44294	37350	2498	2283
	2009	291418	251794	430	381	225208	34782	26156	21747	1671	1518
	2010	366447	312951	518	468	283215	45282	29217	24484	2154	1937
	2011	471740	384048	656	588	349772	56374	33619	27450	3393	2893
France	2000	8183	7258	28	13	6660	1009	570	561	16	15
	2008	30139	24863	56	50	21753	2959	3054	2863	8	8
	2009	16389	12901	39	35	11701	1629	1161	1098	17	16
	2010	18717	14723	42	39	13341	1826	1340	1227	10	10
	2011	26539	20190	26	22	18545	2288	1619	1405	17	15
Germany	2000	7757	5384	13	9	4961	.	410	406	35	33
	2008	37526	27977	30	20	26347	.	1601	1564	204	173
	2009	23147	21626	26	18	21060	.	539	536	190	161
	2010	23907	22555	37	24	22294	.	225	213	320	279
	2011	33312	22493	52	34	22117	.	323	281	474	408
Developed Economies - North America 2/	2000	49685	41512	1485	1328	2019	97	38009	35232	8	8
	2008	202339	158240	3918	3511	20920	941	133401	116912	201	196
	2009	126736	92722	2809	2500	14219	526	75694	66022	121	111
	2010	172794	118231	3964	3677	16628	1188	97639	85148	492	446
	2011	245086	159991	5274	4787	31512	1594	123205	105235	1113	1045
United States	2000	13340	5570	1001	845	1793	80	2776	.	8	7
	2008	76533	35577	1722	1319	17367	635	16488	.	189	185
	2009	54720	23616	1189	884	12755	357	9672	.	117	108
	2010	80728	29744	2097	1815	15156	931	12491	.	483	439
	2011	129233	49609	2988	2517	28653	1347	17968	.	1088	1021
South-Eastern Europe	2000	1442	243	...	.	231	6	12	12	243	170
	2008	9342	2570	0	0	2440	118	130	130	1483	1145
	2009	5550	1875	0	0	1798	85	77	77	787	526
	2010	6943	2476	0	0	2405	120	71	71	1042	716
	2011	9351	3328	0	0	3257	213	72	71	1595	1098
Commonwealth of Independent States	2000	62943	41876	302	302	40040	3736	1534	215	10354	9064
	2008	424345	304217	6687	6684	284529	15714	13001	11383	44769	36332
	2009	250975	179771	5793	5687	165671	10037	8307	6004	28675	23400
	2010	334403	236293	11508	11402	213599	12205	11186	8120	32824	27955
	2011	397180	287665	11907	11900	259822	20811	15935	12273	23575	19889
Russian Federation 4/	2000	52166	36681	302	302	36076	3554	303	189	6979	6287
	2008	307371	225989	6538	6538	213437	14285	6014	5267	29946	23365
	2009	190171	141687	5791	5687	131599	8743	4296	3903	18741	15121
	2010	257616	187565	11477	11402	169513	11096	6575	5989	25235	22200
	2011	282392	212520	11900	11900	190880	17461	9740	9395	9198	8123

For general note and footnotes see end of table

Exportations mondiales en provenance et de destination (Tableau D)

En millions de dollars E.-U. f.o.b.

South-Eastern Europe Europe du Sud-Est	Northern Africa Afrique septentrionale	Sub-Saharan Africa Afrique subsaharienne	Latin America and the Caribbean Amérique latine et Caraïbes	Eastern Asia Asie orientale	Southern Asia Asie méridionale	South-eastern Asia Asie du Sud-Est	Western Asia Asie occidentale	Oceania Océanie	Other 3/ Autres 3/	Année	← Exportations vers Exportations en provence de ↓
			Combustibles minéraux et produits assimiles (CTCI, Rev. 3, 3)								
3229	7442	5752	33958	88964	11886	25846	12503	1115	12433	2000	Monde 1/
26107	25215	42608	140093	508463	71510	139144	63190	3260	77933	2008	
11507	18499	32514	89379	355839	60814	99432	41138	2798	47062	2009	
15331	22590	40470	116485	482330	69170	133262	50507	3509	52066	2010	
16074	27039	53123	157714	615776	75469	167203	66389	4562	264694	2011	
0	8	65	320	3610	499	1633	112	421	706	2000	Economies développées -
83	74	471	2782	19001	5589	9475	835	401	2594	2008	Asie-Pacifique 2/
17	62	123	1429	18152	4473	7112	229	508	406	2009	
0	11	353	2427	23609	7195	8694	289	550	601	2010	
0	1	347	2294	24514	7813	11190	321	557	12370	2011	
...	0	2	42	701	27	220	4	0	...	2000	Japon
1	1	12	1349	7588	595	4781	160	5	...	2008	
17	1	15	395	3604	148	3956	35	0	...	2009	
0	1	14	1068	4577	186	4232	32	0	...	2010	
0	1	84	668	6441	213	5375	79	38	...	2011	
784	1350	1171	767	506	436	286	1983	6	4373	2000	Economies développées -
3546	6730	9765	6562	1319	564	1828	8154	20	26114	2008	Europe 2/
2293	4617	7969	4263	1162	732	1374	6252	18	9273	2009	
3103	6634	11568	6384	1476	441	1844	7406	47	12441	2010	
5134	6954	16330	7944	2841	947	2927	13574	42	27606	2011	
8	212	257	130	23	21	19	204	3	34	2000	France
30	1296	691	922	111	121	123	1707	4	262	2008	
28	684	705	273	141	83	117	1273	4	163	2009	
21	716	1329	260	49	93	157	875	4	478	2010	
48	829	2030	462	113	193	127	1841	4	684	2011	
22	10	35	117	35	12	13	38	0	2056	2000	Allemagne
83	34	140	89	120	31	50	262	0	8535	2008	
59	49	172	113	132	33	55	191	0	527	2009	
73	58	203	109	179	44	94	218	0	54	2010	
102	31	289	124	198	52	72	277	0	9201	2011	
73	105	134	6228	821	95	419	287	2	0	2000	Economies développées -
470	833	1450	31317	3534	926	2715	2652	1	0	2008	Amérique du Nord 2/
56	919	1108	22825	3716	1047	2724	1497	2	0	2009	
159	1135	1425	38875	5495	1125	4068	1789	2	0	2010	
268	1759	1844	60582	8290	1992	5121	4123	2	...	2011	
61	96	125	6142	582	85	418	251	2	...	2000	Etats-Unis
329	819	1441	30361	1844	887	2674	2411	1	...	2008	
52	866	1095	22238	1836	980	2600	1319	1	...	2009	
159	1133	1411	38100	3025	1101	3965	1606	2	...	2010	
268	1707	1838	59152	4726	1883	5114	3848	2	...	2011	
661	13	65	17	0	1	12	186	...	1	2000	Europe du Sud-Est
2411	112	238	75	1	13	277	2161	1	0	2008	
1447	147	101	12	2	44	304	823	2	7	2009	
2018	45	165	12	3	69	234	840	5	35	2010	
2520	188	139	7	4	72	36	1399	2	60	2011	
1626	28	22	4633	697	251	464	2990	1	2	2000	Communauté d'Etats
18781	719	355	3264	23494	4416	2772	21551	3	4	2008	Indépendants
7209	826	287	1461	16083	3189	2661	10591	76	146	2009	
9658	1131	74	1897	27770	3678	6022	15025	0	31	2010	
7818	2170	319	2991	46207	4054	6633	15617	0	132	2011	
1407	24	15	3416	590	15	428	2611	0	0	2000	Fédération de Russie 4/
16667	567	244	1693	17453	286	1208	13313	3	0	2008	
5759	603	273	1070	12516	700	1540	7206	76	0	2009	
7615	756	24	1188	20055	886	3753	10515	0	24	2010	
4714	1834	251	2056	35001	1111	4904	10684	0	120	2011	

Voir la fin du tableau pour la remarque générale et les notes.

World exports by provenance and destination (Table D)

In million U.S. dollars f.o.b.

Exports to → / ↓ Exports from	Year	World 1/ Monde 1/	Developed economies 2/ Économies développées 2/ Total	Asia-Pacific Asie-Pacifique Total	Asia-Pacific Japan Japon	Europe Total	Europe Germany Allemagne	North America Amérique du Nord Total	North America U.S.A. É.-U.	Commonwealth of Independent States Communauté d'Etats Indépendants Total	Commonwealth of Independent States Europe
		Mineral fuels and related materials (SITC. Rev. 3, 3) *[cont.]*									
Northern Africa	2000	34262	28468	95	95	24088	2706	4285	3508	10	0
	2008	153410	128368	1882	1786	97265	8440	29222	23800	112	19
	2009	89367	71347	417	331	55740	4272	15191	12719	6	6
	2010	110368	88344	611	291	68492	4225	19241	16272	35	0
	2011	138045	109061	834	392	87128	6546	21099	16445	1	1
Sub-Saharan Africa	2000	45328	27709	229	193	9432	279	18048	17393	3	3
	2008	203901	116390	2767	2360	39856	2464	73767	69296	19	19
	2009	123281	61465	1251	1168	24345	1296	35868	32438	29	27
	2010	166714	86336	1684	864	29945	1225	54707	49912	1	1
	2011	238723	122815	2983	1867	45704	2531	74128	66836	3	0
South Africa	2000	2664	1005	72	36	902	32	31	29	0	0
	2008	7120	3035	24	14	2953	100	58	58	19	19
	2009	6023	2134	43	33	2058	78	32	32	17	14
	2010	7198	1443	43	32	1343	121	58	58	0	0
	2011	9706	1991	108	80	1661	168	222	222	0	0
Latin America and the Caribbean	2000	62261	43938	434	371	3985	406	39519	38681	2	1
	2008	206127	124067	145	145	18563	1547	105358	103613	14	14
	2009	140143	80594	160	160	13698	242	66736	51683	3	3
	2010	176787	92365	416	406	13744	337	78205	66045	9	0
	2011	230991	117642	507	507	20049	72	97085	83387	35	7
Brazil	2000	908	600	0	0	66	6	533	529	...	...
	2008	18689	7527	0	0	2552	150	4974	4971	3	3
	2009	13657	4377	0	0	1780	112	2597	2590	0	0
	2010	19843	7330	72	72	2788	247	4470	4136	...	...
	2011	26791	10437	0	0	3918	31	6518	5866	...	...
Eastern Asia	2000	19504	7958	5952	5704	452	46	1553	1477	97	78
	2008	90364	23417	11187	8985	7127	439	5103	4794	467	366
	2009	56624	13681	5992	4091	4518	206	3171	3077	217	178
	2010	75664	17405	7748	5784	4588	276	5069	4852	441	356
	2011	106067	24311	14516	11932	5593	592	4202	4002	643	528
China	2000	7855	3226	2080	1973	436	46	711	689	70	51
	2008	31773	10213	5012	4760	2597	435	2605	2361	367	273
	2009	20383	3511	1945	1617	808	202	758	696	121	90
	2010	26673	4607	2240	2032	1317	273	1050	868	294	222
	2011	32274	6642	3438	3087	1988	497	1216	1067	447	352
Southern Asia	2000	26843	16072	5330	5318	10595	184	147	147	11	3
	2008	115010	27791	1370	1227	26173	39	248	247	101	17
	2009	80957	22430	1393	1236	20754	31	283	278	65	6
	2010	98608	26751	2468	2358	23644	6	640	639	70	8
	2011	144633	39390	3428	3259	35101	8	862	861	107	11
South-Eastern Asia	2000	45413	18800	16753	13540	405	19	1643	1637	2	2
	2008	177147	61874	54225	34932	4818	51	2831	2824	16	15
	2009	123897	36635	31499	20019	3056	30	2081	2075	12	11
	2010	165548	47121	41812	26503	2778	35	2531	2385	37	35
	2011	229250	66745	59991	39477	4138	48	2616	2524	51	45
Western Asia	2000	161909	88233	34692	34555	28385	1172	25155	24686	58	22
	2008	636420	232572	79513	78201	67832	2015	85227	27720	472	268
	2009	389059	107654	29378	28466	38094	1211	40182	14488	242	174
	2010	439865	106941	22964	22350	37311	1614	46666	10493	298	227
	2011	625596	102571	16089	14778	39138	1864	47343	884	328	244
Oceania	2000	699	595	595	0	0	.	0	0	...	...
	2008	1653	1280	1279	239	1	0	0	0	...	...
	2009	959	702	700	91	1	.	0	0	...	...
	2010	1018	553	552	44	1	.	0	0	...	...
	2011	1172	789	776	43	0	0	12	12	0	0

For general note and footnotes see end of table

Exportations mondiales en provenance et de destination (Tableau D)

En millions de dollars E.-U. f.o.b.

South-Eastern Europe Europe du Sud-Est	Northern Africa Afrique septentrio-nale	Sub-Saharan Africa Afrique subsahari-enne	Latin America and the Caribbean Amérique latine et Caraïbes	Eastern Asia Asie orientale	Southern Asia Asie méridionale	South-eastern Asia Asie du Sud-Est	Western Asia Asie occidentale	Oceania Océanie	Other 3/ Autres 3/	Année	← Exportations vers / Exportations en provence de ↓
			Combustibles minéraux et produits assimilés (CTCI, Rev. 3, 3) *[suite]*								
35	472	59	1830	167	173	173	2219	...	656	2000	Afrique septentrionale
203	3239	855	4860	5825	3416	971	3969	...	1591	2008	
188	2056	130	2681	6350	2147	551	3144	...	769	2009	
217	2014	138	3013	7852	3218	686	3884	0	968	2010	
129	2838	158	4067	8462	6437	910	4592	40	1349	2011	
9	37	3591	1794	6333	4023	787	294	28	720	2000	Afrique subsaharienne
41	119	14847	12158	44646	10995	1232	862	19	2571	2008	
138	446	13300	6339	27808	10114	1371	1213	130	927	2009	
12	799	14612	8901	35627	15134	3063	1475	17	737	2010	
20	970	22892	12554	51231	20740	4327	2124	24	1023	2011	
2	35	580	45	129	83	42	168	1	573	2000	Afrique du sud
28	110	1257	414	218	718	262	464	18	579	2008	
13	22	921	115	396	1287	164	476	43	436	2009	
12	74	1044	371	956	1890	405	613	0	388	2010	
20	8	1386	319	2113	1929	523	833	0	584	2011	
3	1	92	15544	438	209	176	105	0	1751	2000	Amérique latine et Caraïbes
4	113	1364	65292	8470	956	3873	961	5	1010	2008	
9	281	429	42736	8358	2185	4631	709	1	207	2009	
18	290	882	42460	17305	2226	5678	613	4	14935	2010	
...	32	935	51922	16057	3848	1298	1490	5	37726	2011	
...	...	25	238	36	1	8	0	...	...	2000	Brésil
...	5	901	7711	1703	20	677	143	...	...	2008	
...	0	315	6183	1365	873	496	49	0	...	2009	
...	0	55	6590	4054	1255	530	29	...	...	2010	
...	0	73	8840	4884	1705	804	48	...	...	2011	
10	7	77	363	6606	489	2581	66	133	1116	2000	Asie orientale
4	30	955	7082	27259	3487	22383	1536	334	3410	2008	
8	81	465	3286	16890	1442	17644	661	455	1794	2009	
0	294	791	4636	22274	1910	23467	1272	651	2523	2010	
45	28	1821	5971	33122	2326	31917	1375	819	3688	2011	
10	6	59	209	2528	334	1360	53	0	...	2000	Chine
4	27	469	3826	10574	1202	4393	632	66	...	2008	
8	6	300	1655	7722	350	6149	495	66	...	2009	
0	10	507	2761	8912	645	8081	735	122	...	2010	
45	27	772	4078	10898	812	7706	622	223	...	2011	
0	2008	8	679	7173	177	502	212	0	0	2000	Asie méridionale
9	3801	4264	2351	53848	4757	6617	10953	26	494	2008	
8	2502	2591	1149	38144	2417	3862	6960	0	829	2009	
7	2895	3874	3654	40430	2783	7870	9866	0	407	2010	
10	4403	5257	4934	61910	3752	10730	13575	0	564	2011	
3	9	28	78	13054	1725	11078	110	523	3	2000	Asie du Sud-est
23	145	970	343	41019	9701	59364	1149	2087	455	2008	
4	82	884	312	33722	7168	42522	597	1351	607	2009	
7	176	1654	463	45823	9517	57561	772	1873	545	2010	
9	135	1567	475	60468	14317	81267	874	2771	570	2011	
25	3405	438	1706	49457	3810	7734	3937	...	3106	2000	Asie occidentale
531	9301	7075	4008	279976	26689	27508	8408	309	39570	2008	
129	6480	5126	2881	185382	25858	14522	8462	250	32073	2009	
132	7166	4933	3764	254430	21876	14059	7276	146	18844	2010	
120	7560	1514	3954	302551	9171	10847	7325	227	179429	2011	
0	...	0	...	101	...	2	...	1	0	2000	Océanie
...	...	0	0	70	0	130	...	52	120	2008	
...	...	0	4	70	0	155	0	5	23	2009	
0	...	1	0	237	0	14	...	213	...	2010	
...	...	0	18	118	0	0	0	71	177	2011	

Voir la fin du tableau pour la remarque générale et les notes.

World exports by provenance and destination (Table D)

In million U.S. dollars f.o.b.

Exports to → / ↓ Exports from	Year	World 1/ Monde 1/	Developed economies 2/ Économies développées 2/ Total	Asia-Pacific Asie-Pacifique Total	Asia-Pacific Japan Japon	Europe Total	Europe Germany Allemagne	North America Amérique du Nord Total	North America U.S.A. É.-U.	Commonwealth of Independent States Communauté d'Etats Indépendants Total	Commonwealth of Independent States Europe
					Chemicals (SITC, Rev. 3, 5)						
World 1/	2000	566099	375659	29219	21276	261094	42954	85346	65987	7364	6175
	2008	1653315	1042187	67987	46900	768767	137945	205434	164590	46721	40470
	2009	1416361	895981	60110	41681	655429	118557	180443	143559	35197	29459
	2010	1658642	999347	73907	52182	720383	127159	205057	163666	44699	38513
	2011	1939686	1143360	88356	62694	821771	141573	233233	186607	55087	48008
Developed Economies - Asia-Pacific 2/	2000	39061	14664	1393	353	6096	976	7176	6972	23	19
	2008	77974	21756	2637	565	9534	1953	9584	9315	154	149
	2009	69110	18517	2215	417	7842	1502	8460	8259	114	109
	2010	86979	21370	2502	524	9026	1715	9841	9586	159	151
	2011	93657	22317	2598	538	9820	2064	9898	9624	186	178
Japan	2000	35160	12405	386	.	5500	899	6520	6354	22	18
	2008	69137	17455	630	.	8410	1769	8414	8261	148	144
	2009	61416	14830	539	.	6794	1342	7497	7379	110	106
	2010	78419	17469	559	.	8145	1570	8765	8594	153	147
	2011	84522	18269	572	.	8893	1860	8804	8625	179	172
Developed Economies - Europe 2/	2000	317507	260854	11752	8614	212637	36874	36465	33723	4371	4039
	2008	927549	747712	24424	16310	629830	116822	93458	84675	30272	28181
	2009	808334	656226	25594	17693	539826	99894	90806	82389	23575	21641
	2010	887433	707217	28024	19030	583093	105851	96101	87122	29755	27470
	2011	1002866	792703	31117	21139	658034	120666	103552	94195	35512	32825
France	2000	40440	32870	1270	908	27982	5990	3618	3362	530	469
	2008	99984	76738	2974	2112	65035	13925	8729	7781	3406	3167
	2009	86490	65083	2897	1947	54520	11108	7667	6751	2501	2297
	2010	91304	67228	3399	2446	56267	11793	7562	6703	3168	2931
	2011	99606	72746	3832	2965	62151	13518	6763	5930	3309	3056
Germany	2000	69666	53574	3003	2398	43607	.	6964	6328	1211	1124
	2008	214293	162543	5129	3695	138515	.	18898	17462	8361	7868
	2009	172088	135754	5056	3735	115023	.	15675	14495	6237	5769
	2010	187400	144104	5597	4143	124276	.	14232	12961	7641	7099
	2011	213341	162725	6429	4752	139701	.	16595	15080	9365	8728
Developed Economies - North America 2/	2000	94865	61283	8502	6582	24815	2845	27966	12116	312	267
	2008	216802	131273	14855	10962	61423	10524	54995	27884	1077	993
	2009	187318	115266	12756	9184	57086	10625	45424	20992	795	701
	2010	221888	129968	15938	12064	60942	11032	53087	24580	1208	1123
	2011	246570	139710	16722	12707	61601	8168	61387	29223	1363	1271
United States	2000	80057	48161	8179	6371	24133	2719	15849	.	302	260
	2008	178881	99536	14255	10621	58176	10199	27104	.	1009	937
	2009	159408	90885	12283	8911	54177	10425	24425	.	755	669
	2010	188730	101947	15415	11738	58031	10638	28500	.	1158	1077
	2011	207030	106512	16109	12386	58245	7790	32158	.	1297	1211
South-Eastern Europe	2000	1338	541	2	2	513	46	26	26	204	195
	2008	6308	2898	44	21	2701	326	153	146	645	577
	2009	4288	1752	13	11	1683	286	56	53	571	510
	2010	5731	2539	14	13	2387	469	138	136	808	733
	2011	8168	4064	18	12	3753	1142	293	291	1018	934
Commonwealth of Independent States	2000	8547	4568	35	33	3214	282	1319	1286	1364	840
	2008	36906	14232	186	103	10736	1107	3309	3011	6819	4821
	2009	21210	7203	92	52	6091	473	1020	887	4752	2978
	2010	28302	9684	126	66	7817	570	1740	1302	5558	4014
	2011	40258	14756	172	102	12054	848	2530	1927	7462	6046
Russian Federation 4/	2000	6181	3740	23	21	2535	218	1183	1165	607	189
	2008	22359	8559	143	91	6531	755	1885	1816	3677	2297
	2009	12482	4172	73	47	3589	278	511	483	2490	1288
	2010	16451	6445	84	55	5512	362	850	749	2609	1689
	2011	21792	8467	112	71	7077	553	1279	1168	3456	2895

For general note and footnotes see end of table

Exportations mondiales en provenance et de destination (Tableau D)

En millions de dollars E.-U. f.o.b.

South-Eastern Europe Europe du Sud-Est	Northern Africa Afrique septentrionale	Sub-Saharan Africa Afrique subsaharienne	Latin America and the Caribbean Amérique latine et Caraïbes	Eastern Asia Asie orientale	Southern Asia Asie méridionale	South-eastern Asia Asie du Sud-Est	Western Asia Asie occidentale	Oceania Océanie	Other 3/ Autres 3/	Année	← Exportations vers Exportations en provence de ↓
				Produits chimiques (CTCI, Rev. 3, 5)							
2698	4514	7673	39093	68064	8957	27525	16990	324	7238	2000	Monde 1/
16118	15881	27094	109981	195361	48052	75753	59059	1452	15655	2008	
13522	14988	23523	90637	179679	40145	63754	52796	1118	5021	2009	
14531	16620	27137	113716	238246	50359	84036	61009	1283	7659	2010	
17675	18920	33599	140872	279418	60689	102468	74177	1513	11907	2011	
2	52	161	1390	16114	491	5662	301	95	107	2000	Économies développées - Asie-Pacifique 2/
28	104	816	1176	41654	1477	9692	899	205	13	2008	
31	101	433	1059	38611	1229	7978	825	190	21	2009	
36	73	560	1272	50079	1513	10795	868	226	29	2010	
36	93	500	1425	54251	1697	11900	970	256	25	2011	
2	45	105	1298	15458	446	5143	230	6	...	2000	Japon
22	92	207	927	40047	971	8496	766	7	...	2008	
16	87	190	791	37025	914	6771	676	6	...	2009	
29	65	249	1038	48084	1155	9441	730	5	...	2010	
32	84	289	1128	52038	1254	10429	814	6	...	2011	
2195	3333	3873	9259	8747	2823	4879	10676	146	6351	2000	Économies développées - Europe 2/
12494	10000	10371	24126	28355	8776	11982	31207	401	11852	2008	
10783	9376	9076	20971	28549	8459	10793	28590	357	1582	2009	
11442	10215	10492	25883	34151	9712	13508	32765	363	1929	2010	
13722	11025	12320	29740	39412	10932	15739	38062	384	3316	2011	
193	1065	1052	1207	1065	286	690	1358	122	2	2000	France
1047	2975	2640	2735	3046	850	2016	4192	324	15	2008	
927	2839	2649	2499	2881	832	1847	4129	293	12	2009	
871	2945	2928	2988	3331	941	2292	4306	301	5	2010	
976	2966	3121	3560	4088	1049	2863	4587	330	11	2011	
423	372	616	2378	2718	681	1316	2344	6	4026	2000	Allemagne
2443	1351	1981	6453	8922	2400	2918	6773	12	10138	2008	
2062	1134	1477	5340	8958	2364	2714	5961	11	77	2009	
2113	1328	1894	6547	10814	2770	3257	6813	6	111	2010	
2400	1431	2245	7588	12564	3054	3776	8007	8	178	2011	
19	215	666	17202	9182	676	3844	1453	13	0	2000	Economies développées - Amérique du Nord 2/
115	675	1593	41553	22705	5809	8057	3905	41	0	2008	
103	743	1437	33906	20747	4142	6643	3501	36	0	2009	
94	851	1595	42784	27389	4646	8856	4441	56	0	2010	
73	849	1998	51215	30630	5216	10705	4787	25	0	2011	
17	207	648	16767	8305	619	3605	1413	12	...	2000	Etats-Unis
109	657	1446	40003	20292	5045	7019	3732	34	...	2008	
61	700	1372	33091	19540	3645	5997	3333	31	...	2009	
58	792	1500	41074	25789	4206	7927	4230	50	...	2010	
67	830	1823	49312	28557	4729	9280	4602	21	...	2011	
223	21	21	18	9	19	19	262	0	1	2000	Europe du Sud-Est
1498	85	84	218	38	116	14	677	0	35	2008	
1209	76	39	51	71	76	18	414	0	12	2009	
1385	73	58	61	88	87	49	577	0	6	2010	
1673	58	71	123	67	153	28	625	1	287	2011	
65	78	40	548	1031	246	118	488	1	1	2000	Communauté d'Etats Indépendants
493	258	604	4889	4413	2482	717	1977	1	21	2008	
244	117	365	2101	3005	1888	453	1068	0	14	2009	
257	121	451	2986	4822	2129	865	1391	0	39	2010	
445	261	574	5200	5793	2461	1359	1870	2	76	2011	
38	48	16	378	889	159	62	243	1	0	2000	Fédération de Russie 4/
287	88	279	3051	2988	1644	650	1134	0	1	2008	
152	82	249	1349	1935	1071	286	696	0	1	2009	
132	45	199	1713	2414	1526	531	819	0	18	2010	
198	74	194	3049	3009	1309	816	1195	0	26	2011	

Voir la fin du tableau pour la remarque générale et les notes.

World exports by provenance and destination (Table D)

In million U.S. dollars f.o.b.

Exports to → / ↓ Exports from	Year	World 1/ Monde 1/	Developed economies 2/ Économies développées 2/ — Total	Asia-Pacific Asie-Pacifique — Total	Asia-Pacific — Japan Japon	Europe — Total	Europe — Germany Allemagne	North America Amérique du Nord — Total	North America — U.S.A. É.-U.	Commonwealth of Independent States Communauté d'Etats Indépendants — Total	CIS — Europe
Chemicals (SITC, Rev. 3, 5) *[cont.]*											
Northern Africa	2000	2350	1095	25	2	1015	49	55	54	3	3
	2008	12175	4694	149	22	4208	165	337	333	16	7
	2009	7560	2647	23	5	2464	112	160	131	10	2
	2010	9901	3786	26	10	3450	158	310	275	24	10
	2011	12193	4590	68	21	4081	137	441	419	33	24
Sub-Saharan Africa	2000	2850	948	141	79	446	64	361	330	38	38
	2008	10141	3089	266	161	1737	191	1086	1040	10	8
	2009	7295	1835	208	115	1007	118	620	608	8	7
	2010	8513	2220	222	117	990	130	1008	989	9	9
	2011	11259	3273	339	235	1339	152	1595	1268	199	190
South Africa	2000	2055	874	137	79	382	57	355	324	1	0
	2008	5724	2182	264	160	1130	172	788	761	3	2
	2009	4100	1411	202	113	698	108	510	499	3	2
	2010	5077	1808	219	115	846	118	743	726	3	3
	2011	6145	2326	334	232	973	136	1018	1005	18	17
Latin America and the Caribbean	2000	16624	7477	325	259	2088	315	5064	4945	12	11
	2008	47261	20519	821	608	6601	785	13097	12465	72	63
	2009	40865	16833	1081	957	5976	686	9776	9394	52	46
	2010	48780	20181	906	729	7373	754	11902	11431	80	74
	2011	62827	27003	1307	1079	9423	891	16273	15566	89	77
Brazil	2000	3565	1471	157	141	649	152	665	641	3	3
	2008	12627	5655	359	312	2970	403	2326	2234	32	30
	2009	10486	4173	357	319	2438	374	1378	1318	16	16
	2010	12235	5080	417	358	2849	377	1814	1744	21	21
	2011	15055	6626	582	509	3458	476	2586	2491	19	18
Eastern Asia	2000	45642	11728	4104	3441	4184	868	3439	3221	444	368
	2008	170774	48668	16418	12931	17729	3905	14521	13419	4307	3483
	2009	140356	36847	11748	9023	13943	3203	11155	10397	2832	2070
	2010	190461	51039	16865	13308	18984	4199	15191	14163	3970	3072
	2011	236069	66180	23272	18356	23597	4737	19311	18005	5145	4032
China	2000	12098	6060	1714	1493	2570	645	1775	1661	131	93
	2008	79313	33571	9410	7566	13599	3282	10562	9740	2891	2271
	2009	62008	25146	6266	4984	10663	2543	8217	7650	1954	1384
	2010	87519	35343	9397	7605	14940	3352	11006	10218	2698	2094
	2011	114723	46294	13765	11024	18423	3731	14107	13140	3539	2772
Southern Asia	2000	5012	1853	170	101	1149	223	534	482	233	152
	2008	31226	10129	679	441	6152	964	3298	2962	1059	621
	2009	26289	8576	553	334	4856	785	3167	2928	864	497
	2010	31844	10674	734	436	5827	965	4112	3875	999	606
	2011	44405	14540	1001	602	8010	1302	5528	5212	1404	823
South-Eastern Asia	2000	21083	6188	2395	1681	2423	199	1369	1309	43	41
	2008	66891	20017	6693	4532	8452	445	4873	3726	273	263
	2009	60214	17184	5339	3681	7538	285	4307	2619	155	146
	2010	81048	22701	8047	5699	10175	591	4479	4056	216	198
	2011	105287	31613	10908	7671	15776	579	4929	4656	352	298
Western Asia	2000	11203	4458	374	128	2513	213	1571	1522	315	201
	2008	49272	17186	806	245	9659	756	6721	5612	2018	1303
	2009	43489	13084	483	207	7111	590	5490	4901	1471	753
	2010	57718	17951	492	187	10314	723	7146	6148	1913	1054
	2011	75936	22467	697	231	14276	885	7494	6219	2325	1309
Oceania	2000	18	3	1	0	2	0	0	0	...	...
	2008	38	14	8	1	5	0	1	1	0	0
	2009	34	11	5	0	4	0	1	1	0	0
	2010	43	17	11	0	5	0	1	1	0	0
	2011	192	144	137	0	6	0	1	1	0	0

For general note and footnotes see end of table

En millions de dollars E.-U. f.o.b.

South-Eastern Europe Europe du Sud-Est	Northern Africa Afrique septentrionale	Sub-Saharan Africa Afrique subsaharienne	Latin America and the Caribbean Amérique latine et Caraïbes	Eastern Asia Asie orientale	Southern Asia Asie méridionale	South-eastern Asia Asie du Sud-Est	Western Asia Asie occidentale	Oceania Océanie	Other 3/ Autres 3/	Année	← Exportations vers Exportations en provence de ↓
				Produits chimiques (CTCI, Rev. 3, 5)*[suite]*							
9	172	44	118	32	545	42	255	0	34	2000	Afrique septentrionale
174	692	371	1233	214	2885	263	1412	0	222	2008	
144	641	383	456	324	1433	152	1174	0	195	2009	
111	748	497	878	204	1885	160	1417	0	190	2010	
134	878	640	1020	221	2164	180	2126	0	206	2011	
5	9	1247	105	116	233	72	69	0	6	2000	Afrique subsaharienne
5	30	4647	232	345	1176	255	316	5	31	2008	
20	26	3795	226	317	634	182	208	10	34	2009	
6	36	3999	290	470	949	256	254	5	18	2010	
6	51	4735	406	682	1244	329	310	7	17	2011	
5	9	658	101	114	160	70	62	0	1	2000	Afrique du sud
2	23	1724	210	305	820	172	263	2	20	2008	
2	19	1481	178	282	373	151	170	3	28	2009	
4	30	1783	239	415	354	208	222	3	8	2010	
4	43	2087	338	384	396	275	266	3	6	2011	
2	19	147	8269	362	66	162	83	0	24	2000	Amérique latine et Caraïbes
23	86	569	23379	1174	566	378	279	0	215	2008	
20	80	459	20422	1615	469	480	242	0	192	2009	
13	98	455	24738	1738	421	459	383	3	211	2010	
27	147	577	31196	2123	340	604	476	1	245	2011	
1	10	88	1693	156	21	80	40	0	...	2000	Brésil
10	54	405	5688	351	171	143	119	0	...	2008	
6	45	335	4594	746	246	220	104	0	...	2009	
2	38	309	5570	657	206	186	164	3	...	2010	
2	53	404	6499	855	147	219	229	1	...	2011	
42	205	628	1318	23683	1634	5179	760	17	3	2000	Asie orientale
341	1377	3608	9194	67936	11110	18630	5520	81	2	2008	
231	1195	3027	6475	58715	10506	15951	4494	81	2	2009	
276	1504	3784	9115	77451	15851	21375	6003	88	5	2010	
407	1751	5219	12328	90131	19830	26831	8147	95	5	2011	
23	91	219	511	2632	779	1356	290	6	...	2000	Chine
205	759	2188	6426	12917	7899	9278	3135	44	...	2008	
154	699	1988	4527	10186	6913	7846	2539	56	...	2009	
191	841	2557	6309	14455	10910	10730	3429	55	...	2010	
289	1018	3709	8529	18225	14198	14061	4800	59	...	2011	
8	65	352	280	647	492	517	560	4	0	2000	Asie méridionale
123	394	2041	1456	5268	3944	2709	4047	15	42	2008	
79	393	2092	1332	4047	3090	2355	3395	16	51	2009	
102	443	2523	1754	4908	3283	3028	4060	17	53	2010	
137	623	3389	2377	7227	4723	4139	5748	22	76	2011	
14	55	275	232	6051	1229	6582	369	43	1	2000	Asie du Sud-est
46	259	1126	1019	15829	4677	21600	1896	138	11	2008	
20	214	1025	2719	15363	4415	17385	1611	115	7	2009	
37	257	1184	2537	22385	6296	23436	1833	151	14	2010	
43	294	1483	4331	28781	7081	28671	2400	222	15	2011	
113	291	211	354	2089	501	445	1714	0	711	2000	Asie occidentale
779	1922	1262	1505	7431	5033	1454	6922	546	3212	2008	
638	2026	1387	920	8315	3804	1363	7273	297	2910	2009	
772	2201	1535	1416	14563	3584	1248	7015	355	5166	2010	
973	2890	2072	1507	20101	4846	1983	8654	477	7639	2011	
0	0	8	0	0	0	3	...	4	0	2000	Océanie
0	...	1	0	0	0	3	0	19	0	2008	
0	...	4	0	1	0	1	1	16	0	2009	
0	0	5	0	1	2	1	1	17	0	2010	
...	0	19	3	1	2	1	1	20	0	2011	

Voir la fin du tableau pour la remarque générale et les notes.

World exports by provenance and destination (Table D)

In million U.S. dollars f.o.b.

Exports to → / ↓ Exports from	Year	World 1/ Monde 1/	Developed economies 2/ Économies développées 2/ Total	Asia-Pacific Asie-Pacifique Total	Asia-Pacific Japan Japon	Europe Total	Europe Germany Allemagne	North America Amérique du Nord Total	North America U.S.A. É.-U.	Commonwealth of Independent States Communauté d'Etats Indépendants Total	CIS Europe
Manufactured goods classified chiefly by material (SITC, Rev. 3, 6)											
World 1/	2000	864586	568114	40353	31010	365647	70986	162114	130428	10966	8899
	2008	2171623	1271535	87497	63547	911712	170319	272326	221387	73423	54425
	2009	1554402	860594	61899	42040	613704	114217	184991	147038	46235	30225
	2010	1935722	1053794	80242	56114	734621	141802	238930	190574	55235	41593
	2011	2343167	1268508	100821	72193	884344	173176	283344	228150	69115	53504
Developed Economies - Asia-Pacific 2/	2000	56349	18592	3850	1805	5447	1114	9295	8627	158	116
	2008	115924	27343	6873	2899	9487	1750	10982	9981	964	836
	2009	87807	18620	4393	1325	6643	1209	7584	6781	555	462
	2010	116364	24525	6227	2398	7786	1474	10512	9603	978	873
	2011	128455	27784	6523	2417	9096	1691	12166	11281	1322	1155
Japan	2000	46676	13690	850	.	4552	1022	8288	7686	157	115
	2008	97630	19472	1810	.	8031	1680	9631	8689	956	831
	2009	74799	14071	1342	.	5722	1125	7007	6255	548	456
	2010	99797	17727	1744	.	6593	1400	9390	8554	971	867
	2011	109712	20519	1865	.	7823	1606	10831	10023	1309	1145
Developed Economies - Europe 2/	2000	388619	324598	7273	4786	285365	59519	31960	29068	4808	4379
	2008	923789	732708	12156	7339	676262	139442	44289	39576	27001	24911
	2009	642480	499957	7974	4414	463396	92962	28588	25417	16949	15027
	2010	745968	581402	9564	5468	534940	112734	36899	32463	20257	18586
	2011	888852	690554	11706	6349	634129	135405	44718	39415	24726	22552
France	2000	41170	35053	654	444	31193	7735	3206	2793	205	180
	2008	79675	64273	1135	707	59413	15291	3724	3273	899	803
	2009	55982	43601	841	522	40099	9941	2662	2283	620	549
	2010	61323	47612	930	543	43629	11462	3054	2718	784	672
	2011	69810	54422	1052	671	49883	13689	3488	3106	947	837
Germany	2000	76521	63845	1352	846	56559	.	5935	5391	1276	1198
	2008	202057	160884	2464	1410	147346	.	11074	10062	7116	6605
	2009	144528	115078	1797	959	105996	.	7285	6593	4452	4034
	2010	165286	131038	2207	1207	119401	.	9430	8532	5335	4986
	2011	198933	157153	2506	1387	142973	.	11674	10580	7026	6601
Developed Economies - North America 2/	2000	111200	77822	5107	4207	13184	1973	59531	34995	124	99
	2008	186914	119397	6967	5179	27203	3943	85227	48792	694	589
	2009	134945	83034	4645	3018	18239	2721	60149	32363	418	342
	2010	169767	103076	5775	3905	23461	3783	73840	39355	494	420
	2011	195508	116094	6578	4367	27039	4225	82478	43916	655	549
United States	2000	71990	40258	4380	3549	11348	1845	24529	.	112	89
	2008	124970	63336	5719	4109	21209	3693	36407	.	594	507
	2009	94619	46733	4109	2605	14865	2577	27759	.	379	313
	2010	119487	58146	5046	3331	18631	3624	34470	.	412	354
	2011	139414	66008	5725	3715	21730	3993	38553	.	547	462
South-Eastern Europe	2000	4672	3293	9	7	2958	442	327	279	121	103
	2008	23047	15820	18	4	15326	2281	475	431	684	589
	2009	13802	9135	15	2	8975	1636	145	126	460	411
	2010	18111	11810	16	7	11421	2305	373	279	661	622
	2011	24899	16462	22	9	15870	3466	570	394	1080	1039
Commonwealth of Independent States	2000	27546	14486	1244	1240	10728	1616	2514	2428	4240	3258
	2008	105401	46719	3606	3533	37239	4497	5874	5730	22608	14489
	2009	63205	25647	1642	1616	20846	2633	3159	3108	13260	7173
	2010	80487	35877	1769	1740	29846	4185	4262	4185	14950	10501
	2011	96571	42673	2259	2203	35805	5400	4609	4511	18471	14090
Russian Federation 4/	2000	18349	11959	1176	1174	8853	1330	1930	1887	1126	399
	2008	56293	31724	2658	2636	24928	3198	4138	4102	8511	3765
	2009	37127	19670	1352	1340	15488	1743	2831	2794	5526	1412
	2010	45822	26445	1139	1126	22018	2654	3288	3246	5123	2316
	2011	50593	29829	1316	1303	25205	3427	3308	3253	4926	2892

For general note and footnotes see end of table

Exportations mondiales en provenance et de destination (Tableau D)

En millions de dollars E.-U. f.o.b.

← Exportations vers

South-Eastern Europe Europe du Sud-Est	Northern Africa Afrique septentrionale	Sub-Saharan Africa Afrique subsaharienne	Latin America and the Caribbean Amérique latine et Caraïbes	Eastern Asia Asie orientale	Southern Asia Asie méridionale	South-eastern Asia Asie du Sud-Est	Western Asia Asie occidentale	Oceania Océanie	Other 3/ Autres 3/	Année	Exportations en provence de ↓
Articles manufacturés classés principalement d'après la matière première (CTCI, Rev. 3, 6)											
6496	9121	11574	47785	109919	18123	42196	36483	1019	2791	2000	Monde 1/
31580	34615	42945	111279	248367	77961	125913	144390	1606	8010	2008	
20453	32021	37687	80757	204464	66529	96022	104065	1447	4130	2009	
23123	32614	43646	110686	263892	94787	127584	123374	1650	5336	2010	
28947	34569	54085	133942	307908	122206	156186	155410	2270	10021	2011	
6	153	545	1540	21933	1109	10187	1524	317	285	2000	Economies développées - Asie-Pacifique 2/
44	372	1194	3049	50227	2590	24510	5048	529	54	2008	
29	444	953	2416	41087	2755	16766	3679	461	44	2009	
39	416	1165	3668	52915	3529	24489	4014	543	82	2010	
114	449	1256	4238	56082	4017	27785	4693	655	60	2011	
6	150	429	1446	19458	961	8894	1421	64	...	2000	Japon
40	300	948	2922	45821	2225	20460	4425	59	...	2008	
27	390	753	2335	36765	2341	14139	3360	70	...	2009	
36	333	919	3450	48197	3098	21282	3713	70	...	2010	
112	339	1030	3770	50811	3567	23791	4358	105	...	2011	
4904	5806	3786	6703	10386	6566	4388	14768	159	1747	2000	Economies développées - Europe 2/
20397	17328	11388	16299	28314	18923	9745	35866	347	5473	2008	
14466	15456	9207	11246	24979	14069	7858	25657	282	2354	2009	
16051	15709	10415	15186	27927	17693	9041	29160	281	2846	2010	
19327	16701	11878	17605	33623	22545	10882	34904	320	5787	2011	
247	1711	670	619	814	243	357	1144	103	4	2000	France
971	3086	1955	1265	2221	942	815	3009	225	12	2008	
711	2817	1319	879	1828	885	660	2483	174	5	2009	
831	2824	1632	1259	2195	803	717	2481	178	5	2010	
985	2932	1586	1417	2566	1076	879	2784	186	29	2011	
1158	761	652	1783	2199	610	950	2114	10	1163	2000	Allemagne
3723	1733	1877	4318	7378	3224	2414	7152	20	2219	2008	
2851	1568	1543	3079	6561	2424	2090	4853	28	3	2009	
3302	1519	1638	4335	7414	2473	2494	5717	17	4	2010	
4081	1485	1852	4909	9229	2679	2969	7018	36	497	2011	
24	187	591	21581	5485	516	2135	2709	25	0	2000	Economies développées - Amérique du Nord 2/
91	627	1252	34561	13820	3310	3336	9782	41	1	2008	
63	608	1200	26760	10945	2694	2833	6369	22	0	2009	
69	519	1242	33733	14303	4544	3571	8169	48	0	2010	
114	597	1517	39661	16564	5745	3942	10569	48	0	2011	
20	139	569	20958	4946	431	1954	2581	24	...	2000	Etats-Unis
71	444	1101	32487	11948	2870	2999	9086	35	...	2008	
52	502	1089	25562	9336	2412	2578	5960	17	...	2009	
48	397	1131	32059	12351	4025	3270	7605	42	...	2010	
80	465	1366	37749	14546	5034	3666	9910	42	...	2011	
462	83	27	82	64	29	16	492	0	2	2000	Europe du Sud-Est
3417	178	97	74	261	271	60	2180	0	5	2008	
2051	275	67	51	149	213	41	1354	0	4	2009	
2520	367	57	84	255	128	43	2184	0	3	2010	
3409	398	103	90	616	181	48	2460	1	53	2011	
549	670	232	540	3149	827	845	2007	1	0	2000	Communauté d'Etats Indépendants
2547	2544	895	1949	6239	5187	3192	13517	0	4	2008	
824	1146	670	783	5984	4505	2249	8134	0	4	2009	
1248	1169	615	1198	6239	5425	2395	11331	2	40	2010	
1880	1041	909	1164	7812	6305	2288	13949	6	72	2011	
160	310	122	368	2218	603	455	1027	...	0	2000	Fédération de Russie 4/
709	850	214	661	3213	3264	1734	5412	...	3	2008	
236	500	214	309	2788	3031	1352	3497	0	3	2009	
342	472	126	694	2924	3407	1397	4851	1	39	2010	
549	445	209	612	3267	4122	1007	5551	5	71	2011	

Voir la fin du tableau pour la remarque générale et les notes.

World exports by provenance and destination (Table D)

In million U.S. dollars f.o.b.

Exports to → / ↓ Exports from	Year	World 1/ Monde 1/	Developed economies 2/ Économies développées 2/ Total	Asia-Pacific Asie-Pacifique Total	Asia-Pacific Asie-Pacifique Japan Japon	Europe Total	Europe Germany Allemagne	North America Amérique du Nord Total	North America Amérique du Nord U.S.A. É.-U.	Commonwealth of Independent States Communauté d'Etats Indépendants Total	Commonwealth of Independent States Communauté d'Etats Indépendants Europe
Manufactured goods classified chiefly by material (SITC, Rev. 3, 6) *[cont.]*											
Northern Africa	2000	1898	1326	21	18	1193	68	112	104	8	1
	2008	8569	4230	34	21	3992	172	204	180	64	62
	2009	7327	2795	18	10	2489	131	288	268	28	27
	2010	8688	3810	29	17	3433	201	349	323	36	34
	2011	9789	4553	28	16	4164	283	361	335	60	54
Sub-Saharan Africa	2000	14289	10001	787	671	8134	262	1080	981	7	7
	2008	44361	29099	5911	5635	18759	1718	4429	4293	58	56
	2009	30060	17102	2951	2786	12244	823	1908	1855	21	20
	2010	46929	27561	4844	4600	18913	1402	3804	3729	37	36
	2011	58419	35303	5627	5378	25221	1751	4455	4389	76	34
South Africa	2000	7487	4495	649	539	2888	176	958	862	2	2
	2008	26946	18674	5817	5550	8773	1653	4085	3952	44	43
	2009	17535	10693	2875	2717	6076	770	1741	1699	16	15
	2010	24584	15940	4634	4442	8089	1341	3217	3155	30	29
	2011	26936	17653	5315	5137	8950	1428	3388	3336	28	26
Latin America and the Caribbean	2000	42090	27537	1561	1446	6859	560	19117	18506	15	13
	2008	108446	57130	3109	2475	20007	2104	34015	32465	244	137
	2009	77269	34873	1718	1248	10614	823	22541	21513	153	75
	2010	98862	45387	2533	1713	14639	1043	28216	26872	108	55
	2011	117702	57265	3416	2484	17857	1944	35992	34538	112	79
Brazil	2000	11043	6548	666	612	2768	273	3114	2909	5	5
	2008	30732	14873	1355	1162	6834	880	6684	6455	107	105
	2009	19746	8198	813	756	3809	358	3576	3400	42	41
	2010	23352	10452	1011	940	4973	487	4468	4225	37	36
	2011	28753	14013	1168	1085	6429	1215	6415	6157	38	37
Eastern Asia	2000	132035	46466	12332	10252	13552	2451	20582	18744	644	459
	2008	405137	148985	33057	25242	58550	8092	57379	51764	15086	9263
	2009	297887	104230	24768	18659	39271	6350	40191	36203	10318	4754
	2010	392614	137313	32809	24360	51231	8372	53273	47785	12792	7882
	2011	494428	174583	44232	33804	66010	11170	64341	57399	16395	10632
China	2000	42546	19264	5932	5145	6238	1178	7093	6500	332	189
	2008	262391	106074	20809	15561	44461	6129	40805	36531	13856	8268
	2009	184775	74183	16006	11734	28694	4871	29484	26484	9496	4176
	2010	249118	97987	20831	14707	39067	6599	38089	33878	11468	6850
	2011	319564	123326	27868	20426	49621	8762	45838	40554	14593	9235
Southern Asia	2000	24552	13682	1222	881	6263	1141	6196	5804	248	135
	2008	67644	27233	1682	1041	14740	1985	10811	10277	1080	435
	2009	58739	20200	1243	679	10533	1641	8424	7996	714	285
	2010	79373	25649	1710	1032	13134	2014	10805	10279	826	376
	2011	106136	33833	2330	1440	17491	2770	14012	13347	1189	499
South-Eastern Asia	2000	34760	14652	6032	4932	4459	660	4161	3876	30	22
	2008	87852	27357	13129	9665	8235	1325	5993	5616	271	210
	2009	72036	22137	11834	7981	5834	958	4469	4146	354	116
	2010	90877	28159	14024	10444	7899	1357	6235	5787	361	230
	2011	108497	33626	16755	13219	9350	1599	7522	7057	526	438
Western Asia	2000	25888	15273	733	609	7352	1172	7188	6965	563	305
	2008	93538	34972	741	321	21633	3011	12598	12236	4668	2846
	2009	68107	22516	561	185	14439	2330	7516	7231	3005	1534
	2010	86799	28725	691	237	17729	2931	10305	9856	3735	1977
	2011	112661	35008	837	256	22129	3473	12043	11492	4502	2383
Oceania	2000	689	387	183	155	153	7	51	50	0	0
	2008	1001	541	213	192	280	0	48	47	0	0
	2009	740	348	138	118	180	1	30	30	0	0
	2010	882	499	252	193	190	0	58	57	0	0
	2011	1251	770	509	251	184	0	77	76	0	0

For general note and footnotes see end of table

Exportations mondiales en provenance et de destination (Tableau D)

En millions de dollars E.-U. f.o.b.

← Exportations vers

South-Eastern Europe / Europe du Sud-Est	Northern Africa / Afrique septentrionale	Sub-Saharan Africa / Afrique subsaharienne	Latin America and the Caribbean / Amérique latine et Caraïbes	Eastern Asia / Asie orientale	Southern Asia / Asie méridionale	South-eastern Asia / Asie du Sud-Est	Western Asia / Asie occidentale	Oceania / Océanie	Other 3/ / Autres 3/	Année	Exportations en provenance de ↓
Articles manufacturés classés principalement d'après la matière première (CTCI, Rev. 3, 6)*[suite]*											
2	208	62	15	40	5	18	167	0	47	2000	Afrique septentrionale
54	1463	615	38	67	67	24	1883	0	65	2008	
14	1446	568	36	258	122	32	1860	1	168	2009	
23	1484	666	57	307	156	35	2046	0	68	2010	
28	1329	709	95	215	129	56	2540	0	74	2011	
4	23	1746	338	1022	157	390	586	1	14	2000	Afrique subsaharienne
29	467	5940	540	4475	751	921	1998	9	73	2008	
42	184	5440	266	4494	460	686	1235	39	91	2009	
6	134	7131	843	7209	1146	695	2100	13	54	2010	
19	142	8574	954	8729	1434	713	2425	16	34	2011	
3	10	819	295	947	114	317	483	1	2	2000	Afrique du sud
15	40	2774	414	2859	509	629	963	3	21	2008	
11	40	2286	203	2837	311	506	608	6	18	2009	
3	40	2994	543	3167	457	501	896	3	10	2010	
13	29	3293	540	3397	468	568	939	3	5	2011	
2	110	254	10543	2545	113	462	461	2	45	2000	Amérique latine et Caraïbes
58	517	1016	31487	13525	504	1986	1627	4	348	2008	
25	459	1002	22097	15533	475	1535	1017	3	97	2009	
21	557	781	27842	20658	544	1959	943	4	59	2010	
85	519	1029	32568	21877	448	2319	1408	7	65	2011	
1	69	138	3135	666	47	255	179	1	...	2000	Brésil
14	136	738	9015	3402	178	1374	890	3	...	2008	
18	161	664	6036	2938	315	940	430	3	...	2009	
14	117	443	7643	2894	323	1096	331	3	...	2010	
17	113	587	8982	3166	262	1198	374	4	...	2011	
153	769	2159	5198	52187	5024	13626	5345	374	90	2000	Asie orientale
1288	5064	13243	18622	100699	24188	47662	29938	355	7	2008	
789	5040	11647	13441	72266	21896	36802	21068	383	6	2009	
963	5698	13852	22669	91245	30803	52150	24734	390	5	2010	
1296	5870	18322	30707	105695	38738	68644	33725	453	2	2011	
68	375	1160	1430	13538	1247	3224	1881	28	...	2000	Chine
1106	4321	11816	14154	50034	14038	25644	21127	220	...	2008	
655	4254	10392	9922	30173	12451	19044	13915	290	...	2009	
778	4723	12608	17463	38712	18435	28636	18016	293	...	2010	
1048	5092	16859	24822	47914	22720	38912	23958	319	...	2011	
12	251	1016	435	3966	992	1173	2764	10	3	2000	Asie méridionale
252	869	3211	2092	9192	5211	4107	13988	19	389	2008	
97	956	2775	1534	10017	5102	3530	13524	16	274	2009	
130	986	3353	2293	16647	6486	3889	18876	18	221	2010	
182	1345	4414	2981	22168	8865	5184	25631	22	322	2011	
11	247	670	605	6882	1589	8267	1691	115	1	2000	Asie du Sud-est
64	878	1809	1761	15523	4554	29129	6246	232	27	2008	
58	841	1928	1536	14218	3887	22293	4561	203	20	2009	
59	871	1934	2090	18535	5150	27878	5526	298	17	2010	
118	872	2176	2553	23462	5947	32502	6022	675	18	2011	
365	613	471	194	2009	1189	687	3969	0	556	2000	Asie occidentale
3337	4309	2235	806	5677	12389	1239	22316	26	1563	2008	
1995	5166	2207	589	4216	10339	1392	15607	7	1067	2009	
1994	4703	2406	1022	7348	19173	1435	14292	24	1942	2010	
2374	5306	3167	1327	10679	27833	1815	17084	33	3533	2011	
1	...	15	11	252	5	2	0	14	1	2000	Océanie
0	0	50	1	347	17	3	1	42	0	2008	
0	0	22	1	318	11	6	1	31	1	2009	
0	0	30	2	305	12	5	0	29	0	2010	
0	0	32	0	384	21	9	0	34	0	2011	

Voir la fin du tableau pour la remarque générale et les notes.

World exports by provenance and destination (Table D)

In million U.S. dollars f.o.b.

Exports from ↓ / Exports to →	Year	World 1/ Monde 1/	Developed economies 2/ Économies développées 2/ — Total	Asia-Pacific Asie-Pacifique — Total	Japan Japon	Europe — Total	Germany Allemagne	North America Amérique du Nord — Total	U.S.A. É.-U.	Commonwealth of Independent States Communauté d'Etats Indépendants — Total	Europe
Machinery and transport equipment (SITC, Rev. 3, 7)											
World 1/	2000	2615661	1795817	137023	102477	982507	187816	676288	554512	19764	15868
	2008	5408632	3127480	235283	153267	1988770	392993	903427	737659	198181	171942
	2009	4209108	2348050	181557	117509	1472425	305580	694068	570952	96370	76023
	2010	5139458	2747603	228676	147193	1651128	354792	867798	712393	131906	111056
	2011	5806997	3075518	256410	162281	1860419	402664	958689	787786	181477	155676
Developed Economies - Asia-Pacific 2/	2000	338298	189906	9501	291	63126	14800	117279	110881	536	422
	2008	500095	211100	16621	188	79525	15646	114954	105806	17773	17253
	2009	349333	135291	12098	136	48724	10247	74469	68107	3238	2943
	2010	471514	170048	15894	217	59112	13145	95042	87425	7623	7150
	2011	495038	181338	16484	217	64344	15268	100511	93205	11790	10791
Japan	2000	329680	185109	7675	.	61931	14533	115503	109214	526	414
	2008	484399	203082	13444	.	77853	15303	111784	102868	17692	17185
	2009	337758	129686	9567	.	47399	10003	72720	66504	3164	2882
	2010	458036	163744	12958	.	57669	12865	93117	85702	7565	7106
	2011	480368	174224	13210	.	62900	14985	98114	91049	11721	10734
Developed Economies - Europe 2/	2000	1015546	832161	24275	16823	693925	126654	113962	104674	11246	9770
	2008	2219167	1629837	43911	22559	1417301	262383	168625	151679	106933	97773
	2009	1661670	1215032	31962	15882	1060073	208937	122998	110767	56776	49159
	2010	1867948	1330465	38540	19313	1147899	234066	144027	128506	69444	62150
	2011	2177305	1534938	47977	24096	1318004	274835	168957	152142	95582	86843
France	2000	132952	103387	1699	1089	86545	19223	15143	14101	962	653
	2008	227846	155196	5227	1765	134883	34606	15086	13741	6456	5616
	2009	174992	116559	2989	1075	101804	29124	11766	10929	4199	3378
	2010	199558	131919	4132	1539	115433	39671	12354	11472	4181	3746
	2011	218936	146087	5730	1828	125490	44985	14867	13808	6004	5541
Germany	2000	272345	223326	8768	6855	175308	.	39250	37072	4105	3664
	2008	677257	487045	15994	9414	403963	.	67088	61746	35889	33203
	2009	501949	356833	13115	7231	297393	.	46324	42001	19743	17654
	2010	584810	396711	15509	8546	322673	.	58529	51928	23995	21368
	2011	696182	464166	18923	11084	377556	.	67687	61417	35744	32466
Developed Economies - North America 2/	2000	523666	335332	36795	28250	99404	18363	199133	101693	1535	1086
	2008	670612	371896	36734	22670	125968	29719	209195	91697	9335	7357
	2009	450980	236528	21213	12055	67762	16797	147553	64564	4209	2980
	2010	550263	283607	24424	13069	72712	17575	186471	80781	4813	3714
	2011	610679	315722	29292	14372	79375	19915	207054	88530	6866	5488
United States	2000	412200	227821	35994	27866	94397	17580	97431	.	1458	1018
	2008	556909	270105	35140	22130	117486	28349	117478	.	8244	6520
	2009	366966	163117	19830	11498	60316	15422	82971	.	3497	2473
	2010	449130	193263	22926	12499	64670	16374	105667	.	3945	2992
	2011	500949	217981	27776	13815	71746	18410	118459	.	5926	4706
South-Eastern Europe	2000	2785	2115	3	0	2009	521	103	93	111	100
	2008	23900	17814	45	26	17404	5812	366	336	1928	1753
	2009	22342	17423	28	15	17057	5767	337	311	1204	1052
	2010	26538	20246	31	17	19801	6422	413	375	1710	1517
	2011	33409	25246	55	22	24615	8567	576	529	2122	1864
Commonwealth of Independent States	2000	10414	3201	38	34	2870	479	293	271	4452	3318
	2008	36592	6525	103	84	5982	959	440	383	23333	16506
	2009	22865	4912	132	101	4435	864	345	315	11868	7391
	2010	28062	5429	250	228	4661	996	519	442	16018	12084
	2011	33536	5994	271	248	5044	986	679	623	20867	17314
Russian Federation 4/	2000	6422	2634	35	34	2410	387	189	179	1573	749
	2008	17233	3577	92	83	3208	447	277	238	8338	3723
	2009	11607	2760	103	89	2396	463	261	241	4381	1390
	2010	12405	3065	236	227	2466	562	362	292	4512	2368
	2011	12391	3171	255	247	2527	465	389	359	4229	2992

For general note and footnotes see end of table

En millions de dollars E.-U. f.o.b.

South-Eastern Europe / Europe du Sud-Est	Northern Africa / Afrique septentrionale	Sub-Saharar Africa / Afrique subsaharienne	Latin America and the Caribbean / Amérique latine et Caraïbes	Eastern Asia / Asie orientale	Southern Asia / Asie méridionale	South-easter Asia / Asie du Sud-Est	Western Asia / Asie occidentale	Oceania / Océanie	Other 3/ / Autres 3/	Année	← Exportations vers / Exportations en provence de ↓
			Machines et matériel de transport (CTCI, Rev. 3, 7)								
7388	17501	28871	158704	287527	22814	198703	71410	2011	5151	2000	Monde 1/
47778	57236	104491	333074	804478	109903	353746	250545	12113	9607	2008	
30119	54089	85958	256907	725778	97604	295579	194655	16043	7956	2009	
32444	56308	99548	348347	984082	120375	375602	222951	14482	5810	2010	
39549	52482	123272	405025	1090760	140918	413335	259433	16564	8663	2011	
76	919	3093	17123	67403	2899	46357	8977	622	389	2000	Economies développées - Asie-Pacifique 2/
544	3355	8324	32640	128767	7957	56318	31115	2120	82	2008	
238	2093	5730	26439	105979	5854	44300	17939	2189	42	2009	
269	2588	7615	34989	150972	8665	62994	21921	3778	51	2010	
393	1828	9361	34245	155256	10219	66098	20722	3749	39	2011	
74	909	2942	16949	66606	2790	45359	8114	304	0	2000	Japon
538	3331	7761	32130	127282	7656	54720	28949	1257	...	2008	
229	2060	5361	26133	104880	5631	42759	16565	1290	...	2009	
264	2566	7166	34611	149507	8405	61397	20237	2574	...	2010	
379	1801	8832	33833	153531	9985	64254	19437	2372	0	2011	
6112	11738	15229	29109	38550	8210	22907	36121	550	3612	2000	Economies développées - Europe 2/
37856	33435	40688	63019	110381	35076	47448	106223	3137	5135	2008	
22892	31386	32743	45190	101512	29377	39778	83422	1232	2329	2009	
24472	31835	34102	59109	140366	32134	44959	96742	1763	2557	2010	
30116	29615	41545	70010	172292	35415	51244	112398	1532	2618	2011	
536	4200	4160	4149	5250	1384	2817	5172	337	600	2000	France
2674	8814	6608	9386	12551	5467	7941	11332	746	674	2008	
1821	8115	5680	5712	9232	3468	7269	11884	588	466	2009	
2141	8564	5485	7480	13680	4041	7781	13296	603	388	2010	
2488	8103	6532	7513	17164	3670	7657	12741	692	287	2011	
1738	1857	3307	7626	12322	1917	5981	9509	102	555	2000	Allemagne
10854	6311	10054	20110	47750	10946	13969	32596	257	1475	2008	
6368	5926	7441	13949	46408	9981	11387	23676	121	116	2009	
6638	6061	8708	19992	67556	10367	13717	30565	476	26	2010	
8799	5310	10730	23138	83991	12258	15855	35918	239	34	2011	
266	2440	3056	84864	48817	2259	32401	12523	171	1	2000	Economies développées - Amérique du Nord 2/
1079	3906	10612	120974	66129	8907	40170	37324	279	0	2008	
588	3400	7315	95602	48129	6312	25444	23246	205	1	2009	
581	2795	8120	120593	64712	7204	31984	25589	266	1	2010	
685	2319	9609	137660	68399	8363	31968	28597	484	6	2011	
244	2348	2934	83422	47397	2166	32085	12159	164	1	2000	Etats-Unis
961	3566	9887	116675	64018	8320	39075	35808	250	...	2008	
532	2924	6758	92065	46017	5818	24395	21663	180	...	2009	
520	2537	7211	116778	62627	6723	30927	24399	198	...	2010	
590	2046	8798	133654	65557	7724	30857	27385	431	...	2011	
193	70	20	25	35	42	17	154	0	2	2000	Europe du Sud-Est
1536	382	258	410	224	293	144	828	82	0	2008	
1335	414	159	303	308	175	100	902	19	0	2009	
1202	480	376	273	409	274	95	1465	8	1	2010	
1599	568	529	360	590	417	143	1816	15	4	2011	
197	155	103	138	842	677	146	496	1	6	2000	Communauté d'Etats Indépendants
605	316	991	408	1398	2013	350	647	2	3	2008	
498	395	138	653	1580	2115	239	464	0	3	2009	
550	489	166	683	1924	1625	410	726	1	40	2010	
614	513	261	824	1494	1751	616	533	3	65	2011	
165	100	84	117	765	568	115	294	1	6	2000	Fédération de Russie 4/
265	243	904	318	1193	1722	293	375	2	2	2008	
252	259	64	433	1311	1667	163	315	0	2	2009	
302	366	84	434	1647	1119	297	540	1	39	2010	
279	443	195	650	1250	1246	570	291	3	63	2011	

Voir la fin du tableau pour la remarque générale et les notes.

World exports by provenance and destination (Table D)

In million U.S. dollars f.o.b.

Exports to → / ↓ Exports from	Year	World 1/ Monde 1/	Developed economies 2/ Économies développées 2/: Total	Asia-Pacific Asie-Pacifique: Total	Asia-Pacific: Japan Japon	Europe: Total	Europe: Germany Allemagne	North America Amérique du Nord: Total	North America: U.S.A. É.-U.	Commonwealth of Independent States Communauté d'Etats Indépendants: Total	CIS: Europe
Machinery and transport equipment (SITC, Rev. 3, 7)*cont.*]											
Northern Africa	2000	1754	1566	1	1	1559	277	6	5	1	1
	2008	8348	6356	25	24	6200	769	131	129	17	16
	2009	7288	5295	29	28	5144	733	121	119	13	7
	2010	9237	6901	52	51	6673	953	175	173	10	5
	2011	10713	7904	63	59	7626	1072	214	213	17	8
Sub-Saharan Africa	2000	5324	3398	403	155	2349	969	647	613	15	14
	2008	23225	12261	1959	896	7250	2271	3052	2886	85	75
	2009	17813	7875	834	405	4709	1502	2331	2166	62	47
	2010	21076	9881	1052	505	5895	2495	2934	2702	72	48
	2011	24967	11442	993	525	6808	2678	3641	3372	403	67
South Africa	2000	4570	3150	390	143	2156	950	604	577	14	14
	2008	16229	10636	1928	869	6075	2213	2633	2486	79	72
	2009	10787	6375	789	371	3428	1462	2158	2019	53	38
	2010	13451	8582	1027	487	4934	2459	2621	2406	69	46
	2011	15931	9767	957	503	5563	2648	3247	2992	75	64
Latin America and the Caribbean	2000	122150	108687	764	615	6608	1776	101316	98437	19	18
	2008	218501	163092	2069	825	15797	6772	145226	140216	648	612
	2009	167965	129450	1375	773	11355	4598	116719	110010	74	56
	2010	221085	167527	1740	1023	13081	5153	152706	144703	326	313
	2011	250853	184475	1997	988	16002	6199	166475	159067	619	494
Brazil	2000	15416	8675	358	290	3065	497	5252	5157	3	3
	2008	41823	15257	819	133	6261	2481	8177	7738	468	448
	2009	26322	9524	450	229	4892	1807	4182	3748	38	29
	2010	33109	9903	436	230	5688	1797	3779	3561	76	74
	2011	38812	11059	434	169	5744	1662	4881	4576	251	141
Eastern Asia	2000	347613	188125	37112	32788	64658	14462	86355	82182	1052	698
	2008	1230382	517062	88789	72837	227040	49480	201233	186977	30140	25142
	2009	1080408	435966	77390	62097	181468	40411	177108	164963	14876	10327
	2010	1414800	565714	99435	78971	237560	54823	228718	213396	25974	20492
	2011	1608737	619056	111454	87182	249685	53273	257917	240618	35679	28298
China	2000	82600	46255	10601	9716	16464	3921	19191	18323	325	217
	2008	674065	333933	55029	45253	149129	32539	129774	121382	18119	14715
	2009	591128	285849	48130	38596	121034	26248	116685	109669	9675	6532
	2010	781074	376271	63827	50927	161483	37055	150961	142241	16412	12828
	2011	902599	419563	73635	57896	174515	36998	171412	161871	22789	17893
Southern Asia	2000	3625	1641	151	104	958	204	532	511	71	33
	2008	28032	11486	644	258	7596	1623	3246	3112	418	292
	2009	29480	10941	675	304	7190	1529	3075	2958	325	219
	2010	34597	12614	735	250	7962	1530	3918	3782	594	507
	2011	46552	16892	979	331	10672	2083	5242	5060	810	684
South-Eastern Asia	2000	225569	118401	27610	23208	38165	7455	52626	51240	145	131
	2008	369761	141659	42006	31014	48805	11623	50848	48930	1550	1442
	2009	325297	116687	35008	25353	40549	10184	41130	39314	799	705
	2010	416914	142660	45764	33210	50272	12881	46625	44485	1395	1281
	2011	416646	135489	45857	33777	47729	12239	41904	39568	1770	1617
Western Asia	2000	18758	11174	341	203	6813	1825	4020	3894	570	265
	2008	79823	38245	2292	1884	29852	5935	6101	5499	6022	3721
	2009	72609	31874	614	279	23448	3948	7812	7292	2925	1136
	2010	77242	32372	692	339	25436	4752	6244	5617	3926	1795
	2011	98335	36892	933	463	30454	5547	5505	4846	4952	2208
Oceania	2000	159	110	30	4	63	31	18	17	11	11
	2008	194	146	85	2	50	1	11	9	0	0
	2009	1058	778	199	80	509	62	69	64	0	0
	2010	182	139	67	1	66	1	6	6	0	0
	2011	228	130	54	0	62	1	13	13	0	0

For general note and footnotes see end of table

Exportations mondiales en provenance et de destination (Tableau D)

En millions de dollars E.-U. f.o.b.

South-Eastern Europe Europe du Sud-Est	Northern Africa Afrique septentrionale	Sub-Saharan Africa Afrique subsaharienne	Latin America and the Caribbean Amérique latine et Caraïbes	Eastern Asia Asie orientale	Southern Asia Asie méridionale	South-eastern Asia Asie du Sud-Est	Western Asia Asie occidentale	Oceania Océanie	Other 3/ Autres 3/	Année	← Exportations vers Exportations en provenance de ↓
Machines et matériel de transport (CTCI, Rev. 3, 7)*[suite]*											
0	62	28	0	1	3	1	66	0	26	2000	Afrique septentrionale
28	516	315	11	13	11	262	661	0	158	2008	
56	661	293	9	22	11	215	561	2	149	2009	
86	705	351	12	38	14	347	623	9	142	2010	
94	658	433	14	107	11	414	898	7	157	2011	
4	25	1372	92	140	40	118	107	3	9	2000	Afrique subsaharienne
96	373	8094	438	278	149	344	938	7	162	2008	
76	353	7110	355	286	249	329	583	112	424	2009	
16	322	8308	558	406	264	314	501	16	419	2010	
25	531	9405	720	381	358	511	576	8	607	2011	
4	21	967	88	136	25	96	65	2	2	2000	Afrique du sud
61	320	3643	249	232	110	225	651	2	20	2008	
8	285	2939	181	167	208	138	413	7	12	2009	
16	221	3407	264	329	169	125	242	13	15	2010	
23	410	4308	365	278	228	211	255	5	6	2011	
3	47	290	11643	631	99	526	174	1	30	2000	Amérique latine et Caraïbes
105	381	2410	45019	3147	578	1704	1266	12	140	2008	
132	439	1613	31055	2539	526	972	1008	31	125	2009	
106	389	1591	44961	3181	521	1241	1184	20	38	2010	
199	311	2192	54596	3980	626	2567	1201	27	60	2011	
1	41	254	6013	131	70	97	130	1	...	2000	Brésil
65	345	2097	20345	914	349	1047	931	7	...	2008	
78	360	1440	12887	740	277	348	615	16	...	2009	
62	313	1166	19351	829	232	360	803	16	...	2010	
38	214	1448	22049	1242	396	1526	573	15	0	2011	
234	1157	3450	11502	92408	4160	37352	7457	528	188	2000	Asie orientale
3479	9422	24654	58733	396454	35502	106660	42467	5566	243	2008	
2571	9529	22372	48448	367126	34343	95520	38192	11437	27	2009	
3233	10903	28495	73327	490467	44723	118779	45414	7742	27	2010	
3597	9119	36080	89285	554403	53485	142286	56043	9687	19	2011	
39	283	1034	2120	21483	1303	7934	1814	10	...	2000	Chine
2246	6195	15449	30983	163421	24439	55681	22970	629	...	2008	
1878	5830	13781	26763	146984	24609	52527	21595	1637	...	2009	
2372	6061	19157	42795	196975	30524	62648	25503	2355	...	2010	
2659	6035	22558	54113	230539	37663	73523	30779	2378	0	2011	
3	69	318	125	154	337	457	448	1	1	2000	Asie méridionale
75	848	2400	1199	960	1822	3442	5159	31	191	2008	
377	985	2651	1014	1408	1568	5373	4668	17	151	2009	
196	1122	4018	1522	1299	2521	5449	5129	17	118	2010	
261	1503	5415	1992	1681	3381	7339	7084	23	171	2011	
31	254	1346	3706	37735	3155	57990	2659	114	32	2000	Asie du Sud-est
175	1860	2794	8644	93955	11679	95642	10977	574	253	2008	
154	1464	2346	6362	94291	10611	81796	10040	685	61	2009	
254	1921	3226	9571	125157	13765	106816	11359	717	73	2010	
303	1801	4014	12081	125782	14690	107586	12080	813	236	2011	
268	563	567	375	809	934	418	2227	7	846	2000	Asie occidentale
2199	2442	2944	1578	2767	5912	1254	12939	284	3238	2008	
1194	2969	3485	1470	2432	6459	1436	13627	98	4641	2009	
1480	2758	3179	2744	5145	8665	2201	12298	128	2344	2010	
1662	3715	4422	3231	6388	12202	2532	17485	172	4680	2011	
0	...	1	1	2	0	13	0	13	10	2000	Océanie
0	0	6	1	4	4	9	2	20	2	2008	
6	0	1	7	165	2	77	4	15	2	2009	
0	0	1	4	8	0	13	1	17	0	2010	
0	0	7	7	6	0	31	1	45	0	2011	

Voir la fin du tableau pour la remarque générale et les notes.

World exports by provenance and destination (Table D)

In million U.S. dollars f.o.b.

Exports from ↓ / Exports to →	Year	World 1/ Monde 1/	Developed economies 2/ Économies développées 2/ Total	Developed economies 2/ Économies développées 2/ Asia-Pacific Asie-Pacifique Total	Developed economies 2/ Économies développées 2/ Asia-Pacific Asie-Pacifique Japan Japon	Developed economies 2/ Économies développées 2/ Europe Total	Developed economies 2/ Économies développées 2/ Europe Germany Allemagne	Developed economies 2/ Économies développées 2/ North America Amérique du Nord Total	Developed economies 2/ Économies développées 2/ North America Amérique du Nord U.S.A. É.-U.	Commonwealth of Independent States Communauté d'Etats Indépendants Total	Commonwealth of Independent States Communauté d'Etats Indépendants Europe
		Miscellaneous manufactured articles (SITC, Rev. 3, 8)									
World 1/	2000	775851	590142	64499	53883	315519	67065	210123	183321	9403	8002
	2008	1630745	1120590	99993	76479	707868	126236	312729	266738	65128	46841
	2009	1425847	974202	91692	69970	613737	113651	268773	228984	40898	28656
	2010	1638700	1082898	103699	78874	664721	124612	314478	269317	49630	36392
	2011	1896773	1229104	121205	91228	761936	148441	345963	296981	59455	45162
Developed Economies - Asia-Pacific 2/	2000	46250	23611	1476	127	8212	2530	13923	13423	60	51
	2008	60955	26358	2451	164	11536	3908	12372	11797	247	229
	2009	49648	21015	2174	158	8962	3152	9879	9390	132	121
	2010	64053	24339	2432	179	10539	3127	11369	10759	214	200
	2011	72329	27078	2960	174	12048	3747	12071	11447	271	253
Japan	2000	43292	21705	525	.	7829	2456	13351	12873	58	49
	2008	55187	22026	610	.	10347	3700	11069	10607	222	207
	2009	44571	17181	508	.	7993	2973	8680	8295	120	111
	2010	58412	20181	531	.	9543	2942	10107	9591	199	187
	2011	66079	22399	993	.	10614	3496	10792	10265	261	244
Developed Economies - Europe 2/	2000	287846	245308	10532	8433	200489	41158	34287	31945	4592	4266
	2008	642940	516222	17528	12511	447394	73977	51299	47093	27877	25822
	2009	542589	439779	14740	10473	383527	66296	41512	38048	17807	15860
	2010	586275	468608	16485	11612	404792	71159	47331	43522	19669	17209
	2011	683169	537504	19068	13334	464443	83556	53993	49652	25136	22254
France	2000	28497	23630	1558	1416	19052	3940	3020	2668	226	204
	2008	61747	48513	2191	1869	41560	7257	4763	4098	1517	1395
	2009	52590	41586	1882	1605	35912	6577	3792	3255	968	836
	2010	54614	42368	1911	1615	36317	6851	4140	3552	1081	944
	2011	62223	47993	2081	1743	41213	7728	4698	4050	1236	1090
Germany	2000	51366	43807	1667	1311	37120	.	5020	4704	988	898
	2008	139318	111605	3481	2421	98279	.	9845	9088	6920	6502
	2009	118976	96692	2880	1997	85763	.	8050	7404	4458	4059
	2010	128975	102527	3327	2333	89828	.	9371	8704	4895	4455
	2011	151588	118008	3752	2590	103157	.	11099	10286	6931	6337
Developed Economies - North America 2/	2000	111721	73202	11744	9881	26290	4281	35168	16863	271	219
	2008	155344	101954	12987	9437	43505	6569	45462	17302	1134	909
	2009	136919	88077	11401	8048	38363	5639	38313	13782	591	470
	2010	152811	94709	13130	9777	39256	6241	42324	15137	712	600
	2011	163632	100188	14538	10467	40745	6720	44905	15977	934	796
United States	2000	93184	55116	11494	9680	25322	4102	18299	.	237	190
	2008	133943	82417	12614	9248	41664	6272	28138	.	986	782
	2009	119758	72466	11092	7890	36862	5407	24511	.	518	411
	2010	133791	77385	12743	9580	37472	5997	27170	.	638	542
	2011	143306	81886	14099	10248	38876	6443	28911	.	829	708
South-Eastern Europe	2000	5919	5677	9	6	5347	1365	322	303	72	63
	2008	16327	14755	18	10	14530	3137	207	184	432	401
	2009	13439	12155	24	10	11983	2746	149	132	294	266
	2010	14267	12947	13	8	12773	3007	161	144	337	319
	2011	17135	15432	19	12	15217	3692	196	172	457	428
Commonwealth of Independent States	2000	3708	1870	6	6	1486	462	377	366	875	708
	2008	7500	2480	15	12	2306	659	159	143	3664	2639
	2009	5972	2029	15	12	1851	533	163	150	2695	1867
	2010	6996	2126	13	10	1961	585	152	132	3308	2589
	2011	7666	2403	29	26	2204	658	170	152	3871	3272
Russian Federation 4/	2000	2063	973	5	5	735	130	233	228	223	87
	2008	2906	761	9	7	653	194	99	90	1143	393
	2009	2293	575	11	10	479	136	84	77	820	224
	2010	2561	670	9	7	564	205	97	81	693	290
	2011	2271	741	18	16	599	225	124	113	539	374

For general note and footnotes see end of table

En millions de dollars E.-U. f.o.b.

← Exportations vers

South-Eastern Europe Europe du Sud-Est	Northern Africa Afrique septentrio-nale	Sub-Saharar Africa Afrique subsahari-enne	Latin America and the Caribbean Amérique latine et Caraïbes	Eastern Asia Asie orientale	Southern Asia Asie méridionale	South-easter Asia Asie du Sud-Est	Western Asia Asie occidentale	Oceania Océanie	Other 3/ Autres 3/	Année	Exportations en provenance de ↓
				Articles manifacturés divers (CTCI, Rev. 3, 8)							
3357	4478	6410	39286	70791	4453	24591	20253	620	2067	2000	Monde 1/
13987	11128	20101	73339	183529	18804	55351	64122	1074	3592	2008	
10226	11349	19531	62856	165252	17886	52082	68039	994	2533	2009	
10586	12059	22967	77685	219304	23232	66637	70056	1164	2481	2010	
12450	12222	27693	92489	266091	29210	77328	85338	1379	4015	2011	
14	52	174	802	15385	388	4933	577	118	133	2000	Economies développées - Asie-Pacifique 2/
29	81	266	1500	23902	813	6582	924	236	14	2008	
24	77	207	1312	19850	704	5377	735	208	7	2009	
21	121	245	1727	27743	841	7753	799	246	4	2010	
17	97	311	2267	31378	966	8755	910	269	11	2011	
12	51	135	765	14980	343	4673	551	20	...	2000	Japon
23	78	178	1411	23482	723	6230	805	11	...	2008	
21	71	137	1249	19473	643	5035	628	13	...	2009	
19	114	151	1650	27294	769	7332	689	13	...	2010	
15	92	192	2192	30896	892	8309	817	13	...	2011	
2801	2668	2335	5400	9429	1360	3373	8790	208	1582	2000	Economies développées - Europe 2/
9992	5890	6128	10590	25783	5484	7779	25865	396	935	2008	
7454	5640	5503	8507	22856	5045	6785	22440	334	440	2009	
7597	5672	5980	10165	30311	5819	8046	23651	322	434	2010	
8891	5496	6999	12405	40731	6972	9721	27691	355	1268	2011	
184	765	524	431	1157	181	296	967	132	4	2000	France
582	1709	1210	920	2647	542	907	2808	301	90	2008	
380	1596	1085	712	2458	514	776	2211	255	48	2009	
425	1587	1095	897	3142	607	868	2242	249	54	2010	
500	1641	1183	1058	4184	649	1070	2393	272	42	2011	
366	283	418	1004	1617	294	717	1320	6	546	2000	Allemagne
1622	769	1222	2575	6455	1599	1891	4324	12	325	2008	
1296	701	1027	2047	5787	1504	1492	3950	16	5	2009	
1375	776	1206	2508	7890	1673	1781	4331	10	3	2010	
1725	743	1456	3007	10378	1906	2075	5332	11	17	2011	
35	510	453	21696	8326	463	4596	2132	38	0	2000	Economies développées - Amérique du Nord 2/
180	647	1089	23965	14344	1897	5158	4924	52	0	2008	
135	660	1002	21852	13332	1801	4452	4963	53	0	2009	
124	813	1193	24141	17935	2251	5572	5294	65	0	2010	
160	522	1295	26268	19182	2735	5991	6291	63	0	2011	
33	502	434	21555	8197	450	4561	2062	37	...	2000	Etats-Unis
165	593	996	23427	13873	1805	4986	4645	48	...	2008	
124	609	928	21452	12876	1724	4297	4717	47	...	2009	
107	765	1117	23651	17385	2175	5411	5095	62	...	2010	
144	493	1169	25693	18561	2633	5808	6030	59	...	2011	
125	2	4	2	2	1	0	31	0	1	2000	Europe du Sud-Est
854	13	9	10	22	23	16	191	0	1	2008	
650	15	12	9	31	15	12	244	0	1	2009	
665	19	13	32	47	25	7	171	1	2	2010	
782	45	10	34	72	42	22	234	0	4	2011	
19	18	30	20	503	223	31	118	0	0	2000	Communauté d'Etats Indépendants
346	57	28	50	163	498	27	176	0	10	2008	
143	69	22	73	238	469	64	164	0	7	2009	
186	76	27	99	244	601	92	215	0	23	2010	
208	106	99	78	219	343	119	189	0	31	2011	
11	9	23	12	492	213	29	76	0	0	2000	Fédération de Russie 4/
188	53	17	38	117	449	21	116	0	4	2008	
38	54	12	58	147	436	52	97	0	3	2009	
61	67	16	58	187	573	80	137	0	19	2010	
26	97	85	69	179	306	104	102	0	22	2011	

Voir la fin du tableau pour la remarque générale et les notes.

World exports by provenance and destination (Table D)

In million U.S. dollars f.o.b.

Exports to → / ↓ Exports from	Year	World 1/ Monde 1/	Developed economies 2/ Économies développées 2/ Total	Asia-Pacific Asie-Pacifique Total	Asia-Pacific Japan Japon	Europe Total	Europe Germany Allemagne	North America Amérique du Nord Total	North America U.S.A. É.-U.	Commonwealth of Independent States Communauté d'Etats Indépendants Total	CIS Europe
					Miscellaneous manufactured articles (SITC, Rev. 3, 8)*[cont.]*						
Northern Africa	2000	6113	5902	6	5	5598	719	297	290	0	0
	2008	10764	9885	9	4	9468	885	408	398	11	8
	2009	10176	9178	10	6	8380	802	788	775	6	4
	2010	10169	9202	10	5	8374	830	818	802	7	4
	2011	11439	10355	12	7	9536	958	808	788	7	5
Sub-Saharan Africa	2000	3655	2663	41	19	1667	357	956	939	1	1
	2008	7054	3740	47	9	2746	537	947	911	5	3
	2009	6259	2848	44	8	1776	398	1027	911	7	4
	2010	7267	3406	48	9	1791	517	1567	1432	4	2
	2011	7883	3753	58	9	1856	434	1840	1692	33	6
South Africa	2000	1101	790	29	14	556	276	204	200	0	0
	2008	1777	927	36	5	717	388	174	154	3	2
	2009	1408	684	28	5	517	298	138	126	5	3
	2010	1700	813	33	4	644	416	135	126	2	1
	2011	1792	733	37	4	542	311	154	145	5	3
Latin America and the Caribbean	2000	31074	27207	182	100	1133	309	25892	25696	6	6
	2008	52909	38458	345	211	3266	577	34846	34297	61	58
	2009	43820	32553	346	237	2710	437	29496	28999	38	36
	2010	49697	36948	320	192	2818	518	33810	33141	54	50
	2011	54454	39282	312	191	2783	587	36187	35514	58	53
Brazil	2000	3455	2315	52	34	590	135	1673	1624	3	3
	2008	5575	2953	82	44	1640	311	1231	1168	40	38
	2009	4407	2309	69	37	1280	225	960	917	26	25
	2010	4689	2278	70	32	1298	296	911	869	34	33
	2011	4926	2063	78	37	1138	305	847	810	39	38
Eastern Asia	2000	195614	139894	31956	28206	38834	8849	69104	65047	2369	1902
	2008	501949	292402	54030	44421	116448	23604	121925	112144	28603	14900
	2009	442316	259449	50970	41848	102198	21782	106281	98001	17012	8792
	2010	547571	307299	56902	46219	121327	25790	129070	119265	22308	13643
	2011	637725	346999	67395	54432	138633	31874	140972	130244	24845	15840
China	2000	85989	57952	18935	17210	13990	3023	25027	23605	2080	1646
	2008	335236	202987	40349	33488	78746	15075	83892	76541	27475	13862
	2009	298986	187314	38468	31839	71169	14473	77677	71343	16091	7964
	2010	376863	229017	42949	34831	88542	18855	97526	89827	20812	12289
	2011	458568	267449	53009	42791	105423	24172	109017	100397	23106	14279
Southern Asia	2000	19654	16403	408	250	7510	1663	8486	7986	597	371
	2008	40671	30996	649	327	18145	4031	12202	11327	418	149
	2009	50247	32183	760	326	19141	4524	12281	11387	326	115
	2010	49304	34215	997	468	20425	4542	12793	11758	439	227
	2011	66135	45614	1489	695	27931	6466	16195	14764	705	390
South-Eastern Asia	2000	49622	37075	7498	6365	11923	2504	17655	16917	118	106
	2008	96198	62457	11526	9175	21768	4092	29164	27647	652	578
	2009	90330	57131	10879	8685	20715	3757	25536	24249	528	474
	2010	112007	69613	12980	10209	24960	4358	31674	30068	637	574
	2011	126922	76647	14834	11604	27296	4969	34517	32759	751	666
Western Asia	2000	13578	10576	123	87	6869	2863	3584	3475	442	309
	2008	36985	20746	315	192	16701	4258	3730	3488	2025	1144
	2009	32830	17589	256	152	14003	3578	3330	3144	1463	647
	2010	37133	19396	308	185	15686	3937	3403	3148	1941	975
	2011	47060	23745	422	277	19221	4780	4102	3815	2387	1199
Oceania	2000	1095	754	518	399	163	4	73	73	0	0
	2008	1148	136	73	6	54	2	8	8	0	0
	2009	1303	216	73	6	125	7	17	17	0	0
	2010	1150	89	62	1	18	0	8	8	0	0
	2011	1223	102	71	0	25	1	7	7	0	0

For general note and footnotes see end of table

Exportations mondiales en provenance et de destination (Tableau D)

En millions de dollars E.-U. f.o.b.

South-Eastern Europe Europe du Sud-Est	Northern Africa Afrique septentrio-nale	Sub-Saharan Africa Afrique subsahari-enne	Latin America and the Caribbean Amérique latine et Caraïbes	Eastern Asia Asie orientale	Southern Asia Asie méridionale	South-eastern Asia Asie du Sud-Est	Western Asia Asie occidentale	Oceania Océanie	Other 3/ Autres 3/	← Exportations vers Année	Exportations en provence de ↓
			Articles manifacturés divers (CTCI, Rev. 3, 8) *[suite]*								
0	52	46	3	1	1	1	53	0	54	2000	Afrique septentrionale
8	245	177	10	18	12	2	352	0	45	2008	
4	271	207	11	20	8	4	408	0	58	2009	
4	235	191	13	30	12	3	366	0	106	2010	
7	212	221	15	37	9	4	456	0	116	2011	
0	4	826	18	16	8	17	93	1	7	2000	Afrique subsaharienne
19	14	2948	45	102	27	19	108	3	24	2008	
16	29	3075	53	42	35	49	77	18	11	2009	
7	26	3405	127	54	54	61	93	19	11	2010	
6	12	3598	172	59	66	70	75	25	15	2011	
0	3	231	10	10	6	15	33	1	1	2000	Afrique du sud
1	8	644	18	76	17	12	61	2	9	2008	
1	6	593	10	11	21	22	47	3	4	2009	
1	20	725	21	15	14	25	60	3	3	2010	
2	6	924	26	17	15	24	37	2	3	2011	
2	10	27	3588	97	18	41	48	1	29	2000	Amérique latine et Caraïbes
12	34	306	12908	195	70	151	166	8	540	2008	
10	25	235	10339	189	64	158	140	2	69	2009	
14	23	198	11767	241	86	161	136	3	67	2010	
12	23	251	14056	283	56	152	162	3	115	2011	
1	4	17	1022	30	13	20	30	0	...	2000	Brésil
8	26	268	1976	76	32	76	118	2	...	2008	
9	19	211	1533	65	27	108	99	1	...	2009	
11	18	167	1886	75	26	95	99	1	...	2010	
9	14	225	2252	88	32	90	113	1	0	2011	
215	740	1632	6514	32754	949	6154	4212	168	14	2000	Asie orientale
1269	2707	6612	21302	106284	5153	21646	15787	176	6	2008	
912	3034	6622	17972	94589	5768	21719	15019	206	14	2009	
993	3605	8869	25879	123594	8272	28314	18148	284	6	2010	
1226	3947	11323	32665	149796	10883	33265	22396	370	10	2011	
184	486	801	2665	17527	283	1857	2137	16	...	2000	Chine
1159	2512	5742	14437	49830	3671	14309	13030	84	...	2008	
830	2809	5938	12533	41555	4056	15056	12710	94	...	2009	
872	3329	8132	20137	52629	6342	20075	15385	133	...	2010	
1097	3690	10573	27184	72683	8438	24854	19312	179	1	2011	
7	23	241	213	345	182	255	1371	14	2	2000	Asie méridionale
39	98	717	536	874	589	686	5605	19	94	2008	
29	115	789	575	1495	540	873	13126	18	177	2009	
48	111	854	784	1683	617	909	9568	21	54	2010	
69	145	1152	1117	2390	859	1365	12618	28	72	2011	
15	102	478	676	3729	624	5075	1660	60	7	2000	Asie du Sud-est
78	199	907	2173	10582	1732	12924	4280	165	51	2008	
47	201	882	1947	11674	1651	12229	3879	135	26	2009	
40	239	1082	2656	15608	2232	15336	4387	153	22	2010	
46	224	1257	3141	19597	2842	17308	4897	188	25	2011	
123	297	161	58	177	234	109	1166	0	237	2000	Asie occidentale
1161	1142	914	244	1239	2506	357	5742	5	904	2008	
800	1214	972	205	898	1784	332	6839	8	726	2009	
886	1118	910	295	1808	2423	372	7223	36	725	2010	
1026	1393	1173	270	2331	3431	535	9415	62	1292	2011	
0	...	2	298	25	0	3	2	10	1	2000	Océanie
0	0	1	5	19	0	3	3	14	967	2008	
1	0	4	2	37	1	29	5	11	997	2009	
0	0	0	0	7	1	11	3	13	1026	2010	
0	0	4	1	16	4	20	3	15	1057	2011	

Voir la fin du tableau pour la remarque générale et les notes.

World exports by provenance and destination (Table D)

In million U.S. dollars f.o.b.

Exports to → / ↓ Exports from	Year	World 1/ Monde 1/	Developed economies 2/ Économies développées 2/ Total	Asia-Pacific Asie-Pacifique Total	Asia-Pacific Asie-Pacifique Japan Japon	Europe Total	Europe Germany Allemagne	North America Amérique du Nord Total	North America Amérique du Nord U.S.A. É.-U.	Commonwealth of Independent States Communauté d'Etats Indépendants Total	Commonwealth of Independent States Communauté d'Etats Indépendants Europe
Commodities and transactions not classified elsewhere in the SITC (SITC, Rev. 3, 9)											
World 1/	2000	260415	179633	7569	4494	127582	42491	44482	37638	7942	2087
	2008	696575	374909	16425	7225	289222	63956	69262	52665	28766	27707
	2009	686515	381685	24818	13104	290837	49040	66031	44681	7102	4967
	2010	754541	418233	24196	12518	317741	60673	76297	49918	6458	5551
	2011	960638	425718	30357	18768	309074	46413	86287	53540	7926	6143
Developed Economies - Asia-Pacific 2/	2000	24052	11394	762	441	3965	977	6667	6529	17	10
	2008	63098	25239	1789	310	14582	1229	8869	8584	164	111
	2009	59190	22353	1146	93	14694	1052	6513	6270	58	31
	2010	70988	25202	1381	131	16877	1351	6945	6650	86	57
	2011	74793	26042	1700	144	17587	1393	6755	6490	109	72
Japan	2000	17490	9032	214	.	3389	974	5429	5296	10	9
	2008	42080	15667	851	.	8146	1220	6671	6391	158	108
	2009	38744	16019	313	.	10079	1041	5627	5387	56	30
	2010	46457	18545	414	.	12028	1314	6102	5812	82	54
	2011	49439	20685	698	.	14061	1295	5927	5664	105	69
Developed Economies - Europe 2/	2000	133373	113334	2398	1455	100485	39094	10450	8935	881	475
	2008	324191	229774	2773	1541	210977	58409	16024	13949	4572	4153
	2009	266025	190303	2695	1463	171105	39262	16503	14681	3775	3311
	2010	284701	208122	3478	1991	186324	49305	18320	16697	4164	3745
	2011	308265	192057	3992	2341	170886	34916	17178	15480	4897	3971
France	2000	6657	5424	194	157	4748	1034	482	440	59	57
	2008	14368	11467	415	320	10434	2683	618	529	231	217
	2009	12232	9457	360	275	8559	2153	538	482	183	166
	2010	13906	10864	459	371	9763	2612	642	583	194	177
	2011	17400	13876	530	425	12509	3169	837	740	261	240
Germany	2000	40968	32604	131	106	31812	.	661	578	272	195
	2008	100105	77702	333	128	76421	.	948	861	2025	1929
	2009	86984	70400	872	455	67309	.	2219	2057	2160	1896
	2010	91891	74153	1084	460	70790	.	2279	2095	2619	2441
	2011	80120	60507	1160	569	56624	.	2723	2455	2435	2170
Developed Economies - North America 2/	2000	50224	36083	2708	1591	11165	1213	22210	17321	208	103
	2008	81500	60388	3198	1456	29183	2051	28007	18213	231	60
	2009	140241	88439	9379	5541	51952	6926	27108	13931	1045	705
	2010	157411	97513	10165	6270	58320	7642	29029	14983	768	519
	2011	185791	113413	10653	5498	72083	7578	30677	15495	1273	864
United States	2000	32007	18124	2589	1504	10659	1116	4876	.	197	98
	2008	56283	36131	3027	1369	23315	1898	9790	.	225	54
	2009	119482	68359	9225	5485	45962	6634	13172	.	1040	701
	2010	131625	72686	10007	6175	48635	7440	14044	.	758	510
	2011	154864	84451	10416	5341	58859	7273	15176	.	1263	853
South-Eastern Europe	2000	385	121	1	0	113	8	8	8	48	47
	2008	1587	1105	0	0	1077	245	28	27	15	2
	2009	2195	1313	3	3	1274	228	36	36	15	10
	2010	2726	1539	4	4	1509	256	26	25	22	18
	2011	2167	1503	0	0	1464	260	39	38	25	23
Commonwealth of Independent States	2000	17287	5097	145	145	4640	549	312	303	6651	1383
	2008	39052	4195	429	427	3394	320	373	270	23294	23039
	2009	29992	12767	209	208	12297	487	262	114	1937	775
	2010	46335	20216	363	324	19591	752	263	133	1168	1009
	2011	80594	7781	174	174	6171	302	1437	1251	1323	987
Russian Federation 4/	2000	12145	2519	63	63	2311	13	145	140	5251	327
	2008	35673	2140	27	27	1866	312	247	247	22509	22507
	2009	26848	10952	25	24	10847	454	81	81	1300	359
	2010	42383	18280	57	19	18191	713	33	33	716	611
	2011	75733	5145	83	83	3829	283	1232	1232	313	34

For general note and footnotes see end of table

En millions de dollars E.-U. f.o.b.

South-Eastern Europe Europe du Sud-Est	Northern Africa Afrique septentrio-nale	Sub-Saharar Africa Afrique subsahari-enne	Latin America and the Caribbean Amérique latine et Caraïbes	Eastern Asia Asie orientale	Southern Asia Asie méridionale	outh-easter Asia Asie du Sud-Est	Western Asia Asie occidentale	Oceania Océanie	Other 3/ Autres 3/	← Exportations vers Année	Exportations en provence de ↓
Articles et transactions non classés ailleurs dans la CTCI (CTCI, Rev. 3, 9)											
529	954	2210	11681	15876	2184	11365	10043	204	17793	2000	Monde 1/
3489	3089	12098	24931	48900	15547	26042	29409	1891	127504	2008	
5473	3441	11879	28317	47937	21383	24056	40538	1242	113462	2009	
6394	3826	14922	32655	61213	23001	30508	46817	1829	108685	2010	
2425	8933	16017	39967	94757	25559	41155	33874	2590	261717	2011	
15	38	65	224	6622	104	4960	567	46	1	2000	Économies développées - Asie-Pacifique 2/
15	34	225	523	18462	4758	9514	3151	718	293	2008	
8	27	207	385	15594	5775	7847	524	214	6198	2009	
30	33	216	449	20450	5430	9487	438	240	8927	2010	
20	29	225	532	20221	4781	12880	642	257	9055	2011	
14	38	50	223	4319	68	3474	251	11	0	2000	Japon
12	34	148	391	17790	218	7112	537	12	...	2008	
8	26	156	375	15143	269	6313	366	12	...	2009	
29	31	150	440	19105	404	7261	397	13	0	2010	
19	28	162	526	18150	529	8677	540	17	0	2011	
392	630	980	1753	2921	869	1584	3241	17	6771	2000	Économies développées - Europe 2/
3215	1823	2772	3408	5978	2917	2485	10870	76	56302	2008	
3860	1886	2231	3546	6633	3001	2664	6879	31	41216	2009	
3967	1766	2832	4125	7434	3735	3482	7313	63	37697	2010	
2014	1975	3296	5342	8842	3794	4631	8815	93	72510	2011	
19	125	133	210	235	80	139	214	7	11	2000	France
77	349	313	326	639	193	258	468	13	34	2008	
83	319	248	340	583	187	265	523	12	31	2009	
72	357	238	381	662	212	280	601	10	36	2010	
87	327	359	423	822	232	348	574	42	49	2011	
92	190	245	317	1089	210	238	502	6	5201	2000	Allemagne
1541	703	616	837	1872	540	335	2083	27	11824	2008	
1874	801	592	1290	3377	1332	775	2473	3	1906	2009	
1622	632	746	1418	3684	1579	1377	2707	16	1338	2010	
1232	466	921	1412	3964	1214	1893	3359	12	2705	2011	
45	77	329	8301	2504	268	1350	1015	44	0	2000	Économies développées - Amérique du Nord 2/
67	200	856	11679	2595	983	1962	2459	78	2	2008	
189	1055	1758	17896	11602	3493	6255	8327	183	0	2009	
123	1731	2186	19369	14933	3340	9351	7967	130	...	2010	
160	1275	2824	22229	21770	2716	9768	10218	147	...	2011	
42	72	311	8210	2437	257	1321	994	43	...	2000	États-Unis
61	193	765	11467	2324	910	1915	2219	71	...	2008	
187	1041	1710	17706	11499	3396	6214	8166	164	...	2009	
117	1716	2145	19134	14597	3216	9240	7895	120	...	2010	
157	1261	2784	22006	20382	2679	9595	10150	135	...	2011	
32	3	10	5	3	8	4	150	0	1	2000	Europe du Sud-Est
111	2	4	3	0	6	23	63	0	255	2008	
532	5	9	3	14	49	5	95	0	155	2009	
673	7	19	6	18	85	8	74	0	275	2010	
169	2	22	6	0	46	8	112	1	274	2011	
12	78	24	51	1416	293	72	3592	0	1	2000	Communauté d'Etats Indépendants
8	142	76	6	175	421	40	686	...	10010	2008	
814	93	71	323	41	822	27	13097	0	1	2009	
1466	47	116	368	35	1013	30	21284	0	591	2010	
6	980	300	906	461	762	269	1425	1	66380	2011	
2	...	0	3	822	18	35	3494	...	...	2000	Fédération de Russie 4/
...	108	...	2	159	182	1	563	...	10010	2008	
809	49	1	303	6	466	4	12957	0	...	2009	
1461	28	0	367	13	531	11	20976	...	...	2010	
4	967	184	905	438	424	133	1235	...	65984	2011	

Voir la fin du tableau pour la remarque générale et les notes.

World exports by provenance and destination (Table D)

In million U.S. dollars f.o.b.

Exports from ↓ / Exports to →	Year	World 1/ Monde 1/	Developed economies 2/ Économies développées 2/ Total	Asia-Pacific Asie-Pacifique Total	Asia-Pacific Asie-Pacifique Japan Japon	Europe Total	Europe Germany Allemagne	North America Amérique du Nord Total	North America Amérique du Nord U.S.A. É.-U.	Commonwealth of Independent States Communauté d'Etats Indépendants Total	Commonwealth of Independent States Communauté d'Etats Indépendants Europe
			Commodities and transactions not classified elsewhere in the SITC (SITC, Rev. 3, 9) *[cont.]*								
Northern Africa	2000	135	114	1	1	17	0	95	95	2	0
	2008	517	230	0	0	142	5	87	87	0	0
	2009	1811	858	0	0	821	7	37	37	1	1
	2010	2282	554	0	0	463	5	91	6	0	0
	2011	4445	373	0	0	370	27	3	3	34	34
Sub-Saharan Africa	2000	5208	1303	2	2	1277	11	24	24	1	0
	2008	6902	1940	12	2	1862	21	66	64	22	21
	2009	10260	4522	19	16	3665	22	837	34	19	19
	2010	11673	4612	27	26	3502	17	1083	154	17	17
	2011	22532	6258	35	30	4599	38	1623	159	30	30
South Africa	2000	3561	14	0	0	14	1	0	0	...	...
	2008	230	80	6	0	67	12	6	5	0	0
	2009	207	35	1	0	35	6	0	0	0	0
	2010	267	30	0	0	29	2	1	1	0	0
	2011	7339	72	4	0	56	12	12	12	...	...
Latin America and the Caribbean	2000	6543	4216	22	22	1852	60	2342	2166	31	0
	2008	23164	17947	31	30	8322	49	9594	6342	4	2
	2009	26741	22476	70	68	9646	255	12760	8121	5	5
	2010	29802	27892	18	17	10228	87	17647	8928	0	0
	2011	46157	38605	19	16	13474	66	25112	11805	6	5
Brazil	2000	1449	1310	9	9	269	19	1031	1031	25	0
	2008	5859	3426	23	23	1611	0	1793	1786	4	2
	2009	4200	3030	13	13	1912	81	1105	1078	2	2
	2010	1819	1670	...	.	1408	0	262	216	0	0
	2011	7406	2454	3	1	2021	7	431	289	4	4
Eastern Asia	2000	3390	1290	442	110	759	15	88	79	1	1
	2008	13602	4487	1419	1157	2266	135	802	529	11	6
	2009	19386	10195	1750	1359	7635	87	810	603	19	13
	2010	19344	5689	1460	1253	3495	100	733	495	18	12
	2011	36303	3471	1518	1435	1162	218	791	493	33	23
China	2000	514	64	37	36	13	0	15	14	0	...
	2008	1710	1078	833	832	56	13	189	175	6	2
	2009	1629	1080	837	834	52	7	191	181	13	9
	2010	1468	1067	858	856	53	14	157	151	11	8
	2011	2343	1266	1016	1014	76	20	175	168	23	16
Southern Asia	2000	1098	721	38	23	307	50	376	359	16	4
	2008	7670	1188	95	50	591	75	502	477	10	6
	2009	11303	869	113	87	462	77	294	281	27	18
	2010	8173	2355	150	72	1074	314	1131	1123	119	102
	2011	11510	720	68	60	435	72	217	190	76	58
South-Eastern Asia	2000	8509	3404	886	589	1777	358	742	695	27	25
	2008	55824	18975	5217	2177	10216	1250	3541	3095	165	158
	2009	30593	13741	4416	758	8802	481	523	284	28	25
	2010	38774	13890	3764	852	9359	757	767	476	45	41
	2011	54690	17114	4296	2527	10799	1445	2018	1721	58	42
Western Asia	2000	10122	2483	124	104	1222	155	1136	1093	58	38
	2008	77770	8056	130	74	6562	167	1364	1025	277	148
	2009	86871	12268	3518	3507	8410	152	340	281	174	55
	2010	80188	8803	1610	1577	6932	87	261	248	50	29
	2011	131665	16968	6555	6541	9979	96	435	413	61	34
Oceania	2000	89	73	40	12	3	0	30	30	1	...
	2008	1699	1386	1333	1	49	.	5	5	0	0
	2009	1907	1582	1501	1	73	5	8	8	...	...
	2010	2147	1845	1776	1	67	0	2	1	0	0
	2011	1725	1413	1346	3	64	0	3	3	0	0

For general note and footnotes see end of table

Exportations mondiales en provenance et de destination (Tableau D)

En millions de dollars E.-U. f.o.b.

South-Eastern Europe Europe du Sud-Est	Northern Africa Afrique septentrio-nale	Sub-Saharan Africa Afrique subsahari-enne	Latin America and the Caribbean Amérique latine et Caraïbes	Eastern Asia Asie orientale	Southern Asia Asie méridionale	South-eastern Asia Asie du Sud-Est	Western Asia Asie occidentale	Oceania Océanie	Other 3/ Autres 3/	Année	← Exportations vers Exportations en provence de ↓
Articles et transactions non classés ailleurs dans la CTCI (CTCI, Rev. 3, 9) [suite]											
0	0	0	0	0	0	0	18	0	0	2000	Afrique septentrionale
1	9	4	1	3	2	1	267	...	1	2008	
0	12	6	0	2	2	1	928	...	0	2009	
0	21	363	27	2	6	1	1307	...	1	2010	
0	16	936	31	1	2	1	3048	...	1	2011	
0	5	309	0	15	12	3	21	0	3539	2000	Afrique subsaharienne
1	7	3534	9	138	4	5	510	0	732	2008	
1	8	4384	24	254	6	1	868	1	173	2009	
1	8	5268	19	249	65	19	1298	5	111	2010	
1	11	6552	28	247	95	30	2222	7	7053	2011	
...	...	1	...	0	10	0	0	...	3535	2000	Afrique du sud
0	0	11	0	132	2	2	2	0	0	2008	
0	0	1	0	170	0	0	0	...	0	2009	
0	0	2	0	235	0	0	0	0	0	2010	
0	0	25	3	226	2	2	9	...	7000	2011	
0	0	80	130	4	4	22	49	0	2006	2000	Amérique latine et Caraïbes
3	0	760	927	23	54	218	729	1	2498	2008	
34	0	319	793	26	77	243	473	1	2293	2009	
1	0	9	90	14	2	19	538	0	1236	2010	
1	1	23	151	75	3	116	463	1	6713	2011	
0	...	54	41	0	1	6	12	0	...	2000	Brésil
2	0	755	809	2	52	203	605	0	...	2008	
19	0	298	404	1	72	237	135	1	...	2009	
...	...	0	2	0	0	0	147	...	...	2010	
0	0	12	40	32	0	2	47	1	4813	2011	
1	10	20	14	971	171	402	437	2	71	2000	Asie orientale
22	8	24	52	6123	558	1836	284	3	194	2008	
3	7	31	73	6669	580	1283	327	3	196	2009	
12	6	30	54	9999	481	2073	156	3	823	2010	
5	6	52	68	28051	448	2976	369	4	819	2011	
0	9	11	1	47	161	8	209	0	2	2000	Chine
1	5	11	20	289	219	79	2	0	...	2008	
0	3	12	26	206	119	80	88	0	...	2009	
1	2	15	24	231	55	56	6	0	...	2010	
0	1	33	23	609	66	311	9	0	...	2011	
0	2	15	14	18	183	38	88	0	1	2000	Asie méridionale
3	12	60	92	602	193	492	4749	44	226	2008	
9	17	25	79	113	268	1013	3259	0	5623	2009	
91	0	117	864	72	630	211	3486	95	132	2010	
1	7	56	69	85	295	1007	966	0	8227	2011	
4	12	307	1054	1062	182	1789	320	80	268	2000	Asie du Sud-est
7	50	2757	8124	13550	616	9232	1272	962	113	2008	
2	129	1951	5149	4711	370	3032	675	803	1	2009	
3	83	3198	7224	6661	492	4970	876	1287	45	2010	
16	4457	865	10535	10890	644	6506	1483	2072	52	2011	
26	99	72	134	340	92	1139	545	1	5133	2000	Asie occidentale
35	800	1027	108	1250	5036	223	4368	8	56583	2008	
20	202	888	45	2273	6939	1670	5086	4	57302	2009	
27	127	569	59	1344	7722	855	2079	5	58549	2010	
32	176	867	70	4113	11972	2962	4110	6	90327	2011	
...	...	0	0	1	0	1	0	13	0	2000	Océanie
0	0	0	0	1	0	13	0	2	296	2008	
0	0	0	0	2	0	16	0	1	304	2009	
...	0	0	0	2	0	0	0	2	298	2010	
0	0	0	0	1	0	1	0	2	307	2011	

Voir la fin du tableau pour la remarque générale et les notes.

World exports by provenance and destination (Table D)
Exportations mondiales en provenance et de destination (Tableau D)

General note:

Table D is based on data of UN Comtrade at the end of May 2012. An updated and more detailed version of this table will be published in Volume II of the 2011 ITSY which will be produced later this year. The totals of imports and exports presented in table A and D are not necessarily identical as table A is mainly based on the data of the IMF's International Financial Statistics (IFS) which is a different data collection system with different aims, procedures, timetable and sources for update and maintenance than UN Comtrade (see the introduction for details). Nevertheless, discrepancies between both tables are in general minor and usually do not affect the overall information provided. A systematic comparison of the figures from both sources (which includes the description of known and relevant conceptual differences) is available at http://unstats.un.org/unsd/trade/imts/annual%20totals.htm. Overall, the discrepancies in the world total or world aggregate of exports in table A and table D is around 0.5 percent or less for all years shown, which is minor, given the differences between the two sources.

Remarque générale:

Tableau D est basé sur les données telles que disponible en fin Mai 2012. Une version antérieure de ce tableau est publiée dans le volume I de l'annuaire 2011 ITSY qui a été produit plus tôt cette année. Les importations et exportations totales présentées dans les tableaux A et D ne sont pas nécessairement identiques du fait que le tableau A est basé principalement sur les données des Statistiques Financières Internationales (IFS) du FMI qui est un différent système de collecte des données avec des objectifs, des procédures, un calendrier et des sources de mise à jour et de maintenance différents de ceux de UN Comtrade sur lequel le tableau D est basé (voir l'introduction pour les détails). Toutefois, les écarts entre les deux tableaux sont en général mineurs et n'affectent pas substantiellement l'information fournie. Une comparaison systématique des données de ces deux sources (incluant une description des différences conceptuelles pertinentes connues) est disponible à http://unstats.un.org/unsd/trade/imts/annual%20totals.htm. En général, la différence entre les totaux des exportations mondiales présentés dans les tableaux A et D est inférieure à 0.5 pour cent pour chacune des années publiées, ce qui est mineur étant donné les différences entre les deux sources.

Footnotes:

1 Exports for which country of destination is not available are included in the totals for the 'World' and in region "Others" (see footnote number 3 for further explanation)

2 This classification is intended for statistical convenience and does not, necessarily, express a judgment about the stage reached by a particular country in the development process.

3 The region "Others" as destination for exports contains the following trading partners: Antarctica, bunkers, free zones, confidential and not elsewhere specified countries.

4 2011 data excludes trading partner Belarus and Kazakhstan

1 Exportations dont les pays de destination n'est pas disponible sont incluses dansles totaux pour le 'Monde ' et dans la région "les autres " (voir note n ° 3 pour plus d'explications)

2 Cette classification est utilisée pour plus de commodité dans la présentation des statistiques et n'implique pas nécessairement un jugement quant au stade de développement auquel est parvenuun pays donné.

3 La région "Autres" comme destination des exportations comprend les partenaires commerciaux suivants: Antarctique, combustibles de soute, zones franches, partenaires confidentiels ou non specifiés ailleurs

4 Données de 2011 exclut partenaire commercial du Bélarus et le Kazakhstan

2011
INTERNATIONAL TRADE
STATISTICS YEARBOOK

VOLUME I
TRADE BY COUNTRY

PART 2 – COUNTRY TRADE PROFILES

173 Countries (or areas)

European Union (EU-27)

Imports: CIF, by origin	Exports: FOB, by last known destination	Trade System: General

Overview:

Following a significant decrease in exports of 25.3 percent in 2009, the value of exports of Afghanistan decreased further by 3.7 percent in 2010 to amount to 388.5 mln US$ (see table 1 and graph 1). Imports, on the other hand, increased by 54.5 percent and amounted to 5.2 bln US$ (see table 2 and graph 1). This resulted in a trade deficit of 4.8 bln US$ in 2010 (see graph 1). Trade was in deficit with almost all of the MDG regions (see graph 2). Large deficits were recorded with the Commonwealth of Independent States (-1.7 bln US$), Southern Asia (-850.0 mln US$) and Eastern Asia (-757.3 mln US$). In 2010, Afghanistan's imports were more diversified across partners than exports: 9 (respectively 5) major partners accounted for 80 percent of imports (respectively exports) (see graph 3).

Graph 1: Total imports, exports and trade balance

(Bln US$ by year)

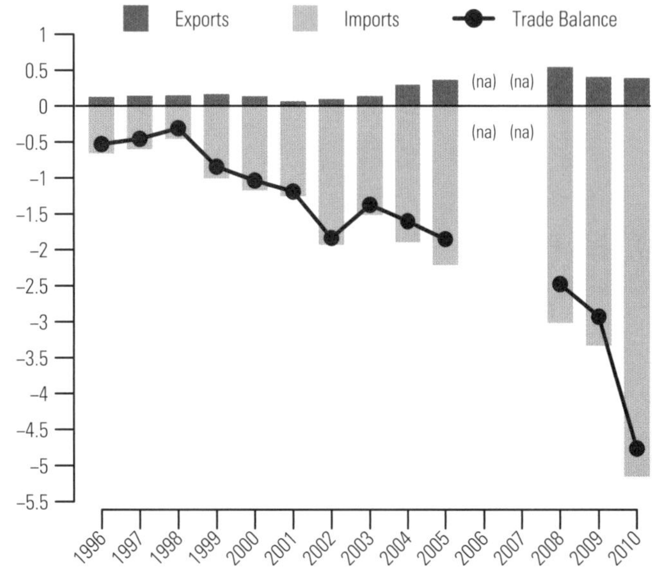

Table 1: Exports by SITC sections

(Value in million US$, growth and shares in percentage)

SITC	2010	Avg. Growth rates (%) 2006-2010	Avg. Growth rates (%) 2009-2010	2010 share
Total	388.5	...	-3.7	100.0
0+1	130.9	...	-36.5	33.7
2+4	67.5	...	48.9	17.4
6	76.2	...	5.0	19.6
8	0.0	...	-85.8	0.0
9	113.8	...	44.0	29.3

Exports Profile:

In 2010, Afghanistan's exports were composed of 33.7 percent of food, live animals, beverages and tobacco (SITC sections 0+1) and 29.3 percent of commodities and transactions not classified elsewhere (SITC section 9) (see table 1). Top partners for exports were Pakistan, India and Turkey (see table 4). From 2008 to 2010, Afghanistan's top products for exports were carpets and other textile floor coverings, knotted (HS code 5701), other nuts, fresh or dried (HS code 0802) and grapes, fresh or dried (HS code 0806) (see table 3).

Table 2: Imports by SITC sections

(Value in million US$, growth and shares in percentage)

SITC	2010	Avg. Growth rates (%) 2006-2010	Avg. Growth rates (%) 2009-2010	2010 share
Total	5154.2	...	54.5	100.0
0+1	586.4	...	3.3	11.4
2+4	123.6	...	181.5	2.4
3	1075.2	...	36.4	20.9
5	82.4	...	124.5	1.6
6	433.2	...	77.6	8.4
7	339.3	...	65.7	6.6
8	138.9	...	81.6	2.7
9	2375.2	...	72.8	46.1

Table 3: Top 10 export commodities 2008 to 2010

(Value in million US$)

HS code	4-digit heading of Harmonized System 2002	Value (million US$) 2008	2009	2010	Unit value 2008	2009	2010	Unit	SITC code
	All Commodities	540.1	403.4	388.5					
5701	Carpets and other textile floor coverings, knotted	149.6	67.9	70.0	*25.0*	22.8		US$/m^2	659
0802	Other nuts, fresh or dried	112.1	104.6	36.1	156.6			thsd US$/kg	057
9999	Commodities not specified according to kind	42.3	79.0	113.8					931
0806	Grapes, fresh or dried	112.0	60.2	62.4	2.7			mln US$/kg	057
1302	Vegetable saps and extracts; pectic substances	22.8	30.3	40.1	735.9			thsd US$/kg	292
1207	Other oil seeds and oleaginous fruits	3.4	14.3	24.6	3.4			mln US$/kg	222
0804	Dates, figs, pineapples, avocados and mangosteens, fresh or dried	16.1	9.8	6.8	1.5			mln US$/kg	057
9706	Antiques of an age exceeding one hundred years	29.9	...	...					896
1214	Swedes, mangolds, fodder roots, hay, lucerne (alfalfa)	1.0	17.1	4.1	333.3			thsd US$/kg	081
0813	Fruit, dried	16.9	...	...	627.4			thsd US$/kg	057

Graph 2: Trade Balance by MDG Regions in 2010

(Bln US$)

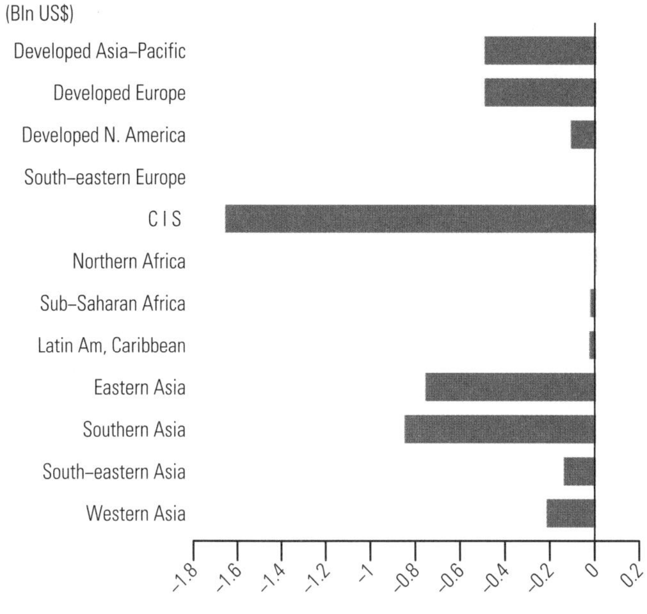

Graph 3: Partner concentration of trade in 2010

(Cumulative share by ranked partners)

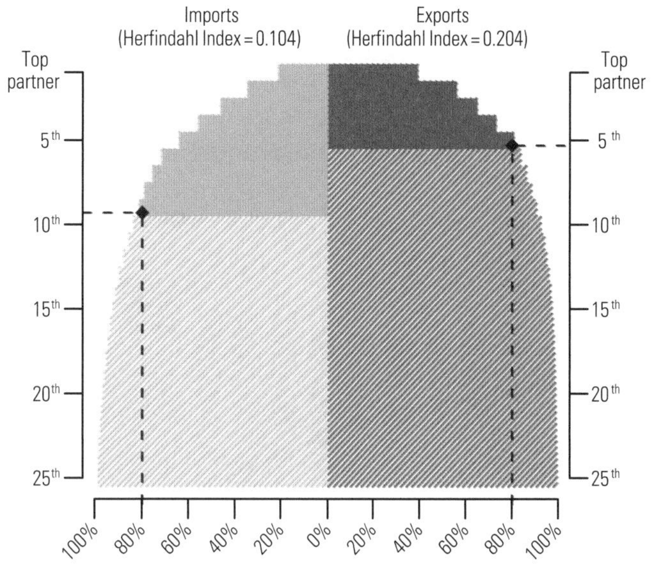

Table 4: Exports by principal countries and SITC sections in 2010

(Value in million US$, percentages of country total)

Country	Total	Shares by SITC sections (%) 0+1	2+4	3	5	6	7	8	9	Total
World	388.5	33.7	17.4	...	...	19.6	...	0.0	29.3	100
Pakistan	151.3	21.6	9.3	...	...	27.1	...	...	42.1	100
India	65.4	61.2	29.2	...	...	2.7	...	...	6.9	100
Turkey	34.8	12.3	9.8	...	...	70.4	...	0.0	7.4	100
Iran	31.7	9.0	65.2	...	...	...	...	...	25.8	100
Russian Federation	29.6	98.1	0.0	...	...	0.9	...	0.0	1.0	100
China	11.7	0.2	4.0	...	...	3.8	...	0.0	92.0	100
Netherlands	9.4	100.0	0.0	...	...	...	...	...	...	100
Iraq	8.7	33.7	31.1	...	...	...	...	...	35.2	100
Turkmenistan	8.6	0.7	0.4	...	...	...	...	0.1	98.8	100
Tajikistan	7.2	3.1	0.0	...	...	85.6	...	...	11.3	100

Imports Profile:

In 2010, Afghanistan's imports were composed of 46.1 percent of commodities and transactions not classified elsewhere (SITC section 9), 20.9 percent of mineral fuels, lubricants and related materials (SITC section 3) and 11.4 percent of food, live animals, beverages and tobacco (SITC sections 0+1) (see table 2). Top imported products for the years 2008 to 2010 were peat (including peat litter) (HS code 2703), wheat or meslin flour (HS code 1101) and paintings, drawings and pastels, executed entirely by hand (HS code 9701) (see table 5).

Table 5: Top 10 import commodities 2008 to 2010

(Value in million US$)

HS code	4-digit heading of Harmonized System 2002	Value (million US$) 2008	2009	2010	Unit value 2008	2009	2010	Unit	SITC code
	All Commodities	3019.9	3336.4	5154.2					
9999	Commodities not specified according to kind	1484.7	1374.7	2375.2					931
2703	Peat (including peat litter)	...	729.9	961.0		0.7	0.7	US$/kg	322
1101	Wheat or meslin flour	162.4	359.9	229.6	40.6			mln US$/kg	046
9701	Paintings, drawings and pastels, executed entirely by hand	409.1	...	...					896
8708	Parts and accessories of the motor vehicles of headings 87.01 to 87.05	91.8	97.3	168.3	*13.3*	*15.9*	*15.1*	US$/kg	784
1518	Animal or vegetable fats and oils	163.2	42.7	119.3	11.7			mln US$/kg	431
5808	Braids in the piece; ornamental trimmings	69.9	108.6	117.8	5.8			mln US$/kg	656
1806	Chocolate and other food preparations containing cocoa	52.1	78.5	107.6	*5.4*	*6.2*	*5.8*	US$/kg	073
6801	Setts, curbstones and flagstones, of natural stone (except slate)	...	38.3	179.0		0.1	0.1	US$/kg	661
4012	Retreaded or used pneumatic tyres of rubber	113.8	38.9	45.4	51.2	58.2	49.5	US$/unit	625

Albania

Imports: CIF, by origin | **Exports: FOB, by last known destination** | **Trade System: Special**

Overview:

From 2007 to 2011, Albania's exports increased on average by 16.0 percent each year and amounted to 1.9 bln US$, reflecting an increase of 25.7 percent in 2011 (see table 1 and graph 1). Imports also increased by 17.2 percent and amounted to 5.4 bln US$ (see table 2 and graph 1). This resulted in a trade deficit of 3.4 bln US$ for 2011, compared to 3.1 bln US$ for the previous year (see graph 1). Trade with Developed Europe accounted for a large part of the 2011 deficit (-2.1 bln US$) (see graph 2). The trade balance also recorded significant deficits with Eastern Asia (-339.5 mln US$) and South-eastern Europe (-251.3 mln US$) among others. Compared to imports, exports were concentrated among a few partners: 6 major partners accounted for 80 percent of exports in 2011 compared to 16 major partners for imports (see graph 3).

Graph 1: Total imports, exports and trade balance

(Bln US$ by year)

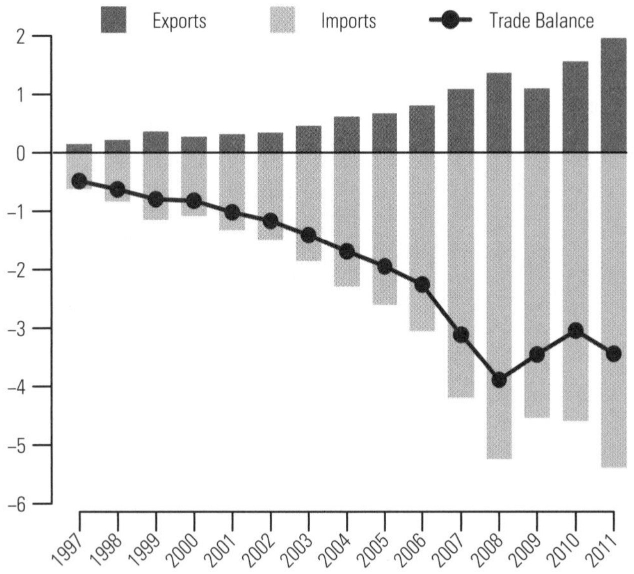

Exports Profile:

In 2011, miscellaneous manufactured articles (SITC section 8) was the largest commodity group for exports and represented 34.5 percent of exported goods (see table 1). In addition to Italy, other major partners for exports in 2011 included Serbia and Turkey (see table 4). Over the last three years, main commodities for exports were petroleum oils and oils obtained from bituminous minerals, crude (HS code 2709), parts of footwear (HS code 6406) and footwear with outer soles of rubber, plastics, leather (HS code 6403) (see table 3).

Table 1: Exports by SITC sections

(Value in million US$, growth and shares in percentage)

SITC	2011	Avg. Growth rates (%) 2007-2011	2010-2011	2011 share
Total	1 948.2	16.0	25.7	100.0
0+1	78.6	8.8	14.2	4.0
2+4	258.1	11.5	21.5	13.3
3	412.7	50.6	48.3	21.2
5	18.7	45.1	151.2	1.0
6	428.7	25.9	25.6	22.0
7	75.9	14.8	18.7	3.9
8	672.8	4.9	17.4	34.5
9	2.6	89.7	-43.3	0.1

Table 2: Imports by SITC sections

(Value in million US$, growth and shares in percentage)

SITC	2011	Avg. Growth rates (%) 2007-2011	2010-2011	2011 share
Total	5 395.9	6.5	17.2	100.0
0+1	831.8	6.6	7.7	15.4
2+4	280.2	18.4	29.8	5.2
3	948.2	11.5	49.2	17.6
5	522.6	9.0	12.5	9.7
6	1 174.1	3.5	5.3	21.8
7	1 064.5	5.2	21.7	19.7
8	570.9	1.5	9.2	10.6
9	3.5	...	24.4	0.1

Table 3: Top 10 export commodities 2009 to 2011

(Value in million US$)

HS code	4-digit heading of Harmonized System 2007	Value (million US$) 2009	2010	2011	Unit value 2009	2010	2011	Unit	SITC code
	All Commodities	1 087.9	1 550.0	1 948.2					
2709	Petroleum oils and oils obtained from bituminous minerals, crude	83.2	162.7	314.1	0.2	0.3	0.5	US$/kg	333
6406	Parts of footwear	86.2	93.9	118.9	15.9	14.7	19.2	US$/kg	851
6403	Footwear with outer soles of rubber, plastics, leather	54.4	95.8	138.5	13.4	*14.4*	16.5	US$/pair	851
6203	Men's or boys' suits, ensembles, jackets, blazers, trousers	65.5	66.1	78.6	8.6	*9.5*	10.6	US$/unit	841
2716	Electrical energy	30.3	101.5	66.1	68.9	57.5	54.0	US$/MWh	351
2610	Chromium ores and concentrates	42.5	78.3	52.0	0.2	0.2	0.1	US$/kg	287
7207	Semi-finished products of iron or non-alloy steel	...	71.4	98.2		0.5	0.6	US$/kg	672
7214	Other bars and rods of iron or non-alloy steel	40.9	51.6	75.2	0.5	0.6	0.7	US$/kg	676
6405	Other footwear	66.0	48.2	33.7	18.9	*17.7*	17.5	US$/pair	851
8301	Padlocks and locks (key, combination or electrically operated)	39.4	43.2	45.0	10.3	9.8	11.0	US$/kg	699

Graph 2: Trade Balance by MDG Regions in 2011

(Bln US$)

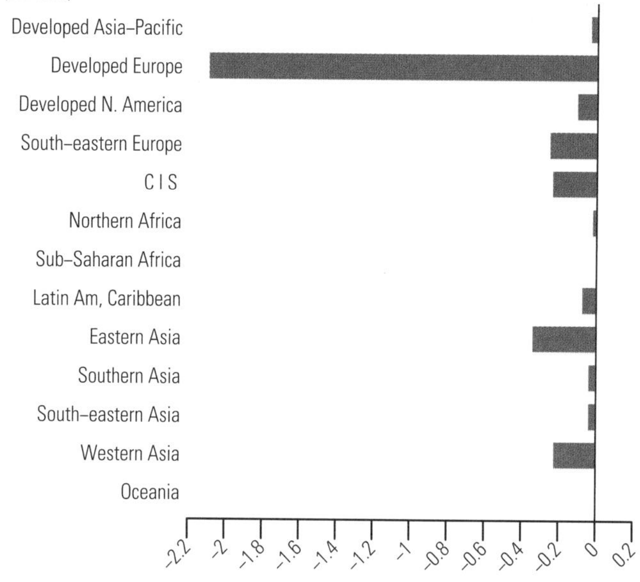

Graph 3: Partner concentration of trade in 2011

(Cumulative share by ranked partners)

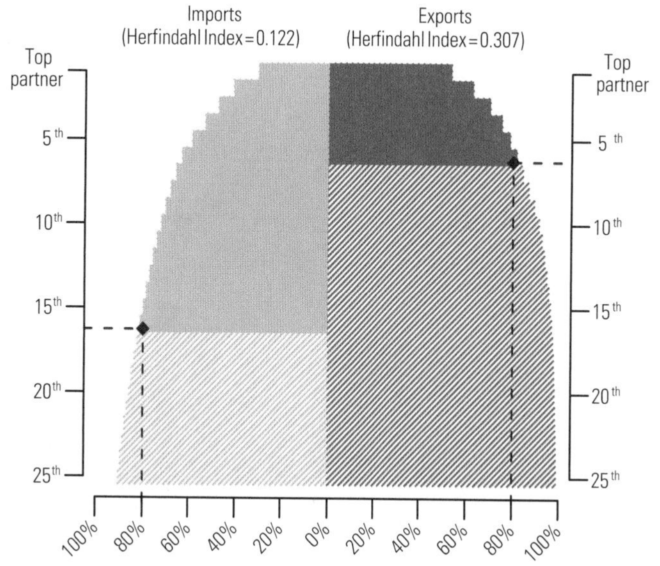

Table 4: Exports by principal countries and SITC sections in 2011

(Value in million US$, percentages of country total)

Country	Total	Shares by SITC sections (%)								
		0+1	2+4	3	5	6	7	8	9	Total
World	1 948.2	4.0	13.3	21.2	1.0	22.0	3.9	34.5	0.1	100
Italy	1 039.9	3.6	4.6	20.2	0.8	12.9	4.7	53.2	0.1	100
Serbia	180.7	5.6	4.8	22.9	2.6	54.8	4.8	4.5	0.0	100
Turkey	143.5	0.0	27.9	0.3	1.1	69.8	0.6	0.3	...	100
Greece	98.9	12.4	36.4	0.8	0.6	11.3	1.8	36.6	...	100
Spain	69.5	4.1	0.3	78.9	0.1	5.5	0.1	11.0	...	100
Germany	56.4	3.2	19.9	7.7	0.6	1.6	1.3	65.8	...	100
Switzerland	52.3	0.5	22.2	72.6	0.1	0.1	0.3	4.3	...	100
China	48.6	0.0	98.7	...	1.3	...	0.0	...	...	100
Malta	46.4	0.0	0.0	99.9	...	0.1	...	0.0	...	100
TFYR of Macedonia	41.1	6.6	28.2	0.1	0.5	51.5	9.3	3.8	...	100

Imports Profile:

In 2011, the majority of imported goods were manufactured goods classified chiefly by material (SITC section 6) and machinery and transport equipment (SITC section 7). They accounted respectively for 21.8 and 19.7 percent of imports (see table 2). Other major commodity groups included mineral fuels, lubricants and related materials (SITC section 3) and food, live animals, beverages and tobacco (SITC sections 0+1). Top products for imports were petroleum oils, other than crude (HS code 2710), motor cars and other motor vehicles principally designed for the transport (HS code 8703) and electrical energy (HS code 2716) (see table 5).

Table 5: Top 10 import commodities 2009 to 2011

(Value in million US$)

HS code	4-digit heading of Harmonized System 2007	Value (million US$)			Unit value				SITC code
		2009	2010	2011	2009	2010	2011	Unit	
	All Commodities	4 548.3	4 602.8	5 395.9					
2710	Petroleum oils, other than crude	274.1	404.9	568.7	0.6	0.8	1.0	US$/kg	334
8703	Motor cars and other motor vehicles principally designed for the transport	159.0	132.9	202.2	4.8	0.2	5.5	thsd US$/unit	781
2716	Electrical energy	152.6	113.9	223.9	71.1	61.5	74.6	US$/MWh	351
3004	Medicaments (excluding goods of heading 30.02, 30.05 or 30.06)	136.8	141.7	141.6	34.8	39.9	45.0	US$/kg	542
7214	Other bars and rods of iron or non-alloy steel	108.8	92.9	105.4	0.5	0.6	0.7	US$/kg	676
7204	Ferrous waste and scrap; remelting scrap ingots of iron or steel	40.3	102.3	142.2	0.3	0.4	0.5	US$/kg	282
2402	Cigars, cheroots, cigarillos and cigarettes	84.8	99.2	80.6	20.9	22.0	24.8	US$/kg	122
1001	Wheat and meslin	56.8	68.5	107.0	0.2	0.3	0.3	US$/kg	041
2523	Portland cement, aluminous cement, slag cement	99.8	61.3	46.7	0.1	0.1	0.1	US$/kg	661
4107	Leather further prepared after tanning or crusting	62.0	66.0	71.4	16.8	16.2	18.2	US$/kg	611

Algeria

Imports: CIF, by origin | **Exports: FOB, by last known destination** | **Trade System: Special**

Overview:

In 2011, the value of the exports of Algeria grew by 28.9 percent and reached 73.6 bln US$ (see table 1 and graph 1). The last five years showed an average annual increase of 5.2 percent in exports, while imports registered an average annual growth of 13.9 percent (see tables 1 and 2 and graph 1). In 2011, imports increased by 13.2 percent to 46.4 bln US$. This resulted in a trade surplus of 27.1 bln US$ in 2011, much higher than the 2010 surplus of 16.1 bln US$ (see graph 1). Two MDG regions accounted for this surplus: Developed North America (+16.9 bln US$) and Developed Europe (+15.2 bln US$) (see graph 2). Compared to imports, exports were less diversified among partners: in 2011, 10 major partners accounted for 80 percent of exports (compared to 19 major partners for imports) (see graph 3).

Graph 1: Total imports, exports and trade balance

(Bln US$ by year)

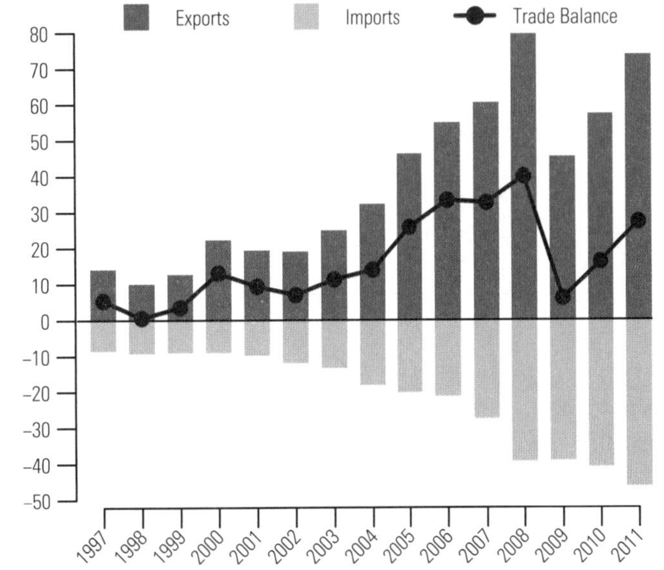

Table 1: Exports by SITC sections

(Value in million US$, growth and shares in percentage)

SITC	2011	Avg. Growth rates (%) 2007-2011	2010-2011	2011 share
Total	73562.0	5.2	28.9	100.0
0+1	350.4	39.2	12.9	0.5
2+4	177.9	-8.2	71.2	0.2
3	72345.0	5.1	29.0	98.3
5	482.6	14.8	54.8	0.7
6	181.7	-12.6	-11.7	0.2
7	17.5	-4.9	24.1	0.0
8	6.0	-25.2	-37.2	0.0
9	0.9	-16.4	-89.2	0.0

Exports Profile:

In 2011, Algeria's exports were almost exclusively (98.3 percent) mineral fuels, lubricants and related materials (SITC section 3) (see table 1). Exports of mineral fuels, lubricants and related materials (SITC section 3) went up by 29.0 percent and amounted to 72.3 bln US$ in 2011. USA, Italy and Spain, the top three markets for exports in 2011 accounted for 43.5 percent of exports (see table 4). Main products were petroleum oils and oils obtained from bituminous minerals, crude (HS code 2709), petroleum gases and other gaseous hydrocarbons (HS code 2711) and petroleum oils, other than crude (HS code 2710) (see table 3).

Table 2: Imports by SITC sections

(Value in million US$, growth and shares in percentage)

SITC	2011	Avg. Growth rates (%) 2007-2011	2010-2011	2011 share
Total	46426.4	13.9	13.2	100.0
0+1	9649.6	18.2	61.3	20.8
2+4	1913.6	9.6	23.0	4.1
3	1011.6	35.2	16.6	2.2
5	5344.3	13.3	20.1	11.5
6	9149.9	10.8	-6.9	19.7
7	17291.3	13.3	3.4	37.2
8	2065.7	13.5	29.7	4.4
9	0.4	-58.9	...	0.0

Table 3: Top 10 export commodities 2009 to 2011

(Value in million US$)

HS code	4-digit heading of Harmonized System 2007	Value (million US$) 2009	2010	2011	Unit value 2009	2010	2011	Unit	SITC code
	All Commodities	45193.9	57051.0	73562.0					
2709	Petroleum oils and oils obtained from bituminous minerals, crude	21284.5	24779.4	35985.2	0.4	0.6	0.8	US$/kg	333
2711	Petroleum gases and other gaseous hydrocarbons	17855.4	22461.9	26086.4	*0.5*	*0.2*	*0.4*	US$/kg	343
2710	Petroleum oils, other than crude	4976.5	8282.0	8488.3	*0.5*	0.7	0.9	US$/kg	334
2707	Oils and other products of high temperature coal tar	311.8	558.4	1785.1	*0.4*	0.7	3.3	US$/kg	335
2814	Ammonia, anhydrous or in aqueous solution	147.0	195.9	374.7	0.2	0.4	0.5	US$/kg	522
1701	Cane or beet sugar and chemically pure sucrose, in solid form	6.6	231.4	269.4	0.5	0.6	0.8	US$/kg	061
2510	Natural calcium phosphates	75.8	44.0	128.3	0.1	0.1	0.1	US$/kg	272
7901	Unwrought zinc	36.8	61.4	36.4	1.6	2.2	2.1	US$/kg	686
2804	Hydrogen, rare gases and other non-metals	45.8	43.4	40.3					522
7204	Ferrous waste and scrap; remelting scrap ingots of iron or steel	83.0	33.7	...	0.1	0.1		US$/kg	282

Graph 2: Trade Balance by MDG Regions in 2011

(Bln US$)

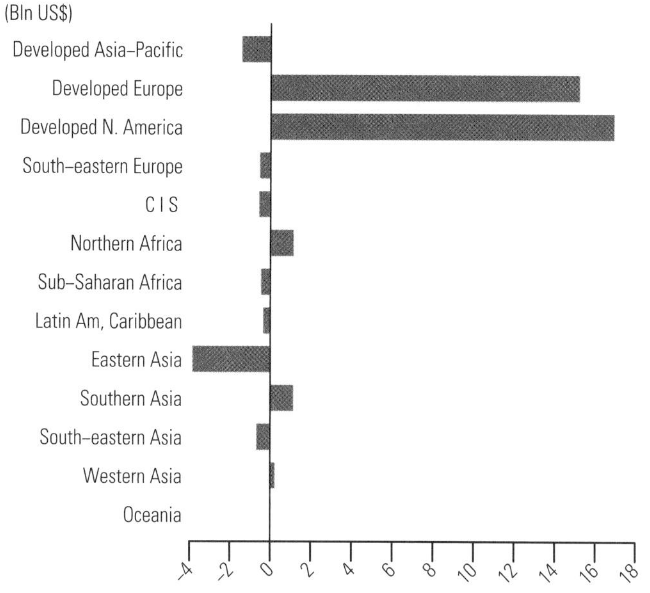

Graph 3: Partner concentration of trade in 2011

(Cumulative share by ranked partners)

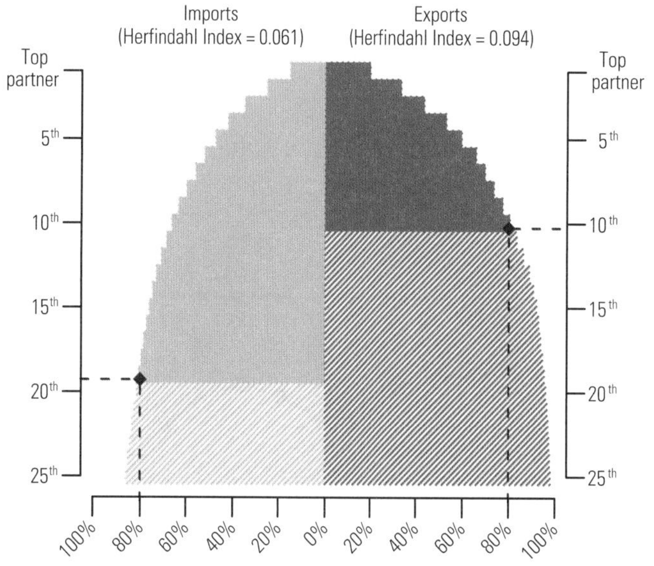

Table 4: Exports by principal countries and SITC sections in 2011

(Value in million US$, percentages of country total)

Country	Total	Shares by SITC sections (%) 0 + 1	2 + 4	3	5	6	7	8	9	Total
World	73562.0	0.5	0.2	98.3	0.7	0.2	0.0	0.0	0.0	100
USA	14657.2	0.0	0.0	100.0	0.0	0.0	0.0	0.0	...	100
Italy	10022.2	0.3	0.1	98.8	0.3	0.5	0.0	0.0	...	100
Spain	7296.0	0.3	0.1	96.2	3.1	0.3	0.0	0.0	...	100
France	6943.3	0.3	0.1	97.6	1.9	0.1	0.0	0.0	...	100
Netherlands	4847.5	0.4	0.4	99.2	...	0.1	0.0	...	...	100
Canada	4656.8	0.0	0.0	99.9	0.0	0.0	0.0	0.0	...	100
Brazil	2870.8	0.0	0.7	99.3	...	0.0	...	...	...	100
United Kingdom	2825.0	0.1	0.0	99.4	0.5	0.0	0.0	0.0	...	100
Turkey	2782.4	0.0	0.0	99.5	0.2	0.3	0.0	0.0	...	100
India	2304.1	0.0	0.4	99.2	0.0	0.3	...	...	...	100

Imports Profile:

Machinery and transport equipment (SITC section 7) accounted for 37.2 percent of imported goods in 2011 (see table 2). Other major commodity groups were food, live animals, beverages and tobacco (SITC sections 0+1) and manufactured goods classified chiefly by material (SITC section 6) respectively with 20.8 percent and 19.7 percent of imports. From 2009 to 2011, top imported products were wheat and meslin (HS code 1001), motor cars and other motor vehicles principally designed for the transport (HS code 8703) and tubes, pipes and hollow profiles, seamless, of iron (other than cast iron) (HS code 7304) (see table 5).

Table 5: Top 10 import commodities 2009 to 2011

(Value in million US$)

HS code	4-digit heading of Harmonized System 2007	Value (million US$) 2009	2010	2011	Unit value 2009	2010	2011	Unit	SITC code
	All Commodities	39258.3	40999.9	46426.4					
1001	Wheat and meslin	1830.3	1251.6	2821.1	0.3	0.2	0.4	US$/kg	041
8703	Motor cars and other motor vehicles principally designed for the transport	1524.0	1455.7	2108.1	*9.8*	8.5	*9.4*	thsd US$/unit	781
7304	Tubes, pipes and hollow profiles, seamless, of iron (other than cast iron)	1982.4	2015.7	699.9	3.7	3.2	*4.1*	US$/kg	679
3004	Medicaments (excluding goods of heading 30.02, 30.05 or 30.06)	1509.4	1459.4	1614.7	62.9	69.8	*75.9*	US$/kg	542
8704	Motor vehicles for the transport of goods	1465.6	1303.6	1540.2	*5.7*	*14.2*	*7.8*	thsd US$/unit	782
7214	Other bars and rods of iron or non-alloy steel	1487.2	1093.9	1684.4	0.5	0.6	0.7	US$/kg	676
0402	Milk and cream, concentrated or containing added sugar	799.7	903.1	1342.9	2.7	3.4	4.1	US$/kg	022
7308	Structures (excluding prefabricated buildings of heading 94.06)	849.5	956.0	712.4	3.5	3.3	4.0	US$/kg	691
8411	Turbo-jets, turbo-propellers and other gas turbines	647.3	1191.2	642.6					714
8481	Taps, cocks, valves and similar appliances for pipes, boiler shells	584.3	689.4	1059.3	*21.0*	*21.4*	*32.7*	US$/kg	747

Anguilla

Imports: CIF, by origin	Exports: FOB, by last known destination	Trade System: General

Overview:

From 2004 to 2008, Anguilla's exports increased on average by 18.9 percent each year and amounted to 11.5 mln US$ in 2008 (see table 1 and graph 1). Imports increased on average by 27.6 percent each year and reached 271.7 mln US$ (see table 2 and graph 1). This resulted in a trade deficit of 260.3 mln US$ (see graph 1). By MDG regions, trade with Developed North America accounted for a large part of this deficit (-165.2 mln US$) (see graph 2). Significant deficits were also recorded with Latin America and the Caribbean (-69.3 mln US$) and Developed Europe (-16.3 mln US$). Anguilla's trade was highly concentrated among a few partners: in 2008, 3 major partners accounted for 80 percent of exports and imports (see graph 3).

Graph 1: Total imports, exports and trade balance

(Mln US$ by year)

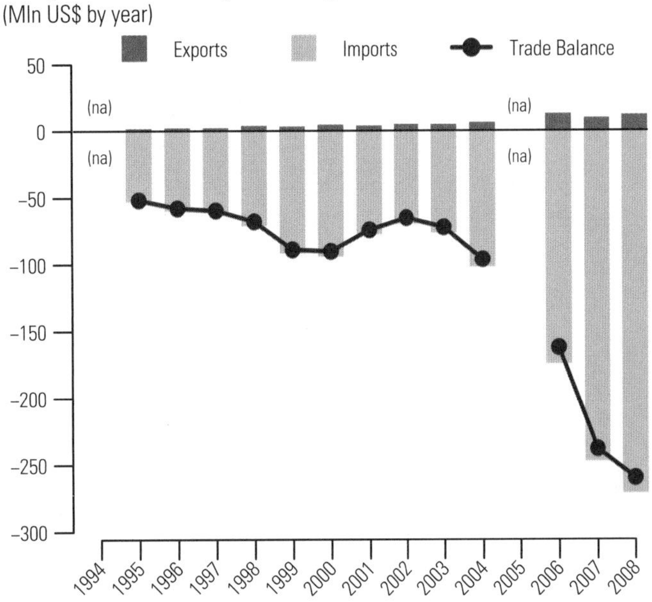

Exports Profile:

In 2008, food, live animals, beverages and tobacco (SITC sections 0+1) accounted for 41.5 percent of exported goods (see table 1). Commodities and transactions not classified elsewhere (SITC section 9) and machinery and transport equipment (SITC section 7) accounted respectively for 21.4 and 19.7 percent of exports. Guyana, the major partner for exports, was the destination of 38.3 percent of exports in 2008 (see table 4). Other major markets included Netherlands Antilles and USA. From 2006 to 2008, top exported products were liqueur, spirits and undenatured ethyl alcohol <80% (HS code 2208), solid cane or beet sugar and chemically pure sucrose (HS code 1701) and motor vehicles for transport of persons (except buses) (HS code 8703) (see table 3).

Table 1: Exports by SITC sections

(Value in million US$, growth and shares in percentage)

SITC	2008	Avg. Growth rates (%) 2004-2008	2007-2008	2008 share
Total	11.5	18.9	24.9	100.0
0+1	4.8	86.4	10.2	41.5
2+4	0.0	26.1	11.5	0.1
3	0.0	-51.1	-67.7	0.3
5	0.0	8.7	37.6	0.3
6	1.6	47.8	133.5	13.9
7	2.3	-1.9	-26.5	19.7
8	0.3	-34.3	-27.7	2.8
9	2.5	86.5	377.0	21.4

Table 2: Imports by SITC sections

(Value in million US$, growth and shares in percentage)

SITC	2008	Avg. Growth rates (%) 2004-2008	2007-2008	2008 share
Total	271.7	27.6	9.6	100.0
0+1	28.4	15.6	-2.5	10.4
2+4	2.0	16.9	17.2	0.7
3	38.8	41.0	53.1	14.3
5	9.1	25.4	-0.2	3.3
6	49.7	47.3	22.7	18.3
7	45.3	11.8	-22.1	16.7
8	25.1	33.7	20.3	9.2
9	73.4	31.4	16.2	27.0

Table 3: Top 10 export commodities 2006 to 2008

(Value in million US$)

HS code	4-digit heading of Harmonized System 1992	Value (million US$) 2006	2007	2008	Unit value 2006	2007	2008	Unit	SITC code
	All Commodities	12.2	9.2	11.5					
2208	Liqueur, spirits and undenatured ethyl alcohol <80%	4.4	4.1	4.7					112
1701	Solid cane or beet sugar and chemically pure sucrose	5.4	0.2	0.0	0.5	0.5	1.2	US$/kg	061
9999	Commodities not specified according to kind	0.3	0.5	2.5					931
8703	Motor vehicles for transport of persons (except buses)	0.3	1.6	0.6	*12.8*	*16.5*	*15.9*	thsd US$/unit	781
8429	Self-propelled earth moving, road making, etc machine	0.2	0.1	0.3	*48.9*		*69.4*	thsd US$/unit	723
7308	Structures, parts of structures of iron or steel, nes	0.0	0.5	0.0	4.5	8.1	6.6	US$/kg	691
7007	Safety glass (toughened, tempered, laminated)	0.0	...	0.5					664
9405	Lamps and lighting fittings, illuminated signs, etc	0.3	0.1	0.2	25.0	61.7	62.4	US$/kg	813
8426	Derricks, cranes, straddle carriers, crane trucks	...	0.0	0.4					744
8705	Special purpose motor vehicles	0.1	0.2	0.1			*93.8*	thsd US$/unit	782

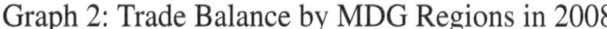

Graph 2: Trade Balance by MDG Regions in 2008

(Mln US$)

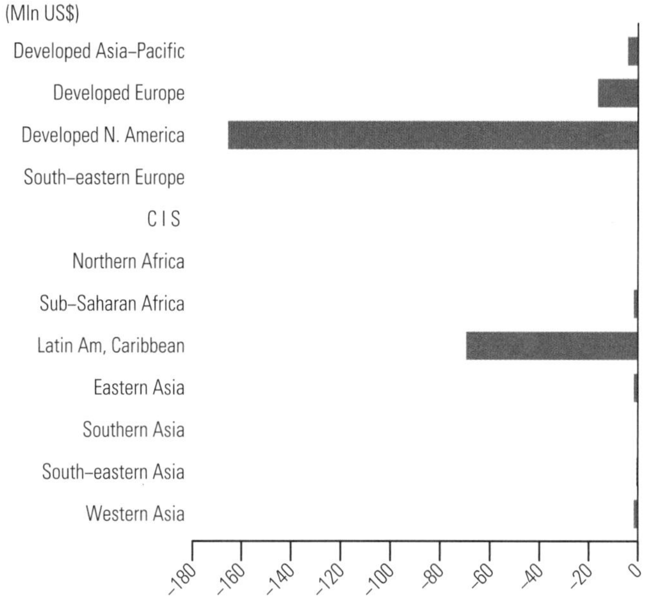

Graph 3: Partner concentration of trade in 2008

(Cumulative share by ranked partners)

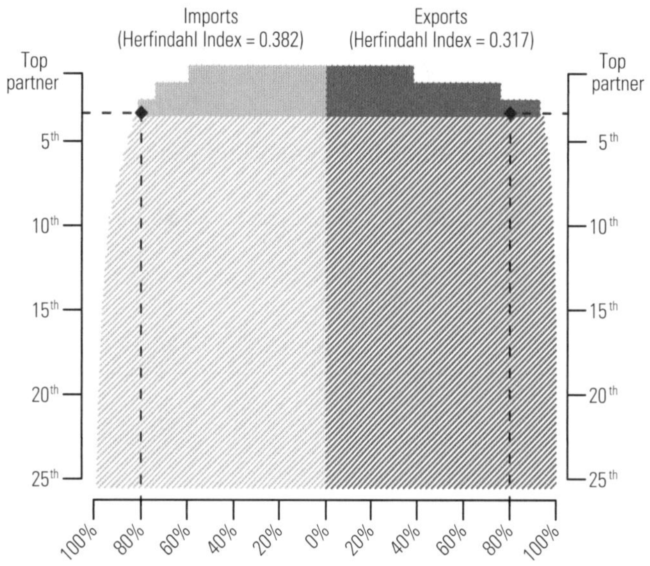

Table 4: Exports by principal countries and SITC sections in 2008

(Value in million US$, percentages of country total)

Country	Total	Shares by SITC sections (%)								
		0 + 1	2 + 4	3	5	6	7	8	9	Total
World	11.5	41.5	0.1	0.3	0.3	13.9	19.7	2.8	21.4	100
Guyana	4.4	100.0	0.0	...	...	...	...	...	...	100
Neth. Antilles	4.3	0.1	0.0	0.7	0.4	33.2	17.2	4.5	43.9	100
USA	2.0	5.1	0.2	0.2	0.7	6.7	55.9	3.8	27.5	100
United Kingdom	0.2	98.1	0.0	...	...	...	1.9	...	...	100
France	0.1	3.7	0.0	...	...	2.6	85.0	...	8.7	100
Israel	0.1	0.0	0.0	...	...	...	100.0	...	...	100
Canada	0.1	0.0	0.0	...	...	...	100.0	...	...	100
Switzerland	0.0	0.0	0.0	...	...	...	...	100.0	...	100
Br. Virgin Isds	0.0	22.2	0.1	...	13.4	1.7	48.9	1.7	12.0	100
Netherlands	0.0	95.5	0.0	...	...	1.8	...	...	2.8	100

Imports Profile:

In 2008, commodities and transactions not classified elsewhere (SITC section 9) accounted for 27.0 percent of imports (see table 2). Other major commodity groups included manufactured goods classified chiefly by material (SITC section 6) and machinery and transport equipment (SITC section 7), respectively with 18.3 and 16.7 percent of imports. From 2006 to 2008, top imported products included oils petroleum, bituminous, distillates, except crude (HS code 2710), motor vehicles for transport of persons (except buses) (HS code 8703) and aluminium structures, parts nes, for construction (HS code 7610) (see table 5).

Table 5: Top 10 import commodities 2006 to 2008

(Value in million US$)

HS code	4-digit heading of Harmonized System 1992	Value (million US$)			Unit value				SITC code
		2006	2007	2008	2006	2007	2008	Unit	
	All Commodities	174.9	247.9	271.7					
9999	Commodities not specified according to kind	37.3	63.2	73.4					931
2710	Oils petroleum, bituminous, distillates, except crude	23.1	23.9	36.8	2.0	1.3	4.8	US$/kg	334
8703	Motor vehicles for transport of persons (except buses)	16.7	20.1	11.3	*14.9*	*15.3*	*15.9*	thsd US$/unit	781
7610	Aluminium structures, parts nes, for construction	2.6	6.7	15.7	6.7	8.5	11.0	US$/kg	691
2208	Liqueur, spirits and undenatured ethyl alcohol <80%	7.2	7.7	6.9					112
9403	Other furniture and parts thereof	4.1	7.1	9.3					821
7228	Bar, rod, angle etc nes, hollow steel drill bars	1.7	5.3	3.5	1.0	0.6	*2.1*	US$/kg	676
2202	Waters, non-alcoholic sweetened or flavoured beverages	2.5	3.1	2.9	*1.3*	*1.4*	*0.8*	US$/litre	111
7308	Structures, parts of structures of iron or steel, nes	0.8	5.1	2.6	4.6	4.7	3.2	US$/kg	691
6810	Articles of cement, concrete or artificial stone	1.5	2.8	3.2	0.2	0.2	0.3	US$/kg	663

Antigua and Barbuda

Imports: CIF, by origin | **Exports: FOB, by last known destination** | **Trade System: General**

Overview:

After reaching a peak of 205.7 mln US$ in 2009, the value of exports of Antigua and Barbuda dropped in 2010 and 2011 to reach 29.0 mln US$ (see table 1 and graph 1). Imports, on the other hand, increased in 2011 by 30.4 percent and amounted to 471.1 mln US$ (see table 2 and graph 1). The trade balance recorded a deficit of 442.1 mln US$ in 2011 (see graph 1). By MDG regions, trade recorded a deficit amounting to 150.1 mln US$ with Developed North America (see graph 2). Other deficits were also recorded with Latin America and the Caribbean (-55.2 mln US$), Developed Europe (-36.4 mln US$) and Eastern Asia (-17.3 mln US$). Antigua and Barbuda's trade was relatively concentrated among a few partners in 2011: respectively 10 and 6 major partners accounted for 80 percent of exports and imports (see graph 3).

Graph 1: Total imports, exports and trade balance

(Mln US$ by year)

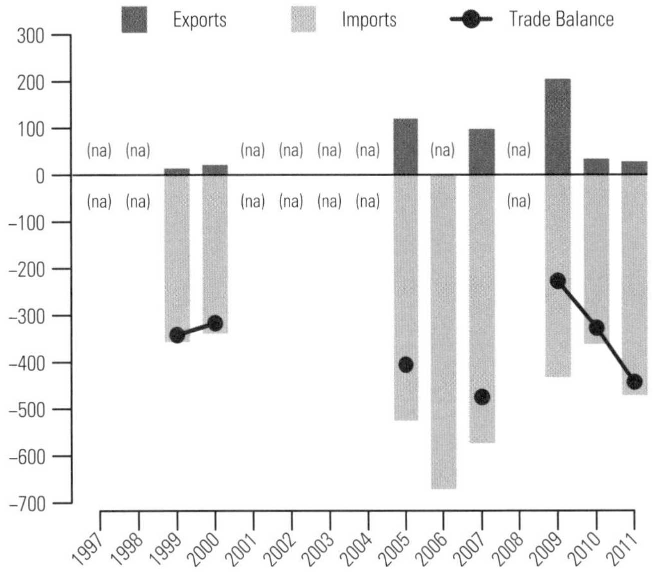

Exports Profile:

In 2011, machinery and transport equipment (SITC section 7) and manufactured goods classified chiefly by material (SITC section 6) accounted respectively for 37.9 and 33.6 percent of exports (see table 1). Other major commodity groups included food, live animals, beverages and tobacco (SITC sections 0+1) and miscellaneous manufactured articles (SITC section 8): they accounted respectively for 12.7 and 10.1 percent of exports. The three largest markets for exports were USA, United Kingdom and Barbados (see table 4). Over the last three years, main commodities for exports included oils petroleum, bituminous, distillates, except crude (HS code 2710), textile tarpaulin, sail, awning, tent, camping goods (HS code 6306) and radio and TV transmitters, television cameras (HS code 8525) (see table 3).

Table 1: Exports by SITC sections

(Value in million US$, growth and shares in percentage)

SITC	2011	Avg. Growth rates (%) 2007-2011	2010-2011	2011 share
Total	29.0	-26.3	-16.7	100.0
0+1	3.7	10.8	47.2	12.7
2+4	0.2	-26.3	120.9	0.6
3	0.7	-66.6	-44.8	2.4
5	0.8	-11.0	-9.3	2.6
6	9.8	1.0	1.0	33.6
7	11.0	-13.6	-16.5	37.9
8	2.9	-23.3	-59.7	10.1
9	0.0	189.6	-69.3	0.0

Table 2: Imports by SITC sections

(Value in million US$, growth and shares in percentage)

SITC	2011	Avg. Growth rates (%) 2007-2011	2010-2011	2011 share
Total	471.1	-4.8	30.4	100.0
0+1	111.2	-0.5	5.2	23.6
2+4	9.5	-13.2	-2.7	2.0
3	2.9	-46.8	13.5	0.6
5	30.0	-8.8	-9.3	6.4
6	44.6	-16.9	-22.2	9.5
7	56.3	-23.4	-42.9	12.0
8	50.5	-17.0	-6.2	10.7
9	166.1	577.2	45549.6	35.3

Table 3: Top 10 export commodities 2009 to 2011

(Value in million US$)

HS code	4-digit heading of Harmonized System 1996	Value (million US$) 2009	2010	2011	Unit value 2009	2010	2011	Unit	SITC code
	All Commodities	205.7	34.8	29.0					
2710	Oils petroleum, bituminous, distillates, except crude	168.1	1.3	0.7					334
6306	Textile tarpaulin, sail, awning, tent, camping goods	2.5	6.1	6.3	229.3	79.3	80.0	US$/kg	658
8525	Radio and TV transmitters, television cameras	10.1	0.2	2.6					764
7113	Jewellery and parts, containing precious metal	4.4	0.9	0.3	33.5	12.4	3.6	thsd US$/kg	897
8409	Parts for internal combustion spark ignition engines	5.3	0.1	0.1	41.5	11.2	23.5	US$/kg	713
8903	Yachts, pleasure, sports vessels, rowing boats, canoes	1.1	1.3	1.5					793
8501	Electric motors and generators, except generating sets	0.1	3.6	0.0					716
2208	Liqueur, spirits and undenatured ethyl alcohol <80%	0.7	1.3	1.0	*4.2*	*5.7*	*3.6*	US$/litre	112
8502	Electric generating sets and rotary converters	1.1	1.1	0.0					716
8703	Motor vehicles for transport of persons (except buses)	0.5	1.0	0.5	*14.2*	*14.8*		thsd US$/unit	781

Graph 2: Trade Balance by MDG Regions in 2011

(Mln US$)

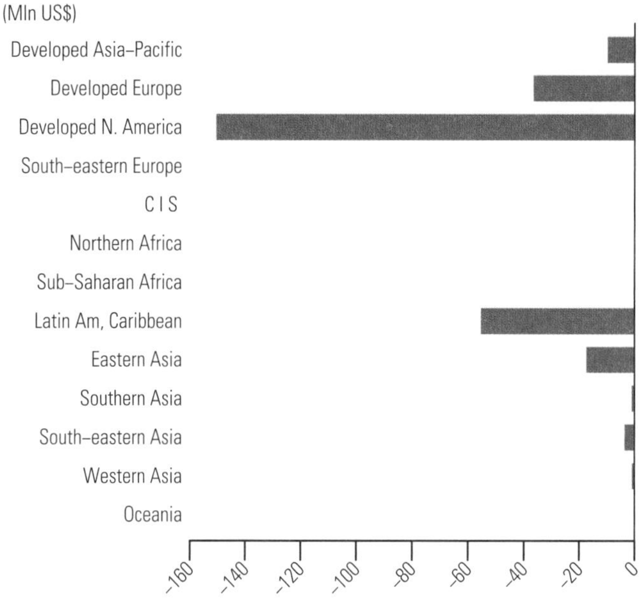

Graph 3: Partner concentration of trade in 2011

(Cumulative share by ranked partners)

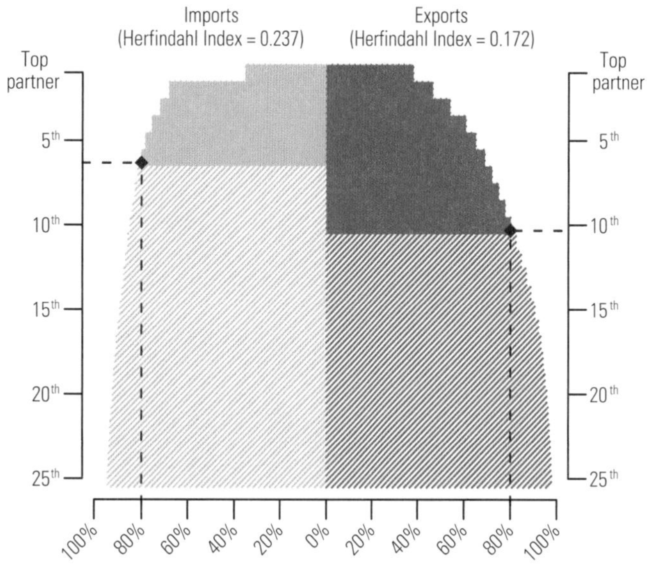

Table 4: Exports by principal countries and SITC sections in 2011

(Value in million US$, percentages of country total)

Country	Total	Shares by SITC sections (%)								
		0 + 1	2 + 4	3	5	6	7	8	9	Total
World	29.0	12.7	0.6	2.4	2.6	33.6	37.9	10.1	0.0	100
USA	11.1	11.9	0.1	1.5	0.8	42.7	34.6	8.5	...	100
United Kingdom	2.4	0.1	0.0	0.0	0.1	80.1	17.0	2.6	...	100
Barbados	2.2	1.0	0.0	12.1	0.1	0.2	81.2	5.3	0.0	100
Trinidad and Tobago	2.0	19.6	0.0	3.0	0.4	26.0	49.9	1.1	...	100
Jamaica	1.2	0.0	0.0	...	0.1	4.4	89.9	5.6	...	100
Montserrat	1.1	5.3	0.5	0.6	8.3	4.2	26.5	54.6	...	100
France	0.9	97.3	0.0	...	0.2	0.0	0.4	2.1	...	100
Areas, nes	0.8	0.7	0.7	...	3.7	19.9	67.8	7.3	...	100
Dominica	0.8	1.7	0.2	0.7	30.1	5.8	47.7	13.8	...	100
Saint Vincent and the Grenadines	0.7	20.0	0.0	...	0.1	70.1	9.8	0.1	...	100

Imports Profile:

In 2011, Antigua and Barbuda's imports were composed of 35.3 percent of commodities and transactions not classified elsewhere (SITC section 9), 23.6 percent of food, live animals, beverages and tobacco (SITC sections 0+1) and 12.0 percent of machinery and transport equipment (SITC section 7) (see table 2). From 2009 to 2011, top imported products included motor vehicles for transport of persons (except buses) (HS code 8703), meat, edible offal of domestic poultry (HS code 0207) and waters, non-alcoholic sweetened or flavoured beverages (HS code 2202) (see table 5).

Table 5: Top 10 import commodities 2009 to 2011

(Value in million US$)

HS code	4-digit heading of Harmonized System 1996	Value (million US$)			Unit value				SITC code
		2009	2010	2011	2009	2010	2011	Unit	
	All Commodities	432.1	361.3	471.1					
9999	Commodities not elsewhere specified	0.5	0.4	166.1					931
8703	Motor vehicles for transport of persons (except buses)	24.6	14.3	8.8	*13.0*	*15.1*		thsd US$/unit	781
0207	Meat, edible offal of domestic poultry	11.2	10.3	11.0	0.8	*1.6*	1.9	US$/kg	012
2202	Waters, non-alcoholic sweetened or flavoured beverages	11.0	8.3	8.7	*1.1*	*0.8*	*1.0*	US$/litre	111
3004	Medicaments, therapeutic, prophylactic use, in dosage	8.4	7.7	6.6	27.4	*27.1*	18.4	US$/kg	542
7113	Jewellery and parts, containing precious metal	7.5	7.2	7.5	2.2	*2.9*	3.9	thsd US$/kg	897
8407	Spark-ignition internal combustion engines	0.7	20.3	0.8					713
6306	Textile tarpaulin, sail, awning, tent, camping goods	6.4	8.3	4.4	53.2	56.0	51.5	US$/kg	658
8525	Radio and TV transmitters, television cameras	7.6	4.7	6.3					764
2106	Food preparations, nes	6.2	5.7	5.8	1.2	*2.0*	2.2	US$/kg	098

Argentina

Imports: CIF, by origin | **Exports: FOB, by last known destination** | **Trade System: Special**

Overview:

From 2007 to 2011, despite a decline of 20.5 percent in 2009, Argentina's exports increased on average by 10.8 percent each year and amounted to 84.0 bln US$ in 2011, a 23.2 percent increase from 2010 (see table 1 and graph 1). During the same period, imports increased on average by 14.5 percent each year and amounted to 76.9 bln US$ in 2011 (see table 2 and graph 1). This resulted in a trade surplus amounting to 7.0 bln US$ in 2011 (see graph 1). By MDG regions, large surpluses were recorded with Latin America and the Caribbean (+4.8 bln US$), Northern Africa (+4.0 bln US$) and South-eastern Asia (+2.3 bln US$) (see graph 2). Trade deficits were recorded with Eastern Asia (-6.1 bln US$) and Developed North America (-2.2 bln US$). Compared to imports, exports were diversified among partners: 25 major partners accounted for 80 percent of exports compared to 12 major partners for imports (see graph 3).

Graph 1: Total imports, exports and trade balance

(Bln US$ by year)

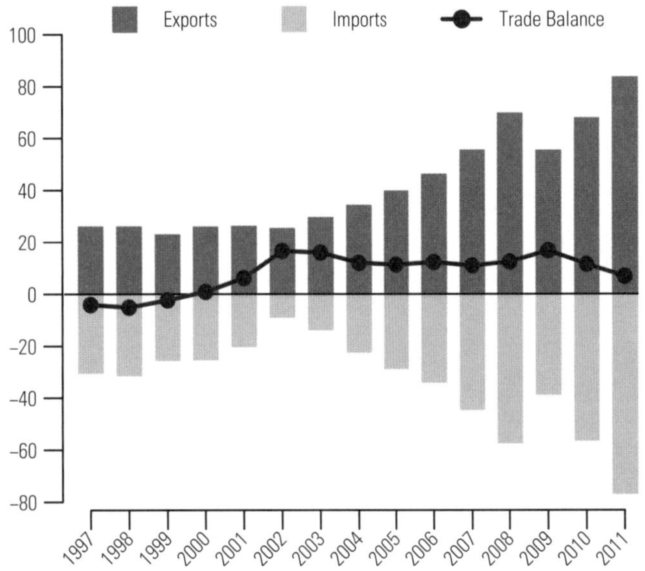

Table 1: Exports by SITC sections

(Value in million US$, growth and shares in percentage)

SITC	2011	Avg. Growth rates (%) 2007-2011	2010-2011	2011 share
Total	83950.2	10.8	23.2	100.0
0+1	31437.0	13.3	33.8	37.4
2+4	15740.0	8.9	20.8	18.7
3	4955.8	-5.0	-8.0	5.9
5	7433.9	15.8	26.3	8.9
6	5971.6	3.6	11.9	7.1
7	13361.0	14.9	23.6	15.9
8	965.8	1.0	3.4	1.2
9	4085.2	28.8	25.7	4.9

Exports Profile:

In 2011, food, live animals, beverages and tobacco (SITC sections 0+1) accounted for 37.4 percent of exports (see table 1). Other major commodity groups included inedible crude materials (except fuels), animal and vegetable oils, fats and waxes (SITC sections 2+4) and machinery and transport equipment (SITC section 7) respectively with 18.7 and 15.9 percent of exports. Brazil, China and Chile were the top markets for exports (see table 4). From 2009 to 2011, top exported products were oil-cake and other solid residues (HS code 2304), soya-bean oil and its fractions (HS code 1507) and soya beans, whether or not broken (HS code 1201) (see table 3).

Table 2: Imports by SITC sections

(Value in million US$, growth and shares in percentage)

SITC	2011	Avg. Growth rates (%) 2007-2011	2010-2011	2011 share
Total	76949.2	14.5	36.2	100.0
0+1	1760.1	16.8	25.2	2.3
2+4	2686.5	6.2	34.1	3.5
3	9021.8	35.3	115.4	11.7
5	12977.2	12.0	27.3	16.9
6	9242.9	10.3	26.6	12.0
7	35024.4	13.4	29.4	45.5
8	5613.0	17.0	43.1	7.3
9	623.3	23.7	49.8	0.8

Table 3: Top 10 export commodities 2009 to 2011

(Value in million US$)

HS code	4-digit heading of Harmonized System 2007	Value (million US$) 2009	2010	2011	Unit value 2009	2010	2011	Unit	SITC code
	All Commodities	55672.1	68134.1	83950.2					
2304	Oil-cake and other solid residues	8053.0	8194.9	9906.7	0.4	0.3	0.4	US$/kg	081
1507	Soya-bean oil and its fractions	3261.2	4135.9	5196.7	0.7	0.8	1.2	US$/kg	421
1201	Soya beans, whether or not broken	1675.5	4986.3	5457.2	*0.4*	0.4	0.5	US$/kg	222
8703	Motor cars and other motor vehicles principally designed for the transport	2759.9	3923.1	4712.1	11.3	12.1	13.3	thsd US$/unit	781
1005	Maize (corn)	1613.4	3145.3	4518.8	0.2	0.2	0.3	US$/kg	044
8704	Motor vehicles for the transport of goods	1465.2	2479.8	3480.8	20.4	22.0	24.1	thsd US$/unit	782
2709	Petroleum oils and oils obtained from bituminous minerals, crude	2466.4	2582.0	2182.2	0.4	0.5	0.7	US$/kg	333
7108	Gold (including gold plated with platinum)	1040.4	2009.0	2325.7		8.7	11.1	thsd US$/kg	971
2710	Petroleum oils, other than crude	1635.8	1593.8	1416.9	*0.5*	0.7	*0.9*	US$/kg	334
1001	Wheat and meslin	1002.0	901.8	2508.7	0.2	0.2	0.3	US$/kg	041

Graph 2: Trade Balance by MDG Regions in 2011

(Bln US$)

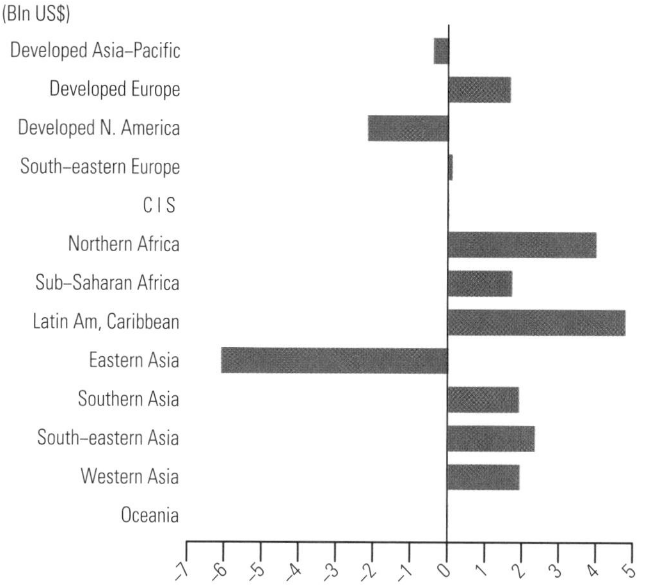

Graph 3: Partner concentration of trade in 2011

(Cumulative share by ranked partners)

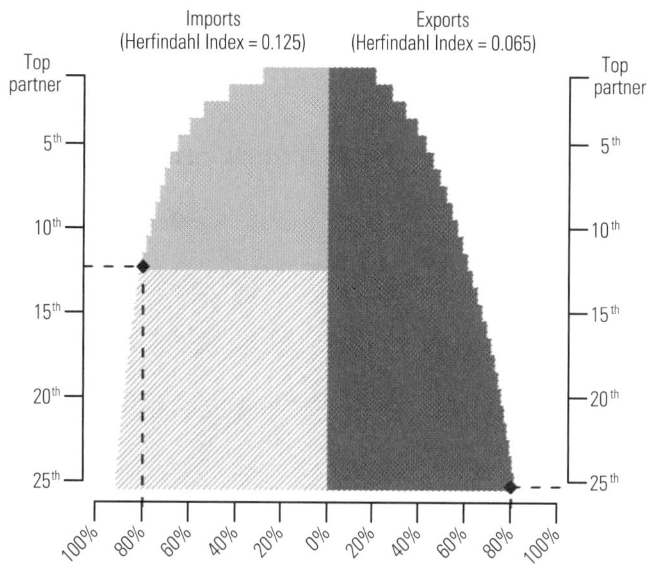

Table 4: Exports by principal countries and SITC sections in 2011

(Value in million US$, percentages of country total)

Country	Total	Shares by SITC sections (%) 0 + 1	2 + 4	3	5	6	7	8	9	Total
World	83950.2	37.4	18.7	5.9	8.9	7.1	15.9	1.2	4.9	100
Brazil	17344.8	22.2	2.0	9.3	10.3	7.2	47.7	1.4	0.0	100
China	6237.8	6.4	82.0	6.8	2.0	2.3	0.4	0.1	0.0	100
Chile	4839.7	28.5	8.4	27.0	13.0	9.8	10.8	2.6	0.0	100
USA	4303.5	31.1	5.1	23.3	8.6	22.1	8.2	1.5	0.0	100
Spain	3081.3	43.0	8.0	0.5	36.7	1.3	10.2	0.4	0.0	100
Netherlands	2655.4	71.2	14.4	2.1	10.2	1.8	0.2	0.1	0.0	100
Germany	2473.4	26.4	28.9	0.0	3.8	11.7	28.5	0.3	0.4	100
Canada	2391.4	8.0	1.5	...	2.1	4.8	4.3	0.1	79.1	100
Italy	2024.2	63.3	7.0	...	25.2	3.1	1.2	0.2	0.0	100
Uruguay	1995.3	22.5	3.5	7.5	22.7	15.7	20.5	7.6	0.0	100

Imports Profile:

Machinery and transport equipment (SITC section 7) accounted for 45.5 percent of imported goods in 2011 (see table 2). Other major commodity groups included chemicals and related products, n.e.s. (SITC section 5) and manufactured goods classified chiefly by material (SITC section 6), respectively with 16.9 and 12.0 percent of imports. From 2009 to 2011, top imported products were motor cars and other motor vehicles principally designed for the transport (HS code 8703), parts and accessories of the motor vehicles of headings 87.01 to 87.05 (HS code 8708) and petroleum oils, other than crude (HS code 2710) (see table 5).

Table 5: Top 10 import commodities 2009 to 2011

(Value in million US$)

HS code	4-digit heading of Harmonized System 2007	Value (million US$) 2009	2010	2011	Unit value 2009	2010	2011	Unit	SITC code
	All Commodities	38786.2	56501.3	76949.2					
8703	Motor cars and other motor vehicles principally designed for the transport	2513.6	4482.7	5882.7	9.7	10.7	10.9	thsd US$/unit	781
8708	Parts and accessories of the motor vehicles of headings 87.01 to 87.05	2133.2	3360.7	4148.0	*8.1*	*8.5*	*9.1*	US$/kg	784
2710	Petroleum oils, other than crude	1483.0	2567.7	5517.0	*0.6*	*0.7*	*1.0*	US$/kg	334
8517	Electrical apparatus for line telephony or line telegraphy	1633.9	1896.3	2495.6					764
2711	Petroleum gases and other gaseous hydrocarbons	411.7	802.3	2499.4	0.2	0.3	*0.5*	US$/kg	343
8802	Other aircraft (for example, helicopters, aeroplanes); spacecraft	1115.7	1350.5	955.4	6.5	5.3	3.3	mln US$/unit	792
8471	Automatic data processing machines and units thereof	680.8	1021.5	1296.1	51.5	75.2	63.6	US$/unit	752
8704	Motor vehicles for the transport of goods	495.6	950.3	1438.6	19.5	20.2	21.1	thsd US$/unit	782
3004	Medicaments (excluding goods of heading 30.02, 30.05 or 30.06)	658.8	794.8	1023.5	*53.3*	*51.0*	*57.3*	US$/kg	542
2601	Iron ores and concentrates, including roasted iron pyrites	282.5	826.5	1246.4	*0.1*	*0.1*	*0.2*	US$/kg	281

Armenia

Imports: CIF, by origin | **Exports: FOB, by last known destination** | **Trade System: General**

Overview:

From 2007 to 2011, Armenia's exports increased on average by 4.2 percent each year despite a decline of 35.2 percent in 2009 and amounted to 1.3 bln US$ (see table 1 and graph 1). During the same period, imports also increased on average by 7.7 percent each year to 4.1 bln US$ (see table 2 and graph 1). This resulted in a trade deficit amounting to 2.8 bln US$ in 2011 (see graph 1). Trade was in deficit with almost all of the MDG regions (see graph 2). The largest deficit was recorded with the Commonwealth of Independent States and amounted to 957.2 mln US$. Trade with Developed Europe and Eastern Asia recorded deficits of 450.2 and 435.8 mln US$ respectively. Compared to exports, imports were diversified across partners: 19 major partners accounted for 80 percent of imports compared to 9 major partners for exports (see graph 3).

Graph 1: Total imports, exports and trade balance

(Bln US$ by year)

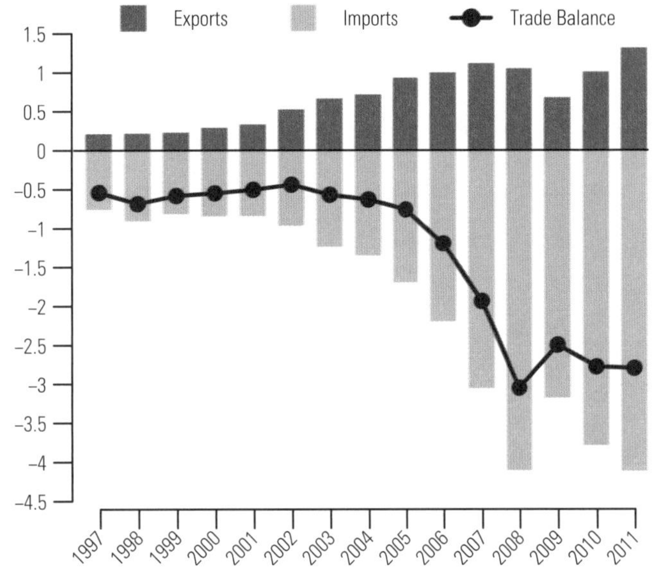

Table 1: Exports by SITC sections

(Value in million US$, growth and shares in percentage)

SITC	2011	Avg. Growth rates (%) 2007-2011	Avg. Growth rates (%) 2010-2011	2011 share
Total	1 320.4	4.2	30.5	100.0
0+1	223.3	7.2	42.7	16.9
2+4	315.3	16.3	18.9	23.9
3	101.5	66.9	148.5	7.7
5	15.0	6.6	21.1	1.1
6	484.6	-5.1	14.6	36.7
7	57.4	8.2	76.0	4.3
8	41.9	-18.8	27.7	3.2
9	81.5	45.2	68.9	6.2

Table 2: Imports by SITC sections

(Value in million US$, growth and shares in percentage)

SITC	2011	Avg. Growth rates (%) 2007-2011	Avg. Growth rates (%) 2010-2011	2011 share
Total	4 109.3	7.7	8.7	100.0
0+1	716.8	9.8	16.0	17.4
2+4	114.4	5.2	21.4	2.8
3	806.2	13.7	21.8	19.6
5	395.8	7.5	11.9	9.6
6	775.1	2.4	6.6	18.9
7	779.0	4.7	-7.0	19.0
8	312.4	11.3	7.9	7.6
9	209.6	12.5	5.2	5.1

Exports Profile:

In 2011, manufactured goods classified chiefly by material (SITC section 6) was the largest commodity group for exports (see table 1) and accounted for 36.7 percent of exports. Other major commodity groups included inedible crude materials (except fuels), animal and vegetable oils, fats and waxes (SITC sections 2+4) and food, live animals, beverages and tobacco (SITC sections 0+1) respectively with 23.9 and 16.9 percent of exports. The top three markets for exports were Russian Federation, Germany and Bulgaria (see table 4). The majority of exports to Russian Federation (67.7 percent) were in food, live animals, beverages and tobacco (SITC sections 0+1). Over the last three years, top products for exports included copper ores and concentrates (HS code 2603), ferro-alloys (HS code 7202) and alcohol of a strength by volume of less than 80 % vol (HS code 2208) (see table 3).

Table 3: Top 10 export commodities 2009 to 2011

(Value in million US$)

HS code	4-digit heading of Harmonized System 2007	Value (million US$) 2009	2010	2011	Unit value 2009	2010	2011	Unit	SITC code
	All Commodities	684.0	1011.4	1320.4					
2603	Copper ores and concentrates	98.8	210.6	260.6	1.2	1.8	2.2	US$/kg	283
7202	Ferro-alloys	86.5	119.6	121.3					671
2208	Alcohol of a strength by volume of less than 80 % vol	71.6	95.7	131.2	14.2	12.6	13.7	US$/litre	112
7402	Unrefined copper; copper anodes for electrolytic refining	60.5	92.6	114.6	8.7	12.0	12.8	US$/kg	682
7102	Diamonds, whether or not worked, but not mounted or set	59.8	90.3	113.7					667
7607	Aluminium foil (whether or not printed or backed with paper, paperboard	58.1	78.5	87.0	2.5	3.2	3.5	US$/kg	684
7108	Gold (including gold plated with platinum)	32.8	28.6	67.3	17.7	17.6	28.8	thsd US$/kg	971
2716	Electrical energy	0.5	26.2	87.5	1.6	34.6	57.1	US$/MWh	351
8102	Molybdenum and articles thereof, including waste and scrap	9.5	15.5	15.4	23.8	33.1	32.0	US$/kg	699
7113	Articles of jewellery and parts thereof, of precious metal	10.8	13.2	12.2	7.4	28.4	37.8	thsd US$/kg	897

Graph 2: Trade Balance by MDG Regions in 2011

(Mln US$)

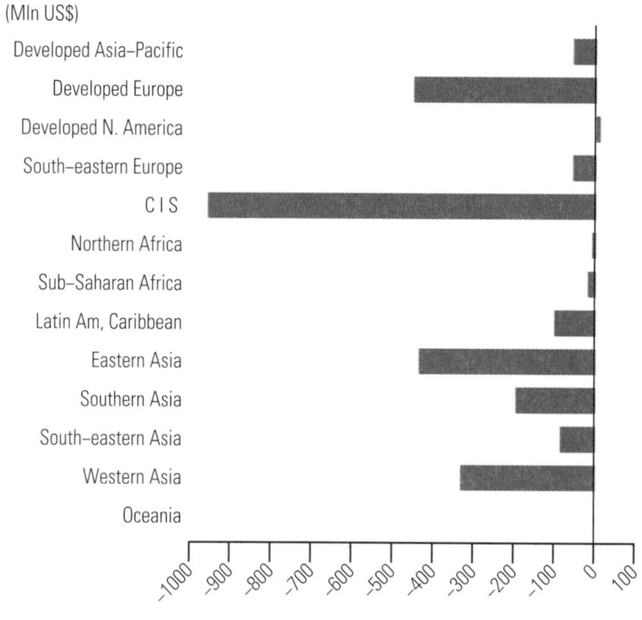

Graph 3: Partner concentration of trade in 2011

(Cumulative share by ranked partners)

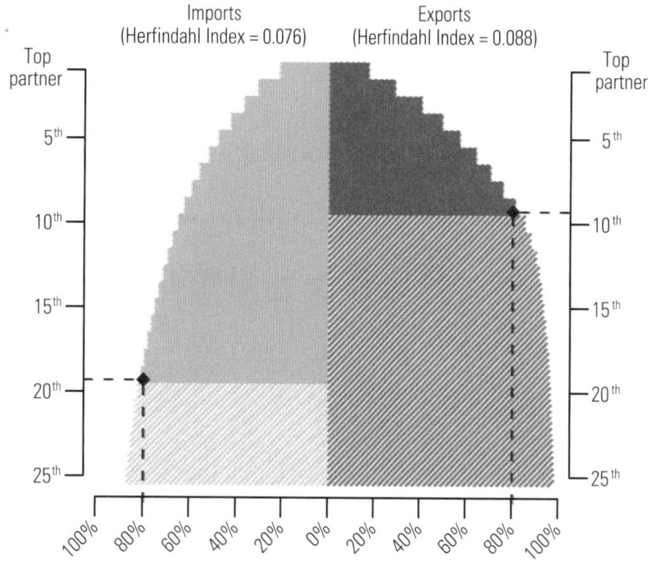

Table 4: Exports by principal countries and SITC sections in 2011

(Value in million US$, percentages of country total)

Country	Total	Shares by SITC sections (%) 0+1	2+4	3	5	6	7	8	9	Total
World	1320.4	16.9	23.9	7.7	1.1	36.7	4.3	3.2	6.2	100
Russian Federation	220.9	67.7	0.8	0.0	1.0	12.8	14.6	2.9	0.0	100
Germany	157.8	1.6	0.8	...	0.1	93.7	0.7	3.0	...	100
Bulgaria	152.2	0.0	99.7	...	0.2	0.0	0.1	0.0	...	100
Netherlands	117.2	0.0	10.9	...	...	87.6	1.4	0.0	...	100
USA	100.4	6.5	3.2	...	0.0	86.2	1.1	3.0	...	100
Iran	94.3	0.5	6.3	88.1	0.2	0.8	4.0	0.2	...	100
Spain	82.5	0.0	95.4	...	...	0.2	4.2	0.2	...	100
Belgium	70.5	1.5	0.0	...	0.1	98.3	0.1	0.0	...	100
Canada	70.3	0.0	0.0	...	...	6.5	0.0	0.8	92.6	100
Georgia	55.0	26.0	2.4	12.9	11.7	33.5	3.4	10.1	...	100

Imports Profile:

The major imports in 2011 were composed of 19.6 percent of mineral fuels, lubricants and related materials (SITC section 3), 19.0 percent of machinery and transport equipment (SITC section 7) and 18.9 percent of manufactured goods classified chiefly by material (SITC section 6) (see table 2). From 2009 to 2011, the three main products for imports were petroleum gases and other gaseous hydrocarbons (HS code 2711), petroleum oils, other than crude (HS code 2710) and diamonds, whether or not worked, but not mounted or set (HS code 7102) (see table 5).

Table 5: Top 10 import commodities 2009 to 2011

(Value in million US$)

HS code	4-digit heading of Harmonized System 2007	Value (million US$) 2009	2010	2011	Unit value 2009	2010	2011	Unit	SITC code
	All Commodities	3174.6	3781.8	4109.3					
2711	Petroleum gases and other gaseous hydrocarbons	235.2	339.5	411.7	0.2	0.2	0.3	US$/kg	343
2710	Petroleum oils, other than crude	238.1	304.1	370.9	0.7	0.8	1.0	US$/kg	334
7102	Diamonds, whether or not worked, but not mounted or set	65.5	93.9	126.7					667
1001	Wheat and meslin	94.7	87.9	90.6	0.3	0.3	0.3	US$/kg	041
9999	Commodities not specified according to kind	1.2	139.0	131.2					931
7601	Unwrought aluminium	97.0	92.6	71.6	4.4	4.4	3.2	US$/kg	684
3004	Medicaments (excluding goods of heading 30.02, 30.05 or 30.06)	75.2	80.2	91.5	65.0	65.0	73.8	US$/kg	542
8517	Electrical apparatus for line telephony or line telegraphy	70.4	81.4	79.1					764
8703	Motor cars and other motor vehicles principally designed for the transport	48.4	59.2	76.7	16.7	18.9	19.0	thsd US$/unit	781
7108	Gold (including gold plated with platinum)	38.2	60.1	78.4	31.8	39.9	51.5	thsd US$/kg	971

Aruba

Imports: CIF, by origin | **Exports: FOB, by last known destination** | **Trade System: General**

Overview:

From 2007 to 2011, Aruba's exports increased on average by 10.9 percent each year and amounted to 148.0 mln US$ in 2011 (see table 1 and graph 1). Imports increased on average by 1.8 percent each year and reached 1,195.8 mln US$ (see table 2 and graph 1). This resulted in a trade deficit 1,047.8 mln US$ (see graph 1). This deficit was accounted for largely by trade with Developed North America (-597.7 mln US$), Developed Europe (-287.7 mln US$) and Latin America and the Caribbean (-82.5 mln US$) (see graph 2). Aruba's trade in 2011 was highly concentrated among a few partners. The top 4 partners (respectively top 8 partners) accounted for 80 percent of exports (respectively imports) (see graph 3).

Graph 1: Total imports, exports and trade balance

(Bln US$ by year)

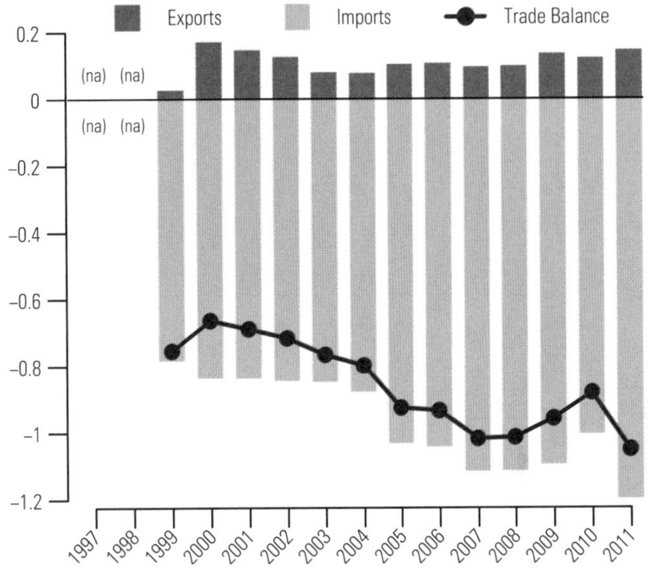

Table 1: Exports by SITC sections

(Value in million US$, growth and shares in percentage)

SITC	2011	Avg. Growth rates (%) 2007-2011	Avg. Growth rates (%) 2010-2011	2011 share
Total	148.0	10.9	18.9	100.0
0+1	117.6	56.1	14.7	79.5
2+4	2.0	6.7	340.2	1.3
3	0.0	...	...	0.0
5	3.0	-51.2	6.1	2.0
6	3.0	-21.7	-5.9	2.0
7	7.3	1.2	51.1	4.9
8	9.9	32.1	58.5	6.7
9	5.3	-2.1	16.9	3.6

Table 2: Imports by SITC sections

(Value in million US$, growth and shares in percentage)

SITC	2011	Avg. Growth rates (%) 2007-2011	Avg. Growth rates (%) 2010-2011	2011 share
Total	1 195.8	1.8	19.2	100.0
0+1	350.1	13.1	3.8	29.3
2+4	28.4	-18.9	41.8	2.4
3	8.1	...	...	0.7
5	118.6	-10.5	18.5	9.9
6	142.6	-7.5	30.2	11.9
7	281.0	5.1	40.9	23.5
8	259.1	6.7	12.9	21.7
9	7.9	-24.7	11.0	0.7

Exports Profile:

Food, live animals, beverages and tobacco (SITC sections 0+1) was the largest commodity group for exports in 2011. It represented 79.5 percent of exported goods (see table 1). Major markets for exports were Colombia, Venezuela and Curacao (see table 4). Exports to these countries were chiefly food, live animals, beverages and tobacco (SITC sections 0+1). From 2009 to 2011, the top three exported products were alcohol of a strength by volume of less than 80 % vol (HS code 2208), cigars, cheroots, cigarillos and cigarettes (HS code 2402) and articles of jewellery and parts thereof, of precious metal (HS code 7113) (see table 3).

Table 3: Top 10 export commodities 2009 to 2011

(Value in million US$)

HS code	4-digit heading of Harmonized System 2007	Value (million US$) 2009	Value (million US$) 2010	Value (million US$) 2011	Unit value 2009	Unit value 2010	Unit value 2011	Unit	SITC code
	All Commodities	137.7	124.5	148.0					
2208	Alcohol of a strength by volume of less than 80 % vol	67.1	61.3	65.6	*10.0*	*10.4*	*10.9*	US$/litre	112
2402	Cigars, cheroots, cigarillos and cigarettes	28.9	38.4	49.0	9.6	10.1	10.8	US$/kg	122
9999	Commodities not specified according to kind	5.2	4.4	4.7					931
7113	Articles of jewellery and parts thereof, of precious metal	1.2	3.9	6.1	3.9	4.2	16.4	thsd US$/kg	897
1701	Cane or beet sugar and chemically pure sucrose, in solid form	4.3	0.0	0.0	0.5	36.0	3.3	US$/kg	061
3303	Perfumes and toilet waters	1.0	1.3	1.6	80.8	85.0	52.4	US$/kg	553
8703	Motor cars and other motor vehicles principally designed for the transport	1.7	1.1	0.8		*9.9*		thsd US$/unit	781
2202	Waters with added sugar	0.8	1.1	1.1	*0.9*	*1.1*	*1.0*	US$/litre	111
9403	Other furniture and parts thereof	2.0	0.1	0.1					821
7326	Other articles of iron or steel	1.1	0.8	0.2	0.4	0.2	0.1	US$/kg	699

Graph 2: Trade Balance by MDG Regions in 2011

(Mln US$)

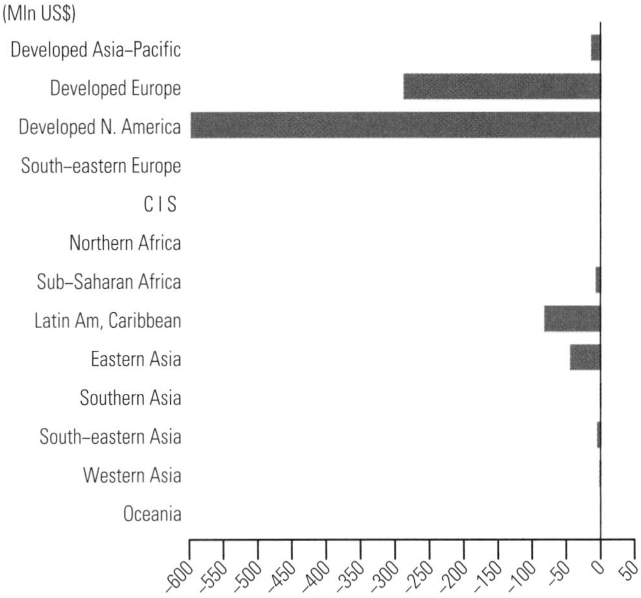

Graph 3: Partner concentration of trade in 2011

(Cumulative share by ranked partners)

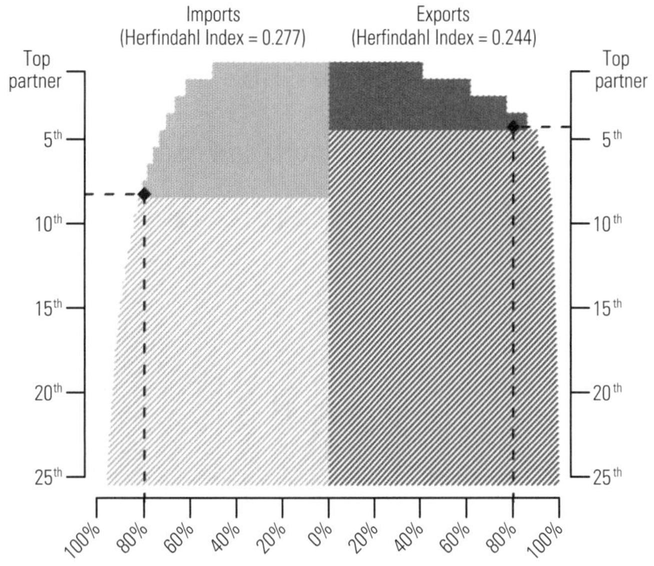

Table 4: Exports by principal countries and SITC sections in 2011

(Value in million US$, percentages of country total)

Country	Total	Shares by SITC sections (%) 0+1	2+4	3	5	6	7	8	9	Total
World	148.0	79.5	1.3	0.0	2.0	2.0	4.9	6.7	3.6	100
Colombia	60.3	99.4	0.1	...	0.0	0.1	0.3	0.0	0.1	100
Venezuela	30.3	96.1	0.1	0.0	0.1	1.4	2.2	0.1	0.0	100
Curaçao	23.0	75.3	0.2	0.0	2.1	2.9	5.0	10.6	3.9	100
USA	13.1	19.0	1.0	0.0	7.3	7.8	22.1	38.0	4.7	100
Netherlands	6.7	11.8	3.0	0.1	19.2	4.3	15.0	10.2	36.4	100
Areas, nes	4.8	63.3	1.0	0.0	4.2	1.8	7.7	13.4	8.6	100
Suriname	1.8	93.1	0.0	...	0.1	0.7	4.2	1.8	0.1	100
Other Asia, nes	1.2	0.0	73.7	...	...	25.3	0.0	1.0	...	100
Mexico	1.1	91.5	2.0	...	...	...	0.0	0.1	6.4	100
United Kingdom	0.5	66.2	19.8	0.1	0.0	0.0	0.2	3.1	10.6	100

Imports Profile:

In 2011, Aruba's imports were composed of 29.3 percent of food, live animals, beverages and tobacco (SITC sections 0+1), 23.5 percent of machinery and transport equipment and 21.7 percent of miscellaneous manufactured articles (SITC section 8) (SITC section 7) (see table 2). From 2009 to 2011, top imported products were alcohol of a strength by volume of less than 80% vol (HS code 2208), cigars, cheroots, cigarillos and cigarettes (HS code 2402) and motor cars and other motor vehicles principally designed for the transport (HS code 8703) (see table 5).

Table 5: Top 10 import commodities 2009 to 2011

(Value in million US$)

HS code	4-digit heading of Harmonized System 2007	Value (million US$) 2009	2010	2011	Unit value 2009	2010	2011	Unit	SITC code
	All Commodities	1 093.5	1 002.9	1 195.8					
2208	Alcohol of a strength by volume of less than 80 % vol	63.7	71.1	68.9	*8.1*	*9.2*	*9.3*	US$/litre	112
2402	Cigars, cheroots, cigarillos and cigarettes	32.2	43.1	45.2	10.5	10.5	10.9	US$/kg	122
8703	Motor cars and other motor vehicles principally designed for the transport	34.2	34.4	45.4		*15.3*		thsd US$/unit	781
7113	Articles of jewellery and parts thereof, of precious metal	32.9	37.7	41.6	1.8	1.7	2.3	thsd US$/kg	897
8502	Electric generating sets and rotary converters	54.4	4.2	4.3					716
8517	Electrical apparatus for line telephony or line telegraphy	18.9	18.1	20.8					764
3004	Medicaments (excluding goods of heading 30.02, 30.05 or 30.06)	15.4	17.6	18.2	57.2	56.6	54.5	US$/kg	542
9102	Wrist-watches, pocket-watches and other watches, including stop-watches	7.2	15.0	21.9					885
9403	Other furniture and parts thereof	14.7	12.6	16.0					821
0202	Meat of bovine animals, frozen	11.9	15.3	15.8	4.3	4.9	5.6	US$/kg	011

Australia

Imports: FOB, by origin | **Exports: FOB, by last known destination** | **Trade System: General**

Overview:

After reaching a peak of 206.7 bln US$ in 2010, the value of exports of Australia continued to grow in 2011 by 18.8 percent to reach 245.6 bln US$ (see table 1 and graph 1). Imports also increased in 2011 by 24.1 percent and amounted to 234.3 bln US$ (see table 2 and graph 1). The trade balance recorded a surplus of 11.3 bln US$ in 2011 (see graph 1). By MDG regions, trade with Eastern Asia recorded a surplus of 45.2 bln US$ in 2011 (see graph 2). Major trade surpluses were also recorded with Developed Asia-Pacific (+27.5 bln US$) and Southern Asia (+13.0 bln US$). Deficits were recorded with Developed Europe (-27.1 bln US$), Developed North America (-18.3 bln US$) and South-eastern Asia (-17.6 bln US$). Australia's trade in 2011 was diversified across partners: respectively 11 and 17 major partners accounted for 80 percent of exports and imports (see graph 3).

Graph 1: Total imports, exports and trade balance

(Bln US$ by year)

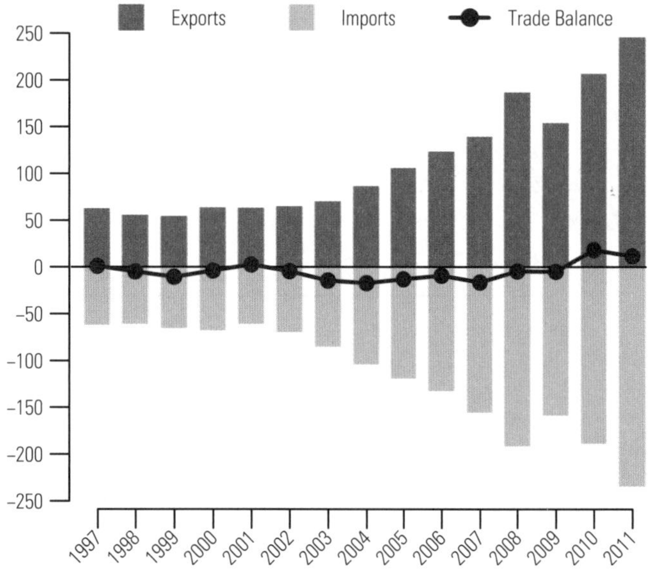

Exports Profile:

In 2011, Australia's exports were composed of 36.4 percent of inedible crude materials (except fuels), animal and vegetable oils, fats and waxes (SITC sections 2+4), 28.0 percent of mineral fuels, lubricants and related materials (SITC section 3) and 10.1 percent of food, live animals, beverages and tobacco (SITC sections 0+1) (see table 1). Major destinations for exported goods were China, Japan and Republic of Korea (see table 4). From 2009 to 2011, main exported products were iron ores and concentrates, including roasted iron pyrites (HS code 2601), coal; briquettes, ovoids and similar solid fuels manufactured from coal (HS code 2701) and gold (including gold plated with platinum) (HS code 7108) (see table 3).

Table 1: Exports by SITC sections

(Value in million US$, growth and shares in percentage)

SITC	2011	Avg. Growth rates (%) 2007-2011	2010-2011	2011 share
Total	245631.0	15.3	18.8	100.0
0+1	24764.3	9.6	18.6	10.1
2+4	89297.6	27.1	33.5	36.4
3	68670.3	21.4	14.9	28.0
5	7482.5	3.6	3.9	3.0
6	15377.2	0.0	12.7	6.3
7	11708.6	0.7	6.5	4.8
8	4859.4	3.8	11.1	2.0
9	23471.1	6.0	2.2	9.6

Table 2: Imports by SITC sections

(Value in million US$, growth and shares in percentage)

SITC	2011	Avg. Growth rates (%) 2007-2011	2010-2011	2011 share
Total	234319.3	10.8	24.1	100.0
0+1	11419.9	12.4	22.8	4.9
2+4	3429.3	8.3	33.3	1.5
3	39608.3	18.4	52.8	16.9
5	24653.2	10.4	22.4	10.5
6	25651.3	9.9	24.8	10.9
7	86785.2	7.3	17.2	37.0
8	28921.3	9.3	18.1	12.3
9	13850.9	24.5	18.1	5.9

Table 3: Top 10 export commodities 2009 to 2011

(Value in million US$)

HS code	4-digit heading of Harmonized System 2007	Value (million US$) 2009	2010	2011	Unit value 2009	2010	2011	Unit	SITC code
	All Commodities	153766.6	206705.1	245631.0					
2601	Iron ores and concentrates, including roasted iron pyrites	23573.3	44290.2	61195.1	0.1	0.1	0.1	US$/kg	281
2701	Coal; briquettes, ovoids and similar solid fuels manufactured from coal	30941.6	38572.8	43661.3	0.1	0.1	0.2	US$/kg	321
7108	Gold (including gold plated with platinum)	11760.4	12816.1	13502.6					971
2711	Petroleum gases and other gaseous hydrocarbons	6771.1	9452.4	11275.0	*0.5*	*0.4*	*0.4*	US$/kg	343
9999	Commodities not specified according to kind	7483.3	9996.0	9838.5					931
2709	Petroleum oils and oils obtained from bituminous minerals, crude	5628.5	9385.3	10739.6	*0.4*	*0.6*	0.8	US$/kg	333
2818	Artificial corundum, whether or not chemically defined	3732.2	4687.1	5038.3	0.2	0.3	0.3	US$/kg	285
1001	Wheat and meslin	3730.9	3754.5	5713.7	*0.2*	0.2	0.3	US$/kg	041
2603	Copper ores and concentrates	2973.5	4467.9	5082.1	1.7	2.4	3.1	US$/kg	283
7601	Unwrought aluminium	2880.5	3750.3	3962.2	1.7	2.2	2.5	US$/kg	684

Graph 2: Trade Balance by MDG Regions in 2011

(Bln US$)

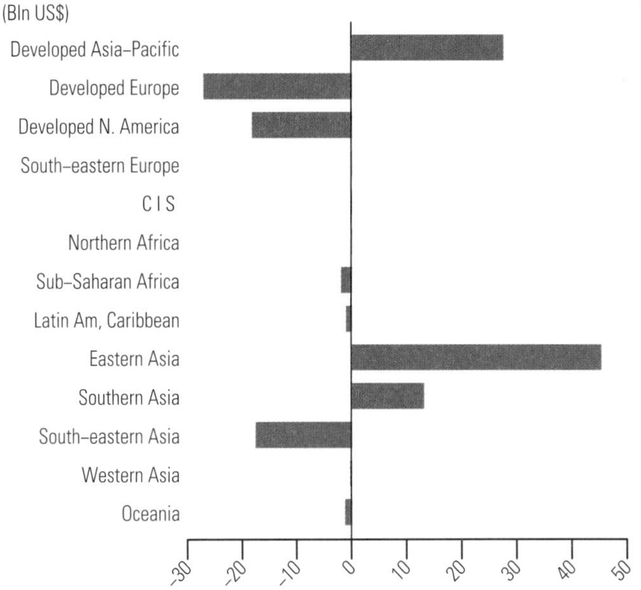

Graph 3: Partner concentration of trade in 2011

(Cumulative share by ranked partners)

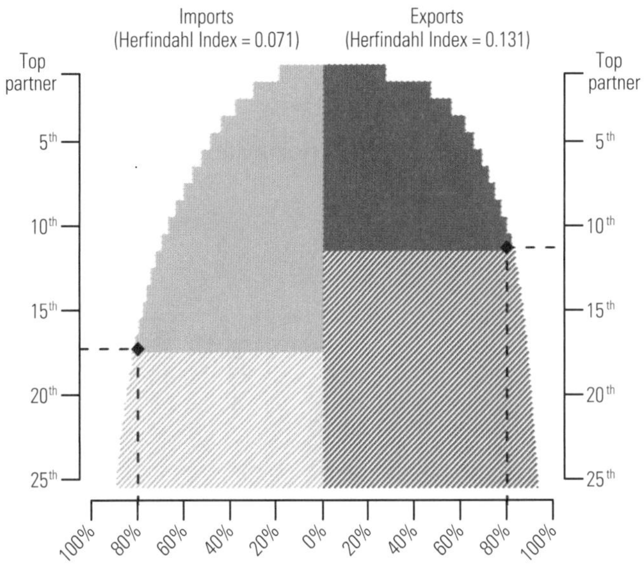

Table 4: Exports by principal countries and SITC sections in 2011

(Value in million US$, percentages of country total)

Country	Total	Shares by SITC sections (%)								
		0 + 1	2 + 4	3	5	6	7	8	9	Total
World	245631.0	10.1	36.4	28.0	3.0	6.3	4.8	2.0	9.6	100
China	67589.4	2.1	80.0	10.4	1.2	3.1	1.2	0.3	1.8	100
Japan	47215.6	10.6	36.5	46.6	1.0	4.5	0.4	0.4	0.0	100
Rep. of Korea	21882.8	8.1	44.2	35.9	2.5	5.8	1.6	0.3	1.6	100
India	14587.5	1.7	12.5	53.1	1.5	2.4	1.0	0.4	27.4	100
USA	9035.3	24.1	1.8	4.0	8.7	13.7	23.5	13.3	11.0	100
Other Asia, nes	8741.7	6.6	26.8	45.4	4.8	15.3	0.6	0.3	0.1	100
New Zealand	7307.2	18.0	1.4	3.3	15.2	15.5	26.9	15.9	3.8	100
Thailand	6524.8	7.9	7.0	22.4	5.4	14.0	2.9	0.8	39.6	100
United Kingdom	6440.9	9.7	1.2	14.9	2.8	6.6	5.3	6.0	53.5	100
Singapore	6106.1	12.4	2.9	41.9	3.4	5.9	11.1	3.3	19.0	100

Imports Profile:

Machinery and transport equipment (SITC section 7) accounted for a large share of imported goods and represented 37.0 percent of total imports in 2011 (see table 2). Other major commodity groups included mineral fuels, lubricants and related materials (SITC section 3) and miscellaneous manufactured articles (SITC section 8). They represented, respectively, 16.9 and 12.3 percent of imports. In addition to petroleum oils and oils obtained from bituminous minerals, crude (HS code 2709), other major products for imports over the last three years included motor cars and other motor vehicles principally designed for the transport (HS code 8703) and petroleum oils, other than crude (HS code 2710) (see table 5).

Table 5: Top 10 import commodities 2009 to 2011

(Value in million US$)

HS code	4-digit heading of Harmonized System 2007	Value (million US$)			Unit value				SITC code
		2009	2010	2011	2009	2010	2011	Unit	
	All Commodities	158941.1	188740.7	234319.3					
2709	Petroleum oils and oils obtained from bituminous minerals, crude	9760.4	14576.0	21515.0	*0.5*	*0.6*	*0.9*	US$/kg	333
8703	Motor cars and other motor vehicles principally designed for the transport	9252.9	14300.1	14612.1	15.1	17.3	20.0	thsd US$/unit	781
2710	Petroleum oils, other than crude	8143.0	8961.9	14841.4			*0.9*	US$/kg	334
3004	Medicaments (excluding goods of heading 30.02, 30.05 or 30.06)	6001.5	7071.9	8739.9					542
7108	Gold (including gold plated with platinum)	7286.4	6329.6	6554.7					971
9999	Commodities not specified according to kind	4656.9	5392.4	7242.3					931
8471	Automatic data processing machines and units thereof	4428.7	5861.8	6792.2	230.6	248.8	251.6	US$/unit	752
8517	Electrical apparatus for line telephony or line telegraphy	4064.1	5075.4	6618.3					764
8704	Motor vehicles for the transport of goods	3392.3	5351.7	6259.9		*26.4*	*31.3*	thsd US$/unit	782
8528	Reception apparatus for television	2576.3	2552.0	2362.5	264.6	269.0	252.4	US$/unit	761

Austria

Imports: CIF, by origin | **Exports: FOB, by last known destination** | **Trade System: Special**

Overview:

Following the decline in exports of 23.7 percent in 2009, the value of Austria's exports increased by 10.3 percent in 2010 and amounted to 144.9 bln US$ (see table 1 and graph 1). Imports increased by 10.4 percent and amounted to 150.6 bln US$ in 2010 (see table 2 and graph 1). This resulted in a trade deficit of 5.7 bln US$ in 2010 (see graph 2). Trade with Developed Europe and Eastern Asia recorded deficits respectively of 8.5 and 2.9 bln US$ in 2010 (see graph 2). Major trade surpluses were recorded with Developed North America (+2.8 bln US$) and South-eastern Europe (+1.9 bln US$). Trade was relatively diversified across partners: in 2010, 17 major partners accounted for 80 percent of exports and 14 major partners accounted for 80 percent of imports (see graph 3). However, Germany, the top partner for Austria's exports, was the destination for 31.6 percent of exports (see table 4).

Graph 1: Total imports, exports and trade balance

(Bln US$ by year)

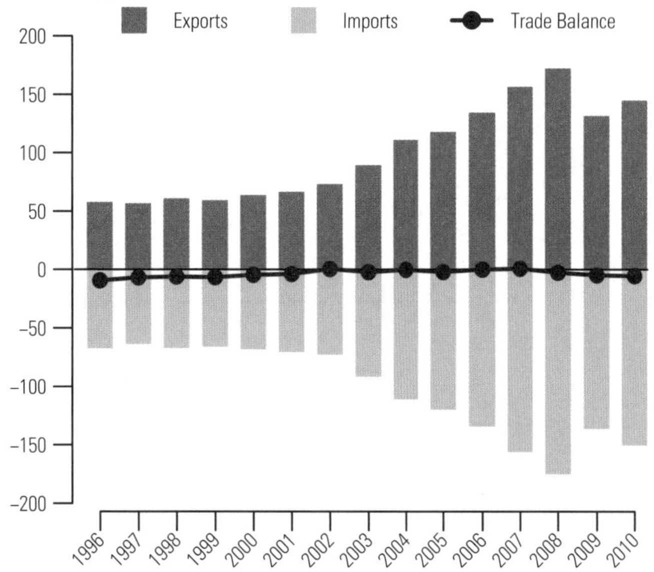

Exports Profile:

In 2010, Austria's exports were composed largely of machinery and transport equipment (SITC section 7) and manufactured goods classified chiefly by material (SITC section 6) (see table 1). They represented respectively 37.8 and 21.9 percent of total exports. In addition to Germany, other major markets for exports included Italy and Switzerland (see table 4). Over the last three years, top export commodities were motor cars and other motor vehicles principally designed for the transport (HS code 8703), medicaments (excluding goods of heading 30.02, 30.05 or 30.06) (HS code 3004) and parts and accessories of the motor vehicles of headings 87.01 to 87.05 (HS code 8708) (see table 3).

Table 1: Exports by SITC sections

(Value in million US$, growth and shares in percentage)

SITC	2010	Avg. Growth rates (%) 2006-2010	2009-2010	2010 share
Total	144882.0	1.9	10.3	100.0
0+1	9559.5	4.9	3.0	6.6
2+4	4261.5	4.3	20.9	2.9
3	4650.9	-9.9	2.9	3.2
5	16693.6	8.0	9.3	11.5
6	31767.5	2.4	12.8	21.9
7	54763.3	0.0	11.2	37.8
8	16399.6	2.1	3.8	11.3
9	6785.9	9.9	22.0	4.7

Table 2: Imports by SITC sections

(Value in million US$, growth and shares in percentage)

SITC	2010	Avg. Growth rates (%) 2006-2010	2009-2010	2010 share
Total	150592.7	2.9	10.4	100.0
0+1	9996.6	7.6	2.3	6.6
2+4	7993.1	9.2	39.2	5.3
3	16121.8	-3.4	13.3	10.7
5	18850.8	6.7	10.9	12.5
6	23900.5	2.1	15.0	15.9
7	49051.3	0.9	9.2	32.6
8	21659.3	4.9	4.8	14.4
9	3019.3	29.8	-8.9	2.0

Table 3: Top 10 export commodities 2008 to 2010

(Value in million US$)

HS code	4-digit heading of Harmonized System 2007	Value (million US$) 2008	2009	2010	Unit value 2008	2009	2010	Unit	SITC code
	All Commodities	172228.0	131387.2	144882.0					
9999	Commodities not specified according to kind	6275.8	4904.7	5445.7					931
8703	Motor cars and other motor vehicles principally designed for the transport	6617.2	3449.1	4063.4	32.4	28.3	26.5	thsd US$/unit	781
3004	Medicaments (excluding goods of heading 30.02, 30.05 or 30.06)	4207.7	4575.0	4973.4	*67.6*	*61.5*	*70.8*	US$/kg	542
8708	Parts and accessories of the motor vehicles of headings 87.01 to 87.05	4687.0	3386.7	3909.1	*11.2*	*12.2*	*10.6*	US$/kg	784
3002	Human blood; animal blood prepared for therapeutic uses	2268.1	2277.3	2207.1	*407.2*	*410.8*	*348.8*	US$/kg	541
8407	Spark-ignition reciprocating or rotary internal combustion piston engines	2024.4	1894.2	2824.9	2.4	2.4		thsd US$/unit	713
8408	Compression-ignition internal combustion piston engines	2341.1	2055.7	2324.9	5.0	4.7	*4.1*	thsd US$/unit	713
8504	Electrical transformers, static converters	1951.6	1692.6	1957.4					771
8704	Motor vehicles for the transport of goods	2375.4	1454.0	1629.8	*64.4*	60.6	58.8	thsd US$/unit	782
2202	Waters with added sugar	1903.1	1593.5	1749.8	1.4	1.4	1.4	US$/litre	111

Graph 2: Trade Balance by MDG Regions in 2010

(Bln US$)

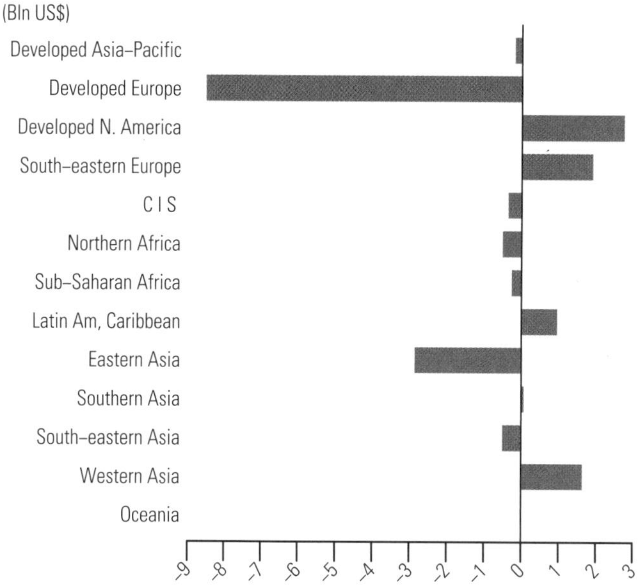

Graph 3: Partner concentration of trade in 2010

(Cumulative share by ranked partners)

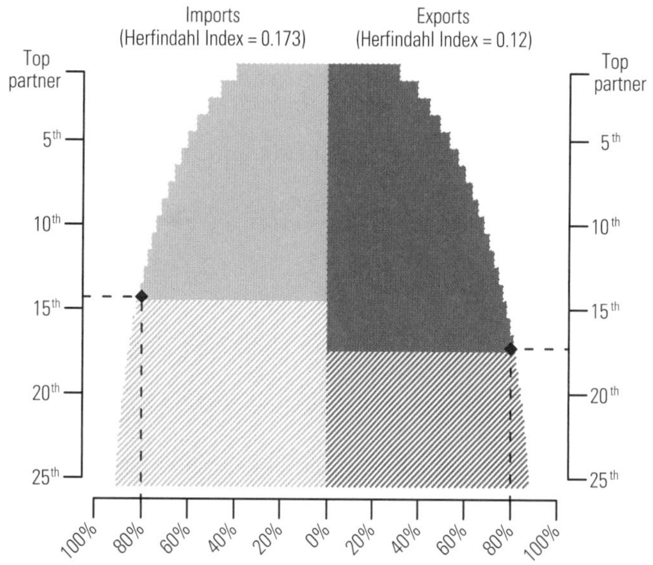

Table 4: Exports by principal countries and SITC sections in 2010

(Value in million US$, percentages of country total)

Country	Total	Shares by SITC sections (%)								
		0 + 1	2 + 4	3	5	6	7	8	9	Total
World	144882.0	6.6	2.9	3.2	11.5	21.9	37.8	11.3	4.7	100
Germany	45740.0	7.0	2.6	3.7	7.2	22.2	40.8	12.1	4.5	100
Italy	11359.7	13.3	14.3	0.9	8.2	27.1	23.4	9.0	3.8	100
Switzerland	7449.8	4.7	2.6	1.4	19.9	25.3	26.6	15.3	4.3	100
USA	6568.4	7.3	0.1	0.0	10.9	14.4	50.1	9.5	7.6	100
France	6037.1	3.7	1.5	0.1	13.0	23.5	35.2	18.1	5.1	100
Czech Rep.	5490.4	5.3	2.3	9.6	11.4	22.4	30.0	14.1	4.9	100
Hungary	4431.1	9.9	2.7	10.3	9.7	21.8	32.7	10.5	2.4	100
United Kingdom	4396.5	4.7	0.4	1.5	8.5	17.0	43.5	19.2	5.1	100
China	3718.9	0.4	0.8	0.0	11.1	7.9	66.0	8.8	5.1	100
Poland	3636.4	4.8	1.1	0.9	14.5	28.2	36.0	9.9	4.6	100

Imports Profile:

By commodity groups, Austria's imports profile in 2010 was similar to the profile for exports: machinery and transport equipment (SITC section 7) accounted for the largest share (32.6 percent) followed by manufactured goods classified chiefly by material (SITC section 6) and miscellaneous manufactured articles (SITC section 8) with 15.9 and 14.4 percent of total imports (see table 2). Over the last three years, top imported goods were motor cars and other motor vehicles principally designed for the transport (HS code 8703), petroleum oils, other than crude (HS code 2710) and petroleum oils and oils obtained from bituminous minerals, crude (HS code 2709) (see table 5).

Table 5: Top 10 import commodities 2008 to 2010

(Value in million US$)

HS code	4-digit heading of Harmonized System 2007	Value (million US$)			Unit value				SITC code
		2008	2009	2010	2008	2009	2010	Unit	
	All Commodities	175025.8	136418.4	150592.7					
8703	Motor cars and other motor vehicles principally designed for the transport	8518.7	7312.3	7909.0	22.9	19.9	20.8	thsd US$/unit	781
2710	Petroleum oils, other than crude	7021.7	4850.9	5859.4	*1.1*	*0.7*	*0.8*	US$/kg	334
2709	Petroleum oils and oils obtained from bituminous minerals, crude	6039.9	3406.9	4039.6	0.8	0.5	*0.6*	US$/kg	333
8708	Parts and accessories of the motor vehicles of headings 87.01 to 87.05	4868.3	3021.1	3737.1	*10.4*	*10.5*	*9.2*	US$/kg	784
2711	Petroleum gases and other gaseous hydrocarbons	4372.2	3380.0	3872.6	*0.6*	*0.4*	*0.4*	US$/kg	343
3004	Medicaments (excluding goods of heading 30.02, 30.05 or 30.06)	3596.3	3308.2	3005.9	*69.3*	*68.1*	*64.3*	US$/kg	542
7108	Gold (including gold plated with platinum)	2073.9	2749.4	2300.5	28.6	31.7	39.9	thsd US$/kg	971
8517	Electrical apparatus for line telephony or line telegraphy	2461.7	1956.5	2074.4					764
8409	Parts suitable for use with the engines of heading 84	2256.9	1752.8	2077.1	*17.6*	*17.6*	*14.0*	US$/kg	713
8471	Automatic data processing machines and units thereof	1869.0	1526.9	1759.5	190.2	*168.8*	197.7	US$/unit	752

Imports: CIF, by origin | Exports: FOB, by last known destination | Trade System: General

Overview:

After reaching a peak of 47.8 bln US$ in 2008, the value of exports of Azerbaijan contracted sharply by 69.2 percent in 2009 but increased again in 2010 and 2011 by respectively 44.9 and 24.4 percent to amount to 26.5 bln US$ (see table 1 and graph 1). Imports increased by 47.5 percent in 2011 to 9.7 bln US$ (see table 2 and graph 1). The trade surplus went up from 14.7 bln US$ in 2010 to 16.7 bln US$ in 2011 (see graph 1). By MDG regions, large surpluses were recorded with Developed Europe (+12.4 bln US$), South-eastern Asia (+1.6 bln US$) and Developed North America (+1.6 bln US$). Trade was in deficit with Sub-Saharan Africa (-0.6 bln US$) and Latin America and the Caribbean (-0.2 bln US$). In 2011, imports were more diversified across partners than exports: 14 major partners accounted for 80 percent of imports (compared to 10 major partners for exports) (see graph 3).

Graph 1: Total imports, exports and trade balance

(Bln US$ by year)

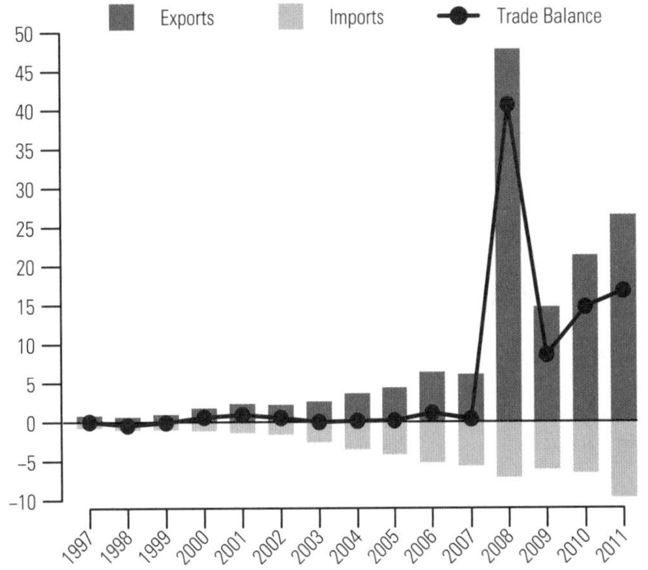

Table 1: Exports by SITC sections

(Value in million US$, growth and shares in percentage)

SITC	2011	Avg. Growth rates (%) 2007-2011	2010-2011	2011 share
Total	26480.2	44.6	24.4	100.0
0+1	572.8	7.1	31.0	2.2
2+4	178.8	0.7	0.5	0.7
3	25089.3	50.2	24.8	94.7
5	242.3	25.1	86.2	0.9
6	303.7	8.3	77.8	1.1
7	56.6	-21.3	-74.0	0.2
8	22.0	-6.7	0.0	0.1
9	14.8	-8.8	16.7	0.1

Exports Profile:

In 2011, Azerbaijan's exports were almost exclusively (94.7 percent) mineral fuels, lubricants and related materials (SITC section 3) (see table 1). Their exports increased on average by 50.2 percent each year since 2007. The top three markets for exports in 2011 were Italy, France and USA and accounted for 59.1 percent of exports (see table 4). Main exported products were petroleum oils and oils obtained from bituminous minerals, crude (HS code 2709), petroleum oils, other than crude (HS code 2710) and petroleum gases and other gaseous hydrocarbons (HS code 2711) (see table 3).

Table 2: Imports by SITC sections

(Value in million US$, growth and shares in percentage)

SITC	2011	Avg. Growth rates (%) 2007-2011	2010-2011	2011 share
Total	9732.9	14.3	47.5	100.0
0+1	1283.1	10.8	13.7	13.2
2+4	345.1	15.2	30.8	3.5
3	83.8	-12.5	13.8	0.9
5	856.2	18.9	46.6	8.8
6	1920.8	15.6	34.8	19.7
7	4729.6	16.0	76.0	48.6
8	500.1	9.7	28.3	5.1
9	14.0	-30.0	-67.7	0.1

Table 3: Top 10 export commodities 2009 to 2011

(Value in million US$)

HS code	4-digit heading of Harmonized System 2007	Value (million US$) 2009	2010	2011	Unit value 2009	2010	2011	Unit	SITC code
	All Commodities	14688.7	21278.4	26480.2					
2709	Petroleum oils and oils obtained from bituminous minerals, crude	11989.7	18489.6	22911.0	0.4	0.6	0.8	US$/kg	333
2710	Petroleum oils, other than crude	1482.8	1284.0	1527.7	0.5	0.6	0.8	US$/kg	334
2711	Petroleum gases and other gaseous hydrocarbons	131.8	303.9	587.1	0.2	0.2	0.3	US$/kg	343
1701	Cane or beet sugar and chemically pure sucrose, in solid form	102.1	145.9	198.4	0.6	0.7	0.9	US$/kg	061
1516	Animal or vegetable fats and oils	54.4	87.6	77.3	2.5	2.5	2.5	US$/kg	431
8901	Cruise ships, excursion boats, ferry-boats, cargo ships, barges	30.6	173.8	0.0	3.4	173.8		mln US$/unit	793
0810	Other fruit, fresh	46.1	51.9	63.1	0.4	0.4	0.6	US$/kg	057
3901	Polymers of ethylene, in primary forms	34.6	49.2	72.2	0.9	1.1	1.2	US$/kg	571
7207	Semi-finished products of iron or non-alloy steel	6.7	48.4	92.0	0.4	0.5	0.5	US$/kg	672
0802	Other nuts, fresh or dried, whether or not shelled or peeled	52.5	35.3	57.2	4.3	4.1	4.4	US$/kg	057

Graph 2: Trade Balance by MDG Regions in 2011

(Bln US$)

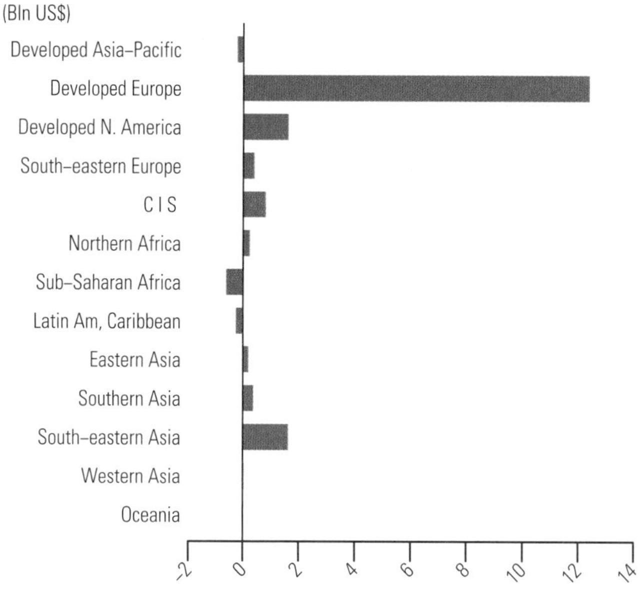

Graph 3: Partner concentration of trade in 2011

(Cumulative share by ranked partners)

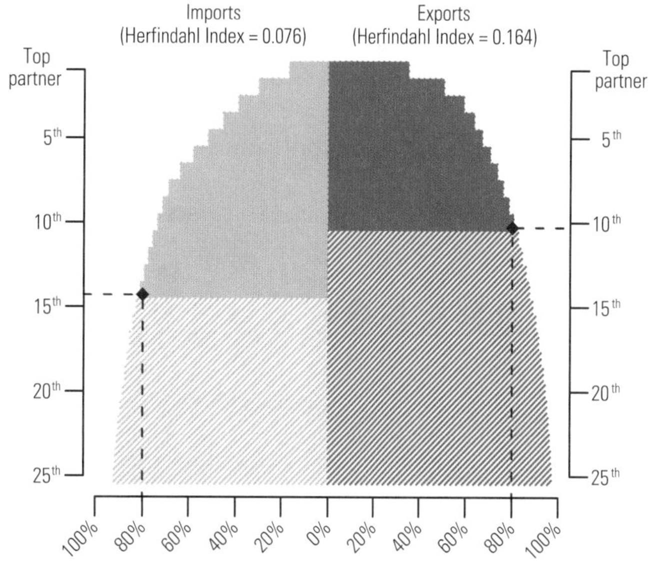

Table 4: Exports by principal countries and SITC sections in 2011

(Value in million US$, percentages of country total)

Country	Total	Shares by SITC sections (%)								
		0 + 1	2 + 4	3	5	6	7	8	9	Total
World	26480.2	2.2	0.7	94.7	0.9	1.1	0.2	0.1	0.1	100
Italy	9341.0	0.1	0.0	99.7	0.1	0.0	0.0	0.0	...	100
France	4036.7	0.0	0.0	99.9	0.0	0.0	0.0	0.0	...	100
USA	2274.5	0.0	0.0	99.9	0.0	0.0	0.0	0.0	0.0	100
Russian Federation	1187.4	29.1	11.0	42.5	2.3	12.2	0.5	1.0	1.2	100
Indonesia	913.2	0.0	0.0	100.0	...	0.0	0.0	0.0	...	100
Ukraine	909.3	0.7	0.0	97.4	1.5	0.2	0.1	0.0	...	100
Israel	817.6	0.0	0.0	99.9	0.0	0.0	0.0	0.0	...	100
Belarus	666.8	1.1	0.1	98.5	0.2	0.1	0.0	...	...	100
Malaysia	664.0	0.0	0.0	100.0	...	0.0	0.0	0.0	...	100
Georgia	535.3	3.4	1.7	84.9	6.6	1.2	1.8	0.4	0.0	100

Imports Profile:

Machinery and transport equipment (SITC section 7) represented nearly half of imported goods (48.6 percent) in 2011 (see table 2). Other major commodity groups included manufactured goods classified chiefly by material (SITC section 6) and food, live animals, beverages and tobacco (SITC sections 0+1) respectively with 19.7 and 13.2 percent of imports. Over the last three years, top imported products were other aircraft (for example, helicopters, aeroplanes); spacecraft (HS code 8802), motor cars and other motor vehicles principally designed for the transport (HS code 8703) and wheat and meslin (HS code 1001) (see table 5).

Table 5: Top 10 import commodities 2009 to 2011

(Value in million US$)

HS code	4-digit heading of Harmonized System 2007	Value (million US$)			Unit value				SITC code
		2009	2010	2011	2009	2010	2011	Unit	
	All Commodities	6119.1	6596.8	9732.9					
8802	Other aircraft (for example, helicopters, aeroplanes); spacecraft	128.4	58.7	863.9	2.6	4.9	23.3	mln US$/unit	792
8703	Motor cars and other motor vehicles principally designed for the transport	254.4	275.0	379.7	9.0	9.5	10.8	thsd US$/unit	781
1001	Wheat and meslin	194.8	285.4	282.0	0.2	0.2	0.2	US$/kg	041
2402	Cigars, cheroots, cigarillos and cigarettes	217.7	221.3	241.2	16.4	17.6	19.7	US$/kg	122
7304	Tubes, pipes and hollow profiles, seamless, of iron (other than cast iron)	114.0	145.6	213.1	3.1	2.5	2.6	US$/kg	679
8517	Electrical apparatus for line telephony or line telegraphy	186.1	110.4	168.4					764
1701	Cane or beet sugar and chemically pure sucrose, in solid form	105.7	180.1	167.0	0.3	0.5	0.5	US$/kg	061
3004	Medicaments (excluding goods of heading 30.02, 30.05 or 30.06)	112.1	120.7	211.5	9.5	10.2	16.2	US$/kg	542
8431	Parts suitable for use principally with the machinery of headings 84.25	102.3	137.1	197.8	22.0	19.3	16.0	US$/kg	723
7308	Structures (excluding prefabricated buildings of heading 94.06)	66.3	196.9	144.6	1.7	3.0	2.5	US$/kg	691

Bahamas

Imports: CIF, by origin | **Exports: FOB, by last known destination** | **Trade System: General**

Overview:

From 2007 to 2011, Bahamas' exports increased on average by 2.1 percent each year to reach 726.9 mln US$ in 2011 (see table 1 and graph 1). During the same period, imports also increased on average by 2.4 percent each year to 3.4 bln US$ (see table 2 and graph 1). This resulted in a trade deficit amounting to 2.7 bln US$ in 2011 (see graph 1). This deficit was largely accounted for by trade with Developed North America which recorded a deficit of 2.5 bln US$ (see graph 2). Trade also recorded a deficit of 187.0 mln US$ with Latin America and the Caribbean. Bahamas' trade was concentrated with very few partners: in 2011, 1 single partner accounted for more than 80 percent of imported goods compared to 2 partners for exports (see graph 3).

Graph 1: Total imports, exports and trade balance

(Bln US$ by year)

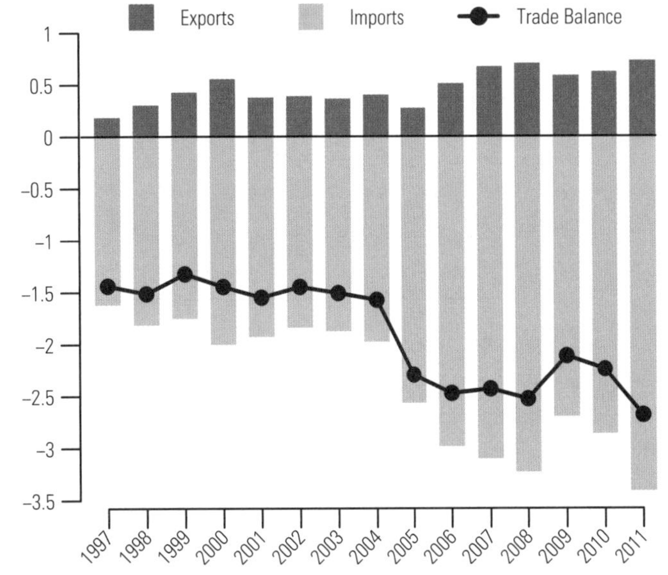

Table 1: Exports by SITC sections

(Value in million US$, growth and shares in percentage)

SITC	2011	Avg. Growth rates (%) 2007-2011	2010-2011	2011 share
Total	726.9	2.1	17.2	100.0
0+1	77.4	-8.0	0.7	10.7
2+4	45.4	-1.4	2.2	6.2
3	216.1	6.6	35.3	29.7
5	250.4	0.4	15.7	34.5
6	42.9	13.5	18.6	5.9
7	86.3	6.1	17.1	11.9
8	8.3	10.1	-34.3	1.1
9	0.0	15.2	-81.0	0.0

Exports Profile:

In 2011, Bahamas' exports were composed of 34.5 percent of chemicals and related products, n.e.s. (SITC section 5), 29.7 percent of mineral fuels, lubricants and related materials (SITC section 3) and 11.9 percent of machinery and transport equipment (SITC section 7) (see table 1). In addition to USA, which accounted for 78.3 percent of total exports, other major partners for exports included the United Kingdom and France (see table 4). From 2009 to 2011, top exported commodities included petroleum oils, other than crude (HS code 2710), polymers of styrene, in primary forms (HS code 3903) and heterocyclic compounds with nitrogen hetero-atom(s) only (HS code 2933) (see table 3).

Table 2: Imports by SITC sections

(Value in million US$, growth and shares in percentage)

SITC	2011	Avg. Growth rates (%) 2007-2011	2010-2011	2011 share
Total	3410.3	2.4	19.2	100.0
0+1	531.0	3.0	7.5	15.6
2+4	64.5	-7.9	-10.1	1.9
3	930.0	10.9	35.4	27.3
5	385.9	8.5	18.4	11.3
6	445.5	-2.0	19.1	13.1
7	583.3	-4.1	18.1	17.1
8	338.5	-0.6	4.1	9.9
9	131.6	0.7	46.4	3.9

Table 3: Top 10 export commodities 2009 to 2011

(Value in million US$)

HS code	4-digit heading of Harmonized System 2007	Value (million US$) 2009	2010	2011	Unit value 2009	2010	2011	Unit	SITC code
	All Commodities	584.9	620.1	726.9					
2710	Petroleum oils, other than crude	112.1	159.7	216.1					334
3903	Polymers of styrene, in primary forms	122.5	104.1	135.8	2.4	2.2	3.4	US$/kg	572
2933	Heterocyclic compounds with nitrogen hetero-atom(s) only	106.9	81.7	73.8	810.1	549.4	741.8	US$/kg	515
0306	Crustaceans, whether in shell or not	61.0	70.5	70.5	25.7	32.2	33.1	US$/kg	036
3303	Perfumes and toilet waters	14.7	23.8	32.9	48.3	79.6	*46.2*	US$/kg	553
2517	Pebbles, gravel, broken or crushed stone	15.9	12.4	12.3	0.0	0.0	0.0	US$/kg	273
2501	Salt (including table salt)	11.2	16.4	12.0	0.0	0.0	0.0	US$/kg	278
8903	Yachts and other vessels for pleasure or sports; rowing boats and canoes	1.8	19.5	13.1	1.1	177.4	23.2	thsd US$/unit	793
7326	Other articles of iron or steel	5.0	11.1	12.3	2.5	6.2	6.8	US$/kg	699
8205	Hand tools (including glaziers' diamonds)	9.9	6.9	7.7	11.3	17.0	14.5	US$/kg	695

Graph 2: Trade Balance by MDG Regions in 2011

(Bln US$)

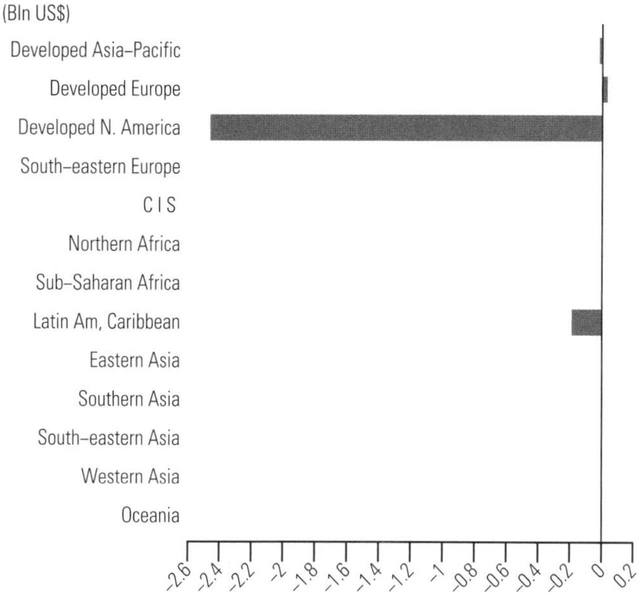

Graph 3: Partner concentration of trade in 2011

(Cumulative share by ranked partners)

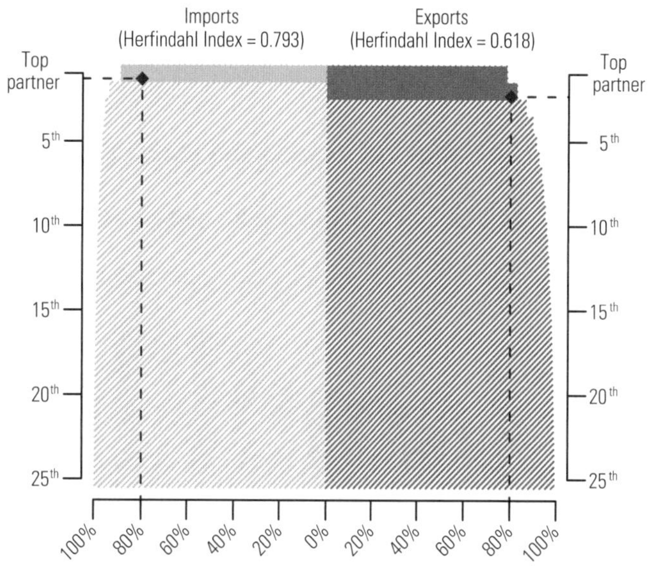

Table 4: Exports by principal countries and SITC sections in 2011

(Value in million US$, percentages of country total)

Country	Total	Shares by SITC sections (%)								
		0 + 1	2 + 4	3	5	6	7	8	9	Total
World	726.9	10.7	6.2	29.7	34.5	5.9	11.9	1.1	0.0	100
USA	569.2	8.5	5.2	37.6	29.9	5.5	12.0	1.2	0.0	100
United Kingdom	31.6	0.0	2.0	...	88.3	5.9	2.6	1.2	...	100
France	26.9	99.4	0.5	...	0.0	...	0.0	0.0	...	100
Canada	21.8	7.6	5.1	...	81.7	2.6	1.6	1.4	0.0	100
Germany	11.3	0.3	0.6	...	97.8	0.0	1.2	0.1	...	100
Panama	8.4	0.0	0.1	...	34.2	6.0	58.0	1.7	...	100
Belgium	8.1	0.0	0.0	...	...	0.1	98.9	1.0	...	100
China, Hong Kong SAR	6.7	0.0	94.5	...	1.0	4.3	0.2	...	...	100
China	5.4	0.0	1.3	...	0.1	94.3	4.2	...	...	100
Argentina	4.8	0.0	0.0	...	99.5	0.0	...	0.5	...	100

Imports Profile:

Imports were composed of 27.3 percent of mineral fuels, lubricants and related materials (SITC section 3), 17.1 percent of machinery and transport equipment (SITC section 7) and 15.6 percent of food, live animals, beverages and tobacco (SITC sections 0+1) (see table 2). In addition to petroleum oils, other than crude (HS code 2710), other major imported products from 2009 to 2011 were motor cars and other motor vehicles principally designed for the transport (HS code 8703) and medicaments (excluding goods of heading 30.02, 30.05 or 30.06) (HS code 3004) (see table 5).

Table 5: Top 10 import commodities 2009 to 2011

(Value in million US$)

HS code	4-digit heading of Harmonized System 2007	Value (million US$)			Unit value				SITC code
		2009	2010	2011	2009	2010	2011	Unit	
	All Commodities	2 698.5	2 861.9	3 410.3					
2710	Petroleum oils, other than crude	537.9	667.4	908.7					334
9999	Commodities not specified according to kind	104.2	89.7	131.2					931
8703	Motor cars and other motor vehicles principally designed for the transport	55.4	57.5	62.0	3.8	*5.2*	5.8	thsd US$/unit	781
3004	Medicaments (excluding goods of heading 30.02, 30.05 or 30.06)	27.5	61.1	55.9	36.3	42.7	41.6	US$/kg	542
9403	Other furniture and parts thereof	47.2	40.9	44.8					821
2106	Food preparations not elsewhere specified or included	29.4	31.3	49.3	4.9	*5.0*	5.6	US$/kg	098
7326	Other articles of iron or steel	29.2	26.3	43.3	8.3	7.3	7.4	US$/kg	699
3303	Perfumes and toilet waters	19.2	28.8	49.3	27.3	30.0	25.0	US$/kg	553
0207	Meat and edible offal, of the poultry of heading 01.05	29.4	29.9	32.0	4.0	4.1	4.1	US$/kg	012
3915	Waste, parings and scrap, of plastics	10.6	21.6	59.0	6.2	6.9	4.4	US$/kg	579

Imports: CIF, by origin | **Exports: FOB, by last known destination** | **Trade System: General**

Overview:

Bahrain's trade data for 2011 excludes exports and imports of petroleum oils. Exports amounted to 7.1 bln US$ in 2011 and imports to 10.2 bln US$ (see tables 1 and 2). In 2011, trade recorded a deficit of 3.1 bln US$ (see graph 1). By MDG regions, large deficits were recorded with Developed Europe (-1.7 bln US$), Latin America and the Caribbean (-1.2 bln US$) and Eastern Asia (-1.2 bln US$) (see graph 2). Trade with Western Asia showed a significant surplus of 2.6 bln US$. Bahrain's trade was diversified across partners in 2011: respectively 13 and 16 major partners accounted for 80 percent of exports and imports (see graph 3).

Graph 1: Total imports, exports and trade balance

(Bln US$ by year)

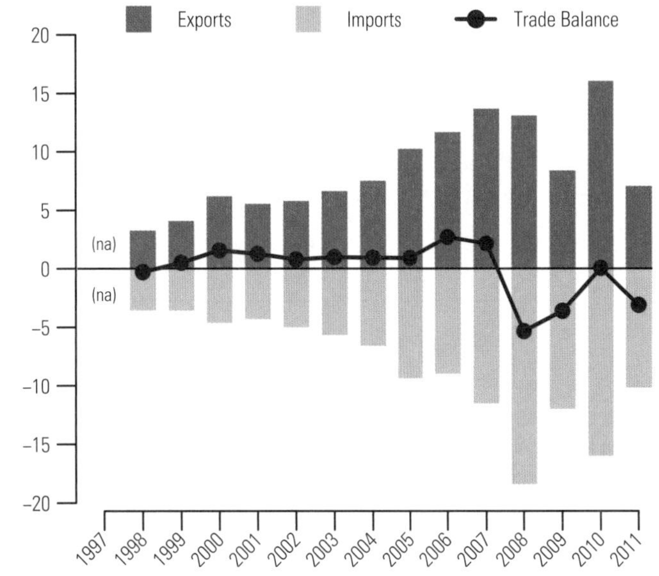

Table 1: Exports by SITC sections

(Value in million US$, growth and shares in percentage)

SITC	2011	Avg. Growth rates (%) 2007-2011	Avg. Growth rates (%) 2010-2011	2011 share
Total	7071.3	-15.2	-56.0	100.0
0+1	437.7	61.1	43.2	6.2
2+4	2808.3	87.7	126.6	39.7
3	96.9	-69.2	-99.2	1.4
5	171.7	-27.2	54.6	2.4
6	2596.6	13.9	22.8	36.7
7	788.9	31.2	46.3	11.2
8	170.4	5.0	-21.0	2.4
9	0.7	-24.6	-92.2	0.0

Exports Profile:

With the exclusion of petroleum oils exports in the 2011 data, inedible crude materials (except fuels), animal and vegetable oils, fats and waxes (SITC sections 2+4) and manufactured goods classified chiefly by material (SITC section 6) accounted for large shares of Bahrain's exports during the year at 39.7 and 36.7 percent, respectively (see table 1). Major trading partners included Saudi Arabia, Qatar and Oman (see table 4). In 2011, major commodities for exports included iron ores and concentrates, including roasted iron pyrites (HS code 2601), aluminium bars, rods and profiles (HS code 7604) and aluminium plates, sheets and strip, of a thickness exceeding 0.2 mm (HS code 7606) (see table 3).

Table 2: Imports by SITC sections

(Value in million US$, growth and shares in percentage)

SITC	2011	Avg. Growth rates (%) 2007-2011	Avg. Growth rates (%) 2010-2011	2011 share
Total	10173.9	-3.0	-36.4	100.0
0+1	1419.1	25.4	20.1	13.9
2+4	1813.0	21.5	-24.6	17.8
3	275.9	-53.7	-95.5	2.7
5	830.4	16.2	21.6	8.2
6	1631.9	9.5	22.0	16.0
7	3392.0	12.3	-5.6	33.3
8	811.1	19.5	13.3	8.0
9	0.5	-39.3	-78.2	0.0

Table 3: Top 10 export commodities 2009 to 2011

(Value in million US$)

HS code	4-digit heading of Harmonized System 2007	Value (million US$) 2009	2010	2011	Unit value 2009	2010	2011	Unit	SITC code
	All Commodities	8384.0	16059.2	7071.3					
2710	Petroleum oils, other than crude	5372.4	11507.9	35.4	*1.0*	*0.7*	0.7	US$/kg	334
2601	Iron ores and concentrates, including roasted iron pyrites	260.6	1187.3	2611.2	0.1	0.2	0.2	US$/kg	281
7604	Aluminium bars, rods and profiles	563.9	825.4	1030.2	2.3	2.4	2.6	US$/kg	684
7606	Aluminium plates, sheets and strip, of a thickness exceeding 0.2 mm	234.4	480.5	535.3	2.5	2.8	3.4	US$/kg	684
7614	Stranded wire, cables, plaited bands and the like, of aluminium	199.7	172.5	212.5	2.8	2.8	3.0	US$/kg	693
8703	Motor cars and other motor vehicles principally designed for the transport	153.5	171.4	253.8	13.1	32.4	30.5	thsd US$/unit	781
7605	Aluminium wire	82.4	165.8	222.2	2.4	2.5	2.8	US$/kg	684
0406	Cheese and curd	136.4	114.8	167.4	6.3	6.4	6.7	US$/kg	024
8415	Air conditioning machines, comprising a motor-driven fan	92.9	86.5	133.2					741
2106	Food preparations not elsewhere specified or included	69.0	110.4	128.5	3.2	3.2	3.2	US$/kg	098

Graph 2: Trade Balance by MDG Regions in 2011

(Bln US$)

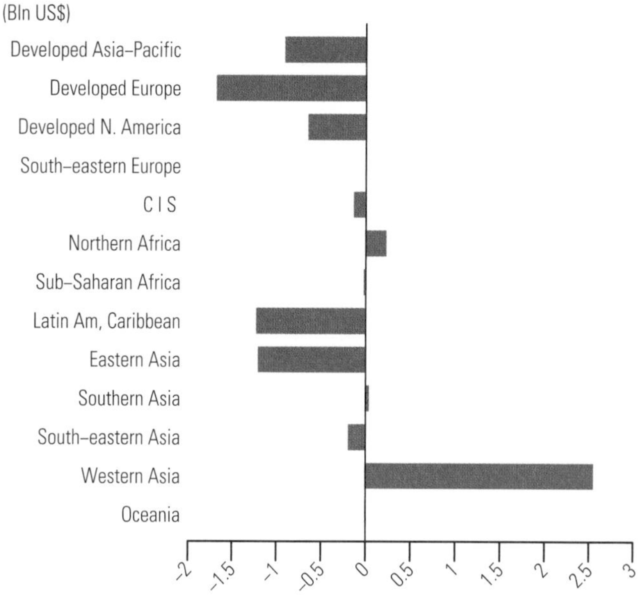

Graph 3: Partner concentration of trade in 2011

(Cumulative share by ranked partners)

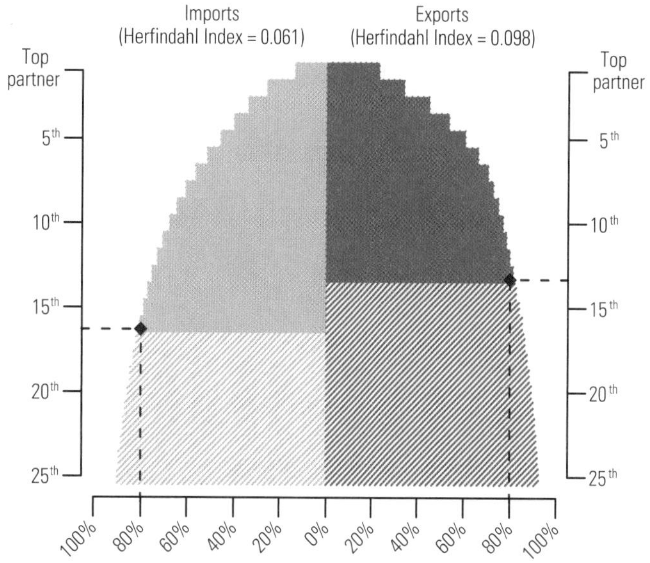

Table 4: Exports by principal countries and SITC sections in 2011

(Value in million US$, percentages of country total)

Country	Total	Shares by SITC sections (%)								
		0 + 1	2 + 4	3	5	6	7	8	9	Total
World	7 071.3	6.2	39.7	1.4	2.4	36.7	11.2	2.4	0.0	100
Saudi Arabia	1 643.1	11.5	14.1	0.0	3.6	42.4	25.2	3.1	0.0	100
Qatar	778.2	4.9	85.2	0.5	1.8	3.1	3.4	1.0	0.0	100
Oman	768.2	3.1	88.5	0.0	0.6	6.6	1.1	0.2	0.0	100
United Arab Emirates	599.5	8.8	45.8	3.5	2.5	19.9	17.4	2.1	0.0	100
India	492.9	0.3	77.8	0.8	0.9	19.2	0.9	0.1	0.0	100
China	397.0	0.1	59.2	3.2	3.0	7.5	27.0	0.0	...	100
USA	301.1	0.2	0.0	0.0	2.2	70.1	6.6	20.7	0.0	100
Kuwait	162.2	44.6	0.1	0.1	5.2	30.9	16.0	3.1	0.0	100
Italy	158.9	0.0	0.0	...	0.0	98.7	0.8	0.5	...	100
Netherlands	141.8	0.0	0.0	0.0	0.9	98.5	0.5	0.0	...	100

Imports Profile:

With the exclusion of petroleum oils imports in the 2011 data, major commodity groups included machinery and transport equipment (SITC section 7), inedible crude materials (except fuels), animal and vegetable oils, fats and waxes (SITC sections 2+4) and manufactured goods classified chiefly by material (SITC section 6): they accounted respectively for 33.3, 17.8 and 16.0 percent of imported goods. Top products for imports in 2011 were iron ores and concentrates, including roasted iron pyrites (HS code 2601), motor cars and other motor vehicles principally designed for the transport (HS code 8703) and artificial corundum, whether or not chemically defined (HS code 2818) (see table 5).

Table 5: Top 10 import commodities 2009 to 2011

(Value in million US$)

HS code	4-digit heading of Harmonized System 2007	Value (million US$)			Unit value				SITC code
		2009	2010	2011	2009	2010	2011	Unit	
	All Commodities	11 993.4	16 001.6	10 173.9					
2709	Petroleum oils and oils obtained from bituminous minerals, crude	5 147.4	5 858.9	0.1	*0.7*	*0.4*	0.2	US$/kg	333
2601	Iron ores and concentrates, including roasted iron pyrites	211.5	1 784.6	1 349.6	0.1	0.4	0.3	US$/kg	281
8703	Motor cars and other motor vehicles principally designed for the transport	728.8	924.0	855.8	22.2	0.0	23.1	thsd US$/unit	781
2818	Artificial corundum, whether or not chemically defined	462.7	433.8	241.3	0.3	0.5	0.5	US$/kg	285
8517	Electrical apparatus for line telephony or line telegraphy	109.6	142.2	230.4					764
8471	Automatic data processing machines and units thereof	126.5	148.9	177.9	447.1	116.2	469.7	US$/unit	752
2713	Petroleum coke and other residues	147.9	116.9	178.0	0.3	0.3	0.4	US$/kg	335
3004	Medicaments (excluding goods of heading 30.02, 30.05 or 30.06)	90.7	161.5	173.0	43.4	66.3	83.0	US$/kg	542
8544	Insulated (including enamelled or anodised) wire, cable	144.6	155.6	113.8	5.3	3.5	5.8	US$/kg	773
8504	Electrical transformers, static converters	84.9	221.2	92.9					771

Imports: CIF, by consignment | **Exports: FOB, by last known destination** | **Trade System: General**

Overview:

From 2003 to 2007, exports of Bangladesh increased on average by 19.7 percent each year and amounted to 13.1 bln US$ (see table 1 and graph 1). During the same period, imports increased on average by 14.8 percent each year to 17.6 bln US$ (see table 2 and graph 1). The trade balance recorded a deficit amounting to 4.5 bln US$ compared to 3.7 bln US$ in 2003 (see graph 1). Trade recorded surpluses with Developed Europe (+4.9 bln US$) and Developed North America (+2.8 bln US$) (see graph 2). Significant deficits were recorded with Eastern Asia (-3.6 bln US$), South-eastern Asia (-2.4 bln US$) and Southern Asia (-2.0 bln US$) among others. Trade, especially imports, was diversified across partners: in 2007, 11 (respectively 18) major partners accounted for 80 percent of exports (respectively imports) (see graph 3).

Graph 1: Total imports, exports and trade balance

(Bln US$ by year)

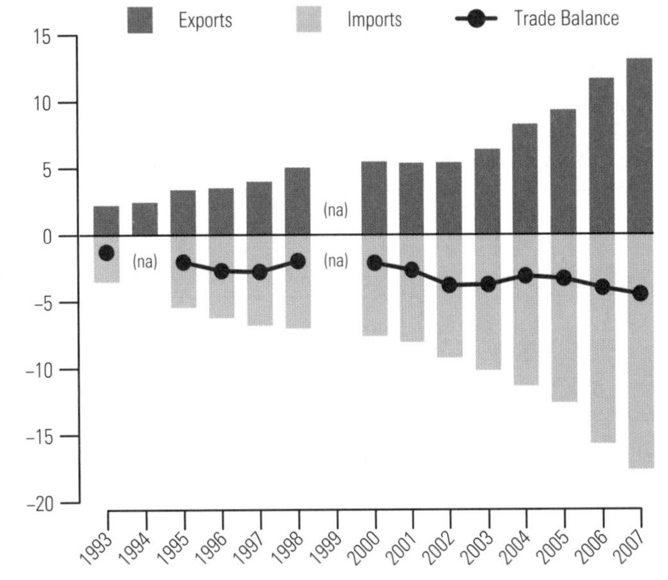

Table 1: Exports by SITC sections

(Value in million US$, growth and shares in percentage)

SITC	2007	Avg. Growth rates (%) 2003-2007	Avg. Growth rates (%) 2006-2007	2007 share
Total	13143.0	19.7	12.4	100.0
0+1	856.1	23.4	23.7	6.5
2+4	452.6	64.0	104.5	3.4
3	213.3	79.2	139.5	1.6
5	176.4	19.2	22.0	1.3
6	1406.8	23.0	-23.1	10.7
7	335.4	51.2	72.5	2.6
8	9698.7	17.0	13.8	73.8
9	3.7	38.1	3368.3	0.0

Exports Profile:

In 2007, miscellaneous manufactured articles (SITC section 8) accounted for 73.8 percent of Bangladesh's exports (see table 1). Other major commodity groups for exports were manufactured goods classified chiefly by material (SITC section 6) and food, live animals, beverages and tobacco (SITC sections 0+1) respectively with 10.7 and 6.5 percent of exported goods. Major partners for exports were USA, Germany and United Kingdom (see table 4). From 2005 to 2007, top exported products included men's or boys' suits, ensembles, jackets, blazers, trousers (HS code 6203), t-shirts, singlets and other vests, knitted or crocheted (HS code 6109) and jerseys, pullovers, cardigans, waist-coats and similar articles (HS code 6110) (see table 3).

Table 2: Imports by SITC sections

(Value in million US$, growth and shares in percentage)

SITC	2007	Avg. Growth rates (%) 2003-2007	Avg. Growth rates (%) 2006-2007	2007 share
Total	17622.9	14.8	12.3	100.0
0+1	2222.4	20.2	44.5	12.6
2+4	3416.3	19.8	38.3	19.4
3	1842.3	13.7	-7.9	10.5
5	2110.8	20.9	25.0	12.0
6	2965.6	3.6	-2.5	16.8
7	4064.3	20.2	-5.0	23.1
8	727.5	-2.5	8.0	4.1
9	273.6	433.9	921106.5	1.6

Table 3: Top 10 export commodities 2005 to 2007

(Value in million US$)

HS code	4-digit heading of Harmonized System 2002	Value (million US$) 2005	2006	2007	Unit value 2005	2006	2007	Unit	SITC code
	All Commodities	9331.6	11696.7	13143.0					
6203	Men's or boys' suits, ensembles, jackets, blazers, trousers	1399.1	1923.5	2183.8	1.7	2.6	3.9	US$/unit	841
6109	T-shirts, singlets and other vests, knitted or crocheted	1474.9	1886.6	2087.1	1.1	1.0	1.2	US$/unit	845
6110	Jerseys, pullovers, cardigans, waist-coats and similar articles	995.0	1209.4	1300.0	4.3	3.9	3.9	US$/unit	845
6204	Women's or girls' suits, ensembles, jackets, blazers, dresses, skirts	807.7	935.3	1033.6	3.5	4.4	4.3	US$/unit	842
6205	Men's or boys' shirts	821.4	849.1	841.3	3.6	2.9	3.1	US$/unit	841
0306	Crustaceans, whether in shell or not	354.9	482.6	612.6	8.7	8.7	8.2	US$/kg	036
6105	Men's or boys' shirts, knitted or crocheted	286.3	307.9	359.6	2.9	3.3	3.3	US$/unit	843
5209	Woven fabrics of cotton, containing 85 % or more by weight of cotton	12.7	692.1	12.3	6.9	5.4	4.0	US$/kg	652
6108	Women's or girls' slips, petticoats, briefs, panties, knitted or crocheted	107.3	140.8	389.6	2.0	1.0	2.3	US$/unit	844
6302	Bed linen, table linen, toilet linen and kitchen linen	148.3	201.5	247.1	4.9	4.6	5.1	US$/kg	658

Graph 2: Trade Balance by MDG Regions in 2007

(Bln US$)

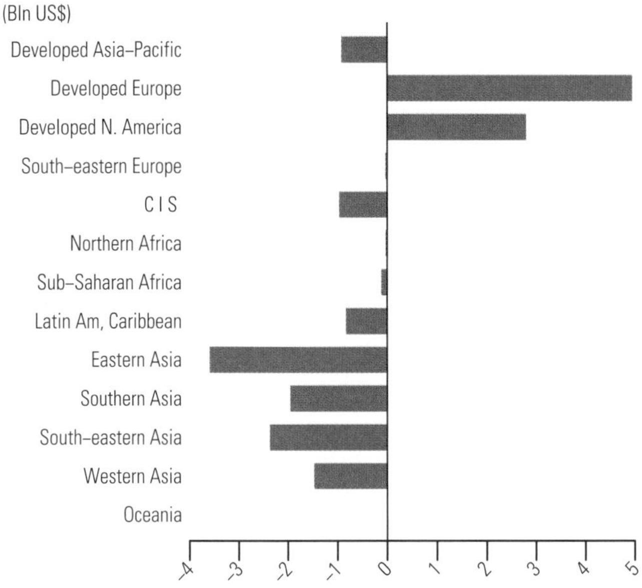

Graph 3: Partner concentration of trade in 2007

(Cumulative share by ranked partners)

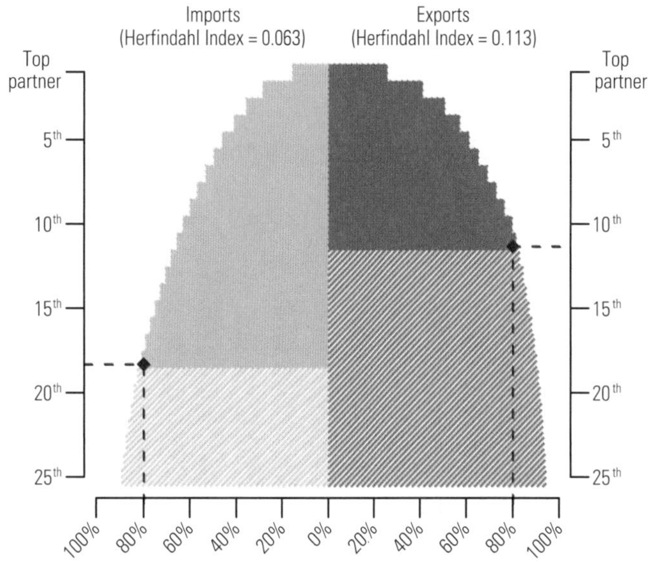

Table 4: Exports by principal countries and SITC sections in 2007

(Value in million US$, percentages of country total)

Country	Total	Shares by SITC sections (%)								
		0 + 1	2 + 4	3	5	6	7	8	9	Total
World	13 143.0	6.5	3.4	1.6	1.3	10.7	2.6	73.8	0.0	100
USA	3 374.5	6.6	0.1	0.0	0.3	3.5	0.1	89.4	0.0	100
Germany	2 002.5	1.8	0.1	...	0.3	2.0	0.4	95.4	0.0	100
United Kingdom	1 253.5	8.7	1.0	0.0	0.1	9.5	2.7	78.1	0.0	100
France	855.7	2.2	0.1	...	0.1	3.0	0.1	94.6	0.0	100
Italy	529.3	2.0	1.2	...	0.0	14.3	3.3	79.2	0.0	100
India	523.7	4.2	39.1	18.0	19.9	13.2	4.4	1.2	0.0	100
Spain	506.2	0.4	0.8	...	0.1	8.7	0.1	90.0	0.0	100
Belgium	504.2	37.1	0.0	0.0	0.0	9.1	1.5	52.3	0.0	100
Canada	454.8	1.2	0.1	...	0.0	9.0	0.4	89.3	0.0	100
Netherlands	440.5	5.9	0.6	...	0.2	5.3	0.3	87.8	0.0	100

Imports Profile:

In 2007, Bangladesh's imports were composed of 23.1 percent of machinery and transport equipment (SITC section 7), 19.4 percent of inedible crude materials (except fuels), animal and vegetable oils, fats and waxes (SITC sections 2+4) and 16.8 percent of manufactured goods classified chiefly by material (SITC section 6) (see table 2). From 2005 to 2007, top imported products included petroleum oils, other than crude (HS code 2710), cotton, not carded or combed (HS code 5201) and palm oil and its fractions (HS code 1511) (see table 5).

Table 5: Top 10 import commodities 2005 to 2007

(Value in million US$)

HS code	4-digit heading of Harmonized System 2002	Value (million US$)			Unit value				SITC code
		2005	2006	2007	2005	2006	2007	Unit	
	All Commodities	12 630.5	15 688.5	17 622.9					
2710	Petroleum oils, other than crude	1 089.9	1 717.3	1 558.8	0.2	0.2	0.3	US$/kg	334
5201	Cotton, not carded or combed	664.0	837.2	1 041.1	1.2	1.4	1.3	US$/kg	263
1511	Palm oil and its fractions	482.9	697.3	906.1	0.4	0.4	0.6	US$/kg	422
8525	Transmission apparatus for radio-telephony, radio-broadcasting	496.3	708.9	522.8	*96.7*	*111.6*		US$/unit	764
1001	Wheat and meslin	267.8	394.5	590.4	0.2	0.2	0.3	US$/kg	041
8908	Vessels and other floating structures for breaking up	322.8	484.6	401.8		334.4		thsd US$/unit	793
1507	Soya-bean oil and its fractions	150.9	238.9	621.5	0.5	0.5	0.7	US$/kg	421
1701	Cane or beet sugar and pure sucrose, in solid form	203.2	311.6	305.6	0.3	0.4	0.3	US$/kg	061
2523	Portland cement, aluminous cement, slag cement	237.2	249.1	324.3	*0.0*	0.0	0.0	US$/kg	661
1006	Rice	109.4	220.6	393.9	0.2	0.2	0.3	US$/kg	042

Barbados

Imports: CIF, by origin | **Exports: FOB, by last known destination** | **Trade System: General**

Overview:

Since 2006, Barbados' exports decreased on average by 8.2 percent each year to 313.7 mln US$ in 2010 (see table 1 and graph 1). During the same period, imports decreased on average by 7.4 percent each year and amounted to 1.2 bln US$ (see table 2 and graph 1). The trade deficit dropped from 1.2 bln US$ in 2006 to 0.9 bln US$ in 2010 (see graph 1). By MDG regions, large deficits were recorded with Developed North America (-491.3 mln US$) and Developed Europe (131.9 mln US$) (see graph 2). Trade was relatively diversified across partners: 11 and 12 major partners accounted for 80 percent respectively of exports and imports (see graph 3).

Graph 1: Total imports, exports and trade balance

(Bln US$ by year)

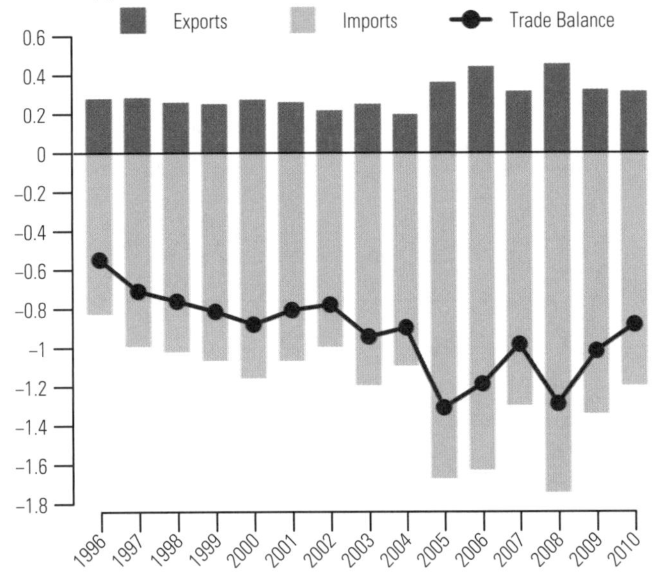

Exports Profile:

In 2010, exports were composed of 28.6 percent of chemicals and related products, n.e.s. (SITC section 5), 28.1 percent of food, live animals, beverages and tobacco (SITC sections 0+1) and 20.7 percent of miscellaneous manufactured articles (SITC section 8) (see table 1). The three largest markets for exported goods were USA, United Kingdom and Trinidad and Tobago (see table 4). From 2008 to 2010, top exported goods included medicaments (excluding goods of heading 30.02, 30.05 or 30.06) (HS code 3004), alcohol of a strength by volume of less than 80 % vol (HS code 2208) and petroleum oils, other than crude (HS code 2710) (see table 3).

Table 1: Exports by SITC sections

(Value in million US$, growth and shares in percentage)

SITC	2010	Avg. Growth rates (%) 2006-2010	2009-2010	2010 share
Total	313.7	-8.2	-2.8	100.0
0+1	88.2	3.8	-3.4	28.1
2+4	6.0	-12.0	-23.1	1.9
3	0.1	-86.0	-99.5	0.0
5	89.6	18.9	34.5	28.6
6	38.5	-4.7	-7.6	12.3
7	23.1	-19.9	-20.1	7.4
8	64.9	-1.1	-10.1	20.7
9	3.2	9.6	15.6	1.0

Table 2: Imports by SITC sections

(Value in million US$, growth and shares in percentage)

SITC	2010	Avg. Growth rates (%) 2006-2010	2009-2010	2010 share
Total	1196.2	-7.4	-10.8	100.0
0+1	279.5	4.4	8.6	23.4
2+4	43.4	-5.7	-10.9	3.6
3	19.5	-49.5	-89.1	1.6
5	176.3	3.3	-0.5	14.7
6	192.7	-4.5	0.3	16.1
7	288.5	-9.5	-2.0	24.1
8	190.8	-2.8	2.4	16.0
9	5.6	-7.0	0.9	0.5

Table 3: Top 10 export commodities 2008 to 2010

(Value in million US$)

HS code	4-digit heading of Harmonized System 2002	Value (million US$) 2008	2009	2010	Unit value 2008	2009	2010	Unit	SITC code
	All Commodities	454.2	322.7	313.7					
3004	Medicaments (excluding goods of heading 30.02, 30.05 or 30.06)	41.4	41.0	64.4	*37.5*	*39.3*	*47.1*	US$/kg	542
2208	Alcohol of a strength by volume of less than 80 % vol	39.5	35.7	44.0	2.8	3.1	3.0	US$/litre	112
2710	Petroleum oils, other than crude	91.6	1.7	0.0	0.7	0.3	2.1	US$/kg	334
1701	Cane or beet sugar and pure sucrose, in solid form	22.6	18.1	9.7	0.8	1.1	0.1	US$/kg	061
2523	Portland cement, aluminous cement, slag cement	14.5	16.9	15.5	*3.8*	1.3	0.1	US$/kg	661
7113	Articles of jewellery and parts thereof, of precious metal	18.7	14.2	8.1	*3.1*	*3.9*		thsd US$/kg	897
2709	Petroleum oils, crude	22.3	9.7	...	0.7	0.3		US$/kg	333
1517	Margarine; edible mixtures	9.9	9.3	9.4	2.3	2.5	2.4	US$/kg	091
9102	Wrist-watches, pocket-watches and other watches, including stop-watches	12.4	7.9	7.9	296.9	148.0	279.9	US$/unit	885
4821	Paper or paperboard lables of all kinds, whether or not printed	9.4	7.9	10.1	20.3	*22.8*	20.7	US$/kg	892

Graph 2: Trade Balance by MDG Regions in 2010

(Mln US$)

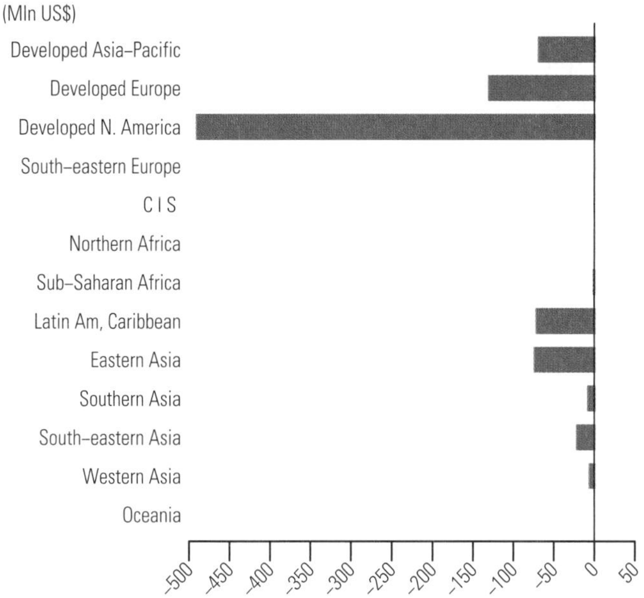

Graph 3: Partner concentration of trade in 2010

(Cumulative share by ranked partners)

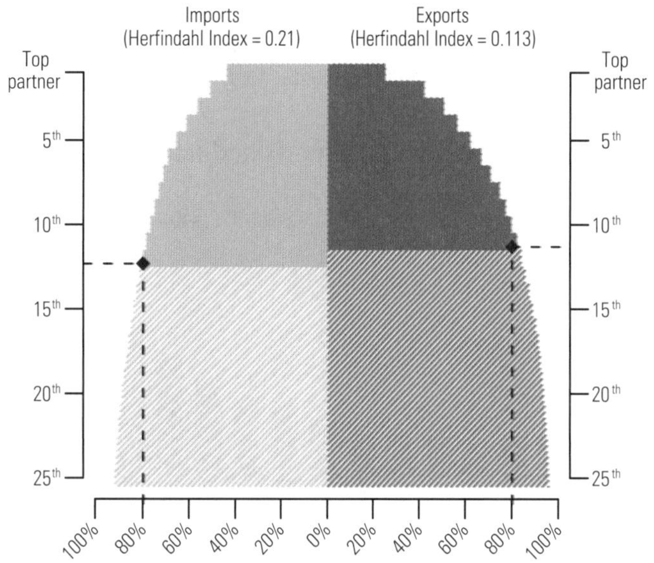

Table 4: Exports by principal countries and SITC sections in 2010

(Value in million US$, percentages of country total)

Country	Total	Shares by SITC sections (%) 0 + 1	2 + 4	3	5	6	7	8	9	Total
World	313.7	28.1	1.9	0.0	28.6	12.3	7.4	20.7	1.0	100
USA	78.2	32.7	0.2	0.0	6.8	4.0	13.8	41.8	0.8	100
United Kingdom	52.6	32.1	0.3	0.1	57.0	0.1	8.6	1.1	0.8	100
Trinidad and Tobago	26.5	24.9	2.0	0.0	38.6	15.1	7.9	10.4	1.1	100
Saint Lucia	18.2	36.4	5.2	0.0	22.7	19.6	2.8	13.0	0.2	100
Jamaica	17.7	17.0	0.0	...	36.3	20.4	2.1	23.1	1.0	100
Guyana	14.9	14.1	0.3	...	13.3	50.6	1.1	15.3	5.3	100
Saint Vincent and the Grenadines	12.5	20.5	8.1	0.0	34.6	19.3	4.4	11.9	1.2	100
Grenada	12.4	17.2	6.2	0.0	33.1	31.6	3.3	8.2	0.3	100
Canada	8.1	69.7	4.3	0.0	3.0	14.7	1.7	3.7	2.9	100
Antigua and Barbuda	7.7	37.2	3.1	...	39.4	5.3	2.7	11.9	0.2	100

Imports Profile:

In 2010, imports of machinery and transport equipment (SITC section 7) decreased by 2.0 percent and accounted for 24.1 percent of imported goods (see table 2). Imports of food, live animals, beverages and tobacco (SITC sections 0+1), on the other hand, increased by 8.6 percent and represented 23.4 percent of imported goods. From 2008 to 2010, top imported products included petroleum oils, other than crude (HS code 2710), medicaments (excluding goods of heading 30.02, 30.05 or 30.06) (HS code 3004) and motor cars and other motor vehicles principally designed for the transport (HS code 8703) (see table 5).

Table 5: Top 10 import commodities 2008 to 2010

(Value in million US$)

HS code	4-digit heading of Harmonized System 2002	Value (million US$) 2008	2009	2010	Unit value 2008	2009	2010	Unit	SITC code
	All Commodities	1 744.3	1 340.7	1 196.2					
2710	Petroleum oils, other than crude	294.1	159.9	6.9	*0.8*	*0.5*	*2.2*	US$/kg	334
3004	Medicaments (excluding goods of heading 30.02, 30.05 or 30.06)	62.5	66.6	65.4	*40.3*	38.3	*40.3*	US$/kg	542
8703	Motor cars and other motor vehicles principally designed for the transport	54.4	34.2	41.7	12.2	10.9	*10.7*	thsd US$/unit	781
8471	Automatic data processing machines and units thereof	32.0	30.1	24.6	419.1	320.8	261.3	US$/unit	752
9403	Other furniture and parts thereof	24.5	14.0	16.4					821
8704	Motor vehicles for the transport of goods	28.3	9.2	13.9	17.7	15.0	14.5	thsd US$/unit	782
2106	Food preparations not elsewhere specified or included	16.4	15.0	16.2	*2.9*	*2.6*	3.0	US$/kg	098
7113	Articles of jewellery and parts thereof, of precious metal	21.6	14.2	11.8	*3.3*	*3.0*		thsd US$/kg	897
2202	Waters with added sugar	15.4	15.7	16.4	0.6	0.6	0.5	US$/litre	111
3923	Articles for the conveyance or packing of goods, of plastics	15.1	14.3	13.9	*3.4*	*3.3*	*3.1*	US$/kg	893

Belarus

Imports: CIF, by origin	Exports: FOB, by last known destination	Trade System: General

Overview:

From 2007 to 2011, Belarus' exports increased on average by 13.5 percent each year and reached its peak of 40.3 bln US$ in 2011 (see table 1 and graph 1). Similarly, imports increased on average by 12.4 percent each year and reached 45.7 bln US$ (see table 2 and graph 1). This resulted in a trade deficit of 5.5 bln US$ in 2011 (see graph 1). This deficit is reflected largely in trade with two MDG regions: Commonwealth of Independent States (-8.6 bln US$) and Eastern Asia (-1.7 bln US$) (see graph 2). Trade, however, recorded surpluses with Developed Europe (+6.7 bln US$), Southern Asia (+0.6 bln US$) and South-eastern Asia (+0.2 bln US$) among others. In 2011, trade was concentrated among a few partners: 8 major partners accounted for 80 percent of imports (compared to 9 major partners for exports) (see graph 3).

Graph 1: Total imports, exports and trade balance

(Bln US$ by year)

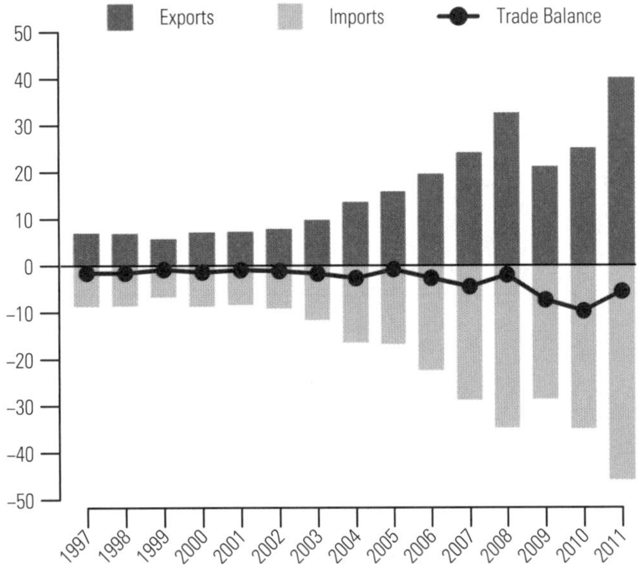

Exports Profile:

Mineral fuels, lubricants and related materials (SITC section 3) was the largest commodity group for exports in 2011 with 35.5 percent of total exports (see table 1). Other major commodity groups were chemicals and related products, n.e.s. (SITC section 5) and machinery and transport equipment (SITC section 7), respectively with 17.6 and 15.8 percent of exports. Major markets for exports were Russian Federation, the Netherlands and Ukraine (see table 4). From 2009 to 2011, top exported products were petroleum oils, other than crude (HS code 2710), mineral or chemical fertilisers, potassic (HS code 3104) and tractors (other than tractors of heading 87.09) (HS code 8701) (see table 3).

Table 1: Exports by SITC sections

(Value in million US$, growth and shares in percentage)

SITC	2011	Avg. Growth rates (%) 2007-2011	2010-2011	2011 share
Total	40294.0	13.5	59.7	100.0
0+1	3748.8	21.2	20.0	9.3
2+4	811.8	8.1	18.0	2.0
3	14322.7	13.9	101.8	35.5
5	7107.8	30.3	90.5	17.6
6	4844.8	5.3	28.1	12.0
7	6354.0	5.8	46.7	15.8
8	1881.0	5.8	18.6	4.7
9	1223.3	27.2	38.0	3.0

Table 2: Imports by SITC sections

(Value in million US$, growth and shares in percentage)

SITC	2011	Avg. Growth rates (%) 2007-2011	2010-2011	2011 share
Total	45747.1	12.4	31.2	100.0
0+1	2856.8	10.5	11.4	6.2
2+4	1855.2	14.4	29.0	4.1
3	18736.4	16.8	55.7	41.0
5	4078.4	12.0	13.0	8.9
6	6107.5	6.9	15.9	13.4
7	7963.9	7.5	17.9	17.4
8	1591.4	8.6	12.7	3.5
9	2557.4	20.2	43.1	5.6

Table 3: Top 10 export commodities 2009 to 2011

(Value in million US$)

HS code	4-digit heading of Harmonized System 2007	Value (million US$) 2009	2010	2011	Unit value 2009	2010	2011	Unit	SITC code
	All Commodities	21282.2	25225.9	40294.0					
2710	Petroleum oils, other than crude	7005.1	6751.7	12537.4	0.5	0.6	0.8	US$/kg	334
3104	Mineral or chemical fertilisers, potassic	1357.9	2225.6	3351.4	0.5	0.3	0.4	US$/kg	562
8701	Tractors (other than tractors of heading 87.09)	626.7	790.2	1390.2	15.2	18.2	21.7	thsd US$/unit	722
8704	Motor vehicles for the transport of goods	410.9	813.3	1369.8	137.6	118.4	116.5	thsd US$/unit	782
9999	Commodities not specified according to kind	445.0	886.2	1223.3					931
3814	Organic composite solvents and thinners	549.6	158.6	1570.6	0.4	0.7	0.8	US$/kg	533
2709	Petroleum oils and oils obtained from bituminous minerals, crude	738.1	...	1319.6	0.4		0.8	US$/kg	333
0406	Cheese and curd	394.7	524.5	557.3	3.3	4.4	4.6	US$/kg	024
4011	New pneumatic tyres, of rubber	346.1	464.0	634.3	90.9	124.9	170.7	US$/unit	625
7214	Other bars and rods of iron or non-alloy steel	356.9	411.0	567.6	0.4	0.5	0.7	US$/kg	676

Graph 2: Trade Balance by MDG Regions in 2011

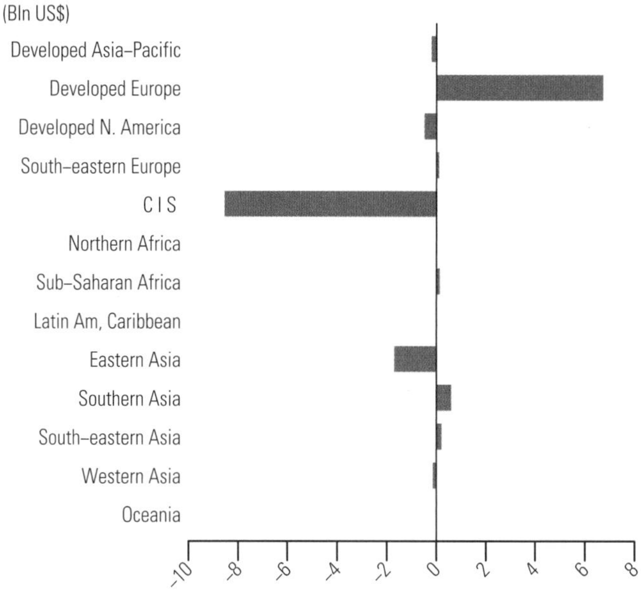

Graph 3: Partner concentration of trade in 2011

(Cumulative share by ranked partners)

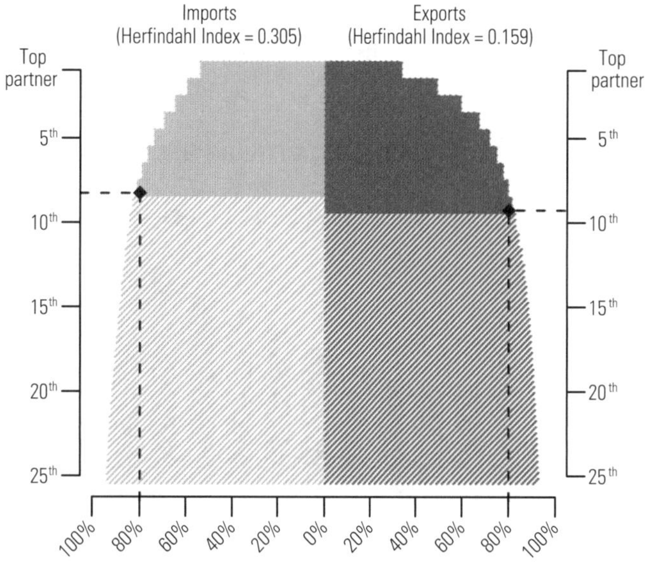

Table 4: Exports by principal countries and SITC sections in 2011

(Value in million US$, percentages of country total)

Country	Total	Shares by SITC sections (%) 0 + 1	2 + 4	3	5	6	7	8	9	Total
World	40294.0	9.3	2.0	35.5	17.6	12.0	15.8	4.7	3.0	100
Russian Federation	13574.0	23.2	1.7	0.8	5.3	19.4	33.3	10.1	6.3	100
Netherlands	6157.8	0.1	0.2	88.9	9.7	0.9	0.0	0.2	...	100
Ukraine	4154.9	2.3	0.9	69.6	6.1	7.4	11.7	2.0	...	100
Latvia	3150.6	0.3	0.9	53.5	38.5	5.9	0.6	0.3	...	100
Germany	1819.3	1.2	4.0	71.8	3.1	11.6	2.0	6.3	...	100
Brazil	1224.1	0.0	0.0	...	99.0	1.0	0.0	0.0	...	100
Poland	1122.1	2.1	12.4	41.5	22.1	12.5	8.7	0.7	...	100
Lithuania	859.3	7.4	8.0	35.8	19.3	18.4	7.1	3.9	...	100
China	632.1	0.1	2.4	...	84.9	2.2	10.0	0.5	...	100
Kazakhstan	625.9	27.8	0.8	0.1	6.4	19.0	33.5	11.9	0.5	100

Imports Profile:

Similar to exports, mineral fuels, lubricants and related materials (SITC section 3) was the largest commodity group for imports in 2011 with 41.0 percent of total imports (see table 2). Other major commodity groups were machinery and transport equipment (SITC section 7) and manufactured goods classified chiefly by material (SITC section 6), respectively with 17.4 and 13.4 percent of imports. In addition to petroleum oils and oils obtained from bituminous minerals, crude (HS code 2709), other major products for imports over the last three years included petroleum gases and other gaseous hydrocarbons (HS code 2711) and petroleum oils, other than crude (HS code 2710) (see table 5).

Table 5: Top 10 import commodities 2009 to 2011

(Value in million US$)

HS code	4-digit heading of Harmonized System 2007	Value (million US$) 2009	2010	2011	Unit value 2009	2010	2011	Unit	SITC code
	All Commodities	28563.6	34868.2	45747.1					
2709	Petroleum oils and oils obtained from bituminous minerals, crude	7065.0	6757.7	9387.5	0.3	0.5	0.5	US$/kg	333
2711	Petroleum gases and other gaseous hydrocarbons	2676.3	4188.0	5434.4	0.2	0.3	*0.4*	US$/kg	343
2710	Petroleum oils, other than crude	1320.8	903.2	3487.4	*0.3*	0.6	*0.6*	US$/kg	334
9999	Commodities not specified according to kind	992.2	1787.1	2557.4					931
7204	Ferrous waste and scrap; remelting scrap ingots of iron or steel	277.9	475.5	580.3	0.2	0.3	*0.4*	US$/kg	282
8703	Motor cars and other motor vehicles principally designed for the transport	578.6	140.4	571.9	6.6	14.9	19.3	thsd US$/unit	781
3004	Medicaments (excluding goods of heading 30.02, 30.05 or 30.06)	408.8	401.8	417.4	51.2	54.4	65.2	US$/kg	542
8408	Compression-ignition internal combustion piston engines	189.3	347.2	468.3	7.2	9.1	9.0	thsd US$/unit	713
8708	Parts and accessories of the motor vehicles of headings 87.01 to 87.05	206.3	277.2	342.3	*4.4*	*4.8*	*4.8*	US$/kg	784
7208	Flat-rolled products of iron or non-alloy steel	152.0	285.4	351.8	0.5	0.6	0.8	US$/kg	673

Belgium

Imports: CIF, by origin/consignment for intra-eu | **Exports: FOB, by last known destination** | **Trade System: Special**

Overview:

From 2007 to 2011, Belgium's exports increased on average by 2.6 percent each year and amounted to 477.9 bln US$ in 2011 (see table 1 and graph 1). Similarly, imports increased on average by 3.0 percent each year and reached 465.2 bln US$ (see table 2 and graph 1). This resulted in a trade surplus of 12.7 bln US$ (see graph 1). This surplus was accounted for largely by trade with Developed Europe: trade with this region recorded a surplus of 27.3 bln US$ (see graph 2). Large deficits were recorded with Eastern Asia (-7.9 bln US$), Commonwealth of Independent States (-5.0 bln US$) and South-eastern Asia (-4.2 bln US$). In 2011, both exports and imports were diversified across partners: 17 major partners accounted for 80 percent of exports and 15 partners accounted for 80 percent of imports (see graph 3).

Graph 1: Total imports, exports and trade balance

(Bln US$ by year)

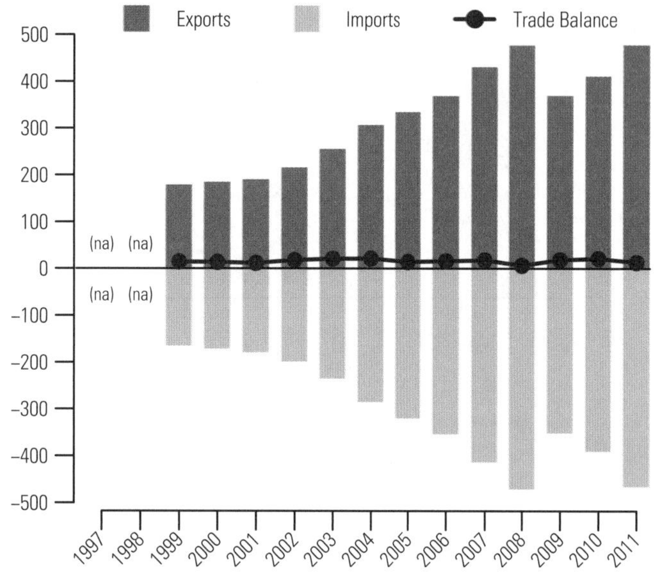

Exports Profile:

In 2011, chemicals and related products, n.e.s. (SITC section 5) accounted for 28.3 percent of exported goods (see table 1). Other major commodity groups included machinery and transport equipment (SITC section 7) and manufactured goods classified chiefly by material (SITC section 6), respectively with 20.6 and 17.8 percent of exported goods. Germany, France and the Netherlands were the top three partners for exports (see table 4). They accounted jointly for nearly half of exported goods in 2011 (46.8 percent). Over the last three years, the main products for exports were medicaments (excluding goods of heading 30.02, 30.05 or 30.06) (HS code 3004), petroleum oils, other than crude (HS code 2710) and motor cars and other motor vehicles principally designed for the transport (HS code 8703) (see table 3).

Table 1: Exports by SITC sections

(Value in million US$, growth and shares in percentage)

SITC	2011	Avg. Growth rates (%) 2007-2011	2010-2011	2011 share
Total	477925.2	2.6	16.3	100.0
0+1	39784.4	4.8	14.4	8.3
2+4	15063.4	5.2	21.3	3.2
3	51670.3	16.0	42.6	10.8
5	135468.3	2.7	8.0	28.3
6	85120.0	-0.6	18.6	17.8
7	98468.1	-0.9	17.7	20.6
8	40880.5	3.2	12.0	8.6
9	11470.1	4.0	11.2	2.4

Table 2: Imports by SITC sections

(Value in million US$, growth and shares in percentage)

SITC	2011	Avg. Growth rates (%) 2007-2011	2010-2011	2011 share
Total	465216.1	3.0	19.3	100.0
0+1	34513.0	4.4	17.3	7.4
2+4	23169.1	5.7	25.7	5.0
3	76371.5	12.7	40.6	16.4
5	104853.5	0.9	5.7	22.5
6	74041.2	0.7	29.2	15.9
7	105455.8	0.3	16.4	22.7
8	39836.9	2.0	12.0	8.6
9	6975.0	11.8	32.5	1.5

Table 3: Top 10 export commodities 2009 to 2011

(Value in million US$)

HS code	4-digit heading of Harmonized System 2007	Value (million US$) 2009	2010	2011	Unit value 2009	2010	2011	Unit	SITC code
	All Commodities	369950.1	411084.8	477925.2					
3004	Medicaments (excluding goods of heading 30.02, 30.05 or 30.06)	38992.1	35929.6	35160.0	*186.7*	*187.0*	*181.1*	US$/kg	542
2710	Petroleum oils, other than crude	17301.6	23715.3	35776.9	*0.5*	*0.6*	*0.9*	US$/kg	334
8703	Motor cars and other motor vehicles principally designed for the transport	23989.1	23487.9	28473.2	17.1	17.8	19.3	thsd US$/unit	781
7102	Diamonds, whether or not worked, but not mounted or set	11092.8	16546.2	20286.5	111.9	128.0	190.5	US$/carat	667
2933	Heterocyclic compounds with nitrogen hetero-atom(s) only	10065.8	9303.4	9648.2	*22.2*	*19.2*	*19.6*	US$/kg	515
3002	Human blood; animal blood prepared for therapeutic uses	9421.8	8740.7	9430.0	*1.1*	*0.8*	*1.0*	thsd US$/kg	541
9999	Commodities not specified according to kind	8464.8	9400.8	9367.3					931
2711	Petroleum gases and other gaseous hydrocarbons	5100.3	7208.1	9678.4	*0.6*	*0.5*	*0.4*	US$/kg	343
8708	Parts and accessories of the motor vehicles of headings 87.01 to 87.05	5378.8	6253.3	7084.6	*8.5*	*8.6*	*8.8*	US$/kg	784
3901	Polymers of ethylene, in primary forms	4742.8	6172.8	6875.4	1.4	*1.7*	2.0	US$/kg	571

Graph 2: Trade Balance by MDG Regions in 2011

(Bln US$)

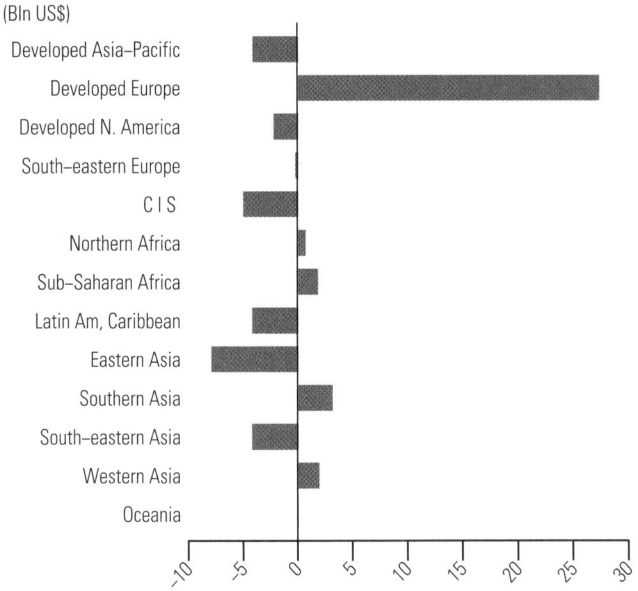

Graph 3: Partner concentration of trade in 2011

(Cumulative share by ranked partners)

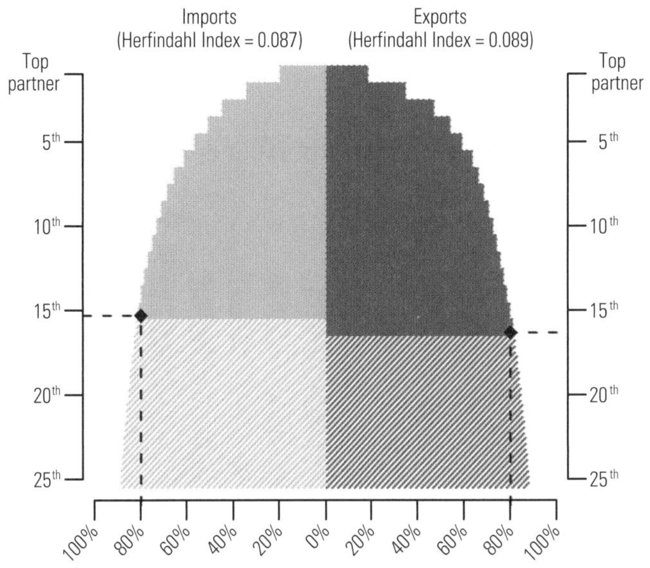

Table 4: Exports by principal countries and SITC sections in 2011

(Value in million US$, percentages of country total)

Country	Total	Shares by SITC sections (%) 0+1	2+4	3	5	6	7	8	9	Total
World	477925.2	8.3	3.2	10.8	28.3	17.8	20.6	8.6	2.4	100
Germany	87014.4	7.3	3.3	9.6	35.2	17.9	18.8	5.9	2.0	100
France	78493.0	11.4	3.4	11.0	22.1	18.0	18.2	14.6	1.3	100
Netherlands	58140.3	14.5	4.5	22.9	16.6	14.8	16.1	8.0	2.6	100
United Kingdom	33344.5	9.0	1.7	7.4	25.1	14.0	31.8	8.6	2.4	100
USA	24205.4	2.0	0.7	9.2	49.0	10.5	20.3	6.6	1.7	100
Italy	21427.0	7.2	2.2	1.0	45.2	12.2	18.2	11.8	2.2	100
Spain	12721.3	8.4	2.7	2.5	36.5	12.8	20.0	15.1	1.9	100
India	11092.5	0.2	1.6	1.0	5.7	83.8	4.4	2.1	1.2	100
China	10219.9	0.9	10.7	5.8	21.7	23.0	31.4	3.1	3.5	100
Luxembourg	8654.0	11.6	6.0	33.0	9.6	13.3	20.0	5.5	1.0	100

Imports Profile:

Imports were composed of 22.7 percent of machinery and transport equipment (SITC section 7), 22.5 percent of chemicals and related products, n.e.s. (SITC section 5) and 16.4 percent of mineral fuels, lubricants and related materials (SITC section 3) (see table 2) The three main products for imports over the last three years were medicaments (excluding goods of heading 30.02, 30.05 or 30.06) (HS code 3004), motor cars and other motor vehicles principally designed for the transport (HS code 8703) and petroleum oils and oils obtained from bituminous minerals, crude (HS code 2709) (see table 5).

Table 5: Top 10 import commodities 2009 to 2011

(Value in million US$)

HS code	4-digit heading of Harmonized System 2007	Value (million US$) 2009	2010	2011	Unit value 2009	2010	2011	Unit	SITC code
	All Commodities	351781.0	390091.1	465216.1					
3004	Medicaments (excluding goods of heading 30.02, 30.05 or 30.06)	33484.0	30789.6	25590.4	*165.3*	*162.4*	*128.3*	US$/kg	542
8703	Motor cars and other motor vehicles principally designed for the transport	22679.5	24619.6	26623.3	18.1	18.2	20.3	thsd US$/unit	781
2709	Petroleum oils and oils obtained from bituminous minerals, crude	14511.0	20459.3	27400.2	*0.4*	0.6	*0.8*	US$/kg	333
2710	Petroleum oils, other than crude	15050.4	17841.9	27820.9	*0.5*	*0.7*	*0.9*	US$/kg	334
7102	Diamonds, whether or not worked, but not mounted or set	10064.0	14321.0	21458.3	111.4	124.5	186.2	US$/carat	667
2711	Petroleum gases and other gaseous hydrocarbons	9361.1	12594.0	16824.0	*0.3*	*0.4*	*0.5*	US$/kg	343
8708	Parts and accessories of the motor vehicles of headings 87.01 to 87.05	7836.2	9030.5	10766.0	*8.4*	*8.1*	*8.4*	US$/kg	784
2933	Heterocyclic compounds with nitrogen hetero-atom(s) only	8652.3	7845.4	10883.0	*93.3*	*71.5*	*92.8*	US$/kg	515
3002	Human blood; animal blood prepared for therapeutic uses	5367.2	6418.6	6392.5	*1.1*	*1.1*	*1.0*	thsd US$/kg	541
9999	Commodities not specified according to kind	3587.2	4396.6	5649.6					931

Belize

Imports: CIF, by origin | **Exports: FOB, by last known destination** | **Trade System: General**

Overview:

In 2010, Belize's exports increased by 13.0 percent and amounted to 282.0 mln US$ (see table 1 and graph 1). Imports increased by 5.2 percent and amounted to 700.0 mln US$ (see table 2 and graph 1). This resulted in a trade deficit of 417.9 mln US$ in 2010 (see graph 1). By MDG regions, the trade balance recorded a surplus amounting to 53.6 mln US$ with Developed Europe (see graph 2). Large deficits were recorded with Developed North America (-201.7 mln US$), Latin America and the Caribbean (-181.2 mln US$) and Eastern Asia (-83.6 mln US$). Both imports and exports were concentrated among a few partners: 4 (respectively 5) major partners accounted for 80 percent of exports (respectively imports) (see graph 3).

Graph 1: Total imports, exports and trade balance

(Mln US$ by year)

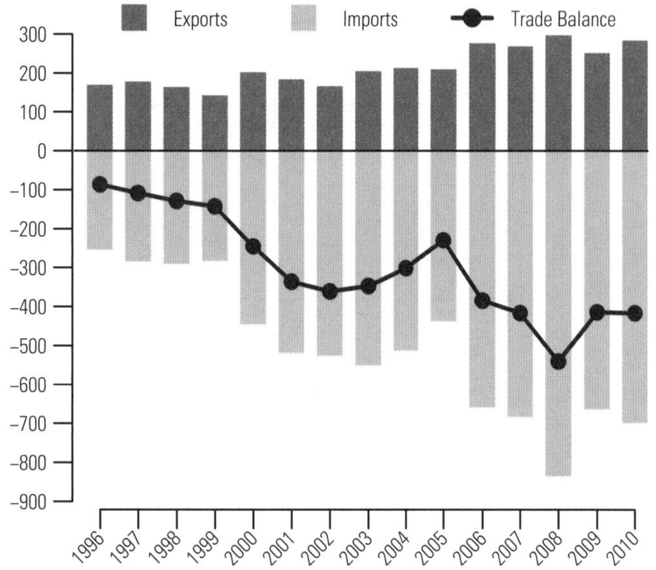

Table 1: Exports by SITC sections

(Value in million US$, growth and shares in percentage)

SITC	2010	Avg. Growth rates (%) 2006-2010	2009-2010	2010 share
Total	282.0	0.7	13.0	100.0
0+1	171.6	-3.7	-1.6	60.9
2+4	4.1	48.3	118.5	1.4
3	102.0	22.7	46.0	36.2
5	2.2	-6.7	-4.2	0.8
6	1.4	-17.7	36.9	0.5
7	0.0	-61.6	18.5	0.0
8	0.2	-39.7	150.2	0.1
9	0.5	-61.0	567.2	0.2

Table 2: Imports by SITC sections

(Value in million US$, growth and shares in percentage)

SITC	2010	Avg. Growth rates (%) 2006-2010	2009-2010	2010 share
Total	700.0	1.5	5.2	100.0
0+1	112.6	9.4	17.1	16.1
2+4	10.7	9.6	12.7	1.5
3	114.6	1.8	9.4	16.4
5	66.3	9.1	3.7	9.5
6	102.0	5.7	11.5	14.6
7	122.1	2.8	-9.9	17.4
8	138.9	28.3	66.2	19.8
9	32.8	-34.6	-59.1	4.7

Exports Profile:

In 2010, food, live animals, beverages and tobacco (SITC sections 0+1) accounted for the majority of exported goods representing 60.9 percent of total exports (see table 1). Exports of mineral fuels, lubricants and related materials (SITC section 3) increased by 46.0 percent and represented 36.2 percent of exports. Top partners for exports in 2010 were the USA, the United Kingdom and Costa Rica (see table 4). Exports to the United Kingdom were exclusively food, live animals, beverages and tobacco (SITC sections 0+1) while exports to Costa Rica were exclusively mineral fuels, lubricants and related materials (SITC section 3). Top products for exports from 2008 to 2010 included petroleum oils, crude (HS code 2709), fruit juices (including grape must) and vegetable juices (HS code 2009) and bananas, including plantains (HS code 0803) (see table 3).

Table 3: Top 10 export commodities 2008 to 2010

(Value in million US$)

HS code	4-digit heading of Harmonized System 2002	Value (million US$) 2008	2009	2010	Unit value 2008	2009	2010	Unit	SITC code
	All Commodities	295.1	249.7	282.0					
2709	Petroleum oils, crude	118.3	63.6	100.6	0.3	0.4	0.6	US$/kg	333
2009	Fruit juices (including grape must) and vegetable juices	57.5	50.5	42.8	0.7	0.9	1.6	US$/kg	059
0803	Bananas, including plantains	33.4	33.3	41.3	0.2	0.4	0.7	US$/kg	057
1701	Cane or beet sugar and pure sucrose, in solid form	35.7	38.8	29.4	0.2	0.6	0.5	US$/kg	061
0306	Crustaceans, whether in shell or not	21.5	24.9	26.7	2.5	4.6	4.7	US$/kg	036
0807	Melons (including watermelons) and papaws (papayas), fresh	11.3	16.5	12.7	0.2	0.5	0.4	US$/kg	057
0713	Dried leguminous vegetables, shelled	4.0	4.4	5.6	0.4	0.6	0.8	US$/kg	054
2710	Petroleum oils, other than crude	0.5	6.3	1.4	0.3	0.5	*0.6*	US$/kg	334
0303	Fish, frozen, excluding fish fillets	2.0	0.9	3.6	0.7	1.4	3.0	US$/kg	034
3301	Essential oils (terpeneless or not), including concretes	2.0	2.3	2.2	1.1	1.5	1.9	US$/kg	551

Graph 2: Trade Balance by MDG Regions in 2010

(Mln US$)

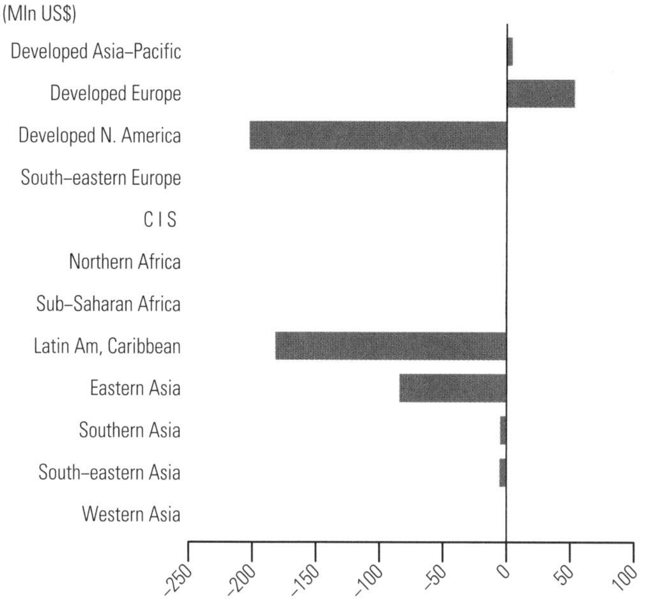

Graph 3: Partner concentration of trade in 2010

(Cumulative share by ranked partners)

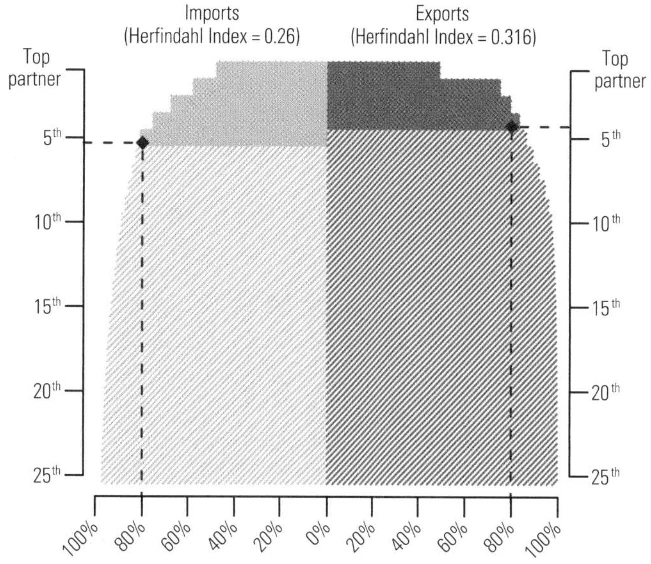

Table 4: Exports by principal countries and SITC sections in 2010

(Value in million US$, percentages of country total)

Country	Total	Shares by SITC sections (%)								
		0 + 1	2 + 4	3	5	6	7	8	9	Total
World	282.0	60.9	1.4	36.2	0.8	0.5	0.0	0.1	0.2	100
USA	138.5	32.8	1.4	63.5	1.3	0.8	0.0	0.1	0.2	100
United Kingdom	73.6	100.0	0.0	...	...	...	...	0.0	...	100
Costa Rica	12.6	0.0	0.0	100.0	...	...	...	...	...	100
Netherlands	10.3	95.7	2.6	...	...	...	...	...	1.8	100
Japan	8.2	99.7	0.0	...	...	0.3	...	...	...	100
Mexico	7.9	93.9	5.8	...	0.2	...	...	0.1	...	100
Trinidad and Tobago	7.6	98.6	0.0	...	0.1	1.4	...	...	...	100
Jamaica	7.3	98.5	0.7	...	0.1	0.4	...	0.0	0.3	100
Guatemala	4.4	65.1	1.7	32.6	0.5	...	0.0	...	...	100
Spain	3.5	100.0	0.0	...	...	...	...	...	...	100

Imports Profile:

In 2010, Belize's imports were composed of 19.8 percent of miscellaneous manufactured articles (SITC section 8), 17.4 percent of machinery and transport equipment (SITC section 7) and 16.4 percent of mineral fuels, lubricants and related materials (SITC section 3). From 2008 to 2010, major products for imports were petroleum oils, other than crude (HS code 2710), motor vehicles for the transport of goods (HS code 8704) and motor cars and other motor vehicles principally designed for the transport (HS code 8703) (see table 5).

Table 5: Top 10 import commodities 2008 to 2010

(Value in million US$)

HS code	4-digit heading of Harmonized System 2002	Value (million US$)			Unit value				SITC code
		2008	2009	2010	2008	2009	2010	Unit	
	All Commodities	836.5	665.1	700.0					
2710	Petroleum oils, other than crude	120.6	95.9	104.3	0.5	0.6	0.8	US$/kg	334
9999	Commodities not specified according to kind	187.5	80.2	32.8					931
8704	Motor vehicles for the transport of goods	17.1	9.8	8.2	*16.7*			thsd US$/unit	782
8703	Motor cars and other motor vehicles principally designed for the transport	15.0	10.6	8.7	*17.9*	*18.7*	*18.1*	thsd US$/unit	781
2711	Petroleum gases and other gaseous hydrocarbons	14.5	8.7	10.2	0.4	0.7	0.9	US$/kg	343
8517	Electrical apparatus for line telephony or line telegraphy	18.1	7.0	8.1					764
2523	Portland cement, aluminous cement, slag cement	9.3	10.4	10.1	0.0	0.1	0.1	US$/kg	661
2208	Alcohol of a strength by volume of less than 80 % vol	12.9	5.2	10.1	*1.2*	*7.9*	*16.8*	US$/litre	112
3808	Insecticides, rodenticides, fungicides, herbicides	9.4	9.4	9.2	1.9	3.9	4.3	US$/kg	591
4819	Cartons, boxes, cases, bags and other packing containers, of paper	7.7	8.4	11.3	0.4	0.9	1.3	US$/kg	642

Imports: CIF, by origin | **Exports: FOB, by last known destination** | **Trade System: General**

Overview:

From 2006 to 2010, exports of Benin increased on average by 17.9 percent each year and amounted to 434.5 mln US$ in 2010 (see table 1 and graph 1). During the same period, imports increased on average by 10.5 percent each year and reached 1.5 bln US$ resulting in a trade deficit of 1.1 bln US$ (see table 2 and graph 1). By MDG regions, Developed Europe accounted for a large share of this deficit with 622.2 mln US$. Trade deficits were also recorded with Eastern Asia (-155.1 mln US$) and South-eastern Asia (-95.8 mln US$) (see graph 2). In 2010, trade was diversified across partners: 8 major partners accounted for 80 percent of exports and 15 major partners accounted for 80 percent of imports (see graph 3).

Graph 1: Total imports, exports and trade balance

(Bln US$ by year)

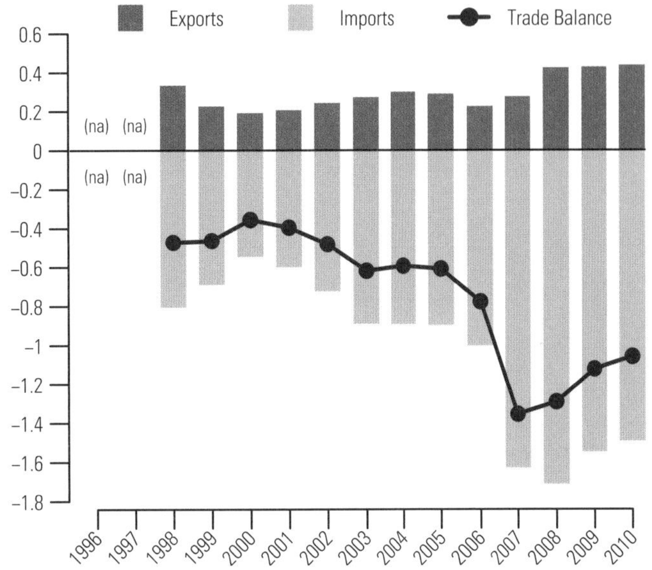

Table 1: Exports by SITC sections

(Value in million US$, growth and shares in percentage)

SITC	2010	Avg. Growth rates (%) 2006-2010	Avg. Growth rates (%) 2009-2010	2010 share
Total	434.5	17.9	2.1	100.0
0+1	241.4	38.2	37.9	55.6
2+4	129.0	1.8	-24.7	29.7
3	0.0	-52.5	23.4	0.0
5	3.8	12.2	-1.3	0.9
6	34.8	9.5	-34.6	8.0
7	23.8	68.9	21.1	5.5
8	1.6	8.2	-29.4	0.4

Exports Profile:

In 2010, exports of food, live animals, beverages and tobacco (SITC sections 0+1) increased by 37.9 percent and accounted for 55.6 percent of exported goods (see table 1). Meanwhile, inedible crude materials (except fuels), animal and vegetable oils, fats and waxes (SITC sections 2+4) dropped by 24.7 percent and still accounted for 29.7 percent of exported goods. Nigeria, China and India were the three major partners for exports in 2010 (see table 4). Exports to Nigeria were almost exclusively food, live animals, beverages and tobacco at 87.4 percent (SITC sections 0+1). Exports to China were almost exclusively inedible crude materials (except fuels), animal and vegetable oils, fats and waxes (SITC sections 2+4) at 94.7 percent. From 2008 to 2010, top exported products were cotton, not carded or combed (HS code 5201), meat and edible offal, of the poultry of heading 01.05 (HS code 0207) and rice (HS code 1006) (see table 3).

Table 2: Imports by SITC sections

(Value in million US$, growth and shares in percentage)

SITC	2010	Avg. Growth rates (%) 2006-2010	Avg. Growth rates (%) 2009-2010	2010 share
Total	1 494.3	10.5	-3.5	100.0
0+1	384.4	8.7	-5.7	25.7
2+4	153.6	15.8	12.0	10.3
3	308.8	9.2	19.7	20.7
5	110.8	12.1	-21.4	7.4
6	230.8	8.0	-10.6	15.4
7	214.6	17.3	-11.2	14.4
8	91.3	7.1	-13.7	6.1
9	0.1	-61.9	53.3	0.0

Table 3: Top 10 export commodities 2008 to 2010

(Value in million US$)

HS code	4-digit heading of Harmonized System 2002	Value (million US$) 2008	2009	2010	Unit value 2008	2009	2010	Unit	SITC code
	All Commodities	421.1	425.3	434.5					
5201	Cotton, not carded or combed	156.6	128.3	97.5	1.4	1.5	1.4	US$/kg	263
0207	Meat and edible offal, of the poultry of heading 01.05	...	67.0	93.2		1.8	1.7	US$/kg	012
1006	Rice	11.2	38.1	90.6	0.4	0.3	0.2	US$/kg	042
0801	Coconuts, Brazil nuts and cashew nuts, fresh or dried	28.0	29.5	23.7	0.5	0.5	0.4	US$/kg	057
7215	Other bars and rods of iron or non-alloy steel	30.0	16.2	12.7	1.0	0.7	0.7	US$/kg	676
1516	Animal or vegetable fats and oils	27.0	16.1	4.2	1.5	1.1	1.0	US$/kg	431
8905	Light-vessels, fire-floats, dredgers, floating cranes and other vessels	43.4	...	...					793
7213	Bars and rods, hot-rolled, in irregularly wound coils	10.9	16.4	10.2	0.9	0.7	0.6	US$/kg	676
1511	Palm oil and its fractions	10.3	15.8	5.1	1.4	0.6	0.9	US$/kg	422
2402	Cigars, cheroots, cigarillos and cigarettes	14.1	14.5	...	18.7	17.7		US$/kg	122

Graph 2: Trade Balance by MDG Regions in 2010

(Mln US$)

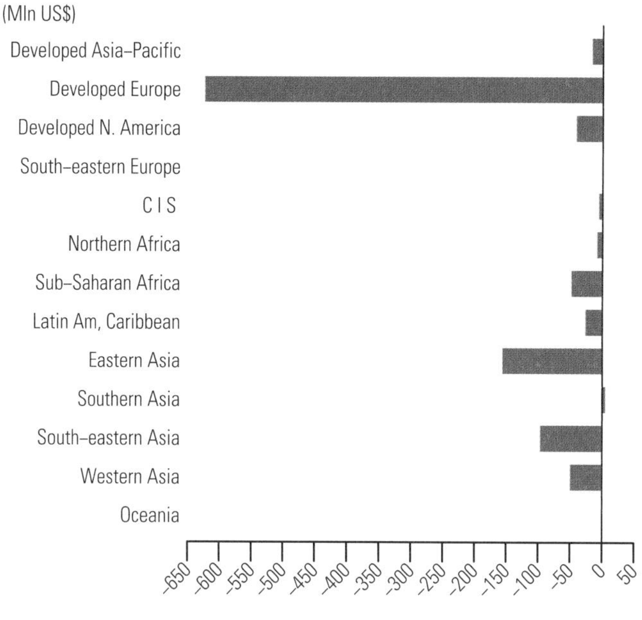

Graph 3: Partner concentration of trade in 2010

(Cumulative share by ranked partners)

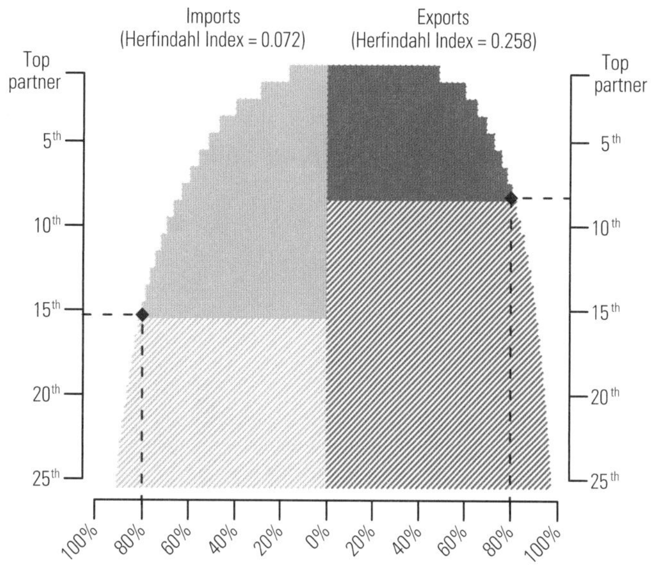

Table 4: Exports by principal countries and SITC sections in 2010

(Value in million US$, percentages of country total)

Country	Total	Shares by SITC sections (%)								
		0+1	2+4	3	5	6	7	8	9	Total
World	434.5	55.6	29.7	0.0	0.9	8.0	5.5	0.4	...	100
Nigeria	210.8	87.4	7.3	0.0	0.3	3.6	1.4	0.0	...	100
China	50.6	2.6	94.7	...	...	2.5	0.0	0.2	...	100
India	22.5	69.2	26.2	...	0.2	4.4	...	...	...	100
Chad	17.7	0.0	0.0	...	1.3	93.0	5.7	...	...	100
Indonesia	14.7	0.0	99.6	...	...	0.3	...	0.1	...	100
Niger	14.0	73.1	3.0	...	0.2	22.4	0.9	0.4	...	100
Viet Nam	10.0	5.2	94.5	...	...	0.2	...	0.2	...	100
Togo	8.8	56.5	5.4	0.4	9.0	3.6	23.7	1.5	...	100
Portugal	7.8	57.1	42.8	...	...	0.0	...	0.1	...	100
Malaysia	7.6	0.0	99.8	...	...	0.1	...	0.1	...	100

Imports Profile:

In 2010, Benin's imports were composed of 25.7 percent of food, live animals, beverages and tobacco (SITC sections 0+1), 20.7 percent of mineral fuels, lubricants and related materials (SITC section 3) and 15.4 percent of manufactured goods classified chiefly by material (SITC section 6) (see table 2). From 2008 to 2010, top imported products included petroleum oils, other than crude (HS code 2710), meat and edible offal, of the poultry of heading 01.05 (HS code 0207) and rice (HS code 1006) (see table 5).

Table 5: Top 10 import commodities 2008 to 2010

(Value in million US$)

HS code	4-digit heading of Harmonized System 2002	Value (million US$)			Unit value				SITC code
		2008	2009	2010	2008	2009	2010	Unit	
	All Commodities	1713.6	1549.0	1494.3					
2710	Petroleum oils, other than crude	170.2	153.2	182.1	0.4	0.3	0.6	US$/kg	334
0207	Meat and edible offal, of the poultry of heading 01.05	123.5	144.6	138.8	1.3	1.3	1.2	US$/kg	012
1006	Rice	184.7	91.5	78.6	0.3	0.1	0.1	US$/kg	042
2716	Electrical energy	74.3	96.9	113.4	*53.2*	*82.5*	*57.1*	US$/MWh	351
1511	Palm oil and its fractions	76.9	67.2	72.6	0.5	0.4	0.4	US$/kg	422
7213	Bars and rods, hot-rolled, in irregularly wound coils	82.3	58.0	39.7	0.9	0.5	0.6	US$/kg	676
3004	Medicaments (excluding goods of heading 30.02, 30.05 or 30.06)	50.3	57.1	56.9	21.3	15.7	20.1	US$/kg	542
6309	Worn clothing and other worn articles	58.2	51.6	52.0	1.1	1.1	1.0	US$/kg	269
8703	Motor cars and other motor vehicles principally designed for the transport	53.9	50.4	48.0		*12.3*	*13.1*	thsd US$/unit	781
2523	Portland cement, aluminous cement, slag cement	27.0	39.5	45.7	0.0	0.1	0.1	US$/kg	661

Imports: CIF, by origin | **Exports: FOB, by last known destination** | **Trade System: General**

Overview:

In 2010, the value of Bhutan's exports decreased by 16.6 percent and amounted to 413.5 mln US$ (see table 1 and graph 1). On the other hand, the value of imports increased by 61.3 percent amounted to 853.8 mln US$ in 2010 (see table 2 and graph 1). The trade balance recorded a deficit of 440.3 mln US$ in 2010 with Southern Asia accounting for the majority of the deficit with 296.4 mln US$ (see graph 2). Trade was also in deficit with South-eastern Asia (-57.0 mln US$) and Developed Europe (-46.2 mln US$). Trade was highly concentrated among a few partners: in 2010, 1 major partner accounted for 80 percent of exports compared to 2 major partners for imports (see graph 3).

Graph 1: Total imports, exports and trade balance

(Mln US$ by year)

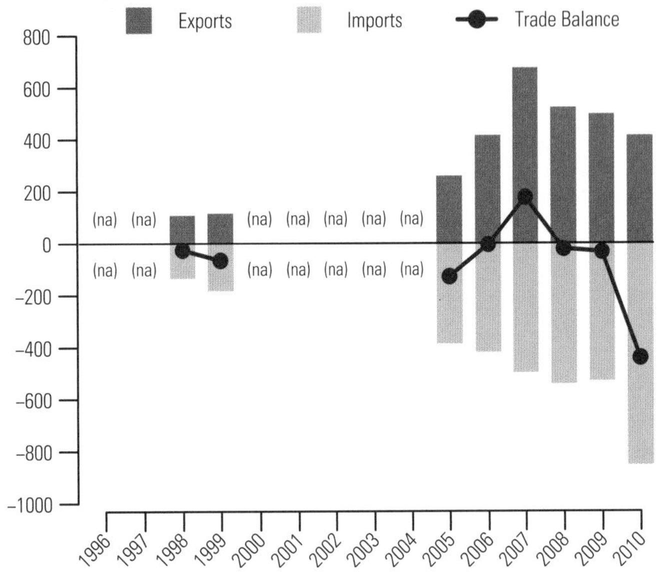

Exports Profile:

In 2010, Bhutan's exports were composed largely of manufactured goods classified chiefly by material (SITC section 6) at 62.2 percent (see table 1). India was the destination of 82.4 percent of Bhutan's exports (see table 4). In addition to India, other major markets for exports included China, Hong Kong SAR, Bangladesh and Japan (see table 4). From 2008 to 2010, top exported commodities were electrical energy (HS code 2716), ginger, saffron, turmeric (curcuma), thyme and other spices (HS code 0910) and ferro-alloys (HS code 7202) (see table 3).

Table 1: Exports by SITC sections

(Value in million US$, growth and shares in percentage)

SITC	2010	Avg. Growth rates (%) 2006-2010	Avg. Growth rates (%) 2009-2010	2010 share
Total	413.5	0.0	-16.6	100.0
0+1	29.3	8.3	-2.6	7.1
2+4	36.6	-7.0	26.2	8.9
3	4.9	-54.4	-97.7	1.2
5	36.9	22.4	32.0	8.9
6	257.4	20.8	39.7	62.2
7	0.1	-53.1	-68.8	0.0
8	48.3	-13.1	249.6	11.7
9	0.0	-72.9	48.0	0.0

Table 2: Imports by SITC sections

(Value in million US$, growth and shares in percentage)

SITC	2010	Avg. Growth rates (%) 2006-2010	Avg. Growth rates (%) 2009-2010	2010 share
Total	853.8	19.5	61.3	100.0
0+1	86.0	13.9	26.4	10.1
2+4	73.2	15.2	59.2	8.6
3	130.1	18.7	40.2	15.2
5	40.7	9.9	48.4	4.8
6	200.2	14.9	85.9	23.4
7	287.2	29.7	79.4	33.6
8	35.9	22.3	44.4	4.2
9	0.3	32.3	-86.0	0.0

Table 3: Top 10 export commodities 2008 to 2010

(Value in million US$)

HS code	4-digit heading of Harmonized System 2007	Value (million US$) 2008	2009	2010	Unit value 2008	2009	2010	Unit	SITC code
	All Commodities	521.4	495.8	413.5					
2716	Electrical energy	254.6	208.5	...	*49.9*	38.6		US$/MWh	351
0910	Ginger, saffron, turmeric (curcuma), thyme, bay leaves, curry and other spices	236.1	0.5	0.5	*0.1*	0.3	0.5	US$/kg	075
7202	Ferro-alloys	2.1	90.3	124.9	2.0	1.0	1.3	US$/kg	671
8523	Prepared unrecorded media for sound recording	0.0	12.8	46.9	0.0	1.4	5.1	thsd US$/unit	898
2523	Portland cement, aluminous cement, slag cement	0.1	29.5	30.0	0.1	0.1	0.1	US$/kg	661
7408	Copper wire	...	20.1	37.7		4.0	3.8	US$/kg	682
2849	Carbides, whether or not chemically defined	...	21.0	31.0		0.7	0.8	US$/kg	524
7214	Other bars and rods of iron or non-alloy steel	0.0	18.0	16.1	1.0	0.5	0.7	US$/kg	676
2518	Dolomite, whether or not calcined or sintered	2.7	11.8	16.1	0.0	0.0	0.0	US$/kg	278
0805	Citrus fruit, fresh or dried	5.7	8.0	7.3	0.3	0.3	0.3	US$/kg	057

Graph 2: Trade Balance by MDG Regions in 2010

(Mln US$)

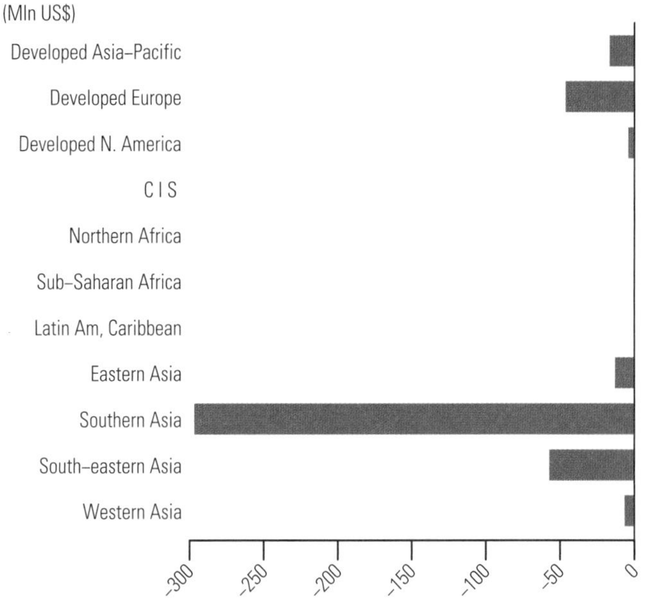

Graph 3: Partner concentration of trade in 2010

(Cumulative share by ranked partners)

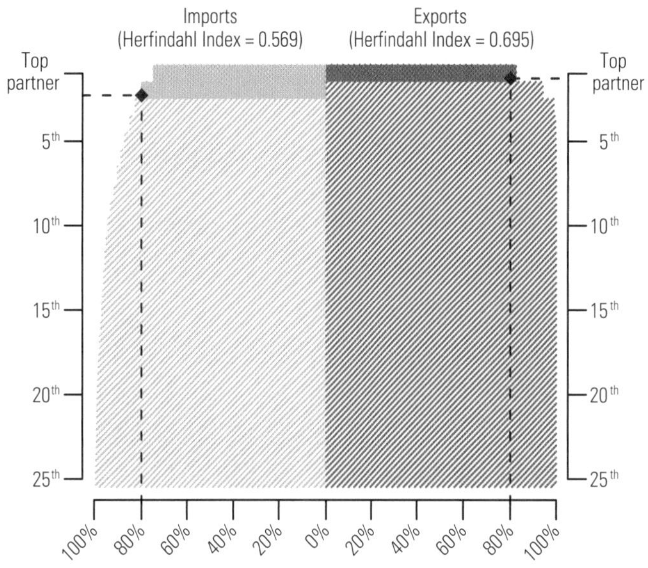

Table 4: Exports by principal countries and SITC sections in 2010

(Value in million US$, percentages of country total)

Country	Total	Shares by SITC sections (%) 0 + 1	2 + 4	3	5	6	7	8	9	Total
World	413.5	7.1	8.9	1.2	8.9	62.2	0.0	11.7	0.0	100
India	340.8	4.9	8.2	1.4	10.8	74.3	0.0	0.4	...	100
China, Hong Kong SAR	47.8	1.9	0.0	...	...	0.0	...	98.1	...	100
Bangladesh	19.8	54.1	42.3	...	...	3.6	...	...	...	100
Japan	2.9	1.9	0.0	...	0.0	98.0	...	...	...	100
Nepal	0.9	34.8	39.7	16.6	...	8.8	...	...	...	100
Singapore	0.4	38.1	0.0	...	0.1	61.6	...	0.1	0.1	100
Italy	0.3	0.0	0.0	...	...	100.0	...	0.0	...	100
USA	0.2	86.0	0.0	...	1.0	2.0	...	3.7	7.3	100
Thailand	0.1	81.5	18.3	...	...	0.1	...	...	...	100
Other Asia, nes	0.1	43.7	0.0	...	10.8	7.4	...	37.8	0.3	100

Imports Profile:

In 2010, imports of machinery and transport equipment (SITC section 7) represented 33.6 percent of imported goods (see table 2). Other major commodity groups included manufactured goods classified chiefly by material (SITC section 6) and mineral fuels, lubricants and related materials (SITC section 3) respectively with 23.4 and 15.2 percent of imports. From 2008 to 2010, top imported products were petroleum oils, other than crude (HS code 2710), motor cars and other motor vehicles principally designed for the transport (HS code 8703) and ferrous products obtained by direct reduction of iron ore (HS code 7203) (see table 5).

Table 5: Top 10 import commodities 2008 to 2010

(Value in million US$)

HS code	4-digit heading of Harmonized System 2007	Value (million US$) 2008	2009	2010	Unit value 2008	2009	2010	Unit	SITC code
	All Commodities	543.3	529.4	853.8					
2710	Petroleum oils, other than crude	64.8	62.4	91.9	*1.0*			US$/kg	334
8703	Motor cars and other motor vehicles principally designed for the transport	35.8	24.7	31.2	9.4	6.8	9.0	thsd US$/unit	781
7203	Ferrous products obtained by direct reduction of iron ore	15.7	20.6	26.9	0.4	0.3	0.4	US$/kg	671
8429	Self-propelled bulldozers, angledozers, graders, levellers, scrapers	10.0	15.2	36.8	*25.0*	10.8	11.1	thsd US$/unit	723
7408	Copper wire	8.4	12.2	40.5	3.4	3.4	5.0	US$/kg	682
8704	Motor vehicles for the transport of goods	6.3	12.8	31.6	17.8	0.0	20.5	thsd US$/unit	782
1006	Rice	16.1	14.9	18.5	0.3	0.3	0.4	US$/kg	042
7204	Ferrous waste and scrap; remelting scrap ingots of iron or steel	12.2	10.7	15.4	*0.5*	0.3	0.4	US$/kg	282
7308	Structures (excluding prefabricated buildings of heading 94.06)	8.4	9.7	19.6	2.0	1.2	1.5	US$/kg	691
4402	Wood charcoal (including shell or nut charcoal), whether or not agglomerated	10.0	11.9	15.5	0.2	0.2	0.2	US$/kg	245

Bolivia (Plurinational State of)

Imports: CIF, by origin | **Exports: FOB, by last known destination** | **Trade System: Special**

Overview:

From 2007 to 2011, the Plurinational State of Bolivia's exports increased on average by 17.3 percent each year and reached its peak of 9.1 bln US$ in 2011 (see table 1 and graph 1). Similarly, imports increased on average by 21.5 percent each year and reached 7.7 bln US$ (see table 2 and graph 1). The trade balance recorded a surplus of 1.4 bln US$ in 2011 (see graph 1). Trade with Latin America and the Caribbean accounted for a large part of this surplus (+1.3 bln US$) (see graph 2). Trade also recorded surpluses with Developed Europe (+388.7 mln US$) and Developed North America (+169.5 mln US$). However, trade recorded a deficit of 300.1 mln US$ with Eastern Asia. Trade was relatively concentrated among a few partners: 9 major partners accounted for 80 percent of both exports and imports (see graph 3).

Graph 1: Total imports, exports and trade balance

(Bln US$ by year)

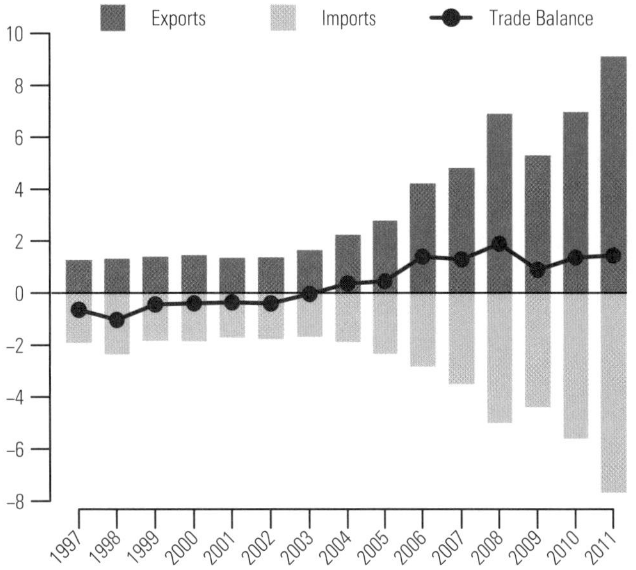

Table 1: Exports by SITC sections

(Value in million US$, growth and shares in percentage)

SITC	2011	Avg. Growth rates (%) 2007-2011	2010-2011	2011 share
Total	9112.7	17.3	30.8	100.0
0+1	745.1	12.5	9.0	8.2
2+4	2901.7	20.1	25.3	31.8
3	4148.7	15.8	37.6	45.5
5	127.8	20.1	-23.2	1.4
6	799.0	26.8	52.6	8.8
7	8.5	82.5	37.2	0.1
8	116.4	-6.2	-27.6	1.3
9	265.4	20.4	180.8	2.9

Exports Profile:

In 2011, mineral fuels, lubricants and related materials (SITC section 3), inedible crude materials (except fuels), animal and vegetable oils, fats and waxes (SITC sections 2+4) and manufactured goods classified chiefly by material (SITC section 6) accounted respectively for 45.5, 31.8 and 8.8 percent of exports (see table 1). Top partners for exports were Brazil, Argentina and USA (see table 4). From 2009 to 2011, the top three commodities for exports were petroleum gases and other gaseous hydrocarbons (HS code 2711), zinc ores and concentrates (HS code 2608) and precious metal ores and concentrates (HS code 2616) (see table 3).

Table 2: Imports by SITC sections

(Value in million US$, growth and shares in percentage)

SITC	2011	Avg. Growth rates (%) 2007-2011	2010-2011	2011 share
Total	7672.7	21.5	36.9	100.0
0+1	613.1	19.7	46.8	8.0
2+4	85.5	-6.7	40.0	1.1
3	1073.5	39.5	56.2	14.0
5	1120.2	16.7	17.3	14.6
6	1360.0	18.4	23.7	17.7
7	2889.4	22.9	51.2	37.7
8	503.0	20.3	13.3	6.6
9	28.0	4.0	-1.2	0.4

Table 3: Top 10 export commodities 2009 to 2011

(Value in million US$)

HS code	4-digit heading of Harmonized System 2007	Value (million US$) 2009	2010	2011	Unit value 2009	2010	2011	Unit	SITC code
	All Commodities	5296.7	6965.4	9112.7					
2711	Petroleum gases and other gaseous hydrocarbons	1967.3	2797.8	3884.9	0.3	0.3	0.4	US$/kg	343
2608	Zinc ores and concentrates	688.8	892.5	944.2	0.9	1.2	1.2	US$/kg	287
2616	Precious metal ores and concentrates	596.2	687.3	1091.1	58.7	58.0	83.8	US$/kg	289
2304	Oil-cake and other solid residues	326.4	321.6	372.8	0.3	0.3	0.4	US$/kg	081
8001	Unwrought tin	205.6	290.1	392.6	13.3	19.7	26.3	US$/kg	687
1507	Soya-bean oil and its fractions	155.7	189.3	261.1	0.8	0.9	1.2	US$/kg	421
2607	Lead ores and concentrates	138.1	156.8	241.0	1.0	1.3	1.4	US$/kg	287
2709	Petroleum oils and oils obtained from bituminous minerals, crude	77.5	186.6	227.6	0.4	0.6	0.8	US$/kg	333
7106	Silver (including silver plated with gold or platinum)	13.8	113.4	291.8	0.4	0.6	1.1	thsd US$/kg	681
0801	Coconuts, Brazil nuts and cashew nuts, fresh or dried	72.8	95.1	148.3	3.4	5.2	8.0	US$/kg	057

Graph 2: Trade Balance by MDG Regions in 2011

(Bln US$)

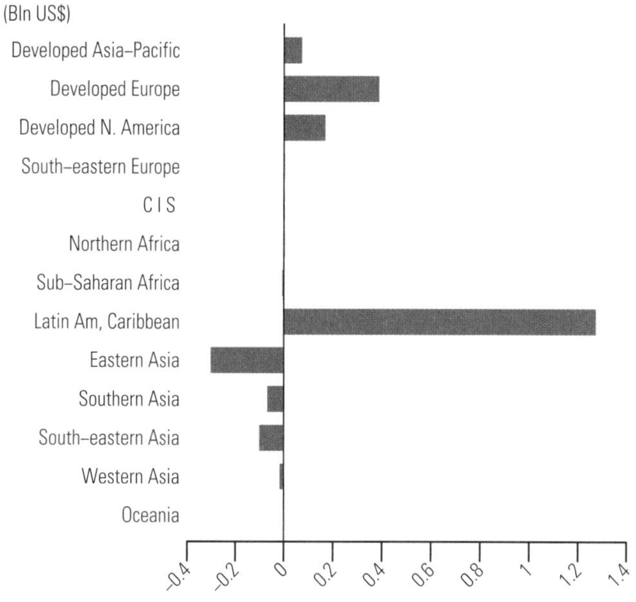

Graph 3: Partner concentration of trade in 2011

(Cumulative share by ranked partners)

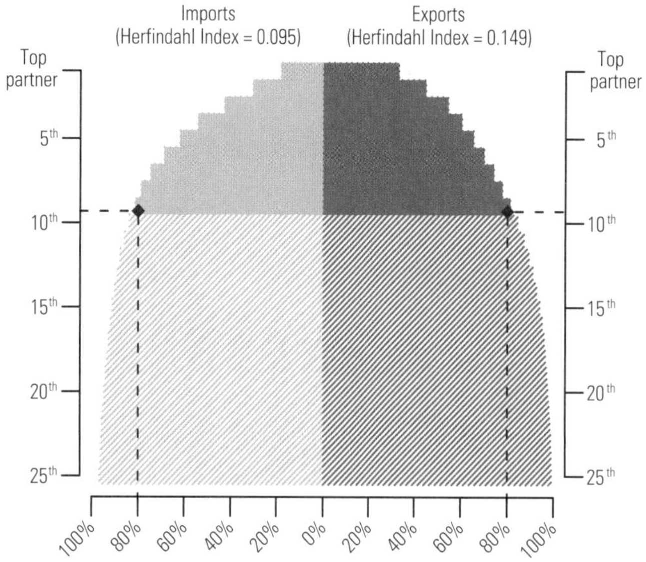

Table 4: Exports by principal countries and SITC sections in 2011

(Value in million US$, percentages of country total)

Country	Total	Shares by SITC sections (%) 0 + 1	2 + 4	3	5	6	7	8	9	Total
World	9112.7	8.2	31.8	45.5	1.4	8.8	0.1	1.3	2.9	100
Brazil	3030.1	0.6	2.0	95.7	0.2	1.4	0.0	0.1	...	100
Argentina	1056.5	2.7	2.4	93.6	0.2	0.6	0.0	0.5	...	100
USA	876.4	9.1	3.0	18.2	3.9	38.2	0.1	7.3	20.3	100
Japan	539.8	0.4	98.5	...	0.0	1.0	...	0.1	...	100
Peru	457.1	18.5	76.0	1.4	2.0	1.3	0.0	0.7	...	100
Rep. of Korea	419.1	0.0	99.5	...	0.0	0.3	...	0.1	...	100
Belgium	375.7	1.7	97.6	...	0.6	0.1	...	0.0	...	100
China	332.9	0.2	73.9	...	0.9	25.0	...	0.0	...	100
Switzerland	306.0	0.4	21.6	0.0	0.0	49.5	...	0.0	28.5	100
Venezuela	290.3	62.3	29.0	0.2	0.8	1.7	1.0	5.1	...	100

Imports Profile:

In 2011, imports were composed of 37.7 percent of machinery and transport equipment (SITC section 7), 17.7 percent of manufactured goods classified chiefly by material (SITC section 6) and 14.6 percent of chemicals and related products, n.e.s. (SITC section 5) (see table 2). From 2009 to 2011, top imported products were petroleum oils, other than crude (HS code 2710), motor cars and other motor vehicles principally designed for the transport (HS code 8703) and motor vehicles for the transport of goods (HS code 8704) (see table 5).

Table 5: Top 10 import commodities 2009 to 2011

(Value in million US$)

HS code	4-digit heading of Harmonized System 2007	Value (million US$) 2009	2010	2011	Unit value 2009	2010	2011	Unit	SITC code
	All Commodities	4409.0	5603.9	7672.7					
2710	Petroleum oils, other than crude	433.0	623.1	967.9	*0.7*	0.8	1.0	US$/kg	334
8703	Motor cars and other motor vehicles principally designed for the transport	187.8	209.7	489.2	*15.7*	*11.7*	*9.4*	thsd US$/unit	781
8704	Motor vehicles for the transport of goods	142.4	155.3	262.8		15.3	12.5	thsd US$/unit	782
3808	Insecticides, rodenticides, fungicides, herbicides	162.4	158.0	162.8	5.2	4.5	4.3	US$/kg	591
7214	Other bars and rods of iron or non-alloy steel	134.2	140.0	189.1	0.7	0.7	0.8	US$/kg	676
8429	Self-propelled bulldozers, angledozers, graders, levellers, scrapers	86.5	133.4	163.5		7.6	4.2	thsd US$/unit	723
8701	Tractors (other than tractors of heading 87.09)	87.4	85.5	133.2		21.5	21.2	thsd US$/unit	722
8517	Electrical apparatus for line telephony or line telegraphy	67.9	96.2	103.5					764
1101	Wheat or meslin flour	103.8	75.9	78.4	0.3	0.4	0.4	US$/kg	046
3004	Medicaments (excluding goods of heading 30.02, 30.05 or 30.06)	64.3	84.6	98.7	*21.9*	25.0	24.9	US$/kg	542

Bosnia and Herzegovina

Imports: CIF, by origin | **Exports: FOB, by last known destination** | **Trade System: Special**

Overview:

After a big drop of 21.3 percent in 2009, the value of exports of Bosnia and Herzegovina bounced back in 2010 by 21.5 percent and continued to rise by 21.8 percent to reach its peak of 5.9 bln US$ in 2011 (see table 1 and graph 1). Imports also showed an increase of 19.8 percent in 2011 and amounted to 11.1 bln US$ (see table 2 and graph 1). This resulted in a trade deficit of 5.2 bln US$ (see graph 1). By MDG regions, the largest deficit was recorded with Developed Europe (-2.3 bln US$) (see graph 2). Significant deficits were also recorded with Commonwealth of Independent States (-1.2 bln US$), Eastern Asia (-0.6 bln US$) and Developed North America (-0.4 bln US$). Compared to imports, exports were concentrated among partners: in 2011, 10 major partners accounted for 80 percent of exports compared to 13 major partners for imports (see graph 3).

Graph 1: Total imports, exports and trade balance

(Bln US$ by year)

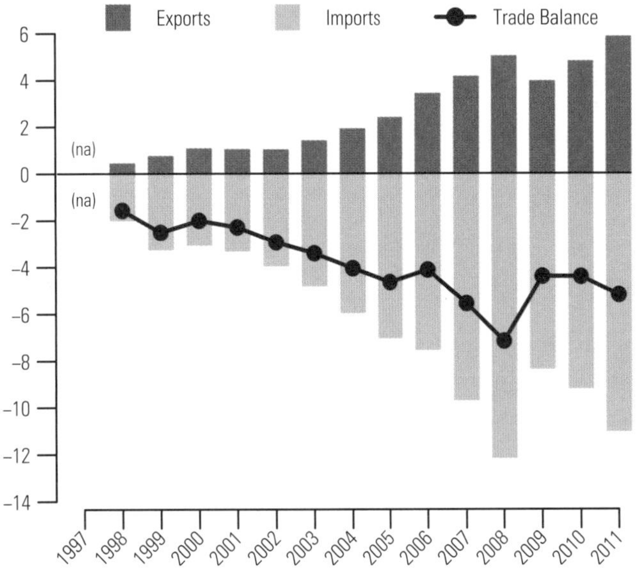

Table 1: Exports by SITC sections

(Value in million US$, growth and shares in percentage)

SITC	2011	Avg. Growth rates (%) 2007-2011	2010-2011	2011 share
Total	5850.0	8.9	21.8	100.0
0+1	387.1	17.8	22.8	6.6
2+4	838.3	5.4	31.0	14.3
3	838.3	26.4	15.7	14.3
5	323.8	17.6	33.2	5.5
6	1525.9	3.7	28.1	26.1
7	706.1	3.9	25.6	12.1
8	1196.8	9.0	19.6	20.5
9	33.8	88.5	-73.3	0.6

Table 2: Imports by SITC sections

(Value in million US$, growth and shares in percentage)

SITC	2011	Avg. Growth rates (%) 2007-2011	2010-2011	2011 share
Total	11050.1	3.3	19.8	100.0
0+1	1812.7	5.7	16.4	16.4
2+4	448.7	1.3	18.6	4.1
3	2376.4	14.9	33.5	21.5
5	1271.3	5.6	14.4	11.5
6	2152.8	0.1	19.1	19.5
7	2056.7	-3.0	20.1	18.6
8	928.4	0.0	7.0	8.4
9	3.2	-51.3	-61.4	0.0

Exports Profile:

In 2011, exports were composed of 26.1 percent of manufactured goods classified chiefly by material (SITC section 6), 20.5 percent miscellaneous manufactured articles (SITC section 8) and 14.3 percent of both inedible crude materials (except fuels), animal and vegetable oils, fats and waxes (SITC sections 2+4) and mineral fuels, lubricants and related materials (SITC section 3) (see table 1). Top partners for exports were Germany, Croatia and Serbia (see table 4). From 2009 to 2011, top products for exports were electrical energy (HS code 2716), seats (other than those of heading 94.02) (HS code 9401) and unwrought aluminium (HS code 7601) (see table 3).

Table 3: Top 10 export commodities 2009 to 2011

(Value in million US$)

HS code	4-digit heading of Harmonized System 2007	Value (million US$) 2009	2010	2011	Unit value 2009	2010	2011	Unit	SITC code
	All Commodities	3953.9	4803.1	5850.0					
2716	Electrical energy	326.2	328.4	262.0	*79.0*	*54.8*	*60.9*	US$/MWh	351
9401	Seats (other than those of heading 94.02)	247.3	306.1	357.0					821
7601	Unwrought aluminium	189.3	288.4	336.1	1.8	2.3	2.7	US$/kg	684
2704	Coke and semi-coke of coal, of lignite or of peat	86.3	198.4	187.4	0.2	0.4	0.4	US$/kg	325
2710	Petroleum oils, other than crude	62.0	126.1	270.2	0.4	0.7	1.0	US$/kg	334
6403	Footwear with outer soles of rubber, plastics, leather	128.2	149.4	177.3	*34.8*	*35.4*	*35.1*	US$/pair	851
4407	Wood sawn or chipped lengthwise, sliced or peeled	129.4	133.2	177.6					248
9403	Other furniture and parts thereof	88.8	101.9	124.0					821
2818	Artificial corundum, whether or not chemically defined	53.6	110.7	115.4	0.2	0.4	0.4	US$/kg	285
8409	Parts suitable for use with the engines of heading 84	94.3	84.9	90.4	33.8	36.1	45.4	US$/kg	713

Graph 2: Trade Balance by MDG Regions in 2011

(Bln US$)

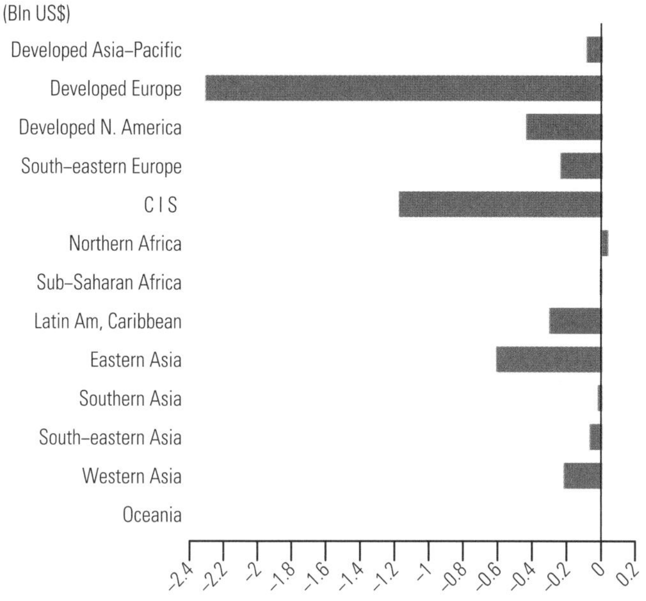

Graph 3: Partner concentration of trade in 2011

(Cumulative share by ranked partners)

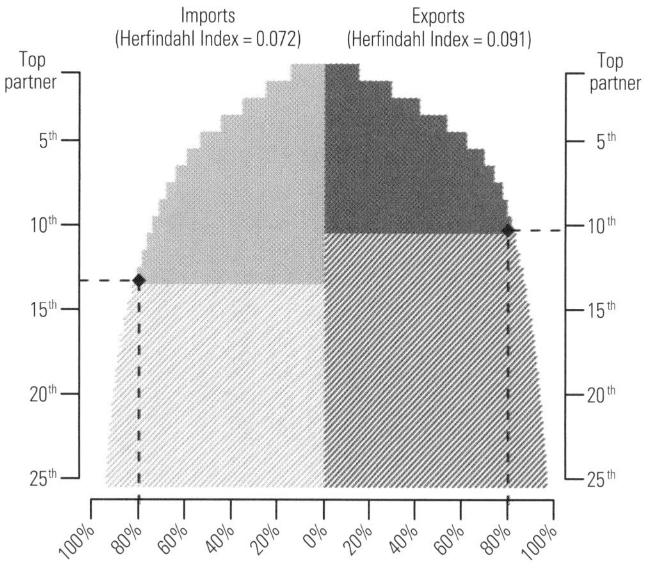

Table 4: Exports by principal countries and SITC sections in 2011

(Value in million US$, percentages of country total)

Country	Total	Shares by SITC sections (%) 0+1	2+4	3	5	6	7	8	9	Total
World	5850.0	6.6	14.3	14.3	5.5	26.1	12.1	20.5	0.6	100
Germany	862.7	0.7	10.9	3.1	1.0	19.2	12.8	52.3	...	100
Croatia	856.8	13.7	10.3	19.7	2.8	41.8	3.3	8.4	...	100
Serbia	711.4	9.0	10.8	48.3	4.0	19.6	4.0	4.2	...	100
Italy	685.6	2.6	13.5	0.9	8.6	32.6	7.0	34.7	...	100
Slovenia	502.8	5.1	23.2	1.5	2.4	14.9	40.9	11.7	0.3	100
Austria	440.3	3.1	15.8	4.0	2.7	20.9	25.5	28.0	...	100
Areas, nes	246.2	12.2	12.5	9.6	30.3	20.5	0.9	1.0	13.0	100
Montenegro	213.7	10.9	33.2	22.1	2.5	22.4	4.4	4.5	...	100
Hungary	118.0	2.9	18.2	4.5	7.1	50.3	7.5	9.5	...	100
Turkey	106.7	1.4	56.6	4.2	7.7	24.0	5.1	1.0	0.1	100

Imports Profile:

Mineral fuels, lubricants and related materials (SITC section 3), manufactured goods classified chiefly by material (SITC section 6) and machinery and transport equipment (SITC section 7) accounted respectively for 21.5, 19.5 and 18.6 percent of imports (see table 2). From 2009 to 2011, top imported goods were petroleum oils and oils obtained from bituminous minerals, crude (HS code 2709), petroleum oils, other than crude (HS code 2710) and motor cars and other motor vehicles principally designed for the transport (HS code 8703) (see table 5).

Table 5: Top 10 import commodities 2009 to 2011

(Value in million US$)

HS code	4-digit heading of Harmonized System 2007	Value (million US$) 2009	2010	2011	Unit value 2009	2010	2011	Unit	SITC code
	All Commodities	8363.7	9223.0	11050.1					
2709	Petroleum oils and oils obtained from bituminous minerals, crude	450.1	628.7	915.8	0.4	0.6	0.8	US$/kg	333
2710	Petroleum oils, other than crude	447.1	538.0	721.0	*0.6*	*0.8*	1.0	US$/kg	334
8703	Motor cars and other motor vehicles principally designed for the transport	283.1	262.2	371.8	*17.8*	*18.0*	*18.4*	thsd US$/unit	781
2701	Coal; briquettes, ovoids and similar solid fuels manufactured from coal	147.7	304.1	401.4	0.2	0.2	0.3	US$/kg	321
3004	Medicaments (excluding goods of heading 30.02, 30.05 or 30.06)	247.3	243.9	271.0	*40.1*	*37.5*	43.0	US$/kg	542
2711	Petroleum gases and other gaseous hydrocarbons	126.4	135.7	188.2	0.6	*0.6*	0.8	US$/kg	343
1701	Cane or beet sugar and chemically pure sucrose, in solid form	69.1	98.9	153.8	0.4	*0.6*	0.7	US$/kg	061
2716	Electrical energy	65.9	133.3	83.2	*82.5*	*57.1*	*60.4*	US$/MWh	351
2203	Beer made from malt	89.9	88.3	96.9	*0.7*	*0.7*	*0.7*	US$/litre	112
8517	Electrical apparatus for line telephony or line telegraphy	92.6	83.8	94.7					764

Imports: CIF, by origin	Exports: FOB, by last known destination	Trade System: General

Overview:

In 2011, the value of the exports of Botswana grew by 25.3 percent and reached 5.9 bln US$ (see table 1 and graph 1). The last five years showed an average annual increase of 3.8 percent in exports, while imports registered an average annual growth of 16.2 percent (see tables 1 and 2 and graph 1). In 2011, imports increased by 28.6 percent to 7.3 bln US$. This resulted in a trade deficit of 1.4 bln US$ in 2011, higher than the 2010 surplus of 1.0 bln US$ (see graph 1). By MDG regions, trade recorded a surplus of 3.2 bln US$ with Developed Europe and a deficit of 3.9 bln US$ with Sub-Saharan Africa (see graph 2). Botswana's trade was highly concentrated among a few partners: in 2011, 3 major partners accounted for 80 percent of both imports and exports (see graph 3).

Graph 1: Total imports, exports and trade balance

(Bln US$ by year)

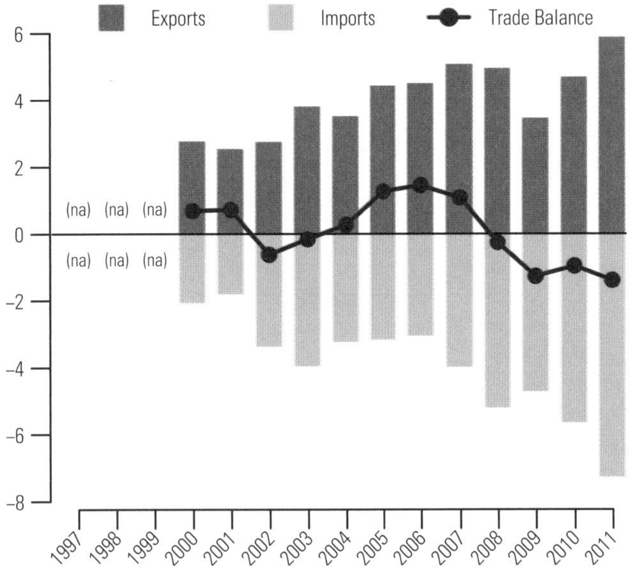

Table 1: Exports by SITC sections

(Value in million US$, growth and shares in percentage)

SITC	2011	Avg. Growth rates (%) 2007-2011	2010-2011	2011 share
Total	5881.9	3.8	25.3	100.0
0+1	123.6	-3.2	-46.0	2.1
2+4	505.9	-19.2	-26.6	8.6
3	23.4	16.6	40.2	0.4
5	82.8	19.8	-14.7	1.4
6	4502.3	8.8	38.8	76.5
7	280.9	33.4	55.2	4.8
8	264.7	-7.5	63.2	4.5
9	98.3	43.4	32.4	1.7

Table 2: Imports by SITC sections

(Value in million US$, growth and shares in percentage)

SITC	2011	Avg. Growth rates (%) 2007-2011	2010-2011	2011 share
Total	7272.0	16.2	28.6	100.0
0+1	715.6	10.1	7.5	9.8
2+4	127.9	-2.4	-22.8	1.8
3	1189.3	17.6	43.5	16.4
5	487.5	7.3	8.0	6.7
6	1847.8	25.2	23.7	25.4
7	2311.2	17.7	54.9	31.8
8	508.5	7.2	5.7	7.0
9	84.2	28.9	7.2	1.2

Exports Profile:

Exports of Botswana were mostly manufactured goods classified chiefly by material (SITC section 6). In 2011, it represented 76.5 percent of exported goods and amounted to 4.5 bln US$ (see table 1). The largest market for exports was the United Kingdom which accounted for 62.4 percent of exported goods (see table 4). Other major markets for exports were South Africa and Israel. Exports to the United Kingdom and Israel were almost exclusively manufactured goods classified chiefly by material (SITC section 6), representing 99.6 and 100 percent respectively. Over the last three years, main products were diamonds, not mounted or set (HS code 7102), nickel matte, interim products of nickel metallurgy (HS code 7501) and gold (including gold plated with platinum) (HS code 7108) (see table 3).

Table 3: Top 10 export commodities 2009 to 2011

(Value in million US$)

HS code	4-digit heading of Harmonized System 2002	Value (million US$) 2009	2010	2011	Unit value 2009	2010	2011	Unit	SITC code
	All Commodities	3455.7	4693.2	5881.9					
7102	Diamonds, whether or not worked, but not mounted or set	2165.1	3208.4	4448.5					667
7501	Nickel mattes, nickel oxide sinters and other intermediate products	425.0	512.5	354.6	4.9	8.2	8.7	US$/kg	284
7108	Gold (including gold plated with platinum)	75.6	61.1	79.5	25.8	33.0	46.8	thsd US$/kg	971
2603	Copper ores and concentrates	75.3	43.4	74.5			2.0	US$/kg	283
6204	Women's or girls' suits, ensembles, jackets, blazers, dresses, skirts	63.3	49.2	73.8	*5.4*	4.7		US$/unit	842
0201	Meat of bovine animals, fresh or chilled	64.4	97.8	19.4	5.9	5.3	4.9	US$/kg	011
6203	Men's or boys' suits, ensembles, jackets, blazers, trousers	31.6	43.8	74.7		5.1		US$/unit	841
2836	Carbonates; peroxocarbonates (percarbonates)	28.4	68.5	40.8	0.1	*0.2*	0.2	US$/kg	523
0202	Meat of bovine animals, frozen	49.1	60.6	27.4	3.5	3.4	4.4	US$/kg	011
8544	Insulated (including enamelled or anodised) wire, cable	18.8	39.7	46.7	*15.7*	19.0	*12.3*	US$/kg	773

Graph 2: Trade Balance by MDG Regions in 2011

(Bln US$)

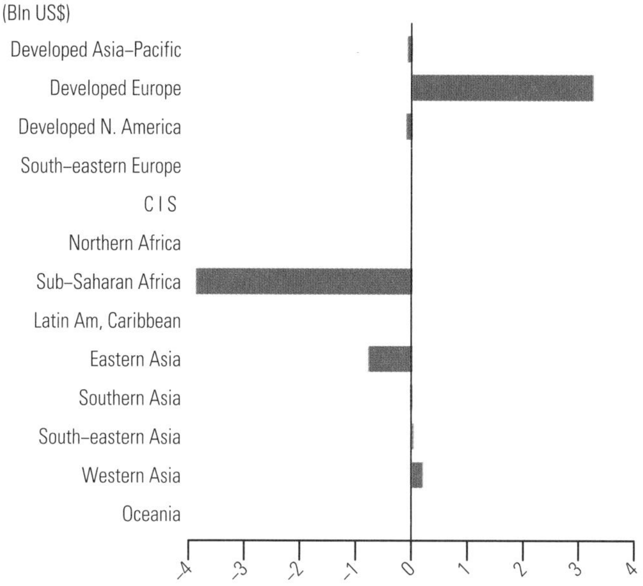

Graph 3: Partner concentration of trade in 2011

(Cumulative share by ranked partners)

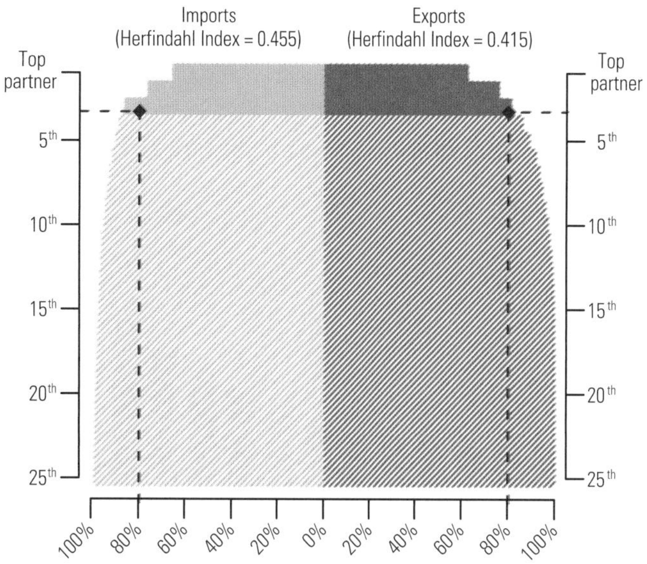

Table 4: Exports by principal countries and SITC sections in 2011

(Value in million US$, percentages of country total)

Country	Total	Shares by SITC sections (%)								
		0 + 1	2 + 4	3	5	6	7	8	9	Total
World	5881.9	2.1	8.6	0.4	1.4	76.5	4.8	4.5	1.7	100
United Kingdom	3671.0	0.0	0.4	...	0.0	99.6	0.0	0.0	0.0	100
South Africa	794.0	9.0	15.1	0.2	7.9	7.3	19.3	29.8	11.5	100
Israel	304.3	0.0	0.0	...	...	100.0	0.0	0.0	...	100
Norway	280.4	0.0	100.0	...	...	...	...	...	...	100
Zimbabwe	173.1	17.5	45.0	12.3	4.0	3.3	15.4	1.6	0.9	100
Belgium	159.8	0.0	0.0	...	...	99.9	0.0	0.0	0.1	100
Switzerland	89.6	0.0	0.0	0.0	0.0	99.4	0.0	0.6	0.0	100
Zambia	76.8	16.7	6.3	0.3	4.3	3.6	65.8	1.9	1.1	100
India	75.4	0.0	0.0	...	0.0	99.7	0.1	0.0	0.2	100
USA	62.7	0.0	1.0	...	0.0	63.0	5.1	29.3	1.5	100

Imports Profile:

In 2011, machinery and transport equipment (SITC section 7), manufactured goods classified chiefly by material (SITC section 6) and mineral fuels, lubricants and related materials (SITC section 3) accounted respectively for 31.8, 25.4 and 16.4 percent of imported goods (see table 2). From 2009 to 2011, top imported products were oils petroleum, bituminous, distillates, except crude (HS code 2710), diamonds, not mounted or set (HS code 7102) and motor vehicles for the transport of goods (except buses) (HS code 8704) (see table 5).

Table 5: Top 10 import commodities 2009 to 2011

(Value in million US$)

HS code	4-digit heading of Harmonized System 2002	Value (million US$)			Unit value				SITC code
		2009	2010	2011	2009	2010	2011	Unit	
	All Commodities	4728.0	5656.8	7272.0					
2710	Petroleum oils, other than crude	513.5	705.5	930.7	*0.6*	0.8	0.3	US$/kg	334
7102	Diamonds, whether or not worked, but not mounted or set	367.8	659.4	861.6					667
8704	Motor vehicles for the transport of goods	150.3	146.8	233.4	*11.7*	*4.3*		thsd US$/unit	782
8703	Motor cars and other motor vehicles principally designed for the transport	153.3	181.9	188.7	*7.6*	*7.2*		thsd US$/unit	781
2716	Electrical energy	73.1	89.3	228.9	0.1	0.0	*9.0*	US$/MWh	351
8502	Electric generating sets and rotary converters	16.8	43.1	238.2	709.1	684.3		US$/unit	716
2523	Portland cement, aluminous cement, slag cement	74.9	91.4	83.5	0.1	*0.1*	*0.1*	US$/kg	661
3004	Medicaments (excluding goods of heading 30.02, 30.05 or 30.06)	73.0	66.2	101.6	*23.7*	*13.3*	*32.2*	US$/kg	542
8708	Parts and accessories of the motor vehicles of headings 87.01 to 87.05	69.8	76.8	89.6	*12.1*	*14.8*	*15.6*	US$/kg	784
7308	Structures (excluding prefabricated buildings of heading 94.06)	46.5	64.5	114.1	1.7	1.4	2.6	US$/kg	691

Brazil

Imports: FOB, by origin | **Exports: FOB, by last known destination** | **Trade System: Special**

Overview:

From 2007 to 2011, Brazil's exports increased on average by 12.4 percent each year and amounted to 256.0 bln US$ in 2011, surpassing its previous peak of 197.9 bln US$ in 2008 (see table 1 and graph 1). Imports increased on average by 17.0 percent each year and reached 226.2 bln US$ (see table 2 and graph 1). This resulted in a trade surplus of 29.8 bln US$ in 2011 (see graph 1). The trade balance recorded a surplus amounting to 18.2 bln US$ with Latin America and the Caribbean and 6.1 bln US$ with Eastern Asia (see graph 2). A deficit of 8.7 bln US$ was recorded with Developed North America. Brazil's trade was highly diversified across partners: in 2011, 21 major partners accounted for 80 percent of imports and 25 major partners accounted for less than 80 percent of exports (see graph 3).

Graph 1: Total imports, exports and trade balance

(Bln US$ by year)

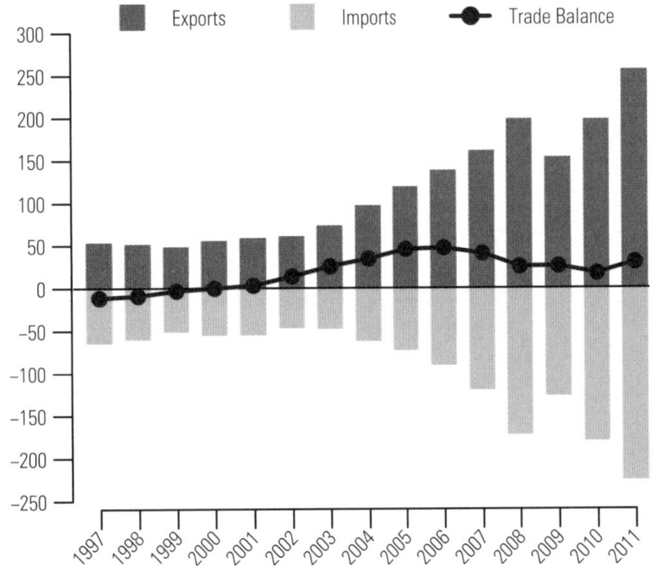

Table 1: Exports by SITC sections

(Value in million US$, growth and shares in percentage)

SITC	2011	Avg. Growth rates (%) 2007-2011	Avg. Growth rates (%) 2010-2011	2011 share
Total	256038.7	12.4	29.7	100.0
0+1	58414.8	15.0	21.6	22.8
2+4	75880.1	27.1	39.9	29.6
3	26791.0	19.1	35.0	10.5
5	15055.0	9.0	23.0	5.9
6	28753.2	1.3	23.1	11.2
7	38812.0	1.7	17.2	15.2
8	4926.5	-2.2	5.1	1.9
9	7406.2	9.9	307.1	2.9

Exports Profile:

Inedible crude materials (except fuels), animal and vegetable oils, fats and waxes (SITC sections 2+4), food, live animals, beverages and tobacco (SITC sections 0+1) and machinery and transport equipment (SITC section 7) accounted respectively for 29.6, 22.8 and 15.2 percent of exports in 2011 (see table 1). China, USA and Argentina were the three largest markets for exports (see table 4). The majority of exports to China (76.9 percent) were inedible crude materials (except fuels), animal and vegetable oils, fats and waxes (SITC sections 2+4). From 2009 to 2011, the main commodities for exports included iron ores and concentrates (HS code 2601), petroleum oils and oils obtained from bituminous minerals, crude (HS code 2709) and soya beans, whether or not broken (HS code 1201) (see table 3).

Table 2: Imports by SITC sections

(Value in million US$, growth and shares in percentage)

SITC	2011	Avg. Growth rates (%) 2007-2011	Avg. Growth rates (%) 2010-2011	2011 share
Total	226243.4	17.0	25.4	100.0
0+1	9121.4	15.9	20.7	4.0
2+4	7065.2	12.0	35.1	3.1
3	41967.6	17.1	40.1	18.5
5	41846.8	16.2	29.5	18.5
6	25812.9	16.5	12.9	11.4
7	86733.4	24.1	22.2	38.3
8	13692.4	17.5	18.5	6.1
9	3.8	-85.3	62.9	0.0

Table 3: Top 10 export commodities 2009 to 2011

(Value in million US$)

HS code	4-digit heading of Harmonized System 2007	Value (million US$) 2009	2010	2011	Unit value 2009	2010	2011	Unit	SITC code
	All Commodities	152994.7	197356.4	256038.7					
2601	Iron ores and concentrates, including roasted iron pyrites	13246.9	28911.9	41817.3	*0.0*	0.1	0.1	US$/kg	281
2709	Petroleum oils and oils obtained from bituminous minerals, crude	9351.0	16293.4	21603.3	*0.3*	0.5	0.7	US$/kg	333
1201	Soya beans, whether or not broken	11424.3	11043.0	16327.3	0.4	0.4	0.5	US$/kg	222
1701	Cane or beet sugar and chemically pure sucrose, in solid form	8377.8	12761.4	14941.7	*0.3*	0.5	0.6	US$/kg	061
0207	Meat and edible offal, of the poultry of heading 01.05	4945.4	5952.0	7242.6	1.5	1.7	2.0	US$/kg	012
0901	Coffee, whether or not roasted or decaffeinated	3791.2	5203.3	8026.4	2.3	2.9	4.5	US$/kg	071
2304	Oil-cake and other solid residues	4592.7	4719.4	5697.9	0.4	0.3	0.4	US$/kg	081
4703	Chemical wood pulp, soda or sulphate, other than dissolving grades	3073.1	4434.2	4609.7	0.4	0.5	0.5	US$/kg	251
8703	Motor cars and other motor vehicles principally designed for the transport	3244.9	4416.1	4375.7	10.4	*13.7*	10.0	thsd US$/unit	781
8802	Other aircraft (for example, helicopters, aeroplanes); spacecraft	3870.8	3999.1	3939.5	5.6		19.7	mln US$/unit	792

Graph 2: Trade Balance by MDG Regions in 2011

(Bln US$)

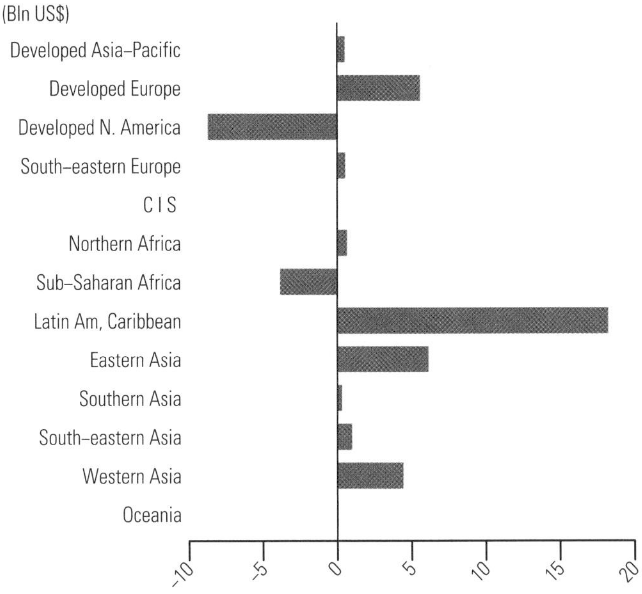

Graph 3: Partner concentration of trade in 2011

(Cumulative share by ranked partners)

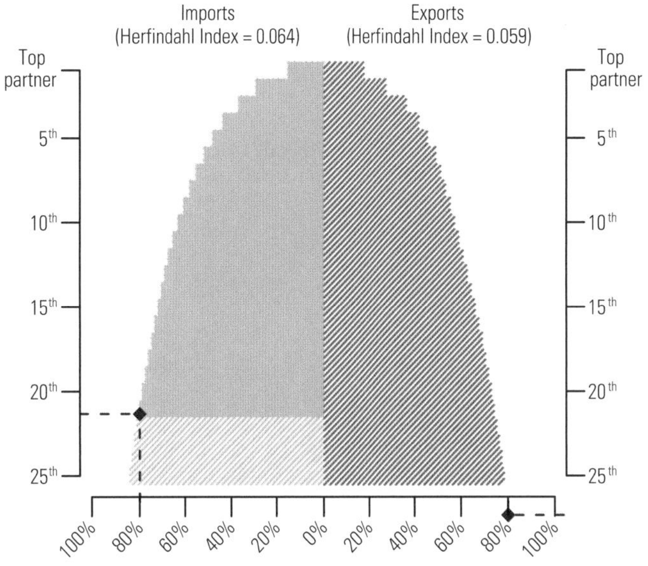

Table 4: Exports by principal countries and SITC sections in 2011

(Value in million US$, percentages of country total)

Country	Total	Shares by SITC sections (%)								
		0 + 1	2 + 4	3	5	6	7	8	9	Total
World	256038.7	22.8	29.6	10.5	5.9	11.2	15.2	1.9	2.9	100
China	44314.6	5.0	76.9	11.0	1.2	3.4	2.3	0.1	0.1	100
USA	25943.0	14.6	7.6	22.6	9.6	23.7	17.6	3.1	1.1	100
Argentina	22709.3	2.9	7.6	5.8	10.9	14.9	53.8	3.9	0.0	100
Netherlands	13639.7	31.3	30.7	11.1	6.0	14.3	6.0	0.5	0.0	100
Japan	9473.1	28.2	52.8	0.0	5.4	11.5	1.8	0.4	0.0	100
Germany	9039.1	32.1	27.0	0.3	5.3	13.4	18.4	3.4	0.1	100
Italy	5440.9	21.2	44.3	0.0	4.3	18.4	9.9	2.0	0.1	100
Chile	5418.1	8.5	0.7	40.4	9.9	11.6	25.7	3.1	0.0	100
United Kingdom	5229.8	20.4	25.2	4.3	6.1	6.2	9.4	4.2	24.1	100
Bunkers	4813.1	0.0	0.0	...	...	...	...	...	100.0	100

Imports Profile:

In 2011, Brazil's imports were composed of 38.3 percent of machinery and transport equipment (SITC section 7) and 18.5 percent of both mineral fuels, lubricants and related materials (SITC section 3) and chemicals and related products, n.e.s. (SITC section 5) (see table 2). The top three commodities for imports over the last three years were petroleum oils and oils obtained from bituminous minerals, crude (HS code 2709), petroleum oils, other than crude (HS code 2710) and motor cars and other motor vehicles principally designed for the transport (HS code 8703) (see table 5).

Table 5: Top 10 import commodities 2009 to 2011

(Value in million US$)

HS code	4-digit heading of Harmonized System 2007	Value (million US$)			Unit value				SITC code
		2009	2010	2011	2009	2010	2011	Unit	
	All Commodities	127647.3	180458.8	226243.4					
2709	Petroleum oils and oils obtained from bituminous minerals, crude	9206.4	10097.4	14080.6	*0.5*	0.6	0.9	US$/kg	333
2710	Petroleum oils, other than crude	4538.0	11125.9	16905.1	*0.6*	0.7	*1.0*	US$/kg	334
8703	Motor cars and other motor vehicles principally designed for the transport	5466.4	8305.0	11891.4	13.1	*14.6*	13.8	thsd US$/unit	781
8708	Parts and accessories of the motor vehicles of headings 87.01 to 87.05	3652.4	4928.5	6317.6	*8.5*	7.8	*8.0*	US$/kg	784
8542	Electronic integrated circuits	2865.5	3913.5	4258.7					776
2711	Petroleum gases and other gaseous hydrocarbons	2358.7	4038.3	4592.4	*0.3*	0.4	*0.5*	US$/kg	343
8517	Electrical apparatus for line telephony or line telegraphy	2847.5	3359.4	4599.6					764
2701	Coal; briquettes, ovoids and similar solid fuels manufactured from coal	2066.6	2929.9	4302.8	0.1	0.2	0.2	US$/kg	321
3004	Medicaments (excluding goods of heading 30.02, 30.05 or 30.06)	2633.2	3144.9	3490.5	*113.4*	*122.7*	*151.1*	US$/kg	542
3104	Mineral or chemical fertilisers, potassic	2112.5	2263.3	3533.0	*0.6*	0.4	*0.5*	US$/kg	562

Bulgaria

Imports: CIF, by origin	Exports: FOB, by consignment	Trade System: Special

Overview:

After a big drop of 26.6 percent in 2009, the value of exports of Bulgaria bounced back in 2010 by 24.9 percent and continued to rise by 36.7 percent to reach its peak of 28.2 bln US$ in 2011 (see table 1 and graph 1). Imports showed an increase of 28.1 percent in 2011 and amounted to 32.5 bln US$ (see table 2 and graph 1). This resulted in a trade deficit of 4.3 bln US$ (see graph 1). By MDG regions, the largest deficit was recorded with Commonwealth of Independent States (-5.9 bln US$) (see graph 2). Significant deficits were also recorded with Developed Europe (-1.1 bln US$) and Eastern Asia (-0.6 bln US$). Bulgaria's trade was diversified across partners: in 2011, 20 (respectively 15) major partners accounted for 80 percent of exports (respectively imports) (see graph 3).

Graph 1: Total imports, exports and trade balance

(Bln US$ by year)

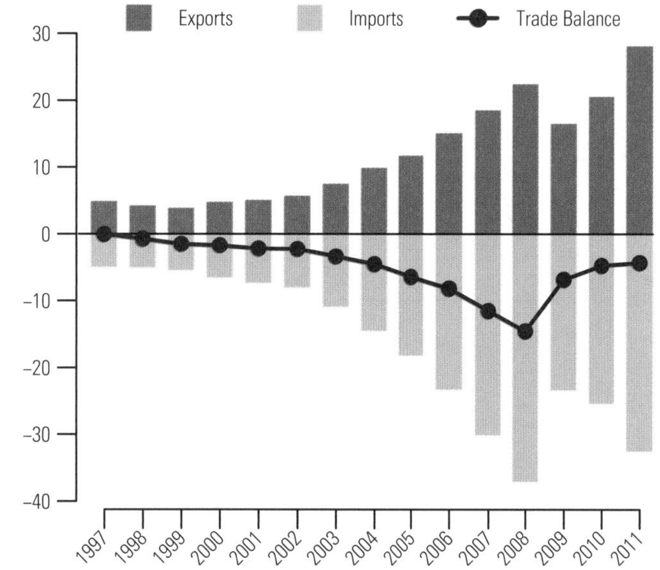

Table 1: Exports by SITC sections

(Value in million US$, growth and shares in percentage)

SITC	2011	Avg. Growth rates (%) 2007-2011	2010-2011	2011 share
Total	28 165.2	11.0	36.7	100.0
0+1	3 171.2	23.4	22.0	11.3
2+4	3 011.2	23.6	57.3	10.7
3	3 698.0	8.1	35.0	13.1
5	2 183.8	11.8	35.5	7.8
6	6 953.2	6.6	47.0	24.7
7	4 665.8	14.0	37.5	16.6
8	3 644.0	2.4	22.7	12.9
9	838.1	25.1	29.4	3.0

Table 2: Imports by SITC sections

(Value in million US$, growth and shares in percentage)

SITC	2011	Avg. Growth rates (%) 2007-2011	2010-2011	2011 share
Total	32 493.6	1.9	28.1	100.0
0+1	2 796.4	14.9	25.0	8.6
2+4	3 338.8	9.6	48.9	10.3
3	7 481.3	6.0	33.1	23.0
5	3 577.0	8.3	23.5	11.0
6	5 360.9	-3.2	28.4	16.5
7	7 094.4	-4.8	27.0	21.8
8	1 963.4	-1.5	11.1	6.0
9	881.4	2.2	5.7	2.7

Exports Profile:

In 2011, exports were composed of 24.7 percent of manufactured goods classified chiefly by material (SITC section 6), 16.6 percent of machinery and transport equipment (SITC section 7) and 13.1 percent of mineral fuels, lubricants and related materials (SITC section 3) (see table 1). The top three markets for exports in 2011 were Germany, Romania and Turkey (see table 4). Over the last three years, top products for exports were petroleum oils, other than crude (HS code 2710), refined copper and copper alloys, unwrought (HS code 7403) and unrefined copper; copper anodes for electrolytic refining (HS code 7402) (see table 3).

Table 3: Top 10 export commodities 2009 to 2011

(Value in million US$)

HS code	4-digit heading of Harmonized System 2007	Value (million US$) 2009	2010	2011	Unit value 2009	2010	2011	Unit	SITC code
	All Commodities	16 502.5	20 608.0	28 165.2					
2710	Petroleum oils, other than crude	1 681.3	2 240.3	3 028.3	0.5	*0.6*	0.8	US$/kg	334
7403	Refined copper and copper alloys, unwrought	778.6	1 359.4	1 839.6	5.1	7.4	6.5	US$/kg	682
9999	Commodities not specified according to kind	333.3	634.3	813.3					931
7402	Unrefined copper; copper anodes for electrolytic refining	445.8	233.8	864.4	6.1	7.9	10.9	US$/kg	682
3004	Medicaments (excluding goods of heading 30.02, 30.05 or 30.06)	365.9	493.6	624.7	*36.8*	*42.0*	*49.8*	US$/kg	542
2716	Electrical energy	359.7	444.7	602.2	68.6	61.6	67.2	US$/MWh	351
1206	Sunflower seeds, whether or not broken	350.7	329.6	676.3	0.3	0.6	0.6	US$/kg	222
1001	Wheat and meslin	302.5	451.9	577.5	0.2	0.2	0.3	US$/kg	041
8544	Insulated (including enamelled or anodised) wire, cable	264.2	359.1	425.9	*13.9*	*12.7*	*14.8*	US$/kg	773
7112	Waste and scrap of precious metal or of metal clad with precious metal	144.4	192.5	573.1	115.6	156.6		US$/kg	289

Graph 2: Trade Balance by MDG Regions in 2011

(Bln US$)

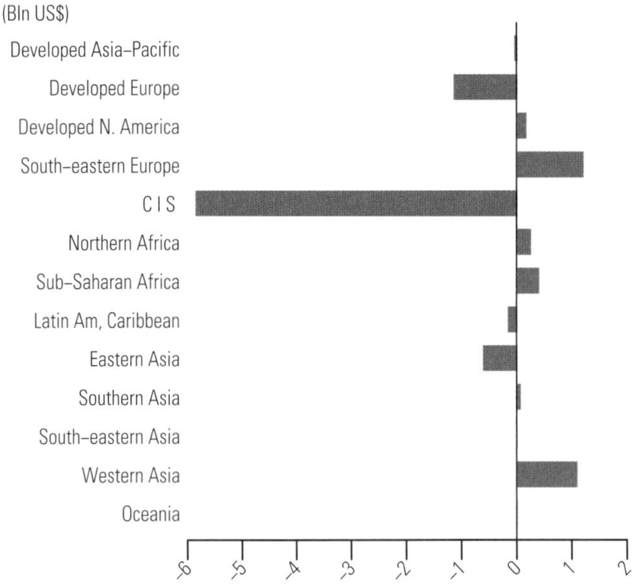

Graph 3: Partner concentration of trade in 2011

(Cumulative share by ranked partners)

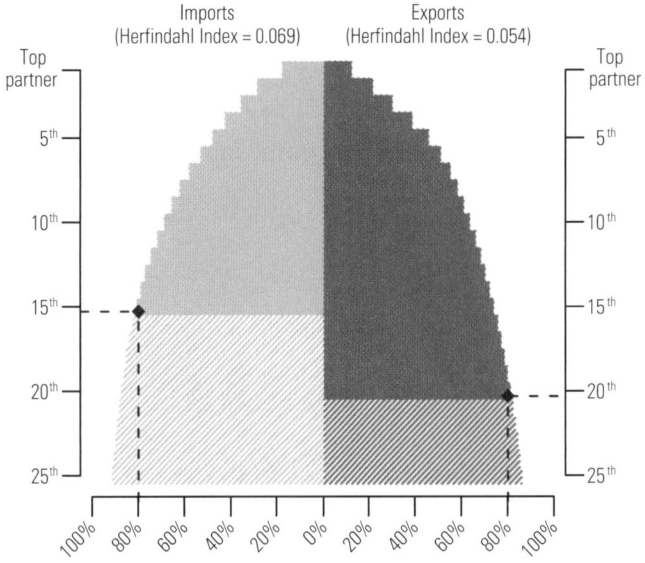

Table 4: Exports by principal countries and SITC sections in 2011

(Value in million US$, percentages of country total)

Country	Total	Shares by SITC sections (%)								
		0 + 1	2 + 4	3	5	6	7	8	9	Total
World	28 165.2	11.3	10.7	13.1	7.8	24.7	16.6	12.9	3.0	100
Germany	3 360.1	3.9	5.1	1.1	3.7	34.0	27.2	22.2	2.7	100
Romania	2 691.3	20.8	10.8	3.7	10.9	26.0	20.7	3.8	3.3	100
Turkey	2 400.3	9.9	19.9	21.5	6.2	33.6	6.2	2.0	0.6	100
Italy	2 396.1	8.0	3.7	1.9	3.4	29.1	18.1	33.6	2.1	100
Greece	1 984.8	24.0	10.4	13.5	4.7	22.5	4.5	15.6	4.7	100
Belgium	1 439.8	6.2	28.8	0.1	0.7	43.4	5.5	14.8	0.6	100
France	1 193.8	9.4	11.1	0.5	7.4	9.3	31.5	27.6	3.1	100
Gibraltar	869.8	0.0	0.0	99.7	0.2	...	...	...	0.0	100
Spain	757.2	39.0	10.6	6.6	4.7	15.5	11.8	10.7	1.1	100
Russian Federation	732.2	8.5	1.1	1.4	39.1	7.4	33.5	6.5	2.5	100

Imports Profile:

In 2011, Bulgaria's imports were composed of 23.0 percent of mineral fuels, lubricants and related materials (SITC section 3), 21.8 percent of machinery and transport equipment (SITC section 7) and 16.5 percent of manufactured goods classified chiefly by material (SITC section 6) (see table 2). From 2009 to 2011, top imported products were petroleum oils and oils obtained from bituminous minerals, crude (HS code 2709), copper ores and concentrates (HS code 2603) and petroleum oils, other than crude (HS code 2710) (see table 5).

Table 5: Top 10 import commodities 2009 to 2011

(Value in million US$)

HS code	4-digit heading of Harmonized System 2007	Value (million US$)			Unit value				SITC code
		2009	2010	2011	2009	2010	2011	Unit	
	All Commodities	23 340.8	25 359.9	32 493.6					
2709	Petroleum oils and oils obtained from bituminous minerals, crude	2 719.3	3 080.8	4 022.5	0.4	0.6	0.8	US$/kg	333
2603	Copper ores and concentrates	719.2	1 044.8	1 772.2	1.1	1.8	*2.1*	US$/kg	283
2710	Petroleum oils, other than crude	683.8	1 100.3	1 585.5	0.6	*0.7*	*0.9*	US$/kg	334
2711	Petroleum gases and other gaseous hydrocarbons	889.2	1 000.2	1 310.1	*0.4*	*0.4*	*0.5*	US$/kg	343
9999	Commodities not specified according to kind	847.6	830.9	870.7					931
3004	Medicaments (excluding goods of heading 30.02, 30.05 or 30.06)	727.8	785.6	947.6	90.8	*54.2*	*62.5*	US$/kg	542
8703	Motor cars and other motor vehicles principally designed for the transport	459.3	476.7	651.7	8.2	*8.6*		thsd US$/unit	781
8517	Electrical apparatus for line telephony or line telegraphy	376.8	410.0	441.6					764
2701	Coal; briquettes, ovoids and similar solid fuels manufactured from coal	329.5	327.4	422.6	0.1	0.1	0.1	US$/kg	321
8528	Reception apparatus for television	312.3	276.7	255.0	250.6	213.2		US$/unit	761

Burkina Faso

Imports: CIF, by origin | **Exports: FOB, by consumption** | **Trade System: General**

Overview:

In 2010, exports of Burkina Faso went up by 61.9 percent to amount to 1.3 bln US$ (see table 1 and graph 1). This is largely due to an increase of 132.7 percent in commodities and transactions not classified elsewhere (SITC section 9) which is essentially exports of gold (including gold plated with platinum) (see tables 1 and 3). Imports increased by 9.5 percent and amounted to 2.0 bln US$ (see table 2 and graph 1). The trade balance recorded a deficit of 0.8 bln US$ in 2010 (see graph 1). Trade was in deficit with all MDG regions except Developed Europe (+311.9 mln US$) (see graph 2). Large deficits were recorded with Sub-Saharan Africa (-379.4 mln US$), Eastern Asia (-227.7 mln US$) and Developed North America (-125.4 mln US$) among others. In 2010, Burkina Faso's trade was concentrated among a few partners: 4 major partners accounted for 80 percent of exports compared to 21 major partners for imports (see graph 3).

Graph 1: Total imports, exports and trade balance

(Bln US$ by year)

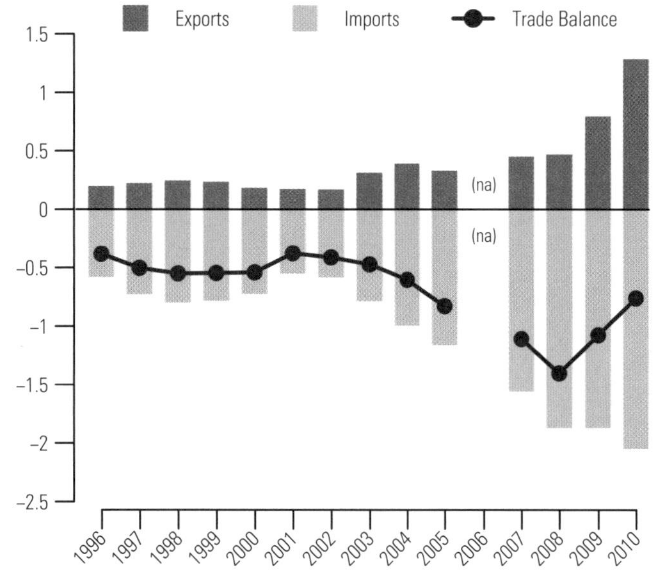

Table 1: Exports by SITC sections

(Value in million US$, growth and shares in percentage)

SITC	2010	Avg. Growth rates (%) 2006-2010	2009-2010	2010 share
Total	1 288.1	...	61.9	100.0
0+1	59.8	...	24.6	4.6
2+4	307.7	...	-3.0	23.9
3	0.2	...	122.6	0.0
5	5.4	...	108.2	0.4
6	17.1	...	-42.6	1.3
7	10.8	...	-19.7	0.8
8	3.5	...	-23.0	0.3
9	883.7	...	132.7	68.6

Table 2: Imports by SITC sections

(Value in million US$, growth and shares in percentage)

SITC	2010	Avg. Growth rates (%) 2006-2010	2009-2010	2010 share
Total	2 048.2	...	9.5	100.0
0+1	289.2	...	0.9	14.1
2+4	48.8	...	70.3	2.4
3	450.3	...	2.2	22.0
5	283.5	...	11.6	13.8
6	382.1	...	17.2	18.7
7	469.2	...	12.5	22.9
8	125.1	...	7.0	6.1
9	0.0	...	-88.8	0.0

Exports Profile:

In 2010, majority of Burkina Faso's exports were of commodities and transactions not classified elsewhere (SITC section 9) and inedible crude materials (except fuels), animal and vegetable oils, fats and waxes (SITC sections 2+4), representing 68.6 and 23.9 percent of exports respectively (see table 1). Major destinations for exports were Switzerland, South Africa and Singapore (see table 4). In 2010, gold (including gold plated with platinum) (HS code 7108) accounted for 68.6 percent of exported goods (see table 3). Other major products for exports were cotton, not carded or combed (HS code 5201) and other oil seeds and oleaginous fruits (HS code 1207).

Table 3: Top 10 export commodities 2008 to 2010

(Value in million US$)

HS code	4-digit heading of Harmonized System 2002	Value (million US$) 2008	2009	2010	Unit value 2008	2009	2010	Unit	SITC code
	All Commodities	470.1	795.5	1 288.1					
7108	Gold (including gold plated with platinum)	121.5	379.8	883.7	21.4	24.8	31.8	thsd US$/kg	971
5201	Cotton, not carded or combed	196.4	249.4	223.4	1.4	1.3	1.4	US$/kg	263
1207	Other oil seeds and oleaginous fruits	41.2	60.4	71.1	0.3	0.5	0.5	US$/kg	222
0102	Live bovine animals	20.7	14.3	8.2	*736.5*	*816.2*	*824.1*	US$/unit	001
2402	Cigars, cheroots, cigarillos and cigarettes	9.6	2.9	6.8	18.5	16.6	15.9	US$/kg	122
0801	Coconuts, Brazil nuts and cashew nuts, fresh or dried	4.0	3.0	8.1	0.2	0.3	0.4	US$/kg	057
0804	Dates, figs, pineapples, avocados and mangosteens, fresh or dried	4.4	3.3	5.4	0.7	0.6	0.8	US$/kg	057
1005	Maize (corn)	2.3	4.1	6.1	0.2	0.3	0.3	US$/kg	044
2306	Oil-cake and other solid residues	2.9	4.2	4.6	0.2	0.2	0.2	US$/kg	081
7214	Other bars and rods of iron or non-alloy steel	3.2	5.4	2.9	0.8	0.8	0.7	US$/kg	676

Graph 2: Trade Balance by MDG Regions in 2010

(Mln US$)

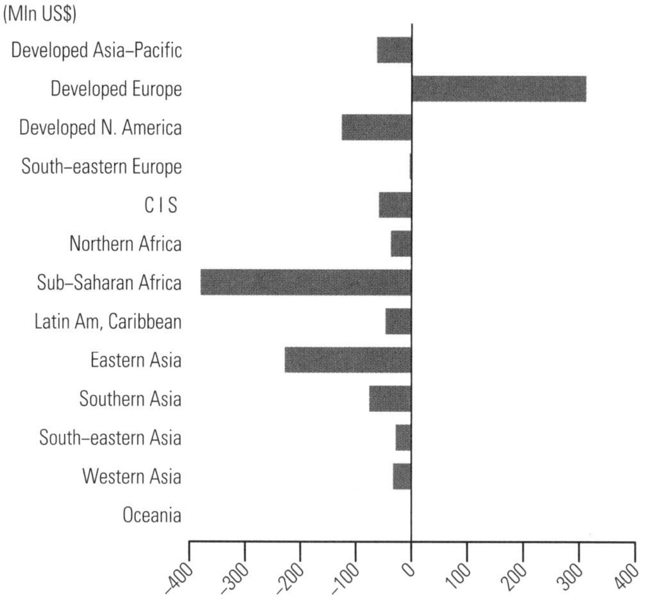

Graph 3: Partner concentration of trade in 2010

(Cumulative share by ranked partners)

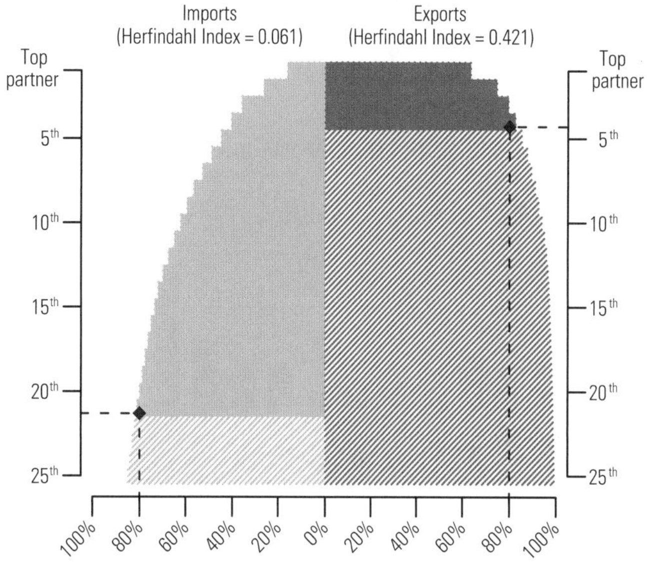

Table 4: Exports by principal countries and SITC sections in 2010

(Value in million US$, percentages of country total)

Country	Total	Shares by SITC sections (%)								
		0 + 1	2 + 4	3	5	6	7	8	9	Total
World	1 288.1	4.6	23.9	0.0	0.4	1.3	0.8	0.3	68.6	100
Switzerland	817.3	0.0	11.1	...	0.0	0.0	...	0.0	88.9	100
South Africa	144.3	0.0	0.0	...	...	...	0.1	0.0	99.9	100
Singapore	62.8	7.6	92.4	...	...	0.0	...	...	...	100
United Kingdom	38.1	0.0	99.7	...	...	0.1	0.2	...	...	100
Ghana	35.1	17.6	79.4	0.4	0.1	1.2	1.1	0.3	...	100
France	29.9	6.0	89.3	...	0.1	0.1	1.5	2.7	0.3	100
Niger	23.4	54.9	0.2	0.3	6.4	31.5	5.9	0.9	...	100
Netherlands	20.4	15.5	81.0	...	0.0	...	1.2	2.3	...	100
Côte d'Ivoire	18.9	71.3	9.9	...	4.8	11.2	2.5	0.3	...	100
Belgium	18.0	0.3	80.9	...	0.0	0.1	0.0	0.5	18.2	100

Imports Profile:

In 2010, imports were composed of 22.9 percent of machinery and transport equipment (SITC section 7), 22.0 percent of mineral fuels, lubricants and related materials (SITC section 3) and 18.7 percent of manufactured goods classified chiefly by material (SITC section 6) (see table 2). Top imported products over the period from 2008 to 2010 included petroleum oils, other than crude (HS code 2710), medicaments (excluding goods of heading 30.02, 30.05 or 30.06) (HS code 3004) and rice (HS code 1006) (see table 5).

Table 5: Top 10 import commodities 2008 to 2010

(Value in million US$)

HS code	4-digit heading of Harmonized System 2002	Value (million US$)			Unit value				SITC code
		2008	2009	2010	2008	2009	2010	Unit	
	All Commodities	1 870.1	1 870.3	2 048.2					
2710	Petroleum oils, other than crude	417.2	419.8	424.8	0.7	0.9	0.8	US$/kg	334
3004	Medicaments (excluding goods of heading 30.02, 30.05 or 30.06)	89.2	89.6	80.2	15.9	15.5	16.6	US$/kg	542
1006	Rice	90.9	69.6	63.7	0.4	0.3	0.3	US$/kg	042
2523	Portland cement, aluminous cement, slag cement	68.8	69.7	73.7	0.1	0.1	0.1	US$/kg	661
8703	Motor cars and other motor vehicles principally designed for the transport	45.8	51.7	51.0			*19.7*	thsd US$/unit	781
8711	Motorcycles (including mopeds) and cycles fitted with an auxiliary motor	37.5	36.4	48.9					785
3105	Mineral or chemical fertilisers	44.8	34.4	32.4	0.7	0.6	0.5	US$/kg	562
2403	Other manufactured tobacco and tobacco substitutes	32.8	34.5	36.9	17.6	17.9	17.2	US$/kg	122
7308	Structures (excluding prefabricated buildings of heading 94.06)	43.3	26.6	19.9	3.3	3.3	3.4	US$/kg	691
1001	Wheat and meslin	33.0	24.7	19.9	0.5	0.4	0.3	US$/kg	041

Burundi

Imports: CIF, by origin	Exports: FOB, by last known destination	Trade System: General

Overview:

After three years of continuously decreasing exports, Burundi's exports increased by 4.6 percent and amounted to 118.2 mln US$ in 2010 while imports increased by 17.2 percent to 404.1 mln US$ (see tables 1, 2 and graph 1). The trade balance recorded a deficit of 285.9 mln US$ in 2010, compared to 231.9 mln US$ in 2009. By MDG regions, deficits were recorded with Sub-Saharan Africa (-100.6 mln US$), Eastern Asia (-48.5 mln US$) and Developed Europe (-43.4 mln US$) (see graph 2). A surplus of 2.6 mln US$ was recorded with South-eastern Asia. Compared to exports, imports were diversified across partners: in 2010, 11 major partners accounted for 80 percent of imports compared to 7 major partners for exports (see graph 3).

Graph 1: Total imports, exports and trade balance

(Mln US$ by year)

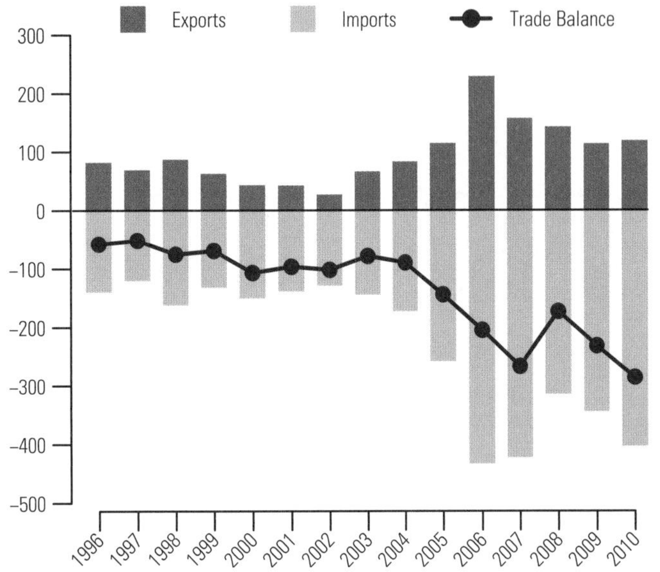

Exports Profile:

In 2010, food, live animals, beverages and tobacco (SITC sections 0+1) was the largest commodity group for exports with 72.3 percent of total exports (see table 1). Other major commodity groups were commodities and transactions not classified elsewhere in the SITC (SITC section 9) and inedible crude materials (except fuels), animal and vegetable oils, fats and waxes (SITC sections 2+4), respectively with 11.2 and 9.1 percent of exports. Exports to Switzerland and United Kingdom, the top markets, were almost exclusively food, live animals, beverages and tobacco (SITC sections 0+1) (see table 4). From 2008 to 2010, the top three commodities for exports were coffee, whether or not roasted or decaffeinated (HS code 0901), gold (including gold plated with platinum) (HS code 7108) and tea, whether or not flavoured (HS code 0902) (see table 3).

Table 1: Exports by SITC sections

(Value in million US$, growth and shares in percentage)

SITC	2010	Avg. Growth rates (%) 2006-2010	Avg. Growth rates (%) 2009-2010	2010 share
Total	118.2	-15.2	4.6	100.0
0+1	85.5	19.6	50.8	72.3
2+4	10.7	12.1	32.8	9.1
3	2.4	62.4	55.0	2.1
5	1.5	43.5	7.4	1.3
6	1.0	-19.3	-1.3	0.8
7	2.7	-55.4	-79.0	2.3
8	1.1	-53.1	-45.7	0.9
9	13.2	-37.3	-54.8	11.2

Table 2: Imports by SITC sections

(Value in million US$, growth and shares in percentage)

SITC	2010	Avg. Growth rates (%) 2006-2010	Avg. Growth rates (%) 2009-2010	2010 share
Total	404.1	-1.8	17.2	100.0
0+1	51.7	-13.9	26.6	12.8
2+4	11.5	10.1	48.7	2.9
3	8.5	20.3	6.9	2.1
5	69.1	11.0	25.0	17.1
6	106.8	9.5	22.8	26.4
7	121.4	-4.8	8.3	30.0
8	33.2	-13.6	24.6	8.2
9	1.7	...	-76.3	0.4

Table 3: Top 10 export commodities 2008 to 2010

(Value in million US$)

HS code	4-digit heading of Harmonized System 2002	Value (million US$) 2008	2009	2010	Unit value 2008	2009	2010	Unit	SITC code
	All Commodities	141.8	112.9	118.2					
0901	Coffee, whether or not roasted or decaffeinated	39.5	39.7	70.4	2.4	2.2	3.4	US$/kg	071
7108	Gold (including gold plated with platinum)	61.0	29.0	13.0	28.2	29.5	41.5	thsd US$/kg	971
0902	Tea, whether or not flavoured	6.8	7.6	10.1	1.1	1.2	1.3	US$/kg	074
2611	Tungsten ores and concentrates	3.4	1.5	3.0	3.7	5.9	5.9	US$/kg	287
8704	Motor vehicles for the transport of goods	0.8	5.2	0.4					782
8703	Motor cars and other motor vehicles principally designed for the transport	3.8	1.5	0.6		*15.0*	*14.6*	thsd US$/unit	781
7204	Ferrous waste and scrap; remelting scrap ingots of iron or steel	1.8	2.0	2.0	*0.2*	0.2	0.2	US$/kg	282
2710	Petroleum oils, other than crude	1.1	1.6	2.4	1.6	1.2	1.4	US$/kg	334
2203	Beer made from malt	1.5	1.4	1.8	*0.4*	*0.5*	*0.5*	US$/litre	112
2402	Cigars, cheroots, cigarillos and cigarettes	1.6	1.4	1.4	5.3	5.4	5.8	US$/kg	122

Graph 2: Trade Balance by MDG Regions in 2010

(Mln US$)

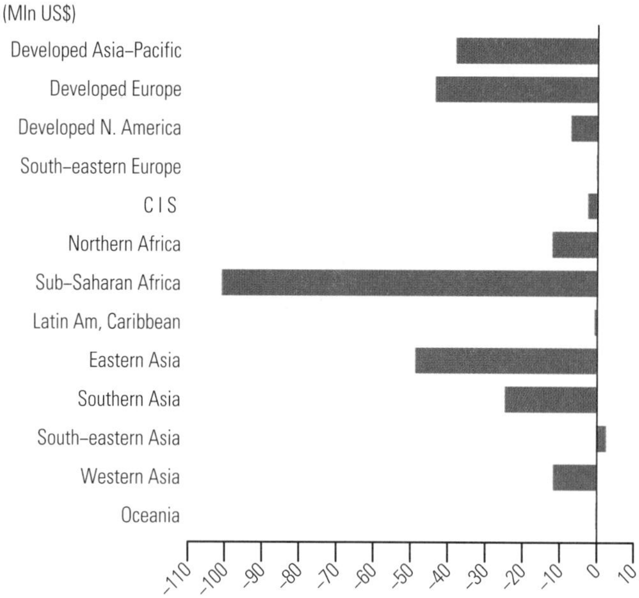

Graph 3: Partner concentration of trade in 2010

(Cumulative share by ranked partners)

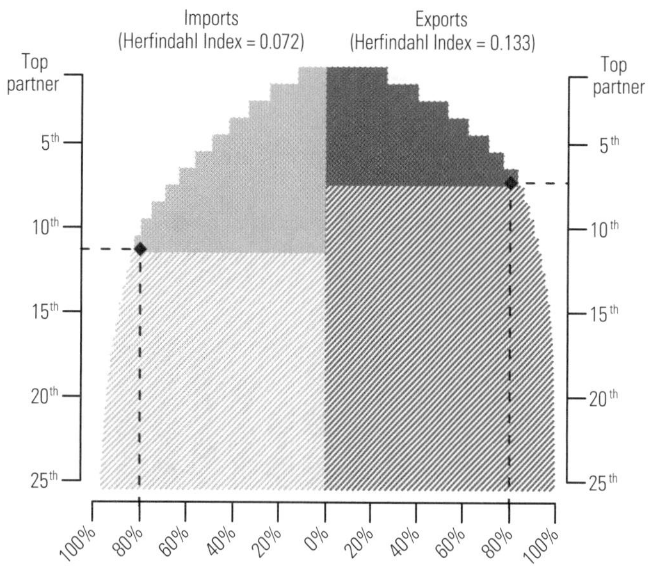

Table 4: Exports by principal countries and SITC sections in 2010

(Value in million US$, percentages of country total)

Country	Total	Shares by SITC sections (%)								
		0 + 1	2 + 4	3	5	6	7	8	9	Total
World	118.2	72.3	9.1	2.1	1.3	0.8	2.3	0.9	11.2	100
Switzerland	31.8	95.5	4.4	...	...	0.0	0.0	0.0	...	100
United Kingdom	15.8	99.8	0.2	...	...	...	0.0	...	...	100
Belgium	15.4	74.6	3.1	...	0.0	0.1	2.3	2.1	17.9	100
United Arab Emirates	10.5	0.0	1.0	...	...	0.0	0.2	...	98.7	100
Kenya	10.3	80.6	16.3	...	...	1.7	1.2	0.3	0.0	100
Dem.Rep. of the Congo	7.3	33.4	0.0	33.6	6.6	4.6	19.9	1.4	0.4	100
Singapore	7.2	100.0	0.0	...	...	...	...	...	...	100
Rwanda	3.0	39.0	20.5	0.0	28.3	5.0	5.4	1.4	0.3	100
Uganda	2.9	57.7	34.4	...	...	2.1	4.2	1.5	0.1	100
Germany	2.5	97.4	0.0	...	...	0.0	0.9	1.6	...	100

Imports Profile:

Burundi's imports in 2010 were composed of 30.0 percent of machinery and transport equipment (SITC section 7), 26.4 percent of manufactured goods classified chiefly by material (SITC section 6) and 17.1 percent of chemicals and related products (SITC section 5) (see table 2). Over the last three years, the top three imported products were medicaments (excluding goods of heading 30.02, 30.05 or 30.06) (HS code 3004), portland cement, aluminous cement, slag cement (HS code 2523) and motor cars and other motor vehicles principally designed for the transport (HS code 8703) (see table 5).

Table 5: Top 10 import commodities 2008 to 2010

(Value in million US$)

HS code	4-digit heading of Harmonized System 2002	Value (million US$)			Unit value				SITC code
		2008	2009	2010	2008	2009	2010	Unit	
	All Commodities	315.2	344.8	404.1					
3004	Medicaments (excluding goods of heading 30.02, 30.05 or 30.06)	22.5	27.7	36.4	12.5	12.0	9.9	US$/kg	542
2523	Portland cement, aluminous cement, slag cement	21.0	0.3	34.9	0.3	0.2	0.2	US$/kg	661
8703	Motor cars and other motor vehicles principally designed for the transport	10.1	16.8	20.2		*11.5*	*10.2*	thsd US$/unit	781
1107	Malt, whether or not roasted	12.2	12.7	10.2	1.1	1.0	0.7	US$/kg	048
4804	Uncoated kraft paper and paperboard, in rolls or sheets	0.0	26.1	0.1	1.2	0.3	1.4	US$/kg	641
8704	Motor vehicles for the transport of goods	8.1	8.5	7.1					782
8517	Electrical apparatus for line telephony or line telegraphy	2.0	10.6	9.3					764
7210	Flat-rolled products of iron or non-alloy steel	7.4	4.4	7.6	1.6	1.0	1.0	US$/kg	674
8708	Parts and accessories of the motor vehicles of headings 87.01 to 87.05	5.6	5.3	7.4	11.0	6.7	7.8	US$/kg	784
1006	Rice	0.2	6.8	10.0	0.3	8.3	1.8	US$/kg	042

Imports: CIF, by origin | **Exports: FOB, by last known destination** | **Trade System: General**

Overview:

From 2006 to 2010, Cambodia's exports increased on average by 11.9 percent each year and amounted to 5.6 bln US$ in 2010 (see table 1 and graph 1). During the same period, imports increased on average by 13.2 percent each year and amounted to 4.9 bln US$ (see table 2 and graph 1). The trade balance recorded a surplus amounting to 687.6 mln US$, compared to a surplus of 1.1 bln US$ in 2009 (see graph 1). Large surpluses were recorded with Developed North America (+2.0 bln US$) and Developed Europe (+0.6 bln US$) (see graph 2). Significant deficits were recorded with Eastern Asia (-992.1 mln US$) and South-eastern Asia (-980.6 mln US$) . In 2010, trade was concentrated among a few partners: 7 (respectively 8) major partners accounted for 80 percent of exports (respectively imports) (see graph 3).

Graph 1: Total imports, exports and trade balance

(Bln US$ by year)

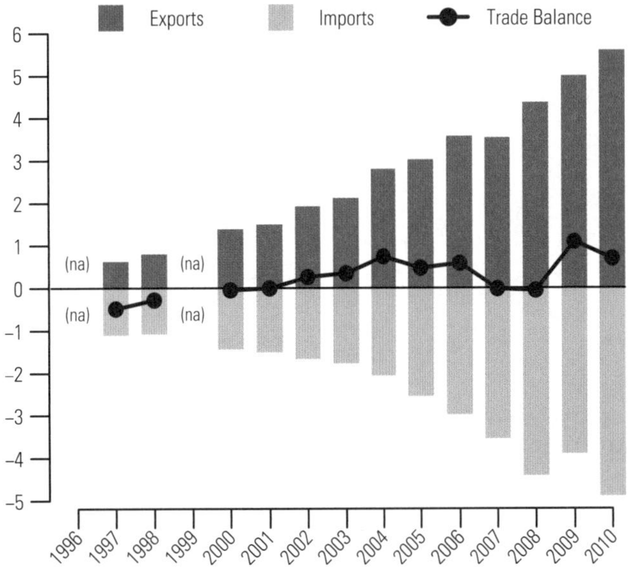

Table 1: Exports by SITC sections

(Value in million US$, growth and shares in percentage)

SITC	2010	Avg. Growth rates (%) 2006-2010	2009-2010	2010 share
Total	5590.1	11.9	12.0	100.0
0+1	68.2	39.6	120.9	1.2
2+4	147.0	24.0	43.5	2.6
3	0.0	...	...	0.0
5	15.0	24.5	-33.6	0.3
6	39.3	0.4	43.4	0.7
7	269.1	44.5	138.5	4.8
8	5047.8	10.7	9.6	90.3
9	3.7	-31.3	-95.9	0.1

Table 2: Imports by SITC sections

(Value in million US$, growth and shares in percentage)

SITC	2010	Avg. Growth rates (%) 2006-2010	2009-2010	2010 share
Total	4902.5	13.2	25.5	100.0
0+1	341.4	14.1	10.8	7.0
2+4	110.5	12.8	12.5	2.3
3	346.4	10.0	-9.4	7.1
5	308.3	14.4	13.8	6.3
6	2252.2	11.2	33.8	45.9
7	1016.9	17.3	26.6	20.7
8	360.2	8.7	17.9	7.3
9	166.7	48.8	205.7	3.4

Exports Profile:

Miscellaneous manufactured articles (SITC section 8) accounted for 90.3 percent of Cambodia's exports in 2010 (see table 1). The USA, the top partner for Cambodia's exports, was the destination of 34.1 percent of exported goods (see table 4). Other major export partners were China, Hong Kong SAR and Singapore (see table 4). Top exported products from 2008 to 2010 included unused postage, revenue or similar stamps of current or new issue (HS code 4907),women's or girl's suits, ensembles, jackets, blazers, dresses, skirts (HS code 6104) and jerseys, pullovers, cardigans, waist-coats and similar articles (HS code 6110) (see table 3).

Table 3: Top 10 export commodities 2008 to 2010

(Value in million US$)

HS code	4-digit heading of Harmonized System 2007	Value (million US$) 2008	2009	2010	Unit value 2008	2009	2010	Unit	SITC code
	All Commodities	4358.2	4992.0	5590.1					
4907	Unused postage, revenue or similar stamps of current or new issue	902.5	2001.6	1777.0	38.9	46.9	53.3	thsd US$/kg	892
6104	Women's or girls' suits, ensembles, jackets, blazers, dresses, skirts	703.1	625.1	819.9					844
6110	Jerseys, pullovers, cardigans, waist-coats and similar articles	722.8	652.3	641.6	*18.8*	*23.0*	*19.3*	US$/unit	845
6103	Men's, boys' suits,jackets,trousers etc knitted or crocheted	463.0	393.2	485.0					843
6109	T-shirts, singlets and other vests, knitted or crocheted	158.5	165.8	307.9	*6.1*	*6.9*	*6.4*	US$/unit	845
6106	Women's or girls' blouses, shirts and shirt-blouses, knitted or crocheted	276.8	135.2	146.3					844
6108	Women's or girls' slips, petticoats, briefs, panties, knitted or crocheted	151.6	130.2	186.2					844
6105	Men's or boys' shirts, knitted or crocheted	164.0	103.4	102.9					843
6403	Footwear with outer soles of rubber, plastics, leather	75.0	81.2	114.1	*14.3*	*16.8*	*17.7*	US$/pair	851
6107	Men's or boys' underpants, briefs, nightshirts, pyjamas, bathrobes	68.0	58.7	76.5	*4.7*			US$/unit	843

Graph 2: Trade Balance by MDG Regions in 2010

(Bln US$)

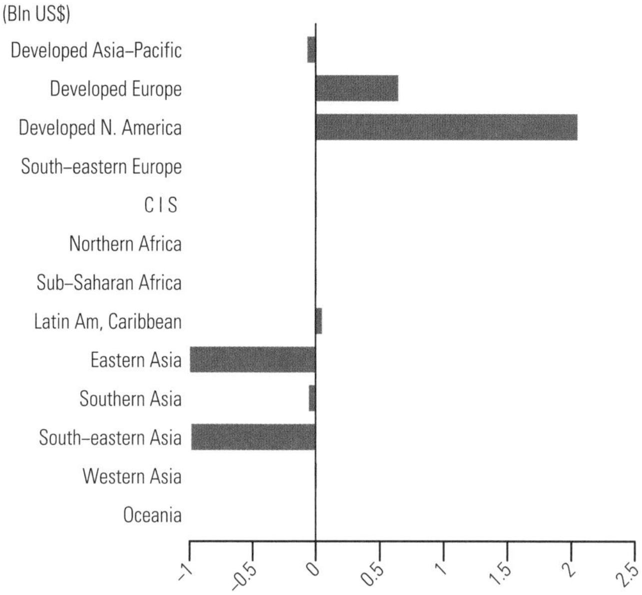

Graph 3: Partner concentration of trade in 2010

(Cumulative share by ranked partners)

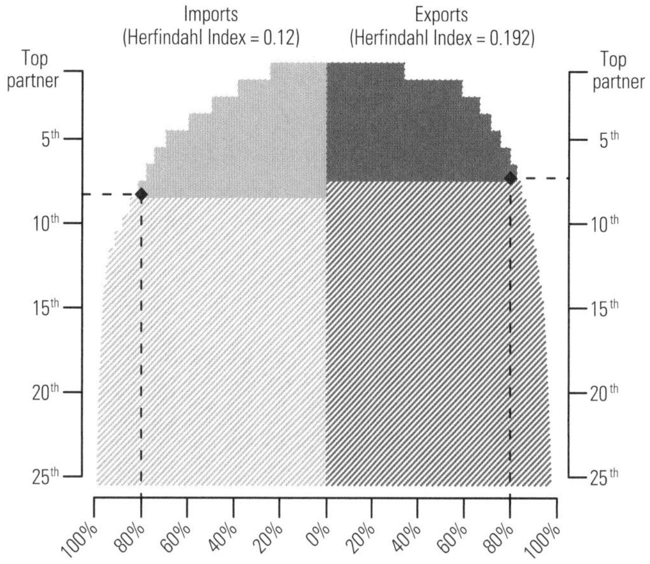

Table 4: Exports by principal countries and SITC sections in 2010

(Value in million US$, percentages of country total)

Country	Total	Shares by SITC sections (%) 0 + 1	2 + 4	3	5	6	7	8	9	Total
World	5590.1	1.2	2.6	0.0	0.3	0.7	4.8	90.3	0.1	100
USA	1905.6	0.4	0.0	...	0.0	0.5	0.4	98.7	0.0	100
China, Hong Kong SAR	1386.4	0.0	0.1	...	0.0	0.1	0.2	99.5	0.0	100
Singapore	430.0	0.8	0.7	0.0	0.0	0.5	2.3	95.7	0.0	100
Canada	274.4	0.0	0.0	...	...	0.5	1.5	98.0	0.0	100
Netherlands	235.8	0.3	0.0	...	2.9	0.2	1.9	94.6	0.0	100
United Kingdom	235.5	2.1	0.0	...	0.0	0.5	9.1	88.2	0.0	100
Thailand	150.1	1.9	3.6	...	0.1	1.1	92.8	0.5	0.0	100
Germany	112.4	0.5	0.0	...	...	2.1	12.2	85.0	0.2	100
Spain	101.3	0.1	0.0	...	...	0.1	5.9	94.0	...	100
Viet Nam	96.1	7.2	70.3	0.0	2.7	5.4	12.1	1.8	0.5	100

Imports Profile:

Manufactured goods classified chiefly by material (SITC section 6) accounted for 45.9 percent of imported goods in 2010 (see table 2). Other major commodity groups for imports were machinery and transport equipment (SITC section 7) and miscellaneous manufactured articles (SITC section 8) respectively with 20.7 and 7.3 percent of imports. Top imported products in 2010 included other knitted or crocheted fabric (HS code 6006), petroleum oils, other than crude (HS code 2710) and other woven fabric of synthetic staple fibres (HS code 5515) (see table 5).

Table 5: Top 10 import commodities 2008 to 2010

(Value in million US$)

HS code	4-digit heading of Harmonized System 2007	Value (million US$) 2008	2009	2010	Unit value 2008	2009	2010	Unit	SITC code
	All Commodities	4416.7	3905.7	4902.5					
6006	Other knitted or crocheted fabrics	770.5	546.9	623.3	4.1	5.2	5.5	US$/kg	655
2710	Petroleum oils, other than crude	307.6	350.7	316.8	0.2	0.3	0.3	US$/kg	334
5515	Other woven fabrics of synthetic staple fibres	315.9	263.3	377.8	4.7	5.7	7.1	US$/kg	653
6004	Knitted or crocheted fabrics of a width exceeding 30 cm	104.1	161.6	334.6	3.8	4.2	4.5	US$/kg	655
2402	Cigars, cheroots, cigarillos and cigarettes	117.1	144.1	143.9	4.5	4.5	4.6	US$/kg	122
8517	Electrical apparatus for line telephony or line telegraphy	119.6	181.2	96.8					764
8703	Motor cars and other motor vehicles principally designed for the transport	153.7	98.1	130.4	*21.0*		*19.8*	thsd US$/unit	781
5509	Yarn (other than sewing thread) of synthetic staple fibres	82.8	99.2	119.2	3.9	4.7	4.8	US$/kg	651
7108	Gold (including gold plated with platinum)	35.7	52.5	164.5	24.7	27.7	36.6	thsd US$/kg	971
8704	Motor vehicles for the transport of goods	115.6	53.1	76.9					782

Cameroon

Imports: CIF, by origin | **Exports: FOB, by last known destination** | **Trade System: Special**

Overview:

From 2006 to 2010, exports of Cameroon increased on average by 2.0 percent each year and amounted to 3.9 bln US$ in 2010, reflecting an increase of 123.9 percent over 2009 (see table 1 and graph 1). During the same period, imports increased on average by 13.0 percent each year and amounted to 5.1 bln US$ in 2010 (see table 2 and graph 1). The trade balance recorded a deficit of 1.3 bln US$ in 2010 (see graph 1). By MDG regions, trade recorded a surplus of 456.4 mln US$ with Developed Europe and a deficit of 673.3 mln US$ with Sub-Saharan Africa (see graph 2). In 2010, exports were concentrated among fewer partners while imports were more diversified: 10 major partners accounted for 80 percent of exports compared to 18 major partners for imports (see graph 3).

Graph 1: Total imports, exports and trade balance

(Bln US$ by year)

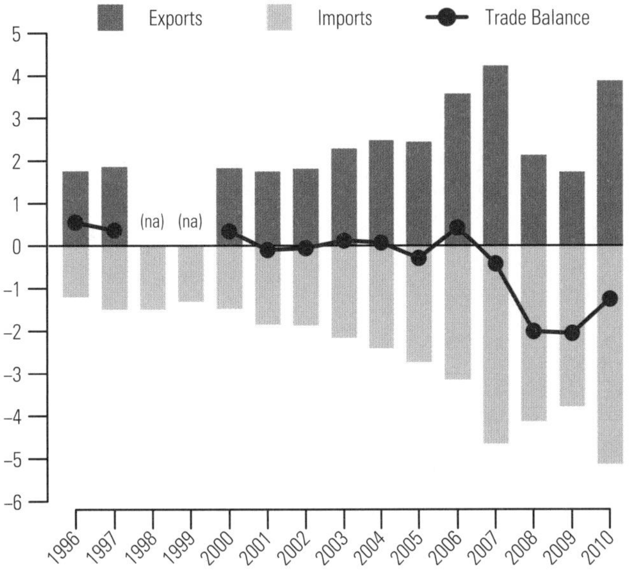

Table 1: Exports by SITC sections

(Value in million US$, growth and shares in percentage)

SITC	2010	Avg. Growth rates (%) 2006-2010	Avg. Growth rates (%) 2009-2010	2010 share
Total	3878.4	2.0	123.9	100.0
0+1	939.8	21.7	15.0	24.2
2+4	609.8	0.6	18.1	15.7
3	1921.7	-3.4	11634.7	49.5
5	55.7	46.0	4.3	1.4
6	216.8	-2.4	10.6	5.6
7	78.9	50.7	-10.0	2.0
8	27.7	52.1	36.3	0.7
9	28.2	-22.4	12.8	0.7

Table 2: Imports by SITC sections

(Value in million US$, growth and shares in percentage)

SITC	2010	Avg. Growth rates (%) 2006-2010	Avg. Growth rates (%) 2009-2010	2010 share
Total	5133.3	13.0	35.5	100.0
0+1	875.7	13.6	-9.7	17.1
2+4	195.3	4.1	-6.6	3.8
3	1421.0	8.9	960.4	27.7
5	536.8	11.4	4.9	10.5
6	676.3	14.0	12.4	13.2
7	1160.3	21.2	3.1	22.6
8	267.9	14.1	13.0	5.2
9	0.0	-67.9	236.2	0.0

Exports Profile:

In 2010, Cameroon's exports were composed of 49.5 percent mineral fuels, lubricants and related materials (SITC section 3), 24.2 percent of food, live animals, beverages and tobacco (SITC sections 0+1) and 15.7 percent of inedible crude materials (except fuels), animal and vegetable oils, fats and waxes (SITC sections 2+4) (see table 1). Spain, Netherlands and Italy were the three major export markets (see table 4). From 2008 to 2010, top exported products included cocoa beans, whole or broken, raw or roasted (HS code 1801), petroleum oils, crude (HS code 2709) and wood sawn or chipped lengthwise, sliced or peeled (HS code 4407) (see table 3).

Table 3: Top 10 export commodities 2008 to 2010

(Value in million US$)

HS code	4-digit heading of Harmonized System 2002	Value (million US$) 2008	2009	2010	Unit value 2008	2009	2010	Unit	SITC code
	All Commodities	2126.7	1732.4	3878.4					
1801	Cocoa beans, whole or broken, raw or roasted	400.3	543.4	611.0	2.2	2.8	3.2	US$/kg	072
2709	Petroleum oils, crude	0.0	0.0	1415.7	7.9	3.6	0.5	US$/kg	333
4407	Wood sawn or chipped lengthwise, sliced or peeled	378.2	212.7	249.4					248
2710	Petroleum oils, other than crude	3.0	4.8	496.8	2.5	2.5	0.6	US$/kg	334
4403	Wood in the rough, whether or not stripped of bark or sapwood	142.2	96.3	144.4			*948.2*	US$/m³	247
7601	Unwrought aluminium	165.1	68.5	98.2	2.5	1.6	2.1	US$/kg	684
0803	Bananas, including plantains	81.4	71.4	82.1	0.3	0.3	0.3	US$/kg	057
5201	Cotton, not carded or combed	60.8	89.9	81.3	1.6	1.6	1.5	US$/kg	263
4001	Natural rubber, balata, gutta-percha, guayule, chicle	65.6	56.9	95.6	2.0	1.5	2.5	US$/kg	231
8905	Light-vessels, fire-floats, dredgers, floating cranes and other vessels	160.6	33.2	1.4					793

Graph 2: Trade Balance by MDG Regions in 2010

(Mln US$)

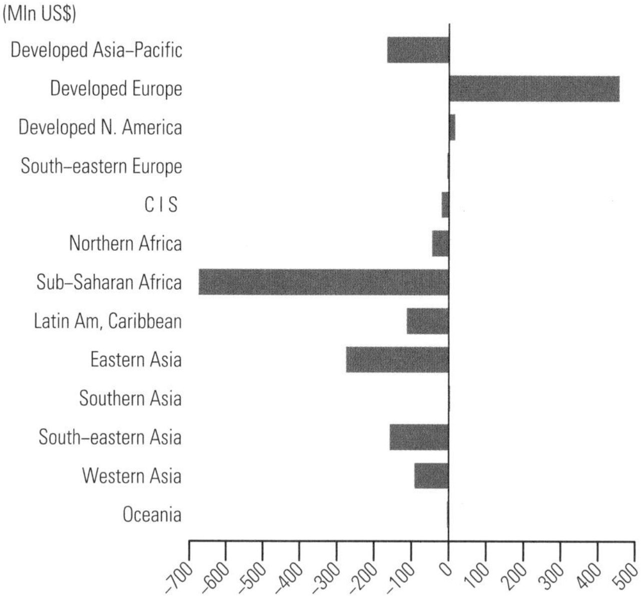

Graph 3: Partner concentration of trade in 2010

(Cumulative share by ranked partners)

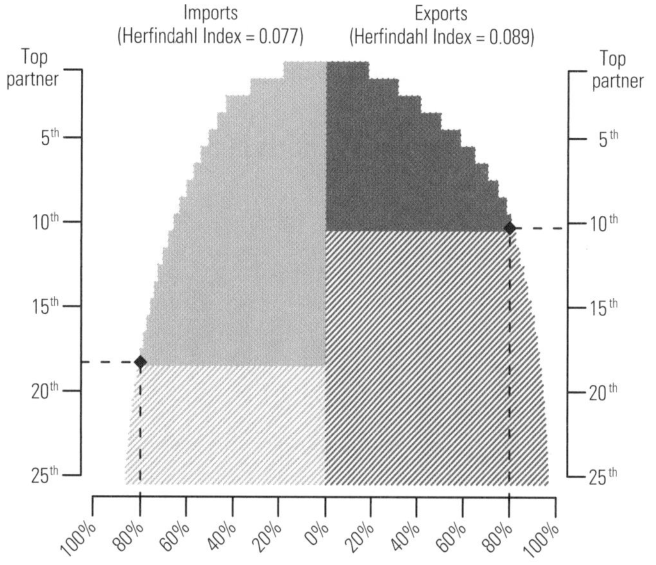

Table 4: Exports by principal countries and SITC sections in 2010

(Value in million US$, percentages of country total)

Country	Total	Shares by SITC sections (%) 0+1	2+4	3	5	6	7	8	9	Total
World	3878.4	24.2	15.7	49.5	1.4	5.6	2.0	0.7	0.7	100
Spain	716.6	11.7	3.2	84.7	0.0	0.2	0.0	0.0	0.1	100
Netherlands	508.6	85.8	8.0	5.6	0.0	0.5	0.1	0.1	0.0	100
Italy	376.6	6.2	12.5	60.1	0.2	14.9	0.1	0.0	6.0	100
Chad	337.8	6.2	0.2	84.3	6.1	1.6	0.8	0.4	0.4	100
China	329.6	0.3	45.1	54.3	0.0	0.1	0.1	0.1	0.0	100
France	242.7	36.3	27.5	3.7	0.8	28.4	2.3	0.9	0.0	100
USA	219.7	19.6	14.2	65.5	0.0	0.2	0.4	0.0	0.1	100
Dem.Rep. of the Congo	173.0	7.3	0.3	68.3	3.4	6.2	14.1	0.4	0.1	100
India	138.4	0.0	7.9	90.8	0.1	1.1	0.1	0.0	...	100
Uruguay	78.7	0.0	0.0	100.0	...	...	...	...	...	100

Imports Profile:

In 2010, imports were composed of 27.7 percent of mineral fuels, lubricants and related materials (SITC section 3), 22.6 percent of machinery and transport equipment (SITC section 7) and 17.1 percent of food, live animals, beverages and tobacco (SITC sections 0+1) (see table 2). From 2008 to 2010, top imported products included petroleum oils, oils from bituminous minerals, crude (HS code 2709), rice (HS code 1006) and fish, frozen, excluding fish fillets (HS code 0303) (see table 5).

Table 5: Top 10 import commodities 2008 to 2010

(Value in million US$)

HS code	4-digit heading of Harmonized System 2002	Value (million US$) 2008	2009	2010	Unit value 2008	2009	2010	Unit	SITC code
	All Commodities	4137.9	3788.6	5133.3					
2709	Petroleum oils, crude	0.0	0.0	1231.8	13.8	3.4	0.6	US$/kg	333
1006	Rice	236.7	252.4	196.0	0.6	0.5	0.5	US$/kg	042
0303	Fish, frozen, excluding fish fillets	173.0	240.0	188.7	1.2	1.2	1.1	US$/kg	034
1001	Wheat and meslin	185.6	124.0	123.9	0.5	0.3	0.3	US$/kg	041
3004	Medicaments (excluding goods of heading 30.02, 30.05 or 30.06)	116.9	130.8	135.2	23.0	18.1	*17.6*	US$/kg	542
8703	Motor cars and other motor vehicles principally designed for the transport	113.1	115.8	129.8		*18.6*	*19.4*	thsd US$/unit	781
2523	Portland cement, aluminous cement, slag cement	99.1	117.2	122.5	0.1	0.1	0.1	US$/kg	661
8905	Light-vessels, fire-floats, dredgers, floating cranes and other vessels	234.7	60.2	38.9					793
8704	Motor vehicles for the transport of goods	91.9	90.0	120.0	*27.1*			thsd US$/unit	782
2710	Petroleum oils, other than crude	44.8	66.9	111.1	1.1	0.5	*0.8*	US$/kg	334

Canada

Imports: FOB, by origin | **Exports: FOB, by last known destination** | **Trade System: General**

Overview:

From 2007 to 2011, the value of exports of Canada increased on average by 1.8 percent each year despite a big drop of 30.8 percent in 2009 and amounted to 450.4 bln US$ (see table 1 and graph 1). During the same period, imports increased on average by 4.3 percent each year and amounted to 450.5 bln US$ (see table 2 and graph 1). This resulted in a trade deficit of 0.1 bln US$ in 2011, much lower than the 2010 deficit of 5.5 bln US$ (see graph 1). By MDG regions, large deficits were recorded with Eastern Asia (-33.9 bln US$), Latin America and the Caribbean (-29.4 bln US$) and Developed Europe (-15.5 bln US$) (see graph 2). The trade balance also recorded a surplus of 104.7 bln US$ with Developed North America. In 2011, 3 (respectively 11) major partners accounted for 80 percent of exports (respectively imports) (see graph 3).

Graph 1: Total imports, exports and trade balance

(Bln US$ by year)

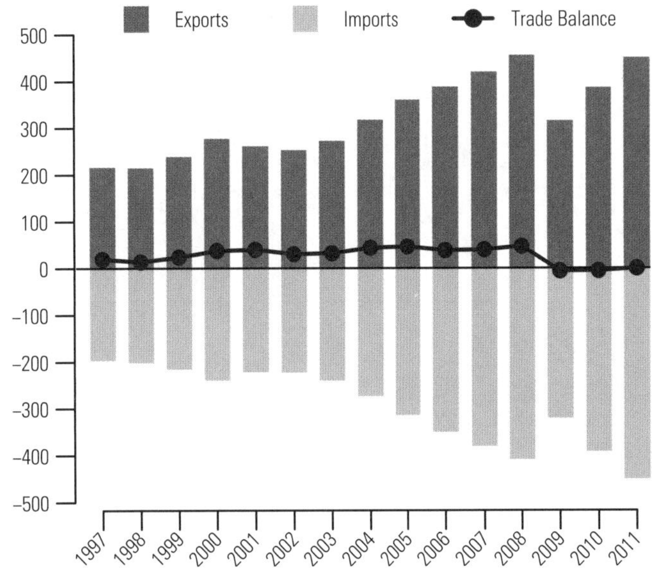

Table 1: Exports by SITC sections

(Value in million US$, growth and shares in percentage)

SITC	2011	Avg. Growth rates (%) 2007-2011	2010-2011	2011 share
Total	450396.9	1.8	16.5	100.0
0+1	33383.5	5.2	13.2	7.4
2+4	44700.4	6.3	25.1	9.9
3	115852.0	7.4	25.9	25.7
5	39533.0	3.3	19.2	8.8
6	56084.8	-3.0	11.6	12.5
7	109679.4	-3.7	8.5	24.4
8	20264.1	-2.5	6.6	4.5
9	30899.7	8.3	19.9	6.9

Table 2: Imports by SITC sections

(Value in million US$, growth and shares in percentage)

SITC	2011	Avg. Growth rates (%) 2007-2011	2010-2011	2011 share
Total	450536.9	4.3	14.9	100.0
0+1	30451.2	8.1	14.2	6.8
2+4	13913.3	4.2	19.9	3.1
3	53134.4	10.6	34.6	11.8
5	45802.5	4.0	10.1	10.2
6	55082.1	3.8	14.4	12.2
7	180607.8	1.8	12.0	40.1
8	52397.9	3.6	8.8	11.6
9	19147.7	15.8	26.0	4.2

Exports Profile:

Canada's exports in 2011 were mainly composed of 25.7 percent of mineral fuels, lubricants and related materials (SITC section 3), 24.4 percent of machinery and transport equipment (SITC section 7) and 12.5 percent of manufactured goods classified chiefly by material (SITC section 6) (see table 1). In addition to USA, other major partners for exports in 2011 included United Kingdom and China (see table 4). From 2009 to 2011, Canada's major commodities for exports included petroleum oils and oils obtained from bituminous minerals, crude (HS code 2709), motor cars and other motor vehicles principally designed for the transport (HS code 8703) and petroleum gases and other gaseous hydrocarbons (HS code 2711) (see table 3).

Table 3: Top 10 export commodities 2009 to 2011

(Value in million US$)

HS code	4-digit heading of Harmonized System 2007	Value (million US$) 2009	2010	2011	Unit value 2009	2010	2011	Unit	SITC code
	All Commodities	315176.8	386579.9	450396.9					
2709	Petroleum oils and oils obtained from bituminous minerals, crude	37619.2	50458.8	69477.2	*0.7*	*0.4*	*0.6*	US$/kg	333
8703	Motor cars and other motor vehicles principally designed for the transport	23342.1	36898.9	39772.2	*18.6*	*20.0*	*20.4*	thsd US$/unit	781
2711	Petroleum gases and other gaseous hydrocarbons	16113.0	17841.5	16537.7					343
2710	Petroleum oils, other than crude	10528.5	14424.3	17744.3					334
9999	Commodities not specified according to kind	13013.7	11934.4	13052.4					931
7108	Gold (including gold plated with platinum)	7347.1	13436.7	16980.9	30.9	39.3	49.0	thsd US$/kg	971
8708	Parts and accessories of the motor vehicles of headings 87.01 to 87.05	6120.2	8799.5	9368.0			*8.7*	US$/kg	784
8802	Other aircraft (for example, helicopters, aeroplanes); spacecraft	6893.9	6742.6	6597.3					792
2701	Coal; briquettes, ovoids and similar solid fuels manufactured from coal	4354.4	5815.8	8089.8	0.2	0.2	*0.2*	US$/kg	321
7601	Unwrought aluminium	4271.5	5853.1	6460.9	1.7	2.3	2.6	US$/kg	684

Graph 2: Trade Balance by MDG Regions in 2011

(Bln US$)

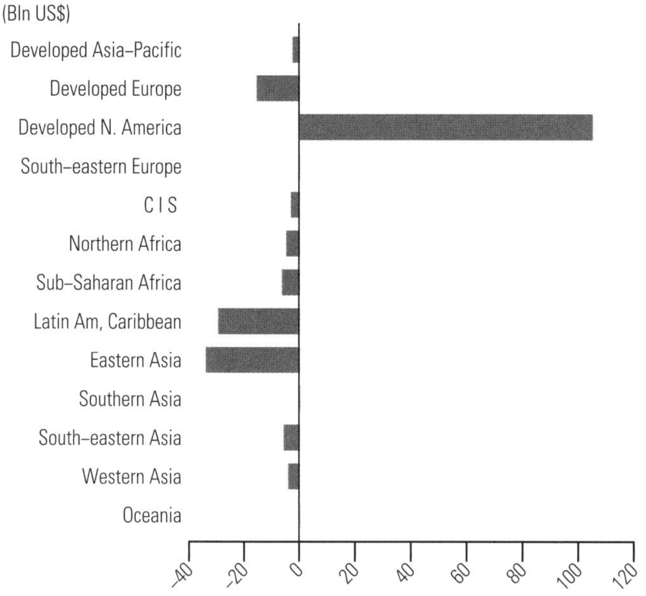

Graph 3: Partner concentration of trade in 2011

(Cumulative share by ranked partners)

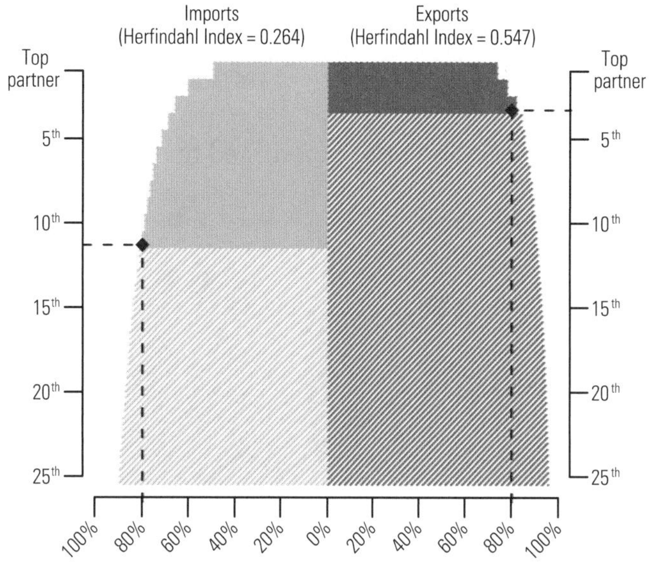

Table 4: Exports by principal countries and SITC sections in 2011

(Value in million US$, percentages of country total)

Country	Total	Shares by SITC sections (%) 0 + 1	2 + 4	3	5	6	7	8	9	Total
World	450396.9	7.4	9.9	25.7	8.8	12.5	24.4	4.5	6.9	100
USA	331737.9	5.7	4.3	31.7	8.8	13.2	26.7	4.8	4.7	100
United Kingdom	18976.7	1.9	6.8	1.2	7.0	10.2	7.5	2.2	63.2	100
China	16957.1	6.9	57.1	7.8	9.5	5.8	9.8	1.8	1.3	100
Japan	10776.0	20.2	41.1	21.1	3.0	6.1	5.2	2.0	1.5	100
Mexico	5529.6	14.2	19.8	2.5	8.5	14.6	35.0	4.0	1.3	100
Rep. of Korea	5135.3	17.1	23.7	37.6	4.2	6.0	8.2	2.3	0.8	100
Netherlands	4851.3	2.4	24.1	31.0	8.7	21.4	8.4	3.3	0.7	100
Germany	3859.5	4.0	19.7	6.4	9.8	6.0	39.0	7.2	7.9	100
France	3111.1	4.6	19.3	7.7	9.6	6.9	44.1	7.0	0.7	100
China, Hong Kong SAR	2989.7	10.9	14.8	0.0	4.1	9.8	18.6	4.8	37.0	100

Imports Profile:

In 2011, machinery and transport equipment (SITC section 7) accounted for a large part of Canada's imports with 40.1 percent of imported goods (see table 2). Other major commodity groups were manufactured goods classified chiefly by material (SITC section 6) and mineral fuels, lubricants and related materials (SITC section 3), respectively with 12.2 and 11.8 percent of imports. Top products for imports were petroleum oils and oils obtained from bituminous minerals, crude (HS code 2709), motor cars and other motor vehicles principally designed for the transport (HS code 8703) and parts and accessories of the motor vehicles of headings 87.01 to 87.05 (HS code 8708) (see table 5).

Table 5: Top 10 import commodities 2009 to 2011

(Value in million US$)

HS code	4-digit heading of Harmonized System 2007	Value (million US$) 2009	2010	2011	Unit value 2009	2010	2011	Unit	SITC code
	All Commodities	321227.6	392108.7	450536.9					
2709	Petroleum oils and oils obtained from bituminous minerals, crude	18503.7	23082.1	28832.2	*0.7*	*0.4*	*0.6*	US$/kg	333
8703	Motor cars and other motor vehicles principally designed for the transport	17062.2	22359.2	23562.1	*16.9*	*19.5*	*20.5*	thsd US$/unit	781
8708	Parts and accessories of the motor vehicles of headings 87.01 to 87.05	13128.0	17824.6	19419.7			*10.5*	US$/kg	784
2710	Petroleum oils, other than crude	6249.1	9462.6	16580.4					334
8704	Motor vehicles for the transport of goods	7554.7	11247.9	12308.7	*26.2*	*29.9*	*33.3*	thsd US$/unit	782
3004	Medicaments (excluding goods of heading 30.02, 30.05 or 30.06)	8567.9	8899.2	9398.2					542
8471	Automatic data processing machines and units thereof	6519.6	8117.5	9443.7					752
8517	Electrical apparatus for line telephony or line telegraphy	5475.3	7325.7	9277.3					764
7108	Gold (including gold plated with platinum)	3968.6	7358.6	10194.8	*23.6*	*26.4*	30.8	thsd US$/kg	971
9999	Commodities not specified according to kind	5287.6	6222.0	7137.4					931

Cape Verde

Imports: CIF, by origin	Exports: FOB, by last known destination	Trade System: Special

Overview:

In 2011, exports of Cape Verde increased by a significant 48.0 percent to 68.9 mln US$ (see table 1 and graph 1). During the same period, imports increased by 31.5 percent to 961.3 mln US$ (see table 2 and graph 1). This resulted in a trade deficit of 892.4 mln US$ in 2011, higher than the 2010 deficit of 684.2 mln US$ (see graph 1). By MDG regions, trade with Developed Europe alone accounted for a large part of this deficit (-713.0 mln US$) (see graph 2). Significant deficits were also recorded with Latin America and the Caribbean (-53.3 mln US$) and Eastern Asia (-26.1 mln US$). Trade was concentrated among a few partners: in 2011, 2 (respectively 8) major partners accounted for 80 percent of exports (respectively imports) (see graph 3). See footnote*.

Graph 1: Total imports, exports and trade balance

(Mln US$ by year)

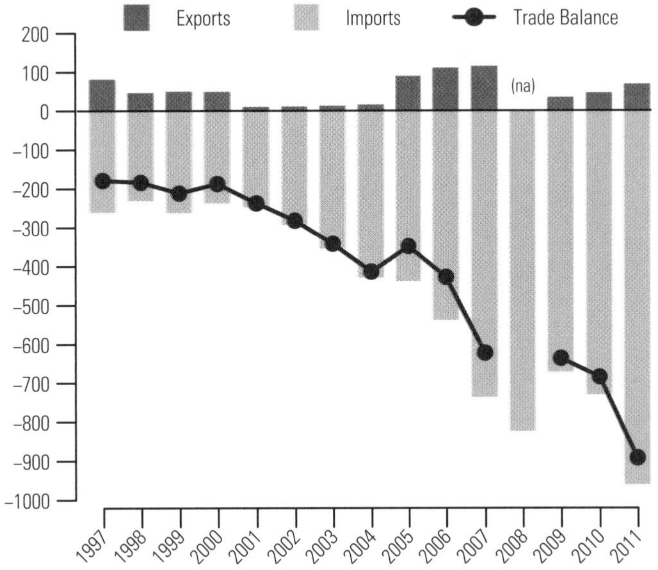

Exports Profile:

In 2011, major bulk of exports came from food, live animals, beverages and tobacco (SITC sections 0+1) with 83.7 percent of total exports (see table 1). The other major commodity group was miscellaneous manufactured articles (SITC section 8) with 14.5 percent of exports. Major markets for exports included Spain, Portugal and Germany (see table 4). Exports to Spain were almost exclusively food, live animals, beverages and tobacco (SITC sections 0+1). From 2009 to 2011, top products for exports were prepared or preserved fish; caviar (HS code 1604), fish, frozen, excluding fish fillets and other fish meat of heading 03.04 (HS code 0303) and parts of footwear (HS code 6406) (see table 3).

Table 1: Exports by SITC sections

(Value in million US$, growth and shares in percentage)

SITC	2011	Avg. Growth rates (%) 2007-2011	2010-2011	2011 share
Total	68.9	-12.0	48.0	100.0
0+1	57.7	45.8	52.0	83.7
2+4	0.7	28.4	41.4	0.9
3	0.0	-94.8	...	0.0
5	0.5	5.7	4140.0	0.7
6	0.1	-53.1	408.6	0.1
8	10.0	-5.8	23.2	14.5

Table 2: Imports by SITC sections

(Value in million US$, growth and shares in percentage)

SITC	2011	Avg. Growth rates (%) 2007-2011	2010-2011	2011 share
Total	961.3	6.9	31.5	100.0
0+1	229.3	6.6	20.2	23.8
2+4	28.1	2.2	9.9	2.9
3	185.1	22.8	112.1	19.3
5	54.7	6.7	20.0	5.7
6	150.2	3.7	19.3	15.6
7	250.6	2.7	23.4	26.1
8	63.3	7.3	20.9	6.6

Table 3: Top 10 export commodities 2009 to 2011

(Value in million US$)

HS code	4-digit heading of Harmonized System 2007	Value (million US$) 2009	2010	2011	Unit value 2009	2010	2011	Unit	SITC code
	All Commodities	35.2	46.6	68.9					
1604	Prepared or preserved fish; caviar	10.5	18.2	30.6	5.7	6.3	7.2	US$/kg	037
0303	Fish, frozen, excluding fish fillets and other fish meat of heading 03.04	13.4	18.0	24.9	1.2	1.4	1.8	US$/kg	034
6406	Parts of footwear	3.7	4.2	4.7	81.3	72.9	76.3	US$/kg	851
6203	Men's or boys' suits, ensembles, jackets, blazers, trousers	3.3	1.6	2.0					841
6109	T-shirts, singlets and other vests, knitted or crocheted	1.2	1.2	1.8	*6.3*	*6.0*	*5.5*	US$/unit	845
6107	Men's or boys' underpants, briefs, nightshirts, pyjamas, bathrobes	1.2	1.1	1.5					843
2208	Alcohol of a strength by volume of less than 80 % vol	0.8	0.7	0.7	*3.6*	*3.7*	*4.1*	US$/litre	112
0306	Crustaceans, whether in shell or not	0.4	0.4	0.9	49.7	56.2	54.4	US$/kg	036
7204	Ferrous waste and scrap; remelting scrap ingots of iron or steel	0.2	0.4	0.5	0.1	0.1	0.1	US$/kg	282
0307	Molluscs, whether in shell or not	0.3	0.5	...	1.4	1.7		US$/kg	036

*2009, 2010 and 2011 exports do not include mineral fuels, lubricants and related materials (SITC section 3)

Graph 2: Trade Balance by MDG Regions in 2011

(Mln US$)

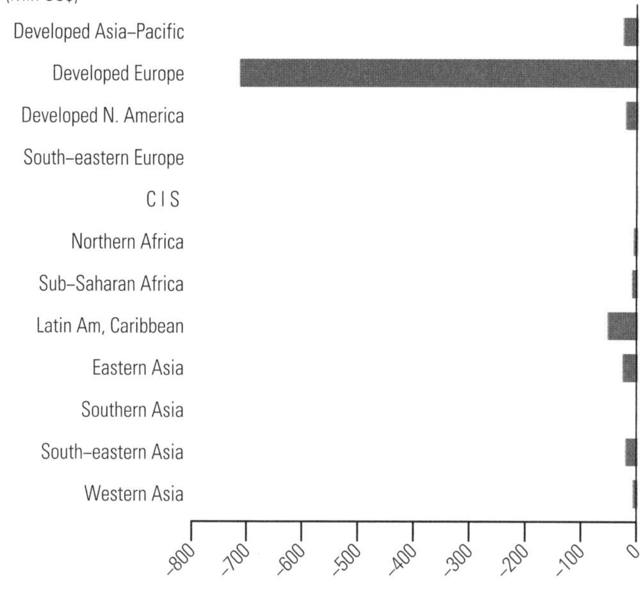

Graph 3: Partner concentration of trade in 2011

(Cumulative share by ranked partners)

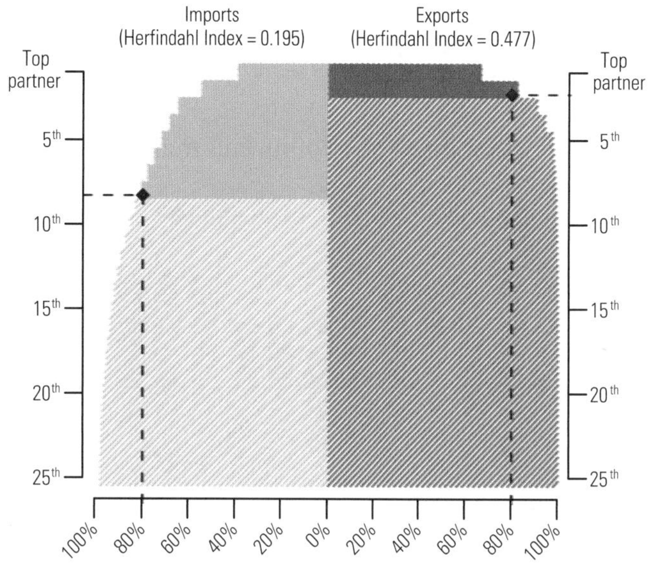

Table 4: Exports by principal countries and SITC sections in 2011

(Value in million US$, percentages of country total)

Country	Total	Shares by SITC sections (%) 0+1	2+4	3	5	6	7	8	9	Total
World	68.9	83.7	0.9	0.0	0.7	0.1	...	14.5	...	100
Spain	45.9	99.9	0.1	...	...	0.0	...	0.0	...	100
Portugal	10.8	13.5	0.2	...	0.0	0.6	...	85.8	...	100
Germany	5.8	84.6	1.6	...	1.1	0.0	...	12.7	...	100
El Salvador	2.4	100.0	0.0	...	...	...	...	...	...	100
France	2.3	100.0	0.0	...	...	...	...	...	...	100
Sao Tome and Principe	0.4	0.0	0.0	...	100.0	...	...	...	...	100
USA	0.3	100.0	0.0	...	...	...	...	...	...	100
India	0.2	0.0	100.0	...	...	...	...	...	...	100
Libya	0.2	100.0	0.0	...	...	...	...	...	...	100
Guinea-Bissau	0.1	26.3	28.2	...	42.5	...	...	3.1	...	100

Imports Profile:

In 2011, Cape Verde's imports were mainly composed of 26.1 percent of machinery and transport equipment (SITC section 7), 23.8 percent of food, live animals, beverages and tobacco (SITC sections 0+1) and 19.3 percent of mineral fuels, lubricants and related materials (SITC section 3) (see table 2). Over the last three years, top imported products included petroleum oils, other than crude (HS code 2710), portland cement, aluminous cement, slag cement (HS code 2523) and rice (HS code 1006) (see table 5).

Table 5: Top 10 import commodities 2009 to 2011

(Value in million US$)

HS code	4-digit heading of Harmonized System 2007	Value (million US$) 2009	2010	2011	Unit value 2009	2010	2011	Unit	SITC code
	All Commodities	671.0	730.8	961.3					
2710	Petroleum oils, other than crude	68.7	76.3	169.2	0.6	0.6	0.8	US$/kg	334
2523	Portland cement, aluminous cement, slag cement	28.1	27.9	30.0	0.1	0.1	0.1	US$/kg	661
1006	Rice	29.1	24.8	25.1	0.3	0.7	0.8	US$/kg	042
8703	Motor cars and other motor vehicles principally designed for the transport	16.0	15.8	19.0	*16.8*	*17.2*	*16.6*	thsd US$/unit	781
8704	Motor vehicles for the transport of goods	16.5	15.4	17.8					782
0402	Milk and cream, concentrated or containing added sugar	13.3	15.8	19.4	3.2	3.7	5.1	US$/kg	022
7214	Other bars and rods of iron or non-alloy steel	13.3	12.4	13.1	0.8	0.7	0.8	US$/kg	676
7308	Structures (excluding prefabricated buildings of heading 94.06)	7.8	11.6	16.9	1.5	1.9	2.2	US$/kg	691
1701	Cane or beet sugar and chemically pure sucrose, in solid form	9.5	8.9	16.9	0.5	0.7	0.9	US$/kg	061
8471	Automatic data processing machines and units thereof	8.5	17.8	7.7					752

Imports: CIF, by origin | **Exports: FOB, by last known destination** | **Trade System: Special**

Overview:

From 2005 to 2009, exports of Central African Republic decreased on average by 7.7 percent each year. It experienced a significant drop of 29.5 percent in 2009 and amounted to 80.5 mln US$ (see table 1 and graph 1). During the same period, imports increased on average by 3.4 percent each year to 211.7 mln US$ (see table 2 and graph 1). The trade balance recorded a significant deficit of 131.2 mln US$ compared to a deficit of 70.8 mln US$ in 2008 (see graph 1). Trade with all MDG regions were in deficit, with Sub-Saharan Africa recording the largest deficit amounting to 33.9 mln US$ (see graph 2). In 2009, trade was concentrated among a few partners: 4 (respectively 12) major partners accounted for 80 percent of exports (respectively imports) (see graph 3).

Graph 1: Total imports, exports and trade balance

(Mln US$ by year)

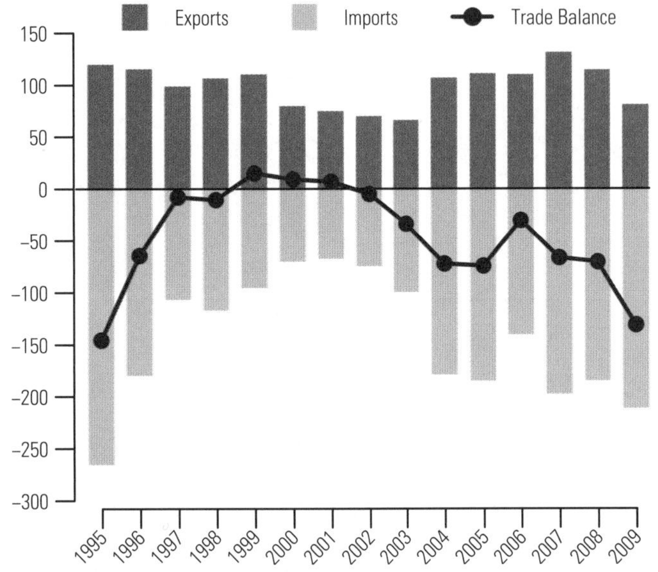

Table 1: Exports by SITC sections

(Value in million US$, growth and shares in percentage)

SITC	2009	Avg. Growth rates (%) 2005-2009	2008-2009	2009 share
Total	80.5	-7.7	-29.5	100.0
0+1	2.7	33.9	67.8	3.3
2+4	75.1	2.7	-24.3	93.3
6	0.3	-70.9	-96.9	0.4
7	0.7	-18.2	-79.8	0.8
8	1.2	66.8	531.9	1.5
9	0.6	94.2	16.0	0.7

Table 2: Imports by SITC sections

(Value in million US$, growth and shares in percentage)

SITC	2009	Avg. Growth rates (%) 2005-2009	2008-2009	2009 share
Total	211.7	3.4	14.4	100.0
0+1	76.0	26.4	70.1	35.9
2+4	13.3	-29.5	45.5	6.3
3	1.3	-54.9	-47.7	0.6
5	30.8	24.4	23.8	14.6
6	29.8	12.4	-8.8	14.1
7	46.5	10.2	-16.3	22.0
8	13.6	17.6	-11.8	6.4
9	0.3	...	245.7	0.1

Exports Profile:

In 2009, exports of inedible crude materials (excluding fuels), animal and vegetable oils, fats, waxes (SITC sections 2+4) dropped by 24.3 percent and accounted for 93.3 percent of exported goods (see table 1). Exports of miscellaneous manufactured articles (SITC section 8) increased by 531.9 percent and represented 1.5 percent of exports. Belgium, China and France were the top three markets for exports in 2009 (see table 4). Inedible crude materials (except fuels), animal and vegetable oils, fats and waxes (SITC sections 2+4) represented all exports to China and the majority of exports to Belgium and France. From 2007 to 2009, top exported products included diamonds, whether or not worked, but not mounted or set (HS code 7102), wood in the rough, whether or not stripped of bark or sapwood (HS code 4403) and wood sawn or chipped lengthwise, sliced or peeled (HS code 4407) (see table 3). They accounted respectively for 61.9, 20.4 and 10.5 percent of exports in 2009.

Table 3: Top 10 export commodities 2007 to 2009

(Value in million US$)

HS code	4-digit heading of Harmonized System 2002	Value (million US$) 2007	2008	2009	Unit value 2007	2008	2009	Unit	SITC code
	All Commodities	131.1	114.2	80.5					
7102	Diamonds, whether or not worked, but not mounted or set	62.4	49.4	49.8					667
4403	Wood in the rough, whether or not stripped of bark or sapwood	38.9	36.6	16.4					247
4407	Wood sawn or chipped lengthwise, sliced or peeled	24.0	20.2	8.5	*0.6*	*0.8*	*1.1*	thsd US$/m³	248
0901	Coffee, whether or not roasted or decaffeinated	3.4	0.6	1.8	0.6	0.7	0.9	US$/kg	071
5201	Cotton, not carded or combed	1.0	1.7	0.4	1.1	1.0	0.9	US$/kg	263
8705	Special purpose motor vehicles	...	1.1	0.1			*112.1*	thsd US$/unit	782
8704	Motor vehicles for the transport of goods	0.1	1.0	0.0		*27.2*	*0.0*	thsd US$/unit	782
7108	Gold (including gold plated with platinum)	0.2	0.3	0.5	12.9	16.0	19.9	US$/kg	971
2104	Soups and broths and preparations therefor	0.1	0.6	0.1	2.7	2.4	0.8	US$/kg	098
8431	Parts suitable for use principally with the machinery of headings 84.25	...	0.6	...		9.0		US$/kg	723

Graph 2: Trade Balance by MDG Regions in 2009

(Mln US$)

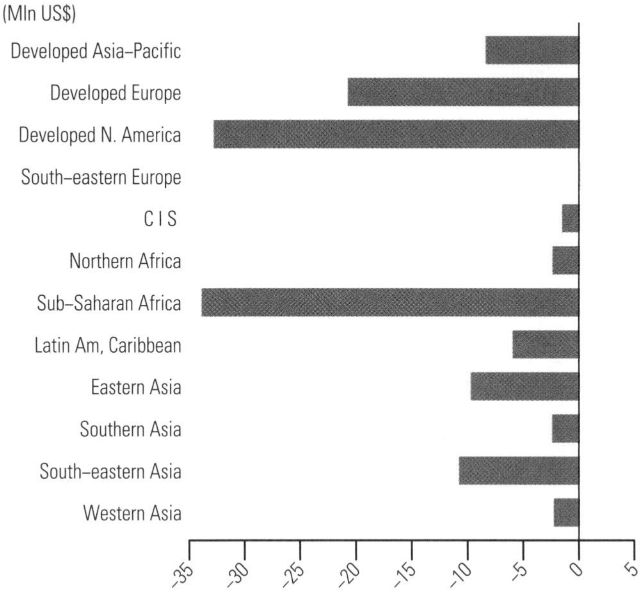

Graph 3: Partner concentration of trade in 2009

(Cumulative share by ranked partners)

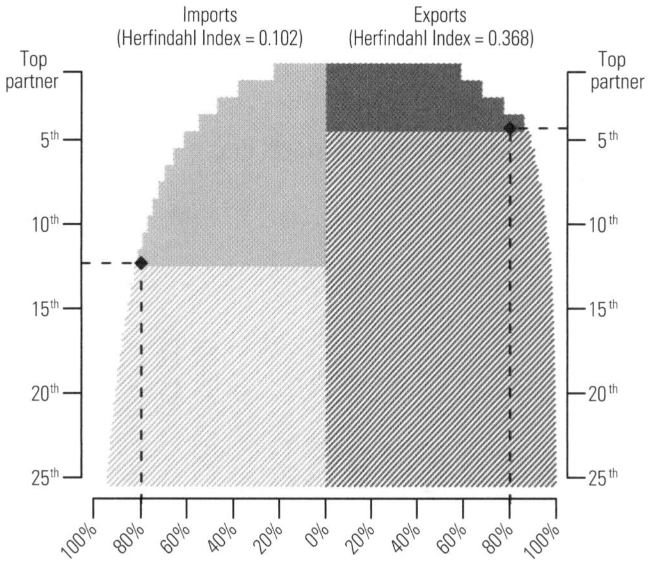

Table 4: Exports by principal countries and SITC sections in 2009

(Value in million US$, percentages of country total)

Country	Total	Shares by SITC sections (%) 0 + 1	2 + 4	3	5	6	7	8	9	Total
World	80.5	3.3	93.3	...	...	0.4	0.8	1.5	0.7	100
Belgium	47.1	0.0	99.6	...	...	...	...	...	0.4	100
China	7.5	0.0	100.0	...	...	...	...	...	...	100
France	7.5	19.9	68.8	...	...	...	3.0	7.3	1.1	100
Germany	6.8	0.0	99.5	...	...	...	0.1	...	0.4	100
Saudi Arabia	2.3	0.0	100.0	...	...	...	...	...	...	100
Italy	1.3	0.0	100.0	...	...	...	...	...	...	100
Turkey	1.2	0.0	100.0	...	...	...	...	...	...	100
Cameroon	1.1	27.3	40.1	...	...	8.7	21.7	1.1	1.0	100
Spain	0.9	0.0	100.0	...	...	...	...	...	...	100
Switzerland	0.8	30.5	69.3	...	...	...	0.1	...	...	100

Imports Profile:

Imports were composed of 35.9 percent of food, live animals, beverages and tobacco (SITC sections 0+1), 22.0 percent of machinery and transport equipment (SITC section 7) and 14.6 percent of chemicals and related products, n.e.s. (SITC section 5) (see table 2). From 2007 to 2009, top imported products included medicaments (excluding goods of heading 30.02, 30.05 or 30.06) (HS code 3004), diamonds, whether or not worked, but not mounted or set (HS code 7102) and wheat or meslin flour (HS code 1101) (see table 5).

Table 5: Top 10 import commodities 2007 to 2009

(Value in million US$)

HS code	4-digit heading of Harmonized System 2002	Value (million US$) 2007	2008	2009	Unit value 2007	2008	2009	Unit	SITC code
	All Commodities	197.8	185.0	211.7					
3004	Medicaments (excluding goods of heading 30.02, 30.05 or 30.06)	16.6	16.1	20.7	12.2	16.7	22.8	US$/kg	542
7102	Diamonds, whether or not worked, but not mounted or set	51.6	...	...					667
1101	Wheat or meslin flour	7.3	12.3	13.1	0.4	0.6	0.6	US$/kg	046
0713	Dried leguminous vegetables, shelled	0.9	0.9	23.4	0.5	0.6	12.7	US$/kg	054
8517	Electrical apparatus for line telephony or line telegraphy	8.8	5.4	6.4					764
1102	Cereal flours other than of wheat or meslin	4.6	4.3	8.6	0.8	0.5	0.5	US$/kg	047
1701	Cane or beet sugar and pure sucrose, in solid form	3.7	4.8	5.7	0.5	0.4	0.6	US$/kg	061
8703	Motor cars and other motor vehicles principally designed for the transport	4.2	4.5	5.3	*17.0*	*15.6*	*19.6*	thsd US$/unit	781
2523	Portland cement, aluminous cement, slag cement	2.6	4.4	5.7	0.2	0.3	0.2	US$/kg	661
2403	Other manufactured tobacco and tobacco substitutes	3.1	4.2	5.5	14.1	15.3	15.6	US$/kg	122

Chile

Imports: CIF, by origin | **Exports: FOB, by consignment** | **Trade System: General**

Overview:

From 2007 to 2011, Chile's exports increased on average by 4.6 percent each year to reach 81.4 bln US$ in 2011, surpassing its previous peak in 2010 and overcoming the sharp decline in 2009 (see table 1 and graph 1). During the same period, imports increased on average by 12.3 percent each year and reached 74.9 bln US$ in 2011 (see table 2 and graph 1). This resulted in a trade surplus of 6.5 bln US$, much lower than the surplus of 14.4 bln US$ in 2010 (see graph 1). By MDG regions, major surpluses were recorded with Eastern Asia (+9.5 bln US$), Developed Asia-Pacific (+6.5 bln US$) and Developed Europe (+4.2 bln US$) (see graph 2). The trade balance showed deficits with Latin America and the Caribbean (-6.6 bln US$) and Developed North America (-5.5 bln US$). By partners, both exports and imports were diversified: in 2011, 15 major partners accounted for 80 percent of exports (compared to 13 major partners for imports) (see graph 3).

Graph 1: Total imports, exports and trade balance

(Bln US$ by year)

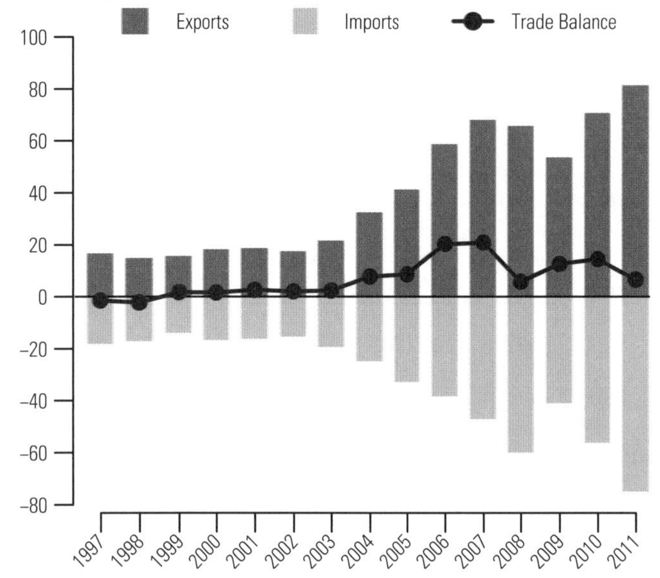

Exports Profile:

In 2011, Chile's exports were composed of 41.9 percent of manufactured goods classified chiefly by material (SITC section 6), 29.2 percent of inedible crude materials (except fuels), animal and vegetable oils, fats and waxes (SITC sections 2+4) and 17.4 percent of food, live animals, beverages and tobacco (SITC sections 0+1) (see table 1). Top markets for exports included China, USA and Japan (see table 4). From 2009 to 2011, top products for exports included refined copper and copper alloys, unwrought (HS code 7403), copper ores and concentrates (HS code 2603) and chemical wood pulp, soda or sulphate, other than dissolving grades (HS code 4703) (see table 3).

Table 1: Exports by SITC sections

(Value in million US$, growth and shares in percentage)

SITC	2011	Avg. Growth rates (%) 2007-2011	2010-2011	2011 share
Total	81 411.1	4.6	15.3	100.0
0+1	14 138.1	8.4	21.6	17.4
2+4	23 806.3	0.8	9.4	29.2
3	820.3	-0.3	198.5	1.0
5	3 535.1	9.7	25.8	4.3
6	34 089.6	5.6	12.6	41.9
7	2 366.7	22.9	19.6	2.9
8	1 204.7	38.1	36.2	1.5
9	1 450.2	-13.5	41.5	1.8

Table 2: Imports by SITC sections

(Value in million US$, growth and shares in percentage)

SITC	2011	Avg. Growth rates (%) 2007-2011	2010-2011	2011 share
Total	74 907.1	12.3	33.2	100.0
0+1	5 132.0	15.6	28.6	6.9
2+4	2 353.3	6.7	56.1	3.1
3	17 987.6	12.1	54.9	24.0
5	7 452.7	12.2	24.6	9.9
6	8 268.6	15.9	17.0	11.0
7	26 479.0	18.3	30.4	35.3
8	7 233.8	19.7	25.6	9.7
9	0.1	-93.4	-42.7	0.0

Table 3: Top 10 export commodities 2009 to 2011

(Value in million US$)

HS code	4-digit heading of Harmonized System 2007	Value (million US$) 2009	2010	2011	Unit value 2009	2010	2011	Unit	SITC code
	All Commodities	53 592.2	70 631.5	81 411.1					
7403	Refined copper and copper alloys, unwrought	16 657.5	24 108.7	26 030.7	5.2	7.6	8.5	US$/kg	682
2603	Copper ores and concentrates	9 413.7	13 745.1	14 304.5	1.6	2.2	8.1	US$/kg	283
4703	Chemical wood pulp, soda or sulphate, other than dissolving grades	2 011.9	2 422.8	2 855.1	0.5	0.7	0.7	US$/kg	251
7402	Unrefined copper; copper anodes for electrolytic refining	1 631.1	2 403.2	3 199.8	4.8	7.4	9.4	US$/kg	682
2204	Wine of fresh grapes, including fortified wines	1 381.3	1 547.3	1 696.3	2.0	2.1	2.5	US$/litre	112
0806	Grapes, fresh or dried	1 323.0	1 486.7	1 673.4	1.4	1.8	1.8	US$/kg	057
2613	Molybdenum ores and concentrates	1 147.6	1 228.9	1 471.9	15.9	19.0	19.9	US$/kg	287
0304	Fish fillets and other fish meat (whether or not minced)	1 152.3	1 007.3	1 449.6	6.7	8.0	9.1	US$/kg	034
0303	Fish, frozen, excluding fish fillets and other fish meat of heading 03.04	1 042.0	1 029.2	1 440.8	3.2	4.4	5.0	US$/kg	034
7108	Gold (including gold plated with platinum)	879.7	1 019.0	1 450.2	29.8	37.1	47.0	thsd US$/kg	971

Graph 2: Trade Balance by MDG Regions in 2011

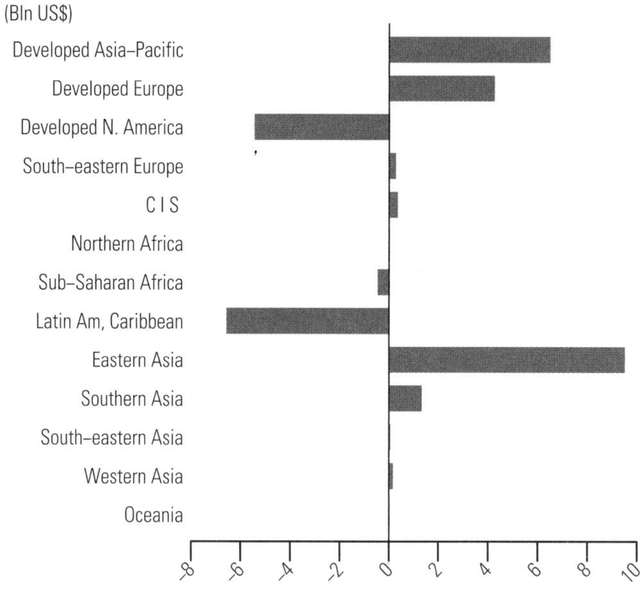

Graph 3: Partner concentration of trade in 2011

(Cumulative share by ranked partners)

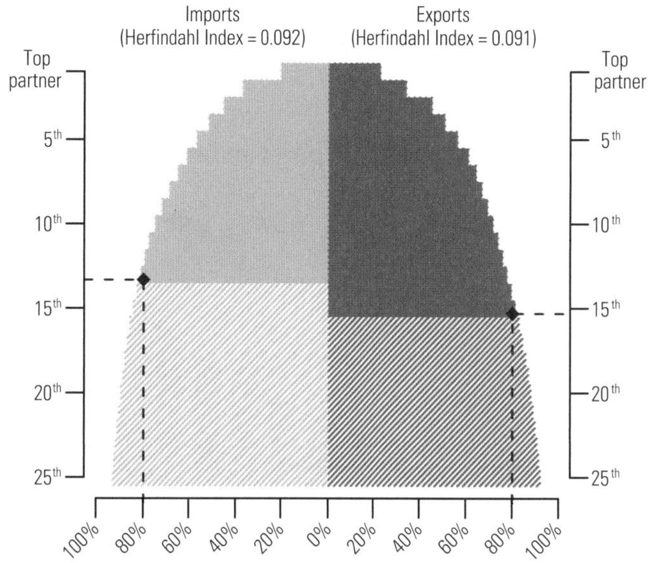

Table 4: Exports by principal countries and SITC sections in 2011

(Value in million US$, percentages of country total)

Country	Total	Shares by SITC sections (%) 0 + 1	2 + 4	3	5	6	7	8	9	Total
World	81411.1	17.4	29.2	1.0	4.3	41.9	2.9	1.5	1.8	100
China	18600.9	3.6	34.7	0.0	1.1	60.5	0.1	0.0	...	100
USA	9087.7	36.4	8.8	0.9	5.2	43.2	1.9	0.5	3.1	100
Japan	9009.4	21.1	69.5	0.1	1.3	8.0	0.0	0.0	...	100
Brazil	4489.6	13.8	22.6	0.1	12.1	47.6	3.1	0.8	...	100
Rep. of Korea	4448.4	8.9	39.3	...	2.1	49.6	0.0	0.0	0.0	100
Netherlands	3813.5	14.9	23.8	0.1	2.5	58.6	0.1	0.0	...	100
Italy	2670.7	8.1	14.5	0.0	0.9	76.3	0.2	0.0	...	100
Other Asia, nes	2063.1	9.3	9.9	...	0.1	80.7	0.0	0.0	...	100
Peru	2017.0	16.2	7.4	7.1	12.8	18.5	19.6	18.5	...	100
India	1913.5	1.4	95.0	0.0	2.7	0.7	0.2	0.0	...	100

Imports Profile:

In 2011, machinery and transport equipment (SITC section 7) and mineral fuels, lubricants and related materials (SITC section 3) accounted respectively for 35.3 and 24.0 percent of total imported goods. From 2009 to 2011, top products for imports included petroleum oils, other than crude (HS code 2710), petroleum oils and oils obtained from bituminous minerals, crude (HS code 2709) and motor cars and other motor vehicles principally designed for the transport (HS code 8703) (see table 5).

Table 5: Top 10 import commodities 2009 to 2011

(Value in million US$)

HS code	4-digit heading of Harmonized System 2007	Value (million US$) 2009	2010	2011	Unit value 2009	2010	2011	Unit	SITC code
	All Commodities	41062.5	56220.8	74907.1					
2710	Petroleum oils, other than crude	3275.8	4670.2	7730.4	*0.6*	*0.7*	*0.6*	US$/kg	334
2709	Petroleum oils and oils obtained from bituminous minerals, crude	3975.7	4340.8	6498.0	0.4	0.5	0.7	US$/kg	333
8703	Motor cars and other motor vehicles principally designed for the transport	1431.9	3132.0	3793.2	*12.6*	*13.5*	0.2	thsd US$/unit	781
8704	Motor vehicles for the transport of goods	998.6	2183.7	2646.8	*30.3*	*23.7*		thsd US$/unit	782
2711	Petroleum gases and other gaseous hydrocarbons	1079.1	1724.4	2387.5	*0.5*	*0.5*	0.5	US$/kg	343
8517	Electrical apparatus for line telephony or line telegraphy	1074.3	1532.0	1945.8					764
8471	Automatic data processing machines and units thereof	804.3	1084.3	1266.5	*123.3*	*123.6*	61.1	US$/unit	752
2701	Coal; briquettes, ovoids and similar solid fuels manufactured from coal	692.1	713.7	1144.7	*0.1*	*0.1*	0.1	US$/kg	321
8429	Self-propelled bulldozers, angledozers, graders, levellers, scrapers	409.5	891.6	1197.1	*226.6*	*172.4*		thsd US$/unit	723
4011	New pneumatic tyres, of rubber	476.8	591.9	1207.4	*121.7*	*108.8*	*47.8*	US$/unit	625

China

Imports: CIF, by origin | **Exports: FOB, by last known destination** | **Trade System: General**

Overview:

After a drop of 16.0 percent in 2009, the value of exports of China bounced back in 2010 by 31.3 percent and continued to rise by 20.3 percent to reach its peak of 1,898.4 bln US$ in 2011 (see table 1 and graph 1). Imports also showed an increase of 24.9 percent in 2011 and amounted to 1,743.4 bln US$ (see table 2 and graph 1). This resulted in a trade surplus of 155.0 bln US$ in 2011, lower than the 2010 surplus of 181.8 bln US$ (see graph 1). Two MDG regions accounted for a large part of this surplus: Developed North America (+205.3 bln US$) and Developed Europe (+119.0 bln US$) (see graph 2). Trade recorded significant deficits with Developed Asia-Pacific (-96.3 bln US$), Eastern Asia (-37.8 bln US$) and Sub-Saharan Africa (-30.7 bln US$). In 2011, China's trade was diversified across partners: 24 (respectively 22) major partners accounted for 80 percent of exports (respectively imports) (see graph 3).

Graph 1: Total imports, exports and trade balance

(Bln US$ by year)

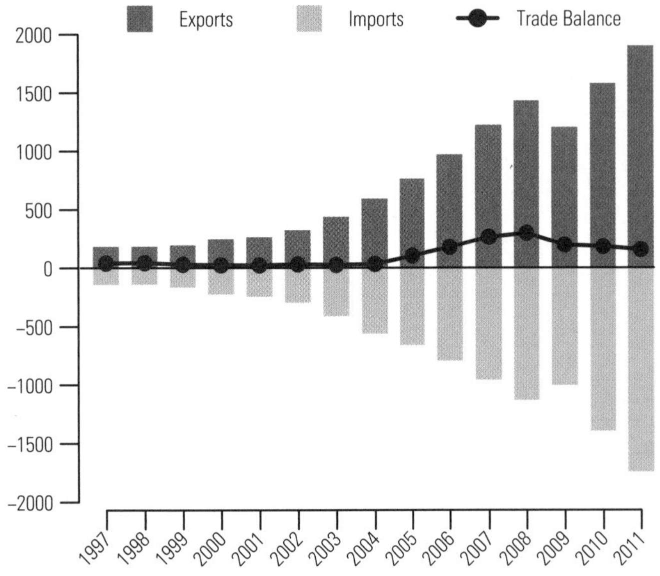

Table 1: Exports by SITC sections

(Value in million US$, growth and shares in percentage)

SITC	2011	Avg. Growth rates (%) 2007-2011	Avg. Growth rates (%) 2010-2011	2011 share
Total	1 898 388.4	11.7	20.3	100.0
0+1	52 770.5	13.2	22.6	2.8
2+4	15 546.3	13.3	29.6	0.8
3	32 274.1	11.5	21.0	1.7
5	114 723.0	17.4	31.1	6.0
6	319 564.3	9.8	28.3	16.8
7	902 599.3	11.8	15.6	47.5
8	458 568.3	11.5	21.7	24.2
9	2 342.5	1.8	59.6	0.1

Exports Profile:

In 2011, China's exports were mainly composed of 47.5 percent of machinery and transport equipment (SITC section 7), 24.2 percent of miscellaneous manufactured articles (SITC section 8) and 16.8 percent of manufactured goods classified chiefly by material (SITC section 6) (see table 1). USA, China, Hong Kong SAR and Japan were the three largest markets for exports in 2011 (see table 4). From 2009 to 2011, top exported commodities were automatic data processing machines and units thereof (HS code 8471), electrical apparatus for line telephony or line telegraphy (HS code 8517) and cruise ships, excursion boats, ferry-boats, cargo ships, barges (HS code 8901) (see table 3).

Table 2: Imports by SITC sections

(Value in million US$, growth and shares in percentage)

SITC	2011	Avg. Growth rates (%) 2007-2011	Avg. Growth rates (%) 2010-2011	2011 share
Total	1 743 394.9	16.2	24.9	100.0
0+1	32 455.6	25.9	35.2	1.9
2+4	296 543.8	24.0	34.2	17.0
3	275 727.8	27.3	45.9	15.8
5	180 542.3	13.9	20.8	10.4
6	150 314.9	9.9	14.5	8.6
7	630 916.7	11.2	14.8	36.2
8	127 380.9	9.9	12.5	7.3
9	49 513.0	111.7	168.6	2.8

Table 3: Top 10 export commodities 2009 to 2011

(Value in billion US$)

HS code	4-digit heading of Harmonized System 2007	Value (billion US$) 2009	2010	2011	Unit value 2009	2010	2011	Unit	SITC code
	All Commodities	1 201.6	1 577.8	1 898.4					
8471	Automatic data processing machines and units thereof	101.6	139.1	152.0	87.7	93.3	*91.1*	US$/unit	752
8517	Electrical apparatus for line telephony or line telegraphy	86.5	106.0	133.4					764
8901	Cruise ships, excursion boats, ferry-boats, cargo ships, barges	23.9	35.2	37.1	12.2	16.7	15.7	mln US$/unit	793
8528	Reception apparatus for television	26.7	31.9	30.3	100.2	116.6	111.2	US$/unit	761
8473	Parts and accessories for use with machines of heading 84.69 to 84.72	26.2	31.3	30.6	*26.9*	*31.1*	*30.7*	US$/kg	759
8542	Electronic integrated circuits	23.6	29.6	32.9					776
8541	Diodes, transistors and similar semiconductor devices	15.5	32.0	35.4					776
9013	Liquid crystal devices	20.3	27.9	31.7					871
8443	Printing machinery used for printing by means of the printing type, blocks	17.1	23.6	25.1					726
8504	Electrical transformers, static converters	14.7	20.2	22.3					771

Graph 2: Trade Balance by MDG Regions in 2011

(Bln US$)

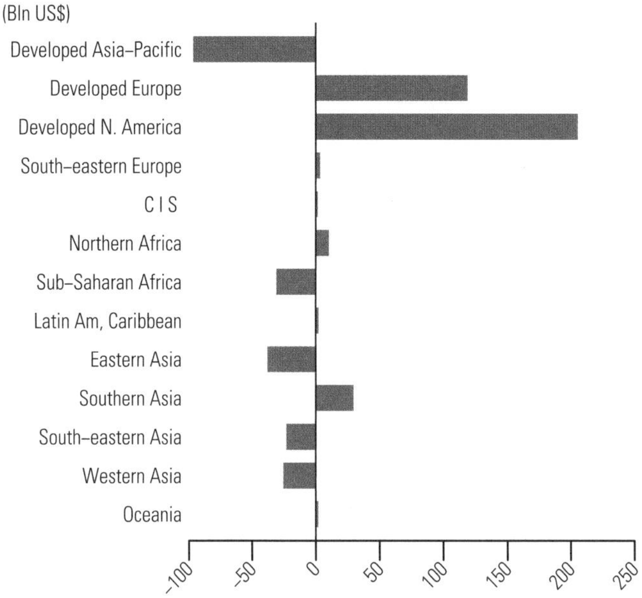

Graph 3: Partner concentration of trade in 2011

(Cumulative share by ranked partners)

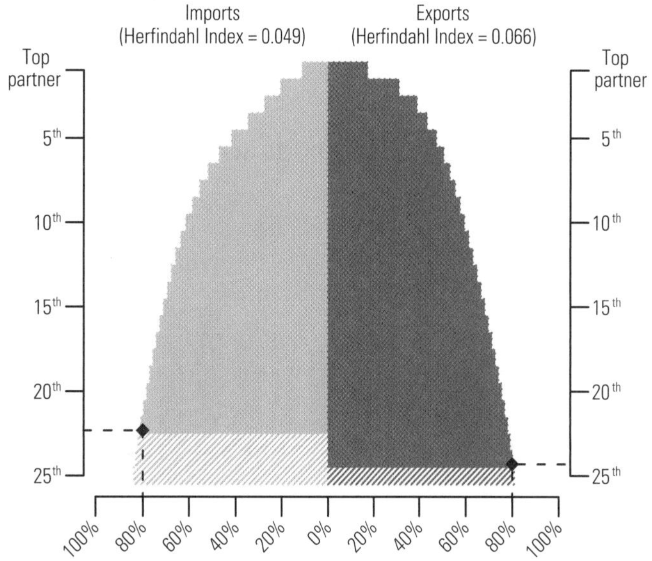

Table 4: Exports by principal countries and SITC sections in 2011

(Value in million US$, percentages of country total)

Country	Total	Shares by SITC sections (%) 0 + 1	2 + 4	3	5	6	7	8	9	Total
World	1 898 388.4	2.8	0.8	1.7	6.0	16.8	47.5	24.2	0.1	100
USA	325 011.0	1.9	0.5	0.3	4.0	12.5	49.8	30.9	0.1	100
China, Hong Kong SAR	267 983.7	2.0	0.2	2.4	2.0	7.4	65.6	20.2	0.2	100
Japan	148 268.7	6.7	1.4	2.1	7.4	13.8	39.0	28.9	0.7	100
Rep. of Korea	82 920.3	4.3	1.7	2.9	8.9	24.7	43.2	14.3	0.0	100
Germany	76 400.0	1.9	1.0	0.7	4.9	11.5	48.4	31.6	0.0	100
Netherlands	59 499.7	1.5	1.3	0.5	5.2	9.5	64.9	17.1	0.0	100
India	50 536.4	0.5	1.3	1.3	20.8	20.3	48.1	7.6	0.1	100
United Kingdom	44 122.1	1.9	0.6	0.5	4.0	15.5	39.6	37.9	0.0	100
Russian Federation	38 903.0	4.6	0.7	0.9	5.3	19.3	38.1	31.1	0.0	100
Singapore	35 570.1	1.5	0.3	4.7	4.4	13.2	64.0	11.1	0.8	100

Imports Profile:

Machinery and transport equipment (SITC section 7) accounted for more than a third of China's imports (36.2 percent) (see table 2). Other major commodity groups included inedible crude materials (except fuels), animal and vegetable oils, fats and waxes (SITC sections 2+4) and mineral fuels, lubricants and related materials (SITC section 3), respectively with 17.0 and 15.8 percent of imports. From 2009 to 2011, top imported products were electronic integrated circuits (HS code 8542), petroleum oils and oils obtained from bituminous minerals, crude (HS code 2709) and iron ores and concentrates, including roasted iron pyrites (HS code 2601) (see table 5).

Table 5: Top 10 import commodities 2009 to 2011

(Value in billion US$)

HS code	4-digit heading of Harmonized System 2007	Value (billion US$) 2009	2010	2011	Unit value 2009	2010	2011	Unit	SITC code
	All Commodities	1 005.6	1 396.0	1 743.4					
8542	Electronic integrated circuits	120.8	158.0	171.1					776
2709	Petroleum oils and oils obtained from bituminous minerals, crude	89.3	135.3	196.8	0.4	0.6	0.8	US$/kg	333
2601	Iron ores and concentrates, including roasted iron pyrites	50.1	79.7	112.4	0.1	0.1	0.2	US$/kg	281
9013	Liquid crystal devices	38.3	51.5	53.1					871
8703	Motor cars and other motor vehicles principally designed for the transport	14.4	28.9	41.0	34.6	36.4	40.3	thsd US$/unit	781
8471	Automatic data processing machines and units thereof	21.8	26.9	29.4	37.6	37.6	41.2	US$/unit	752
1201	Soya beans, whether or not broken	18.8	25.1	29.7	0.4	*0.5*	0.6	US$/kg	222
8517	Electrical apparatus for line telephony or line telegraphy	19.1	22.5	30.9					764
2710	Petroleum oils, other than crude	17.0	22.4	32.8	*0.5*	*0.6*	*0.8*	US$/kg	334
9999	Commodities not specified according to kind	3.3	18.4	49.5					931

China, Hong Kong SAR

Imports: CIF, by consignment | **Exports: FOB, by last known destination** | **Trade System: General**

Overview:

From 2007 to 2011, China, Hong Kong SAR's exports increased on average by 6.9 percent each year despite a decline of 11.0 percent in 2009 and reached a peak of 455.6 bln US$ in 2011 (see table 1 and graph 1). Imports showed a similar development with an increase of 15.7 percent in 2011 and amounted to 510.9 bln US$ in 2011 (see table 2 and graph 1). This resulted in a trade deficit of 55.2 bln US$ in 2011 (see graph 1). By MDG regions, trade recorded surpluses with Developed North America (+11.9 bln US$) and Latin America and the Caribbean (+2.4 bln US$) (see graph 2). The trade balance was in deficit with South-eastern Asia (-37.3 bln US$), Developed Asia-Pacific (-22.9 bln US$) and Developed Europe (-8.7 bln US$). In 2011, both imports and exports were concentrated among a few partners: 9 (respectively 8) major partners accounted for 80 percent of exports (respectively imports) (see graph 3).

Graph 1: Total imports, exports and trade balance

(Bln US$ by year)

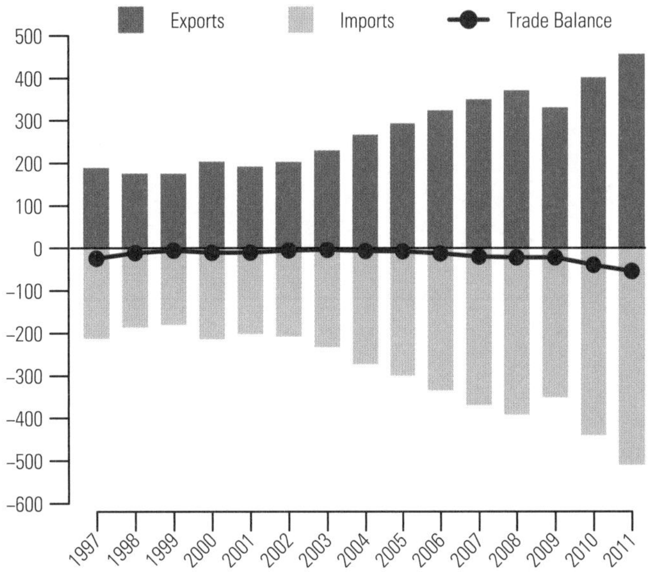

Exports Profile:

In 2011, exports of China, Hong Kong SAR were largely various kinds of manufactured goods: machinery and transport equipment (SITC section 7), accounting for more than half of total exported goods (56.6 percent) (see table 1). Miscellaneous manufactured articles (SITC section 8) accounted for 20.2 percent of exports. In addition to China, other major markets for exports were USA and Japan (see table 4). From 2009 to 2011, top exported commodities included electronic integrated circuits (HS code 8542), electrical apparatus for line telephony or line telegraphy (HS code 8517) and parts and accessories for use with machines of heading 84.69 to 84.72 (HS code 8473) (see table 3).

Table 1: Exports by SITC sections

(Value in million US$, growth and shares in percentage)

SITC	2011	Avg. Growth rates (%) 2007-2011	Avg. Growth rates (%) 2010-2011	2011 share
Total	455 649.7	6.9	13.7	100.0
0+1	7 076.4	17.5	16.7	1.6
2+4	3 424.1	6.2	9.3	0.8
3	899.0	1.5	29.8	0.2
5	19 951.4	4.0	8.3	4.4
6	49 125.5	5.4	19.0	10.8
7	257 843.1	8.0	9.8	56.6
8	91 848.7	0.3	7.8	20.2
9	25 481.5	48.5	131.7	5.6

Table 2: Imports by SITC sections

(Value in million US$, growth and shares in percentage)

SITC	2011	Avg. Growth rates (%) 2007-2011	Avg. Growth rates (%) 2010-2011	2011 share
Total	510 854.7	8.4	15.7	100.0
0+1	21 039.2	18.0	18.4	4.1
2+4	4 354.2	4.9	12.3	0.9
3	18 782.9	13.4	22.4	3.7
5	24 471.3	3.4	5.5	4.8
6	55 693.1	2.9	13.5	10.9
7	271 961.0	8.3	9.7	53.2
8	87 509.2	4.7	15.5	17.1
9	27 043.8	78.2	219.7	5.3

Table 3: Top 10 export commodities 2009 to 2011

(Value in million US$)

HS code	4-digit heading of Harmonized System 2007	Value (million US$) 2009	2010	2011	Unit value 2009	2010	2011	Unit	SITC code
	All Commodities	329 421.9	400 692.0	455 649.7					
8542	Electronic integrated circuits	45 726.9	55 254.3	59 169.3					776
8517	Electrical apparatus for line telephony or line telegraphy	28 073.2	37 275.2	45 258.0					764
8473	Parts and accessories for use with machines of heading 84.69 to 84.72	16 170.5	21 096.5	22 605.5	45.8	51.1	*48.4*	US$/kg	759
7108	Gold (including gold plated with platinum)	10 047.6	10 091.3	24 727.1	31.6	39.1	*0.0*	thsd US$/kg	971
8471	Automatic data processing machines and units thereof	9 521.2	12 734.1	16 286.4	26.5	34.9	*38.7*	US$/unit	752
8529	Parts suitable for use with the apparatus of headings 85.25 to 85.28	10 469.2	12 365.0	12 216.3	40.3	52.8	*60.1*	US$/kg	764
7102	Diamonds, whether or not worked, but not mounted or set	8 123.6	11 163.1	14 848.6	253.4	336.5	*434.2*	US$/carat	667
8504	Electrical transformers, static converters	6 820.3	9 881.6	10 423.5					771
8443	Printing machinery used for printing by means of the printing type, blocks	6 212.2	8 721.0	9 657.6					726
8541	Diodes, transistors and similar semiconductor devices	5 868.5	8 650.9	9 647.6					776

Graph 2: Trade Balance by MDG Regions in 2011

(Bln US$)

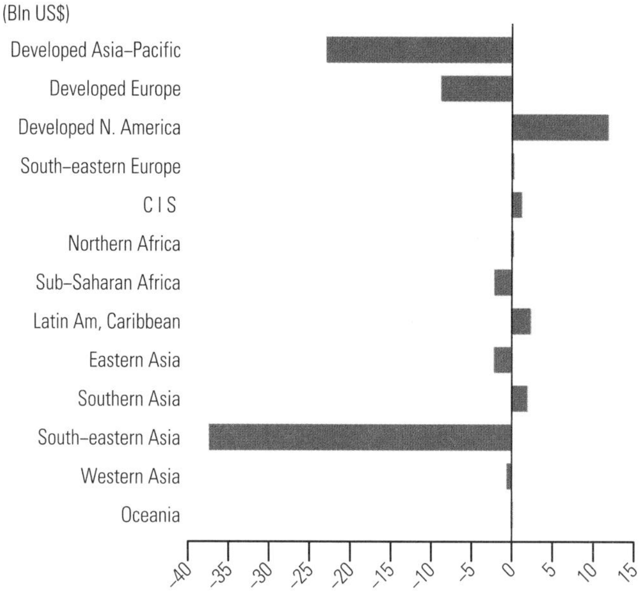

Graph 3: Partner concentration of trade in 2011

(Cumulative share by ranked partners)

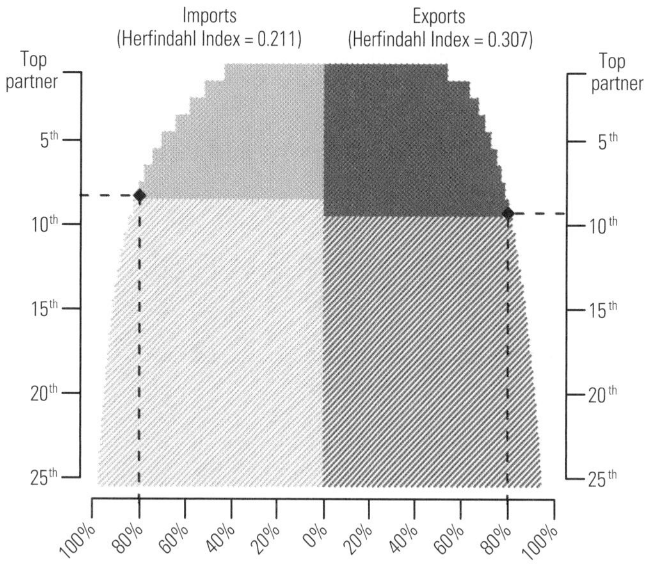

Table 4: Exports by principal countries and SITC sections in 2011

(Value in million US$, percentages of country total)

Country	Total	Shares by SITC sections (%) 0 + 1	2 + 4	3	5	6	7	8	9	Total
World	455 649.7	1.6	0.8	0.2	4.4	10.8	56.6	20.2	5.6	100
China	246 464.0	1.2	0.9	0.2	6.2	9.1	65.7	8.0	8.6	100
USA	42 653.0	0.4	0.1	0.0	0.7	6.7	39.7	52.3	0.1	100
Japan	17 792.8	0.3	0.5	0.0	2.8	5.2	54.2	36.7	0.3	100
India	12 330.6	0.3	0.1	0.0	0.5	56.5	32.8	7.3	2.5	100
Other Asia, nes	11 671.2	3.9	2.1	0.1	3.9	18.3	53.4	14.1	4.1	100
Germany	11 625.9	0.1	0.1	0.0	0.3	4.5	42.7	51.0	1.4	100
Rep. of Korea	8 447.2	0.7	1.4	0.0	2.1	3.6	62.8	23.0	6.4	100
Singapore	7 689.6	2.2	0.3	0.0	4.1	5.8	64.7	17.1	5.8	100
United Kingdom	7 533.1	0.4	0.2	0.0	1.1	10.6	27.3	60.2	0.2	100
Thailand	6 182.6	0.4	0.5	0.0	2.2	16.2	57.4	11.6	11.5	100

Imports Profile:

By SITC sections, imports and exports had similar profiles in 2011: machinery and transport equipment (SITC section 7) accounted for more than a half of imported goods in 2011 (53.2 percent) followed by miscellaneous manufactured articles (SITC section 8) and manufactured goods classified chiefly by material (SITC section 6), respectively with 17.1 and 10.9 percent (see table 2). The three main goods for imports over the last three years were electronic integrated circuits (HS code 8542), electrical apparatus for line telephony or line telegraphy (HS code 8517) and parts and accessories for use with machines of heading 84.69 to 84.72 (HS code 8473) (see table 5).

Table 5: Top 10 import commodities 2009 to 2011

(Value in million US$)

HS code	4-digit heading of Harmonized System 2007	Value (million US$) 2009	2010	2011	Unit value 2009	2010	2011	Unit	SITC code
	All Commodities	352 240.7	441 369.2	510 854.7					
8542	Electronic integrated circuits	54 637.5	69 791.8	72 144.3					776
8517	Electrical apparatus for line telephony or line telegraphy	25 553.4	33 234.4	42 349.0					764
8473	Parts and accessories for use with machines of heading 84.69 to 84.72	16 228.5	20 481.9	20 323.6	41.8	49.6	52.5	US$/kg	759
7102	Diamonds, whether or not worked, but not mounted or set	10 706.1	14 688.0	19 226.4	273.0	358.2	467.6	US$/carat	667
8471	Automatic data processing machines and units thereof	10 491.2	13 520.4	17 735.6	31.6	40.5	43.9	US$/unit	752
2710	Petroleum oils, other than crude	9 165.3	12 748.6	15 841.0	*1.4*	*1.2*	*1.3*	US$/kg	334
7108	Gold (including gold plated with platinum)	3 988.7	7 223.2	24 951.5	18.9	26.0	42.7	thsd US$/kg	971
8541	Diodes, transistors and similar semiconductor devices	7 726.2	11 205.4	12 203.7					776
8529	Parts suitable for use with the apparatus of headings 85.25 to 85.28	7 950.2	9 564.6	9 936.1	44.7	55.2	54.2	US$/kg	764
8504	Electrical transformers, static converters	5 848.5	8 832.5	9 110.6					771

China, Macao SAR

Imports: CIF, by origin | **Exports: FOB, by last known destination** | **Trade System: General**

Overview:

From 2007 to 2011, the value of exports of China, Macao SAR decreased on average by 23.5 percent each year (see table 1 and graph 1). Exports in 2011 remained constant with 2010 at 870.0 mln US$. Imports, on the other hand, registered an annual average growth of 7.0 percent and amounted to 7.9 bln US$, a 40.8 percent increase over 2010 (see table 2 and graph 1). This resulted in a trade deficit of 7.1 bln US$ in 2011, much higher than the 2010 deficit of 4.8 bln US$ (see graph 1). By MDG regions, trade deficits were recorded with Eastern Asia (-3.2 bln US$), Developed Europe (-2.4 bln US$) and Developed Asia-Pacific (-0.6 bln US$) (see graph 2). Trade, especially exports, was highly concentrated among a few partners: 2 major partners accounted for over 80 percent of exports compared to 8 major partners for imports in 2011 (see graph 3).

Graph 1: Total imports, exports and trade balance

(Bln US$ by year)

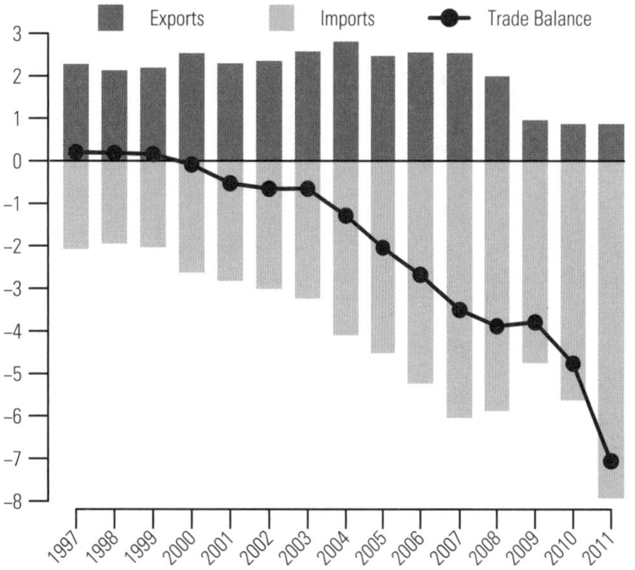

Exports Profile:

In 2011, a large part of exports had no commodity and partner details provided. Therefore, commodities and transactions not classified elsewhere (SITC section 9) accounted for the overwhelming majority of exports (70.6 percent) (see table 1). Other major commodity groups included miscellaneous manufactured articles (SITC section 8) and machinery and transport equipment (SITC section 7); they accounted respectively for 14.0 and 9.4 percent of exports. Major markets for exports in 2011 included China, Hong Kong SAR, China and USA (see table 4). Exports to USA were almost exclusively miscellaneous manufactured articles (SITC section 8). Major exported commodities over the last three years were articles of jewellery and parts thereof, of precious metal (HS code 7113), jerseys, pullovers, cardigans, waist-coats and similar articles (HS code 6110) and petroleum oils, other than crude (HS code 2710) (see table 3).

Table 1: Exports by SITC sections

(Value in million US$, growth and shares in percentage)

SITC	2011	Avg. Growth rates (%) 2007-2011	2010-2011	2011 share
Total	870.0	-23.5	0.0	100.0
0+1	20.7	-17.0	10.7	2.4
2+4	7.3	-6.7	525.0	0.8
5	5.9	-32.0	259.5	0.7
6	17.8	-49.9	-42.6	2.0
7	81.7	-29.2	31.5	9.4
8	122.0	-48.3	-19.0	14.0
9	614.5	2183.8	1.7	70.6

Table 2: Imports by SITC sections

(Value in million US$, growth and shares in percentage)

SITC	2011	Avg. Growth rates (%) 2007-2011	2010-2011	2011 share
Total	7 926.8	7.0	40.8	100.0
0+1	1 224.4	18.4	31.1	15.4
2+4	44.4	-0.2	53.8	0.6
3	646.6	1.4	5.7	8.2
5	437.3	13.6	22.1	5.5
6	386.3	-21.5	11.0	4.9
7	1 678.9	2.8	37.7	21.2
8	2 905.9	10.0	63.3	36.7
9	602.9	384.4	72.4	7.6

Table 3: Top 10 export commodities 2009 to 2011

(Value in million US$)

HS code	4-digit heading of Harmonized System 2007	Value (million US$) 2009	2010	2011	Unit value 2009	2010	2011	Unit	SITC code
	All Commodities	960.7	869.8	870.0					
9999	Commodities not specified according to kind	...	604.5	614.5					931
7113	Articles of jewellery and parts thereof, of precious metal	85.6	...	29.6			118.5	thsd US$/kg	897
6110	Jerseys, pullovers, cardigans, waist-coats and similar articles	57.0	24.8	9.9	5.4	*11.7*	6.3	US$/unit	845
2710	Petroleum oils, other than crude	87.4	...	...	0.6			US$/kg	334
6204	Women's or girls' suits, ensembles, jackets, blazers, dresses, skirts	53.1	28.7	3.2	8.4		12.6	US$/unit	842
8528	Reception apparatus for television	19.3	22.7	11.4	32.7		30.0	US$/unit	761
9504	Articles for funfair, table or parlour games, including pintables	48.0	...	...					894
6109	T-shirts, singlets and other vests, knitted or crocheted	15.6	15.4	11.3	4.0	*5.4*	4.4	US$/unit	845
6203	Men's or boys' suits, ensembles, jackets, blazers, trousers	17.2	11.9	9.7	9.6		15.9	US$/unit	841
9101	Wrist-watches, pocket-watches and other watches, including stop-watches	36.9	...	...	15.8			thsd US$/unit	885

Graph 2: Trade Balance by MDG Regions in 2011

(Bln US$)

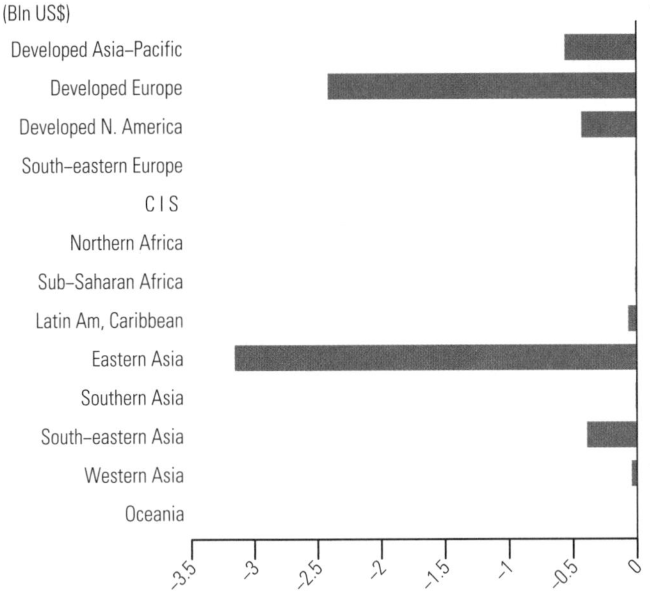

Graph 3: Partner concentration of trade in 2011

(Cumulative share by ranked partners)

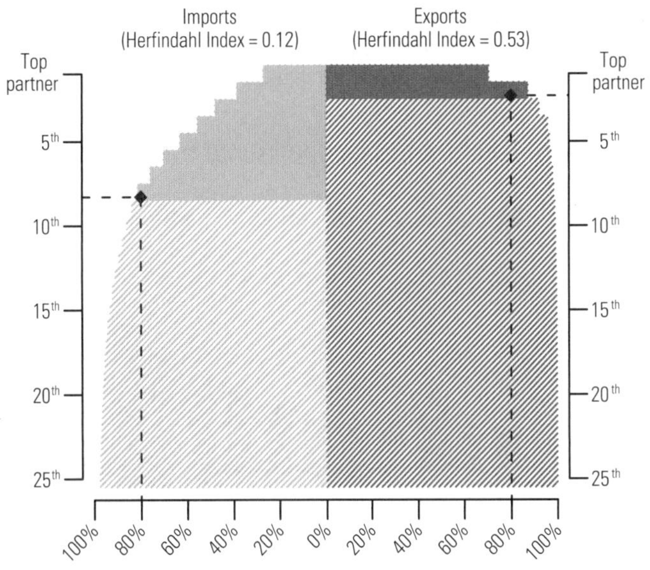

Table 4: Exports by principal countries and SITC sections in 2011

(Value in million US$, percentages of country total)

Country	Total	Shares by SITC sections (%) 0+1	2+4	3	5	6	7	8	9	Total
World	870.0	2.4	0.8	...	0.7	2.0	9.4	14.0	70.6	100
Areas, nes	614.5	0.0	0.0	...	...	...	...	...	100.0	100
China, Hong Kong SAR	144.4	12.9	4.8	...	3.5	4.1	38.0	36.5	...	100
China	42.6	4.2	0.2	...	1.8	27.1	50.5	16.3	...	100
USA	32.0	0.0	0.0	...	...	0.0	5.5	94.5	...	100
Netherlands	6.9	0.0	0.0	...	...	0.6	0.1	99.3	...	100
France	5.8	0.1	0.0	...	...	0.7	0.5	98.7	...	100
Other Asia, nes	5.5	0.0	4.9	...	0.4	1.6	18.0	75.0	...	100
Mexico	4.8	0.0	0.0	...	...	0.1	0.5	99.4	...	100
United Kingdom	3.6	1.7	0.0	...	...	1.8	0.6	95.9	...	100
Japan	2.0	0.1	0.0	...	0.5	0.2	13.7	85.6	...	100

Imports Profile:

In 2011, imports of miscellaneous manufactured articles (SITC section 8), machinery and transport equipment (SITC section 7) and food, live animals, beverages and tobacco (SITC sections 0+1) represented respectively 36.7, 21.2 and 15.4 percent of imported goods (see table 2). Top imported products included articles of jewellery and parts thereof, of precious metal (HS code 7113), electrical apparatus for line telephony or line telegraphy (HS code 8517) and petroleum oils, other than crude (HS code 2710) (see table 5).

Table 5: Top 10 import commodities 2009 to 2011

(Value in million US$)

HS code	4-digit heading of Harmonized System 2007	Value (million US$) 2009	2010	2011	Unit value 2009	2010	2011	Unit	SITC code
	All Commodities	4750.9	5629.5	7926.8					
7113	Articles of jewellery and parts thereof, of precious metal	304.1	487.7	939.1		*36.6*	*57.4*	thsd US$/kg	897
8517	Electrical apparatus for line telephony or line telegraphy	243.1	340.7	573.6					764
2710	Petroleum oils, other than crude	335.0	320.8	298.6	0.6	0.8	1.0	US$/kg	334
9999	Commodities not specified according to kind	...	349.3	602.5					931
4202	Trunks, suit-cases, vanity-cases, executive-cases, brief-cases	134.8	226.5	476.5					831
9101	Wrist-watches, pocket-watches and other watches, including stop-watches	193.1	240.3	342.3	6.9		7.6	thsd US$/unit	885
2716	Electrical energy	195.3	254.1	299.9	87.7	*57.1*	94.8	US$/MWh	351
8703	Motor cars and other motor vehicles principally designed for the transport	122.4	224.4	288.2	26.7	*21.8*	37.2	thsd US$/unit	781
2204	Wine of fresh grapes, including fortified wines	117.7	179.8	284.4	24.4	*29.3*	36.9	US$/litre	112
9504	Articles for funfair, table or parlour games, including pintables	171.9	141.4	197.2					894

Colombia

Imports: CIF, by origin | **Exports: FOB, by last known destination** | **Trade System: Special**

Overview:

From 2007 to 2011, Colombia's exports increased on average by 17.4 percent each year and reached its peak of 57.0 bln US$ in 2011 (see table 1 and graph 1). Imports showed a similar development with an average increase of 13.5 percent to 54.7 bln US$ (see table 2 and graph 1). This resulted in a trade surplus of 2.3 bln US$ in 2011 compared to deficits experienced in the previous years (see graph 1). By MDG regions, the trade balance recorded surpluses with Developed North America (+7.9 bln US$) and Developed Europe (+2.0 bln US$) (see graph 2). The trade balance recorded a deficit with Eastern Asia amounting to 7.6 bln US$. Colombia's trade was diversified across partners in 2011: 17 major partners accounted for 80 percent of exports and 14 for imports (see graph 3).

Graph 1: Total imports, exports and trade balance

(Bln US$ by year)

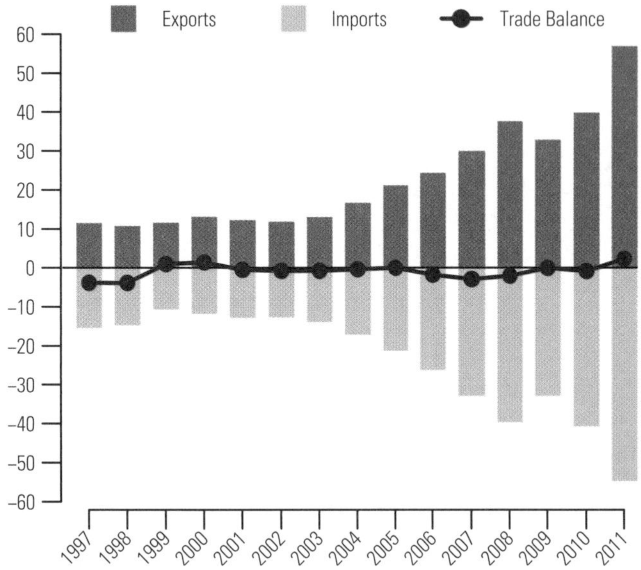

Table 1: Exports by SITC sections

(Value in million US$, growth and shares in percentage)

SITC	2011	Avg. Growth rates (%) 2007-2011	2010-2011	2011 share
Total	56 953.5	17.4	43.0	100.0
0+1	5 426.3	5.9	26.0	9.5
2+4	2 152.8	1.1	11.7	3.8
3	36 481.8	35.3	61.7	64.1
5	3 312.1	8.2	16.3	5.8
6	3 472.1	-7.5	4.0	6.1
7	1 721.0	-6.0	36.0	3.0
8	1 590.3	-11.3	10.2	2.8
9	2 797.1	36.5	31.3	4.9

Table 2: Imports by SITC sections

(Value in million US$, growth and shares in percentage)

SITC	2011	Avg. Growth rates (%) 2007-2011	2010-2011	2011 share
Total	54 674.8	13.5	34.4	100.0
0+1	4 280.7	12.8	29.3	7.8
2+4	1 620.7	12.4	23.2	3.0
3	3 853.2	43.3	85.2	7.0
5	9 202.7	10.9	23.4	16.8
6	8 552.0	10.2	33.8	15.6
7	22 262.3	13.1	36.8	40.7
8	4 399.8	14.7	25.0	8.0
9	503.4	13.8	49.1	0.9

Exports Profile:

Mineral fuels, lubricants and related materials (SITC section 3) accounted for a major bulk of exported goods in 2011. It accounted for 64.1 percent of total exports (see table 1). Other major commodity groups included food, live animals, beverages and tobacco (SITC sections 0+1) and manufactured goods classified chiefly by material (SITC section 6), which accounted for 9.5 and 6.1 percent of exports, respectively. In 2011, exports to USA, the top partner, were largely mineral fuels, lubricants and related materials (SITC section 3) (73.3 percent). Other major partners included the Netherlands and Chile (see table 4). Petroleum oils and oils obtained from bituminous minerals, crude (HS code 2709), the top product for exports over the last three years, accounted for 40.4 percent of exports in 2011. Other major products for exports included coal; briquettes, ovoids and similar solid fuels manufactured from coal (HS code 2701) and petroleum oils, other than crude (HS code 2710) (see table 3).

Table 3: Top 10 export commodities 2009 to 2011

(Value in million US$)

HS code	4-digit heading of Harmonized System 2007	Value (million US$) 2009	2010	2011	Unit value 2009	2010	2011	Unit	SITC code
	All Commodities	32 853.0	39 819.5	56 953.5					
2709	Petroleum oils and oils obtained from bituminous minerals, crude	8 053.5	13 394.0	23 020.1	0.4	0.5	0.7	US$/kg	333
2701	Coal; briquettes, ovoids and similar solid fuels manufactured from coal	5 257.0	5 520.8	7 856.4	0.1	0.1	0.1	US$/kg	321
2710	Petroleum oils, other than crude	1 911.6	2 872.2	4 564.5	0.4	0.5	0.7	US$/kg	334
7108	Gold (including gold plated with platinum)	1 537.2	2 094.6	2 774.9	26.8	33.3	41.7	thsd US$/kg	971
0901	Coffee, whether or not roasted or decaffeinated	1 574.7	1 913.7	2 657.5	3.4	4.6	6.1	US$/kg	071
0603	Cut flowers and flower buds of a kind suitable for bouquets	1 049.2	1 240.5	1 251.3	5.1	5.6	6.1	US$/kg	292
7202	Ferro-alloys	726.2	967.8	827.2	4.3	6.9	7.4	US$/kg	671
0803	Bananas, including plantains, fresh or dried	837.0	748.1	815.3	0.4	0.4	0.4	US$/kg	057
1701	Cane or beet sugar and chemically pure sucrose, in solid form	381.8	450.3	593.9	0.4	0.6	0.7	US$/kg	061
2704	Coke and semi-coke of coal, of lignite or of peat	159.4	494.4	540.4	0.2	0.3	0.4	US$/kg	325

Graph 2: Trade Balance by MDG Regions in 2011

(Bln US$)

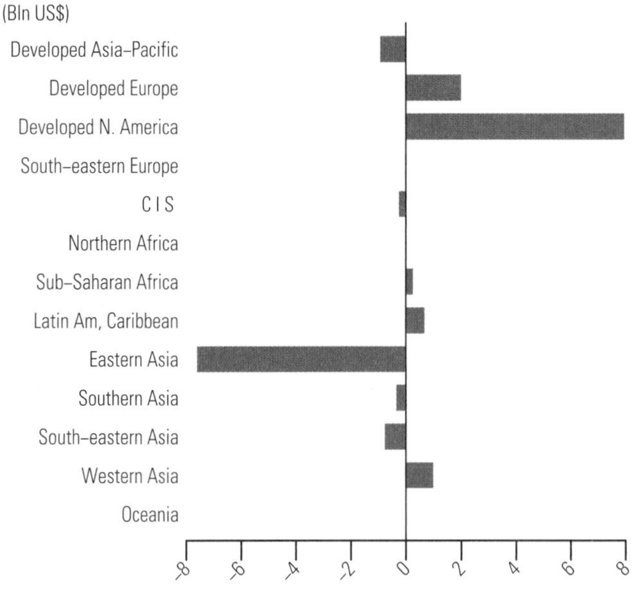

Graph 3: Partner concentration of trade in 2011

(Cumulative share by ranked partners)

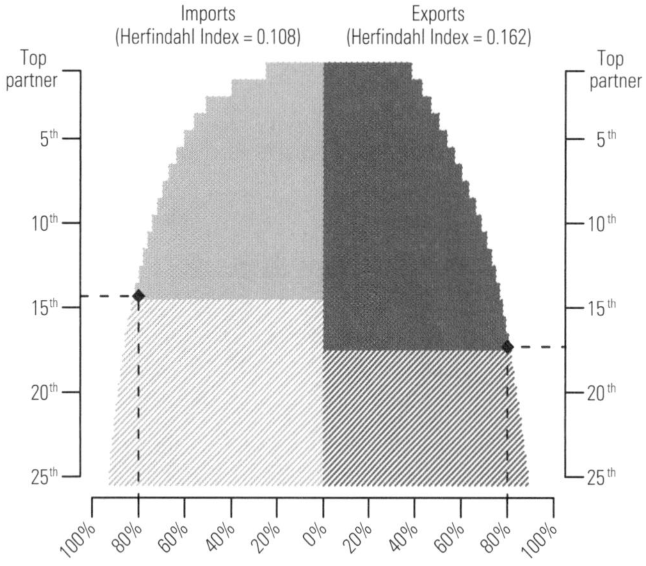

Table 4: Exports by principal countries and SITC sections in 2011

(Value in million US$, percentages of country total)

Country	Total	Shares by SITC sections (%)								
		0 + 1	2 + 4	3	5	6	7	8	9	Total
World	56 953.5	9.5	3.8	64.1	5.8	6.1	3.0	2.8	4.9	100
USA	21 948.5	7.6	4.6	73.3	1.0	2.6	0.6	1.7	8.5	100
Netherlands	2 524.1	1.7	5.6	82.6	0.3	9.0	0.4	0.4	0.0	100
Chile	2 205.0	8.5	1.1	75.8	6.1	3.5	2.6	2.4	0.0	100
China	1 989.1	0.3	13.0	67.6	1.1	17.9	0.0	0.0	0.0	100
Panama	1 956.8	1.1	0.6	78.2	5.8	4.5	5.2	4.4	0.1	100
Ecuador	1 908.6	8.1	0.6	8.7	27.1	23.9	20.6	11.0	0.0	100
Venezuela	1 750.4	9.3	1.4	22.0	19.7	22.7	9.7	15.2	0.0	100
Aruba	1 724.1	0.3	0.0	98.9	0.1	0.5	0.0	0.2	...	100
Spain	1 720.2	7.4	4.0	82.0	2.1	3.4	0.2	0.8	0.0	100
Peru	1 396.9	10.4	0.4	21.4	28.4	17.5	14.2	7.6	0.0	100

Imports Profile:

In 2011, imports were mainly composed of 40.7 percent of machinery and transport equipment (SITC section 7), 16.8 percent of chemicals and related products, n.e.s. (SITC section 5) and 15.6 percent of manufactured goods classified chiefly by material (SITC section 6) (see table 2). From 2009 to 2011, top products for imports were petroleum oils, other than crude (HS code 2710), other aircraft (for example, helicopters, aeroplanes); spacecraft (HS code 8802) and motor cars and other motor vehicles principally designed for the transport (HS code 8703) (see table 5).

Table 5: Top 10 import commodities 2009 to 2011

(Value in million US$)

HS code	4-digit heading of Harmonized System 2007	Value (million US$)			Unit value				SITC code
		2009	2010	2011	2009	2010	2011	Unit	
	All Commodities	32 897.7	40 682.5	54 674.8					
2710	Petroleum oils, other than crude	1 163.9	2 023.8	3 794.2	0.6	0.7	0.9	US$/kg	334
8802	Other aircraft (for example, helicopters, aeroplanes); spacecraft	2 460.4	1 720.1	2 659.1			13.0	mln US$/unit	792
8703	Motor cars and other motor vehicles principally designed for the transport	1 266.4	2 121.5	2 790.1	*14.9*	*16.0*	12.7	thsd US$/unit	781
8517	Electrical apparatus for line telephony or line telegraphy	863.6	1 260.0	1 688.6					764
8471	Automatic data processing machines and units thereof	926.0	1 183.6	1 356.0			232.7	US$/unit	752
8704	Motor vehicles for the transport of goods	659.8	985.5	1 688.6			10.9	thsd US$/unit	782
3004	Medicaments (excluding goods of heading 30.02, 30.05 or 30.06)	774.3	864.6	1 008.3	42.3	40.5	44.4	US$/kg	542
1005	Maize (corn)	671.2	805.8	926.9	0.2	0.2	0.3	US$/kg	044
8528	Reception apparatus for television	449.2	654.3	696.4			244.2	US$/unit	761
8429	Self-propelled bulldozers, angledozers, graders, levellers, scrapers	497.8	547.5	739.0		*70.6*	47.8	thsd US$/unit	723

Imports: CIF, by consignment | **Exports: FOB, by last known destination** | **Trade System: General**

Overview:

From 2005 to 2009, Comoros's exports increased on average by 35.4 percent each year, amounting to 12.6 mln US$ in 2009 (see table 1 and graph 1). Over the same period, imports increased on average by 20.8 percent each year, and reached 181.5 mln US$ in 2009 (see table 2 and graph 1). This resulted in a trade deficit of 169.0 mln US$ in 2009 compared to the deficit of 81.4 mln US$ in 2005 (see graph 1). Deficit with Western Asia alone amounted to 57.0 mln US$ (see graph 2). Trade also recorded significant deficits with Developed Europe (-35.2 mln US$) and Southern Asia (-32.1 mln US$). Trade, especially exports were highly concentrated among few partners: 5 partners accounted for nearly 80 percent of exports and 7 major partners accounted for 80 percent of imports (see graph 3).

Graph 1: Total imports, exports and trade balance
(Mln US$ by year)

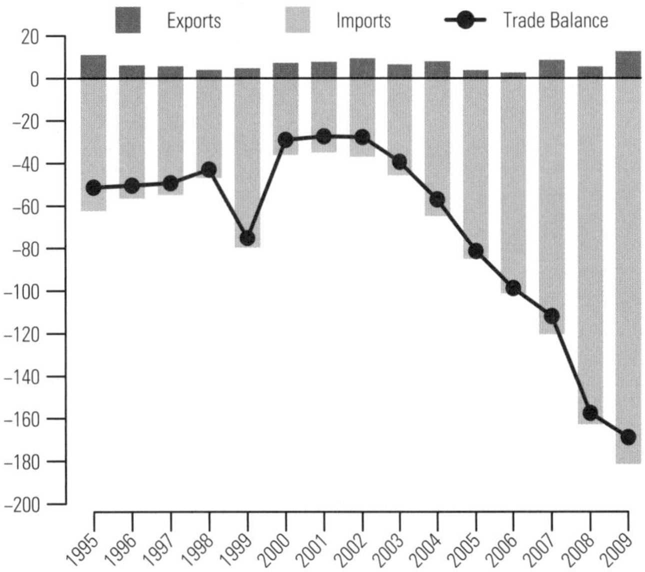

Table 1: Exports by SITC sections
(Value in million US$, growth and shares in percentage)

SITC	2009	Avg. Growth rates (%) 2005-2009	2008-2009	2009 share
Total	12.6	35.4	132.2	100.0
0+1	9.2	29.6	143.1	72.7
2+4	0.0	12.1	-71.0	0.1
3	0.0	...	...	0.0
5	2.4	88.9	95.2	19.0
6	0.3	220.4	9.6	2.0
7	0.5	15.6	361.4	4.0
8	0.3	120.5	542.5	2.1

Table 2: Imports by SITC sections
(Value in million US$, growth and shares in percentage)

SITC	2009	Avg. Growth rates (%) 2005-2009	2008-2009	2009 share
Total	181.5	20.8	11.4	100.0
0+1	66.2	24.3	3.9	36.4
2+4	4.9	28.4	10.3	2.7
3	0.8	-47.3	22.9	0.5
5	6.4	17.4	-51.1	3.5
6	44.9	33.8	67.4	24.7
7	44.1	21.4	6.4	24.3
8	14.3	18.6	11.6	7.9

Exports Profile:

In 2009, Comoros's exports were composed of 72.7 percent of food, live animals, beverages and tobacco (SITC sections 0+1) and 19.0 percent of chemicals and related products, n.e.s. (SITC section 5) (see table 1). Major destinations for exports in 2009 included France, Singapore and Netherlands (see table 4). Exports to Singapore and Netherlands were exclusively food, live animals, beverages and tobacco (SITC sections 0+1). From 2007 to 2009, major products for exports were cloves (whole fruit, cloves and stems) (HS code 0907), essential oils, resinoids and terpenic by-products (HS code 3301) and vanilla beans (HS code 0905) (see table 3).

Table 3: Top 10 export commodities 2007 to 2009
(Value in million US$)

HS code	4-digit heading of Harmonized System 1992	Value (million US$) 2007	2008	2009	Unit value 2007	2008	2009	Unit	SITC code
	All Commodities	8.5	5.4	12.6					
0907	Cloves (whole fruit, cloves and stems)	0.6	3.0	6.8	2.8	2.7	2.3	US$/kg	075
9999	Commodities not specified according to kind	6.8	...	...					931
3301	Essential oils, resinoids and terpenic by-products	0.5	1.2	2.3	107.0	61.8	47.7	US$/kg	551
0905	Vanilla beans	0.6	0.8	2.3	25.4		22.1	US$/kg	075
7311	Containers for compressed, liquefied gas, iron, steel	...	0.2	0.0		0.8	0.6	US$/kg	692
9617	Vacuum flasks etc, parts thereof except inner	...	...	0.1			0.1	US$/kg	899
9018	Instruments etc for medical, surgical, dental, etc use	...	...	0.1					774
8517	Electric apparatus for line telephony, telegraphy	...	...	0.1					764
3006	Special pharmaceutical goods	...	...	0.1			264.7	US$/kg	541
8703	Motor vehicles for transport of persons (except buses)	...	0.0	0.1		*0.0*	*7.0*	thsd US$/unit	781

Graph 2: Trade Balance by MDG Regions in 2009

(Mln US$)

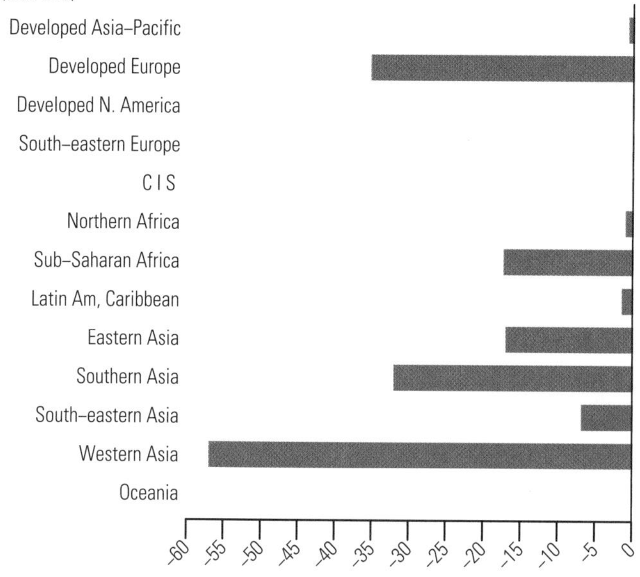

Graph 3: Partner concentration of trade in 2009

(Cumulative share by ranked partners)

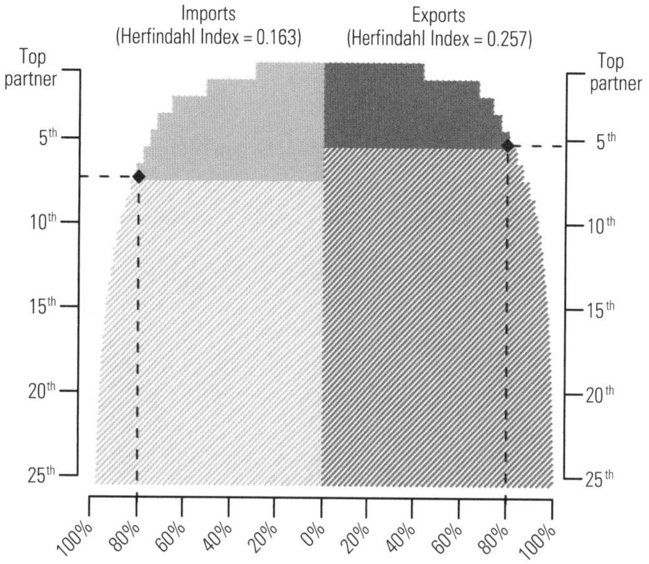

Table 4: Exports by principal countries and SITC sections in 2009

(Value in million US$, percentages of country total)

Country	Total	Shares by SITC sections (%)								
		0 + 1	2 + 4	3	5	6	7	8	9	Total
World	12.6	72.7	0.1	0.0	19.0	2.0	4.0	2.1	...	100
France	5.5	53.3	0.2	...	41.1	0.5	3.1	1.8	...	100
Singapore	3.0	100.0	0.0	...	...	...	...	...	...	100
Netherlands	0.8	100.0	0.0	...	...	...	...	...	...	100
Germany	0.4	100.0	0.0	...	...	...	...	...	...	100
USA	0.4	100.0	0.0	...	...	...	...	...	...	100
Mauritius	0.4	10.8	0.0	0.1	24.3	22.4	38.5	3.8	...	100
Viet Nam	0.3	100.0	0.0	...	...	...	...	...	...	100
Madagascar	0.3	0.0	0.7	0.0	13.2	25.7	20.8	39.6	...	100
China	0.3	100.0	0.0	...	...	...	...	...	...	100
United Arab Emirates	0.2	96.4	0.0	...	...	1.3	1.3	1.1	...	100

Imports Profile:

In 2009, Comoros's imports were mainly composed of 36.4 percent of food, live animals, beverages and tobacco (SITC sections 0+1), 24.7 percent of manufactured goods classified chiefly by material (SITC section 6) and 24.3 percent of machinery and transport equipment (SITC section 7) (see table 2). From 2007 to 2009, the three major products for imports were rice (HS code 1006), motor vehicles for transport of persons (except buses) (HS code 8703) and cement (portland, aluminous, slag or hydraulic) (HS code 2523) (see table 5).

Table 5: Top 10 import commodities 2007 to 2009

(Value in million US$)

HS code	4-digit heading of Harmonized System 1992	Value (million US$)			Unit value				SITC code
		2007	2008	2009	2007	2008	2009	Unit	
	All Commodities	120.5	163.0	181.5					
1006	Rice	8.5	14.0	27.7	0.4	0.6	0.6	US$/kg	042
8703	Motor vehicles for transport of persons (except buses)	3.7	24.1	13.1	*19.6*	*12.1*	*6.2*	thsd US$/unit	781
9999	Commodities not specified according to kind	31.1	0.0	...					931
2523	Cement (portland, aluminous, slag or hydraulic)	2.8	9.4	18.6	0.1	0.1	0.1	US$/kg	661
8414	Air or vacuum pumps, compressors, ventilating fans, etc.	20.8	0.1	0.1					743
0207	Meat, edible offal of domestic poultry	2.7	7.7	7.7	1.7	1.9	1.2	US$/kg	012
0804	Dates, figs, pineapple, avocado, guava, fresh or dried	0.1	15.8	0.4	0.8		1.4	US$/kg	057
7214	Iron/steel bar, only forged hot-rolled drawn, extrude	1.0	4.6	9.0	0.9	1.1	1.0	US$/kg	676
8517	Electric apparatus for line telephony, telegraphy	1.7	3.6	9.4					764
3004	Medicaments, therapeutic, prophylactic use, in dosage	1.0	9.3	1.6	13.1	1.7	6.5	US$/kg	542

 Source: UN Comtrade

Imports: CIF, by origin | **Exports: FOB, by last known destination** | **Trade System: Special**

Overview:

In 2010, Congo's exports dropped by 15.7 percent and amounted to 6.9 bln US$ (see table 1 and graph 1). Similarly, imports dropped by 1.7 percent and amounted to 4.4 bln US$ (see table 2 and graph 1). This resulted in a trade surplus of 2.5 bln US$ (see graph 1). By MDG regions, trade surpluses were recorded with Eastern Asia (+1.9 bln US$), Developed North America (+622.4 mln US$) and Developed Europe (+296.5 mln US$) (see graph 2). Trade deficits were recorded with South-eastern Asia (-308.3 mln US$) and Sub-Saharan Africa (-262.0 mln US$). Congo's trade was diversified among a few partners: in 2010: 9 (respectively 13) major partners accounted for 80 percent of exports (respectively imports) (see graph 3).

Graph 1: Total imports, exports and trade balance

(Bln US$ by year)

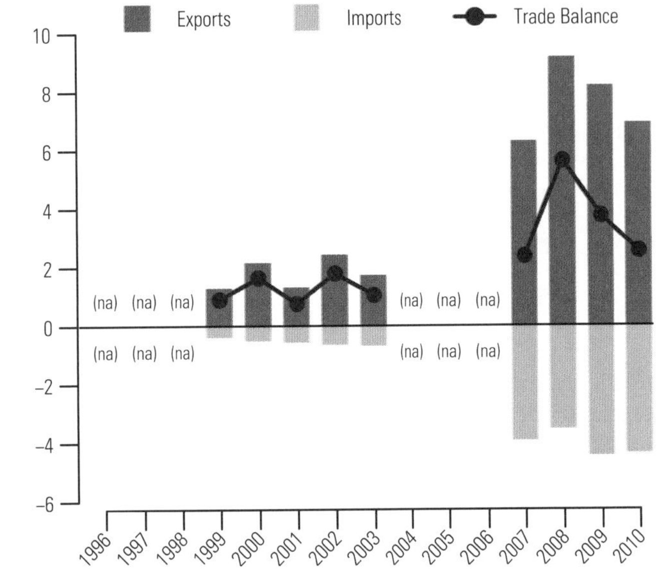

Table 1: Exports by SITC sections

(Value in million US$, growth and shares in percentage)

SITC	2010	Avg. Growth rates (%) 2006-2010	2009-2010	2010 share
Total	6917.6	...	-15.7	100.0
0+1	32.3	...	-5.9	0.5
2+4	111.1	...	-30.5	1.6
3	4684.6	...	-19.2	67.7
5	6.2	...	-5.1	0.1
6	73.8	...	-12.0	1.1
7	1931.4	...	-5.3	27.9
8	78.1	...	-5.1	1.1
9	0.0	...	-5.1	0.0

Exports Profile:

In 2010, Congo's exports in all commodity groups decreased. Exports of mineral fuels, lubricants and related materials (SITC section 3) decreased by 19.2 percent and accounted for 67.7 percent of total exports (see table 1). Top export partners were China, Angola and France (see table 4). Exports to China were almost exclusively composed of mineral fuels, lubricants and related materials (SITC section 3) while exports to Angola were almost exclusively composed of machinery and transport equipment (SITC section 7). From 2008 to 2010, top exported products included petroleum oils, crude (HS code 2709), light-vessels, fire-floats, dredgers, floating cranes and other vessels (HS code 8905) and cruise ships, excursion boats, ferry-boats, cargo ships, barges (HS code 8901) (see table 3).

Table 2: Imports by SITC sections

(Value in million US$, growth and shares in percentage)

SITC	2010	Avg. Growth rates (%) 2006-2010	2009-2010	2010 share
Total	4369.4	...	-1.7	100.0
0+1	286.8	...	-22.7	6.6
2+4	41.2	...	-12.7	0.9
3	248.6	...	126.2	5.7
5	122.5	...	-7.2	2.8
6	301.9	...	-5.0	6.9
7	3249.3	...	-2.9	74.4
8	119.1	...	-2.2	2.7
9	0.0	...	614.8	0.0

Table 3: Top 10 export commodities 2008 to 2010

(Value in million US$)

HS code	4-digit heading of Harmonized System 2002	Value (million US$) 2008	2009	2010	Unit value 2008	2009	2010	Unit	SITC code
	All Commodities	9169.7	8201.5	6917.6					
2709	Petroleum oils, crude	7486.8	5550.1	4481.1	0.7	0.5	0.3	US$/kg	333
8905	Light-vessels, fire-floats, dredgers, floating cranes and other vessels	541.4	1169.4	1107.3					793
8901	Cruise ships, excursion boats, ferry-boats, cargo ships, barges	478.5	717.9	679.7					793
2711	Petroleum gases and other gaseous hydrocarbons	112.8	93.2	143.2	0.8	0.5	0.9	US$/kg	343
4403	Wood in the rough, whether or not stripped of bark or sapwood	140.3	114.3	89.6					247
2710	Petroleum oils, other than crude	111.7	150.6	59.2	0.4	0.4	1.3	US$/kg	334
9015	Surveying (including photogrammetrical surveying), hydrographic	3.6	67.3	63.8					874
8904	Tugs and pusher craft	10.4	43.3	41.0					793
7326	Other articles of iron or steel	2.2	37.7	35.8	7.3	33.8	32.0	US$/kg	699
1701	Cane or beet sugar and pure sucrose, in solid form	23.7	24.1	22.6	0.6	0.6	0.6	US$/kg	061

Graph 2: Trade Balance by MDG Regions in 2010

(Bln US$)

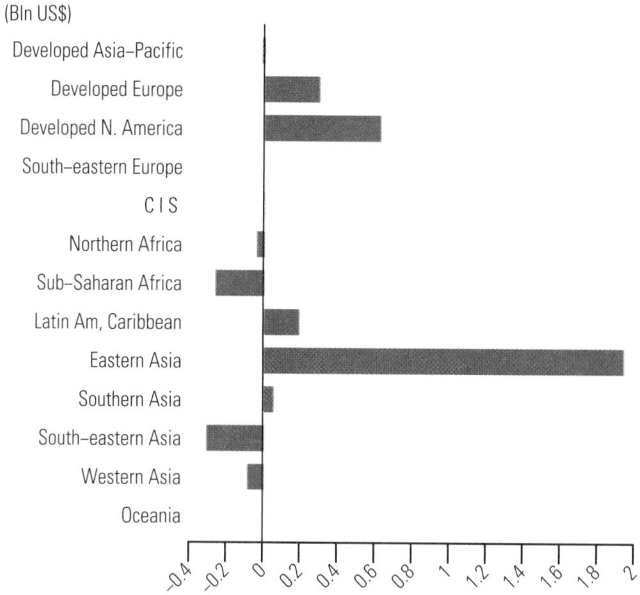

Graph 3: Partner concentration of trade in 2010

(Cumulative share by ranked partners)

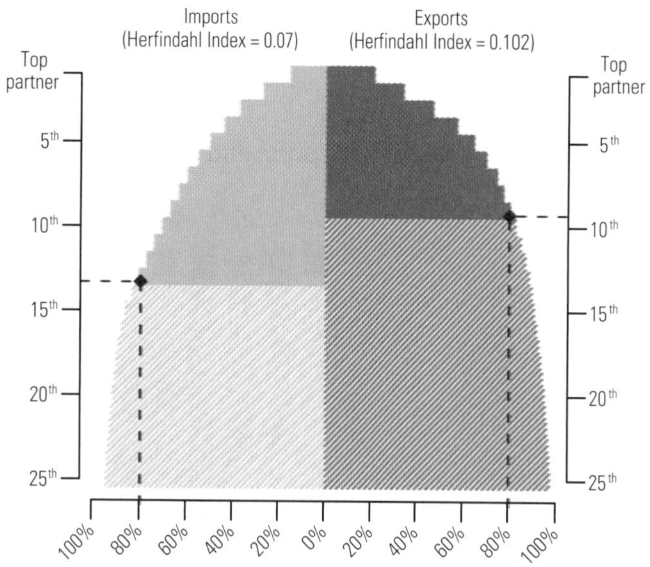

Table 4: Exports by principal countries and SITC sections in 2010

(Value in million US$, percentages of country total)

Country	Total	Shares by SITC sections (%)								
		0 + 1	2 + 4	3	5	6	7	8	9	Total
World	6917.6	0.5	1.6	67.7	0.1	1.1	27.9	1.1	0.0	100
China	1446.7	0.0	4.4	95.5	...	0.1	0.0	0.0	...	100
Angola	903.4	0.5	0.1	0.4	0.2	1.2	97.4	0.2	...	100
France	867.7	0.4	0.4	97.4	0.3	0.8	0.4	0.4	0.0	100
USA	716.3	0.0	0.0	91.3	0.0	0.1	0.7	7.8	...	100
Other Asia, nes	513.9	0.0	0.1	99.9	...	...	...	...	...	100
Bunkers	373.6	0.0	0.0	0.0	...	0.2	99.7	...	...	100
Gabon	327.4	0.0	0.0	0.3	0.2	10.9	88.0	0.6	...	100
Netherlands	197.0	0.1	0.0	99.2	0.1	0.0	0.6	0.0	...	100
Singapore	193.6	0.0	0.0	25.4	...	0.1	73.9	0.6	...	100
Brazil	163.3	0.0	0.0	92.9	...	0.2	6.8	0.2	...	100

Imports Profile:

In 2010, Congo's imports were mainly composed of 74.4 percent machinery and transport equipment (SITC section 7), 6.9 percent manufactured goods classified chiefly by material (SITC section 6) and 6.6 percent food, live animals, beverages and tobacco (SITC sections 0+1) (see table 2). From 2008 to 2010, top imported products were light-vessels, fire-floats, dredgers, floating cranes and other vessels (HS code 8905), cruise ships, excursion boats, ferry-boats, cargo ships, barges (HS code 8901) and petroleum oils, other than crude (HS code 2710) (see table 5).

Table 5: Top 10 import commodities 2008 to 2010

(Value in million US$)

HS code	4-digit heading of Harmonized System 2002	Value (million US$)			Unit value				SITC code
		2008	2009	2010	2008	2009	2010	Unit	
	All Commodities	3539.6	4447.1	4369.4					
8905	Light-vessels, fire-floats, dredgers, floating cranes and other vessels	1110.6	1910.0	1824.9					793
8901	Cruise ships, excursion boats, ferry-boats, cargo ships, barges	693.3	810.0	773.9					793
2710	Petroleum oils, other than crude	189.9	98.1	221.9	0.9	0.7	3.9	US$/kg	334
2523	Portland cement, aluminous cement, slag cement	65.2	72.1	67.8	0.2	0.2	0.5	US$/kg	661
3004	Medicaments (excluding goods of heading 30.02, 30.05 or 30.06)	48.3	57.8	55.2	22.9	20.3	19.5	US$/kg	542
8431	Parts suitable for use principally with the machinery of headings 84.25	23.4	63.4	71.5	30.2	45.9	30.3	US$/kg	723
8411	Turbo-jets, turbo-propellers and other gas turbines	6.4	55.4	62.5					714
0207	Meat and edible offal, of the poultry of heading 01.05	37.9	60.0	26.0	1.3	1.1	1.1	US$/kg	012
8307	Flexible tubing of base metal, with or without fittings	30.1	45.5	41.4	13.5	32.0	29.9	US$/kg	699
8904	Tugs and pusher craft	17.0	50.5	48.3					793

Source: UN Comtrade

Cook Islands

Imports: CIF, by origin | Exports: FOB, by last known destination | Trade System: General

Overview:

In 2008, exports of Cook Islands amounted to 4.1 mln US$ (see table 1 and graph 1). In 2007, imports reached 103.2 mln US$ (see table 2 and graph 1). The trade balance recorded a deficit of 76.0 mln US$ in 2005 (see graph 1). In 2008, exports were concentrated among few partners: 3 major partners accounted for 80 percent of exported goods (see graph 3).

Graph 1: Total imports, exports and trade balance

(Mln US$ by year)

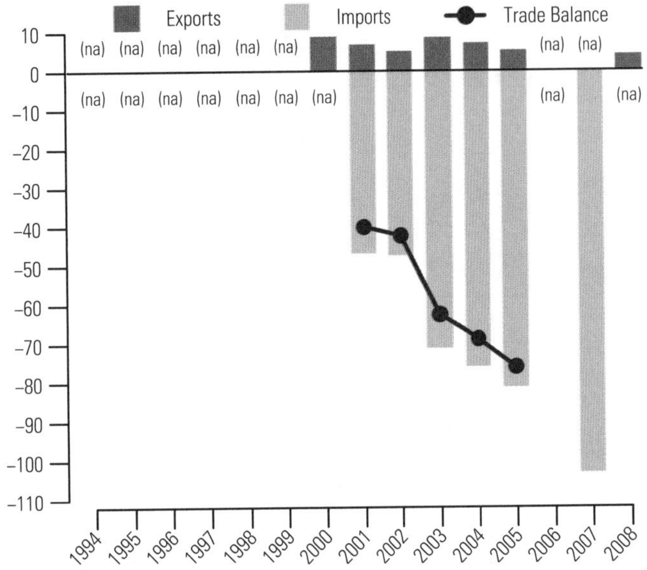

Table 1: Exports by SITC sections

(Value in million US$, growth and shares in percentage)

SITC	2008	Avg. Growth rates (%) 2004-2008	2007-2008	2008 share
Total	4.1	-12.8	...	100.0
0+1	0.9	-32.2	...	22.8
2+4	0.1	17.5	...	1.9
5	0.0	-20.9	...	0.0
6	1.1	-15.1	...	27.2
9	2.0	...	...	48.1

Exports Profile:

In 2008, commodities and transactions not classified elsewhere (SITC section 9) accounted for a large part of exported goods; they represented 48.1 percent of total exports (see table 1). Manufactured goods classified chiefly by material (SITC section 6) and food, live animals, beverages and tobacco (SITC sections 0+1) accounted for 27.2 and 22.8 percent of exports respectively. Japan, China and New Zealand were the top partners for exported goods (see table 4). In 2008, top exported products were pearls, natural or cultured (HS code 7101), fruit and vegetable juices, not fermented or spirited (HS code 2009) and live fish (HS code 0301) (see table 3).

Table 2: Imports by SITC sections

(Value in million US$, growth and shares in percentage)

SITC	2007	Avg. Growth rates (%) 2004-2007	2006-2007	2007 share
Total	103.2	10.8	...	100.0
0+1	15.5	-2.5	...	15.0
2+4	1.6	-11.5	...	1.6
3	19.4	48.8	...	18.8
5	1.7	-27.6	...	1.6
6	6.6	-19.0	...	6.4
7	11.0	-12.7	...	10.7
8	5.5	-14.8	...	5.4
9	41.9	69.2	...	40.6

Table 3: Top 10 export commodities 2006 to 2008

(Value in million US$)

HS code	4-digit heading of Harmonized System 1992	Value (million US$) 2006	2007	2008	Unit value 2006	2007	2008	Unit	SITC code
	All Commodities	...	...	4.1					
9999	Commodities not specified according to kind	...	...	2.0					931
7101	Pearls, natural or cultured, not mounted or set	...	...	1.0					667
2009	Fruit and vegetable juices, not fermented or spirited	...	...	0.8			*3.9*	US$/kg	059
0301	Live fish	...	...	0.1			20.3	US$/kg	034
8106	Bismuth, articles thereof, waste or scrap	...	...	0.1			*27.5*	US$/kg	689
0508	Coral, shell, cuttle bone, etc, unworked, and waste	...	...	0.1					291
0807	Melons, watermelons and papaws (papayas), fresh	...	...	0.0			1.7	US$/kg	057
4811	Paper, board, etc coated, impregnated, coloured, nes	...	...	0.0			*1.5*	US$/kg	641
3401	Soaps	...	...	0.0			*6.5*	US$/kg	554
0709	Vegetables nes, fresh or chilled	...	...	0.0			3.0	US$/kg	054

Graph 2: Trade Balance by MDG Regions in 2007

(Mln US$)

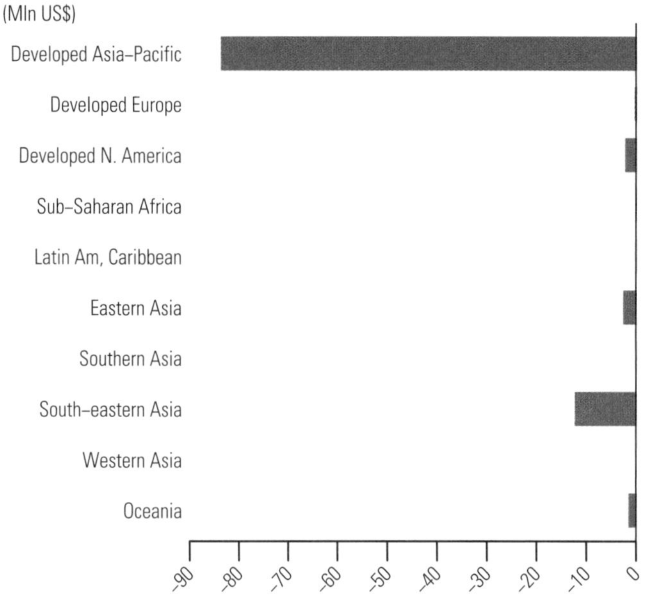

Graph 3: Partner concentration of trade in 2008

(Cumulative share by ranked partners)

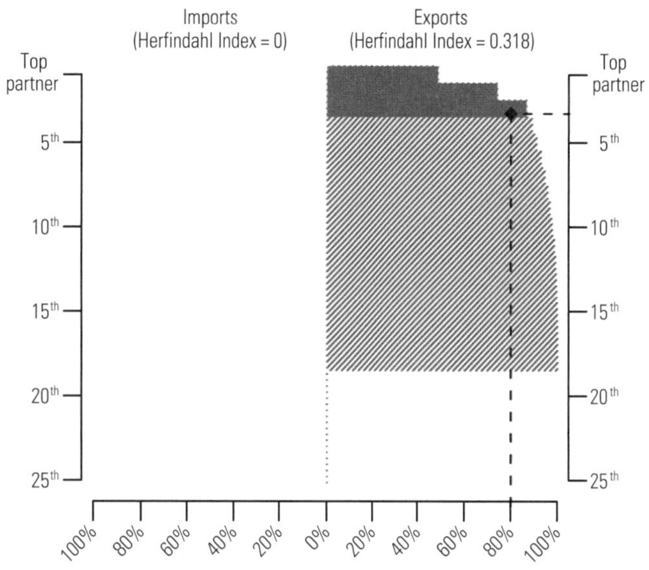

Table 4: Exports by principal countries and SITC sections in 2008

(Value in million US$, percentages of country total)

Country	Total	Shares by SITC sections (%)								
		0 + 1	2 + 4	3	5	6	7	8	9	Total
World	4.1	22.8	1.9	...	0.0	27.2	...	...	48.1	100
Japan	2.0	37.1	0.0	...	0.0	36.1	...	...	26.8	100
China	1.1	0.0	0.0	...	...	13.1	...	...	86.9	100
New Zealand	0.5	21.3	0.2	...	0.0	27.2	...	...	51.3	100
Australia	0.1	0.0	0.0	...	...	51.0	...	...	49.0	100
USA	0.1	78.4	0.0	...	...	...	...	...	21.6	100
Fiji	0.1	0.0	0.0	...	...	1.8	...	...	98.2	100
Indonesia	0.1	0.0	53.4	...	...	46.6	...	...	...	100
Thailand	0.0	0.0	0.0	...	...	...	...	...	100.0	100
American Samoa	0.0	0.0	0.0	...	...	...	...	...	100.0	100
Italy	0.0	0.0	100.0	...	...	...	...	...	...	100

Imports Profile:

In 2007, imports were composed of 40.6 percent of commodities and transactions not classified elsewhere (SITC section 9) (see table 2). Other top commodity groups included mineral fuels, lubricants and related materials (SITC section 3) and food, live animals, beverages and tobacco (SITC sections 0+1), which represented respectively 18.8 and 15.0 percent of total imports. Top imported products in 2007 were oils petroleum, bituminous, distillates, except crude (HS code 2710), motor vehicles for transport of persons (except buses) (HS code 8703) and motor vehicles for the transport of goods (HS code 8704) (see table 5).

Table 5: Top 10 import commodities 2005 to 2007

(Value in million US$)

HS code	4-digit heading of Harmonized System 1992	Value (million US$)			Unit value				SITC code
		2005	2006	2007	2005	2006	2007	Unit	
	All Commodities	81.3	...	103.2					
9999	Commodities not specified according to kind	0.0	...	41.9					931
2710	Oils petroleum, bituminous, distillates, except crude	6.8	...	18.6	*0.4*			US$/kg	334
8703	Motor vehicles for transport of persons (except buses)	2.6	...	3.5	*10.0*		*8.9*	thsd US$/unit	781
8704	Motor vehicles for the transport of goods	1.4	...	1.7	*19.6*		*13.3*	thsd US$/unit	782
1602	Prepared or preserved meat, meat offal and blood, nes	1.7	...	1.1	*6.4*		*11.4*	US$/kg	017
2203	Beer made from malt	1.1	...	1.5	*1.0*		*1.1*	US$/litre	112
4409	Wood continuously shaped along any edges	1.0	...	1.4	*1.4*		*1.3*	US$/kg	248
8711	Motorcycles, bicycles etc with auxiliary motor	1.1	...	1.3	*2.4*		*0.9*	thsd US$/unit	785
9403	Other furniture and parts thereof	1.1	...	1.3					821
9406	Prefabricated buildings	0.8	...	1.5	*2.3*		*2.9*	US$/kg	811

Costa Rica

Imports: CIF, by origin | **Exports: FOB, by last known destination** | **Trade System: Special**

Overview:

From 2007 to 2011, Costa Rica's exports increased on average by 3.4 percent each year and amounted to 10.2 bln US$ in 2011 (see table 1 and graph 1). Imports increased on average by 9.4 percent each year and reached 18.3 bln US$ (see table 2 and graph 1). This resulted in a trade deficit of 8.0 bln US$ (see graph 1). This deficit was accounted for largely by trade with Developed North America which recorded a deficit of 4.5 bln US$ (see graph 2). Other deficits were recorded with Latin America and the Caribbean (-1.4 bln US$) and Eastern Asia (-1.0 bln US$). In 2011, both exports and imports were relatively diversified across partners: 12 major partners accounted for 80 percent of both exports and imports (see graph 3).

Graph 1: Total imports, exports and trade balance

(Bln US$ by year)

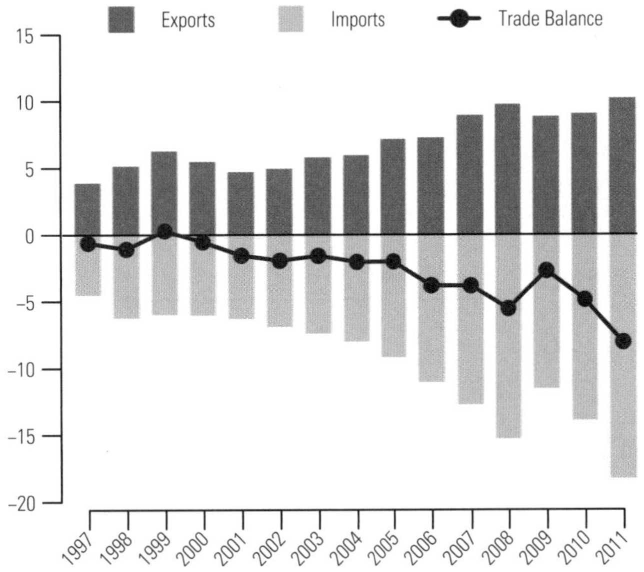

Exports Profile:

In 2011, exports of food, live animals, beverages and tobacco (SITC sections 0+1) accounted for 32.4 percent of exported goods (see table 1). Other major commodity groups included machinery and transport equipment (SITC section 7) and miscellaneous manufactured articles (SITC section 8) respectively with 27.0 and 16.2 percent of exports. Major partners for exports were USA, the Netherlands and Panama (see table 4). From 2009 to 2011, top products for exports were electronic integrated circuits (HS code 8542), instruments and appliances used in medical, surgical, dental or veterinary (HS code 9018) and bananas, including plantains, fresh or dried (HS code 0803) (see table 3).

Table 1: Exports by SITC sections

(Value in million US$, growth and shares in percentage)

SITC	2011	Avg. Growth rates (%) 2007-2011	2010-2011	2011 share
Total	10222.2	3.4	13.0	100.0
0+1	3313.9	7.2	11.7	32.4
2+4	620.9	9.8	32.8	6.1
3	33.3	-10.3	-34.8	0.3
5	814.9	9.4	17.8	8.0
6	986.1	6.1	17.9	9.6
7	2755.6	-2.9	12.3	27.0
8	1654.5	8.1	7.0	16.2
9	43.1	-37.6	39.9	0.4

Table 2: Imports by SITC sections

(Value in million US$, growth and shares in percentage)

SITC	2011	Avg. Growth rates (%) 2007-2011	2010-2011	2011 share
Total	18263.8	9.4	31.2	100.0
0+1	1407.3	12.5	28.8	7.7
2+4	454.6	9.7	25.8	2.5
3	2272.9	10.6	34.7	12.4
5	2414.8	7.9	14.2	13.2
6	2915.5	8.2	31.2	16.0
7	6754.8	9.8	44.4	37.0
8	2033.0	14.9	50.6	11.1
9	10.9	-57.0	-97.4	0.1

Table 3: Top 10 export commodities 2009 to 2011

(Value in million US$)

HS code	4-digit heading of Harmonized System 2007	Value (million US$) 2009	2010	2011	Unit value 2009	2010	2011	Unit	SITC code
	All Commodities	8836.3	9044.8	10222.2					
8542	Electronic integrated circuits	661.0	930.7	1888.8					776
9999	Commodities not specified according to kind	2293.1	0.1	...					931
9018	Instruments and appliances used in medical, surgical, dental or veterinary	538.0	750.8	837.6					872
0803	Bananas, including plantains, fresh or dried	448.2	702.0	722.1	0.4	0.4	0.4	US$/kg	057
0804	Dates, figs, pineapples, avocados and mangosteens, fresh or dried	454.6	682.0	727.5	0.4	0.4	0.4	US$/kg	057
8473	Parts and accessories for use with machines of heading 84.69 to 84.72	856.8	810.3	20.9	822.4	472.9	98.8	US$/kg	759
0901	Coffee, whether or not roasted or decaffeinated	218.3	265.5	379.4	3.0	3.5	4.9	US$/kg	071
9021	Orthopaedic appliances, including crutches, surgical belts and trusses	186.9	299.8	289.3					899
3004	Medicaments (excluding goods of heading 30.02, 30.05 or 30.06)	256.5	280.9	232.1	72.4	43.4	37.0	US$/kg	542
2106	Food preparations not elsewhere specified or included	167.9	277.0	295.9	12.4	13.2	6.3	US$/kg	098

Graph 2: Trade Balance by MDG Regions in 2011

(Bln US$)

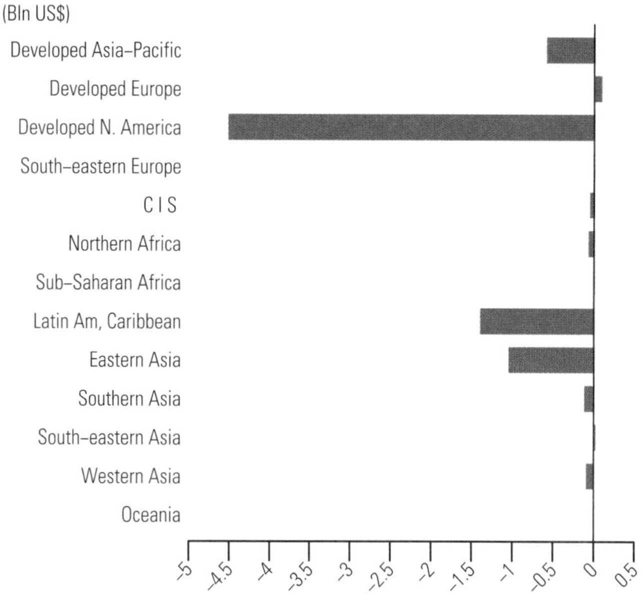

Graph 3: Partner concentration of trade in 2011

(Cumulative share by ranked partners)

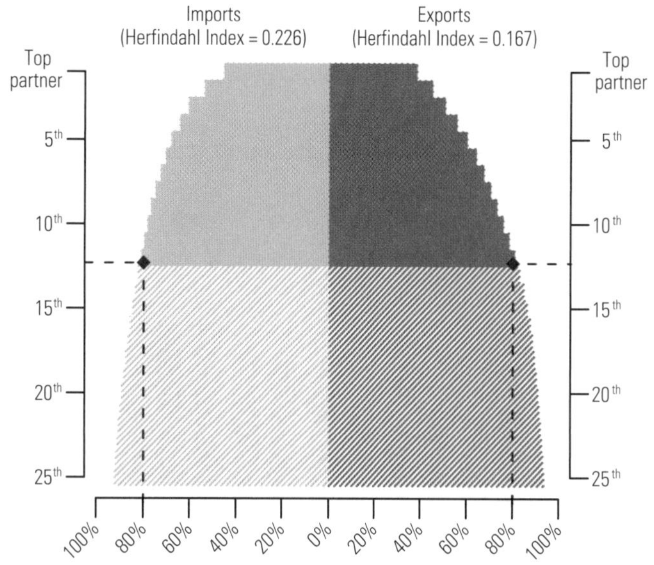

Table 4: Exports by principal countries and SITC sections in 2011

(Value in million US$, percentages of country total)

Country	Total	Shares by SITC sections (%)								
		0+1	2+4	3	5	6	7	8	9	Total
World	10222.2	32.4	6.1	0.3	8.0	9.6	27.0	16.2	0.4	100
USA	3911.3	32.8	3.0	0.0	1.9	5.8	25.4	30.2	1.0	100
Netherlands	686.2	29.3	8.9	0.0	2.1	0.5	54.3	5.0	...	100
Panama	559.9	20.6	3.3	0.5	41.4	17.3	9.5	7.3	...	100
China, Hong Kong SAR	517.0	2.7	1.0	0.0	0.5	0.6	94.6	0.6	...	100
Nicaragua	455.8	32.3	6.9	0.2	18.2	27.2	8.6	6.6	0.0	100
Guatemala	407.5	37.6	1.5	0.0	18.6	25.3	11.1	5.9	...	100
Honduras	336.2	32.4	3.4	0.0	25.6	17.7	14.3	6.6	0.0	100
Mexico	307.1	12.7	55.5	0.0	4.1	14.5	6.0	7.1	0.0	100
El Salvador	285.8	32.1	3.8	0.0	16.7	29.3	12.3	5.7	...	100
Belgium	274.3	74.1	8.7	0.0	0.2	0.2	1.4	15.2	0.2	100

Imports Profile:

In 2011, Costa Rica's imports were mainly composed of 37.0 percent of machinery and transport equipment (SITC section 7), 16.0 percent of manufactured goods classified chiefly by material (SITC section 6) and 13.2 percent of chemicals and related products, n.e.s. (SITC section 5) (see table 2). From 2009 to 2011, top imported products were petroleum oils, other than crude (HS code 2710), electronic integrated circuits (HS code 8542) and printed circuits (HS code 8534) (see table 5).

Table 5: Top 10 import commodities 2009 to 2011

(Value in million US$)

HS code	4-digit heading of Harmonized System 2007	Value (million US$)			Unit value				SITC code
		2009	2010	2011	2009	2010	2011	Unit	
	All Commodities	11550.5	13920.2	18263.8					
2710	Petroleum oils, other than crude	792.7	1291.6	1991.2	0.6	0.7	1.0	US$/kg	334
8542	Electronic integrated circuits	1018.6	1164.9	1297.0					776
9999	Commodities not specified according to kind	2593.0	390.9	...					931
8534	Printed circuits	370.4	406.8	604.5	420.8	281.2	347.2	US$/kg	772
8703	Motor cars and other motor vehicles principally designed for the transport	172.2	399.0	739.9		*17.9*		thsd US$/unit	781
3004	Medicaments (excluding goods of heading 30.02, 30.05 or 30.06)	347.4	450.6	432.5	78.8	55.3	56.4	US$/kg	542
8517	Electrical apparatus for line telephony or line telegraphy	151.6	216.6	472.0					764
8471	Automatic data processing machines and units thereof	136.8	196.6	390.0					752
2709	Petroleum oils and oils obtained from bituminous minerals, crude	115.1	300.8	160.4	0.5	0.6	0.8	US$/kg	333
8473	Parts and accessories for use with machines of heading 84.69 to 84.72	143.0	212.7	174.5	86.0	96.4	70.2	US$/kg	759

Côte d'Ivoire

Imports: CIF, by origin | **Exports: FOB, by last known destination** | **Trade System: Special**

Overview:

In 2011, the value of Côte d'Ivoire's exports increased by 7.4 percent and amounted to 11.0 bln US$ (see table 1 and graph 1). The value of imports, on the other hand, decreased by 14.4 percent and amounted to 6.7 bln US$ in 2011. The trade balance recorded a surplus of 4.3 bln US$ in 2011 compared to 1.4 bln US$ in 2007 (see graph 1). By MDG regions, trade surpluses were recorded with Developed Europe (+2.5 bln US$), Developed North America (+1.9 bln US$) and Sub-Saharan Africa (+1.2 bln US$) in 2011 (see graph 2). Trade deficits were recorded with Eastern Asia (-0.4 bln US$) and Latin America and the Caribbean (-0.2 bln US$) among others. Côte d'Ivoire's trade was diversified across partners: in 2011,18 (respectively 19) major partners accounted for 80 percent of exports (respectively imports) (see graph 3).

Graph 1: Total imports, exports and trade balance

(Bln US$ by year)

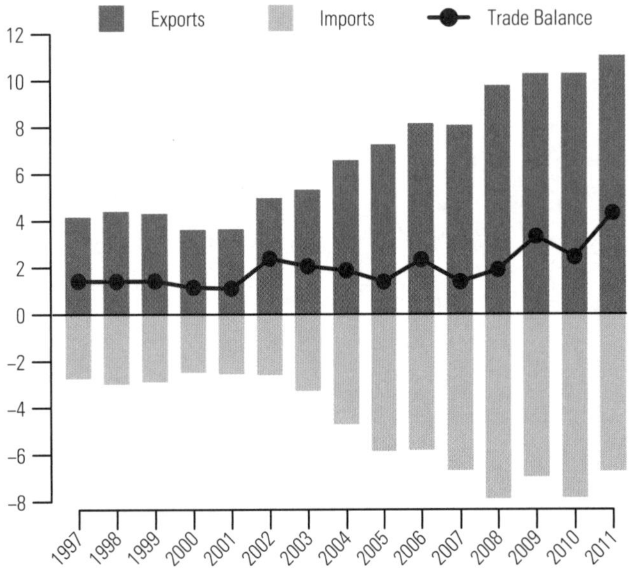

Exports Profile:

In 2011, exports were composed of 45.1 percent of food, live animals, beverages and tobacco (SITC sections 0+1), 24.3 percent of mineral fuels, lubricants and related materials (SITC section 3) and 15.9 percent of inedible crude materials (excluding fuels), animal and vegetable oils, fats and waxes (SITC sections 2+4) (see table 1). Major markets for exported goods were USA, Netherlands and Germany (see table 4). Top exported products over the last three years included cocoa beans, whole or broken, raw or roasted (HS code 1801), petroleum oils, other than crude (HS code 2710) and petroleum oils and oils obtained from bituminous minerals, crude (HS code 2709) (see table 3).

Table 1: Exports by SITC sections

(Value in million US$, growth and shares in percentage)

SITC	2011	Avg. Growth rates (%) 2007-2011	2010-2011	2011 share
Total	11 049.1	8.2	7.4	100.0
0+1	4 983.5	12.8	3.6	45.1
2+4	1 752.1	20.2	46.5	15.9
3	2 688.1	0.6	10.5	24.3
5	331.2	2.0	3.3	3.0
6	283.9	-4.8	-1.1	2.6
7	270.1	-8.9	-69.1	2.4
8	163.8	-21.1	-6.9	1.5
9	576.4	83.7	210.8	5.2

Table 2: Imports by SITC sections

(Value in million US$, growth and shares in percentage)

SITC	2011	Avg. Growth rates (%) 2007-2011	2010-2011	2011 share
Total	6 720.0	0.1	-14.4	100.0
0+1	1 631.9	9.4	14.1	24.3
2+4	169.3	9.7	-18.4	2.5
3	1 924.3	-1.2	3.4	28.6
5	955.3	6.8	3.2	14.2
6	680.9	-2.1	-18.7	10.1
7	1 059.0	-5.3	-54.2	15.8
8	289.8	-13.2	8.2	4.3
9	9.3	-45.8	2.4	0.1

Table 3: Top 10 export commodities 2009 to 2011

(Value in million US$)

HS code	4-digit heading of Harmonized System 2007	Value (million US$) 2009	2010	2011	Unit value 2009	2010	2011	Unit	SITC code
	All Commodities	10 280.1	10 283.5	11 049.1					
1801	Cocoa beans, whole or broken, raw or roasted	2 596.1	2 492.5	3 017.4	2.8	3.2	2.8	US$/kg	072
2710	Petroleum oils, other than crude	1 409.3	1 206.6	1 289.2	0.5	0.7	0.9	US$/kg	334
2709	Petroleum oils and oils obtained from bituminous minerals, crude	1 141.1	1 091.3	1 306.0	0.4	0.5	0.7	US$/kg	333
4001	Natural rubber, balata, gutta-percha, guayule, chicle	344.8	680.4	1 136.4	1.6	2.8	4.9	US$/kg	231
1803	Cocoa paste, whether or not defatted	488.4	601.8	539.2	3.5	4.1	3.8	US$/kg	072
8905	Light-vessels, fire-floats, dredgers, floating cranes and other vessels	338.6	726.2	...					793
7108	Gold (including gold plated with platinum)	210.7	183.3	573.3	26.4	33.8	43.7	thsd US$/kg	971
1804	Cocoa butter, fat and oil	323.3	302.2	218.9	4.8	4.8	3.9	US$/kg	072
0801	Coconuts, Brazil nuts and cashew nuts, fresh or dried	178.0	320.6	279.0	0.5	0.9	0.9	US$/kg	057
2713	Petroleum coke and other residues	456.6	131.8	91.3	1.8	0.5	0.6	US$/kg	335

Graph 2: Trade Balance by MDG Regions in 2011

(Bln US$)

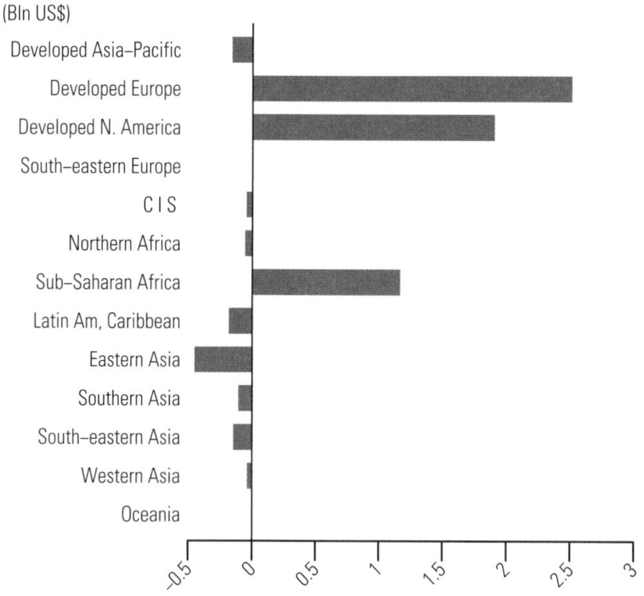

Graph 3: Partner concentration of trade in 2011

(Cumulative share by ranked partners)

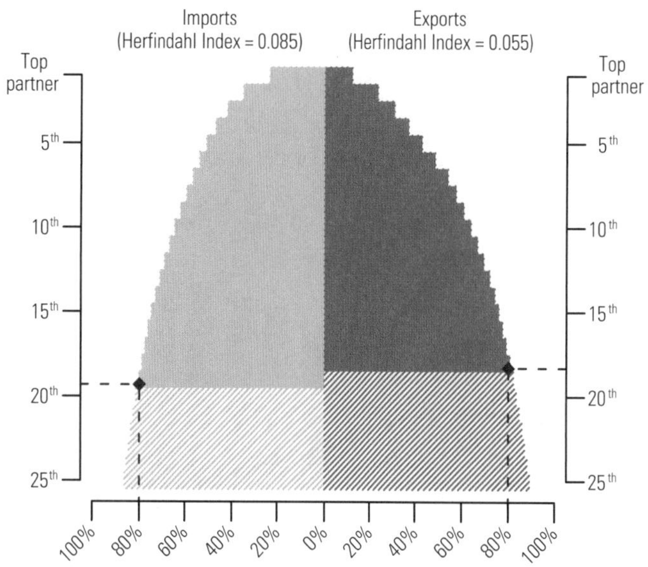

Table 4: Exports by principal countries and SITC sections in 2011

(Value in million US$, percentages of country total)

Country	Total	Shares by SITC sections (%) 0+1	2+4	3	5	6	7	8	9	Total
World	11049.1	45.1	15.9	24.3	3.0	2.6	2.4	1.5	5.2	100
USA	1318.5	64.5	10.7	23.8	0.1	0.4	0.5	0.0	...	100
Netherlands	1296.4	89.7	3.9	6.2	0.1	0.1	0.1	0.0	0.0	100
Germany	818.9	39.3	24.2	35.6	0.0	0.8	0.0	0.0	0.0	100
Nigeria	663.9	0.9	8.7	79.9	6.6	1.2	0.0	2.7	...	100
Canada	634.1	13.9	1.6	84.3	0.0	0.2	0.1	...	...	100
France	630.1	67.2	12.2	0.0	1.0	2.4	14.2	2.9	0.0	100
South Africa	605.4	1.0	30.0	...	0.3	0.0	0.4	0.0	68.3	100
Malaysia	386.8	53.1	46.9	...	...	0.0	0.0	...	...	100
Belgium	361.5	83.0	12.6	0.1	0.1	3.9	0.3	0.0	...	100
Burkina Faso	343.9	36.0	7.7	17.2	17.1	10.0	2.3	9.6	0.0	100

Imports Profile:

In 2011, imports of mineral fuels, lubricants and related materials (SITC section 3) increased by 3.4 percent and accounted for 28.6 percent of imported goods (see table 2). Other major commodity groups imported included food, live animals, beverages and tobacco (SITC sections 0+1) and machinery and transport equipment (SITC section 7), respectively with 24.3 and 15.8 percent of imports. Top imported products over the last three years were petroleum oils and oils obtained from bituminous minerals, crude (HS code 2709), rice (HS code 1006) and fish, frozen, excluding fish fillets and other fish meat of heading 03.04 (HS code 0303) (see table 5).

Table 5: Top 10 import commodities 2009 to 2011

(Value in million US$)

HS code	4-digit heading of Harmonized System 2007	Value (million US$) 2009	2010	2011	Unit value 2009	2010	2011	Unit	SITC code
	All Commodities	6959.9	7849.3	6720.0					
2709	Petroleum oils and oils obtained from bituminous minerals, crude	1622.9	1689.7	1749.4	0.5	0.6	0.8	US$/kg	333
1006	Rice	597.3	460.2	567.9	0.5	0.5	0.6	US$/kg	042
0303	Fish, frozen, excluding fish fillets and other fish meat of heading 03.04	353.5	277.7	326.2	1.0	0.9	1.1	US$/kg	034
8905	Light-vessels, fire-floats, dredgers, floating cranes and other vessels	3.2	841.9	...					793
3004	Medicaments (excluding goods of heading 30.02, 30.05 or 30.06)	212.4	208.5	231.3	22.4	27.1	26.7	US$/kg	542
8703	Motor cars and other motor vehicles principally designed for the transport	175.1	183.8	134.3	*20.1*	*19.7*		thsd US$/unit	781
1001	Wheat and meslin	129.3	147.5	185.3	0.3	0.3	0.4	US$/kg	041
8517	Electrical apparatus for line telephony or line telegraphy	148.5	152.2	96.0					764
3901	Polymers of ethylene, in primary forms	108.5	95.8	100.6	1.3	1.4	1.6	US$/kg	571
2523	Portland cement, aluminous cement, slag cement	102.9	102.4	87.4	0.1	0.1	0.1	US$/kg	661

Croatia

Imports: CIF, by origin	Exports: FOB, by last known destination	Trade System: Special

Overview:

In 2011, Croatia's exports increased by 4.0 percent and amounted to 12.3 bln US$, despite contracting sharply by 25.7 percent in 2009 (see table 1 and graph 1). Imports increased by 1.6 percent and amounted to 20.4 bln US$ in 2011 (see table 2 and graph 1). The trade balance recorded a deficit of 8.1 bln US$ in 2011 (see graph 1). By MDG regions, trade deficits were recorded with Developed Europe (-5.1 bln US$), the Commonwealth of Independent States (-2.1 bln US$) and Eastern Asia (-1.6 bln US$) (see graph 2). A trade surplus of 896.2 mln US$ was recorded with South-eastern Europe. Croatia's trade was diversified across partners: in 2011, 19 (respectively 17) major partners accounted for 80 percent of exports (respectively imports) (see graph 3).

Graph 1: Total imports, exports and trade balance

(Bln US$ by year)

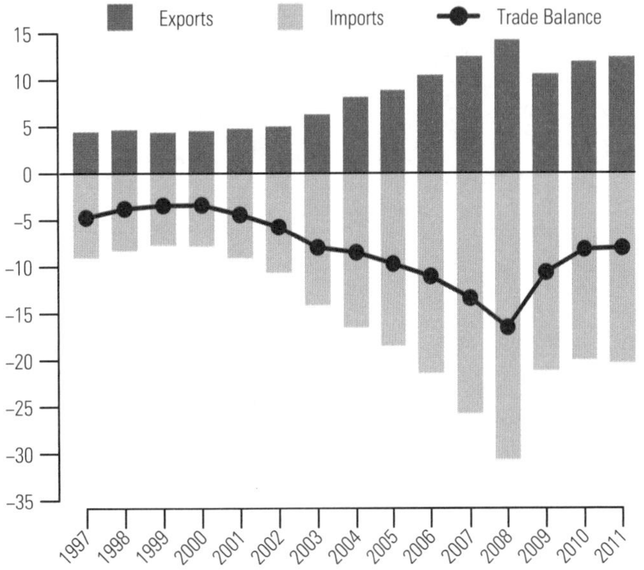

Table 1: Exports by SITC sections

(Value in million US$, growth and shares in percentage)

SITC	2011	Avg. Growth rates (%) 2007-2011	Avg. Growth rates (%) 2010-2011	2011 share
Total	12 288.8	-0.1	4.0	100.0
0+1	1 292.2	1.0	2.5	10.5
2+4	972.8	4.6	17.9	7.9
3	1 515.2	-1.3	2.9	12.3
5	1 388.4	4.5	3.6	11.3
6	1 807.6	-1.3	8.3	14.7
7	3 733.9	-0.7	-0.4	30.4
8	1 518.9	-4.1	2.2	12.4
9	59.9	88.9	549.5	0.5

Table 2: Imports by SITC sections

(Value in million US$, growth and shares in percentage)

SITC	2011	Avg. Growth rates (%) 2007-2011	Avg. Growth rates (%) 2010-2011	2011 share
Total	20 396.9	-5.7	1.6	100.0
0+1	2 050.8	1.0	3.5	10.1
2+4	431.7	-4.2	3.8	2.1
3	4 435.2	3.1	17.3	21.7
5	2 810.1	-0.2	-0.6	13.8
6	3 683.6	-7.8	2.0	18.1
7	4 622.9	-13.9	-10.2	22.7
8	2 362.2	-6.2	2.9	11.6
9	0.4	-61.4	-93.7	0.0

Exports Profile:

In 2011, machinery and transport equipment (SITC section 7), the largest commodity group, accounted for 30.4 percent of exports followed by manufactured goods classified chiefly by material (SITC section 6) and miscellaneous manufactured articles (SITC section 8), respectively with 14.7 and 12.4 percent (see table 1). Three major partners for exports in 2011 were Italy, Bosnia Herzegovina and Germany (see table 4). Top products for exports over the last three years included petroleum oils, other than crude (HS code 2710), cruise ships, excursion boats, ferry-boats, cargo ships, barges (HS code 8901) and electrical transformers, static converters (HS code 8504) (see table 3).

Table 3: Top 10 export commodities 2009 to 2011

(Value in million US$)

HS code	4-digit heading of Harmonized System 2007	Value (million US$) 2009	Value (million US$) 2010	Value (million US$) 2011	Unit value 2009	Unit value 2010	Unit value 2011	Unit	SITC code
	All Commodities	10 491.8	11 810.7	12 288.8					
2710	Petroleum oils, other than crude	872.3	1 112.6	1 209.0	0.5	0.6	0.9	US$/kg	334
8901	Cruise ships, excursion boats, ferry-boats, cargo ships, barges	690.5	841.8	882.8			*44.1*	mln US$/unit	793
8504	Electrical transformers, static converters	454.8	383.8	354.7					771
3004	Medicaments (excluding goods of heading 30.02, 30.05 or 30.06)	307.7	400.3	441.0	*104.9*	*137.5*	*137.0*	US$/kg	542
2711	Petroleum gases and other gaseous hydrocarbons	379.5	284.7	231.9	0.5	0.6	0.8	US$/kg	343
8905	Light-vessels, fire-floats, dredgers, floating cranes and other vessels	43.4	428.8	328.0	10.9		3.5	mln US$/unit	793
4407	Wood sawn or chipped lengthwise, sliced or peeled	182.8	206.9	225.9		*375.7*	*397.7*	US$/m³	248
9401	Seats (other than those of heading 94.02)	173.4	205.5	200.5					821
3102	Mineral or chemical fertilisers, nitrogenous	127.9	163.1	199.3	0.2	0.3	0.4	US$/kg	562
3901	Polymers of ethylene, in primary forms	117.6	190.1	132.3	1.1	1.5	1.7	US$/kg	571

Graph 2: Trade Balance by MDG Regions in 2011

(Bln US$)

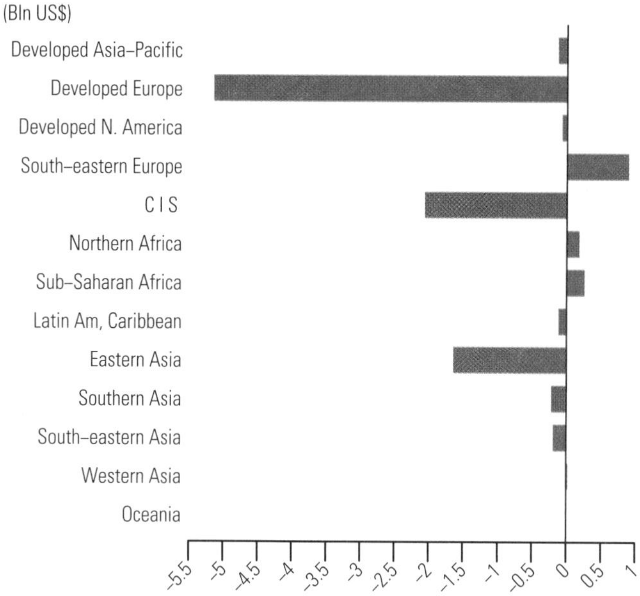

Graph 3: Partner concentration of trade in 2011

(Cumulative share by ranked partners)

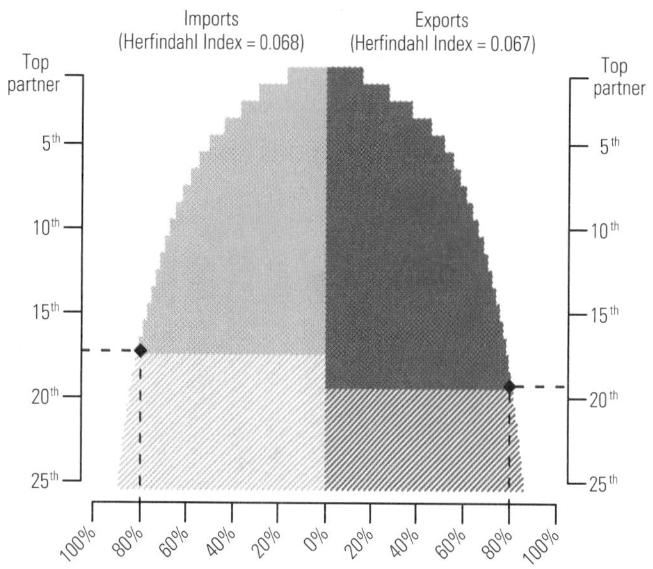

Table 4: Exports by principal countries and SITC sections in 2011

(Value in million US$, percentages of country total)

Country	Total	Shares by SITC sections (%)								
		0 + 1	2 + 4	3	5	6	7	8	9	Total
World	12288.8	10.5	7.9	12.3	11.3	14.7	30.4	12.4	0.5	100
Italy	1934.9	6.7	15.2	8.9	7.8	15.2	23.0	22.4	0.8	100
Bosnia Herzegovina	1489.8	27.0	4.2	34.9	9.3	12.7	6.9	4.9	...	100
Germany	1220.1	4.8	5.8	0.9	3.1	21.3	29.5	34.1	0.7	100
Slovenia	1001.0	13.1	17.7	5.4	10.9	23.1	21.0	8.5	0.3	100
Austria	686.5	4.1	9.0	0.5	3.8	16.8	45.0	15.9	4.8	100
Serbia	479.1	15.5	8.5	7.6	18.5	25.7	15.7	8.6	...	100
France	366.3	0.9	1.3	0.2	6.4	13.2	69.2	8.9	...	100
Luxembourg	330.7	0.0	0.0	...	...	0.5	99.1	0.4	...	100
USA	329.8	5.7	0.3	0.2	50.8	16.7	10.5	15.7	...	100
Hungary	306.0	21.2	9.7	27.8	10.2	20.4	8.2	2.6	...	100

Imports Profile:

In 2011, machinery and transport equipment (SITC section 7) accounted for 22.7 percent of total imports followed by mineral fuels, lubricants and related materials (SITC section 3) and manufactured goods classified chiefly by material (SITC section 6), respectively with 21.7 and 18.1 percent (see table 2). Three major products for imports over the last three years were petroleum oils and oils obtained from bituminous minerals, crude (HS code 2709), petroleum oils, other than crude (HS code 2710) and motor cars and other motor vehicles principally designed for the transport (HS code 8703) (see table 5).

Table 5: Top 10 import commodities 2009 to 2011

(Value in million US$)

HS code	4-digit heading of Harmonized System 2007	Value (million US$)			Unit value				SITC code
		2009	2010	2011	2009	2010	2011	Unit	
	All Commodities	21204.9	20067.0	20396.9					
2709	Petroleum oils and oils obtained from bituminous minerals, crude	1792.2	2034.4	2199.3	0.4	0.6	0.8	US$/kg	333
2710	Petroleum oils, other than crude	602.8	842.8	1067.4	*0.6*	*0.8*	*1.0*	US$/kg	334
8703	Motor cars and other motor vehicles principally designed for the transport	713.9	608.0	636.4	14.2	*12.8*	*13.3*	thsd US$/unit	781
3004	Medicaments (excluding goods of heading 30.02, 30.05 or 30.06)	618.9	590.5	601.2	*88.2*	*78.8*	*82.3*	US$/kg	542
2716	Electrical energy	570.7	381.2	578.0	73.6	56.5	67.0	US$/MWh	351
2711	Petroleum gases and other gaseous hydrocarbons	454.1	328.9	405.7	0.6	*0.5*	*0.7*	US$/kg	343
8517	Electrical apparatus for line telephony or line telegraphy	354.8	316.0	264.9					764
8471	Automatic data processing machines and units thereof	248.6	242.4	216.2	130.1	127.0	84.8	US$/unit	752
9403	Other furniture and parts thereof	241.1	188.0	179.7					821
7208	Flat-rolled products of iron or non-alloy steel	185.2	149.7	190.1	*0.8*	*0.8*	*0.9*	US$/kg	673

Cyprus

Imports: CIF, by origin/consignment for intra-eu | **Exports: FOB, by last known destination** | **Trade System: General**

Overview:

After a big drop of 21.2 percent in 2009, the value of Cyprus's exports bounced back in 2010 by 11.5 percent and continued to rise by 29.9 percent to reach its peak of 2.0 bln US$ in 2011 (see table 1 and graph 1). Imports showed a slight increase of 0.9 percent and amounted to 8.7 bln US$ (see table 2 and graph 1). This resulted in a trade deficit of 6.8 bln US$ in 2011, slightly higher than the 2009 deficit of 6.6 bln US$ but less than the 2010 deficit of 7.1 bln US$ (see graph 1). Although trade was in deficit with almost all MDG regions, this deficit reflected largely trade with Developed Europe (-5.0 bln US$) (see graph 2). Deficits were also recorded with Western Asia (-0.8 bln US$) and Eastern Asia (-0.4 bln US$) (see graph 2). In 2011, exports were well diversified across partners: 20 major partners accounted for 80 percent of exports compared to 12 major partners for imports (see graph 3).

Graph 1: Total imports, exports and trade balance

(Bln US$ by year)

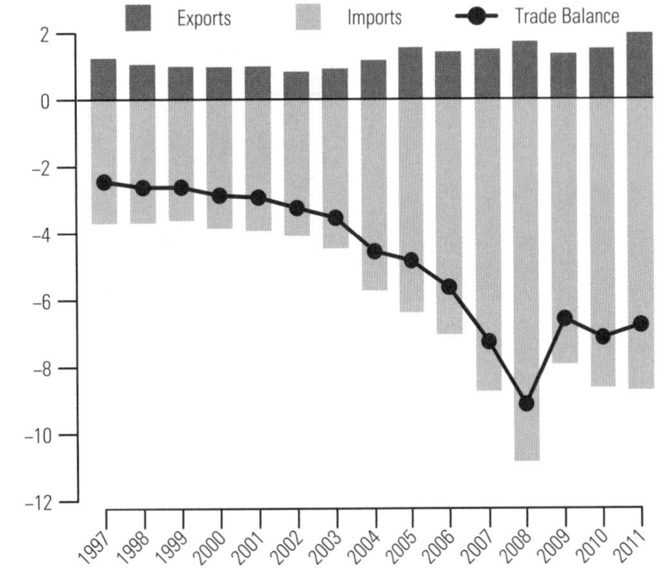

Table 1: Exports by SITC sections

(Value in million US$, growth and shares in percentage)

SITC	2011	Avg. Growth rates (%) 2007-2011	Avg. Growth rates (%) 2010-2011	2011 share
Total	1 957.5	7.1	29.9	100.0
0+1	395.3	3.4	16.1	20.2
2+4	137.2	14.8	41.1	7.0
3	347.6	10.8	61.6	17.8
5	491.1	22.0	37.9	25.1
6	85.1	4.0	27.3	4.3
7	293.3	-5.1	15.6	15.0
8	169.2	-0.6	3.5	8.6
9	38.6	149.6	189.2	2.0

Table 2: Imports by SITC sections

(Value in million US$, growth and shares in percentage)

SITC	2011	Avg. Growth rates (%) 2007-2011	Avg. Growth rates (%) 2010-2011	2011 share
Total	8 718.9	-0.1	0.9	100.0
0+1	1 334.4	5.0	7.6	15.3
2+4	130.3	-5.6	6.0	1.5
3	2 203.6	10.7	26.6	25.3
5	891.3	3.1	6.2	10.2
6	1 025.9	-6.0	-6.4	11.8
7	1 807.0	-8.3	-19.3	20.7
8	1 230.1	-2.1	1.6	14.1
9	96.3	39.0	-38.2	1.1

Exports Profile:

In 2011, the major exports of Cyprus were chemicals and related products, n.e.s. (SITC section 5), food, live animals, beverages and tobacco (SITC sections 0+1) and mineral fuels, lubricants and related materials (SITC section 3), respectively with 25.1, 20.2 and 17.8 percent of exports (see table 1). Major partners for exports included Greece, United Kingdom and Germany (see table 4). A large share of exported goods, almost exclusively mineral fuels, lubricants and related materials (SITC section 3) was reported to be supplied to foreign vessels and aircrafts and the partner was unknown. In addition to petroleum oils, other than crude (HS code 2710), other major exported products over the last three years included medicaments (excluding goods of heading 30.02, 30.05 or 30.06) (HS code 3004) and diodes, transistors and similar semiconductor devices (HS code 8541) (see table 3).

Table 3: Top 10 export commodities 2009 to 2011

(Value in million US$)

HS code	4-digit heading of Harmonized System 2007	Value (million US$) 2009	2010	2011	Unit value 2009	2010	2011	Unit	SITC code
	All Commodities	1 350.9	1 506.5	1 957.5					
2710	Petroleum oils, other than crude	188.1	215.1	347.5	0.6	0.7	1.0	US$/kg	334
3004	Medicaments (excluding goods of heading 30.02, 30.05 or 30.06)	164.0	187.6	230.5	51.2	51.0	62.7	US$/kg	542
8541	Diodes, transistors and similar semiconductor devices	91.1	115.7	84.1					776
2402	Cigars, cheroots, cigarillos and cigarettes	77.7	86.0	68.5	21.1	20.7	*23.9*	US$/kg	122
0406	Cheese and curd	58.8	64.6	77.4	*8.6*	8.1	8.5	US$/kg	024
0701	Potatoes, fresh or chilled	53.1	44.1	74.0	0.7	0.8	0.7	US$/kg	054
9021	Orthopaedic appliances, including crutches, surgical belts and trusses	66.0	36.0	12.0					899
7204	Ferrous waste and scrap; remelting scrap ingots of iron or steel	20.3	33.3	58.8	0.3	0.3	0.4	US$/kg	282
0805	Citrus fruit, fresh or dried	32.2	37.6	37.0	0.8	0.7	0.7	US$/kg	057
9018	Instruments and appliances used in medical, surgical, dental or veterinary	44.5	26.7	24.8					872

Graph 2: Trade Balance by MDG Regions in 2011

(Bln US$)

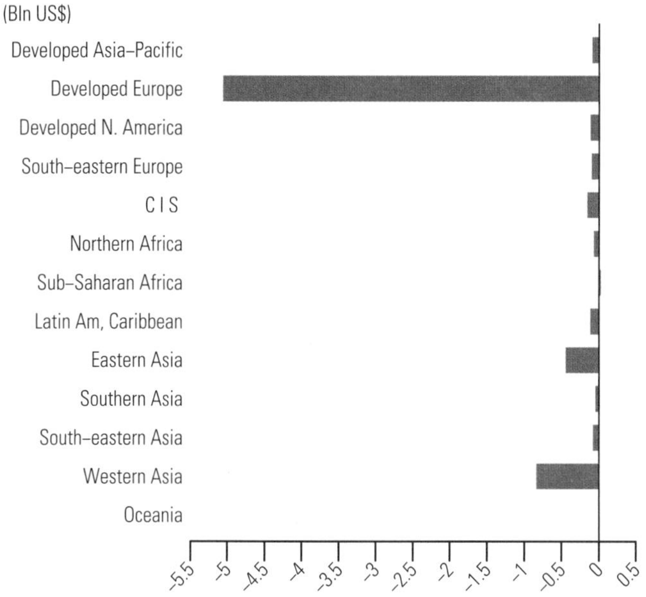

Graph 3: Partner concentration of trade in 2011

(Cumulative share by ranked partners)

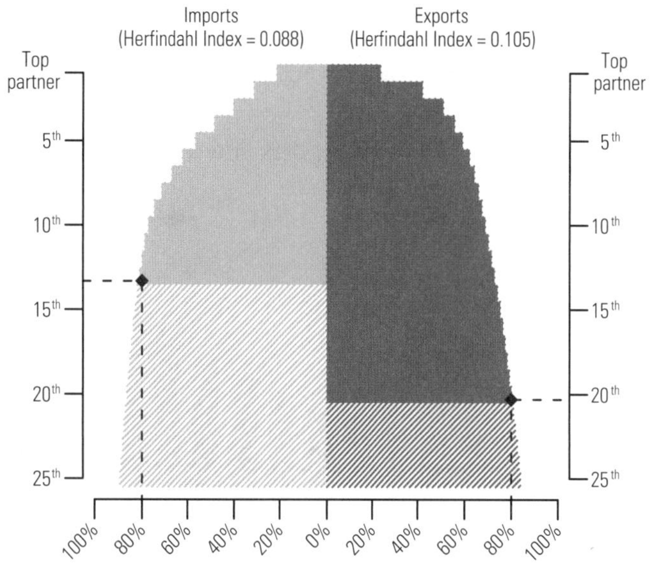

Table 4: Exports by principal countries and SITC sections in 2011

(Value in million US$, percentages of country total)

Country	Total	Shares by SITC sections (%) 0 + 1	2 + 4	3	5	6	7	8	9	Total
World	1957.5	20.2	7.0	17.8	25.1	4.3	15.0	8.6	2.0	100
Greece	465.3	11.7	12.2	0.2	45.3	1.1	13.4	16.2	0.0	100
Bunkers	356.4	2.3	0.0	97.3	0.0	0.0	0.3	0.1	...	100
United Kingdom	174.0	32.6	3.6	...	16.1	3.8	25.4	5.0	13.4	100
Germany	94.0	23.7	1.2	...	3.7	1.8	67.3	2.2	0.0	100
Lebanon	66.1	39.4	8.0	0.0	12.1	0.6	7.2	9.7	23.0	100
Italy	58.5	16.7	2.9	...	1.3	59.1	15.8	4.3	0.0	100
Israel	40.5	57.1	11.6	0.1	6.3	6.6	17.0	1.3	...	100
United Arab Emirates	35.0	52.7	5.3	...	15.2	2.4	14.5	9.9	...	100
Egypt	29.0	42.6	0.4	...	0.8	1.6	11.6	43.1	...	100
China, Hong Kong SAR	28.4	20.8	28.1	...	15.4	0.1	18.9	16.3	0.4	100

Imports Profile:

In 2011, imports of Cyprus were mainly composed of 25.3 percent of mineral fuels, lubricants and related materials (SITC section 3), 20.7 percent of machinery and transport equipment (SITC section 7) and 15.3 percent of food, live animals, beverages and tobacco (SITC sections 0+1) (see table 2). In addition to petroleum oils, other than crude (HS code 2710), other major products for imports over the last three years included motor cars and other motor vehicles principally designed for the transport (HS code 8703) and medicaments (excluding goods of heading 30.02, 30.05 or 30.06) (HS code 3004) (see table 5).

Table 5: Top 10 import commodities 2009 to 2011

(Value in million US$)

HS code	4-digit heading of Harmonized System 2007	Value (million US$) 2009	2010	2011	Unit value 2009	2010	2011	Unit	SITC code
	All Commodities	7933.4	8644.7	8718.9					
2710	Petroleum oils, other than crude	1316.9	1643.1	2094.8	0.5	0.6	0.8	US$/kg	334
8703	Motor cars and other motor vehicles principally designed for the transport	425.6	479.0	434.1	14.7	14.8	*16.6*	thsd US$/unit	781
3004	Medicaments (excluding goods of heading 30.02, 30.05 or 30.06)	236.1	229.5	245.9	64.1	64.8	69.2	US$/kg	542
9403	Other furniture and parts thereof	142.4	126.0	110.7					821
2402	Cigars, cheroots, cigarillos and cigarettes	120.6	130.6	119.4	25.3	24.1	31.5	US$/kg	122
7214	Other bars and rods of iron or non-alloy steel	102.4	144.1	112.4	0.5	0.6	0.7	US$/kg	676
8802	Other aircraft (for example, helicopters, aeroplanes); spacecraft	3.5	286.7	29.0	1.2	31.9	3.2	mln US$/unit	792
8517	Electrical apparatus for line telephony or line telegraphy	118.4	105.0	83.1					764
9999	Commodities not specified according to kind	12.5	155.3	95.7					931
8471	Automatic data processing machines and units thereof	85.0	87.5	83.5	195.6	179.5	215.6	US$/unit	752

Imports: CIF, by origin | **Exports: FOB, by last known destination** | **Trade System: Special**

Overview:

From 2007 to 2011, despite a decline of 22.7 percent in 2009, the value of the exports of Czech Republic increased on average by 7.6 percent each year and reached its peak of 162.1 bln US$ in 2011 (see table 1 and graph 1). Imports showed a similar development with an increase of 19.8 percent and amounted to 150.5 bln US$ in 2011 (see table 2 and graph 1).The trade balance recorded a surplus of 11.6 bln US$ (see graph 1). By MDG regions, trade recorded a surplus of 38.4 bln US$ with Developed Europe (see graph 2). Significant deficits were recorded with Eastern Asia (-20.2 bln US$), Commonwealth of Independent States (-4.3 bln US$) and South-eastern Asia (-3.9 bln US$). Both imports and exports were diversified across partners: in 2011, 13 (respectively 15) major partners accounted for 80 percent of exports (respectively imports) (see graph 3).

Graph 1: Total imports, exports and trade balance

(Bln US$ by year)

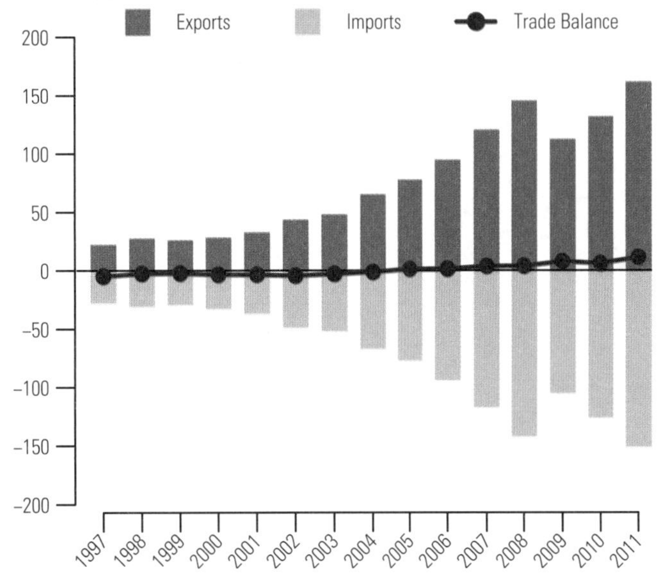

Table 1: Exports by SITC sections

(Value in million US$, growth and shares in percentage)

SITC	2011	Avg. Growth rates (%) 2007-2011	Avg. Growth rates (%) 2010-2011	2011 share
Total	162111.7	7.6	22.7	100.0
0+1	6147.6	9.7	30.5	3.8
2+4	4916.0	11.1	21.2	3.0
3	6135.9	17.9	26.2	3.8
5	9987.3	9.6	21.3	6.2
6	28721.0	4.0	29.2	17.7
7	88602.8	7.7	25.5	54.7
8	17344.8	8.1	22.7	10.7
9	256.4	29.0	-92.3	0.2

Table 2: Imports by SITC sections

(Value in million US$, growth and shares in percentage)

SITC	2011	Avg. Growth rates (%) 2007-2011	Avg. Growth rates (%) 2010-2011	2011 share
Total	150542.4	6.5	19.8	100.0
0+1	7863.4	7.8	22.2	5.2
2+4	4910.5	13.1	43.1	3.3
3	15154.6	13.3	26.6	10.1
5	16445.5	8.0	29.3	10.9
6	27554.6	3.1	28.4	18.3
7	63537.4	5.8	19.3	42.2
8	14783.2	6.1	20.4	9.8
9	293.1	46.8	-92.9	0.2

Exports Profile:

In 2011, machinery and transport equipment (SITC section 7) accounted for more than half (54.7 percent) of total exports (see table 1). Other major commodity groups included manufactured goods classified chiefly by material (SITC section 6) and miscellaneous manufactured articles (SITC section 8) respectively with 17.7 and 10.7 percent. The main partners for exports in 2011 were Germany, Slovakia and Poland (see table 4). From 2009 to 2011, top exported products were motor cars and other motor vehicles principally designed for the transport (HS code 8703), parts and accessories of the motor vehicles of headings 87.01 to 87.05 (HS code 8708) and automatic data processing machines and units thereof (HS code 8471) (see table 3).

Table 3: Top 10 export commodities 2009 to 2011

(Value in million US$)

HS code	4-digit heading of Harmonized System 2007	Value (million US$) 2009	2010	2011	Unit value 2009	2010	2011	Unit	SITC code
	All Commodities	112884.3	132140.9	162111.7					
8703	Motor cars and other motor vehicles principally designed for the transport	10596.2	12490.0	15484.0	12.3	13.1	14.6	thsd US$/unit	781
8708	Parts and accessories of the motor vehicles of headings 87.01 to 87.05	7409.2	8530.2	10512.2	8.4	8.1	*8.8*	US$/kg	784
8471	Automatic data processing machines and units thereof	6174.6	8333.0	10223.7	159.3	174.1	204.5	US$/unit	752
8528	Reception apparatus for television	2899.2	3334.3	3469.6	339.3	324.2	263.3	US$/unit	761
8517	Electrical apparatus for line telephony or line telegraphy	1783.2	2149.1	3569.9					764
8544	Insulated (including enamelled or anodised) wire, cable	1609.8	2185.4	2592.6	9.1	10.2	*11.1*	US$/kg	773
4011	New pneumatic tyres, of rubber	1643.5	1929.5	2360.0	63.1	63.0	74.2	US$/unit	625
9999	Commodities not specified according to kind	2317.9	3233.9	119.3					931
2716	Electrical energy	1814.2	1449.0	2159.0	69.9	62.5	72.4	US$/MWh	351
9401	Seats (other than those of heading 94.02)	1380.8	1660.2	1971.3					821

Graph 2: Trade Balance by MDG Regions in 2011

(Bln US$)

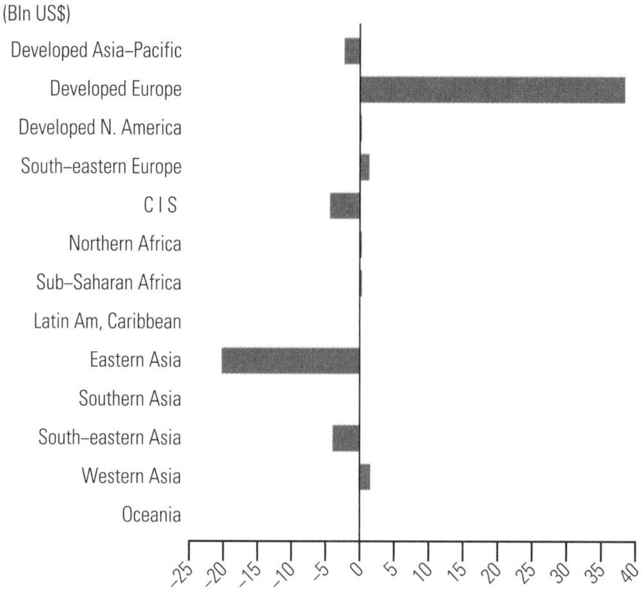

Graph 3: Partner concentration of trade in 2011

(Cumulative share by ranked partners)

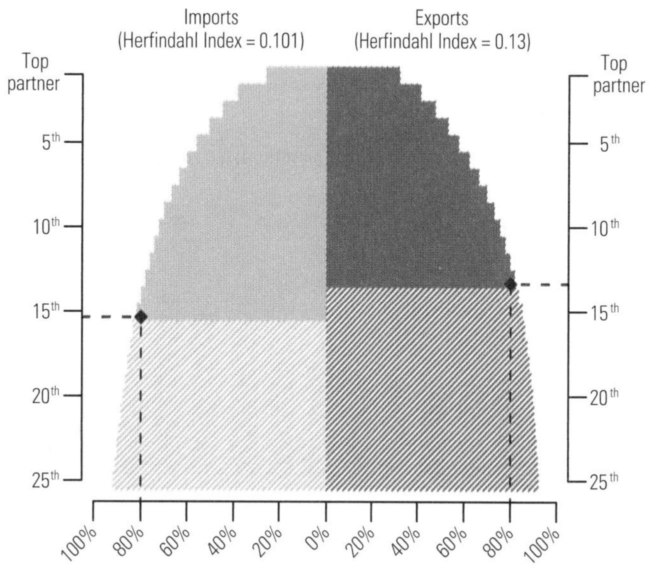

Table 4: Exports by principal countries and SITC sections in 2011

(Value in million US$, percentages of country total)

Country	Total	Shares by SITC sections (%) 0 + 1	2 + 4	3	5	6	7	8	9	Total
World	162111.7	3.8	3.0	3.8	6.2	17.7	54.7	10.7	0.2	100
Germany	52114.2	2.3	2.9	3.2	4.1	17.5	58.0	11.9	0.1	100
Slovakia	14550.9	12.1	3.4	14.7	8.6	18.4	31.3	11.1	0.4	100
Poland	10182.6	6.1	6.2	5.8	12.3	27.0	34.9	7.8	0.0	100
France	8848.1	1.5	1.3	0.3	3.5	12.1	71.5	9.6	0.1	100
Austria	7441.1	4.1	8.9	11.5	5.3	18.5	38.6	12.9	0.2	100
United Kingdom	7368.4	2.4	0.4	2.6	2.2	13.1	68.8	10.4	0.1	100
Italy	6685.5	7.3	6.5	0.6	5.9	22.6	47.5	9.7	0.0	100
Netherlands	5677.0	1.8	1.5	0.3	3.1	14.2	69.5	9.6	0.0	100
Russian Federation	5215.5	1.8	0.3	0.2	10.2	10.1	68.6	8.8	...	100
Belgium	3991.2	2.7	1.3	0.2	6.6	18.4	57.7	13.0	0.1	100

Imports Profile:

Similar to exports, machinery and transport equipment (SITC section 7) accounted for a large share of imports: 42.4 percent (see table 2). Other major commodity groups included manufactured goods classified chiefly by material (SITC section 6) and chemicals and related products, n.e.s. (SITC section 5), accounting respectively for 18.3 and 10.9 percent. From 2009 to 2011, top imported products were parts and accessories of the motor vehicles of headings 87.01 to 87.05 (HS code 8708), automatic data processing machines and units thereof (HS code 8471) and petroleum oils and oils obtained from bituminous minerals, crude (HS code 2709) (see table 5).

Table 5: Top 10 import commodities 2009 to 2011

(Value in million US$)

HS code	4-digit heading of Harmonized System 2007	Value (million US$) 2009	2010	2011	Unit value 2009	2010	2011	Unit	SITC code
	All Commodities	104849.5	125690.7	150542.4					
8708	Parts and accessories of the motor vehicles of headings 87.01 to 87.05	4854.6	5674.0	7049.4	7.1	6.9	*6.8*	US$/kg	784
8471	Automatic data processing machines and units thereof	3733.7	5737.9	7263.2	45.6	79.2	101.7	US$/unit	752
2709	Petroleum oils and oils obtained from bituminous minerals, crude	3222.3	4433.8	5576.2	0.4	0.6	0.8	US$/kg	333
2711	Petroleum gases and other gaseous hydrocarbons	3170.9	4074.5	4145.7	0.4	0.5	*0.6*	US$/kg	343
3004	Medicaments (excluding goods of heading 30.02, 30.05 or 30.06)	2992.0	2856.7	3294.7	84.6	84.8	*92.7*	US$/kg	542
8473	Parts and accessories for use with machines of heading 84.69 to 84.72	2599.1	3221.4	3321.4	41.9	41.7	*34.8*	US$/kg	759
8703	Motor cars and other motor vehicles principally designed for the transport	2410.0	2339.4	2840.2	15.8	15.6	17.4	thsd US$/unit	781
8529	Parts suitable for use with the apparatus of headings 85.25 to 85.28	1972.1	2742.2	2385.4	26.6	24.8	*19.9*	US$/kg	764
8517	Electrical apparatus for line telephony or line telegraphy	1481.1	2160.9	3355.0					764
8542	Electronic integrated circuits	1846.9	2326.3	2582.7					776

Imports: CIF, by origin/consignment for intra-eu | **Exports: FOB, by last known destination** | **Trade System: General**

Overview:

Since 2006, the value of the exports of Denmark increased on average by 1.4 percent each year and amounted to 96.8 bln US$ in 2010 (see table 1 and graph 1). Imports, on the other hand, decreased on average by 0.2 percent each year to reach 84.5 bln US$ in 2010 (see table 2 and graph 1). The trade balance registered a surplus of 12.3 bln US$ in 2010 compared to 10.9 bln US$ in 2009 (see graph 1). By MDG regions, trade surpluses with Developed North America, Developed Asia-Pacific and Western Asia amounted respectively to 3.3, 1.7 and 1.1 bln US$ in 2010 (see graph 2). A deficit of 3.1 bln US$ was recorded in trade with Eastern Asia. In 2010, trade was diversified across partners: respectively 16 and 15 major partners accounted for 80 percent of exports and imports (see graph 3).

Graph 1: Total imports, exports and trade balance

(Bln US$ by year)

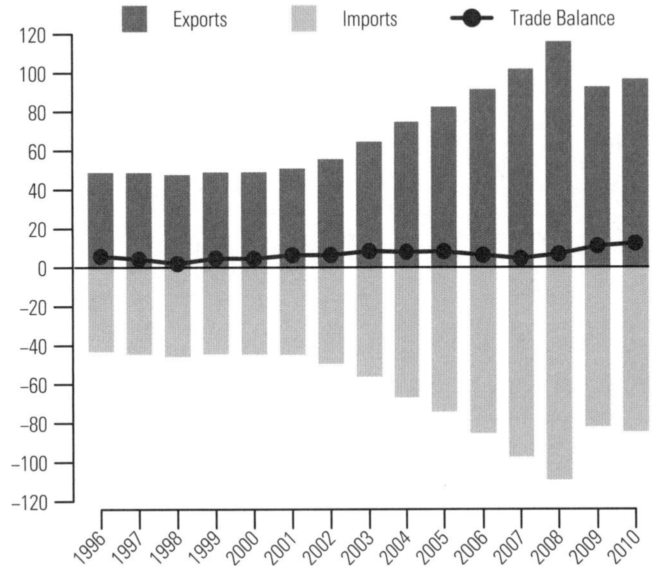

Table 1: Exports by SITC sections

(Value in million US$, growth and shares in percentage)

SITC	2010	Avg. Growth rates (%) 2006-2010	Avg. Growth rates (%) 2009-2010	2010 share
Total	96 811.6	1.4	4.3	100.0
0+1	17 152.4	2.8	1.1	17.7
2+4	4 502.3	2.8	24.2	4.7
3	7 987.1	-3.3	14.2	8.3
5	10 983.1	0.3	-18.2	11.3
6	8 542.8	-1.9	-9.9	8.8
7	24 118.7	-0.1	2.4	24.9
8	15 222.5	2.7	8.4	15.7
9	8 302.7	13.2	74.7	8.6

Exports Profile:

In 2010, exports were composed of 24.9 percent of machinery and transport equipment (SITC section 7), 17.7 percent of food, live animals, beverages and tobacco (SITC sections 0+1) and 15.7 percent of miscellaneous manufactured articles (SITC section 8) (see table 1). Top partners for exports were Germany, Sweden and the United Kingdom (see table 4). By commodities, top exported products over the last three years included petroleum oils and oils obtained from bituminous minerals, crude (HS code 2709), medicaments (excluding goods of heading 30.02, 30.05 or 30.06) (HS code 3004) and meat of swine, fresh, chilled or frozen (HS code 0203) (see table 3).

Table 2: Imports by SITC sections

(Value in million US$, growth and shares in percentage)

SITC	2010	Avg. Growth rates (%) 2006-2010	Avg. Growth rates (%) 2009-2010	2010 share
Total	84 468.3	-0.2	3.1	100.0
0+1	10 576.6	4.5	6.7	12.5
2+4	3 292.6	2.8	19.6	3.9
3	6 320.6	6.2	20.8	7.5
5	9 781.6	1.8	6.2	11.6
6	12 094.9	-4.1	4.1	14.3
7	26 535.4	-3.6	-5.0	31.4
8	14 152.0	2.9	6.2	16.8
9	1 714.5	-1.1	-11.4	2.0

Table 3: Top 10 export commodities 2008 to 2010

(Value in million US$)

HS code	4-digit heading of Harmonized System 2007	Value (million US$) 2008	2009	2010	Unit value 2008	2009	2010	Unit	SITC code
	All Commodities	116 016.1	92 833.3	96 811.6					
9999	Commodities not specified according to kind	6 957.8	4 740.6	8 291.3					931
2709	Petroleum oils and oils obtained from bituminous minerals, crude	6 118.8	3 882.7	4 374.6	0.7	0.5	0.6	US$/kg	333
3004	Medicaments (excluding goods of heading 30.02, 30.05 or 30.06)	5 791.9	5 666.5	2 840.5	257.9	265.4	184.2	US$/kg	542
0203	Meat of swine, fresh, chilled or frozen	3 787.6	3 165.1	3 138.0	3.2	2.9	2.7	US$/kg	012
2710	Petroleum oils, other than crude	4 011.3	2 404.3	2 790.6	0.7	0.5	0.6	US$/kg	334
9403	Other furniture and parts thereof	1 944.9	1 486.8	1 347.1					821
3002	Human blood; animal blood prepared for therapeutic uses	1 401.1	1 473.0	1 568.4	478.8	496.6	408.2	US$/kg	541
0406	Cheese and curd	1 491.3	1 363.3	1 343.5	6.3	5.2	5.1	US$/kg	024
8502	Electric generating sets and rotary converters	1 277.0	1 220.5	1 638.6					716
7308	Structures (excluding prefabricated buildings of heading 94.06)	1 513.5	1 332.0	953.7	4.8	4.6	4.3	US$/kg	691

Graph 2: Trade Balance by MDG Regions in 2010

(Bln US$)

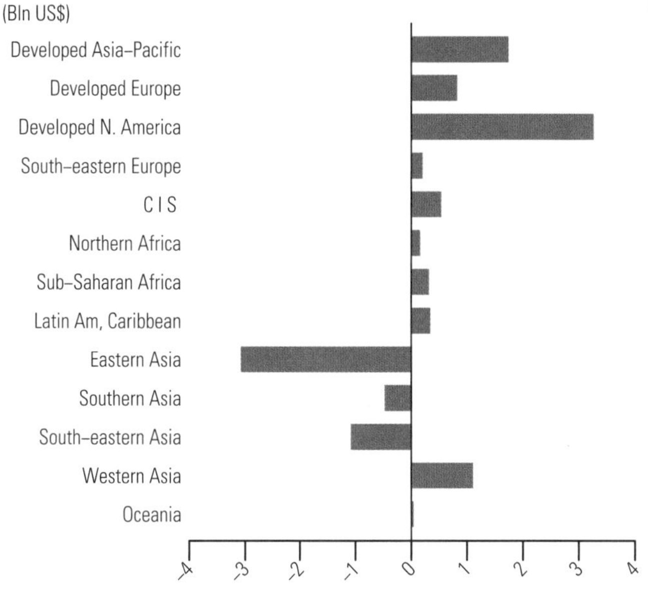

Graph 3: Partner concentration of trade in 2010

(Cumulative share by ranked partners)

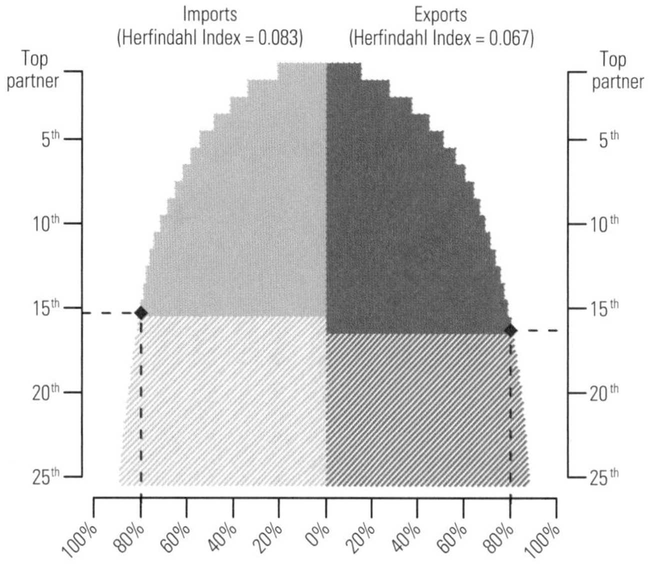

Table 4: Exports by principal countries and SITC sections in 2010

(Value in million US$, percentages of country total)

Country	Total	Shares by SITC sections (%)								
		0 + 1	2 + 4	3	5	6	7	8	9	Total
World	96811.6	17.7	4.7	8.3	11.3	8.8	24.9	15.7	8.6	100
Germany	14484.3	24.4	6.0	6.2	7.5	11.9	24.4	18.8	0.8	100
Sweden	12357.5	14.8	3.9	25.7	10.7	10.9	18.5	15.0	0.6	100
Special Categories	9273.0	1.6	1.6	...	9.3	1.1	2.9	7.1	76.3	100
United Kingdom	7228.8	26.7	1.8	18.2	4.7	9.2	25.1	13.7	0.7	100
Norway	5898.5	10.4	4.3	10.1	9.3	13.0	24.7	25.5	2.7	100
USA	5095.9	7.8	0.7	7.6	20.1	4.0	42.6	16.6	0.7	100
Netherlands	4028.9	14.7	4.9	16.6	10.3	9.1	18.8	24.5	1.1	100
France	3653.8	15.1	2.7	8.0	14.1	12.8	27.1	19.5	0.6	100
Italy	2543.4	36.7	3.9	0.8	12.2	7.2	22.2	16.4	0.6	100
Finland	2211.5	16.4	3.9	5.8	19.0	9.6	21.8	23.2	0.3	100

Imports Profile:

Machinery and transport equipment (SITC section 7) accounted for 31.4 percent of imports in 2010 (see table 2). Other major commodity groups included miscellaneous manufactured articles (SITC section 8) and manufactured goods classified chiefly by material (SITC section 6) respectively with 16.8 percent and 14.3 percent of imports. Over the last three years, top products for imports were petroleum oils, other than crude (HS code 2710), motor cars and other motor vehicles principally designed for the transport (HS code 8703) and medicaments (excluding goods of heading 30.02, 30.05 or 30.06) (HS code 3004) (see table 5).

Table 5: Top 10 import commodities 2008 to 2010

(Value in million US$)

HS code	4-digit heading of Harmonized System 2007	Value (million US$)			Unit value				SITC code
		2008	2009	2010	2008	2009	2010	Unit	
	All Commodities	109166.1	81916.9	84468.3					
2710	Petroleum oils, other than crude	5446.6	3024.4	3962.9	0.7	0.5	0.6	US$/kg	334
8703	Motor cars and other motor vehicles principally designed for the transport	3725.4	2359.5	2868.9			*16.6*	thsd US$/unit	781
3004	Medicaments (excluding goods of heading 30.02, 30.05 or 30.06)	2604.9	2492.8	2658.1	135.7	118.1	135.3	US$/kg	542
9999	Commodities not specified according to kind	2286.4	1923.8	1696.4					931
8471	Automatic data processing machines and units thereof	2095.3	1792.1	1900.3					752
2709	Petroleum oils and oils obtained from bituminous minerals, crude	1648.8	1628.8	1603.4	0.7	0.5	0.6	US$/kg	333
8901	Cruise ships, excursion boats, ferry-boats, cargo ships, barges	1693.5	1364.6	1297.7					793
8517	Electrical apparatus for line telephony or line telegraphy	1446.9	1345.2	1492.9					764
8528	Reception apparatus for television	1204.4	1000.9	743.8					761
8483	Transmission shafts (including cam shafts and crank shafts) and cranks	1045.1	1009.3	766.6					748

Dominica

Imports: CIF, by origin | **Exports: FOB, by last known destination** | **Trade System: Special**

Overview:

From 2006 to 2010, Dominica's exports dropped on average by 4.8 percent each year and amounted to 34.1 mln US$ in 2010 (see table 1 and graph 1). During the same period, imports increased on average by 7.7 percent to 224.6 mln US$ (see table 2 and graph 1). The trade balance recorded a deficit of 190.5 mln US$, slightly higher than the 188.7 mln US$ deficit in 2009 (see graph 1). Two MDG regions accounted for a large part of this deficit: Developed North America (-96.7 mln US$) and Latin America and the Caribbean (-59.6 mln US$) (see graph 2). By partners, trade was relatively concentrated: in 2010, 7 (respectively 8) major partners accounted for 80 percent of exports (respectively imports) (see graph 3).

Graph 1: Total imports, exports and trade balance

(Mln US$ by year)

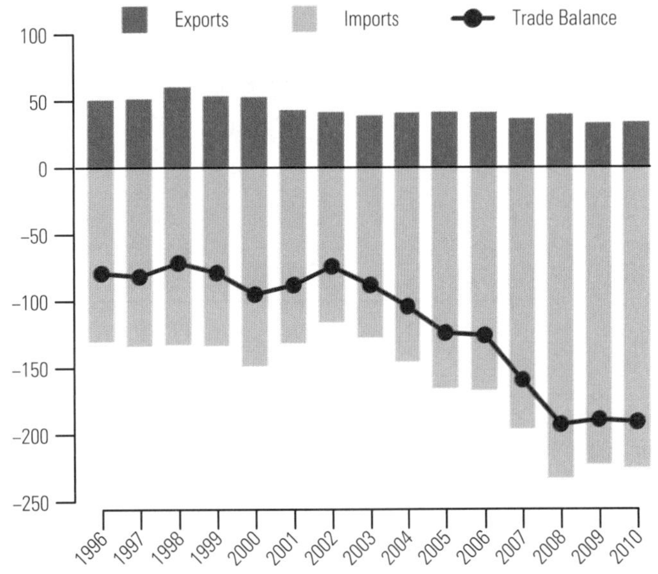

Table 1: Exports by SITC sections

(Value in million US$, growth and shares in percentage)

SITC	2010	Avg. Growth rates (%) 2006-2010	Avg. Growth rates (%) 2009-2010	2010 share
Total	34.1	-4.8	1.9	100.0
0+1	7.7	-14.4	-52.1	22.6
2+4	1.9	-9.6	-29.2	5.5
3	0.0	18.9	35.9	0.1
5	16.5	-8.4	25.2	48.4
6	0.4	25.4	195.7	1.2
7	2.6	56.2	171.1	7.6
8	5.0	115.9	1310.8	14.5
9	0.0	277.7	-64.2	0.1

Exports Profile:

In 2010, chemicals and related products, n.e.s. (SITC section 5) accounted for 48.4 percent of total exports (see table 1). Other major commodity groups included food, live animals, beverages and tobacco (SITC sections 0+1) and miscellaneous manufactured articles (SITC section 8) respectively with 22.6 and 14.5 percent of exports. Major destinations for exports in 2010 were Saint Kitts and Nevis, Jamaica and Trinidad and Tobago (see table 4). Exports to Jamaica were almost exclusively chemicals and related products, n.e.s. (SITC section 5) while exports to Saint Kitts and Nevis were largely miscellaneous manufactured articles (SITC section 8). From 2008 to 2010, top exported products included soap; organic surface-active products (HS code 3401), bananas, including plantains (HS code 0803) and manioc, arrowroot, sweet potatoes and similar roots (HS code 0714) (see table 3).

Table 2: Imports by SITC sections

(Value in million US$, growth and shares in percentage)

SITC	2010	Avg. Growth rates (%) 2006-2010	Avg. Growth rates (%) 2009-2010	2010 share
Total	224.6	7.7	1.1	100.0
0+1	43.7	9.8	0.6	19.5
2+4	13.2	12.4	21.4	5.9
3	38.8	10.8	11.8	17.3
5	17.9	-3.1	-4.9	8.0
6	33.8	7.4	0.3	15.1
7	51.0	6.8	-6.8	22.7
8	25.8	10.0	1.7	11.5
9	0.2	53.5	-41.6	0.1

Table 3: Top 10 export commodities 2008 to 2010

(Value in million US$)

HS code	4-digit heading of Harmonized System 2002	Value (million US$) 2008	2009	2010	Unit value 2008	2009	2010	Unit	SITC code
	All Commodities	40.0	33.5	34.1					
3401	Soap; organic surface-active products	13.2	9.7	13.8	1.6	1.5	*3.9*	US$/kg	554
0803	Bananas, including plantains	8.0	7.3	3.1	0.7	0.7	*0.8*	US$/kg	057
0714	Manioc, arrowroot, sweet potatoes and similar roots	2.4	3.2	1.7	2.2	2.4	*3.2*	US$/kg	054
3210	Other paints and varnishes	2.7	2.9	1.8	2.5	2.7	*4.3*	US$/kg	533
2517	Pebbles, gravel, broken or crushed stone	3.2	1.4	0.9	0.0	0.0	*0.0*	US$/kg	273
4907	Unused postage, revenue or similar stamps of current or new issue	...	...	4.5					892
2505	Natural sands of all kinds	2.2	1.2	0.9	0.0	0.0	*0.0*	US$/kg	273
0804	Dates, figs, pineapples, avocados and mangosteens, fresh or dried	1.2	1.5	0.5	2.0	2.2	*2.5*	US$/kg	057
0805	Citrus fruit, fresh or dried	1.0	1.5	0.6	1.1	1.4	*1.6*	US$/kg	057
3301	Essential oils (terpeneless or not), including concretes	0.5	0.1	0.6	36.6	32.4	*52.8*	US$/kg	551

Graph 2: Trade Balance by MDG Regions in 2010

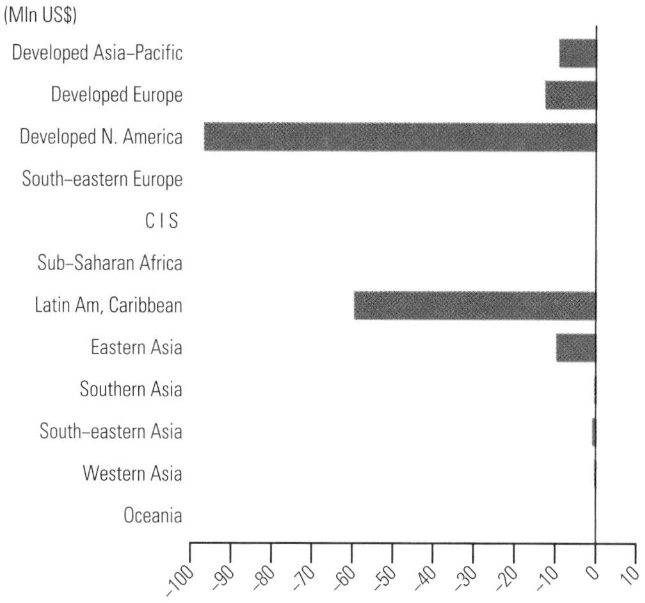

Graph 3: Partner concentration of trade in 2010

(Cumulative share by ranked partners)

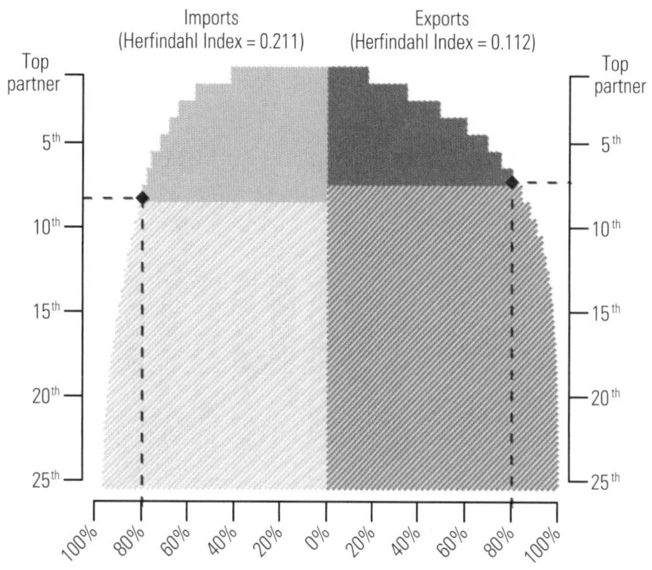

Table 4: Exports by principal countries and SITC sections in 2010

(Value in million US$, percentages of country total)

Country	Total	Shares by SITC sections (%) 0+1	2+4	3	5	6	7	8	9	Total
World	34.1	22.6	5.5	0.1	48.4	1.2	7.6	14.5	0.1	100
Saint Kitts and Nevis	6.0	13.9	1.5	0.0	8.7	0.3	0.6	74.9	0.0	100
Jamaica	5.9	0.3	0.0	...	99.7	...	...	0.0	...	100
Trinidad and Tobago	4.7	1.9	0.5	...	68.0	4.7	24.7	0.2	...	100
France	3.9	48.7	29.7	0.0	0.6	0.4	19.4	0.6	0.6	100
Antigua and Barbuda	3.1	58.6	0.0	0.1	40.4	0.4	0.1	0.3	0.1	100
Guyana	2.0	0.0	2.7	...	97.3	...	...	...	0.1	100
United Kingdom	1.7	78.8	4.4	...	12.9	0.1	0.3	3.6	...	100
USA	1.3	6.1	0.1	...	45.3	1.9	35.7	11.0	...	100
Areas, nes	1.3	76.5	13.2	1.1	6.9	0.0	1.2	1.0	0.1	100
Barbados	1.0	2.6	9.9	...	85.1	0.1	1.6	0.6	...	100

Imports Profile:

In 2010, imports were composed of machinery and transport equipment (SITC section 7), food, live animals, beverages and tobacco (SITC sections 0+1) and mineral fuels, lubricants and related materials (SITC section 3) respectively with 22.7, 19.5 and 17.3 percent of imports (see table 2). In addition to petroleum oils, other than crude (HS code 2710), other major imported products from 2008 to 2010 were meat and edible offal, of the poultry of heading 01.05 (HS code 0207) and motor cars and other motor vehicles principally designed for the transport (HS code 8703) (see table 5).

Table 5: Top 10 import commodities 2008 to 2010

(Value in million US$)

HS code	4-digit heading of Harmonized System 2002	Value (million US$) 2008	2009	2010	Unit value 2008	2009	2010	Unit	SITC code
	All Commodities	232.4	222.2	224.6					
2710	Petroleum oils, other than crude	33.6	32.6	35.3	0.9	0.5	*1.2*	US$/kg	334
0207	Meat and edible offal, of the poultry of heading 01.05	5.2	5.5	5.5	1.6	1.7	*3.9*	US$/kg	012
8703	Motor cars and other motor vehicles principally designed for the transport	4.8	5.1	5.5	*16.0*	*15.6*	*16.3*	thsd US$/unit	781
1502	Fats of bovine animals, sheep or goats	5.0	3.6	5.2	1.1	0.6	3.5	US$/kg	411
8704	Motor vehicles for the transport of goods	3.8	3.9	3.7	*16.3*			thsd US$/unit	782
0402	Milk and cream, concentrated or containing added sugar	4.3	2.9	3.7	2.2	2.1	*4.2*	US$/kg	022
1101	Wheat or meslin flour	3.4	3.5	3.1	0.8	0.8	*1.6*	US$/kg	046
8502	Electric generating sets and rotary converters	8.2	0.5	0.6					716
8471	Automatic data processing machines and units thereof	2.8	3.1	2.9					752
2202	Waters with added sugar	2.8	3.1	2.9	*1.0*	*1.1*	*2.2*	US$/litre	111

Dominican Republic

Imports: CIF, by origin	Exports: FOB, by last known destination	Trade System: General

Overview:

After a big drop of 31.9 percent in 2009, the value of Dominican Republic's exports bounced back in 2010 by 9.0 percent and continued to rise by 28.2 percent to reach 6.1 bln US$ in 2011 (see table 1 and graph 1). Imports showed a continuous growth in 2011 with an increase of 19.9 percent to 18.2 bln US$ (see table 2 and graph 1). This resulted in a trade deficit of 12.1 bln US$ in 2011, slightly higher than the 2010 deficit of 10.4 bln US$ (see graph 1). Trade was in deficit with almost all of the MDG regions (see graph 2). Large deficits were recorded with Developed North America (-4.4 bln US$), Latin America and the Caribbean (-4.1 bln US$) and Eastern Asia (-1.6 bln US$). Imports were more diversified across partners than exports in 2011: 10 major partners accounted for 80 percent of imports (compared to 5 major partners for exports) (see graph 3).

Graph 1: Total imports, exports and trade balance

(Bln US$ by year)

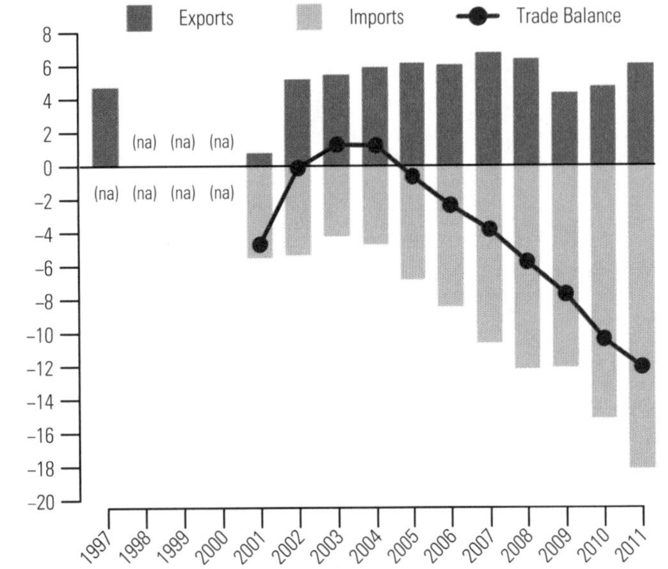

Table 1: Exports by SITC sections

(Value in million US$, growth and shares in percentage)

SITC	2011	Avg. Growth rates (%) 2007-2011	2010-2011	2011 share
Total	6 112.5	-2.6	28.2	100.0
0+1	1 468.7	10.8	14.1	24.0
2+4	253.9	18.2	51.1	4.2
3	179.1	-17.9	3668.6	2.9
5	371.5	20.6	16.1	6.1
6	1 228.7	-10.0	67.2	20.1
7	520.8	-16.3	13.6	8.5
8	2 077.4	-1.2	15.9	34.0
9	12.4	30.5	740.4	0.2

Exports Profile:

Dominican Republic's exports in 2011 were composed of 34.0 percent of miscellaneous manufactured articles (SITC section 8), 24.0 percent of food, live animals, beverages and tobacco (SITC sections 0+1) and 20.1 percent of manufactured goods classified chiefly by material (SITC section 6) (see table 1). USA, Haiti and China were the major destinations for exports (see table 4). From 2009 to 2011, top export commodities were instruments and appliances used in medical, surgical, dental or veterinary (HS code 9018), cigars, cheroots, cigarillos and cigarettes (HS code 2402) and articles of jewellery and parts thereof, of precious metal (HS code 7113) (see table 3).

Table 2: Imports by SITC sections

(Value in million US$, growth and shares in percentage)

SITC	2011	Avg. Growth rates (%) 2007-2011	2010-2011	2011 share
Total	18 156.1	14.4	19.9	100.0
0+1	2 133.2	14.2	28.9	11.7
2+4	680.5	8.0	15.1	3.7
3	4 669.7	129.8	25.9	25.7
5	1 981.7	13.1	24.0	10.9
6	3 474.9	8.8	32.9	19.1
7	3 330.5	-0.2	-6.0	18.3
8	1 767.3	4.4	30.0	9.7
9	118.3	-2.7	80.2	0.7

Table 3: Top 10 export commodities 2009 to 2011

(Value in million US$)

HS code	4-digit heading of Harmonized System 2007	Value (million US$) 2009	2010	2011	Unit value 2009	2010	2011	Unit	SITC code
	All Commodities	4 374.4	4 766.7	6 112.5					
9018	Instruments and appliances used in medical, surgical, dental or veterinary	634.6	670.2	662.4					872
2402	Cigars, cheroots, cigarillos and cigarettes	244.2	290.1	324.4	20.3	19.7	11.8	US$/kg	122
7113	Articles of jewellery and parts thereof, of precious metal	219.3	215.0	197.0					897
5208	Woven fabrics of cotton, containing 85 % or more by weight of cotton	280.9	228.6	0.1		4.3	6.7	US$/kg	652
6405	Other footwear	127.4	164.7	184.9					851
1801	Cocoa beans, whole or broken, raw or roasted	143.7	164.5	165.2	2.5	3.2	3.4	US$/kg	072
8536	Electrical apparatus for switching or protecting electrical circuits	172.1	211.8	40.5					772
0803	Bananas, including plantains, fresh or dried	108.9	154.8	153.9	0.4	0.4	0.4	US$/kg	057
1701	Cane or beet sugar and chemically pure sucrose, in solid form	93.6	137.5	132.4	0.5	0.6	0.6	US$/kg	061
7214	Other bars and rods of iron or non-alloy steel	86.4	90.6	173.0	0.6	0.6	0.7	US$/kg	676

Graph 2: Trade Balance by MDG Regions in 2011

(Bln US$)

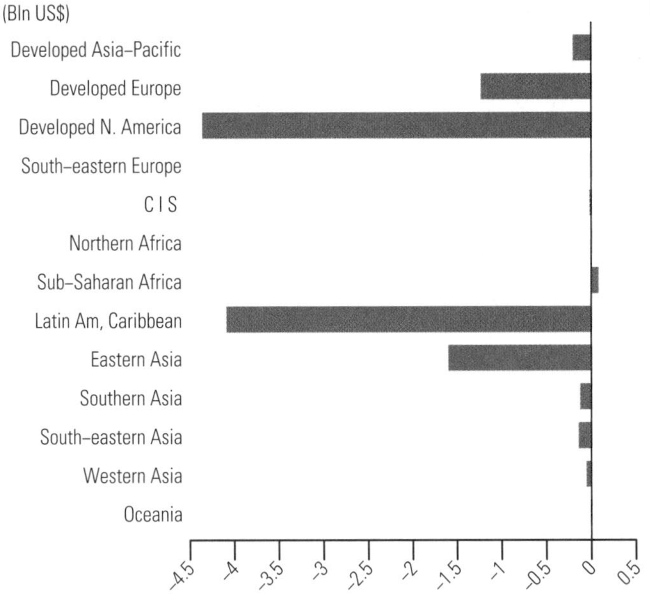

Graph 3: Partner concentration of trade in 2011

(Cumulative share by ranked partners)

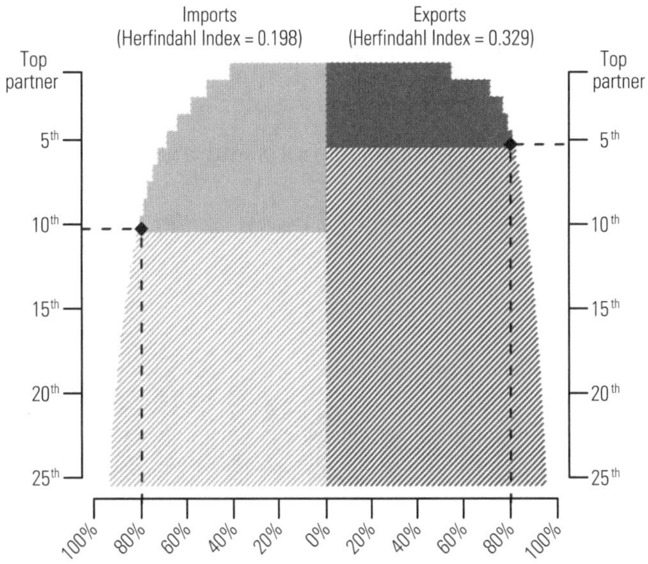

Table 4: Exports by principal countries and SITC sections in 2011

(Value in million US$, percentages of country total)

Country	Total	Shares by SITC sections (%) 0 + 1	2 + 4	3	5	6	7	8	9	Total
World	6112.5	24.0	4.2	2.9	6.1	20.1	8.5	34.0	0.2	100
USA	3330.9	21.1	1.5	0.1	4.9	10.2	13.3	48.5	0.4	100
Haiti	1013.6	26.9	2.6	1.3	8.6	42.0	1.2	17.4	...	100
China	330.3	0.5	15.5	0.0	0.6	76.6	0.4	6.4	...	100
Netherlands	128.3	45.2	1.4	...	0.2	0.7	2.7	49.8	...	100
United Kingdom	117.4	86.9	1.8	...	0.5	0.2	0.2	10.5	...	100
Belgium	84.8	52.5	0.1	...	9.7	0.1	0.0	37.5	...	100
Venezuela	80.2	62.3	6.7	0.4	15.2	13.0	0.9	1.4	...	100
Nigeria	73.8	0.0	0.0	100.0	...	...	0.0	...	...	100
Germany	59.1	56.3	2.2	0.0	0.2	1.8	31.3	8.0	...	100
Honduras	54.4	7.9	9.7	13.7	4.8	50.4	0.8	12.7	...	100

Imports Profile:

In 2011, mineral fuels, lubricants and related materials (SITC section 3) accounted for 25.7 percent of imports in 2011 (see table 2). Other major commodity groups included manufactured goods classified chiefly by material (SITC section 6) and machinery and transport equipment (SITC section 7) respectively with 19.1 percent and 18.3 percent of imports. Over the last three years, top products for imports were petroleum oils, other than crude (HS code 2710), petroleum oils and oils obtained from bituminous minerals, crude (HS code 2709) and petroleum gases and other gaseous hydrocarbons (HS code 2711) (see table 5).

Table 5: Top 10 import commodities 2009 to 2011

(Value in million US$)

HS code	4-digit heading of Harmonized System 2007	Value (million US$) 2009	2010	2011	Unit value 2009	2010	2011	Unit	SITC code
	All Commodities	12054.4	15138.2	18156.1					
2710	Petroleum oils, other than crude	1426.5	1993.2	2508.6	*1.0*			US$/kg	334
2709	Petroleum oils and oils obtained from bituminous minerals, crude	435.3	863.9	979.5	*0.7*	*0.4*	*0.6*	US$/kg	333
2711	Petroleum gases and other gaseous hydrocarbons	504.4	627.6	801.4					343
8703	Motor cars and other motor vehicles principally designed for the transport	345.9	567.3	373.7	*24.6*	*25.4*		thsd US$/unit	781
3004	Medicaments (excluding goods of heading 30.02, 30.05 or 30.06)	335.7	360.5	382.2					542
8517	Electrical apparatus for line telephony or line telegraphy	285.4	387.1	306.4					764
3926	Other articles of plastics	256.7	186.4	357.8	*11.6*	*11.2*	*11.1*	US$/kg	893
1005	Maize (corn)	165.7	236.4	327.4		*0.2*		US$/kg	044
8536	Electrical apparatus for switching or protecting electrical circuits	158.5	175.3	258.7					772
7206	Iron and non-alloy steel in ingots or other primary forms	139.3	190.9	158.5	*1.2*	*0.9*	*0.7*	US$/kg	672

Ecuador

Imports: CIF, by origin | **Exports: FOB, by last known destination** | **Trade System: Special**

Overview:

From 2007 to 2011, Ecuador's exports increased on average by 12.8 percent each year despite a sharp decline in 2009 (see table 1 and graph 1). In 2011, exports increased by 27.8 percent to reach its peak of 22.3 bln US$ in 2011. Imports also showed a similar development with an increase of 17.9 percent to reach its peak of 24.3 bln US$ in 2011 (see table 2 and graph 1). The trade balance registered a deficit of 2.0 bln US$ in 2011 (see graph 1). Trade with Developed North America recorded a surplus amounting to 4.7 bln US$ in 2011 (see graph 2). Significant deficits were recorded with Eastern Asia (-4.3 bln US$) and Latin America and the Caribbean (-2.0 bln US$). Trade was relatively diversified across partners: in 2011, 9 (respectively 13) major partners accounted for 80 percent of exports (respectively imports) (see graph 3). However, the USA, the top partner for Ecuador's exports, accounted for 44.9 percent of exported goods in 2011 (see table 4).

Graph 1: Total imports, exports and trade balance
(Bln US$ by year)

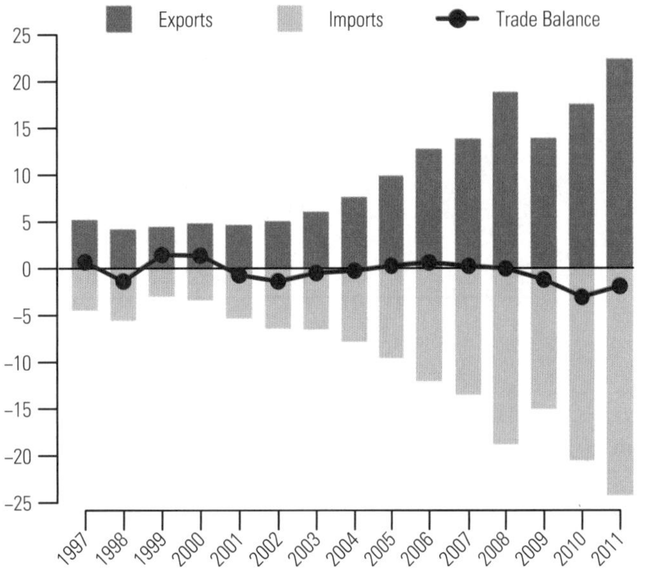

Table 1: Exports by SITC sections
(Value in million US$, growth and shares in percentage)

SITC	2011	Avg. Growth rates (%) 2007-2011	2010-2011	2011 share
Total	22345.2	12.8	27.8	100.0
0+1	6263.3	14.9	24.7	28.0
2+4	1328.3	15.7	29.3	5.9
3	12911.9	11.8	33.5	57.8
5	305.8	16.7	9.9	1.4
6	624.1	13.2	7.6	2.8
7	570.3	8.9	1.5	2.6
8	207.7	7.1	-25.1	0.9
9	133.8	13.3	87.5	0.6

Table 2: Imports by SITC sections
(Value in million US$, growth and shares in percentage)

SITC	2011	Avg. Growth rates (%) 2007-2011	2010-2011	2011 share
Total	24286.1	15.7	17.9	100.0
0+1	1882.7	15.9	21.1	7.8
2+4	606.9	20.9	33.5	2.5
3	5403.6	17.6	23.4	22.2
5	3723.6	15.3	17.9	15.3
6	3569.1	14.1	24.2	14.7
7	7407.3	16.2	8.3	30.5
8	1604.7	12.5	29.3	6.6
9	88.0	-10.4	-1.5	0.4

Exports Profile:

Ecuador's exports were dominated by mineral fuels, lubricants and related materials (SITC section 3) and food, live animals, beverages and tobacco (SITC sections 0+1) with 57.8 percent and 28.0 percent of total exports respectively (see table 1). The majority of exports to the USA, the top partner, were mineral fuels, lubricants and related materials (SITC section 3) at 79.6 percent (see table 4). Other major destinations for Ecuador's exports were Peru and Venezuela. From 2009 to 2011, the three major exported commodities were petroleum oils and oils obtained from bituminous minerals, crude (HS code 2709), bananas, including plantains, fresh or dried (HS code 0803) and crustaceans, whether in shell or not (HS code 0306) (see table 3).

Table 3: Top 10 export commodities 2009 to 2011
(Value in million US$)

HS code	4-digit heading of Harmonized System 2007	Value (million US$) 2009	2010	2011	Unit value 2009	2010	2011	Unit	SITC code
	All Commodities	13863.0	17489.9	22345.2					
2709	Petroleum oils and oils obtained from bituminous minerals, crude	6284.1	8951.9	11802.7	0.4	0.5	0.7	US$/kg	333
0803	Bananas, including plantains, fresh or dried	1995.9	2033.8	2246.4	0.3	0.4	0.4	US$/kg	057
0306	Crustaceans, whether in shell or not	666.0	850.7	1176.5	4.9	5.6	6.3	US$/kg	036
2710	Petroleum oils, other than crude	594.9	677.2	1033.9	0.4	0.5	0.6	US$/kg	334
1604	Prepared or preserved fish; caviar	626.4	598.3	870.3	3.5	3.5	4.1	US$/kg	037
0603	Cut flowers and flower buds of a kind suitable for bouquets	546.7	607.8	679.9	5.4	5.7	5.8	US$/kg	292
1801	Cocoa beans, whole or broken, raw or roasted	342.6	350.2	471.7	2.7	3.0	3.0	US$/kg	072
1511	Palm oil and its fractions	141.3	140.5	302.2	0.8	1.0	1.2	US$/kg	422
8703	Motor cars and other motor vehicles principally designed for the transport	123.3	179.9	153.8	*14.3*	*13.5*		thsd US$/unit	781
8704	Motor vehicles for the transport of goods	101.9	147.6	192.9					782

Graph 2: Trade Balance by MDG Regions in 2011

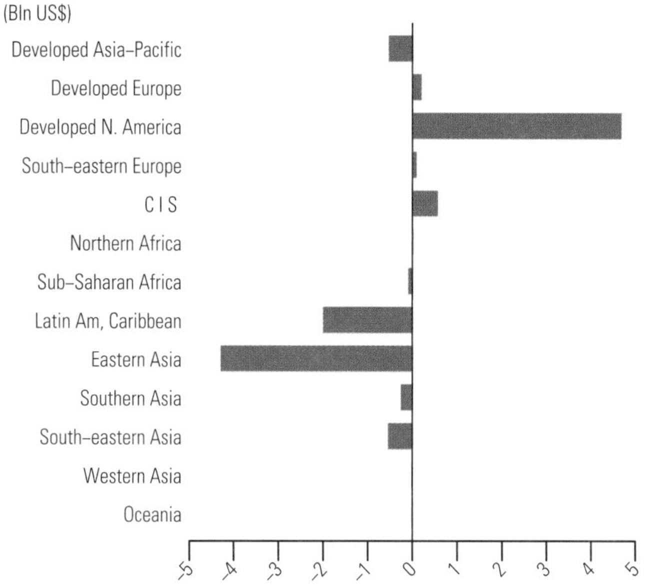

Graph 3: Partner concentration of trade in 2011

(Cumulative share by ranked partners)

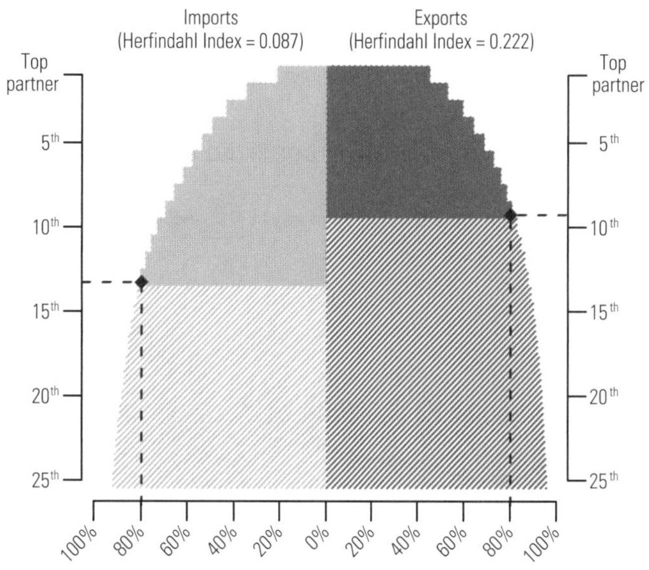

Table 4: Exports by principal countries and SITC sections in 2011

(Value in million US$, percentages of country total)

Country	Total	Shares by SITC sections (%)								
		0 + 1	2 + 4	3	5	6	7	8	9	Total
World	22345.2	28.0	5.9	57.8	1.4	2.8	2.6	0.9	0.6	100
USA	10034.7	16.0	3.1	79.6	0.1	0.5	0.3	0.2	0.3	100
Peru	1724.4	2.9	3.7	81.9	2.6	5.3	1.7	1.6	0.3	100
Venezuela	1473.9	14.2	8.6	46.7	7.4	8.4	13.3	1.4	0.0	100
Panama	1035.8	0.5	0.1	96.9	0.7	1.0	0.3	0.5	0.0	100
Colombia	1023.2	28.2	7.9	0.3	8.3	21.0	27.9	6.4	0.0	100
Chile	899.2	25.8	5.1	63.7	1.1	2.7	0.7	0.9	0.0	100
Russian Federation	699.9	77.9	22.1	...	...	0.0	...	0.0	...	100
Italy	580.4	92.5	5.1	...	0.0	1.5	0.1	0.7	0.0	100
Germany	491.9	84.2	14.0	0.0	0.1	0.7	0.1	0.9	0.0	100
Curaçao	470.7	0.4	0.1	99.3	0.0	0.1	...	0.1	0.0	100

Imports Profile:

Machinery and transport equipment (SITC section 7), the top commodity group for imports, accounted for 30.5 percent of imported goods in 2011 (see table 2). Other major commodity groups for imports included mineral fuels, lubricants and related materials (SITC section 3) and chemicals and related products, n.e.s. (SITC section 5) respectively with 22.2 and 15.3 percent of imports. From 2009 to 2011, top products for imports were petroleum oils, other than crude (HS code 2710), oils and other products of high temperature coal tar (HS code 2707) and motor cars and other motor vehicles principally designed for the transport (HS code 8703) (see table 5).

Table 5: Top 10 import commodities 2009 to 2011

(Value in million US$)

HS code	4-digit heading of Harmonized System 2007	Value (million US$)			Unit value				SITC code
		2009	2010	2011	2009	2010	2011	Unit	
	All Commodities	15089.9	20590.8	24286.1					
2710	Petroleum oils, other than crude	1381.8	2663.2	2857.3	*0.6*	0.7	1.0	US$/kg	334
2707	Oils and other products of high temperature coal tar	738.7	968.5	1533.7	0.7	0.8	1.1	US$/kg	335
8703	Motor cars and other motor vehicles principally designed for the transport	632.6	1068.5	876.9	*16.3*	*16.0*		thsd US$/unit	781
3004	Medicaments (excluding goods of heading 30.02, 30.05 or 30.06)	577.7	640.2	762.0	*29.7*	27.9	29.3	US$/kg	542
2711	Petroleum gases and other gaseous hydrocarbons	403.2	575.4	858.6	0.5	0.7	0.9	US$/kg	343
8704	Motor vehicles for the transport of goods	479.6	699.8	610.8					782
8517	Electrical apparatus for line telephony or line telegraphy	306.6	387.9	500.1					764
7304	Tubes, pipes and hollow profiles, seamless, of iron (other than cast iron)	255.9	265.3	352.4	*2.9*	2.4	1.9	US$/kg	679
8471	Automatic data processing machines and units thereof	223.0	291.4	330.8					752
0303	Fish, frozen, excluding fish fillets and other fish meat of heading 03.04	213.9	211.9	275.3	1.3	1.4	1.7	US$/kg	034

Egypt

Imports: CIF, by consignment | **Exports: FOB, by last known destination** | **Trade System: General**

Overview:

From 2007 to 2011, Egypt's exports increased on average by 17.5 percent each year to reach 30.8 bln US$ in 2011(see table 1 and graph 1). During the same period, imports increased on average by 21.7 percent each year and reached 59.3 bln US$ in 2011 (see table 2 and graph 1). This resulted in a trade deficit of 28.5 bln US$ (see graph 1). The largest deficit was recorded with Developed Europe (-8.1 bln US$) (see graph 2). Deficits were also recorded with Eastern Asia (-6.2 bln US$), Developed North America (-5.2 bln US$) and the Commonwealth of Independent States (-3.8 bln US$). In 2011, trade was highly diversified across partners: 25 major partners (respectively 21) accounted for 80 percent of exports (respectively imports) (see graph 3). See footnote*.

Graph 1: Total imports, exports and trade balance

(Bln US$ by year)

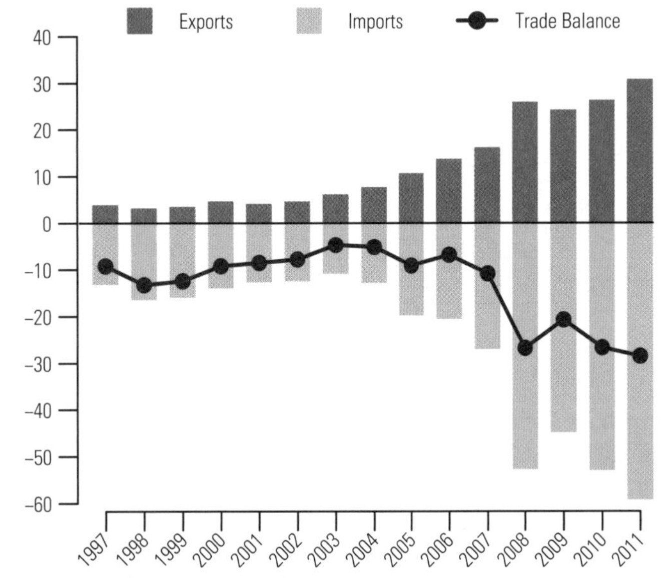

Table 1: Exports by SITC sections

(Value in million US$, growth and shares in percentage)

SITC	2011	Avg. Growth rates (%) 2007-2011	Avg. Growth rates (%) 2010-2011	2011 share
Total	30782.0	17.5	16.9	100.0
0+1	4051.7	34.2	-1.6	13.2
2+4	1649.8	34.9	13.3	5.4
3	9220.1	2.2	22.1	30.0
5	4450.8	56.5	26.1	14.5
6	6013.4	32.6	10.8	19.5
7	1467.6	125.1	29.6	4.8
8	2174.0	44.6	7.8	7.1
9	1754.7	-10.5	59.1	5.7

Exports Profile:

Mineral fuels, lubricants and related materials (SITC section 3) accounted for 30.0 percent of Egypt's exports in 2011 (see table 1). Other major commodity groups included manufactured goods classified chiefly by material (SITC section 6) and chemicals and related products, n.e.s. (SITC section 5) representing 19.5 and 14.5 percent of total exports. Top partners for exports in 2011 were Italy, India and Saudi Arabia (see table 4). From 2009 to 2011, Egypt's main exported commodities were petroleum products: petroleum oils, other than crude (HS code 2710), petroleum gases and other gaseous hydrocarbons (HS code 2711) and petroleum oils and oils obtained from bituminous minerals, crude (HS code 2709) (see table 3).

Table 2: Imports by SITC sections

(Value in million US$, growth and shares in percentage)

SITC	2011	Avg. Growth rates (%) 2007-2011	Avg. Growth rates (%) 2010-2011	2011 share
Total	59269.0	21.7	11.8	100.0
0+1	10844.9	23.1	30.2	18.3
2+4	6651.0	28.9	35.1	11.2
3	9316.5	23.6	30.7	15.7
5	7471.4	29.6	18.5	12.6
6	11192.5	36.0	2.9	18.9
7	11887.2	23.6	-8.2	20.1
8	1873.6	24.4	-23.2	3.2
9	31.8	-70.4	-39.7	0.1

Table 3: Top 10 export commodities 2009 to 2011

(Value in million US$)

HS code	4-digit heading of Harmonized System 2007	Value (million US$) 2009	2010	2011	Unit value 2009	2010	2011	Unit	SITC code
	All Commodities	24182.3	26331.8	30782.0					
2710	Petroleum oils, other than crude	2064.0	2962.0	3525.9	0.5	0.7		US$/kg	334
2711	Petroleum gases and other gaseous hydrocarbons	2414.2	2266.6	2012.6	0.2	0.2	*0.4*	US$/kg	343
2709	Petroleum oils and oils obtained from bituminous minerals, crude	1568.3	1777.5	3030.0	0.3	0.5	*0.6*	US$/kg	333
7108	Gold (including gold plated with platinum)	906.3	1033.8	1710.3		15.1		thsd US$/kg	971
3102	Mineral or chemical fertilisers, nitrogenous	1081.9	1080.8	1290.6	0.2	0.3		US$/kg	562
8544	Insulated (including enamelled or anodised) wire, cable	434.3	603.5	915.2	5.4	*6.7*		US$/kg	773
7409	Copper plates, sheets and strip, of a thickness exceeding 0.15 mm	527.7	633.4	500.5	5.2	7.6	*8.5*	US$/kg	682
0805	Citrus fruit, fresh or dried	532.1	518.4	571.5	0.6	*0.6*	*0.7*	US$/kg	057
0406	Cheese and curd	424.8	471.7	482.6	3.3	3.0	*4.9*	US$/kg	024
7208	Flat-rolled products of iron or non-alloy steel	308.1	457.7	450.3	0.5	0.7	*0.7*	US$/kg	673

*Special trade system up to 2007

Graph 2: Trade Balance by MDG Regions in 2011

(Bln US$)

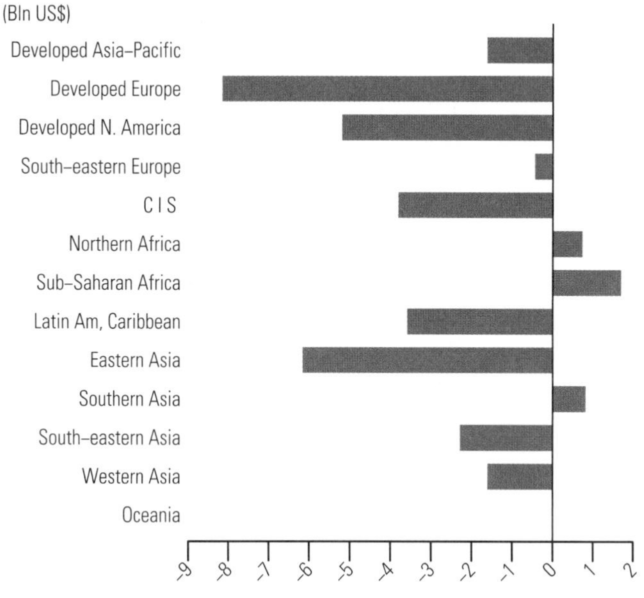

Graph 3: Partner concentration of trade in 2011

(Cumulative share by ranked partners)

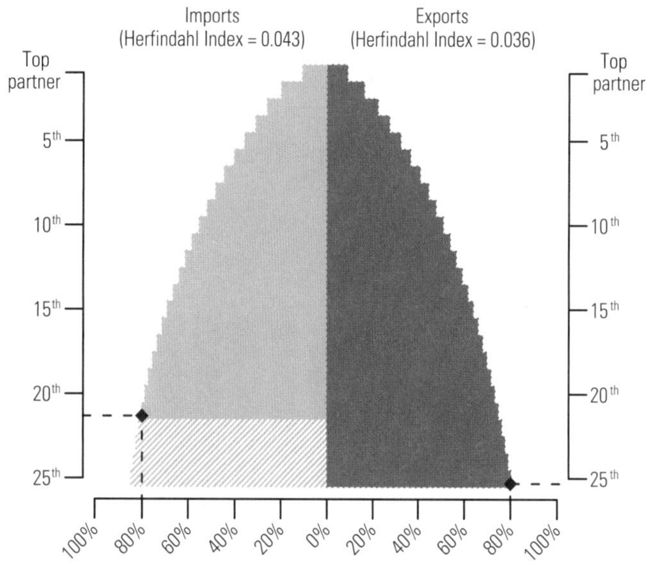

Table 4: Exports by principal countries and SITC sections in 2011

(Value in million US$, percentages of country total)

Country	Total	Shares by SITC sections (%)								
		0 + 1	2 + 4	3	5	6	7	8	9	Total
World	30 782.0	13.2	5.4	30.0	14.5	19.5	4.8	7.1	5.7	100
Italy	2 682.3	6.8	2.8	46.2	11.5	27.4	1.4	3.7	0.2	100
India	2 261.2	0.2	8.2	87.3	1.5	2.5	0.1	0.2	0.1	100
Saudi Arabia	1 892.3	31.0	2.5	1.0	6.1	43.5	8.4	6.6	0.9	100
USA	1 605.2	3.8	3.6	14.7	14.5	19.6	0.9	42.9	0.0	100
Turkey	1 520.7	2.2	4.3	16.4	40.7	31.2	1.1	4.0	0.3	100
Spain	1 297.1	3.1	1.8	51.8	16.5	17.9	1.5	7.3	0.1	100
France	1 289.7	2.3	2.8	25.3	49.9	9.0	5.4	5.2	0.0	100
Bunkers	1 120.0	0.0	0.0	100.0	...	0.0	...	0.0	...	100
South Africa	1 000.1	1.8	0.2	1.3	2.4	1.1	0.2	0.4	92.7	100
United Kingdom	966.4	18.9	3.3	2.3	19.2	16.1	14.9	25.3	0.0	100

Imports Profile:

In 2011, imports of machinery and transport equipment (SITC section 7) and manufactured goods classified chiefly by material (SITC section 6) accounted respectively for 20.1 and 18.9 percent of total imports (see table 2). Over the last three years, the three main products for imports were petroleum oils, other than crude (HS code 2710), wheat and meslin (HS code 1001) and petroleum gases and other gaseous hydrocarbons (HS code 2711) (see table 5).

Table 5: Top 10 import commodities 2009 to 2011

(Value in million US$)

HS code	4-digit heading of Harmonized System 2007	Value (million US$)			Unit value				SITC code
		2009	2010	2011	2009	2010	2011	Unit	
	All Commodities	44 912.5	53 003.4	59 269.0					
2710	Petroleum oils, other than crude	1 888.9	3 656.7	5 146.4	0.5	0.6		US$/kg	334
1001	Wheat and meslin	1 576.1	2 181.9	2 841.1	0.4	0.2	*0.3*	US$/kg	041
2711	Petroleum gases and other gaseous hydrocarbons	1 287.2	1 806.2	2 066.5	0.6	0.8	*0.7*	US$/kg	343
1005	Maize (corn)	833.7	1 270.6	2 096.1	0.4	0.2		US$/kg	044
2709	Petroleum oils and oils obtained from bituminous minerals, crude	1 079.0	1 321.2	1 709.2	0.4	0.5	*0.6*	US$/kg	333
7326	Other articles of iron or steel	885.8	1 401.1	1 149.8	5.1	2.1	*6.6*	US$/kg	699
8703	Motor cars and other motor vehicles principally designed for the transport	842.1	1 348.7	1 138.2	15.6	0.4		thsd US$/unit	781
8517	Electrical apparatus for line telephony or line telegraphy	709.7	1 095.7	1 127.9					764
3004	Medicaments (excluding goods of heading 30.02, 30.05 or 30.06)	874.9	897.7	1 148.3	341.3	4.2		US$/kg	542
7207	Semi-finished products of iron or non-alloy steel	827.2	867.8	1 102.4	0.6	0.6		US$/kg	672

El Salvador

Imports: CIF, by origin | **Exports: FOB, by last known destination** | **Trade System: General**

Overview:

After several years of continuous growth marked by a peak of 4.6 bln US$ in 2008, the value of El Salvador's exports dropped in 2009 (by 16.7 percent), but bounced back in 2010 by 16.4 percent to amount to 4.5 bln US$ (see table 1 and graph 1). Imports showed a similar development with an increase of 16.1 percent to 8.5 bln US$ in 2010. This resulted in a trade deficit of 4.0 bln US$ in 2010, slightly higher than the 2009 deficit of 3.4 bln US$ (see graph 1). By MDG regions, trade recorded large deficits with Latin America and the Caribbean (-1.6 bln US$), Developed North America (-0.9 bln US$) and Eastern Asia (-0.7 bln US$) (see graph 2). By partners, exports were more concentrated than imports: in 2010, 4 major partners accounted for 80 percent of exports (compared to 12 major partners for imports) (see graph 3).

Graph 1: Total imports, exports and trade balance

(Bln US$ by year)

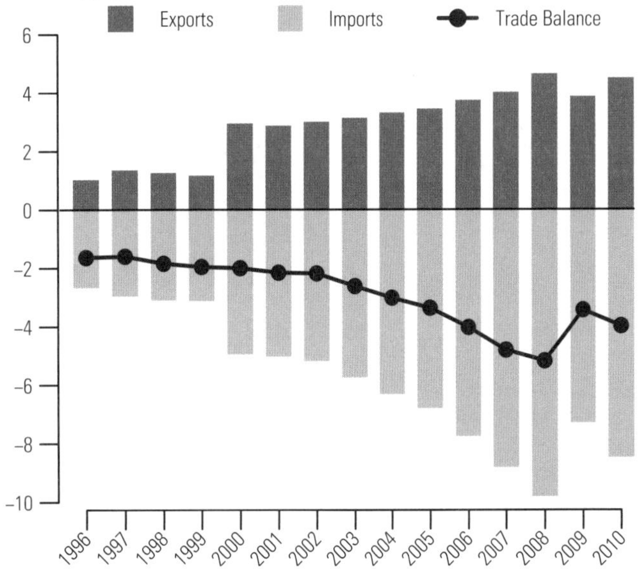

Table 1: Exports by SITC sections

(Value in million US$, growth and shares in percentage)

SITC	2010	Avg. Growth rates (%) 2006-2010	2009-2010	2010 share
Total	4499.2	4.8	16.4	100.0
0+1	939.0	9.4	9.6	20.9
2+4	91.6	16.0	59.9	2.0
3	131.5	11.7	23.4	2.9
5	287.5	-8.0	-15.5	6.4
6	658.9	8.2	15.3	14.6
7	273.4	5.6	34.2	6.1
8	2028.0	2.8	21.4	45.1
9	89.5	41.7	48.4	2.0

Table 2: Imports by SITC sections

(Value in million US$, growth and shares in percentage)

SITC	2010	Avg. Growth rates (%) 2006-2010	2009-2010	2010 share
Total	8484.6	2.2	16.1	100.0
0+1	1255.7	7.1	-0.1	14.8
2+4	329.9	10.1	26.0	3.9
3	1376.4	6.3	23.4	16.2
5	1332.8	3.0	15.6	15.7
6	1890.8	0.0	29.3	22.3
7	1396.0	0.6	11.0	16.5
8	888.9	1.4	13.2	10.5
9	14.2	-50.2	8.3	0.2

Exports Profile:

In 2010, major exports were composed of 45.1 percent of miscellaneous manufactured articles (SITC section 8), 20.9 percent of food, live animals, beverages and tobacco (SITC sections 0+1) and 14.6 percent of manufactured goods classified chiefly by material (SITC section 6) (see table 1). USA, Guatemala and Honduras were the three largest markets for exports and accounted jointly for 75.2 percent of exported goods in 2010 (see table 4). By commodity, top products for exports over the last three years included t-shirts, singlets and other vests, knitted or crocheted (HS code 6109), coffee, whether or not roasted or decaffeinated (HS code 0901) and electrical capacitors, fixed, variable or adjustable (pre-set) (HS code 8532) (see table 3).

Table 3: Top 10 export commodities 2008 to 2010

(Value in million US$)

HS code	4-digit heading of Harmonized System 2007	Value (million US$) 2008	2009	2010	Unit value 2008	2009	2010	Unit	SITC code
	All Commodities	4641.1	3866.1	4499.2					
6109	T-shirts, singlets and other vests, knitted or crocheted	905.7	622.0	739.5	*5.0*	*5.4*	*5.1*	US$/unit	845
0901	Coffee, whether or not roasted or decaffeinated	258.7	230.3	213.2	2.9	2.8	3.3	US$/kg	071
8532	Electrical capacitors, fixed, variable or adjustable (pre-set)	148.4	134.7	190.0	153.2	185.5	196.1	US$/kg	778
6110	Jerseys, pullovers, cardigans, waist-coats and similar articles	152.9	135.4	175.5	*12.9*	*12.6*	*11.7*	US$/unit	845
2710	Petroleum oils, other than crude	143.1	95.7	119.0	0.8	0.7	0.7	US$/kg	334
1701	Cane or beet sugar and chemically pure sucrose, in solid form	87.3	101.6	160.6	0.3	0.3	0.4	US$/kg	061
6115	Panty hose, tights, stockings, socks and other hosiery	60.5	83.8	167.7	17.7	10.9	9.4	US$/kg	846
3004	Medicaments (excluding goods of heading 30.02, 30.05 or 30.06)	107.4	97.7	104.8	5.5	4.8	4.3	US$/kg	542
4818	Toilet paper and similar paper	106.1	104.4	98.7	1.5	1.6	1.5	US$/kg	642
3923	Articles for the conveyance or packing of goods, of plastics	90.4	90.5	118.5	2.2	1.9	2.2	US$/kg	893

Graph 2: Trade Balance by MDG Regions in 2010

(Bln US$)

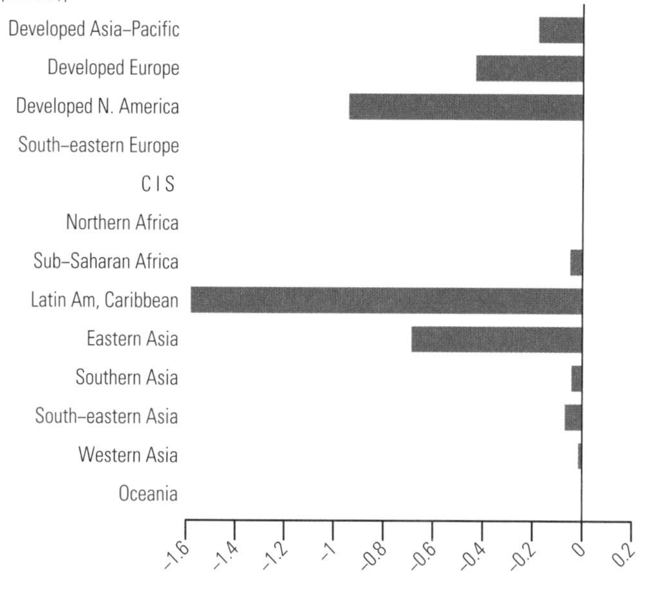

Graph 3: Partner concentration of trade in 2010

(Cumulative share by ranked partners)

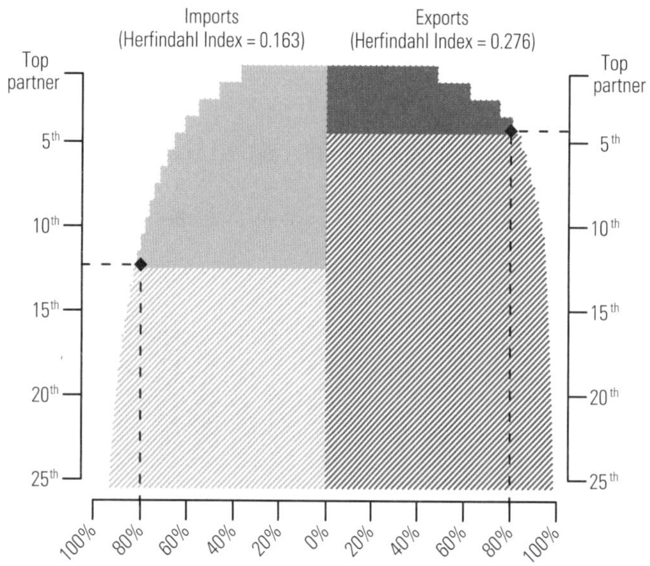

Table 4: Exports by principal countries and SITC sections in 2010

(Value in million US$, percentages of country total)

Country	Total	Shares by SITC sections (%)								
		0 + 1	2 + 4	3	5	6	7	8	9	Total
World	4 499.2	20.9	2.0	2.9	6.4	14.6	6.1	45.1	2.0	100
USA	2 176.0	9.6	1.0	1.0	0.3	2.8	9.0	72.2	4.1	100
Guatemala	628.9	29.9	2.9	6.8	11.8	31.9	2.5	14.2	0.0	100
Honduras	579.4	14.7	1.5	3.2	11.9	29.4	3.7	35.6	0.0	100
Nicaragua	244.0	18.2	0.2	4.6	20.0	29.2	4.5	23.3	0.0	100
Costa Rica	161.4	15.4	0.1	8.5	16.3	36.1	6.3	17.3	0.0	100
Panama	102.4	16.0	1.1	15.0	24.0	23.7	5.0	15.2	0.0	100
Dominican Rep.	84.2	45.1	0.0	6.1	14.9	22.0	3.0	8.9	0.0	100
Germany	81.9	95.8	1.7	...	0.0	0.4	0.9	1.2	0.0	100
Mexico	76.2	23.8	1.8	0.0	11.6	31.6	3.6	27.5	0.0	100
Canada	67.7	85.9	1.7	...	0.0	0.1	0.0	12.2	0.0	100

Imports Profile:

The major imports in 2010 were composed of 22.3 percent of manufactured goods classified chiefly by material (SITC section 6), 16.5 percent of machinery and transport equipment (SITC section 7) and 16.2 percent of mineral fuels, lubricants and related materials (SITC section 3) (see table 2). Over the last three years, top imported products included petroleum oils, other than crude (HS code 2710), petroleum oils and oils obtained from bituminous minerals, crude (HS code 2709) and other knitted or crocheted fabrics (HS code 6006) (see table 5).

Table 5: Top 10 import commodities 2008 to 2010

(Value in million US$)

HS code	4-digit heading of Harmonized System 2007	Value (million US$)			Unit value				SITC code
		2008	2009	2010	2008	2009	2010	Unit	
	All Commodities	9 817.7	7 306.2	8 484.6					
2710	Petroleum oils, other than crude	1 037.2	592.6	683.7	0.9	0.6	0.7	US$/kg	334
2709	Petroleum oils and oils obtained from bituminous minerals, crude	572.9	367.7	473.3	0.7	0.4	0.6	US$/kg	333
6006	Other knitted or crocheted fabrics	403.8	236.3	300.5	4.2	4.6	4.6	US$/kg	655
3004	Medicaments (excluding goods of heading 30.02, 30.05 or 30.06)	260.3	257.9	277.9	27.6	25.0	21.7	US$/kg	542
8517	Electrical apparatus for line telephony or line telegraphy	219.8	166.9	198.9					764
2711	Petroleum gases and other gaseous hydrocarbons	183.2	123.9	184.4	0.9	0.6	0.8	US$/kg	343
1005	Maize (corn)	170.4	115.8	117.6	0.3	0.3	0.3	US$/kg	044
2106	Food preparations not elsewhere specified or included	105.7	114.0	108.0	6.5	7.0	6.1	US$/kg	098
2207	Alcohol of a strength by volume of 80 % vol or higher	222.8	43.7	7.3	*0.8*	*0.9*	*0.8*	US$/litre	512
8703	Motor cars and other motor vehicles principally designed for the transport	110.5	77.4	79.4		*17.5*	*18.9*	thsd US$/unit	781

 Source: UN Comtrade

Imports: CIF, by origin/consignment for intra-eu **Exports: FOB, by last known destination** **Trade System: General**

Overview:

From 2007 to 2011, Estonia's exports increased on average by 11.5 percent each year despite a sharp decline in 2009 (see table 1 and graph 1). In 2011, exports increased by 41.6 percent and amounted to 18.2 bln US$. Imports showed a similar development with an increase of 42.5 percent in 2011 and amounted to 18.8 bln US$ (see table 2 and graph 1). In 2011, the trade deficit amounted to 622.0 mln US$ as compared to 359.4 mln US$ in 2010 (see graph 1). This deficit is reflected largely in trade with Eastern Asia (-1.3 bln US$) and Developed Europe (-1.2 bln US$) (see graph 2). Trade with Developed North America and Commonwealth of Independent States recorded a surplus of 837.1 mln US$ and 662.4 mln US$, respectively. Trade was relatively diversified across partners: approximately 13 major partners (16 major partners) accounted for 80 percent of exports (respectively imports) (see graph 3).

Graph 1: Total imports, exports and trade balance

(Bln US$ by year)

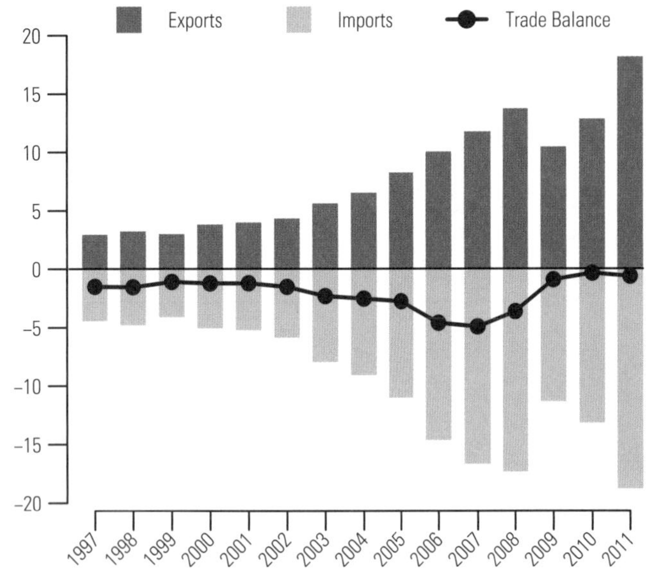

Exports Profile:

Machinery and transport equipment (SITC section 7), the largest commodity group for exports, accounted for 30.0 percent of exports in 2011 (see table 1). Other major commodity groups for exports included mineral fuels, lubricants and related materials (SITC section 3) and manufactured goods classified chiefly by material (SITC section 6) respectively with 16.9 and 14.1 percent of total exports in 2011. Russian Federation, Sweden and Finland were the top three markets for exports (see table 4). Over the last three years, top products for exports were petroleum oils, other than crude (HS code 2710), electrical apparatus for line telephony or line telegraphy (HS code 8517) and motor cars and other motor vehicles principally designed for the transport (HS code 8703) (see table 3).

Table 1: Exports by SITC sections

(Value in million US$, growth and shares in percentage)

SITC	2011	Avg. Growth rates (%) 2007-2011	2010-2011	2011 share
Total	18158.3	11.5	41.6	100.0
0+1	1496.2	9.5	28.5	8.2
2+4	1261.4	5.2	17.0	6.9
3	3075.7	20.6	52.4	16.9
5	1000.8	11.9	46.5	5.5
6	2562.3	5.4	34.6	14.1
7	5451.9	14.0	55.0	30.0
8	2455.4	9.7	34.4	13.5
9	854.5	10.2	35.3	4.7

Table 2: Imports by SITC sections

(Value in million US$, growth and shares in percentage)

SITC	2011	Avg. Growth rates (%) 2007-2011	2010-2011	2011 share
Total	18780.3	3.0	42.5	100.0
0+1	1766.0	5.7	22.5	9.4
2+4	507.1	-4.4	27.0	2.7
3	3348.5	8.6	52.9	17.8
5	1748.7	4.7	29.2	9.3
6	2804.0	-0.9	32.5	14.9
7	5977.3	2.7	61.6	31.8
8	1434.5	-0.5	13.6	7.6
9	1194.2	3.6	65.7	6.4

Table 3: Top 10 export commodities 2009 to 2011

(Value in million US$)

HS code	4-digit heading of Harmonized System 2007	Value (million US$) 2009	2010	2011	Unit value 2009	2010	2011	Unit	SITC code
	All Commodities	10445.8	12823.0	18158.3					
2710	Petroleum oils, other than crude	1460.7	1621.8	2591.8	0.5	0.6	*0.8*	US$/kg	334
8517	Electrical apparatus for line telephony or line telegraphy	328.2	804.8	1819.0					764
9999	Commodities not specified according to kind	491.8	622.7	800.8					931
8703	Motor cars and other motor vehicles principally designed for the transport	618.5	293.0	334.8	19.1	15.6	25.3	thsd US$/unit	781
8544	Insulated (including enamelled or anodised) wire, cable	179.9	296.2	408.3	*10.8*	*13.9*	*17.5*	US$/kg	773
2716	Electrical energy	155.5	277.8	322.6	52.8	63.8	*60.9*	US$/MWh	351
4418	Builders' joinery and carpentry of wood	190.9	224.5	282.2	1.9	1.9	2.2	US$/kg	635
4407	Wood sawn or chipped lengthwise, sliced or peeled	169.8	240.8	247.7		*316.5*	*332.7*	US$/m^3	248
7308	Structures (excluding prefabricated buildings of heading 94.06)	221.4	164.8	200.4	3.2	3.0	3.5	US$/kg	691
7204	Ferrous waste and scrap; remelting scrap ingots of iron or steel	112.6	206.4	263.7	0.3	0.4	0.5	US$/kg	282

Graph 2: Trade Balance by MDG Regions in 2011

(Bln US$)

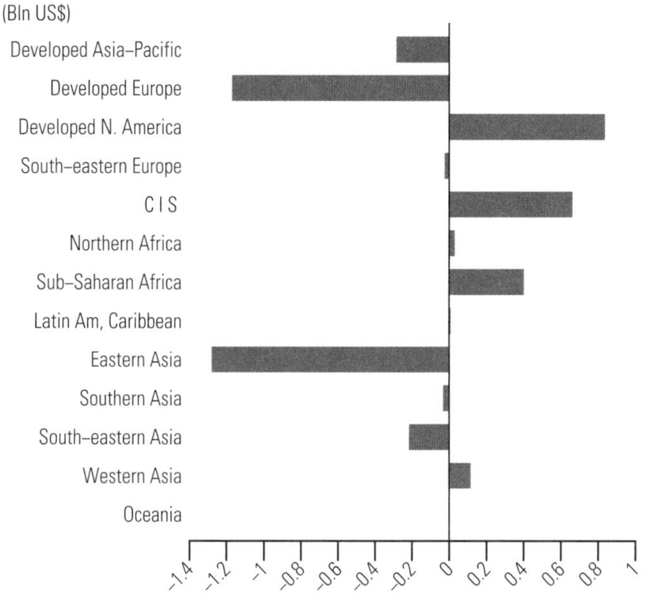

Graph 3: Partner concentration of trade in 2011

(Cumulative share by ranked partners)

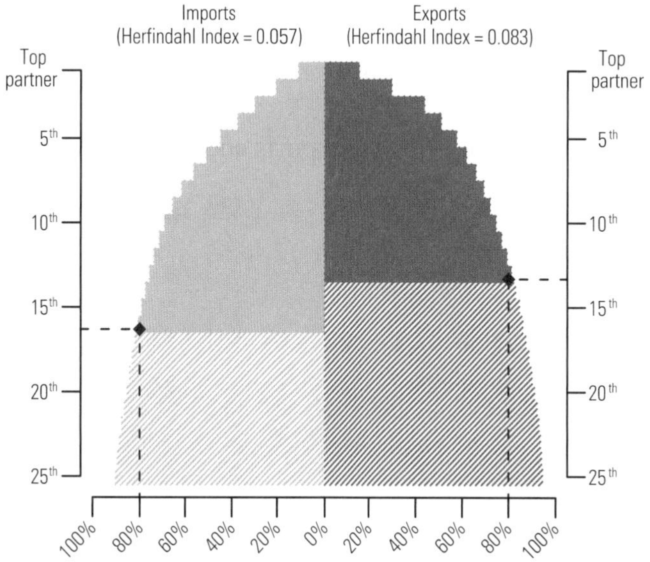

Table 4: Exports by principal countries and SITC sections in 2011

(Value in million US$, percentages of country total)

Country	Total	Shares by SITC sections (%) 0+1	2+4	3	5	6	7	8	9	Total
World	18158.3	8.2	6.9	16.9	5.5	14.1	30.0	13.5	4.7	100
Russian Federation	2848.0	16.2	0.8	2.0	11.2	16.9	35.2	17.6	0.0	100
Sweden	2590.6	1.9	5.6	3.9	1.1	11.7	59.3	12.9	3.6	100
Finland	2495.7	8.0	8.1	5.6	2.4	18.8	28.3	18.7	10.0	100
Latvia	1305.5	13.6	6.8	13.1	7.7	12.8	23.7	8.9	13.2	100
USA	1202.1	0.7	0.3	59.5	5.7	3.7	25.6	4.6	0.0	100
Lithuania	771.7	16.1	4.8	14.8	9.9	13.1	19.8	10.3	11.1	100
Germany	758.6	8.3	13.7	1.1	4.9	18.8	22.2	23.7	7.4	100
Nigeria	615.2	0.1	0.0	99.2	0.5	0.0	0.1	0.0	0.0	100
Norway	504.6	2.9	8.9	0.9	2.2	21.9	23.7	38.6	0.9	100
Netherlands	463.4	8.8	11.9	48.9	5.0	5.9	7.6	8.5	3.6	100

Imports Profile:

Machinery and transport equipment (SITC section 7) accounted for a large share of imports: 31.8 percent in 2011 (see table 2). Other major commodity groups were mineral fuels, lubricants and related materials (SITC section 3) and manufactured goods classified chiefly by material (SITC section 6) respectively with 17.8 and 14.9 percent of total imports. In addition to petroleum oils, other than crude (HS code 2710), other major products for imports over the last three years were electrical apparatus for line telephony or line telegraphy (HS code 8517) and motor cars and other motor vehicles principally designed for the transport (HS code 8703) (see table 5).

Table 5: Top 10 import commodities 2009 to 2011

(Value in million US$)

HS code	4-digit heading of Harmonized System 2007	Value (million US$) 2009	2010	2011	Unit value 2009	2010	2011	Unit	SITC code
	All Commodities	11360.0	13182.5	18780.3					
2710	Petroleum oils, other than crude	1707.5	1797.0	2828.3	0.5	0.6	*0.8*	US$/kg	334
9999	Commodities not specified according to kind	612.0	682.8	1094.9					931
8517	Electrical apparatus for line telephony or line telegraphy	165.3	564.1	1183.0					764
8703	Motor cars and other motor vehicles principally designed for the transport	550.1	339.4	594.5	14.1	18.4	21.2	thsd US$/unit	781
3004	Medicaments (excluding goods of heading 30.02, 30.05 or 30.06)	254.7	251.5	289.6	73.7	58.6	*72.4*	US$/kg	542
2711	Petroleum gases and other gaseous hydrocarbons	226.8	220.8	258.0	0.5	0.4	0.5	US$/kg	343
8542	Electronic integrated circuits	111.5	199.2	308.4					776
4011	New pneumatic tyres, of rubber	157.3	184.7	273.1	62.0	65.0	72.5	US$/unit	625
8544	Insulated (including enamelled or anodised) wire, cable	108.5	203.0	253.0	*7.6*	*9.9*	*11.8*	US$/kg	773
4407	Wood sawn or chipped lengthwise, sliced or peeled	113.1	164.0	204.3		*251.9*	*282.0*	US$/m^3	248

Ethiopia

Imports: CIF, by origin | **Exports: FOB, by last known destination** | **Trade System: General**

Overview:

From 2007 to 2011, Ethiopia's exports increased on average by 19.6 percent each year and amounted to 2.6 bln US$ in 2011 (see table 1 and graph 1). Imports showed a similar development with an average growth rate of 11.2 percent each year to reach 8.9 bln US$ in 2011 (see table 2 and graph 1). This resulted in a trade deficit of 6.3 bln US$ in 2011 (see graph 1). Except for Sub-Saharan Africa (surplus of 240.0 mln US$) and Oceania (surplus of 0.1 mln US $), trade was in deficit with all MDG regions (see graph 2). Large deficits were recorded with Western Asia (-1.8 bln US$), Eastern Asia (-1.6 bln US$) and Southern Asia (-0.9 bln US$). Ethiopia's trade was diversified across partners: in 2011, 15 (respectively 17) major partners accounted for 80 percent of exports (respectively imports) (see graph 3).

Graph 1: Total imports, exports and trade balance

(Bln US$ by year)

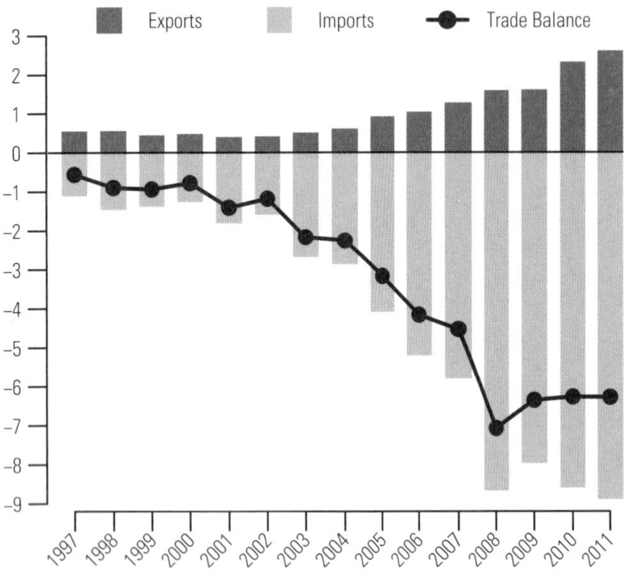

Table 1: Exports by SITC sections

(Value in million US$, growth and shares in percentage)

SITC	2011	Avg. Growth rates (%) 2007-2011	2010-2011	2011 share
Total	2614.9	19.6	12.2	100.0
0+1	1619.9	27.1	19.3	62.0
2+4	609.2	9.5	10.3	23.3
3	0.0	-76.1	-99.7	0.0
5	6.6	37.5	12.3	0.3
6	175.6	12.9	66.3	6.7
7	28.6	-5.4	-68.9	1.1
8	50.3	-0.5	49.1	1.9
9	124.6	37.5	-31.7	4.8

Table 2: Imports by SITC sections

(Value in million US$, growth and shares in percentage)

SITC	2011	Avg. Growth rates (%) 2007-2011	2010-2011	2011 share
Total	8896.3	11.2	3.4	100.0
0+1	907.6	31.4	33.0	10.2
2+4	524.7	30.1	45.5	5.9
3	1575.3	19.5	-1.0	17.7
5	1026.4	10.8	3.6	11.5
6	1479.0	4.3	7.5	16.6
7	2771.8	6.5	-9.7	31.2
8	607.7	7.2	15.1	6.8
9	3.8	165.0	117.2	0.0

Exports Profile:

Food, live animals, beverages and tobacco (SITC sections 0+1) and inedible crude materials (except fuels), animal and vegetable oils, fats and waxes (SITC sections 2+4) accounted for a large part of Ethiopia's exports in 2011: respectively 62.0 and 23.3 percent of exported goods (see table 1). In 2011, Germany, China and Somalia were the top three partners for exports (see table 4). Food, live animals, beverages and tobacco (SITC sections 0+1) accounted respectively for 82.5 and 99.7 percent of exports to Germany and Somalia. Inedible crude materials (except fuels), animal and vegetable oils, fats and waxes (SITC sections 2+4) accounted for 85.5 percent of exports to China. From 2009 to 2011, the top products for exports were coffee, whether or not roasted or decaffeinated (HS code 0901), other oil seeds and oleaginous fruits, whether or not broken (HS code 1207) and other vegetables, fresh or chilled (HS code 0709) (see table 3).

Table 3: Top 10 export commodities 2009 to 2011

(Value in million US$)

HS code	4-digit heading of Harmonized System 2007	Value (million US$) 2009	2010	2011	Unit value 2009	2010	2011	Unit	SITC code
	All Commodities	1618.2	2329.8	2614.9					
0901	Coffee, whether or not roasted or decaffeinated	369.8	699.1	846.9	2.8	3.3	5.3	US$/kg	071
1207	Other oil seeds and oleaginous fruits, whether or not broken	380.3	338.8	363.8	1.2	1.2	1.3	US$/kg	222
0709	Other vegetables, fresh or chilled	168.5	245.1	238.1	5.7	5.5	5.6	US$/kg	054
0603	Cut flowers and flower buds of a kind suitable for bouquets	131.5	143.8	168.9	4.2	3.9	3.9	US$/kg	292
7108	Gold (including gold plated with platinum)	92.5	182.3	124.6	23.7	32.0	40.0	thsd US$/kg	971
0713	Dried leguminous vegetables, shelled, whether or not skinned or split	104.1	136.5	139.3	0.6	0.6	0.7	US$/kg	054
0102	Live bovine animals	36.7	77.6	137.8	*808.9*	*823.9*	*811.0*	US$/unit	001
0204	Meat of sheep or goats, fresh, chilled or frozen	22.8	39.6	67.6	3.7	4.1	4.6	US$/kg	012
4105	Tanned or crust skins of sheep or lambs, without wool on	20.7	33.7	64.7	22.7	23.8	26.3	US$/kg	611
0106	Other live animals	17.4	48.9	36.6					001

Graph 2: Trade Balance by MDG Regions in 2011

(Bln US$)

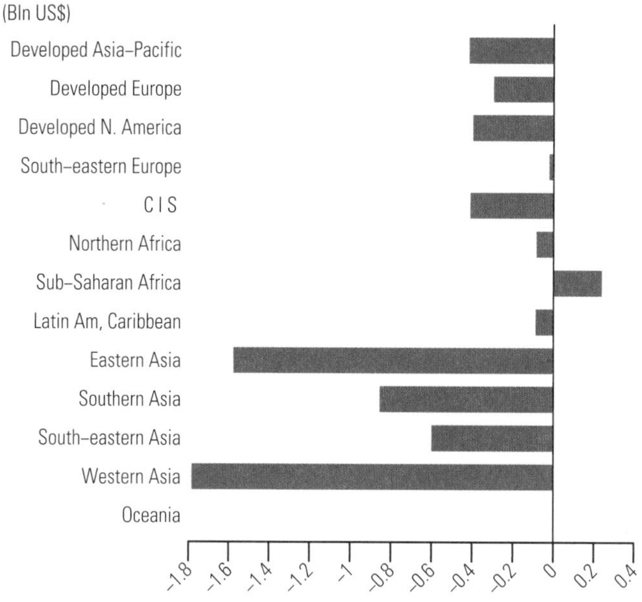

Graph 3: Partner concentration of trade in 2011

(Cumulative share by ranked partners)

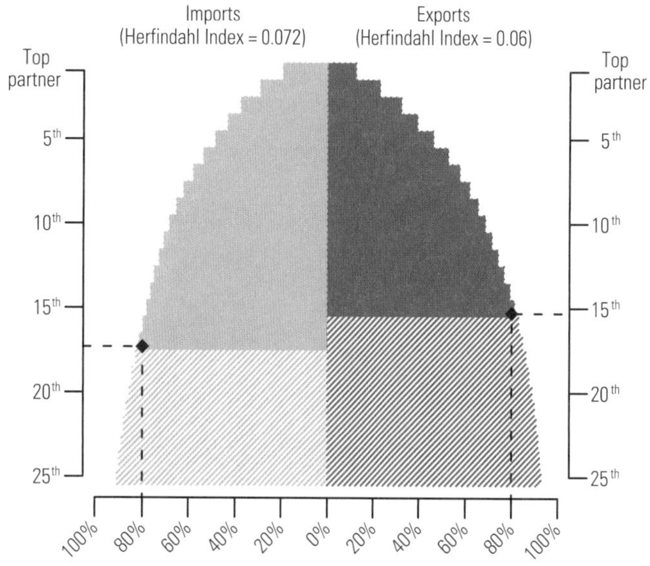

Table 4: Exports by principal countries and SITC sections in 2011

(Value in million US$, percentages of country total)

Country	Total	Shares by SITC sections (%)								
		0 + 1	2 + 4	3	5	6	7	8	9	Total
World	2614.9	62.0	23.3	0.0	0.3	6.7	1.1	1.9	4.8	100
Germany	318.8	82.5	3.6	...	0.0	3.6	0.6	9.6	0.0	100
China	283.4	3.9	85.5	...	0.1	10.2	0.1	0.1	0.0	100
Somalia	243.3	99.7	0.0	...	0.0	...	0.3	0.0	...	100
Netherlands	181.2	8.5	90.2	...	0.0	1.0	0.1	0.1	...	100
Sudan	178.4	87.9	6.8	...	2.1	0.5	0.2	2.5	...	100
Saudi Arabia	167.4	95.6	4.2	...	0.0	0.0	0.1	0.1	0.0	100
Switzerland	129.4	2.6	0.9	...	0.0	0.1	0.0	0.1	96.3	100
Italy	111.2	56.0	1.7	...	0.0	39.6	0.3	2.4	...	100
USA	98.0	81.4	10.4	...	0.1	2.1	1.4	4.7	0.0	100
United Arab Emirates	82.5	84.8	6.6	...	0.0	1.8	6.8	0.2	...	100

Imports Profile:

Machinery and transport equipment (SITC section 7) and mineral fuels, lubricants and related materials (SITC section 3) accounted respectively for 31.2 and 17.7 percent of imports in 2011 (see table 2). In addition to petroleum oils, other than crude (HS code 2710), other major imported products over the period from 2009 to 2011 were electrical apparatus for line telephony or line telegraphy (HS code 8517) and wheat and meslin (HS code 1001) (see table 5).

Table 5: Top 10 import commodities 2009 to 2011

(Value in million US$)

HS code	4-digit heading of Harmonized System 2007	Value (million US$)			Unit value				SITC code
		2009	2010	2011	2009	2010	2011	Unit	
	All Commodities	7973.9	8601.8	8896.3					
2710	Petroleum oils, other than crude	1222.5	1544.4	1484.3	0.6	0.7	0.9	US$/kg	334
8517	Electrical apparatus for line telephony or line telegraphy	414.0	529.3	107.0					764
1001	Wheat and meslin	321.6	304.3	402.6	0.3	0.3	0.4	US$/kg	041
8704	Motor vehicles for the transport of goods	206.0	382.2	357.6					782
1511	Palm oil and its fractions	204.8	222.7	330.9	1.0	1.0	1.4	US$/kg	422
3105	Mineral or chemical fertilisers	250.3	168.9	250.2	0.5	0.5	0.6	US$/kg	562
3004	Medicaments (excluding goods of heading 30.02, 30.05 or 30.06)	256.5	204.2	110.5	27.7	26.2	16.4	US$/kg	542
8703	Motor cars and other motor vehicles principally designed for the transport	141.5	197.5	192.9		*20.5*		thsd US$/unit	781
8429	Self-propelled bulldozers, angledozers, graders, levellers, scrapers	183.4	146.9	195.4		*65.0*	*69.5*	thsd US$/unit	723
7308	Structures (excluding prefabricated buildings of heading 94.06)	159.4	149.4	55.4	1.8	1.9	1.9	US$/kg	691

Faeroe Islands

Imports: CIF, by origin | **Exports: FOB, by last known destination** | **Trade System: General**

Overview:

After several years of continuous growth, the value of the exports of Faeroe Islands dropped by 10.6 percent in 2009 and amounted to 761.7 mln US$ (see table 1 and graph 1). Imports showed a more pronounced development with a decline by 20.7 percent in 2009 to 783.4 mln US$ (see table 2 and graph 1). The trade deficit narrowed for the second consecutive year to 21.7 mln US$ in 2009 (see graph 1). Deficits were recorded with Developed Europe (-76.7 mln US$), Latin America and the Caribbean (-46.9 mln US$) and Eastern Asia (-10.5 mln US$) (see graph 2). However, trade recorded significant surpluses with Developed North America (+54.2 mln US$), Commonwealth of Independent States (+36.7 mln US$) and Sub-Saharan Africa (+32.7 mln US$). In 2009, trade was relatively concentrated among a few partners: 11 (respectively 9) major partners accounted for 80 percent of exports (respectively imports) (see graph 3).

Graph 1: Total imports, exports and trade balance

(Bln US$ by year)

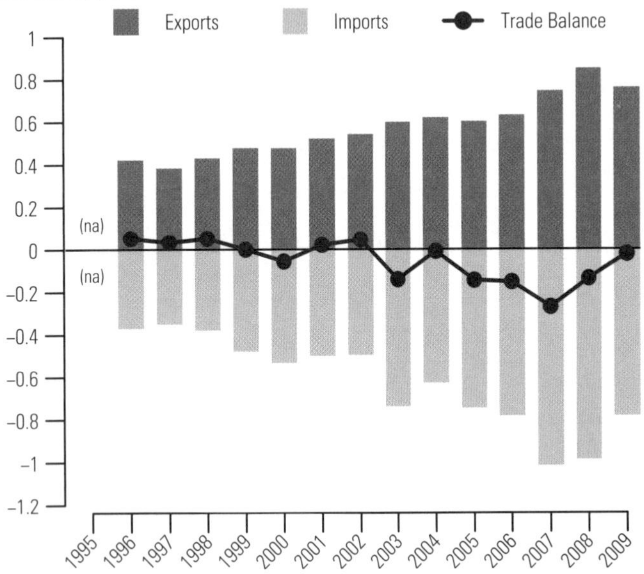

Exports Profile:

Food, live animals, beverages and tobacco (SITC sections 0+1) accounted for 88.0 percent of exported goods in 2009 (see table 1). Major markets for exports included United Kingdom, Denmark and France (see table 4). From 2007 to 2009, top exported products were fish fillets and other fish meat (whether or not minced) (HS code 0304), fish, fresh or chilled, excluding fish fillets (HS code 0302) and fish, dried, salted or in brine (HS code 0305) (see table 3).

Table 1: Exports by SITC sections

(Value in million US$, growth and shares in percentage)

SITC	2009	Avg. Growth rates (%) 2005-2009	Avg. Growth rates (%) 2008-2009	2009 share
Total	761.7	6.1	-10.6	100.0
0+1	670.0	5.1	-0.6	88.0
2+4	14.2	5.2	-44.8	1.9
3	21.3	...	17.8	2.8
5	1.0	13.4	9.1	0.1
6	5.7	35.5	-25.4	0.7
7	47.9	10.1	-61.3	6.3
8	1.7	-29.2	-3.2	0.2

Table 2: Imports by SITC sections

(Value in million US$, growth and shares in percentage)

SITC	2009	Avg. Growth rates (%) 2005-2009	Avg. Growth rates (%) 2008-2009	2009 share
Total	783.4	1.2	-20.7	100.0
0+1	123.7	6.2	-6.7	15.8
2+4	38.0	13.0	-18.5	4.9
3	123.2	0.4	-40.5	15.7
5	70.5	10.1	-4.4	9.0
6	91.0	1.0	-34.4	11.6
7	232.7	-4.1	-8.5	29.7
8	97.3	4.1	-22.1	12.4
9	6.9	-12.0	-32.7	0.9

Table 3: Top 10 export commodities 2007 to 2009

(Value in million US$)

HS code	4-digit heading of Harmonized System 2007	Value (million US$) 2007	2008	2009	Unit value 2007	2008	2009	Unit	SITC code
	All Commodities	746.2	852.1	761.7					
0304	Fish fillets and other fish meat (whether or not minced)	228.9	223.0	221.7	4.2	4.7	3.9	US$/kg	034
0302	Fish, fresh or chilled, excluding fish fillets	169.5	209.3	249.5	2.1	2.4	2.3	US$/kg	034
0305	Fish, dried, salted or in brine	100.9	106.8	82.0	6.3	7.3	5.3	US$/kg	035
0303	Fish, frozen, excluding fish fillets and other fish meat of heading 03.04	67.3	69.2	74.1	1.2	2.0	2.0	US$/kg	034
8902	Fishing vessels; factory ships and other vessels for processing	14.3	110.9	42.2					793
2301	Flours, meals and pellets, of meat or meat offal	51.6	28.7	4.6	1.5	1.1	1.1	US$/kg	081
0306	Crustaceans, whether in shell or not	19.8	26.4	20.9	2.9	2.9	2.7	US$/kg	036
0511	Animal products not elsewhere specified or included	28.5	23.4	8.3					291
2710	Petroleum oils, other than crude	12.9	18.1	21.3	0.7	0.7	0.5	US$/kg	334
2309	Preparations of a kind used in animal feeding	26.1	3.8	10.4	1.2	1.3	1.6	US$/kg	081

Graph 2: Trade Balance by MDG Regions in 2009

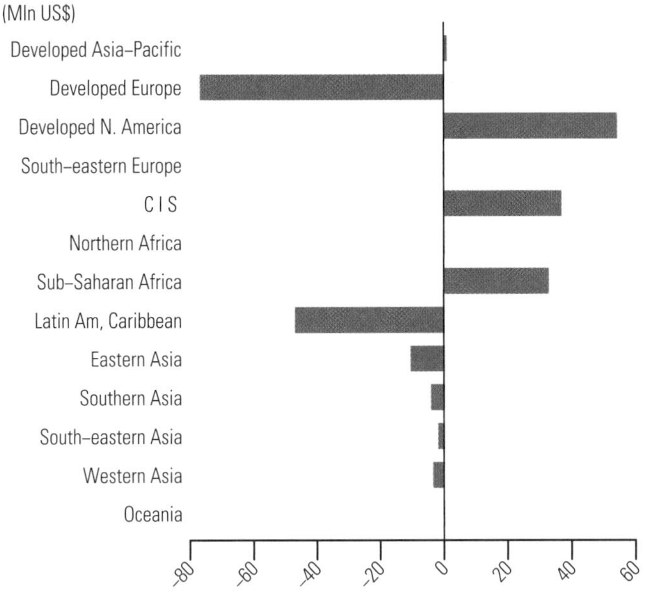

Graph 3: Partner concentration of trade in 2009

(Cumulative share by ranked partners)

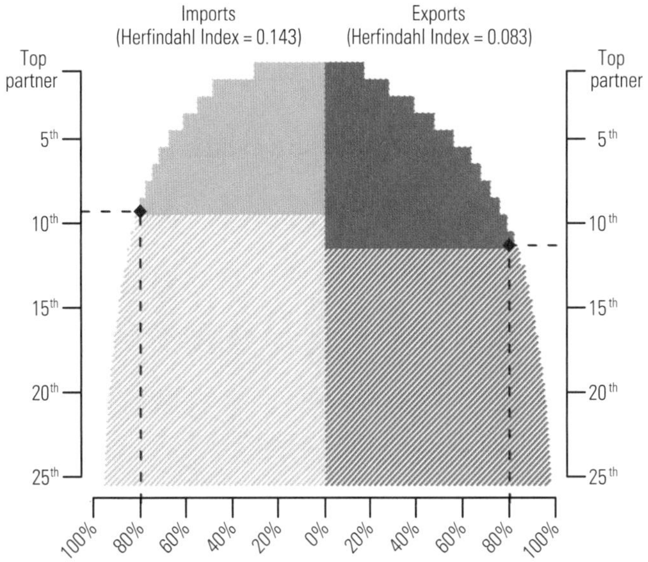

Table 4: Exports by principal countries and SITC sections in 2009

(Value in million US$, percentages of country total)

Country	Total	Shares by SITC sections (%) 0+1	2+4	3	5	6	7	8	9	Total
World	761.7	88.0	1.9	2.8	0.1	0.7	6.3	0.2	...	100
United Kingdom	131.9	99.6	0.1	0.0	0.0	0.0	0.1	0.1	...	100
Denmark	83.8	80.9	10.1	1.6	0.5	0.5	5.4	1.0	...	100
France	82.3	100.0	0.0	...	...	0.0	...	...	...	100
Germany	65.8	99.3	0.3	0.3	0.0	0.1	0.0	...	...	100
Norway	62.4	93.3	2.7	1.6	0.3	1.0	0.6	0.4	...	100
USA	57.3	99.5	0.0	0.5	...	...	...	...	...	100
Spain	31.3	100.0	0.0	...	...	...	0.0	...	...	100
Nigeria	31.2	100.0	0.0	...	...	...	...	...	...	100
Russian Federation	30.7	39.1	0.1	50.5	0.0	0.5	9.9	0.0	...	100
Italy	24.4	100.0	0.0	...	...	...	...	...	...	100

Imports Profile:

In 2009, imports were composed of 29.7 percent of machinery and transport equipment (SITC section 7), 15.8 percent of food, live animals, beverages and tobacco (SITC sections 0+1) and 15.7 percent of mineral fuels, lubricants and related materials (SITC section 3) (see table 2). From 2007 to 2009, top imported products included petroleum oils, other than crude (HS code 2710), fishing vessels; factory ships and other vessels for processing (HS code 8902) and motor cars and other motor vehicles principally designed for the transport (HS code 8703) (see table 5).

Table 5: Top 10 import commodities 2007 to 2009

(Value in million US$)

HS code	4-digit heading of Harmonized System 2007	Value (million US$) 2007	2008	2009	Unit value 2007	2008	2009	Unit	SITC code
	All Commodities	1 015.8	988.1	783.4					
2710	Petroleum oils, other than crude	158.7	206.5	121.6	0.6	0.8	0.5	US$/kg	334
8902	Fishing vessels; factory ships and other vessels for processing	71.7	2.2	50.6					793
8703	Motor cars and other motor vehicles principally designed for the transport	47.5	33.4	10.8	*14.4*	*16.1*	*16.2*	thsd US$/unit	781
3004	Medicaments (excluding goods of heading 30.02, 30.05 or 30.06)	18.9	22.2	20.4	213.3	232.0	230.1	US$/kg	542
9403	Other furniture and parts thereof	16.7	17.0	11.3					821
8471	Automatic data processing machines and units thereof	18.7	15.1	10.9					752
8901	Cruise ships, excursion boats, ferry-boats, cargo ships, barges	1.9	0.0	41.1					793
1504	Fats and oils and their fractions, of fish or marine mammals	5.6	19.1	9.0	0.9	1.3	0.9	US$/kg	411
2309	Preparations of a kind used in animal feeding	16.6	9.6	7.4	0.9	0.9	0.9	US$/kg	081
4418	Builders' joinery and carpentry of wood	11.3	11.4	6.4	6.7	6.9	6.4	US$/kg	635

Imports: CIF, by purchase | **Exports: FOB, by sale** | **Trade System: General**

Overview:

Following a significant decrease of 31.8 percent in 2009, the value of exports of Fiji increased by 34.7 percent in 2010 and amounted to 846.6 mln US$ (see table 1 and graph 1). Imports showed a similar development, with an increase of 26.7 percent and amounted to 1.8 bln US$ (see table 2 and graph 1). This resulted in a trade deficit of 974.0 mln US$ in 2010 (see graph 1). Trade was in deficit with almost all of the MDG regions (see graph 2). Large deficits were recorded with the South-eastern Asia (-0.7 bln US$), Developed Asia-Pacific (-0.4 bln US$) and Eastern Asia (-0.1 bln US$). Trade surpluses were recorded with Oceania (+163.1 mln US$) and Developed North America (+28.8 mln US$). In 2010, Fiji's trade was concentrated among a few partners: 11 partners accounted for 80 percent of exports while 6 partners accounted for 80 percent of imports (see graph 3).

Graph 1: Total imports, exports and trade balance

(Bln US$ by year)

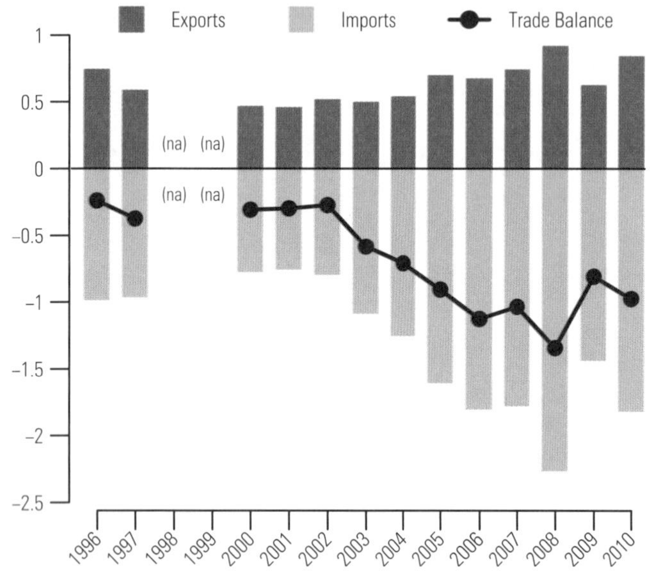

Table 1: Exports by SITC sections

(Value in million US$, growth and shares in percentage)

SITC	2010	Avg. Growth rates (%) 2006-2010	2009-2010	2010 share
Total	846.6	5.7	34.7	100.0
0+1	338.1	2.2	6.5	39.9
2+4	56.4	13.0	91.0	6.7
3	212.7	6.1	67.5	25.1
5	25.3	19.7	27.6	3.0
6	45.7	5.6	35.8	5.4
7	23.6	8.7	9.8	2.8
8	64.9	-1.3	18.0	7.7
9	80.1	26.0	223.4	9.5

Table 2: Imports by SITC sections

(Value in million US$, growth and shares in percentage)

SITC	2010	Avg. Growth rates (%) 2006-2010	2009-2010	2010 share
Total	1 820.7	0.2	26.7	100.0
0+1	318.8	7.2	13.7	17.5
2+4	30.3	6.6	15.8	1.7
3	576.9	-0.6	56.2	31.7
5	150.9	3.4	27.6	8.3
6	247.4	-2.0	20.2	13.6
7	332.1	-4.1	7.1	18.2
8	155.6	1.5	28.9	8.5
9	8.8	0.5	43.2	0.5

Exports Profile:

Food, live animals, beverages and tobacco (SITC sections 0+1) accounted for 39.9 percent of exports in 2010 (see table 1). Mineral fuels, lubricants and related materials (SITC section 3), in majority non crude petroleum oils, accounted for 25.1 percent of exports. In 2010, major partners for exports were Australia, USA and Japan (see table 4). From 2008 to 2010, major commodities for exports were petroleum oils, other than crude (HS code 2710), cane or beet sugar and pure sucrose, in solid form (HS code 1701) and fish, frozen, excluding fish fillets and other fish meat of heading 03.04 (HS code 0303) (see table 3).

Table 3: Top 10 export commodities 2008 to 2010

(Value in million US$)

HS code	4-digit heading of Harmonized System 2007	Value (million US$) 2008	2009	2010	Unit value 2008	2009	2010	Unit	SITC code
	All Commodities	921.9	628.7	846.6					
2710	Petroleum oils, other than crude	258.8	126.9	212.5	*0.8*	*1.0*	*0.7*	US$/kg	334
1701	Cane or beet sugar and chemically pure sucrose, in solid form	155.6	95.8	37.3	0.6	0.5	0.4	US$/kg	061
0303	Fish, frozen, excluding fish fillets and other fish meat of heading 03.04	52.3	61.3	88.9	2.0	2.0	1.9	US$/kg	034
2201	Waters, including natural or artificial mineral waters	69.0	41.5	62.5	*22.3*			US$/litre	111
7108	Gold (including gold plated with platinum)	17.1	21.8	77.8	27.5	30.2	38.6	thsd US$/kg	971
1905	Bread, pastry, cakes, biscuits and other bakers' wares	22.5	25.6	26.8	1.9	1.8	2.1	US$/kg	048
6210	Garments, made up of fabrics of heading 56.02, 56.03, 59.03, 59.06 or 59.07	20.7	14.2	18.2					845
0302	Fish, fresh or chilled, excluding fish fillets	21.7	11.9	18.3	2.1	2.3	2.1	US$/kg	034
6203	Men's or boys' suits, ensembles, jackets, blazers, trousers	19.1	12.6	16.8	10.8		9.4	US$/unit	841
4401	Fuel wood, in logs, in billets, in twigs, in faggots or in similar forms	17.3	5.7	22.7					246

Graph 2: Trade Balance by MDG Regions in 2010

(Mln US$)

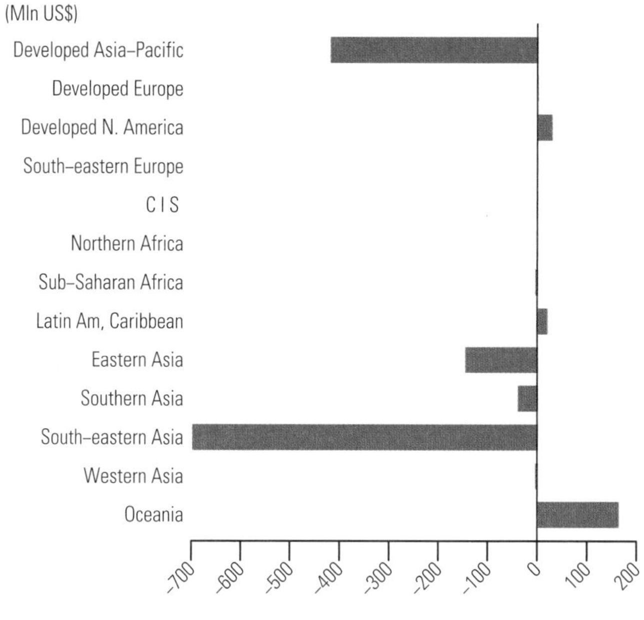

Graph 3: Partner concentration of trade in 2010

(Cumulative share by ranked partners)

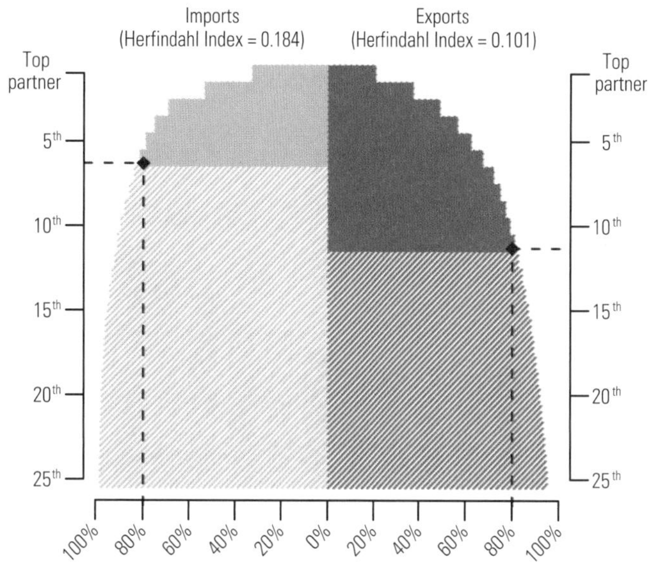

Table 4: Exports by principal countries and SITC sections in 2010

(Value in million US$, percentages of country total)

Country	Total	Shares by SITC sections (%)								
		0 + 1	2 + 4	3	5	6	7	8	9	Total
World	846.6	39.9	6.7	25.1	3.0	5.4	2.8	7.7	9.5	100
Australia	175.5	14.1	2.2	0.0	2.4	8.7	1.9	26.1	44.5	100
Bunkers	141.1	0.0	0.0	100.0	...	...	...	...	...	100
USA	96.5	87.1	5.6	0.0	0.9	0.5	4.2	1.5	0.2	100
Japan	64.3	63.9	35.5	...	0.0	0.3	0.2	0.1	0.0	100
New Zealand	49.2	57.3	6.3	0.0	7.1	7.2	7.0	14.1	0.9	100
United Kingdom	42.3	96.5	1.3	...	0.1	0.5	0.4	1.2	0.0	100
Tonga	39.0	14.4	0.4	71.6	2.5	6.3	2.8	1.9	0.1	100
American Samoa	24.0	75.5	0.0	0.2	5.5	17.0	0.0	1.7	0.0	100
Vanuatu	19.2	50.8	0.8	6.9	14.6	12.6	7.0	7.0	0.3	100
Kiribati	16.1	28.1	1.6	37.8	5.2	14.3	6.2	6.4	0.3	100

Imports Profile:

Mineral fuels, lubricants and related materials (SITC section 3, largely non crude petroleum oils) accounted for 31.7 percent of imports in 2010 (see table 2). Other major commodity groups included machinery and transport equipment (SITC section 7) and food, live animals, beverages and tobacco (SITC sections 0+1) respectively with 18.2 and 17.5 percent of imports. From 2008 to 2010, top products for imports were petroleum oils, other than crude (HS code 2710), wheat and meslin (HS code 1001) and electrical apparatus for line telephony or line telegraphy (HS code 8517) (see table 5).

Table 5: Top 10 import commodities 2008 to 2010

(Value in million US$)

HS code	4-digit heading of Harmonized System 2007	Value (million US$)			Unit value				SITC code
		2008	2009	2010	2008	2009	2010	Unit	
	All Commodities	2 263.9	1 437.0	1 820.7					
2710	Petroleum oils, other than crude	748.7	355.6	555.0	*0.8*	*1.0*	*0.6*	US$/kg	334
1001	Wheat and meslin	59.3	38.9	50.0	0.5	0.4	0.6	US$/kg	041
8517	Electrical apparatus for line telephony or line telegraphy	57.4	27.0	24.4					764
8803	Parts of goods of heading 88.01 or 88.02	31.9	29.6	25.6	509.3	446.0	*326.2*	US$/kg	792
8703	Motor cars and other motor vehicles principally designed for the transport	27.9	23.5	23.5	6.3	*14.9*	*15.7*	thsd US$/unit	781
0303	Fish, frozen, excluding fish fillets and other fish meat of heading 03.04	17.7	16.3	30.9	1.2	1.3	1.3	US$/kg	034
1006	Rice	25.0	17.7	19.9	0.5	0.6	0.4	US$/kg	042
1701	Cane or beet sugar and chemically pure sucrose, in solid form	30.7	15.3	9.3	0.4	0.6	0.8	US$/kg	061
2711	Petroleum gases and other gaseous hydrocarbons	19.2	13.5	21.5	1.1	0.8	1.0	US$/kg	343
8802	Other aircraft (for example, helicopters, aeroplanes); spacecraft	44.8	0.3	3.9			138.5	thsd US$/unit	792

Finland

Imports: CIF, by origin | **Exports: FOB, by consignment** | **Trade System: General**

Overview:

In 2011, the value of Finland's exports increased by 12.4 percent and amounted to 78.8 bln US$ (see table 1 and graph 1). While still well below its 2008 level, the value of exports reflected continuous growth after the sharp decline experienced in 2009. Imports showed a similar development with an increase of 22.0 percent in 2011 and amounted to 83.9 bln US$ (see table 2 and graph 1). This resulted in a trade deficit of 5.1 bln US$ in 2011 (see graph 1). By MDG regions, large surpluses were recorded with Developed North America (+2.4 bln US$) and Western Asia (+2.0 bln US$) (see graph 2). Trade was in deficit with Developed Europe (-8.7 bln US$) and the Commonwealth of Independent States (-7.7 bln US$). Trade was diversified across partners: respectively 20 and 14 major partners accounted for 80 percent of exports and imports (see graph 3).

Graph 1: Total imports, exports and trade balance

(Bln US$ by year)

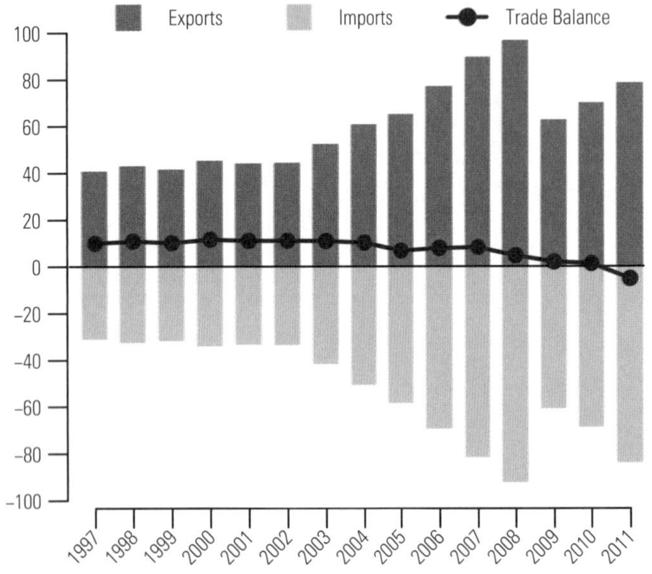

Exports Profile:

In 2011, manufactured goods classified chiefly by material (SITC section 6) was the largest commodity group for exports and represented 31.9 percent of exported goods (see table 1). Exports of machinery and transport equipment (SITC section 7) still accounted for 29.4 percent of total exports despite its trade dropping by 11.6 percent. Major destinations for exports were Sweden, Germany and Russian Federation (see table 4). Over the last three years, top export commodities were petroleum oils, other than crude (HS code 2710), paper and paperboard, coated on one or both sides with kaolin (HS code 4810) and electrical apparatus for line telephony or line telegraphy (HS code 8517) (see table 3).

Table 1: Exports by SITC sections

(Value in million US$, growth and shares in percentage)

SITC	2011	Avg. Growth rates (%) 2007-2011	2010-2011	2011 share
Total	78794.2	-3.2	12.4	100.0
0+1	2104.2	5.1	24.4	2.7
2+4	5771.1	1.7	18.7	7.3
3	7477.5	11.6	33.2	9.5
5	8727.3	6.7	12.6	11.1
6	25104.0	-2.4	12.7	31.9
7	23144.0	-11.6	1.7	29.4
8	4336.9	-0.2	11.0	5.5
9	2129.3	17.4	69.5	2.7

Table 2: Imports by SITC sections

(Value in million US$, growth and shares in percentage)

SITC	2011	Avg. Growth rates (%) 2007-2011	2010-2011	2011 share
Total	83861.7	0.7	22.0	100.0
0+1	5253.6	8.0	18.5	6.3
2+4	7581.3	-3.7	15.8	9.0
3	18188.0	12.9	44.5	21.7
5	9203.1	2.8	17.0	11.0
6	9860.9	-1.7	15.6	11.8
7	23309.8	-5.8	17.7	27.8
8	7667.3	2.4	13.8	9.1
9	2797.7	5.8	23.3	3.3

Table 3: Top 10 export commodities 2009 to 2011

(Value in million US$)

HS code	4-digit heading of Harmonized System 2007	Value (million US$) 2009	2010	2011	Unit value 2009	2010	2011	Unit	SITC code
	All Commodities	62860.5	70116.5	78794.2					
2710	Petroleum oils, other than crude	3737.6	5106.2	7065.3	*0.6*	*0.8*	*1.0*	US$/kg	334
4810	Paper and paperboard, coated on one or both sides with kaolin	4558.2	5140.5	5652.8	0.9	0.9	*1.0*	US$/kg	641
8517	Electrical apparatus for line telephony or line telegraphy	5666.8	3445.8	2833.5					764
7219	Flat-rolled products of stainless steel, of a width of 600 mm or more	1578.2	2431.4	2900.8	*2.7*	3.3	3.7	US$/kg	675
9999	Commodities not specified according to kind	3893.0	968.3	1706.5					931
4802	Uncoated paper and paperboard, of a kind used for writing	2125.4	2103.6	2107.5	*0.8*	*0.7*	*0.8*	US$/kg	641
4407	Wood sawn or chipped lengthwise, sliced or peeled	1240.7	1556.9	1643.8		*266.7*	*269.1*	US$/$m^3$	248
4703	Chemical wood pulp, soda or sulphate, other than dissolving grades	739.9	1518.7	1829.2	0.5	0.8	0.8	US$/kg	251
8504	Electrical transformers, static converters	1169.8	1198.5	1443.0					771
8901	Cruise ships, excursion boats, ferry-boats, cargo ships, barges	1878.1	1347.8	249.6			*124.8*	mln US$/unit	793

Graph 2: Trade Balance by MDG Regions in 2011

(Bln US$)

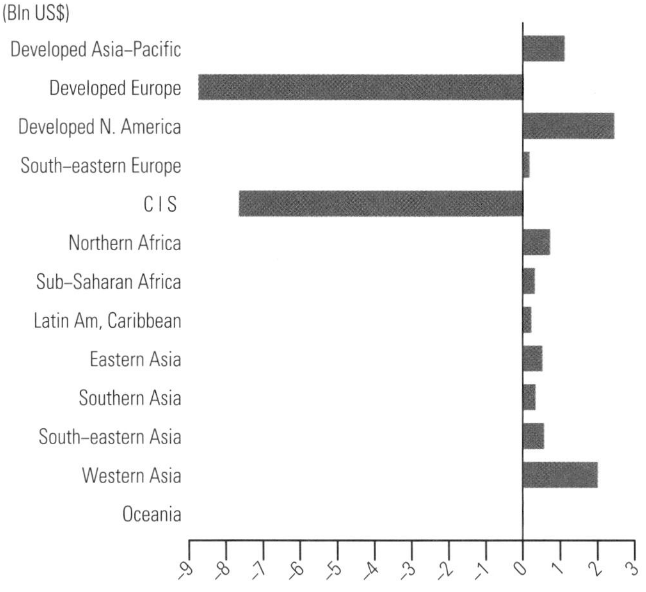

Graph 3: Partner concentration of trade in 2011

(Cumulative share by ranked partners)

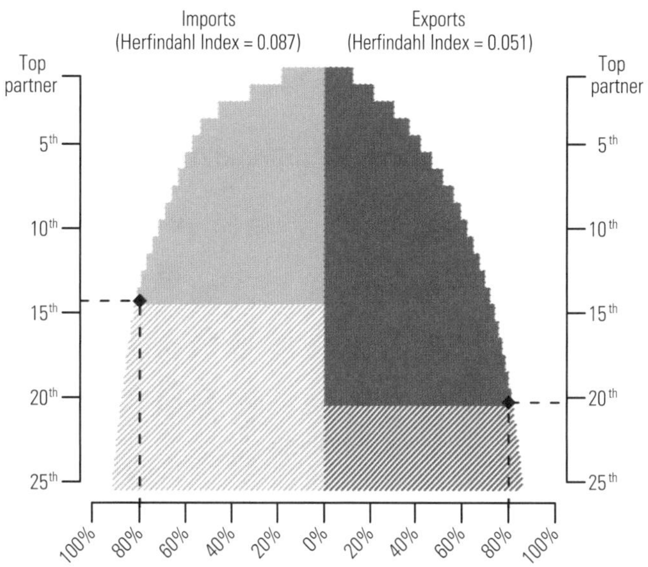

Table 4: Exports by principal countries and SITC sections in 2011

(Value in million US$, percentages of country total)

Country	Total	Shares by SITC sections (%)								
		0 + 1	2 + 4	3	5	6	7	8	9	Total
World	78794.2	2.7	7.3	9.5	11.1	31.9	29.4	5.5	2.7	100
Sweden	9274.1	3.3	3.1	26.9	9.1	27.7	20.0	6.3	3.6	100
Germany	7410.0	1.5	8.6	4.8	10.2	45.8	22.1	4.5	2.5	100
Russian Federation	7321.4	7.4	4.4	4.9	22.0	18.0	35.9	7.5	0.0	100
Netherlands	5223.9	1.0	3.3	15.5	8.4	52.7	15.2	1.7	2.1	100
United Kingdom	3796.3	1.2	9.5	6.6	8.5	40.4	27.5	4.1	2.3	100
USA	3793.1	1.9	0.5	11.8	10.6	26.8	34.8	13.6	0.0	100
Areas, nes	3734.7	3.3	2.9	0.0	19.0	70.5	0.0	0.9	3.4	100
China	3640.4	1.3	25.2	0.0	3.8	13.5	52.0	4.1	...	100
France	2385.0	1.5	11.4	4.9	10.7	25.6	33.3	9.0	3.5	100
Norway	2179.6	2.1	4.3	3.2	10.4	29.6	40.0	8.5	1.8	100

Imports Profile:

In 2011, machinery and transport equipment (SITC section 7) was the largest commodity group accounting for 27.8 percent of total imports (see table 2). Other major commodity groups included mineral fuels, lubricants and related materials (SITC section 3) and manufactured goods classified chiefly by material (SITC section 6) respectively with 21.7 and 11.8 percent of imports. Major imported products over the last three years were petroleum oils and oils obtained from bituminous minerals, crude (HS code 2709), petroleum oils, other than crude (HS code 2710) and motor cars and other motor vehicles principally designed for the transport (HS code 8703) (see table 5).

Table 5: Top 10 import commodities 2009 to 2011

(Value in million US$)

HS code	4-digit heading of Harmonized System 2007	Value (million US$)			Unit value				SITC code
		2009	2010	2011	2009	2010	2011	Unit	
	All Commodities	60830.3	68767.1	83861.7					
2709	Petroleum oils and oils obtained from bituminous minerals, crude	5234.7	6559.0	9456.1	0.5	*0.6*	0.8	US$/kg	333
2710	Petroleum oils, other than crude	2174.3	2608.1	4410.5	*0.5*	*0.7*	*0.9*	US$/kg	334
9999	Commodities not specified according to kind	3993.8	2238.0	2773.7					931
8703	Motor cars and other motor vehicles principally designed for the transport	1997.6	2529.0	3107.0	17.9	17.9	19.9	thsd US$/unit	781
8517	Electrical apparatus for line telephony or line telegraphy	2705.7	2207.3	2400.9					764
3004	Medicaments (excluding goods of heading 30.02, 30.05 or 30.06)	1989.3	1806.0	1874.5	*145.6*	*131.8*	*151.9*	US$/kg	542
7204	Ferrous waste and scrap; remelting scrap ingots of iron or steel	694.7	1463.1	1526.2	1.5	*1.9*	2.1	US$/kg	282
2711	Petroleum gases and other gaseous hydrocarbons	143.7	1534.4	1792.5	*0.5*	*0.4*	*0.5*	US$/kg	343
8471	Automatic data processing machines and units thereof	1011.3	1170.3	1284.7	211.4	224.1	256.0	US$/unit	752
2716	Electrical energy	672.1	913.2	1102.4	44.0	59.0	62.6	US$/MWh	351

France including Monaco

Imports: CIF, by origin | **Exports: FOB, by last known destination** | **Trade System: Special**

Overview:

In 2011, the value of the exports of France grew by 13.7 percent and reached 581.5 bln US$ (see table 1 and graph 1). The last five years showed an average annual increase of 1.9 percent in exports, while imports registered an average annual growth of 3.5 percent (see tables 1 and 2 and graph 1). In 2011, imports increased by 17.0 percent to 700.8 bln US$. This resulted in a trade deficit of 119.3 bln US$ in 2011, much higher than the 2010 deficit of 87.5 bln US$ (see graph 1). By MDG regions, the trade balance recorded large deficits with Developed Europe (-62.8 bln US$), Eastern Asia (-31.6 bln US$) and Commonwealth of Independent States (-19.1 bln US$) (see graph 2). By partners, 2011 trade was highly diversified: 24 major partners (respectively 23) accounted for 80 percent of exports (respectively imports) (see graph 3).

Graph 1: Total imports, exports and trade balance

(Bln US$ by year)

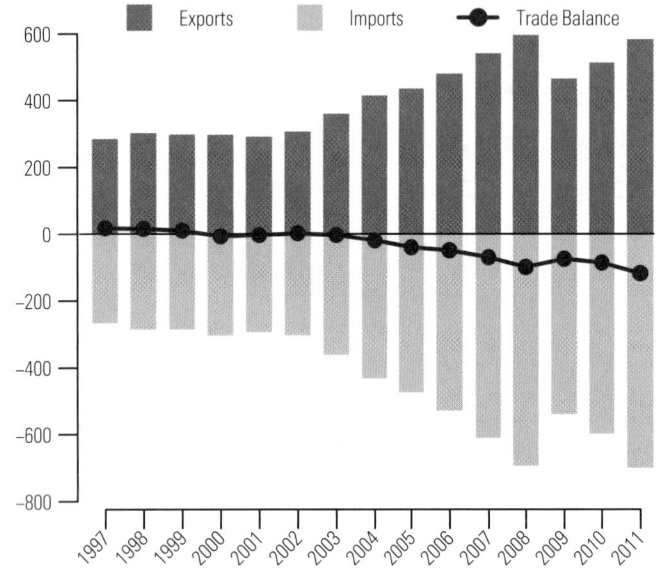

Exports Profile:

In 2011, exports were composed of 37.6 percent of machinery and transport equipment (SITC section 7), 17.1 percent of chemicals and related products, n.e.s. (SITC section 5) and 12.0 percent of both food, live animals, beverages and tobacco (SITC sections 0+1) and manufactured goods classified chiefly by material (SITC section 6) (see table 1). In addition to Germany, other major markets for exports in 2011 were Italy and Spain (see table 4). From 2009 to 2011, the major products for exports were other aircraft (for example, helicopters, aeroplanes); spacecraft (HS code 8802), medicaments (excluding goods of heading 30.02, 30.05 or 30.06) (HS code 3004) and motor cars and other motor vehicles principally designed for the transport (HS code 8703) (see table 3).

Table 1: Exports by SITC sections

(Value in million US$, growth and shares in percentage)

SITC	2011	Avg. Growth rates (%) 2007-2011	2010-2011	2011 share
Total	581 541.9	1.9	13.7	100.0
0+1	69 712.2	5.3	18.6	12.0
2+4	17 316.0	6.4	28.5	3.0
3	26 538.9	6.4	41.8	4.6
5	99 605.6	3.2	9.1	17.1
6	69 809.8	-2.3	13.8	12.0
7	218 936.5	0.5	9.7	37.6
8	62 222.7	2.4	13.9	10.7
9	17 400.2	8.0	25.1	3.0

Table 2: Imports by SITC sections

(Value in million US$, growth and shares in percentage)

SITC	2011	Avg. Growth rates (%) 2007-2011	2010-2011	2011 share
Total	700 851.6	3.5	17.0	100.0
0+1	54 263.1	5.0	13.1	7.7
2+4	20 699.9	5.1	20.5	3.0
3	114 752.5	8.8	38.7	16.4
5	96 937.2	4.7	14.5	13.8
6	89 747.3	-0.4	16.6	12.8
7	230 066.2	1.8	12.5	32.8
8	93 260.2	3.4	10.3	13.3
9	1 125.2	16.7	57.2	0.2

Table 3: Top 10 export commodities 2009 to 2011

(Value in million US$)

HS code	4-digit heading of Harmonized System 2007	Value (million US$) 2009	2010	2011	Unit value 2009	2010	2011	Unit	SITC code
	All Commodities	464 112.8	511 651.0	581 541.9					
8802	Other aircraft (for example, helicopters, aeroplanes); spacecraft	29 184.4	40 818.5	43 346.6	33.3	32.9	12.8	mln US$/unit	792
3004	Medicaments (excluding goods of heading 30.02, 30.05 or 30.06)	27 922.8	27 170.7	26 428.1	*98.9*	*94.1*	*87.6*	US$/kg	542
8703	Motor cars and other motor vehicles principally designed for the transport	19 901.6	21 089.0	23 163.1	*11.6*	13.5	15.0	thsd US$/unit	781
8708	Parts and accessories of the motor vehicles of headings 87.01 to 87.05	14 912.8	16 978.6	18 816.9	*8.9*	*8.4*	*9.0*	US$/kg	784
2710	Petroleum oils, other than crude	10 459.2	12 439.6	16 782.9	*0.5*	*0.7*	*0.9*	US$/kg	334
9999	Commodities not specified according to kind	11 533.3	12 592.7	14 877.9					931
8411	Turbo-jets, turbo-propellers and other gas turbines	9 303.5	9 819.3	10 307.6					714
2204	Wine of fresh grapes, including fortified wines	7 690.8	8 388.0	9 974.4	6.1	*6.2*	*7.2*	US$/litre	112
8542	Electronic integrated circuits	4 569.5	7 086.0	8 460.3					776
3304	Beauty or make-up preparations	5 532.7	6 047.3	7 060.5	*28.9*	*27.5*	*30.9*	US$/kg	553

Graph 2: Trade Balance by MDG Regions in 2011

(Bln US$)

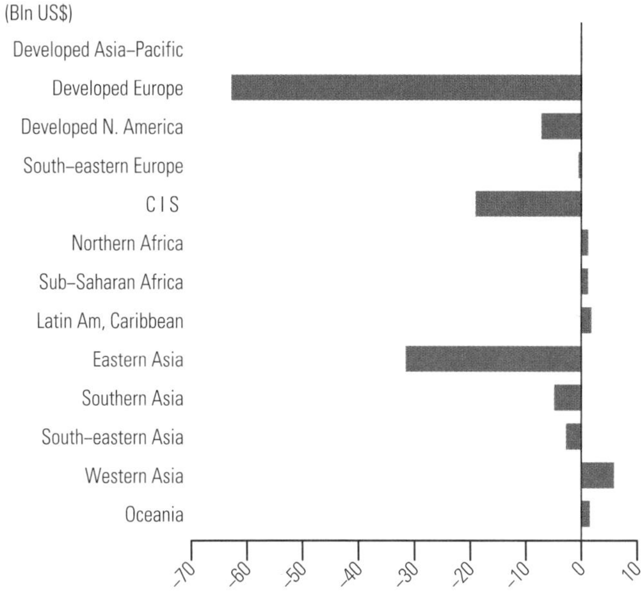

Graph 3: Partner concentration of trade in 2011

(Cumulative share by ranked partners)

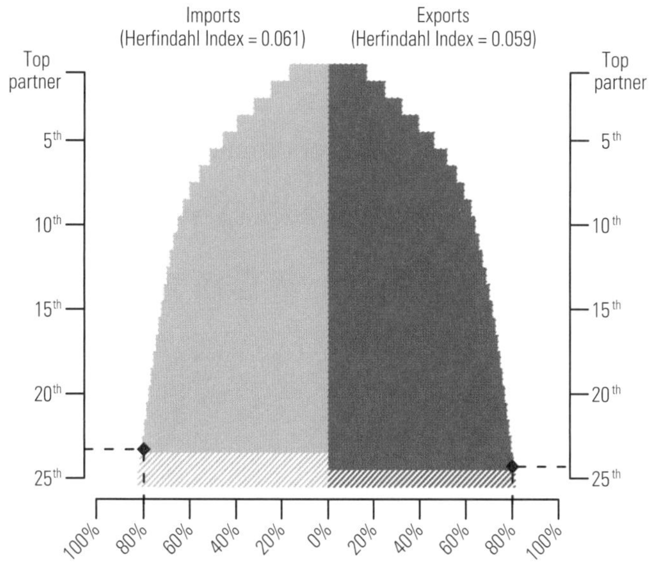

Table 4: Exports by principal countries and SITC sections in 2011

(Value in million US$, percentages of country total)

Country	Total	Shares by SITC sections (%) 0 + 1	2 + 4	3	5	6	7	8	9	Total
World	581541.9	12.0	3.0	4.6	17.1	12.0	37.6	10.7	3.0	100
Germany	96159.8	8.2	3.1	2.4	14.1	14.2	46.8	8.0	3.3	100
Italy	47455.9	15.6	4.3	7.4	16.3	13.3	25.6	12.7	5.0	100
Spain	42281.3	14.2	5.1	4.9	14.9	13.8	32.4	11.7	3.0	100
Belgium	41857.9	17.2	7.4	5.4	20.0	14.7	22.8	10.0	2.5	100
United Kingdom	38470.7	16.0	1.6	4.5	18.3	12.6	33.0	11.7	2.3	100
USA	32468.2	9.7	0.8	4.3	18.3	9.6	42.5	12.5	2.3	100
Netherlands	24888.3	15.4	5.2	12.8	17.5	9.9	24.0	12.1	3.1	100
China	18716.1	9.6	5.0	0.4	11.9	7.2	57.1	6.0	2.8	100
Switzerland	18229.4	10.0	1.8	9.9	13.5	11.0	23.6	25.0	5.1	100
Russian Federation	10352.9	7.3	1.5	0.1	24.7	7.1	48.2	9.3	1.8	100

Imports Profile:

Similar to exports, machinery and transport equipment (SITC section 7) also accounted for a large share of imports: 32.8 percent in 2011 (see table 2). Other major commodity groups included mineral fuels, lubricants and related materials (SITC section 3) and chemicals and related products, n.e.s. (SITC section 5) respectively with 16.4 percent and 13.8 percent of imports. Over the last three years, top products for imports were petroleum oils and oils obtained from bituminous minerals, crude (HS code 2709), motor cars and other motor vehicles principally designed for the transport (HS code 8703) and petroleum oils, other than crude (HS code 2710) (see table 5).

Table 5: Top 10 import commodities 2009 to 2011

(Value in million US$)

HS code	4-digit heading of Harmonized System 2007	Value (million US$) 2009	2010	2011	Unit value 2009	2010	2011	Unit	SITC code
	All Commodities	540502.3	599171.5	700851.6					
2709	Petroleum oils and oils obtained from bituminous minerals, crude	31789.7	35319.2	52125.9	*0.5*	*0.6*	*0.8*	US$/kg	333
8703	Motor cars and other motor vehicles principally designed for the transport	30481.1	31166.6	35698.9	*16.0*	15.4	18.3	thsd US$/unit	781
2710	Petroleum oils, other than crude	17664.3	23518.0	32993.4	*0.5*	*0.7*	*0.9*	US$/kg	334
2711	Petroleum gases and other gaseous hydrocarbons	17690.2	18163.8	23755.7	*0.5*	*0.4*	*0.4*	US$/kg	343
3004	Medicaments (excluding goods of heading 30.02, 30.05 or 30.06)	19609.0	19237.5	19654.6	*98.9*	*94.8*	*103.9*	US$/kg	542
8803	Parts of goods of heading 88.01 or 88.02	12124.5	12317.3	13141.8	*331.0*	*320.8*		US$/kg	792
8708	Parts and accessories of the motor vehicles of headings 87.01 to 87.05	10994.9	12105.6	13721.6	*8.0*	*7.5*	*7.9*	US$/kg	784
8802	Other aircraft (for example, helicopters, aeroplanes); spacecraft	4032.5	12096.0	14031.4	*14.9*	19.8	31.4	mln US$/unit	792
8471	Automatic data processing machines and units thereof	9132.8	9819.9	10678.9	149.8	*162.8*	172.1	US$/unit	752
8517	Electrical apparatus for line telephony or line telegraphy	8429.6	9700.1	10324.8					764

French Polynesia

Imports: CIF, by origin | **Exports: FOB, by last known destination** | **Trade System: Special**

Overview:

From 2007 to 2011, exports of French Polynesia decreased on average by 2.7 percent each year and amounted to 149.8 mln US$ (see table 1 and graph 1). During the same period, imports increased on average by 0.5 percent each year to 1.6 bln US$ in 2011 (see table 2 and graph 1). This resulted in a trade deficit of 1.5 bln US$ in 2011 (see graph 1). Deficit with Developed Europe was 632.7 mln US$ (see graph 2). Large deficits were also recorded with South-eastern Asia (-310.1 mln US$) and Developed Asia-Pacific (-186.9 mln US$). 2011 trade, especially exports, was very concentrated among a few partners (see graph 3): 4 major partners accounted for 80 percent of exports compared to 9 major partners for imports.

Graph 1: Total imports, exports and trade balance

(Bln US$ by year)

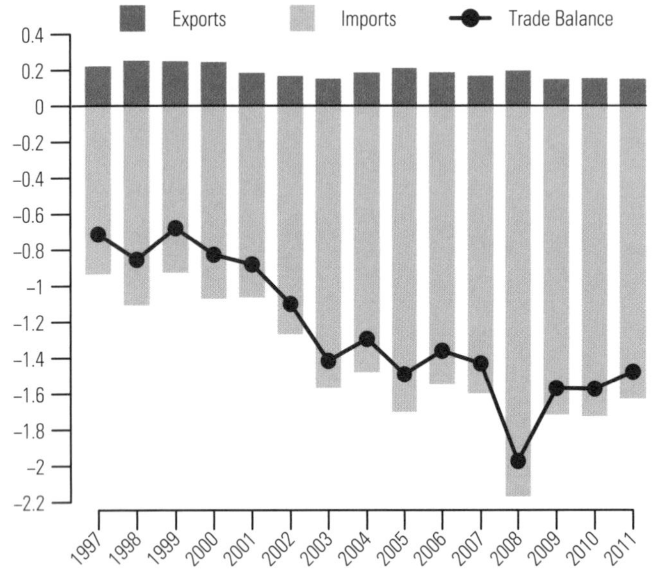

Table 1: Exports by SITC sections

(Value in million US$, growth and shares in percentage)

SITC	2011	Avg. Growth rates (%) 2007-2011	2010-2011	2011 share
Total	149.8	-2.7	-2.2	100.0
0+1	20.4	5.3	3.5	13.6
2+4	12.5	9.2	35.9	8.4
3	0.1	-12.7	-14.4	0.0
5	3.2	1.3	11.9	2.1
6	76.9	-8.0	-8.9	51.3
7	26.7	30.3	-3.3	17.8
8	8.9	-20.2	-4.8	5.9
9	1.2	327.7	97795.9	0.8

Table 2: Imports by SITC sections

(Value in million US$, growth and shares in percentage)

SITC	2011	Avg. Growth rates (%) 2007-2011	2010-2011	2011 share
Total	1627.7	0.5	-5.7	100.0
0+1	396.6	4.9	-0.5	24.4
2+4	29.3	-1.9	-4.9	1.8
3	260.4	8.2	16.1	16.0
5	168.1	2.4	-2.1	10.3
6	190.7	-2.9	-6.1	11.7
7	391.7	-4.5	-18.9	24.1
8	190.9	-2.3	-10.8	11.7
9	0.2	-31.8	-2.6	0.0

Exports Profile:

Exports were largely composed of manufactured goods classified chiefly by material (SITC section 6), mainly pearls, natural or cultured (see tables 1 and 3). On average, their exports dropped 8.0 percent each year since 2007 but still accounted for more than half of all exports (51.3 percent) (see table 1). China, Hong Kong SAR, the top market for exports, accounted for 39.8 mln US$ of exported goods (see table 4). Other major markets for exports in 2011 were Japan and France. Pearls, natural or cultured (HS code 7101), the top commodity for exports over the last three years, accounted for 50.9 percent of exports in 2011 (see table 3). Other major exported products were jams, fruit jellies, marmalades, fruit or nut pastes (HS code 2007) and other aircraft (for example, helicopters, aeroplanes); spacecraft (HS code 8802).

Table 3: Top 10 export commodities 2009 to 2011

(Value in million US$)

HS code	4-digit heading of Harmonized System 2007	Value (million US$) 2009	2010	2011	Unit value 2009	2010	2011	Unit	SITC code
	All Commodities	148.3	153.2	149.8					
7101	Pearls, natural or cultured	91.0	83.1	76.2	*5.7*	*5.1*	*5.1*	thsd US$/kg	667
2007	Jams, fruit jellies, marmalades, fruit or nut pastes	7.5	6.7	6.9	3.3	3.1	2.9	US$/kg	058
8802	Other aircraft (for example, helicopters, aeroplanes); spacecraft	6.6	0.9	9.6					792
8901	Cruise ships, excursion boats, ferry-boats, cargo ships, barges	...	15.9	...					793
1513	Coconut (copra), palm kernel or babassu oil	3.1	4.4	7.7	0.6	0.7	1.3	US$/kg	422
0302	Fish, fresh or chilled, excluding fish fillets	2.5	3.9	3.7	7.3	7.7	7.0	US$/kg	034
8411	Turbo-jets, turbo-propellers and other gas turbines	1.1	2.8	6.3					714
0508	Coral and similar materials, unworked or simply prepared	2.6	2.8	3.1	1.4	1.3	1.1	US$/kg	291
7113	Articles of jewellery and parts thereof, of precious metal	3.5	3.1	1.4	*4.6*	*2.2*	*2.6*	thsd US$/kg	897
0304	Fish fillets and other fish meat (whether or not minced)	2.8	2.1	2.9	11.3	12.0	10.1	US$/kg	034

Graph 2: Trade Balance by MDG Regions in 2011

(Mln US$)

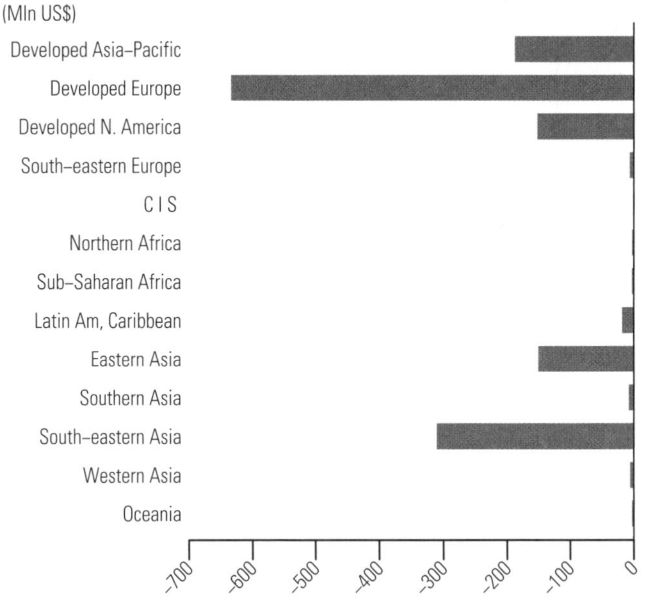

Graph 3: Partner concentration of trade in 2011

(Cumulative share by ranked partners)

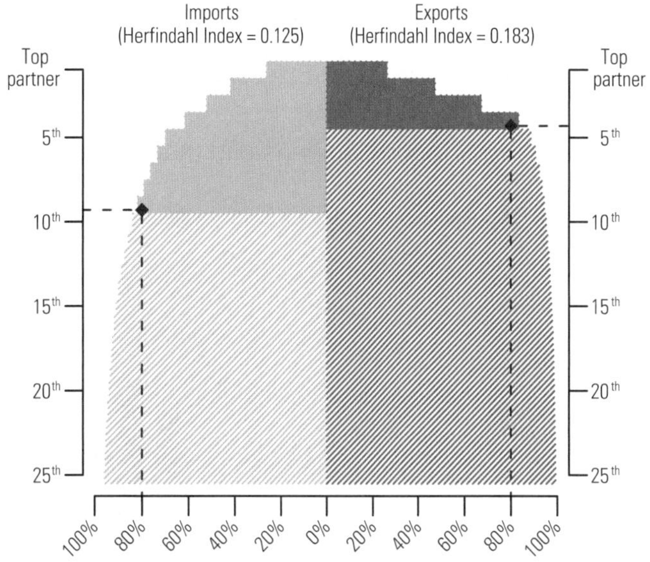

Table 4: Exports by principal countries and SITC sections in 2011

(Value in million US$, percentages of country total)

Country	Total	Shares by SITC sections (%) 0 + 1	2 + 4	3	5	6	7	8	9	Total
World	149.8	13.6	8.4	0.0	2.1	51.3	17.8	5.9	0.8	100
China, Hong Kong SAR	39.8	2.0	0.3	...	0.0	95.9	0.0	1.4	0.3	100
Japan	31.1	3.9	0.2	...	0.1	95.7	0.0	0.0	...	100
France	29.9	14.7	26.1	0.0	8.6	5.7	28.7	15.6	0.5	100
USA	24.1	45.3	0.5	0.0	0.8	16.2	26.1	7.8	3.3	100
Indonesia	7.9	0.0	1.3	...		0.0	98.7	...	...	100
China	2.9	0.5	68.6	...	3.3	24.9	1.0	1.8	...	100
New Caledonia	2.5	3.1	0.3	0.0	6.6	43.6	19.6	26.8	...	100
Guyana	1.6	0.0	0.0	...	...	...	100.0	...	...	100
New Zealand	1.5	2.7	30.6	3.1	1.1	3.7	50.9	2.1	5.7	100
Germany	1.3	92.1	0.0	0.0	...	0.1	7.3	0.6	...	100

Imports Profile:

Imports were composed of 24.4 percent of food, live animals, beverages and tobacco (SITC sections 0+1), 24.1 percent of machinery and transport equipment (SITC section 7), and 16.0 percent of mineral fuels, lubricants and related materials (SITC section 3) (see table 2). Petroleum oils, other than crude (HS code 2710), motor cars and other motor vehicles principally designed for the transport (HS code 8703) and medicaments (excluding goods of heading 30.02, 30.05 or 30.06) (HS code 3004) were the top products for imports over the last three years (see table 5).

Table 5: Top 10 import commodities 2009 to 2011

(Value in million US$)

HS code	4-digit heading of Harmonized System 2007	Value (million US$) 2009	2010	2011	Unit value 2009	2010	2011	Unit	SITC code
	All Commodities	1717.1	1725.8	1627.7					
2710	Petroleum oils, other than crude	182.9	212.0	245.8	0.6	0.7	*0.9*	US$/kg	334
8703	Motor cars and other motor vehicles principally designed for the transport	87.7	84.9	65.6	*18.0*	*18.1*		thsd US$/unit	781
3004	Medicaments (excluding goods of heading 30.02, 30.05 or 30.06)	78.2	70.6	67.9	*68.6*	*62.5*	*63.3*	US$/kg	542
0207	Meat and edible offal, of the poultry of heading 01.05	27.5	26.4	29.3	2.1	2.0	2.0	US$/kg	012
1905	Bread, pastry, cakes, biscuits and other bakers' wares	25.2	26.1	25.1	5.2	5.4	5.1	US$/kg	048
8471	Automatic data processing machines and units thereof	25.7	24.2	25.1					752
0201	Meat of bovine animals, fresh or chilled	20.4	22.3	20.7	8.0	8.7	8.6	US$/kg	011
8517	Electrical apparatus for line telephony or line telegraphy	20.8	21.4	18.7					764
0202	Meat of bovine animals, frozen	17.2	18.3	22.2	3.7	4.4	4.8	US$/kg	011
8704	Motor vehicles for the transport of goods	21.6	15.7	13.2					782

Imports: CIF, by origin | **Exports: FOB, by last known destination** | **Trade System: Special**

Overview:

After reaching a peak of 9.6 bln US$ in 2008, the value of the exports of Gabon dropped in 2009 by 44.0 percent to 5.4 bln US$ (see table 1 and graph 1). Imports also decreased in 2009 by 2.4 percent and amounted to 2.5 bln US$ (see table 2 and graph 1). The trade balance recorded a surplus of 2.9 bln US$ in 2009 (see graph 1). By MDG regions, a large surplus was recorded with Developed North America (+3.0 bln US$) (see graph 2). Significant surpluses were recorded with Eastern Asia (+0.4 bln US$) and South-eastern Asia (+0.2 bln US$). Developed Europe recorded a deficit of 0.6 bln US$. Trade, especially exports, was concentrated among a few partners: in 2009, 5 major partners accounted for 80 percent of exports compared to 11 major partners for imports (see graph 3).

Graph 1: Total imports, exports and trade balance

(Bln US$ by year)

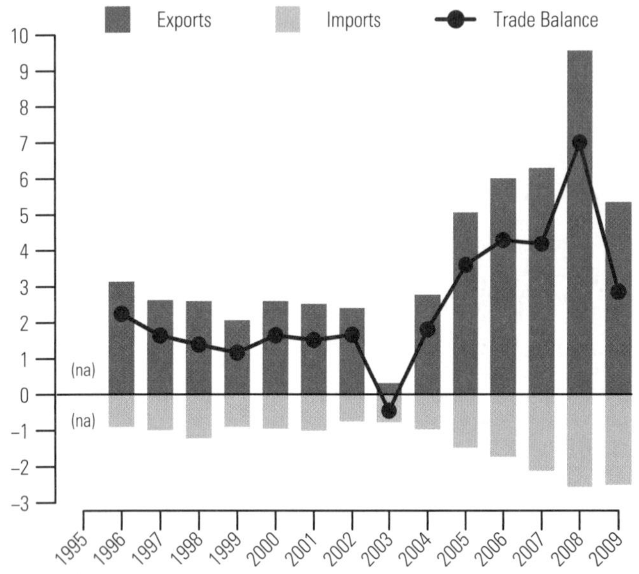

Table 1: Exports by SITC sections

(Value in million US$, growth and shares in percentage)

SITC	2009	Avg. Growth rates (%) 2005-2009	2008-2009	2009 share
Total	5356.0	1.4	-44.0	100.0
0+1	38.1	-9.4	-3.6	0.7
2+4	640.3	3.2	-13.9	12.0
3	4452.7	1.1	-47.8	83.1
5	4.2	21.0	100.9	0.1
6	121.6	1.8	-28.6	2.3
7	88.8	8.9	33.6	1.7
8	10.1	2.0	-23.5	0.2
9	0.2	49.4	224.5	0.0

Table 2: Imports by SITC sections

(Value in million US$, growth and shares in percentage)

SITC	2009	Avg. Growth rates (%) 2005-2009	2008-2009	2009 share
Total	2500.9	14.2	-2.4	100.0
0+1	407.0	12.1	-1.6	16.3
2+4	42.9	6.5	-39.6	1.7
3	182.2	36.1	50.4	7.3
5	243.7	14.6	-26.7	9.7
6	562.9	21.4	32.4	22.5
7	884.5	10.6	-11.2	35.4
8	170.7	7.8	-12.7	6.8
9	6.9	-8.3	-6.3	0.3

Exports Profile:

Exports of Gabon in 2009 were largely mineral fuels, lubricants and related materials (SITC section 3): they accounted for 83.1 percent of exported goods (see table 1). Major markets for exports included USA, China and Spain (see table 4). Exports to USA were almost exclusively mineral fuels, lubricants and related materials (SITC section 3). From 2007 to 2009, the top product for exports included petroleum oils, crude (HS code 2709), wood in the rough, whether or not stripped of bark or sapwood (HS code 4403) and manganese ores and concentrates (HS code 2602) (see table 3).

Table 3: Top 10 export commodities 2007 to 2009

(Value in million US$)

HS code	4-digit heading of Harmonized System 2002	Value (million US$) 2007	2008	2009	Unit value 2007	2008	2009	Unit	SITC code
	All Commodities	6302.0	9565.9	5356.0					
2709	Petroleum oils, crude	5179.6	8329.1	4347.2	0.5	0.8	0.4	US$/kg	333
4403	Wood in the rough, whether or not stripped of bark or sapwood	399.8	370.7	377.2	*159.4*		*911.2*	US$/m³	247
2602	Manganese ores and concentrates	223.0	206.9	157.5	0.1	0.1	0.1	US$/kg	287
4408	Sheets for veneering	154.7	138.1	98.6	1.3	1.4	1.2	US$/kg	634
2710	Petroleum oils, other than crude	75.8	200.0	105.4	0.4	0.6	0.4	US$/kg	334
4407	Wood sawn or chipped lengthwise, sliced or peeled	95.2	101.6	64.3	*0.6*	*0.8*	*1.1*	thsd US$/m³	248
4001	Natural rubber, balata, gutta-percha, guayule, chicle	27.6	55.4	28.2	2.1	3.0	0.1	US$/kg	231
8802	Other aircraft (for example, helicopters, aeroplanes); spacecraft	37.9	37.4	...					792
2403	Other manufactured tobacco and tobacco substitutes	13.2	17.2	22.3	14.7	16.8	16.6	US$/kg	122
8481	Taps, cocks, valves and similar appliances for pipes, boiler shells	0.3	0.2	45.0	0.0	0.1	1.4	thsd US$/kg	747

Graph 2: Trade Balance by MDG Regions in 2009

(Bln US$)

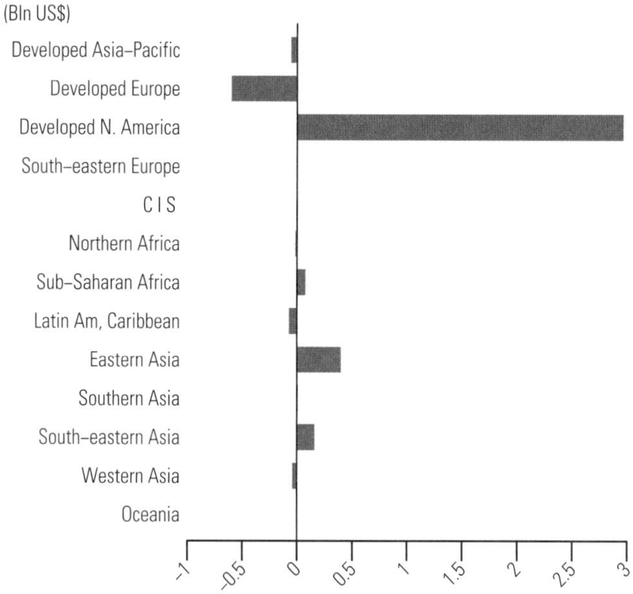

Graph 3: Partner concentration of trade in 2009

(Cumulative share by ranked partners)

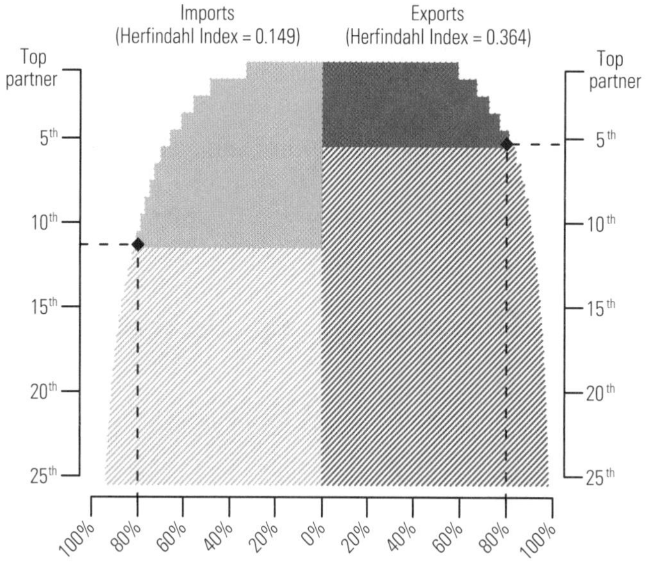

Table 4: Exports by principal countries and SITC sections in 2009

(Value in million US$, percentages of country total)

Country	Total	Shares by SITC sections (%)								
		0 + 1	2 + 4	3	5	6	7	8	9	Total
World	5356.0	0.7	12.0	83.1	0.1	2.3	1.7	0.2	0.0	100
USA	3160.4	0.0	0.3	99.5	0.0	0.0	0.1	0.0	...	100
China	427.9	0.4	84.1	15.2	...	0.2	0.0	0.0	...	100
Spain	282.1	0.0	5.6	93.5	...	0.8	0.0	0.0	...	100
France	244.9	0.1	19.4	49.9	0.0	24.3	4.8	1.4	0.1	100
Malaysia	215.3	0.0	2.1	97.8	...	...	0.0	...	...	100
Netherlands	159.3	0.0	5.6	84.3	0.0	10.0	0.0	0.0	...	100
United Kingdom	112.4	0.0	0.3	96.9	0.0	0.2	2.5	0.2	0.0	100
Rep. of Korea	86.1	0.0	7.4	92.6	...	...	...	...	...	100
Congo	82.4	23.6	2.2	3.8	2.5	2.1	63.9	1.9	...	100
South Africa	60.1	0.0	15.6	79.4	0.1	1.9	3.0	0.0	...	100

Imports Profile:

In 2009, imports of Gabon were composed of 35.4 percent of machinery and transport equipment (SITC section 7), 22.5 percent of manufactured goods classified chiefly by material (SITC section 6) and 16.3 percent of food, live animals, beverages and tobacco (SITC sections 0+1) (see table 2). From 2007 to 2009, top imported products included petroleum oils, other than crude (HS code 2710), tubes, pipes and hollow profiles, seamless, of iron (other than cast iron) (HS code 7304) and medicaments (excluding goods of heading 30.02, 30.05 or 30.06) (HS code 3004) (see table 5).

Table 5: Top 10 import commodities 2007 to 2009

(Value in million US$)

HS code	4-digit heading of Harmonized System 2002	Value (million US$)			Unit value				SITC code
		2007	2008	2009	2007	2008	2009	Unit	
	All Commodities	2110.2	2563.1	2500.9					
2710	Petroleum oils, other than crude	80.9	104.6	158.7	0.7	0.8	0.7	US$/kg	334
7304	Tubes, pipes and hollow profiles, seamless, of iron (other than cast iron)	114.9	62.2	140.4	1.1	2.3	1.8	US$/kg	679
3004	Medicaments (excluding goods of heading 30.02, 30.05 or 30.06)	63.3	174.2	68.3	27.9	73.8	29.0	US$/kg	542
8703	Motor cars and other motor vehicles principally designed for the transport	82.0	91.7	83.9	*17.3*		*20.1*	thsd US$/unit	781
8481	Taps, cocks, valves and similar appliances for pipes, boiler shells	41.1	107.3	61.6	0.6	9.7	14.2	US$/kg	747
0207	Meat and edible offal, of the poultry of heading 01.05	55.2	70.1	57.6	1.2	1.5	1.2	US$/kg	012
1006	Rice	40.0	72.2	40.8	0.6	1.1	0.8	US$/kg	042
8431	Parts suitable for use principally with the machinery of headings 84.25	44.9	41.0	65.5	14.8	19.8	16.5	US$/kg	723
7308	Structures (excluding prefabricated buildings of heading 94.06)	22.4	17.5	95.9	3.1	3.1	9.8	US$/kg	691
8704	Motor vehicles for the transport of goods	49.1	42.5	36.3		*33.9*		thsd US$/unit	782

Gambia

Imports: CIF, by origin | **Exports: FOB, by last known destination** | **Trade System: General**

Overview:

After a big drop of 47.0 percent in 2010, the value of exports of Gambia bounced back in 2011 by 170.8 percent to reach its peak of 94.7 mln US$(see table 1 and graph 1). Imports also showed an increase of 20.6 percent in 2011 and amounted to 343.7 mln US$ (see table 2 and graph 1). This resulted in a trade deficit of 249.0 mln US$ (see graph 1). By MDG regions, trade was in deficit with most of the regions (see graph 2). The largest deficits were recorded with Developed Europe (-83.0 mln US$), Latin America and the Caribbean (-34.9 mln US$) and Eastern Asia (-31.2 mln US$). Compared to imports, exports were concentrated among partners: in 2011, 4 major partners accounted for 80 percent of exports compared to 16 major partners for imports (see graph 3). See footnote*.

Graph 1: Total imports, exports and trade balance

(Mln US$ by year)

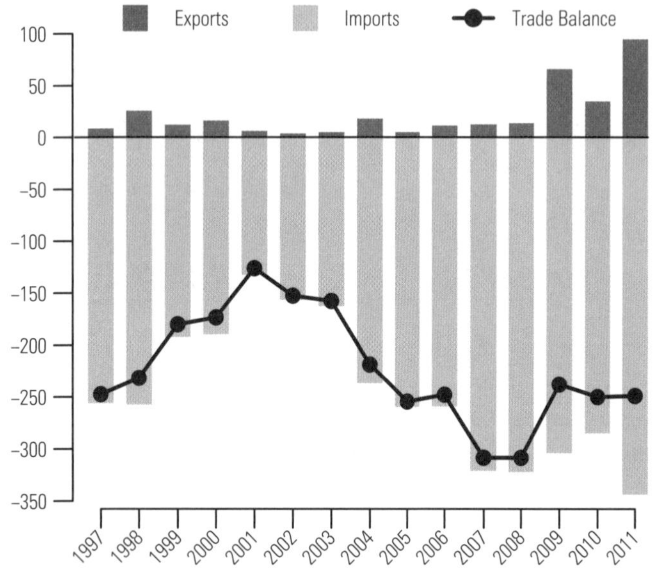

Table 1: Exports by SITC sections

(Value in million US$, growth and shares in percentage)

SITC	2011	Avg. Growth rates (%) 2007-2011	2010-2011	2011 share
Total	94.7	65.9	170.8	100.0
0+1	25.9	43.2	98.0	27.3
2+4	12.6	26.6	-29.9	13.3
3	0.7	...	436.6	0.8
5	1.3	57.7	406.6	1.3
6	44.7	259.5	9695.5	47.2
7	2.8	37.8	121.1	3.0
8	6.8	135.8	297.4	7.1
9	0.0	...	-81.0	0.0

Exports Profile:

Manufactured goods classified chiefly by material (SITC section 6) increased by 9695.5 percent in 2011 and accounted for 47.2 percent of exported goods (see table 1). Other major commodity groups included food, live animals, beverages and tobacco (SITC sections 0+1) and inedible crude materials (except fuels), animal and vegetable oils, fats and waxes (SITC sections 2+4) respectively with 27.3 and 13.3 percent. Top markets for exports in 2011 included Senegal, Guinea and Mali (see table 4). From 2009 to 2011, top exported products included woven fabric of artificial filament, monofilament yarn (HS code 5408), ground-nut oil, fractions, not chemically modified (HS code 1508) and ground-nuts, not roasted or otherwise cooked (HS code 1202) (see table 3).

Table 2: Imports by SITC sections

(Value in million US$, growth and shares in percentage)

SITC	2011	Avg. Growth rates (%) 2007-2011	2010-2011	2011 share
Total	343.7	1.7	20.6	100.0
0+1	92.9	3.4	4.7	27.0
2+4	21.0	-5.3	48.3	6.1
3	75.7	8.7	29.7	22.0
5	19.1	4.4	126.0	5.6
6	51.9	7.1	42.1	15.1
7	59.4	-7.2	-5.5	17.3
8	23.8	-0.2	48.8	6.9
9	0.0	28.1	...	0.0

Table 3: Top 10 export commodities 2009 to 2011

(Value in million US$)

HS code	4-digit heading of Harmonized System 1996	Value (million US$) 2009	2010	2011	Unit value 2009	2010	2011	Unit	SITC code
	All Commodities	66.0	35.0	94.7					
5408	Woven fabric of artificial filament, monofilament yarn	15.9	...	41.3	3.4		4.5	US$/kg	653
1508	Ground-nut oil, fractions, not chemically modified	6.6	6.7	...	1.1	1.1		US$/kg	421
1202	Ground-nuts, not roasted or otherwise cooked	3.1	7.1	1.9	0.8	0.8	0.8	US$/kg	222
0801	Coconuts, Brazil nuts and cashew nuts, fresh or dried	3.3	3.3	2.1	0.1	0.2	0.1	US$/kg	057
0303	Fish, frozen, whole	3.3	3.6	1.7	*1.2*	1.0	1.5	US$/kg	034
2505	Natural sand except sand for mineral extraction	3.5	2.7	0.8	0.1	0.1	0.1	US$/kg	273
3923	Containers, bobbins and packages, of plastics	1.4	1.2	3.9		2.3	3.1	US$/kg	893
6309	Worn clothing and other worn articles	0.6	0.5	5.2	0.7	0.7	3.3	US$/kg	269
0402	Milk and cream, concentrated or sweetened	3.7	0.1	1.6	*9.7*	2.8	0.1	US$/kg	022
0902	Tea	3.2	0.1	1.6		2.7	2.9	US$/kg	074

*2009 exports include re-exports previously not available

Graph 2: Trade Balance by MDG Regions in 2011

(Mln US$)

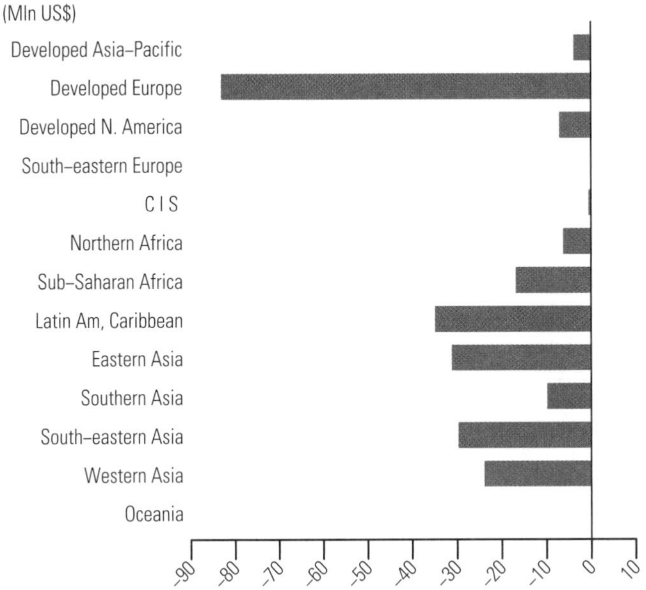

Graph 3: Partner concentration of trade in 2011

(Cumulative share by ranked partners)

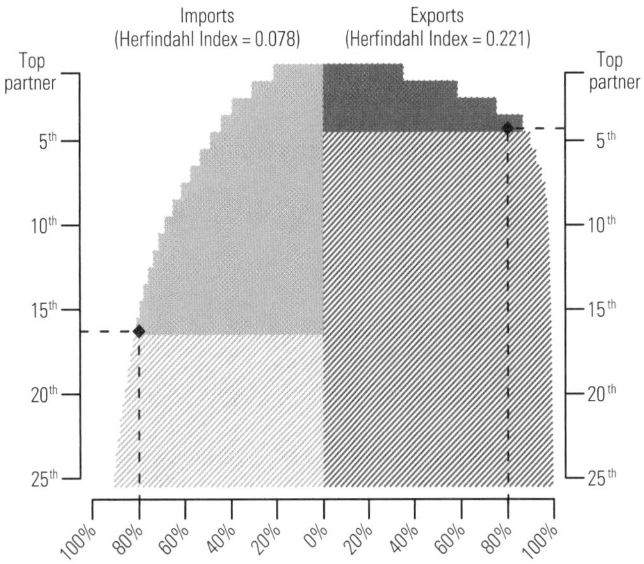

Table 4: Exports by principal countries and SITC sections in 2011

(Value in million US$, percentages of country total)

Country	Total	Shares by SITC sections (%)								
		0 + 1	2 + 4	3	5	6	7	8	9	Total
World	94.7	27.3	13.3	0.8	1.3	47.2	3.0	7.1	0.0	100
Senegal	33.4	35.0	8.6	0.2	1.4	36.4	3.0	15.5	...	100
Guinea	21.9	22.7	2.3	...	1.8	69.6	1.2	2.3	...	100
Mali	15.8	6.6	2.0	3.5	0.2	84.7	2.5	0.5	...	100
Guinea-Bissau	10.7	25.2	32.8	0.8	3.0	23.7	6.9	7.5	...	100
China	3.0	6.2	55.3	...	...	37.9	0.5	...	...	100
India	2.4	92.7	6.1	...	...	0.9	0.3	...	...	100
United Kingdom	2.2	4.4	86.7	...	...	0.5	1.5	6.8	...	100
France	1.5	0.0	99.1	...	...	...	0.6	0.3	...	100
Netherlands	0.7	89.5	0.8	...	0.1	2.1	0.1	3.2	4.2	100
Spain	0.5	99.8	0.0	...	...	...	...	0.2	...	100

Imports Profile:

In 2011, imports were composed of 27.0 percent of food, live animals, beverages and tobacco (SITC sections 0+1), 22.0 percent of mineral fuels, lubricants and related materials (SITC section 3) and 17.3 percent of machinery and transport equipment (SITC section 7) (see table 2). From 2009 to 2011, top imported goods were oils petroleum, bituminous, distillates, except crude (HS code 2710), rice (HS code 1006) and motor vehicles for transport of persons (except buses) (HS code 8703) (see table 5).

Table 5: Top 10 import commodities 2009 to 2011

(Value in million US$)

HS code	4-digit heading of Harmonized System 1996	Value (million US$)			Unit value				SITC code
		2009	2010	2011	2009	2010	2011	Unit	
	All Commodities	303.9	285.0	343.7					
2710	Oils petroleum, bituminous, distillates, except crude	47.0	57.9	75.5	*0.6*	0.8	1.0	US$/kg	334
1006	Rice	30.5	21.4	30.6	*0.2*	0.3	0.7	US$/kg	042
8703	Motor vehicles for transport of persons (except buses)	21.5	18.8	16.3	2.3		*1.8*	thsd US$/unit	781
1515	Fixed veg fat, oil, fractions, not chemically modified	21.6	11.1	17.3	*0.6*	0.5	0.4	US$/kg	422
1701	Solid cane or beet sugar and chemically pure sucrose	12.4	22.4	13.7	*0.1*	0.2	0.2	US$/kg	061
2523	Cement (portland, aluminous, slag or hydraulic)	14.2	9.1	10.7	*0.1*	0.1	0.4	US$/kg	661
1101	Wheat or meslin flour	6.8	11.9	11.0	0.1	0.2	0.2	US$/kg	046
5408	Woven fabric of artificial filament, monofilament yarn	8.5	7.1	9.5	*0.6*	0.6	0.5	US$/kg	653
8503	Parts for electric motors and generators	0.2	16.7	2.1	*17.0*	26.9	94.6	US$/kg	716
3004	Medicaments, therapeutic, prophylactic use, in dosage	7.6	2.0	5.5	*11.7*	4.8	6.5	US$/kg	542

Georgia

Imports: CIF, by purchase | **Exports: FOB, by last known destination** | **Trade System: General**

Overview:

From 2006 to 2010, Georgia's exports increased on average by 14.1 percent each year and reached 1.6 bln US$ in 2010 (see table 1 and graph 1). During the same period, imports increased on average by 8.5 percent each year and amounted to 5.1 bln US$ in 2010 (see table 2 and graph 1). This recorded a trade deficit of 3.5 bln US$ (see graph 1). This deficit reflected largely trade with three MDG regions: Developed Europe (-1.0 bln US$), Commonwealth of Independent States (-0.9 bln US$) and Western Asia (-0.8 bln US$) (see graph 2). In 2010, imports were more diversified across partners than exports: 18 major partners accounted for 80 percent of imports (compared to 14 major partners for exports) (see graph 3).

Graph 1: Total imports, exports and trade balance

(Bln US$ by year)

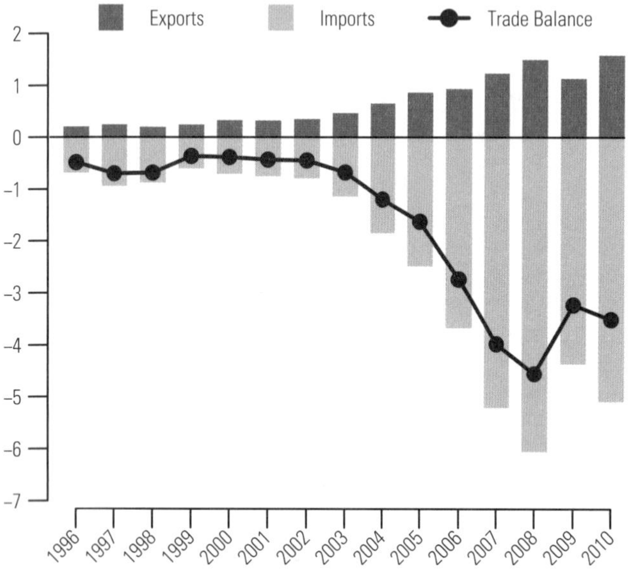

Table 1: Exports by SITC sections

(Value in million US$, growth and shares in percentage)

SITC	2010	Avg. Growth rates (%) 2006-2010	2009-2010	2010 share
Total	1 583.3	14.1	39.7	100.0
0+1	305.9	7.1	4.7	19.3
2+4	267.2	4.7	33.6	16.9
3	69.7	24.0	57.2	4.4
5	127.1	13.0	20.7	8.0
6	343.1	25.5	89.4	21.7
7	334.0	21.1	120.5	21.1
8	47.0	11.0	23.4	3.0
9	89.2	16.2	-26.2	5.6

Table 2: Imports by SITC sections

(Value in million US$, growth and shares in percentage)

SITC	2010	Avg. Growth rates (%) 2006-2010	2009-2010	2010 share
Total	5 095.2	8.5	16.7	100.0
0+1	869.3	11.1	25.0	17.1
2+4	185.9	31.4	49.6	3.6
3	929.9	6.9	20.9	18.2
5	532.0	12.7	14.4	10.4
6	806.4	13.9	37.6	15.8
7	1 233.7	3.9	19.1	24.2
8	520.0	9.1	34.5	10.2
9	18.1	-33.3	-94.1	0.4

Exports Profile:

Exports of manufactured goods classified chiefly by material (SITC section 6) increased on average by 25.5 percent since 2006 and represented 21.7 percent of total exports in 2010 (see table 1). Other major commodity groups for exports were machinery and transport equipment (SITC section 7), and food, live animals, beverages and tobacco (SITC sections 0+1): they represented respectively 21.1 and 19.3 percent of exports. In 2010, exports of machinery and transport equipment (SITC section 7) increased by 120.5 percent while exports of food, live animals, beverages and tobacco (SITC sections 0+1) increased by 4.7 percent. Azerbaijan, Turkey and USA were the three largest markets for exports (see table 4). From 2008 to 2010, top exported goods were ferro-alloys (HS code 7202), motor cars and other motor vehicles principally designed for the transport (HS code 8703) and gold (including gold plated with platinum) (HS code 7108) (see table 3).

Table 3: Top 10 export commodities 2008 to 2010

(Value in million US$)

HS code	4-digit heading of Harmonized System 2002	Value (million US$) 2008	2009	2010	Unit value 2008	2009	2010	Unit	SITC code
	All Commodities	1 497.5	1 133.6	1 583.3					
7202	Ferro-alloys	267.2	130.1	263.9	2.1	0.9	1.3	US$/kg	671
8703	Motor cars and other motor vehicles principally designed for the transport	113.3	78.5	227.3		24.7	9.8	thsd US$/unit	781
7108	Gold (including gold plated with platinum)	100.1	116.2	85.8	12.7	17.9	16.2	thsd US$/kg	971
7204	Ferrous waste and scrap; remelting scrap ingots of iron or steel	128.5	63.6	109.4	0.3	0.2	0.3	US$/kg	282
2603	Copper ores and concentrates	118.3	61.9	70.7	1.2	0.8	1.4	US$/kg	283
3102	Mineral or chemical fertilisers, nitrogenous	105.5	60.2	72.1	0.3	0.2	0.2	US$/kg	562
2208	Alcohol of a strength by volume of less than 80 % vol	59.0	54.0	54.6	4.4	3.6	*5.0*	US$/litre	112
0802	Other nuts, fresh or dried	31.7	70.0	64.0	3.9	3.9	4.2	US$/kg	057
2204	Wine of fresh grapes, including fortified wines	36.9	32.0	39.3	*3.5*	3.3	3.2	US$/litre	112
2523	Portland cement, aluminous cement, slag cement	80.1	22.4	5.6	0.1	0.1	0.1	US$/kg	661

Graph 2: Trade Balance by MDG Regions in 2010

(Bln US$)

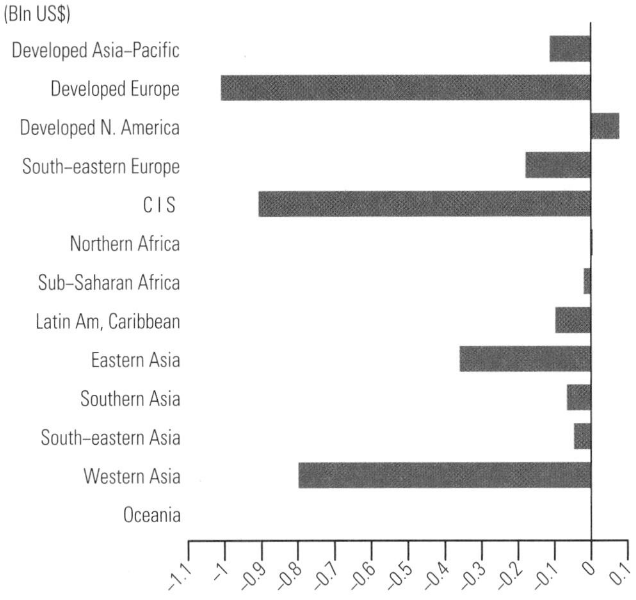

Graph 3: Partner concentration of trade in 2010

(Cumulative share by ranked partners)

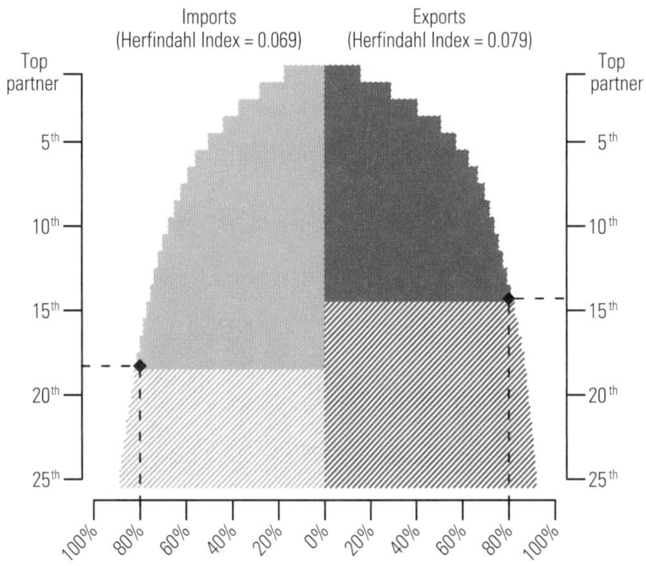

Table 4: Exports by principal countries and SITC sections in 2010

(Value in million US$, percentages of country total)

Country	Total	Shares by SITC sections (%) 0+1	2+4	3	5	6	7	8	9	Total
World	1583.3	19.3	16.9	4.4	8.0	21.7	21.1	3.0	5.6	100
Azerbaijan	244.0	20.1	0.6	0.4	5.9	14.2	57.7	1.0	...	100
Turkey	216.0	4.7	48.3	4.8	8.2	13.4	9.7	10.9	...	100
USA	180.5	2.0	2.4	1.3	2.4	91.0	0.9	0.0	...	100
Armenia	160.2	18.0	1.7	2.2	12.9	11.1	52.5	1.5	...	100
Ukraine	103.3	75.2	0.6	0.3	0.8	15.2	7.7	0.3	...	100
Canada	86.7	0.6	0.0	...	0.3	0.0	0.1	0.0	99.0	100
Bulgaria	62.1	0.5	81.6	0.8	16.6	0.1	0.3	0.1	...	100
Kazakhstan	47.9	32.9	0.1	0.2	2.4	1.4	54.0	8.9	...	100
Russian Federation	33.9	1.4	7.2	66.7	2.2	15.8	6.5	0.2	...	100
Spain	32.6	6.1	67.5	...	24.8	0.1	1.3	0.2	...	100

Imports Profile:

Georgia's imports were composed of 24.2 percent of machinery and transport equipment (SITC section 7), 18.2 percent of mineral fuels, lubricants and related materials (SITC section 3) and 17.1 percent of food, live animals, beverages and tobacco (SITC sections 0+1) (see table 2). From 2008 to 2010, top products for imports were petroleum oils, other than crude (HS code 2710), motor cars and other motor vehicles principally designed for the transport (HS code 8703) and medicaments (excluding goods of heading 30.02, 30.05 or 30.06) (HS code 3004) (see table 5).

Table 5: Top 10 import commodities 2008 to 2010

(Value in million US$)

HS code	4-digit heading of Harmonized System 2002	Value (million US$) 2008	2009	2010	Unit value 2008	2009	2010	Unit	SITC code
	All Commodities	6055.7	4365.7	5095.2					
2710	Petroleum oils, other than crude	762.5	555.3	694.6	0.9	0.6	0.7	US$/kg	334
8703	Motor cars and other motor vehicles principally designed for the transport	463.3	254.7	309.6		6.7	6.6	thsd US$/unit	781
3004	Medicaments (excluding goods of heading 30.02, 30.05 or 30.06)	189.9	175.2	188.4	*38.4*	37.5	37.2	US$/kg	542
2711	Petroleum gases and other gaseous hydrocarbons	204.7	151.9	133.6	0.2	0.2	0.2	US$/kg	343
1001	Wheat and meslin	108.9	104.1	171.7	0.3	0.2	0.2	US$/kg	041
9999	Commodities not specified according to kind	34.6	303.9	17.6					931
8525	Transmission apparatus for radio-telephony, radio-broadcasting	148.2	45.4	70.3					764
7214	Other bars and rods of iron or non-alloy steel	111.1	35.1	56.4	0.8	0.5	0.6	US$/kg	676
2402	Cigars, cheroots, cigarillos and cigarettes	60.0	57.4	79.0	16.2	16.4	14.8	US$/kg	122
8471	Automatic data processing machines and units thereof	92.8	41.8	61.4		51.6		US$/unit	752

Germany

Imports: CIF, by origin	Exports: FOB, by last known destination	Trade System: Special

Overview:

From 2007 to 2011, despite a sharp decline of 23.1 percent in 2009, Germany's exports increased on average by 2.8 percent each year and amounted to 1,482.2 bln US$ in 2011, surpassing its previous peak of 1,466.1 bln US$ in 2008 (see table 1 and graph 1). Imports showed a similar development with an increase of 18.1 percent and amounted to 1,260.3 bln US$ in 2011 (see table 2 and graph 1). This resulted in a trade surplus of 221.9 bln US$ (see graph 1). By MDG regions, surpluses were recorded with Developed Europe (+186.2 bln US$), Western Asia (+39.6 bln US$) and Developed North America (+37.4 bln US$) (see graph 2). Trade deficits were recorded with Eastern Asia (-13.6 bln US$), South-eastern Asia (-8.7 bln US$) and Developed Asia-Pacific (-5.4 bln US$). In 2011, trade was highly diversified across partners: respectively 22 and 21 major partners accounted for 80 percent of respectively exports and imports (see graph 3).

Graph 1: Total imports, exports and trade balance

(Bln US$ by year)

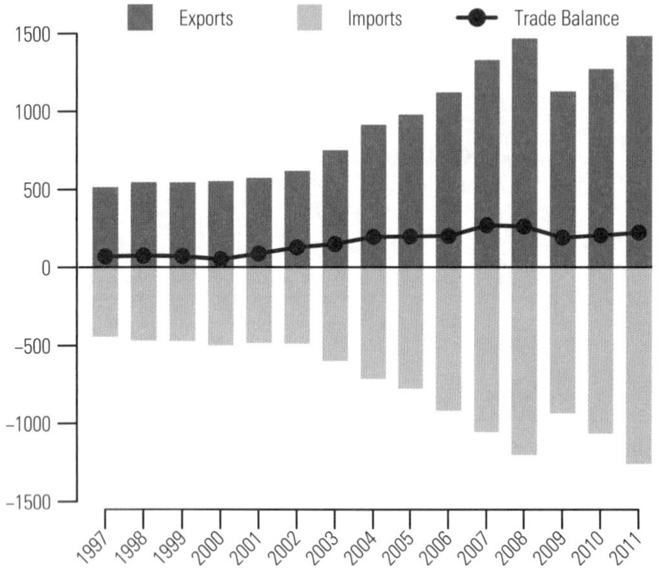

Exports Profile:

In 2011, nearly half of Germany's exports (47.0 percent) were composed of machinery and transport equipment (SITC section 7) (see table 1). Other major commodity groups included chemicals and related products, n.e.s. (SITC section 5) and manufactured goods classified chiefly by material (SITC section 6) respectively with 14.4 and 13.4 percent of exports. France, USA and Netherlands were the top three destinations for Germany's exports (see table 4). Over the last three years, major products for exports included motor cars and other motor vehicles principally designed for the transport (HS code 8703), medicaments (excluding goods of heading 30.02, 30.05 or 30.06) (HS code 3004) and parts and accessories of the motor vehicles of headings 87.01 to 87.05 (HS code 8708) (see table 3).

Table 1: Exports by SITC sections

(Value in million US$, growth and shares in percentage)

SITC	2011	Avg. Growth rates (%) 2007-2011	2010-2011	2011 share
Total	1 482 202.3	2.8	16.6	100.0
0+1	75 568.0	8.2	20.1	5.1
2+4	33 157.9	6.5	28.0	2.2
3	33 312.5	2.4	39.3	2.2
5	213 341.4	3.8	13.8	14.4
6	198 932.9	1.4	20.4	13.4
7	696 181.6	2.5	19.0	47.0
8	151 588.2	4.7	17.5	10.2
9	80 119.8	-2.9	-12.8	5.4

Table 2: Imports by SITC sections

(Value in million US$, growth and shares in percentage)

SITC	2011	Avg. Growth rates (%) 2007-2011	2010-2011	2011 share
Total	1 260 297.5	4.4	18.1	100.0
0+1	82 026.6	6.9	19.8	6.5
2+4	58 188.2	8.3	30.4	4.6
3	166 614.9	10.5	36.6	13.2
5	157 988.3	5.9	17.6	12.5
6	170 953.3	2.8	27.1	13.6
7	416 198.2	4.0	14.9	33.0
8	140 156.9	6.6	19.8	11.1
9	68 171.2	-9.2	-18.4	5.4

Table 3: Top 10 export commodities 2009 to 2011

(Value in billion US$)

HS code	4-digit heading of Harmonized System 2007	Value (billion US$) 2009	2010	2011	Unit value 2009	2010	2011	Unit	SITC code
	All Commodities	1 127.8	1 271.1	1 482.2					
8703	Motor cars and other motor vehicles principally designed for the transport	102.4	128.7	154.3		*18.9*		thsd US$/unit	781
9999	Commodities not specified according to kind	84.0	84.8	70.2					931
3004	Medicaments (excluding goods of heading 30.02, 30.05 or 30.06)	44.3	43.9	45.9	*95.4*	*88.0*	*82.7*	US$/kg	542
8708	Parts and accessories of the motor vehicles of headings 87.01 to 87.05	33.1	43.2	53.4	*10.6*	*10.0*	10.4	US$/kg	784
8802	Other aircraft (for example, helicopters, aeroplanes); spacecraft	24.0	23.2	28.1					792
3002	Human blood; animal blood prepared for therapeutic uses	12.4	15.4	17.3	*1.1*	*1.2*	*1.1*	thsd US$/kg	541
8443	Printing machinery used for printing by means of the printing type, blocks	13.0	14.0	15.1					726
2710	Petroleum oils, other than crude	12.5	12.4	16.4	*0.6*	0.8	1.0	US$/kg	334
8409	Parts suitable for use with the engines of heading 84	9.8	12.1	15.3	*14.6*	*13.2*	*14.2*	US$/kg	713
8471	Automatic data processing machines and units thereof	11.6	12.1	12.3					752

Graph 2: Trade Balance by MDG Regions in 2011

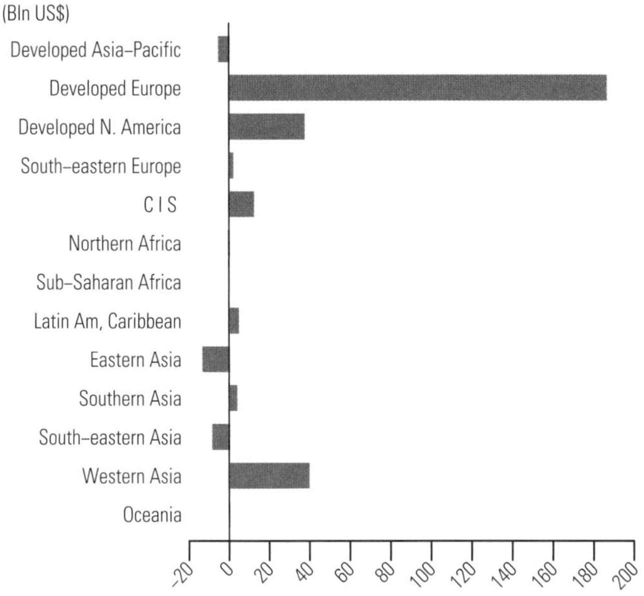

Graph 3: Partner concentration of trade in 2011

(Cumulative share by ranked partners)

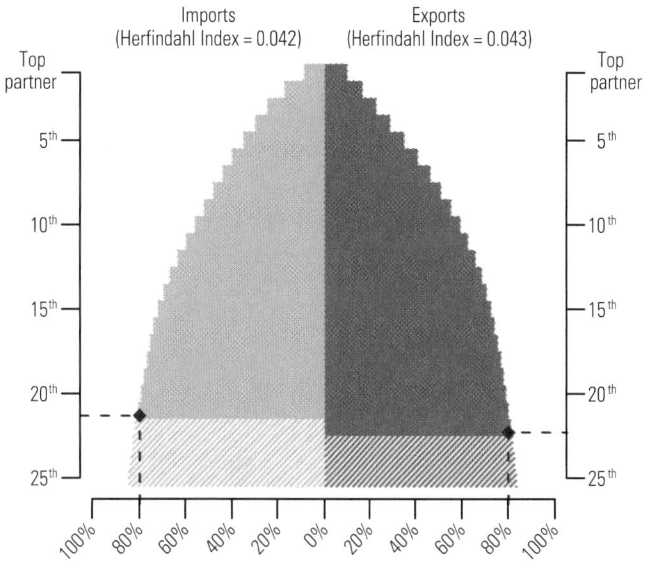

Table 4: Exports by principal countries and SITC sections in 2011

(Value in million US$, percentages of country total)

Country	Total	Shares by SITC sections (%)								
		0 + 1	2 + 4	3	5	6	7	8	9	Total
World	1 482 202.3	5.1	2.2	2.2	14.4	13.4	47.0	10.2	5.4	100
France	140 672.0	5.1	1.8	0.5	12.5	14.4	50.6	10.6	4.4	100
USA	103 075.2	1.9	1.0	0.3	14.6	10.3	59.6	10.0	2.4	100
Netherlands	93 493.2	10.7	5.0	5.0	20.4	14.2	26.5	12.3	6.0	100
China	90 496.7	0.5	2.1	0.2	7.6	7.2	72.5	7.1	2.8	100
United Kingdom	89 304.4	5.3	1.1	0.9	12.4	13.3	51.5	9.3	6.2	100
Italy	85 818.5	9.1	3.2	0.3	15.6	14.5	43.0	9.0	5.3	100
Austria	79 049.7	6.4	3.4	6.9	10.1	17.0	33.3	14.8	8.2	100
Switzerland	67 079.4	3.1	1.5	5.9	15.5	16.7	30.8	16.5	10.0	100
Belgium	64 441.9	5.5	5.4	1.4	30.7	13.0	30.1	9.4	4.5	100
Poland	60 146.4	6.5	2.6	3.8	14.6	20.9	34.2	10.3	7.1	100

Imports Profile:

In 2011, Germany's imports were composed of 33.0 percent of machinery and transport equipment (SITC section 7) and 13.6 of manufactured goods classified chiefly by material (SITC section 6) and 13.2 percent mineral fuels, lubricants and related materials (SITC section 3) (see table 2). From 2009 to 2011, top products for imports were petroleum oils and oils obtained from bituminous minerals, crude (HS code 2709), motor cars and other motor vehicles principally designed for the transport (HS code 8703) and petroleum gases and other gaseous hydrocarbons (HS code 2711) (see table 5).

Table 5: Top 10 import commodities 2009 to 2011

(Value in billion US$)

HS code	4-digit heading of Harmonized System 2007	Value (billion US$)			Unit value				SITC code
		2009	2010	2011	2009	2010	2011	Unit	
	All Commodities	938.4	1 066.8	1 260.3					
9999	Commodities not specified according to kind	82.0	77.2	59.2					931
2709	Petroleum oils and oils obtained from bituminous minerals, crude	43.4	52.6	70.9	0.4	0.6	0.8	US$/kg	333
8703	Motor cars and other motor vehicles principally designed for the transport	39.0	35.2	43.9		*16.8*		thsd US$/unit	781
2711	Petroleum gases and other gaseous hydrocarbons	34.1	32.7	45.4	0.4	0.4	0.5	US$/kg	343
8708	Parts and accessories of the motor vehicles of headings 87.01 to 87.05	22.4	27.1	33.7	*8.3*	*8.0*	*8.3*	US$/kg	784
2710	Petroleum oils, other than crude	18.0	26.0	36.0	*0.6*	0.7	*1.0*	US$/kg	334
3004	Medicaments (excluding goods of heading 30.02, 30.05 or 30.06)	20.5	21.9	27.4	*105.0*	*105.1*	*113.4*	US$/kg	542
8471	Automatic data processing machines and units thereof	17.0	20.3	20.7					752
8802	Other aircraft (for example, helicopters, aeroplanes); spacecraft	15.3	16.3	16.1					792
8541	Diodes, transistors and similar semiconductor devices	11.0	18.3	16.2					776

Ghana

Imports: CIF, by origin | **Exports: FOB, by last known destination** | **Trade System: General**

Overview:

There is a huge overall increase in Ghana's exports due to the significant trade in mineral fuels, lubricants and related materials (SITC section 3) in 2011 (see table 1 and graph 1). During this period, Ghana started exporting crude oil which also caused significant increase in overall trade. Exports in 2011 increased by 251.6 percent and amounted to 18.4 bln US$. Imports also increased by 68.5 percent to 13.6 bln US$ (see table 2 and graph 1). The trade balance recorded, for the first time, a surplus amounting to 4.8 bln US$ (see graph 1). By MDG regions, a large surplus was recorded with Sub-Saharan Africa (+8.6 bln US$) (see graph 2). Large deficits were recorded with Eastern Asia (-2.3 bln US$) and Developed North America (-1.0 bln US$). Compared to exports, imports were diversified across partners: in 2011, 18 major partners accounted for 80 percent of imports compared to 10 major partners for exports (see graph 3).

Graph 1: Total imports, exports and trade balance

(Bln US$ by year)

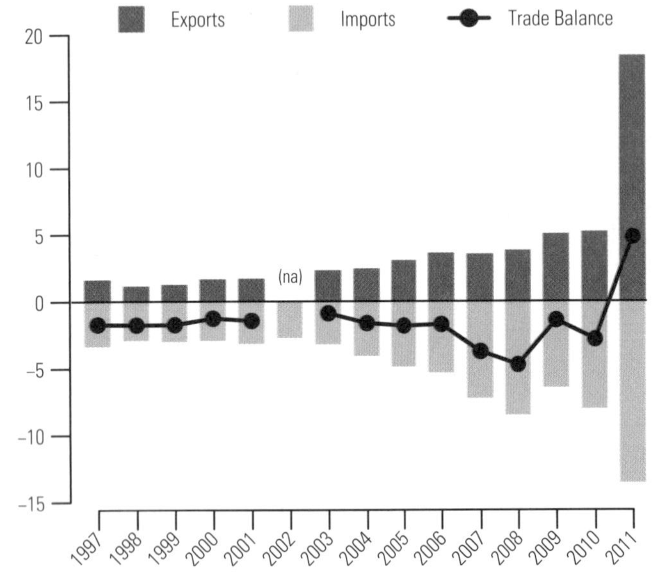

Exports Profile:

In 2011, mineral fuels, lubricants and related materials (SITC section 3) was the largest commodity group for exports and represented 39.9 percent of exported goods (see table 1). Other major commodity groups for exports included commodities and transactions not classified elsewhere (SITC section 9), food, live animals, beverages and tobacco (SITC section 0+1). Togo, South Africa and France were the three largest markets for exports in 2011(see table 4). Over the last three years, top exported products were gold (including gold plated with platinum) (HS code 7108), petroleum gases and other gaseous hydrocarbons (HS code 2711) and coco beans, whole or broken, raw or roasted (HS code 1801) (see table 3).

Table 1: Exports by SITC sections

(Value in million US$, growth and shares in percentage)

SITC	2011	Avg. Growth rates (%) 2007-2011	2010-2011	2011 share
Total	18400.6	51.1	251.6	100.0
0+1	3587.4	30.7	226.0	19.5
2+4	887.2	25.9	238.3	4.8
3	7335.2	306.7	122532.8	39.9
5	336.3	44.4	262.1	1.8
6	677.4	27.9	129.5	3.7
7	140.6	19.6	110.5	0.8
8	597.8	73.7	1367.2	3.2
9	4838.6	34.9	43.6	26.3

Table 2: Imports by SITC sections

(Value in million US$, growth and shares in percentage)

SITC	2011	Avg. Growth rates (%) 2007-2011	2010-2011	2011 share
Total	13573.3	16.9	68.5	100.0
0+1	1836.6	17.3	58.1	13.5
2+4	279.1	13.1	46.8	2.1
3	116.4	-40.1	49.0	0.9
5	1691.4	19.4	56.0	12.5
6	2294.2	15.5	25.6	16.9
7	4963.0	16.6	51.5	36.6
8	2390.9	54.6	460.1	17.6
9	1.7	-27.0	-86.2	0.0

Table 3: Top 10 export commodities 2009 to 2011

(Value in million US$)

HS code	4-digit heading of Harmonized System 2002	Value (million US$) 2009	2010	2011	Unit value 2009	2010	2011	Unit	SITC code
	All Commodities	5070.5	5233.4	18400.6					
7108	Gold (including gold plated with platinum)	2944.9	3367.9	4836.6	27.0	35.1	41.7	thsd US$/kg	971
2711	Petroleum gases and other gaseous hydrocarbons	1.0	3.4	4330.8					343
1801	Cocoa beans, whole or broken, raw or roasted	1088.8	847.4	2071.6	2.8	3.0	3.3	US$/kg	072
2709	Petroleum oils, crude	...	...	2862.0			0.7	US$/kg	333
0801	Coconuts, Brazil nuts and cashew nuts, fresh or dried	18.9	15.2	512.4	0.4	0.4	3.2	US$/kg	057
0714	Manioc, arrowroot, sweet potatoes and similar roots	7.4	4.2	422.0	0.7	0.6	19.6	US$/kg	054
3924	Tableware, kitchenware, other household articles and toilet articles	79.6	12.9	187.6	2.4	0.8	0.3	US$/kg	893
4407	Wood sawn or chipped lengthwise, sliced or peeled	70.8	65.8	127.8	*604.6*			US$/$m^3$	248
4907	Unused postage, revenue or similar stamps of current or new issue	...	...	253.9			26.0	thsd US$/kg	892
2602	Manganese ores and concentrates	46.8	77.3	107.4	65.3	56.3	62.1	US$/kg	287

Graph 2: Trade Balance by MDG Regions in 2011

(Bln US$)

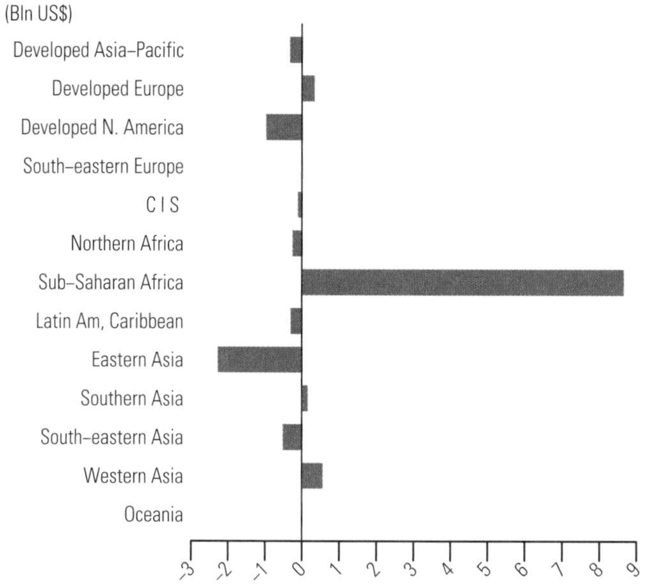

Graph 3: Partner concentration of trade in 2011

(Cumulative share by ranked partners)

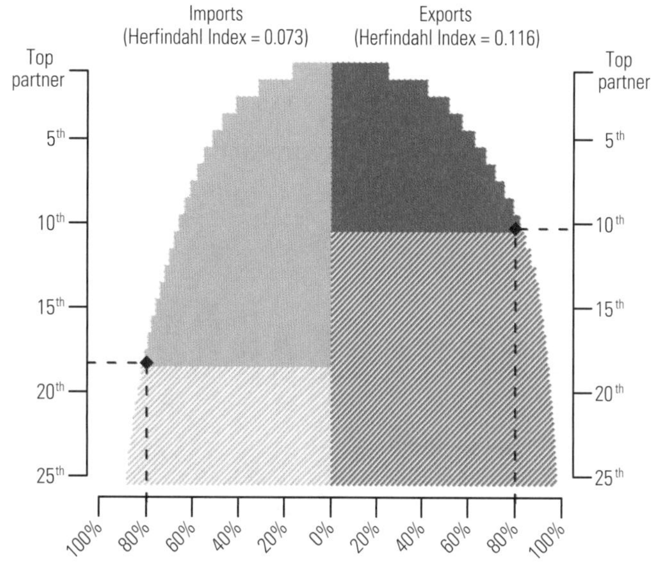

Table 4: Exports by principal countries and SITC sections in 2011

(Value in million US$, percentages of country total)

Country	Total	Shares by SITC sections (%)								
		0 + 1	2 + 4	3	5	6	7	8	9	Total
World	18400.6	19.5	4.8	39.9	1.8	3.7	0.8	3.2	26.3	100
Togo	4594.0	0.3	0.1	94.1	1.4	1.0	0.0	3.1	0.0	100
South Africa	3146.8	3.9	0.1	0.0	0.1	0.2	0.2	0.1	95.5	100
France	1722.4	6.8	0.7	92.1	0.0	0.3	0.0	0.0	...	100
Italy	1041.5	4.7	10.6	81.7	0.0	2.9	0.1	0.0	0.1	100
United Arab Emirates	993.9	0.6	1.1	0.0	0.1	1.4	1.0	0.0	95.7	100
Switzerland	865.9	0.4	0.3	...	4.9	0.0	0.1	0.0	94.4	100
India	722.2	65.7	32.3	0.0	0.0	1.9	0.1	0.0	...	100
Côte d'Ivoire	717.4	41.5	1.5	0.1	2.1	17.4	4.1	33.5	...	100
Netherlands	710.7	73.5	3.3	10.0	0.0	7.5	0.3	4.2	1.2	100
Burkina Faso	500.6	2.7	0.6	2.5	32.1	38.6	2.0	21.6	...	100

Imports Profile:

In 2011, imports were composed of 36.6 percent of machinery and transport equipment (SITC section 7), 17.6 percent of miscellaneous manufactured articles (SITC section 8) and 16.9 percent of manufactured goods classified chiefly by material (SITC section 6) (see table 2). Trade in these commodity groups increased respectively by 51.5, 460.1 and 25.6 percent in 2011. From 2009 to 2011, the three major products for imports were motor cars and other motor vehicles principally designed for the transport (HS code 8703), unused postage, revenue or similar stamps of current or new issue (HS code 4907) and motor vehicles for the transport of goods (HS code 8704) (see table 5).

Table 5: Top 10 import commodities 2009 to 2011

(Value in million US$)

HS code	4-digit heading of Harmonized System 2002	Value (million US$)			Unit value				SITC code
		2009	2010	2011	2009	2010	2011	Unit	
	All Commodities	6464.8	8057.1	13573.3					
8703	Motor cars and other motor vehicles principally designed for the transport	498.8	525.1	860.4	*19.0*	*19.4*		thsd US$/unit	781
4907	Unused postage, revenue or similar stamps of current or new issue	...	...	1758.9			5.0	thsd US$/kg	892
8704	Motor vehicles for the transport of goods	286.0	334.0	628.0					782
1006	Rice	224.6	201.4	390.6	0.6	0.6	0.7	US$/kg	042
3808	Insecticides, rodenticides, fungicides, herbicides	164.5	255.4	370.9	4.1	5.1	5.0	US$/kg	591
2523	Portland cement, aluminous cement, slag cement	167.3	209.4	308.0	0.1	0.1	0.0	US$/kg	661
8517	Electrical apparatus for line telephony or line telegraphy	26.8	213.5	278.0					764
1701	Cane or beet sugar and pure sucrose, in solid form	116.6	183.9	186.7	0.4	0.5	0.7	US$/kg	061
0303	Fish, frozen, excluding fish fillets	97.8	128.4	237.1	0.4	0.7	0.8	US$/kg	034
1001	Wheat and meslin	125.3	117.2	150.2	0.4	0.4	0.5	US$/kg	041

Greece

Imports: CIF, by origin/consignment for intra-eu | **Exports: FOB, by last known destination** | **Trade System: Special**

Overview:

From 2007 to 2011, despite a sharp decline of 21.4 percent in 2009, Greece's exports increased on average by 7.8 percent each year and amounted to 31.7 bln US$ in 2011, surpassing its previous peak of 25.5 bln US$ in 2008 (see table 1 and graph 1). During the same period imports decreased by 3.9 percent and amounted to 60.8 bln US$ in 2011 (see table 2 and graph 1). This resulted in a trade deficit of 29.1 bln US$ (see graph 1). While this deficit reflected largely by trade with Developed Europe (-17.2 bln US$), trade deficits were also recorded with Commonwealth of Independent States (-6.7 bln US$) and Eastern Asia (-4.8 bln US$) in 2011(see graph 2). Trade surpluses were recorded with South-eastern Europe (+1.7 bln US$) and Developed North America (+0.7 bln US$). In 2011, trade was highly diversified across partners: respectively 23 and 21 major partners accounted for 80 percent of respectively exports and imports (see graph 3).

Graph 1: Total imports, exports and trade balance

(Bln US$ by year)

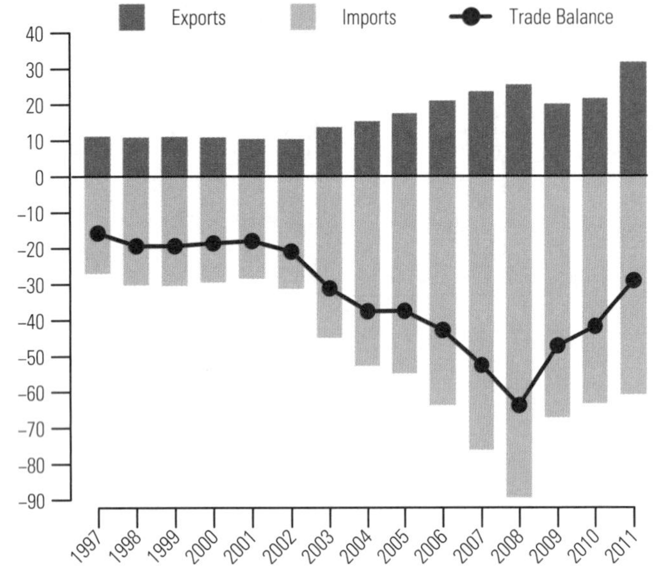

Table 1: Exports by SITC sections

(Value in million US$, growth and shares in percentage)

SITC	2011	Avg. Growth rates (%) 2007-2011	2010-2011	2011 share
Total	31711.1	7.8	47.1	100.0
0+1	5284.6	6.3	10.9	16.7
2+4	1660.5	1.9	1.3	5.2
3	9577.3	35.3	302.9	30.2
5	3261.3	0.2	4.1	10.3
6	5777.3	3.1	33.8	18.2
7	2979.3	-1.7	15.5	9.4
8	2234.8	-4.1	4.3	7.0
9	936.1	4.4	55.1	3.0

Table 2: Imports by SITC sections

(Value in million US$, growth and shares in percentage)

SITC	2011	Avg. Growth rates (%) 2007-2011	2010-2011	2011 share
Total	60832.2	-5.4	-3.9	100.0
0+1	7878.1	0.1	7.4	13.0
2+4	2357.8	-1.2	24.7	3.9
3	16698.4	9.8	12.1	27.5
5	9542.7	-2.5	-1.1	15.7
6	6727.5	-11.7	0.1	11.1
7	11234.6	-16.0	-26.7	18.5
8	6366.4	-9.5	-14.6	10.5
9	26.5	-54.2	-41.5	0.0

Exports Profile:

In 2011, exports were composed of 30.2 percent of mineral fuels, lubricants and related materials (SITC section 3), 18.2 percent of manufactured goods classified chiefly by material (SITC section 6) and 16.7 percent of food, live animals, beverages and tobacco (SITC sections 0+1) (see table 1). Major markets were Italy, Turkey and Germany (see table 4). In addition to petroleum oils, other than crude (HS code 2710), other major commodities for exports from 2009 to 2011 were medicaments (excluding goods of heading 30.02, 30.05 or 30.06) (HS code 3004) and fish, fresh or chilled, excluding fish fillets (HS code 0302) (see table 3).

Table 3: Top 10 export commodities 2009 to 2011

(Value in million US$)

HS code	4-digit heading of Harmonized System 2007	Value (million US$) 2009	2010	2011	Unit value 2009	2010	2011	Unit	SITC code
	All Commodities	20052.5	21559.7	31711.1					
2710	Petroleum oils, other than crude	1690.6	2139.4	9030.1	0.6	0.7	0.9	US$/kg	334
3004	Medicaments (excluding goods of heading 30.02, 30.05 or 30.06)	1233.8	1277.7	1139.6	90.0	74.6	42.4	US$/kg	542
9999	Commodities not specified according to kind	379.1	602.0	913.1					931
0302	Fish, fresh or chilled, excluding fish fillets	522.9	559.5	647.3	5.5	5.3	7.5	US$/kg	034
7606	Aluminium plates, sheets and strip, of a thickness exceeding 0.2 mm	335.9	451.1	782.7	3.4	3.6	4.1	US$/kg	684
5201	Cotton, not carded or combed	402.9	487.8	326.6	1.3	2.2	2.4	US$/kg	263
2008	Fruit, nuts and other edible parts of plants	338.5	357.5	409.4	1.2	1.1	1.2	US$/kg	058
7411	Copper tubes and pipes	213.3	383.9	474.2	6.3	8.4	10.0	US$/kg	682
7214	Other bars and rods of iron or non-alloy steel	183.0	255.4	526.4	0.5	0.6	0.7	US$/kg	676
2005	Other vegetables prepared or preserved	267.4	321.8	375.3	3.3	3.0	3.1	US$/kg	056

Graph 2: Trade Balance by MDG Regions in 2011

(Bln US$)

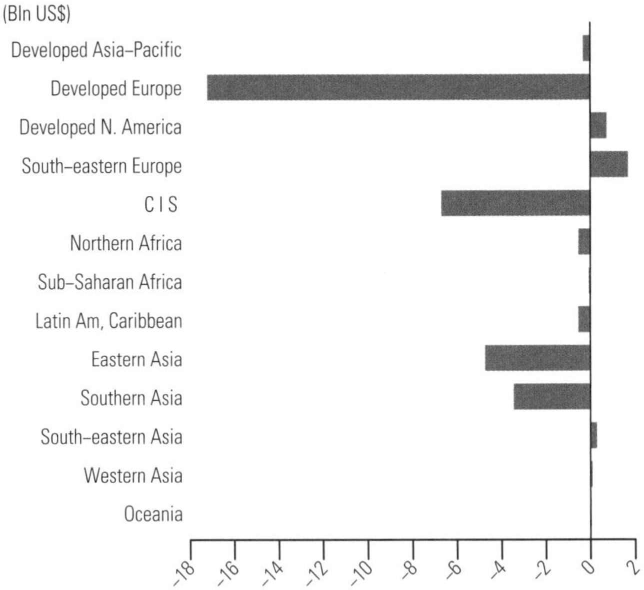

Graph 3: Partner concentration of trade in 2011

(Cumulative share by ranked partners)

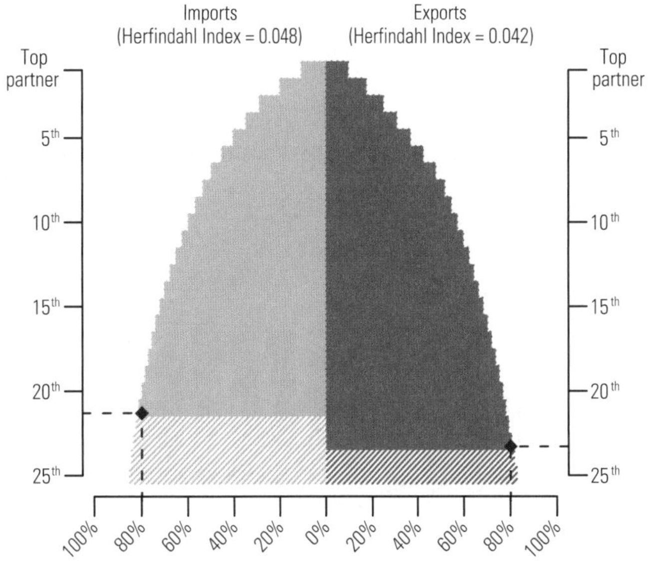

Table 4: Exports by principal countries and SITC sections in 2011

(Value in million US$, percentages of country total)

Country	Total	Shares by SITC sections (%) 0 + 1	2 + 4	3	5	6	7	8	9	Total
World	31 711.1	16.7	5.2	30.2	10.3	18.2	9.4	7.0	3.0	100
Italy	2 955.0	22.9	13.4	10.2	9.6	30.2	5.7	4.8	3.2	100
Turkey	2 485.4	3.6	6.9	62.2	10.4	9.5	5.4	1.8	0.2	100
Germany	2 453.8	30.7	3.4	0.6	18.3	19.7	12.4	13.2	1.8	100
Cyprus	1 903.1	14.7	0.8	24.0	13.6	12.3	17.4	17.2	0.1	100
Bunkers	1 890.6	0.9	0.0	81.6	1.3	1.0	5.7	0.4	9.2	100
Bulgaria	1 724.2	23.6	6.7	10.9	10.8	24.4	10.4	13.0	0.1	100
USA	1 711.6	10.7	2.4	57.2	1.3	10.6	11.1	1.9	4.6	100
United Kingdom	1 239.1	25.7	1.6	12.7	16.3	21.6	14.8	7.2	0.1	100
France	905.8	22.2	3.6	3.1	19.8	31.4	6.6	9.8	3.5	100
Romania	829.9	22.0	1.6	1.7	19.6	32.4	11.6	11.1	0.1	100

Imports Profile:

Imports were composed of 27.5 percent of mineral fuels, lubricants and related materials (SITC section 3) , 18.5 percent of machinery and transport equipment (SITC section 7), and 15.7 percent of chemicals and related products, n.e.s. (SITC section 5) (see table 2). From 2009 to 2011, the three major products for imports were petroleum oils and oils obtained from bituminous minerals, crude (HS code 2709), medicaments (excluding goods of heading 30.02, 30.05 or 30.06) (HS code3004) and cruise ships, excursion boats, ferry-boats, cargo ships, barges (HS code 8901) (see table 5).

Table 5: Top 10 import commodities 2009 to 2011

(Value in million US$)

HS code	4-digit heading of Harmonized System 2007	Value (million US$) 2009	2010	2011	Unit value 2009	2010	2011	Unit	SITC code
	All Commodities	67 192.0	63 320.7	60 832.2					
2709	Petroleum oils and oils obtained from bituminous minerals, crude	6 250.9	10 680.3	10 016.1	0.4	0.6	0.8	US$/kg	333
3004	Medicaments (excluding goods of heading 30.02, 30.05 or 30.06)	4 487.2	3 894.7	3 528.8	161.2	154.1	121.3	US$/kg	542
8901	Cruise ships, excursion boats, ferry-boats, cargo ships, barges	5 008.4	3 827.7	1 664.3					793
2710	Petroleum oils, other than crude	2 379.7	2 559.1	4 301.2	0.5	0.6	0.9	US$/kg	334
8703	Motor cars and other motor vehicles principally designed for the transport	3 206.9	1 557.8	1 160.0	11.1	*4.4*		thsd US$/unit	781
2711	Petroleum gases and other gaseous hydrocarbons	1 024.8	1 197.7	1 886.3	0.3	0.3	0.4	US$/kg	343
8517	Electrical apparatus for line telephony or line telegraphy	1 207.6	895.6	737.4					764
8471	Automatic data processing machines and units thereof	766.4	592.1	482.2	127.6			US$/unit	752
8802	Other aircraft (for example, helicopters, aeroplanes); spacecraft	619.4	830.8	138.9	13.2			mln US$/unit	792
0406	Cheese and curd	503.8	515.3	565.7	4.0	4.3	5.0	US$/kg	024

Greenland

Imports: CIF, by origin | **Exports: FOB, by last known destination** | **Trade System: General**

Overview:

From 2003 to 2007, Greenland's exports dropped on average by 2.1 percent each year to 319.8 mln US$ in 2007 (see table 1 and graph 1). During the same period, imports dropped on average by 1.6 percent each year to 432.3 mln US$ (see table 2 and graph 1). These averages reflected drops mainly in 2007. The trade balance recorded a deficit of 112.5 mln US$ and was essentially identical to the deficit in 2003 (see graph 1). By MDG regions, trade with Developed Europe recorded a deficit of 111.1 mln US$ in 2007 (see graph 2). However, trade recorded a surplus of 23.5 mln US$ with Developed North America. Trade was highly concentrated among a few partners: Denmark accounted for more than 80 percent of exported goods in 2007 (see graph 3). On the imports side, two major partners accounted for 80 percent of imports.

Graph 1: Total imports, exports and trade balance

(Mln US$ by year)

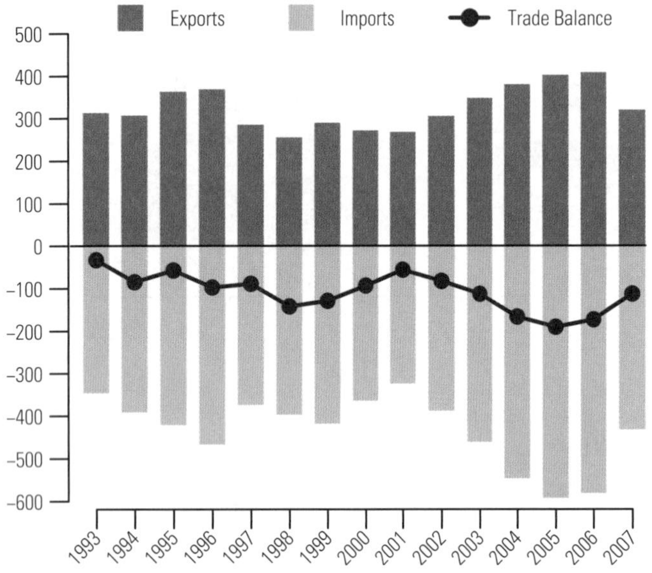

Table 1: Exports by SITC sections

(Value in million US$, growth and shares in percentage)

SITC	2007	Avg. Growth rates (%) 2003-2007	Avg. Growth rates (%) 2006-2007	2007 share
Total	319.8	-2.1	-21.7	100.0
0+1	230.8	-8.2	-33.0	72.2
2+4	38.0	88.6	26.2	11.9
3	0.0	-83.5	-99.8	0.0
5	0.0	-44.9	-53.5	0.0
6	12.8	138.8	100.8	4.0
7	3.2	-2.1	-29.5	1.0
8	2.5	-8.5	-55.9	0.8
9	32.6	27.0	89.0	10.2

Exports Profile:

Exports were driven by food, live animals, beverages and tobacco (SITC sections 0+1), largely crustaceans and fish products (see table 1). In spite of a drop by 33.0 percent in 2007, they accounted for 72.2 percent of exports. Other major commodity groups included inedible crude materials (except fuels), animal and vegetable oils, fats and waxes (SITC sections 2+4) with 11.9 percent of exports. In 2007, major partners were Denmark, Canada and Iceland (see table 4). Exports to Canada were exclusively inedible crude materials (except fuels), animal and vegetable oils, fats and waxes (SITC sections 2+4) while exports to Denmark and Iceland were mainly food, live animals, beverages and tobacco (SITC sections 0+1). From 2005 to 2007, the three major products for exports were crustaceans, molluscs and other aquatic invertebrates (HS code 1605), crustaceans, whether in shell or not (HS code 0306) and fish, frozen, excluding fish fillets (HS code 0303) (see table 3).

Table 2: Imports by SITC sections

(Value in million US$, growth and shares in percentage)

SITC	2007	Avg. Growth rates (%) 2003-2007	Avg. Growth rates (%) 2006-2007	2007 share
Total	432.3	-1.6	-25.6	100.0
0+1	91.0	-2.4	-19.9	21.1
2+4	6.0	-16.8	-9.6	1.4
3	61.5	1.4	-51.7	14.2
5	25.0	0.2	-16.9	5.8
6	59.5	-5.9	-34.4	13.8
7	111.3	-0.4	-12.8	25.8
8	73.1	0.9	-11.1	16.9
9	4.8	-2.7	69.9	1.1

Table 3: Top 10 export commodities 2005 to 2007

(Value in million US$)

HS code	4-digit heading of Harmonized System 2002	Value (million US$) 2005	2006	2007	Unit value 2005	2006	2007	Unit	SITC code
	All Commodities	402.4	408.4	319.8					
1605	Crustaceans, molluscs and other aquatic invertebrates	118.3	112.1	77.1	5.3	5.1	5.5	US$/kg	037
0306	Crustaceans, whether in shell or not	119.8	98.9	71.2	1.9	1.8	2.0	US$/kg	036
0303	Fish, frozen, excluding fish fillets	47.0	63.3	54.1	3.1	3.2	3.5	US$/kg	034
0304	Fish fillets and other fish meat (whether or not minced)	46.5	47.0	13.2	3.8	4.4	5.0	US$/kg	034
2616	Precious metal ores and concentrates	23.7	28.4	32.0	0.2	0.3	0.3	US$/kg	289
9999	Commodities not specified according to kind	14.0	17.2	32.6					931
0305	Fish, dried, salted or in brine	11.3	8.8	4.9	6.7	4.9	4.5	US$/kg	035
0307	Molluscs, whether in shell or not	5.2	7.2	4.5	14.5	16.6	14.4	US$/kg	036
0302	Fish, fresh or chilled, excluding fish fillets	2.8	6.8	5.4	*0.9*	*0.6*	0.3	US$/kg	034
4302	Tanned or dressed furskins (including heads, tails, paws)	4.8	6.2	1.4	111.2	128.9	56.2	US$/kg	613

Graph 2: Trade Balance by MDG Regions in 2007

(Mln US$)

Graph 3: Partner concentration of trade in 2007

(Cumulative share by ranked partners)

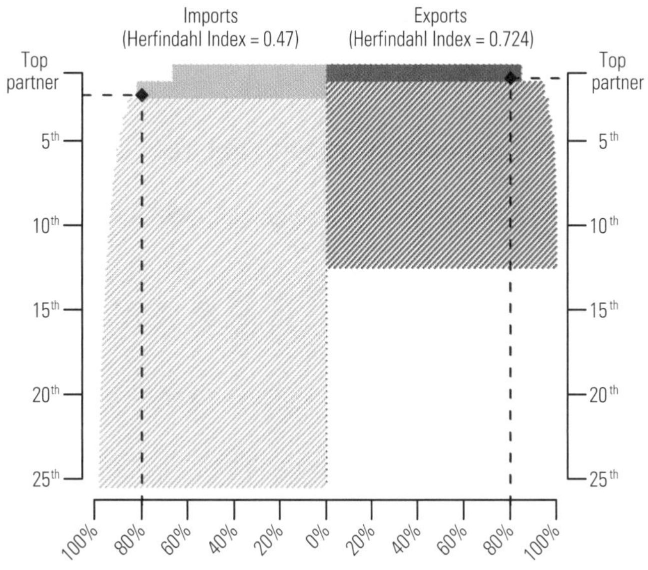

Table 4: Exports by principal countries and SITC sections in 2007

(Value in million US$, percentages of country total)

Country	Total	Shares by SITC sections (%)								
		0 + 1	2 + 4	3	5	6	7	8	9	Total
World	319.8	72.2	11.9	0.0	0.0	4.0	1.0	0.8	10.2	100
Denmark	270.0	80.8	0.3	0.0	0.0	4.7	1.2	0.9	12.1	100
Canada	32.0	0.0	100.0	...	...	...	...	...	...	100
Iceland	5.5	99.7	0.0	...	...	...	...	0.3	...	100
United Kingdom	4.5	100.0	0.0	...	...	...	...	...	...	100
Norway	3.1	0.2	99.8	...	...	...	...	...	...	100
Faeroe Isds	1.6	100.0	0.0	...	...	...	...	...	...	100
Germany	1.0	4.2	95.8	...	...	...	...	...	...	100
Netherlands	0.9	0.0	100.0	...	...	...	...	...	...	100
Spain	0.9	100.0	0.0	...	...	...	...	...	...	100
Switzerland	0.3	0.0	100.0	...	...	...	...	...	...	100

Imports Profile:

In 2007, imports were composed of 25.8 percent of machinery and transport equipment (SITC section 7), 21.1 percent of food, live animals, beverages and tobacco (SITC sections 0+1) and 16.9 percent of miscellaneous manufactured articles (SITC section 8) (see table 2). Mineral fuels, lubricants and related materials (SITC section 3) accounted for 14.2 percent of imports. In addition to petroleum oils, other than crude (HS code 2710), other major products for imports over the period from 2005 to 2007 included parts and accessories for use with machines of heading 84.69 to 84.72 (HS code 8473) and other furniture and parts thereof (HS code 9403) (see table 5).

Table 5: Top 10 import commodities 2005 to 2007

(Value in million US$)

HS code	4-digit heading of Harmonized System 2002	Value (million US$)			Unit value				SITC code
		2005	2006	2007	2005	2006	2007	Unit	
	All Commodities	592.5	581.2	432.3					
2710	Petroleum oils, other than crude	105.5	126.4	60.4	0.5	0.6	0.7	US$/kg	334
8473	Parts and accessories for use with machines of heading 84.69 to 84.72	13.5	15.5	9.8	67.6	60.4	59.9	US$/kg	759
9403	Other furniture and parts thereof	13.4	13.5	9.8					821
6810	Articles of cement, of concrete or of artificial stone	9.0	9.9	5.1	1.2	2.1	1.5	US$/kg	663
3004	Medicaments (excluding goods of heading 30.02, 30.05 or 30.06)	9.8	7.2	5.9	68.9	46.9	39.0	US$/kg	542
9406	Prefabricated buildings	4.5	8.3	9.5	3.3	3.6		US$/kg	811
1905	Bread, pastry, cakes, biscuits and other bakers' wares	8.1	7.8	5.9	4.2	4.2	4.7	US$/kg	048
8517	Electrical apparatus for line telephony or line telegraphy	4.7	5.8	10.7					764
8703	Motor cars and other motor vehicles principally designed for the transport	7.8	5.5	5.6	17.1	14.5	18.6	thsd US$/unit	781
0203	Meat of swine, fresh, chilled or frozen	6.7	6.6	5.0	4.8	4.6	4.9	US$/kg	012

Imports: CIF, by origin | **Exports: FOB, by last known destination** | **Trade System: Special**

Overview:

From 2005 to 2008, Grenada's exports increased on average by 3.4 percent each year despite a drop of 8.6 percent in 2008 and amounted to 30.5 mln US$ (see table 1 and graph 1). From 2005 to 2009, imports decreased on average by 4.2 percent each year to 281.8 mln US$ with a sharp decrease of 22.4 percent in 2009(see table 2 and graph 1). Trade recorded a deficit of 332.8 mln US$ in 2008 (see graph 1). Two MDG regions accounted for a large part of this deficit: Latin America and the Caribbean (-144.8 mln US$) and Developed North America (-116.4 mln US$) (see graph 2). In 2009, imports were relatively concentrated among a few partners: 10 major partners accounted for 80 percent of imported goods (see graph 3).

Graph 1: Total imports, exports and trade balance

(Mln US$ by year)

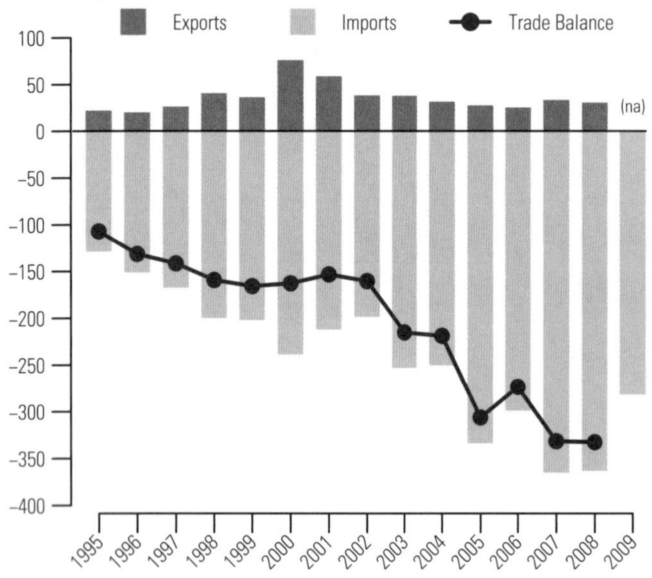

Exports Profile:

The drop of exports by 8.6 percent in 2008 was caused largely by manufactured goods: exports of machinery and transport equipment (SITC section 7) and manufactured goods classified chiefly by material (SITC section 6) dropped respectively by 37.7 and 41.8 percent and represented respectively 19.0 and 14.0 percent of exported goods (see table 1). On the contrary, exports of food, live animals, beverages and tobacco (SITC sections 0+1) increased by 23.8 percent and accounted for 58.4 percent of exports. Dominica, USA and Saint Lucia were the three largest markets for exports (see table 4). From 2006 to 2008, top exported products included wheat or meslin flour (HS code 1101), fish, frozen, whole (HS code 0303) and nutmeg, mace and cardamoms (HS code 0908) (see table 3).

Table 1: Exports by SITC sections

(Value in million US$, growth and shares in percentage)

SITC	2008	Avg. Growth rates (%) 2005-2008	2007-2008	2008 share
Total	30.5	3.4	-8.6	100.0
0+1	17.8	0.2	23.8	58.4
2+4	0.1	47.4	154.7	0.5
3	0.0	27.3	-84.1	0.0
5	0.9	-10.6	-10.9	2.8
6	4.3	9.4	-41.8	14.0
7	5.8	11.7	-37.7	19.0
8	1.6	9.3	32.1	5.3

Table 2: Imports by SITC sections

(Value in million US$, growth and shares in percentage)

SITC	2009	Avg. Growth rates (%) 2005-2009	2008-2009	2009 share
Total	281.8	-4.2	-22.4	100.0
0+1	66.0	5.1	-10.6	23.4
2+4	8.6	-21.2	-25.0	3.1
3	40.9	14.3	-41.8	14.5
5	25.8	-1.4	-8.0	9.1
6	50.0	-13.2	-22.5	17.7
7	57.3	-7.5	-25.7	20.3
8	33.3	-4.5	-12.7	11.8
9	0.0	-26.5	682.5	0.0

Table 3: Top 10 export commodities 2006 to 2008

(Value in million US$)

HS code	4-digit heading of Harmonized System 1996	Value (million US$) 2006	2007	2008	Unit value 2006	2007	2008	Unit	SITC code
	All Commodities	25.4	33.4	30.5					
1101	Wheat or meslin flour	4.1	4.4	7.5	0.5	0.6	0.8	US$/kg	046
0303	Fish, frozen, whole	3.0	3.3	2.6	8.3	9.2	7.8	US$/kg	034
0908	Nutmeg, mace and cardamoms	2.8	2.8	2.6	4.2	4.6	7.5	US$/kg	075
4818	Household, sanitary, hospital paper articles, clothing	2.2	2.5	3.0	1.8	1.9	2.3	US$/kg	642
8525	Radio and TV transmitters, television cameras	0.3	6.8	0.1					764
2309	Animal feed preparations, nes	1.8	1.5	1.5	0.3	0.4	0.5	US$/kg	081
6306	Textile tarpaulin, sail, awning, tent, camping goods	...	3.9	0.0		70.0	22.2	US$/kg	658
1801	Cocoa beans, whole or broken, raw or roasted	0.3	0.9	2.3	3.5	4.0	6.8	US$/kg	072
3210	Paints and varnishes nes, water pigments for leather	0.7	0.8	0.8	2.3	2.2	2.4	US$/kg	533
7210	Flat-rolled iron/steel, >600mm, clad, plated or coated	1.0	0.5	0.7	1.6	1.7	1.7	US$/kg	674

Graph 2: Trade Balance by MDG Regions in 2008

(Mln US$)

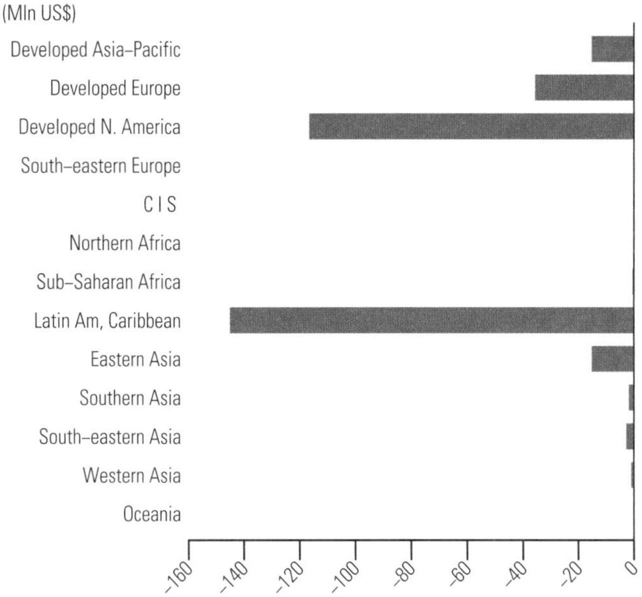

Graph 3: Partner concentration of trade in 2009

(Cumulative share by ranked partners)

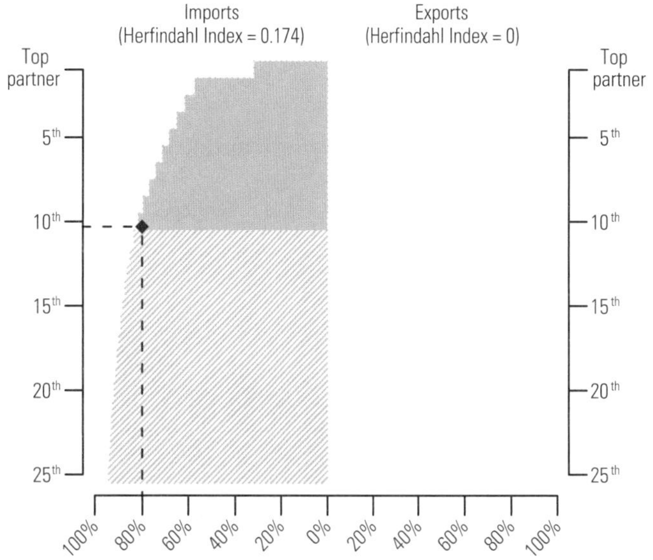

Table 4: Exports by principal countries and SITC sections in 2008

(Value in million US$, percentages of country total)

Country	Total	Shares by SITC sections (%)								
		0 + 1	2 + 4	3	5	6	7	8	9	Total
World	30.5	58.4	0.5	0.0	2.8	14.0	19.0	5.3	...	100
Dominica	5.0	69.6	0.0	...	1.1	11.7	17.6	0.1	...	100
USA	5.0	62.8	0.1	...	0.3	3.0	24.8	9.0	...	100
Saint Lucia	3.4	73.4	0.0	...	9.4	15.2	1.9	0.1	...	100
Barbados	2.9	38.4	0.0	...	0.2	36.8	1.1	23.5	...	100
Saint Kitts and Nevis	2.6	89.9	1.7	...	0.1	8.3	...	0.0	...	100
Germany	1.8	30.1	0.0	0.3	...	...	69.2	0.5	...	100
Japan	1.1	0.0	0.0	...	...	0.2	95.3	4.5	...	100
Belgium	1.0	100.0	0.0	...	...	...	...	...	...	100
Antigua and Barbuda	1.0	65.0	0.0	...	0.1	33.5	0.1	1.2	...	100
Netherlands	1.0	63.6	0.0	...	...	2.0	30.7	3.7	...	100

Imports Profile:

In 2009, imports of food, live animals, beverages and tobacco (SITC sections 0+1) dropped by 10.6 percent and represented 23.4 percent of imports. Machinery and transport equipment (SITC section 7) and manufactured goods classified chiefly by material (SITC section 6) dropped respectively by 25.7 and 22.5 percent, representing respectively 20.3 and 17.7 percent of imports (see table 2). From 2007 to 2009, top imported products were oils petroleum, bituminous, distillates, except crude (HS code 2710), motor vehicles for transport of persons (except buses) (HS code 8703) and meat, edible offal of domestic poultry (HS code 0207) (see table 5).

Table 5: Top 10 import commodities 2007 to 2009

(Value in million US$)

HS code	4-digit heading of Harmonized System 1996	Value (million US$)			Unit value				SITC code
		2007	2008	2009	2007	2008	2009	Unit	
	All Commodities	365.1	363.3	281.8					
2710	Oils petroleum, bituminous, distillates, except crude	58.3	67.7	35.4	0.7	0.7	0.6	US$/kg	334
8703	Motor vehicles for transport of persons (except buses)	10.8	10.8	7.8	7.6	2.2	0.7	thsd US$/unit	781
0207	Meat, edible offal of domestic poultry	8.5	9.0	8.9	1.5	1.8	1.7	US$/kg	012
2523	Cement (portland, aluminous, slag or hydraulic)	9.2	9.1	7.4	0.1	0.1	0.1	US$/kg	661
3004	Medicaments, therapeutic, prophylactic use, in dosage	7.1	6.6	6.5	38.0	27.7	31.6	US$/kg	542
8471	Automatic data processing machines (computers)	6.6	6.4	5.1	356.0	71.9	165.4	US$/unit	752
8525	Radio and TV transmitters, television cameras	11.3	3.0	2.2					764
4901	Printed reading books, brochures, leaflets etc	8.1	4.0	4.1	21.4	13.7	13.4	US$/kg	892
0402	Milk and cream, concentrated or sweetened	4.7	5.9	4.9	2.4	2.2	2.6	US$/kg	022
7214	Iron/steel bar, only forged hot-rolled drawn, extruded	4.8	5.3	2.9	0.9	1.2	0.9	US$/kg	676

Guatemala

Imports: CIF, by origin | **Exports: FOB, by last known destination** | **Trade System: General**

Overview:

In 2011, Guatemala's exports increased by 20.1 percent and amounted to 10.2 bln US$ (see table 1 and graph 1). During the same period, imports increased on average by 5.2 percent each year to reach 16.6 bln US$ in 2011 (see table 2 and graph 1). The trade balance registered a deficit of 6.4 bln US$ in 2011 compared to 4.3 bln US$ deficit in 2009 (see graph 1). Deficits with Developed North America, Eastern Asia and Latin America and the Caribbean amounted respectively to 2.2 bln, 1.6 bln and 1.4 bln US$ in 2011 (see graph 2). Exports were relatively more concentrated among partners: 10 major partners accounted for 80 percent of exports and 12 major partners accounted for 80 percent of imports (see graph 3).

Graph 1: Total imports, exports and trade balance

(Bln US$ by year)

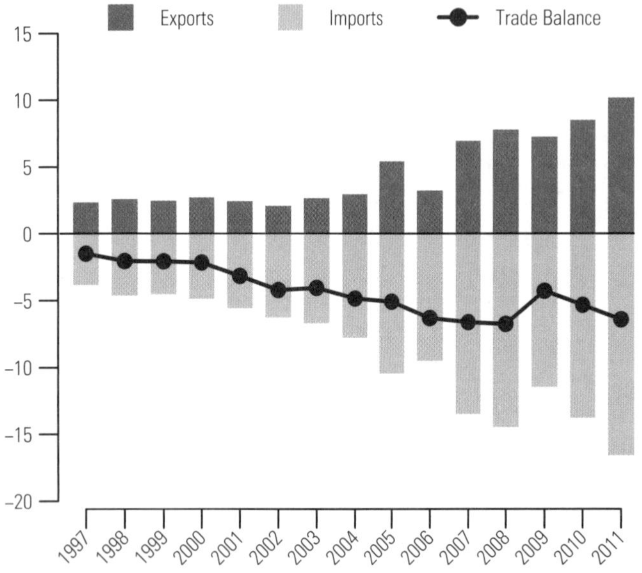

Table 1: Exports by SITC sections

(Value in million US$, growth and shares in percentage)

SITC	2011	Avg. Growth rates (%) 2007-2011	2010-2011	2011 share
Total	10161.0	10.2	20.1	100.0
0+1	3773.9	11.8	13.2	37.1
2+4	1844.1	28.9	63.8	18.1
3	516.0	10.3	35.0	5.1
5	1079.5	9.8	11.8	10.6
6	1027.0	7.6	20.8	10.1
7	261.1	3.4	-7.4	2.6
8	1628.7	-1.3	7.4	16.0
9	30.8	50.2	425.5	0.3

Table 2: Imports by SITC sections

(Value in million US$, growth and shares in percentage)

SITC	2011	Avg. Growth rates (%) 2007-2011	2010-2011	2011 share
Total	16610.8	5.2	20.1	100.0
0+1	1940.4	9.7	19.7	11.7
2+4	562.6	8.7	25.3	3.4
3	3310.0	7.9	32.4	19.9
5	2810.4	8.0	16.7	16.9
6	3193.3	3.3	17.9	19.2
7	3550.5	1.9	17.7	21.4
8	1226.3	1.5	10.0	7.4
9	17.2	-13.3	23.2	0.1

Exports Profile:

In 2011, Guatemala's exports were composed of 37.1 percent of food, live animals, beverages and tobacco (SITC sections 0+1), 18.1 percent of inedible crude materials (except fuels), animal and vegetable oils, fats and waxes (SITC sections 2+4) and 16.0 percent of miscellaneous manufactured articles (SITC section 8) (see table 1). Major destinations in 2011 were USA, El Salvador and Honduras (see table 4). Over the last three years, top exported products included coffee, whether or not roasted or decaffeinated (HS code 0901), cane or beet sugar and chemically pure sucrose, in solid form (HS code 1701) and precious metal ores and concentrates (HS code 2616) (see table 3).

Table 3: Top 10 export commodities 2009 to 2011

(Value in million US$)

HS code	4-digit heading of Harmonized System 2007	Value (million US$) 2009	2010	2011	Unit value 2009	2010	2011	Unit	SITC code
	All Commodities	7208.6	8460.2	10161.0					
0901	Coffee, whether or not roasted or decaffeinated	582.5	714.3	1063.9	2.5	3.0	4.1	US$/kg	071
1701	Cane or beet sugar and chemically pure sucrose, in solid form	507.7	725.2	647.8	0.3	0.4	0.5	US$/kg	061
2616	Precious metal ores and concentrates	335.5	499.7	909.3	2.1	2.2	2.9	thsd US$/kg	289
6106	Women's or girls' blouses, shirts and shirt-blouses, knitted or crocheted	468.4	518.4	445.4					844
0803	Bananas, including plantains, fresh or dried	441.8	385.4	476.3	0.3	0.3	0.3	US$/kg	057
0908	Nutmeg, mace and cardamoms	304.0	308.1	249.1	12.8	13.9	12.0	US$/kg	075
4001	Natural rubber, balata, gutta-percha, guayule, chicle	136.2	236.8	396.5	1.5	2.6	3.8	US$/kg	231
2709	Petroleum oils and oils obtained from bituminous minerals, crude	191.7	227.8	335.5	0.3	0.4	0.6	US$/kg	333
6105	Men's or boys' shirts, knitted or crocheted	160.1	186.5	252.5					843
3004	Medicaments (excluding goods of heading 30.02, 30.05 or 30.06)	157.2	172.0	202.5	26.4	31.3	*27.8*	US$/kg	542

Graph 2: Trade Balance by MDG Regions in 2011

(Bln US$)

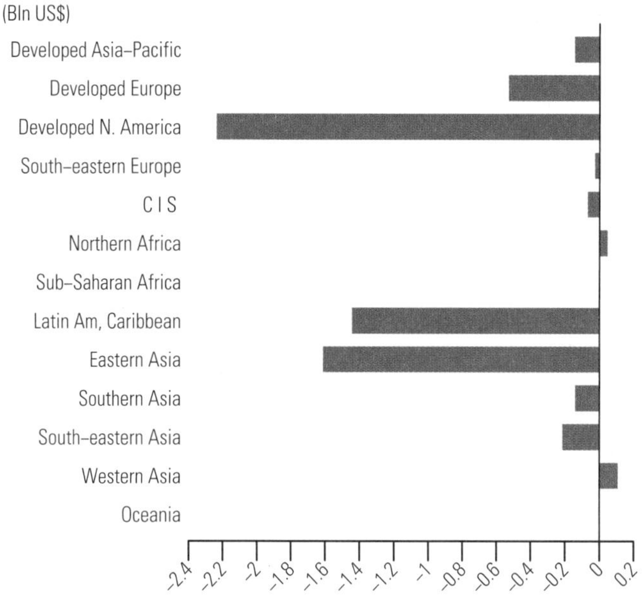

Graph 3: Partner concentration of trade in 2011

(Cumulative share by ranked partners)

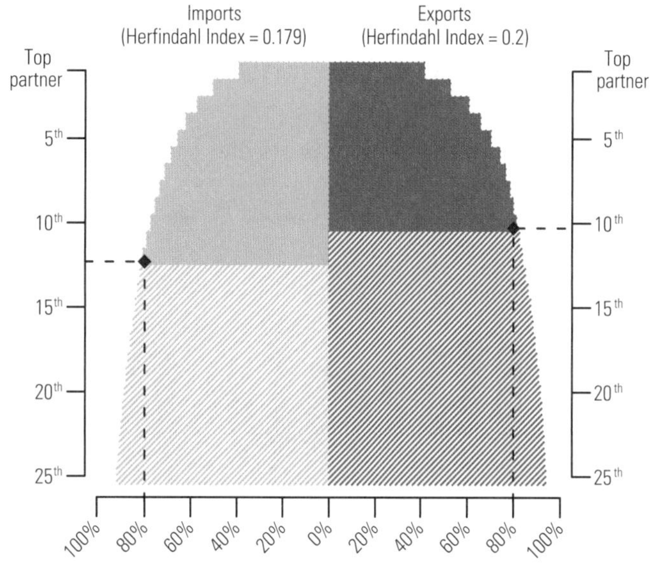

Table 4: Exports by principal countries and SITC sections in 2011

(Value in million US$, percentages of country total)

Country	Total	Shares by SITC sections (%)								
		0 + 1	2 + 4	3	5	6	7	8	9	Total
World	10161.0	37.1	18.1	5.1	10.6	10.1	2.6	16.0	0.3	100
USA	4224.8	33.6	25.1	8.0	1.0	2.2	0.5	29.0	0.5	100
El Salvador	1125.9	22.9	10.1	7.7	21.2	25.2	4.4	8.4	0.0	100
Honduras	813.7	22.3	2.7	5.4	25.6	28.0	6.4	9.6	0.0	100
Mexico	510.8	17.1	58.8	0.0	3.3	13.2	2.0	5.3	0.3	100
Nicaragua	458.9	16.7	4.9	3.9	29.1	27.9	7.3	10.3	...	100
Costa Rica	403.5	18.8	9.4	0.0	30.6	24.9	5.1	11.1	...	100
Panama	247.5	14.4	10.2	4.8	45.2	13.1	5.2	7.1	...	100
Japan	187.5	93.5	5.5	...	0.1	0.1	0.0	0.8	0.1	100
Canada	150.5	88.8	2.6	...	0.2	0.9	0.2	7.2	0.1	100
Germany	136.5	91.0	4.0	0.0	0.9	0.1	2.4	0.9	0.6	100

Imports Profile:

In 2011, imports were composed of 21.4 percent of machinery and transport equipment (SITC section 7), 19.9 percent of mineral fuels, lubricants and related materials (SITC section 3) and 19.2 percent of manufactured goods classified chiefly by material (SITC section 6) (see table 2). Over the last three years, top imported products were petroleum oils, other than crude (HS code 2710), electrical apparatus for line telephony or line telegraphy (HS code 8517) and medicaments (excluding goods of heading 30.02, 30.05 or 30.06) (HS code 3004) (see table 5).

Table 5: Top 10 import commodities 2009 to 2011

(Value in million US$)

HS code	4-digit heading of Harmonized System 2007	Value (million US$)			Unit value				SITC code
		2009	2010	2011	2009	2010	2011	Unit	
	All Commodities	11521.4	13830.3	16610.8					
2710	Petroleum oils, other than crude	1990.6	2110.1	2795.5	0.6		*1.0*	US$/kg	334
8517	Electrical apparatus for line telephony or line telegraphy	279.5	456.5	456.9					764
3004	Medicaments (excluding goods of heading 30.02, 30.05 or 30.06)	346.9	351.2	398.6	35.6	*32.5*	*31.7*	US$/kg	542
8703	Motor cars and other motor vehicles principally designed for the transport	249.8	308.5	368.9		*19.6*		thsd US$/unit	781
2711	Petroleum gases and other gaseous hydrocarbons	165.5	247.5	305.3	0.6	0.8	0.9	US$/kg	343
5205	Cotton yarn (other than sewing thread), containing 85 % or more	188.3	234.0	245.4	2.9	*3.4*	4.6	US$/kg	651
8704	Motor vehicles for the transport of goods	157.3	235.5	249.3					782
1005	Maize (corn)	151.7	149.4	234.8	0.2	0.2	0.3	US$/kg	044
6006	Other knitted or crocheted fabrics	179.3	170.5	173.8	8.2	*8.9*	10.5	US$/kg	655
8471	Automatic data processing machines and units thereof	133.3	154.8	200.2					752

Guinea

Imports: CIF, by origin	Exports: FOB, by last known destination	Trade System: Special

Overview:

From 2004 to 2008, Guinea's exports increased on average by 22.8 percent each year and amounted to 1.4 bln US$ in 2008 (see table 1 and graph 1). During the same period, imports increased on average by 17.7 percent each year to 1.8 bln US$ (see table 2 and graph 1). This resulted in a trade deficit of 404.9 mln US$ in 2008 (see graph 1). Eastern Asia, Developed Asia-Pacific and Sub-Saharan Africa recorded deficits amounting respectively to 119.6, 119.0 and 112.7 mln US$ (see graph 2). Trade with Commonwealth of Independent States showed a surplus of 174.1 mln US$. By partners, imports were more diversified than exports: 16 major partners accounted for 80 percent of imports compared to 7 major partners for exports (see graph 3).

Graph 1: Total imports, exports and trade balance

(Bln US$ by year)

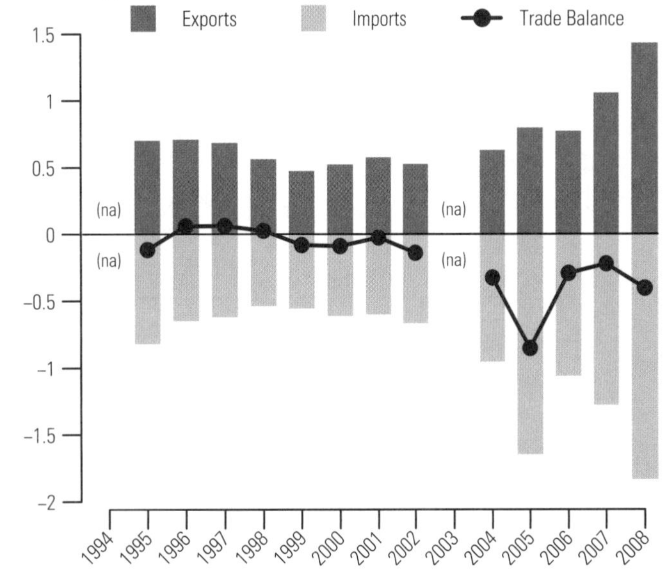

Exports Profile:

In 2008, exports were composed of 54.9 percent of inedible crude materials (except fuels), animal and vegetable oils, fats and waxes (SITC sections 2+4) and 32.0 percent of commodities and transactions not classified elsewhere (SITC section 9) (see table 1). Major markets were France, Switzerland and Russian Federation (see table 4). Exports to the Russian Federation were almost exclusively inedible crude materials (except fuels), animal and vegetable oils, fats and waxes (SITC sections 2+4). In addition to aluminium ores and concentrates (HS code 2606), other major commodities for exports from 2006 to 2008 were gold (including gold plated with platinum) (HS code 7108) and artificial corundum, whether or not chemically defined (HS code 2818) (see table 3).

Table 1: Exports by SITC sections

(Value in million US$, growth and shares in percentage)

SITC	2008	Avg. Growth rates (%) 2004-2008	2007-2008	2008 share
Total	1 430.5	22.8	35.1	100.0
0+1	23.9	8.4	-30.4	1.7
2+4	785.3	12.1	-0.9	54.9
3	14.7	72.0	60.8	1.0
5	6.2	-49.4	-50.8	0.4
6	11.8	14.7	697.1	0.8
7	11.2	13.5	73.8	0.8
8	119.5	226.6	453.9	8.4
9	458.0	219.9	152.7	32.0

Table 2: Imports by SITC sections

(Value in million US$, growth and shares in percentage)

SITC	2008	Avg. Growth rates (%) 2004-2008	2007-2008	2008 share
Total	1 835.5	17.7	43.2	100.0
0+1	225.4	7.6	12.5	12.3
2+4	26.0	0.3	15.6	1.4
3	605.0	26.5	80.9	33.0
5	136.3	12.2	55.4	7.4
6	233.3	8.1	50.5	12.7
7	538.6	26.3	26.1	29.3
8	70.9	8.2	30.7	3.9
9	0.0	-71.5	414.9	0.0

Table 3: Top 10 export commodities 2006 to 2008

(Value in million US$)

HS code	4-digit heading of Harmonized System 2002	Value (million US$) 2006	2007	2008	Unit value 2006	2007	2008	Unit	SITC code
	All Commodities	770.5	1 059.0	1 430.5					
2606	Aluminium ores and concentrates	429.9	719.3	573.0	32.6	34.0	5.3	US$/kg	285
7108	Gold (including gold plated with platinum)	11.3	181.2	458.0	14.4			thsd US$/kg	971
2818	Artificial corundum, whether or not chemically defined	...	68.3	166.9		228.0	6.5	US$/kg	285
9999	Commodities not specified according to kind	195.8	...	...					931
4907	Unused postage, revenue or similar stamps of current or new issue	0.0	18.8	112.7	0.0	35.7	67.4	thsd US$/kg	892
1801	Cocoa beans, whole or broken, raw or roasted	47.3	10.3	5.5	2.6	0.8	0.5	US$/kg	072
4001	Natural rubber, balata, gutta-percha, guayule, chicle	11.3	12.9	22.3	1.7	1.7	2.2	US$/kg	231
0901	Coffee, whether or not roasted or decaffeinated	19.1	15.7	4.0	0.9	0.6	0.5	US$/kg	071
4407	Wood sawn or chipped lengthwise, sliced or peeled	14.6	0.1	15.1		*565.6*	*608.6*	US$/m³	248
2710	Petroleum oils, other than crude	2.4	9.1	14.3	1.7	0.6	0.4	US$/kg	334

Graph 2: Trade Balance by MDG Regions in 2008

(Mln US$)

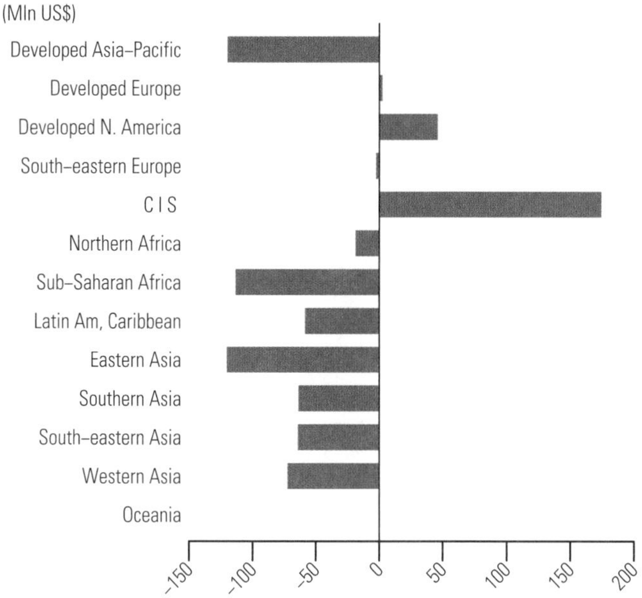

Graph 3: Partner concentration of trade in 2008

(Cumulative share by ranked partners)

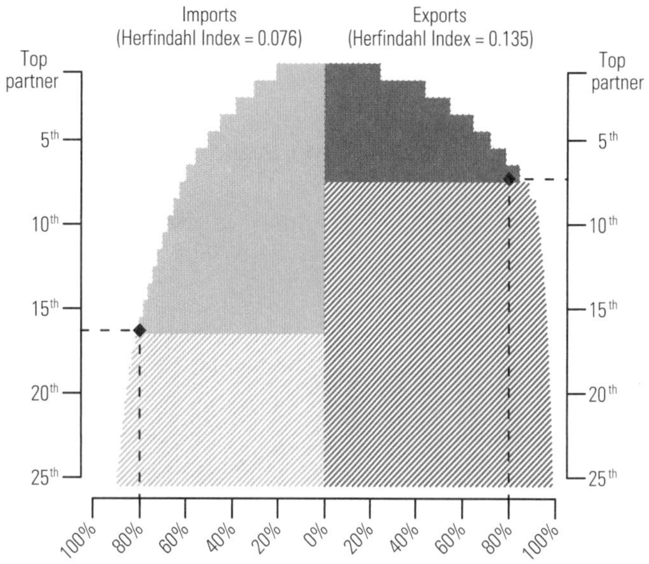

Table 4: Exports by principal countries and SITC sections in 2008

(Value in million US$, percentages of country total)

Country	Total	Shares by SITC sections (%) 0 + 1	2 + 4	3	5	6	7	8	9	Total
World	1 430.5	1.7	54.9	1.0	0.4	0.8	0.8	8.4	32.0	100
France	349.8	2.1	16.3	2.3	0.0	0.0	0.3	0.0	79.0	100
Switzerland	278.4	0.1	0.0	...	...	0.0	0.0	34.6	65.3	100
Russian Federation	151.3	0.0	96.3	...	3.6	0.1	...	...	...	100
Spain	141.5	0.4	99.5	...	...	...	0.0	0.1	...	100
Ireland	106.3	0.0	100.0	...	...	...	...	...	...	100
USA	96.1	0.2	84.7	...	0.0	0.1	0.6	14.3	...	100
Germany	83.9	0.2	99.7	0.0	...	...	0.1	...	...	100
Canada	57.7	0.0	99.9	...	...	0.0	0.1	...	...	100
Ukraine	40.7	0.0	99.4	...	...	0.6	...	...	...	100
China	19.9	0.6	90.9	...	...	8.3	0.1	0.1	...	100

Imports Profile:

In 2008, mineral fuels, lubricants and related materials (SITC section 3) accounted for 33.0 percent of total imports (see table 2). Other major commodity groups included machinery and transport equipment (SITC section 7) and manufactured goods classified chiefly by material (SITC section 6) respectively with 29.3 and 12.7 percent of imports. From 2006 to 2008, top imported products included petroleum oils, other than crude (HS code 2710), rice (HS code 1006) and parts suitable for use principally with the machinery of headings 84.25 (HS code 8431) (see table 5).

Table 5: Top 10 import commodities 2006 to 2008

(Value in million US$)

HS code	4-digit heading of Harmonized System 2002	Value (million US$) 2006	2007	2008	Unit value 2006	2007	2008	Unit	SITC code
	All Commodities	1 063.9	1 281.5	1 835.5					
2710	Petroleum oils, other than crude	257.4	331.0	601.1	0.6	0.2	0.6	US$/kg	334
1006	Rice	133.5	76.3	75.3	0.3	0.2	0.4	US$/kg	042
8431	Parts suitable for use principally with the machinery of headings 84.25	41.4	80.3	96.0	9.3	14.5	16.9	US$/kg	723
8517	Electrical apparatus for line telephony or line telegraphy	20.9	51.9	57.0					764
2523	Portland cement, aluminous cement, slag cement	28.3	23.4	68.4	0.1	0.1	0.2	US$/kg	661
2402	Cigars, cheroots, cigarillos and cigarettes	39.3	29.7	32.8	3.7	2.9	3.6	US$/kg	122
8703	Motor cars and other motor vehicles principally designed for the transport	17.5	33.5	48.9	*17.1*	*17.0*		thsd US$/unit	781
2815	Sodium hydroxide (caustic soda)	26.7	13.4	39.6	0.5	0.2	0.6	US$/kg	522
8429	Self-propelled bulldozers, angledozers, graders, levellers, scrapers	11.8	26.9	34.5	*39.4*		*52.6*	thsd US$/unit	723
1701	Cane or beet sugar and pure sucrose, in solid form	18.1	19.5	28.3	0.2	0.2	0.2	US$/kg	061

Guyana

Imports: CIF, by origin	Exports: FOB, by last known destination	Trade System: Special

Overview:

From 2007 to 2011, Guyana's exports increased on average by 7.5 percent each year to reach 1.0 bln US$ in 2011 (see table 1 and graph 1). During the same period, imports also increased on average by 13.1 percent each year to 1.7 bln US$ (see table 2 and graph 1). This resulted in a trade deficit amounting to 635.3 mln US$ in 2011 (see graph 1). This deficit was largely accounted for by trade with Latin America and the Caribbean (-336.2 mln US$), Eastern Asia (-124.3 mln US$) and Developed Asia-Pacific (-55.3 mln US$) (see graph 2). Trade was in a surplus with Developed Europe (+78.1 mln US$). In 2011, trade was relatively concentrated among a few partners: 9 major partners accounted for 80 percent of exports compared to 11 major partners for imports (see graph 3)

Graph 1: Total imports, exports and trade balance

(Bln US$ by year)

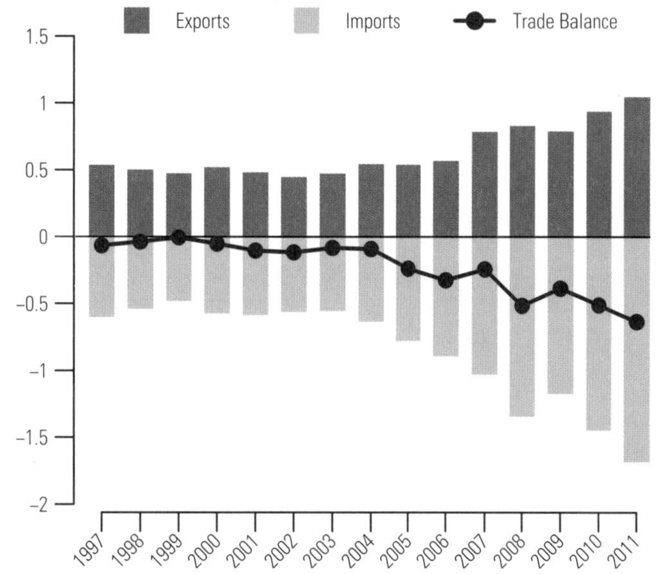

Table 1: Exports by SITC sections

(Value in million US$, growth and shares in percentage)

SITC	2011	Avg. Growth rates (%) 2007-2011	2010-2011	2011 share
Total	1 048.7	7.5	11.9	100.0
0+1	432.6	6.5	7.6	41.3
2+4	197.1	7.6	-14.0	18.8
3	0.0	-46.0	78.1	0.0
5	4.8	2.5	1.4	0.5
6	30.4	-18.8	-3.8	2.9
7	55.1	26.7	877.7	5.3
8	13.2	-27.2	-6.7	1.3
9	315.4	18.8	26.4	30.1

Table 2: Imports by SITC sections

(Value in million US$, growth and shares in percentage)

SITC	2011	Avg. Growth rates (%) 2007-2011	2010-2011	2011 share
Total	1 683.9	13.1	16.3	100.0
0+1	230.9	14.3	13.5	13.7
2+4	26.7	14.9	17.3	1.6
3	494.3	19.0	17.0	29.4
5	162.9	12.8	1.8	9.7
6	195.5	4.4	13.2	11.6
7	463.9	12.6	29.1	27.6
8	109.7	9.0	1.9	6.5
9	0.0	14.2	2302.9	0.0

Exports Profile:

In 2011, food, live animals, beverages and tobacco (SITC sections 0+1) accounted for 41.3 percent of exports (see table 1). Other major commodity groups were commodities and transactions not classified elsewhere (SITC section 9) and inedible crude materials (except fuels), animal and vegetable oils, fats and waxes (SITC sections 2+4). They accounted respectively for 30.1 and 18.8 percent of exports. Major markets for exports included USA, Canada and United Kingdom (see table 4). From 2009 to 2011, the three major products for exports were gold (including gold plated with platinum) (HS code 7108), rice (HS code 1006) and aluminium ores and concentrates (HS code 2606) (see table 3).

Table 3: Top 10 export commodities 2009 to 2011

(Value in million US$)

HS code	4-digit heading of Harmonized System 2007	Value (million US$) 2009	2010	2011	Unit value 2009	2010	2011	Unit	SITC code
	All Commodities	788.4	936.7	1 048.7					
7108	Gold (including gold plated with platinum)	279.7	249.4	315.4	9.0	23.4	32.2	thsd US$/kg	971
1006	Rice	113.4	173.3	148.1	0.4	1.1	1.7	US$/kg	042
2606	Aluminium ores and concentrates	79.4	169.2	151.5	0.1	0.9	0.3	US$/kg	285
1701	Cane or beet sugar and chemically pure sucrose, in solid form	119.7	116.6	155.8	0.6	0.8	0.6	US$/kg	061
2208	Alcohol of a strength by volume of less than 80 % vol	25.0	29.5	34.6	1.7	*1.9*	*2.8*	US$/litre	112
0306	Crustaceans, whether in shell or not	30.8	29.4	25.0	2.3	2.5	2.4	US$/kg	036
4407	Wood sawn or chipped lengthwise, sliced or peeled	23.3	25.5	21.8	*2.1*	*2.7*	*12.6*	US$/m³	248
8609	Containers (including containers for the transport of fluids)	0.1	0.2	43.3	126.8	8.1	*798.9*	US$/unit	786
4409	Wood (including strips and friezes for parquet flooring, not assembled)	5.5	23.5	13.9	0.6	1.7	1.0	US$/kg	248
1703	Molasses resulting from the extraction or refining of sugar	7.8	10.1	19.7	0.4	0.2	0.2	US$/kg	061

Graph 2: Trade Balance by MDG Regions in 2011

(Mln US$)

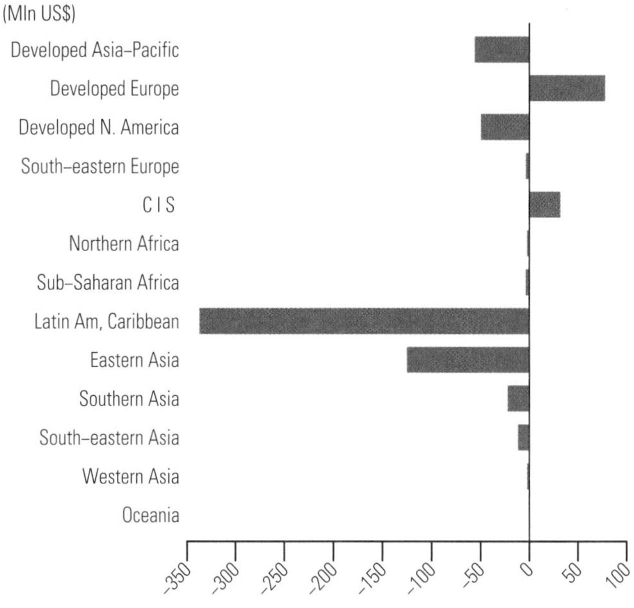

Graph 3: Partner concentration of trade in 2011

(Cumulative share by ranked partners)

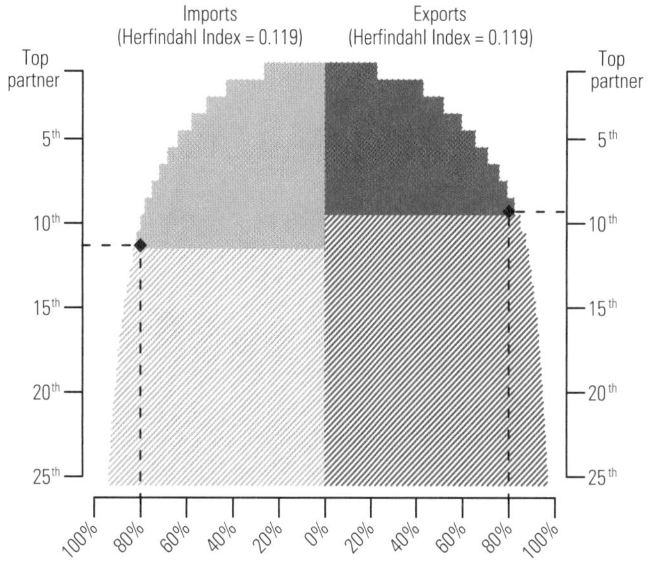

Table 4: Exports by principal countries and SITC sections in 2011

(Value in million US$, percentages of country total)

Country	Total	Shares by SITC sections (%) 0 + 1	2 + 4	3	5	6	7	8	9	Total
World	1 048.7	41.3	18.8	0.0	0.5	2.9	5.3	1.3	30.1	100
USA	238.9	21.4	14.2	0.0	0.3	1.4	9.3	3.9	49.6	100
Canada	211.0	4.5	3.5	...	0.0	0.0	0.4	0.1	91.5	100
United Kingdom	91.7	95.6	1.7	0.0	0.2	0.1	2.3	0.2	...	100
Venezuela	81.9	96.8	3.2	...	...	0.0	0.0	0.0	...	100
Germany	61.8	5.4	94.4	...	0.0	0.0	0.2	0.0	...	100
Jamaica	56.4	86.4	0.8	...	0.7	0.4	11.6	0.0	...	100
Trinidad and Tobago	52.9	60.7	3.8	0.0	2.5	2.9	29.8	0.3	...	100
Ukraine	36.2	0.0	100.0	...	...	0.0	0.0	0.0	...	100
Portugal	32.4	100.0	0.0	...	...	...	0.0	0.0	...	100
Netherlands	25.9	77.5	16.6	...	0.0	1.0	4.8	0.1	...	100

Imports Profile:

Imports of Guyana in 2011 were composed of 29.4 percent of mineral fuels, lubricants and related materials (SITC section 3), 27.6 percent of machinery and transport equipment (SITC section 7) and 13.7 percent of food, live animals, beverages and tobacco (SITC sections 0+1) (see table 2). From 2009 to 2011, in addition to petroleum oils, other than crude (HS code 2710), other major imported goods were self-propelled bulldozers, angledozers, graders, levellers, scrapers (HS code 8429) and medicaments (excluding goods of heading 30.02, 30.05 or 30.06) (HS code 3004) (see table 5).

Table 5: Top 10 import commodities 2009 to 2011

(Value in million US$)

HS code	4-digit heading of Harmonized System 2007	Value (million US$) 2009	2010	2011	Unit value 2009	2010	2011	Unit	SITC code
	All Commodities	1 175.3	1 448.3	1 683.9					
2710	Petroleum oils, other than crude	278.9	405.7	472.9	0.5	1.3	1.8	US$/kg	334
8429	Self-propelled bulldozers, angledozers, graders, levellers, scrapers	27.8	54.2	80.2	*49.0*	51.4	*69.4*	thsd US$/unit	723
3004	Medicaments (excluding goods of heading 30.02, 30.05 or 30.06)	66.1	40.7	39.3	82.3	19.6	39.4	US$/kg	542
8703	Motor cars and other motor vehicles principally designed for the transport	32.5	35.9	36.6	*5.5*	*4.3*	*4.4*	thsd US$/unit	781
8704	Motor vehicles for the transport of goods	23.6	29.6	39.7	*7.5*	*12.7*	*11.2*	thsd US$/unit	782
1001	Wheat and meslin	11.4	29.1	24.0	1.2	0.7	0.8	US$/kg	041
0402	Milk and cream, concentrated or containing added sugar	17.3	22.7	23.8	2.1	0.7	4.1	US$/kg	022
2523	Portland cement, aluminous cement, slag cement	21.5	16.5	18.2	0.1	0.0	0.1	US$/kg	661
3923	Articles for the conveyance or packing of goods, of plastics	16.7	17.7	21.2	2.7	2.6	3.1	US$/kg	893
8517	Electrical apparatus for line telephony or line telegraphy	14.5	15.9	22.6					764

Honduras

Imports: CIF, by origin | **Exports: FOB, by last known destination** | **Trade System: Special**

Overview:

Since 2005, the value of the exports of Honduras increased on average by 19.4 percent each year and amounted to 2.6 bln US$ in 2009 (see table 1 and graph 1). Imports showed a less pronounced pattern with an average annual increase of 7.7 percent to reach 6.0 bln US$ in 2009 (see table 2 and graph 1). This resulted in a trade deficit of 3.3 bln US$ (see graph 1). Two MDG regions accounted for a large part of this deficit: Latin America and the Caribbean (-2.1 bln US$) and Developed North America (-0.9 bln US$) (see graph 2). By partners, 9 major partners accounted for 80 percent of exports compared to 11 major partners for imports (see graph 3).

Graph 1: Total imports, exports and trade balance

(Bln US$ by year)

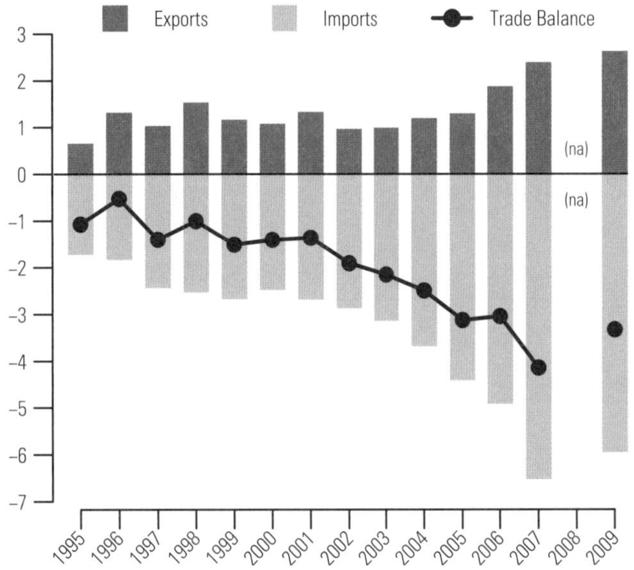

Table 1: Exports by SITC sections

(Value in million US$, growth and shares in percentage)

SITC	2009	Avg. Growth rates (%) 2005-2009	2008-2009	2009 share
Total	2 628.3	19.4	...	100.0
0+1	1 209.8	12.4	...	46.0
2+4	258.7	7.1	...	9.8
3	106.8	90.8	...	4.1
5	128.1	13.1	...	4.9
6	111.3	2.6	...	4.2
7	179.9	33.7	...	6.8
8	461.1	61.5	...	17.5
9	172.6	55.2	...	6.6

Exports Profile:

Food, live animals, beverages and tobacco (SITC sections 0+1) accounted for 46.0 percent of exported goods in 2009 (see table 1). Other major commodity groups included miscellaneous manufactured articles (SITC section 8) and inedible crude materials (except fuels), animal and vegetable oils, fats and waxes (SITC sections 2+4) respectively with 17.5 and 9.8 percent of exported goods. USA, the top partner, accounted for 47.7 percent of exported goods in 2009 (see table 4). Other major destinations for exports in 2009 were El Salvador and Germany. From 2007 to 2009, coffee, whether or not roasted or decaffeinated (HS code 0901), unused postage, revenue or similar stamps of current or new issue (HS code 4907) and bananas, including plantains (HS code 0803) were the three major products for exports (see table 3). They accounted respectively for 19.6, 13.9 and 6.9 percent of exported goods in 2009.

Table 2: Imports by SITC sections

(Value in million US$, growth and shares in percentage)

SITC	2009	Avg. Growth rates (%) 2005-2009	2008-2009	2009 share
Total	5 953.5	7.7	...	100.0
0+1	1 062.9	13.8	...	17.9
2+4	147.1	18.3	...	2.5
3	1 144.3	4.5	...	19.2
5	1 032.0	9.0	...	17.3
6	796.1	3.5	...	13.4
7	1 269.7	7.4	...	21.3
8	498.6	7.8	...	8.4
9	2.8	64.1	...	0.0

Table 3: Top 10 export commodities 2007 to 2009

(Value in million US$)

HS code	4-digit heading of Harmonized System 2007	Value (million US$) 2007	2008	2009	Unit value 2007	2008	2009	Unit	SITC code
	All Commodities	2 391.4	...	2 628.3					
0901	Coffee, whether or not roasted or decaffeinated	500.1	...	515.8	2.4		2.6	US$/kg	071
4907	Unused postage, revenue or similar stamps of current or new issue	1.5	...	366.1	0.3		19.9	thsd US$/kg	892
0803	Bananas, including plantains, fresh or dried	153.9	...	180.4	0.3		0.3	US$/kg	057
8544	Insulated (including enamelled or anodised) wire, cable	229.9	...	102.1	10.0		10.5	US$/kg	773
0306	Crustaceans, whether in shell or not	129.1	...	118.6	6.2		5.0	US$/kg	036
1511	Palm oil and its fractions	110.5	...	123.8	0.6		0.7	US$/kg	422
2711	Petroleum gases and other gaseous hydrocarbons	110.3	...	104.0	0.8		0.6	US$/kg	343
2402	Cigars, cheroots, cigarillos and cigarettes	81.5	...	77.6	10.4		10.6	US$/kg	122
7108	Gold (including gold plated with platinum)	50.9	...	66.8	4.9		5.5	thsd US$/kg	971
3401	Soap; organic surface-active products	41.7	...	48.6	0.7		0.9	US$/kg	554

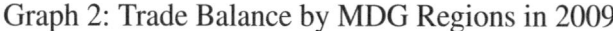

Graph 2: Trade Balance by MDG Regions in 2009

(Bln US$)

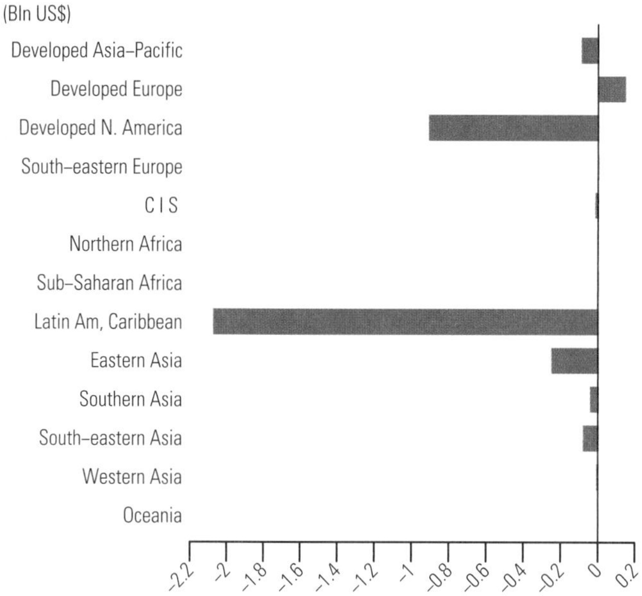

Graph 3: Partner concentration of trade in 2009

(Cumulative share by ranked partners)

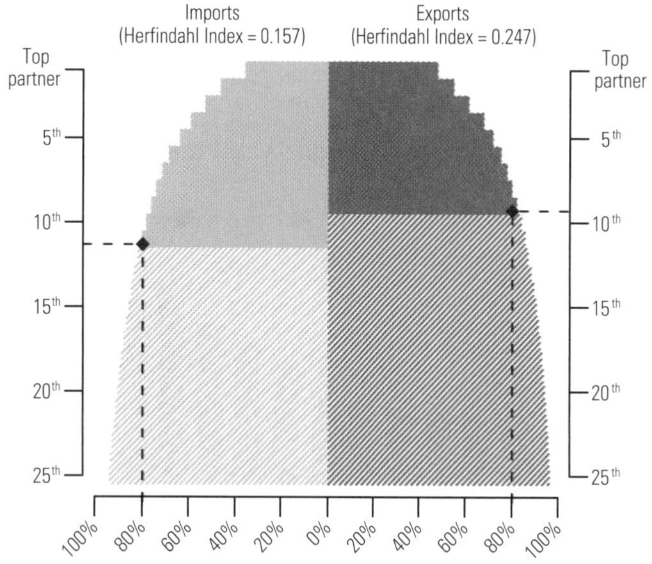

Table 4: Exports by principal countries and SITC sections in 2009

(Value in million US$, percentages of country total)

Country	Total	Shares by SITC sections (%)								
		0 + 1	2 + 4	3	5	6	7	8	9	Total
World	2628.3	46.0	9.8	4.1	4.9	4.2	6.8	17.5	6.6	100
USA	1253.7	37.2	1.0	2.4	0.4	1.7	11.6	32.0	13.7	100
El Salvador	182.9	27.7	20.0	5.7	23.8	9.7	3.2	9.9	0.0	100
Germany	170.2	84.0	14.8	...	0.3	0.6	0.2	0.0	0.1	100
Guatemala	168.4	24.5	10.7	23.7	18.9	9.7	2.8	9.8	0.0	100
Nicaragua	102.4	37.1	15.9	2.7	14.4	14.4	2.8	12.7	0.1	100
Belgium	90.6	89.3	10.7	...	0.0	...	0.0	...	...	100
United Kingdom	69.2	73.0	26.9	0.0	0.0	0.0	0.0	0.0	...	100
Costa Rica	55.2	31.6	3.8	1.1	17.0	32.9	5.3	8.3	0.0	100
Mexico	53.8	10.8	76.1	...	7.7	1.6	3.0	0.7	0.0	100
Rep. of Korea	52.3	98.0	1.5	...	0.2	0.0	0.3	0.0	0.0	100

Imports Profile:

In 2009, machinery and transport equipment (SITC section 7) accounted for 21.3 percent of Honduras' imports (see table 2). Other major commodity groups included mineral fuels, lubricants and related materials (SITC section 3) and food, live animals, beverages and tobacco (SITC sections 0+1) respectively with 19.2 and 17.9 percent of imports. From 2007 to 2009, the major imported products were petroleum oils, other than crude (HS code 2710), medicaments (excluding goods of heading 30.02, 30.05 or 30.06) (HS code 3004) and motor vehicles for the transport of goods (HS code 8704) (see table 5).

Table 5: Top 10 import commodities 2007 to 2009

(Value in million US$)

HS code	4-digit heading of Harmonized System 2007	Value (million US$)			Unit value				SITC code
		2007	2008	2009	2007	2008	2009	Unit	
	All Commodities	6530.4	...	5953.5					
2710	Petroleum oils, other than crude	1234.4	...	1088.8	0.5		0.7	US$/kg	334
3004	Medicaments (excluding goods of heading 30.02, 30.05 or 30.06)	308.7	...	321.9	29.7		35.6	US$/kg	542
8704	Motor vehicles for the transport of goods	203.2	...	141.2					782
8517	Electrical apparatus for line telephony or line telegraphy	139.2	...	163.2					764
8703	Motor cars and other motor vehicles principally designed for the transport	186.4	...	112.6	*15.9*			thsd US$/unit	781
8471	Automatic data processing machines and units thereof	83.3	...	72.5					752
1005	Maize (corn)	49.7	...	90.5	0.2		0.2	US$/kg	044
2106	Food preparations not elsewhere specified or included	61.7	...	75.3	5.4		2.8	US$/kg	098
4818	Toilet paper and similar paper	59.8	...	74.6	1.7		2.0	US$/kg	642
3923	Articles for the conveyance or packing of goods, of plastics	62.6	...	63.6	2.3		2.1	US$/kg	893

Hungary

Imports: CIF, by consignment | **Exports: FOB, by last known destination** | **Trade System: Special**

Overview:

From 2007 to 2011, Hungary's exports increased on average by 4.1 percent each year and amounted to 111.1 bln US$ in 2011, surpassing its previous peak of 108.2 bln US$ in 2008 (see table 1 and graph 1). During the same period, imports increased at an average annual rate of 1.8 percent and amounted to 101.5 bln US$ in 2011 (see table 2 and graph 1). This resulted in a trade surplus of 9.6 bln US$ for the year (see graph 1). Large trade deficits were recorded with Eastern Asia (-8.1 bln US$) and Commonwealth of Independent States (-3.9 bln US$) (see graph 2). Trade recorded large surpluses with Developed Europe (+11.8 bln US$), South-Eastern Europe (+5.3 bln US$) and Western Asia (+4.1 bln US$). By partners, both exports and imports were diversified: in 2011, 17 (respectively 14) major partners accounted for 80 percent of exports (respectively imports) (see graph 3).

Graph 1: Total imports, exports and trade balance

(Bln US$ by year)

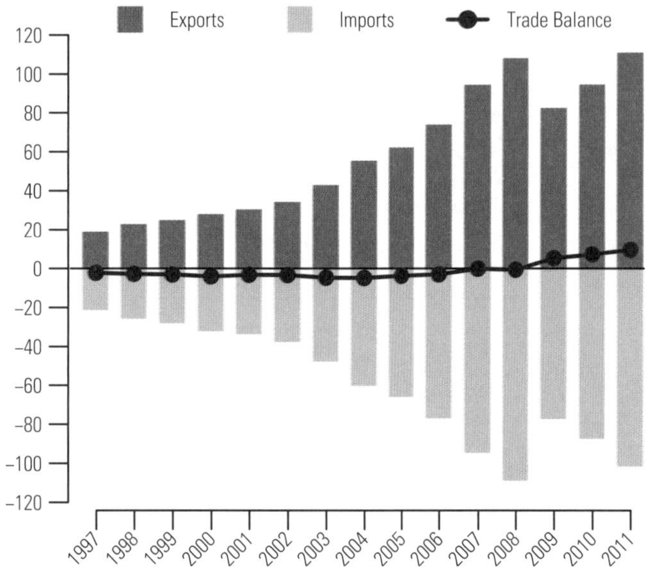

Table 1: Exports by SITC sections

(Value in million US$, growth and shares in percentage)

SITC	2011	Avg. Growth rates (%) 2007-2011	Avg. Growth rates (%) 2010-2011	2011 share
Total	111125.0	4.1	17.3	100.0
0+1	7507.7	7.9	19.1	6.8
2+4	3077.4	16.3	39.5	2.8
3	3851.4	9.9	53.1	3.5
5	10222.3	10.6	25.7	9.2
6	10914.3	5.8	23.7	9.8
7	60430.0	2.4	10.9	54.4
8	9139.6	6.0	21.1	8.2
9	5982.4	-3.7	26.4	5.4

Table 2: Imports by SITC sections

(Value in million US$, growth and shares in percentage)

SITC	2011	Avg. Growth rates (%) 2007-2011	Avg. Growth rates (%) 2010-2011	2011 share
Total	101519.8	1.8	16.1	100.0
0+1	4535.3	5.5	15.3	4.5
2+4	2344.3	15.2	34.4	2.3
3	12379.9	8.5	33.1	12.2
5	10715.8	7.1	24.5	10.6
6	13100.2	-0.4	20.8	12.9
7	42943.0	-1.8	6.8	42.3
8	5996.4	-1.2	12.8	5.9
9	9504.9	8.6	26.9	9.4

Exports Profile:

In 2011, more than half of Hungary's exports were machinery and transport equipment (SITC section 7), accounting for 54.4 percent of total exports (see table 1). Other major commodity groups included manufactured goods classified chiefly by material (SITC section 6) and chemicals and related products, n.e.s. (SITC section 5) respectively with 9.8 and 9.2 percent of exported goods. In 2011, Germany, the top partner for exports was the destination for 25.2 percent of exported goods (see table 4). Other major partners were Romania and Austria. From 2009 to 2011, top exported commodities were electrical apparatus for line telephony or line telegraphy (HS code 8517), reception apparatus for television (HS code 8528) and motor cars and other motor vehicles principally designed for the transport (HS code 8703) (see table 3).

Table 3: Top 10 export commodities 2009 to 2011

(Value in million US$)

HS code	4-digit heading of Harmonized System 2007	Value (million US$) 2009	2010	2011	Unit value 2009	2010	2011	Unit	SITC code
	All Commodities	82571.8	94748.7	111125.0					
8517	Electrical apparatus for line telephony or line telegraphy	9805.6	11246.6	12080.5					764
8528	Reception apparatus for television	5286.0	5883.5	4219.6					761
9999	Commodities not specified according to kind	4776.2	4677.3	5865.9					931
8703	Motor cars and other motor vehicles principally designed for the transport	3932.8	4146.0	4895.1		13.8		thsd US$/unit	781
8708	Parts and accessories of the motor vehicles of headings 87.01 to 87.05	2660.4	3380.9	4130.3	*10.9*	*9.8*	*10.4*	US$/kg	784
3004	Medicaments (excluding goods of heading 30.02, 30.05 or 30.06)	2581.9	2747.7	3715.3	*101.9*	*90.0*	*110.7*	US$/kg	542
8407	Spark-ignition reciprocating or rotary internal combustion piston engines	2723.5	2825.8	3372.9					713
8471	Automatic data processing machines and units thereof	2628.3	2636.2	2982.9					752
8408	Compression-ignition internal combustion piston engines	2043.6	2156.9	2700.3					713
8544	Insulated (including enamelled or anodised) wire, cable	1501.5	1837.5	2432.1	*12.2*	*13.6*	*16.6*	US$/kg	773

Graph 2: Trade Balance by MDG Regions in 2011

(Bln US$)

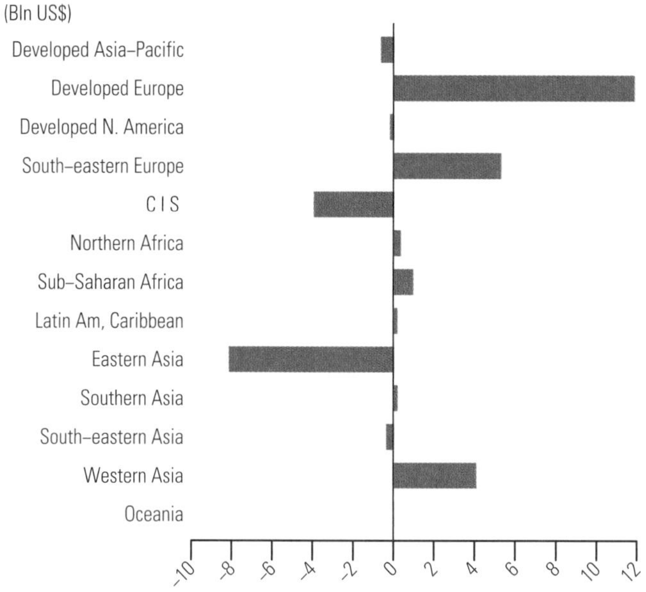

Graph 3: Partner concentration of trade in 2011

(Cumulative share by ranked partners)

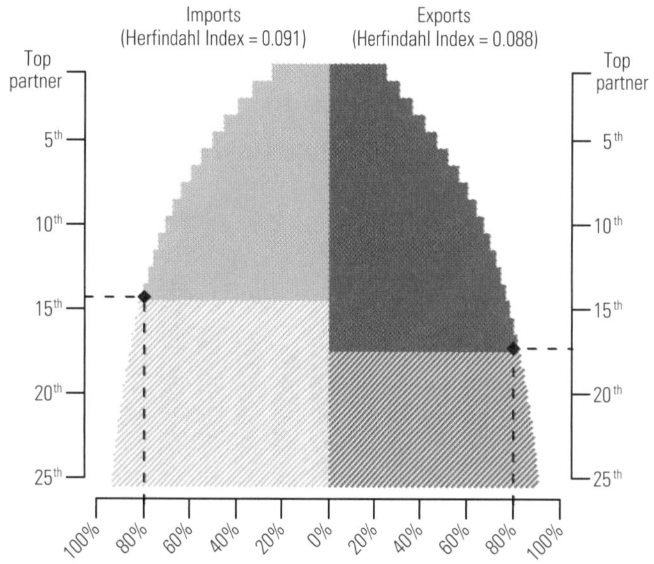

Table 4: Exports by principal countries and SITC sections in 2011

(Value in million US$, percentages of country total)

Country	Total	Shares by SITC sections (%) 0+1	2+4	3	5	6	7	8	9	Total
World	111125.0	6.8	2.8	3.5	9.2	9.8	54.4	8.2	5.4	100
Germany	28047.8	3.3	2.0	0.6	3.6	11.3	64.9	14.2	0.1	100
Romania	6367.0	13.9	4.9	12.7	20.0	10.3	32.4	5.7	0.2	100
Austria	6049.8	10.6	7.5	13.3	5.5	14.7	36.4	11.2	0.9	100
Slovakia	5968.4	14.4	6.5	3.9	11.2	11.0	48.2	4.3	0.5	100
Italy	5613.1	14.5	9.5	0.4	12.4	11.7	42.3	9.0	0.2	100
France	5331.6	4.6	1.1	0.6	9.9	12.5	60.9	10.3	0.1	100
United Kingdom	5140.8	4.4	0.8	0.2	4.0	7.5	77.0	6.1	0.0	100
Poland	4347.7	8.8	1.8	2.3	23.5	16.3	41.6	5.6	0.1	100
Czech Rep.	4132.2	7.2	2.1	1.6	17.8	16.3	46.7	8.1	0.1	100
Russian Federation	3574.6	7.0	0.8	1.0	24.0	9.3	54.5	3.3	0.0	100

Imports Profile:

In 2011, nearly half of Hungary's imported goods were machinery and transport equipment (SITC section 7) accounting for 42.3 percent of total imports (see table 2). Other major commodity groups included manufactured goods classified chiefly by material (SITC section 6) and mineral fuels, lubricants and related materials (SITC section 3) respectively with 12.9 and 12.2 percent of imported goods. From 2009 to 2011, top imported products were electrical apparatus for line telephony or line telegraphy (HS code 8517), petroleum gases and other gaseous hydrocarbons (HS code 2711) and electronic integrated circuits (HS code 8542) (see table 5).

Table 5: Top 10 import commodities 2009 to 2011

(Value in million US$)

HS code	4-digit heading of Harmonized System 2007	Value (million US$) 2009	2010	2011	Unit value 2009	2010	2011	Unit	SITC code
	All Commodities	77272.4	87432.1	101519.8					
9999	Commodities not specified according to kind	9516.6	7473.6	9426.1					931
8517	Electrical apparatus for line telephony or line telegraphy	4114.1	5087.7	5915.7					764
2711	Petroleum gases and other gaseous hydrocarbons	2935.8	3230.8	3433.4	*0.5*	*0.5*	*0.6*	US$/kg	343
8542	Electronic integrated circuits	2914.0	3375.5	3109.6					776
8529	Parts suitable for use with the apparatus of headings 85.25 to 85.28	3208.0	3671.0	2495.4	*34.2*	*35.9*	*32.6*	US$/kg	764
3004	Medicaments (excluding goods of heading 30.02, 30.05 or 30.06)	2293.9	2382.2	3016.5	*83.9*	*78.7*	*88.5*	US$/kg	542
2709	Petroleum oils and oils obtained from bituminous minerals, crude	...	2949.6	4628.8		0.6	0.8	US$/kg	333
8708	Parts and accessories of the motor vehicles of headings 87.01 to 87.05	2018.8	2378.1	2862.1	*9.2*	*8.4*	*8.9*	US$/kg	784
8409	Parts suitable for use with the engines of heading 84	1664.6	1729.2	2295.0	*10.4*	*8.9*		US$/kg	713
2710	Petroleum oils, other than crude	1255.6	1795.1	2191.6	*0.6*	0.7	*1.0*	US$/kg	334

Imports: CIF, by origin | **Exports: FOB, by last known destination** | **Trade System: Special**

Overview:

From 2007 to 2011, Iceland's exports increased on average by 2.9 percent each year despite a decline of 24.2 percent in 2009 and amounted to 5.3 bln US$ in 2011 (see table 1 and graph 1). Imports, on the other hand, decreased on average by 7.7 percent each year and reached 4.8 bln US$ (see table 2 and graph 1). The trade balance recorded a surplus of 503.0 mln US$, slightly below the 2010 surplus of 688.7 mln US$ (see graph 1). By MDG regions, trade with Developed Europe and Commonwealth of Independent States accounted for a large part of this surplus (1.4 bln US$ and 143.0 mln US$, respectively) (see graph 2). Large surpluses were also recorded with Sub-Sahara Africa (+94.3 mln US$) and Developed Asia-Pacific (+62.7 mln US$). By partners, exports were more concentrated than imports in 2011: 10 major partners accounted for 80 percent of exports compared to 15 major partners for imports (see graph 3).

Graph 1: Total imports, exports and trade balance

(Bln US$ by year)

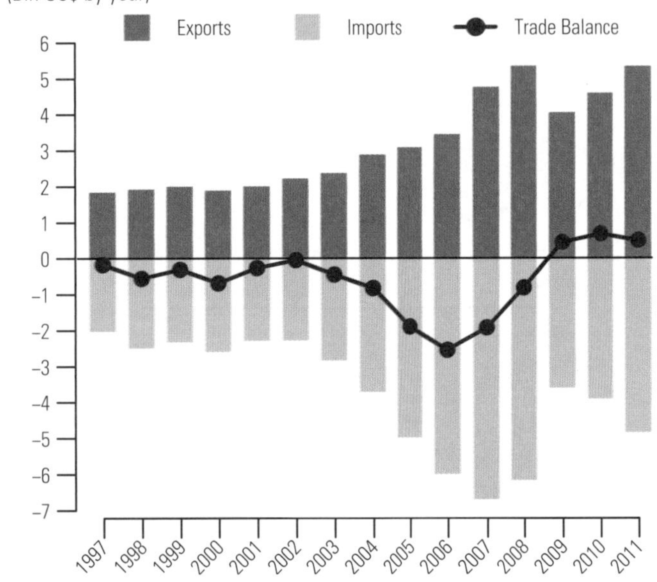

Table 1: Exports by SITC sections

(Value in million US$, growth and shares in percentage)

SITC	2011	Avg. Growth rates (%) 2007-2011	2010-2011	2011 share
Total	5348.8	2.9	16.2	100.0
0+1	2173.4	2.2	18.7	40.6
2+4	179.6	9.7	39.3	3.4
3	103.4	10.5	118.4	1.9
5	159.4	10.5	-1.6	3.0
6	2349.0	13.6	12.3	43.9
7	245.3	-28.3	8.8	4.6
8	112.7	6.5	13.8	2.1
9	25.9	-15.9	36.9	0.5

Table 2: Imports by SITC sections

(Value in million US$, growth and shares in percentage)

SITC	2011	Avg. Growth rates (%) 2007-2011	2010-2011	2011 share
Total	4845.8	-7.7	23.8	100.0
0+1	475.5	-0.6	16.4	9.8
2+4	704.8	10.3	13.9	14.5
3	700.1	4.1	36.8	14.4
5	449.3	-2.6	13.5	9.3
6	576.1	-11.7	24.7	11.9
7	1434.4	-15.3	34.5	29.6
8	499.4	-13.5	11.8	10.3
9	6.3	3.5	67.5	0.1

Exports Profile:

In 2011, the exports of Iceland were composed of 43.9 percent of manufactured goods classified chiefly by material (SITC section 6) and 40.6 percent of food, live animals, beverages and tobacco (SITC sections 0+1) (see table 1). Top markets for exports were Netherlands, Germany and United Kingdom (see table 4). Exports to Netherlands and Germany were largely manufactured goods classified chiefly by material (SITC section 6) while 78.6 percent of exports to United Kingdom were food, live animals, beverages and tobacco (SITC sections 0+1). From 2009 to 2011, top products for exports were unwrought aluminium (HS code 7601), fish fillets and other fish meat (whether or not minced) (HS code 0304) and fish, dried, salted or in brine (HS code 0305) (see table 3).

Table 3: Top 10 export commodities 2009 to 2011

(Value in million US$)

HS code	4-digit heading of Harmonized System 2007	Value (million US$) 2009	2010	2011	Unit value 2009	2010	2011	Unit	SITC code
	All Commodities	4057.0	4603.1	5348.8					
7601	Unwrought aluminium	1382.4	1825.0	1954.1	1.7	2.2	2.6	US$/kg	684
0304	Fish fillets and other fish meat (whether or not minced)	639.8	677.0	844.8	*3.9*	4.1	5.1	US$/kg	034
0305	Fish, dried, salted or in brine	376.4	371.8	348.9	*5.1*	5.3	6.0	US$/kg	035
0303	Fish, frozen, excluding fish fillets and other fish meat of heading 03.04	225.6	345.1	503.1	2.0	1.8	2.2	US$/kg	034
7202	Ferro-alloys	145.1	166.9	206.8	1.2	1.4	1.7	US$/kg	671
2301	Flours, meals and pellets, of meat or meat offal	135.6	115.8	147.3	1.2	1.7	1.6	US$/kg	081
0302	Fish, fresh or chilled, excluding fish fillets	132.6	99.7	96.0	2.2	2.6	3.2	US$/kg	034
3004	Medicaments (excluding goods of heading 30.02, 30.05 or 30.06)	77.1	118.9	118.2	131.0	133.0	126.0	US$/kg	542
8802	Other aircraft (for example, helicopters, aeroplanes); spacecraft	182.9	59.1	65.6					792
1504	Fats and oils and their fractions, of fish or marine mammals	79.5	73.2	104.2	0.9	1.2	1.7	US$/kg	411

Graph 2: Trade Balance by MDG Regions in 2011

(Bln US$)

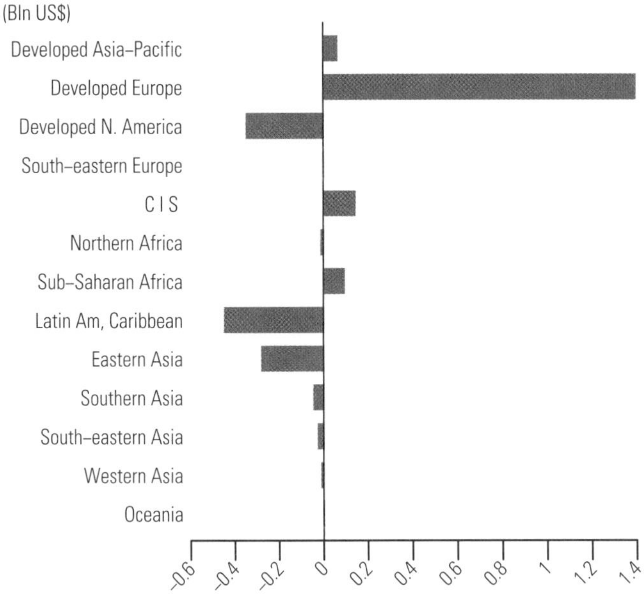

Graph 3: Partner concentration of trade in 2011

(Cumulative share by ranked partners)

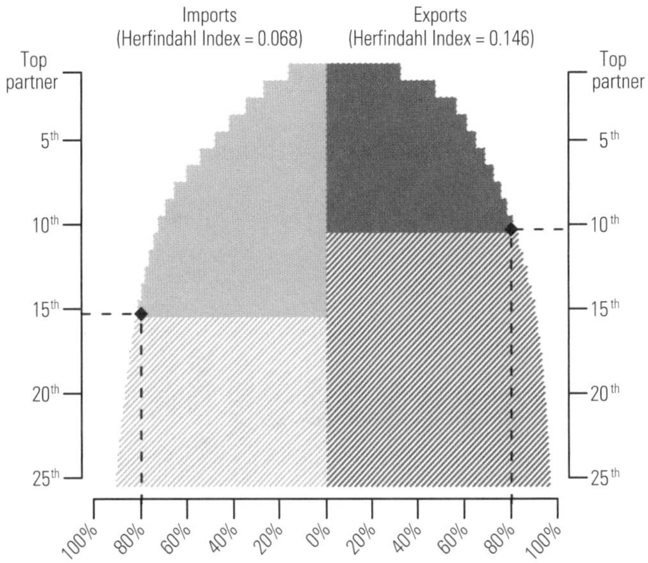

Table 4: Exports by principal countries and SITC sections in 2011

(Value in million US$, percentages of country total)

Country	Total	Shares by SITC sections (%)								
		0 + 1	2 + 4	3	5	6	7	8	9	Total
World	5348.8	40.6	3.4	1.9	3.0	43.9	4.6	2.1	0.5	100
Netherlands	1732.7	8.5	0.8	0.2	3.9	82.9	1.9	1.3	0.5	100
Germany	800.4	13.0	0.7	1.2	2.7	79.0	2.4	0.8	0.2	100
United Kingdom	482.0	78.6	5.1	5.5	0.4	6.5	2.8	0.5	0.6	100
Norway	236.2	48.4	24.0	2.8	0.8	2.2	17.9	3.0	1.0	100
France	209.2	72.7	1.3	0.6	3.5	20.3	1.3	0.2	0.1	100
Spain	206.1	92.8	3.1	0.0	1.8	1.6	0.5	0.2	0.0	100
USA	199.4	52.2	1.7	2.5	5.8	3.5	5.4	28.3	0.6	100
Russian Federation	167.3	93.5	0.1	3.6	0.0	1.3	1.3	0.1	...	100
Italy	135.7	18.1	0.0	0.5	1.9	78.5	0.1	0.9	0.1	100
Japan	133.2	78.2	1.6	0.1	1.3	17.6	0.8	0.4	...	100

Imports Profile:

Machinery and transport equipment (SITC section 7) accounted for 29.6 percent of imports in 2011 (see table 2). Other major commodity groups for imports were inedible crude materials (except fuels), animal and vegetable oils, fats and waxes (SITC sections 2+4) and mineral fuels, lubricants and related materials (SITC section 3) respectively accounting for 14.5 and 14.4 percent of imports. From 2009 to 2011, major products for imports were artificial corundum, whether or not chemically defined (HS code 2818), petroleum oils, other than crude (HS code 2710) and carbon electrodes, carbon brushes, lamp carbons, battery carbons (HS code 8545) (see table 5).

Table 5: Top 10 import commodities 2009 to 2011

(Value in million US$)

HS code	4-digit heading of Harmonized System 2007	Value (million US$)			Unit value				SITC code
		2009	2010	2011	2009	2010	2011	Unit	
	All Commodities	3604.0	3914.3	4845.8					
2818	Artificial corundum, whether or not chemically defined	425.1	515.5	576.0	0.3	0.3	*0.4*	US$/kg	285
2710	Petroleum oils, other than crude	401.0	461.7	648.1	0.5	0.7	1.0	US$/kg	334
8545	Carbon electrodes, carbon brushes, lamp carbons, battery carbons	320.4	307.6	399.3	*0.7*	*0.7*	0.9	US$/kg	778
3004	Medicaments (excluding goods of heading 30.02, 30.05 or 30.06)	113.7	113.2	121.4	*165.0*	*143.0*	*144.6*	US$/kg	542
8703	Motor cars and other motor vehicles principally designed for the transport	70.0	68.9	122.0		*16.7*	*17.4*	thsd US$/unit	781
8802	Other aircraft (for example, helicopters, aeroplanes); spacecraft	104.3	32.1	69.6					792
8471	Automatic data processing machines and units thereof	45.8	59.3	79.3					752
0306	Crustaceans, whether in shell or not	45.9	57.8	59.7	1.8	1.9	2.7	US$/kg	036
8517	Electrical apparatus for line telephony or line telegraphy	38.5	38.5	54.9					764
8902	Fishing vessels; factory ships and other vessels for processing	29.8	22.8	47.6					793

Imports: CIF, by origin	Exports: FOB, by last known destination	Trade System: General

Overview:

After several years of continuous growth, the value of the India's exports dropped by 2.8 percent in 2009 and bounced back by 24.7 percent in 2010 to reach its peak of 220.4 bln US$ (see table 1 and graph 1). Imports showed a similar development with an increase of 31.4 percent in 2010 to reach 350.0 bln US$ (see table 2 and graph 1). This resulted in a trade deficit of 129.6 bln US$ in 2010 (see graph 1). Trade recorded deficits with Western Asia (-41.3 bln US$), Eastern Asia (-29.4 bln US$) and Developed Europe (-22.8 bln US$) (see graph 2). Trade was in a surplus with Developed North America (+3.7 bln US$). India's imports and exports were well diversified across partners: in 2010, 24 major partners accounted for 80 percent of imports and even the top 25 partners could not account for 80 percent of exports (see graph 3).

Graph 1: Total imports, exports and trade balance

(Bln US$ by year)

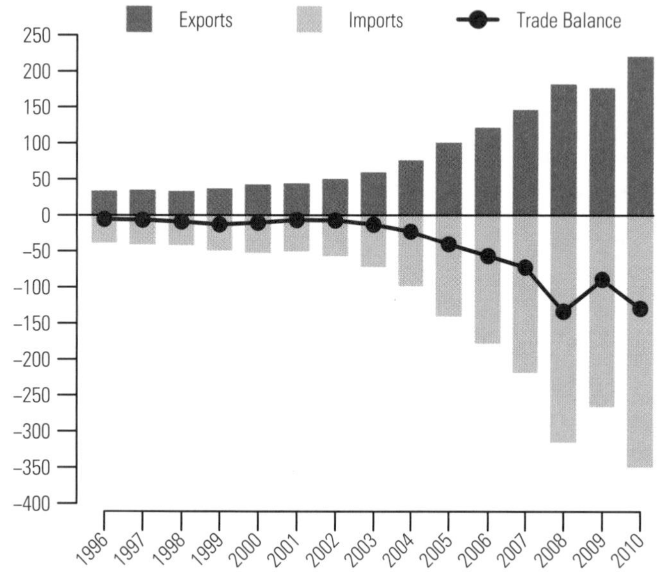

Table 1: Exports by SITC sections

(Value in million US$, growth and shares in percentage)

SITC	2010	Avg. Growth rates (%) 2006-2010	2009-2010	2010 share
Total	220408.5	16.1	24.7	100.0
0+1	16500.0	14.3	27.4	7.5
2+4	16236.8	16.7	53.3	7.4
3	37975.6	20.5	58.1	17.2
5	23576.8	13.7	27.3	10.7
6	62438.9	14.1	42.5	28.3
7	31930.6	24.6	18.2	14.5
8	27173.8	8.9	-14.8	12.3
9	4575.9	37.5	-42.5	2.1

Table 2: Imports by SITC sections

(Value in million US$, growth and shares in percentage)

SITC	2010	Avg. Growth rates (%) 2006-2010	2009-2010	2010 share
Total	350029.4	18.4	31.4	100.0
0+1	5617.8	21.8	11.7	1.6
2+4	23533.2	15.0	39.0	6.7
3	110830.7	15.9	34.1	31.7
5	34449.3	21.0	26.5	9.8
6	54352.7	25.5	43.7	15.5
7	63751.5	11.8	9.6	18.2
8	10354.6	12.8	5.7	3.0
9	47139.6	31.9	63.5	13.5

Exports Profile:

In 2010, exports were composed of 28.3 percent of manufactured goods classified chiefly by material (SITC section 6), 17.2 percent of mineral fuels, lubricants and related materials (SITC section 3) and 14.5 percent of machinery and transport equipment (SITC section 7) (see table 1). The three major partners for exports were United Arab Emirates, USA and China (see table 4). From 2008 to 2010, top exported products were petroleum oils, other than crude (HS code 2710), diamonds, whether or not worked, but not mounted or set (HS code 7102) and articles of jewellery and parts thereof, of precious metal (HS code 7113) (see table 3).

Table 3: Top 10 export commodities 2008 to 2010

(Value in million US$)

HS code	4-digit heading of Harmonized System 2002	Value (million US$) 2008	2009	2010	Unit value 2008	2009	2010	Unit	SITC code
	All Commodities	181860.9	176765.0	220408.5					
2710	Petroleum oils, other than crude	31558.8	23226.0	36641.3	*0.8*	*0.5*		US$/kg	334
7102	Diamonds, whether or not worked, but not mounted or set	14886.8	16689.2	22269.7	*277.6*			US$/carat	667
7113	Articles of jewellery and parts thereof, of precious metal	4608.1	10604.1	7833.7	*0.7*	*3.4*		thsd US$/kg	897
2601	Iron ores and concentrates	5638.1	5298.6	6146.9	0.1	*0.1*	*0.0*	US$/kg	281
9999	Commodities not specified according to kind	2862.2	7719.4	4229.5					931
3004	Medicaments (excluding goods of heading 30.02, 30.05 or 30.06)	4128.4	3969.4	5151.3	*14.9*	9.5		US$/kg	542
8703	Motor cars and other motor vehicles principally designed for the transport	2219.8	2940.8	4510.6	*5.0*	4.7	*8.8*	thsd US$/unit	781
1006	Rice	2843.3	2398.2	2295.8	0.8	*1.1*	*0.9*	US$/kg	042
7403	Refined copper and copper alloys, unwrought	1283.6	1048.1	4628.4	7.3	5.6		US$/kg	682
2942	Other organic compounds	2390.9	2185.4	2216.2	27.5	*26.2*		US$/kg	516

Graph 2: Trade Balance by MDG Regions in 2010

(Bln US$)

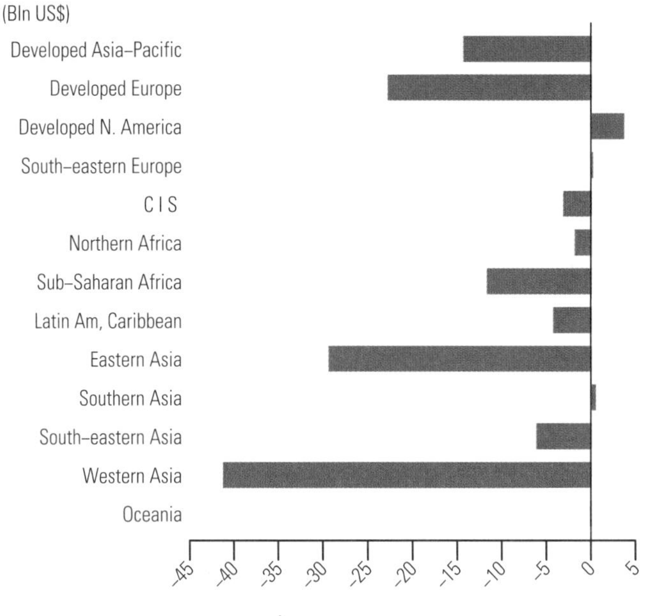

Graph 3: Partner concentration of trade in 2010

(Cumulative share by ranked partners)

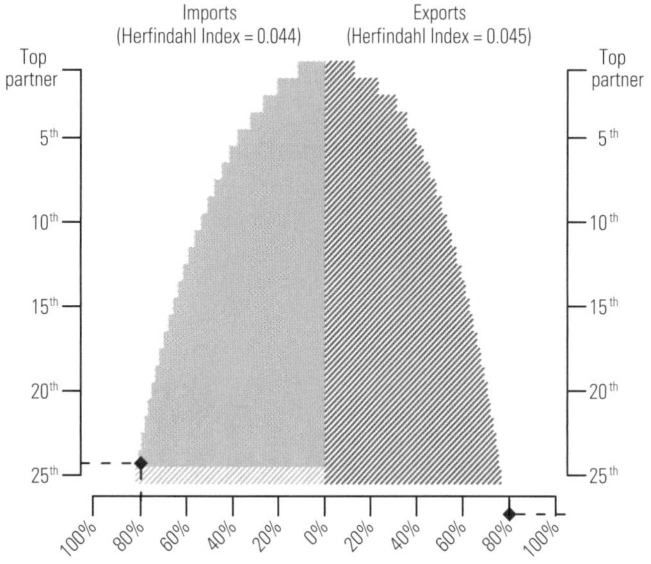

Table 4: Exports by principal countries and SITC sections in 2010

(Value in million US$, percentages of country total)

Country	Total	Shares by SITC sections (%) 0+1	2+4	3	5	6	7	8	9	Total
World	220408.5	7.5	7.4	17.2	10.7	28.3	14.5	12.3	2.1	100
United Arab Emirates	27412.3	5.5	0.8	19.5	2.8	38.8	5.7	24.6	2.4	100
USA	23587.4	4.3	2.6	2.7	16.2	34.7	15.8	23.2	0.6	100
China	17440.0	2.7	52.5	2.1	7.8	30.3	3.3	1.1	0.1	100
China, Hong Kong SAR	9508.3	1.9	1.3	0.0	1.1	79.2	3.7	12.7	0.1	100
Singapore	9066.2	1.8	0.5	53.9	4.9	6.5	19.2	5.7	7.4	100
Netherlands	6572.9	5.0	3.3	52.7	8.5	7.8	11.4	10.9	0.4	100
United Kingdom	6436.4	6.9	2.1	4.3	11.4	19.7	19.5	35.6	0.7	100
Germany	5989.5	4.1	3.4	0.1	15.5	22.3	24.5	29.3	0.9	100
Belgium	5025.9	6.3	5.2	8.4	8.2	55.9	6.9	8.3	0.7	100
France	4903.0	3.8	2.8	41.5	6.5	7.9	14.3	22.7	0.5	100

Imports Profile:

Imports were composed of 31.7 percent of mineral fuels, lubricants and related materials (SITC section 3), 18.2 percent of machinery and transport equipment (SITC section 7) and 15.5 percent of manufactured goods classified chiefly by material (SITC section 6) (see table 2). From 2008 to 2010, top imported products were petroleum oils, crude (HS code 2709), gold (including gold plated with platinum) (HS code 7108) and diamonds, whether or not worked, but not mounted or set (HS code 7102) (see table 5).

Table 5: Top 10 import commodities 2008 to 2010

(Value in million US$)

HS code	4-digit heading of Harmonized System 2002	Value (million US$) 2008	2009	2010	Unit value 2008	2009	2010	Unit	SITC code
	All Commodities	315712.1	266401.6	350029.4					
2709	Petroleum oils, crude	86582.5	64899.5	88611.0	0.7	*0.4*	0.6	US$/kg	333
7108	Gold (including gold plated with platinum)	19875.5	23365.1	38352.4	*27.5*	*31.7*		thsd US$/kg	971
7102	Diamonds, whether or not worked, but not mounted or set	12119.7	15226.4	27879.0	100.1			US$/carat	667
2701	Coal; briquettes, ovoids and similar solid fuels manufactured from coal	9048.8	7589.5	9379.8	0.2	0.1	0.1	US$/kg	321
9999	Commodities not specified according to kind	11505.0	5457.2	8785.3					931
2710	Petroleum oils, other than crude	12133.5	4563.2	5785.0	*0.9*	*0.5*		US$/kg	334
8802	Other aircraft (for example, helicopters, aeroplanes); spacecraft	11366.1	4292.3	2427.6	3.3	17.9		mln US$/unit	792
2711	Petroleum gases and other gaseous hydrocarbons	5662.4	4097.0	5406.4	0.5	0.3		US$/kg	343
8525	Transmission apparatus for radio-telephony, radio-broadcasting	4180.4	3598.2	5795.8	74.7	*58.0*		US$/unit	764
3105	Mineral or chemical fertilisers	7002.8	2320.4	3129.4	1.2	0.4	0.5	US$/kg	562

Imports: CIF, by origin | **Exports: FOB, by last known destination** | **Trade System: General**

Overview:

From 2007 to 2011, Indonesia's exports increased on average by 15.6 percent each year and amounted to 203.5 bln US$ in 2011 (see table 1 and graph 1). During the same period, imports increased at an average annual rate of 24.2 percent and amounted to 177.4 bln US$ in 2011 (see table 2 and graph 1). This resulted in a trade surplus of 26.1 bln US$ for the year (see graph 1). Large surpluses were recorded with Developed Asia-Pacific (+14.3 bln US$), Southern Asia (+11.1 bln US$), Developed Europe (+7.3 bln US$) and Developed North America (+4.6 bln US$) (see graph 2). Trade recorded large deficits with South-eastern Asia (-9.0 bln US$) and Western Asia (-3.9 bln US$). Indonesia's trade was diversified across partners: 14 major partners accounted for 80 percent of both exports and imports (see graph 3). See footnote*.

Graph 1: Total imports, exports and trade balance

(Bln US$ by year)

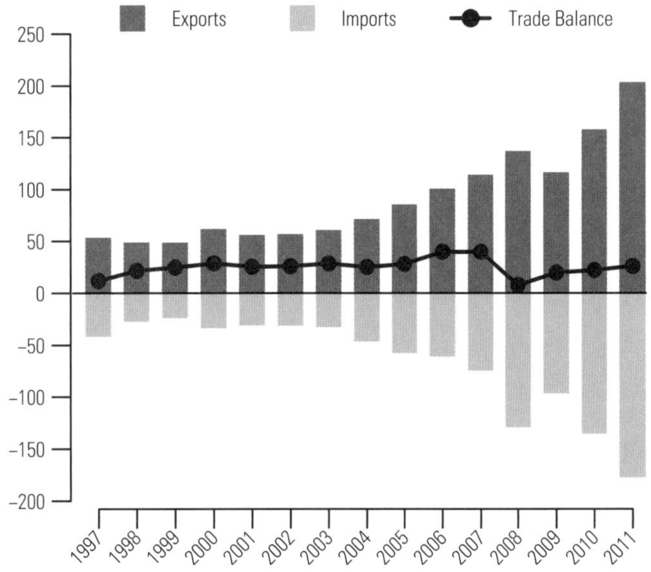

Table 1: Exports by SITC sections

(Value in million US$, growth and shares in percentage)

SITC	2011	Avg. Growth rates (%) 2007-2011	2010-2011	2011 share
Total	203 496.6	15.6	29.0	100.0
0+1	10 922.2	14.6	21.5	5.4
2+4	46 168.2	16.2	25.2	22.7
3	68 912.3	23.9	47.4	33.9
5	11 568.2	15.8	41.7	5.7
6	25 485.6	7.7	16.1	12.5
7	21 770.6	9.3	10.9	10.7
8	16 444.4	8.2	15.6	8.1
9	2 225.2	33.7	88.4	1.1

Exports Profile:

In 2011, exports of mineral fuels, lubricants and related materials (SITC section 3) accounted for 33.9 percent of exported goods (see table 1). Other major commodity groups included inedible crude materials (except fuels), animal and vegetable oils, fats and waxes (SITC sections 2+4), manufactured goods classified chiefly by material (SITC section 6) and machinery and transport equipment (SITC section 7) respectively with 22.7, 12.5 and 10.7 percent of exports. Japan, China and Singapore were the top three trading partners for exports (see table 4). Top exported products over the last three years were coal, briquettes, ovoids etc, made from coal (HS code 2701), petroleum gases and other gaseous hydrocarbons (HS code 2711) and palm oil and its fractions, not chemically modified (HS code 1511) (see table 3).

Table 2: Imports by SITC sections

(Value in million US$, growth and shares in percentage)

SITC	2011	Avg. Growth rates (%) 2007-2011	2010-2011	2011 share
Total	177 435.6	24.2	30.8	100.0
0+1	14 992.1	20.1	46.8	8.4
2+4	10 210.2	22.3	36.7	5.8
3	40 821.0	16.7	48.4	23.0
5	22 207.8	21.9	33.2	12.5
6	25 864.7	28.1	26.4	14.6
7	56 060.9	30.9	19.4	31.6
8	5 411.9	29.2	16.5	3.1
9	1 866.9	284.3	6.3	1.1

Table 3: Top 10 export commodities 2009 to 2011

(Value in million US$)

HS code	4-digit heading of Harmonized System 1996	Value (million US$) 2009	2010	2011	Unit value 2009	2010	2011	Unit	SITC code
	All Commodities	116 510.0	157 779.1	203 496.6					
2701	Coal, briquettes, ovoids etc, made from coal	13 799.1	18 169.7	25 523.2	0.1	0.1	0.1	US$/kg	321
2711	Petroleum gases and other gaseous hydrocarbons	8 935.7	13 669.5	22 871.5	0.4	0.4	0.7	US$/kg	343
1511	Palm oil and its fractions, not chemically modified	10 367.6	13 469.0	17 261.2	0.6	0.8	1.1	US$/kg	422
2709	Petroleum oils, oils from bituminous minerals, crude	7 820.3	10 402.9	13 828.7	0.4	0.6	0.8	US$/kg	333
4001	Natural rubber and gums, in primary form, plates, etc	3 244.0	7 329.1	11 766.2	1.6	3.1	4.6	US$/kg	231
2603	Copper ores and concentrates	5 101.3	6 882.2	4 700.4	2.2	2.6	3.2	US$/kg	283
1513	Coconut, palm kernel, babassu oil, fractions, refined	1 479.2	2 293.8	3 051.6	0.7	1.1	1.5	US$/kg	422
7403	Refined copper and copper alloys, unwrought	1 731.0	2 262.1	2 544.4	8.8	14.0	19.3	US$/kg	682
2710	Oils petroleum, bituminous, distillates, except crude	866.2	2 190.9	2 901.7	0.5	0.6	0.8	US$/kg	334
4802	Uncoated paper for writing, printing, office machines	1 708.6	2 111.5	2 106.1	0.8	0.9	0.9	US$/kg	641

*Imports data has special trade system

Graph 2: Trade Balance by MDG Regions in 2011

(Bln US$)

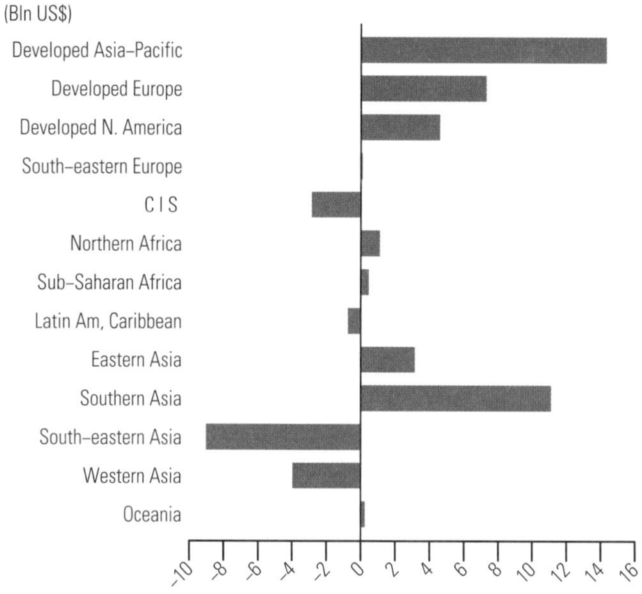

Graph 3: Partner concentration of trade in 2011

(Cumulative share by ranked partners)

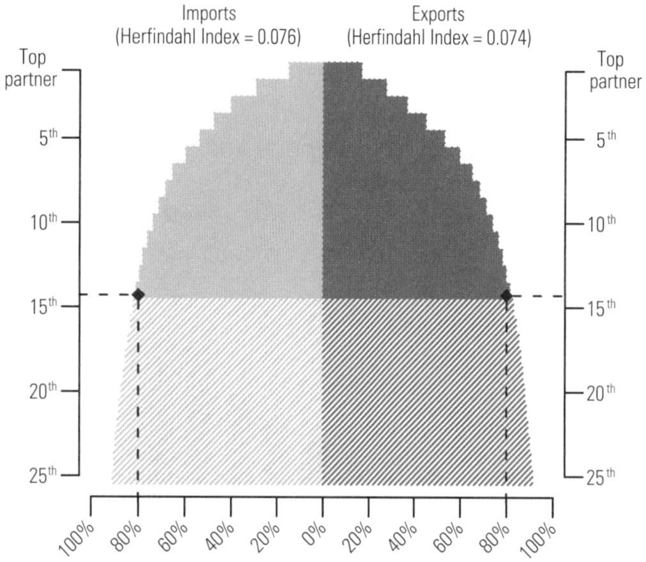

Table 4: Exports by principal countries and SITC sections in 2011

(Value in million US$, percentages of country total)

Country	Total	Shares by SITC sections (%) 0+1	2+4	3	5	6	7	8	9	Total
World	203496.6	5.4	22.7	33.9	5.7	12.5	10.7	8.1	1.1	100
Japan	33714.7	3.2	13.4	56.8	2.2	13.6	7.3	3.4	0.0	100
China	22941.0	3.2	39.6	38.9	9.3	4.9	3.0	1.0	0.0	100
Singapore	18443.9	3.8	7.8	39.8	3.2	13.8	24.3	3.4	3.9	100
USA	16497.6	11.3	19.2	5.0	3.0	11.5	11.1	38.9	0.0	100
Rep. of Korea	16388.8	1.3	13.6	71.2	2.5	6.1	3.1	2.2	0.0	100
India	13335.7	1.3	53.7	35.5	4.0	2.5	2.7	0.3	0.0	100
Malaysia	10995.8	9.6	24.5	30.5	6.0	17.5	9.5	2.3	0.0	100
Other Asia, nes	6584.9	1.9	5.1	72.6	6.1	9.2	3.2	1.9	0.0	100
Thailand	5896.7	5.6	2.6	26.4	10.3	22.0	31.5	1.6	0.0	100
Australia	5582.5	2.9	3.3	44.9	5.1	14.6	16.8	4.9	7.5	100

Imports Profile:

Machinery and transport equipment (SITC section 7) was the largest commodity group for imports in 2011 and accounted for 31.6 percent (see table 2). Imports of mineral fuels, lubricants and related materials (SITC section 3) accounted for 23.0 percent of imported goods. Over the last three years, oils petroleum, bituminous, distillates, except crude (HS code 2710), petroleum oils, oils from bituminous minerals, crude (HS code 2709) and aircraft, spacecraft, satellites (HS code 8802) were the three major imported product groups (see table 5).

Table 5: Top 10 import commodities 2009 to 2011

(Value in million US$)

HS code	4-digit heading of Harmonized System 1996	Value (million US$) 2009	2010	2011	Unit value 2009	2010	2011	Unit	SITC code
	All Commodities	96829.2	135663.3	177435.6					
2710	Oils petroleum, bituminous, distillates, except crude	10841.0	17654.3	27721.8	0.6	0.7	1.0	US$/kg	334
2709	Petroleum oils, oils from bituminous minerals, crude	7362.2	8531.2	11154.5	0.5	0.6	0.8	US$/kg	333
8802	Aircraft, spacecraft, satellites	3125.5	3140.8	2880.7					792
8525	Radio and TV transmitters, television cameras	1995.6	2389.0	2472.5					764
8471	Automatic data processing machines (computers)	1442.2	2219.9	2631.4					752
8708	Parts and accessories for motor vehicles	1031.6	1963.3	2276.7	7.3	8.3	8.8	US$/kg	784
1001	Wheat and meslin	1316.1	1424.3	2194.0	0.3	0.3	0.4	US$/kg	041
8704	Motor vehicles for the transport of goods	1209.9	1389.9	2326.0					782
8517	Electric apparatus for line telephony, telegraphy	890.3	1471.2	2172.3					764
8542	Electronic integrated circuits and microassemblies	1132.2	1582.3	1725.6					776

Source: UN Comtrade

Iran (Islamic Republic of)

Imports: CIF, by origin | **Exports: FOB, by last known destination** | **Trade System: Special**

Overview:

From 2006 to 2010, exports of the Islamic Republic of Iran increased on average by 7.3 percent each year and amounted to 83.8 bln US$ (see table 1 and graph 1). During the same period, imports increased on average by 7.7 percent and amounted to 54.7 bln US$ (see table 2 and graph 1). The trade balance recorded a surplus amounting to 29.1 bln US$ (see graph 1). Large surpluses were recorded with Eastern Asia (+31.8 bln US$), Northern Africa (+2.4 bln US$), Developed Europe (+2.1 bln US$) and Southern Asia (+1.8 bln US$) (see graph 2). In 2010, imports were more diversified across partners than exports: 13 major partners accounted for 80 percent of imports while 6 major partners accounted for 80 percent of exports (see graph 3).

Graph 1: Total imports, exports and trade balance

(Bln US$ by year)

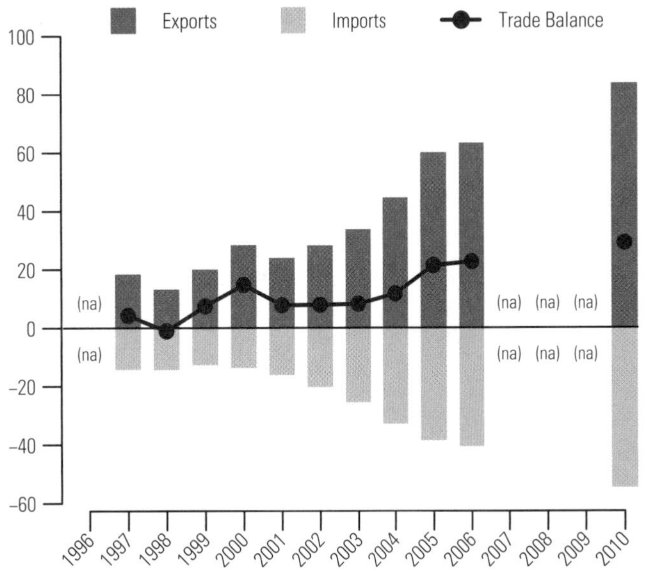

Table 1: Exports by SITC sections

(Value in million US$, growth and shares in percentage)

SITC	2010	Avg. Growth rates (%) 2006-2010	2009-2010	2010 share
Total	83785.0	7.3	...	100.0
0+1	5092.3	18.4	...	6.1
2+4	1881.4	22.5	...	2.2
3	59321.3	3.0	...	70.8
5	7209.5	37.2	...	8.6
6	4584.8	5.6	...	5.5
7	1518.4	19.8	...	1.8
8	841.5	7.4	...	1.0
9	3335.8	173.9	...	4.0

Exports Profile:

In 2010, exports of the Islamic Republic of Iran were composed of 70.8 percent of mineral fuels, lubricants and related materials (SITC section 3), largely crude petroleum oils (see table 1). Major partners were Other Asia, nes and Other Europe, nes and Iraq (see table 4). In 2010, top exported commodities included petroleum oils, crude (HS code 2709), petroleum oils, other than crude (HS code 2710) and petroleum gases and other gaseous hydrocarbons (HS code 2711) (see table 3). In 2010, petroleum oils, crude (HS code 2709) accounted for 55.7 percent of exports.

Table 2: Imports by SITC sections

(Value in million US$, growth and shares in percentage)

SITC	2010	Avg. Growth rates (%) 2006-2010	2009-2010	2010 share
Total	54697.2	7.7	...	100.0
0+1	6729.7	84.8	...	12.3
2+4	3160.9	58.5	...	5.8
3	1472.5	-2.4	...	2.7
5	6650.4	56.4	...	12.2
6	13414.6	61.7	...	24.5
7	16833.6	50.5	...	30.8
8	2006.0	52.4	...	3.7
9	4429.4	-38.6	...	8.1

Table 3: Top 10 export commodities 2008 to 2010

(Value in million US$)

HS code	4-digit heading of Harmonized System 2002	Value (million US$) 2008	2009	2010	Unit value 2008	2009	2010	Unit	SITC code
	All Commodities	...	...	83785.0					
2709	Petroleum oils, crude	...	...	46709.4			0.4	US$/kg	333
2710	Petroleum oils, other than crude	...	...	8482.5			*0.7*	US$/kg	334
9999	Commodities not specified according to kind	...	...	3326.2					931
2711	Petroleum gases and other gaseous hydrocarbons	...	...	3167.2			0.7	US$/kg	343
3901	Polymers of ethylene, in primary forms	...	...	1814.4			1.1	US$/kg	571
2905	Acyclic alcohols and their derivatives	...	...	1220.1			0.3	US$/kg	512
0802	Other nuts, fresh or dried	...	...	1175.3			7.6	US$/kg	057
2601	Iron ores and concentrates	...	...	1124.3			0.1	US$/kg	281
2902	Cyclic hydrocarbons	...	...	831.6			1.0	US$/kg	511
2713	Petroleum coke and other residues	...	...	668.1			0.5	US$/kg	335

Graph 2: Trade Balance by MDG Regions in 2010

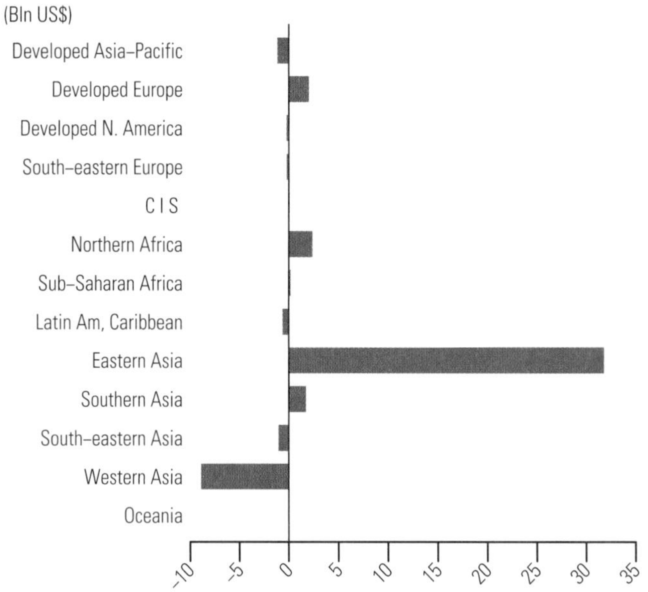

Graph 3: Partner concentration of trade in 2010

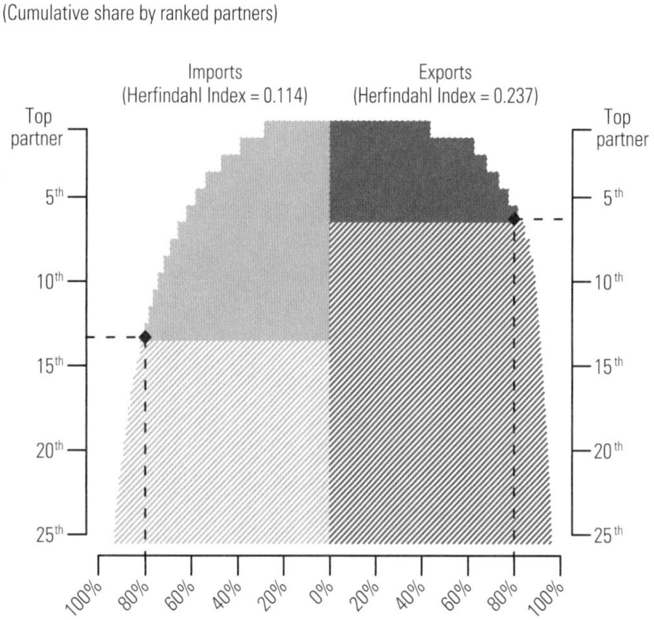

Table 4: Exports by principal countries and SITC sections in 2010

(Value in million US$, percentages of country total)

Country	Total	Shares by SITC sections (%) 0+1	2+4	3	5	6	7	8	9	Total
World	83785.0	6.1	2.2	70.8	8.6	5.5	1.8	1.0	4.0	100
Other Asia, nes	36469.0	0.1	0.0	99.1	0.5	0.4	0.0	0.0	...	100
Other Europe, nes	15874.3	0.0	0.0	100.0	...	...	...	...	...	100
Iraq	4601.6	43.4	1.3	4.1	5.8	23.1	15.6	6.7	0.1	100
China	4450.4	0.7	29.5	18.4	50.2	1.1	0.0	0.0	0.0	100
United Arab Emirates	3484.4	15.6	1.5	39.4	20.5	14.2	1.5	7.2	0.0	100
Areas, nes	3400.4	0.0	0.0	2.3	0.0	0.6	...	...	97.1	100
Other Africa, nes	2451.8	0.0	0.0	100.0	...	...	...	...	...	100
India	1673.4	4.7	6.0	18.6	62.6	8.1	0.0	0.0	...	100
Afghanistan	1315.7	19.5	3.3	10.9	16.0	36.5	6.7	7.1	0.0	100
Turkey	828.8	7.2	3.7	3.1	41.4	40.8	3.3	0.6	0.0	100

Imports Profile:

In 2010, machinery and transport equipment (SITC section 7) accounted for 30.8 percent of imports of the Islamic Republic of Iran (see table 2). In 2010, major products for imports included iron and non-alloy steel in ingots or other primary forms (HS code 7206), flat-rolled products of iron or non-alloy steel (HS code 7208) and turbo-jets, turbo-propellers and other gas turbines (HS code 8411) (see table 5).

Table 5: Top 10 import commodities 2008 to 2010

(Value in million US$)

HS code	4-digit heading of Harmonized System 2002	Value (million US$) 2008	2009	2010	Unit value 2008	2009	2010	Unit	SITC code
	All Commodities	...	...	54697.2					
9999	Commodities not specified according to kind	...	...	3977.2					931
7206	Iron and non-alloy steel in ingots or other primary forms	...	...	2479.3			0.6	US$/kg	672
7208	Flat-rolled products of iron or non-alloy steel	...	...	1977.8			0.7	US$/kg	673
8411	Turbo-jets, turbo-propellers and other gas turbines	...	...	1192.2					714
2710	Petroleum oils, other than crude	...	...	1019.2			0.6	US$/kg	334
3004	Medicaments (excluding goods of heading 30.02, 30.05 or 30.06)	...	...	943.4			130.5	US$/kg	542
1006	Rice	...	...	942.0			0.8	US$/kg	042
1005	Maize (corn)	...	...	919.6			0.3	US$/kg	044
8471	Automatic data processing machines and units thereof	...	...	873.0					752
0202	Meat of bovine animals, frozen	...	...	777.4			4.1	US$/kg	011

Imports: CIF, by origin **Exports: FOB, by last known destination** **Trade System: General**

Overview:

From 2007 to 2011, Ireland's exports increased on average by 1.4 percent each year to reach 129.3 bln US$ in 2011 (see table 1 and graph 1). During the same period, imports decreased on average by 6.3 percent each year to 67.1 bln US$ (see table 2 and graph 1). This resulted in a trade surplus amounting to 62.3 bln US$ in 2011 (see graph 1). This surplus was largely accounted for by trade with Developed Europe which recorded a surplus of 34.6 bln US$ (see graph 2). Trade also recorded surpluses with Developed North America (+22.2 bln US$), Western Asia (+2.6 bln US$) and Developed Asia-Pacific (+2.3 bln US$). Both exports and imports were relatively diversified across partners in 2011: 10 (respectively 11) major partners accounted for 80 percent of exports (respectively imports) (see graph 3).

Graph 1: Total imports, exports and trade balance

(Bln US$ by year)

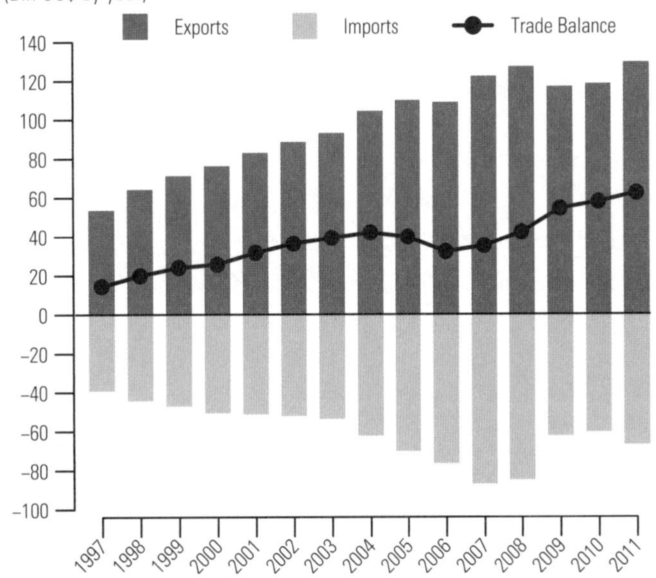

Table 1: Exports by SITC sections

(Value in million US$, growth and shares in percentage)

SITC	2011	Avg. Growth rates (%) 2007-2011	Avg. Growth rates (%) 2010-2011	2011 share
Total	129346.4	1.4	9.3	100.0
0+1	12566.7	0.4	15.9	9.7
2+4	2466.0	3.5	28.0	1.9
3	1883.1	19.0	38.2	1.5
5	77742.0	7.1	12.5	60.1
6	2340.6	-1.5	21.7	1.8
7	15634.2	-15.0	7.1	12.1
8	15582.6	7.8	10.7	12.0
9	1131.3	-26.2	-74.8	0.9

Table 2: Imports by SITC sections

(Value in million US$, growth and shares in percentage)

SITC	2011	Avg. Growth rates (%) 2007-2011	Avg. Growth rates (%) 2010-2011	2011 share
Total	67075.9	-6.3	10.8	100.0
0+1	8071.2	1.7	12.9	12.0
2+4	1385.3	-5.7	24.9	2.1
3	9441.1	4.7	27.6	14.1
5	14540.2	7.0	25.5	21.7
6	5160.2	-11.3	11.2	7.7
7	17327.0	-16.0	6.1	25.8
8	8295.9	-5.6	1.5	12.4
9	2855.0	-13.9	-31.5	4.3

Exports Profile:

In 2011, exports of chemicals and related products, n.e.s. (SITC section 5) increased by 12.5 percent and continued to account for the majority of exported goods (60.1 percent) (see table 1). Other major commodities were machinery and transport equipment (SITC section 7), miscellaneous manufactured articles (SITC section 8) and food, live animals, beverages and tobacco (SITC section 0+1). The top three partners for exports were USA, United Kingdom and Belgium (see table 4). The majority of exports to these countries were chemicals and related products, n.e.s. (SITC section 5). From 2009 to 2011, top exported products were medicaments (excluding goods of heading 30.02, 30.05 or 30.06) (HS code 3004), heterocyclic compounds with nitrogen hetero-atom(s) only (HS code 2933) and nucleic acids and their salts (HS code 2934) (see table 3).

Table 3: Top 10 export commodities 2009 to 2011

(Value in million US$)

HS code	4-digit heading of Harmonized System 2007	Value (million US$) 2009	Value (million US$) 2010	Value (million US$) 2011	Unit value 2009	Unit value 2010	Unit value 2011	Unit	SITC code
	All Commodities	116894.7	118337.5	129346.4					
3004	Medicaments (excluding goods of heading 30.02, 30.05 or 30.06)	21230.5	23410.4	25469.8	*150.8*	*141.5*	*169.0*	US$/kg	542
2933	Heterocyclic compounds with nitrogen hetero-atom(s) only	12997.4	13053.0	14246.4	*4.1*	*3.3*	*4.4*	thsd US$/kg	515
2934	Nucleic acids and their salts	6729.7	7443.6	7574.6	15.3	*17.8*	*28.9*	thsd US$/kg	515
3302	Mixtures of odoriferous substances and mixtures	6590.3	6475.0	6925.5	*54.2*	*51.4*	*51.6*	US$/kg	551
3002	Human blood; animal blood prepared for therapeutic uses	5465.3	5829.6	8594.4	*3.6*	*5.6*	*8.3*	thsd US$/kg	541
9021	Orthopaedic appliances, including crutches, surgical belts and trusses	4108.3	4494.6	4791.5					899
8471	Automatic data processing machines and units thereof	5680.6	3323.9	3490.3	*667.4*	*530.1*	*603.7*	US$/unit	752
9018	Instruments and appliances used in medical, surgical, dental or veterinary	3124.0	3204.6	3790.7					872
9999	Commodities not specified according to kind	4486.4	4483.6	1098.7					931
8542	Electronic integrated circuits	3016.4	2503.0	2318.7					776

Graph 2: Trade Balance by MDG Regions in 2011

(Bln US$)

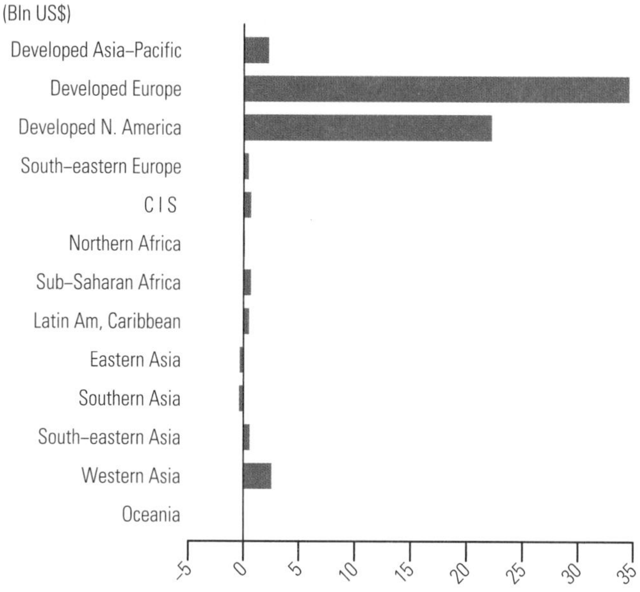

Graph 3: Partner concentration of trade in 2011

(Cumulative share by ranked partners)

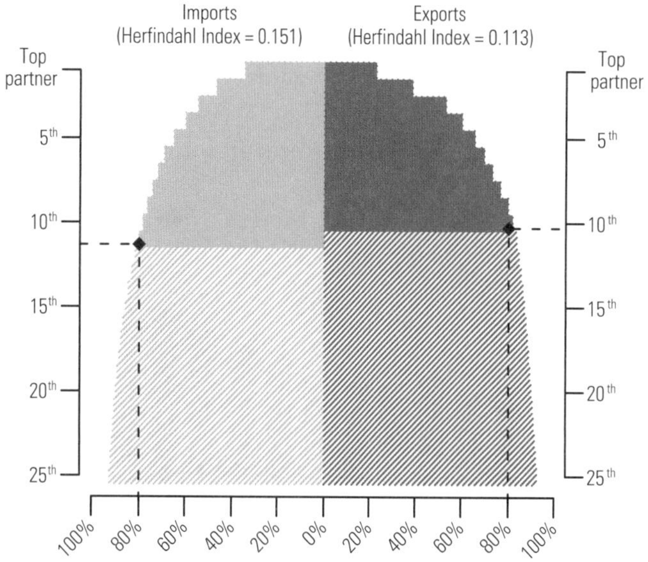

Table 4: Exports by principal countries and SITC sections in 2011

(Value in million US$, percentages of country total)

Country	Total	Shares by SITC sections (%) 0+1	2+4	3	5	6	7	8	9	Total
World	129346.4	9.7	1.9	1.5	60.1	1.8	12.1	12.0	0.9	100
USA	29854.1	1.8	0.1	0.8	76.2	0.6	4.6	15.8	0.1	100
United Kingdom	20127.8	26.7	3.5	4.6	35.4	5.4	10.6	10.8	3.0	100
Belgium	18819.0	1.6	0.7	0.1	90.2	0.3	2.0	5.0	0.1	100
Germany	9099.7	7.6	1.7	1.5	46.1	3.5	24.5	14.0	1.1	100
France	6987.4	12.7	2.6	3.3	58.2	1.3	12.0	9.1	0.8	100
Switzerland	5137.1	1.0	0.1	0.0	93.9	0.2	3.1	1.5	0.0	100
Netherlands	4434.9	14.7	5.8	1.9	20.7	1.8	14.9	39.2	0.9	100
Spain	4387.8	7.0	2.4	0.1	74.8	1.1	5.7	8.1	0.7	100
Italy	4296.2	12.8	1.4	0.2	62.6	2.4	9.6	10.2	0.8	100
Japan	2472.3	2.2	0.7	0.0	44.6	0.9	12.0	39.6	0.0	100

Imports Profile:

Imports of Ireland in 2011 were composed of 25.8 percent of machinery and transport equipment (SITC section 7), 21.7 percent of chemicals and related products, n.e.s. (SITC section 5) and 14.1 percent of mineral fuels, lubricants and related materials (SITC section 3) (see table 2). From 2009 to 2011, top imported goods were petroleum oils, other than crude (HS code 2710), other aircraft (for example, helicopters, aeroplanes); spacecraft (HS code 8802) and medicaments (excluding goods of heading 30.02, 30.05 or 30.06) (HS code 3004) (see table 5).

Table 5: Top 10 import commodities 2009 to 2011

(Value in million US$)

HS code	4-digit heading of Harmonized System 2007	Value (million US$) 2009	2010	2011	Unit value 2009	2010	2011	Unit	SITC code
	All Commodities	62566.4	60549.6	67075.9					
9999	Commodities not specified according to kind	4791.6	4162.7	2845.3					931
2710	Petroleum oils, other than crude	3124.3	3640.3	4803.4	0.6	0.7	1.0	US$/kg	334
8802	Other aircraft (for example, helicopters, aeroplanes); spacecraft	5106.3	3167.9	2777.5	51.6	55.6		mln US$/unit	792
3004	Medicaments (excluding goods of heading 30.02, 30.05 or 30.06)	2186.0	2683.5	3751.1	30.3	48.3	56.1	US$/kg	542
8471	Automatic data processing machines and units thereof	2171.0	2003.6	2408.5	125.0	200.9	206.5	US$/unit	752
2709	Petroleum oils and oils obtained from bituminous minerals, crude	1317.4	1814.9	2180.6	0.5	0.6	0.9	US$/kg	333
8473	Parts and accessories for use with machines of heading 84.69 to 84.72	2742.4	1340.9	1228.6	38.8	30.1	27.8	US$/kg	759
2711	Petroleum gases and other gaseous hydrocarbons	1264.2	1504.7	1882.2	0.3	0.3	0.4	US$/kg	343
8703	Motor cars and other motor vehicles principally designed for the transport	674.0	1457.5	1632.1	17.3	15.7	11.4	thsd US$/unit	781
8542	Electronic integrated circuits	1143.1	846.5	781.6					776

Imports: CIF, by origin **Exports: FOB, by sale** **Trade System: Special**

Overview:

From 2007 to 2011, Israel's exports increased on average by 5.8 percent each year and reached its peak of 67.8 bln US$ in 2011 (see table 1 and graph 1). Similarly, imports increased on average by 6.8 percent each year and reached 73.5 bln US$ (see table 2 and graph 1). This resulted in a trade deficit of 5.7 bln US$ in 2011, much higher than the 0.8 bln US$ deficit in 2010 (see graph 1). By MDG regions, trade with Developed North America recorded a surplus of 11.1 bln US$ (see graph 2). However, trade recorded a deficit amounting to 9.8 bln US$ with Developed Europe. Israel's trade was diversified across partners: in 2011, 17 (respectively 14) major partners accounted for 80 percent of exports (respectively imports) (see graph 3).

Graph 1: Total imports, exports and trade balance

(Bln US$ by year)

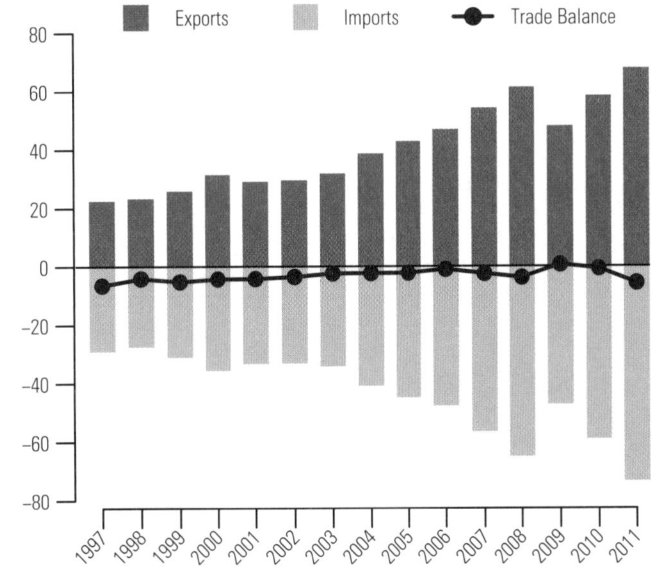

Table 1: Exports by SITC sections

(Value in million US$, growth and shares in percentage)

SITC	2011	Avg. Growth rates (%) 2007-2011	Avg. Growth rates (%) 2010-2011	2011 share
Total	67796.3	5.8	16.1	100.0
0+1	1960.3	8.0	11.5	2.9
2+4	1180.7	13.8	6.9	1.7
3	658.7	68.3	30.3	1.0
5	18738.0	23.2	19.1	27.6
6	24345.6	3.3	22.9	35.9
7	15113.4	18.0	3.1	22.3
8	5599.8	9.2	18.7	8.3
9	200.0	-62.9	43.9	0.3

Exports Profile:

In 2011, exports were composed of 35.9 percent of manufactured goods classified chiefly by material (SITC section 6), 27.6 percent of chemicals and related products, n.e.s. (SITC section 5) and 22.3 percent of machinery and transport equipment (SITC section 7) (see table 1). In addition to the USA, other major partners for exports in 2011 included China, Hong Kong SAR and Belgium (see table 4). Exports to these countries were in majority manufactured goods classified chiefly by material (SITC section 6). From 2009 to 2011, top commodities for exports were diamonds, whether or not worked, but not mounted or set (HS code 7102), medicaments (excluding goods of heading 30.02, 30.05 or 30.06) (HS code 3004) and electronic integrated circuits (HS code 8542) (see table 3).

Table 2: Imports by SITC sections

(Value in million US$, growth and shares in percentage)

SITC	2011	Avg. Growth rates (%) 2007-2011	Avg. Growth rates (%) 2010-2011	2011 share
Total	73526.1	6.8	24.2	100.0
0+1	4732.6	12.9	23.9	6.4
2+4	1685.3	6.6	15.1	2.3
3	13635.9	11.2	30.6	18.5
5	7885.0	6.8	16.6	10.7
6	18053.5	2.8	24.8	24.6
7	21147.9	7.0	26.3	28.8
8	6010.8	6.7	16.7	8.2
9	374.9	-5.3	10.7	0.5

Table 3: Top 10 export commodities 2009 to 2011

(Value in million US$)

HS code	4-digit heading of Harmonized System 2007	Value (million US$) 2009	2010	2011	Unit value 2009	2010	2011	Unit	SITC code
	All Commodities	47934.6	58413.0	67796.3					
7102	Diamonds, whether or not worked, but not mounted or set	11597.9	16401.5	20656.2					667
3004	Medicaments (excluding goods of heading 30.02, 30.05 or 30.06)	4257.3	5343.1	4891.8					542
8542	Electronic integrated circuits	3596.9	2358.9	1787.1					776
3824	Prepared binders for foundry moulds or cores	1955.3	2315.3	3409.4					598
8517	Electrical apparatus for line telephony or line telegraphy	2183.0	2206.0	2190.2					764
8803	Parts of goods of heading 88.01 or 88.02	1661.6	1499.5	1753.6					792
3105	Mineral or chemical fertilisers	1004.3	1535.4	1798.9	*1.7*	*1.8*	*1.2*	US$/kg	562
3003	Medicaments (excluding goods of heading 30.02, 30.05 or 30.06)	166.3	963.0	1987.9					542
9018	Instruments and appliances used in medical, surgical, dental or veterinary	867.0	957.0	1112.7					872
9031	Measuring or checking instruments, appliances and machines	583.5	1018.4	1251.6					874

Graph 2: Trade Balance by MDG Regions in 2011

(Bln US$)

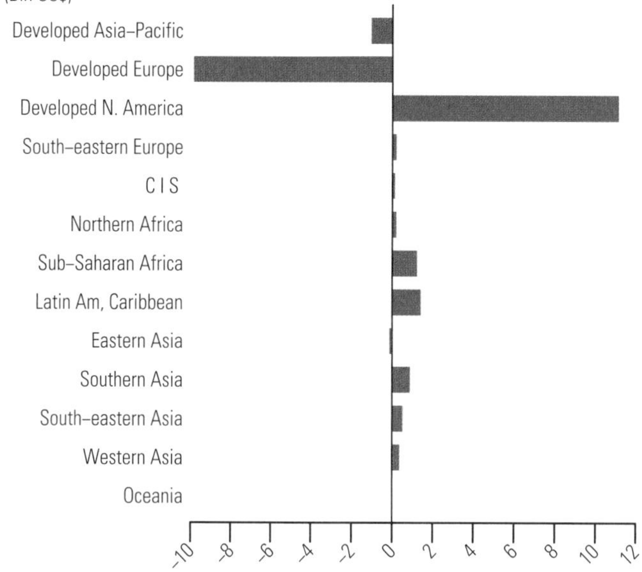

Graph 3: Partner concentration of trade in 2011

(Cumulative share by ranked partners)

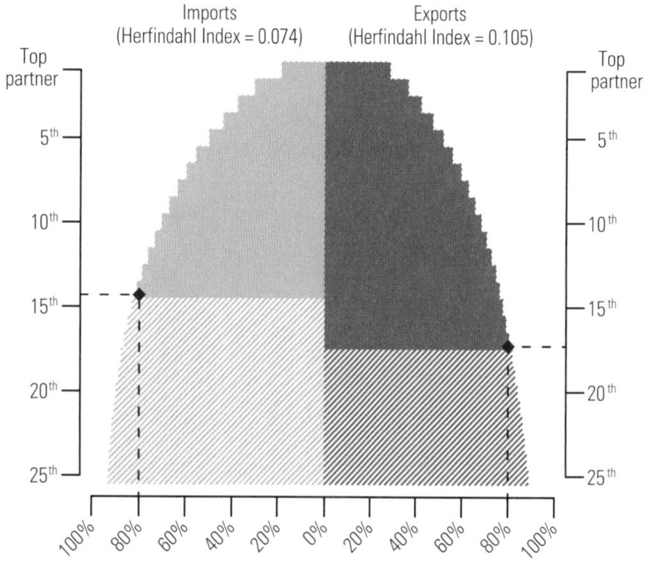

Table 4: Exports by principal countries and SITC sections in 2011

(Value in million US$, percentages of country total)

Country	Total	Shares by SITC sections (%) 0 + 1	2 + 4	3	5	6	7	8	9	Total
World	67 796.3	2.9	1.7	1.0	27.6	35.9	22.3	8.3	0.3	100
USA	19 433.1	1.2	0.5	0.0	26.8	46.7	15.6	9.2	0.0	100
China, Hong Kong SAR	5 338.9	0.1	0.1	0.0	0.5	91.5	5.3	2.6	0.0	100
Belgium	3 767.4	2.0	2.2	0.0	9.5	78.2	4.8	3.3	0.1	100
United Kingdom	3 424.7	4.6	1.0	2.3	59.4	13.3	11.5	8.0	0.0	100
India	3 036.4	0.2	2.8	0.0	21.1	52.5	18.3	5.2	0.0	100
China	2 718.2	1.3	3.3	0.0	28.8	19.0	42.0	5.6	...	100
Areas, nes	2 612.4	0.0	0.0	21.0	0.1	5.4	70.4	3.0	...	100
Netherlands	2 160.5	12.1	6.6	0.1	45.6	3.0	26.6	5.0	1.0	100
Germany	1 948.9	4.9	3.2	0.0	18.3	15.3	36.6	21.4	0.2	100
Turkey	1 855.7	1.0	8.2	0.2	71.2	8.4	6.9	3.9	0.3	100

Imports Profile:

Machinery and transport equipment (SITC section 7), manufactured goods classified chiefly by material (SITC section 6) and mineral fuels, lubricants and related materials (SITC section 3) accounted respectively for 28.8, 24.6 and 18.5 percent of imported goods in 2011 (see table 2). During the last three years, top imported products were diamonds, whether or not worked, but not mounted or set (HS code 7102), petroleum oils and oils obtained from bituminous minerals, crude (HS code 2709) and motor cars and other motor vehicles principally designed for the transport (HS code 8703) (see table 5).

Table 5: Top 10 import commodities 2009 to 2011

(Value in million US$)

HS code	4-digit heading of Harmonized System 2007	Value (million US$) 2009	2010	2011	Unit value 2009	2010	2011	Unit	SITC code
	All Commodities	47 362.7	59 193.9	73 526.1					
7102	Diamonds, whether or not worked, but not mounted or set	5 317.8	8 392.2	10 773.0					667
2709	Petroleum oils and oils obtained from bituminous minerals, crude	5 119.8	6 675.8	8 645.7	*0.7*	*0.4*	0.1	US$/kg	333
8703	Motor cars and other motor vehicles principally designed for the transport	2 444.7	3 056.6	3 360.1	*13.7*	*14.1*	*14.9*	thsd US$/unit	781
2710	Petroleum oils, other than crude	1 395.8	1 946.8	2 985.2					334
8517	Electrical apparatus for line telephony or line telegraphy	1 203.1	1 239.2	1 841.3					764
2701	Coal; briquettes, ovoids and similar solid fuels manufactured from coal	1 153.6	1 225.7	1 573.3	*0.1*	*0.1*	*0.1*	US$/kg	321
3004	Medicaments (excluding goods of heading 30.02, 30.05 or 30.06)	1 147.1	1 186.2	1 327.6					542
8471	Automatic data processing machines and units thereof	959.0	1 204.5	1 307.8					752
8542	Electronic integrated circuits	774.0	1 134.3	1 407.6					776
8486	Machines and apparatus used for the manufacture of semiconductor devices	177.1	169.8	1 608.9					728

Imports: CIF, by origin/consignment for intra-eu **Exports: FOB, by last known destination** **Trade System: Special**

Overview:

From 2007 to 2011, Italy's exports increased on average by 1.1 percent each year to reach 523.2 bln US$ (see table 1 and graph 1). During the same period, imports increased on average by 2.2 percent each year to 557.5 bln US$ (see table 2 and graph 1). The trade balance recorded a deficit of 34.3 bln US$ in 2011 (see graph 1). Large deficits were recorded with the Commonwealth of Independent States (-27.7 bln US$), Eastern Asia (-23.1 bln US$), and Northern Africa (-10.1 bln US$) (see graph 2). However, trade recorded surpluses with Developed North America (+15.0 bln US$) and Developed Europe (+6.8 bln US$). In 2011, Italy's trade was highly diversified across partners: even the 25 major partners could not account for 80 percent of both exports and imports (see graph 3).

Graph 1: Total imports, exports and trade balance

(Bln US$ by year)

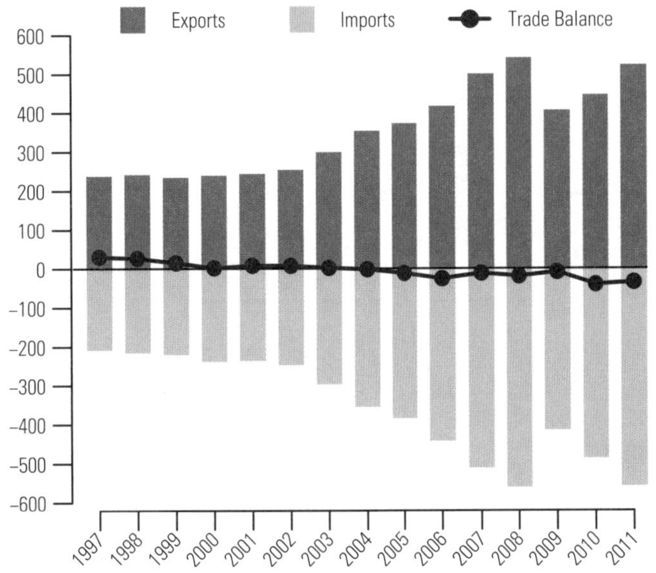

Exports Profile:

In 2011, exports were composed of 35.1 percent of machinery and transport equipment (SITC section 7), 19.4 percent of manufactured goods classified chiefly by material (SITC section 6) and 16.8 percent of miscellaneous manufactured articles (SITC section 8) (see table 1). The top three destinations for exported goods were Germany, France and USA; they accounted jointly for nearly a third (30.7 percent) of exports in 2011 (see table 4). Over the last three years, top products for exports were petroleum oils, other than crude (HS code 2710), medicaments (excluding goods of heading 30.02, 30.05 or 30.06) (HS code 3004) and parts and accessories of the motor vehicles of headings 87.01 to 87.05 (HS code 8708) (see table 3).

Table 1: Exports by SITC sections

(Value in million US$, growth and shares in percentage)

SITC	2011	Avg. Growth rates (%) 2007-2011	2010-2011	2011 share
Total	523179.1	1.1	17.1	100.0
0+1	37143.3	6.0	13.3	7.1
2+4	9174.9	5.2	16.4	1.8
3	24811.6	6.6	19.7	4.7
5	59120.5	4.2	15.2	11.3
6	101482.2	-0.8	19.0	19.4
7	183630.0	-0.7	15.4	35.1
8	88012.4	0.4	15.0	16.8
9	19804.2	9.8	50.5	3.8

Table 2: Imports by SITC sections

(Value in million US$, growth and shares in percentage)

SITC	2011	Avg. Growth rates (%) 2007-2011	2010-2011	2011 share
Total	557510.7	2.2	14.5	100.0
0+1	45882.3	4.9	16.2	8.2
2+4	29603.5	4.3	23.6	5.3
3	110524.0	16.2	23.0	19.8
5	77131.6	4.5	17.2	13.8
6	82941.4	-2.0	19.2	14.9
7	138380.0	-1.3	2.9	24.8
8	58681.0	3.0	11.3	10.5
9	14366.9	-20.3	29.3	2.6

Table 3: Top 10 export commodities 2009 to 2011

(Value in million US$)

HS code	4-digit heading of Harmonized System 2007	Value (million US$) 2009	2010	2011	Unit value 2009	2010	2011	Unit	SITC code
	All Commodities	406479.1	446839.8	523179.1					
2710	Petroleum oils, other than crude	12060.4	18367.4	21959.8	*0.5*	0.7	0.9	US$/kg	334
3004	Medicaments (excluding goods of heading 30.02, 30.05 or 30.06)	12591.8	14027.6	16437.7	77.5	*81.1*	86.8	US$/kg	542
8708	Parts and accessories of the motor vehicles of headings 87.01 to 87.05	10367.9	12887.7	15489.8	*8.4*	*7.7*	*7.9*	US$/kg	784
9999	Commodities not specified according to kind	11264.8	9130.9	11406.2					931
8703	Motor cars and other motor vehicles principally designed for the transport	7946.5	8569.3	9085.1	17.9	19.0	21.1	thsd US$/unit	781
6403	Footwear with outer soles of rubber, plastics, leather	6803.7	7122.1	8413.4	54.4	52.5	61.0	US$/pair	851
8481	Taps, cocks, valves and similar appliances for pipes, boiler shells	7202.1	6806.9	7959.9	*22.0*	*19.5*	*21.6*	US$/kg	747
9403	Other furniture and parts thereof	6824.1	7049.3	7736.5					821
8422	Dish washing machines; machinery for cleaning or drying bottles	5197.9	5613.3	6641.3					745
8479	Machines and mechanical appliances having individual functions	5017.1	5255.5	5959.2					728

Graph 2: Trade Balance by MDG Regions in 2011

(Bln US$)

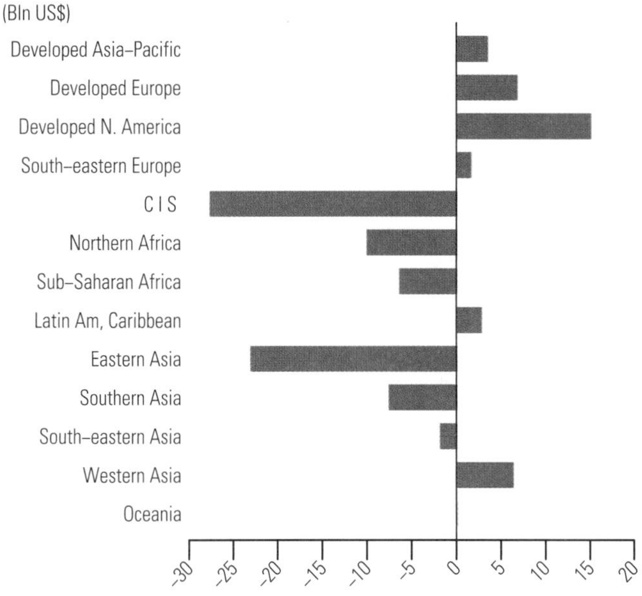

Graph 3: Partner concentration of trade in 2011

(Cumulative share by ranked partners)

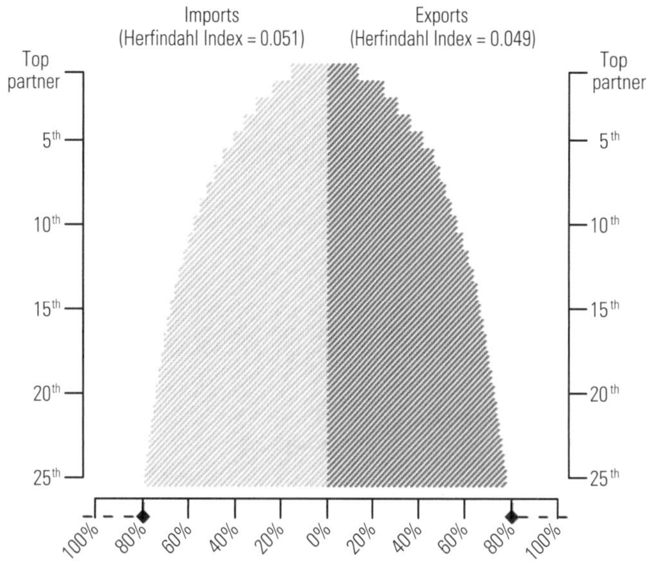

Table 4: Exports by principal countries and SITC sections in 2011

(Value in million US$, percentages of country total)

Country	Total	Shares by SITC sections (%) 0+1	2+4	3	5	6	7	8	9	Total
World	523179.1	7.1	1.8	4.7	11.3	19.4	35.1	16.8	3.8	100
Germany	68338.7	10.6	1.9	0.9	13.2	25.3	34.1	12.9	1.2	100
France	60397.9	7.3	1.4	1.9	10.7	22.1	33.2	20.2	3.2	100
USA	31694.3	9.0	2.3	3.3	9.3	13.8	41.7	20.4	0.0	100
Switzerland	28756.6	5.3	0.8	2.9	15.6	12.4	16.9	25.3	20.8	100
Spain	27443.1	5.3	1.6	11.4	12.8	20.8	30.0	16.2	1.9	100
United Kingdom	24140.2	13.5	1.2	0.7	11.3	17.1	33.7	21.0	1.6	100
China	13866.2	1.6	6.0	0.4	9.0	13.7	56.5	12.8	0.0	100
Belgium	13387.1	8.3	1.3	1.3	21.8	16.8	29.4	16.4	4.7	100
Turkey	13268.9	1.2	1.6	15.4	11.6	17.3	42.1	10.8	0.1	100
Russian Federation	12937.5	5.6	0.7	0.2	7.8	12.4	41.5	31.8	0.0	100

Imports Profile:

Machinery and transport equipment (SITC section 7) accounted for 24.8 percent of imports in 2011 (see table 2). Other major commodity groups included mineral fuels, lubricants and related materials (SITC section 3) and manufactured goods classified chiefly by material (SITC section 6) respectively with 19.3 and 14.9 percent of imported goods. Major imported products were petroleum oils and oils obtained from bituminous minerals, crude (HS code 2709), motor cars and other motor vehicles principally designed for the transport (HS code 8703) and petroleum gases and other gaseous hydrocarbons (HS code 2711) (see table 5).

Table 5: Top 10 import commodities 2009 to 2011

(Value in million US$)

HS code	4-digit heading of Harmonized System 2007	Value (million US$) 2009	2010	2011	Unit value 2009	2010	2011	Unit	SITC code
	All Commodities	414783.6	486984.4	557510.7					
2709	Petroleum oils and oils obtained from bituminous minerals, crude	33540.4	46054.3	58067.0	0.4	0.6	0.8	US$/kg	333
8703	Motor cars and other motor vehicles principally designed for the transport	29673.6	28056.7	29647.4	16.4	16.0	17.7	thsd US$/unit	781
2711	Petroleum gases and other gaseous hydrocarbons	25273.3	27103.0	31208.4	*0.5*	*0.5*	*0.6*	US$/kg	343
3004	Medicaments (excluding goods of heading 30.02, 30.05 or 30.06)	13591.6	13761.8	15765.4	*137.1*	126.8	*125.2*	US$/kg	542
2710	Petroleum oils, other than crude	6825.5	9283.5	11950.7	*0.5*	0.6	0.9	US$/kg	334
8541	Diodes, transistors and similar semiconductor devices	3130.2	12240.2	10098.2					776
9999	Commodities not specified according to kind	8210.4	6484.7	7693.0					931
8517	Electrical apparatus for line telephony or line telegraphy	5524.9	7401.1	6580.3					764
8708	Parts and accessories of the motor vehicles of headings 87.01 to 87.05	5713.2	6297.4	7111.7	*9.6*	*8.7*	*8.8*	US$/kg	784
8471	Automatic data processing machines and units thereof	4937.3	5722.2	5580.9	182.6	194.2	193.1	US$/unit	752

Jamaica

Imports: CIF, by origin | **Exports: FOB, by last known destination** | **Trade System: Special**

Overview:

After several years of continuous growth marked by a peak of 2.4 bln US$ in 2008, the value of the exports of Jamaica contracted sharply in 2009 (by 46.0 percent) but slightly increased again in 2010 by 0.9 percent to amount to 1.3 bln US$, still well below its 2008 level (see table 1 and graph 1). Imports showed a similar development with an increase by 3.2 percent to 5.2 bln US$ in 2010 (see table 2 and graph 1). This resulted in a trade deficit of 3.9 bln US$ in 2010, a bit higher than the deficit of 3.7 bln US$ in 2009 (see graph 1). Two MDG regions accounted for a large part of this deficit: Latin America and the Caribbean (-2.0 bln US$) and Developed North America (-1.1 bln US$). In 2010, 6 (respectively 10) major partners accounted for 80 percent of exports (respectively imports) (see graph 3).

Graph 1: Total imports, exports and trade balance

(Bln US$ by year)

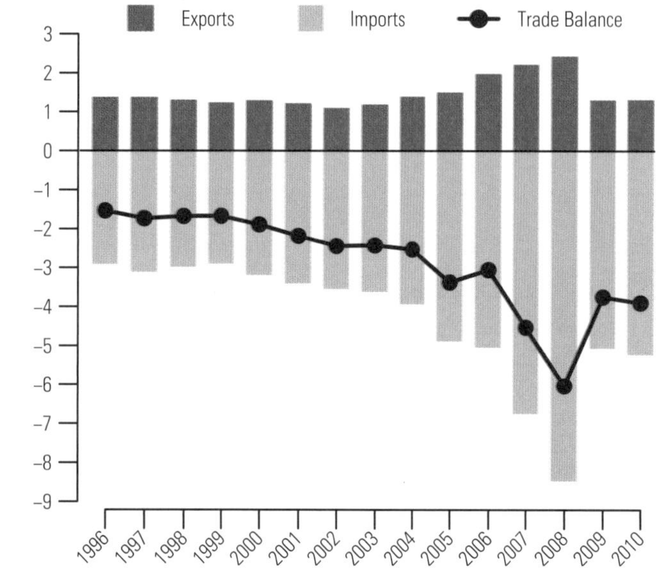

Table 1: Exports by SITC sections

(Value in million US$, growth and shares in percentage)

SITC	2010	Avg. Growth rates (%) 2006-2010	2009-2010	2010 share
Total	1 327.6	-9.6	0.9	100.0
0+1	312.7	-1.3	-7.7	23.6
2+4	555.8	-18.5	19.2	41.9
3	282.0	1.2	31.9	21.2
5	83.3	2.9	-59.2	6.3
6	16.3	0.4	-36.4	1.2
7	35.1	12.0	-14.4	2.6
8	23.3	4.3	13.7	1.8
9	19.1	...	223.0	1.4

Table 2: Imports by SITC sections

(Value in million US$, growth and shares in percentage)

SITC	2010	Avg. Growth rates (%) 2006-2010	2009-2010	2010 share
Total	5 225.2	0.9	3.2	100.0
0+1	888.9	6.2	0.8	17.0
2+4	94.7	-3.7	5.6	1.8
3	1 585.6	6.5	13.5	30.3
5	699.1	5.2	-5.4	13.4
6	587.1	-4.4	5.6	11.2
7	795.2	-8.6	-3.1	15.2
8	481.2	-1.3	4.4	9.2
9	93.3	3.9	-21.5	1.8

Exports Profile:

In 2010, top commodity groups for Jamaica's exports were inedible crude materials (except fuels), animal and vegetable oils, fats and waxes (SITC sections 2+4), food, live animals, beverages and tobacco (SITC sections 0+1) and mineral fuels, lubricants and related materials (SITC section 3), accounting respectively for 41.9, 23.6 and 21.2 percent of total exports (see table 1). The three largest markets for exported goods were USA, Canada and United Kingdom (see table 4). Over the last three years, top exported products were artificial corundum, whether or not chemically defined (HS code 2818), petroleum oils, other than crude (HS code 2710) and alcohol of a strength by volume of 80% vol or higher (HS code 2207) (see table 3).

Table 3: Top 10 export commodities 2008 to 2010

(Value in million US$)

HS code	4-digit heading of Harmonized System 2007	Value (million US$) 2008	2009	2010	Unit value 2008	2009	2010	Unit	SITC code
	All Commodities	2 438.8	1 316.0	1 327.6					
2818	Artificial corundum, whether or not chemically defined	1 246.6	368.8	404.6	0.3	0.2	0.3	US$/kg	285
2710	Petroleum oils, other than crude	435.4	213.8	282.0	0.7	0.4	0.6	US$/kg	334
2207	Alcohol of a strength by volume of 80 % vol or higher	151.5	170.4	48.1	*0.6*	*0.8*	0.4	US$/litre	512
2606	Aluminium ores and concentrates	114.5	84.9	128.7	0.0	0.0	0.0	US$/kg	285
1701	Cane or beet sugar and chemically pure sucrose, in solid form	104.3	72.4	44.9	0.8	0.6	0.5	US$/kg	061
2208	Alcohol of a strength by volume of less than 80 % vol	48.1	51.6	50.6	*2.7*	*2.7*	1.0	US$/litre	112
2203	Beer made from malt	33.1	37.8	39.8	*1.0*	*0.8*	0.9	US$/litre	112
0901	Coffee, whether or not roasted or decaffeinated	27.8	35.1	21.9	*2.4*			US$/kg	071
0714	Manioc, arrowroot, sweet potatoes and similar roots	25.1	23.0	24.6	2.6	2.4	2.1	US$/kg	054
7204	Ferrous waste and scrap; remelting scrap ingots of iron or steel	20.1	12.1	16.7	0.2	0.1	0.2	US$/kg	282

Graph 2: Trade Balance by MDG Regions in 2010

(Bln US$)

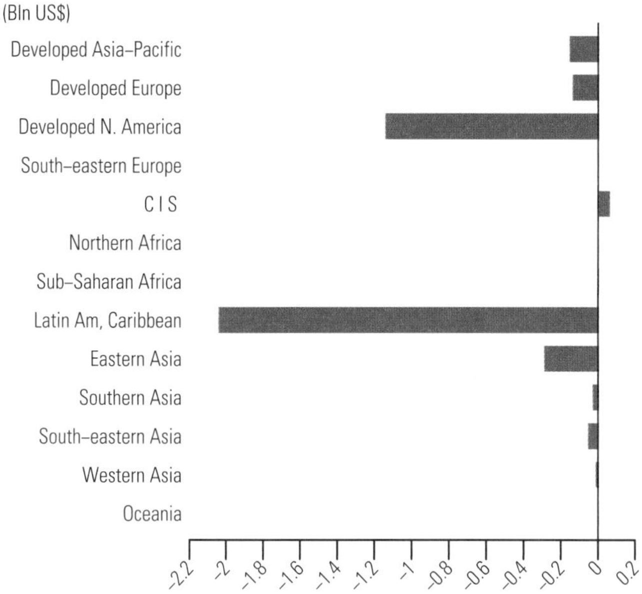

Graph 3: Partner concentration of trade in 2010

(Cumulative share by ranked partners)

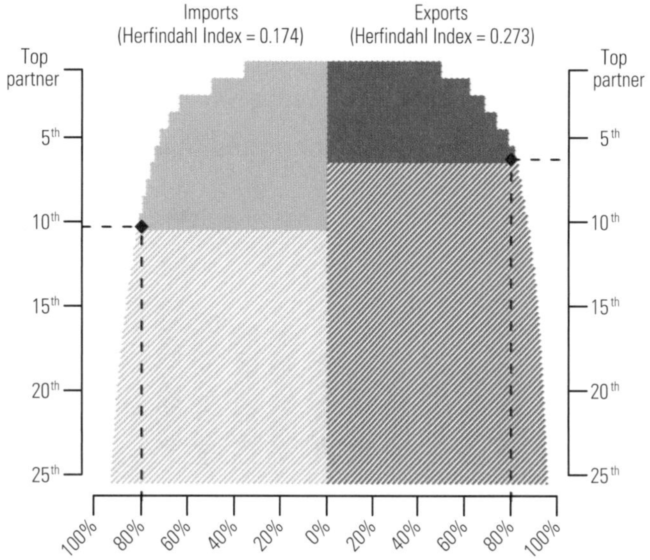

Table 4: Exports by principal countries and SITC sections in 2010

(Value in million US$, percentages of country total)

Country	Total	Shares by SITC sections (%) 0+1	2+4	3	5	6	7	8	9	Total
World	1327.6	23.6	41.9	21.2	6.3	1.2	2.6	1.8	1.4	100
USA	659.1	18.8	25.8	42.8	4.5	0.6	2.9	2.1	2.5	100
Canada	163.4	15.6	83.4	0.0	0.1	0.1	0.2	0.2	0.4	100
United Kingdom	83.9	83.1	0.3	...	14.8	0.1	0.9	0.4	0.4	100
Norway	68.5	0.2	99.8	...	...	0.0	0.0	0.0	...	100
Netherlands	68.3	3.9	93.2	...	0.1	0.3	2.4	0.1	...	100
Russian Federation	37.3	0.1	99.9	...	...	...	...	...	0.0	100
Trinidad and Tobago	19.1	40.9	1.9	0.4	41.3	4.8	3.8	5.8	1.0	100
Iceland	18.3	0.0	100.0	...	...	...	...	...	...	100
Rep. of Korea	17.3	2.4	5.6	...	91.0	0.8	0.0	0.1	...	100
France	16.1	43.9	53.2	0.1	1.0	0.0	1.3	0.2	0.3	100

Imports Profile:

In 2010, Jamaica's imports were mostly composed of mineral fuels, lubricants and related materials (SITC section 3), food, live animals, beverages and tobacco (SITC sections 0+1) and machinery and transport equipment (SITC section 7) (see table 2). They accounted respectively for 30.3, 17.0 and 15.2 percent of imported goods. From 2008 to 2010, petroleum oils, both refined oil and crude (HS code 2710 and 2709), together with medicaments (excluding goods of heading 30.02, 30.05 or 30.06) (HS code 3004), were the top products for imports (see table 5).

Table 5: Top 10 import commodities 2008 to 2010

(Value in million US$)

HS code	4-digit heading of Harmonized System 2007	Value (million US$) 2008	2009	2010	Unit value 2008	2009	2010	Unit	SITC code
	All Commodities	8465.4	5064.3	5225.2					
2710	Petroleum oils, other than crude	2496.7	851.2	895.9	0.2	0.5	0.6	US$/kg	334
2709	Petroleum oils and oils obtained from bituminous minerals, crude	866.1	498.4	627.7	0.8	0.4	0.5	US$/kg	333
3004	Medicaments (excluding goods of heading 30.02, 30.05 or 30.06)	183.5	144.6	145.8	71.8	45.0	*58.9*	US$/kg	542
2207	Alcohol of a strength by volume of 80 % vol or higher	139.7	150.3	175.4	*0.8*	*0.9*	*0.8*	US$/litre	512
8703	Motor cars and other motor vehicles principally designed for the transport	176.2	99.3	106.6			*15.8*	thsd US$/unit	781
9999	Commodities not specified according to kind	116.5	118.9	93.3					931
8517	Electrical apparatus for line telephony or line telegraphy	134.3	81.0	102.9					764
4901	Printed books, brochures, leaflets and similar printed matter	182.2	56.0	72.8	33.2	17.4	22.6	US$/kg	892
2815	Sodium hydroxide (caustic soda)	153.2	80.4	53.5	0.3	0.8	0.5	US$/kg	522
7228	Other bars and rods of other alloy steel	116.9	36.2	43.0	1.1	0.1	0.7	US$/kg	676

Imports: CIF, by origin	Exports: FOB, by last known destination	Trade System: General

Overview:

From 2007 to 2011, Japan's exports increased on average by 3.6 percent each year and amounted to 823.3 bln US$ in 2011, reflecting a 7.0 percent increase from 2010 and surpassing its previous peak of 781.4 bln US$ in 2008 (see table 1 and graph 1). During the same period, imports increased at an average annual rate of 8.3 percent and amounted to 854.6 bln US$ in 2011 (see table 2 and graph 1). This resulted in a trade deficit of 31.3 bln US$ for the year (see graph 1). Trade surpluses were recorded with Eastern Asia (+74.2 bln US$), Developed North America (+47.4 bln US$) and Developed Europe (+15.8 bln US$) (see graph 2). Trade deficits were recorded with Western Asia (-122.7 bln US$) and Developed Asia-Pacific (-39.8 bln US$). Japan's trade was diversified across partners: in 2011, 16 (respectively 17) major partners accounted for 80 percent of exports (respectively imports) (see graph 3).

Graph 1: Total imports, exports and trade balance

(Bln US$ by year)

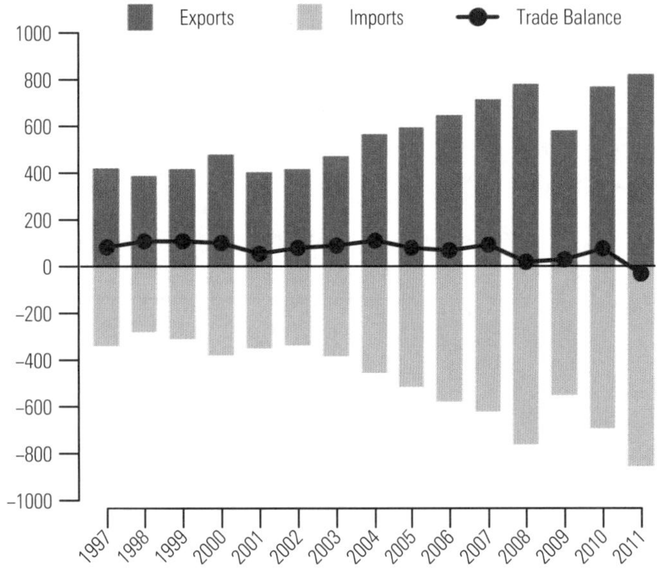

Table 1: Exports by SITC sections

(Value in million US$, growth and shares in percentage)

SITC	2011	Avg. Growth rates (%) 2007-2011	Avg. Growth rates (%) 2010-2011	2011 share
Total	823 292.5	3.6	7.0	100.0
0+1	4 489.1	6.2	-2.7	0.5
2+4	12 380.4	8.2	12.6	1.5
3	16 303.0	15.1	24.9	2.0
5	84 521.8	6.7	7.8	10.3
6	109 712.4	7.0	9.9	13.3
7	480 368.0	1.5	4.9	58.3
8	66 078.7	5.9	13.1	8.0
9	49 439.1	6.0	6.4	6.0

Table 2: Imports by SITC sections

(Value in million US$, growth and shares in percentage)

SITC	2011	Avg. Growth rates (%) 2007-2011	Avg. Growth rates (%) 2010-2011	2011 share
Total	854 626.4	8.3	23.1	100.0
0+1	73 235.4	9.3	23.5	8.6
2+4	69 110.5	8.1	21.2	8.1
3	274 244.6	12.2	37.7	32.1
5	75 573.2	13.5	24.2	8.8
6	73 392.3	5.0	24.8	8.6
7	178 179.0	4.3	10.4	20.8
8	97 609.0	5.3	15.5	11.4
9	13 282.3	4.4	2.0	1.6

Exports Profile:

Japan's exports were largely machinery and transport equipment (SITC section 7) (see table 1). It accounted for 58.3 percent of exports in 2011. Other major commodity groups included manufactured goods classified chiefly by material (SITC section 6) and chemicals and related products, n.e.s. (SITC section 5), accounting respectively for 13.3 and 10.3 percent of exports. China, USA and the Republic of Korea were the top three markets for exports in 2011 (see table 4). From 2007 to 2011, top exported products were motor cars and other motor vehicles principally designed for the transport (HS code 8703), parts and accessories of the motor vehicles of headings 87.01 to 87.05 (HS code 8708) and electronic integrated circuits (HS code 8542) (see table 3).

Table 3: Top 10 export commodities 2009 to 2011

(Value in million US$)

HS code	4-digit heading of Harmonized System 2007	Value (million US$) 2009	Value (million US$) 2010	Value (million US$) 2011	Unit value 2009	Unit value 2010	Unit value 2011	Unit	SITC code
	All Commodities	580 718.7	769 773.8	823 292.5					
8703	Motor cars and other motor vehicles principally designed for the transport	62 268.3	90 372.8	87 344.8	*16.5*	*18.1*	*18.8*	thsd US$/unit	781
9999	Commodities not specified according to kind	34 258.5	40 038.7	39 375.7					931
8708	Parts and accessories of the motor vehicles of headings 87.01 to 87.05	24 657.2	35 090.9	37 488.2	11.8	12.3	13.5	US$/kg	784
8542	Electronic integrated circuits	27 429.8	34 532.1	32 013.1					776
8901	Cruise ships, excursion boats, ferry-boats, cargo ships, barges	21 614.6	25 592.4	25 682.6	27.9		*0.0*	mln US$/unit	793
8486	Machines and apparatus used for the manufacture of semiconductor devices	8 260.4	19 083.2	20 933.0					728
8443	Printing machinery used for printing by means of the printing type, blocks	13 139.6	15 204.2	15 145.1					726
2710	Petroleum oils, other than crude	9 360.6	11 655.2	14 593.1	0.5	0.7	0.9	US$/kg	334
8541	Diodes, transistors and similar semiconductor devices	8 879.9	12 444.7	12 257.2					776
8704	Motor vehicles for the transport of goods	6 558.7	10 279.4	11 266.6	*15.8*	*20.7*	*23.9*	thsd US$/unit	782

Graph 2: Trade Balance by MDG Regions in 2011

(Bln US$)

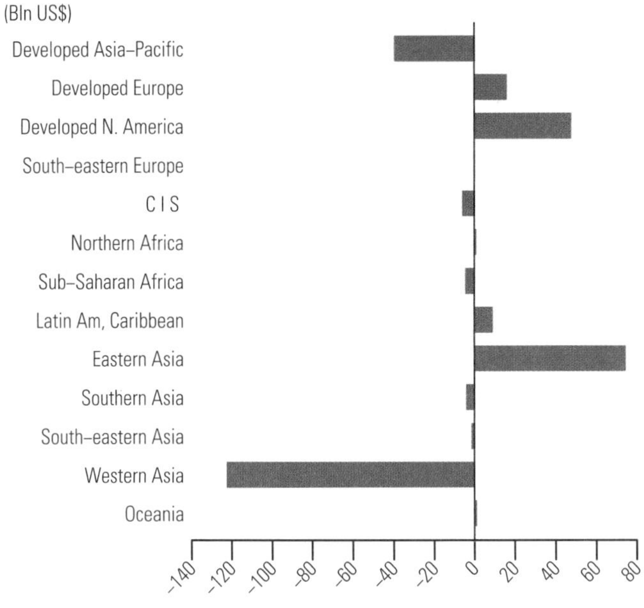

Graph 3: Partner concentration of trade in 2011

(Cumulative share by ranked partners)

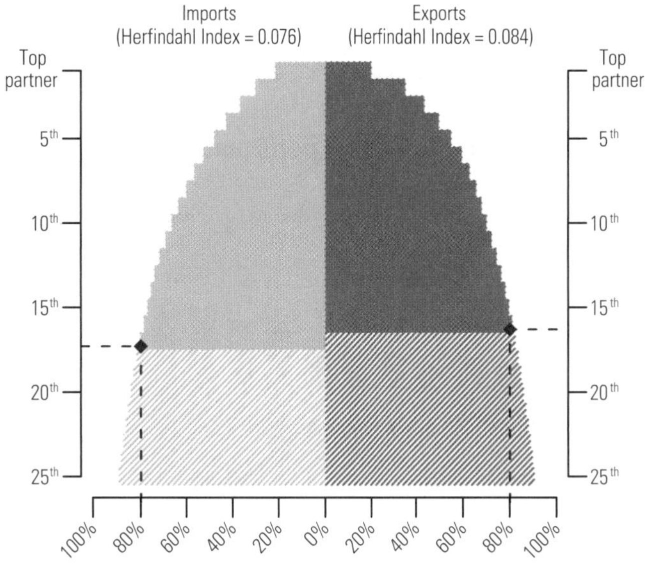

Table 4: Exports by principal countries and SITC sections in 2011

(Value in million US$, percentages of country total)

Country	Total	Shares by SITC sections (%)								
		0+1	2+4	3	5	6	7	8	9	Total
World	823292.5	0.5	1.5	2.0	10.3	13.3	58.3	8.0	6.0	100
China	162062.1	0.2	3.3	1.3	13.0	14.1	54.9	9.0	4.2	100
USA	127679.0	0.5	0.5	0.5	6.8	7.9	71.3	8.0	4.4	100
Rep. of Korea	66167.5	0.6	3.4	3.1	24.1	22.6	34.1	8.4	3.7	100
Other Asia, nes	50960.9	1.3	0.9	0.5	21.8	17.8	44.2	8.8	4.8	100
China, Hong Kong SAR	42954.4	2.6	0.8	4.6	9.1	9.1	44.6	14.2	15.0	100
Thailand	37530.6	0.6	1.5	0.4	9.5	23.1	52.9	6.4	5.6	100
Singapore	27264.6	0.6	0.2	16.5	6.6	8.8	48.3	5.4	13.5	100
Germany	23505.5	0.1	1.0	0.0	7.9	6.8	63.8	14.9	5.5	100
Malaysia	18796.0	0.3	1.1	1.5	7.9	19.8	50.8	10.8	7.8	100
Netherlands	17945.8	0.2	0.6	0.1	8.9	5.5	70.5	10.4	3.8	100

Imports Profile:

In 2011, Japan's imports were composed of 32.1 percent of mineral fuels, lubricants and related materials (SITC section 3), 20.8 percent of machinery and transport equipment (SITC section 7) and 11.4 percent of miscellaneous manufactured articles (SITC section 8) (see table 2). From 2009 to 2011, top imported products were petroleum oils and oils obtained from bituminous minerals, crude (HS code 2709), petroleum gases and other gaseous hydrocarbons (HS code 2711) and coal; briquettes. ovoids and similar solid fuels manufactured from coal (HS code 2701) (see table 5).

Table 5: Top 10 import commodities 2009 to 2011

(Value in million US$)

HS code	4-digit heading of Harmonized System 2007	Value (million US$)			Unit value				SITC code
		2009	2010	2011	2009	2010	2011	Unit	
	All Commodities	551984.8	694059.2	854626.4					
2709	Petroleum oils and oils obtained from bituminous minerals, crude	79973.9	105814.3	142094.4	0.5	0.6	0.8	US$/kg	333
2711	Petroleum gases and other gaseous hydrocarbons	36643.9	48560.8	71140.9					343
2701	Coal; briquettes, ovoids and similar solid fuels manufactured from coal	22052.0	24117.9	30729.6	0.1	0.1	*0.2*	US$/kg	321
2710	Petroleum oils, other than crude	12726.4	18761.2	27844.1	*0.5*	0.7	0.9	US$/kg	334
8542	Electronic integrated circuits	16299.3	20419.5	17961.8					776
2601	Iron ores and concentrates, including roasted iron pyrites	8692.1	15494.9	21442.4	0.1	*0.1*	*0.2*	US$/kg	281
8471	Automatic data processing machines and units thereof	11345.7	14467.0	17028.2	118.8	136.6	179.2	US$/unit	752
8517	Electrical apparatus for line telephony or line telegraphy	10266.5	13451.8	18750.0					764
3004	Medicaments (excluding goods of heading 30.02, 30.05 or 30.06)	9506.2	11548.1	13858.4	*212.2*	*261.8*	*294.7*	US$/kg	542
9999	Commodities not specified according to kind	10238.5	11961.6	12330.9					931

Jordan

Imports: CIF, by origin | **Exports: FOB, by last known destination** | **Trade System: Special**

Overview:

From 2007 to 2011, Jordan's exports increased on average by 8.7 percent each year and amounted to 8.0 bln US$ in 2011, reflecting a 13.4 percent increase from 2010 (see table 1 and graph 1). During the same period, imports increased at an average annual rate of 7.8 percent and amounted to 18.3 bln US$ in 2011 (see table 2 and graph 1). This resulted in a trade deficit of 10.3 bln US$ for the year (see graph 1). By MDG regions, trade recorded deficits with Developed Europe, Western Asia and Eastern Asia amounting to 3.4, 3.2 and 2.4 bln US$ respectively (see graph 2). In 2011, trade was diversified across partners: 15 major partners accounted for 80 percent of exports (compared to 18 major partners for imports) (see graph 3).

Graph 1: Total imports, exports and trade balance

(Bln US$ by year)

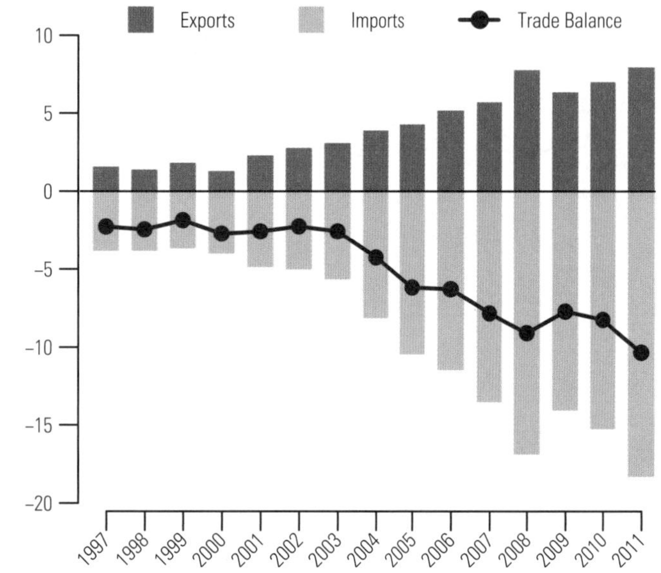

Table 1: Exports by SITC sections

(Value in million US$, growth and shares in percentage)

SITC	2011	Avg. Growth rates (%) 2007-2011	Avg. Growth rates (%) 2010-2011	2011 share
Total	7963.5	8.7	13.4	100.0
0+1	1234.1	14.5	12.4	15.5
2+4	827.3	26.2	63.6	10.4
3	18.0	-17.6	-72.9	0.2
5	2565.4	14.4	8.2	32.2
6	803.3	13.8	4.0	10.1
7	798.2	-5.6	8.6	10.0
8	1446.1	-1.9	14.3	18.2
9	271.2	39.6	28.8	3.4

Table 2: Imports by SITC sections

(Value in million US$, growth and shares in percentage)

SITC	2011	Avg. Growth rates (%) 2007-2011	Avg. Growth rates (%) 2010-2011	2011 share
Total	18301.1	7.8	19.9	100.0
0+1	2703.6	9.4	17.0	14.8
2+4	548.4	12.8	35.6	3.0
3	5283.9	15.8	56.9	28.9
5	2010.9	12.5	16.7	11.0
6	2870.5	4.0	9.7	15.7
7	3390.7	-0.4	-3.4	18.5
8	1192.1	6.5	11.2	6.5
9	301.0	1.8	16.7	1.6

Exports Profile:

In 2011, exports of chemicals and related products, n.e.s. (SITC section 5), the largest commodity group, increased by 8.2 percent and accounted for 32.2 percent of exported goods (see table 1). Other major commodity groups for exports included miscellaneous manufactured articles (SITC section 8) and food, live animals, beverages and tobacco (SITC sections 0+1), representing 18.2 and 15.5 percent of exports, respectively. Iraq, USA and India were the three largest markets for exports (see table 4). Exports to USA were almost exclusively miscellaneous manufactured articles (SITC section 8) while exports to India were in majority chemicals and related products, n.e.s. (SITC section 5) (see table 4). From 2009 to 2011, top products for exports were mineral or chemical fertilisers, potassic (HS code 3104), other garments, knitted or crocheted (HS code 6114) and medicaments (excluding goods of heading 30.02, 30.05 or 30.06) (HS code 3004) (see table 3).

Table 3: Top 10 export commodities 2009 to 2011

(Value in million US$)

HS code	4-digit heading of Harmonized System 2007	Value (million US$) 2009	Value (million US$) 2010	Value (million US$) 2011	Unit value 2009	Unit value 2010	Unit value 2011	Unit	SITC code
	All Commodities	6365.7	7023.1	7963.5					
3104	Mineral or chemical fertilisers, potassic	455.8	691.7	846.4	*0.8*	*0.8*	*0.7*	US$/kg	562
6114	Other garments, knitted or crocheted	441.5	539.7	742.3	*42.7*	15.7	19.4	US$/kg	845
3004	Medicaments (excluding goods of heading 30.02, 30.05 or 30.06)	409.6	541.9	452.9		63.0	57.5	US$/kg	542
2510	Natural calcium phosphates	371.8	372.5	630.0	*0.2*	0.1	0.1	US$/kg	272
3102	Mineral or chemical fertilisers, nitrogenous	206.0	316.2	319.8		0.4	0.6	US$/kg	562
7108	Gold (including gold plated with platinum)	237.1	200.2	263.0	*27.6*	27.0	41.0	thsd US$/kg	971
0702	Tomatoes, fresh or chilled	169.0	232.4	224.8	*1.2*	0.6	0.5	US$/kg	054
8544	Insulated (including enamelled or anodised) wire, cable	148.3	168.4	198.9		5.0	6.0	US$/kg	773
7612	Aluminium casks, drums, cans, boxes and similar containers	139.8	121.9	100.3	*9.7*	7.3	6.1	US$/kg	692
3003	Medicaments (excluding goods of heading 30.02, 30.05 or 30.06)	101.5	133.8	121.8		6.6	15.4	US$/kg	542

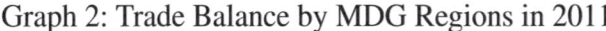

Graph 2: Trade Balance by MDG Regions in 2011

(Bln US$)

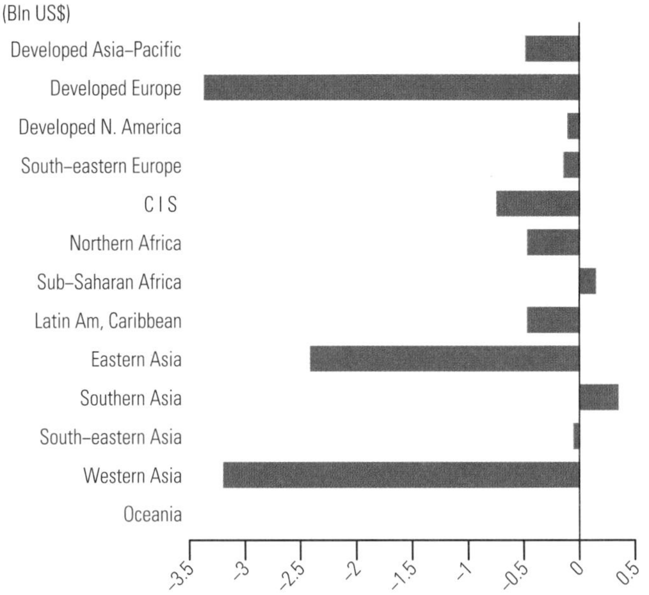

Graph 3: Partner concentration of trade in 2011

(Cumulative share by ranked partners)

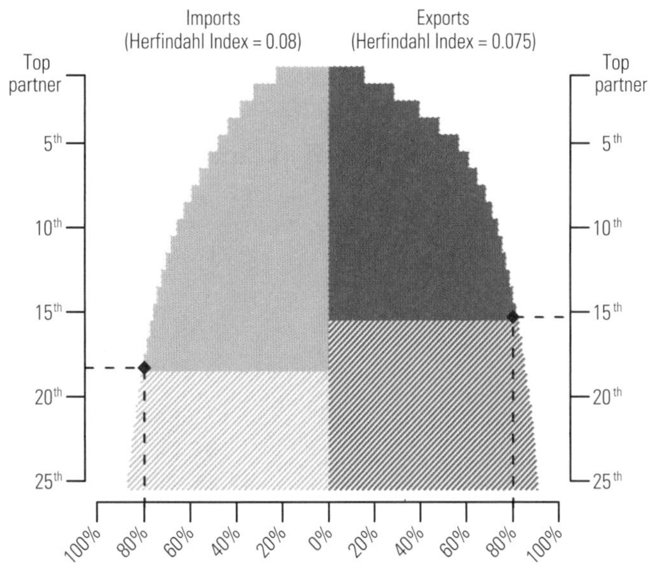

Table 4: Exports by principal countries and SITC sections in 2011

(Value in million US$, percentages of country total)

Country	Total	Shares by SITC sections (%) 0 + 1	2 + 4	3	5	6	7	8	9	Total
World	7963.5	15.5	10.4	0.2	32.2	10.1	10.0	18.2	3.4	100
Iraq	1214.3	30.9	2.5	0.4	17.8	25.8	14.6	7.8	0.0	100
USA	1040.5	0.7	0.1	...	2.9	1.0	0.8	94.4	0.1	100
India	871.2	0.3	46.6	0.0	52.9	0.1	0.1	0.0	...	100
Free Zones	691.4	10.6	4.2	0.5	24.3	10.7	41.8	7.9	0.0	100
Saudi Arabia	679.8	23.2	2.4	0.2	34.0	19.6	13.6	6.4	0.5	100
Lebanon	335.7	9.1	0.7	0.0	15.7	10.8	1.0	11.4	51.1	100
United Arab Emirates	291.0	35.5	4.9	0.0	22.8	10.1	15.5	7.4	3.8	100
Syria	286.8	51.6	1.2	0.1	14.4	19.8	10.3	2.6	0.0	100
Indonesia	221.2	0.1	28.9	...	67.8	0.0	3.2	0.0	...	100
China	203.5	0.1	6.3	0.0	91.0	0.6	0.3	1.8	0.0	100

Imports Profile:

Jordan's imports were composed of 28.9 percent of mineral fuels, lubricants and related materials (SITC section 3), 18.5 percent of machinery and transport equipment (SITC section 7), and 15.7 percent of manufactured goods classified chiefly by material (SITC section 6) (see table 2). The three main imported goods over the last three years were petroleum oils and oils obtained from bituminous minerals, crude (HS code 2709), petroleum oils, other than crude (HS code 2710) and motor cars and other motor vehicles principally designed for the transport (HS code 8703) (see table 5).

Table 5: Top 10 import commodities 2009 to 2011

(Value in million US$)

HS code	4-digit heading of Harmonized System 2007	Value (million US$) 2009	2010	2011	Unit value 2009	2010	2011	Unit	SITC code
	All Commodities	14075.3	15262.0	18301.1					
2709	Petroleum oils and oils obtained from bituminous minerals, crude	1502.1	1866.1	2485.2	*0.7*	0.6	0.8	US$/kg	333
2710	Petroleum oils, other than crude	416.9	932.9	2124.0		0.7	0.9	US$/kg	334
8703	Motor cars and other motor vehicles principally designed for the transport	845.0	782.8	629.0	*10.1*	*16.7*		thsd US$/unit	781
2711	Petroleum gases and other gaseous hydrocarbons	540.0	475.8	354.3		0.2	0.3	US$/kg	343
3004	Medicaments (excluding goods of heading 30.02, 30.05 or 30.06)	334.4	363.1	380.5		47.0	51.5	US$/kg	542
8517	Electrical apparatus for line telephony or line telegraphy	328.6	327.4	382.8					764
9999	Commodities not specified according to kind	257.5	243.6	269.6					931
6006	Other knitted or crocheted fabrics	157.1	213.9	248.6	*10.8*	6.8	8.6	US$/kg	655
1701	Cane or beet sugar and chemically pure sucrose, in solid form	115.0	200.1	211.7	*0.7*	0.7	0.9	US$/kg	061
1005	Maize (corn)	154.2	157.2	196.6		0.3	0.4	US$/kg	044

Kazakhstan

Imports: CIF, by origin | **Exports: FOB, by last known destination** | **Trade System: General**

Overview:

After several years of continuous growth marked by a peak of 71.2 bln US$ in 2008, the value of the exports of Kazakhstan contracted sharply in 2009 (by 39.3 percent) but bounced back in 2010 by 32.5 percent to amount to 57.2 bln US$, still well below its 2008 level (see table 1 and graph 1). Imports, on the other hand, continued to decrease in 2010 (by 15.4 percent) to reach 24.0 bln US$ (see table 2 and graph 1). This resulted in a trade surplus of 33.2 bln US$, higher than the 2009 surplus of 14.8 bln US$ (see graph 1). This surplus is largely accounted for by trade with Developed Europe (+23.3 bln US$) (see graph 2). However, trade recorded a deficit of 1.9 bln US$ with the Commonwealth of Independent States. By partner, trade was relatively diversified in 2010: 15 (respectively 13) major partners accounted for 80 percent of exports (respectively imports) (see graph 3).

Graph 1: Total imports, exports and trade balance

(Bln US$ by year)

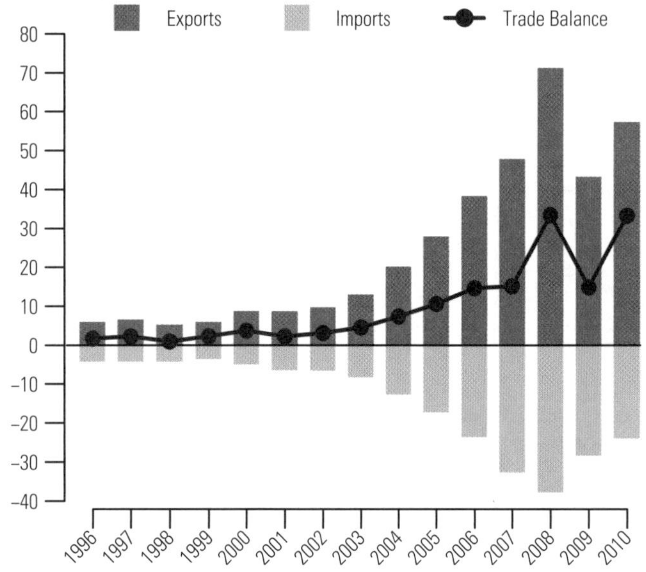

Exports Profile:

Since 2006, exports of mineral fuels, lubricants and related materials (SITC section 3) increased on average by 11.8 percent each year and accounted for more than two-thirds (71.7 percent) of exported goods in 2010 (see table 1). Another major commodity group for exports were manufactured goods classified chiefly by material (SITC section 6); it accounted for 13.0 percent of exports. In 2010, major destinations for exports were China, Italy and France; the combined value accounted for 42.2 percent of total exports (see table 4). Petroleum oils, crude (HS code 2709), the top export commodity accounted for 64.6 percent of exports in 2010 (see table 3). Other major products in the last three years were refined ferro-alloys (HS code 7202) and copper and copper alloys, unwrought (HS code 7403).

Table 1: Exports by SITC sections

(Value in million US$, growth and shares in percentage)

SITC	2010	Avg. Growth rates (%) 2006-2010	2009-2010	2010 share
Total	57244.1	10.6	32.5	100.0
0+1	1861.5	15.9	18.3	3.3
2+4	3125.5	7.8	19.9	5.5
3	41032.9	11.8	36.7	71.7
5	2510.0	24.6	28.8	4.4
6	7430.2	3.5	25.1	13.0
7	345.8	-14.7	-8.4	0.6
8	55.9	4.6	2.9	0.1
9	882.1	21.6	32.0	1.5

Table 2: Imports by SITC sections

(Value in million US$, growth and shares in percentage)

SITC	2010	Avg. Growth rates (%) 2006-2010	2009-2010	2010 share
Total	24023.6	0.4	-15.4	100.0
0+1	2156.5	8.4	-4.4	9.0
2+4	423.8	-1.6	-7.5	1.8
3	2379.6	-6.0	-16.1	9.9
5	2857.7	8.9	0.7	11.9
6	4345.9	-2.8	-42.2	18.1
7	9726.6	-1.1	-7.6	40.5
8	2084.3	8.2	8.2	8.7
9	49.3	161.3	7.0	0.2

Table 3: Top 10 export commodities 2008 to 2010

(Value in million US$)

HS code	4-digit heading of Harmonized System 2002	Value (million US$) 2008	2009	2010	Unit value 2008	2009	2010	Unit	SITC code
	All Commodities	71172.0	43195.8	57244.1					
2709	Petroleum oils, crude	43507.9	26206.9	36982.3	0.7	0.4		US$/kg	333
7202	Ferro-alloys	2959.9	1187.8	1825.7	2.4	1.1		US$/kg	671
7403	Refined copper and copper alloys, unwrought	2502.1	1407.1	1866.4	7.0	4.4		US$/kg	682
2711	Petroleum gases and other gaseous hydrocarbons	1978.7	1802.2	1677.5	0.1	0.1		US$/kg	343
2844	Radioactive chemical elements and radioactive isotopes	1303.5	1618.7	2093.0	98.2	78.6		US$/kg	525
2710	Petroleum oils, other than crude	2003.2	1191.4	1755.1	0.5	0.3		US$/kg	334
2601	Iron ores and concentrates	1279.2	936.1	1189.7	0.1	0.1		US$/kg	281
1001	Wheat and meslin	1458.8	632.9	911.5	0.3	0.2		US$/kg	041
7108	Gold (including gold plated with platinum)	551.9	652.9	865.2	19.8	22.0		thsd US$/kg	971
1101	Wheat or meslin flour	849.2	574.5	535.9	0.5	0.3		US$/kg	046

Graph 2: Trade Balance by MDG Regions in 2010

(Bln US$)

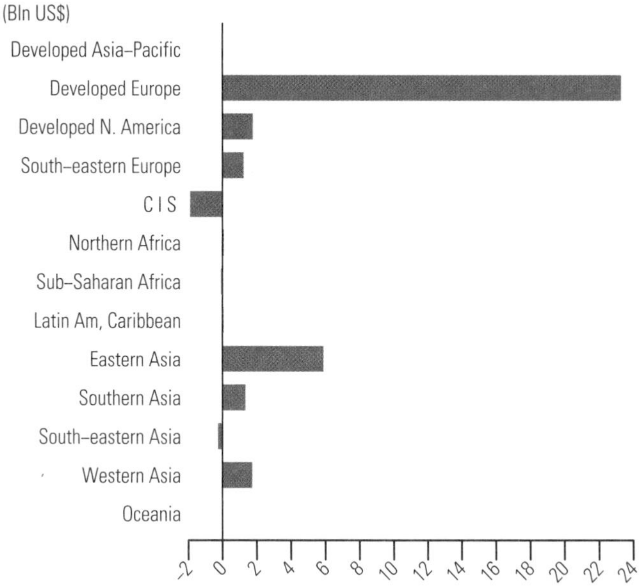

Graph 3: Partner concentration of trade in 2010

(Cumulative share by ranked partners)

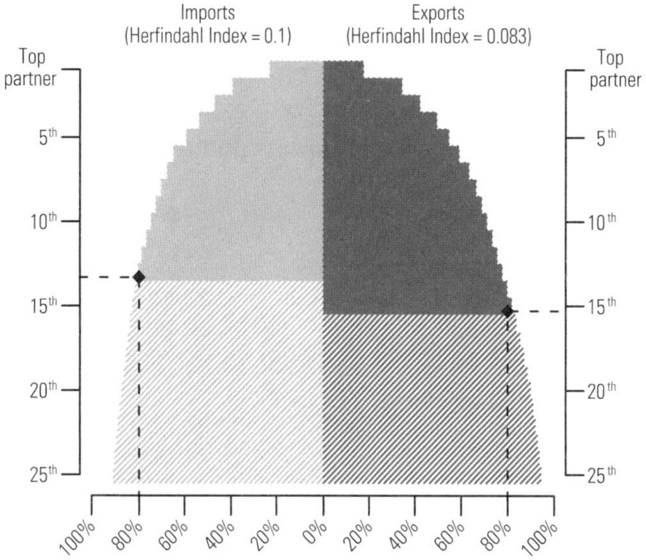

Table 4: Exports by principal countries and SITC sections in 2010

(Value in million US$, percentages of country total)

Country	Total	Shares by SITC sections (%) 0 + 1	2 + 4	3	5	6	7	8	9	Total
World	57244.1	3.3	5.5	71.7	4.4	13.0	0.6	0.1	1.5	100
China	10122.1	0.1	14.3	54.7	9.5	21.4	0.0	0.0	0.0	100
Italy	9576.8	0.1	0.1	97.3	0.0	2.0	0.1	0.0	0.4	100
France	4433.1	0.1	0.0	93.4	6.4	0.0	0.1	0.0	...	100
Netherlands	4161.0	0.1	0.2	96.5	0.2	2.8	0.2	0.0	0.0	100
Russian Federation	3006.5	1.8	38.5	28.3	8.6	19.9	2.8	0.2	0.0	100
Austria	2528.7	0.0	0.0	99.8	0.0	0.2	0.0	0.0	...	100
Canada	2439.1	0.1	0.0	87.8	12.1	0.0	0.0	0.0	...	100
Germany	1749.7	2.6	2.0	55.8	3.3	35.9	0.2	0.1	0.2	100
United Kingdom	1379.5	0.7	0.7	48.0	1.0	48.6	0.6	0.3	0.0	100
Romania	1281.9	0.0	0.0	99.2	0.5	0.2	0.0	0.0	0.0	100

Imports Profile:

In 2010, Kazakhstan imports were mostly composed of machinery and transport equipment (SITC section 7), manufactured goods classified chiefly by material (SITC section 6) and chemicals and related products, n.e.s. (SITC section 5) (see table 2). They accounted respectively for 40.5, 18.1 and 11.9 percent of imports. Top imported products over the last three years were petroleum oils, crude (HS code 2709), other tubes and pipes (for example, welded, riveted or similarly closed) (HS code 7305) and petroleum oils, other than crude (HS code 2710) (see table 5).

Table 5: Top 10 import commodities 2008 to 2010

(Value in million US$)

HS code	4-digit heading of Harmonized System 2002	Value (million US$) 2008	2009	2010	Unit value 2008	2009	2010	Unit	SITC code
	All Commodities	37815.4	28408.7	24023.6					
2709	Petroleum oils, crude	2772.9	1446.1	1340.9	0.4	0.2		US$/kg	333
7305	Other tubes and pipes (for example, welded, riveted or similarly closed)	1358.5	2291.3	200.9	2.4	2.7		US$/kg	679
2710	Petroleum oils, other than crude	1563.4	779.8	472.1	0.7	0.5		US$/kg	334
8703	Motor cars and other motor vehicles principally designed for the transport	1228.3	771.3	403.6	7.9	6.9		thsd US$/unit	781
3004	Medicaments (excluding goods of heading 30.02, 30.05 or 30.06)	597.8	611.9	745.7	27.4	28.3		US$/kg	542
7304	Tubes, pipes and hollow profiles, seamless, of iron (other than cast iron)	712.2	563.6	444.0	2.4	2.8		US$/kg	679
7308	Structures (excluding prefabricated buildings of heading 94.06)	741.8	624.9	334.3	4.6	5.0		US$/kg	691
8802	Other aircraft (for example, helicopters, aeroplanes); spacecraft	752.3	281.9	622.4	5.6	5.0		mln US$/unit	792
8481	Taps, cocks, valves and similar appliances for pipes, boiler shells	598.7	638.7	335.4	22.4	23.2		US$/kg	747
8413	Pumps for liquids, whether or not fitted with a measuring device	639.8	286.8	280.1					742

Kenya

Imports: CIF, by origin | **Exports: FOB, by last known destination** | **Trade System: General**

Overview:

From 2006 to 2010, Kenya's exports increased on average by 10.2 percent each year and amounted to 5.2 bln US$ (see table 1 and graph 1). During the same period, imports increased on average by 13.7 percent each year to 12.1 bln US$ (see table 2 and graph 1). This resulted in a trade deficit of 6.9 bln US$ for 2010, compared to 5.7 bln US$ for the previous year (see graph 1). Trade with Eastern Asia accounted for a large part of the 2010 deficit (-1.8 bln US$) (see graph 2). The trade balance also recorded significant deficits with Western Asia (-1.8 bln US$), Developed Europe (-1.1 bln US$) and Southern Asia (-0.9 bln US$). Trade was diversified across partners: in 2010, 18 major partners accounted for 80 percent of both exports and imports (see graph 3).

Graph 1: Total imports, exports and trade balance

(Bln US$ by year)

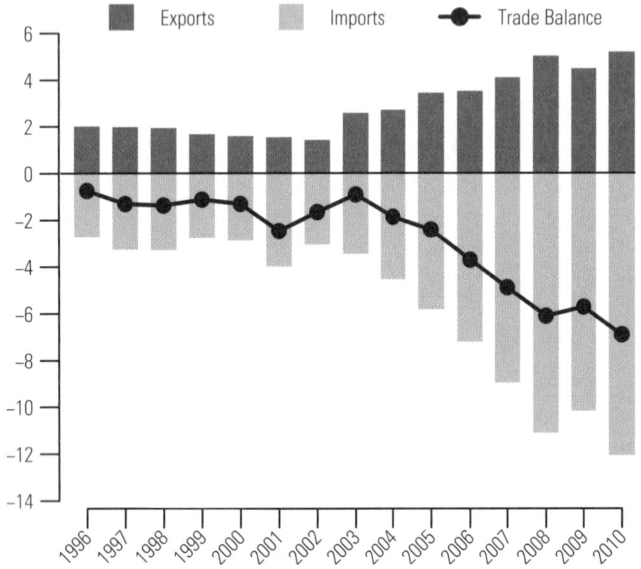

Exports Profile:

In 2010, Kenya's exports were composed of 44.3 percent of food, live animals, beverages and tobacco (SITC sections 0+1), 14.3 percent of inedible crude materials (except fuels), animal and vegetable oils, fats and waxes (SITC sections 2+4) and 12.1 percent of manufactured goods classified chiefly by material (SITC section 6) (see table 1). Major destinations for exports were Uganda, the United Kingdom and the United Republic of Tanzania (see table 4). The majority (70.4 percent) of exports to the United Kingdom were food, live animals, beverages and tobacco (SITC sections 0+1). From 2008 to 2010, top exported products were tea, whether or not flavoured (HS code 0902), cut flowers and flower buds of a kind suitable for bouquets (HS code 0603) and Coffee, whether or not roasted or decaffeinated (HS code 0901) (see table 3).

Table 1: Exports by SITC sections

(Value in million US$, growth and shares in percentage)

SITC	2010	Avg. Growth rates (%) 2006-2010	2009-2010	2010 share
Total	5169.1	10.2	15.8	100.0
0+1	2291.2	12.1	22.6	44.3
2+4	738.0	9.3	3.1	14.3
3	216.9	-3.9	15.6	4.2
5	466.5	16.5	2.0	9.0
6	625.6	8.4	14.2	12.1
7	263.0	17.5	14.2	5.1
8	449.2	1.0	4.6	8.7
9	118.7	103.2	335.1	2.3

Table 2: Imports by SITC sections

(Value in million US$, growth and shares in percentage)

SITC	2010	Avg. Growth rates (%) 2006-2010	2009-2010	2010 share
Total	12092.9	13.7	18.5	100.0
0+1	946.0	21.9	-20.1	7.8
2+4	753.6	17.4	29.7	6.2
3	2670.2	11.1	22.1	22.1
5	1602.7	12.4	20.9	13.3
6	1774.6	13.0	26.0	14.7
7	3841.1	14.3	24.0	31.8
8	504.0	12.7	20.8	4.2
9	0.7	44.7	-14.5	0.0

Table 3: Top 10 export commodities 2008 to 2010

(Value in million US$)

HS code	4-digit heading of Harmonized System 2007	Value (million US$) 2008	2009	2010	Unit value 2008	2009	2010	Unit	SITC code
	All Commodities	5000.9	4463.4	5169.1					
0902	Tea, whether or not flavoured	931.6	894.0	1163.6	2.4	2.7	2.8	US$/kg	074
0603	Cut flowers and flower buds of a kind suitable for bouquets	446.0	421.5	396.2	4.1	3.7	3.6	US$/kg	292
0901	Coffee, whether or not roasted or decaffeinated	152.8	201.2	207.5	3.5	3.2	4.7	US$/kg	071
2710	Petroleum oils, other than crude	173.3	177.9	205.2	0.8			US$/kg	334
0709	Other vegetables, fresh or chilled	206.4	175.4	150.3	3.6	3.4	*3.5*	US$/kg	054
2836	Carbonates; peroxocarbonates (percarbonates)	193.9	109.5	95.5	0.3	0.2	0.2	US$/kg	523
2523	Portland cement, aluminous cement, slag cement	117.2	104.5	94.6	0.1	0.1	0.1	US$/kg	661
2402	Cigars, cheroots, cigarillos and cigarettes	91.4	85.8	92.7	6.1		*12.3*	US$/kg	122
7210	Flat-rolled products of iron or non-alloy steel	99.2	69.7	77.3	1.5	1.1	1.2	US$/kg	674
3923	Articles for the conveyance or packing of goods, of plastics	69.5	59.8	68.4	2.8	2.3	2.4	US$/kg	893

Graph 2: Trade Balance by MDG Regions in 2010

(Bln US$)

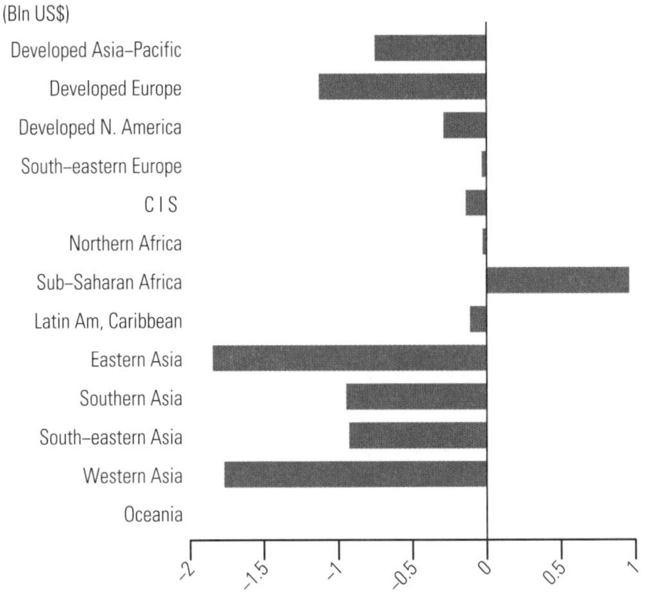

Graph 3: Partner concentration of trade in 2010

(Cumulative share by ranked partners)

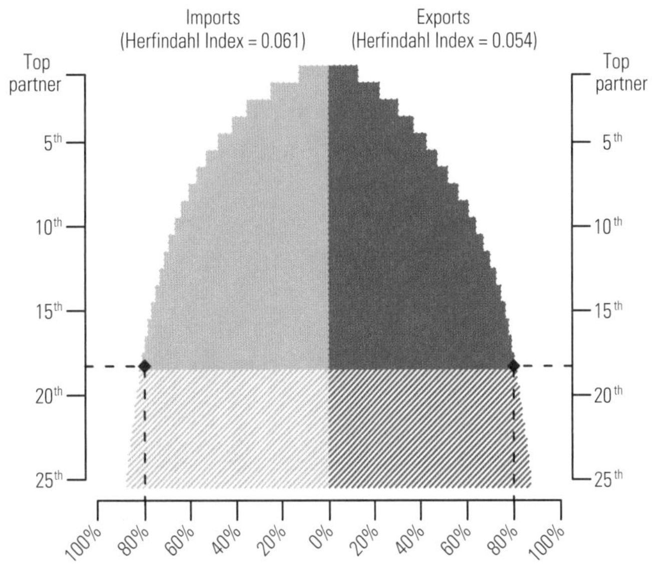

Table 4: Exports by principal countries and SITC sections in 2010

(Value in million US$, percentages of country total)

Country	Total	Shares by SITC sections (%)								
		0 + 1	2 + 4	3	5	6	7	8	9	Total
World	5169.1	44.3	14.3	4.2	9.0	12.1	5.1	8.7	2.3	100
Uganda	657.3	14.0	5.6	12.7	19.8	28.8	10.8	8.3	0.0	100
United Kingdom	507.2	70.4	24.5	0.0	0.1	2.8	0.2	1.7	0.3	100
United Rep. of Tanzania	420.2	14.7	12.4	1.9	20.2	27.1	12.3	11.3	0.0	100
Netherlands	338.9	22.2	76.5	0.0	0.0	0.2	0.7	0.1	0.2	100
USA	284.9	22.2	1.7	0.0	0.4	2.6	0.3	61.9	10.9	100
United Arab Emirates	237.8	37.5	2.2	14.0	3.1	1.0	8.0	0.4	33.8	100
Sudan	237.5	50.6	10.1	1.7	6.0	13.1	12.3	6.3	0.0	100
Egypt	228.5	97.2	0.6	...	0.4	1.4	0.3	0.2	...	100
Pakistan	227.9	92.9	0.1	0.0	3.4	3.1	0.0	0.4	...	100
Somalia	164.7	38.7	21.8	0.2	6.2	8.9	6.9	14.8	2.5	100

Imports Profile:

Imports of Kenya in 2010 were composed of 31.8 percent of machinery and transport equipment (SITC section 7), 22.1 percent of mineral fuels, lubricants and related materials (SITC section 3) and 14.7 percent of manufactured goods classified chiefly by material (SITC section 6) (see table 2). From 2008 to 2010, top imported products were petroleum oils, other than crude (HS code 2710), petroleum oils, crude (HS code 2709) and palm oil and its fractions (HS code 1511) (see table 5).

Table 5: Top 10 import commodities 2008 to 2010

(Value in million US$)

HS code	4-digit heading of Harmonized System 2007	Value (million US$)			Unit value				SITC code
		2008	2009	2010	2008	2009	2010	Unit	
	All Commodities	11127.8	10202.0	12092.9					
2710	Petroleum oils, other than crude	1769.6	1399.2	1646.3	1.0			US$/kg	334
2709	Petroleum oils and oils obtained from bituminous minerals, crude	1176.5	705.8	915.2	0.7	0.4	0.6	US$/kg	333
1511	Palm oil and its fractions	458.8	332.6	452.0	1.1	0.7	0.8	US$/kg	422
8517	Electrical apparatus for line telephony or line telegraphy	319.3	342.1	520.0					764
8703	Motor cars and other motor vehicles principally designed for the transport	311.9	296.0	345.5	6.7	6.2	5.9	thsd US$/unit	781
8802	Other aircraft (for example, helicopters, aeroplanes); spacecraft	157.4	305.4	453.2	3.2	3.2	2.2	mln US$/unit	792
7208	Flat-rolled products of iron or non-alloy steel	315.3	213.9	269.0	1.0	0.6	0.7	US$/kg	673
3004	Medicaments (excluding goods of heading 30.02, 30.05 or 30.06)	236.5	233.7	269.6	23.0	26.1	22.6	US$/kg	542
1005	Maize (corn)	96.3	439.6	69.0	0.4	0.3	0.3	US$/kg	044
1001	Wheat and meslin	201.3	179.3	219.7	0.4	0.2	0.3	US$/kg	041

Korea, Republic of

Imports: CIF, by origin | **Exports: FOB, by last known destination** | **Trade System: General**

Overview:

After several years of continuous growth marked by a peak of 422.0 bln US$ in 2008, the exports of the Republic of Korea dropped by 13.9 percent in 2009 and bounced back for two consecutive years to reach 555.2 bln US$ in 2011 (see table 1 and graph 1). Imports showed a similar development with an increase of 23.3 percent in 2011 to 524.4 bln US$ (see table 2 and graph 1). This resulted in a trade surplus of 30.8 bln US$ in 2011 compared to a deficit of 13.3 bln US$ in 2008 (see graph 1). By MDG regions, trade recorded large surpluses with Eastern Asia (+80.2 bln US$), South-eastern Asia (+18.6 bln US$) and Latin America and the Caribbean (+18.4 bln US$) (see graph 2). Trade deficits were recorded with Western Asia (-78.8 bln US$) and Developed Asia-Pacific (-47.2 bln US$). Exports were more diversified across partners: in 2011, 22 (respectively 17) major partners accounted for 80 percent of exports (respectively imports) (see graph 3).

Graph 1: Total imports, exports and trade balance

(Bln US$ by year)

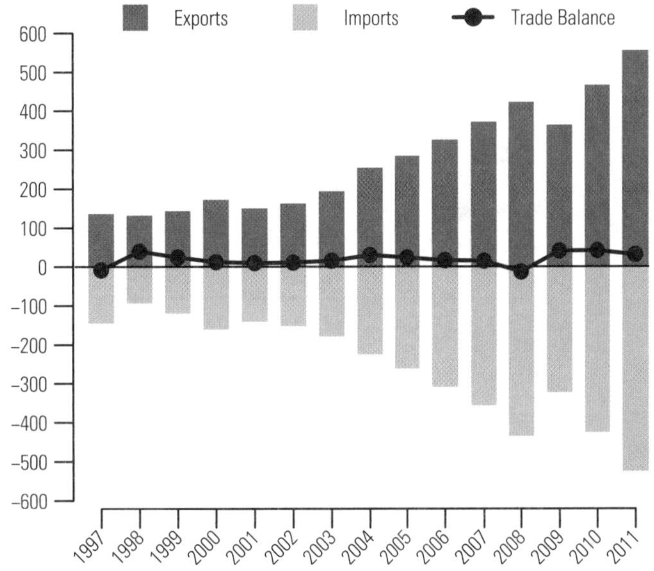

Table 1: Exports by SITC sections

(Value in million US$, growth and shares in percentage)

SITC	2011	Avg. Growth rates (%) 2007-2011	Avg. Growth rates (%) 2010-2011	2011 share
Total	555 208.9	10.6	19.0	100.0
0+1	6 076.1	16.3	23.2	1.1
2+4	8 310.1	18.5	46.2	1.5
3	53 086.9	21.2	62.9	9.6
5	60 704.0	12.8	24.0	10.9
6	76 748.8	10.2	27.0	13.8
7	300 094.4	8.5	13.7	54.1
8	46 982.1	9.9	0.3	8.5
9	3 206.5	43.3	5.4	0.6

Table 2: Imports by SITC sections

(Value in million US$, growth and shares in percentage)

SITC	2011	Avg. Growth rates (%) 2007-2011	Avg. Growth rates (%) 2010-2011	2011 share
Total	524 405.2	10.1	23.3	100.0
0+1	22 760.8	12.2	32.4	4.3
2+4	43 951.4	15.2	38.1	8.4
3	173 673.7	15.8	41.7	33.1
5	47 969.1	10.4	17.1	9.1
6	64 231.1	5.5	14.4	12.2
7	133 322.7	5.5	8.0	25.4
8	36 780.1	7.5	16.7	7.0
9	1 716.3	0.1	9.1	0.3

Exports Profile:

In 2011, machinery and transport equipment (SITC section 7) accounted for the majority of exported goods with a share of 54.1 percent (see table 1). Other major commodity groups for exports included manufactured goods classified chiefly by material (SITC section 6) and chemicals and related products, n.e.s. (SITC section 5) respectively with 13.8 and 10.9 percent of exports. China, USA and Japan were the three major markets for exported goods in 2011. Over the last three years, top exported products included cruise ships, excursion boats, ferry-boats, cargo ships, barges (HS code 8901), petroleum oils, other than crude (HS code 2710) and electronic integrated circuits (HS code 8542) (see table 3).

Table 3: Top 10 export commodities 2009 to 2011

(Value in million US$)

HS code	4-digit heading of Harmonized System 2007	Value (million US$) 2009	2010	2011	Unit value 2009	2010	2011	Unit	SITC code
	All Commodities	363 531.1	466 380.6	555 208.9					
8901	Cruise ships, excursion boats, ferry-boats, cargo ships, barges	37 223.2	37 208.1	37 969.8					793
2710	Petroleum oils, other than crude	22 145.4	30 163.3	50 371.1	0.5	*0.7*	*1.0*	US$/kg	334
8542	Electronic integrated circuits	24 384.4	37 904.5	39 664.8					776
8703	Motor cars and other motor vehicles principally designed for the transport	22 399.2	31 781.7	40 909.9		*15.6*		thsd US$/unit	781
8517	Electrical apparatus for line telephony or line telegraphy	29 530.6	25 881.6	25 802.4					764
9013	Liquid crystal devices	23 390.0	30 076.5	27 656.2					871
8708	Parts and accessories of the motor vehicles of headings 87.01 to 87.05	10 926.0	17 821.9	21 583.4	7.3	*7.7*	*8.1*	US$/kg	784
8905	Light-vessels, fire-floats, dredgers, floating cranes and other vessels	5 207.9	9 407.7	16 043.7					793
8529	Parts suitable for use with the apparatus of headings 85.25 to 85.28	5 704.2	8 266.8	8 444.3	18.7	*22.3*	*24.3*	US$/kg	764
8473	Parts and accessories for use with machines of heading 84.69 to 84.72	5 074.9	8 037.2	5 090.1	180.8	*262.2*	*218.2*	US$/kg	759

Graph 2: Trade Balance by MDG Regions in 2011

(Bln US$)

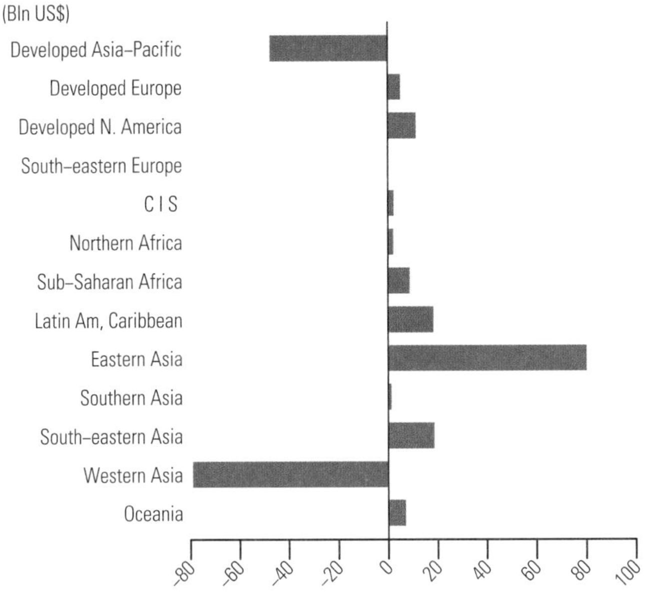

Graph 3: Partner concentration of trade in 2011

(Cumulative share by ranked partners)

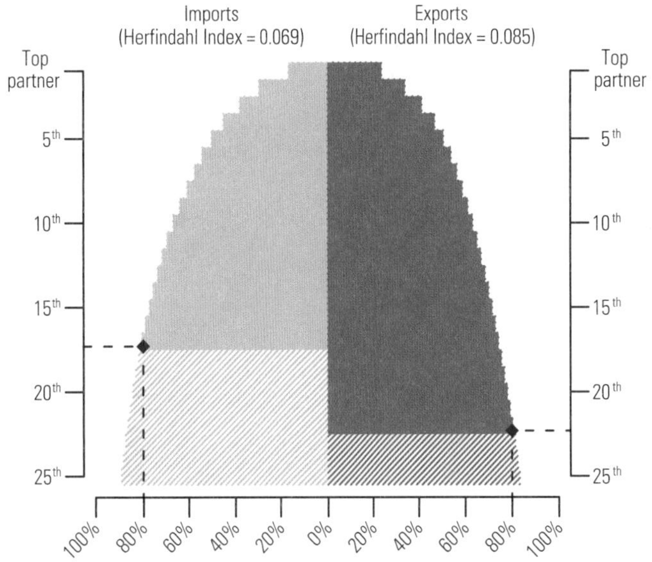

Table 4: Exports by principal countries and SITC sections in 2011

(Value in million US$, percentages of country total)

Country	Total	Shares by SITC sections (%) 0+1	2+4	3	5	6	7	8	9	Total
World	555208.9	1.1	1.5	9.6	10.9	13.8	54.1	8.5	0.6	100
China	134185.0	0.7	1.6	8.6	18.9	9.2	42.1	18.8	0.1	100
USA	56421.4	0.9	0.9	4.7	5.3	14.0	69.6	4.6	0.0	100
Japan	39679.5	5.1	2.9	22.1	10.8	23.0	29.2	6.5	0.3	100
China, Hong Kong SAR	30967.4	0.8	0.4	8.3	6.3	8.2	64.3	6.3	5.3	100
Singapore	20839.0	0.4	0.2	29.2	3.2	5.0	57.6	1.3	3.2	100
Other Asia, nes	18206.0	0.9	1.6	13.6	22.2	12.7	41.4	6.1	1.5	100
Indonesia	13564.5	0.7	3.8	47.8	8.7	21.7	14.5	2.9	0.0	100
Viet Nam	13464.9	1.5	2.8	8.3	12.6	31.5	38.6	4.6	0.1	100
India	12654.1	0.1	4.3	6.4	16.2	23.2	47.4	2.5	0.0	100
Brazil	11821.4	0.1	0.7	10.4	5.5	6.8	71.0	5.4	0.0	100

Imports Profile:

In 2011, imports were composed of 33.1 percent of mineral fuels, lubricants and related materials (SITC Section 3), 25.4 percent of machinery and transport equipment (SITC section 7) and 12.2 percent of manufactured goods classified chiefly by material (SITC section 6) (see table 2). Over the last three years, petroleum oils and oils obtained from bituminous minerals, crude (HS code 2709), electronic integrated circuits (HS code 8542) and petroleum gases and other gaseous hydrocarbons (HS code 2711) were the three major imported goods (see table 5).

Table 5: Top 10 import commodities 2009 to 2011

(Value in million US$)

HS code	4-digit heading of Harmonized System 2007	Value (million US$) 2009	2010	2011	Unit value 2009	2010	2011	Unit	SITC code
	All Commodities	323081.7	425208.0	524405.2					
2709	Petroleum oils and oils obtained from bituminous minerals, crude	50757.4	68662.2	100805.6	0.4	0.6	0.8	US$/kg	333
8542	Electronic integrated circuits	21596.4	23836.3	25369.8					776
2711	Petroleum gases and other gaseous hydrocarbons	17146.7	21788.7	30182.7	0.5	0.6	*0.7*	US$/kg	343
2710	Petroleum oils, other than crude	12431.3	17330.4	22029.9	0.5	0.7	*0.9*	US$/kg	334
2701	Coal; briquettes, ovoids and similar solid fuels manufactured from coal	9896.7	12863.1	18283.7	*0.1*	0.1	0.1	US$/kg	321
8486	Machines and apparatus used for the manufacture of semiconductor devices	4020.2	11076.1	10336.2					728
7208	Flat-rolled products of iron or non-alloy steel	7090.4	7718.1	7775.2	0.7	0.7	0.8	US$/kg	673
2601	Iron ores and concentrates, including roasted iron pyrites	3538.3	6646.5	11380.8	0.1	*0.1*	*0.2*	US$/kg	281
8517	Electrical apparatus for line telephony or line telegraphy	4518.6	5898.0	8492.5					764
2603	Copper ores and concentrates	3293.5	4536.9	5634.0	*2.1*	2.6	*3.3*	US$/kg	283

Imports: CIF, by origin | **Exports: FOB, by last known destination** | **Trade System: Special**

Overview:

After two years of continuous growth marked by a peak of 87.5 bln US$ in 2008, the value of the exports of Kuwait dropped in 2009 to reach 51.9 bln US$ (see table 1 and graph 1). Imports increased in 2008 by 16.3 percent to amount to 24.8 bln US$ (see table 2 and graph 1). Trade balance recorded a surplus of 62.6 bln US$ in 2008 (see graph 1). In 2008, the deficit with Developed Europe amounted to 6.5 bln US$ (see graph 2). In the same year large deficits were also recorded with Eastern Asia (-3.8 bln US$), Developed Asia-Pacific (-3.0 bln US$), Developed North America (-2.6 bln US$) and Western Asia (-1.4 bln US$). In 2009, exports were concentrated among partners: 90.3 percent of exported goods were classified as exports to Areas, nes (see graph 3 and table 4).

Graph 1: Total imports, exports and trade balance

(Bln US$ by year)

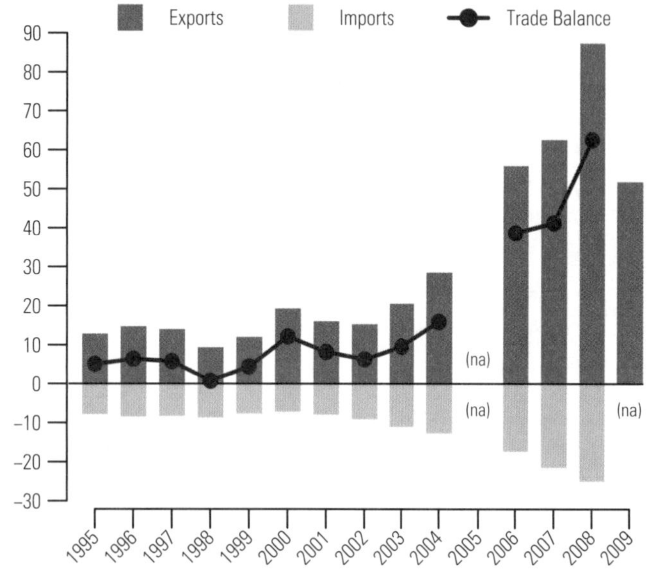

Table 1: Exports by SITC sections

(Value in million US$, growth and shares in percentage)

SITC	2009	Avg. Growth rates (%) 2005-2009	Avg. Growth rates (%) 2008-2009	2009 share
Total	51 936.6	...	-40.6	100.0
0+1	178.7	...	-4.1	0.3
2+4	159.3	...	-4.4	0.3
3	46 898.6	...	-43.3	90.3
5	2 665.2	...	22.2	5.1
6	321.1	...	-23.3	0.6
7	1 509.2	...	-7.5	2.9
8	202.5	...	48.3	0.4
9	1.9	...	75.4	0.0

Table 2: Imports by SITC sections

(Value in million US$, growth and shares in percentage)

SITC	2008	Avg. Growth rates (%) 2005-2008	Avg. Growth rates (%) 2007-2008	2008 share
Total	24 839.6	...	16.3	100.0
0+1	3 491.4	...	31.3	14.1
2+4	521.3	...	22.2	2.1
3	146.9	...	22.1	0.6
5	2 048.4	...	21.7	8.2
6	5 478.1	...	11.8	22.1
7	10 137.7	...	13.6	40.8
8	2 817.8	...	11.4	11.3
9	198.2	...	65.8	0.8

Exports Profile:

In 2009, exports were composed of 90.3 percent of mineral fuels, lubricants and related materials (SITC section 3) (see table 1). Major destinations for exports in 2009 included China, the United Arab Emirates and Saudi Arabia (see table 4). From 2007 to 2009, top exported products were petroleum oils, oils from bituminous minerals, crude (HS code 2709), oils petroleum, bituminous, distillates, except crude (HS code 2710) and petroleum gases and other gaseous hydrocarbons (HS code 2711) (see table 3).

Table 3: Top 10 export commodities 2007 to 2009

(Value in million US$)

HS code	4-digit heading of Harmonized System 2002	Value (million US$) 2007	2008	2009	Unit value 2007	2008	2009	Unit	SITC code
	All Commodities	62 691.2	87 457.0	51 936.6					
2709	Petroleum oils, crude	38 610.9	57 754.5	29 658.9					333
2710	Petroleum oils, other than crude	18 660.8	22 309.1	15 651.6					334
2711	Petroleum gases and other gaseous hydrocarbons	1 937.9	2 650.8	1 571.8					343
3901	Polymers of ethylene, in primary forms	1 085.8	583.2	2 201.8	0.8	1.0	1.3	US$/kg	571
8703	Motor cars and other motor vehicles principally designed for the transport	366.7	512.4	400.0	16.0	3.7	14.0	thsd US$/unit	781
3102	Mineral or chemical fertilisers, nitrogenous	290.2	479.1	194.7	0.3	0.6	0.3	US$/kg	562
2905	Acyclic alcohols and their derivatives	0.0	875.0	4.3	0.9	2.2	0.5	US$/kg	512
8803	Parts of goods of heading 88.01 or 88.02	7.4	210.3	403.7	0.3	1.0	1.0	thsd US$/kg	792
8704	Motor vehicles for the transport of goods	105.2	111.2	153.8	17.0	3.9	10.2	thsd US$/unit	782
8544	Insulated (including enamelled or anodised) wire, cable	93.1	171.2	94.4	4.7	5.0	3.6	US$/kg	773

Graph 2: Trade Balance by MDG Regions in 2008

(Bln US$)

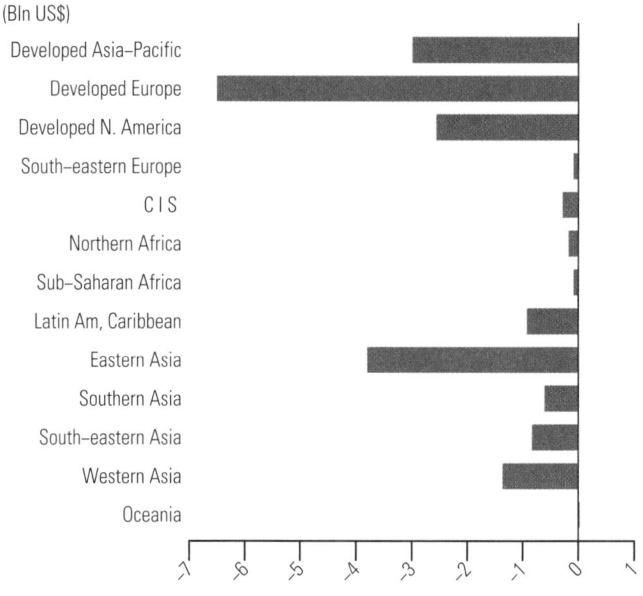

Graph 3: Partner concentration of trade in 2009

(Cumulative share by ranked partners)

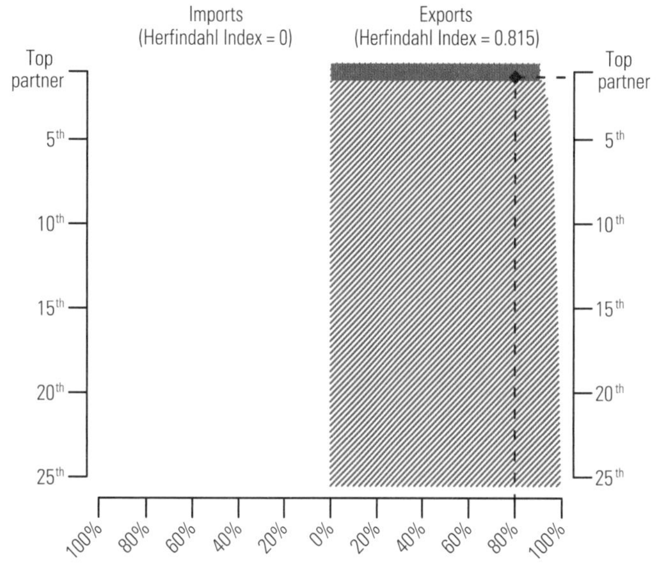

Table 4: Exports by principal countries and SITC sections in 2009

(Value in million US$, percentages of country total)

Country	Total	Shares by SITC sections (%)								
		0 + 1	2 + 4	3	5	6	7	8	9	Total
World	51 936.6	0.3	0.3	90.3	5.1	0.6	2.9	0.4	0.0	100
Areas, nes	46 873.2	0.0	0.0	100.0	...	0.0	...	0.0	...	100
China	1 135.0	0.0	0.1	0.2	99.0	0.1	0.5	0.0	...	100
United Arab Emirates	585.9	3.8	1.7	1.9	29.1	8.4	42.6	12.4	0.1	100
Saudi Arabia	441.7	20.5	0.9	0.8	13.5	26.3	32.9	5.2	0.0	100
India	328.4	0.1	27.6	1.3	65.0	2.1	2.7	1.1	...	100
Turkey	229.1	0.1	0.1	...	99.2	0.1	0.4	0.1	...	100
Jordan	225.3	3.4	0.1	0.5	14.6	3.3	75.5	2.5	0.0	100
USA	180.1	0.1	1.8	0.0	30.6	0.2	64.4	2.6	0.3	100
Qatar	147.1	9.5	0.3	0.5	17.3	20.4	46.6	4.9	0.4	100
Indonesia	145.4	0.0	0.3	...	98.7	0.9	0.0	0.0	...	100

Imports Profile:

In 2008, machinery and transport equipment (SITC section 7) accounted for 40.8 percent of imported goods (see table 2). Other major commodity groups included manufactured goods classified chiefly by material (SITC section 6) and food, live animals, beverages and tobacco (SITC sections 0+1), accounting respectively for 22.1 and 14.1 percent of imports. From 2007 to 2009, top imported products were motor vehicles for transport of persons (except buses) (HS code 8703), iron and non-alloy steel in ingots or other primary forms (HS code 7206) and machinery, plant or laboratory equipment (HS code 8419) (see table 5).

Table 5: Top 10 import commodities 2006 to 2008

(Value in million US$)

HS code	4-digit heading of Harmonized System 2002	Value (million US$)			Unit value				SITC code
		2006	2007	2008	2006	2007	2008	Unit	
	All Commodities	17 239.7	21 362.5	24 839.6					
8703	Motor cars and other motor vehicles principally designed for the transport	2 044.8	2 610.1	3 159.1	18.4	20.3	22.2	thsd US$/unit	781
7206	Iron and non-alloy steel in ingots or other primary forms	263.5	321.7	711.3	0.4	0.5	1.3	US$/kg	672
8419	Machinery, plant or laboratory equipment	60.7	472.5	608.8					741
7304	Tubes, pipes and hollow profiles, seamless, of iron (other than cast iron)	339.9	327.2	394.2	1.4	1.2	2.0	US$/kg	679
3004	Medicaments (excluding goods of heading 30.02, 30.05 or 30.06)	320.7	249.6	484.5	16.1	70.1	86.3	US$/kg	542
8544	Insulated (including enamelled or anodised) wire, cable	238.5	400.0	321.5	5.8	7.5	7.7	US$/kg	773
8525	Transmission apparatus for radio-telephony, radio-broadcasting	80.8	341.1	533.5	138.9	140.0	130.1	US$/unit	764
8481	Taps, cocks, valves and similar appliances for pipes, boiler shells	182.8	343.1	328.8	13.4	18.3	20.3	US$/kg	747
8471	Automatic data processing machines and units thereof	180.0	236.5	361.7	161.7	205.6	251.5	US$/unit	752
8704	Motor vehicles for the transport of goods	313.7	234.8	217.5	13.0	14.7	17.0	thsd US$/unit	782

Imports: CIF, by origin | **Exports: FOB, by last known destination** | **Trade System: General**

Overview:

From 2007 to 2011, despite a decline of 27.2 percent in 2009, Kyrgyzstan's exports increased on average by 14.9 percent each year and amounted to 2.0 bln US$ in 2011, reflecting an increase of 33.0 percent from 2010 (see table 1 and graph 1). Imports showed a similar development and increased by 32.2 percent in 2011 to 4.3 bln US$ (see table 2 and graph 1). This resulted in a trade deficit of 2.3 bln US$ in 2011, compared to 1.7 bln US$ in 2010 (see graph 1). The deficit with the Commonwealth of Independent States alone amounted to 1.4 bln US$ (see graph 2). A major deficit was also recorded with Eastern Asia (-947.6 mln US$). Trade was concentrated among a few partners: in 2011, 4 (respectively 8) major partners accounted for 80 percent of exports (respectively imports) (see graph 3).

Graph 1: Total imports, exports and trade balance

(Bln US$ by year)

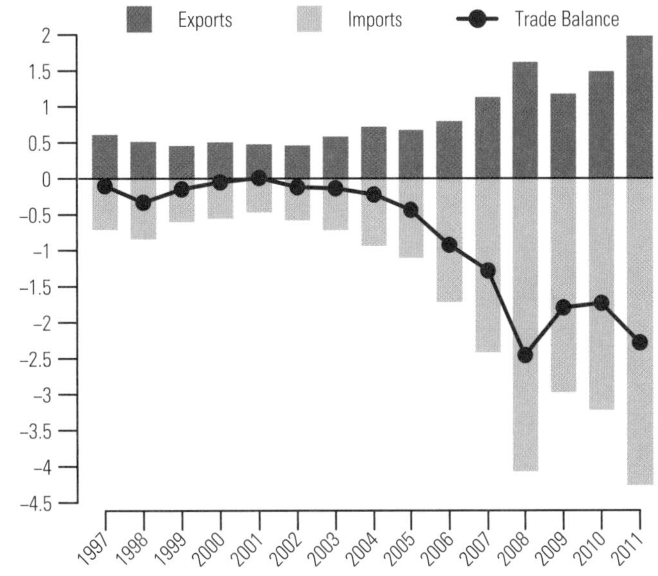

Table 1: Exports by SITC sections

(Value in million US$, growth and shares in percentage)

SITC	2011	Avg. Growth rates (%) 2007-2011	2010-2011	2011 share
Total	1 978.9	14.9	33.0	100.0
0+1	220.3	9.1	15.4	11.1
2+4	87.8	2.2	64.9	4.4
3	184.3	-9.9	56.9	9.3
5	18.9	11.1	126.1	1.0
6	105.0	-6.9	105.2	5.3
7	125.0	2.7	44.3	6.3
8	171.3	12.3	21.2	8.7
9	1 066.3	44.2	27.1	53.9

Table 2: Imports by SITC sections

(Value in million US$, growth and shares in percentage)

SITC	2011	Avg. Growth rates (%) 2007-2011	2010-2011	2011 share
Total	4 260.7	15.2	32.2	100.0
0+1	647.3	16.6	30.8	15.2
2+4	142.3	10.3	36.5	3.3
3	971.8	7.0	13.8	22.8
5	453.0	15.3	40.6	10.6
6	662.7	16.8	44.7	15.6
7	971.1	18.6	39.8	22.8
8	387.8	34.6	42.1	9.1
9	24.8	25.7	11.1	0.6

Exports Profile:

In 2011, 53.9 percent of exports were reported as commodities and transactions not classified elsewhere (SITC section 9) (see table 1). Other major commodity groups for exports included food, live animals, beverages and tobacco (SITC sections 0+1) and mineral fuels, lubricants and related materials (SITC section 3), respectively with 11.1 and 9.3 percent of exported goods. Major destinations for exports were Switzerland, Kazakhstan and Russian Federation (see table 4). Exports to Switzerland were almost exclusively commodities and transactions not classified elsewhere (SITC section 9). Over the last three years, top products for exports were gold (including gold plated with platinum) (HS code 7108), petroleum oils, other than crude (HS code 2710) and electrical energy (HS code 2716) (see table 3).

Table 3: Top 10 export commodities 2009 to 2011

(Value in million US$)

HS code	4-digit heading of Harmonized System 2007	Value (million US$) 2009	2010	2011	Unit value 2009	2010	2011	Unit	SITC code
	All Commodities	1 178.3	1 488.4	1 978.9					
7108	Gold (including gold plated with platinum)	529.5	668.3	1 006.2	32.4	39.0	49.7	thsd US$/kg	971
9999	Commodities not specified according to kind	187.1	170.9	60.1					931
2710	Petroleum oils, other than crude	...	67.1	101.0		0.6	0.9	US$/kg	334
2716	Electrical energy	37.3	48.4	80.4	40.9	29.6	28.8	US$/MWh	351
6204	Women's or girls' suits, ensembles, jackets, blazers, dresses, skirts	30.1	45.7	49.0	1.8	1.9	1.9	US$/unit	842
0713	Dried leguminous vegetables, shelled, whether or not skinned or split	30.1	35.3	51.8	0.5	0.6	0.7	US$/kg	054
5201	Cotton, not carded or combed	21.5	27.8	31.0	1.0	1.4	1.5	US$/kg	263
6206	Women's or girls' blouses, shirts and shirt-blouses	23.4	28.8	21.4	1.6	1.6	1.5	US$/unit	842
8539	Electric filament or discharge lamps, including sealed beam lamp units	18.5	19.7	21.5					778
8708	Parts and accessories of the motor vehicles of headings 87.01 to 87.05	13.1	14.5	23.1	*2.8*	2.3	4.3	US$/kg	784

Graph 2: Trade Balance by MDG Regions in 2011

(Bln US$)

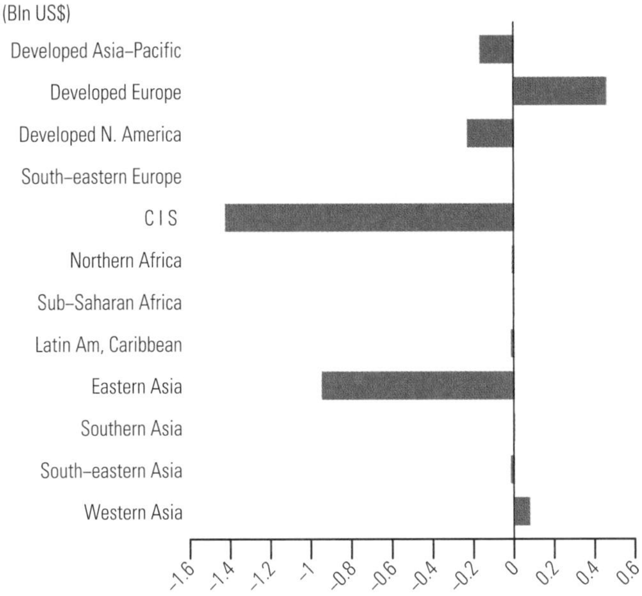

Graph 3: Partner concentration of trade in 2011

(Cumulative share by ranked partners)

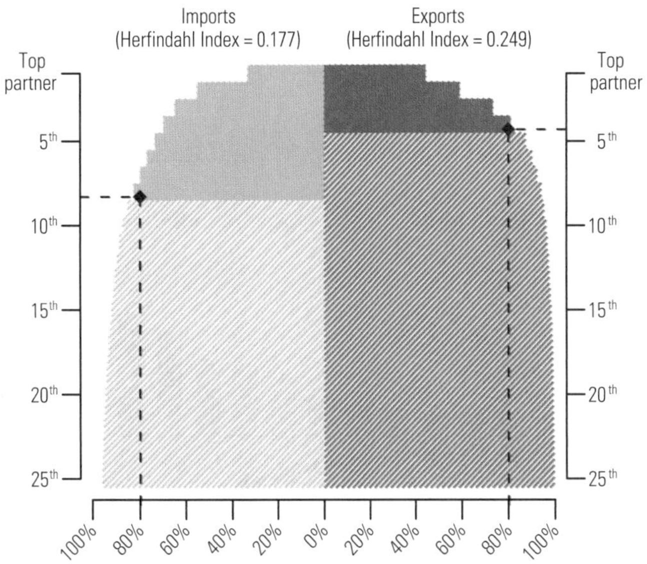

Table 4: Exports by principal countries and SITC sections in 2011

(Value in million US$, percentages of country total)

Country	Total	Shares by SITC sections (%) 0+1	2+4	3	5	6	7	8	9	Total
World	1978.9	11.1	4.4	9.3	1.0	5.3	6.3	8.7	53.9	100
Switzerland	873.6	0.0	0.0	0.0	...	0.7	0.0	0.0	99.3	100
Kazakhstan	289.7	34.6	2.8	24.0	2.2	9.9	10.8	6.1	9.5	100
Russian Federation	284.4	12.6	11.0	11.3	0.7	1.9	8.0	51.5	3.0	100
United Arab Emirates	150.0	2.4	0.1	4.8	...	0.6	0.2	0.3	91.6	100
Uzbekistan	124.4	3.8	11.8	14.5	5.5	32.9	30.6	1.0	...	100
Turkey	54.5	65.2	5.9	22.4	0.1	1.9	1.1	1.4	2.0	100
China	42.0	1.4	49.9	15.1	1.0	16.8	13.7	0.7	1.4	100
Tajikistan	36.3	32.8	0.9	27.5	1.4	27.8	5.5	4.1	0.0	100
Afghanistan	23.5	1.2	0.9	89.3	2.3	3.0	2.7	0.7	...	100
India	18.3	0.0	0.1	0.8	0.0	0.4	0.4	0.0	98.3	100

Imports Profile:

In 2011, imports were composed of 22.8 percent of mineral fuels, lubricants and related materials (SITC section 3), 22.8 percent of machinery and transport equipment (SITC section 7) and 15.6 percent of manufactured goods classified chiefly by material (SITC section 6) (see table 2). In addition to petroleum oils, other than crude (HS code 2710), other major imported goods over the last three years were motor cars and other motor vehicles principally designed for the transport (HS code 8703) and medicaments (excluding goods of heading 30.02, 30.05 or 30.06) (HS code 3004) (see table 5).

Table 5: Top 10 import commodities 2009 to 2011

(Value in million US$)

HS code	4-digit heading of Harmonized System 2007	Value (million US$) 2009	2010	2011	Unit value 2009	2010	2011	Unit	SITC code
	All Commodities	2973.9	3222.6	4260.7					
2710	Petroleum oils, other than crude	0.1	730.9	833.6	0.2	0.6	0.7	US$/kg	334
9999	Commodities not specified according to kind	807.9	21.8	24.1					931
8703	Motor cars and other motor vehicles principally designed for the transport	14.4	119.6	236.9	17.0	4.6	4.3	thsd US$/unit	781
3004	Medicaments (excluding goods of heading 30.02, 30.05 or 30.06)	77.4	97.6	148.7	*16.6*	*20.1*	26.5	US$/kg	542
8704	Motor vehicles for the transport of goods	34.5	87.4	113.5	20.3	24.5	15.2	thsd US$/unit	782
2711	Petroleum gases and other gaseous hydrocarbons	71.6	62.7	74.7	*0.4*	*0.4*	*0.4*	US$/kg	343
8517	Electrical apparatus for line telephony or line telegraphy	31.8	53.8	110.0					764
1001	Wheat and meslin	62.7	62.3	67.0	0.2	0.2	0.2	US$/kg	041
1701	Cane or beet sugar and chemically pure sucrose, in solid form	46.1	46.5	77.9	*0.6*	0.8	0.9	US$/kg	061
1806	Chocolate and other food preparations containing cocoa	45.1	48.7	67.2	*2.9*	3.2	3.5	US$/kg	073

Imports: CIF, by origin/consignment for intra-eu **Exports: FOB, by last known destination** **Trade System: Special**

Overview:

From 2007 to 2011, Latvia's exports increased on average by 11.1 percent each year, despite a decline of 22.7 percent in 2009, and amounted to 12.0 bln US$ in 2011, a 35.8 percent increase from 2010 (see table 1 and graph 1). Imports showed a similar development with an increase of 36.1 percent and amounted to 15.2 bln US$ in 2011 (see table 2 and graph 1). This resulted in a trade deficit of 3.2 bln US$ (see graph 1). Developed Europe (-2.9 bln US$) accounted for the largest share of the overall trade deficit (see graph 2). Significant deficits were also recorded with the Commonwealth of Independent States (-0.5 bln US$) and Eastern Asia (-0.4 bln US$). Latvia's trade was relatively diversified across partners: 13 major partners accounted for 80 percent of both exports and imports (see graph 3).

Graph 1: Total imports, exports and trade balance

(Bln US$ by year)

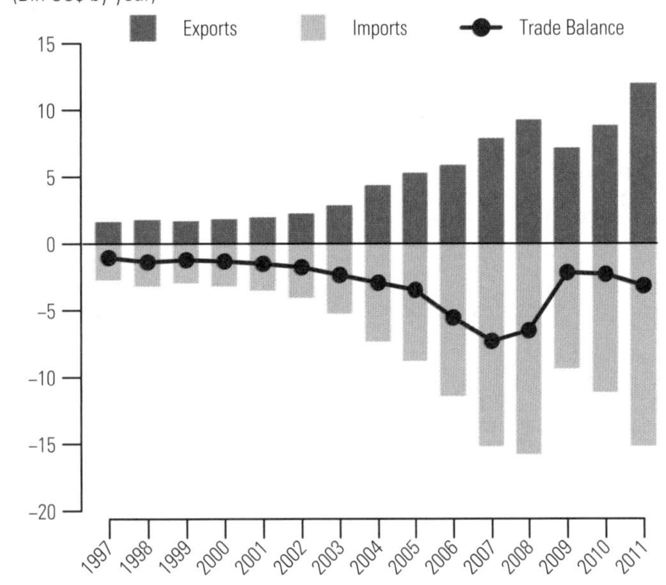

Table 1: Exports by SITC sections

(Value in million US$, growth and shares in percentage)

SITC	2011	Avg. Growth rates (%) 2007-2011	2010-2011	2011 share
Total	12015.1	11.1	35.8	100.0
0+1	1628.0	13.0	18.0	13.5
2+4	1831.6	5.9	21.1	15.2
3	948.1	34.6	101.9	7.9
5	1010.2	12.2	38.0	8.4
6	2562.1	6.1	29.6	21.3
7	2108.6	11.7	29.5	17.5
8	1011.9	4.8	19.1	8.4
9	914.6	32.8	203.3	7.6

Table 2: Imports by SITC sections

(Value in million US$, growth and shares in percentage)

SITC	2011	Avg. Growth rates (%) 2007-2011	2010-2011	2011 share
Total	15167.2	0.0	36.1	100.0
0+1	1741.4	3.7	13.7	11.5
2+4	628.2	-1.5	30.2	4.1
3	2519.8	11.5	53.4	16.6
5	1691.3	3.3	15.4	11.2
6	2388.0	-2.3	37.7	15.7
7	3441.9	-9.3	41.7	22.7
8	1211.0	-6.7	20.9	8.0
9	1545.7	27.3	80.7	10.2

Exports Profile:

In 2011, the majority of exports were composed of 21.3 percent of manufactured goods classified chiefly by material (SITC section 6), 17.5 percent of machinery and transport equipment (SITC section 7) and 15.2 percent of inedible crude materials (except fuels), animal and vegetable oils, fats and waxes (SITC sections 2+4) (see table 1). Top markets for exports were Lithuania, Estonia and Russian Federation (see table 4). Over the last three years, top commodities for exports included wood sawn or chipped lengthwise, sliced or peeled (HS code 4407), other bars and rods of iron or non-alloy steel (HS code 7214) and petroleum oils, other than crude (HS code 2710) (see table 3).

Table 3: Top 10 export commodities 2009 to 2011

(Value in million US$)

HS code	4-digit heading of Harmonized System 2007	Value (million US$) 2009	2010	2011	Unit value 2009	2010	2011	Unit	SITC code
	All Commodities	7171.5	8850.8	12015.1					
9999	Commodities not specified according to kind	298.1	299.1	902.9					931
4407	Wood sawn or chipped lengthwise, sliced or peeled	351.8	524.4	576.6	*215.1*	*244.0*	*261.7*	US$/m³	248
7214	Other bars and rods of iron or non-alloy steel	328.0	370.8	434.6	*0.5*	0.6	0.8	US$/kg	676
2710	Petroleum oils, other than crude	174.6	211.5	579.2	*0.7*	*0.8*	*1.0*	US$/kg	334
3004	Medicaments (excluding goods of heading 30.02, 30.05 or 30.06)	255.8	305.9	392.8	*66.2*	*91.8*	*115.4*	US$/kg	542
8703	Motor cars and other motor vehicles principally designed for the transport	220.4	248.9	396.9	17.1	18.0	25.1	thsd US$/unit	781
4401	Fuel wood, in logs, in billets, in twigs, in faggots or in similar forms	199.6	263.8	290.0	0.1	0.1	0.1	US$/kg	246
4403	Wood in the rough, whether or not stripped of bark or sapwood	140.7	264.3	314.1	56.2	63.6	73.8	US$/m³	247
2208	Alcohol of a strength by volume of less than 80 % vol	122.7	215.3	319.8	*8.1*	*11.8*	*14.5*	US$/litre	112
8528	Reception apparatus for television	167.8	244.0	226.7	365.6	376.8	441.5	US$/unit	761

Graph 2: Trade Balance by MDG Regions in 2011

(Bln US$)

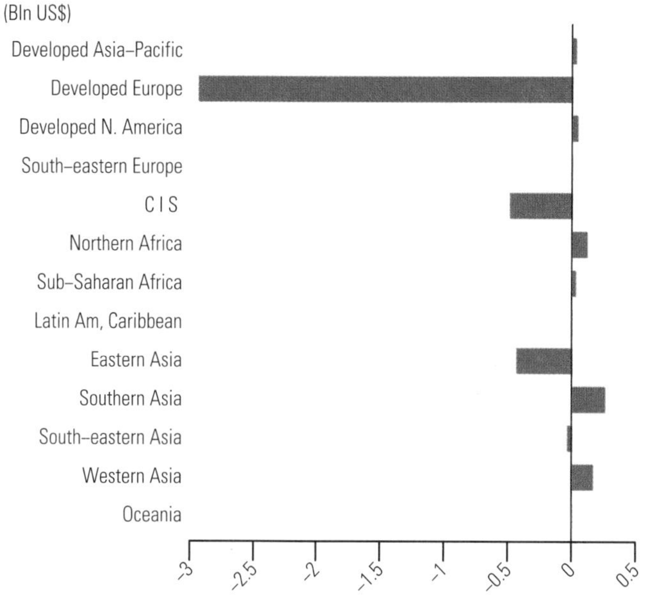

Graph 3: Partner concentration of trade in 2011

(Cumulative share by ranked partners)

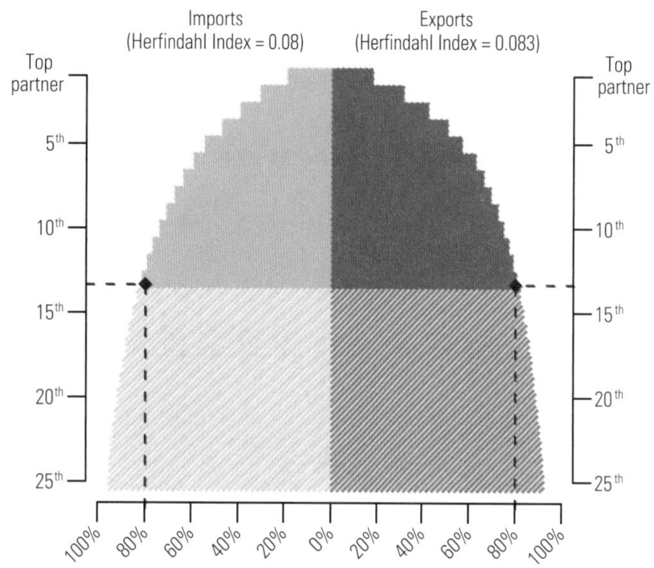

Table 4: Exports by principal countries and SITC sections in 2011

(Value in million US$, percentages of country total)

Country	Total	Shares by SITC sections (%) 0+1	2+4	3	5	6	7	8	9	Total
World	12015.1	13.5	15.2	7.9	8.4	21.3	17.5	8.4	7.6	100
Lithuania	2144.5	17.4	6.1	10.5	12.9	12.7	24.9	4.7	10.9	100
Estonia	1670.0	16.1	7.7	3.0	11.8	15.3	22.8	11.3	12.2	100
Russian Federation	1272.9	34.6	3.5	0.7	15.1	14.1	23.3	8.6	0.0	100
Germany	1001.9	8.5	15.6	4.5	7.2	28.5	15.4	10.2	10.1	100
Sweden	727.4	2.9	41.9	0.2	1.6	23.1	11.9	10.7	7.8	100
Poland	714.6	4.5	5.8	18.9	2.3	52.7	6.1	1.3	8.4	100
Denmark	411.3	6.0	21.1	1.7	2.4	27.9	9.2	22.4	9.2	100
United Kingdom	372.9	2.4	50.6	1.5	2.1	21.5	4.2	6.8	10.9	100
Finland	367.0	3.5	32.8	0.5	2.0	40.5	5.2	8.0	7.4	100
Norway	286.4	2.7	10.8	3.4	1.5	37.1	15.1	29.5	0.0	100

Imports Profile:

In 2011, imports were composed of 22.7 percent of machinery and transport equipment (SITC section 7), 16.6 percent of mineral fuels, lubricants and related materials (SITC section 3) and 15.7 percent of manufactured goods classified chiefly by material (SITC section 6) (see table 2). From 2009 to 2011, top imported products were petroleum oils, other than crude (HS code 2710), petroleum gases and other gaseous hydrocarbons (HS code 2711) and medicaments (excluding goods of heading 30.02, 30.05 or 30.06) (HS code 3004) (see table 5).

Table 5: Top 10 import commodities 2009 to 2011

(Value in million US$)

HS code	4-digit heading of Harmonized System 2007	Value (million US$) 2009	2010	2011	Unit value 2009	2010	2011	Unit	SITC code
	All Commodities	9336.9	11143.3	15167.2					
2710	Petroleum oils, other than crude	784.5	902.5	1568.0	*0.6*	*0.7*	*1.0*	US$/kg	334
9999	Commodities not specified according to kind	706.1	853.0	1514.9					931
2711	Petroleum gases and other gaseous hydrocarbons	540.2	539.4	632.9	*0.5*	*0.4*	*0.5*	US$/kg	343
3004	Medicaments (excluding goods of heading 30.02, 30.05 or 30.06)	442.5	473.5	484.7	*83.5*	*84.2*	*79.7*	US$/kg	542
8703	Motor cars and other motor vehicles principally designed for the transport	200.2	311.4	538.6	19.3	20.6	22.0	thsd US$/unit	781
8528	Reception apparatus for television	165.3	242.5	227.7	296.1	239.8	339.9	US$/unit	761
8517	Electrical apparatus for line telephony or line telegraphy	124.5	178.0	242.6					764
2716	Electrical energy	160.7	131.0	225.2	56.6	61.8	65.5	US$/MWh	351
7207	Semi-finished products of iron or non-alloy steel	79.2	98.6	252.1	0.4	0.5	0.6	US$/kg	672
8471	Automatic data processing machines and units thereof	92.4	118.4	150.1	66.8	80.2	129.9	US$/unit	752

Lebanon

Imports: CIF, by origin | **Exports: FOB, by last known destination** | **Trade System: Special**

Overview:

From 2006 to 2010, Lebanon's exports increased on average by 16.8 percent each year and amounted to 4.3 bln US$ in 2010 (see table 1 and graph 1). During the same period, imports increased on average by 17.6 percent each year and amounted to 18.0 bln US$ (see table 2 and graph 1). The trade balance recorded a deficit of 13.7 bln US$ in 2010 compared to 12.7 bln US$ in 2009 (see graph 1). Trade was in deficit with nearly all MDG regions (see graph 2). In 2010, deficit with Developed Europe alone was 5.5 bln US$. Major deficits were also recorded with Eastern Asia (-2.0 bln US$) and Developed North America (-1.9 bln US$). Lebanon's trade was well diversified across partners: in 2010, 18 major partners accounted for 80 percent of exports compared to 23 major partners for imports (see graph 3).

Graph 1: Total imports, exports and trade balance

(Bln US$ by year)

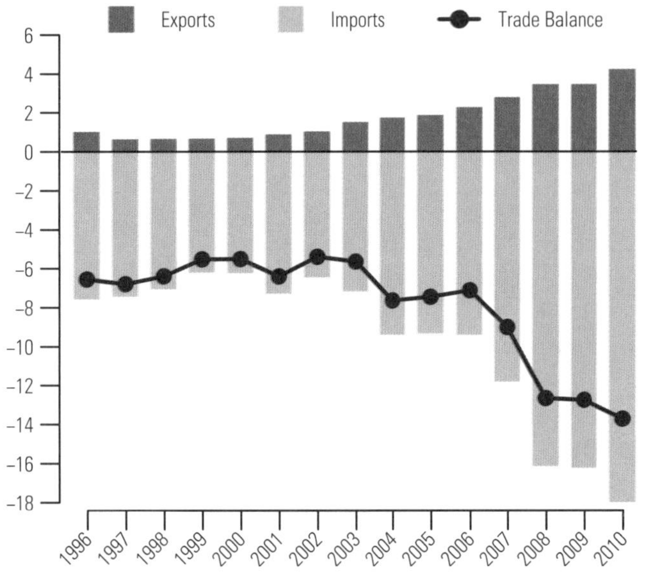

Exports Profile:

In 2010, major commodity groups for export include commodities and transactions not classified elsewhere (SITC section 9), miscellaneous manufactured articles (SITC section 8) and machinery and transport equipment (SITC section 7), accounting respectively for 19.7, 18.9 and 17.6 percent of exports (see table 1). Switzerland, United Arab Emirates and France were the three major markets for exported goods in 2010 (see table 4). Exports to Switzerland were largely commodities and transactions not classified elsewhere in the SITC (SITC section 9). From 2008 to 2010, the three major exported products were gold (including gold plated with platinum) (HS code 7108), ferrous waste and scrap; remelting scrap ingots of iron or steel (HS code 7204) and diamonds, whether or not worked, but not mounted or set (HS code 7102) (see table 3).

Table 1: Exports by SITC sections

(Value in million US$, growth and shares in percentage)

SITC	2010	Avg. Growth rates (%) 2006-2010	2009-2010	2010 share
Total	4254.2	16.8	22.1	100.0
0+1	486.8	15.3	17.8	11.4
2+4	368.4	12.9	81.4	8.7
3	5.6	-4.7	-52.3	0.1
5	382.3	16.8	21.6	9.0
6	620.6	10.5	-4.4	14.6
7	749.6	19.6	35.4	17.6
8	803.9	24.8	64.7	18.9
9	836.9	16.5	-1.6	19.7

Table 2: Imports by SITC sections

(Value in million US$, growth and shares in percentage)

SITC	2010	Avg. Growth rates (%) 2006-2010	2009-2010	2010 share
Total	17969.7	17.6	10.7	100.0
0+1	2617.2	19.2	16.5	14.6
2+4	502.9	14.1	7.0	2.8
3	3674.0	11.8	13.7	20.4
5	1918.1	15.0	15.4	10.7
6	2735.7	17.8	15.4	15.2
7	4100.0	21.1	-5.3	22.8
8	1612.7	16.4	10.3	9.0
9	809.0	52.6	76.0	4.5

Table 3: Top 10 export commodities 2008 to 2010

(Value in million US$)

HS code	4-digit heading of Harmonized System 2007	Value (million US$) 2008	2009	2010	Unit value 2008	2009	2010	Unit	SITC code
	All Commodities	3478.3	3484.2	4254.2					
7108	Gold (including gold plated with platinum)	319.0	842.0	830.1	26.0	27.0	33.3	thsd US$/kg	971
7204	Ferrous waste and scrap; remelting scrap ingots of iron or steel	199.6	91.6	182.6	0.5	0.3	0.3	US$/kg	282
7102	Diamonds, whether or not worked, but not mounted or set	122.5	151.2	170.2					667
8710	Tanks and other armoured fighting vehicles, motorised	15.7	50.3	332.4					891
3103	Mineral or chemical fertilisers, phosphatic	214.5	73.4	97.8	0.8	0.3	0.4	US$/kg	562
8502	Electric generating sets and rotary converters	135.4	105.3	122.7					716
7113	Articles of jewellery and parts thereof, of precious metal	115.4	89.3	84.0	*23.2*	*23.8*	*29.0*	thsd US$/kg	897
7404	Copper waste and scrap	86.2	49.8	100.7	6.4	4.6	5.8	US$/kg	288
2523	Portland cement, aluminous cement, slag cement	114.2	71.6	44.5	0.1	0.1	0.1	US$/kg	661
9403	Other furniture and parts thereof	82.7	71.9	73.7					821

Graph 2: Trade Balance by MDG Regions in 2010

(Bln US$)

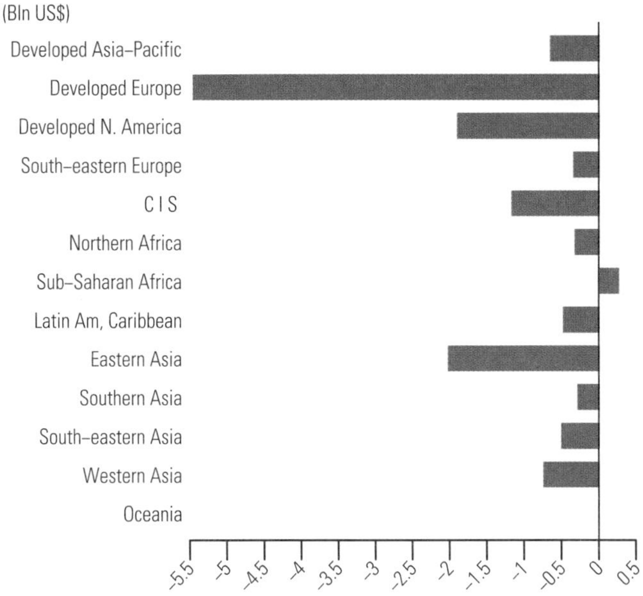

Graph 3: Partner concentration of trade in 2010

(Cumulative share by ranked partners)

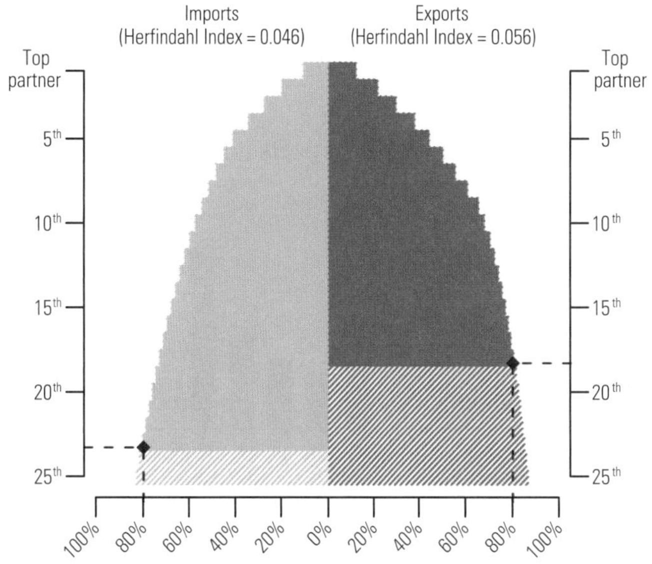

Table 4: Exports by principal countries and SITC sections in 2010

(Value in million US$, percentages of country total)

Country	Total	Shares by SITC sections (%)								
		0 + 1	2 + 4	3	5	6	7	8	9	Total
World	4254.2	11.4	8.7	0.1	9.0	14.6	17.6	18.9	19.7	100
Switzerland	502.6	0.2	0.0	...	0.1	2.2	0.1	0.6	96.8	100
United Arab Emirates	418.6	7.5	0.9	0.0	5.1	25.0	34.7	26.4	0.5	100
France	349.0	2.3	0.8	0.0	0.7	3.2	4.1	88.9	0.1	100
South Africa	344.4	0.2	0.0	0.0	0.3	0.2	0.7	0.1	98.6	100
Iraq	267.0	13.2	3.5	0.0	11.4	8.8	41.5	21.4	0.1	100
Saudi Arabia	246.0	27.9	2.2	0.0	11.3	20.0	12.6	25.9	0.0	100
Turkey	230.7	2.2	74.5	...	17.6	3.5	1.4	0.8	0.0	100
Syria	220.8	36.5	2.2	0.0	13.2	30.5	8.7	8.9	0.1	100
Egypt	201.1	11.9	1.1	...	10.2	9.1	62.5	5.0	0.0	100
Jordan	103.7	28.3	4.2	0.0	10.1	24.6	10.0	20.6	2.1	100

Imports Profile:

In 2010, Lebanon's imports were composed of 22.8 percent of machinery and transport equipment (SITC section 7), 20.4 percent of mineral fuels, lubricants and related materials (SITC section 3) and 15.2 percent of manufactured goods classified chiefly by material (SITC section 6) (see table 2). From 2008 to 2010, the three major imported products were petroleum oils, other than crude (HS code 2710), motor cars and other motor vehicles principally designed for the transport (HS code 8703), medicaments (excluding goods of heading 30.02, 30.05 or 30.06) (HS code 3004) (see table 5).

Table 5: Top 10 import commodities 2008 to 2010

(Value in million US$)

HS code	4-digit heading of Harmonized System 2007	Value (million US$)			Unit value				SITC code
		2008	2009	2010	2008	2009	2010	Unit	
	All Commodities	16136.5	16231.6	17969.7					
2710	Petroleum oils, other than crude	3807.3	3014.2	3400.9	*0.9*	0.5	*0.7*	US$/kg	334
8703	Motor cars and other motor vehicles principally designed for the transport	1359.8	1463.1	1428.6			*20.5*	thsd US$/unit	781
3004	Medicaments (excluding goods of heading 30.02, 30.05 or 30.06)	625.9	675.3	756.0	110.6	107.5	99.8	US$/kg	542
7108	Gold (including gold plated with platinum)	512.5	449.8	801.9	*26.3*	*30.5*	*24.7*	thsd US$/kg	971
7214	Other bars and rods of iron or non-alloy steel	420.5	311.8	349.3	0.8	0.4	0.5	US$/kg	676
7102	Diamonds, whether or not worked, but not mounted or set	248.9	258.6	255.1					667
0102	Live bovine animals	150.8	207.9	275.4	*793.8*	*936.4*	*804.6*	US$/unit	001
2402	Cigars, cheroots, cigarillos and cigarettes	150.2	173.4	210.9	16.5	16.9	19.0	US$/kg	122
8704	Motor vehicles for the transport of goods	113.2	174.6	184.0	*14.0*			thsd US$/unit	782
8802	Other aircraft (for example, helicopters, aeroplanes); spacecraft	...	458.6	...					792

Lesotho

Imports: CIF, by consignment **Exports: FOB, by last known destination** **Trade System: General**

Overview:

In 2009, the exports of Lesotho increased by 156.7 percent to 628.1 mln US$ (see table 1 and graph 1). During the same period, imports increased by 27.2 percent to 1,356.1 mln US$ (see table 2 and graph 1). This resulted in a trade deficit of 727.9 mln US$ in 2009 (see graph 1). By MDG regions, trade with Sub-Saharan Africa alone accounted for a large part of this deficit (-982.3 mln US$) (see graph 2). Significant surplus was recorded with Developed North America at 293.2 mln US$. Trade was highly concentrated among partners: in 2009, 2 (respectively 1) major partners accounted for 80 percent of exports (respectively imports) (see graph 3).

Graph 1: Total imports, exports and trade balance

(Bln US$ by year)

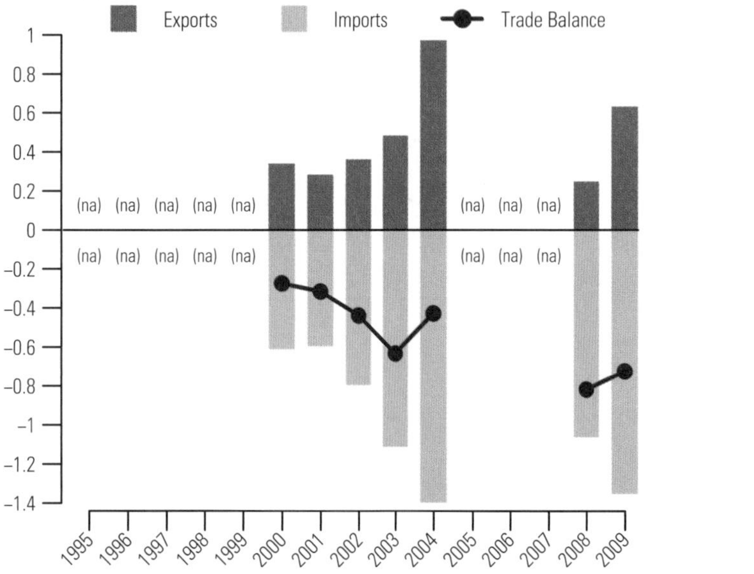

Exports Profile:

In 2009, exports were mainly composed of 62.6 percent of miscellaneous manufactured articles (SITC section 8), 12.7 percent of machinery and transport equipment (SITC section 7) and 8.9 percent of food, live animals, beverages and tobacco (SITC sections 0+1) (see table 1). The major partners for exports in 2009 were South Africa, USA and Canada (see table 4). From 2008 to 2009, top exported products were men's or boys' suits, jackets, trousers etc (HS code 6203), television receivers, video monitors, projectors (HS code 8528) and jerseys, pullovers, cardigans, etc, knitted or crocheted (HS code 6110) (see table 3).

Table 1: Exports by SITC sections

(Value in million US$, growth and shares in percentage)

SITC	2009	Avg. Growth rates (%) 2005-2009	2008-2009	2009 share
Total	628.1	...	156.7	100.0
0+1	56.1	...	70.4	8.9
2+4	22.4	...	-20.4	3.6
3	0.1	...	-88.7	0.0
5	3.6	...	188.9	0.6
6	49.2	...	202.5	7.8
7	80.0	...	-20.0	12.7
8	393.0	...	506.4	62.6
9	23.6	...	7287.2	3.8

Table 2: Imports by SITC sections

(Value in million US$, growth and shares in percentage)

SITC	2009	Avg. Growth rates (%) 2005-2009	2008-2009	2009 share
Total	1 356.1	...	27.2	100.0
0+1	345.9	...	65.2	25.5
2+4	66.2	...	112.5	4.9
3	147.3	...	29.5	10.9
5	115.5	...	28.4	8.5
6	228.0	...	89.7	16.8
7	274.8	...	32.0	20.3
8	157.0	...	3.0	11.6
9	21.3	...	-84.9	1.6

Table 3: Top 10 export commodities 2007 to 2009

(Value in million US$)

HS code	4-digit heading of Harmonized System 1996	Value (million US$) 2007	2008	2009	Unit value 2007	2008	2009	Unit	SITC code
	All Commodities	...	244.7	628.1					
6203	Men's or boys' suits, jackets, trousers etc	...	13.7	86.7					841
8528	Television receivers, video monitors, projectors	...	50.9	35.2					761
6110	Jerseys, pullovers, cardigans, etc, knitted or crocheted	...	4.8	77.9		*13.0*	*12.6*	US$/unit	845
8538	Parts for electrical switches, protectors, connectors	...	34.1	36.7					772
6204	Women's or girls' suits, jacket, dress, skirt, etc	...	6.8	61.9					842
6104	Womens, girls suit, dress, skirt, etc, knit or crocheted	...	8.6	34.8					844
6103	Men's, boys' suits,jackets,trousers etc knitted or crocheted	...	2.1	38.9					843
6404	Footwear with uppers of textile materials	...	13.4	20.5					851
2201	Unsweetened beverage waters, ice and snow	...	0.0	32.4					111
5101	Wool, not carded or combed	...	14.9	15.2					268

Graph 2: Trade Balance by MDG Regions in 2009

(Mln US$)

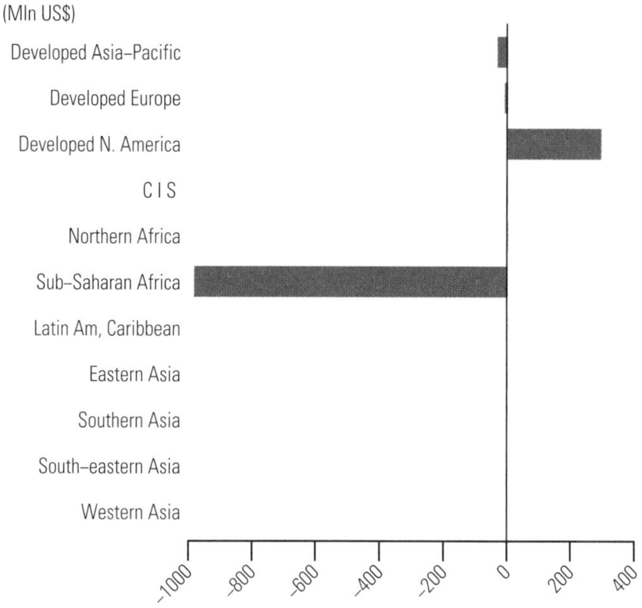

Graph 3: Partner concentration of trade in 2009

(Cumulative share by ranked partners)

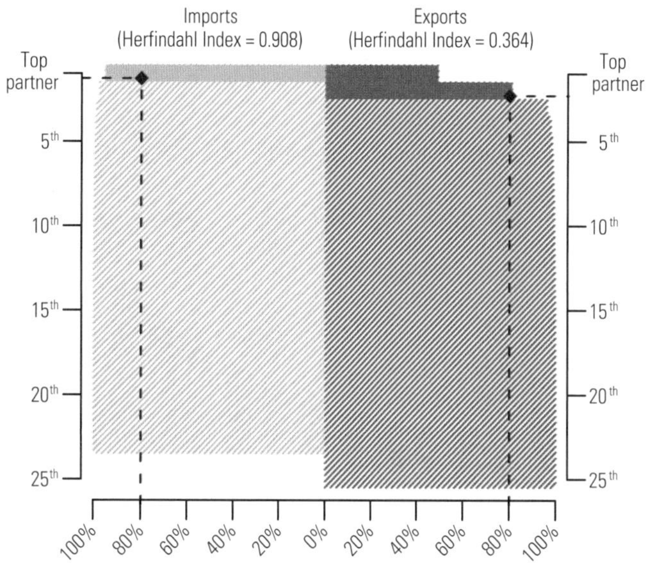

Table 4: Exports by principal countries and SITC sections in 2009

(Value in million US$, percentages of country total)

Country	Total	Shares by SITC sections (%)								
		0 + 1	2 + 4	3	5	6	7	8	9	Total
World	628.1	8.9	3.6	0.0	0.6	7.8	12.7	62.6	3.8	100
South Africa	307.4	18.1	7.2	0.0	1.2	7.2	26.0	32.6	7.7	100
USA	200.0	0.0	0.0	...	...	1.3	...	98.6	...	100
Canada	95.0	0.0	0.1	...	...	4.9	...	95.0	...	100
Belgium	10.2	0.0	0.0	...	...	100.0	...	...	...	100
Madagascar	3.6	0.0	0.0	...	...	95.9	...	4.1	...	100
China	2.2	0.0	4.5	...	...	62.5	...	33.0	...	100
Japan	1.3	0.0	0.0	...	...	9.5	...	90.5	...	100
Egypt	1.1	0.0	0.0	...	...	91.4	...	8.6	...	100
Kenya	1.1	0.0	0.0	...	...	100.0	...	...	...	100
Netherlands	0.9	0.0	0.0	...	...	...	...	100.0	...	100

Imports Profile:

In 2009, imports were mainly composed of 25.5 percent of food, live animals, beverages and tobacco (SITC sections 0+1), 20.3 percent of machinery and transport equipment (SITC section 7) and 16.8 percent of manufactured goods classified chiefly by material (SITC section 6) (see table 2). From 2008 to 2009, top imported products included oils petroleum, bituminous, distillates, except crude (HS code 2710), public-transport type passenger motor vehicles (HS code 8702) and other furniture and parts thereof (HS code 9403) (see table 5).

Table 5: Top 10 import commodities 2007 to 2009

(Value in million US$)

HS code	4-digit heading of Harmonized System 1996	Value (million US$)			Unit value				SITC code
		2007	2008	2009	2007	2008	2009	Unit	
	All Commodities	...	1 066.2	1 356.1					
9999	Commodities not elsewhere specified	...	141.1	21.3					931
2710	Oils petroleum, bituminous, distillates, except crude	...	70.3	79.2		*0.9*	*1.3*	US$/kg	334
8702	Public-transport type passenger motor vehicles	...	38.1	75.5			*25.8*	thsd US$/unit	783
9403	Other furniture and parts thereof	...	24.8	29.9					821
2711	Petroleum gases and other gaseous hydrocarbons	...	19.0	31.9					343
3304	Beauty, make-up and skin care preparations	...	36.5	13.5		*16.8*	*18.9*	US$/kg	553
0207	Meat, edible offal of domestic poultry	...	15.3	27.6		*1.7*	*2.0*	US$/kg	012
8708	Parts and accessories for motor vehicles	...	12.0	24.2		*10.2*	*12.2*	US$/kg	784
1102	Cereal flours other than of wheat or meslin	...	10.2	23.3		*0.6*		US$/kg	047
1005	Maize (corn)	...	16.8	14.9					044

Lithuania

Imports: CIF, by origin | **Exports: FOB, by last known destination** | **Trade System: Special**

Overview:

From 2007 to 2011, despite a decline of 30.6 percent in 2009, Lithuania's exports increased on average by 13.2 percent each year and amounted to 28.2 bln US$ in 2011, reflecting an increase of 35.3 percent from 2010 (see table 1 and graph 1). Imports showed a similar development with an increase of 34.6 percent to reach 31.5 bln US$ in 2011 (see table 2 and graph 1). This recorded a trade deficit of 3.3 bln US$ in 2011 (see graph 1). The Commonwealth of Independent States accounted for a large share of this deficit: 3.7 bln US$ (see graph 2). Trade was relatively diversified across partners: 13 (respectively 11) major partners accounted for 80 percent of exports (respectively imports) in 2011 (see graph 3).

Graph 1: Total imports, exports and trade balance

(Bln US$ by year)

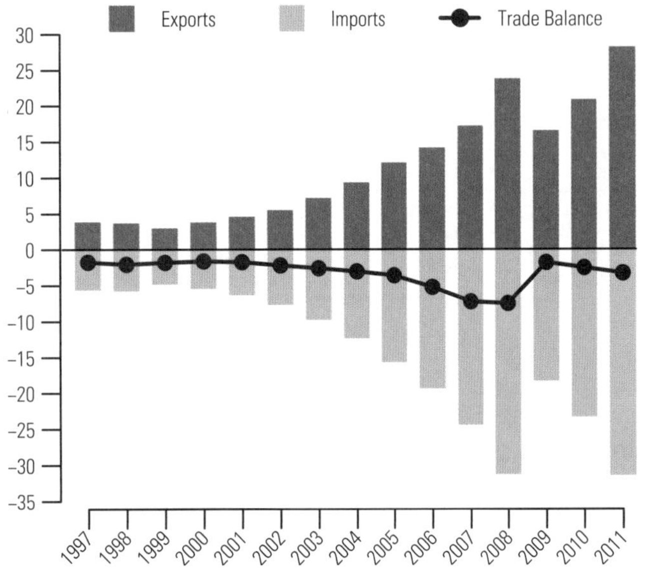

Exports Profile:

In 2011, exports of mineral fuels, lubricants and related materials (SITC section 3), increased by 47.6 percent and accounted for 25.5 percent of exported goods (see table 1). Other major commodity groups for exports included machinery and transport equipment (SITC section 7) and food, live animals, beverages and tobacco (SITC sections 0+1), respectively with 17.4 and 15.1 percent of exported goods (see table 1). Russian Federation, Latvia and Germany were the top three destinations for exports (see table 4). From 2009 to 2011, the top three products for exports were petroleum oils, other than crude (HS code 2710), motor cars and other motor vehicles principally designed for the transport (HS code 8703) and other furniture and parts thereof (HS code 9403) (see table 3).

Table 1: Exports by SITC sections

(Value in million US$, growth and shares in percentage)

SITC	2011	Avg. Growth rates (%) 2007-2011	2010-2011	2011 share
Total	28153.8	13.2	35.3	100.0
0+1	4242.4	11.7	24.6	15.1
2+4	1261.4	6.6	32.6	4.5
3	7175.8	33.1	47.6	25.5
5	3794.3	13.4	41.7	13.5
6	2678.1	7.4	28.8	9.5
7	4909.4	5.6	33.2	17.4
8	3554.1	6.6	25.5	12.6
9	538.3	33.5	66.0	1.9

Table 2: Imports by SITC sections

(Value in million US$, growth and shares in percentage)

SITC	2011	Avg. Growth rates (%) 2007-2011	2010-2011	2011 share
Total	31469.2	6.5	34.6	100.0
0+1	3437.4	12.3	25.9	10.9
2+4	1222.5	8.7	38.9	3.9
3	10602.3	27.9	41.5	33.7
5	3980.2	6.6	27.1	12.6
6	3419.0	-3.4	30.3	10.9
7	6090.4	-7.3	34.0	19.4
8	1728.3	-2.3	20.3	5.5
9	989.1	34.6	83.0	3.1

Table 3: Top 10 export commodities 2009 to 2011

(Value in million US$)

HS code	4-digit heading of Harmonized System 2007	Value (million US$) 2009	2010	2011	Unit value 2009	2010	2011	Unit	SITC code
	All Commodities	16496.3	20813.9	28153.8					
2710	Petroleum oils, other than crude	3210.4	4518.3	6695.7	0.5	0.6	0.9	US$/kg	334
8703	Motor cars and other motor vehicles principally designed for the transport	530.1	649.5	1075.6	3.3	4.3	5.2	thsd US$/unit	781
9403	Other furniture and parts thereof	615.4	677.8	844.8					821
3907	Polyacetals, other polyethers and epoxide resins, in primary forms	474.7	639.6	762.6	1.3	1.4	1.9	US$/kg	574
3102	Mineral or chemical fertilisers, nitrogenous	353.0	383.8	795.0	0.2	0.2	0.3	US$/kg	562
3105	Mineral or chemical fertilisers	356.1	404.9	552.4	0.3	0.4	0.6	US$/kg	562
9999	Commodities not specified according to kind	281.6	322.6	532.3					931
0406	Cheese and curd	261.9	274.9	328.2	3.8	4.6	5.0	US$/kg	024
3004	Medicaments (excluding goods of heading 30.02, 30.05 or 30.06)	232.3	271.5	333.3	190.3	158.6	170.1	US$/kg	542
3923	Articles for the conveyance or packing of goods, of plastics	236.3	247.8	312.2	2.1	2.1	2.6	US$/kg	893

Graph 2: Trade Balance by MDG Regions in 2011

(Bln US$)

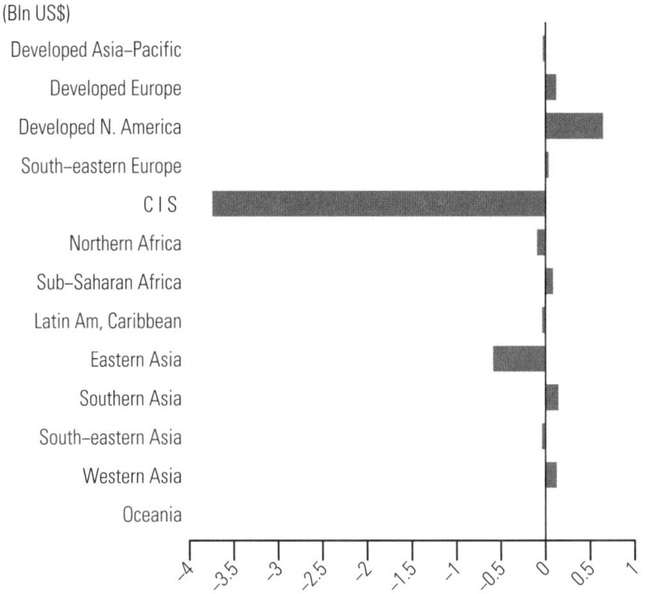

Graph 3: Partner concentration of trade in 2011

(Cumulative share by ranked partners)

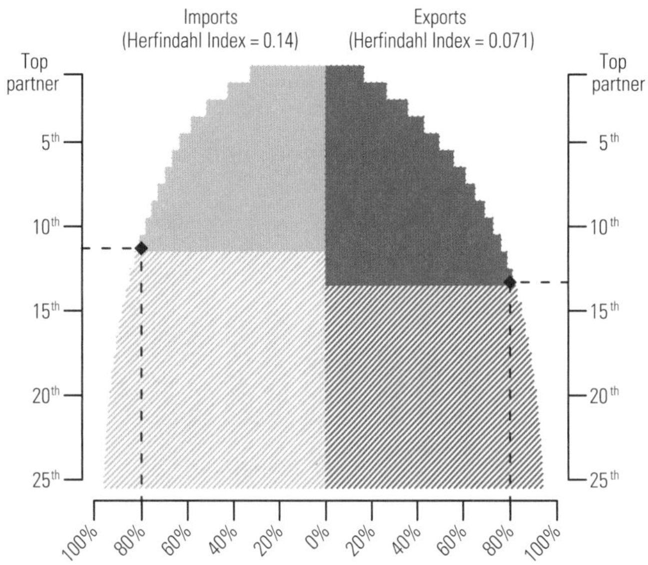

Table 4: Exports by principal countries and SITC sections in 2011

(Value in million US$, percentages of country total)

Country	Total	Shares by SITC sections (%)								
		0 + 1	2 + 4	3	5	6	7	8	9	Total
World	28153.8	15.1	4.5	25.5	13.5	9.5	17.4	12.6	1.9	100
Russian Federation	4653.1	28.4	2.2	1.4	7.7	10.8	33.7	15.7	0.1	100
Latvia	2873.2	18.3	6.4	32.3	9.8	7.5	15.1	5.1	5.4	100
Germany	2611.2	16.5	6.1	12.6	22.8	9.5	11.9	18.5	2.2	100
Poland	1962.6	12.5	6.3	39.9	14.4	11.2	6.7	6.6	2.3	100
Estonia	1866.8	11.1	1.3	54.5	9.4	6.9	10.0	3.9	2.9	100
Netherlands	1778.0	7.8	2.0	72.0	5.9	2.4	3.3	5.9	0.8	100
Belarus	1461.0	7.1	1.9	0.6	13.1	11.2	60.7	5.0	0.3	100
United Kingdom	1164.8	11.5	3.1	37.6	16.8	7.1	3.2	19.0	1.7	100
France	1155.3	5.9	2.2	39.9	23.3	6.4	7.2	13.9	1.2	100
Sweden	1001.3	14.3	5.7	0.0	14.3	18.0	11.3	34.1	2.3	100

Imports Profile:

Imports of mineral fuels, lubricants and related materials (SITC section 3), machinery and transport equipment (SITC section 7) and chemicals and related products, n.e.s. (SITC section 5) accounted for 33.7, 19.4 and 12.6 percent of imported goods, respectively (see table 2). From 2009 to 2011, top imported products were: petroleum oils and oils obtained from bituminous minerals, crude (HS code 2709), petroleum gases and other gaseous hydrocarbons (HS code 2711) and motor cars and other motor vehicles principally designed for the transport (HS code 8703) (see table 5).

Table 5: Top 10 import commodities 2009 to 2011

(Value in million US$)

HS code	4-digit heading of Harmonized System 2007	Value (million US$)			Unit value				SITC code
		2009	2010	2011	2009	2010	2011	Unit	
	All Commodities	18340.6	23378.0	31469.2					
2709	Petroleum oils and oils obtained from bituminous minerals, crude	3935.8	5566.1	7638.4	0.5	0.6	0.9	US$/kg	333
2711	Petroleum gases and other gaseous hydrocarbons	820.8	1047.5	1530.0	0.4	0.5	0.6	US$/kg	343
8703	Motor cars and other motor vehicles principally designed for the transport	568.2	745.7	1138.5	4.5	5.7	7.0	thsd US$/unit	781
3004	Medicaments (excluding goods of heading 30.02, 30.05 or 30.06)	668.0	647.9	759.0	86.5	82.3	88.2	US$/kg	542
9999	Commodities not specified according to kind	387.5	534.7	977.2					931
2710	Petroleum oils, other than crude	245.8	442.5	790.2	0.6	0.7	1.0	US$/kg	334
2917	Polycarboxylic acids, their anhydrides	340.3	436.2	557.7	0.9	1.0	1.3	US$/kg	513
2716	Electrical energy	31.5	353.9	513.2	46.8	50.3	58.9	US$/MWh	351
8701	Tractors (other than tractors of heading 87.09)	125.6	263.6	483.9	32.3	39.1	49.5	thsd US$/unit	722
8517	Electrical apparatus for line telephony or line telegraphy	169.8	243.9	291.1					764

Luxembourg

Imports: CIF, by origin/consignment for intra-eu **Exports: FOB, by last known destination** **Trade System: Special**

Overview:

After several years of continuous growth marked by a peak of 17.4 bln US$ in 2008, the value of the exports of Luxembourg contracted sharply in 2009 (by 27.8 percent) but bounced back in 2010 and continued to rise in 2011 by 18.0 percent to amount to 16.4 bln US$, still below its 2008 level (see table 1 and graph 1). Imports showed a similar development with an increase of 24.0 percent to 25.3 bln US$ in 2011 (see table 2 and graph 1). This resulted in a trade deficit of 8.9 bln US$ in 2011, well above the 2010 deficit of 6.5 bln US$ (see graph 1). This deficit resulted largely from trade with Developed Europe (-7.7 bln US$) (see graph 2). Trade, however, recorded surpluses with Commonwealth of Independent States (+302.1 mln US$) and Western Asia (+298.9 mln US$) among others. Compared to imports, exports were more diversified across partners: 12 major partners accounted for 80 percent of exports compared to 8 major partners for imports (see graph 3).

Graph 1: Total imports, exports and trade balance

(Bln US$ by year)

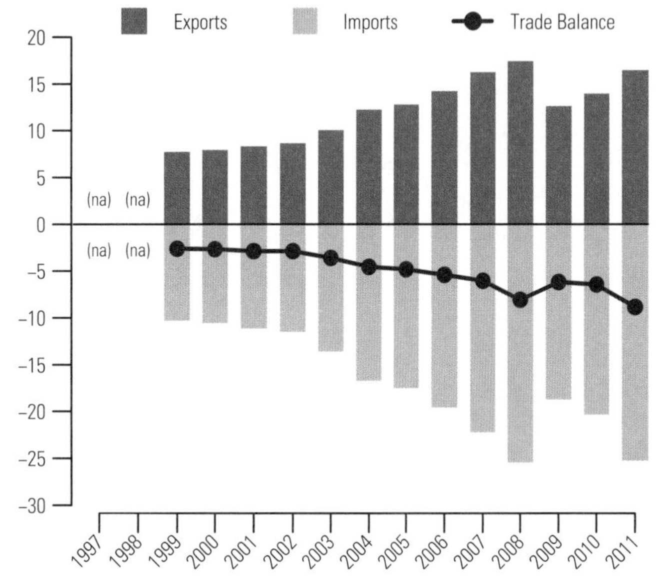

Table 1: Exports by SITC sections

(Value in million US$, growth and shares in percentage)

SITC	2011	Avg. Growth rates (%) 2007-2011	2010-2011	2011 share
Total	16413.0	0.3	18.0	100.0
0+1	1277.9	6.8	12.6	7.8
2+4	705.6	20.6	37.8	4.3
3	132.8	1.5	1.0	0.8
5	1149.5	3.9	9.2	7.0
6	7272.4	-1.0	15.2	44.3
7	3794.4	-1.2	21.2	23.1
8	1296.3	-4.2	4.9	7.9
9	784.1	3.7	94.6	4.8

Table 2: Imports by SITC sections

(Value in million US$, growth and shares in percentage)

SITC	2011	Avg. Growth rates (%) 2007-2011	2010-2011	2011 share
Total	25299.8	3.2	24.0	100.0
0+1	2454.1	4.2	8.9	9.7
2+4	2451.0	8.8	55.0	9.7
3	2406.8	5.1	19.7	9.5
5	2370.8	4.1	19.1	9.4
6	4135.3	0.3	22.1	16.3
7	7059.2	0.8	20.1	27.9
8	2273.2	2.1	14.4	9.0
9	2149.4	10.1	63.6	8.5

Exports Profile:

In 2011, exports were mainly composed of 44.3 percent of manufactured goods classified chiefly by material (SITC section 6) and 23.1 percent of machinery and transport equipment (SITC section 7) (see table 1). The three largest markets for exported goods were Germany, France and Belgium (see table 4). From 2009 to 2011, the top three commodities for exports were angles, shapes and sections of iron or non-alloy steel (HS code 7216), sheet piling of iron or steel (HS code 7301) and new pneumatic tyres, of rubber (HS code 4011) (see table 3).

Table 3: Top 10 export commodities 2009 to 2011

(Value in million US$)

HS code	4-digit heading of Harmonized System 2007	Value (million US$) 2009	2010	2011	Unit value 2009	2010	2011	Unit	SITC code
	All Commodities	12542.1	13911.3	16413.0					
7216	Angles, shapes and sections of iron or non-alloy steel	773.1	954.7	1236.1	0.8	0.8	0.8	US$/kg	676
7301	Sheet piling of iron or steel	534.3	583.7	638.8	1.3	1.2	1.1	US$/kg	676
4011	New pneumatic tyres, of rubber	373.1	553.9	793.3	*268.1*	*277.1*	346.0	US$/unit	625
7210	Flat-rolled products of iron or non-alloy steel	483.5	585.7	578.2	0.9	0.8	1.0	US$/kg	674
8703	Motor cars and other motor vehicles principally designed for the transport	461.8	455.4	533.9	*15.6*	9.2	13.9	thsd US$/unit	781
4811	Paper, paperboard, cellulose wadding and webs of cellulose fibres	404.6	386.4	402.9	3.2	2.9	2.9	US$/kg	641
9999	Commodities not specified according to kind	355.7	370.2	463.9					931
7601	Unwrought aluminium	260.8	362.4	414.5	2.2	2.3	2.7	US$/kg	684
5902	Tyre cord fabric of high tenacity yarn of nylon or other polyamides	249.9	308.3	352.8	5.0	4.6	4.9	US$/kg	657
5603	Nonwovens, whether or not impregnated, coated, covered or laminated	252.1	251.2	260.4	8.4	7.4	6.3	US$/kg	657

Graph 2: Trade Balance by MDG Regions in 2011

(Bln US$)

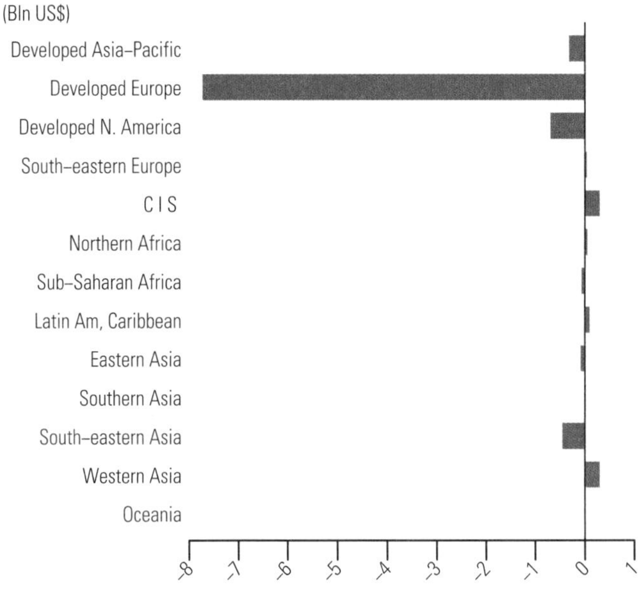

Graph 3: Partner concentration of trade in 2011

(Cumulative share by ranked partners)

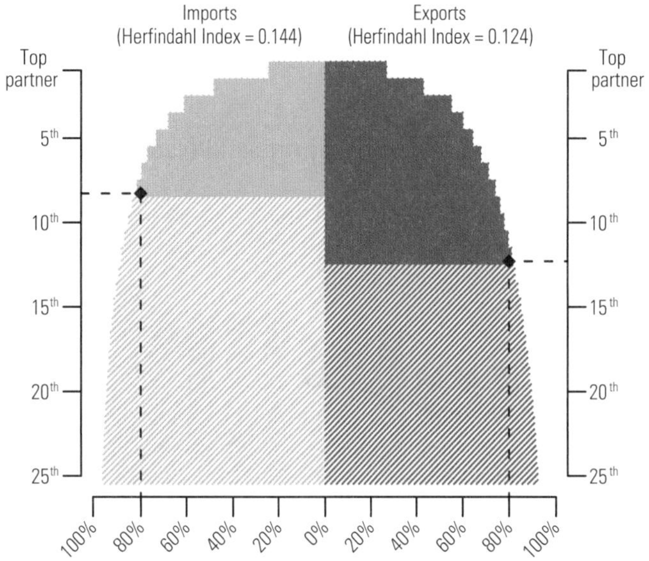

Table 4: Exports by principal countries and SITC sections in 2011

(Value in million US$, percentages of country total)

Country	Total	Shares by SITC sections (%)								
		0 + 1	2 + 4	3	5	6	7	8	9	Total
World	16 413.0	7.8	4.3	0.8	7.0	44.3	23.1	7.9	4.8	100
Germany	4 462.9	13.2	10.1	0.1	8.7	44.6	15.4	6.4	1.6	100
France	2 602.2	10.5	4.7	0.2	5.8	44.0	23.1	10.4	1.3	100
Belgium	1 994.1	10.0	3.8	6.2	11.9	31.7	24.3	9.8	2.3	100
Netherlands	815.3	9.7	1.0	0.0	4.0	59.7	14.7	10.9	0.0	100
Italy	693.9	3.5	0.4	0.0	11.2	50.2	22.0	11.6	1.1	100
USA	574.4	0.0	0.4	0.0	1.6	39.0	55.3	3.5	0.2	100
United Kingdom	539.8	1.5	4.0	0.0	7.7	52.4	17.0	14.5	2.8	100
Switzerland	472.4	0.3	0.0	0.0	2.8	16.8	22.7	3.4	54.0	100
Poland	341.1	1.0	0.0	0.2	6.2	67.7	15.6	8.2	1.1	100
Spain	294.6	8.7	0.3	0.0	8.5	43.3	23.1	14.1	2.1	100

Imports Profile:

In 2011, machinery and transport equipment (SITC section 7) and manufactured goods classified chiefly by material (SITC section 6) accounted respectively for 27.9 and 16.3 percent of imported goods (see table 2). From 2009 to 2011, top imported goods were petroleum oils, other than crude (HS code 2710), motor cars and other motor vehicles principally designed for the transport (HS code 8703) and ferrous waste and scrap; remelting scrap ingots of iron or steel (HS code 7204) (see table 5).

Table 5: Top 10 import commodities 2009 to 2011

(Value in million US$)

HS code	4-digit heading of Harmonized System 2007	Value (million US$)			Unit value				SITC code
		2009	2010	2011	2009	2010	2011	Unit	
	All Commodities	18 770.6	20 400.0	25 299.8					
2710	Petroleum oils, other than crude	1 441.1	1 964.3	2 346.8	0.5	0.7	0.9	US$/kg	334
8703	Motor cars and other motor vehicles principally designed for the transport	1 758.4	1 828.9	1 996.3	25.5	*25.2*		thsd US$/unit	781
9999	Commodities not specified according to kind	1 242.8	1 153.0	1 452.1					931
7204	Ferrous waste and scrap; remelting scrap ingots of iron or steel	512.6	918.9	1 121.5	0.3	0.3	0.4	US$/kg	282
8802	Other aircraft (for example, helicopters, aeroplanes); spacecraft	243.1	438.4	1 075.4	8.4	18.3	46.8	mln US$/unit	792
3004	Medicaments (excluding goods of heading 30.02, 30.05 or 30.06)	396.3	374.1	395.0	148.0	110.0	126.7	US$/kg	542
7108	Gold (including gold plated with platinum)	160.2	155.0	688.6	3.8	3.7	3.8	thsd US$/kg	971
0406	Cheese and curd	291.1	311.1	327.8	6.2	5.9	6.6	US$/kg	024
7207	Semi-finished products of iron or non-alloy steel	279.1	249.6	285.4	0.6	0.6	0.8	US$/kg	672
8517	Electrical apparatus for line telephony or line telegraphy	250.2	265.3	284.4					764

Madagascar

Imports: CIF, by origin | **Exports: FOB, by consumption** | **Trade System: General**

Overview:

In 2010, the value of Madagascar's exports dropped by 1.3 percent and amounted to 1.1 bln US$ (see table 1 and graph 1). Imports showed a more pronounced development with a drop of 19.4 percent in 2010 and amounted to 2.5 bln US$ (see table 2 and graph 1). This resulted in a trade deficit of 1.5 bln US$ (see graph 1). Large deficits were recorded with Eastern Asia (-374.1 mln US$), Western Asia (-320.5 mln US$) and Sub-Saharan Africa (-238.7 mln US$) (see graph 2). In 2010, trade was relatively diversified across partners: 13 major partners accounted for 80 percent of exports and 16 major partners for 80 percent of imports (see graph 3).

Graph 1: Total imports, exports and trade balance

(Bln US$ by year)

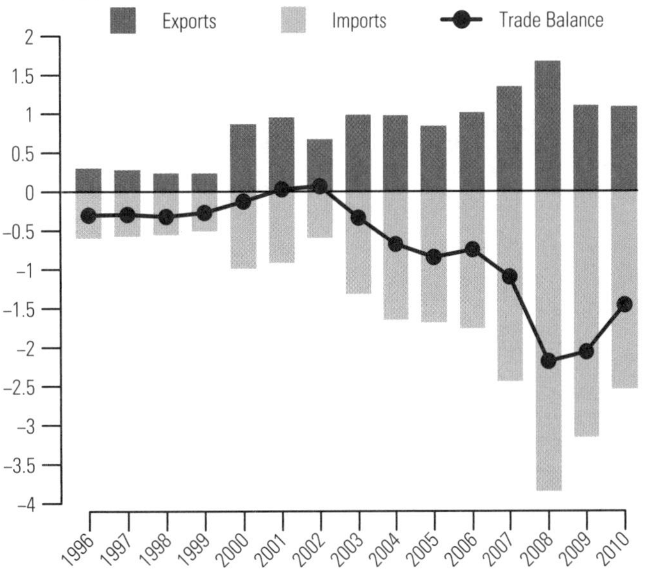

Table 1: Exports by SITC sections

(Value in million US$, growth and shares in percentage)

SITC	2010	Avg. Growth rates (%) 2006-2010	2009-2010	2010 share
Total	1 082.2	1.8	-1.3	100.0
0+1	251.9	-6.4	-12.4	23.3
2+4	120.8	12.4	46.9	11.2
3	62.7	-6.0	28.0	5.8
5	32.3	20.6	49.6	3.0
6	72.8	1.1	-24.3	6.7
7	120.3	47.8	77.4	11.1
8	363.4	3.8	-23.4	33.6
9	57.9	-12.7	238.4	5.4

Table 2: Imports by SITC sections

(Value in million US$, growth and shares in percentage)

SITC	2010	Avg. Growth rates (%) 2006-2010	2009-2010	2010 share
Total	2 545.8	9.7	-19.4	100.0
0+1	284.2	8.4	12.4	11.2
2+4	89.8	4.9	-16.5	3.5
3	386.0	4.1	17.9	15.2
5	221.0	10.0	14.6	8.7
6	634.2	5.0	-44.4	24.9
7	751.8	22.2	-14.7	29.5
8	171.4	6.4	-31.4	6.7
9	7.4	-3.3	-9.5	0.3

Exports Profile:

Madagascar's exports were composed largely of miscellaneous manufactured articles (SITC section 8). While its exports dropped by 23.4 percent, it represented 33.6 percent of total exports in 2010 (see table 1). Other major commodity groups for exports were food, live animals, beverages and tobacco (SITC sections 0+1) and inedible crude materials (except fuels), animal and vegetable oils, fats and waxes (SITC sections 2+4), respectively with 23.3 and 11.2 percent of exports. France, Germany and China were the three largest markets for exports (see table 4). Over the last three years, top exported products were jerseys, pullovers, cardigans, waist-coats and similar articles (HS code 6110), men's or boys' suits, ensembles, jackets, blazers, trousers (HS code 6203) and women's or girls' suits, ensembles, jackets, blazers, dresses, skirts (HS code 6204) (see table 3).

Table 3: Top 10 export commodities 2008 to 2010

(Value in million US$)

HS code	4-digit heading of Harmonized System 2007	Value (million US$) 2008	2009	2010	Unit value 2008	2009	2010	Unit	SITC code
	All Commodities	1 667.4	1 095.9	1 082.2					
6110	Jerseys, pullovers, cardigans, waist-coats and similar articles	187.6	134.0	126.6	*22.2*	*22.1*	*22.1*	US$/unit	845
6203	Men's or boys' suits, ensembles, jackets, blazers, trousers	289.3	43.4	27.3					841
6204	Women's or girls' suits, ensembles, jackets, blazers, dresses, skirts	182.5	89.5	27.7					842
0306	Crustaceans, whether in shell or not	116.9	82.6	66.0	10.2	8.8	8.6	US$/kg	036
2710	Petroleum oils, other than crude	90.2	48.3	62.3	1.3	0.9	1.0	US$/kg	334
0905	Vanilla	50.1	44.2	17.6	22.5	21.6	26.4	US$/kg	075
0907	Cloves (whole fruit, cloves and stems)	30.1	48.4	31.7	3.6	3.1	3.8	US$/kg	075
1604	Prepared or preserved fish; caviar	32.4	23.0	37.5	4.3	3.7	3.6	US$/kg	037
6214	Shawls, scarves, mufflers, mantillas, veils and the like	29.4	26.4	33.7					846
6206	Women's or girls' blouses, shirts and shirt-blouses	63.0	12.4	12.8					842

Graph 2: Trade Balance by MDG Regions in 2010

(Mln US$)

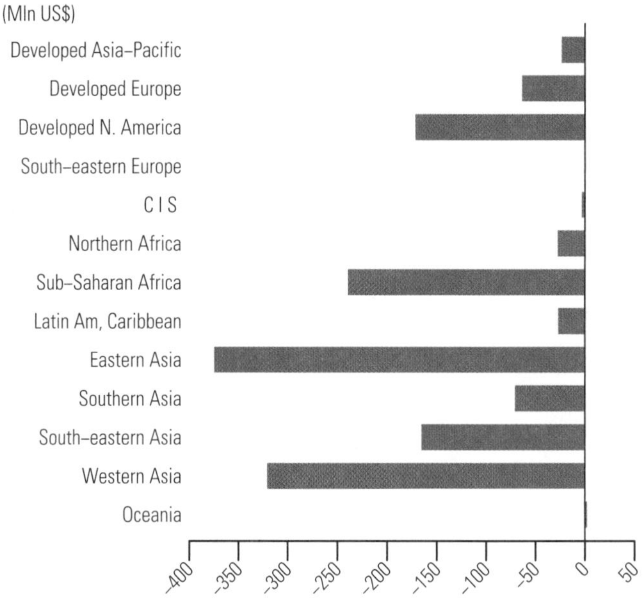

Graph 3: Partner concentration of trade in 2010

(Cumulative share by ranked partners)

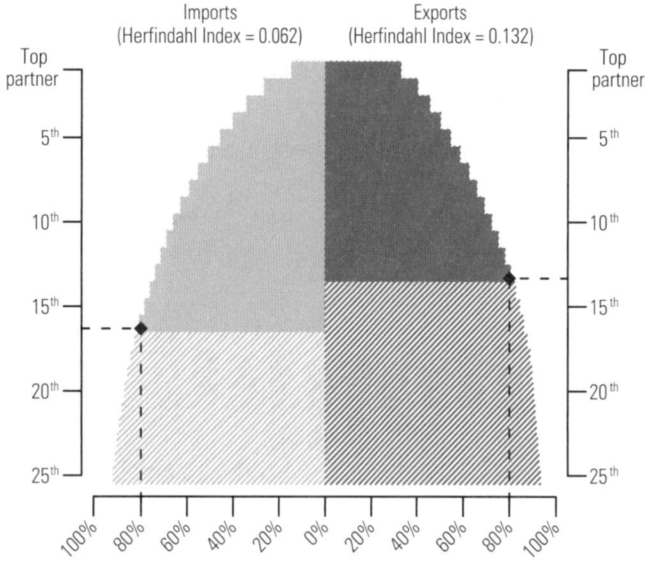

Table 4: Exports by principal countries and SITC sections in 2010

(Value in million US$, percentages of country total)

Country	Total	Shares by SITC sections (%)								
		0 + 1	2 + 4	3	5	6	7	8	9	Total
World	1 082.2	23.3	11.2	5.8	3.0	6.7	11.1	33.6	5.4	100
France	358.6	32.3	1.2	8.9	3.1	7.4	0.9	45.5	0.7	100
Germany	78.9	10.7	7.7	0.0	2.9	2.2	1.5	75.0	0.0	100
China	56.7	1.1	69.2	...	4.7	10.4	3.9	10.7	0.0	100
Côte d'Ivoire	49.2	0.0	0.2	...	...	...	0.0	...	99.8	100
India	46.1	14.6	22.6	0.0	3.3	4.4	54.2	0.7	0.2	100
USA	44.5	14.3	5.0	0.1	4.0	5.4	3.7	67.3	0.2	100
Canada	42.3	3.1	85.4	0.0	0.1	0.1	2.4	8.5	0.3	100
Areas, nes	36.6	7.6	1.6	27.3	6.4	41.9	5.6	8.6	0.9	100
United Kingdom	35.3	2.2	3.2	0.0	0.7	1.0	1.0	91.8	0.0	100
United Arab Emirates	34.9	7.4	0.0	0.2	0.1	2.4	87.2	2.7	...	100

Imports Profile:

In 2010, machinery and transport equipment (SITC section 7) and manufactured goods classified chiefly by material (SITC section 6) accounted respectively for 29.5 and 24.9 percent of imported goods (see table 2). Other major commodity groups included mineral fuels, lubricants and related materials (SITC section 3) (15.2 percent) and food, live animals, beverages and tobacco (SITC sections 0+1) (11.2 percent). Over the last three years, top imported products were petroleum oils, other than crude (HS code 2710), structures (excluding prefabricated buildings of heading 94.06) (HS code 7308) and yarn of carded wool, not put up for retail sale (HS code 5106) (see table 5).

Table 5: Top 10 import commodities 2008 to 2010

(Value in million US$)

HS code	4-digit heading of Harmonized System 2007	Value (million US$)			Unit value				SITC code
		2008	2009	2010	2008	2009	2010	Unit	
	All Commodities	3 850.6	3 159.3	2 545.8					
2710	Petroleum oils, other than crude	490.8	315.0	368.8	0.9	0.6	0.7	US$/kg	334
7308	Structures (excluding prefabricated buildings of heading 94.06)	76.6	493.8	38.7	3.0	17.0	2.5	US$/kg	691
5106	Yarn of carded wool, not put up for retail sale	61.6	54.7	62.5	42.9	37.2	40.8	US$/kg	651
1006	Rice	74.0	47.2	53.5	0.5	0.4	0.4	US$/kg	042
8481	Taps, cocks, valves and similar appliances for pipes, boiler shells	13.2	44.4	105.6	7.9	46.4	41.5	US$/kg	747
8703	Motor cars and other motor vehicles principally designed for the transport	66.0	47.7	43.7		*18.5*	*18.8*	thsd US$/unit	781
8419	Machinery, plant or laboratory equipment	43.2	89.1	22.7					741
1701	Cane or beet sugar and chemically pure sucrose, in solid form	47.9	54.2	50.1	0.4	0.4	0.5	US$/kg	061
8517	Electrical apparatus for line telephony or line telegraphy	72.4	47.1	31.7					764
8704	Motor vehicles for the transport of goods	75.5	38.5	35.1					782

Malawi

Imports: CIF, by origin **Exports: FOB, by last known destination** **Trade System: General**

Overview:

From 2006 to 2010, Malawi's exports increased on average by 12.5 percent each year and amounted to 1.1 bln US$, despite a drop of 10.2 percent in 2010 (see table 1 and graph 1). During the same period, imports increased on average by 15.8 percent each year to 2.2 bln US$ (see table 2 and graph 1). The trade deficit increased to 1.1 bln US$ in 2010 as compared to 0.8 bln US$ in 2009 (see graph 1). By MDG regions, the largest deficit was recorded with Sub-Saharan Africa and amounted to 743.0 mln US$ in 2010 (see graph 2). Other major deficits were recorded with Eastern Asia (-200.1 mln US$) and Southern Asia (-156.4 mln US$). Malawi's trade was diversified across partners in 2010: 15 major partners accounted for 80 percent of both exports and imports (see graph 3).

Graph 1: Total imports, exports and trade balance

(Bln US$ by year)

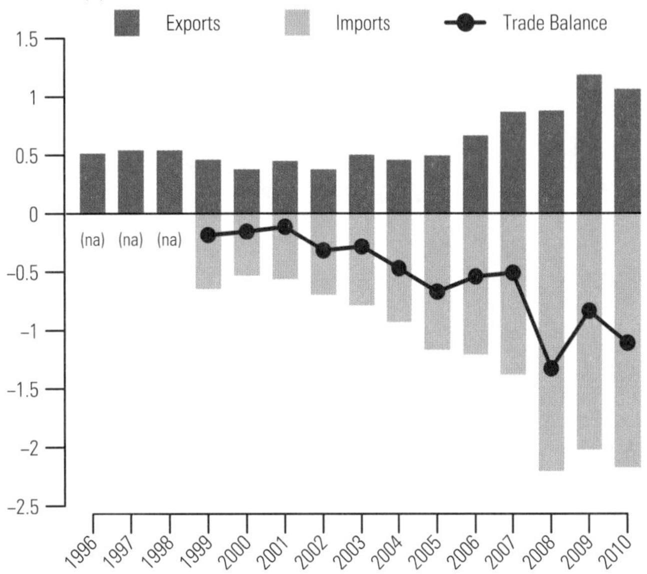

Table 1: Exports by SITC sections

(Value in million US$, growth and shares in percentage)

SITC	2010	Avg. Growth rates (%) 2006-2010	2009-2010	2010 share
Total	1066.2	12.5	-10.2	100.0
0+1	796.9	10.4	-18.2	74.7
2+4	170.5	47.2	54.5	16.0
3	2.0	19.3	46.3	0.2
5	15.7	43.4	89.8	1.5
6	16.0	2.3	32.3	1.5
7	27.1	12.4	-3.7	2.5
8	38.1	-9.8	-28.4	3.6

Table 2: Imports by SITC sections

(Value in million US$, growth and shares in percentage)

SITC	2010	Avg. Growth rates (%) 2006-2010	2009-2010	2010 share
Total	2173.0	15.8	7.5	100.0
0+1	246.4	12.4	11.2	11.3
2+4	90.5	18.0	19.5	4.2
3	217.1	12.0	3.1	10.0
5	532.4	24.2	14.7	24.5
6	346.6	18.6	5.4	15.9
7	515.2	9.7	-2.7	23.7
8	222.0	18.6	16.2	10.2
9	2.8	116.8	583.8	0.1

Exports Profile:

Malawi's exports were largely food, live animals, beverages and tobacco (SITC sections 0+1); they accounted for 74.7 percent of exported goods in 2010 (see table 1). Other major commodity groups for exports included inedible crude materials (except fuels), animal and vegetable oils, fats and waxes (SITC sections 2+4) and miscellaneous manufactured articles (SITC section 8), respectively with 16.0 and 3.6 percent of exports. Major markets for exports were Belgium, Canada and Egypt (see table 4). Exports to Belgium and Egypt were almost exclusively food, live animals, beverages and tobacco (SITC sections 0+1). The major product for exports was unmanufactured tobacco; tobacco refuse (HS code 2401), representing 54.9 percent of exports in 2010 (see table 3). Other top products were tea, whether or not flavoured (HS code 0902) and cane or beet sugar and pure sucrose, in solid form (HS code 1701) (see table 3).

Table 3: Top 10 export commodities 2008 to 2010

(Value in million US$)

HS code	4-digit heading of Harmonized System 2007	Value (million US$) 2008	2009	2010	Unit value 2008	2009	2010	Unit	SITC code
	All Commodities	879.0	1187.9	1066.2					
2401	Unmanufactured tobacco; tobacco refuse	590.0	759.5	585.2	4.2	4.1	4.0	US$/kg	121
0902	Tea, whether or not flavoured	36.9	78.3	80.8	1.2	1.7	1.6	US$/kg	074
1701	Cane or beet sugar and chemically pure sucrose, in solid form	50.7	70.2	69.4	0.6	0.6	0.7	US$/kg	061
2612	Uranium or thorium ores and concentrates	...	8.5	114.3		122.0	121.6	US$/kg	286
0713	Dried leguminous vegetables, shelled, whether or not skinned or split	16.3	32.9	27.6	*1.7*	0.9	0.9	US$/kg	054
5201	Cotton, not carded or combed	21.8	24.3	11.7	1.6	0.7	1.2	US$/kg	263
1208	Flours and meals of oil seeds or oleaginous fruits	1.0	26.6	4.4	0.6	4.2	0.4	US$/kg	223
1202	Ground-nuts, not roasted or otherwise cooked, whether or not shelled or broken	3.2	18.1	6.0	0.2	0.9	0.3	US$/kg	222
0802	Other nuts, fresh or dried, whether or not shelled or peeled	5.2	6.7	10.2	4.7	4.5	5.6	US$/kg	057
4001	Natural rubber, balata, gutta-percha, guayule, chicle	7.4	4.2	9.6	2.8	1.9	3.2	US$/kg	231

Graph 2: Trade Balance by MDG Regions in 2010

(Mln US$)

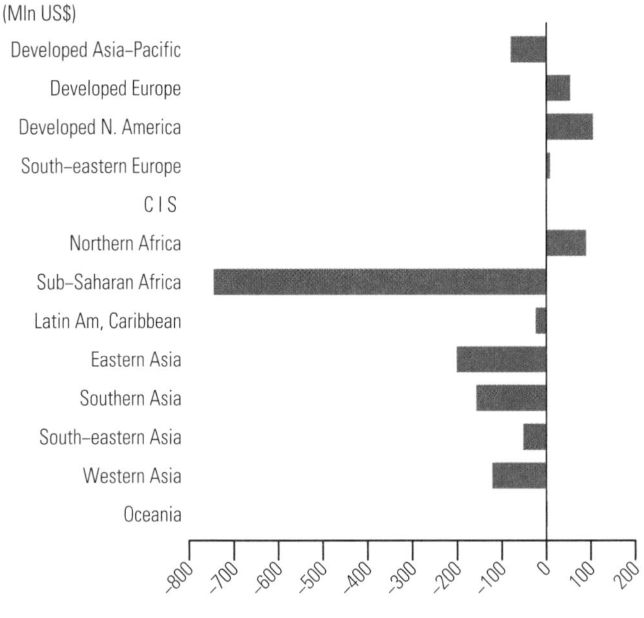

Graph 3: Partner concentration of trade in 2010

(Cumulative share by ranked partners)

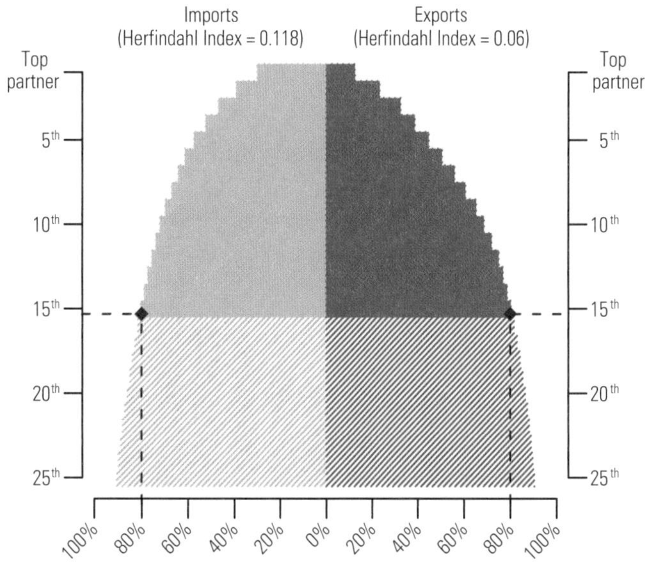

Table 4: Exports by principal countries and SITC sections in 2010

(Value in million US$, percentages of country total)

Country	Total	Shares by SITC sections (%)								
		0 + 1	2 + 4	3	5	6	7	8	9	Total
World	1 066.2	74.7	16.0	0.2	1.5	1.5	2.5	3.6	...	100
Belgium	132.5	99.9	0.0	...	0.0	0.0	0.0	0.0	...	100
Canada	117.6	2.8	97.2	...	...	0.0	0.0	0.0	...	100
Egypt	98.3	100.0	0.0	...	...	...	...	...	...	100
Germany	65.7	94.6	0.2	...	...	0.9	4.1	0.2	...	100
USA	63.7	80.9	0.2	...	0.0	0.1	0.4	18.4	...	100
South Africa	61.6	61.9	19.6	0.0	0.7	6.0	5.9	5.9	...	100
Zimbabwe	57.9	69.8	12.0	...	7.0	1.9	1.5	7.8	...	100
Netherlands	49.8	99.4	0.2	...	...	0.0	0.3	0.1	...	100
United Kingdom	49.1	96.5	2.1	...	0.0	0.1	0.3	1.1	...	100
Mozambique	36.2	24.9	27.8	...	10.5	4.6	7.8	24.3	...	100

Imports Profile:

In 2010, imports of chemicals and related products, n.e.s. (SITC section 5) increased by 14.7 percent and accounted for 24.5 percent of imported goods (see table 2). Other major commodity goods for imports were machinery and transport equipment (SITC section 7) and manufactured goods classified chiefly by material (SITC section 6) respectively with 23.7 and 15.9 percent of imports. Top imported goods from 2008 to 2010 were petroleum oils, other than crude (HS code 2710), mineral or chemical fertilisers, nitrogenous (HS code 3102) and mineral or chemical fertilisers (HS code 3105) (see table 5).

Table 5: Top 10 import commodities 2008 to 2010

(Value in million US$)

HS code	4-digit heading of Harmonized System 2007	Value (million US$)			Unit value				SITC code
		2008	2009	2010	2008	2009	2010	Unit	
	All Commodities	2 203.7	2 021.7	2 173.0					
2710	Petroleum oils, other than crude	202.0	198.3	198.6	0.7	0.7	0.7	US$/kg	334
3102	Mineral or chemical fertilisers, nitrogenous	228.7	90.7	130.3	1.1	0.6	0.6	US$/kg	562
3105	Mineral or chemical fertilisers	136.5	80.1	66.3	1.9	0.8	0.7	US$/kg	562
3004	Medicaments (excluding goods of heading 30.02, 30.05 or 30.06)	71.0	86.1	101.0	14.7	24.6	33.4	US$/kg	542
4907	Unused postage, revenue or similar stamps of current or new issue	84.0	54.7	104.0	345.5	271.8	372.5	US$/kg	892
1001	Wheat and meslin	74.4	66.1	81.1	0.3	0.5	0.5	US$/kg	041
8701	Tractors (other than tractors of heading 87.09)	183.9	15.9	14.8		1.6	30.9	thsd US$/unit	722
2401	Unmanufactured tobacco; tobacco refuse	66.8	53.5	89.3	3.2	2.5	2.9	US$/kg	121
8703	Motor cars and other motor vehicles principally designed for the transport	59.3	66.5	57.5		*0.2*	*3.2*	thsd US$/unit	781
8517	Electrical apparatus for line telephony or line telegraphy	36.9	61.9	65.0					764

Imports: CIF, by origin | **Exports: FOB, by last known destination** | **Trade System: General**

Overview:

From 2007 to 2011, despite a significant decline of 20.9 percent in 2009, Malaysia's exports increased on average by 6.6 percent each year and amounted to 227.0 bln US$ in 2011, well above its previous peak level of 2008 (see table 1 and graph 1). Imports increased on average by 6.4 percent each year and reached 187.6 bln US$ in 2011 (see table 2 and graph 1). This resulted in a trade surplus of 39.4 bln US$ in 2011, higher than the surplus in 2010 of 34.2 bln US$ (see graph 1). Trade was in surplus with most MDG regions. Large surpluses were recorded with Southern Asia (+11.0 bln US$), Eastern Asia (+10.4 bln US$), Developed Asia-Pacific (+9.0 bln US$) and South-eastern Asia (+4.0 bln US$) among others (see graph 2). In 2011, trade was relatively diversified across partners: 14 major partners accounted for 80 percent of both exports and imports (see graph 3).

Graph 1: Total imports, exports and trade balance

(Bln US$ by year)

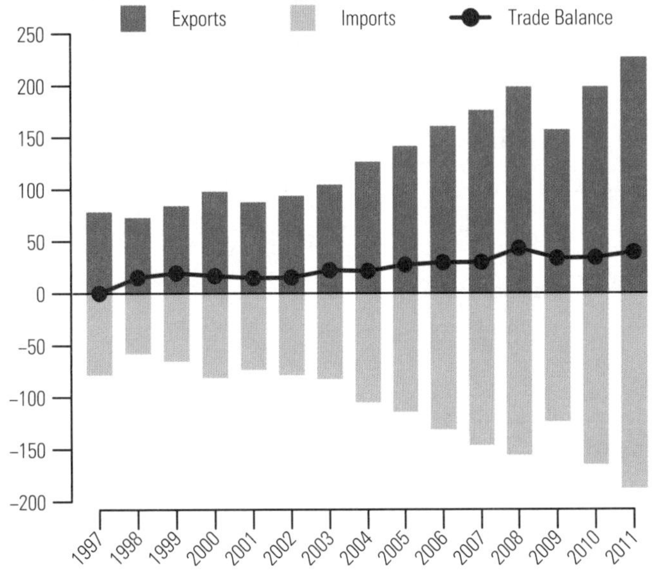

Table 1: Exports by SITC sections

(Value in million US$, growth and shares in percentage)

SITC	2011	Avg. Growth rates (%) 2007-2011	Avg. Growth rates (%) 2010-2011	2011 share
Total	226 992.7	6.6	14.2	100.0
0+1	7 745.5	13.5	18.7	3.4
2+4	32 058.7	18.5	39.4	14.1
3	40 265.6	12.3	27.8	17.7
5	15 102.0	9.4	19.2	6.7
6	21 294.8	8.6	21.5	9.4
7	88 089.3	0.6	0.9	38.8
8	21 069.5	8.6	11.6	9.3
9	1 367.2	-14.4	1.1	0.6

Table 2: Imports by SITC sections

(Value in million US$, growth and shares in percentage)

SITC	2011	Avg. Growth rates (%) 2007-2011	Avg. Growth rates (%) 2010-2011	2011 share
Total	187 573.0	6.4	14.0	100.0
0+1	12 283.2	13.8	21.0	6.5
2+4	11 854.1	20.1	42.9	6.3
3	22 054.8	14.4	34.5	11.8
5	17 598.4	10.3	17.5	9.4
6	24 523.0	7.3	20.1	13.1
7	83 747.5	1.8	2.8	44.6
8	11 700.4	12.9	18.0	6.2
9	3 811.7	-5.6	29.3	2.0

Exports Profile:

In 2011, machinery and transport equipment (SITC section 7) represented the largest commodity group for exports with 38.8 percent of total exports (see table 1). The second largest commodity group, mineral fuels, lubricants and related materials (SITC section 3), increased by 27.8 percent and represented 17.7 percent of exports. Top markets for exported goods were China, Singapore and Japan (see table 4). Exports to China and Singapore were mostly machinery and transport equipment (SITC section 7). From 2009 to 2011, the top exported products were electronic integrated circuits (HS code 8542), petroleum gases and other gaseous hydrocarbons (HS code 2711) and palm oil and its fractions (HS code 1511) (see table 3).

Table 3: Top 10 export commodities 2009 to 2011

(Value in million US$)

HS code	4-digit heading of Harmonized System 2007	Value (million US$) 2009	2010	2011	Unit value 2009	2010	2011	Unit	SITC code
	All Commodities	157 194.8	198 790.7	226 992.7					
8542	Electronic integrated circuits	21 218.8	22 809.4	27 239.5					776
2711	Petroleum gases and other gaseous hydrocarbons	10 126.9	13 371.9	18 210.2	0.4	0.5	0.7	US$/kg	343
1511	Palm oil and its fractions	9 262.8	12 405.4	17 446.9	0.7	0.8	1.1	US$/kg	422
8471	Automatic data processing machines and units thereof	9 654.5	11 018.9	9 691.2		36.4	76.2	US$/unit	752
2709	Petroleum oils and oils obtained from bituminous minerals, crude	7 265.4	9 646.1	10 760.3	0.4	0.6	0.8	US$/kg	333
8473	Parts and accessories for use with machines of heading 84.69 to 84.72	9 240.8	10 787.4	6 318.7	4.8	0.1	35.3	US$/kg	759
2710	Petroleum oils, other than crude	5 512.1	7 941.2	10 797.4	0.5	0.7	0.9	US$/kg	334
8541	Diodes, transistors and similar semiconductor devices	4 792.4	7 201.6	7 480.6					776
8528	Reception apparatus for television	2 919.5	5 283.5	4 832.9	246.2	183.4	289.7	US$/unit	761
4001	Natural rubber, balata, gutta-percha, guayule, chicle	1 267.1	2 863.6	4 339.7	1.8	3.2	4.6	US$/kg	231

Graph 2: Trade Balance by MDG Regions in 2011

(Bln US$)

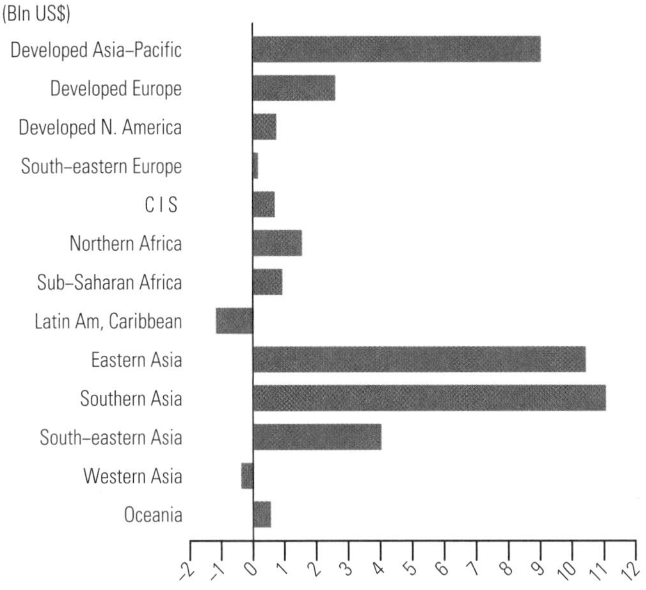

Graph 3: Partner concentration of trade in 2011

(Cumulative share by ranked partners)

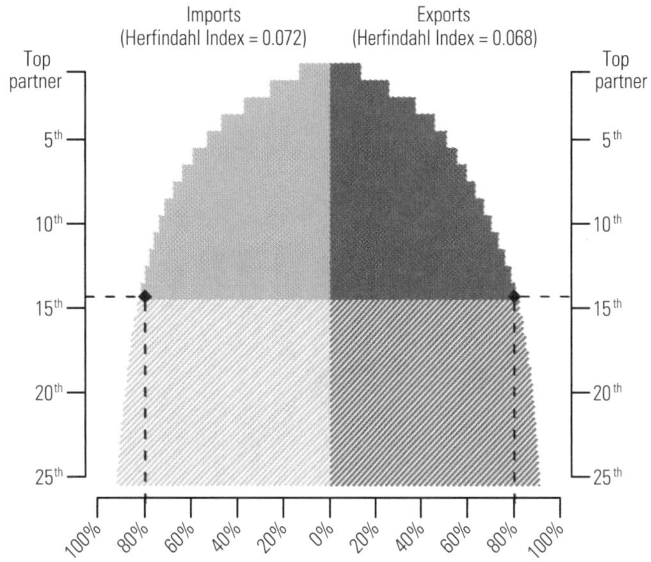

Table 4: Exports by principal countries and SITC sections in 2011

(Value in million US$, percentages of country total)

Country	Total	Shares by SITC sections (%) 0 + 1	2 + 4	3	5	6	7	8	9	Total
World	226992.7	3.4	14.1	17.7	6.7	9.4	38.8	9.3	0.6	100
China	29821.4	1.2	25.0	6.3	8.7	8.6	47.4	2.5	0.3	100
Singapore	28812.6	5.5	3.4	22.8	4.4	9.9	43.4	9.9	0.6	100
Japan	26134.5	1.5	5.5	48.5	4.9	8.4	23.9	7.2	0.2	100
USA	18850.4	3.2	10.1	0.4	2.4	4.9	57.0	21.7	0.3	100
Thailand	11674.0	3.8	5.2	19.4	11.7	10.4	36.1	12.9	0.5	100
China, Hong Kong SAR	10210.5	3.2	0.7	1.9	4.7	4.6	78.6	5.4	1.0	100
India	9209.5	0.7	25.1	25.3	9.5	9.2	27.6	2.5	0.2	100
Rep. of Korea	8438.4	2.8	8.8	41.2	6.5	12.4	23.6	4.0	0.7	100
Australia	8206.2	3.3	4.1	46.8	4.7	9.3	23.6	6.5	1.7	100
Other Asia, nes	7421.0	2.1	5.2	39.1	7.2	8.8	30.8	6.3	0.5	100

Imports Profile:

In 2011, similar to exports, the largest commodity group for imports was machinery and transport equipment (SITC section 7) and accounted for 44.6 percent of total imports (see table 2). Other major commodity groups included manufactured goods classified chiefly by material (SITC section 6) and mineral fuels, lubricants and related materials (SITC section 3), respectively with 13.1 and 11.8 percent of total imports. From 2009 to 2011, the major imported goods were electronic integrated circuits (HS code 8542), petroleum oils, other than crude (HS code 2710) and petroleum oils and oils obtained from bituminous minerals, crude (HS code 2709) (see table 5).

Table 5: Top 10 import commodities 2009 to 2011

(Value in million US$)

HS code	4-digit heading of Harmonized System 2007	Value (million US$) 2009	2010	2011	Unit value 2009	2010	2011	Unit	SITC code
	All Commodities	123575.3	164586.3	187573.0					
8542	Electronic integrated circuits	19932.3	28459.2	26631.6					776
2710	Petroleum oils, other than crude	4095.8	7887.4	10632.4	0.5	0.6	0.8	US$/kg	334
2709	Petroleum oils and oils obtained from bituminous minerals, crude	4231.7	5688.2	7846.4	0.5	0.6	0.8	US$/kg	333
8473	Parts and accessories for use with machines of heading 84.69 to 84.72	5816.1	5310.8	4693.2	44.5	5.5	56.2	US$/kg	759
8541	Diodes, transistors and similar semiconductor devices	2277.5	3245.7	3539.5					776
8529	Parts suitable for use with the apparatus of headings 85.25 to 85.28	1689.1	3181.6	3386.5	27.5	24.5	30.0	US$/kg	764
8471	Automatic data processing machines and units thereof	2093.8	2722.8	3170.1	80.2	55.1	91.4	US$/unit	752
8517	Electrical apparatus for line telephony or line telegraphy	1573.0	2242.0	2806.3					764
8703	Motor cars and other motor vehicles principally designed for the transport	1581.6	2508.2	2526.5	4.7	5.5	6.3	thsd US$/unit	781
7108	Gold (including gold plated with platinum)	1713.5	1757.6	2545.7					971

Maldives

Imports: CIF, by consignment | **Exports: FOB, by last known destination** | **Trade System: General**

Overview:

From 2007 to 2011, Maldives's exports dropped on average by 6.3 percent each year and amounted to 83.3 mln US$ in 2011 (see table 1 and graph 1). During the same period, imports demonstrated an average increase of 6.5 percent in the last 5 years and reached 1.4 bln US$ in 2011, despite the sharp decline in 2009 (see table 2 and graph 1). This resulted in a trade deficit amounting to 1.3 bln US$ in 2011 (see graph 1). By MDG regions, trade deficits were recorded with South-eastern Asia (-444.2 mln US$), Western Asia (-341.5 mln US$) and Southern Asia (-215.0 mln US$) (see graph 2). Trade was concentrated among few partners: 8 (respectively 10) major partners accounted for 80 percent of exports (respectively imports) (see graph 3).

Graph 1: Total imports, exports and trade balance

(Bln US$ by year)

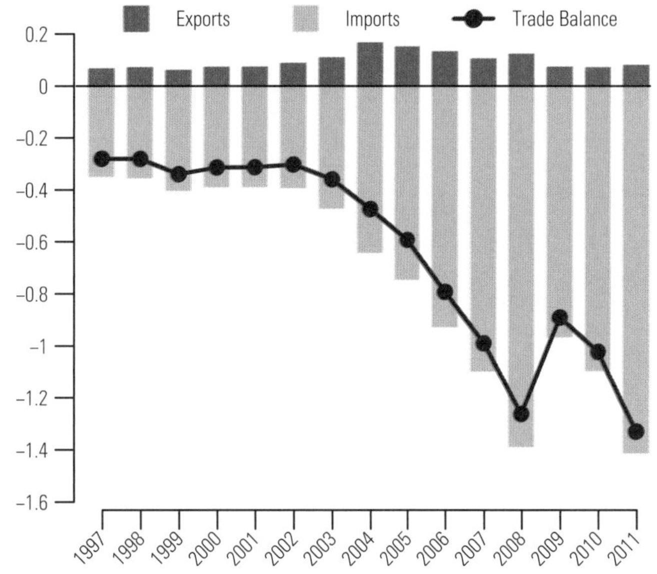

Exports Profile:

Food, live animals, beverages and tobacco (SITC sections 0+1) accounted for the majority of Maldives' exports (see table 1). In 2011, their exports increased by 13.0 percent and accounted for 96.8 percent of exported goods. Thailand, France and Sri Lanka were the three major export destinations in 2011 (see table 4). Over the last three years, top products for exports included fish, frozen, excluding fish fillets and other fish meat of heading 03.04 (HS code 0303), fish fillets and other fish meat (whether or not minced) (HS code 0304) and fish, dried, salted or in brine (HS code 0305) (see table 3).

Table 1: Exports by SITC sections

(Value in million US$, growth and shares in percentage)

SITC	2011	Avg. Growth rates (%) 2007-2011	2010-2011	2011 share
Total	83.3	-6.3	12.2	100.0
0+1	80.6	-6.6	13.0	96.8
2+4	2.5	4.4	-9.1	3.1
3	0.0	...	40.9	0.0
5	0.1	116.0	1000.1	0.1
6	0.0	...	-64.2	0.0
7	0.0	...	...	0.0
8	0.0	129.8	67.8	0.0

Table 2: Imports by SITC sections

(Value in million US$, growth and shares in percentage)

SITC	2011	Avg. Growth rates (%) 2007-2011	2010-2011	2011 share
Total	1411.7	6.5	28.9	100.0
0+1	288.5	12.9	20.7	20.4
2+4	55.4	-8.5	7.3	3.9
3	352.0	14.7	39.4	24.9
5	78.1	5.8	19.1	5.5
6	176.9	-0.7	28.0	12.5
7	332.6	4.0	34.2	23.6
8	128.3	4.4	27.8	9.1
9	0.0	-2.1	25.3	0.0

Table 3: Top 10 export commodities 2009 to 2011

(Value in million US$)

HS code	4-digit heading of Harmonized System 2007	Value (million US$) 2009	2010	2011	Unit value 2009	2010	2011	Unit	SITC code
	All Commodities	76.7	74.2	83.3					
0303	Fish, frozen, excluding fish fillets and other fish meat of heading 03.04	24.2	25.6	22.0	0.9	1.1	1.4	US$/kg	034
0304	Fish fillets and other fish meat (whether or not minced)	21.1	16.1	23.3	7.0	8.3	*7.8*	US$/kg	034
0305	Fish, dried, salted or in brine	11.5	13.2	8.7	1.8	2.1	2.4	US$/kg	035
0302	Fish, fresh or chilled, excluding fish fillets	7.8	7.8	17.5	3.6	5.1	4.8	US$/kg	034
1604	Prepared or preserved fish; caviar	7.6	5.8	7.0	3.6	4.3	5.6	US$/kg	037
7204	Ferrous waste and scrap; remelting scrap ingots of iron or steel	1.3	2.0	1.3	0.2	0.2	0.2	US$/kg	282
0301	Live fish	1.3	1.4	0.8					034
2301	Flours, meals and pellets, of meat or meat offal	0.9	0.8	0.5	0.6	1.0	0.8	US$/kg	081
7404	Copper waste and scrap	0.3	0.7	1.1	2.5	2.5	3.4	US$/kg	288
0307	Molluscs, whether in shell or not	0.3	0.6	0.7	*5.7*	2.8	3.0	US$/kg	036

Graph 2: Trade Balance by MDG Regions in 2011

(Mln US$)

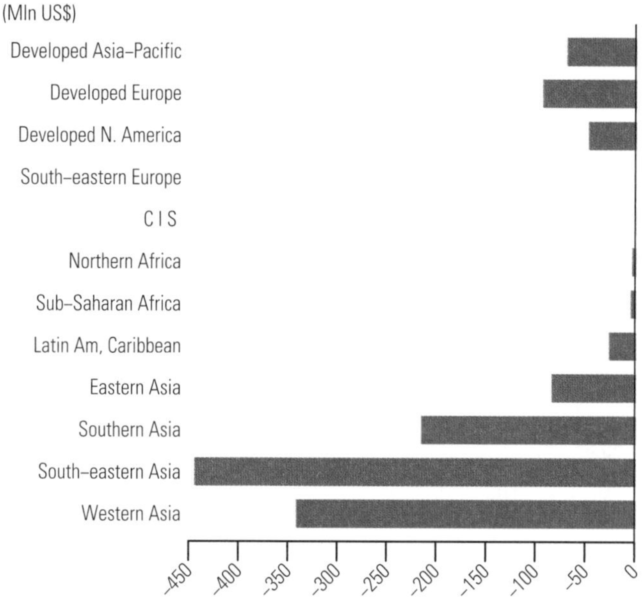

Graph 3: Partner concentration of trade in 2011

(Cumulative share by ranked partners)

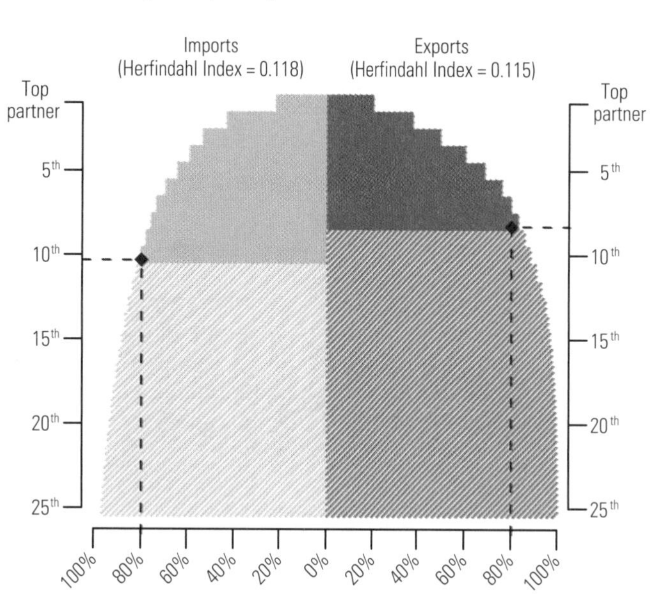

Table 4: Exports by principal countries and SITC sections in 2011

(Value in million US$, percentages of country total)

Country	Total	Shares by SITC sections (%) 0 + 1	2 + 4	3	5	6	7	8	9	Total
World	83.3	96.8	3.1	0.0	0.1	0.0	0.0	0.0	...	100
Thailand	16.9	100.0	0.0	...	...	...	...	...	...	100
France	14.7	100.0	0.0	...	...	...	...	...	...	100
Sri Lanka	9.8	99.8	0.2	...	...	...	...	...	...	100
Italy	8.7	100.0	0.0	...	...	...	...	...	...	100
United Kingdom	6.8	100.0	0.0	...	...	...	...	...	...	100
Other Asia, nes	6.1	100.0	0.0	...	...	...	...	...	...	100
Ireland	3.4	100.0	0.0	...	...	...	...	...	...	100
Japan	2.5	100.0	0.0	...	...	...	...	...	...	100
Netherlands	2.4	100.0	0.0	...	...	...	...	...	...	100
Spain	2.2	100.0	0.0	...	...	...	...	...	...	100

Imports Profile:

In 2011, mineral fuels, lubricants and related materials (SITC section 3) increased by 39.4 percent and accounted for 24.9 percent of imported goods (see table 2). Other major commodity groups for imports were machinery and transport equipment (SITC section 7) and food, live animals, beverages and tobacco (SITC sections 0+1) respectively with 23.6 and 20.4 percent of total imports. In addition to petroleum oils, other than crude (HS code 2710), top products for imports over the last three years included petroleum gases and other gaseous hydrocarbons (HS code 2711) and electrical apparatus for line telephony or line telegraphy (HS code 8517) (see table 5).

Table 5: Top 10 import commodities 2009 to 2011

(Value in million US$)

HS code	4-digit heading of Harmonized System 2007	Value (million US$) 2009	2010	2011	Unit value 2009	2010	2011	Unit	SITC code
	All Commodities	966.1	1 095.1	1 411.7					
2710	Petroleum oils, other than crude	173.1	217.1	308.3	*0.5*	*0.7*	*0.9*	US$/kg	334
2711	Petroleum gases and other gaseous hydrocarbons	26.2	34.4	42.9	*0.7*	*0.8*	*1.0*	US$/kg	343
8517	Electrical apparatus for line telephony or line telegraphy	29.5	30.1	33.2					764
8802	Other aircraft (for example, helicopters, aeroplanes); spacecraft	17.1	16.0	28.9	1.7	2.3	4.1	mln US$/unit	792
9403	Other furniture and parts thereof	13.7	13.5	17.8					821
2517	Pebbles, gravel, broken or crushed stone	12.6	14.8	16.5					273
0402	Milk and cream, concentrated or containing added sugar	11.9	13.2	18.5	*2.3*	*2.6*	*2.9*	US$/kg	022
8471	Automatic data processing machines and units thereof	12.1	14.7	15.9	207.9	208.5	200.1	US$/unit	752
1006	Rice	13.8	12.9	15.0	0.5	0.6	0.6	US$/kg	042
4407	Wood sawn or chipped lengthwise, sliced or peeled	12.3	14.2	13.2	*722.4*	*696.8*		US$/m³	248

Mali

Imports: CIF, by origin | **Exports: FOB, by last known destination** | **Trade System: General**

Overview:

From 2006 to 2010, Mali's exports increased on average by 6.9 percent each year to amount to 2.0 bln US$ in 2010 (see table 1 and graph 1). During the same period, imports increased on average by 26.8 percent each year to reach 4.7 bln US$ (see table 2 and graph 1). The trade balance recorded a deficit of 2.7 bln US$ in 2010 as compared to 0.3 bln US$ in 2006 (see graph 1). Deficit with Developed Europe alone amounted to 722.9 mln US$ (see graph 2). Significant deficits were also recorded with Sub-Saharan Africa (-652.1 mln US$) and Eastern Asia (-429.9 mln US$). Mali's exports were concentrated among a few partners: 5 major partners accounted for 80 percent of exports compared to 12 major partners for imports (see graph 3).

Graph 1: Total imports, exports and trade balance

(Bln US$ by year)

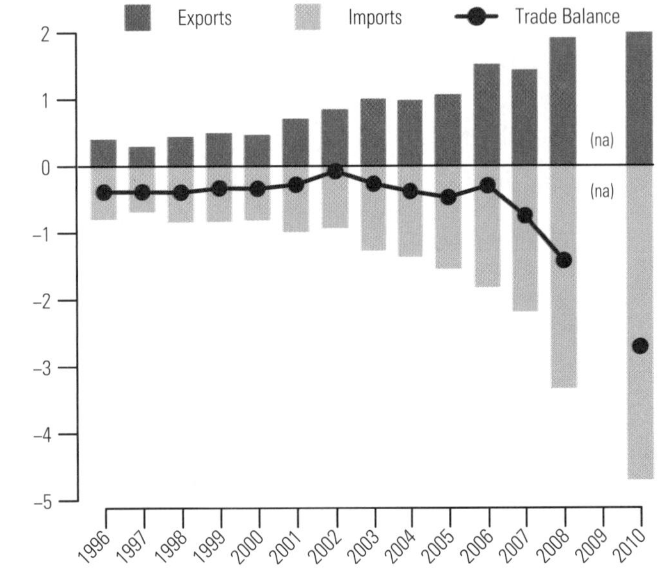

Exports Profile:

Commodities and transactions not classified elsewhere (SITC section 9), almost exclusively gold, was the largest commodity group for exports and accounted for 79.3 percent of Mali's exports in 2010 (see table 1). Other major commodity groups included inedible crude materials (except fuels), animal and vegetable oils, fats and waxes (SITC sections 2+4) and food, live animals, beverages and tobacco (SITC sections 0+1) respectively with 8.9 and 5.2 percent of exports. South Africa, Switzerland and Italy were the top three markets for exports in 2010 (see table 4). Trade with South Africa accounted for over 50 percent of exports and was almost exclusively gold. From 2008 to 2010, major products for exports were gold (including gold plated with platinum) (HS code 7108), cotton, not carded or combed (HS code 5201) and Cotton, carded or combed (HS code 5203) (see table 3).

Table 1: Exports by SITC sections

(Value in million US$, growth and shares in percentage)

SITC	2010	Avg. Growth rates (%) 2006-2010	2009-2010	2010 share
Total	1 996.3	6.9	...	100.0
0+1	103.4	6.1	...	5.2
2+4	178.1	-9.3	...	8.9
3	28.4	33.8	...	1.4
5	41.9	55.9	...	2.1
6	22.7	35.1	...	1.1
7	30.8	12.2	...	1.5
8	7.9	18.6	...	0.4
9	1 583.0	8.7	...	79.3

Table 2: Imports by SITC sections

(Value in million US$, growth and shares in percentage)

SITC	2010	Avg. Growth rates (%) 2006-2010	2009-2010	2010 share
Total	4 703.5	26.8	...	100.0
0+1	488.0	14.3	...	10.4
2+4	97.3	25.1	...	2.1
3	1 221.0	29.4	...	26.0
5	692.7	28.6	...	14.7
6	850.7	28.5	...	18.1
7	1 121.6	28.8	...	23.8
8	228.6	31.6	...	4.9
9	3.5	-21.7	...	0.1

Table 3: Top 10 export commodities 2008 to 2010

(Value in million US$)

HS code	4-digit heading of Harmonized System 2007	Value (million US$) 2008	2009	2010	Unit value 2008	2009	2010	Unit	SITC code
	All Commodities	1 918.3	...	1 996.3					
7108	Gold (including gold plated with platinum)	1 437.1	...	1 578.7	27.8		32.5	thsd US$/kg	971
5201	Cotton, not carded or combed	202.6	...	27.9	1.4		1.1	US$/kg	263
5203	Cotton, carded or combed	0.1	...	139.4	0.8		1.5	US$/kg	263
0102	Live bovine animals	79.6	...	48.6	*736.2*		*823.1*	US$/unit	001
2710	Petroleum oils, other than crude	28.5	...	28.4	1.1		0.8	US$/kg	334
0104	Live sheep and goats	33.1	...	20.5					001
3105	Mineral or chemical fertilisers	16.8	...	30.0	0.6		0.6	US$/kg	562
0804	Dates, figs, pineapples, avocados and mangosteens, fresh or dried	4.7	...	14.9	0.5		1.1	US$/kg	057
8704	Motor vehicles for the transport of goods	16.7	...	2.3					782
8429	Self-propelled bulldozers, angledozers, graders, levellers, scrapers	13.9	...	2.3	*53.0*		*48.7*	thsd US$/unit	723

Graph 2: Trade Balance by MDG Regions in 2010

(Mln US$)

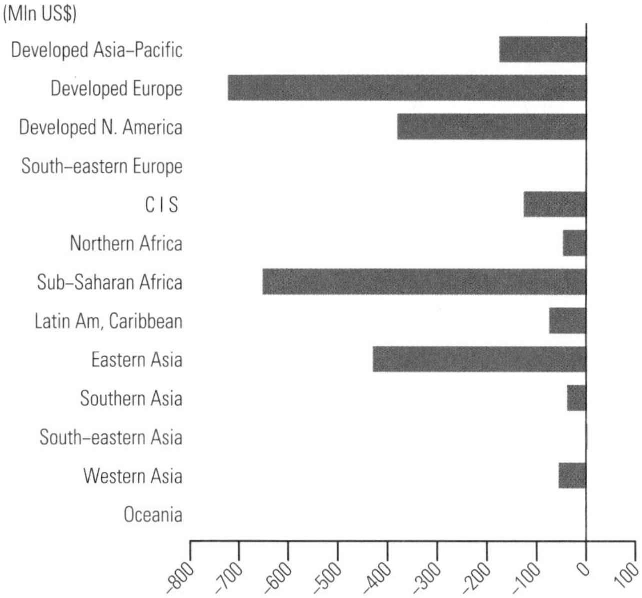

Graph 3: Partner concentration of trade in 2010

(Cumulative share by ranked partners)

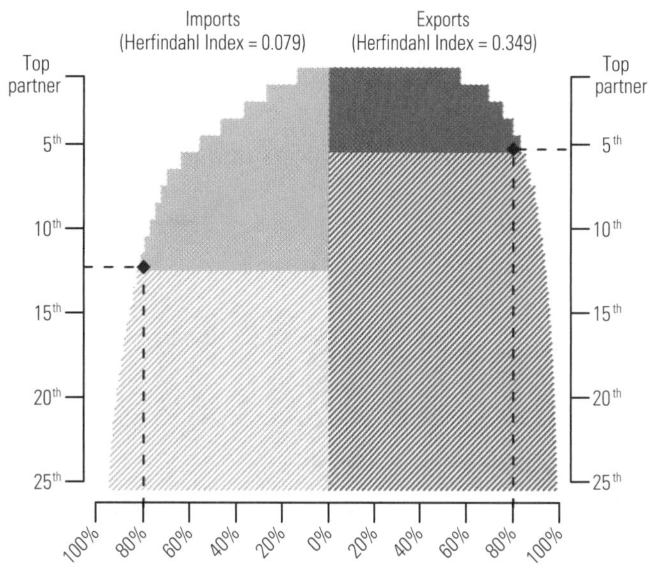

Table 4: Exports by principal countries and SITC sections in 2010

(Value in million US$, percentages of country total)

Country	Total	Shares by SITC sections (%)								
		0 + 1	2 + 4	3	5	6	7	8	9	Total
World	1 996.3	5.2	8.9	1.4	2.1	1.1	1.5	0.4	79.3	100
South Africa	1 139.2	0.0	0.0	...	0.0	0.0	0.2	0.0	99.8	100
Switzerland	241.6	0.4	0.2	...	0.3	0.1	0.8	0.1	98.1	100
Italy	120.0	0.7	3.0	...	0.1	2.5	0.9	0.0	92.8	100
Senegal	87.8	41.8	28.5	24.3	0.7	1.8	1.2	1.1	0.6	100
USA	63.1	0.2	0.0	...	0.3	0.9	6.2	0.3	92.1	100
Burkina Faso	43.1	32.0	0.3	0.2	61.8	2.2	1.9	1.5	0.1	100
China	40.8	1.1	75.7	...	5.7	16.9	0.5	0.2	0.0	100
Côte d'Ivoire	39.9	75.1	2.1	0.0	13.8	4.0	3.1	1.9	0.0	100
Malaysia	24.1	0.6	99.0	...	...	...	...	0.4	...	100
France	22.7	25.7	14.8	0.3	4.1	5.6	38.7	7.5	3.3	100

Imports Profile:

In 2010, mineral fuels, lubricants and related materials (SITC section 3), machinery and transport equipment (SITC section 7) and manufactured goods classified chiefly by material (SITC section 6) accounted respectively for 26.0, 23.8 and 18.1 percent of Mali's imported goods (see table 2). Other major commodity groups for imports included chemicals and related products, n.e.s. (SITC section 5) (14.7 percent) and food, live animals, beverages and tobacco (SITC sections 0+1) (10.4 percent). Top imported goods were petroleum oils, other than crude (HS code 2710), medicaments (excluding goods of heading 30.02, 30.05 or 30.06) (HS code 3004) and portland cement, aluminous cement, slag cement (HS code 2523) (see table 5).

Table 5: Top 10 import commodities 2008 to 2010

(Value in million US$)

HS code	4-digit heading of Harmonized System 2007	Value (million US$)			Unit value				SITC code
		2008	2009	2010	2008	2009	2010	Unit	
	All Commodities	3 338.9	...	4 703.5					
2710	Petroleum oils, other than crude	697.4	...	1 201.2	1.1		0.8	US$/kg	334
3004	Medicaments (excluding goods of heading 30.02, 30.05 or 30.06)	98.7	...	309.5	14.7		43.0	US$/kg	542
2523	Portland cement, aluminous cement, slag cement	175.6	...	185.3	0.2		0.1	US$/kg	661
8703	Motor cars and other motor vehicles principally designed for the transport	72.7	...	101.1			*15.9*	thsd US$/unit	781
8431	Parts suitable for use principally with the machinery of headings 84.25	70.3	...	100.5	16.5		26.6	US$/kg	723
3102	Mineral or chemical fertilisers, nitrogenous	86.4	...	56.2	0.6		0.3	US$/kg	562
8704	Motor vehicles for the transport of goods	60.2	...	81.5					782
7213	Bars and rods, hot-rolled, in irregularly wound coils	49.0	...	73.4	0.9		0.7	US$/kg	676
1006	Rice	66.2	...	50.0	0.4		0.2	US$/kg	042
1701	Cane or beet sugar and chemically pure sucrose, in solid form	44.0	...	54.7	0.3		0.3	US$/kg	061

Imports: CIF, by origin/consignment for intra-eu | **Exports: FOB, by last known destination** | **Trade System: General**

Overview:

After a marked decrease of 24.7 percent in 2009, the value of Malta's exports bounced back by 47.2 percent to amount to 3.4 bln US$ in 2010 (see table 1 and graph 1). Imports showed a less pronounced development with an increase of 5.2 percent to amount to 4.2 bln US$ (see table 2 and graph 1). This resulted in a trade deficit of 0.9 bln US$ in 2010, compared to 1.8 bln US$ in 2009 (see graph 1). By MDG regions, Developed Europe accounted for a large part of the deficit (-1.8 bln US$) (see graph 2). Surpluses were recorded with South-eastern Asia (+269.5 mln US$) and Eastern Asia (+240.7 mln US$). By partners, Malta's trade was relatively diversified: 11 (respectively 15) major partners accounted for 80 percent of exports (respectively imports) (see graph 3).

Graph 1: Total imports, exports and trade balance

(Bln US$ by year)

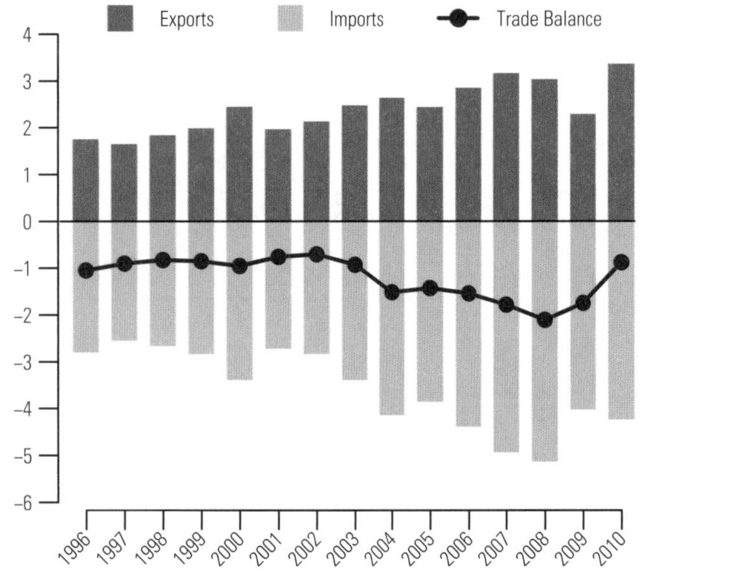

Exports Profile:

Machinery and transport equipment (SITC section 7) accounted for the majority (60.5 percent) of exported goods (see table 1). Its exports increased by 55.0 percent in 2010. Other major commodity groups included miscellaneous manufactured articles (SITC section 8) and food, live animals, beverages and tobacco (SITC sections 0+1) respectively with 11.6 and 8.3 percent of exported goods. Top partners for exports were Singapore, USA and China, Hong Kong SAR (see table 4). Exports to these markets were largely machinery and transport equipment (SITC section 7). From 2008 to 2010, diodes, transistors and similar semiconductor devices (HS code 8541) was the top commodity and accounted for 46.2 percent of exports in 2010 (see table 3). Other major exported products included medicaments (excluding goods of heading 30.02, 30.05 or 30.06) (HS code 3004) and electrical apparatus for switching or protecting electrical circuits (HS code 8536).

Table 1: Exports by SITC sections

(Value in million US$, growth and shares in percentage)

SITC	2010	Avg. Growth rates (%) 2006-2010	2009-2010	2010 share
Total	3357.5	4.2	47.2	100.0
0+1	277.5	12.4	160.1	8.3
2+4	18.1	11.1	34.5	0.5
3	186.5	48.9	432.0	5.6
5	259.0	10.3	-4.6	7.7
6	159.8	2.4	28.8	4.8
7	2029.7	2.8	55.0	60.5
8	388.8	-4.4	-0.7	11.6
9	38.2	15.4	35.3	1.1

Table 2: Imports by SITC sections

(Value in million US$, growth and shares in percentage)

SITC	2010	Avg. Growth rates (%) 2006-2010	2009-2010	2010 share
Total	4245.8	-0.9	5.2	100.0
0+1	548.9	4.3	-10.5	12.9
2+4	45.8	-2.6	-9.4	1.1
3	369.9	-0.9	-13.0	8.7
5	465.1	5.8	8.2	11.0
6	404.0	-1.8	1.9	9.5
7	1923.1	-2.3	20.0	45.3
8	432.1	-5.2	-10.0	10.2
9	56.9	7.0	56.8	1.3

Table 3: Top 10 export commodities 2008 to 2010

(Value in million US$)

HS code	4-digit heading of Harmonized System 2007	Value (million US$) 2008	2009	2010	Unit value 2008	2009	2010	Unit	SITC code
	All Commodities	3028.5	2280.3	3357.5					
8541	Diodes, transistors and similar semiconductor devices	1224.0	905.9	1551.5					776
3004	Medicaments (excluding goods of heading 30.02, 30.05 or 30.06)	248.7	208.0	177.6	126.8	95.2	*106.3*	US$/kg	542
8536	Electrical apparatus for switching or protecting electrical circuits	143.5	114.5	130.0	72.3	70.0		US$/kg	772
4907	Unused postage, revenue or similar stamps of current or new issue	128.4	118.7	90.6	48.8	42.1	*40.1*	US$/kg	892
9503	Tricycles, scooters, wheeled toys; dolls' carriages; dolls; other toys	97.0	92.2	109.0	33.4	31.9	*28.0*	US$/kg	894
2710	Petroleum oils, other than crude	64.4	35.0	186.5	1.1	0.7	*0.6*	US$/kg	334
0302	Fish, fresh or chilled, excluding fish fillets	77.3	20.2	109.2	18.9	8.9		US$/kg	034
2106	Food preparations not elsewhere specified or included	39.4	43.8	93.5	2.1	2.6	*2.8*	US$/kg	098
6005	Warp knit fabrics (including those made on galloon knitting machines)	54.5	49.2	66.0	9.1	8.5		US$/kg	655
4016	Other articles of vulcanised rubber other than hard rubber	53.4	31.7	48.0	94.1	104.1		US$/kg	629

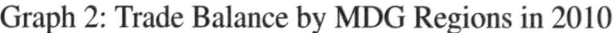

Graph 2: Trade Balance by MDG Regions in 2010

(Bln US$)

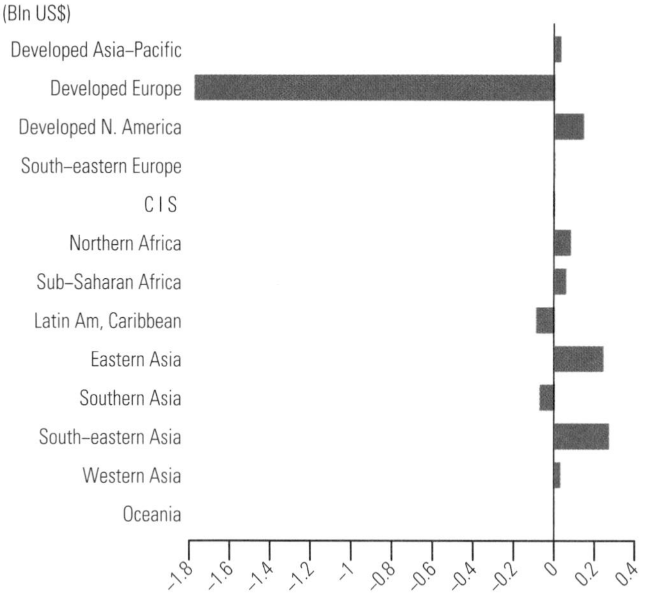

Graph 3: Partner concentration of trade in 2010

(Cumulative share by ranked partners)

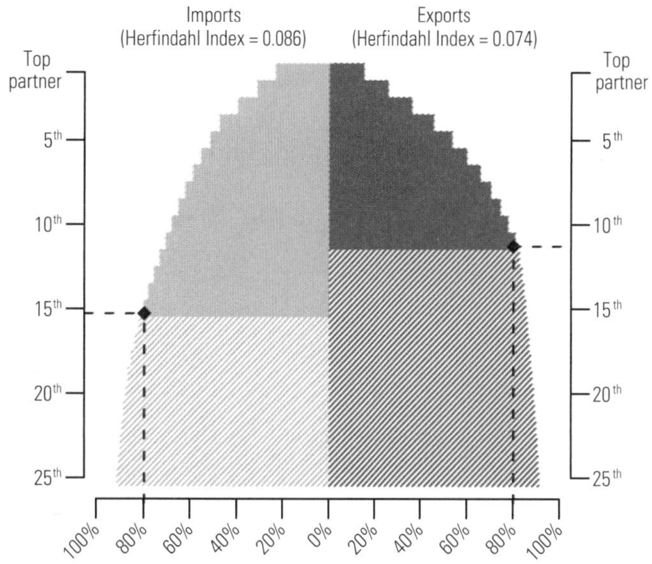

Table 4: Exports by principal countries and SITC sections in 2010

(Value in million US$, percentages of country total)

Country	Total	Shares by SITC sections (%) 0+1	2+4	3	5	6	7	8	9	Total
World	3357.5	8.3	0.5	5.6	7.7	4.8	60.5	11.6	1.1	100
Singapore	495.2	0.2	0.0	...	0.0	0.0	99.5	0.3	...	100
USA	370.4	0.4	0.0	0.0	12.4	3.4	79.8	3.9	0.0	100
China, Hong Kong SAR	344.4	0.0	0.1	...	0.5	0.0	98.9	0.5	...	100
Germany	311.2	0.0	0.1	0.1	8.6	21.6	31.7	37.9	0.0	100
France	265.8	0.0	0.4	0.0	5.3	0.8	85.5	7.8	0.0	100
Bunkers	212.4	0.0	0.0	86.9	0.4	0.0	0.4	0.0	12.4	100
Japan	197.3	52.4	0.0	...	0.1	4.3	42.3	0.4	0.4	100
United Kingdom	153.5	1.7	0.5	0.1	8.8	13.7	23.7	51.5	0.0	100
China	137.9	0.1	0.1	...	0.2	4.5	94.2	0.9	...	100
Italy	111.8	9.0	4.8	0.3	8.8	13.2	22.7	36.2	5.1	100

Imports Profile:

Imports of machinery and transport equipment (SITC section 7) increased by 20.0 percent in 2010 and accounted for 45.3 percent of imported goods (see table 2). Imports of food, live animals, beverages and tobacco (SITC sections 0+1) and miscellaneous manufactured articles (SITC section 8) decreased respectively by 10.5 percent and 10.0 percent, and represented 12.9 and 10.2 percent of total imports respectively. From 2008 to 2010, top imported goods included electronic integrated circuits (HS code 8542), petroleum oils, other than crude (HS code 2710) and other aircraft (for example, helicopters, aeroplanes); spacecraft (HS code 8802) (see table 5).

Table 5: Top 10 import commodities 2008 to 2010

(Value in million US$)

HS code	4-digit heading of Harmonized System 2007	Value (million US$) 2008	2009	2010	Unit value 2008	2009	2010	Unit	SITC code
	All Commodities	5140.8	4034.1	4245.8					
8542	Electronic integrated circuits	770.2	433.6	637.6					776
2710	Petroleum oils, other than crude	721.7	412.4	357.3	0.7	0.5	*0.6*	US$/kg	334
8802	Other aircraft (for example, helicopters, aeroplanes); spacecraft	51.3	266.0	167.2	2.3	20.5		mln US$/unit	792
8903	Yachts and other vessels for pleasure or sports; rowing boats and canoes	126.5	116.3	177.3	149.5	125.9		thsd US$/unit	793
8803	Parts of goods of heading 88.01 or 88.02	62.7	103.9	157.7	28.2	283.0	*7.0*	US$/kg	792
3004	Medicaments (excluding goods of heading 30.02, 30.05 or 30.06)	119.4	94.8	97.5	57.4	60.9	*52.0*	US$/kg	542
8703	Motor cars and other motor vehicles principally designed for the transport	134.5	95.8	80.9	11.4	7.7	*12.0*	thsd US$/unit	781
4802	Uncoated paper and paperboard, of a kind used for writing	55.3	51.3	40.5	5.7	6.7	*2.8*	US$/kg	641
2933	Heterocyclic compounds with nitrogen hetero-atom(s) only	36.4	45.6	60.0	305.7	124.4		US$/kg	515
9403	Other furniture and parts thereof	48.9	45.4	38.9					821

Mauritania

Imports: CIF, by origin | **Exports: FOB, by last known destination** | **Trade System: General**

Overview:

In 2010, Mauritania's exports decreased by 37.7 percent and amounted to 725.4 mln US$ (see table 1 and graph 1). Imports showed the opposite development with an increase of 29.1 percent and amounted to 1.7 bln US$ (see table 2 and graph 1). As a result, the trade deficit increased from 172.6 mln US$ in 2009 to 1.0 bln US$ in 2010 (see graph 1). By MDG regions, trade was in surplus with Developed Asia-Pacific (+63.5 mln US$), Sub-Saharan Africa (+56.6 mln US$) and Eastern Asia (+21.9 mln US$) (see graph 2). Trade recorded deficits with the Developed Europe (-535.9 mln US$), Western Asia (-241.2 mln US$) and South-eastern Asia (-127.6 mln US$). Compared to imports, exports were concentrated among a few partners: in 2010, 5 major partners accounted for 80 percent of exports compared to 13 major partners for imports (see graph 3).

Graph 1: Total imports, exports and trade balance

(Bln US$ by year)

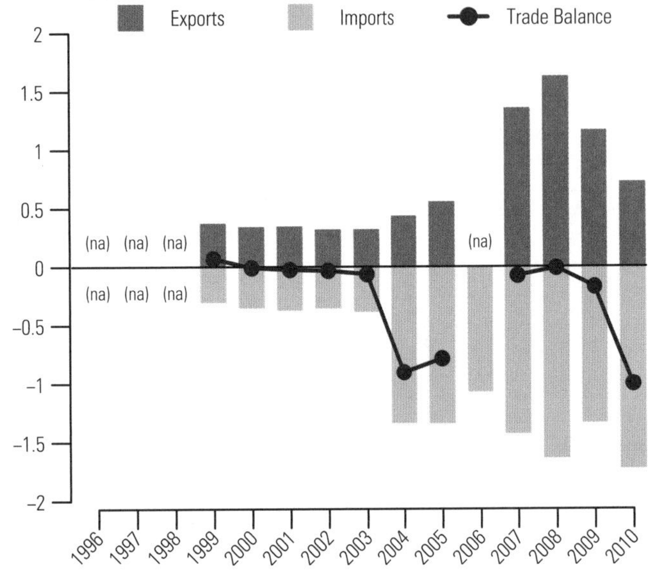

Table 1: Exports by SITC sections

(Value in million US$, growth and shares in percentage)

SITC	2010	Avg. Growth rates (%) 2006-2010	Avg. Growth rates (%) 2009-2010	2010 share
Total	725.4	...	-37.7	100.0
0+1	276.8	...	17.0	38.2
2+4	147.6	...	-78.2	20.4
3	0.0	...	...	0.0
6	0.1	...	326.4	0.0
9	300.8	...	19.8	41.5

Exports Profile:

In 2010, majority of Mauritania's exports were in commodities and transactions not classified elsewhere (SITC section 9); they increased by 19.8 percent to account for 41.5 percent of exported goods (see table 1). Exports of food, live animals, beverages and tobacco (SITC sections 0+1) increased by 17.0 percent and represented 38.2 percent of exported goods, while exports of inedible crude materials (except fuels), animal and vegetable oils, fats and waxes (SITC sections 2+4) decreased by 78.2 percent and accounted for 20.4 percent. In 2010, major destinations for exported goods were China, Switzerland and Japan (see table 4). From 2008 to 2010, top exported products included iron ores and concentrates, roasted iron pyrites (HS code 2601), fish, frozen, whole (HS code 0303) and gold, unwrought, semi-manufactured, powder form (HS code 7108) (see table 3).

Table 2: Imports by SITC sections

(Value in million US$, growth and shares in percentage)

SITC	2010	Avg. Growth rates (%) 2006-2010	Avg. Growth rates (%) 2009-2010	2010 share
Total	1 726.5	12.6	29.1	100.0
0+1	301.3	5.4	-13.0	17.5
2+4	44.9	8.3	-12.0	2.6
3	458.0	12.2	70.1	26.5
5	76.4	12.2	15.2	4.4
6	190.5	4.7	16.2	11.0
7	605.9	23.8	56.3	35.1
8	39.5	-1.8	-23.8	2.3
9	10.1	80.7	1100.8	0.6

Table 3: Top 10 export commodities 2008 to 2010

(Value in million US$)

HS code	4-digit heading of Harmonized System 1996	Value (million US$) 2008	Value (million US$) 2009	Value (million US$) 2010	Unit value 2008	Unit value 2009	Unit value 2010	Unit	SITC code
	All Commodities	1 627.1	1 164.5	725.4					
2601	Iron ores and concentrates, roasted iron pyrites	773.6	519.2	...					281
0303	Fish, frozen, whole	181.3	232.0	122.1	7.3	4.6	2.7	US$/kg	034
7108	Gold, unwrought, semi-manufactured, powder form	120.8	167.2	244.6	26.1	27.9	37.0	thsd US$/kg	971
2603	Copper ores and concentrates	128.1	153.8	122.8	0.9	0.9	0.8	US$/kg	283
2709	Petroleum oils, oils from bituminous minerals, crude	326.4	...	...					333
9999	Commodities not elsewhere specified	89.0	83.9	56.2					931
0307	Molluscs	...	...	109.4			6.6	US$/kg	036
2301	Flour etc of meat, fish or offal for animal feed	...	...	19.7			0.9	US$/kg	081
0302	Fish, fresh or chilled, whole	2.0	1.7	11.9	1.0	0.7	1.5	US$/kg	034
2611	Tungsten ores and concentrates	...	...	12.9			0.1	US$/kg	287

Graph 2: Trade Balance by MDG Regions in 2010

(Mln US$)

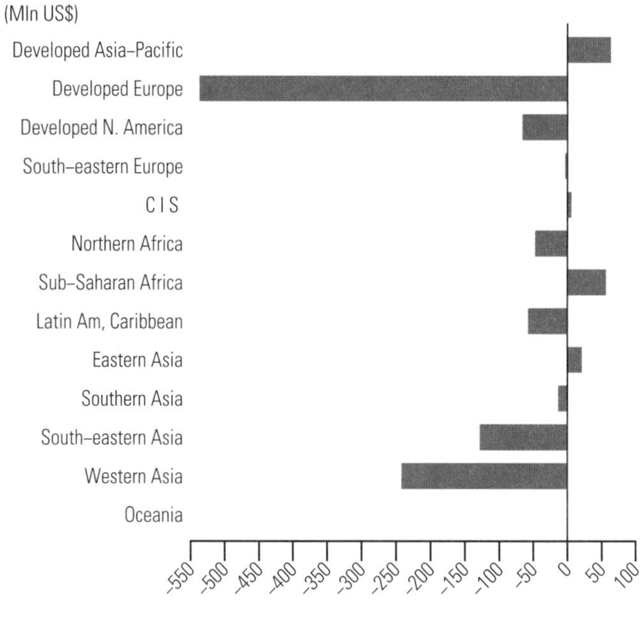

Graph 3: Partner concentration of trade in 2010

(Cumulative share by ranked partners)

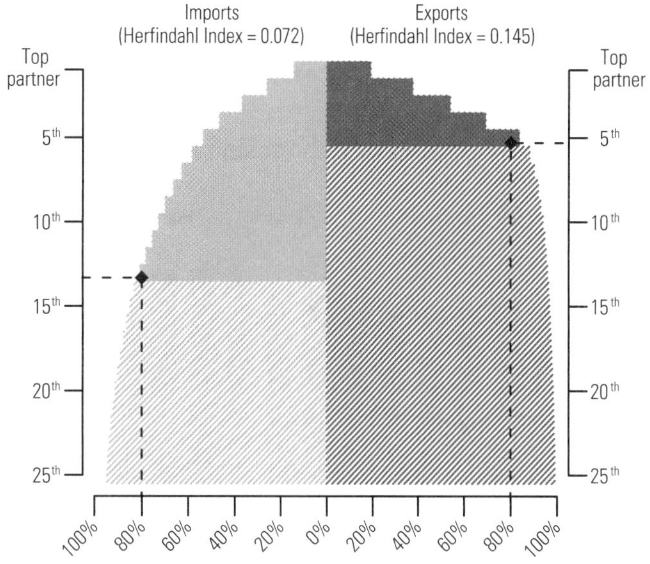

Table 4: Exports by principal countries and SITC sections in 2010

(Value in million US$, percentages of country total)

Country	Total	Shares by SITC sections (%) 0+1	2+4	3	5	6	7	8	9	Total
World	725.4	38.2	20.4	0.0	...	0.0	...	...	41.5	100
China	138.7	1.9	97.7	...	...	...	...	...	0.4	100
Switzerland	135.0	0.0	2.6	...	...	...	...	...	97.4	100
Japan	117.8	99.6	0.0	...	...	...	...	...	0.4	100
Spain	110.7	85.3	0.8	...	...	...	...	...	13.8	100
Swaziland	104.7	0.0	0.0	...	...	...	...	...	100.0	100
Russian Federation	32.5	47.3	0.5	...	...	...	...	...	52.2	100
Italy	13.8	91.1	0.1	...	...	...	...	...	8.8	100
France	13.0	34.9	0.2	...	...	0.0	...	...	64.9	100
Portugal	7.4	69.5	0.0	...	...	...	...	...	30.5	100
Ghana	7.3	46.3	0.0	...	...	...	...	...	53.7	100

Imports Profile:

In 2010, imports of machinery and transport equipment (SITC section 7) increased by 56.3 percent and accounted for 35.1 percent of imported goods (see table 2). Other major commodity groups for imports included mineral fuels, lubricants and related materials (SITC section 3) and food, live animals, beverages and tobacco (SITC sections 0+1) respectively with 26.5 and 17.5 percent of imports. From 2008 to 2010, top imported products were oils petroleum, bituminous, distillates, except crude (HS code 2710), wheat and meslin (HS code 1001) and parts for use with lifting, moving machinery (HS code 8431) (see table 5).

Table 5: Top 10 import commodities 2008 to 2010

(Value in million US$)

HS code	4-digit heading of Harmonized System 1996	Value (million US$) 2008	2009	2010	Unit value 2008	2009	2010	Unit	SITC code
	All Commodities	1 637.6	1 337.1	1 726.5					
2710	Oils petroleum, bituminous, distillates, except crude	545.5	249.9	427.8	0.8	0.5	0.7	US$/kg	334
1001	Wheat and meslin	108.9	77.8	82.4	0.4	0.2	0.3	US$/kg	041
8431	Parts for use with lifting, moving machinery	63.9	94.8	88.5	19.2	12.1	19.4	US$/kg	723
1006	Rice	74.4	74.1	37.9	0.7	0.5	0.4	US$/kg	042
8703	Motor vehicles for transport of persons (except buses)	62.4	53.4	51.8	*17.0*	*16.4*	*17.5*	thsd US$/unit	781
1701	Solid cane or beet sugar and chemically pure sucrose	47.1	46.3	46.3	0.2	0.2	0.2	US$/kg	061
0402	Milk and cream, concentrated or sweetened	53.5	42.9	33.8	2.9	2.2	1.4	US$/kg	022
1507	Soya-bean oil, fractions, not chemically modified	52.5	32.2	24.5	0.8	0.4	0.4	US$/kg	421
2523	Cement (portland, aluminous, slag or hydraulic)	30.7	34.9	37.3	0.1	0.1	0.1	US$/kg	661
8503	Parts for electric motors and generators	6.7	5.5	75.4	34.5	41.9	125.6	US$/kg	716

Mauritius

Imports: CIF, by origin | **Exports: FOB, by last known destination** | **Trade System: General**

Overview:

After reaching a peak of 2.4 bln US$ in 2008, the value of Mauritius's exports dropped in 2009 but increased in 2010 and 2011 by respectively 4.7 and 21.9 percent, to amount to 2.3 bln US$ in 2011 (see table 1 and graph 1). Imports showed a similar development and amounted to 5.2 bln US$ in 2011, reflecting an increase of 17.2 percent from 2010 (see table 2 and graph 1). The trade deficit increased from 2.0 bln US$ in 2009 to 2.9 bln US$ in 2011 (see graph 1). Major deficits were recorded with Southern Asia and Eastern Asia, amounting to 1.2 bln US$ and 873.9 mln US$ respectively. The trade balance also recorded a surplus of 190.7 mln US$ with Developed Europe. In 2011, exports were more concentrated among partners than imports: 8 major partners accounted for 80 percent of exports compared to 16 major partners for imports (see graph 3).

Graph 1: Total imports, exports and trade balance

(Bln US$ by year)

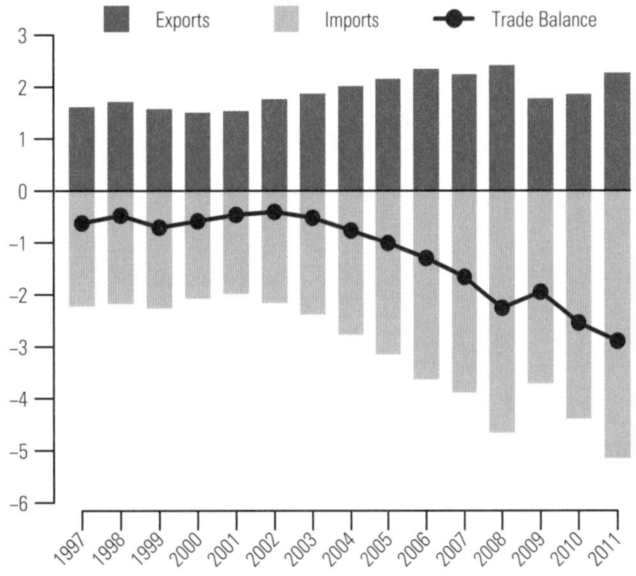

Table 1: Exports by SITC sections

(Value in million US$, growth and shares in percentage)

SITC	2011	Avg. Growth rates (%) 2007-2011	2010-2011	2011 share
Total	2 255.4	0.3	21.9	100.0
0+1	751.9	4.2	10.1	33.3
2+4	44.6	11.3	26.5	2.0
3	2.6	-3.4	-62.9	0.1
5	75.8	15.9	14.4	3.4
6	228.9	5.9	26.8	10.2
7	50.6	-20.9	-6.6	2.2
8	1 090.5	1.6	33.0	48.4
9	10.6	-50.8	226.8	0.5

Exports Profile:

In 2011, two commodity groups accounted for the majority of Mauritius' exports: miscellaneous manufactured articles (SITC section 8) and food, live animals, beverages and tobacco (SITC sections 0+1), respectively with 48.4 and 33.3 percent of exported goods (see table 1). Manufactured goods classified chiefly by material (SITC section 6), another major export commodity group, accounted for 10.2 percent of total exports. In addition to United Kingdom, other major destinations for exports included France and USA (see table 4). Major exported products over the last three years were t-shirts, singlets and other vests, knitted or crocheted (HS code 6109), cane or beet sugar and pure sucrose, in solid form (HS code 1701) and prepared or preserved fish; caviar (HS code 1604) (see table 3).

Table 2: Imports by SITC sections

(Value in million US$, growth and shares in percentage)

SITC	2011	Avg. Growth rates (%) 2007-2011	2010-2011	2011 share
Total	5 158.6	7.2	17.2	100.0
0+1	1 031.2	10.4	16.7	20.0
2+4	234.1	12.8	61.2	4.5
3	1 112.7	11.7	31.9	21.6
5	421.9	8.6	4.1	8.2
6	962.6	4.9	17.9	18.7
7	930.0	1.2	4.5	18.0
8	450.0	10.7	13.7	8.7
9	16.2	-29.3	-30.4	0.3

Table 3: Top 10 export commodities 2009 to 2011

(Value in million US$)

HS code	4-digit heading of Harmonized System 2007	Value (million US$) 2009	2010	2011	Unit value 2009	2010	2011	Unit	SITC code
	All Commodities	1 765.8	1 849.5	2 255.4					
6109	T-shirts, singlets and other vests, knitted or crocheted	303.7	235.3	363.0	3.8	3.8	4.3	US$/unit	845
1701	Cane or beet sugar and chemically pure sucrose, in solid form	214.7	251.7	299.1	0.6	0.6	0.7	US$/kg	061
1604	Prepared or preserved fish; caviar	220.7	250.3	277.5	3.7	3.9	4.3	US$/kg	037
6205	Men's or boys' shirts	107.2	120.8	144.1	9.9	10.1	10.4	US$/unit	841
6203	Men's or boys' suits, ensembles, jackets, blazers, trousers	82.6	76.6	98.6	11.1	11.4	12.5	US$/unit	841
0303	Fish, frozen, excluding fish fillets and other fish meat of heading 03.04	57.8	68.6	48.6	2.1	1.9	2.2	US$/kg	034
6110	Jerseys, pullovers, cardigans, waist-coats and similar articles	57.9	44.8	60.4	10.1	10.3	11.1	US$/unit	845
7102	Diamonds, whether or not worked, but not mounted or set	30.9	48.0	53.6					667
7113	Articles of jewellery and parts thereof, of precious metal	31.0	46.2	46.3			*9.3*	thsd US$/kg	897
6204	Women's or girls' suits, ensembles, jackets, blazers, dresses, skirts	37.8	38.7	40.3	9.3	9.7	9.4	US$/unit	842

Graph 2: Trade Balance by MDG Regions in 2011

(Bln US$)

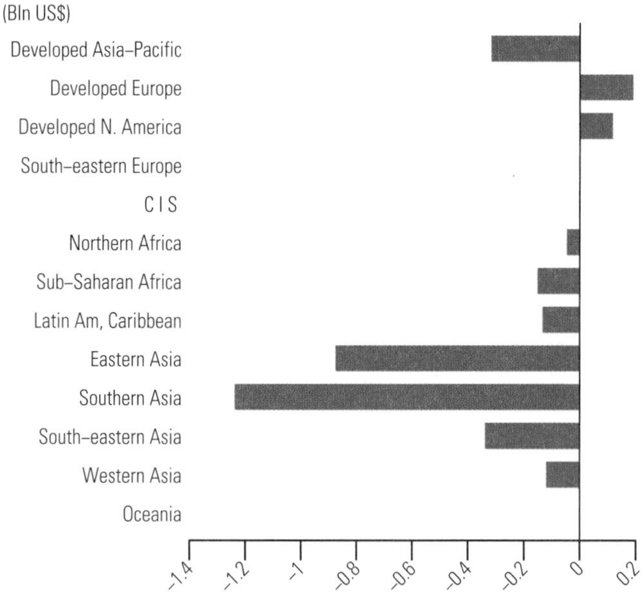

Graph 3: Partner concentration of trade in 2011

(Cumulative share by ranked partners)

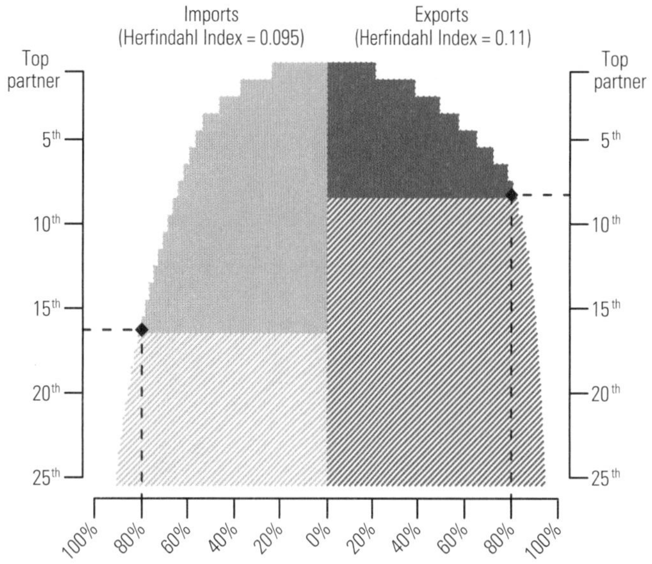

Table 4: Exports by principal countries and SITC sections in 2011

(Value in million US$, percentages of country total)

Country	Total	Shares by SITC sections (%)								
		0+1	2+4	3	5	6	7	8	9	Total
World	2255.4	33.3	2.0	0.1	3.4	10.2	2.2	48.4	0.5	100
United Kingdom	480.8	32.4	0.0	0.0	0.0	1.1	0.6	65.8	0.0	100
France	392.2	13.2	0.5	0.0	7.3	5.3	2.2	69.3	2.2	100
USA	236.5	11.2	0.3	0.0	0.2	14.9	0.1	73.2	...	100
Italy	182.0	86.9	2.3	...	0.0	3.3	0.1	7.4	...	100
South Africa	174.1	1.1	1.7	0.0	1.0	16.3	1.2	78.7	...	100
Spain	160.8	90.5	1.2	0.0	0.0	0.3	0.3	7.7	...	100
Madagascar	140.0	24.3	2.3	0.0	11.1	44.7	7.2	10.4	...	100
Belgium	50.7	22.6	0.3	...	0.0	36.7	0.5	38.9	0.9	100
Germany	48.3	33.8	0.7	0.0	17.2	0.9	3.4	41.9	2.1	100
Switzerland	41.0	3.4	0.2	...	0.1	31.0	0.3	64.1	1.0	100

Imports Profile:

In 2011, imports were composed of 21.6 percent of mineral fuels, lubricants and related materials (SITC section 3), 20.0 percent of food, live animals, beverages and tobacco (SITC sections 0+1) and 18.7 percent of manufactured goods classified chiefly by material (SITC section 6) (see table 2). Over the last three years, top imported products included petroleum oils, other than crude (HS code 2710), fish, frozen, excluding fish fillets and other fish meat of heading 03.04 (HS code 0303) and motor cars and other motor vehicles principally designed for the transport (HS code 8703) (see table 5).

Table 5: Top 10 import commodities 2009 to 2011

(Value in million US$)

HS code	4-digit heading of Harmonized System 2007	Value (million US$)			Unit value				SITC code
		2009	2010	2011	2009	2010	2011	Unit	
	All Commodities	3725.1	4402.3	5158.6					
2710	Petroleum oils, other than crude	482.0	703.6	939.8	*1.5*	*1.2*	*1.4*	US$/kg	334
0303	Fish, frozen, excluding fish fillets and other fish meat of heading 03.04	190.3	219.8	279.3	1.5	1.5	1.8	US$/kg	034
8703	Motor cars and other motor vehicles principally designed for the transport	96.0	122.9	138.4	10.1	12.0	13.7	thsd US$/unit	781
3004	Medicaments (excluding goods of heading 30.02, 30.05 or 30.06)	86.2	118.2	93.2	*19.8*	*24.2*	22.1	US$/kg	542
2701	Coal; briquettes, ovoids and similar solid fuels manufactured from coal	56.5	74.5	92.0	0.1	0.1	0.1	US$/kg	321
8517	Electrical apparatus for line telephony or line telegraphy	57.0	72.9	67.5					764
0402	Milk and cream, concentrated or containing added sugar	49.1	63.8	74.4	3.6	4.4	4.9	US$/kg	022
5208	Woven fabrics of cotton, containing 85 % or more by weight of cotton	49.4	57.5	72.0	14.1	13.7	16.8	US$/kg	652
5205	Cotton yarn (other than sewing thread), containing 85 % or more	42.7	56.1	72.6	3.0	4.0	5.4	US$/kg	651
2711	Petroleum gases and other gaseous hydrocarbons	41.7	53.2	66.0	0.7	0.8	1.0	US$/kg	343

Imports: CIF, by origin | **Exports: FOB, by last known destination** | **Trade System: General**

Overview:

In 2009, the value of the exports of Mayotte dropped by 12.4 percent and amounted to 6.8 mln US$ (see table 1 and graph 1). Imports showed a continuous growth from 2005 to 2009 with a peak of 606.3 mln US$ in 2008 before dropping by 17.2 percent in 2009 to amount to 501.9 mln US$ (see table 2 and graph 1). This resulted in a trade deficit of 495.1 mln US$ in 2009 (see graph 1). By MDG regions, the deficit with Developed Europe alone amounted to 320.5 mln US$ (see graph 2). Significant deficits were also recorded with South-eastern Asia (-40.4 mln US$) and Western Asia (-39.5 mln US$). By partners, exports were highly concentrated: 3 major partners accounted for 80 percent of exports compared to 14 major partners for imports (see graph 3).

Graph 1: Total imports, exports and trade balance

(Mln US$ by year)

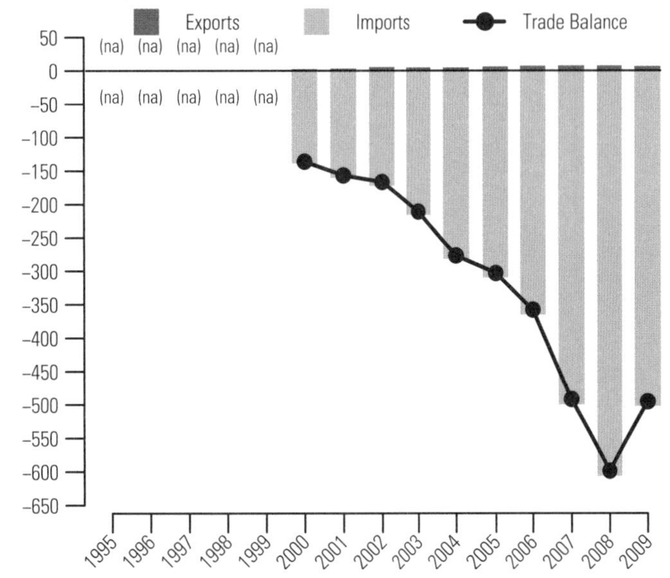

Exports Profile:

In 2009, exports of machinery and transport equipment (SITC section 7) increased by 2.0 percent and accounted for 56.6 percent of exported goods (see table 1). Exports of food, live animals, beverages and tobacco (SITC sections 0+1) decreased by 1.7 percent and represented 15.8 percent of exported goods. France, the top partner, was the destination of 52.9 percent of exports in 2009 (see table 4). Other major markets for exported goods were Comoros and Madagascar. From 2007 to 2009, top exported products included motor cars and other motor vehicles principally designed for the transport (HS code 8703), fish, fresh or chilled, excluding fish fillets (HS code 0302) and essential oils (terpeneless or not), including concretes (HS code 3301) (see table 3).

Table 1: Exports by SITC sections

(Value in million US$, growth and shares in percentage)

SITC	2009	Avg. Growth rates (%) 2005-2009	Avg. Growth rates (%) 2008-2009	2009 share
Total	6.8	1.3	-12.4	100.0
0+1	1.1	-3.7	-1.7	15.8
2+4	0.4	137.9	1592.0	6.6
3	0.0	39.8	-30.1	0.6
5	0.4	-17.5	-68.6	6.6
6	0.4	1.1	-49.8	6.3
7	3.8	4.3	2.0	56.6
8	0.5	-1.3	-2.9	7.6

Table 2: Imports by SITC sections

(Value in million US$, growth and shares in percentage)

SITC	2009	Avg. Growth rates (%) 2005-2009	Avg. Growth rates (%) 2008-2009	2009 share
Total	501.9	12.8	-17.2	100.0
0+1	114.4	14.0	-3.5	22.8
2+4	8.0	5.4	-30.2	1.6
3	43.6	1.3	-52.0	8.7
5	44.9	14.5	1.9	9.0
6	65.3	6.1	-30.8	13.0
7	176.1	20.3	-7.1	35.1
8	49.6	11.6	-13.3	9.9
9	0.0	6.6	-73.9	0.0

Table 3: Top 10 export commodities 2007 to 2009

(Value in million US$)

HS code	4-digit heading of Harmonized System 2007	Value (million US$) 2007	2008	2009	Unit value 2007	2008	2009	Unit	SITC code
	All Commodities	7.8	7.7	6.8					
8703	Motor cars and other motor vehicles principally designed for the transport	0.9	1.3	1.2	*9.2*		*12.9*	thsd US$/unit	781
0302	Fish, fresh or chilled, excluding fish fillets	0.5	0.7	0.7	6.3	9.1	9.1	US$/kg	034
3301	Essential oils (terpeneless or not), including concretes	0.6	0.9	0.2	102.1	135.6	100.6	US$/kg	551
8426	Ships' derricks; cranes, including cable cranes; mobile lifting frames	0.0	0.1	1.0					744
9403	Other furniture and parts thereof	0.4	0.3	0.2					821
7326	Other articles of iron or steel	0.2	0.4	0.1	0.3	0.3	0.4	US$/kg	699
8903	Yachts and other vessels for pleasure or sports; rowing boats and canoes	0.5	0.1	0.0					793
8525	Transmission apparatus for radio-telephony, radio-broadcasting	0.6	...	...					764
9999	Commodities not specified according to kind	0.6	...	...					931
3004	Medicaments (excluding goods of heading 30.02, 30.05 or 30.06)	0.2	0.3	0.0	20.8	41.0	8.0	US$/kg	542

Graph 2: Trade Balance by MDG Regions in 2009

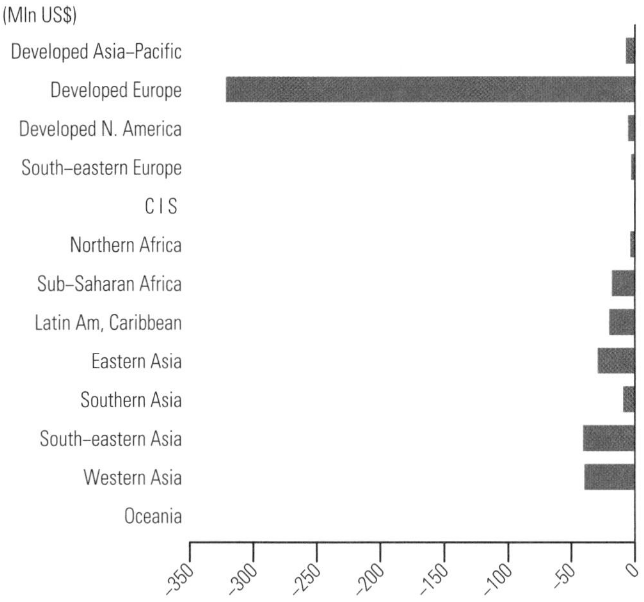

Graph 3: Partner concentration of trade in 2009

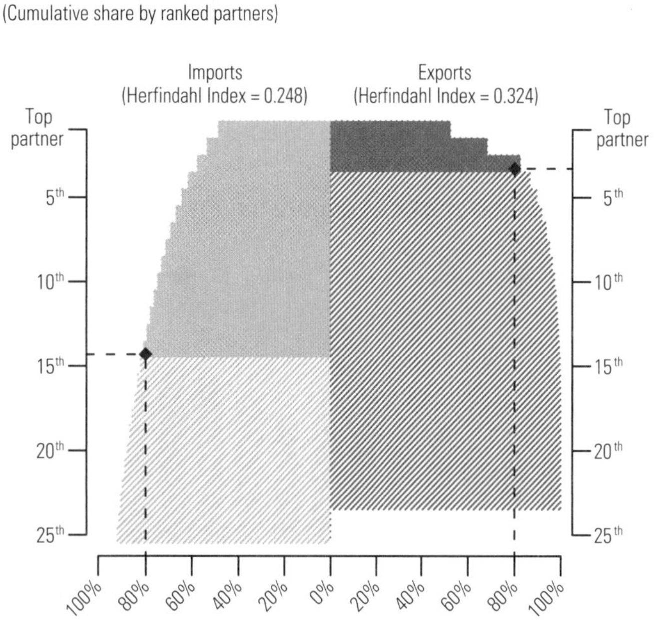

Table 4: Exports by principal countries and SITC sections in 2009

(Value in million US$, percentages of country total)

Country	Total	Shares by SITC sections (%) 0+1	2+4	3	5	6	7	8	9	Total
World	6.8	15.8	6.6	0.6	6.6	6.3	56.6	7.6	...	100
France	3.6	24.3	0.0	1.0	8.4	3.8	57.1	5.4	...	100
Comoros	1.1	18.9	0.1	0.4	11.0	9.2	34.1	26.3	...	100
Madagascar	1.0	0.1	0.5	...	2.0	3.1	93.5	0.8	...	100
Indonesia	0.3	0.0	100.0	...	...	...	...	...	...	100
Mauritius	0.2	1.5	0.4	0.0	...	22.5	73.9	1.7	...	100
India	0.1	0.0	81.2	...	...	18.8	...	...	...	100
Benin	0.1	0.0	0.0	...	...	...	100.0	...	...	100
China	0.1	0.0	0.0	...	...	52.0	46.1	1.9	...	100
Japan	0.1	0.0	0.0	...	...	...	100.0	...	...	100
Singapore	0.1	0.0	43.8	...	...	56.2	...	...	...	100

Imports Profile:

Imports of machinery and transport equipment (SITC section 7) decreased by 7.1 percent in 2009 and represented 35.1 percent of imported goods (see table 2). Other major commodity groups for imports included food, live animals, beverages and tobacco (SITC sections 0+1) and manufactured goods classified chiefly by material (SITC section 6) respectively with 22.8 and 13.0 percent of imports. From 2007 to 2009, top imported products were petroleum oils, other than crude (HS code 2710), motor cars and other motor vehicles principally designed for the transport (HS code 8703) and fishing vessels; factory ships and other vessels for processing (HS code 8902) (see table 5).

Table 5: Top 10 import commodities 2007 to 2009

(Value in million US$)

HS code	4-digit heading of Harmonized System 2007	Value (million US$) 2007	2008	2009	Unit value 2007	2008	2009	Unit	SITC code
	All Commodities	499.4	606.3	501.9					
2710	Petroleum oils, other than crude	62.3	86.2	40.1	0.8	1.0	0.7	US$/kg	334
8703	Motor cars and other motor vehicles principally designed for the transport	27.8	35.5	20.0	*10.4*		*13.6*	thsd US$/unit	781
8902	Fishing vessels; factory ships and other vessels for processing	28.0	0.5	46.7					793
0207	Meat and edible offal, of the poultry of heading 01.05	14.1	18.3	17.6	1.9	2.2	2.0	US$/kg	012
8704	Motor vehicles for the transport of goods	16.2	20.1	8.7					782
1006	Rice	9.8	13.4	16.7	0.6	1.0	1.0	US$/kg	042
2523	Portland cement, aluminous cement, slag cement	10.0	16.7	12.5	0.1	0.1	0.1	US$/kg	661
0202	Meat of bovine animals, frozen	10.3	14.8	13.0	2.9	3.9	3.9	US$/kg	011
3004	Medicaments (excluding goods of heading 30.02, 30.05 or 30.06)	9.1	12.6	14.8	33.8	32.5	35.9	US$/kg	542
8541	Diodes, transistors and similar semiconductor devices	0.8	4.1	17.3					776

Mexico

Imports: CIF, by origin | **Exports: FOB, by last known destination** | **Trade System: General**

Overview:

Following a decline in exports in 2009, Mexico's exports bounced back in 2010 and increased even further in 2011 by 17.2 percent to reach its peak of 349.6 bln US$, surpassing its previous peak of 291.3 bln US$ in 2008 (see table 1 and graph 1). Imports showed a similar development with an increase of 16.4 percent and amounted to 350.8 bln US$ in 2011 (see table 2 and graph 1). This resulted in a trade deficit of 1.3 bln US$ (see graph 1). By MDG regions, major deficits were recorded with Eastern Asia (-63.7 bln US$), Developed Europe (-19.1 bln US$) and Developed Asia-Pacific (-14.7 bln US$) (see graph 2). A trade surplus was recorded with Developed North America (+101.1 bln US$). Trade, especially exports, was highly concentrated among a few partners. USA alone accounted for 78.7 percent of Mexico's exports in 2011. In addition, 7 major partners accounted for 80 percent of imports (see graph 3).

Graph 1: Total imports, exports and trade balance

(Bln US$ by year)

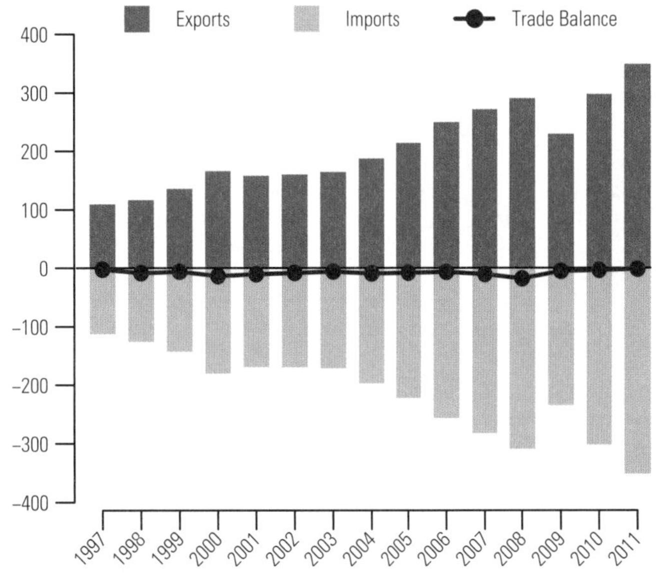

Exports Profile:

The majority of Mexico's exported goods in 2011 were machinery and transport equipment (SITC section 7), representing 52.6 percent of exports (see table 1). Other major commodity groups included mineral fuels, lubricants and related materials (SITC section 3) and miscellaneous manufactured articles (SITC section 8), which accounted respectively for 15.9 and 8.2 percent of exports. The three major markets for exports were USA, Canada and China (see table 4). From 2009 to 2011, top exported products were petroleum oils and oils obtained from bituminous minerals, crude (HS code 2709), motor cars and other motor vehicles principally designed for the transport (HS code 8703) and reception apparatus for television (HS code 8528) (see table 3).

Table 1: Exports by SITC sections

(Value in million US$, growth and shares in percentage)

SITC	2011	Avg. Growth rates (%) 2007-2011	Avg. Growth rates (%) 2010-2011	2011 share
Total	349 569.0	6.5	17.2	100.0
0+1	21 447.3	10.6	22.0	6.1
2+4	7 246.3	14.6	42.7	2.1
3	55 683.6	6.9	35.6	15.9
5	14 187.4	8.9	19.7	4.1
6	28 262.8	5.4	26.1	8.1
7	183 786.7	7.1	10.8	52.6
8	28 745.5	1.7	6.0	8.2
9	10 209.5	-2.7	38.7	2.9

Table 2: Imports by SITC sections

(Value in million US$, growth and shares in percentage)

SITC	2011	Avg. Growth rates (%) 2007-2011	Avg. Growth rates (%) 2010-2011	2011 share
Total	350 842.4	5.6	16.4	100.0
0+1	19 575.1	6.6	26.3	5.6
2+4	12 184.5	7.5	20.3	3.5
3	35 011.1	15.9	45.6	10.0
5	39 547.1	6.9	16.1	11.3
6	47 882.4	3.6	16.8	13.6
7	159 102.6	7.5	11.7	45.3
8	30 011.5	-0.5	5.6	8.6
9	7 528.1	-18.3	26.3	2.1

Table 3: Top 10 export commodities 2009 to 2011

(Value in million US$)

HS code	4-digit heading of Harmonized System 2007	Value (million US$) 2009	Value (million US$) 2010	Value (million US$) 2011	Unit value 2009	Unit value 2010	Unit value 2011	Unit	SITC code
	All Commodities	229 712.3	298 305.1	349 569.0					
2709	Petroleum oils and oils obtained from bituminous minerals, crude	25 693.5	35 907.4	49 363.3	0.4	*0.4*	*0.6*	US$/kg	333
8703	Motor cars and other motor vehicles principally designed for the transport	15 103.3	23 091.1	26 844.1	2.9	14.3	15.4	thsd US$/unit	781
8528	Reception apparatus for television	18 198.7	20 697.7	18 789.6	370.1	345.3	321.1	US$/unit	761
8517	Electrical apparatus for line telephony or line telegraphy	16 158.7	18 292.5	15 971.8					764
8708	Parts and accessories of the motor vehicles of headings 87.01 to 87.05	9 229.4	13 835.3	16 801.3			*9.0*	US$/kg	784
8471	Automatic data processing machines and units thereof	8 094.7	13 331.8	16 501.6	469.1	592.1	567.8	US$/unit	752
8704	Motor vehicles for the transport of goods	6 515.5	10 465.2	12 466.3	16.9	11.5	9.1	thsd US$/unit	782
8544	Insulated (including enamelled or anodised) wire, cable	5 030.1	6 772.2	8 021.0	*14.0*	*14.3*	*15.4*	US$/kg	773
7108	Gold (including gold plated with platinum)	4 003.7	5 753.3	7 721.0	*1.5*	*5.7*	13.2	thsd US$/kg	971
2710	Petroleum oils, other than crude	4 477.3	4 752.4	5 957.9					334

Graph 2: Trade Balance by MDG Regions in 2011

(Bln US$)

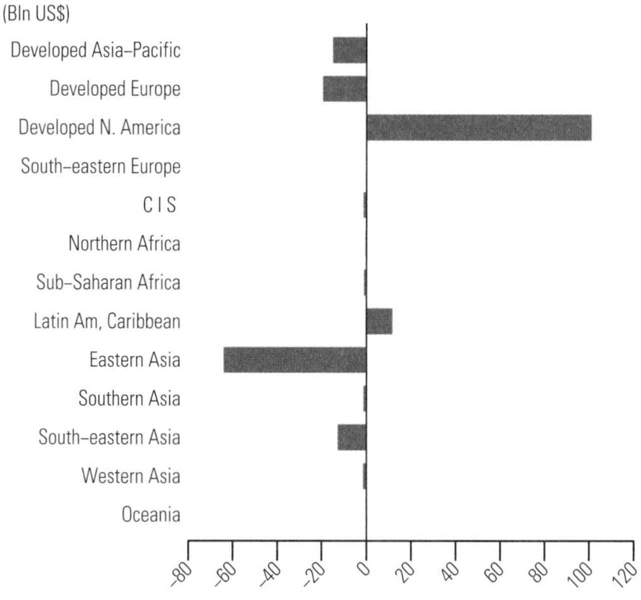

Graph 3: Partner concentration of trade in 2011

(Cumulative share by ranked partners)

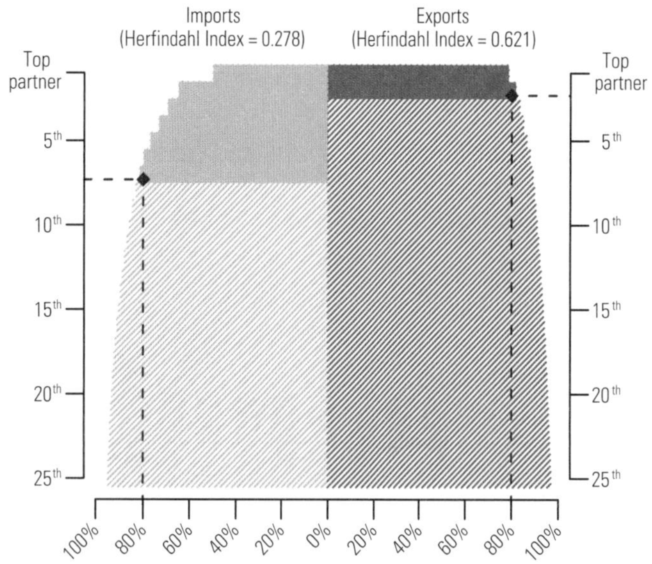

Table 4: Exports by principal countries and SITC sections in 2011

(Value in million US$, percentages of country total)

Country	Total	Shares by SITC sections (%) 0 + 1	2 + 4	3	5	6	7	8	9	Total
World	349569.0	6.1	2.1	15.9	4.1	8.1	52.6	8.2	2.9	100
USA	274992.0	6.0	0.7	16.6	2.0	7.4	55.0	9.5	2.7	100
Canada	10676.1	6.6	1.6	7.0	3.2	4.0	65.1	4.8	7.7	100
China	5965.1	1.3	36.5	22.4	7.0	8.3	23.6	0.9	0.0	100
Colombia	5632.7	1.7	0.7	7.9	14.8	17.7	55.4	1.8	0.1	100
Spain	4902.4	3.5	1.5	85.0	3.5	1.6	4.2	0.5	0.2	100
Brazil	4891.3	1.2	0.8	0.4	19.0	12.5	63.6	2.0	0.5	100
Germany	4315.1	2.8	1.0	0.0	4.2	3.0	85.2	3.5	0.2	100
Japan	2256.8	29.2	11.2	1.0	4.4	15.5	33.3	5.0	0.4	100
United Kingdom	2158.6	7.0	1.6	0.0	6.4	4.4	33.3	3.9	43.3	100
Netherlands	2078.9	7.4	8.1	12.8	5.9	3.1	55.0	7.2	0.6	100

Imports Profile:

In 2011, machinery and transport equipment (SITC section 7) also accounted for a large share of imports, representing 45.3 percent of total imports (see table 2). Manufactured goods classified chiefly by material (SITC section 6), chemicals and related products, n.e.s. (SITC section 5) and mineral fuels, lubricants and related materials (SITC section 3) accounted respectively for 13.6, 11.3 and 10.0 percent of imported goods. From 2009 to 2011, major imported goods were petroleum oils, other than crude (HS code 2710), parts and accessories of the motor vehicles of headings 87.01 to 87.05 (HS code 8708) and electrical apparatus for line telephony or line telegraphy (HS code 8517) (see table 5).

Table 5: Top 10 import commodities 2009 to 2011

(Value in million US$)

HS code	4-digit heading of Harmonized System 2007	Value (million US$) 2009	2010	2011	Unit value 2009	2010	2011	Unit	SITC code
	All Commodities	234384.5	301481.7	350842.4					
2710	Petroleum oils, other than crude	11726.8	18269.7	27872.3					334
8708	Parts and accessories of the motor vehicles of headings 87.01 to 87.05	10793.0	14774.6	17600.9			*10.8*	US$/kg	784
8517	Electrical apparatus for line telephony or line telegraphy	9876.3	12564.4	13653.3					764
8529	Parts suitable for use with the apparatus of headings 85.25 to 85.28	9960.8	11483.3	9812.1	*24.8*			US$/kg	764
8542	Electronic integrated circuits	7754.8	10658.2	12457.6					776
8471	Automatic data processing machines and units thereof	5196.4	6353.1	7638.1	62.4	67.3	68.4	US$/unit	752
8703	Motor cars and other motor vehicles principally designed for the transport	4755.1	6461.2	7264.0	*9.1*	8.8	8.8	thsd US$/unit	781
9999	Commodities not specified according to kind	4461.2	5776.8	7312.4					931
8473	Parts and accessories for use with machines of heading 84.69 to 84.72	3370.0	5420.3	5088.5	*27.1*	*28.4*	28.3	US$/kg	759
8536	Electrical apparatus for switching or protecting electrical circuits	3358.2	4383.2	4724.8	*16.5*	*1.6*	*16.1*	US$/kg	772

Mongolia

Imports: CIF, by origin | **Exports: FOB, by last known destination** | **Trade System: General**

Overview:

From 2003 to 2007, Mongolia's exports increased on average by 32.3 percent each year to reach 1.9 bln US$ in 2007 (see table 1 and graph 1). During the same period, imports increased on average by 27.5 percent each year to 2.1 bln US$ in 2007 (see table 2 and graph 1). The trade balance turned from a surplus of 56.7 mln US$ in 2006 to a deficit of 230.5 mln US$ in 2007, largely due to an increase of imports by 42.5 percent. The trade balance was in surplus with Eastern Asia (+641.6 mln US$) and Developed North America (+181.2 mln US$) (see graph 2). However, trade recorded a deficit of 740.4 mln US$ with the Commonwealth of Independent States. Trade, especially exports, was highly concentrated among a few partners (see graph 3). China alone accounted for 74.2 percent of exported goods in 2007. In addition, 6 major partners accounted for 80 percent of imports.

Graph 1: Total imports, exports and trade balance

(Bln US$ by year)

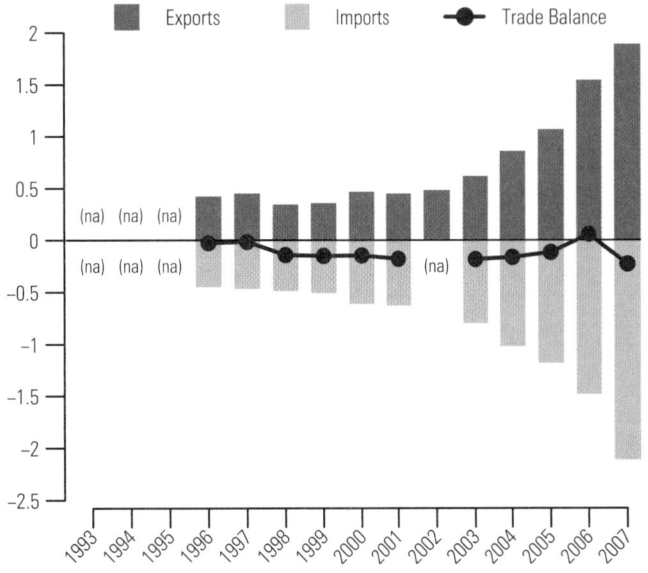

Exports Profile:

Two commodity groups accounted for a large part of Mongolia's exports: inedible crude materials (except fuels), animal and vegetable oils, fats and waxes (SITC sections 2+4) and commodities and transactions not classified elsewhere (SITC section 9) (see table 1). From 2003 to 2007, exports of inedible crude materials (except fuels), animal and vegetable oils, fats and waxes (SITC sections 2+4) increased on average by 50.2 percent each year and accounted for 71.0 percent of total exports in 2007. In addition to China, other major markets for exports were Canada and USA (see table 4). Exports to China were composed of 83.0 percent of inedible crude materials (except fuels), animal and vegetable oils, fats and waxes (SITC sections 2+4) while exports to Canada and USA were largely gold. From 2005 to 2007, the three major exported products were copper ores and concentrates (HS code 2603), gold (including gold plated with platinum) (HS code 7108) and zinc ores and concentrates (HS code 2608) (see table 4). They accounted respectively for 43.0, 12.5 and 9.3 percent of exports in 2007.

Table 1: Exports by SITC sections

(Value in million US$, growth and shares in percentage)

SITC	2007	Avg. Growth rates (%) 2003-2007	2006-2007	2007 share
Total	1 886.6	32.3	22.3	100.0
0+1	28.0	13.9	3.4	1.5
2+4	1 339.0	50.2	34.2	71.0
3	170.1	87.1	141.6	9.0
5	2.6	53.6	67.7	0.1
6	68.1	4.1	2.3	3.6
7	18.1	34.7	5.4	1.0
8	25.8	-31.7	-72.0	1.4
9	234.9	13.8	-13.0	12.4

Table 2: Imports by SITC sections

(Value in million US$, growth and shares in percentage)

SITC	2007	Avg. Growth rates (%) 2003-2007	2006-2007	2007 share
Total	2 117.0	27.5	42.5	100.0
0+1	236.7	22.0	38.9	11.2
2+4	23.7	9.3	25.6	1.1
3	569.3	37.5	31.0	26.9
5	126.5	28.5	56.2	6.0
6	326.4	20.2	46.6	15.4
7	623.6	25.0	48.6	29.5
8	210.7	37.0	52.6	10.0
9	0.1	165.0	15.2	0.0

Table 3: Top 10 export commodities 2005 to 2007

(Value in million US$)

HS code	4-digit heading of Harmonized System 2002	Value (million US$) 2005	2006	2007	Unit value 2005	2006	2007	Unit	SITC code
	All Commodities	1 064.4	1 542.3	1 886.6					
2603	Copper ores and concentrates	326.2	635.4	811.4	0.6	1.1	1.3	US$/kg	283
7108	Gold (including gold plated with platinum)	331.4	270.1	234.9	13.9	17.6	20.3	thsd US$/kg	971
2608	Zinc ores and concentrates	10.2	91.1	175.5	0.4	0.9	1.3	US$/kg	287
5105	Wool and fine or coarse animal hair, carded or combed	62.2	83.0	115.4	56.2	57.0	62.0	US$/kg	268
2701	Coal; briquettes, ovoids and similar solid fuels manufactured from coal	26.6	45.1	115.8	0.0	0.0	0.0	US$/kg	321
2613	Molybdenum ores and concentrates	46.7	47.8	75.9	19.5	14.3	23.8	US$/kg	287
5102	Fine or coarse animal hair, not carded or combed	17.4	66.8	67.3	8.1	18.5	21.1	US$/kg	268
2529	Felspar; leucite and nepheline syenite	25.4	35.1	45.0	0.1	0.1	0.1	US$/kg	278
2709	Petroleum oils, crude	9.3	19.8	53.3	*0.4*	0.4	*0.5*	US$/kg	333
4105	Tanned or crust skins of sheep or lambs, without wool on	16.4	24.5	25.0	*5.9*	5.4	*6.5*	US$/kg	611

Graph 2: Trade Balance by MDG Regions in 2007

(Mln US$)

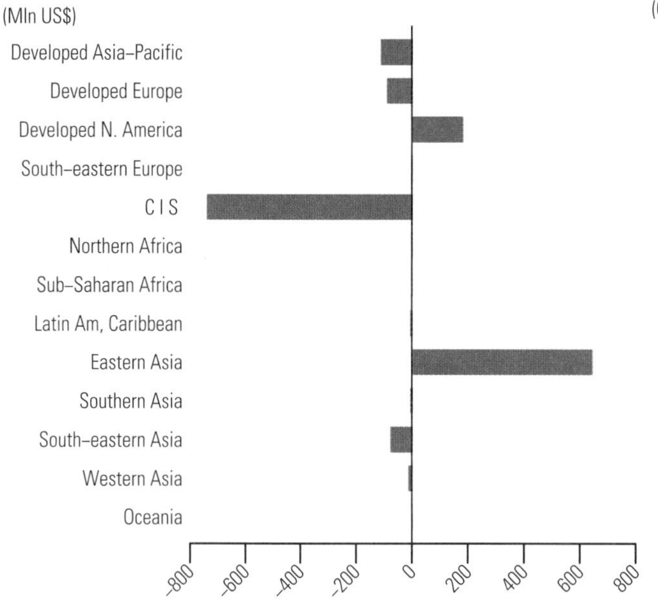

Graph 3: Partner concentration of trade in 2007

(Cumulative share by ranked partners)

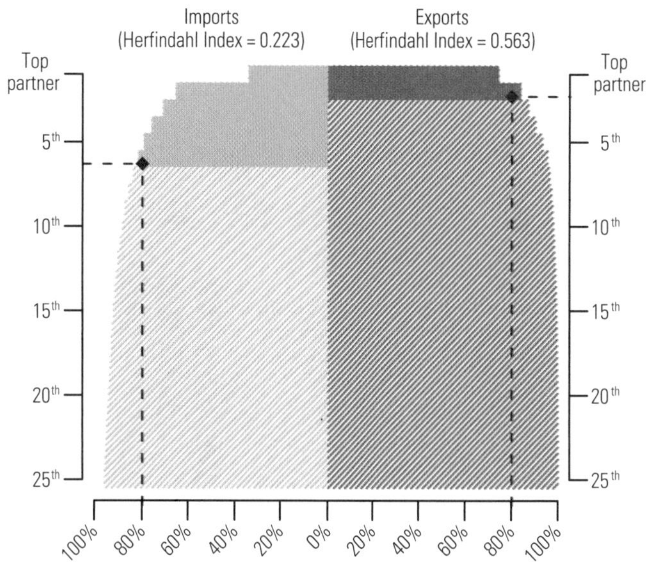

Table 4: Exports by principal countries and SITC sections in 2007

(Value in million US$, percentages of country total)

Country	Total	Shares by SITC sections (%)								
		0 + 1	2 + 4	3	5	6	7	8	9	Total
World	1886.6	1.5	71.0	9.0	0.1	3.6	1.0	1.4	12.4	100
China	1399.8	0.6	83.0	12.1	0.1	4.1	0.2	0.0	...	100
Canada	178.5	0.0	0.0	0.0	...	0.0	0.1	0.2	99.6	100
USA	64.5	0.4	15.9	...	2.1	0.0	0.9	13.1	67.6	100
Russian Federation	57.2	28.6	55.0	2.0	0.0	2.3	10.6	1.5	...	100
Italy	55.8	0.0	87.6	...	...	9.1	0.0	3.3	...	100
Rep. of Korea	40.6	0.7	75.5	0.3	0.0	0.8	0.7	1.2	20.7	100
United Kingdom	17.2	0.0	55.1	...	0.0	2.5	1.5	11.5	29.4	100
Japan	14.4	1.6	76.2	0.0	0.0	16.7	0.1	5.3	...	100
Germany	10.4	0.4	32.7	0.0	0.0	1.9	47.0	18.1	...	100
Netherlands	7.2	0.0	97.7	0.0	...	0.9	0.4	1.0	...	100

Imports Profile:

In 2007, Mongolia's imports increased by 42.5 percent driven largely by machinery and transport equipment (SITC section 7) and manufactured goods classified chiefly by material (SITC section 6) (see table 2). Imports of these commodity groups increased respectively by 48.6 and 46.6 percent and represented 29.5 and 15.4 percent of imports. Mineral fuels, lubricants and related materials (SITC section 3), largely non crude petroleum oils, accounted for 26.9 percent of imported goods. From 2005 to 2007, top imported products were petroleum oils, other than crude (HS code 2710), motor cars and other motor vehicles principally designed for the transport (HS code 8703) and unused postage, revenue or similar stamps of current or new issue (HS code 4907) (see table 5).

Table 5: Top 10 import commodities 2005 to 2007

(Value in million US$)

HS code	4-digit heading of Harmonized System 2002	Value (million US$)			Unit value				SITC code
		2005	2006	2007	2005	2006	2007	Unit	
	All Commodities	1182.6	1485.6	2117.0					
2710	Petroleum oils, other than crude	302.1	422.6	551.3	0.5	0.7	0.7	US$/kg	334
8703	Motor cars and other motor vehicles principally designed for the transport	51.8	81.1	87.3	*3.6*	*3.7*	4.1	thsd US$/unit	781
4907	Unused postage, revenue or similar stamps of current or new issue	10.6	53.8	115.7	*0.0*	1.2		thsd US$/kg	892
8429	Self-propelled bulldozers, angledozers, graders, levellers, scrapers	35.1	16.6	52.7	*98.1*	7.8	43.1	thsd US$/unit	723
8704	Motor vehicles for the transport of goods	22.6	25.3	53.4	*3.6*	*3.4*	4.1	thsd US$/unit	782
8517	Electrical apparatus for line telephony or line telegraphy	19.6	26.6	34.5					764
8474	Machinery for sorting, screening, separating, washing, crushing, grinding	24.7	24.1	23.4					728
8431	Parts suitable for use principally with the machinery of headings 84.25	17.3	21.8	31.3	*6.2*	8.5		US$/kg	723
1101	Wheat or meslin flour	20.0	21.3	26.1	0.2	0.2	0.3	US$/kg	046
1001	Wheat and meslin	15.8	20.1	21.2	0.2	0.2	0.2	US$/kg	041

Montenegro

Imports: CIF, by origin | **Exports: FOB, by last known destination** | **Trade System: Special**

Overview:

After a big drop of 37.2 percent in 2009, the exports of Montenegro bounced back in 2010 by 12.7 percent and continued to grow by 43.7 percent to 627.5 mln US$ in 2011 (see table 1 and graph 1). During the same period, imports showed an increase of 16.6 percent and reached 2.5 bln US$ in 2011 (see table 2 and graph 1). The trade balance recorded a deficit of 1.9 bln US$ in 2011. By MDG regions, trade recorded large deficits with South-eastern Europe (-861.1 mln US$), Developed Europe (-610.1 mln US$) and Eastern Asia (-161.5 mln US$) (see graph 2). By partners, exports were more concentrated than imports: 9 major partners accounted for 80 percent of exports compared to 12 major partners for imports (see graph 3).

Graph 1: Total imports, exports and trade balance

(Bln US$ by year)

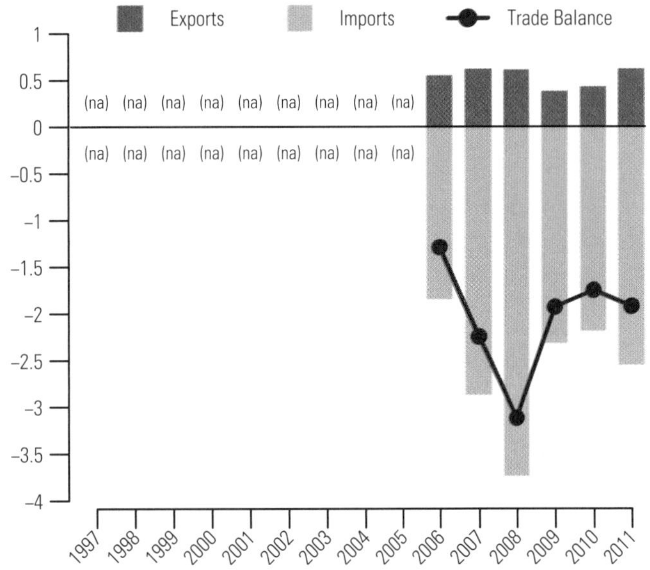

Table 1: Exports by SITC sections

(Value in million US$, growth and shares in percentage)

SITC	2011	Avg. Growth rates (%) 2007-2011	2010-2011	2011 share
Total	627.5	0.0	43.7	100.0
0+1	70.4	8.4	18.3	11.2
2+4	91.2	14.3	50.0	14.5
3	87.5	68.4	98.9	13.9
5	16.8	5.8	-1.6	2.7
6	304.9	-9.7	46.9	48.6
7	33.2	12.2	-7.0	5.3
8	23.5	11.4	98.7	3.7

Table 2: Imports by SITC sections

(Value in million US$, growth and shares in percentage)

SITC	2011	Avg. Growth rates (%) 2007-2011	2010-2011	2011 share
Total	2 544.0	-2.9	16.6	100.0
0+1	583.0	9.0	14.3	22.9
2+4	138.6	14.5	26.9	5.4
3	461.6	1.8	66.9	18.1
5	236.7	2.8	10.1	9.3
6	369.6	-6.4	5.5	14.5
7	442.3	-13.2	-1.6	17.4
8	312.3	-0.3	15.1	12.3
9	0.0	-88.5	...	0.0

Exports Profile:

Manufactured goods classified chiefly by material (SITC section 6) represented 48.6 percent of exported goods in 2011 (see table 1). Other major commodity groups for exports include inedible crude materials (excluding fuels), vegetable and animal oils, fats and waxes (SITC sections 2+4) and mineral fuels, lubricants and related materials (SITC section 3), respectively with 14.5 and 13.9 percent of exports. Major markets for exports included Serbia, Hungary and Croatia (see table 4). Over the last three years, main products for exports included unwrought aluminium (HS code 7601), electrical energy (HS code 2716) and wine of fresh grapes, including fortified wines (HS code 2204) (see table 3).

Table 3: Top 10 export commodities 2009 to 2011

(Value in million US$)

HS code	4-digit heading of Harmonized System 2007	Value (million US$) 2009	2010	2011	Unit value 2009	2010	2011	Unit	SITC code
	All Commodities	387.5	436.6	627.5					
7601	Unwrought aluminium	157.5	172.0	253.1	1.8	2.2	2.6	US$/kg	684
2716	Electrical energy	...	22.5	68.2		*54.8*	64.3	US$/MWh	351
2204	Wine of fresh grapes, including fortified wines	23.2	22.0	25.6			*3.8*	US$/litre	112
4407	Wood sawn or chipped lengthwise, sliced or peeled	14.6	14.4	18.4					248
7224	Other alloy steel in ingots or other primary forms	14.3	16.9	9.1	1.0	0.9	1.3	US$/kg	672
7204	Ferrous waste and scrap; remelting scrap ingots of iron or steel	3.9	9.8	24.9	0.3	0.3	0.4	US$/kg	282
2710	Petroleum oils, other than crude	7.4	14.0	15.7	0.6	0.8	1.0	US$/kg	334
3004	Medicaments (excluding goods of heading 30.02, 30.05 or 30.06)	12.5	8.7	10.7	9.2	7.4	9.2	US$/kg	542
7214	Other bars and rods of iron or non-alloy steel	15.9	4.8	6.2	0.5	0.7	1.2	US$/kg	676
7404	Copper waste and scrap	4.4	10.9	11.3	4.4	6.2	7.0	US$/kg	288

Graph 2: Trade Balance by MDG Regions in 2011

(Mln US$)

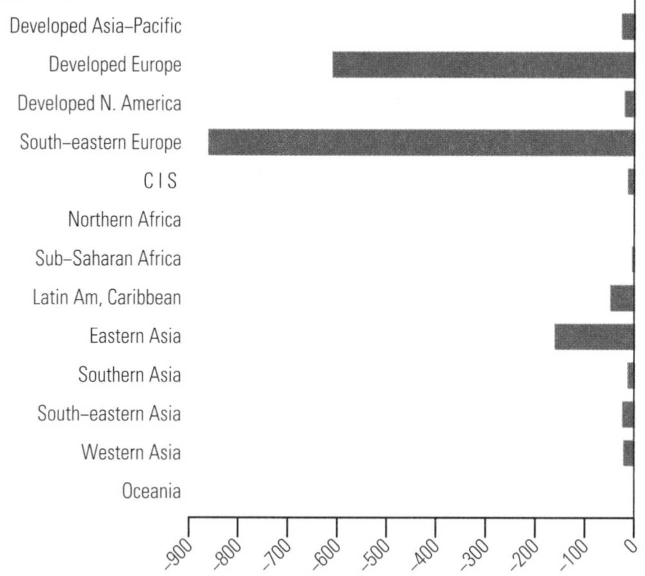

Graph 3: Partner concentration of trade in 2011

(Cumulative share by ranked partners)

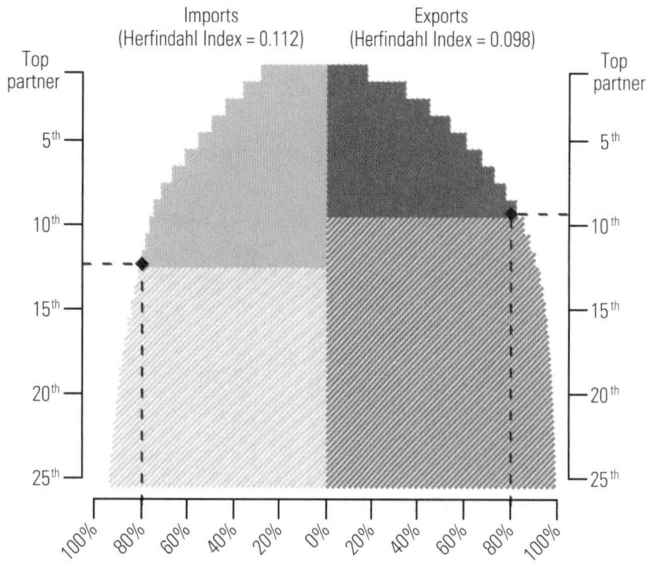

Table 4: Exports by principal countries and SITC sections in 2011

(Value in million US$, percentages of country total)

Country	Total	Shares by SITC sections (%) 0+1	2+4	3	5	6	7	8	9	Total
World	627.5	11.2	14.5	13.9	2.7	48.6	5.3	3.7	...	100
Serbia	110.9	17.6	7.3	41.8	10.6	11.2	7.1	4.4	...	100
Hungary	106.8	0.1	4.3	...	0.0	95.5	0.1	0.0	...	100
Croatia	63.8	1.2	2.1	...	0.7	93.3	2.1	0.6	...	100
Greece	54.6	0.0	1.0	...	0.0	98.9	0.1	0.0	...	100
Italy	43.2	9.0	35.8	0.0	0.0	48.1	6.3	0.7	...	100
Slovenia	42.1	1.5	13.4	37.8	0.8	42.4	3.5	0.6	...	100
Areas, nes	33.5	55.1	28.0	1.6	3.6	6.2	3.6	2.0	...	100
Bosnia Herzegovina	31.1	48.1	23.4	5.1	4.9	7.1	7.3	4.1	...	100
Germany	28.5	5.2	8.2	...	0.0	84.2	1.8	0.6	...	100
Switzerland	20.3	1.2	14.5	80.0	0.0	1.2	2.7	0.4	...	100

Imports Profile:

Montenegro's imports were mainly composed of 22.9 percent of food, live animals, beverages and tobacco (SITC sections 0+1), 18.1 percent of mineral fuels, lubricants and related materials (SITC section 3) and 17.4 percent of machinery and transport equipment (SITC section 7) (see table 2). Over the last three years, top three products for imports were petroleum oils, other than crude (HS code 2710), electrical energy (HS code 2716) and motor cars and other motor vehicles principally designed for the transport (HS code 8703) (see table 5).

Table 5: Top 10 import commodities 2009 to 2011

(Value in million US$)

HS code	4-digit heading of Harmonized System 2007	Value (million US$) 2009	2010	2011	Unit value 2009	2010	2011	Unit	SITC code
	All Commodities	2313.1	2181.9	2544.0					
2710	Petroleum oils, other than crude	157.0	191.3	252.4	0.6	0.7	*1.0*	US$/kg	334
2716	Electrical energy	95.3	39.9	152.1	*82.5*	*57.1*	65.8	US$/MWh	351
8703	Motor cars and other motor vehicles principally designed for the transport	77.0	77.0	89.8	*9.2*	*0.7*	*9.1*	thsd US$/unit	781
3004	Medicaments (excluding goods of heading 30.02, 30.05 or 30.06)	59.4	58.9	62.4	43.7	56.7	58.3	US$/kg	542
2818	Artificial corundum, whether or not chemically defined	17.8	66.1	83.3	0.3	0.4	0.4	US$/kg	285
0203	Meat of swine, fresh, chilled or frozen	54.9	55.2	56.8	3.1	2.9	3.2	US$/kg	012
9403	Other furniture and parts thereof	40.3	34.5	37.3					821
2202	Waters with added sugar	35.1	33.8	40.9	*1.1*	*1.1*	*0.6*	US$/litre	111
2523	Portland cement, aluminous cement, slag cement	44.4	32.6	29.6	0.1	0.1	0.1	US$/kg	661
0901	Coffee, whether or not roasted or decaffeinated	24.8	32.4	31.2	2.0	2.6	3.6	US$/kg	071

Montserrat

Imports: CIF, by origin | **Exports: FOB, by last known destination** | **Trade System: Special**

Overview:

After two years of continuous growth marked by a peak of 4.1 mln US$ in 2008, the value of the exports of Montserrat dropped in 2009 and 2010 to reach 1.1 mln US$ (see table 1 and graph 1). Imports recorded a peak of 38.0 mln US$ in 2008 before dropping by 22.2 percent in 2009 to 29.6 mln US$ (see table 2 and graph 1). The trade balance recorded a deficit of 26.5 mln US$ in 2009 (see graph 1). Developed North America accounted with 20.3 mln US$ for a major part of this deficit (see graph 2). Trade was also in deficit with Latin America and the Caribbean (-2.2 mln US$) and Developed Europe (-2.1 mln US$). Montserrat's trade was highly concentrated among a few countries for exports in 2010: 4 major partners accounted for 80 percent of exports (see graph 3).

Graph 1: Total imports, exports and trade balance

(Mln US$ by year)

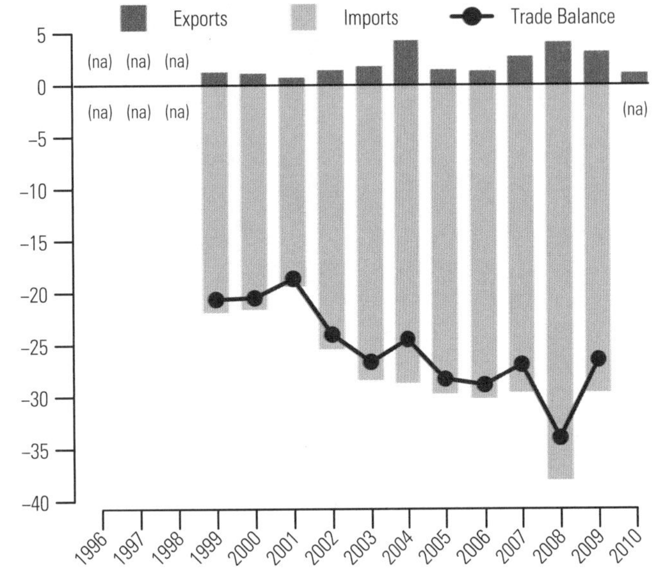

Exports Profile:

In 2010, exported goods were largely inedible crude materials (except fuels), animal and vegetable oils, fats and waxes (SITC sections 2+4) and machinery and transport equipment (SITC section 7) (see table 1). They accounted for, respectively, 56.8 and 31.1 percent of exports in 2010. USA, France and Anguilla were the top three markets for exports (see table 4). From 2008 to 2010, the three major exported products were natural sands of all kinds (HS code 2505), surveying (including photogrammetrical surveying), hydrographic instruments (HS code 9015) and self-propelled bulldozers, angledozers, graders, levellers, scrapers (HS code 8429) (see table 3).

Table 1: Exports by SITC sections

(Value in million US$, growth and shares in percentage)

SITC	2010	Avg. Growth rates (%) 2006-2010	2009-2010	2010 share
Total	1.1	-4.3	-65.1	100.0
0+1	0.0	-58.8	-93.3	0.0
2+4	0.6	-4.9	-42.6	56.8
5	0.0	27.2	473.0	0.1
6	0.0	-17.8	-92.1	0.7
7	0.3	14.2	-72.9	31.1
8	0.0	-48.7	-95.9	1.2
9	0.1	-4.2	-70.9	10.1

Table 2: Imports by SITC sections

(Value in million US$, growth and shares in percentage)

SITC	2009	Avg. Growth rates (%) 2006-2009	2008-2009	2009 share
Total	29.6	-0.7	-22.2	100.0
0+1	5.9	4.7	0.2	19.8
2+4	0.6	-8.5	-22.7	2.0
3	7.9	-3.5	-41.5	26.7
5	1.8	4.3	-6.2	6.1
6	5.2	4.0	-7.9	17.6
7	6.0	-4.9	-20.3	20.2
8	2.2	-0.2	-18.5	7.4
9	0.1	-24.0	-57.3	0.3

Table 3: Top 10 export commodities 2008 to 2010

(Value in million US$)

HS code	4-digit heading of Harmonized System 2002	Value (million US$) 2008	2009	2010	Unit value 2008	2009	2010	Unit	SITC code
	All Commodities	4.1	3.1	1.1					
2505	Natural sands of all kinds	1.5	1.1	0.6	0.0	0.0		US$/kg	273
9999	Commodities not specified according to kind	0.9	0.4	0.1					931
9015	Surveying (including photogrammetrical surveying), hydrographic	0.5	0.0	0.0			*90.0*	US$/kg	874
8429	Self-propelled bulldozers, angledozers, graders, levellers, scrapers	0.0	0.4	...	*0.0*	*105.9*		thsd US$/unit	723
8474	Machinery for sorting, screening, separating, washing, crushing, grinding	0.0	0.3	0.0					728
2804	Hydrogen, rare gases and other non-metals	0.3	...	...					522
8704	Motor vehicles for the transport of goods	...	...	0.2					782
9026	Instruments and apparatus for measuring or checking the flow, level	...	0.2	...					874
8426	Ships' derricks; cranes, including cable cranes; mobile lifting frames	...	0.2	...		*50.3*		thsd US$/unit	744
9027	Instruments and apparatus for physical or chemical analysis	...	0.1	0.0					874

Graph 2: Trade Balance by MDG Regions in 2009

(Mln US$)

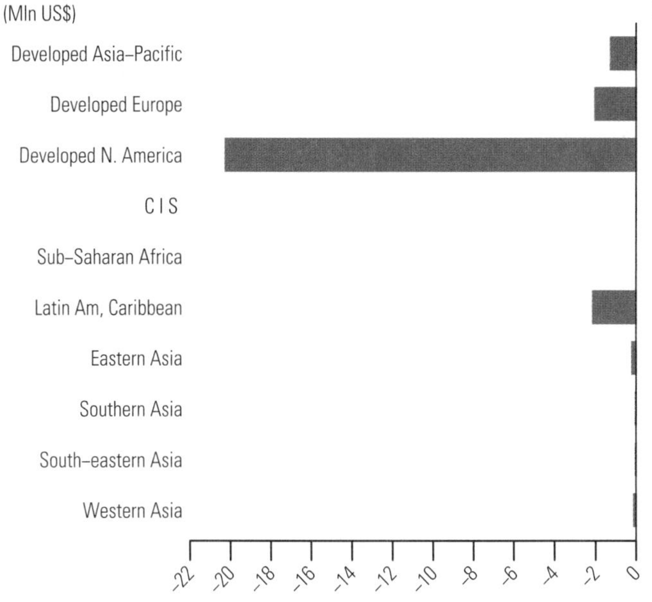

Graph 3: Partner concentration of trade in 2010

(Cumulative share by ranked partners)

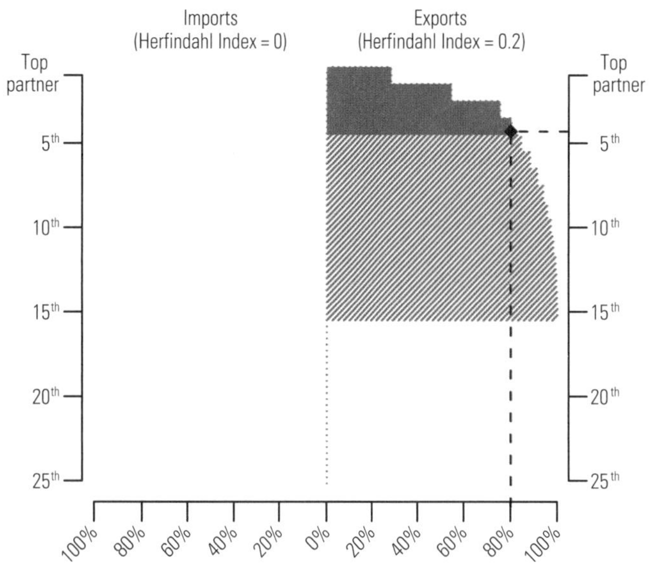

Table 4: Exports by principal countries and SITC sections in 2010

(Value in million US$, percentages of country total)

Country	Total	Shares by SITC sections (%) 0+1	2+4	3	5	6	7	8	9	Total
World	1.1	0.0	56.8	...	0.1	0.7	31.1	1.2	10.1	100
USA	0.3	0.0	0.1	...	...	0.3	87.9	2.0	9.7	100
France	0.3	0.0	100.0	...	...	...	...	...	...	100
Anguilla	0.2	0.0	99.5	...	...	0.3	0.3	...	...	100
United Kingdom	0.1	0.0	0.0	...	...	...	10.6	...	89.4	100
Br. Virgin Isds	0.0	0.0	97.3	...	...	2.7	...	...	...	100
Saint Kitts and Nevis	0.0	0.3	80.0	...	1.7	0.1	2.4	15.6	...	100
Neth. Antilles	0.0	0.0	86.9	...	...	4.5	6.3	...	2.2	100
Antigua and Barbuda	0.0	0.0	3.2	...	...	2.5	94.2	0.1	...	100
Dominica	0.0	0.0	0.3	...	...	...	58.0	0.1	41.6	100
Saint Lucia	0.0	0.0	0.0	...	...	...	33.3	...	66.7	100

Imports Profile:

In 2009, the top commodity group for imports was mineral fuels, lubricants and related materials (SITC section 3) (see table 2). Even though with a decrease of 41.5 percent, it accounted for 26.7 percent of total imports. Other major commodities were machinery and transport equipment (SITC section 7) with 20.2 percent and food, live animals, beverages and tobacco (SITC sections 0+1) with 19.8 percent. In addition to petroleum oils, other than crude (HS code 2710), other major products for imports from 2007 to 2009 included motor cars and other motor vehicles principally designed for the transport (HS code 8703) and meat and edible offal, of the poultry of heading 01.05 (HS code 0207) (see table 5).

Table 5: Top 10 import commodities 2007 to 2009

(Value in million US$)

HS code	4-digit heading of Harmonized System 2002	Value (million US$) 2007	2008	2009	Unit value 2007	2008	2009	Unit	SITC code
	All Commodities	29.6	38.0	29.6					
2710	Petroleum oils, other than crude	8.1	12.8	7.4	0.7	*0.9*	0.5	US$/kg	334
8703	Motor cars and other motor vehicles principally designed for the transport	1.1	1.2	1.4	*13.1*	*15.9*	*15.7*	thsd US$/unit	781
0207	Meat and edible offal, of the poultry of heading 01.05	0.6	0.8	0.8	2.3	2.6	2.8	US$/kg	012
2523	Portland cement, aluminous cement, slag cement	0.7	0.6	0.8	0.1	0.1	0.2	US$/kg	661
8704	Motor vehicles for the transport of goods	0.6	0.8	0.5		*32.3*		thsd US$/unit	782
8471	Automatic data processing machines and units thereof	0.5	0.7	0.6					752
2711	Petroleum gases and other gaseous hydrocarbons	0.4	0.7	0.5	0.7	0.2	0.6	US$/kg	343
2203	Beer made from malt	0.4	0.5	0.5	*1.7*	*1.7*	*1.2*	US$/litre	112
7214	Other bars and rods of iron or non-alloy steel	0.2	0.8	0.4	1.0	1.5	0.8	US$/kg	676
2202	Waters with added sugar	0.5	0.4	0.4	*1.5*	*1.5*	*1.5*	US$/litre	111

Imports: CIF, by origin | **Exports: FOB, by last known destination** | **Trade System: Special**

Overview:

After several years of continuous growth marked by a peak of 20.3 bln US$ in 2008, Morocco's exports decreased sharply in 2009 by 30.7 percent but bounced back in 2010 by 26.3 percent to 17.8 bln US$, still well below it 2008 level (see table 1 and graph 1). Imports exhibited a less pronounced development with an increase of 7.6 percent to reach 35.4 bln US$ in 2010 (see table 2 and graph 1). The trade balance recorded a deficit amounting to 17.6 bln US$ (see graph 1). Trade was in deficit with most of the MDG regions (see graph 2). Significant trade deficits were recorded with Developed Europe (-6.7 bln US$), Western Asia (-3.3 bln US$) and Eastern Asia (-3.2 bln US$) among others (see graph 2). Morocco's trade was diversified across partners: in 2010, 18 major partners accounted for 80 percent of exports and imports (see graph 3).

Graph 1: Total imports, exports and trade balance

(Bln US$ by year)

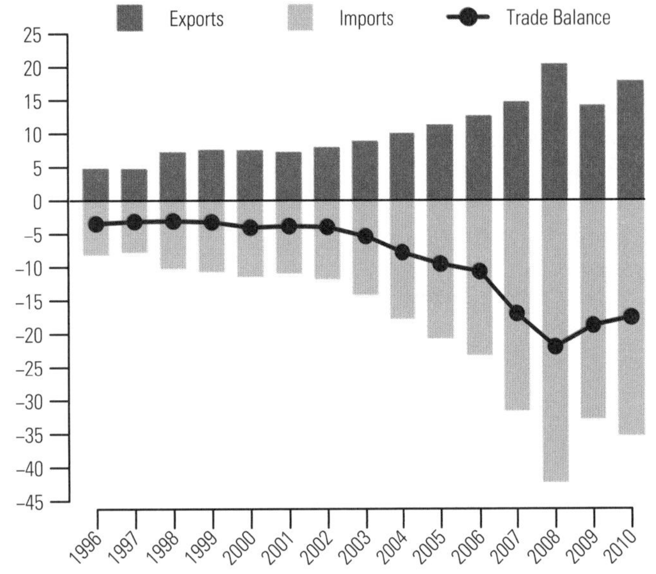

Exports Profile:

In 2010, Morocco's exports were composed of 20.6 percent of miscellaneous manufactured articles (SITC section 8), 19.6 percent of chemical and related products, n.e.s. (SITC section 5) and 19.0 percent of machinery and transport equipment (SITC section 7) (see table 1).The three largest markets for exports were France, Spain and India (see table 4). The majority of exports to India were chemicals and related products, n.e.s. (SITC section 5). From 2008 to 2010, top products for exports were diphosphorus pentaoxide; phosphoric acid (HS code 2809), insulated (including enamelled or anodised) wire, cable (HS code 8544) and natural calcium phosphates (HS code 2510) (see table 3).

Table 1: Exports by SITC sections

(Value in million US$, growth and shares in percentage)

SITC	2010	Avg. Growth rates (%) 2006-2010	2009-2010	2010 share
Total	17764.8	9.1	26.3	100.0
0+1	3205.6	8.6	1.4	18.0
2+4	2146.0	13.5	77.8	12.1
3	588.1	5.7	16.7	3.3
5	3476.6	20.0	77.8	19.6
6	1102.9	6.3	20.6	6.2
7	3377.6	11.9	30.9	19.0
8	3665.9	-0.6	-1.0	20.6
9	202.1	76.0	390.8	1.1

Table 2: Imports by SITC sections

(Value in million US$, growth and shares in percentage)

SITC	2010	Avg. Growth rates (%) 2006-2010	2009-2010	2010 share
Total	35378.9	11.0	7.6	100.0
0+1	3470.8	18.9	14.4	9.8
2+4	1922.0	7.7	11.3	5.4
3	8132.6	12.7	20.6	23.0
5	3504.2	11.6	12.4	9.9
6	6149.2	5.6	1.9	17.4
7	9860.1	11.2	-2.5	27.9
8	2274.4	12.3	14.8	6.4
9	65.6	34.2	-49.9	0.2

Table 3: Top 10 export commodities 2008 to 2010

(Value in million US$)

HS code	4-digit heading of Harmonized System 2002	Value (million US$) 2008	2009	2010	Unit value 2008	2009	2010	Unit	SITC code
	All Commodities	20305.7	14068.9	17764.8					
2809	Diphosphorus pentaoxide; phosphoric acid	2976.7	1002.2	1633.3	1.8	0.5	0.7	US$/kg	522
8544	Insulated (including enamelled or anodised) wire, cable	1491.4	1148.4	1659.5	*20.4*	*17.7*	*19.4*	US$/kg	773
2510	Natural calcium phosphates	2305.6	554.3	1067.0	0.2	0.1	0.1	US$/kg	272
6204	Women's or girls' suits, ensembles, jackets, blazers, dresses, skirts	963.4	933.2	957.9					842
3105	Mineral or chemical fertilisers	926.3	573.0	1268.7	1.0	0.3	0.5	US$/kg	562
1604	Prepared or preserved fish; caviar	589.9	602.2	590.0	4.0	*4.2*	3.9	US$/kg	037
8541	Diodes, transistors and similar semiconductor devices	587.5	486.6	583.8					776
0307	Molluscs, whether in shell or not	585.0	430.6	367.1	6.9	4.4	5.1	US$/kg	036
6203	Men's or boys' suits, ensembles, jackets, blazers, trousers	515.9	438.0	409.5	18.6			US$/unit	841
0805	Citrus fruit, fresh or dried	420.7	312.9	381.5	0.7	0.7	*0.7*	US$/kg	057

Graph 2: Trade Balance by MDG Regions in 2010

(Bln US$)

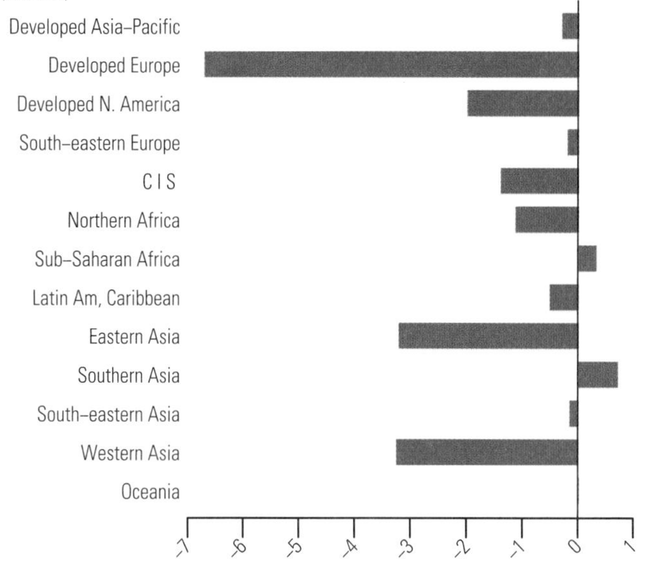

Graph 3: Partner concentration of trade in 2010

(Cumulative share by ranked partners)

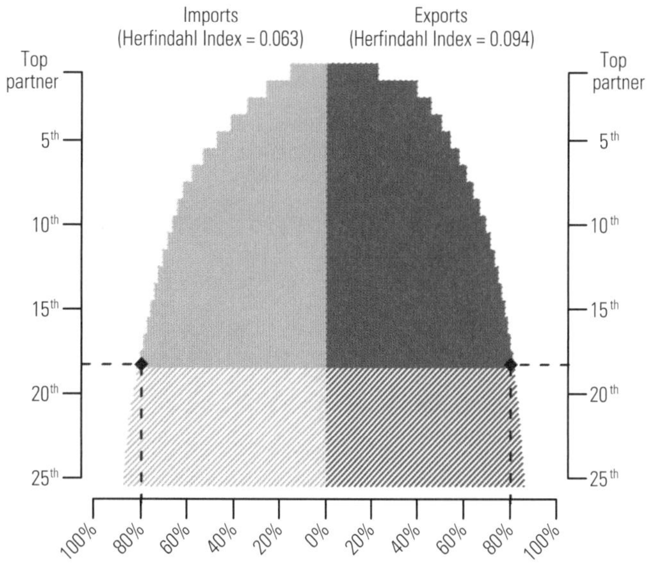

Table 4: Exports by principal countries and SITC sections in 2010

(Value in million US$, percentages of country total)

Country	Total	Shares by SITC sections (%) 0 + 1	2 + 4	3	5	6	7	8	9	Total
World	17764.8	18.0	12.1	3.3	19.6	6.2	19.0	20.6	1.1	100
France	3991.8	16.2	3.2	0.0	6.6	5.6	34.8	33.7	0.0	100
Spain	3004.3	21.2	7.9	0.0	2.4	8.8	15.4	44.2	...	100
India	1075.6	0.0	12.0	...	87.8	0.1	0.1	0.0	...	100
Italy	798.6	22.2	8.2	...	10.1	6.0	33.9	19.5	0.0	100
Brazil	670.4	4.5	7.5	10.7	76.9	0.3	0.0	0.0	...	100
USA	669.9	16.5	47.0	...	12.7	1.9	16.8	5.1	...	100
Germany	556.4	23.5	7.0	...	11.3	7.1	17.5	33.5	...	100
United Kingdom	515.5	17.3	3.4	...	11.7	1.6	16.9	49.2	...	100
Netherlands	501.0	48.6	6.8	23.8	6.2	4.6	3.9	6.2	0.0	100
Belgium	473.3	10.9	16.2	15.1	43.9	4.0	2.8	7.2	...	100

Imports Profile:

In 2010, Morocco's imports were composed of 27.9 percent of machinery and transport equipment (SITC section 7), 23.0 percent of mineral fuels, lubricants and related materials (SITC section 3) and 17.4 percent of manufactured goods classified chiefly by material (SITC section 6) (see table 2). From 2008 to 2010, petroleum products were the top three products for imports: petroleum oils, crude (HS code 2709), petroleum oils, other than crude (HS code 2710) and petroleum gases and other gaseous hydrocarbons (HS code 2711) (see table 5).

Table 5: Top 10 import commodities 2008 to 2010

(Value in million US$)

HS code	4-digit heading of Harmonized System 2002	Value (million US$) 2008	2009	2010	Unit value 2008	2009	2010	Unit	SITC code
	All Commodities	42322.0	32882.1	35378.9					
2709	Petroleum oils, crude	3983.4	2138.6	2979.6	0.7	0.4	0.6	US$/kg	333
2710	Petroleum oils, other than crude	2530.5	2214.4	2633.3	*0.9*	*0.5*	*0.6*	US$/kg	334
2711	Petroleum gases and other gaseous hydrocarbons	1611.5	1266.9	1671.3		*0.5*	0.7	US$/kg	343
8703	Motor cars and other motor vehicles principally designed for the transport	1434.8	1181.7	1279.3	*11.8*	*18.1*	*20.4*	thsd US$/unit	781
1001	Wheat and meslin	1613.5	683.1	878.5	0.4	0.3	0.3	US$/kg	041
2503	Sulphur of all kinds	1608.2	187.2	365.7	0.5	0.1	0.1	US$/kg	274
7207	Semi-finished products of iron or non-alloy steel	781.8	460.9	467.6	0.8	0.4	*0.5*	US$/kg	672
8544	Insulated (including enamelled or anodised) wire, cable	683.5	395.5	478.1	*13.1*	*11.3*	*12.5*	US$/kg	773
2701	Coal; briquettes, ovoids and similar solid fuels manufactured from coal	667.3	490.7	377.7	0.1	0.1	0.1	US$/kg	321
1005	Maize (corn)	530.2	358.0	444.7	0.3	0.2	0.2	US$/kg	044

Mozambique

Imports: CIF, by origin	Exports: FOB, by last known destination	Trade System: General

Overview:

After several years of continuous growth marked by a peak of 2.7 bln US$ in 2008, the value of the exports of Mozambique dropped in 2009 but increased again in 2010 by 4.5 percent to amount to 2.2 bln US$, still well below its 2008 level (see table 1 and graph 1). Imports, on the other hand, continued to decrease (in 2010 by 5.3 percent) to reach 3.6 bln US$. This resulted in a trade deficit of 1.3 bln US$ in 2010, slightly lower than the 2009 deficit of 1.6 bln US$ (see graph 1). This deficit came largely from trade with Sub-Saharan Africa (-0.8 bln US$), Southern Asia (-0.2 bln US$) and Western Asia (-0.2 bln US$) (see graph 2). Trade, however, recorded a surplus with Developed Europe (+0.3 bln US$). Exports were more concentrated among partners: in 2010, 4 major partners accounted for 80 percent of exported goods compared to 11 major partners for imports (see graph 3).

Graph 1: Total imports, exports and trade balance

(Bln US$ by year)

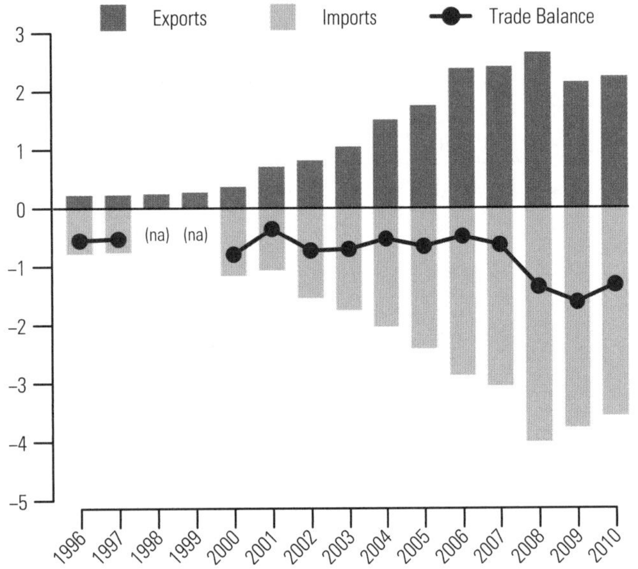

Table 1: Exports by SITC sections

(Value in million US$, growth and shares in percentage)

SITC	2010	Avg. Growth rates (%) 2006-2010	Avg. Growth rates (%) 2009-2010	2010 share
Total	2243.1	-1.5	4.5	100.0
0+1	312.8	-2.3	-29.5	13.9
2+4	163.6	6.5	-18.1	7.3
3	447.4	6.4	19.6	19.9
5	1.6	-2.0	-72.4	0.1
6	1174.3	-4.6	4245.3	52.4
7	38.5	-16.6	-77.8	1.7
8	20.5	-3.1	-58.6	0.9
9	84.2	20.8	-90.4	3.8

Table 2: Imports by SITC sections

(Value in million US$, growth and shares in percentage)

SITC	2010	Avg. Growth rates (%) 2006-2010	Avg. Growth rates (%) 2009-2010	2010 share
Total	3564.2	5.6	-5.3	100.0
0+1	336.4	-0.8	-32.7	9.4
2+4	126.0	11.0	-9.3	3.5
3	710.2	10.0	22.2	19.9
5	240.8	6.4	-11.3	6.8
6	448.7	7.6	-11.9	12.6
7	927.3	6.9	-14.6	26.0
8	157.7	1.7	-24.7	4.4
9	617.2	1.9	31.8	17.3

Exports Profile:

In 2010, manufactured goods classified chiefly by material (SITC section 6) was the largest commodity group for exports and accounted for 52.4 percent of exported goods (see table 1). Other major commodity groups included mineral fuels, lubricants and related materials (SITC section 3) and food, live animals, beverages and tobacco (SITC sections 0+1) with respectively 19.9 percent and 13.9 percent of exports. Netherlands, the top partner for exports, accounted for 52.7 percent of exported goods (see table 4). Other major destinations for exports in 2010 included South Africa and Portugal. A large share of exports to Netherlands (98.1 percent) were manufactured goods classified chiefly by material (SITC section 6). Top exported products over the last three years were unwrought aluminium (HS code 7601), electrical energy (HS code 2716) and unmanufactured tobacco; tobacco refuse (HS code 2401) (see table 3).

Table 3: Top 10 export commodities 2008 to 2010

(Value in million US$)

HS code	4-digit heading of Harmonized System 2002	Value (million US$) 2008	Value (million US$) 2009	Value (million US$) 2010	Unit value 2008	Unit value 2009	Unit value 2010	Unit	SITC code
	All Commodities	2653.3	2147.2	2243.1					
7601	Unwrought aluminium	1451.8	...	1159.6	*2.4*		*1.8*	US$/kg	684
9999	Commodities not specified according to kind	199.0	867.7	83.7					931
2716	Electrical energy	226.4	274.4	276.5	*49.9*	*79.0*	*54.8*	US$/MWh	351
2401	Unmanufactured tobacco; tobacco refuse	193.0	179.3	142.6	*3.4*	*4.1*	*4.8*	US$/kg	121
2711	Petroleum gases and other gaseous hydrocarbons	4.5	90.2	135.4					343
0306	Crustaceans, whether in shell or not	68.7	60.3	52.3	*6.8*	*7.1*	*6.3*	US$/kg	036
1207	Other oil seeds and oleaginous fruits	37.1	45.3	20.1					222
2710	Petroleum oils, other than crude	56.0	8.8	35.0					334
4407	Wood sawn or chipped lengthwise, sliced or peeled	25.9	28.7	43.4	*546.5*		*713.0*	US$/m^3	248
2614	Titanium ores and concentrates	28.8	43.8	19.7		*0.5*	*0.6*	US$/kg	287

Graph 2: Trade Balance by MDG Regions in 2010

(Mln US$)

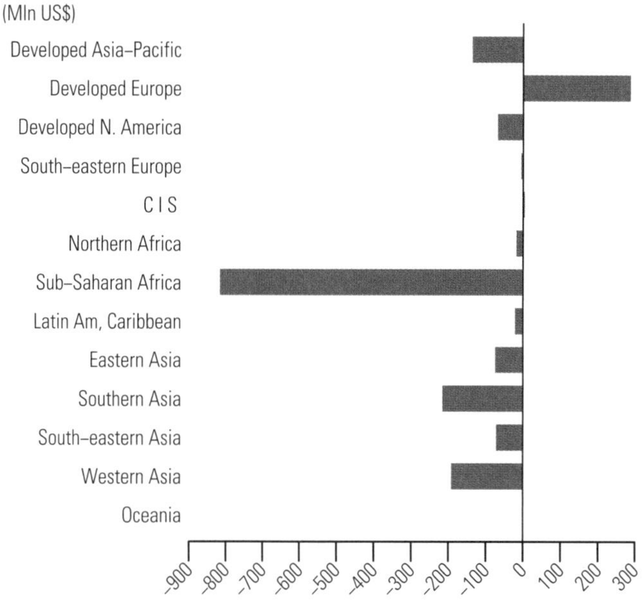

Graph 3: Partner concentration of trade in 2010

(Cumulative share by ranked partners)

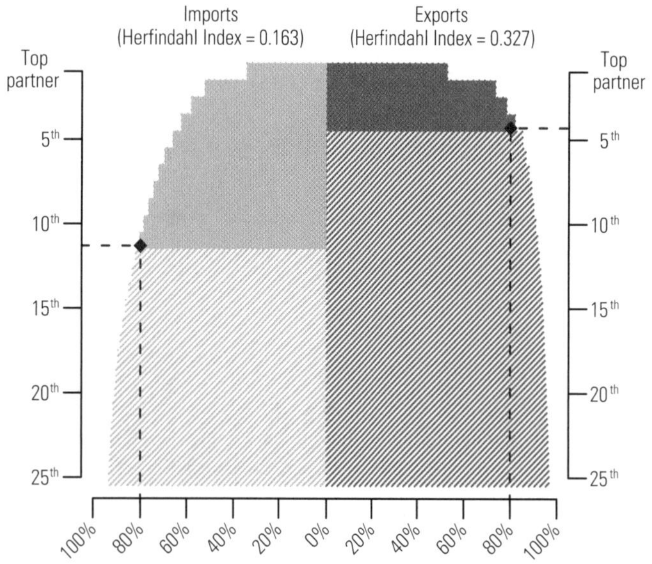

Table 4: Exports by principal countries and SITC sections in 2010

(Value in million US$, percentages of country total)

Country	Total	Shares by SITC sections (%) 0 + 1	2 + 4	3	5	6	7	8	9	Total
World	2243.1	13.9	7.3	19.9	0.1	52.4	1.7	0.9	3.8	100
Netherlands	1181.9	1.9	0.0	...	...	98.1	0.0	...	...	100
South Africa	467.2	8.7	2.3	81.2	0.0	1.0	3.0	3.7	0.0	100
Portugal	108.3	21.4	0.9	...	0.1	0.1	0.3	0.0	77.1	100
China	79.6	8.1	90.6	...	...	1.2	0.1	0.0	...	100
Zimbabwe	72.1	23.8	0.0	74.0	0.4	1.0	0.7	0.0	...	100
Spain	30.6	83.6	14.6	...	...	1.6	0.1	0.0	...	100
India	30.4	81.4	11.5	...	0.0	6.5	0.3	0.3	...	100
Malawi	27.0	53.0	5.1	35.0	0.4	3.4	1.7	1.4	...	100
Germany	20.4	98.8	1.1	...	0.0	0.1	0.0	...	...	100
Areas, nes	19.4	21.6	12.7	14.0	3.1	5.1	36.2	5.8	1.5	100

Imports Profile:

Imports of machinery and transport equipment (SITC section 7) decreased by 14.6 percent and accounted for 26.0 percent of imported goods (see table 2). Imports of mineral fuels, lubricants and related materials (SITC section 3), on the other hand, increased by 22.2 percent and represented 19.9 percent of imported goods. Other major commodity groups included commodities and transactions not classified elsewhere (SITC section 9) and manufactured goods classified chiefly by material (SITC section 6) respectively with 17.3 and 12.6 percent of imports in 2010. Top imported products over the last three years were petroleum oils, other than crude (HS code 2710), motor vehicles for the transport of goods (HS code 8704) and electrical energy (HS code 2716) (see table 5).

Table 5: Top 10 import commodities 2008 to 2010

(Value in million US$)

HS code	4-digit heading of Harmonized System 2002	Value (million US$) 2008	2009	2010	Unit value 2008	2009	2010	Unit	SITC code
	All Commodities	4007.8	3764.2	3564.2					
9999	Commodities not specified according to kind	674.9	468.3	617.2					931
2710	Petroleum oils, other than crude	650.8	411.5	520.6					334
8704	Motor vehicles for the transport of goods	168.9	180.9	146.6					782
2716	Electrical energy	122.1	127.3	157.4	*53.2*	*82.5*	*57.1*	US$/MWh	351
1006	Rice	114.5	152.3	74.1	*0.6*	*1.0*	*0.9*	US$/kg	042
8703	Motor cars and other motor vehicles principally designed for the transport	96.6	102.5	79.3		*17.6*	*17.8*	thsd US$/unit	781
1001	Wheat and meslin	106.2	96.9	64.2	*0.3*	*0.4*	*0.3*	US$/kg	041
2523	Portland cement, aluminous cement, slag cement	53.9	74.8	55.2					661
1511	Palm oil and its fractions	70.9	50.9	52.3	*0.7*		*0.7*	US$/kg	422
8701	Tractors (other than tractors of heading 87.09)	48.3	50.4	37.3					722

Namibia

Imports: CIF, by origin | **Exports: FOB, by last known destination** | **Trade System: General**

Overview:

From 2004 to 2008, both Namibia's exports and imports increased on average by 18.0 percent each year and amounted to 4.7 bln US$ (see tables 1, 2 and graph 1). The trade balance recorded a surplus of 40.8 mln US$ as compared to 14.3 mln US$ in 2007 (see graph 1). By MDG regions, trade recorded a large deficit with Sub-Saharan Africa (-1.2 bln US$) (see graph 2). However, large surpluses were recorded with Developed Europe (+784.2 mln US$) and Developed North America (+493.0 mln US$). In 2008, trade, especially imports, was very concentrated among a few partners: 8 major partners (respectively 5) accounted for 80 percent of exports (respectively imports) (see graph 3).

Graph 1: Total imports, exports and trade balance

(Bln US$ by year)

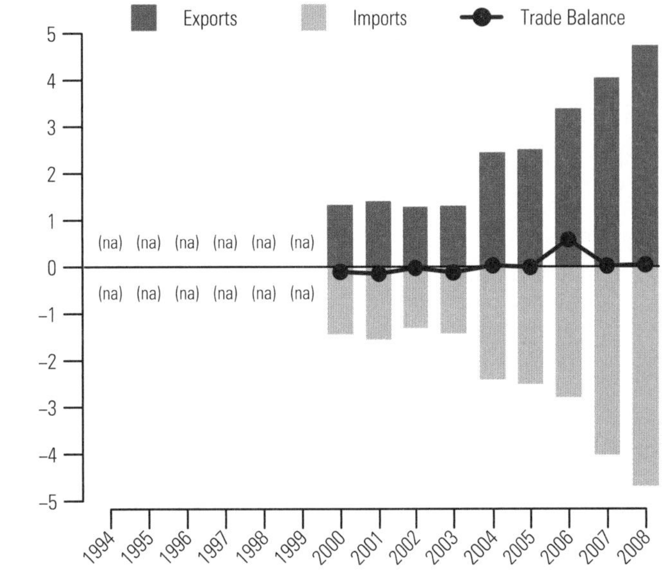

Table 1: Exports by SITC sections

(Value in million US$, growth and shares in percentage)

SITC	2008	Avg. Growth rates (%) 2004-2008	2007-2008	2008 share
Total	4729.3	18.0	17.1	100.0
0+1	1048.4	11.6	10.9	22.2
2+4	1050.6	32.4	60.6	22.2
3	21.0	13.7	26.6	0.4
5	35.6	-16.9	-60.6	0.8
6	1314.7	8.9	-15.5	27.8
7	288.6	21.4	3.0	6.1
8	890.7	41.6	111.0	18.8
9	79.8	14.3	6.8	1.7

Table 2: Imports by SITC sections

(Value in million US$, growth and shares in percentage)

SITC	2008	Avg. Growth rates (%) 2004-2008	2007-2008	2008 share
Total	4688.6	18.0	16.5	100.0
0+1	626.0	9.9	4.4	13.4
2+4	88.8	16.1	54.2	1.9
3	637.7	65.9	53.1	13.6
5	510.7	16.9	38.7	10.9
6	876.5	21.2	30.6	18.7
7	1456.5	14.2	5.3	31.1
8	477.5	12.3	-7.0	10.2
9	14.9	-1.8	-5.8	0.3

Exports Profile:

In 2008, exports of manufactured goods classified chiefly by material (SITC section 6) dropped by 15.5 percent and accounted for 27.8 percent of exported goods (see table 1). Other major commodity groups included food, live animals, beverages and tobacco (SITC sections 0+1) and inedible crude materials (except fuels), animal and vegetable oils, fats and waxes (SITC sections 2+4), and accounted for 22.2 percent of exports each. South Africa, the largest market for exports, was the destination for 31.8 percent of exported goods in 2008 (see table 4). A large share of exports to the United Kingdom (96.5 percent) were manufactured goods classified chiefly by material (SITC section 6). From 2006 to 2008, top exported commodities were diamonds, whether or not worked, but not mounted or set (HS code 7102), unused postage, revenue or similar stamps of current or new issue (HS code 4907) and unwrought zinc (HS code 7901) (see table 3).

Table 3: Top 10 export commodities 2006 to 2008

(Value in million US$)

HS code	4-digit heading of Harmonized System 2002	Value (million US$) 2006	2007	2008	Unit value 2006	2007	2008	Unit	SITC code
	All Commodities	3375.9	4040.3	4729.3					
7102	Diamonds, whether or not worked, but not mounted or set	978.4	805.7	900.2					667
4907	Unused postage, revenue or similar stamps of current or new issue	291.9	356.6	806.5	26.2	23.8	39.4	thsd US$/kg	892
7901	Unwrought zinc	399.1	616.6	276.1	2.9	*3.1*	1.9	US$/kg	686
2612	Uranium or thorium ores and concentrates	163.0	350.3	741.7	70.9		151.3	US$/kg	286
0303	Fish, frozen, excluding fish fillets	327.7	317.7	326.7	0.9	*1.6*	*0.3*	US$/kg	034
7402	Unrefined copper; copper anodes for electrolytic refining	148.9	142.1	153.7	7.1	4.0	1.5	US$/kg	682
2203	Beer made from malt	85.4	110.5	114.8	*0.8*	*0.8*	*0.8*	US$/litre	112
0304	Fish fillets and other fish meat (whether or not minced)	66.7	93.8	149.0	3.4	1.6	2.5	US$/kg	034
2608	Zinc ores and concentrates	2.2	103.2	73.2	0.7	1.1	0.8	US$/kg	287
0102	Live bovine animals	65.8	70.5	39.6	*487.6*	*644.5*	*736.3*	US$/unit	001

Graph 2: Trade Balance by MDG Regions in 2008

(Bln US$)

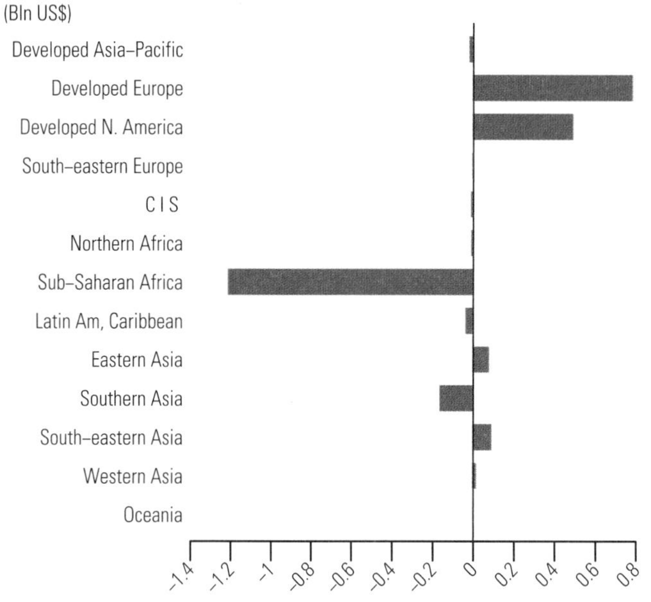

Graph 3: Partner concentration of trade in 2008

(Cumulative share by ranked partners)

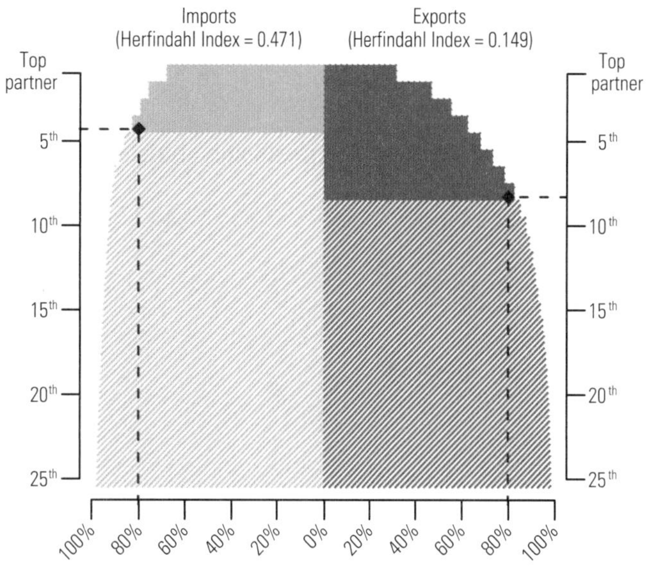

Table 4: Exports by principal countries and SITC sections in 2008

(Value in million US$, percentages of country total)

Country	Total	Shares by SITC sections (%) 0+1	2+4	3	5	6	7	8	9	Total
World	4729.3	22.2	22.2	0.4	0.8	27.8	6.1	18.8	1.7	100
South Africa	1505.0	24.6	7.9	0.1	0.6	4.2	3.5	54.5	4.6	100
United Kingdom	709.7	2.6	0.0	0.0	0.0	96.5	0.3	0.0	0.5	100
Angola	405.6	18.9	1.7	1.0	4.7	15.0	45.1	13.3	0.2	100
Canada	334.2	0.2	99.4	0.0	0.0	0.0	0.2	0.0	0.0	100
USA	260.8	18.4	75.4	0.0	0.0	5.1	0.5	0.5	0.0	100
China	247.7	2.2	59.2	0.0	0.0	37.6	0.5	0.3	0.0	100
Spain	242.4	99.2	0.1	0.1	0.0	0.0	0.1	0.2	0.2	100
Switzerland	196.3	0.9	28.2	0.0	0.0	70.4	0.0	0.4	0.0	100
France	126.7	28.4	70.8	0.0	0.4	0.0	0.0	0.2	0.0	100
Malaysia	113.8	1.7	0.6	...	0.1	97.5	0.0	0.0	0.0	100

Imports Profile:

Namibia's imports were composed of 31.1 percent of machinery and transport equipment (SITC section 7), 18.7 percent of manufactured goods classified chiefly by material (SITC section 6) and 13.6 percent of mineral fuels, lubricants and related materials (SITC section 3) in 2008 (see table 2). From 2006 to 2008, top imported products were petroleum oils, other than crude (HS code 2710), motor cars and other motor vehicles principally designed for the transport (HS code 8703) and motor vehicles for the transport of goods (HS code 8704) (see table 5).

Table 5: Top 10 import commodities 2006 to 2008

(Value in million US$)

HS code	4-digit heading of Harmonized System 2002	Value (million US$) 2006	2007	2008	Unit value 2006	2007	2008	Unit	SITC code
	All Commodities	2798.5	4026.0	4688.6					
2710	Petroleum oils, other than crude	76.1	391.9	602.5	0.9	0.6	0.6	US$/kg	334
8703	Motor cars and other motor vehicles principally designed for the transport	243.8	287.0	287.2	*15.4*	*16.2*		thsd US$/unit	781
8704	Motor vehicles for the transport of goods	61.7	76.5	142.4	*23.6*			thsd US$/unit	782
3004	Medicaments (excluding goods of heading 30.02, 30.05 or 30.06)	69.8	72.4	88.9	30.9	34.3	32.2	US$/kg	542
8708	Parts and accessories of the motor vehicles of headings 87.01 to 87.05	51.3	59.6	69.7	*10.9*	11.8	*12.1*	US$/kg	784
7326	Other articles of iron or steel	23.1	92.5	44.8	1.4	4.4	1.7	US$/kg	699
8429	Self-propelled bulldozers, angledozers, graders, levellers, scrapers	39.6	50.0	69.5	*42.2*		*65.3*	thsd US$/unit	723
7102	Diamonds, whether or not worked, but not mounted or set	1.8	18.3	130.7					667
1702	Other sugars, including pure lactose, glucose and fructose	18.3	96.1	24.5	0.4	1.9	0.5	US$/kg	061
2807	Sulphuric acid; oleum	11.0	27.0	94.5	0.1	0.1	0.3	US$/kg	522

Nepal

Imports: CIF, by origin **Exports: FOB, by last known destination** **Trade System: Special**

Overview:

In 2010, exports of Nepal decreased by 5.9 percent to 834.0 mln US$ (see table 1 and graph 1). During the same period, imports increased by 36.6 percent and amounted to 5.1 bln US$ (see table 2 and graph 1). This resulted in a trade deficit of 4.3 bln US$ in 2010 (see graph 1). By MDG regions, trade with Southern Asia alone accounted for a large part of this deficit (-2.3 bln US$) (see graph 2). Significant deficits were also recorded with Eastern Asia and Western Asia (-0.7 bln US$ and -0.5 bln US$ respectively). Trade was concentrated among a few partners: in 2010, 4 (respectively 5) major partners accounted for 80 percent of exports (respectively imports) (see graph 3). See footnote*.

Graph 1: Total imports, exports and trade balance

(Bln US$ by year)

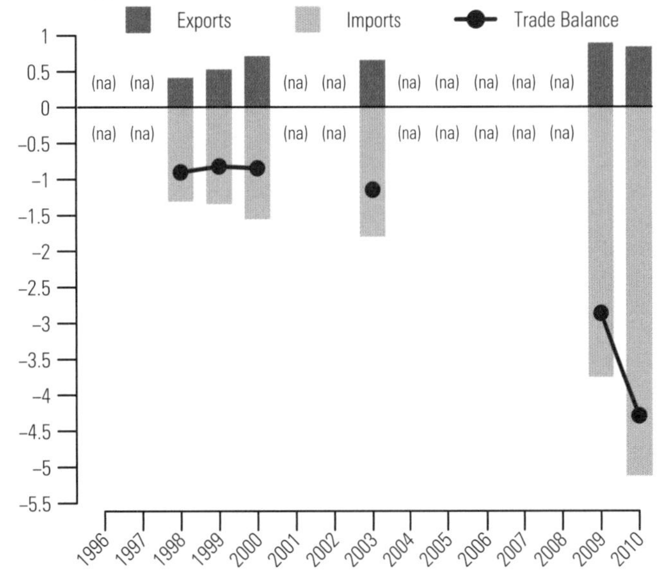

Table 1: Exports by SITC sections

(Value in million US$, growth and shares in percentage)

SITC	2010	Avg. Growth rates (%) 2006-2010	Avg. Growth rates (%) 2009-2010	2010 share
Total	834.0	...	-5.9	100.0
0+1	155.4	...	-28.0	18.6
2+4	53.5	...	-13.5	6.4
3	0.0	...	-94.1	0.0
5	38.1	...	-33.2	4.6
6	451.8	...	9.2	54.2
7	19.6	...	178.5	2.4
8	115.6	...	-11.5	13.9
9	0.0	...	-85.9	0.0

Exports Profile:

Manufactured goods classified chiefly by material (SITC section 6) accounted for 54.2 percent of exports in 2010 (see table 1). Other major commodity groups included food, live animals, beverages and tobacco (SITC sections 0+1) and miscellaneous manufactured articles (SITC section 8), respectively with 18.6 and 13.9 percent of exports. Major markets for exports included India, USA and Bangladesh (see table 4). In 2010, top products for exports were flat-rolled products of iron or non-alloy steel (HS code 7210), carpets and other textile floor coverings, knotted, whether or not made up (HS code 5701) and dried leguminous vegetables, shelled, whether or not skinned or split (HS code 0713) (see table 3).

Table 2: Imports by SITC sections

(Value in million US$, growth and shares in percentage)

SITC	2010	Avg. Growth rates (%) 2006-2010	Avg. Growth rates (%) 2009-2010	2010 share
Total	5 127.5	...	36.6	100.0
0+1	392.8	...	17.8	7.7
2+4	346.7	...	1.7	6.8
3	804.7	...	30.5	15.7
5	477.0	...	13.1	9.3
6	1 012.7	...	30.1	19.8
7	1 256.0	...	47.4	24.5
8	270.5	...	10.7	5.3
9	567.2	...	239.6	11.1

Table 3: Top 10 export commodities 2008 to 2010

(Value in million US$)

HS code	4-digit heading of Harmonized System 2007	Value (million US$) 2008	2009	2010	Unit value 2008	2009	2010	Unit	SITC code
	All Commodities	...	886.0	834.0					
7210	Flat-rolled products of iron or non-alloy steel	...	72.9	81.4		1.0	1.1	US$/kg	674
5701	Carpets and other textile floor coverings, knotted, whether or not made up	...	72.1	59.7			71.3	US$/m²	659
0713	Dried leguminous vegetables, shelled, whether or not skinned or split	...	79.0	51.4		1.3	1.4	US$/kg	054
5509	Yarn (other than sewing thread) of synthetic staple fibres	...	48.4	55.0			2.0	US$/kg	651
5407	Woven fabrics of synthetic filament yarn	...	46.0	52.8					653
6305	Sacks and bags, of a kind used for the packing of goods	...	30.4	37.3			1.2	US$/kg	658
6214	Shawls, scarves, mufflers, mantillas, veils and the like	...	25.8	19.7		13.0		US$/unit	846
7306	Other tubes, pipes and hollow profiles	...	24.0	19.6		0.4	0.4	US$/kg	679
2009	Fruit juices (including grape must) and vegetable juices	...	28.9	14.7		0.6	0.7	US$/kg	059
7217	Wire of iron or non-alloy steel	...	18.1	20.4		0.9	1.0	US$/kg	678

*Fiscal year ends July 15

Graph 2: Trade Balance by MDG Regions in 2010

(Bln US$)

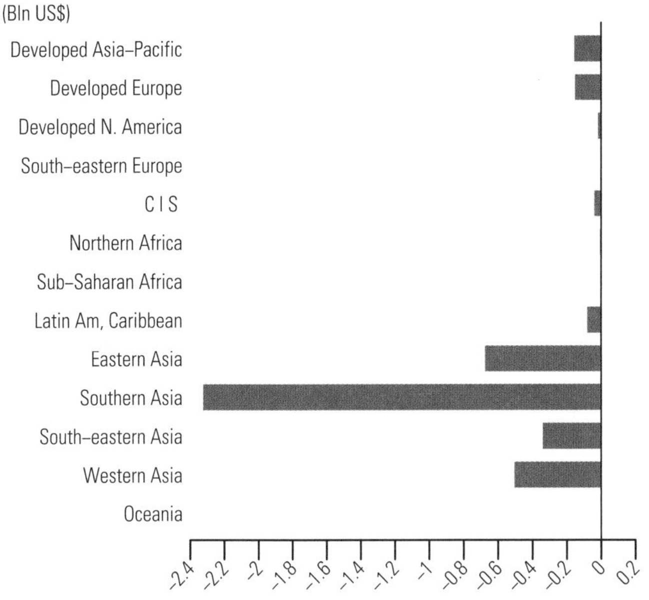

Graph 3: Partner concentration of trade in 2010

(Cumulative share by ranked partners)

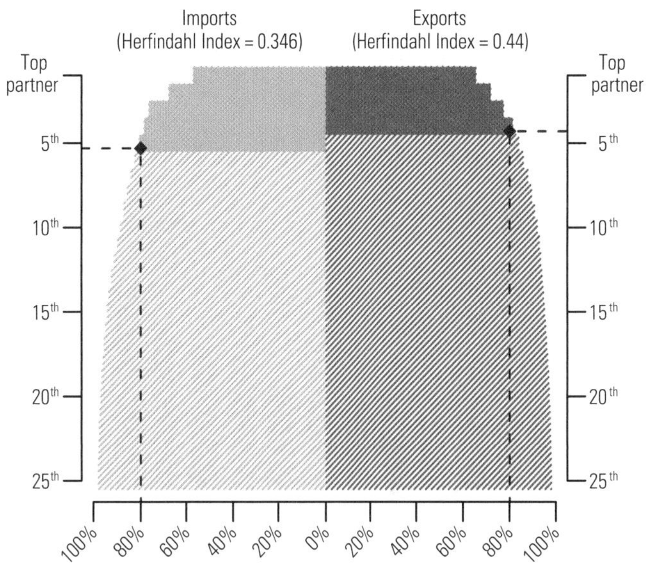

Table 4: Exports by principal countries and SITC sections in 2010

(Value in million US$, percentages of country total)

Country	Total	Shares by SITC sections (%) 0+1	2+4	3	5	6	7	8	9	Total
World	834.0	18.6	6.4	0.0	4.6	54.2	2.4	13.9	0.0	100
India	546.0	17.5	8.7	...	6.4	61.3	0.9	5.2	...	100
USA	52.9	6.8	0.4	...	0.3	54.5	2.8	35.3	...	100
Bangladesh	46.2	94.2	0.7	...	0.2	4.1	...	0.9	...	100
Germany	32.7	1.7	0.6	...	0.4	65.1	2.8	29.4	...	100
Bhutan	21.3	2.5	0.0	...	1.4	81.6	13.7	0.8	...	100
United Kingdom	16.8	2.7	1.3	...	0.6	29.2	5.0	61.3	...	100
France	15.8	0.8	0.3	...	0.5	19.0	0.4	79.0	...	100
China	13.8	12.8	1.9	0.0	9.7	62.6	2.2	10.8	...	100
Canada	10.5	6.2	0.2	...	0.2	41.0	0.0	52.3	0.1	100
Italy	9.8	4.4	0.2	...	0.5	43.5	10.0	41.6	...	100

Imports Profile:

In 2010, imports of machinery and transport equipment (SITC section 7) accounted for 24.5 percent of imported goods (see table 2). Other major commodity groups for imports included manufactured goods classified chiefly by material (SITC section 6) and mineral fuels, lubricants and related materials (SITC section 3), respectively with 19.8 and 15.7 percent of imports. In 2010, top imported products included petroleum oils, other than crude (HS code 2710), gold (including gold plated with platinum) (HS code 7108) and semi-finished products of iron or non-alloy steel (HS code 7207) (see table 5).

Table 5: Top 10 import commodities 2008 to 2010

(Value in million US$)

HS code	4-digit heading of Harmonized System 2007	Value (million US$) 2008	2009	2010	Unit value 2008	2009	2010	Unit	SITC code
	All Commodities	...	3754.4	5127.5					
2710	Petroleum oils, other than crude	...	480.5	599.4					334
7108	Gold (including gold plated with platinum)	...	166.8	567.0		*26.5*	*28.5*	thsd US$/kg	971
7207	Semi-finished products of iron or non-alloy steel	...	109.8	187.9		*1.2*	0.6	US$/kg	672
2523	Portland cement, aluminous cement, slag cement	...	104.2	170.9			0.1	US$/kg	661
8517	Electrical apparatus for line telephony or line telegraphy	...	77.8	177.3					764
2711	Petroleum gases and other gaseous hydrocarbons	...	98.2	152.4					343
8711	Motorcycles (including mopeds) and cycles fitted with an auxiliary motor	...	64.8	118.0					785
1507	Soya-bean oil and its fractions	...	96.7	82.0		1.1	1.0	US$/kg	421
3003	Medicaments (excluding goods of heading 30.02, 30.05 or 30.06)	...	82.6	96.0			0.9	US$/kg	542
7208	Flat-rolled products of iron or non-alloy steel	...	61.3	96.7		*0.9*	0.7	US$/kg	673

Netherlands

Imports: CIF, by origin/consignment for intra-eu **Exports: FOB, by last known destination** **Trade System: Special**

Overview:

In 2010, the value of the Netherlands' exports increased by 14.2 percent and amounted to 492.6 bln US$ (see table 1 and graph 1). Imports showed a similar development with an increase of 15.1 percent in 2010 to 440.0 bln US$ (see table 2 and graph 1). This resulted in a trade surplus of 52.7 bln US$ in 2010 (see graph 1). Trade with Eastern Asia, South-eastern Asia and Developed North America recorded deficits respectively of 33.2, 11.9 and 11.2 bln US$ in 2010 (see graph 2). A major trade surplus was recorded with Developed Europe (+128.3 bln US$). Netherlands' trade was diversified across partners: in 2010, 18 (respectively 20) major partners accounted for 80 percent of exports (respectively imports) (see graph 3).

Graph 1: Total imports, exports and trade balance

(Bln US$ by year)

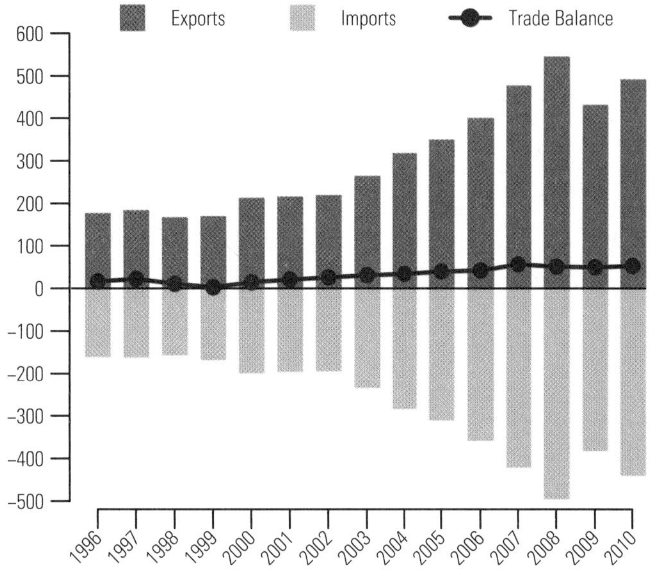

Exports Profile:

In 2010, exports were composed of 27.0 percent of machinery and transport equipment (SITC section 7), 14.8 percent of commodities and transactions not classified elsewhere (SITC section 9) and 14.5 percent of chemicals and related products, n.e.s. (SITC section 5) (see table 1). In addition to Germany, other major markets for exports in 2010 included Belgium and France (see table 4). From 2008 to 2010, top exported commodities were petroleum oils, other than crude (HS code 2710), automatic data processing machines and units thereof (HS code 8471) and printing machinery used for printing by means of the printing type, blocks (HS code 8443) (see table 3).

Table 1: Exports by SITC sections

(Value in million US$, growth and shares in percentage)

SITC	2010	Avg. Growth rates (%) 2006-2010	2009-2010	2010 share
Total	492645.9	5.3	14.2	100.0
0+1	61230.0	7.6	5.3	12.4
2+4	25421.1	6.2	13.8	5.2
3	50071.9	9.7	40.8	10.2
5	71393.6	4.5	18.4	14.5
6	38159.3	2.6	17.6	7.7
7	132769.4	3.6	14.6	27.0
8	40761.3	4.0	9.3	8.3
9	72839.3	6.7	4.6	14.8

Table 2: Imports by SITC sections

(Value in million US$, growth and shares in percentage)

SITC	2010	Avg. Growth rates (%) 2006-2010	2009-2010	2010 share
Total	439986.6	5.3	15.1	100.0
0+1	37387.2	9.0	3.9	8.5
2+4	19850.4	6.9	27.0	4.5
3	71678.2	5.3	41.6	16.3
5	46273.0	2.9	8.6	10.5
6	37534.9	1.3	13.5	8.5
7	125340.1	2.3	16.4	28.5
8	45066.0	6.4	10.3	10.2
9	56856.9	15.5	2.0	12.9

Table 3: Top 10 export commodities 2008 to 2010

(Value in million US$)

HS code	4-digit heading of Harmonized System 2007	Value (million US$) 2008	2009	2010	Unit value 2008	2009	2010	Unit	SITC code
	All Commodities	545853.4	431502.5	492645.9					
9999	Commodities not specified according to kind	87788.9	69208.3	71249.4					931
2710	Petroleum oils, other than crude	53189.2	32019.0	44928.0	*0.8*		*0.6*	US$/kg	334
8471	Automatic data processing machines and units thereof	14583.7	13879.5	16546.9	121.7		167.6	US$/unit	752
8443	Printing machinery used for printing by means of the printing type, blocks	14695.4	12036.7	11254.1					726
8517	Electrical apparatus for line telephony or line telegraphy	12787.4	10767.7	13027.1					764
3004	Medicaments (excluding goods of heading 30.02, 30.05 or 30.06)	8517.0	9430.6	11719.3	193.9		141.9	US$/kg	542
8473	Parts and accessories for use with machines of heading 84.69 to 84.72	9645.9	7966.1	8628.0	113.4		114.6	US$/kg	759
9018	Instruments and appliances used in medical, surgical, dental or veterinary	6175.8	5767.7	6336.2					872
8528	Reception apparatus for television	5914.9	4569.5	4597.4	243.9		175.1	US$/unit	761
8486	Machines and apparatus used for the manufacture of semiconductor devices	4486.4	2177.3	6435.8					728

Graph 2: Trade Balance by MDG Regions in 2010

(Bln US$)

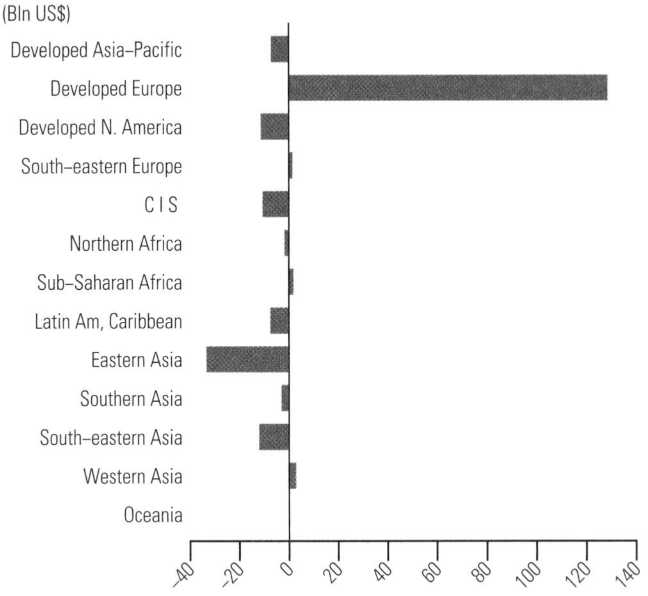

Graph 3: Partner concentration of trade in 2010

(Cumulative share by ranked partners)

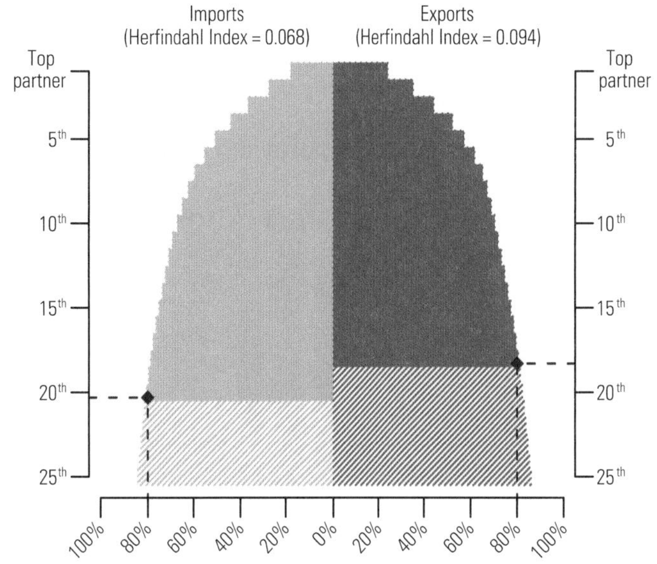

Table 4: Exports by principal countries and SITC sections in 2010

(Value in million US$, percentages of country total)

Country	Total	Shares by SITC sections (%)								
		0 + 1	2 + 4	3	5	6	7	8	9	Total
World	492645.9	12.4	5.2	10.2	14.5	7.7	27.0	8.3	14.8	100
Germany	119690.6	13.8	5.9	10.9	13.3	10.0	23.1	8.5	14.6	100
Belgium	54730.6	12.0	5.8	19.3	19.7	9.7	16.4	8.8	8.4	100
France	43089.3	15.3	4.5	7.8	16.6	8.3	28.0	11.3	8.2	100
United Kingdom	39323.5	16.0	5.1	8.3	16.0	7.6	29.5	9.8	7.7	100
Italy	24664.4	15.3	3.9	0.4	19.0	7.8	29.7	11.3	12.8	100
USA	22351.3	8.4	2.3	14.7	14.2	7.7	29.5	5.1	18.2	100
Spain	16716.3	13.8	5.0	6.9	19.0	7.3	31.5	12.2	4.2	100
Poland	9784.8	13.6	4.9	1.1	17.9	9.2	40.2	10.1	2.9	100
Sweden	8819.2	14.7	4.9	3.6	16.9	9.6	35.8	11.0	3.6	100
Russian Federation	7481.0	16.4	7.3	0.3	15.9	5.4	44.7	6.9	3.1	100

Imports Profile:

Similar to exports, machinery and transport equipment (SITC section 7) accounted for the largest share of imports in 2010: 28.5 percent (see table 2). Other major commodity groups included mineral fuels, lubricants and related materials (SITC section 3) and commodities and transactions not classified elsewhere (SITC section 9) respectively with 16.3 and 12.9 percent of imported goods. From 2008 to 2010, top imported commodities were petroleum oils and oils obtained from bituminous minerals, crude (HS code 2709), petroleum oils, other than crude (HS code 2710) and automatic data processing machines and units thereof (HS code 8471) (see table 5).

Table 5: Top 10 import commodities 2008 to 2010

(Value in million US$)

HS code	4-digit heading of Harmonized System 2007	Value (million US$)			Unit value				SITC code
		2008	2009	2010	2008	2009	2010	Unit	
	All Commodities	494936.6	382190.4	439986.6					
9999	Commodities not specified according to kind	64251.0	54530.8	55275.5					931
2709	Petroleum oils and oils obtained from bituminous minerals, crude	41995.1	25894.7	35933.1	0.7	*0.7*	0.6	US$/kg	333
2710	Petroleum oils, other than crude	26464.9	19547.5	27859.2	*0.7*		*0.6*	US$/kg	334
8471	Automatic data processing machines and units thereof	14739.6	12650.6	17270.7	103.4		117.7	US$/unit	752
8517	Electrical apparatus for line telephony or line telegraphy	14820.2	11953.7	14507.4					764
3004	Medicaments (excluding goods of heading 30.02, 30.05 or 30.06)	10508.0	10336.3	10359.8	165.2		163.4	US$/kg	542
8443	Printing machinery used for printing by means of the printing type, blocks	11903.3	8753.0	9624.7					726
8703	Motor cars and other motor vehicles principally designed for the transport	10979.2	8462.2	9762.6	18.8		15.4	thsd US$/unit	781
8473	Parts and accessories for use with machines of heading 84.69 to 84.72	10161.7	8129.8	8903.3	157.4		136.5	US$/kg	759
8528	Reception apparatus for television	6913.5	5224.4	5707.0	225.2		179.4	US$/unit	761

Netherlands Antilles

Imports: CIF, by consignment **Exports: FOB, by last known destination** **Trade System: Special**

Overview:

In 2008, Netherlands Antilles' exports and imports increased almost at the same rate, on average, respectively by 25.9 and 24.8 percent each year amounting to 0.1 and 1.4 bln US$ (see tables 1, 2 and graph 1). Trade balance recorded a deficit of 1.3 bln US$ (see graph 1). Trade recorded deficits with Developed North America (-0.5 bln US$), Developed Europe (-0.3 bln US$) and Latin America and the Caribbean (-0.2 bln US$) among others. Netherlands Antilles' trade was concentrated across partners: in 2008, 4 (respectively 8) major partners accounted for 80 percent of exports (respectively imports) (see graph 3).

Graph 1: Total imports, exports and trade balance

(Bln US$ by year)

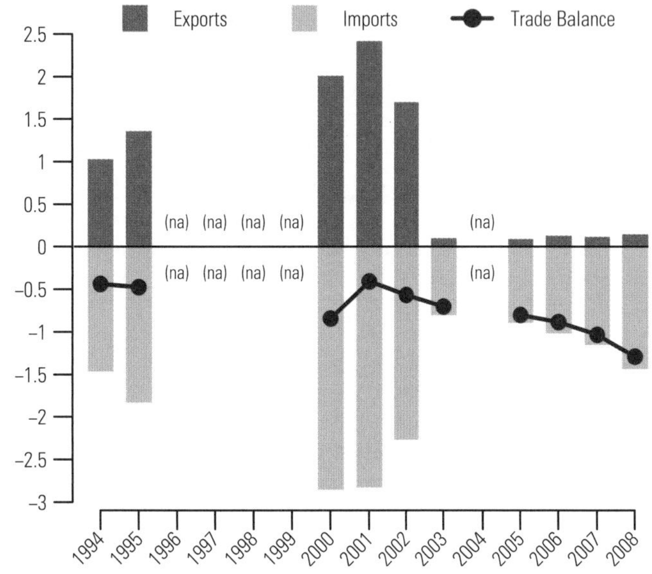

Exports Profile:

In 2008, exports were composed of 33.5 percent of machinery and transport equipment (SITC section 7), 27.5 percent of food, live animals, beverages and tobacco (SITC sections 0+1) and 15.5 percent of miscellaneous manufactured articles (SITC section 8) (see table 1). Major markets for exports in 2008 included Netherlands, USA and Aruba (see table 4). From 2006 to 2008, top exported commodities were articles of jewellery and parts thereof, of precious metal (HS code 7113), chocolate and other food preparations containing cocoa (HS code 1806) and parts of goods of heading 88.01 or 88.02 (HS code 8803) (see table 3).

Table 1: Exports by SITC sections

(Value in million US$, growth and shares in percentage)

SITC	2008	Avg. Growth rates (%) 2004-2008	2007-2008	2008 share
Total	146.2	...	25.9	100.0
0+1	40.2	...	19.6	27.5
2+4	7.5	...	-9.1	5.2
5	9.8	...	25.9	6.7
6	9.0	...	7.6	6.2
7	49.0	...	121.4	33.5
8	22.7	...	-14.7	15.5
9	8.0	...	-14.0	5.5

Table 2: Imports by SITC sections

(Value in million US$, growth and shares in percentage)

SITC	2008	Avg. Growth rates (%) 2004-2008	2007-2008	2008 share
Total	1 437.0	...	24.8	100.0
0+1	288.7	...	15.2	20.1
2+4	25.5	...	19.8	1.8
5	166.1	...	22.2	11.6
6	209.9	...	27.9	14.6
7	464.4	...	30.2	32.3
8	265.3	...	28.6	18.5
9	17.1	...	1.3	1.2

Table 3: Top 10 export commodities 2006 to 2008

(Value in million US$)

HS code	4-digit heading of Harmonized System 2002	Value (million US$) 2006	2007	2008	Unit value 2006	2007	2008	Unit	SITC code
	All Commodities	129.3	116.1	146.2					
7113	Articles of jewellery and parts thereof, of precious metal	24.7	14.1	10.7	103.3	23.5	27.7	thsd US$/kg	897
1806	Chocolate and other food preparations containing cocoa	4.1	10.1	16.0	1.0	1.5	1.6	US$/kg	073
8803	Parts of goods of heading 88.01 or 88.02	5.8	4.6	18.8	361.0	213.2	374.7	US$/kg	792
1701	Cane or beet sugar and pure sucrose, in solid form	9.1	10.6	8.0	0.9	1.1	1.2	US$/kg	061
9999	Commodities not specified according to kind	6.1	6.9	6.8					931
2501	Salt (including table salt)	5.1	7.3	6.1	2.3	5.5	8.9	US$/kg	278
2106	Food preparations not elsewhere specified or included	1.7	5.2	10.3	1.5	1.5	1.9	US$/kg	098
3402	Organic surface-active agents (other than soap)	3.1	3.3	3.0	1.1	1.0	1.2	US$/kg	554
8703	Motor cars and other motor vehicles principally designed for the transport	2.6	2.8	3.9	*6.6*	*6.5*		thsd US$/unit	781
8711	Motorcycles (including mopeds) and cycles fitted with an auxiliary motor	2.4	3.5	1.9	*2.1*			thsd US$/unit	785

Graph 2: Trade Balance by MDG Regions in 2008

(Mln US$)

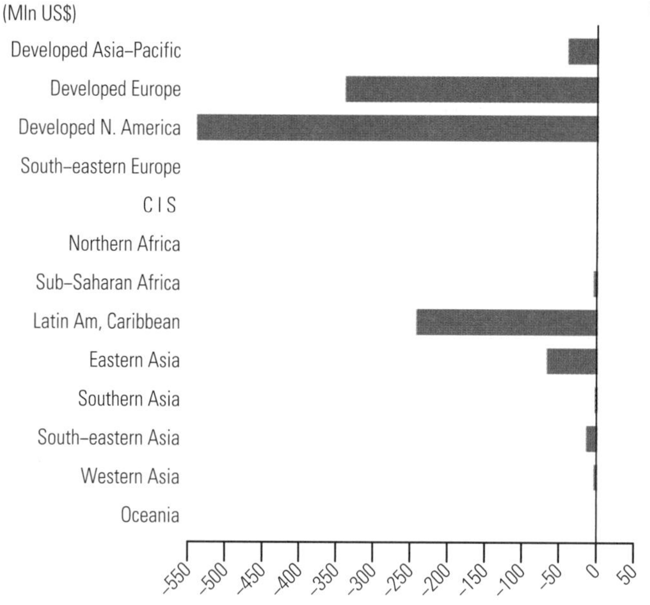

Graph 3: Partner concentration of trade in 2008

(Cumulative share by ranked partners)

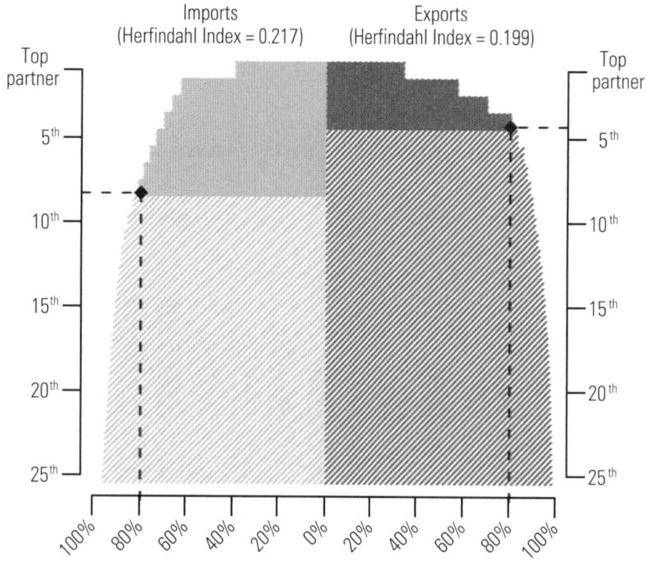

Table 4: Exports by principal countries and SITC sections in 2008

(Value in million US$, percentages of country total)

Country	Total	Shares by SITC sections (%)								
		0 + 1	2 + 4	3	5	6	7	8	9	Total
World	146.2	27.5	5.2	...	6.7	6.2	33.5	15.5	5.5	100
Netherlands	50.0	65.3	1.7	...	1.9	5.0	13.3	4.1	8.6	100
USA	33.6	0.2	8.9	...	6.0	7.0	63.3	13.5	1.0	100
Areas, nes	18.8	8.5	0.4	...	7.5	10.7	19.2	52.0	1.6	100
Aruba	14.9	23.2	1.0	...	17.3	10.6	34.5	11.9	1.5	100
Germany	4.0	0.1	0.0	...	...	0.1	98.6	0.2	0.9	100
Venezuela	3.7	53.5	0.6	...	13.7	0.6	29.2	1.3	1.2	100
Namibia	2.2	0.5	9.7	...	...	0.0	87.3	0.3	2.2	100
Antigua and Barbuda	2.1	0.3	0.0	...	17.7	0.2	10.5	70.5	0.6	100
Canada	1.7	0.0	0.2	...	...	0.0	93.5	0.3	6.0	100
France	1.7	0.9	18.9	...	14.9	...	43.5	19.2	2.5	100

Imports Profile:

Similar to exports, machinery and transport equipment (SITC section 7) accounted for the largest share of imports in 2008: 32.3 percent (see table 2). Other major commodity groups included food, live animals, beverages and tobacco (SITC sections 0+1) and miscellaneous manufactured articles (SITC section 8) respectively with 20.1 and 18.5 percent of imported goods. From 2006 to 2008, top imported commodities were motor cars and other motor vehicles principally designed for the transport (HS code 8703), medicaments (excluding goods of heading 30.02, 30.05 or 30.06) (HS code 3004) and automatic data processing machines and units thereof (HS code 8471) (see table 5).

Table 5: Top 10 import commodities 2006 to 2008

(Value in million US$)

HS code	4-digit heading of Harmonized System 2002	Value (million US$)			Unit value				SITC code
		2006	2007	2008	2006	2007	2008	Unit	
	All Commodities	1016.7	1151.7	1437.0					
8703	Motor cars and other motor vehicles principally designed for the transport	62.8	63.3	76.6	*5.9*	*7.1*		thsd US$/unit	781
3004	Medicaments (excluding goods of heading 30.02, 30.05 or 30.06)	23.8	30.2	32.0	48.6	55.4	55.5	US$/kg	542
8471	Automatic data processing machines and units thereof	23.2	26.4	29.1	*305.7*			US$/unit	752
7113	Articles of jewellery and parts thereof, of precious metal	26.4	17.3	19.6	9.1	3.7	1.6	thsd US$/kg	897
3003	Medicaments (excluding goods of heading 30.02, 30.05 or 30.06)	17.7	18.2	19.3	81.1	110.1	84.5	US$/kg	542
8544	Insulated (including enamelled or anodised) wire, cable	8.3	16.9	25.2	7.9	12.7	10.0	US$/kg	773
8704	Motor vehicles for the transport of goods	15.9	14.7	19.6	*14.2*		*21.2*	thsd US$/unit	782
9999	Commodities not specified according to kind	15.1	15.9	17.0					931
2203	Beer made from malt	13.8	14.4	16.9	*0.7*	*0.7*	*0.9*	US$/litre	112
8525	Transmission apparatus for radio-telephony, radio-broadcasting	15.5	11.8	15.7					764

New Caledonia

Imports: CIF, by consignment	Exports: FOB, by last known destination	Trade System: Special

Overview:

After reaching a peak of 2.1 bln US$ in 2009, the exports of New Caledonia dropped in 2010 but bounced back by 30.8 percent in 2011 and amounted to 1.7 bln US$ (see table 1 and graph1). Imports, on the other hand, increased on average by 11.1 percent over the last five years and reached 3.7 bln US$ in 2011 (see table 2 and graph 1). This resulted in a trade deficit of 2.0 bln US$, the same level as in 2010. The deficit was chiefly recorded with Developed Europe (-949.6 mln US$), South-eastern Asia (-755.4 mln US$) and Developed North America (-126.1 mln US$) (see graph 2). New Caledonia's exports were concentrated among a few partners, 7 major partners accounted for 80 percent of exports compared to 11 major partners for imports (see graph 3).

Graph 1: Total imports, exports and trade balance

(Bln US$ by year)

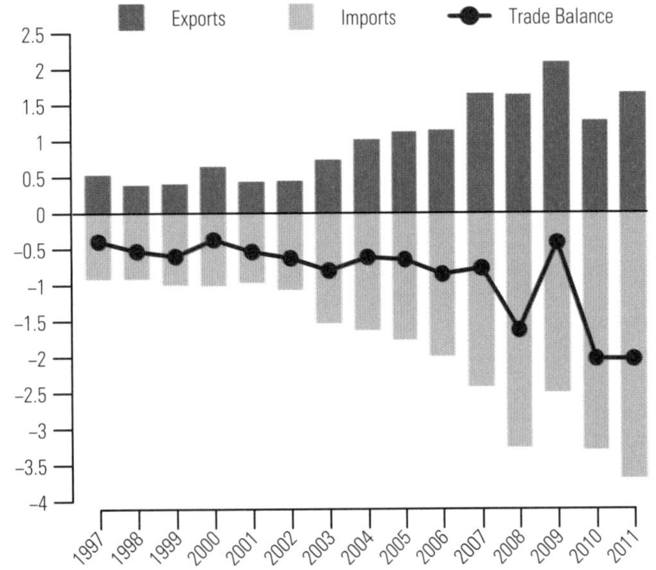

Table 1: Exports by SITC sections

(Value in million US$, growth and shares in percentage)

SITC	2011	Avg. Growth rates (%) 2007-2011	2010-2011	2011 share
Total	1657.5	0.1	30.8	100.0
0+1	24.2	-0.4	10.7	1.5
2+4	581.9	-2.3	12.8	35.1
3	0.2	19.7	-82.3	0.0
5	133.5	159.6	1934.4	8.1
6	852.4	-2.7	23.7	51.4
7	46.8	21.0	185.2	2.8
8	7.9	5.9	-37.3	0.5
9	10.7	42.6	134.2	0.6

Table 2: Imports by SITC sections

(Value in million US$, growth and shares in percentage)

SITC	2011	Avg. Growth rates (%) 2007-2011	2010-2011	2011 share
Total	3696.9	11.1	11.9	100.0
0+1	421.6	13.7	18.0	11.4
2+4	67.0	27.4	33.5	1.8
3	668.4	18.1	27.0	18.1
5	266.9	11.7	4.7	7.2
6	364.4	7.3	-11.1	9.9
7	930.8	3.1	1.0	25.2
8	339.4	10.5	12.5	9.2
9	638.2	20.1	32.8	17.3

Exports Profile:

Two commodity groups accounted for the majority of exports in 2011: manufactured goods classified chiefly by material (SITC section 6) and inedible crude materials (excluding fuels), vegetable and animal oils, fats and waxes (SITC sections 2+4) representing respectively 51.4 and 35.1 percent of exports (see table 1). Major destinations for exports included Japan, France and Australia (see table 4). Exports to France were almost exclusively inedible crude materials (except fuels), vegetable and animal oils, fats and waxes (SITC sections 2+4). Over the last three years, top exported goods included ferro-alloys (HS code 7202), nickel ores and concentrates (HS code 2604) and nickel mattes, nickel oxide sinters and other intermediate products (HS code 7501) (see table 3).

Table 3: Top 10 export commodities 2009 to 2011

(Value in million US$)

HS code	4-digit heading of Harmonized System 2007	Value (million US$) 2009	2010	2011	Unit value 2009	2010	2011	Unit	SITC code
	All Commodities	2082.8	1267.6	1657.5					
7202	Ferro-alloys	548.2	684.1	846.6	5.3	3.9	5.1	US$/kg	671
2604	Nickel ores and concentrates	171.0	283.4	302.1	0.0	0.1	0.1	US$/kg	284
7501	Nickel mattes, nickel oxide sinters and other intermediate products	174.2	227.3	270.7		11.3	13.8	US$/kg	284
8703	Motor cars and other motor vehicles principally designed for the transport	176.6	0.6	1.6		*19.9*		thsd US$/unit	781
2825	Hydrazine and hydroxylamine and their inorganic salts	...	2.0	127.5		2.9	2.8	US$/kg	522
8704	Motor vehicles for the transport of goods	82.8	0.9	0.3					782
9999	Commodities not specified according to kind	53.5	4.6	10.7					931
8429	Self-propelled bulldozers, angledozers, graders, levellers, scrapers	37.7	0.3	1.1		*48.9*	*58.9*	thsd US$/unit	723
0306	Crustaceans, whether in shell or not	15.5	11.3	11.8	14.3	15.2	16.7	US$/kg	036
8802	Other aircraft (for example, helicopters, aeroplanes); spacecraft	8.1	...	28.1					792

Graph 2: Trade Balance by MDG Regions in 2011

(Mln US$)

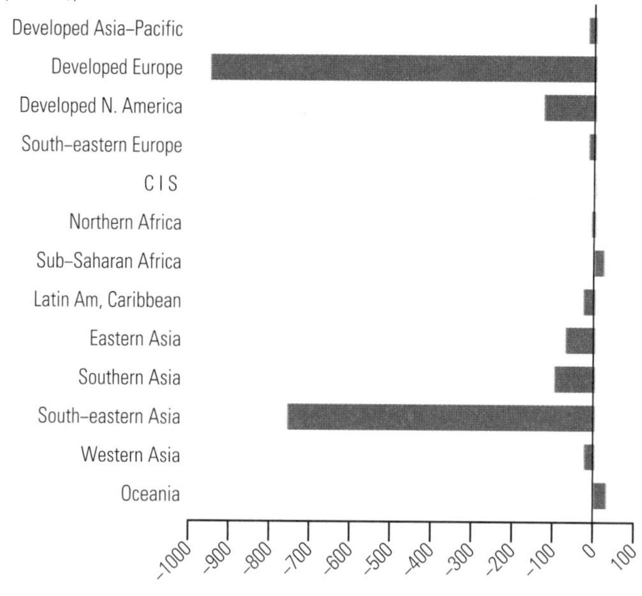

Graph 3: Partner concentration of trade in 2011

(Cumulative share by ranked partners)

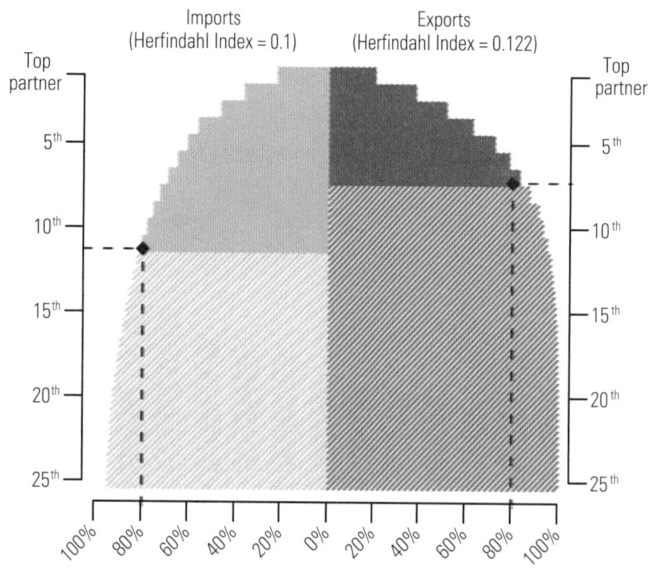

Table 4: Exports by principal countries and SITC sections in 2011

(Value in million US$, percentages of country total)

Country	Total	Shares by SITC sections (%)								
		0 + 1	2 + 4	3	5	6	7	8	9	Total
World	1 657.5	1.5	35.1	0.0	8.1	51.4	2.8	0.5	0.6	100
Japan	332.6	4.1	29.5	...	0.0	66.4	0.0	0.0	0.0	100
France	297.3	0.8	91.1	0.0	1.0	0.2	3.0	1.2	2.8	100
Australia	218.4	0.4	42.8	0.0	52.8	0.6	2.6	0.5	0.3	100
Other Asia, nes	186.7	0.0	0.1	...	...	99.9	0.0	0.0	...	100
Rep. of Korea	160.0	0.0	65.5	...	0.0	34.5	0.0	0.0	0.0	100
China	103.0	0.0	9.4	...	0.0	90.6	0.0	0.0	...	100
Belgium	73.7	0.0	0.0	...	0.0	99.7	0.1	0.0	0.2	100
USA	73.2	1.5	0.0	...	0.0	97.8	0.3	0.3	0.1	100
Spain	64.6	0.2	0.0	...	0.1	99.7	0.0	...	0.0	100
South Africa	31.2	0.0	0.0	0.0	...	99.8	0.0	...	0.1	100

Imports Profile:

In 2011, New Caledonia's imports were composed of 25.2 percent of machinery and transport equipment (SITC section 7), 18.1 percent of mineral fuels, lubricants and related materials (SITC section 3) and 17.3 percent of commodities and transactions not classified elsewhere (SITC section 9) (see table 2). From 2009 to 2011, top imported products were petroleum oils, other than crude (HS code 2710), motor cars and other motor vehicles principally designed for the transport (HS code 8703) and medicaments (excluding goods of heading 30.02, 30.05 or 30.06) (HS code 3004) (see table 5).

Table 5: Top 10 import commodities 2009 to 2011

(Value in million US$)

HS code	4-digit heading of Harmonized System 2007	Value (million US$)			Unit value				SITC code
		2009	2010	2011	2009	2010	2011	Unit	
	All Commodities	2 507.2	3 303.2	3 696.9					
2710	Petroleum oils, other than crude	343.8	442.6	566.1	0.5	0.6	*0.8*	US$/kg	334
9999	Commodities not specified according to kind	51.7	480.1	637.8					931
8703	Motor cars and other motor vehicles principally designed for the transport	175.6	186.0	193.8		*18.3*		thsd US$/unit	781
3004	Medicaments (excluding goods of heading 30.02, 30.05 or 30.06)	84.4	80.9	84.7	56.3	64.9	67.7	US$/kg	542
8704	Motor vehicles for the transport of goods	82.3	77.6	79.9					782
2701	Coal; briquettes, ovoids and similar solid fuels manufactured from coal	21.9	66.6	77.6	0.1	0.1	0.1	US$/kg	321
8429	Self-propelled bulldozers, angledozers, graders, levellers, scrapers	37.5	49.9	48.2		*68.8*	*68.1*	thsd US$/unit	723
8708	Parts and accessories of the motor vehicles of headings 87.01 to 87.05	31.3	31.4	31.6	22.5	20.8	*20.0*	US$/kg	784
8471	Automatic data processing machines and units thereof	25.8	28.0	33.3					752
7308	Structures (excluding prefabricated buildings of heading 94.06)	26.0	39.9	20.5	4.2	3.4	3.1	US$/kg	691

New Zealand

Imports: CIF, by origin | **Exports: FOB, by last known destination** | **Trade System: General**

Overview:

From 2007 to 2011, New Zealand's exports increased on average by 8.7 percent each year and reached its peak of 37.6 bln US$ in 2011 (see table 1 and graph 1). Similarly, imports increased on average by 4.0 percent each year and reached 36.1 bln US$ (see table 2 and graph 1). This resulted in a trade surplus of 1.5 bln US$ in 2011 (see graph 1). By MDG regions, trade balance recorded surpluses with Developed Asia-Pacific (+3.2 bln US$), Oceania (+1.1 bln US$) and Southern Asia (+1.0 bln US$) (see graph 2). Large deficits were recorded with South-eastern Asia (-1.7 bln US$), Developed Europe (-1.6 bln US$) and Western Asia (-1.5 bln US$) (see graph 2). Both imports and exports were diversified across partners: 21 (respectively 16) major partners accounted for 80 percent of exports (respectively imports) in 2011 (see graph 3).

Graph 1: Total imports, exports and trade balance

(Bln US$ by year)

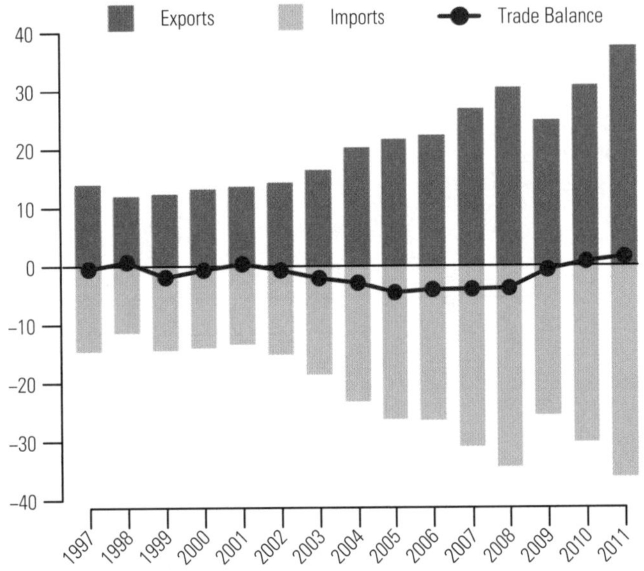

Exports Profile:

In 2011, more than half (53.0 percent) of New Zealand's exported goods were food, live animals, beverages and tobacco (SITC sections 0+1) (see table 1). Other major commodity groups included inedible crude materials (except fuels), animal and vegetable oils, fats and waxes (SITC sections 2+4) and manufactured goods classified chiefly by material (SITC section 6), respectively with 11.9 and 8.9 percent of exports. Top markets for exports included Australia, China and USA (see table 4). From 2009 to 2011, top products for exports included milk and cream, concentrated or containing added sugar (HS code 0402), meat of sheep or goats, fresh, chilled or frozen (HS code 0204) and butter and other fats and oils derived from milk; dairy spreads (HS code 0405) (see table 3).

Table 1: Exports by SITC sections

(Value in million US$, growth and shares in percentage)

SITC	2011	Avg. Growth rates (%) 2007-2011	2010-2011	2011 share
Total	37633.2	8.7	21.7	100.0
0+1	19961.2	10.6	22.8	53.0
2+4	4471.3	10.5	24.2	11.9
3	1948.2	13.4	32.9	5.2
5	1652.4	1.3	21.5	4.4
6	3364.9	1.5	15.0	8.9
7	2961.2	1.8	19.0	7.9
8	1391.4	2.7	9.8	3.7
9	1882.5	29.8	20.3	5.0

Table 2: Imports by SITC sections

(Value in million US$, growth and shares in percentage)

SITC	2011	Avg. Growth rates (%) 2007-2011	2010-2011	2011 share
Total	36111.3	4.0	19.7	100.0
0+1	3691.4	10.3	22.1	10.2
2+4	978.7	6.3	22.9	2.7
3	6230.9	8.7	35.1	17.3
5	4168.8	5.6	17.9	11.5
6	4129.9	0.6	15.1	11.4
7	11858.7	0.5	18.0	32.8
8	4750.8	3.9	11.0	13.2
9	302.1	29.5	13.0	0.8

Table 3: Top 10 export commodities 2009 to 2011

(Value in million US$)

HS code	4-digit heading of Harmonized System 2007	Value (million US$) 2009	2010	2011	Unit value 2009	2010	2011	Unit	SITC code
	All Commodities	24932.6	30931.9	37633.2					
0402	Milk and cream, concentrated or containing added sugar	2704.4	4095.5	5506.0	2.2	3.2	3.7	US$/kg	022
0204	Meat of sheep or goats, fresh, chilled or frozen	1820.6	1942.3	2369.5	4.7	5.5	6.8	US$/kg	012
0405	Butter and other fats and oils derived from milk; dairy spreads	949.7	1545.3	1967.9	2.0	3.9	4.5	US$/kg	023
2709	Petroleum oils and oils obtained from bituminous minerals, crude	1085.0	1378.4	1712.9	0.5	0.6	0.8	US$/kg	333
0202	Meat of bovine animals, frozen	978.0	1176.7	1418.8	2.9	3.5	4.3	US$/kg	011
9999	Commodities not specified according to kind	768.0	1143.1	1387.0					931
0406	Cheese and curd	855.6	1023.5	1077.7	2.8	3.9	*4.1*	US$/kg	024
4403	Wood in the rough, whether or not stripped of bark or sapwood	598.7	962.3	1308.6	67.9	88.3	102.3	US$/m^3	247
2204	Wine of fresh grapes, including fortified wines	637.3	774.2	895.2	5.0	*4.9*	*5.3*	US$/litre	112
0810	Other fruit, fresh	665.0	710.8	848.4	1.6	*1.9*	1.9	US$/kg	057

Graph 2: Trade Balance by MDG Regions in 2011

(Bln US$)

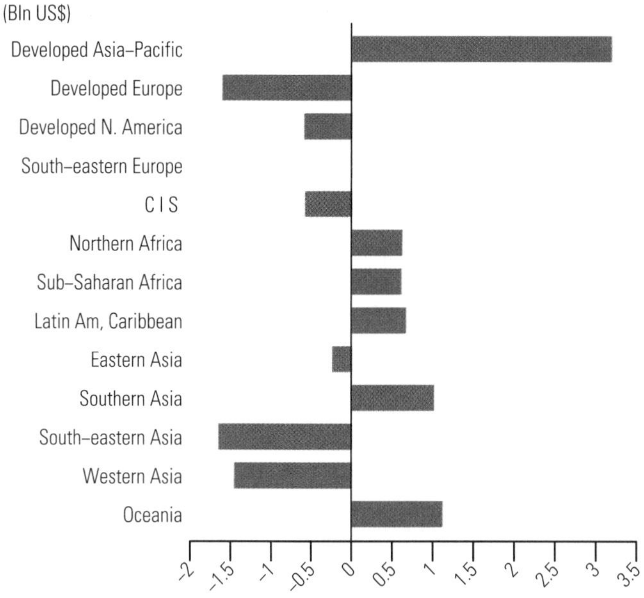

Graph 3: Partner concentration of trade in 2011

(Cumulative share by ranked partners)

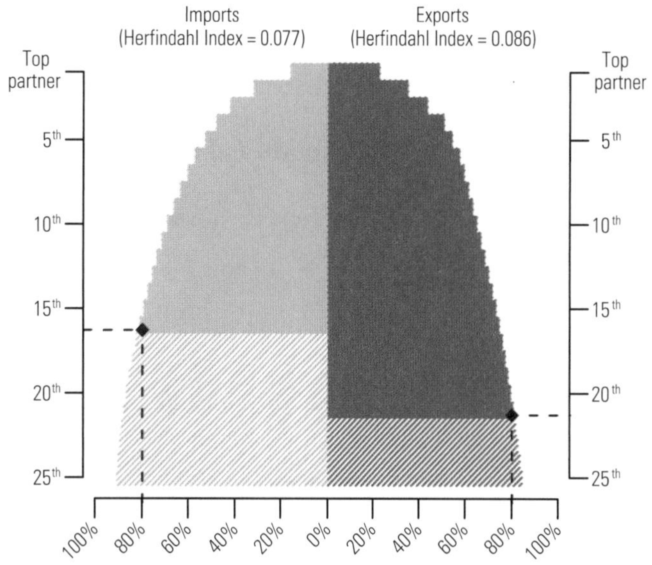

Table 4: Exports by principal countries and SITC sections in 2011

(Value in million US$, percentages of country total)

Country	Total	Shares by SITC sections (%) 0 + 1	2 + 4	3	5	6	7	8	9	Total
World	37633.2	53.0	11.9	5.2	4.4	8.9	7.9	3.7	5.0	100
Australia	8537.9	25.6	3.8	22.3	5.2	13.8	14.1	8.2	7.0	100
China	4647.7	51.5	39.4	0.0	2.7	1.9	1.6	0.6	2.3	100
USA	3150.0	56.3	6.2	0.0	11.1	7.4	12.8	6.1	0.2	100
Japan	2717.1	45.1	11.7	0.7	6.3	28.3	2.1	1.0	4.8	100
Rep. of Korea	1320.1	39.6	34.4	0.0	3.6	9.1	3.0	0.7	9.5	100
United Kingdom	1216.2	73.2	5.3	0.0	2.2	5.4	8.2	5.1	0.6	100
India	739.2	13.2	33.7	0.0	0.7	2.5	3.7	0.9	45.2	100
Other Asia, nes	708.5	77.1	13.5	0.0	1.9	3.0	2.8	0.3	1.4	100
Malaysia	689.8	74.1	10.0	0.0	2.5	6.3	6.2	0.5	0.4	100
Indonesia	674.3	70.4	16.8	...	3.8	5.3	3.1	0.3	0.3	100

Imports Profile:

In 2011, imports were composed of 32.8 percent of machinery and transport equipment (SITC section 7), 17.3 percent of mineral fuels, lubricants and related materials (SITC section 3) and 13.2 percent of miscellaneous manufactured articles (SITC section 8) (see table 2). Over the last three years, top products for imports included petroleum oils and oils obtained from bituminous minerals, crude (HS code 2709), motor cars and other motor vehicles principally designed for the transport (HS code 8703) and petroleum oils, other than crude (HS code 2710) (see table 5).

Table 5: Top 10 import commodities 2009 to 2011

(Value in million US$)

HS code	4-digit heading of Harmonized System 2007	Value (million US$) 2009	2010	2011	Unit value 2009	2010	2011	Unit	SITC code
	All Commodities	25565.9	30157.8	36111.3					
2709	Petroleum oils and oils obtained from bituminous minerals, crude	1867.8	2871.9	4176.8	0.4	0.6	0.8	US$/kg	333
8703	Motor cars and other motor vehicles principally designed for the transport	1244.9	2021.1	1984.5	10.0	11.9	13.1	thsd US$/unit	781
2710	Petroleum oils, other than crude	1690.8	1617.3	1904.7	*0.6*		*1.1*	US$/kg	334
8471	Automatic data processing machines and units thereof	587.0	795.1	899.7					752
8517	Electrical apparatus for line telephony or line telegraphy	533.3	574.8	785.2					764
3004	Medicaments (excluding goods of heading 30.02, 30.05 or 30.06)	567.2	594.9	663.5	*32.5*		*1.7*	US$/kg	542
8802	Other aircraft (for example, helicopters, aeroplanes); spacecraft	672.8	332.9	604.7	4.7	2.3	4.6	mln US$/unit	792
8704	Motor vehicles for the transport of goods	271.2	448.9	502.9	23.3	27.5	32.8	thsd US$/unit	782
8803	Parts of goods of heading 88.01 or 88.02	290.9	208.7	398.7	*836.4*		*851.2*	US$/kg	792
8528	Reception apparatus for television	275.5	304.4	318.0					761

Nicaragua

Imports: CIF, by origin	Exports: FOB, by last known destination	Trade System: Special

Overview:

In 2010, the value of the Nicaragua's exports increased by 32.6 percent and amounted to 1.8 bln US$ (see table 1 and graph 1). Imports showed a similar development with an increase of 20.5 percent in 2010 to 4.2 bln US$ (see table 2 and graph 1). This resulted in a trade deficit of 2.3 bln US$ in 2010 (see graph 1). This deficit came largely from trade with Latin America and the Caribbean (-1.5 bln US$) (see graph 2). Major deficits were also recorded with Eastern Asia (-484.2 mln US$) and Developed North America (-134.9 mln US$). In 2010, exports were more concentrated among partners than imports: 8 major partners accounted for 80 percent of exports compared to 9 major partners for imports (see graph 3).

Graph 1: Total imports, exports and trade balance

(Bln US$ by year)

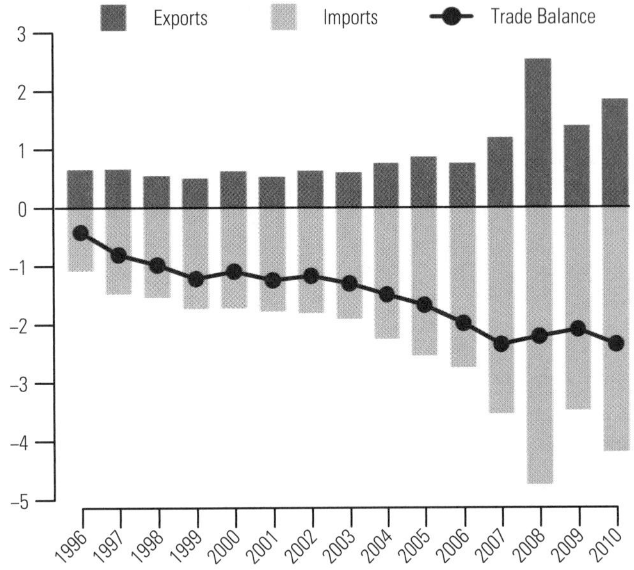

Table 1: Exports by SITC sections

(Value in million US$, growth and shares in percentage)

SITC	2010	Avg. Growth rates (%) 2006-2010	Avg. Growth rates (%) 2009-2010	2010 share
Total	1 847.6	24.9	32.6	100.0
0+1	1 331.9	24.9	27.4	72.1
2+4	148.8	16.5	31.6	8.1
3	22.7	53.5	99.7	1.2
5	26.6	9.0	-58.8	1.4
6	31.9	17.1	23.8	1.7
7	14.1	12.3	-18.0	0.8
8	48.8	20.2	131.9	2.6
9	222.8	39.5	136.2	12.1

Table 2: Imports by SITC sections

(Value in million US$, growth and shares in percentage)

SITC	2010	Avg. Growth rates (%) 2006-2010	Avg. Growth rates (%) 2009-2010	2010 share
Total	4 190.8	11.2	20.5	100.0
0+1	582.0	20.1	9.2	13.9
2+4	138.8	26.3	31.4	3.3
3	909.1	7.1	17.7	21.7
5	756.9	13.4	14.2	18.1
6	532.6	11.1	19.9	12.7
7	915.3	9.9	40.7	21.8
8	350.3	10.0	15.8	8.4
9	5.7	-39.0	-19.1	0.1

Exports Profile:

In 2010, the majority of Nicaragua's exports were food, live animals, beverages and tobacco (SITC sections 0+1): they accounted for 72.1 percent of exported goods. Other major commodity groups included commodities and transactions not classified elsewhere (SITC section 9) and inedible crude materials (except fuels), animal and vegetable oils, fats and waxes (SITC sections 2+4), respectively with 12.1 and 8.1 percent of exports (see table 1). The three major destinations for exports in 2010 were USA, Venezuela and El Salvador (see table 4). From 2008 to 2010, top exported products included coffee, whether or not roasted or decaffeinated (HS code 0901), meat of bovine animals, frozen (HS code 0202) and gold (including gold plated with platinum) (HS code 7108) (see table 3).

Table 3: Top 10 export commodities 2008 to 2010

(Value in million US$)

HS code	4-digit heading of Harmonized System 2007	Value (million US$) 2008	2009	2010	Unit value 2008	2009	2010	Unit	SITC code
	All Commodities	2 537.6	1 393.1	1 847.6					
0901	Coffee, whether or not roasted or decaffeinated	269.9	238.8	343.5	2.9	2.9	3.2	US$/kg	071
0202	Meat of bovine animals, frozen	102.5	142.1	234.9	3.0	3.0	3.6	US$/kg	011
7108	Gold (including gold plated with platinum)	77.6	93.6	222.2	16.3	18.1	20.9	thsd US$/kg	971
9999	Commodities not specified according to kind	310.5	0.8	0.6					931
0306	Crustaceans, whether in shell or not	104.6	82.6	107.6	6.6	4.3	6.1	US$/kg	036
0201	Meat of bovine animals, fresh or chilled	88.4	88.5	72.8	3.8	3.7	4.0	US$/kg	011
1701	Cane or beet sugar and chemically pure sucrose, in solid form	50.4	50.0	126.9	0.4	0.4	0.5	US$/kg	061
1202	Ground-nuts, not roasted or otherwise cooked, whether or not shelled or broken	90.2	65.9	61.8	1.2	0.9	0.9	US$/kg	222
0406	Cheese and curd	65.6	76.8	68.7	2.2	2.7	2.6	US$/kg	024
0713	Dried leguminous vegetables, shelled, whether or not skinned or split	75.5	61.3	59.4	1.4	1.0	1.1	US$/kg	054

Graph 2: Trade Balance by MDG Regions in 2010

(Bln US$)

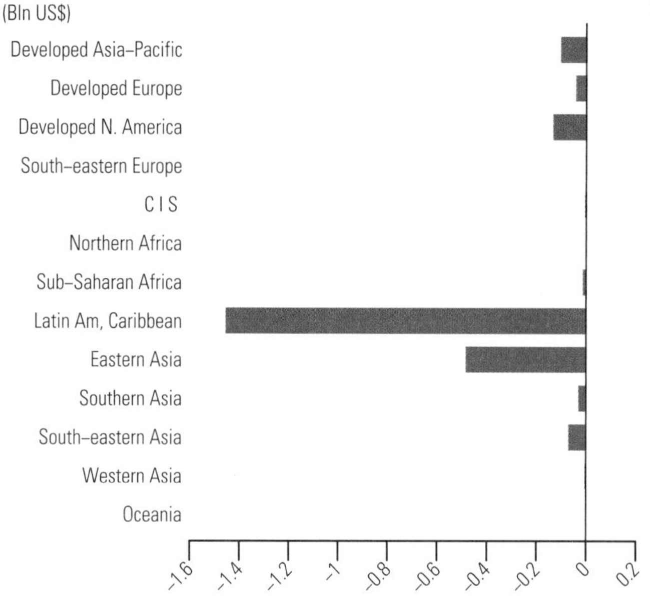

Graph 3: Partner concentration of trade in 2010

(Cumulative share by ranked partners)

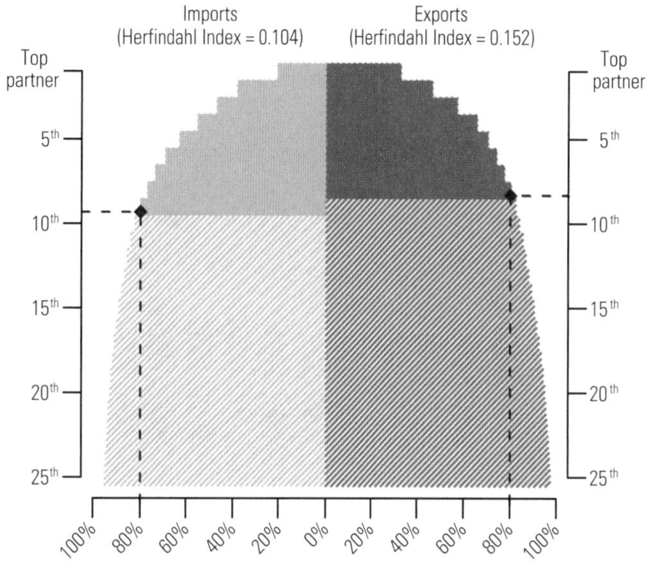

Table 4: Exports by principal countries and SITC sections in 2010

(Value in million US$, percentages of country total)

Country	Total	Shares by SITC sections (%)								
		0 + 1	2 + 4	3	5	6	7	8	9	Total
World	1 847.6	72.1	8.1	1.2	1.4	1.7	0.8	2.6	12.1	100
USA	606.6	75.2	3.6	0.6	0.2	0.7	0.6	4.9	14.1	100
Venezuela	248.6	95.5	4.2	...	0.3	0.0	0.0	0.0	0.0	100
El Salvador	198.2	84.6	3.6	4.4	3.1	1.0	1.4	2.0	0.0	100
Canada	157.4	10.5	1.2	...	...	1.5	0.0	0.0	86.8	100
Costa Rica	87.1	61.3	9.4	8.0	3.8	10.6	2.5	4.3	0.1	100
Guatemala	68.3	73.9	4.9	1.1	8.8	4.7	2.2	4.5	0.0	100
Honduras	61.7	71.8	6.2	2.7	6.6	3.0	1.4	8.1	0.1	100
Mexico	51.6	36.5	59.1	...	0.0	1.3	1.1	1.9	0.0	100
Spain	39.1	99.5	0.1	...	0.2	0.0	0.1	0.1	0.0	100
Other Asia, nes	29.3	66.8	32.5	...	0.1	0.6	0.0	0.0	0.0	100

Imports Profile:

In 2010, Nicaragua's imports were composed of 21.8 percent of machinery and transport equipment (SITC section 7), 21.7 percent of mineral fuels, lubricants and related materials (SITC section 3) and 18.1 percent of chemicals and related products, n.e.s. (SITC section 5) (see table 2). From 2008 to 2010, top imported products were petroleum oils and oils obtained from bituminous minerals, crude (HS code 2709), petroleum oils, other than crude (HS code 2710) and medicaments (excluding goods of heading 30.02, 30.05 or 30.06) (HS code 3004) (see table 5).

Table 5: Top 10 import commodities 2008 to 2010

(Value in million US$)

HS code	4-digit heading of Harmonized System 2007	Value (million US$)			Unit value				SITC code
		2008	2009	2010	2008	2009	2010	Unit	
	All Commodities	4 744.4	3 478.6	4 190.8					
2709	Petroleum oils and oils obtained from bituminous minerals, crude	446.8	371.9	475.5	0.8	0.4	0.6	US$/kg	333
2710	Petroleum oils, other than crude	412.6	366.7	379.1	0.8	0.7	0.7	US$/kg	334
9999	Commodities not specified according to kind	831.9	3.6	5.5					931
3004	Medicaments (excluding goods of heading 30.02, 30.05 or 30.06)	250.2	266.0	311.5	30.8	32.2	33.5	US$/kg	542
8517	Electrical apparatus for line telephony or line telegraphy	93.2	55.9	91.0					764
8704	Motor vehicles for the transport of goods	81.3	61.5	79.1					782
1006	Rice	78.7	53.4	49.0	0.5	0.4	0.4	US$/kg	042
3808	Insecticides, rodenticides, fungicides, herbicides	58.1	52.9	64.2	4.9	4.5	4.1	US$/kg	591
8703	Motor cars and other motor vehicles principally designed for the transport	61.4	45.5	60.6		*15.9*	*16.5*	thsd US$/unit	781
8502	Electric generating sets and rotary converters	53.8	3.5	102.4					716

Niger

Imports: CIF, by origin | **Exports: FOB, by last known destination** | **Trade System: General**

Overview:

In 2011, the value of the exports of Niger grew by 101.4 percent and reached its peak at 973.8 mln US$ (see table 1 and graph 1). The last five years showed an average annual increase of 15.4 percent in exports, while imports registered an average annual growth of 18.8 percent (see tables 1 and 2 and graph 1). In 2011, imports went down by 16.9 percent to 1.9 bln US$. This resulted in a trade deficit of 0.9 bln US$ in 2011, lower than the 2010 deficit of 1.8 bln US$ (see graph 1). By MDG regions, trade recorded deficits with Eastern Asia (-0.5 bln US$) and Sub-Saharan Africa (-0.2 bln US$) (see graph 2). Contrary to imports, exports were concentrated among a few partners: 4 major partners accounted for 80 percent of exports (compared to 12 major partners for imports) (see graph 3).

Graph 1: Total imports, exports and trade balance

(Bln US$ by year)

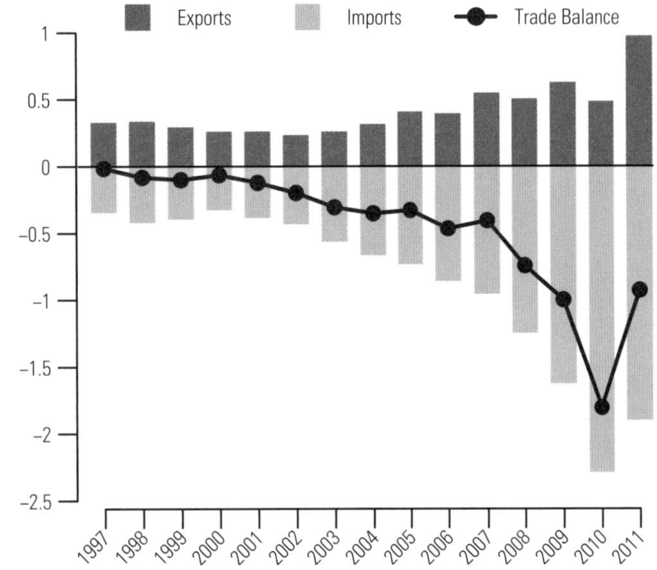

Exports Profile:

In 2011, inedible crude materials (except fuels), animal and vegetable oils, fats and waxes (SITC sections 2+4), largely uranium or thorium ores and concentrates, accounted for the majority of exported goods (see table 2). Their exports rose by 171.6 percent in 2011 and accounted for 72.0 percent of exported goods. Other major commodity group includes food, live animals, beverages and tobacco (SITC sections 0+1) which increased by 35.1 percent and represented 11.8 percent of exports. Major partners for exports included France, Switzerland and Nigeria (see table 4). In addition to uranium or thorium ores and concentrates (HS code 2612), other major commodities for exports from 2009 to 2011 were gold (including gold plated with platinum) (HS code 7108) and live bovine animals (HS code 0102) (see table 3).

Table 1: Exports by SITC sections

(Value in million US$, growth and shares in percentage)

SITC	2011	Avg. Growth rates (%) 2007-2011	Avg. Growth rates (%) 2010-2011	2011 share
Total	973.8	15.4	101.4	100.0
0+1	114.8	5.2	35.1	11.8
2+4	701.3	20.9	171.6	72.0
3	10.8	-7.2	42.7	1.1
5	1.0	-10.3	-8.5	0.1
6	17.5	-2.6	26.1	1.8
7	34.6	8.3	-9.8	3.6
8	3.6	-17.4	-17.9	0.4
9	90.3	10.8	20.2	9.3

Table 2: Imports by SITC sections

(Value in million US$, growth and shares in percentage)

SITC	2011	Avg. Growth rates (%) 2007-2011	Avg. Growth rates (%) 2010-2011	2011 share
Total	1902.1	18.8	-16.9	100.0
0+1	263.8	7.1	-16.3	13.9
2+4	121.1	9.6	22.5	6.4
3	338.7	20.2	18.3	17.8
5	201.4	13.8	41.2	10.6
6	279.7	22.5	-51.0	14.7
7	615.8	30.3	-18.7	32.4
8	81.6	14.9	-31.1	4.3

Table 3: Top 10 export commodities 2009 to 2011

(Value in million US$)

HS code	4-digit heading of Harmonized System 2007	Value (million US$) 2009	2010	2011	Unit value 2009	2010	2011	Unit	SITC code
	All Commodities	628.0	483.5	973.8					
2612	Uranium or thorium ores and concentrates	348.6	242.8	668.8	108.8	61.6	148.9	US$/kg	286
7108	Gold (including gold plated with platinum)	44.1	75.1	90.3					971
0102	Live bovine animals	51.3	26.9	22.1	*810.4*	*827.4*	*844.5*	US$/unit	001
0104	Live sheep and goats	70.2	14.7	13.3					001
0703	Onions, shallots, garlic, leeks and other alliaceous vegetables	32.3	9.6	31.1	0.7	0.2	0.7	US$/kg	054
6309	Worn clothing and other worn articles	11.2	11.0	22.3	0.5	0.5	1.0	US$/kg	269
5208	Woven fabrics of cotton, containing 85 % or more by weight of cotton	12.7	12.9	16.0	21.1	26.5	31.2	US$/kg	652
2710	Petroleum oils, other than crude	7.2	7.6	10.8	1.0	0.8	1.1	US$/kg	334
0713	Dried leguminous vegetables, shelled, whether or not skinned or split	2.8	1.7	16.6	0.7	0.3	0.5	US$/kg	054
8429	Self-propelled bulldozers, angledozers, graders, levellers, scrapers	0.4	12.8	5.0		*52.9*	*45.7*	thsd US$/unit	723

Graph 2: Trade Balance by MDG Regions in 2011

(Mln US$)

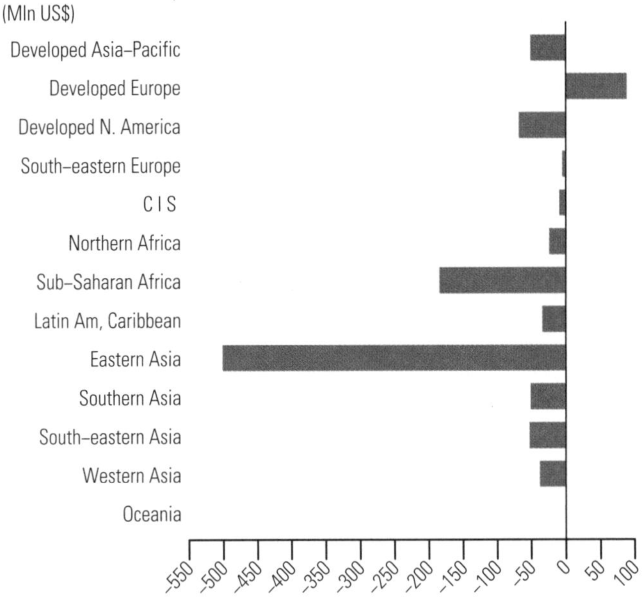

Graph 3: Partner concentration of trade in 2011

(Cumulative share by ranked partners)

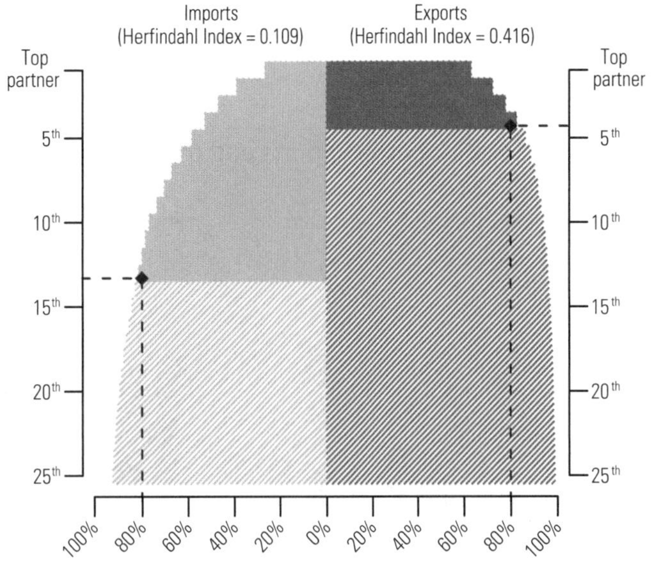

Table 4: Exports by principal countries and SITC sections in 2011

(Value in million US$, percentages of country total)

Country	Total	Shares by SITC sections (%)								
		0 + 1	2 + 4	3	5	6	7	8	9	Total
World	973.8	11.8	72.0	1.1	0.1	1.8	3.6	0.4	9.3	100
France	615.2	0.1	98.4	0.0	0.0	0.0	1.2	0.2	...	100
Switzerland	90.6	0.0	0.1	...	...	0.3	0.0	0.0	99.7	100
Nigeria	52.9	93.1	3.8	2.1	0.0	0.3	0.0	0.7	...	100
USA	45.8	0.1	94.0	3.2	...	0.0	2.1	0.5	...	100
Ghana	35.5	99.4	0.2	...	...	0.4	0.1	0.0	...	100
China	22.2	6.9	12.2	...	0.4	0.4	76.1	4.1	...	100
Japan	16.2	0.0	83.9	...	...	2.5	13.5	0.0	...	100
Spain	13.7	0.1	99.3	...	0.1	0.2	0.4	0.0	...	100
Netherlands	13.1	0.0	14.3	...	...	85.5	0.1	0.1	...	100
Côte d'Ivoire	10.5	30.9	0.0	32.4	...	36.3	...	0.4	...	100

Imports Profile:

In 2011, imports were composed of 32.4 percent of machinery and transport equipment (SITC section 7), 17.8 percent of mineral fuels, lubricants and related materials (SITC section 3) and 14.7 percent of manufactured goods classified chiefly by material (SITC sections 6) (see table 2). By products, top commodities for imports from 2009 to 2011 included petroleum oils, other than crude (HS code 2710), structures (excluding prefabricated buildings of heading 94.06) (HS code 7308) and motor vehicles for the transport of goods (HS code 8704) (see table 5).

Table 5: Top 10 import commodities 2009 to 2011

(Value in million US$)

HS code	4-digit heading of Harmonized System 2007	Value (million US$)			Unit value				SITC code
		2009	2010	2011	2009	2010	2011	Unit	
	All Commodities	1 627.2	2 290.0	1 902.1					
2710	Petroleum oils, other than crude	172.5	258.1	306.2	0.8	0.9	1.2	US$/kg	334
7308	Structures (excluding prefabricated buildings of heading 94.06)	43.6	192.5	15.3	5.0	12.4	3.7	US$/kg	691
8704	Motor vehicles for the transport of goods	55.5	86.7	54.3					782
1006	Rice	68.0	71.6	54.9	0.4	0.5	0.3	US$/kg	042
3004	Medicaments (excluding goods of heading 30.02, 30.05 or 30.06)	54.5	30.5	107.9	21.5	8.0	27.4	US$/kg	542
2523	Portland cement, aluminous cement, slag cement	49.6	59.4	63.5	0.2	0.2	0.2	US$/kg	661
8431	Parts suitable for use principally with the machinery of headings 84.25	55.4	58.1	44.8	13.9	23.0	40.2	US$/kg	723
6309	Worn clothing and other worn articles	49.0	44.3	44.4	1.5	1.4	1.2	US$/kg	269
8429	Self-propelled bulldozers, angledozers, graders, levellers, scrapers	53.4	37.8	37.8		*58.2*	*53.7*	thsd US$/unit	723
2402	Cigars, cheroots, cigarillos and cigarettes	32.3	38.1	46.1	10.0	9.4	10.6	US$/kg	122

Nigeria

Imports: CIF, by origin	Exports: FOB, by last known destination	Trade System: General

Overview:

From 2006 to 2010, Nigeria's exports increased on average by 10.0 percent each year and amounted to 86.6 bln US$ (see table 1 and graph1). During the same period, imports increased on average by 17.9 percent each year to 44.2 bln US$ (see table 2 and graph 1). The trade surplus increased from 16.0 bln US$ in 2009 to 42.3 bln US$ in 2010 (see graph 1). Significant surpluses were recorded with Developed North America (+24.4 bln US$), Developed Europe (+9.4 bln US$) and Sub-Saharan Africa (+7.5 bln US$) (see graph 2). Trade recorded deficits with Eastern Asia (-7.2 bln US$) and Western Asia (-2.5 bln US$). In 2010, exports were concentrated among a few partners while imports were diversified: 12 major partners accounted for 80 percent of exports compared to 16 major partners for imports (see graph 3).

Graph 1: Total imports, exports and trade balance

(Bln US$ by year)

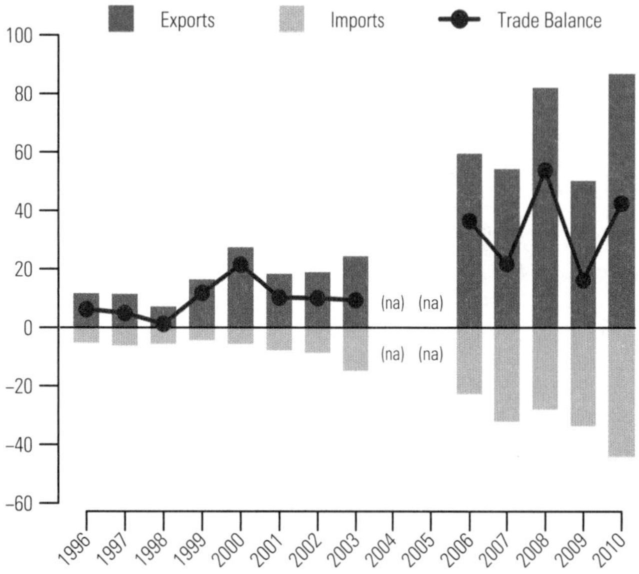

Exports Profile:

Mineral fuels, lubricants and related materials (SITC section 3), largely crude petroleum oils, accounted for 87.1 percent of Nigeria's exports in 2010 (see table 1). Major partners included USA, India and Brazil (see table 4). In 2010, petroleum oils, crude (HS code 2709) represented 70.4 percent of exports (see table 3). Other major commodities for exports included petroleum oils, other than crude (HS code 2710) and petroleum gases and other gaseous hydrocarbons (HS code 2711).

Table 1: Exports by SITC sections

(Value in million US$, growth and shares in percentage)

SITC	2010	Avg. Growth rates (%) 2006-2010	2009-2010	2010 share
Total	86 567.9	10.0	73.4	100.0
0+1	2 246.3	194.5	8.6	2.6
2+4	2 585.3	85.5	234.8	3.0
3	75 428.9	6.7	67.2	87.1
5	527.8	62.4	75.4	0.6
6	3 946.7	146.0	375.9	4.6
7	1 020.8	19.4	84.6	1.2
8	699.4	59.2	252.3	0.8
9	112.7	363.0	24.1	0.1

Table 2: Imports by SITC sections

(Value in million US$, growth and shares in percentage)

SITC	2010	Avg. Growth rates (%) 2006-2010	2009-2010	2010 share
Total	44 235.3	17.9	30.5	100.0
0+1	4 247.5	1.4	8.2	9.6
2+4	769.1	25.1	39.4	1.7
3	580.2	-3.1	73.3	1.3
5	4 766.8	6.4	4.7	10.8
6	9 355.3	24.5	47.6	21.1
7	22 169.0	26.4	36.5	50.1
8	2 337.5	9.9	38.1	5.3
9	9.9	-6.0	-96.3	0.0

Table 3: Top 10 export commodities 2008 to 2010

(Value in million US$)

HS code	4-digit heading of Harmonized System 2002	Value (million US$) 2008	2009	2010	Unit value 2008	2009	2010	Unit	SITC code
	All Commodities	81 820.5	49 937.5	86 567.9					
2709	Petroleum oils, crude	74 832.1	42 212.0	60 904.6					333
2710	Petroleum oils, other than crude	7.9	15.0	9 805.0					334
2711	Petroleum gases and other gaseous hydrocarbons	224.6	2 895.5	4 716.8					343
4113	Leather further prepared after tanning or crusting	468.3	315.1	2 073.8	*44.1*	16.9	10.8	US$/kg	611
1801	Cocoa beans, whole or broken, raw or roasted	510.3	1 250.9	1 048.0	*1.9*	5.2	1.8	US$/kg	072
8905	Light-vessels, fire-floats, dredgers, floating cranes and other vessels	1 561.6	9.5	314.6			2.1	US$/unit	793
4106	Tanned or crust hides and skins of other animals, without wool or hair on	209.4	195.0	956.4		3.8	51.4	US$/kg	611
4001	Natural rubber, balata, gutta-percha, guayule, chicle	420.9	170.4	555.3	*2.1*	1.1	4.7	US$/kg	231
1207	Other oil seeds and oleaginous fruits	153.5	194.7	641.5		1.7	*2.8*	US$/kg	222
3901	Polymers of ethylene, in primary forms	516.0	82.9	138.6	*1.4*	1.6	2.6	US$/kg	571

Graph 2: Trade Balance by MDG Regions in 2010

(Bln US$)

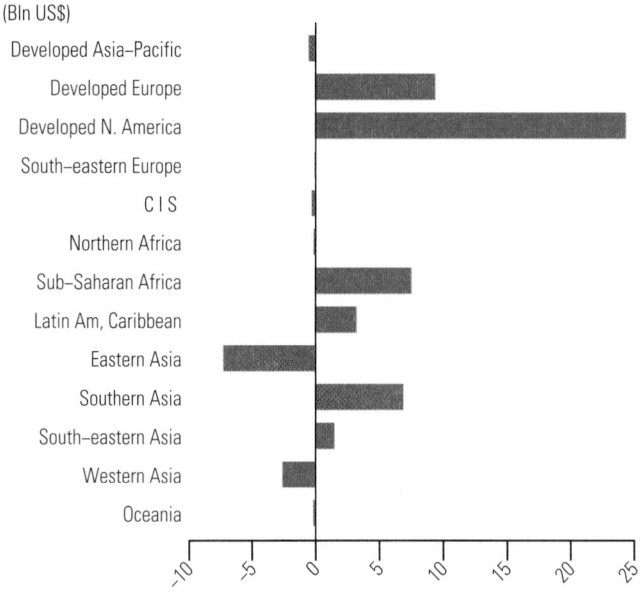

Graph 3: Partner concentration of trade in 2010

(Cumulative share by ranked partners)

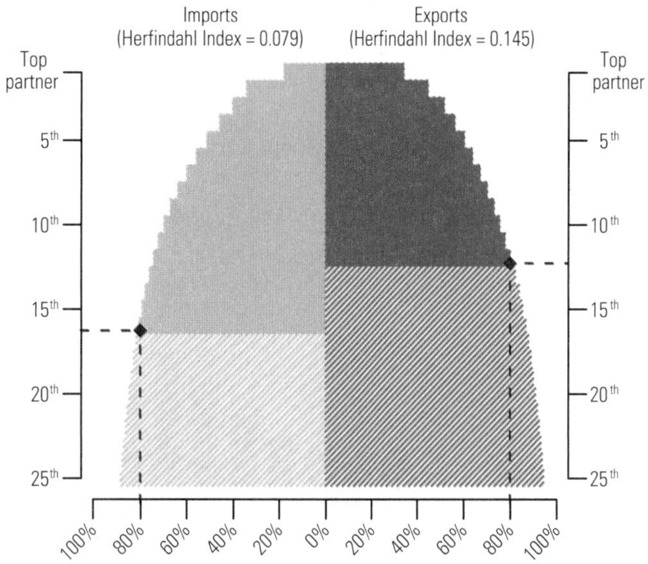

Table 4: Exports by principal countries and SITC sections in 2010

(Value in million US$, percentages of country total)

Country	Total	Shares by SITC sections (%)								
		0 + 1	2 + 4	3	5	6	7	8	9	Total
World	86567.9	2.6	3.0	87.1	0.6	4.6	1.2	0.8	0.1	100
USA	29755.9	0.5	1.0	95.1	0.3	1.0	0.8	1.4	0.0	100
India	9068.5	0.4	0.4	92.1	1.1	5.7	0.2	0.1	0.0	100
Brazil	6042.0	0.2	0.4	98.6	0.0	0.2	0.0	0.6	0.0	100
Netherlands	3936.5	6.8	0.1	90.4	0.0	0.0	2.5	0.0	0.0	100
France	3506.0	4.4	11.2	82.3	0.0	0.8	1.3	0.0	...	100
Italy	3047.9	0.5	2.2	73.9	0.0	22.9	0.1	0.1	0.3	100
Spain	2830.1	1.7	0.2	96.0	...	1.8	0.1	0.0	0.1	100
Equatorial Guinea	2675.2	0.0	0.0	99.8	0.0	0.0	0.0	0.1	...	100
Canada	2544.9	0.6	0.0	99.4	...	0.0	0.0	...	...	100
Belgium	2112.7	6.3	3.7	82.6	0.0	6.1	1.0	0.1	0.2	100

Imports Profile:

In 2010, imports were composed of 50.1 percent of machinery and transport equipment (SITC section 7), 21.1 percent of manufactured goods classified chiefly by material (SITC section 6) and 10.8 percent of chemicals and related products, n.e.s. (SITC section 5) (see table 2). From 2008 to 2010, top imported products included motor cars and other motor vehicles principally designed for the transport (HS code 8703), motor vehicles for the transport of goods (HS code 8704) and motor vehicles for the transport of ten or more persons (HS code 8702) (see table 5).

Table 5: Top 10 import commodities 2008 to 2010

(Value in million US$)

HS code	4-digit heading of Harmonized System 2002	Value (million US$)			Unit value				SITC code
		2008	2009	2010	2008	2009	2010	Unit	
	All Commodities	28193.6	33906.3	44235.3					
8703	Motor cars and other motor vehicles principally designed for the transport	1652.5	2745.9	4137.6			0.3	US$/unit	781
8704	Motor vehicles for the transport of goods	589.1	1117.1	2016.8			0.4	US$/unit	782
8702	Motor vehicles for the transport of ten or more persons	778.8	1222.9	1085.2			0.3	US$/unit	783
1001	Wheat and meslin	671.2	1107.6	839.7	*0.3*	0.8	0.6	US$/kg	041
8708	Parts and accessories of the motor vehicles of headings 87.01 to 87.05	263.1	706.8	939.3	*9.8*	0.5	*0.5*	US$/kg	784
0303	Fish, frozen, excluding fish fillets	535.0	571.9	745.6		1.4	0.4	US$/kg	034
8504	Electrical transformers, static converters (for example, rectifiers)	292.7	269.7	1231.3					771
8525	Transmission apparatus for radio-telephony, radio-broadcasting	1212.4	252.1	159.2			9.7	US$/unit	764
8481	Taps, cocks, valves and similar appliances for pipes, boiler shells	319.8	381.9	895.6	*23.3*	1.8	*3.4*	US$/kg	747
3901	Polymers of ethylene, in primary forms	297.9	633.2	499.0	*1.6*	1.9	1.0	US$/kg	571

Norway, including Svalbard and Jan Mayen Islands

Imports: CIF, by origin | **Exports: FOB, by last known destination** | **Trade System: General**

Overview:

After several years of continuous growth marked by a peak of 173.2 bln US$ in 2008, the value of the exports of Norway, including Svalbard and Jan Mayen Islands, contracted sharply in 2009 (by 33.8 percent) but bounced back in 2010 by 14.6 percent to amount to 131.4 bln US$, still well below its 2008 level (see table 1 and graph 1). Imports showed a similar development with an increase by 12.0 percent to 77.3 bln US$ in 2010. This resulted in a trade surplus of 54.1 bln US$, higher than the 2009 surplus of 45.7 bln US$ (see graph 1). This surplus was accounted for largely by trade with Developed Europe: trade with this region recorded a surplus of 57.9 bln US$ (see graph 2). Norway's trade was relatively diversified across partners: 11 major partners accounted for 80 percent of exports compared to 16 major partners for imports (see graph 3).

Graph 1: Total imports, exports and trade balance

(Bln US$ by year)

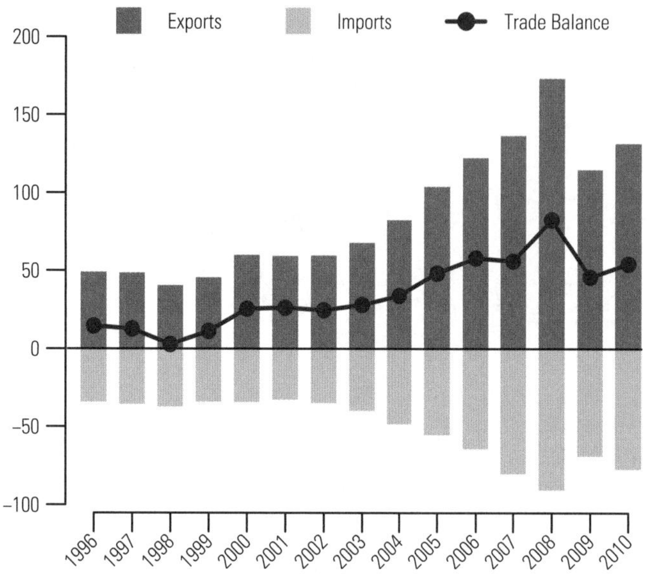

Table 1: Exports by SITC sections

(Value in million US$, growth and shares in percentage)

SITC	2010	Avg. Growth rates (%) 2006-2010	2009-2010	2010 share
Total	131 395.4	1.8	14.6	100.0
0+1	9 217.2	11.8	24.1	7.0
2+4	1 852.2	7.6	31.4	1.4
3	83 931.2	0.3	16.2	63.9
5	4 551.2	11.8	19.7	3.5
6	11 412.6	-1.5	21.6	8.7
7	12 334.2	4.9	-9.6	9.4
8	3 330.4	5.9	3.6	2.5
9	4 766.5	3.2	33.7	3.6

Table 2: Imports by SITC sections

(Value in million US$, growth and shares in percentage)

SITC	2010	Avg. Growth rates (%) 2006-2010	2009-2010	2010 share
Total	77 251.7	4.7	12.0	100.0
0+1	5 348.4	9.0	5.6	6.9
2+4	5 844.6	3.0	31.0	7.6
3	5 055.2	14.6	47.4	6.5
5	7 440.0	6.2	9.5	9.6
6	11 337.5	0.9	9.6	14.7
7	29 767.1	3.7	7.1	38.5
8	11 452.2	4.7	7.1	14.8
9	1 006.6	40.1	150.9	1.3

Exports Profile:

In 2010, mineral fuels, lubricants and related materials (SITC section 3) represented nearly two-thirds (63.9 percent) of Norway's exports (see table 1). Other major commodity groups included machinery and transport equipment (SITC section 7) and manufactured goods classified chiefly by material (SITC section 6) respectively with 9.4 and 8.7 percent of exports. Major markets for exports included United Kingdom, Netherlands and Germany (see table 4). Top exported products over the last three years were petroleum products: petroleum oils and oils obtained from bituminous minerals, crude (HS code 2709), petroleum gases and other gaseous hydrocarbons (HS code 2711) and petroleum oils, other than crude (HS code 2710). They accounted respectively for 35.7, 23.7 and 4.0 percent of exports in 2010 (see table 3).

Table 3: Top 10 export commodities 2008 to 2010

(Value in million US$)

HS code	4-digit heading of Harmonized System 2007	Value (million US$) 2008	2009	2010	Unit value 2008	2009	2010	Unit	SITC code
	All Commodities	173 221.4	114 675.5	131 395.4					
2709	Petroleum oils and oils obtained from bituminous minerals, crude	66 869.1	39 931.8	46 972.5	0.7	0.5	0.6	US$/kg	333
2711	Petroleum gases and other gaseous hydrocarbons	43 550.1	26 854.5	31 168.9	0.6	0.3	0.4	US$/kg	343
2710	Petroleum oils, other than crude	7 678.8	4 717.5	5 246.2	0.8	0.5	0.6	US$/kg	334
9999	Commodities not specified according to kind	6 426.1	3 439.1	4 590.8					931
7601	Unwrought aluminium	4 821.9	2 800.3	3 568.8	3.0	2.1	2.4	US$/kg	684
0302	Fish, fresh or chilled, excluding fish fillets	2 961.8	3 241.4	4 318.7	4.3	4.4	5.1	US$/kg	034
7502	Unwrought nickel	1 892.2	1 254.6	1 964.9	21.3	14.2	21.4	US$/kg	683
8901	Cruise ships, excursion boats, ferry-boats, cargo ships, barges	1 900.8	1 559.5	1 116.0	26.0	22.0	17.4	mln US$/unit	793
0303	Fish, frozen, excluding fish fillets and other fish meat of heading 03.04	1 455.6	1 444.8	1 660.3	1.6	1.3	1.5	US$/kg	034
8431	Parts suitable for use principally with the machinery of headings 84.25	1 150.8	1 415.1	1 357.4	36.5	36.0	41.7	US$/kg	723

Graph 2: Trade Balance by MDG Regions in 2010

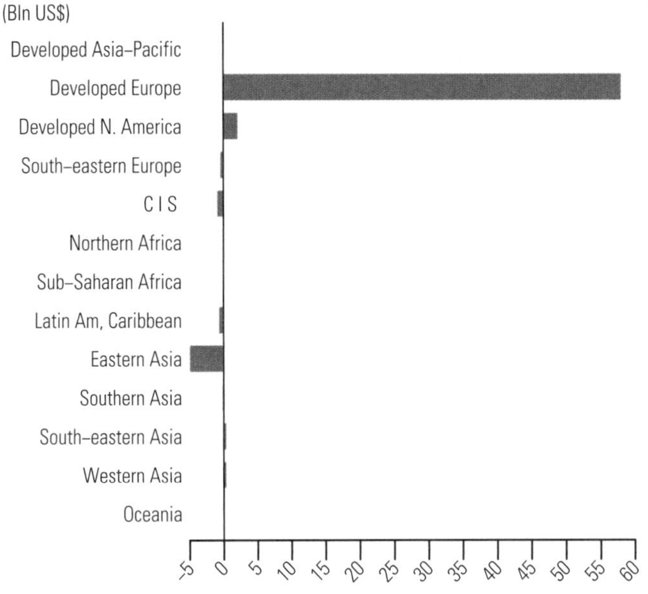

Graph 3: Partner concentration of trade in 2010

(Cumulative share by ranked partners)

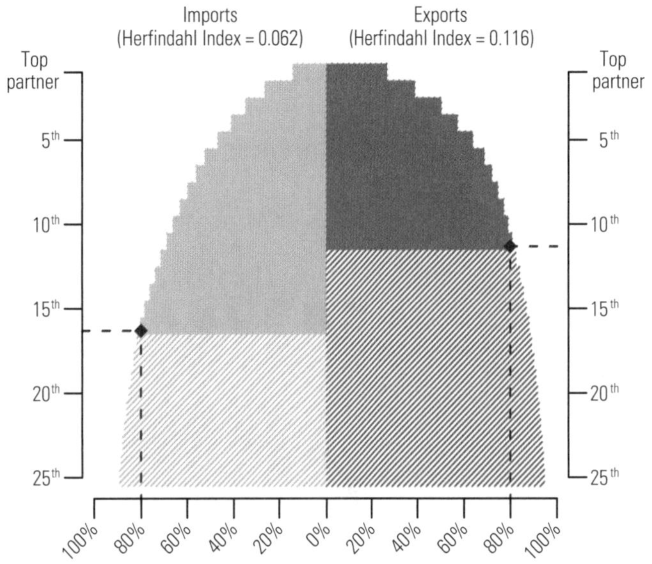

Table 4: Exports by principal countries and SITC sections in 2010

(Value in million US$, percentages of country total)

Country	Total	Shares by SITC sections (%)								
		0 + 1	2 + 4	3	5	6	7	8	9	Total
World	131 395.4	7.0	1.4	63.9	3.5	8.7	9.4	2.5	3.6	100
United Kingdom	35 474.6	1.2	0.2	90.5	0.4	2.6	2.6	0.6	1.8	100
Netherlands	15 703.1	1.9	1.2	79.7	1.8	8.3	3.8	0.9	2.5	100
Germany	14 875.0	2.6	2.0	67.9	3.8	12.4	5.2	1.7	4.5	100
Sweden	9 170.4	5.8	2.9	48.9	3.3	14.4	13.9	4.5	6.3	100
France	8 624.9	10.2	0.6	77.9	0.7	4.5	3.7	1.5	0.9	100
USA	6 586.9	7.6	0.7	45.6	6.1	12.7	15.9	8.0	3.3	100
Denmark	4 232.9	17.6	2.6	47.2	3.3	10.3	11.1	4.6	3.4	100
Belgium	3 468.2	2.1	1.6	68.7	9.4	10.1	3.6	1.2	3.3	100
Italy	3 289.0	7.4	1.6	70.7	1.0	10.7	4.4	1.3	2.9	100
Spain	2 422.9	12.3	0.9	54.4	1.1	15.5	8.9	2.4	4.5	100

Imports Profile:

In 2010, imports were composed of 38.5 percent of machinery and transport equipment (SITC section 7), 14.8 percent of miscellaneous manufactured articles (SITC section 8) and 14.7 percent of manufactured goods classified chiefly by material (SITC section 6) (see table 2). Over the last three years, top imported commodities were motor cars and other motor vehicles principally designed for the transport (HS code 8703), cruise ships, excursion boats, ferry-boats, cargo ships, barges (HS code 8901) and petroleum oils, other than crude (HS code 2710) (see table 5).

Table 5: Top 10 import commodities 2008 to 2010

(Value in million US$)

HS code	4-digit heading of Harmonized System 2007	Value (million US$)			Unit value				SITC code
		2008	2009	2010	2008	2009	2010	Unit	
	All Commodities	90 581.3	68 968.8	77 251.7					
8703	Motor cars and other motor vehicles principally designed for the transport	3 944.6	3 108.6	4 336.7	24.4	22.1	23.6	thsd US$/unit	781
8901	Cruise ships, excursion boats, ferry-boats, cargo ships, barges	3 485.1	1 248.5	2 900.5	51.3	37.8	64.5	mln US$/unit	793
2710	Petroleum oils, other than crude	2 744.6	2 032.3	2 581.1	0.8	0.5	0.7	US$/kg	334
7501	Nickel mattes, nickel oxide sinters and other intermediate products	2 710.5	1 408.2	2 213.4	15.2	9.1	13.0	US$/kg	284
3004	Medicaments (excluding goods of heading 30.02, 30.05 or 30.06)	1 465.6	1 314.5	1 446.0	136.9	118.6	130.8	US$/kg	542
8471	Automatic data processing machines and units thereof	1 527.6	1 273.5	1 416.4	273.7	259.7	259.4	US$/unit	752
8517	Electrical apparatus for line telephony or line telegraphy	1 334.7	1 178.3	1 442.4					764
8906	Other vessels, including warships and lifeboats other than rowing boats	1 307.9	1 646.5	584.0	6.2	10.8	2.9	mln US$/unit	793
8704	Motor vehicles for the transport of goods	1 693.5	752.6	1 032.8	46.4	38.6	38.2	thsd US$/unit	782
9403	Other furniture and parts thereof	1 311.4	1 021.7	1 058.0					821

Occupied Palestinian Territory

Imports: CIF, by origin | **Exports: FOB, by last known destination** | **Trade System: Special**

Overview:

In 2010, the value of the exports of the Occupied Palestinian Territory grew by 11.0 percent and reached 575.5 mln US$ (see table 1 and graph 1). The last five years showed an average annual increase of 11.9 percent in exports, while imports registered an average annual growth of 9.4 percent (see tables 1 and 2 and graph 1). In 2010, imports increased by 9.9 percent to 4.0 bln US$. The trade balance recorded a deficit of 3.4 bln US$ in 2010, slightly higher than the 3.1 bln US$ deficit in 2009 (see graph 1). By MDG regions, deficits were recorded with Western Asia (-2.6 bln US$), Developed Europe (-0.4 bln US$) and Eastern Asia (-0.2 bln US$) (see graph 2). Trade was highly concentrated with top partners: in 2010, 1 major partner accounted for 80 percent of exports compared to 3 major partners for imports (see graph 3).

Graph 1: Total imports, exports and trade balance

(Bln US$ by year)

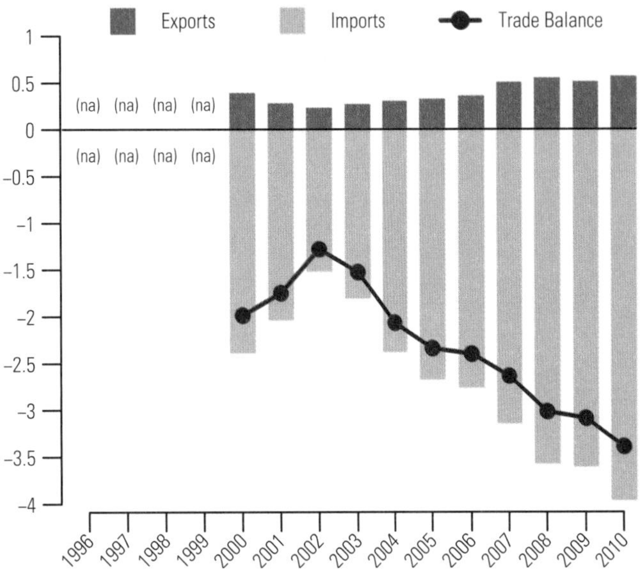

Table 1: Exports by SITC sections

(Value in million US$, growth and shares in percentage)

SITC	2010	Avg. Growth rates (%) 2006-2010	2009-2010	2010 share
Total	575.5	11.9	11.0	100.0
0+1	104.0	20.8	25.4	18.1
2+4	86.6	28.1	95.7	15.1
3	1.5	-17.7	-26.6	0.3
5	46.0	6.9	11.7	8.0
6	190.1	5.2	-0.5	33.0
7	31.7	9.4	10.0	5.5
8	113.3	12.9	-9.1	19.7
9	2.3	340.3	-34.7	0.4

Table 2: Imports by SITC sections

(Value in million US$, growth and shares in percentage)

SITC	2010	Avg. Growth rates (%) 2006-2010	2009-2010	2010 share
Total	3 958.5	9.4	9.9	100.0
0+1	862.3	10.0	16.4	21.8
2+4	84.1	3.8	19.2	2.1
3	1 239.5	7.1	9.1	31.3
5	326.1	13.1	20.4	8.2
6	686.8	13.5	24.1	17.4
7	543.9	13.4	-4.2	13.7
8	211.7	8.4	13.6	5.3
9	4.1	-48.7	-94.6	0.1

Exports Profile:

In 2010, exports were composed of 33.0 percent of manufactured goods classified chiefly by material (SITC section 6), 19.7 percent of miscellaneous manufactured articles (SITC section 8) and 18.1 percent of food, live animals, beverages and tobacco (SITC section 0+1) (see table 1). In addition to Israel, other major partners for exports were Jordan and United Arab Emirates (see table 4). Top exported products included worked monumental or building stone (except slate) and articles thereof (HS code 6802), ferrous waste and scrap; remelting scrap ingots of iron or steel (HS code 7204) and articles for the conveyance or packing of goods, of plastics (HS code 3923) (see table 3).

Table 3: Top 10 export commodities 2008 to 2010

(Value in million US$)

HS code	4-digit heading of Harmonized System 2007	Value (million US$) 2008	2009	2010	Unit value 2008	2009	2010	Unit	SITC code
	All Commodities	558.4	518.4	575.5					
6802	Worked monumental or building stone (except slate) and articles thereof	82.1	97.6	99.6	*0.9*	*0.9*	*0.8*	US$/kg	661
7204	Ferrous waste and scrap; remelting scrap ingots of iron or steel	36.6	17.4	32.6					282
3923	Articles for the conveyance or packing of goods, of plastics	20.2	21.3	24.1	*2.9*	*3.5*	*3.6*	US$/kg	893
9403	Other furniture and parts thereof	16.2	19.7	18.0					821
9404	Mattress supports; articles of bedding and similar furnishing	14.2	24.8	13.1					821
2402	Cigars, cheroots, cigarillos and cigarettes	14.7	17.1	18.6	*11.7*	*13.1*	*12.3*	US$/kg	122
6401	Waterproof footwear with outer soles and uppers of rubber or of plastics	14.4	14.6	15.1		*9.0*		US$/pair	851
4415	Packing cases, boxes, crates, drums and similar packings, of wood	15.3	12.9	13.1					635
1509	Olive oil and its fractions	11.5	7.5	13.8	*4.9*	*5.2*	*4.4*	US$/kg	421
9401	Seats (other than those of heading 94.02)	14.0	7.2	10.2					821

Graph 2: Trade Balance by MDG Regions in 2010

(Bln US$)

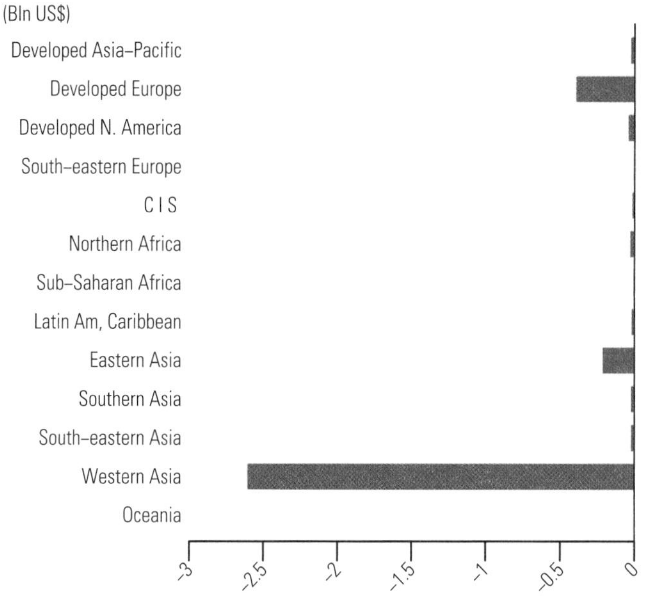

Graph 3: Partner concentration of trade in 2010

(Cumulative share by ranked partners)

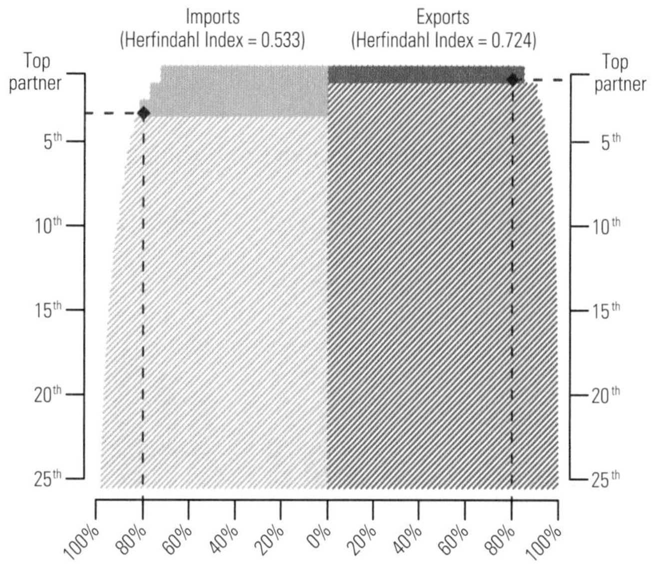

Table 4: Exports by principal countries and SITC sections in 2010

(Value in million US$, percentages of country total)

Country	Total	Shares by SITC sections (%)								
		0+1	2+4	3	5	6	7	8	9	Total
World	575.5	18.1	15.1	0.3	8.0	33.0	5.5	19.7	0.4	100
Israel	488.4	17.5	11.7	0.3	7.0	35.5	5.9	21.8	0.3	100
Jordan	31.2	22.7	22.2	0.0	8.2	30.7	6.9	7.9	1.4	100
United Arab Emirates	11.7	33.4	51.6	...	0.0	13.7	...	0.9	0.3	100
USA	7.3	20.8	67.9	...	0.2	11.0	...	0.2	...	100
Algeria	7.2	2.8	0.0	...	89.6	7.6	...	...	...	100
Saudi Arabia	5.7	17.0	63.0	...	1.9	7.1	...	9.5	1.6	100
Egypt	4.3	0.8	6.9	...	5.7	15.0	0.5	66.8	4.3	100
Netherlands	3.0	16.1	74.0	...	...	0.2	9.7	...	...	100
Kuwait	2.8	40.0	46.7	...	...	13.0	...	0.3	...	100
Germany	2.7	6.3	9.6	...	72.0	5.8	...	6.3	...	100

Imports Profile:

In 2010, imports were composed of 31.3 percent of mineral fuels, lubricants and related materials (SITC section 3), 21.8 percent of food, live animals, beverages and tobacco (SITC sections 0+1) and 17.4 percent of manufactured goods classified chiefly by material (SITC section 6) (see table 2). From 2008 to 2010, top imported products were petroleum oils, other than crude (HS code 2710), electrical energy (HS code 2716) and petroleum gases and other gaseous hydrocarbons (HS code 2711) (see table 5).

Table 5: Top 10 import commodities 2008 to 2010

(Value in million US$)

HS code	4-digit heading of Harmonized System 2007	Value (million US$)			Unit value				SITC code
		2008	2009	2010	2008	2009	2010	Unit	
	All Commodities	3568.7	3600.8	3958.5					
2710	Petroleum oils, other than crude	950.4	697.0	659.2	*1.0*	*1.3*	*0.9*	US$/kg	334
2716	Electrical energy	378.9	354.6	348.0	*53.2*	*82.5*	*57.1*	US$/MWh	351
2711	Petroleum gases and other gaseous hydrocarbons	123.6	75.3	219.8	*0.5*	*0.8*	*0.4*	US$/kg	343
8703	Motor cars and other motor vehicles principally designed for the transport	128.0	148.0	95.2		*14.4*	*13.7*	thsd US$/unit	781
2523	Portland cement, aluminous cement, slag cement	78.0	105.9	114.3	*0.1*		*0.1*	US$/kg	661
3004	Medicaments (excluding goods of heading 30.02, 30.05 or 30.06)	96.4	71.9	72.6					542
2309	Preparations of a kind used in animal feeding	33.9	105.3	69.3	*1.5*	*1.6*	*1.6*	US$/kg	081
2202	Waters with added sugar	50.9	48.1	59.1	*1.1*	*1.2*	*1.1*	US$/litre	111
6802	Worked monumental or building stone (except slate) and articles thereof	62.2	13.2	77.2	*0.7*	*0.8*	*0.7*	US$/kg	661
1006	Rice	52.7	52.7	32.5	*0.6*	*1.0*	*1.0*	US$/kg	042

Oman

Imports: CIF, by origin | **Exports: FOB, by last known destination** | **Trade System: General**

Overview:

Since 2006, Oman's exports increased on average by 14.1 percent each year and amounted to 36.6 bln US$ while imports increased on average by 16.0 percent each year to reach 20.0 bln US$ in 2010 (see tables 1 and 2 and graph 1). This resulted in a trade surplus of 16.6 bln US$ compared to 9.8 bln US$ in 2009. Trade with Southern Asia, Sub-Saharan Africa and South-eastern Asia recorded surpluses amounting respectively to 0.4 bln US$, 0.2 bln US$ and 0.1 bln US$ (see graph 2). Trade recorded significant deficits with Western Asia (-3.3 bln US$) and Developed Europe (-2.2 bln US$), although these numbers are distorted by the lack of partner information for exports. By partners, exports were more concentrated than imports: in 2010, 1 major partner accounted for 80 percent of exports compared to 11 major partners for imports (see graph 3).

Graph 1: Total imports, exports and trade balance

(Bln US$ by year)

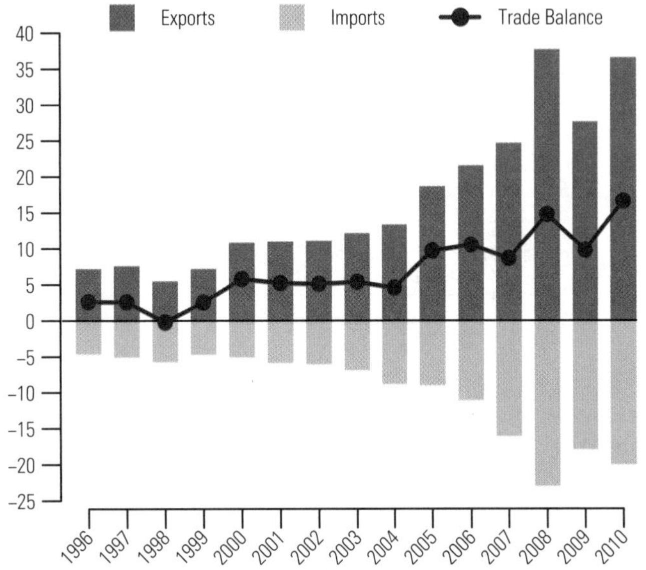

Table 1: Exports by SITC sections

(Value in million US$, growth and shares in percentage)

SITC	2010	Avg. Growth rates (%) 2006-2010	2009-2010	2010 share
Total	36 599.7	14.1	32.4	100.0
0+1	764.5	18.8	18.6	2.1
2+4	335.6	17.9	-4.5	0.9
3	25 347.3	9.1	35.5	69.3
5	2 325.2	52.8	60.9	6.4
6	1 104.2	20.5	-10.9	3.0
7	849.5	15.0	-19.4	2.3
8	294.3	13.2	-16.1	0.8
9	5 579.1	38.7	44.4	15.2

Table 2: Imports by SITC sections

(Value in million US$, growth and shares in percentage)

SITC	2010	Avg. Growth rates (%) 2006-2010	2009-2010	2010 share
Total	19 972.7	16.0	11.9	100.0
0+1	2 086.5	17.9	14.7	10.4
2+4	632.4	11.9	12.1	3.2
3	1 238.3	36.0	22.9	6.2
5	1 617.2	22.4	7.6	8.1
6	3 040.1	10.0	-2.1	15.2
7	3 819.9	-8.4	-54.2	19.1
8	1 086.7	14.9	13.3	5.4
9	6 451.7	107.3	1057.1	32.3

Exports Profile:

In 2010, exports of mineral fuels, lubricants and related materials (SITC section 3) increased by 35.5 percent and accounted for 69.3 percent of total exports (see table 1). Other major commodity groups were commodities and transactions not classified elsewhere (SITC section 9) and chemicals and related products, n.e.s. (SITC section 5) with respectively 15.2 percent and 6.4 percent of exports. Major destinations for exported products were United Arab Emirates, India and China (see table 4). Over the last three years, top products for exports were petroleum products: petroleum oils, crude (HS code 2709), petroleum gases and other gaseous hydrocarbons (HS code 2711) and petroleum oils, other than crude (HS code 2710) (see table 3). In 2010, petroleum oils, crude (HS code 2709) alone accounted for more than half (56.9 percent) of exports.

Table 3: Top 10 export commodities 2008 to 2010

(Value in million US$)

HS code	4-digit heading of Harmonized System 2002	Value (million US$) 2008	2009	2010	Unit value 2008	2009	2010	Unit	SITC code
	All Commodities	37 719.1	27 650.6	36 599.7					
2709	Petroleum oils, crude	21 887.9	13 939.0	20 826.3	0.7	0.1	*0.4*	US$/kg	333
9999	Commodities not specified according to kind	3 940.1	3 846.8	5 543.5					931
2711	Petroleum gases and other gaseous hydrocarbons	4 669.4	2 562.4	3 059.1	*8.2*	*1.6*	*0.4*	US$/kg	343
2710	Petroleum oils, other than crude	2 660.2	2 201.9	1 461.0	*0.8*	*0.7*	*0.6*	US$/kg	334
3102	Mineral or chemical fertilisers, nitrogenous	413.0	494.1	711.2	0.2	0.2	0.2	US$/kg	562
8544	Insulated (including enamelled or anodised) wire, cable	539.3	350.0	225.3	4.6	5.4	4.1	US$/kg	773
7601	Unwrought aluminium	31.0	579.5	497.9	2.7	1.7	0.2	US$/kg	684
2905	Acyclic alcohols and their derivatives	211.5	183.4	339.8	0.4	0.3	0.2	US$/kg	512
0402	Milk and cream, concentrated or containing added sugar	339.1	192.1	185.9	4.4	2.9	3.4	US$/kg	022
3902	Polymers of propylene or of other olefins, in primary forms	294.2	204.0	202.1	0.8	1.4	1.3	US$/kg	575

Graph 2: Trade Balance by MDG Regions in 2010

(Bln US$)

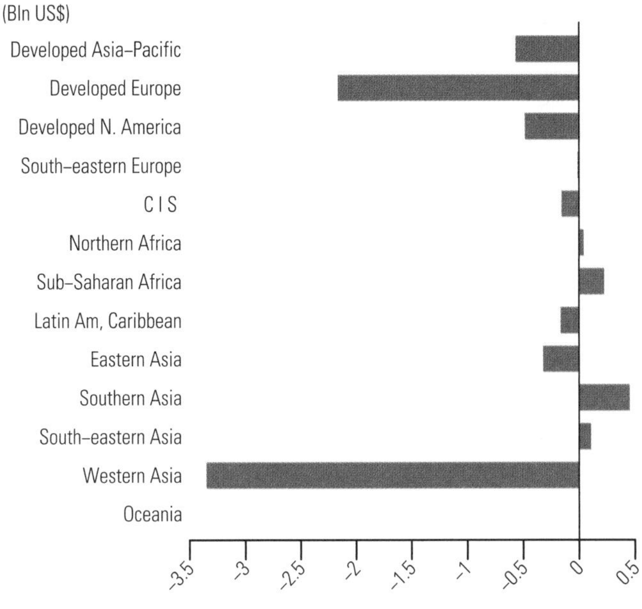

Graph 3: Partner concentration of trade in 2010

(Cumulative share by ranked partners)

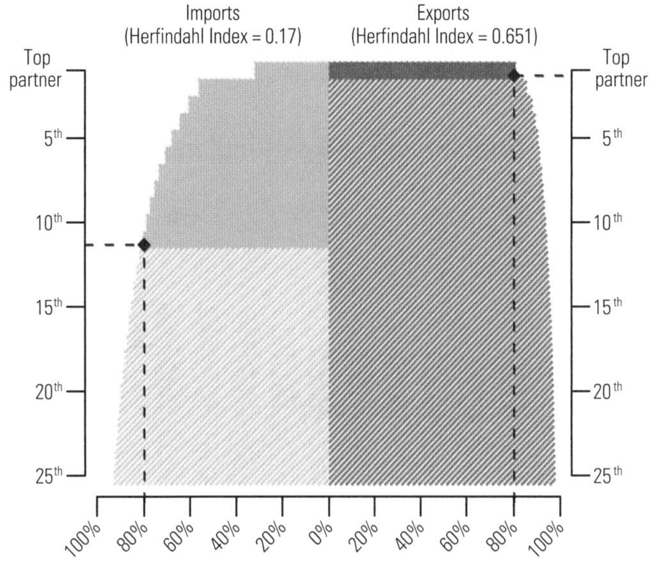

Table 4: Exports by principal countries and SITC sections in 2010

(Value in million US$, percentages of country total)

Country	Total	Shares by SITC sections (%)								
		0 + 1	2 + 4	3	5	6	7	8	9	Total
World	36599.7	2.1	0.9	69.3	6.4	3.0	2.3	0.8	15.2	100
Areas, nes	29449.5	0.0	0.0	81.2	0.0	...	...	...	18.8	100
United Arab Emirates	1702.3	11.9	5.0	36.8	9.4	12.7	19.4	2.9	2.0	100
India	889.7	0.7	5.1	14.0	62.9	8.2	7.2	1.3	0.6	100
China	474.1	1.7	16.9	4.8	64.8	9.7	1.4	0.8	0.0	100
Saudi Arabia	444.0	24.7	15.2	5.6	19.5	20.4	11.5	3.1	0.0	100
Iran	290.2	31.7	0.0	0.0	3.7	5.0	21.7	37.8	0.0	100
USA	275.6	0.1	0.0	0.0	82.8	11.4	4.3	1.2	0.1	100
Other Asia, nes	230.4	0.2	0.0	41.9	47.8	10.0	0.0	0.0	...	100
Rep. of Korea	214.8	0.2	1.4	2.6	18.0	77.4	0.4	0.0	0.0	100
Singapore	205.3	0.5	1.0	61.4	5.5	7.9	23.2	0.4	0.1	100

Imports Profile:

Imports in 2010 were composed of commodities and transactions not classified elsewhere (SITC section 9) with 32.3 percent, machinery and transport equipment (SITC section 7) with 19.1 percent and manufactured goods classified chiefly by material (SITC section 6) with 15.2 percent (see table 2). From 2008 to 2010, top imported products were motor cars and other motor vehicles principally designed for the transport (HS code 8703), petroleum oils, other than crude (HS code 2710) and parts suitable for use principally with the machinery of headings 84.25 (HS code 8431) (see table 5).

Table 5: Top 10 import commodities 2008 to 2010

(Value in million US$)

HS code	4-digit heading of Harmonized System 2002	Value (million US$)			Unit value				SITC code
		2008	2009	2010	2008	2009	2010	Unit	
	All Commodities	22924.7	17851.5	19972.7					
9999	Commodities not specified according to kind	359.8	507.3	6400.7					931
8703	Motor cars and other motor vehicles principally designed for the transport	3795.8	2426.9	...	*23.7*	*26.6*		thsd US$/unit	781
2710	Petroleum oils, other than crude	541.2	768.0	1052.8	0.8	0.7	0.8	US$/kg	334
8431	Parts suitable for use principally with the machinery of headings 84.25	680.5	484.4	383.4	14.0	10.9	7.7	US$/kg	723
7304	Tubes, pipes and hollow profiles, seamless, of iron (other than cast iron)	571.4	411.8	350.0	2.2	2.6	1.7	US$/kg	679
8704	Motor vehicles for the transport of goods	721.3	470.0	...	*13.4*			thsd US$/unit	782
8708	Parts and accessories of the motor vehicles of headings 87.01 to 87.05	505.4	437.6	...	13.2	17.2		US$/kg	784
7408	Copper wire	495.4	147.3	179.5	7.3	5.2	7.3	US$/kg	682
0402	Milk and cream, concentrated or containing added sugar	355.2	222.7	219.4	3.5	2.2	2.8	US$/kg	022
8429	Self-propelled bulldozers, angledozers, graders, levellers, scrapers	426.8	110.6	170.9	*66.6*		*62.3*	thsd US$/unit	723

Imports: CIF, by origin | **Exports: FOB, by last known destination** | **Trade System: General**

Overview:

After a drop of 13.4 percent in 2009, the value of the exports of Pakistan bounced back in 2010 and 2011 to reach 25.3 bln US$, exceeding its previous peak of 20.3 bln US$ in 2008 (see table 1 and graph 1). Imports showed a similar development with an increase by 16.1 percent to 43.6 bln US$ in 2011 (see table 2 and graph 1). This resulted in a trade deficit of 18.2 bln US$, lower than the deficit of 22.0 bln US$ in 2008 (see graph 1). This deficit was accounted for largely by trade with Western Asia (-12.5 bln US$), Eastern Asia (-5.1 bln US$) and South-eastern Asia (-4.4 bln US$) (see graph 2). However, trade with Southern Asia recorded a surplus exceeding 2.1 bln US$ in 2011. Pakistan's trade was well diversified across partners: in 2011, 23 (respectively 15) major partners accounted for 80 percent of exports (respectively imports) (see graph 3).

Graph 1: Total imports, exports and trade balance

(Bln US$ by year)

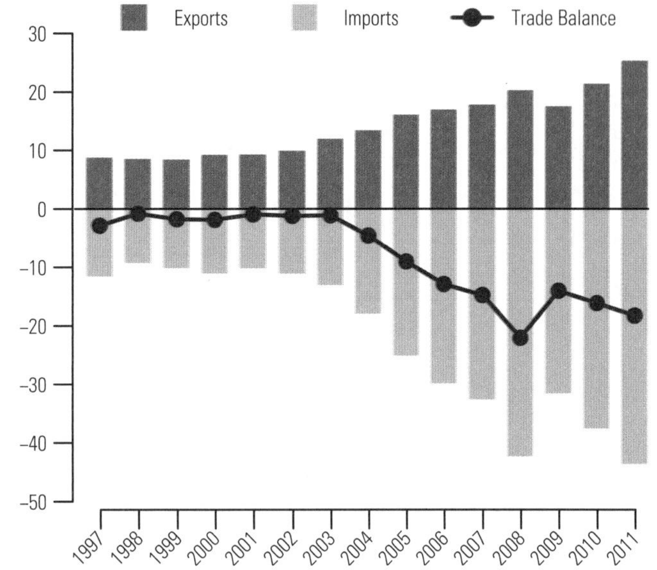

Table 1: Exports by SITC sections

(Value in million US$, growth and shares in percentage)

SITC	2011	Avg. Growth rates (%) 2007-2011	2010-2011	2011 share
Total	25 343.8	9.2	18.4	100.0
0+1	4 681.1	24.1	36.5	18.5
2+4	1 191.2	24.7	50.5	4.7
3	1 311.5	7.2	9.4	5.2
5	1 068.0	23.0	34.1	4.2
6	10 596.3	6.2	15.3	41.8
7	444.2	-13.6	-21.5	1.8
8	6 051.3	6.4	11.3	23.9
9	0.3	-69.5	-69.2	0.0

Table 2: Imports by SITC sections

(Value in million US$, growth and shares in percentage)

SITC	2011	Avg. Growth rates (%) 2007-2011	2010-2011	2011 share
Total	43 578.3	7.5	16.1	100.0
0+1	1 985.9	15.0	-19.1	4.6
2+4	6 096.7	10.1	22.2	14.0
3	14 860.3	15.5	30.4	34.1
5	7 068.1	8.9	22.2	16.2
6	4 569.3	7.3	15.2	10.5
7	7 620.3	-3.6	-1.0	17.5
8	1 208.9	5.1	8.0	2.8
9	168.6	-28.8	31.6	0.4

Exports Profile:

In 2011, Pakistan's exports were mostly composed of 41.8 percent of manufactured goods classified chiefly by material (SITC section 6), 23.9 percent of miscellaneous manufactured articles (SITC section 8) and 18.5 percent of food, live animals, beverages and tobacco (SITC sections 0+1) (see table 1). The three largest markets for exported goods were USA, Afghanistan and the United Arab Emirates (see table 4). Over the last three years, top exported goods included bed linen, table linen, toilet linen and kitchen linen (HS code 6302), rice (HS code 1006) and cotton yarn (other than sewing thread), containing 85 % or more (HS code 5205) (see table 3).

Table 3: Top 10 export commodities 2009 to 2011

(Value in million US$)

HS code	4-digit heading of Harmonized System 2007	Value (million US$) 2009	2010	2011	Unit value 2009	2010	2011	Unit	SITC code
	All Commodities	17 554.7	21 413.1	25 343.8					
6302	Bed linen, table linen, toilet linen and kitchen linen	2 381.8	2 639.2	2 845.0	*4.6*	*5.1*	6.3	US$/kg	658
1006	Rice	1 774.5	2 277.1	2 062.1	0.6	*0.5*	0.6	US$/kg	042
5205	Cotton yarn (other than sewing thread), containing 85 % or more	1 288.0	1 628.7	1 954.7	*2.0*	*3.1*	4.0	US$/kg	651
2710	Petroleum oils, other than crude	709.7	1 196.6	1 309.0	0.5	0.7	0.9	US$/kg	334
6203	Men's or boys' suits, ensembles, jackets, blazers, trousers	706.3	849.2	943.0	*4.7*	*4.8*	*5.8*	US$/unit	841
5209	Woven fabrics of cotton, containing 85 % or more by weight of cotton	539.6	707.9	928.7	*8.4*			US$/kg	652
5208	Woven fabrics of cotton, containing 85 % or more by weight of cotton	538.0	668.6	789.9					652
4203	Articles of apparel and clothing accessories, of leather	552.3	590.7	649.5					848
6105	Men's or boys' shirts, knitted or crocheted	466.3	583.1	626.5	3.8	*3.3*	*4.1*	US$/unit	843
7113	Articles of jewellery and parts thereof, of precious metal	471.0	577.0	448.8	*27.3*			thsd US$/kg	897

Graph 2: Trade Balance by MDG Regions in 2011

(Bln US$)

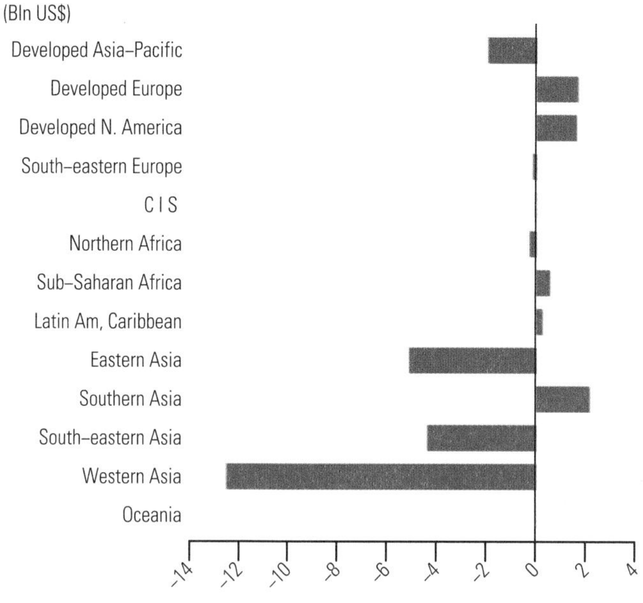

Graph 3: Partner concentration of trade in 2011

(Cumulative share by ranked partners)

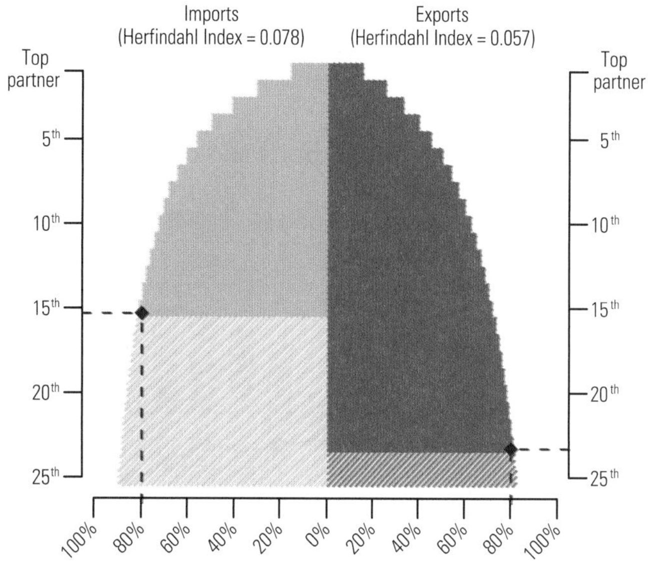

Table 4: Exports by principal countries and SITC sections in 2011

(Value in million US$, percentages of country total)

Country	Total	Shares by SITC sections (%) 0 + 1	2 + 4	3	5	6	7	8	9	Total
World	25343.8	18.5	4.7	5.2	4.2	41.8	1.8	23.9	0.0	100
USA	3839.2	1.4	1.4	0.0	0.6	44.2	0.5	52.0	0.0	100
Afghanistan	2660.3	34.3	7.5	29.1	4.3	18.7	2.8	3.3	0.0	100
United Arab Emirates	1921.0	31.5	0.6	21.1	2.4	11.0	3.7	29.7	0.0	100
China	1679.0	5.1	16.0	2.0	4.8	70.3	0.5	1.3	0.0	100
Germany	1312.2	2.3	2.9	...	0.6	39.1	0.6	54.5	0.0	100
United Kingdom	1258.8	7.6	1.2	0.0	2.0	40.8	3.4	45.0	0.0	100
Bangladesh	947.2	30.7	7.3	0.0	2.9	55.4	3.0	0.7	0.0	100
Italy	777.5	2.6	5.9	...	3.9	63.4	1.5	22.7	0.0	100
Turkey	755.9	6.6	2.7	0.4	20.6	60.7	0.4	8.6	0.0	100
Belgium	657.6	5.8	7.0	...	3.8	42.4	0.3	40.7	0.0	100

Imports Profile:

Mineral fuels, lubricants and related materials (SITC section 3) accounted for 34.1 percent of imported goods in 2011 (see table 2). Other major commodity groups included machinery and transport equipment (SITC section 7) and chemicals and related products (SITC section 5) respectively with 17.5 and 16.2 percent of imports. Over the last three years, top products for imports included petroleum oils, other than crude (HS code 2710), petroleum oils and oils obtained from bituminous minerals, crude (HS code 2709) and palm oil and its fractions (HS code 1511) (see table 5).

Table 5: Top 10 import commodities 2009 to 2011

(Value in million US$)

HS code	4-digit heading of Harmonized System 2007	Value (million US$) 2009	2010	2011	Unit value 2009	2010	2011	Unit	SITC code
	All Commodities	31583.7	37537.0	43578.3					
2710	Petroleum oils, other than crude	5102.8	7238.6	8971.9	0.4	*0.6*	0.8	US$/kg	334
2709	Petroleum oils and oils obtained from bituminous minerals, crude	3132.9	3516.3	5199.4	0.4	0.5	0.8	US$/kg	333
1511	Palm oil and its fractions	1245.8	1659.2	2355.0	0.7	0.9	1.2	US$/kg	422
8517	Electrical apparatus for line telephony or line telegraphy	596.9	835.1	1067.2					764
5201	Cotton, not carded or combed	480.4	760.2	824.8	*1.5*	2.0	3.3	US$/kg	263
8502	Electric generating sets and rotary converters	1081.6	588.4	326.5	2.3	4.3	*2.5*	thsd US$/unit	716
8703	Motor cars and other motor vehicles principally designed for the transport	410.4	618.7	770.9	793.7	797.4	965.9	US$/unit	781
7204	Ferrous waste and scrap; remelting scrap ingots of iron or steel	645.4	557.6	523.7	*0.3*	*0.3*	*0.3*	US$/kg	282
2902	Cyclic hydrocarbons	377.7	440.9	664.4	1.0	1.1	1.5	US$/kg	511
2701	Coal; briquettes, ovoids and similar solid fuels manufactured from coal	466.1	484.2	525.0	0.1	0.1	0.1	US$/kg	321

Imports: CIF, by origin	Exports: FOB, by last known destination	Trade System: Special

Overview:

The value of the exports of Panama continued to grow in 2011 by 32.5 percent to reach 14.6 bln US$ (see table 1 and graph 1). Similarly, imports increased by 30.3 percent to reach 21.8 bln US$ (see table 2 and graph 1). The trade balance registered a deficit of 7.2 bln US$ in 2011, higher than the 2010 deficit of 5.8 bln US$ (see graph 1). The majority of this deficit came from trade with Eastern Asia: deficit with this region amounted to 7.0 bln US$ in 2011 (see graph 2). Trade also recorded significant deficits with South-eastern Asia (-4.2 bln US$) and Developed Europe (-1.9 bln US$). A large surplus was recorded with Latin America and the Caribbean at 6.4 bln US$. Panama's trade was relatively diversified among partners: 11 major partners each accounted for 80 percent of both exports and imports in 2011 (see graph 3). See footnote*.

Graph 1: Total imports, exports and trade balance

(Bln US$ by year)

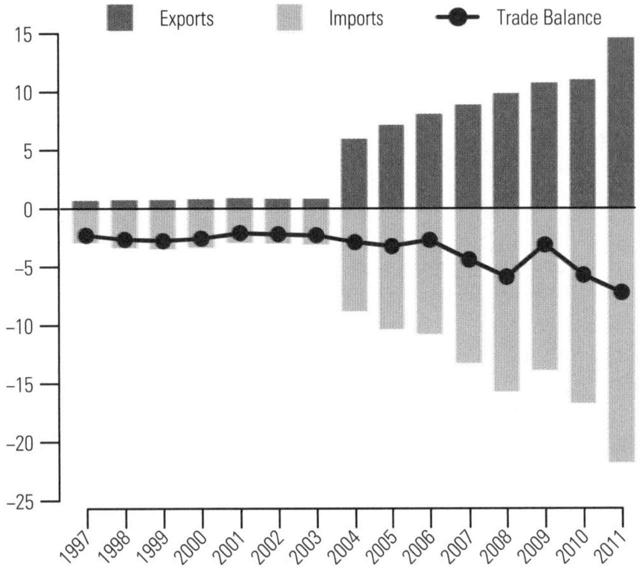

Table 1: Exports by SITC sections

(Value in million US$, growth and shares in percentage)

SITC	2011	Avg. Growth rates (%) 2007-2011	2010-2011	2011 share
Total	14554.8	13.3	32.5	100.0
0+1	776.0	-9.5	-1.2	5.3
2+4	153.5	24.1	41.7	1.1
3	1.3	-41.0	-66.5	0.0
5	5778.1	39.6	63.1	39.7
6	1003.7	8.3	27.2	6.9
7	2222.0	6.8	18.8	15.3
8	4476.6	7.5	17.6	30.8
9	143.8	-14.9	80.5	1.0

Exports Profile:

Top commodity groups for exports in 2011 were chemicals and related products, n.e.s. (SITC section 5), miscellaneous manufactured articles (SITC section 8) and machinery and transport equipment (SITC section 7) (see table 1). They accounted respectively for 39.7, 30.8 and 15.3 percent of exports. The three largest markets for exported goods were USA, Venezuela and Colombia (see table 4). Exports to USA were largely chemicals and related products, n.e.s. (SITC section 5). From 2009 to 2011, top products for exports were antibiotics (HS code 2941), medicaments (excluding goods of heading 30.02, 30.05 or 30.06) (HS code 3004) and other footwear with outer soles and uppers of rubber or plastics (HS code 6402) (see table 3).

Table 2: Imports by SITC sections

(Value in million US$, growth and shares in percentage)

SITC	2011	Avg. Growth rates (%) 2007-2011	2010-2011	2011 share
Total	21801.6	13.2	30.3	100.0
0+1	1547.5	15.0	20.2	7.1
2+4	137.4	15.5	31.3	0.6
3	240.1	-28.2	-2.1	1.1
5	6091.1	36.1	58.9	27.9
6	2521.5	10.8	24.2	11.6
7	5427.6	10.5	19.8	24.9
8	5798.2	9.9	23.7	26.6
9	38.2	-42.4	110.9	0.2

Table 3: Top 10 export commodities 2009 to 2011

(Value in million US$)

HS code	4-digit heading of Harmonized System 2007	Value (million US$) 2009	2010	2011	Unit value 2009	2010	2011	Unit	SITC code
	All Commodities	10716.7	10986.6	14554.8					
2941	Antibiotics	2254.1	1740.2	3554.6	5.2	4.6	6.6	thsd US$/kg	541
3004	Medicaments (excluding goods of heading 30.02, 30.05 or 30.06)	1322.7	1048.5	1290.1	122.8	80.7	82.2	US$/kg	542
6402	Other footwear with outer soles and uppers of rubber or plastics	503.7	538.1	598.4	*8.9*	*9.4*	*8.4*	US$/pair	851
3303	Perfumes and toilet waters	282.9	361.9	512.6	54.6	55.4	59.2	US$/kg	553
6204	Women's or girls' suits, ensembles, jackets, blazers, dresses, skirts	294.1	364.5	409.7					842
6203	Men's or boys' suits, ensembles, jackets, blazers, trousers	242.8	272.3	345.6					841
6403	Footwear with outer soles of rubber, plastics, leather	257.6	296.4	295.1	*28.2*	*34.8*	*32.6*	US$/pair	851
6110	Jerseys, pullovers, cardigans, waist-coats and similar articles	240.4	266.9	290.9	*19.0*	*15.6*	*16.1*	US$/unit	845
8528	Reception apparatus for television	223.4	275.5	284.4					761
2208	Alcohol of a strength by volume of less than 80 % vol	174.9	217.6	252.5	*4.1*	*4.5*	*5.4*	US$/litre	112

*Beginning 2004, Panama trade data is combined with trade data from Zona Libre de Colon

Graph 2: Trade Balance by MDG Regions in 2011

(Bln US$)

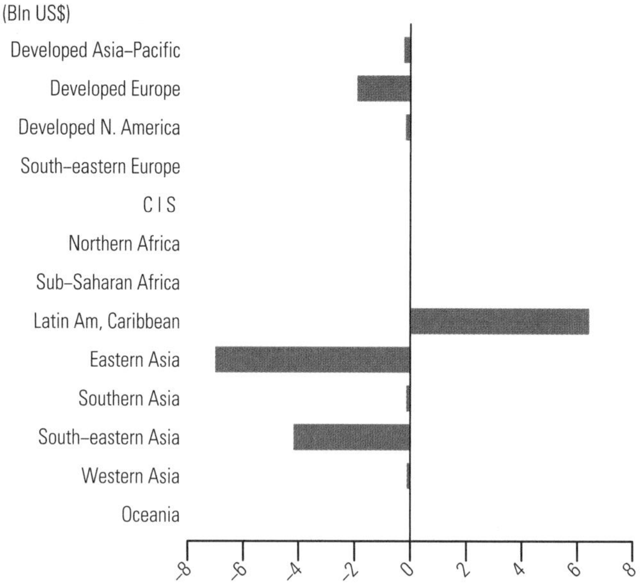

Graph 3: Partner concentration of trade in 2011

(Cumulative share by ranked partners)

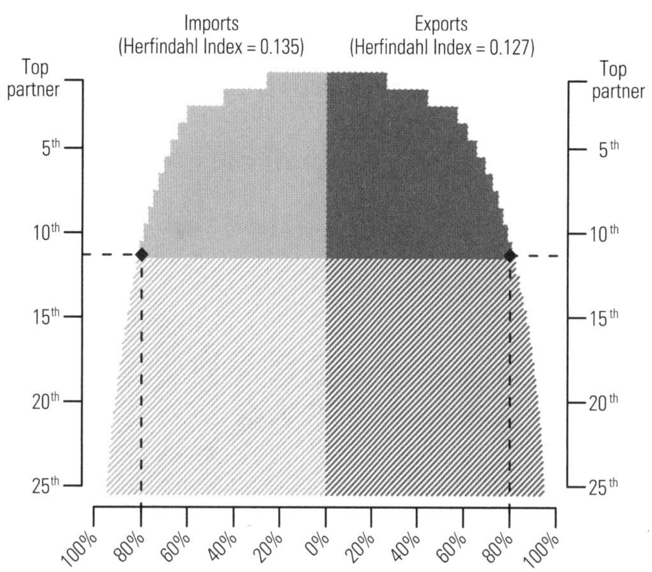

Table 4: Exports by principal countries and SITC sections in 2011

(Value in million US$, percentages of country total)

Country	Total	Shares by SITC sections (%)								
		0 + 1	2 + 4	3	5	6	7	8	9	Total
World	14554.8	5.3	1.1	0.0	39.7	6.9	15.3	30.8	1.0	100
USA	3831.2	4.4	0.3	0.0	89.9	0.3	2.9	1.9	0.4	100
Venezuela	2572.7	3.1	0.1	0.0	8.2	10.8	21.0	56.7	0.0	100
Colombia	1863.9	5.8	0.0	0.0	9.7	11.5	20.1	52.7	0.0	100
Costa Rica	647.4	5.7	0.9	0.1	39.9	10.2	15.2	28.0	0.0	100
Ecuador	583.1	0.6	0.4	0.0	23.4	6.4	39.6	29.5	0.0	100
Dominican Rep.	547.5	5.0	0.2	0.0	24.2	8.9	9.4	52.2	0.0	100
Guatemala	462.4	2.3	0.2	0.0	36.0	7.1	16.1	38.3	0.0	100
Honduras	366.1	4.4	0.9	0.0	40.6	6.2	14.8	33.2	0.0	100
El Salvador	292.7	3.3	0.2	0.0	40.2	6.8	15.9	33.5	0.0	100
Japan	290.5	0.9	0.4	...	98.1	0.0	0.4	0.1	...	100

Imports Profile:

In 2011, imports were composed of 27.9 percent of chemicals and related products, n.e.s. (SITC section 5), 26.6 percent of miscellaneous manufactured articles (SITC section 8) and 24.9 percent of machinery and transport equipment (SITC section 7) (see table 2). The top imported goods from 2009 to 2011 were antibiotics (HS code 2941), medicaments (excluding goods of heading 30.02, 30.05 or 30.06) (HS code 3004) and motor cars and other motor vehicles principally designed for the transport (HS code 8703) (see table 5).

Table 5: Top 10 import commodities 2009 to 2011

(Value in million US$)

HS code	4-digit heading of Harmonized System 2007	Value (million US$)			Unit value				SITC code
		2009	2010	2011	2009	2010	2011	Unit	
	All Commodities	13876.6	16737.1	21801.6					
2941	Antibiotics	1663.5	1719.7	3488.8	6.0	5.6	5.1	thsd US$/kg	541
3004	Medicaments (excluding goods of heading 30.02, 30.05 or 30.06)	927.1	894.5	1087.9	54.8	43.4	49.7	US$/kg	542
8703	Motor cars and other motor vehicles principally designed for the transport	474.0	567.5	642.4	*18.4*	*19.0*		thsd US$/unit	781
6402	Other footwear with outer soles and uppers of rubber or plastics	484.6	579.1	615.1	*8.2*	*8.2*	*7.8*	US$/pair	851
6204	Women's or girls' suits, ensembles, jackets, blazers, dresses, skirts	306.1	449.0	478.4					842
6203	Men's or boys' suits, ensembles, jackets, blazers, trousers	236.6	288.5	425.8					841
6110	Jerseys, pullovers, cardigans, waist-coats and similar articles	238.8	292.9	319.1	*14.2*	*14.1*	*13.6*	US$/unit	845
3303	Perfumes and toilet waters	203.8	261.5	367.2	28.5	29.0	27.1	US$/kg	553
8528	Reception apparatus for television	215.1	283.8	314.5					761
6403	Footwear with outer soles of rubber, plastics, leather	237.5	258.6	307.9	*29.4*	*28.5*	*28.2*	US$/pair	851

Paraguay

Imports: CIF, by origin | Exports: FOB, by last known destination | Trade System: General

Overview:

From 2007 to 2011, Paraguay's exports increased on average by 18.3 percent each year despite a decline of 29.0 percent in 2009 and reached 5.5 bln US$ in 2011 (see table 1 and graph 1). Imports also increased on average by 20.4 percent each year to 12.3 bln US$ in 2011 (see table 2 and graph 1). This resulted in a trade deficit of 6.8 bln US$, the highest in the last five years (see graph 1). The large deficits were recorded chiefly with Eastern Asia (-3.9 bln US$) and Latin America and the Caribbean (-2.3 bln US$) (see graph 2). Trade recorded a surplus of 180.2 mln US$ with the Commonwealth of Independent States. Exports were more diversified across partners than imports: in 2011, 12 major partners accounted for 80 percent of exports compared to 6 major partners for imports (see graph 3).

Graph 1: Total imports, exports and trade balance

(Bln US$ by year)

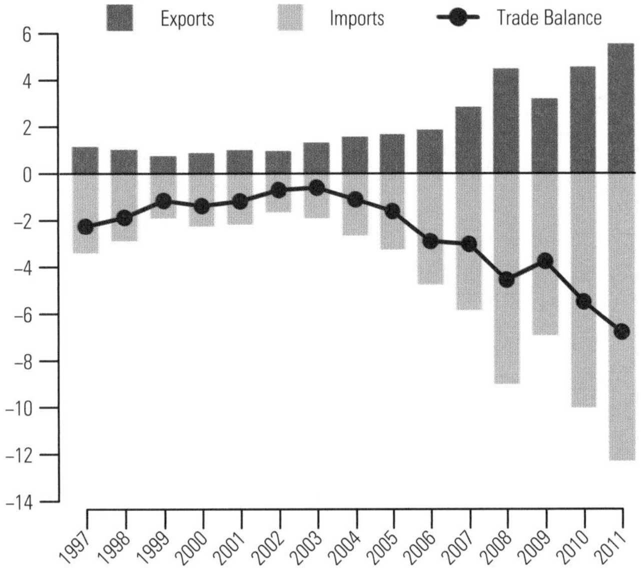

Table 1: Exports by SITC sections

(Value in million US$, growth and shares in percentage)

SITC	2011	Avg. Growth rates (%) 2007-2011	2010-2011	2011 share
Total	5517.4	18.3	21.7	100.0
0+1	1960.1	15.6	1.6	35.5
2+4	2918.1	21.2	37.9	52.9
3	13.2	379.7	983.7	0.2
5	137.4	17.3	18.0	2.5
6	268.1	7.0	25.6	4.9
7	41.1	14.8	25.9	0.7
8	172.4	27.5	39.7	3.1
9	6.9	33.7	416.0	0.1

Table 2: Imports by SITC sections

(Value in million US$, growth and shares in percentage)

SITC	2011	Avg. Growth rates (%) 2007-2011	2010-2011	2011 share
Total	12315.6	20.4	22.7	100.0
0+1	873.3	22.5	20.6	7.1
2+4	135.5	18.0	29.4	1.1
3	1648.1	20.9	37.9	13.4
5	1757.8	17.4	32.5	14.3
6	1487.3	24.9	32.1	12.1
7	5055.9	17.6	17.1	41.1
8	1356.7	33.1	8.8	11.0
9	1.0	-47.7	7408.7	0.0

Exports Profile:

In 2011, inedible crude materials (except fuels), animal and vegetable oils, fats and waxes (SITC sections 2+4) and food, live animals, beverages and tobacco (SITC sections 0+1) accounted for nearly all the exports, respectively 52.9 percent and 35.5 percent (see table 1). Uruguay, Argentina and Brazil were the three major markets for exports (see table 4). The majority of exports to Uruguay and Argentina were composed of inedible crude materials (except fuels), animal and vegetable oils, fats and waxes (SITC sections 2+4), respectively 82.1 and 74.4 percent. Over the last three years, top exported goods were soya beans, whether or not broken (HS code 1201), meat of bovine animals, fresh or chilled (HS code 0201) and oil-cake and other solid residues (HS code 2304) (see table 3).

Table 3: Top 10 export commodities 2009 to 2011

(Value in million US$)

HS code	4-digit heading of Harmonized System 2007	Value (million US$) 2009	2010	2011	Unit value 2009	2010	2011	Unit	SITC code
	All Commodities	3167.0	4533.8	5517.4					
1201	Soya beans, whether or not broken	787.2	1590.8	2294.6	0.4	0.3	0.4	US$/kg	222
0201	Meat of bovine animals, fresh or chilled	278.1	500.1	354.1	3.5	5.1	6.0	US$/kg	011
2304	Oil-cake and other solid residues	365.7	320.1	386.7	0.4	0.3	0.4	US$/kg	081
0202	Meat of bovine animals, frozen	274.9	380.0	368.9	2.7	3.4	4.2	US$/kg	011
1005	Maize (corn)	234.2	239.4	351.9	0.1	0.2	0.2	US$/kg	044
1507	Soya-bean oil and its fractions	204.1	222.8	275.4	0.8	0.9	1.2	US$/kg	421
1001	Wheat and meslin	173.5	246.1	169.6	0.2	0.2	0.3	US$/kg	041
4104	Tanned or crust hides and skins of bovine (including buffalo)	42.7	92.3	98.8	1.6	2.4	3.3	US$/kg	611
1006	Rice	48.6	63.5	85.9	0.3	0.4	0.4	US$/kg	042
1207	Other oil seeds and oleaginous fruits, whether or not broken	77.7	55.1	63.8	1.2	1.4	1.5	US$/kg	222

Graph 2: Trade Balance by MDG Regions in 2011

(Bln US$)

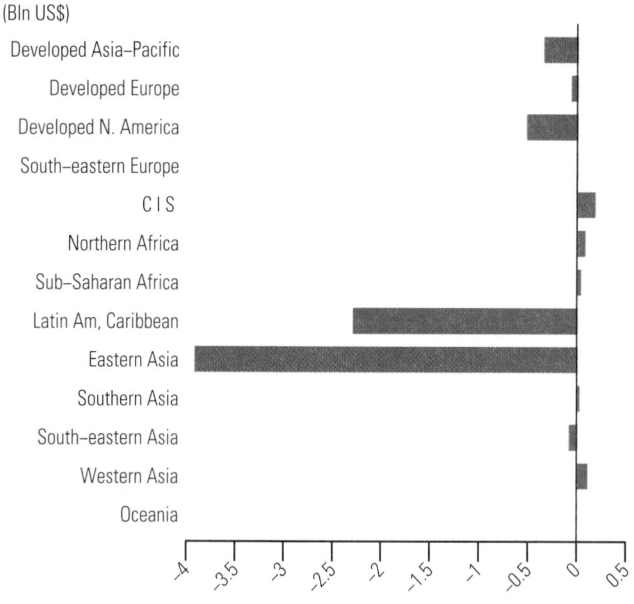

Graph 3: Partner concentration of trade in 2011

(Cumulative share by ranked partners)

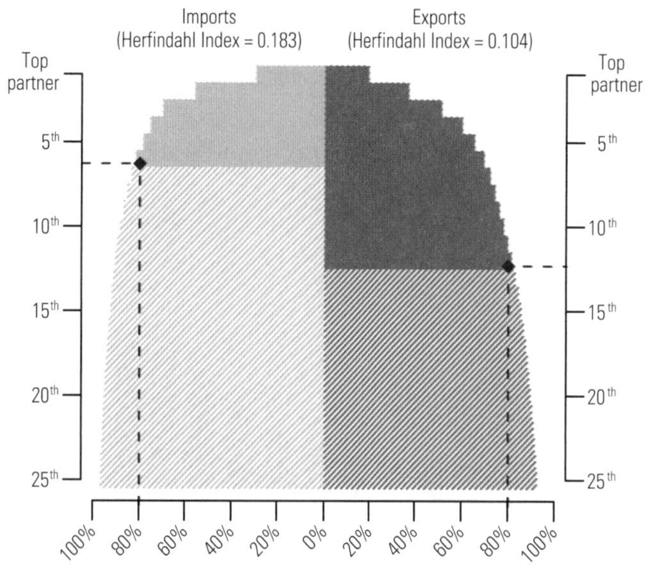

Table 4: Exports by principal countries and SITC sections in 2011

(Value in million US$, percentages of country total)

Country	Total	Shares by SITC sections (%) 0+1	2+4	3	5	6	7	8	9	Total
World	5517.4	35.5	52.9	0.2	2.5	4.9	0.7	3.1	0.1	100
Uruguay	1061.6	14.7	82.1	...	1.0	1.2	0.4	0.7	...	100
Argentina	972.6	15.1	74.4	...	1.1	4.9	0.3	4.3	...	100
Brazil	782.9	49.0	15.0	0.0	6.4	13.9	2.2	13.4	0.0	100
Chile	488.5	93.5	2.0	0.0	2.4	1.7	0.2	0.1	...	100
Switzerland	290.3	14.5	84.7	...	0.2	...	0.0	0.0	0.5	100
Russian Federation	224.9	99.2	0.7	...	0.0	0.0	...	...	...	100
USA	148.0	49.8	37.5	0.0	0.9	4.8	1.1	2.5	3.5	100
Peru	114.2	93.1	3.9	...	2.7	0.1	0.0	0.2	...	100
Israel	104.7	44.6	55.4	...	...	0.0	...	...	...	100
Spain	100.7	6.2	89.3	...	1.8	1.0	1.0	0.6	0.1	100

Imports Profile:

In 2011, the major commodity group for imports, machinery and transport equipment (SITC section 7), accounted for 41.1 percent of total imports (see table 2). Other major commodity groups included chemicals and related products, n.e.s. (SITC section 5) and mineral fuels, lubricants and related materials (SITC section 3) which accounted respectively for 14.3 and 13.4 percent of imports. Over the last three years, major products for imports included petroleum oils, other than crude (HS code 2710), electrical apparatus for line telephony or line telegraphy (HS code 8517) and automatic data processing machines and units thereof (HS code 8471) (see table 5).

Table 5: Top 10 import commodities 2009 to 2011

(Value in million US$)

HS code	4-digit heading of Harmonized System 2007	Value (million US$) 2009	2010	2011	Unit value 2009	2010	2011	Unit	SITC code
	All Commodities	6939.8	10040.2	12315.6					
2710	Petroleum oils, other than crude	947.7	1107.2	1538.8	0.7	0.8	*1.0*	US$/kg	334
8517	Electrical apparatus for line telephony or line telegraphy	240.8	658.4	700.0					764
8471	Automatic data processing machines and units thereof	439.0	468.9	479.0					752
9504	Articles for funfair, table or parlour games, including pintables	323.7	497.8	456.9					894
8703	Motor cars and other motor vehicles principally designed for the transport	261.9	353.7	496.6	*16.4*	*15.5*		thsd US$/unit	781
3105	Mineral or chemical fertilisers	215.5	291.7	429.6	0.5	0.5	0.6	US$/kg	562
8525	Transmission apparatus for radio-telephony, radio-broadcasting	280.2	352.3	254.0					764
3808	Insecticides, rodenticides, fungicides, herbicides	173.7	212.0	258.1	5.7	*5.8*	*7.2*	US$/kg	591
8704	Motor vehicles for the transport of goods	122.6	194.1	261.9					782
4011	New pneumatic tyres, of rubber	115.5	177.4	237.3					625

Imports: CIF, by origin | Exports: FOB, by last known destination | Trade System: Special

Overview:

From 2007 to 2011, Peru's exports increased on average by 12.9 percent each year despite a decline of 14.5 percent in 2009 and reached 45.6 bln US$ in 2011 (see table 1 and graph 1). Similarly, imports increased on average by 16.7 percent each year to 37.7 bln US$ in 2011 (see table 2 and graph 1). This resulted in a significant trade surplus of 7.9 bln US$ in 2011 (see graph 1). The large trade surpluses were mostly recorded with Developed Europe (+9.5 bln US$) and Developed North America (+2.2 bln US$) (see graph 2). Trade, however, recorded deficits with Latin America and the Caribbean (-3.8 bln US$) and Sub-Saharan Africa (-0.7 bln US$) among others. Both imports and exports were diversified across partners: 13 (respectively 15) major partners accounted for 80 percent of exports (respectively imports) (see graph 3).

Graph 1: Total imports, exports and trade balance

(Bln US$ by year)

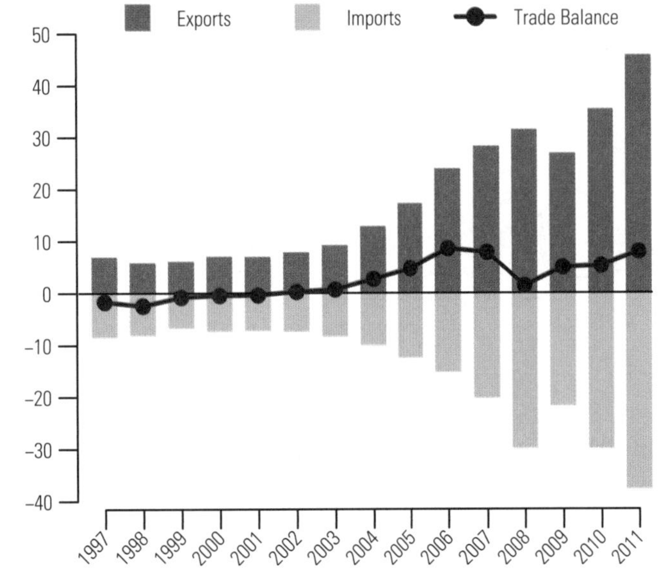

Table 1: Exports by SITC sections

(Value in million US$, growth and shares in percentage)

SITC	2011	Avg. Growth rates (%) 2007-2011	2010-2011	2011 share
Total	45636.1	12.9	29.6	100.0
0+1	7107.1	18.6	34.7	15.6
2+4	14297.4	10.4	29.0	31.3
3	5019.1	20.1	50.0	11.0
5	1372.5	20.6	34.8	3.0
6	5521.3	-0.5	13.5	12.1
7	384.0	24.8	20.6	0.8
8	1998.3	2.6	26.9	4.4
9	9936.4	24.0	28.6	21.8

Table 2: Imports by SITC sections

(Value in million US$, growth and shares in percentage)

SITC	2011	Avg. Growth rates (%) 2007-2011	2010-2011	2011 share
Total	37747.1	16.7	25.7	100.0
0+1	3222.8	15.9	24.0	8.5
2+4	1514.2	19.9	19.9	4.0
3	5935.9	11.6	39.4	15.7
5	5465.3	16.5	24.1	14.5
6	5963.1	17.5	19.8	15.8
7	13084.3	20.5	24.5	34.7
8	2544.4	22.5	27.3	6.7
9	17.1	-58.9	-11.0	0.0

Exports Profile:

In 2011, inedible crude materials (except fuels), animal and vegetable oils, fats and waxes (SITC sections 2+4) accounted for 31.3 percent of Peru's exports (see table 1). Other major commodity groups for exports included commodities and transactions not classified elsewhere (SITC section 9) and food, live animals, beverages and tobacco (SITC sections 0+1). They accounted respectively for 21.8 and 15.6 percent of exports. China, USA and Switzerland were the major partners for exports (see table 4). A large majority (68.3 percent) of exports to China was inedible crude materials (except fuels), animal and vegetable oils, fats and waxes (SITC sections 2+4). Over the last three years, top exported commodities included gold (including gold plated with platinum) (HS code 7108), copper ores and concentrates (HS code 2603) and refined copper and copper alloys, unwrought (HS code 7403) (see table 3).

Table 3: Top 10 export commodities 2009 to 2011

(Value in million US$)

HS code	4-digit heading of Harmonized System 2007	Value (million US$) 2009	2010	2011	Unit value 2009	2010	2011	Unit	SITC code
	All Commodities	26738.3	35205.1	45636.1					
7108	Gold (including gold plated with platinum)	6752.0	7725.5	9930.8	14.9	22.0	28.3	thsd US$/kg	971
2603	Copper ores and concentrates	3920.9	6156.8	7796.7	1.4	2.0	2.5	US$/kg	283
7403	Refined copper and copper alloys, unwrought	1861.5	2527.2	2745.3	4.9	7.4	8.9	US$/kg	682
2710	Petroleum oils, other than crude	1561.0	2300.7	2933.9	0.5	0.6	0.8	US$/kg	334
2301	Flours, meals and pellets, of meat or meat offal	1440.4	1623.0	1781.7	0.9	1.5	1.4	US$/kg	081
2607	Lead ores and concentrates	895.1	1277.3	1783.1	1.8	2.4	4.4	US$/kg	287
2608	Zinc ores and concentrates	1123.1	1478.2	1182.9	0.5	0.7	0.7	US$/kg	287
0901	Coffee, whether or not roasted or decaffeinated	584.4	888.3	1580.8	3.0	3.9	5.4	US$/kg	071
2711	Petroleum gases and other gaseous hydrocarbons	141.8	521.7	1486.9	0.5	0.3	0.3	US$/kg	343
2601	Iron ores and concentrates, including roasted iron pyrites	297.7	523.3	1023.1	0.0	0.1	0.1	US$/kg	281

Graph 2: Trade Balance by MDG Regions in 2011

(Bln US$)

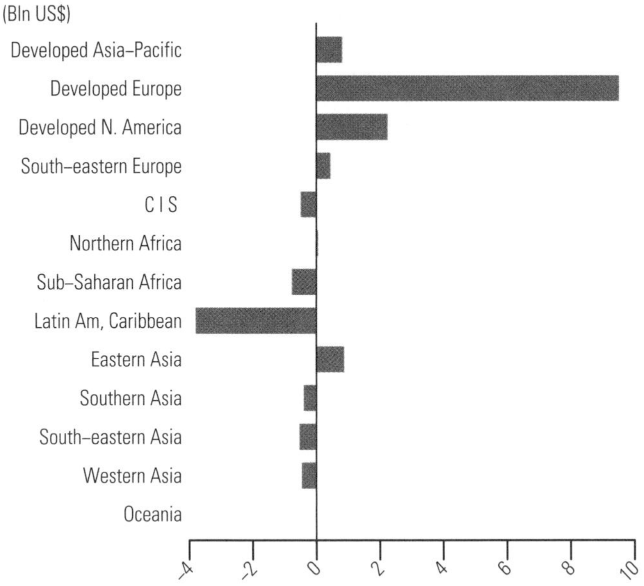

Graph 3: Partner concentration of trade in 2011

(Cumulative share by ranked partners)

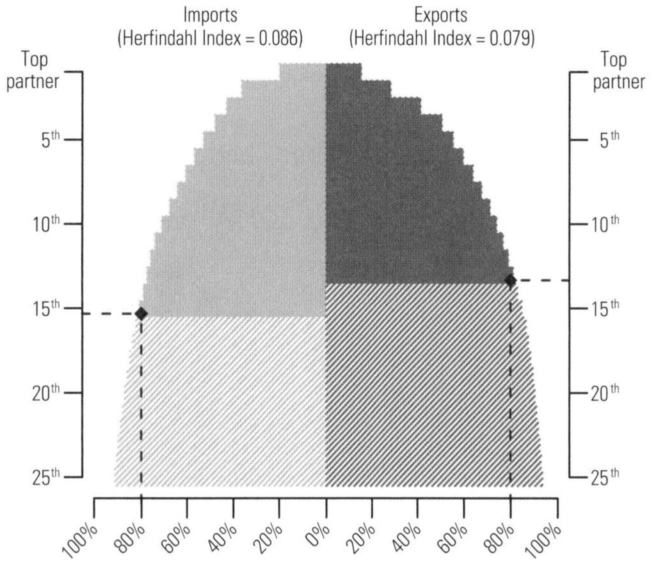

Table 4: Exports by principal countries and SITC sections in 2011

(Value in million US$, percentages of country total)

Country	Total	Shares by SITC sections (%)								
		0 + 1	2 + 4	3	5	6	7	8	9	Total
World	45 636.1	15.6	31.3	11.0	3.0	12.1	0.8	4.4	21.8	100
China	6 961.4	17.5	68.3	1.4	0.6	12.2	0.0	0.0	0.0	100
USA	6 083.9	23.1	7.0	26.6	0.9	14.5	1.0	13.0	13.9	100
Switzerland	5 887.1	0.6	1.7	0.0	0.0	0.3	0.0	0.1	97.3	100
Canada	4 176.3	3.0	13.9	8.6	0.0	0.6	0.1	0.4	73.4	100
Japan	2 174.6	10.6	72.2	10.2	0.4	6.0	0.0	0.7	0.0	100
Chile	1 976.6	8.8	49.1	16.9	9.4	9.7	2.8	3.3	0.0	100
Germany	1 900.2	36.3	58.1	0.0	2.5	1.0	0.2	1.9	0.0	100
Rep. of Korea	1 694.9	7.3	78.3	13.2	0.3	0.7	0.0	0.1	0.0	100
Spain	1 666.2	27.6	33.6	34.7	1.5	1.4	0.1	1.1	0.0	100
Italy	1 297.1	7.6	4.0	...	1.0	61.6	0.6	3.0	22.3	100

Imports Profile:

In 2011, Peru's imports were composed of 34.7 percent of machinery and transport equipment (SITC section 7), 15.8 percent of manufactured goods classified chiefly by material (SITC section 6) and 15.7 percent of mineral fuels, lubricants and related materials (SITC section 3). Over the last three years, major products for imports included petroleum oils and oils obtained from bituminous minerals, crude (HS code 2709), petroleum oils, other than crude (HS code 2710) and motor cars and other motor vehicles principally designed for the transport (HS code 8703) (see table 5).

Table 5: Top 10 import commodities 2009 to 2011

(Value in million US$)

HS code	4-digit heading of Harmonized System 2007	Value (million US$)			Unit value				SITC code
		2009	2010	2011	2009	2010	2011	Unit	
	All Commodities	21 869.7	30 030.5	37 747.1					
2709	Petroleum oils and oils obtained from bituminous minerals, crude	2 210.0	2 689.5	3 642.4	0.4	0.6	0.8	US$/kg	333
2710	Petroleum oils, other than crude	737.2	1 421.9	2 172.0	0.6	0.8	1.0	US$/kg	334
8703	Motor cars and other motor vehicles principally designed for the transport	722.8	1 103.0	1 229.0	8.8	10.2	11.0	thsd US$/unit	781
8704	Motor vehicles for the transport of goods	533.1	980.4	1 156.8	24.8	26.8	13.9	thsd US$/unit	782
8517	Electrical apparatus for line telephony or line telegraphy	606.6	709.1	900.4					764
8429	Self-propelled bulldozers, angledozers, graders, levellers, scrapers	395.9	563.2	742.6	3.6	90.0	99.7	thsd US$/unit	723
8471	Automatic data processing machines and units thereof	385.0	506.6	655.3	80.6	78.0	88.8	US$/unit	752
1001	Wheat and meslin	388.3	429.4	592.0	0.3	0.3	0.4	US$/kg	041
1005	Maize (corn)	324.1	449.6	627.7	0.2	0.2	0.3	US$/kg	044
8528	Reception apparatus for television	248.6	407.3	493.4	109.1	153.0	180.2	US$/unit	761

Philippines

Imports: CIF, by origin | Exports: FOB, by last known destination | Trade System: General

Overview:

After a drop of 21.7 percent in 2009, exports of the Philippines bounced back in 2010 by 33.8 percent but dropped again by 6.6 percent in 2011 to 48.0 bln US$ (see table 1 and graph 1). Imports, on the other hand, continued to grow in 2011 by 9.4 percent and reached 63.7 bln US$ (see table 2 and graph 1). This resulted in a significant trade deficit of 15.7 bln US$ in 2011 (see graph 1). By MDG regions, the large deficits were recorded chiefly with South-eastern Asia (-6.4 bln US$) and Western Asia (-5.2 bln US$) (see graph 2). Trade, on the other hand, also recorded a surplus with Developed Europe (+1.2 bln US$). Philippines' trade, especially exports, was relatively concentrated among a few partners: 10 major partners accounted for 80 percent of exports compared to 13 major partners for imports (see graph 3).

Graph 1: Total imports, exports and trade balance

(Bln US$ by year)

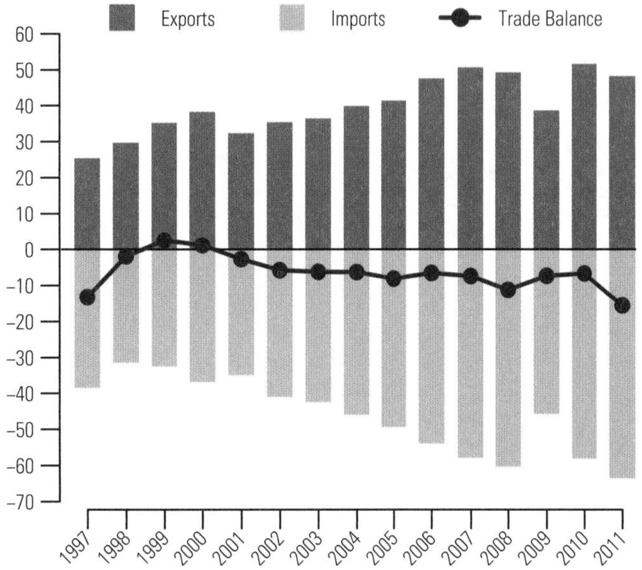

Table 1: Exports by SITC sections

(Value in million US$, growth and shares in percentage)

SITC	2011	Avg. Growth rates (%) 2007-2011	2010-2011	2011 share
Total	48042.1	-1.2	-6.6	100.0
0+1	3453.3	11.8	39.6	7.2
2+4	3238.3	10.4	20.0	6.7
3	1402.9	-0.2	29.9	2.9
5	1874.2	16.4	20.8	3.9
6	4561.5	5.0	36.0	9.5
7	19896.6	-13.3	-44.9	41.4
8	2899.4	-10.1	-24.8	6.0
9	10716.0	163.8	3161.2	22.3

Table 2: Imports by SITC sections

(Value in million US$, growth and shares in percentage)

SITC	2011	Avg. Growth rates (%) 2007-2011	2010-2011	2011 share
Total	63692.7	2.4	9.4	100.0
0+1	5871.8	10.4	-3.8	9.2
2+4	2208.6	10.1	-0.9	3.5
3	12810.4	6.7	30.2	20.1
5	6761.4	12.4	21.7	10.6
6	5800.4	5.2	24.2	9.1
7	18024.7	-13.2	-34.3	28.3
8	2178.5	5.4	13.0	3.4
9	10036.9	158.3	2042.6	15.8

Exports Profile:

In 2011, machinery and transport equipment (SITC section 7) was the largest commodity group for exports, representing 41.4 percent of exported goods. Other major commodity groups for exports included commodities and transactions not classified elsewhere (SITC section 9) and manufactured goods classified chiefly by material (SITC section 6), accounting for 22.3 and 9.5 percent of exports respectively (see table 1). Major partners for exports were Japan, USA and China (see table 4). Over the last three years, top exported commodities were electronic integrated circuits and microassemblies (HS code 8542), automatic data processing machines and units thereof (HS code 8471) and diodes, transistors and similar semiconductor devices (HS code 8541) (see table 3).

Table 3: Top 10 export commodities 2009 to 2011

(Value in million US$)

HS code	4-digit heading of Harmonized System 2002	Value (million US$) 2009	2010	2011	Unit value 2009	2010	2011	Unit	SITC code
	All Commodities	38435.8	51431.7	48042.1					
8542	Electronic integrated circuits and microassemblies	9607.4	13954.5	5476.7					776
8471	Automatic data processing machines and units thereof	5753.1	8207.0	2984.8	20.1	22.4	33.3	US$/unit	752
9999	Commodities not specified according to kind	...	...	10202.4					931
8541	Diodes, transistors and similar semiconductor devices	1459.3	2591.7	2547.0					776
8473	Parts and accessories for use with machines of heading 84.69 to 84.72	2346.9	1981.7	1458.9	6.5	26.5	64.0	US$/kg	759
8708	Parts and accessories of the motor vehicles of headings 87.01 to 87.05	1422.7	1670.5	2069.0	19.6	11.1	18.8	US$/kg	784
4418	Builders' joinery and carpentry of wood	802.1	1008.9	1662.7	3.3	3.4	3.8	US$/kg	635
8504	Electrical transformers, static converters (for example, rectifiers)	948.2	1248.8	1238.4					771
1513	Coconut (copra), palm kernel or babassu oil	594.5	1266.3	1429.5	0.7	0.9	1.7	US$/kg	422
8544	Insulated (including enamelled or anodised) wire, cable	771.7	1144.8	1170.0	14.8	15.1	16.0	US$/kg	773

Graph 2: Trade Balance by MDG Regions in 2011

(Bln US$)

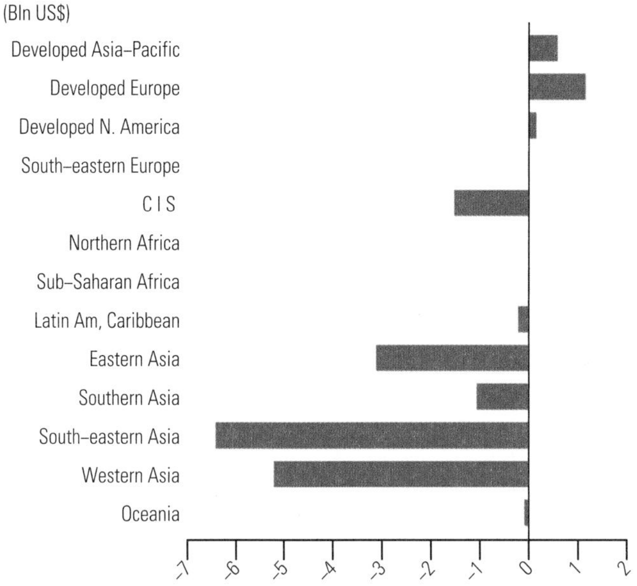

Graph 3: Partner concentration of trade in 2011

(Cumulative share by ranked partners)

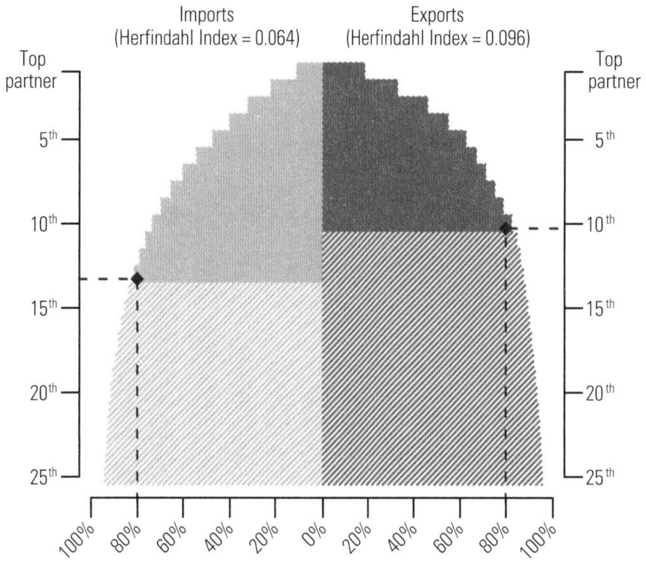

Table 4: Exports by principal countries and SITC sections in 2011

(Value in million US$, percentages of country total)

Country	Total	Shares by SITC sections (%)								
		0 + 1	2 + 4	3	5	6	7	8	9	Total
World	48042.1	7.2	6.7	2.9	3.9	9.5	41.4	6.0	22.3	100
Japan	8866.5	6.3	6.3	0.1	5.9	22.4	37.7	3.6	17.7	100
USA	7106.7	11.7	9.3	...	1.7	4.7	34.6	20.5	17.5	100
China	6102.3	2.5	10.3	2.9	3.6	6.2	49.8	1.3	23.6	100
Singapore	4277.7	3.5	1.1	9.9	0.8	0.9	42.5	0.7	40.5	100
China, Hong Kong SAR	3698.9	3.1	0.3	1.7	0.6	2.7	58.7	1.8	31.1	100
Rep. of Korea	2196.4	12.3	9.3	16.9	4.7	13.6	30.1	2.1	11.1	100
Other Asia, nes	2002.9	3.5	1.7	7.5	6.0	6.1	36.2	1.8	37.3	100
Thailand	1904.0	9.4	2.1	4.5	2.9	21.3	44.0	3.2	12.6	100
Netherlands	1744.8	3.4	33.3	...	3.6	0.6	43.3	6.0	9.8	100
Germany	1729.4	3.7	1.2	...	1.0	3.9	54.8	2.8	32.6	100

Imports Profile:

Imports were composed of 28.3 percent of machinery and transport equipment (SITC section 7), 20.1 percent of mineral fuels, lubricants and related materials (SITC section 3) and 15.8 percent of commodities and transactions not classified elsewhere (SITC section 9) (see table 2). From 2009 to 2011, top imported products were electronic integrated circuits and microassemblies (HS code 8542), petroleum oils, crude (HS code 2709) and petroleum oils, other than crude (HS code 2710) (see table 5).

Table 5: Top 10 import commodities 2009 to 2011

(Value in million US$)

HS code	4-digit heading of Harmonized System 2002	Value (million US$)			Unit value				SITC code
		2009	2010	2011	2009	2010	2011	Unit	
	All Commodities	45877.7	58228.6	63692.7					
8542	Electronic integrated circuits and microassemblies	9620.2	12268.6	4475.4					776
2709	Petroleum oils, crude	3354.6	5504.6	7874.2	0.5	0.6	0.8	US$/kg	333
2710	Petroleum oils, other than crude	3268.3	3234.2	3667.5	0.5	0.7	1.0	US$/kg	334
9999	Commodities not specified according to kind	...	...	9750.9					931
8473	Parts and accessories for use with machines of heading 84.69 to 84.72	3644.7	4082.1	1651.9	39.3	48.7	45.8	US$/kg	759
8703	Motor cars and other motor vehicles principally designed for the transport	955.9	1507.2	1253.7	*7.3*	3.0	*9.7*	thsd US$/unit	781
1006	Rice	1048.9	1652.6	383.2	0.6	0.7	0.5	US$/kg	042
2603	Copper ores and concentrates	909.7	1326.4	757.7	1.3	2.1	1.7	US$/kg	283
8479	Machines and mechanical appliances having individual functions	521.7	916.1	870.7					728
1001	Wheat and meslin	825.3	518.7	955.3	0.3	0.3	0.3	US$/kg	041

Imports: CIF, by origin	Exports: FOB, by last known destination	Trade System: Special

Overview:

From 2007 to 2011, Poland's exports increased on average by 7.2 percent each year despite a decline of 20.5 percent in 2009 and amounted to 183.3 bln US$ in 2011 (see table 1 and graph 1). During the same period, imports also increased on average by 5.5 percent each year to 203.0 bln US$ in 2011 (see table 2 and graph 1). This resulted in a trade deficit amounting to 19.7 bln US$ (see graph 1). By MDG regions, major deficits were recorded with Eastern Asia (-21.2 bln US$) and the Commonwealth of Independent States (-14.1 bln US$) (see graph 2). Major trade surplus was recorded with Developed Europe at 21.5 bln US$. Both exports and imports were diversified across partners: in 2011, 17 major partners accounted for 80 percent of both imports and exports (see graph 3).

Graph 1: Total imports, exports and trade balance

(Bln US$ by year)

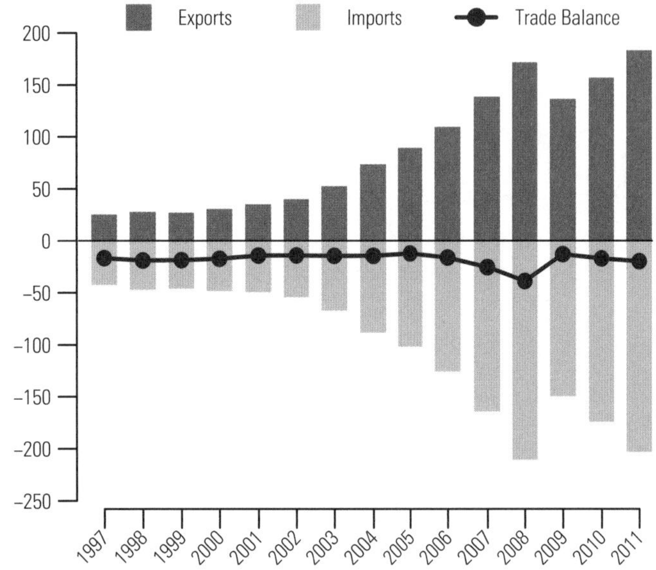

Exports Profile:

In 2011, Poland's exports were composed of 39.3 percent of machinery and transport equipment (SITC section 7), 21.3 percent of manufactured goods classified chiefly by material (SITC section 6) and 12.4 percent of miscellaneous manufactured articles (SITC section 8) (see table 2). In addition to Germany, other major destinations for exports included the United Kingdom, Czech Republic and France (see table 4). From 2009 to 2011, top exported commodities were motor cars and other motor vehicles principally designed for the transport (HS code 8703), parts and accessories of the motor vehicles of headings 87.01 to 87.05 (HS code 8708) and reception apparatus for television (HS code 8528) (see table 3).

Table 1: Exports by SITC sections

(Value in million US$, growth and shares in percentage)

SITC	2011	Avg. Growth rates (%) 2007-2011	2010-2011	2011 share
Total	183292.0	7.2	16.7	100.0
0+1	19144.8	10.9	16.3	10.4
2+4	4549.7	7.6	17.6	2.5
3	9190.8	15.2	40.8	5.0
5	16449.0	13.1	22.4	9.0
6	38960.3	5.4	23.6	21.3
7	72016.3	6.2	10.2	39.3
8	22701.2	6.8	14.9	12.4
9	279.9	-36.3	164.6	0.2

Table 2: Imports by SITC sections

(Value in million US$, growth and shares in percentage)

SITC	2011	Avg. Growth rates (%) 2007-2011	2010-2011	2011 share
Total	203028.0	5.5	16.6	100.0
0+1	14372.5	10.8	15.5	7.1
2+4	7942.8	10.2	36.0	3.9
3	26621.3	13.0	40.4	13.1
5	28724.3	8.2	16.2	14.1
6	36537.8	1.7	19.1	18.0
7	64133.2	2.6	6.8	31.6
8	19520.0	9.0	11.0	9.6
9	5176.0	-4.3	34.7	2.5

Table 3: Top 10 export commodities 2009 to 2011

(Value in million US$)

HS code	4-digit heading of Harmonized System 2007	Value (million US$) 2009	2010	2011	Unit value 2009	2010	2011	Unit	SITC code
	All Commodities	136641.3	157064.9	183292.0					
8703	Motor cars and other motor vehicles principally designed for the transport	9671.8	8786.3	9481.1	11.1	10.7	12.2	thsd US$/unit	781
8708	Parts and accessories of the motor vehicles of headings 87.01 to 87.05	6660.2	7875.3	8843.1	*8.7*	*8.1*	*7.9*	US$/kg	784
8528	Reception apparatus for television	6725.1	7364.7	5974.5	307.5	318.0	297.0	US$/unit	761
9401	Seats (other than those of heading 94.02)	3689.0	4031.7	4722.4					821
9403	Other furniture and parts thereof	2675.4	2920.1	3357.6					821
8471	Automatic data processing machines and units thereof	2884.5	3409.6	2471.3	327.8	324.6	248.2	US$/unit	752
8408	Compression-ignition internal combustion piston engines	2382.6	2700.8	3490.5	2.5	2.4	2.6	thsd US$/unit	713
8901	Cruise ships, excursion boats, ferry-boats, cargo ships, barges	2412.6	2224.1	3650.4			*15.2*	mln US$/unit	793
8544	Insulated (including enamelled or anodised) wire, cable	1895.9	2463.1	2759.9	*9.6*	*9.8*	*11.1*	US$/kg	773
7403	Refined copper and copper alloys, unwrought	1696.8	2402.9	2921.1	5.3	7.6	*8.9*	US$/kg	682

Graph 2: Trade Balance by MDG Regions in 2011

(Bln US$)

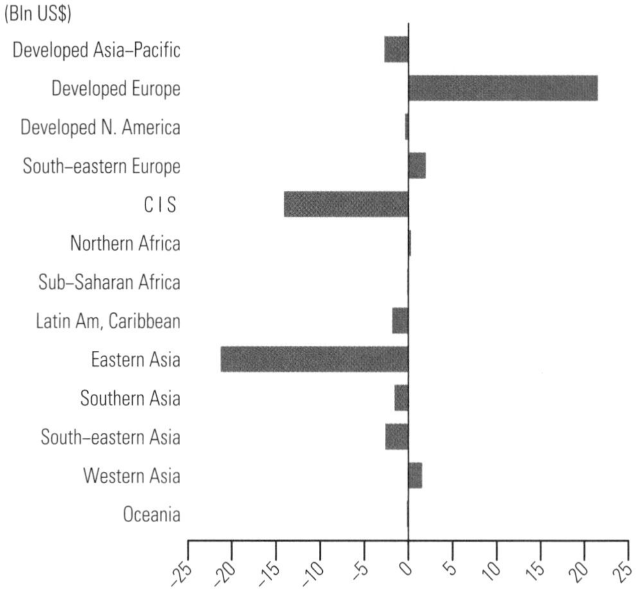

Graph 3: Partner concentration of trade in 2011

(Cumulative share by ranked partners)

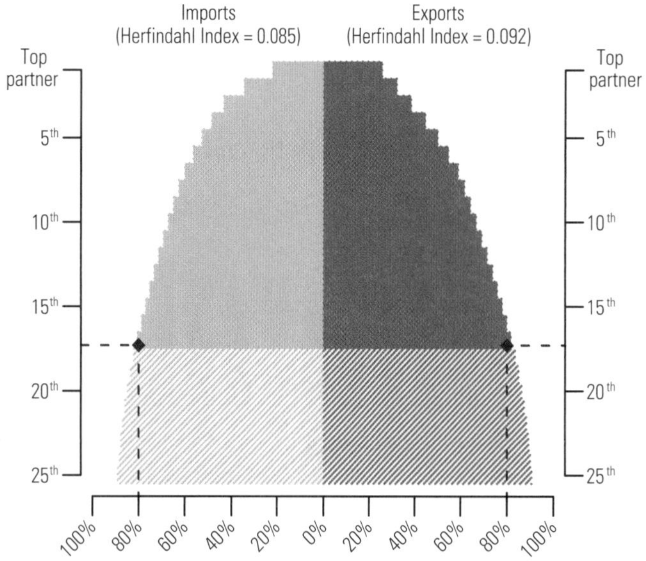

Table 4: Exports by principal countries and SITC sections in 2011

(Value in million US$, percentages of country total)

Country	Total	Shares by SITC sections (%)								
		0 + 1	2 + 4	3	5	6	7	8	9	Total
World	183 292.0	10.4	2.5	5.0	9.0	21.3	39.3	12.4	0.2	100
Germany	47 307.2	8.7	3.7	3.9	7.7	22.9	36.2	16.7	0.1	100
United Kingdom	11 776.4	11.4	0.8	3.2	7.9	20.6	45.4	10.7	0.0	100
Czech Rep.	11 272.5	10.8	3.4	13.0	9.7	27.8	24.5	10.9	0.0	100
France	11 175.2	10.1	1.9	1.7	7.0	18.8	48.0	12.4	0.0	100
Italy	9 873.8	10.4	2.3	0.1	7.8	16.9	54.1	7.3	1.0	100
Russian Federation	8 538.1	12.4	0.9	0.4	15.0	19.6	39.1	12.6	0.0	100
Netherlands	7 797.3	13.9	1.4	7.5	6.9	15.3	40.5	14.3	0.1	100
Sweden	5 151.5	6.4	1.3	7.6	5.1	19.1	45.6	14.9	0.0	100
Ukraine	4 693.5	9.7	1.3	5.1	15.6	29.5	27.5	11.2	0.0	100
Hungary	4 644.8	13.2	1.1	1.9	9.3	21.6	44.7	8.2	0.0	100

Imports Profile:

Machinery and transport equipment (SITC section 7) accounted for 31.6 percent of imported goods in 2011 (see table 2). Other major commodity groups were manufactured goods classified chiefly by material (SITC section 6) and chemicals and related products, n.e.s. (SITC section 5) respectively with 18.0 and 14.1 percent of imports. Over the last three years, top imported products included petroleum oils and oils obtained from bituminous minerals, crude (HS code 2709), parts and accessories of the motor vehicles of headings 87.01 to 87.05 (HS code 8708) and motor cars and other motor vehicles principally designed for the transport (HS code 8703) (see table 5).

Table 5: Top 10 import commodities 2009 to 2011

(Value in million US$)

HS code	4-digit heading of Harmonized System 2007	Value (million US$)			Unit value				SITC code
		2009	2010	2011	2009	2010	2011	Unit	
	All Commodities	149 569.8	174 127.6	203 028.0					
2709	Petroleum oils and oils obtained from bituminous minerals, crude	8 434.9	12 274.0	17 988.4	0.4	0.6	0.8	US$/kg	333
8708	Parts and accessories of the motor vehicles of headings 87.01 to 87.05	4 446.4	5 313.9	6 354.9	*7.7*	*7.4*	*7.6*	US$/kg	784
8703	Motor cars and other motor vehicles principally designed for the transport	5 119.2	5 418.1	5 197.0	14.0	15.6	15.8	thsd US$/unit	781
9999	Commodities not specified according to kind	5 986.7	3 807.5	5 072.5					931
3004	Medicaments (excluding goods of heading 30.02, 30.05 or 30.06)	4 161.5	4 812.3	4 950.0	*63.3*	*69.8*	*79.8*	US$/kg	542
8529	Parts suitable for use with the apparatus of headings 85.25 to 85.28	2 743.9	4 176.1	2 559.2	*22.4*	*28.6*	*26.5*	US$/kg	764
2710	Petroleum oils, other than crude	2 725.1	2 733.4	3 729.4	*0.6*	*0.8*	*1.0*	US$/kg	334
8471	Automatic data processing machines and units thereof	2 345.6	2 803.2	2 674.7	68.2	*73.7*	71.6	US$/unit	752
8517	Electrical apparatus for line telephony or line telegraphy	2 477.2	2 479.4	2 541.8					764
8901	Cruise ships, excursion boats, ferry-boats, cargo ships, barges	1 947.2	2 094.6	2 737.5			892.3	thsd US$/unit	793

Portugal

Imports: CIF, by origin/consignment for intra-eu | **Exports: FOB, by last known destination** | **Trade System: Special**

Overview:

From 2007 to 2011, Portugal's exports increased on average by 3.4 percent each year and reached its peak of 58.9 bln US$ in 2011 (see table 1 and graph 1). Similarly, imports increased on average by 0.6 percent each year and reached 80.3 bln US$ (see table 2 and graph 1). This resulted in a trade deficit of 21.4 bln US$ in 2011 (see graph 1). The majority of this deficit came from trade with Developed Europe: deficit with this region amounted to 15.9 bln US$ in 2011 (see graph 2). Trade recorded significant deficits with Commonwealth of Independent States (-2.4 bln US$), Eastern Asia (-1.7 bln US$) and Latin America and the Caribbean (-1.5 bln US$) among others. Portugal's trade was diversified across partners: in 2011, 13 major partners accounted for 80 percent of both imports and exports (see graph 3).

Graph 1: Total imports, exports and trade balance

(Bln US$ by year)

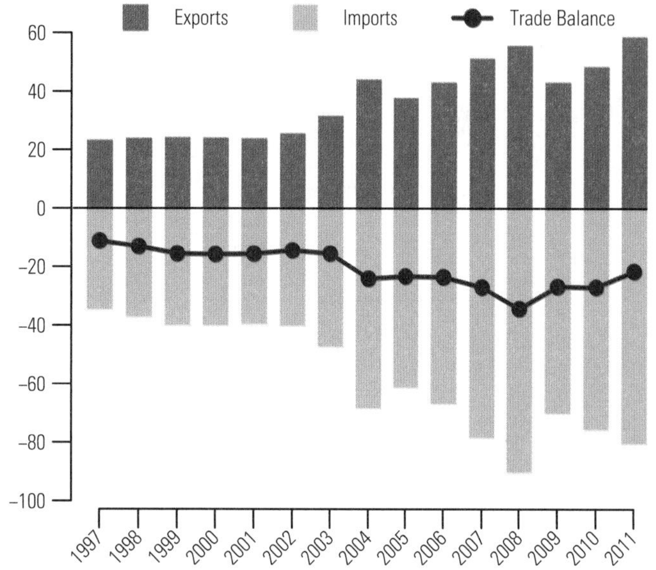

Table 1: Exports by SITC sections

(Value in million US$, growth and shares in percentage)

SITC	2011	Avg. Growth rates (%) 2007-2011	Avg. Growth rates (%) 2010-2011	2011 share
Total	58932.2	3.4	20.9	100.0
0+1	5911.6	8.9	15.5	10.0
2+4	3467.3	10.3	22.1	5.9
3	4268.1	17.0	31.0	7.2
5	5225.8	9.7	29.7	8.9
6	13413.8	4.8	23.4	22.8
7	16256.0	0.3	22.9	27.6
8	9289.8	3.2	15.6	15.8
9	1099.8	-26.2	-19.4	1.9

Exports Profile:

Portugal's exports in 2011 were mainly composed of 27.6 percent of machinery and transport equipment (SITC section 7), 22.8 percent of manufactured goods classified chiefly by material (SITC section 6) and 15.8 percent of miscellaneous manufactured articles (SITC section 8) (see table 1). Major destinations for exported goods were Spain, Germany and France (see table 4). From 2009 to 2011, top exported products were petroleum oils, other than crude (HS code 2710), motor cars and other motor vehicles principally designed for the transport (HS code 8703) and parts and accessories of the motor vehicles of headings 87.01 to 87.05 (HS code 8708) (see table 3).

Table 2: Imports by SITC sections

(Value in million US$, growth and shares in percentage)

SITC	2011	Avg. Growth rates (%) 2007-2011	Avg. Growth rates (%) 2010-2011	2011 share
Total	80324.5	0.6	6.3	100.0
0+1	10320.1	5.1	14.3	12.8
2+4	3867.2	9.0	29.1	4.8
3	14330.7	7.0	30.0	17.8
5	10657.4	6.1	12.4	13.3
6	11957.3	-2.2	5.9	14.9
7	20418.7	-3.6	-10.6	25.4
8	8469.7	1.9	1.0	10.5
9	303.3	-44.7	-43.3	0.4

Table 3: Top 10 export commodities 2009 to 2011

(Value in million US$)

HS code	4-digit heading of Harmonized System 2007	Value (million US$) 2009	2010	2011	Unit value 2009	2010	2011	Unit	SITC code
	All Commodities	43396.5	48743.6	58932.2					
2710	Petroleum oils, other than crude	1916.6	2698.4	3727.1	*0.5*	*0.6*		US$/kg	334
8703	Motor cars and other motor vehicles principally designed for the transport	1998.2	2346.8	3376.3	18.6	*19.4*		thsd US$/unit	781
8708	Parts and accessories of the motor vehicles of headings 87.01 to 87.05	1919.1	2360.8	2740.1	*8.0*	*7.7*	*8.9*	US$/kg	784
6403	Footwear with outer soles of rubber, plastics, leather	1359.4	1507.6	1822.5	*33.3*	*32.2*	*39.4*	US$/pair	851
9999	Commodities not specified according to kind	3085.9	1069.8	374.5					931
8527	Reception apparatus for radio-telephony, radio-telegraphy	908.8	1090.6	1267.8	*121.3*	*135.8*		US$/unit	762
4802	Uncoated paper and paperboard, of a kind used for writing	793.8	871.4	1535.6	*1.0*	*1.0*	*1.0*	US$/kg	641
4011	New pneumatic tyres, of rubber	695.9	798.0	1016.7	*51.8*	*52.3*		US$/unit	625
2204	Wine of fresh grapes, including fortified wines	763.1	807.0	907.6	*3.3*	*3.2*	*3.1*	US$/litre	112
6109	T-shirts, singlets and other vests, knitted or crocheted	752.7	792.2	834.8	6.4	*6.0*	*5.2*	US$/unit	845

Graph 2: Trade Balance by MDG Regions in 2011

(Bln US$)

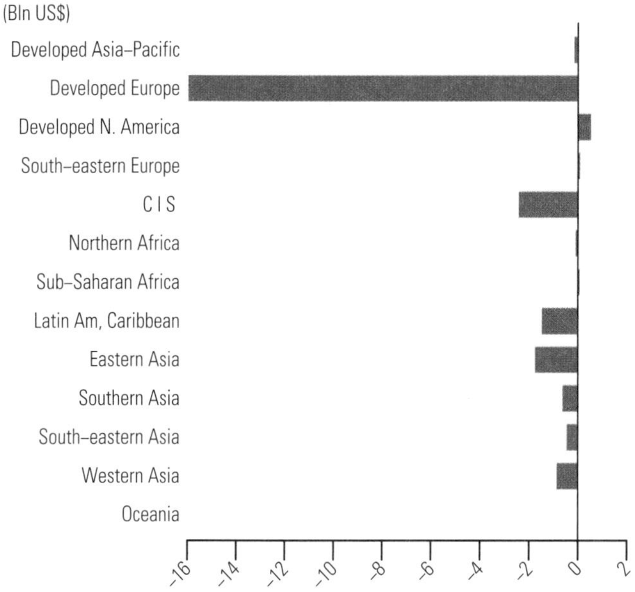

Graph 3: Partner concentration of trade in 2011

(Cumulative share by ranked partners)

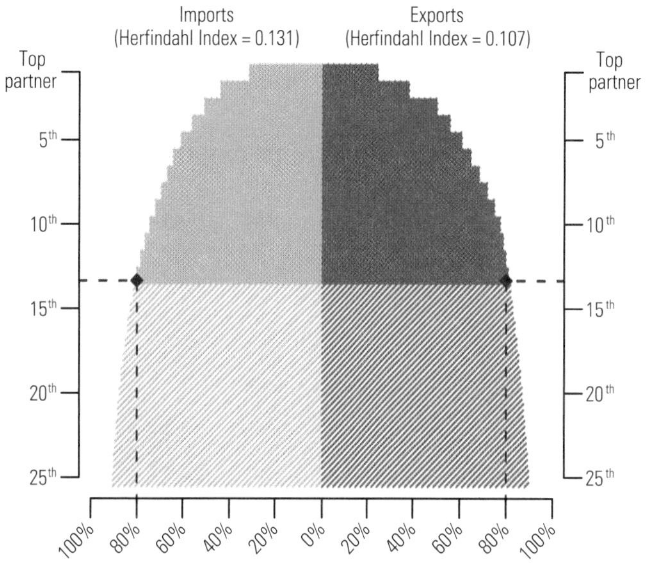

Table 4: Exports by principal countries and SITC sections in 2011

(Value in million US$, percentages of country total)

Country	Total	Shares by SITC sections (%) 0+1	2+4	3	5	6	7	8	9	Total
World	58932.2	10.0	5.9	7.2	8.9	22.8	27.6	15.8	1.9	100
Spain	14615.4	15.8	8.7	3.6	10.9	24.4	17.9	17.5	1.2	100
Germany	7969.6	2.0	3.1	0.2	7.1	17.2	56.4	13.8	0.3	100
France	7065.4	7.7	1.9	0.8	6.4	25.9	30.5	26.7	0.2	100
Angola	3245.1	22.5	3.8	2.3	8.6	21.9	25.7	15.1	0.1	100
United Kingdom	2976.8	10.5	2.4	1.7	7.8	22.6	35.9	19.1	0.1	100
Netherlands	2296.8	8.2	6.4	15.2	18.7	18.0	10.3	22.9	0.1	100
Italy	2130.5	11.8	6.2	0.0	7.7	27.6	26.5	15.5	4.7	100
USA	2069.5	5.6	2.8	26.3	7.8	31.9	18.8	6.1	0.7	100
Belgium	1849.3	7.6	1.3	4.1	11.4	17.1	22.6	12.4	23.5	100
Bunkers	1436.3	1.1	0.0	94.7	0.5	0.2	0.6	0.1	2.8	100

Imports Profile:

In 2011, machinery and transport equipment (SITC section 7) accounted for 25.4 percent of Portugal's imports (see table 2). Other major commodity groups included mineral fuels, lubricants and related materials (SITC section 3) and manufactured goods classified chiefly by material (SITC section 6). They accounted respectively for 17.8 and 14.9 percent of imports. From 2009 to 2011, top imported products were petroleum oils and oils obtained from bituminous minerals, crude (HS code 2709), motor cars and other motor vehicles principally designed for the transport (HS code 8703) and parts and accessories of the motor vehicles of headings 87.01 to 87.05 (HS code 8708) (see table 5).

Table 5: Top 10 import commodities 2009 to 2011

(Value in million US$)

HS code	4-digit heading of Harmonized System 2007	Value (million US$) 2009	2010	2011	Unit value 2009	2010	2011	Unit	SITC code
	All Commodities	69985.0	75572.5	80324.5					
2709	Petroleum oils and oils obtained from bituminous minerals, crude	4733.2	6649.5	8448.6	*0.5*	0.6	*0.8*	US$/kg	333
8703	Motor cars and other motor vehicles principally designed for the transport	3416.1	4689.1	3818.7	*17.6*	*18.1*		thsd US$/unit	781
8708	Parts and accessories of the motor vehicles of headings 87.01 to 87.05	2049.2	2631.0	3095.1	*6.6*	*6.9*	*10.7*	US$/kg	784
3004	Medicaments (excluding goods of heading 30.02, 30.05 or 30.06)	2452.7	2401.3	2407.5	*81.6*	*72.2*	*77.0*	US$/kg	542
9999	Commodities not specified according to kind	5992.9	475.0	214.2					931
2710	Petroleum oils, other than crude	1604.6	1609.9	2457.0	*0.5*	*0.7*		US$/kg	334
2711	Petroleum gases and other gaseous hydrocarbons	1641.0	1825.8	2173.4	*0.4*	*0.4*	*0.5*	US$/kg	343
8517	Electrical apparatus for line telephony or line telegraphy	1000.9	1029.9	909.7					764
8471	Automatic data processing machines and units thereof	975.6	886.8	759.9	*130.0*	*158.3*		US$/unit	752
8528	Reception apparatus for television	595.2	575.6	476.2	*192.6*	*155.7*		US$/unit	761

Qatar

Imports: CIF, by origin | **Exports: FOB, by last known destination** | **Trade System: Special**

Overview:

After several years of continuous growth marked by a peak of 54.9 bln US$ in 2008, the value of exports of Qatar dropped in 2009 by 9.9 percent to reach 49.5 bln US$ (see table 1 and graph 1). From 2005 and 2008, imports increased on average by 40.5 percent each year to 27.9 bln US$ (see table 2 and graph 1). In 2008, trade recorded a surplus of 27.0 bln US$ (see graph 1). This surplus came largely from trade with Developed Asia-Pacific (+17.0 bln US$) (see graph 2). Trade was also in surplus with Eastern Asia (+9.5 bln US$), South-eastern Asia (+7.4 bln US$) and Southern Asia (+2.1 bln US$). Deficits were recorded with Developed Europe (-6.7 bln US$) and Western Asia (-3.9 bln US$). Qatar's exports were concentrated among a few partners in 2009: 8 major partners accounted for 80 percent of exports (see graph 3).

Graph 1: Total imports, exports and trade balance

(Bln US$ by year)

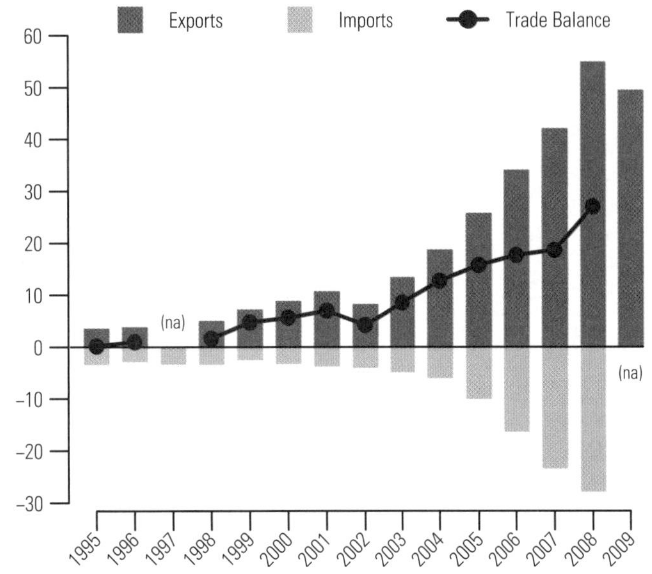

Exports Profile:

Exports of Qatar were mainly composed of 71.1 percent of mineral fuels, lubricants and related materials (SITC section 3), which decreased by 30.6 percent in 2009 (see table 1). Other major commodity groups for exports in 2009 were commodities and transactions not classified elsewhere (SITC section 9) and chemicals and related products, n.e.s. (SITC section 5), respectively 21.2 and 4.5 percent of exports. Major partners for exports included Japan, Republic of Korea and India (see table 4). From 2007 to 2009, top exported products were petroleum products: petroleum gases and other gaseous hydrocarbons (HS code 2711), petroleum oils, crude (HS code 2709) and petroleum oils, other than crude (HS code 2710) (see table 3).

Table 1: Exports by SITC sections

(Value in million US$, growth and shares in percentage)

SITC	2009	Avg. Growth rates (%) 2005-2009	2008-2009	2009 share
Total	49473.4	17.7	-9.9	100.0
0+1	45.3	8.7	71.7	0.1
2+4	67.3	8.2	-47.6	0.1
3	35174.5	13.0	-30.6	71.1
5	2225.6	13.5	8.5	4.5
6	517.7	48.4	21.1	1.0
7	879.4	31.6	16.3	1.8
8	79.9	4.3	55.0	0.2
9	10483.7	45.8	1244.0	21.2

Table 2: Imports by SITC sections

(Value in million US$, growth and shares in percentage)

SITC	2008	Avg. Growth rates (%) 2005-2008	2007-2008	2008 share
Total	27900.0	40.5	19.1	100.0
0+1	1608.4	36.2	48.7	5.8
2+4	732.4	47.0	14.7	2.6
3	185.6	97.1	49.8	0.7
5	1548.8	32.9	31.8	5.6
6	7159.5	43.6	20.3	25.7
7	14354.6	42.7	16.2	51.4
8	2176.7	27.3	5.8	7.8
9	134.1	9.7	155.5	0.5

Table 3: Top 10 export commodities 2007 to 2009

(Value in million US$)

HS code	4-digit heading of Harmonized System 2002	Value (million US$) 2007	2008	2009	Unit value 2007	2008	2009	Unit	SITC code
	All Commodities	42019.9	54912.1	49473.4					
2711	Petroleum gases and other gaseous hydrocarbons	16800.2	23100.8	19493.2	0.4	0.6	*0.4*	US$/kg	343
2709	Petroleum oils, crude	19181.2	25760.6	14053.0	0.5	0.7	0.4	US$/kg	333
9999	Commodities not specified according to kind	269.9	780.0	10483.7					931
2710	Petroleum oils, other than crude	1632.3	1825.4	1622.9	0.7	0.7	0.6	US$/kg	334
3901	Polymers of ethylene, in primary forms	1332.9	1396.6	1133.0	1.4	1.5	1.1	US$/kg	571
3102	Mineral or chemical fertilisers, nitrogenous	896.2	1.1	785.5	0.3	0.4	0.3	US$/kg	562
8703	Motor cars and other motor vehicles principally designed for the transport	137.4	316.8	188.4	*6.0*			thsd US$/unit	781
2903	Halogenated derivatives of hydrocarbons	285.8	309.7	0.2	0.6	0.6	1.5	US$/kg	511
7208	Flat-rolled products of iron or non-alloy steel	187.2	301.5	0.1	0.6	1.1	0.6	US$/kg	673
2905	Acyclic alcohols and their derivatives	453.3	...	0.3	0.5		0.8	US$/kg	512

Graph 2: Trade Balance by MDG Regions in 2008

(Bln US$)

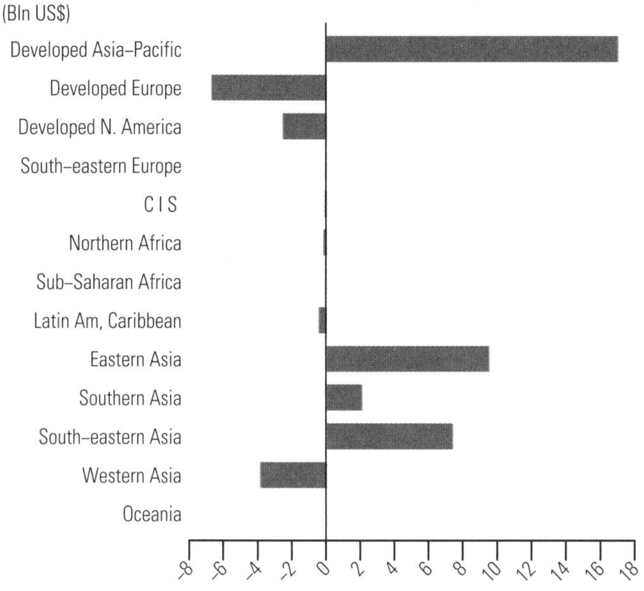

Graph 3: Partner concentration of trade in 2009

(Cumulative share by ranked partners)

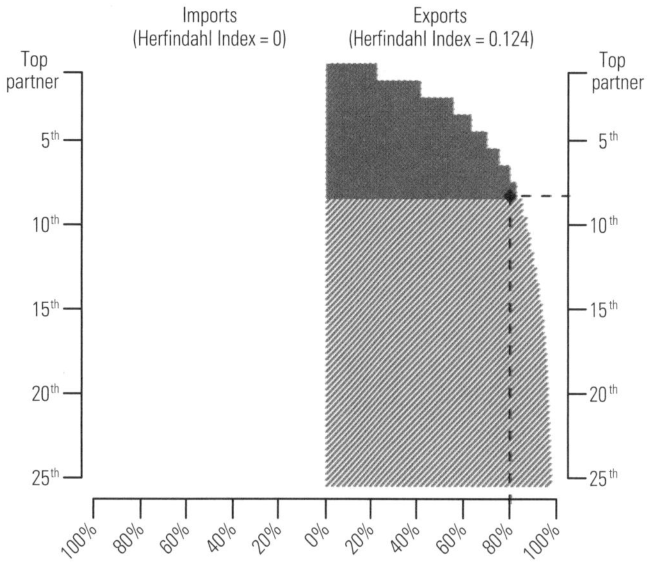

Table 4: Exports by principal countries and SITC sections in 2009

(Value in million US$, percentages of country total)

Country	Total	Shares by SITC sections (%)								
		0 + 1	2 + 4	3	5	6	7	8	9	Total
World	49473.4	0.1	0.1	71.1	4.5	1.0	1.8	0.2	21.2	100
Japan	11076.0	0.0	0.0	68.5	0.0	0.0	0.0	0.0	31.5	100
Areas, nes	9330.5	0.0	0.0	76.3	0.7	...	...	...	23.0	100
Rep. of Korea	6891.9	0.0	0.0	74.8	0.5	0.1	0.1	0.0	24.4	100
India	3828.4	0.0	0.2	81.4	4.4	3.6	0.8	0.0	9.6	100
Singapore	3364.0	0.0	0.0	61.7	0.7	0.0	0.8	0.0	36.8	100
United Arab Emirates	2635.2	0.6	0.4	44.8	6.9	7.5	9.1	0.8	30.0	100
Other Asia, nes	2279.2	0.0	0.0	83.7	12.2	0.0	0.0	...	4.1	100
Thailand	1336.4	0.0	0.0	83.0	9.8	0.1	0.1	0.1	7.0	100
Belgium	1323.7	0.0	0.0	90.8	8.7	0.1	0.3	0.0	...	100
Other Europe, nes	890.5	0.0	0.0	99.5	0.5	...	...	...	...	100

Imports Profile:

In 2008, imports of machinery and transport equipment (SITC section 7) increased by 16.2 percent and accounted for 51.4 percent of imported goods (see table 2). Manufactured goods classified chiefly by material (SITC section 6) increased by 20.3 percent and accounted for 25.7 percent. From 2006 to 2008, top imported products included motor cars and other motor vehicles principally designed for the transport (HS code 8703), tubes, pipes and hollow profiles, seamless, of iron (other than cast iron) (HS code 7304) and insulated (including enamelled or anodised) wire, cable (HS code 8544) (see table 5).

Table 5: Top 10 import commodities 2006 to 2008

(Value in million US$)

HS code	4-digit heading of Harmonized System 2002	Value (million US$)			Unit value				SITC code
		2006	2007	2008	2006	2007	2008	Unit	
	All Commodities	16440.1	23429.2	27900.0					
8703	Motor cars and other motor vehicles principally designed for the transport	144.9	1583.8	2080.2	*6.6*	*6.4*		thsd US$/unit	781
7304	Tubes, pipes and hollow profiles, seamless, of iron (other than cast iron)	1053.0	1038.3	774.3	2.0	0.9	1.4	US$/kg	679
8544	Insulated (including enamelled or anodised) wire, cable	586.3	911.6	1236.9	4.9	*6.3*	*7.7*	US$/kg	773
8481	Taps, cocks, valves and similar appliances for pipes, boiler shells	374.4	687.1	859.7	13.0	17.4	23.0	US$/kg	747
8431	Parts suitable for use principally with the machinery of headings 84.25	467.8	530.6	696.9	15.1	1.3	16.5	US$/kg	723
7308	Structures (excluding prefabricated buildings of heading 94.06)	355.8	596.6	726.2	1.6	1.6	2.1	US$/kg	691
9999	Commodities not specified according to kind	1306.8	11.5	129.3					931
8419	Machinery, plant or laboratory equipment	200.3	552.2	658.6					741
8413	Pumps for liquids, whether or not fitted with a measuring device	314.2	732.9	356.0					742
8704	Motor vehicles for the transport of goods	366.7	428.8	537.1	*16.3*			thsd US$/unit	782

Republic of Moldova

Imports: CIF, by origin | Exports: FOB, by last known destination | Trade System: General

Overview:

From 2007 to 2011, Republic of Moldova's exports increased on average by 13.4 percent each year despite a decline of 19.4 percent in 2009 and amounted to 2.2 bln US$ in 2011 (see table 1 and graph 1). Similarly, imports increased on average by 8.9 percent each year and reached 5.2 bln US$ (see table 2 and graph 1). This resulted in a trade deficit of 3.0 bln US$ in 2011, well above the 2010 deficit of 2.3 bln US$ (see graph 1). This deficit came largely from trade with Developed Europe (-1.0 bln US$), Commonwealth of Independent States (-0.8 bln US$) and Eastern Asia (-0.4 bln US$) (see graph 2). By partners, exports were more concentrated than imports: 9 major partners accounted for 80 percent of exports compared to 13 major partners for imports (see graph 3).

Graph 1: Total imports, exports and trade balance

(Bln US$ by year)

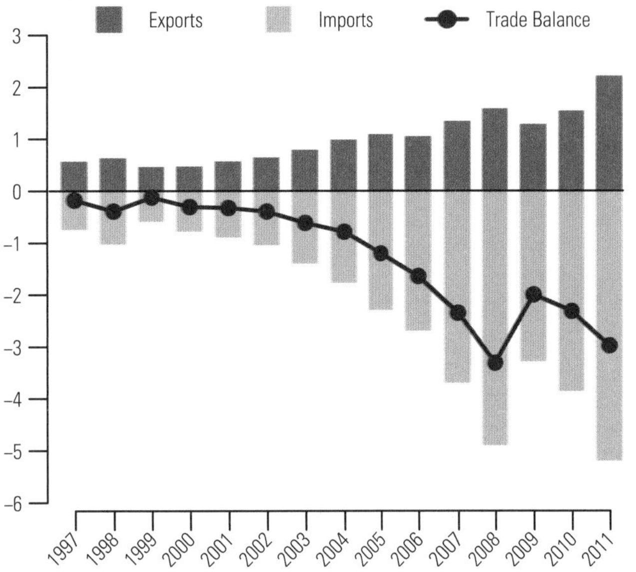

Table 1: Exports by SITC sections

(Value in million US$, growth and shares in percentage)

SITC	2011	Avg. Growth rates (%) 2007-2011	Avg. Growth rates (%) 2010-2011	2011 share
Total	2 216.8	13.4	43.8	100.0
0+1	655.9	13.0	10.7	29.6
2+4	362.9	17.5	88.4	16.4
3	24.0	51.4	211.3	1.1
5	124.3	42.1	56.7	5.6
6	213.7	-0.3	82.0	9.6
7	328.0	31.6	70.3	14.8
8	502.8	6.7	40.1	22.7
9	5.1	...	1914.1	0.2

Table 2: Imports by SITC sections

(Value in million US$, growth and shares in percentage)

SITC	2011	Avg. Growth rates (%) 2007-2011	Avg. Growth rates (%) 2010-2011	2011 share
Total	5 191.3	8.9	34.7	100.0
0+1	641.6	11.5	17.4	12.4
2+4	119.0	2.7	24.9	2.3
3	733.7	-1.4	-7.2	14.1
5	673.1	11.3	29.3	13.0
6	975.9	5.2	32.2	18.8
7	1 159.5	9.1	43.7	22.3
8	451.0	7.5	26.9	8.7
9	437.4	280.3	30925.4	8.4

Exports Profile:

Food, live animals, beverages and tobacco (SITC sections 0+1) represented 29.6 percent of exported goods in 2011 (see table 1). Another major commodity group for exports, miscellaneous manufactured articles (SITC section 8), accounted for 22.7 percent of exports. Major markets for exports included Russian Federation, Romania and Italy (see table 4). They accounted jointly for more than half of exports (54.9 percent). Over the last three years, main products for exports included wine of fresh grapes, including fortified wines (HS code 2204), insulated (including enamelled or anodised) wire, cable (HS code 8544) and sunflower seeds, whether or not broken (HS code 1206) (see table 3).

Table 3: Top 10 export commodities 2009 to 2011

(Value in million US$)

HS code	4-digit heading of Harmonized System 2007	Value (million US$) 2009	2010	2011	Unit value 2009	2010	2011	Unit	SITC code
	All Commodities	1 283.0	1 541.5	2 216.8					
2204	Wine of fresh grapes, including fortified wines	128.7	137.9	132.5	1.3	1.1	1.1	US$/litre	112
8544	Insulated (including enamelled or anodised) wire, cable	94.0	91.1	140.9	*16.4*	*16.6*	*18.2*	US$/kg	773
1206	Sunflower seeds, whether or not broken	37.8	57.3	123.7	0.3	0.5	0.6	US$/kg	222
3004	Medicaments (excluding goods of heading 30.02, 30.05 or 30.06)	44.7	59.8	76.4	*61.1*	*62.4*	65.2	US$/kg	542
0802	Other nuts, fresh or dried, whether or not shelled or peeled	45.8	59.8	71.5	4.2	6.1	7.3	US$/kg	057
0808	Apples, pears and quinces, fresh	44.8	51.3	58.0	0.3	0.3	0.3	US$/kg	057
1512	Sunflower-seed, safflower or cotton-seed oil	41.3	41.1	69.3	0.8	1.0	1.2	US$/kg	421
6204	Women's or girls' suits, ensembles, jackets, blazers, dresses, skirts	32.7	32.7	47.3	12.7	11.7	12.7	US$/unit	842
6203	Men's or boys' suits, ensembles, jackets, blazers, trousers	33.2	33.3	40.1	16.7	15.9	18.2	US$/unit	841
2208	Alcohol of a strength by volume of less than 80 % vol	26.2	36.2	42.7	7.7	*7.0*	6.9	US$/litre	112

Graph 2: Trade Balance by MDG Regions in 2011

(Mln US$)

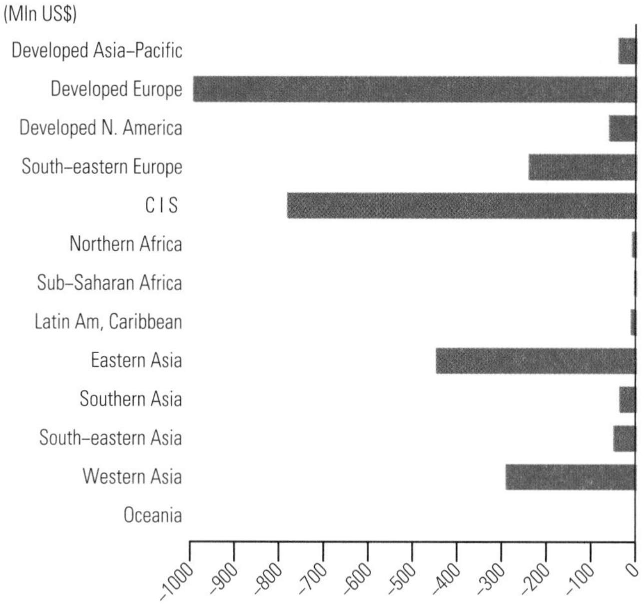

Graph 3: Partner concentration of trade in 2011

(Cumulative share by ranked partners)

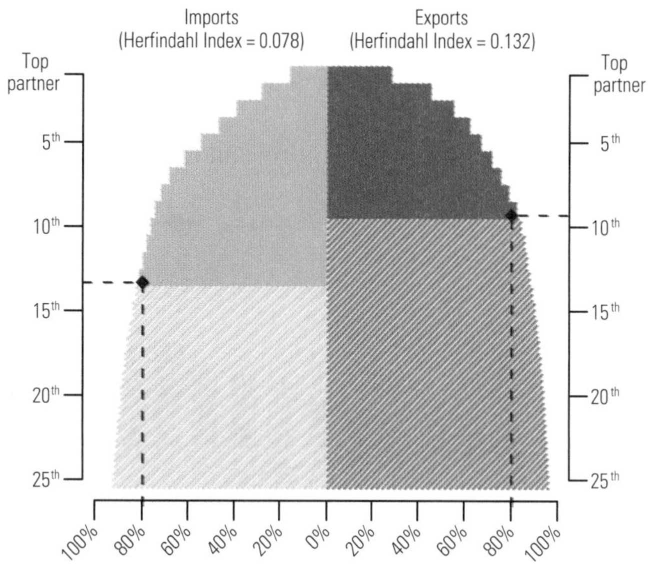

Table 4: Exports by principal countries and SITC sections in 2011

(Value in million US$, percentages of country total)

Country	Total	Shares by SITC sections (%) 0+1	2+4	3	5	6	7	8	9	Total
World	2216.8	29.6	16.4	1.1	5.6	9.6	14.8	22.7	0.2	100
Russian Federation	625.5	38.0	2.6	0.0	15.2	17.3	16.1	10.7	...	100
Romania	376.4	10.0	18.7	2.9	0.7	8.0	42.5	17.1	...	100
Italy	215.1	9.0	13.9	0.0	0.0	4.8	2.1	70.1	...	100
Ukraine	153.0	35.4	26.2	4.0	5.0	10.5	13.0	6.0	0.0	100
Germany	106.5	26.2	38.8	...	0.4	1.5	1.4	31.6	0.0	100
United Kingdom	101.7	10.6	37.8	...	0.1	0.8	0.2	50.5	...	100
Poland	85.9	32.5	16.8	...	0.5	1.1	4.3	44.9	...	100
Belarus	75.6	80.5	8.2	...	3.9	3.4	2.2	1.8	...	100
Turkey	73.4	10.2	37.1	0.1	0.3	17.2	0.7	33.8	0.6	100
Kazakhstan	45.5	59.0	0.1	...	2.1	13.7	16.0	9.1	...	100

Imports Profile:

Republic of Moldova's imports were composed of 22.3 percent of machinery and transport equipment (SITC section 7), 18.8 percent of manufactured goods classified chiefly by material (SITC section 6) and 14.1 percent of mineral fuels, lubricants and related materials (SITC section 3) (see table 2). Over the last three years, top three products for imports were petroleum oils, other than crude (HS code 2710), petroleum gases and other gaseous hydrocarbons (HS code 2711) and medicaments (excluding goods of heading 30.02, 30.05 or 30.06) (HS code 3004) (see table 5).

Table 5: Top 10 import commodities 2009 to 2011

(Value in million US$)

HS code	4-digit heading of Harmonized System 2007	Value (million US$) 2009	2010	2011	Unit value 2009	2010	2011	Unit	SITC code
	All Commodities	3278.3	3855.3	5191.3					
2710	Petroleum oils, other than crude	360.6	417.1	623.4	*0.6*	0.8	*1.0*	US$/kg	334
2711	Petroleum gases and other gaseous hydrocarbons	326.0	340.4	67.0	0.4	0.4	*0.9*	US$/kg	343
3004	Medicaments (excluding goods of heading 30.02, 30.05 or 30.06)	158.0	163.9	197.8	*30.1*	*27.4*	*31.4*	US$/kg	542
9999	Commodities not specified according to kind	1.4	1.3	436.7					931
8703	Motor cars and other motor vehicles principally designed for the transport	78.8	88.6	137.4	16.0	17.1	19.3	thsd US$/unit	781
8517	Electrical apparatus for line telephony or line telegraphy	79.2	79.0	92.1					764
8544	Insulated (including enamelled or anodised) wire, cable	58.4	64.5	116.0	*7.0*	*7.5*	*10.1*	US$/kg	773
2402	Cigars, cheroots, cigarillos and cigarettes	76.8	69.8	73.6		*11.8*	*13.5*	US$/kg	122
9403	Other furniture and parts thereof	35.3	39.7	46.9					821
3808	Insecticides, rodenticides, fungicides, herbicides	27.2	35.3	55.5	*9.9*	*9.6*	*10.9*	US$/kg	591

Imports: CIF, by origin	Exports: FOB, by last known destination	Trade System: Special

Overview:

In 2011, the value of the exports of Romania increased by 26.9 percent to reach 62.7 bln US$ (see table 1 and graph1). Imports showed a similar development with an increase by 23.2 percent to 76.4 bln US$ in 2011 (see table 2 and graph 1). This resulted in a trade deficit of 13.7 bln US$, higher than the 2010 deficit of 12.6 bln US$ (see graph 1). Large deficits were recorded with Developed Europe (-10.6 bln US$), Commonwealth of Independent States (-4.0 bln US$) and Eastern Asia (-3.4 bln US$) (see graph 2). Trade recorded a surplus of 2.9 bln US$ with Western Asia. Exports were more diversified across partners than imports: in 2011, 18 major partners accounted for 80 percent of exports compared to 15 major partners for imports (see graph 3).

Graph 1: Total imports, exports and trade balance

(Bln US$ by year)

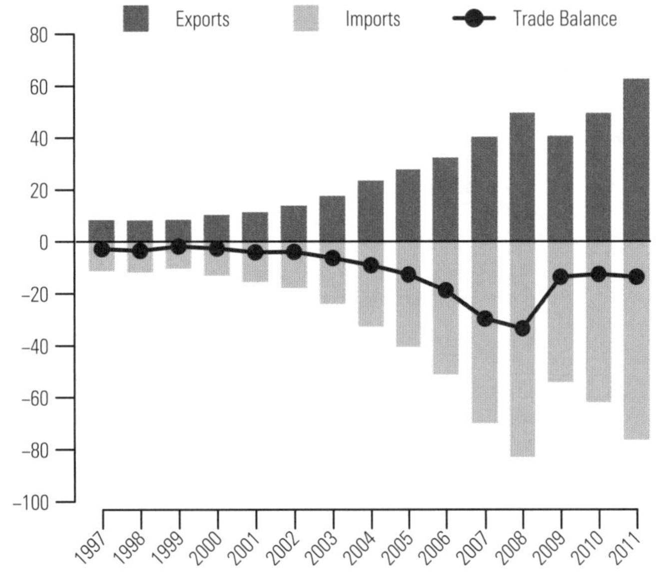

Exports Profile:

Machinery and transport equipment (SITC section 7) accounted for most of exports (40.9 percent) in 2011 (see table 1). Other important commodity groups included manufactured goods classified chiefly by material (SITC section 6) and miscellaneous manufactured articles (SITC section 8) respectively with 17.5 and 14.8 percent. In 2011, Germany, Italy and France were the three largest markets for exports (see table 4). From 2009 to 2011, major commodities for exports included motor cars and other motor vehicles principally designed for transport (HS code 8703), insulated (including enamelled or anodised) wire, cable (HS code 8544) and parts and accessories of the motor vehicles of headings 87.01 to 87.05 (HS code 8708) (see table 3).

Table 1: Exports by SITC sections

(Value in million US$, growth and shares in percentage)

SITC	2011	Avg. Growth rates (%) 2007-2011	2010-2011	2011 share
Total	62692.0	11.7	26.9	100.0
0+1	3931.9	35.9	29.0	6.3
2+4	4408.0	19.2	31.9	7.0
3	3445.8	3.1	31.6	5.5
5	3880.1	14.2	37.1	6.2
6	10974.0	6.1	31.5	17.5
7	25613.6	17.5	23.6	40.9
8	9256.0	1.4	22.2	14.8
9	1182.5	14.0	25.7	1.9

Table 2: Imports by SITC sections

(Value in million US$, growth and shares in percentage)

SITC	2011	Avg. Growth rates (%) 2007-2011	2010-2011	2011 share
Total	76365.3	2.2	23.2	100.0
0+1	5038.2	6.0	19.2	6.6
2+4	2617.7	7.2	23.3	3.4
3	8632.2	3.5	38.9	11.3
5	9861.9	9.0	23.4	12.9
6	16304.0	0.8	24.2	21.3
7	25811.1	-0.3	20.9	33.8
8	6127.4	0.8	16.4	8.0
9	1972.8	5.1	15.6	2.6

Table 3: Top 10 export commodities 2009 to 2011

(Value in million US$)

HS code	4-digit heading of Harmonized System 2007	Value (million US$) 2009	2010	2011	Unit value 2009	2010	2011	Unit	SITC code
	All Commodities	40620.9	49413.4	62692.0					
8703	Motor cars and other motor vehicles principally designed for the transport	2357.5	2711.3	3286.8	8.7	8.8	11.0	thsd US$/unit	781
8544	Insulated (including enamelled or anodised) wire, cable	2213.4	2574.0	3360.2	13.8	13.3	*15.3*	US$/kg	773
8708	Parts and accessories of the motor vehicles of headings 87.01 to 87.05	2004.7	2681.2	3459.4	9.9	*9.4*	*10.0*	US$/kg	784
8517	Electrical apparatus for line telephony or line telegraphy	1740.2	2790.3	3008.9					764
2710	Petroleum oils, other than crude	2004.6	2084.8	2849.2		0.7		US$/kg	334
8901	Cruise ships, excursion boats, ferry-boats, cargo ships, barges	1233.7	969.9	1171.8					793
4011	New pneumatic tyres, of rubber	840.9	1013.8	1371.0	*41.2*	43.7	52.4	US$/unit	625
9999	Commodities not specified according to kind	905.2	941.0	1182.5					931
7204	Ferrous waste and scrap; remelting scrap ingots of iron or steel	687.5	958.7	1065.2	0.3	0.4	0.5	US$/kg	282
9401	Seats (other than those of heading 94.02)	725.1	813.8	1030.4					821

Graph 2: Trade Balance by MDG Regions in 2011

(Bln US$)

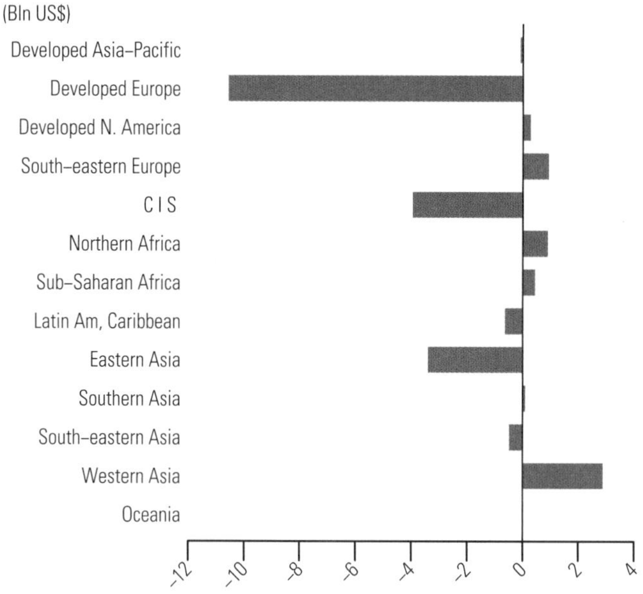

Graph 3: Partner concentration of trade in 2011

(Cumulative share by ranked partners)

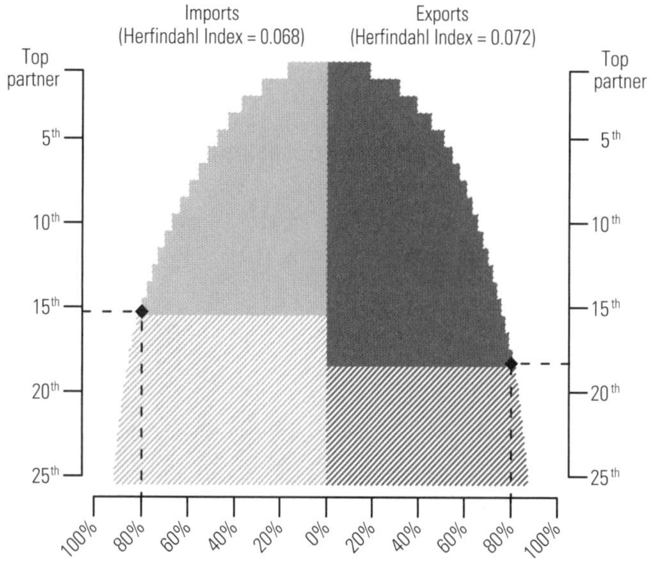

Table 4: Exports by principal countries and SITC sections in 2011

(Value in million US$, percentages of country total)

Country	Total	Shares by SITC sections (%) 0+1	2+4	3	5	6	7	8	9	Total
World	62692.0	6.3	7.0	5.5	6.2	17.5	40.9	14.8	1.9	100
Germany	11687.9	2.4	1.9	1.1	3.5	14.7	59.4	15.6	1.4	100
Italy	8054.2	8.0	2.8	0.3	2.7	19.2	24.9	37.7	4.5	100
France	4688.0	1.7	3.9	0.1	3.9	14.7	53.1	20.9	1.8	100
Turkey	3863.4	3.7	27.7	8.0	10.0	25.0	23.2	1.4	1.0	100
Hungary	3501.2	9.3	8.5	7.4	5.7	20.1	39.1	7.2	2.7	100
Bulgaria	2270.3	20.4	11.3	18.6	13.4	20.4	8.3	4.6	3.0	100
United Kingdom	2015.1	2.8	2.2	1.0	7.7	11.4	41.6	31.6	1.7	100
Netherlands	1952.8	8.5	13.5	0.8	2.2	14.7	46.2	12.3	1.8	100
Spain	1522.7	14.2	5.0	1.2	7.1	17.0	38.2	15.4	2.0	100
Poland	1491.1	3.1	2.2	0.3	10.3	33.5	40.6	8.7	1.2	100

Imports Profile:

Machinery and transport equipment (SITC section 7) and manufactured goods classified chiefly by material (SITC section 6) accounted for large shares of imports: respectively 33.8 and 21.3 percent in 2011 (see table 2). Over the last three years, top imported products were petroleum oils and oils obtained from bituminous minerals, crude (HS code 2709), medicaments (excluding goods of heading 30.02, 30.05 or 30.06) (HS code 3004) and electrical apparatus for line telephony or line telegraphy (HS code 8517) (see table 5).

Table 5: Top 10 import commodities 2009 to 2011

(Value in million US$)

HS code	4-digit heading of Harmonized System 2007	Value (million US$) 2009	2010	2011	Unit value 2009	2010	2011	Unit	SITC code
	All Commodities	54256.3	62006.6	76365.3					
2709	Petroleum oils and oils obtained from bituminous minerals, crude	3108.3	3360.8	4418.9	0.5	0.6	0.8	US$/kg	333
3004	Medicaments (excluding goods of heading 30.02, 30.05 or 30.06)	2184.4	2341.3	2676.6	67.9	70.4	*82.0*	US$/kg	542
8517	Electrical apparatus for line telephony or line telegraphy	1953.7	2670.2	2450.7					764
8708	Parts and accessories of the motor vehicles of headings 87.01 to 87.05	1545.1	1914.4	2297.9	*8.1*	*7.5*	*7.8*	US$/kg	784
9999	Commodities not specified according to kind	1605.7	1707.3	1972.8					931
8703	Motor cars and other motor vehicles principally designed for the transport	1109.7	1264.3	1532.9	15.2	16.0	18.0	thsd US$/unit	781
2710	Petroleum oils, other than crude	718.4	1260.3	1695.3		0.8		US$/kg	334
8544	Insulated (including enamelled or anodised) wire, cable	898.6	1126.1	1468.9	*7.8*	*7.9*	*10.4*	US$/kg	773
2711	Petroleum gases and other gaseous hydrocarbons	722.4	903.9	1504.3	*0.5*		*0.4*	US$/kg	343
8536	Electrical apparatus for switching or protecting electrical circuits	611.9	742.0	895.0	*21.4*	*16.8*	*25.8*	US$/kg	772

Russian Federation

Imports: CIF, by origin | **Exports: FOB, by last known destination** | **Trade System: General**

Overview:

From 2007 to 2011, exports of Russian Federation increased on average by 7.9 percent each year and reached its peak of 478.0 bln US$ in 2011 (see table 1 and graph 1). Similarly, imports increased on average by 9.3 percent each year and reached 284.7 bln US$ (see table 2 and graph 2). This resulted in a trade surplus of 193.3 bln US$ in 2011 (see graph 1). By MDG regions, the largest surplus was recorded with Developed Europe (+112.1 bln US$) (see graph 2). Significant surpluses were also recorded with Western Asia (+15.4 bln US$), Northern Africa (+5.4 bln US$) and Southern Asia (+5.2 bln US$). Trade recorded significant deficit with Eastern Asia (-9.3 bln US$). Trade was well diversified across partners: in 2011, 19 major partners accounted for 80 percent of both exports and imports (see graph 3). See footnote*.

Graph 1: Total imports, exports and trade balance

(Bln US$ by year)

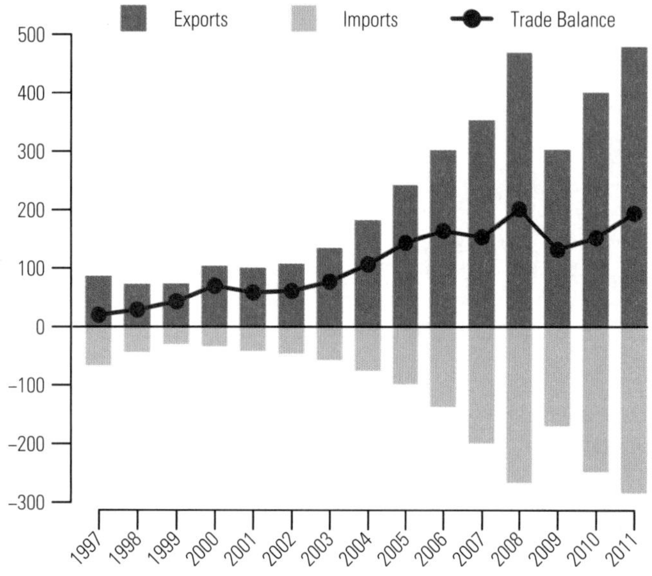

Table 1: Exports by SITC sections

(Value in million US$, growth and shares in percentage)

SITC	2011	Avg. Growth rates (%) 2007-2011	Avg. Growth rates (%) 2010-2011	2011 share
Total	478009.2	7.9	19.5	100.0
0+1	10084.1	7.2	38.1	2.1
2+4	18016.9	4.8	35.7	3.8
3	282391.9	6.9	9.6	59.1
5	21792.2	10.4	32.5	4.6
6	50593.3	-1.7	10.4	10.6
7	11766.3	-2.9	-0.4	2.5
8	2271.4	-2.9	-11.3	0.5
9	81092.9	29.9	79.2	17.0

Table 2: Imports by SITC sections

(Value in million US$, growth and shares in percentage)

SITC	2011	Avg. Growth rates (%) 2007-2011	Avg. Growth rates (%) 2010-2011	2011 share
Total	284736.9	9.3	14.5	100.0
0+1	35024.9	10.0	16.1	12.3
2+4	8298.9	5.4	8.8	2.9
3	4711.0	16.8	39.4	1.7
5	35666.6	14.2	21.2	12.5
6	35451.0	8.7	28.0	12.5
7	128173.5	8.7	43.5	45.0
8	30626.0	15.1	21.1	10.8
9	6784.9	-11.6	-81.0	2.4

Exports Profile:

In 2011, mineral fuels, lubricants and related materials (SITC section 3) accounted for more than half (59.1 percent) of exported goods (see table 1). Other major commodity groups for exports included commodities and transactions not classified elsewhere (SITC section 9) and manufactured goods classified chiefly by material (SITC section 6): they accounted respectively for 17.0 and 10.6 percent of exports. Major markets for exports included the Netherlands, China and Italy (see table 4). The majority of exports to these countries were largely mineral fuels, lubricants and related materials (SITC section 3). Over the last three years, petroleum products were the main products for exports: petroleum oils and oils obtained from bituminous minerals, crude (HS code 2709), petroleum oils, other than crude (HS code 2710) and petroleum gases and other gaseous hydrocarbons (HS code 2711) (see table 3).

Table 3: Top 10 export commodities 2009 to 2011

(Value in million US$)

HS code	4-digit heading of Harmonized System 2007	Value (million US$) 2009	2010	2011	Unit value 2009	2010	2011	Unit	SITC code
	All Commodities	301796.1	400100.0	478009.2					
2709	Petroleum oils and oils obtained from bituminous minerals, crude	93569.6	129126.3	171695.8	0.4	0.6	0.8	US$/kg	333
2710	Petroleum oils, other than crude	46890.3	69550.7	91476.9	0.4	0.5	0.7	US$/kg	334
9999	Commodities not specified according to kind	30510.3	45258.5	81092.7					931
2711	Petroleum gases and other gaseous hydrocarbons	40924.5	47767.4	5528.9	*0.6*	*0.5*	0.4	US$/kg	343
2701	Coal; briquettes, ovoids and similar solid fuels manufactured from coal	7367.4	9180.6	11372.3	0.1	0.1	0.1	US$/kg	321
7207	Semi-finished products of iron or non-alloy steel	4808.0	6978.4	7723.3	0.3	0.4	0.6	US$/kg	672
7601	Unwrought aluminium	5157.2	5989.5	6811.4	1.4	1.8	2.0	US$/kg	684
7502	Unwrought nickel	3560.4	5237.5	4494.0	14.6	21.8	23.0	US$/kg	683
7208	Flat-rolled products of iron or non-alloy steel	2833.8	3225.7	3759.5	0.4	0.5	0.7	US$/kg	673
4407	Wood sawn or chipped lengthwise, sliced or peeled	2605.8	3023.2	3384.8		*170.9*		US$/m^3	248

*2011 excludes trade with Belarus and Kazakhstan

Graph 2: Trade Balance by MDG Regions in 2011

(Bln US$)

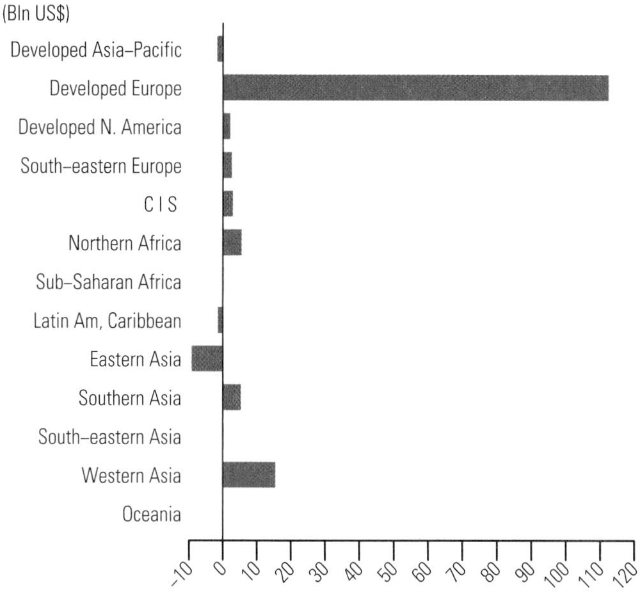

Graph 3: Partner concentration of trade in 2011

(Cumulative share by ranked partners)

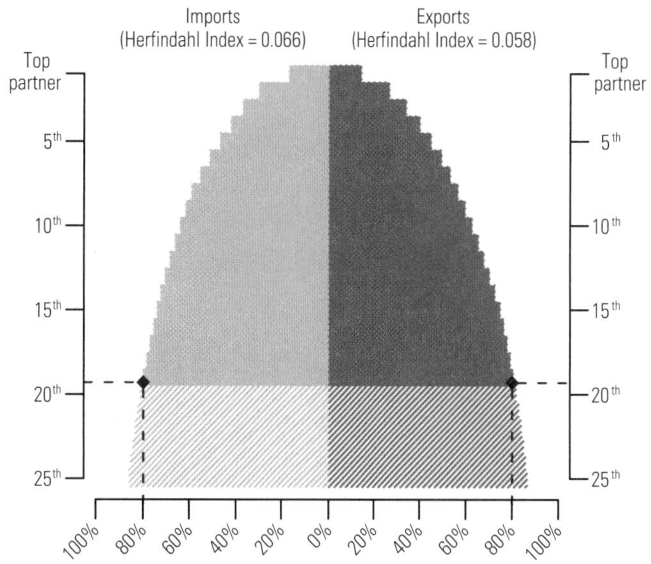

Table 4: Exports by principal countries and SITC sections in 2011

(Value in million US$, percentages of country total)

Country	Total	Shares by SITC sections (%)								
		0 + 1	2 + 4	3	5	6	7	8	9	Total
World	478009.2	2.1	3.8	59.1	4.6	10.6	2.5	0.5	17.0	100
Areas, nes	66691.7	0.1	0.0	0.2	0.0	0.1	0.1	0.0	99.4	100
Netherlands	61224.5	0.4	0.6	87.6	0.5	10.9	0.1	0.0	0.0	100
China	34707.6	2.8	18.1	65.5	7.6	1.9	2.3	0.3	1.6	100
Italy	27898.7	0.8	1.4	81.6	2.5	13.4	0.2	0.1	0.0	100
Germany	22959.6	0.5	1.9	76.1	2.4	14.9	1.9	1.0	1.4	100
Poland	21194.5	0.1	2.5	90.1	2.5	3.2	1.5	0.2	0.0	100
Ukraine	18125.0	3.8	2.3	44.5	15.6	15.5	16.0	2.0	0.3	100
USA	16028.5	0.3	1.0	58.6	7.3	20.3	1.7	0.7	10.1	100
Turkey	15110.8	5.2	7.9	53.8	7.5	25.2	0.3	0.0	0.0	100
Japan	14317.0	1.5	3.3	83.1	0.5	9.1	1.7	0.1	0.6	100

Imports Profile:

In 2011, machinery and transport equipment (SITC section 7) accounted for 45.0 percent of imported goods (see table 2). Other major commodity groups included chemicals and related products, n.e.s. (SITC section 5) and manufactured goods classified chiefly by material (SITC section 6) each making 12.5 percent of imports. From 2009 to 2011, the three main imported products were motor cars and other motor vehicles principally designed for the transport (HS code 8703), medicaments (excluding goods of heading 30.02, 30.05 or 30.06) (HS code 3004) and electrical apparatus for line telephony or line telegraphy (HS code 8517) (see table 5).

Table 5: Top 10 import commodities 2009 to 2011

(Value in million US$)

HS code	4-digit heading of Harmonized System 2007	Value (million US$)			Unit value				SITC code
		2009	2010	2011	2009	2010	2011	Unit	
	All Commodities	170826.6	248700.0	284736.9					
9999	Commodities not specified according to kind	13673.4	35802.0	6784.9					931
8703	Motor cars and other motor vehicles principally designed for the transport	8513.8	11391.6	18591.7	16.3	16.6		thsd US$/unit	781
3004	Medicaments (excluding goods of heading 30.02, 30.05 or 30.06)	7048.0	9217.7	10835.9	69.7	80.7	87.3	US$/kg	542
8517	Electrical apparatus for line telephony or line telegraphy	4223.6	6604.9	7737.9					764
8708	Parts and accessories of the motor vehicles of headings 87.01 to 87.05	2802.7	5496.9	8788.1	6.8	7.2	7.6	US$/kg	784
8471	Automatic data processing machines and units thereof	2855.9	4812.4	5262.6	59.2	76.6		US$/unit	752
2710	Petroleum oils, other than crude	1028.8	1965.0	3632.1	1.0	0.9	1.1	US$/kg	334
0202	Meat of bovine animals, frozen	2255.4	2076.2	2235.0	3.5	3.4	3.9	US$/kg	011
8707	Bodies (including cabs), for the motor vehicles of headings 87.01 to 87.05	891.8	2235.2	2927.6	7.8	8.1		thsd US$/unit	784
0203	Meat of swine, fresh, chilled or frozen	1914.8	1924.9	2138.3	2.9	3.0	3.2	US$/kg	012

Imports: CIF, by origin | **Exports: FOB, by last known destination** | **Trade System: General**

Overview:

Since 2007, Rwanda's exports increased on average by 22.9 percent each year and amounted to 417.3 mln US$ in 2011 (see table 1 and graph 1). During the same period, imports increased on average by 18.9 percent each year and amounted to 1.4 bln US$ (see table 2 and graph 1). In 2011, the trade balance recorded a deficit of 0.9 bln US$ compared to 0.5 bln US$ deficit in 2007 (see graph 1). Trade was in deficit with all MDG regions in 2011 (see graph 2). The largest deficit was recorded with Sub-Saharan Africa and amounted to 319.4 mln US$. Trade with Eastern Asia and Western Asia recorded deficits of 156.7 and 108.6 mln US$ respectively. Exports were more concentrated among partners than imports: in 2011, 9 major partners accounted for 80 percent of exports compared to 17 major partners for imports (see graph 3).

Graph 1: Total imports, exports and trade balance

(Bln US$ by year)

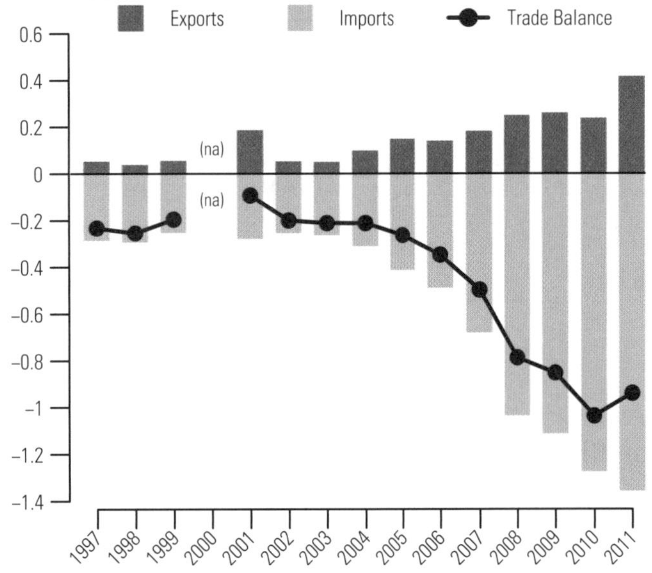

Exports Profile:

In 2011, inedible crude materials (except fuels), animal and vegetable oils, fats and waxes (SITC sections 2+4) accounted for 43.3 percent of exports. Food, live animals, beverages and tobacco (SITC sections 0+1) accounted for 37.2 percent of exported goods. These two commodities formed the major part of exports. Major markets for exported products were Switzerland, Democratic Republic of Congo and Kenya (see table 4). Exports to Kenya were largely food, live animals, beverages and tobacco (SITC sections 0+1). From 2009 to 2011, tin ores and concentrates (HS code 2609), coffee, whether or not roasted or decaffeinated (HS code 0901) and tea, whether or not flavoured (HS code 0902) were the top exported products (see table 3). They jointly accounted for 55.4 percent of exported goods in 2011.

Table 1: Exports by SITC sections

(Value in million US$, growth and shares in percentage)

SITC	2011	Avg. Growth rates (%) 2007-2011	2010-2011	2011 share
Total	417.3	22.9	75.5	100.0
0+1	155.3	22.3	46.2	37.2
2+4	180.8	19.1	72.1	43.3
3	20.2	114.0	1096.3	4.9
5	3.6	10.5	51.8	0.9
6	9.6	26.4	63.9	2.3
7	22.7	14.0	111.0	5.4
8	25.1	71.4	339.0	6.0
9	0.0	...	-95.6	0.0

Table 2: Imports by SITC sections

(Value in million US$, growth and shares in percentage)

SITC	2011	Avg. Growth rates (%) 2007-2011	2010-2011	2011 share
Total	1356.6	18.9	6.5	100.0
0+1	168.0	19.8	19.7	12.4
2+4	101.0	23.0	10.2	7.4
3	113.0	20.8	113.7	8.3
5	199.8	14.9	17.3	14.7
6	290.3	21.1	9.4	21.4
7	369.8	18.3	-17.7	27.3
8	114.1	16.6	9.7	8.4
9	0.5	...	1451.6	0.0

Table 3: Top 10 export commodities 2009 to 2011

(Value in million US$)

HS code	4-digit heading of Harmonized System 2007	Value (million US$) 2009	2010	2011	Unit value 2009	2010	2011	Unit	SITC code
	All Commodities	260.7	237.8	417.3					
2609	Tin ores and concentrates	34.2	66.9	101.9	6.6	10.3	13.9	US$/kg	287
0901	Coffee, whether or not roasted or decaffeinated	33.6	58.4	76.3	2.5	3.1	4.8	US$/kg	071
0902	Tea, whether or not flavoured	75.6	34.4	52.8	4.6	1.6	2.3	US$/kg	074
2615	Niobium, tantalum, vanadium or zirconium ores and concentrates	18.1	20.3	39.0	18.9	24.6	42.6	US$/kg	287
8703	Motor cars and other motor vehicles principally designed for the transport	11.2	2.9	15.3		*24.8*	33.4	thsd US$/unit	781
2611	Tungsten ores and concentrates	6.3	7.4	11.7	6.7	8.4	14.9	US$/kg	287
2710	Petroleum oils, other than crude	0.5	1.7	20.1	0.7	0.6	1.2	US$/kg	334
6405	Other footwear	0.0	0.0	16.8		*0.0*	2.7	thsd US$/pair	851
2610	Chromium ores and concentrates	0.2	2.4	11.9	6.9	10.5	17.7	US$/kg	287
0102	Live bovine animals	2.6	3.9	5.2	*0.8*	*0.8*	1.5	thsd US$/unit	001

Graph 2: Trade Balance by MDG Regions in 2011

(Mln US$)

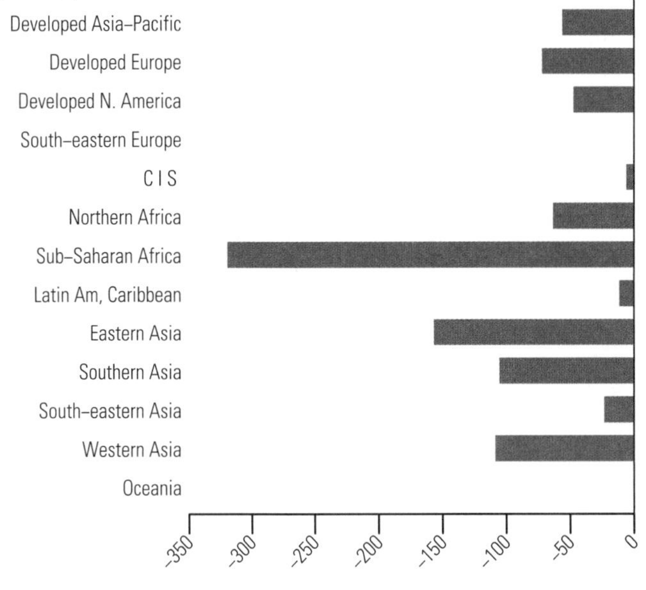

Graph 3: Partner concentration of trade in 2011

(Cumulative share by ranked partners)

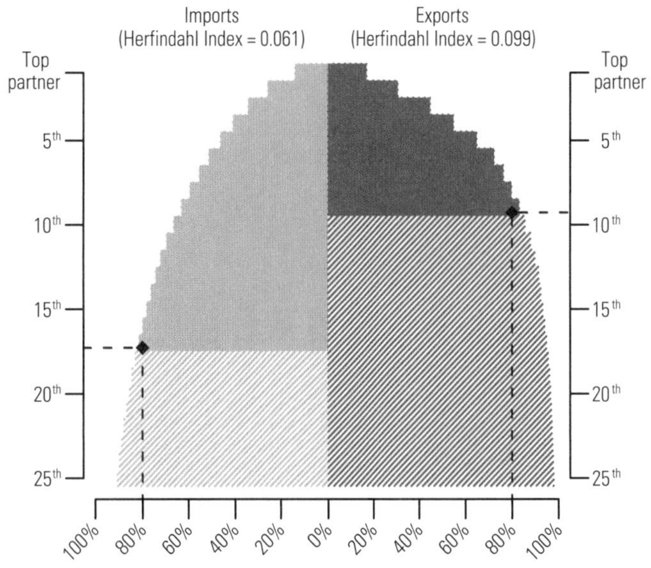

Table 4: Exports by principal countries and SITC sections in 2011

(Value in million US$, percentages of country total)

Country	Total	Shares by SITC sections (%) 0+1	2+4	3	5	6	7	8	9	Total
World	417.3	37.2	43.3	4.9	0.9	2.3	5.4	6.0	0.0	100
Switzerland	70.6	55.0	44.6	0.4	...	0.0	0.0	0.0	...	100
Dem.Rep. of the Congo	58.5	32.8	1.0	18.9	1.4	7.7	7.8	30.3	...	100
Kenya	58.0	84.9	5.4	5.8	0.0	1.0	1.3	1.6	...	100
Belgium	42.0	32.1	67.4	0.1	0.0	0.0	0.1	0.3	...	100
France	41.7	0.1	98.9	0.0	0.0	0.7	0.2	0.0	...	100
Areas, nes	30.8	35.0	59.1	0.0	0.6	2.5	1.3	1.4	...	100
United Kingdom	16.8	34.8	64.5	0.0	0.1	0.0	0.1	0.5	...	100
China	14.5	0.0	99.1	...	...	0.4	0.5	0.0	...	100
China, Hong Kong SAR	13.8	0.9	97.6	...	...	1.5	...	0.0	...	100
Sudan	10.2	0.0	0.1	...	0.1	1.1	98.6	...	...	100

Imports Profile:

In 2011, Rwanda's imports were composed of 27.3 percent of machinery and transport equipment (SITC section 7), 21.4 percent of manufactured goods classified chiefly by material (SITC section 6) and 14.7 percent of chemicals and related products, n.e.s. (SITC section 5) (see table 2). In addition to petroleum oils, other than crude (HS code 2710), other major products for imports from 2009 to 2011 were motor cars and other motor vehicles principally designed for the transport (HS code 8703) and portland cement, aluminous cement, slag cement (HS code 2523) (see table 5).

Table 5: Top 10 import commodities 2009 to 2011

(Value in million US$)

HS code	4-digit heading of Harmonized System 2007	Value (million US$) 2009	2010	2011	Unit value 2009	2010	2011	Unit	SITC code
	All Commodities	1 112.0	1 273.8	1 356.6					
2710	Petroleum oils, other than crude	87.5	47.6	105.6	0.5	0.7	1.2	US$/kg	334
8703	Motor cars and other motor vehicles principally designed for the transport	27.0	64.7	51.8		3.4	5.4	thsd US$/unit	781
2523	Portland cement, aluminous cement, slag cement	39.1	42.9	51.8	0.2	0.2	0.2	US$/kg	661
8517	Electrical apparatus for line telephony or line telegraphy	61.5	31.8	30.3					764
3004	Medicaments (excluding goods of heading 30.02, 30.05 or 30.06)	33.4	35.7	32.9	16.1	13.8	8.8	US$/kg	542
1701	Cane or beet sugar and chemically pure sucrose, in solid form	20.0	35.5	37.3	0.7	0.8	0.8	US$/kg	061
8705	Special purpose motor vehicles	5.5	78.8	2.8	*0.1*	1.9	0.1	mln US$/unit	782
3002	Human blood; animal blood prepared for therapeutic uses	36.4	15.9	33.6	250.2	77.5	100.4	US$/kg	541
8471	Automatic data processing machines and units thereof	18.5	24.7	31.7			509.8	US$/unit	752
7308	Structures (excluding prefabricated buildings of heading 94.06)	26.8	21.6	26.4	4.5	3.1	4.9	US$/kg	691

Saint Kitts and Nevis

Imports: CIF, by origin | **Exports: FOB, by last known destination** | **Trade System: Special**

Overview:

From 2004 to 2008, exports of Saint Kitts and Nevis increased on average by 6.2 percent each year and amounted to 51.2 mln US$ in 2008 (see table 1 and graph 1). Imports increased on average by 15.5 percent each year to reach 324.8 mln US$ (see table 2 and graph 1). The trade deficit increased from 142.4 mln US$ in 2004 to 273.6 mln US$ in 2008. The largest deficit was recorded with Developed North America (-161.5 mln US$) (see graph 2). Significant deficits were recorded with Latin America and the Caribbean (-70.3 mln US$) and Developed Europe (-20.5 mln US$). Trade was highly concentrated: USA, the top partner for exports accounted for 84.7 percent of exports and 4 major partners accounted for 80 percent of imports (see graph 3).

Graph 1: Total imports, exports and trade balance

(Mln US$ by year)

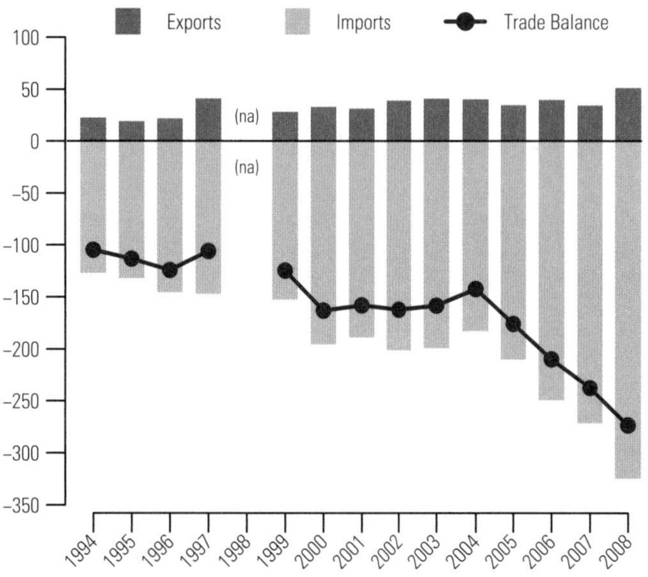

Exports Profile:

In 2008, a large share of exported goods were machinery and transport equipment (SITC section 7) (see table 1). It increased by 46.0 percent in 2008 and accounted for 81.4 percent of exports. In addition to USA, other major partners for exports were United Kingdom and Netherlands Antilles (see table 4). From 2006 to 2008, the three major commodities for exports were electrical switches, connectors, etc, for < 1kV (HS code 8536), parts for radio, tv transmission, receive equipment (HS code 8529) and electric generating sets and rotary converters (HS code 8502) (see table 3).

Table 1: Exports by SITC sections

(Value in million US$, growth and shares in percentage)

SITC	2008	Avg. Growth rates (%) 2004-2008	Avg. Growth rates (%) 2007-2008	2008 share
Total	51.2	6.2	50.1	100.0
0+1	4.7	-19.5	37.8	9.1
2+4	0.6	-4.7	4658.9	1.2
3	0.0	24.2	-84.9	0.0
5	0.5	61.2	362.4	1.0
6	0.5	8.8	-27.3	1.1
7	41.6	11.8	46.0	81.4
8	3.2	26.1	146.2	6.3

Table 2: Imports by SITC sections

(Value in million US$, growth and shares in percentage)

SITC	2008	Avg. Growth rates (%) 2004-2008	Avg. Growth rates (%) 2007-2008	2008 share
Total	324.8	15.5	19.6	100.0
0+1	56.8	13.1	13.0	17.5
2+4	7.7	12.7	22.8	2.4
3	26.2	9.7	40.5	8.1
5	21.5	14.4	13.1	6.6
6	58.8	15.6	19.4	18.1
7	77.6	10.5	-8.3	23.9
8	76.1	29.0	74.8	23.4
9	0.0	34.0	1750.8	0.0

Table 3: Top 10 export commodities 2006 to 2008

(Value in million US$)

HS code	4-digit heading of Harmonized System 1996	Value (million US$) 2006	2007	2008	Unit value 2006	2007	2008	Unit	SITC code
	All Commodities	39.7	34.1	51.2					
8536	Electrical switches, connectors, etc, for < 1kV	17.4	12.1	20.9	18.3	15.6	27.2	US$/kg	772
8529	Parts for radio, tv transmission, receive equipment	10.0	11.5	12.8	39.6	57.2	55.7	US$/kg	764
8502	Electric generating sets and rotary converters	3.9	0.0	1.4	653.5	7.5		thsd US$/unit	716
2203	Beer made from malt	1.1	1.5	1.6	0.5	1.4	*0.5*	US$/litre	112
8504	Electric transformers,static converters and rectifiers	0.4	1.2	1.7					771
4907	Documents of title (bonds etc), unused stamps etc	0.2	0.4	1.8	74.6	72.2	175.8	US$/kg	892
2202	Waters, non-alcoholic sweetened or flavoured beverages	0.8	0.7	0.9	0.7	1.4	*0.7*	US$/litre	111
8429	Self-propelled earth moving, road making, etc machines	0.6	1.7	0.1	*49.0*	*39.0*	*43.6*	thsd US$/unit	723
8707	Bodies (including cabs), for motor vehicles	...	...	1.8					784
2208	Liqueur, spirits and undenatured ethyl alcohol <80%	0.1	0.3	0.7	1.6	11.2	*6.5*	US$/litre	112

Graph 2: Trade Balance by MDG Regions in 2008

(Mln US$)

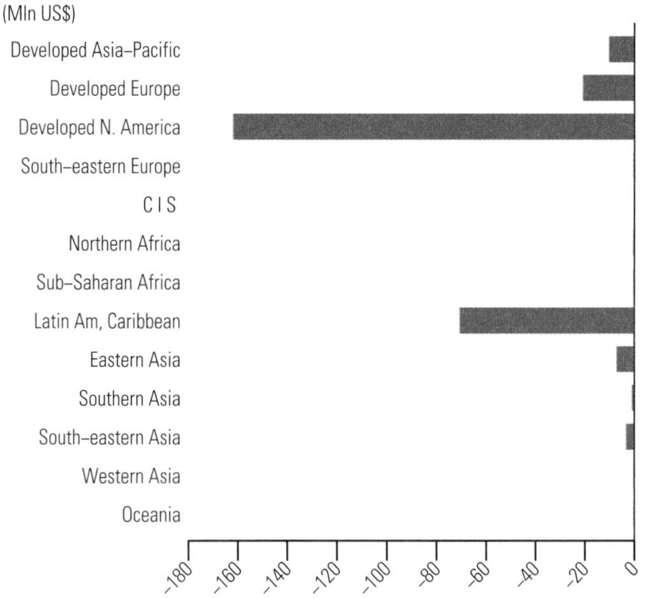

Graph 3: Partner concentration of trade in 2008

(Cumulative share by ranked partners)

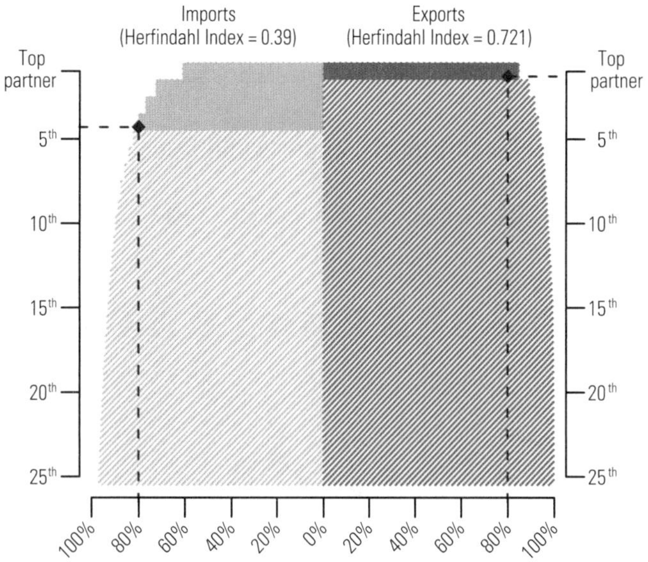

Table 4: Exports by principal countries and SITC sections in 2008

(Value in million US$, percentages of country total)

Country	Total	Shares by SITC sections (%)								
		0+1	2+4	3	5	6	7	8	9	Total
World	51.2	9.1	1.2	0.0	1.0	1.1	81.4	6.3	...	100
USA	43.3	2.3	0.0	...	1.0	0.9	94.4	1.3	...	100
United Kingdom	2.3	11.3	0.0	...	...	1.4	9.8	77.5	...	100
Neth. Antilles	1.2	40.2	49.6	0.0	0.0	0.3	8.0	1.8	...	100
Antigua and Barbuda	0.8	69.5	0.1	...	...	0.3	0.9	29.2	...	100
Grenada	0.6	99.7	0.0	...	...	...	0.3	...	...	100
Saint Lucia	0.5	78.2	0.0	...	...	5.2	1.4	15.2	...	100
Barbados	0.4	52.6	0.0	0.0	...	0.0	...	47.4	...	100
France	0.3	98.9	0.0	...	...	0.5	0.2	0.4	...	100
Br. Virgin Isds	0.2	36.5	0.5	...	0.1	1.7	59.4	1.9	...	100
Saint Vincent and the Grenadines	0.2	84.4	0.1	...	...	4.0	0.7	10.9	...	100

Imports Profile:

In 2008, machinery and transport equipment (SITC section 7), miscellaneous manufactured articles (SITC section 8) and manufactured goods classified chiefly by material (SITC section 6) accounted respectively for 23.9, 23.4 and 18.1 percent of imports. From 2006 to 2008, major products for imports included oils petroleum, bituminous, distillates, except crude (HS code 2710), jewellery and parts, containing precious metal (HS code 7113) and motor vehicles for transport of persons (except buses) (HS code 8703) (see table 5).

Table 5: Top 10 import commodities 2006 to 2008

(Value in million US$)

HS code	4-digit heading of Harmonized System 1996	Value (million US$)			Unit value				SITC code
		2006	2007	2008	2006	2007	2008	Unit	
	All Commodities	249.5	271.7	324.8					
2710	Oils petroleum, bituminous, distillates, except crude	16.5	16.3	22.4	0.5	0.7	0.8	US$/kg	334
7113	Jewellery and parts, containing precious metal	4.3	7.8	27.5	2.9	0.7	10.9	thsd US$/kg	897
8703	Motor vehicles for transport of persons (except buses)	10.2	11.4	13.1	2.3	*4.0*	*16.1*	thsd US$/unit	781
9403	Other furniture and parts thereof	5.7	5.2	6.6					821
2523	Cement (portland, aluminous, slag or hydraulic)	4.4	4.9	6.1	0.1	0.1	0.1	US$/kg	661
2106	Food preparations, nes	3.2	5.7	5.3	3.2	3.6	3.4	US$/kg	098
0207	Meat, edible offal of domestic poultry	3.9	4.4	5.4	1.4	1.4	1.6	US$/kg	012
7326	Articles of iron or steel nes	3.9	3.4	6.3	14.1	11.4	21.3	US$/kg	699
8544	Insulated wire and cable, optical fibre cable	5.4	3.4	4.6	9.2	6.8	9.1	US$/kg	773
7214	Iron/steel bar, only forged hot-rolled drawn, extruded	2.4	4.3	5.1	0.6	0.7	0.7	US$/kg	676

Saint Lucia

Imports: CIF, by origin | **Exports: FOB, by last known destination** | **Trade System: General**

Overview:

Since 2004, exports of Saint Lucia increased on average by 19.7 percent each year and amounted to 164.0 mln US$ in 2008 (see table 1 and graph 1). This increase occurred largely in 2008 as exports increased by 212.7 percent. During the same period, imports increased on average by 11.7 percent each year to 655.7 mln US$ in 2008 (see table 2 and graph 1). The trade balance recorded a deficit of 491.7 mln US$ compared to 341.8 mln US$ in 2004 (see graph 2). Large deficits were recorded with Developed North America (-234.5 mln US$) and Latin America and the Caribbean (-167.4 mln US$). Trade was concentrated among a few partners: in 2008, 4 (respectively 6) major partners accounted for 80 percent of exports (respectively imports) (see graph 3).

Graph 1: Total imports, exports and trade balance

(Mln US$ by year)

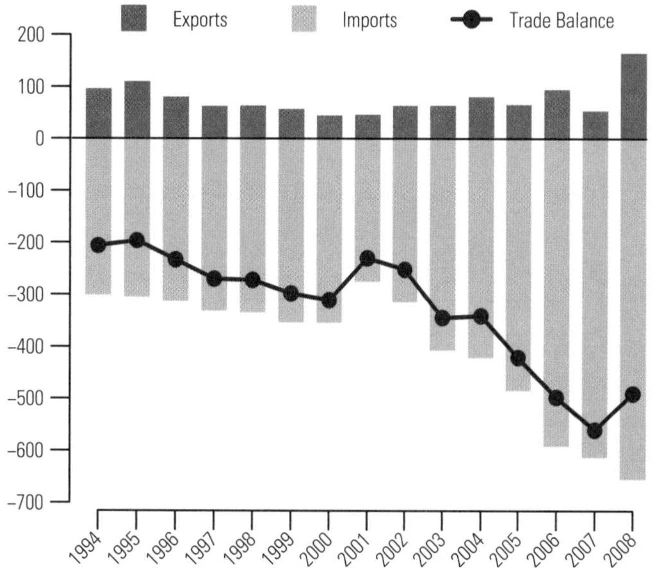

Table 1: Exports by SITC sections

(Value in million US$, growth and shares in percentage)

SITC	2008	Avg. Growth rates (%) 2004-2008	2007-2008	2008 share
Total	164.0	19.7	212.7	100.0
0+1	47.0	9.0	36.6	28.7
2+4	5.2	37.2	184.1	3.1
3	31.2	14.0	602061.2	19.0
5	7.7	40.3	326.5	4.7
6	11.4	17.7	117.9	6.9
7	27.3	20.9	269.9	16.6
8	32.8	60.1	1867.1	20.0
9	1.6	15.5	711.3	0.9

Exports Profile:

In 2008, exports of Saint Lucia were composed of 28.7 percent of food, live animals, beverages and tobacco (SITC sections 0+1), 20.0 percent of miscellaneous manufactured articles (SITC section 8), 19.0 percent of mineral fuels, lubricants and related materials (SITC section 3) and 16.6 percent of machinery and transport equipment (SITC section 7) (see table 1). Major partners for exports included USA, Trinidad and Tobago and United Kingdom (see table 4). From 2006 to 2008, top exported products included bananas, including plantains, fresh or dried (HS code 0803), oils petroleum, bituminous, distillates, except crude (HS code 2710) and beer made from malt (HS code 2203) (see table 3).

Table 2: Imports by SITC sections

(Value in million US$, growth and shares in percentage)

SITC	2008	Avg. Growth rates (%) 2004-2008	2007-2008	2008 share
Total	655.7	11.7	6.8	100.0
0+1	136.3	8.5	10.4	20.8
2+4	13.6	5.2	-3.0	2.1
3	169.9	32.7	30.3	25.9
5	40.7	5.2	11.5	6.2
6	88.3	6.7	14.8	13.5
7	127.1	10.6	-16.4	19.4
8	78.4	3.5	-2.3	11.9
9	1.5	-11.2	433.4	0.2

Table 3: Top 10 export commodities 2006 to 2008

(Value in million US$)

HS code	4-digit heading of Harmonized System 1996	Value (million US$) 2006	2007	2008	Unit value 2006	2007	2008	Unit	SITC code
	All Commodities	93.7	52.5	164.0					
0803	Bananas, including plantains, fresh or dried	17.8	13.3	21.8	0.5	0.5	0.5	US$/kg	057
2710	Oils petroleum, bituminous, distillates, except crude	20.3	0.0	31.2	0.7	1.6	1.1	US$/kg	334
2203	Beer made from malt	13.1	15.7	13.4	2.7	1.1	*1.1*	US$/litre	112
7113	Jewellery and parts, containing precious metal	5.5	0.0	10.6	14.9	3.1	4.0	thsd US$/kg	897
4819	Paper, board containers, packing items, box files, etc.	4.7	4.2	5.4	0.9	1.2	1.3	US$/kg	642
8525	Radio and TV transmitters, television cameras	1.8	1.7	3.7					764
8533	Electrical resistors and rheostats except for heating	2.9	2.4	0.9	194.8	265.3	92.9	US$/kg	772
9101	Watches with case of, or clad with, precious metal	2.1	0.0	4.0	1.6	1.2		thsd US$/unit	885
2202	Waters, non-alcoholic sweetened or flavoured beverages	1.2	1.7	2.3	0.6	2.7	4.1	US$/litre	111
2517	Pebbles, gravels, aggregates and macadam	0.5	1.5	2.6					273

Graph 2: Trade Balance by MDG Regions in 2008

(Mln US$)

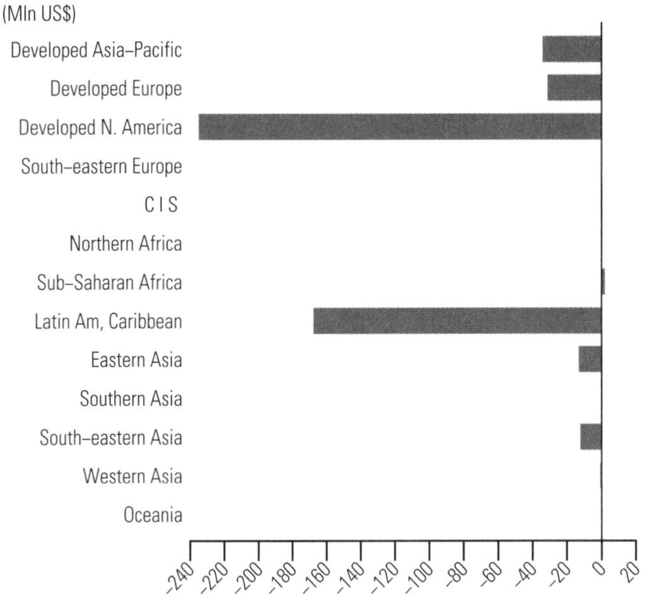

Graph 3: Partner concentration of trade in 2008

(Cumulative share by ranked partners)

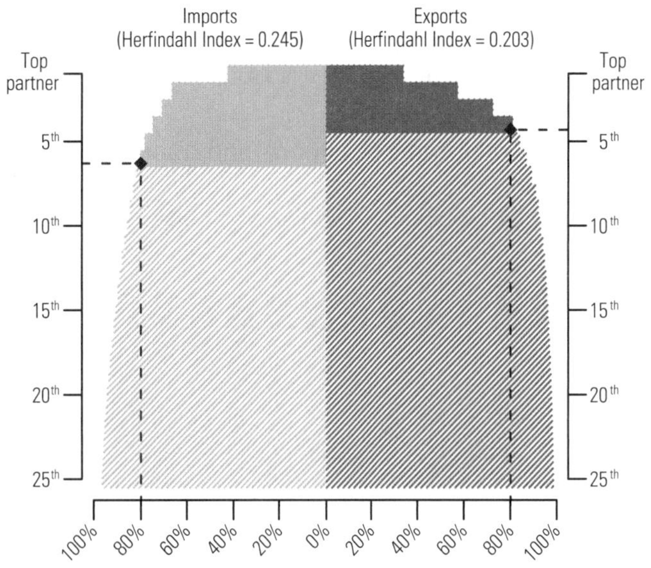

Table 4: Exports by principal countries and SITC sections in 2008

(Value in million US$, percentages of country total)

Country	Total	Shares by SITC sections (%) 0+1	2+4	3	5	6	7	8	9	Total
World	164.0	28.7	3.1	19.0	4.7	6.9	16.6	20.0	0.9	100
USA	55.8	6.4	0.6	0.2	10.1	7.4	24.5	50.3	0.4	100
Trinidad and Tobago	38.1	11.2	6.2	71.2	1.3	7.4	1.6	0.9	0.2	100
United Kingdom	24.8	92.6	0.7	0.0	0.5	0.2	2.0	3.0	0.9	100
Barbados	13.9	50.8	0.0	...	0.9	6.5	35.2	6.3	0.2	100
Saint Vincent and the Grenadines	4.9	34.5	0.0	20.4	4.9	8.8	27.6	3.8	0.1	100
Dominica	4.6	27.7	0.0	4.1	5.1	32.4	25.1	4.6	1.2	100
Antigua and Barbuda	3.7	36.2	0.2	52.0	1.1	3.5	2.2	4.3	0.5	100
Grenada	3.0	39.2	1.0	0.2	5.3	8.4	33.3	11.6	1.2	100
France	1.9	45.9	19.4	...	1.1	20.3	10.1	2.0	1.1	100
Guyana	1.7	57.1	0.8	17.6	15.9	...	6.7	1.6	0.3	100

Imports Profile:

In 2008, imports of Saint Lucia were composed of 25.9 percent of mineral fuels, lubricants and related materials (SITC section 3), 20.8 percent of food, live animals, beverages and tobacco (SITC sections 0+1) and 19.4 percent of machinery and transport equipment (SITC section 7) (see table 2). From 2006 to 2008, top imported products included oils petroleum, bituminous, distillates, except crude (HS code 2710), motor vehicles for transport of persons (except buses) (HS code 8703) and motor vehicles for the transport of goods (HS code 8704) (see table 5).

Table 5: Top 10 import commodities 2006 to 2008

(Value in million US$)

HS code	4-digit heading of Harmonized System 1996	Value (million US$) 2006	2007	2008	Unit value 2006	2007	2008	Unit	SITC code
	All Commodities	592.4	613.9	655.7					
2710	Oils petroleum, bituminous, distillates, except crude	70.4	122.4	157.6	1.1	1.0	1.5	US$/kg	334
8703	Motor vehicles for transport of persons (except buses)	29.0	37.9	29.4	*12.4*	12.2	*13.0*	thsd US$/unit	781
8704	Motor vehicles for the transport of goods	15.8	20.6	17.2	14.8	15.8	16.4	thsd US$/unit	782
7113	Jewellery and parts, containing precious metal	8.7	13.1	11.3	2.2	3.2	2.6	thsd US$/kg	897
0207	Meat, edible offal of domestic poultry	9.2	11.5	12.3	1.1	1.4	1.5	US$/kg	012
2523	Cement (portland, aluminous, slag or hydraulic)	10.3	9.0	10.3	0.1	0.1	0.1	US$/kg	661
8471	Automatic data processing machines (computers)	9.1	10.3	9.6	*285.6*	275.6	263.7	US$/unit	752
2711	Petroleum gases and other gaseous hydrocarbons	4.9	7.9	11.9	0.9	0.9	1.2	US$/kg	343
4407	Wood sawn, chipped lengthwise, sliced or peeled	8.7	8.0	7.5					248
2202	Waters, non-alcoholic sweetened or flavoured beverages	7.1	8.6	7.9	1.6	1.0	2.3	US$/litre	111

Saint Vincent and the Grenadines

Imports: CIF, by origin | **Exports: FOB, by last known destination** | **Trade System: Special**

Overview:

From 2006 to 2010, the exports of Saint Vincent and the Grenadines increased on average by 2.2 percent each year despite a drop of 15.4 percent in 2010 and amounted to 41.5 mln US$ (see table 1 and graph1). During the same period, imports increased on average by 8.8 percent each year to 379.5 mln US$ (see table 2 and graph 1). The trade deficit increased from 233.2 mln US$ in 2006 to 338.0 mln US$ in 2010 (see graph 1). By MDG regions, the largest deficit was recorded with Developed North America to 142.5 mln US$ in 2010 (see graph 2). Other major deficits were recorded with Latin America and the Caribbean (-125.2 mln US$) and Developed Europe (-31.8 mln US$). By partners, both imports and exports were concentrated: 8 (respectively 7) major partners accounted for 80 percent of exports (respectively imports) in 2010 (see graph 3).

Graph 1: Total imports, exports and trade balance

(Mln US$ by year)

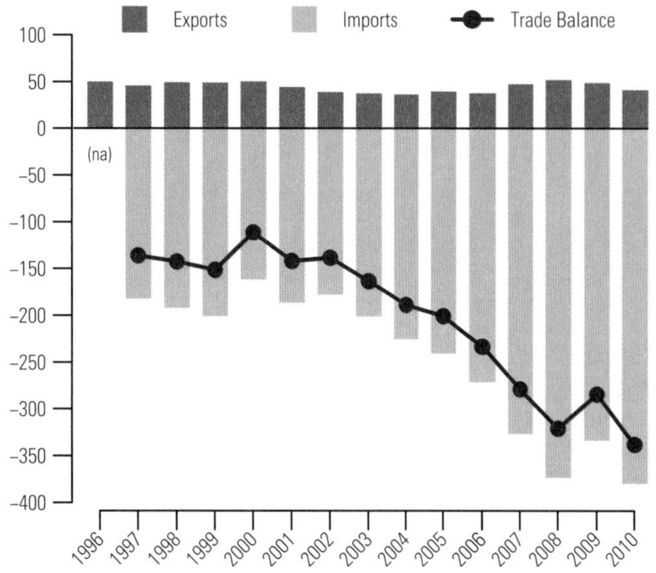

Exports Profile:

In 2010, food, live animals, beverages and tobacco (SITC sections 0+1) accounted for over two-thirds (69.9 percent) of export goods and amounted to 29.0 mln US$ (see table 1). Other major commodity groups included manufactured goods classified chiefly by material (SITC section 6) and machinery and transport equipment (SITC section 7) which accounted respectively for 12.7 and 10.3 percent of exports. Saint Lucia, Trinidad and Tobago and Barbados were the three main markets for exports in 2010 (see table 4). From 2008 to 2010, the top three products for exports were wheat or meslin flour (HS code 1101), bananas, including plantains, fresh or dried (HS code 0803) and rice (HS code 1006) (see table 3).

Table 1: Exports by SITC sections

(Value in million US$, growth and shares in percentage)

SITC	2010	Avg. Growth rates (%) 2006-2010	2009-2010	2010 share
Total	41.5	2.2	-15.4	100.0
0+1	29.0	-0.3	-10.0	69.9
2+4	0.9	46.3	24.1	2.2
3	0.2	72.5	-39.0	0.5
5	0.2	1.3	-19.8	0.5
6	5.3	11.8	0.0	12.7
7	4.3	5.1	-49.0	10.3
8	1.6	2.5	-11.6	3.9

Table 2: Imports by SITC sections

(Value in million US$, growth and shares in percentage)

SITC	2010	Avg. Growth rates (%) 2006-2010	2009-2010	2010 share
Total	379.5	8.8	13.8	100.0
0+1	82.1	11.2	7.6	21.6
2+4	10.6	6.3	7.9	2.8
3	83.1	20.4	37.3	21.9
5	27.1	5.9	-0.7	7.2
6	57.6	0.8	-5.3	15.2
7	76.6	5.2	24.8	20.2
8	42.4	9.0	13.7	11.2
9	0.0	-71.7	559.1	0.0

Table 3: Top 10 export commodities 2008 to 2010

(Value in million US$)

HS code	4-digit heading of Harmonized System 1996	Value (million US$) 2008	2009	2010	Unit value 2008	2009	2010	Unit	SITC code
	All Commodities	52.2	49.1	41.5					
1101	Wheat or meslin flour	7.9	8.5	8.6	0.8	0.8	0.7	US$/kg	046
0803	Bananas, including plantains, fresh or dried	8.3	7.8	5.9	0.4	0.4	0.5	US$/kg	057
1006	Rice	6.3	4.3	3.8	1.1	1.2	1.1	US$/kg	042
0714	Manioc, arrowroot, salep etc, fresh, dried, sago pith	3.7	5.2	3.9	0.6	0.6	0.6	US$/kg	054
2202	Waters, non-alcoholic sweetened or flavoured beverages	1.9	2.7	2.2	*1.2*	*1.1*	*1.3*	US$/litre	111
8531	Electric sound or visual signal equipment nes	5.6	0.0	...					778
8525	Radio and TV transmitters, television cameras	0.1	4.9	0.4					764
7210	Flat-rolled iron/steel, >600mm, clad, plated or coated	1.6	1.9	1.8	1.9	2.1	2.1	US$/kg	674
2309	Animal feed preparations, nes	1.6	1.5	1.8	0.4	0.4	0.4	US$/kg	081
4819	Paper, board containers, packing items, box files, etc	1.4	1.6	1.8	1.5	1.8	1.7	US$/kg	642

Graph 2: Trade Balance by MDG Regions in 2010

(Mln US$)

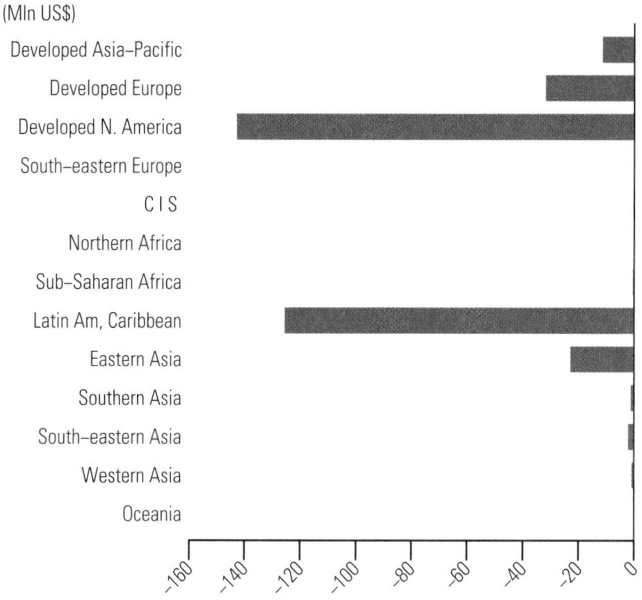

Graph 3: Partner concentration of trade in 2010

(Cumulative share by ranked partners)

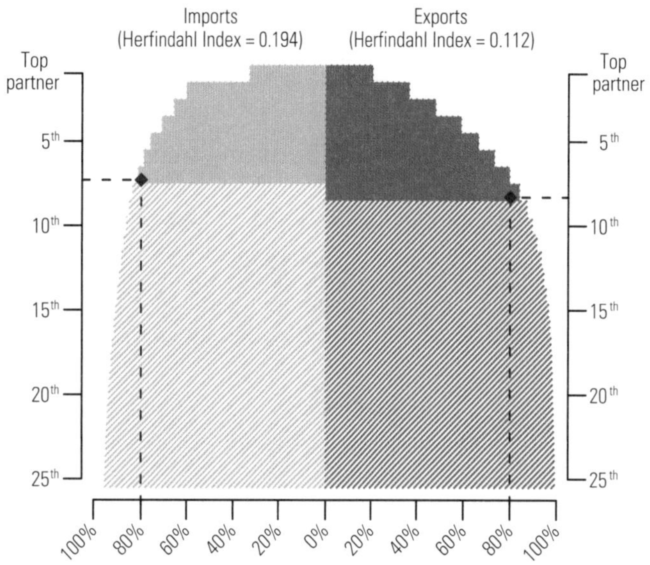

Table 4: Exports by principal countries and SITC sections in 2010

(Value in million US$, percentages of country total)

Country	Total	Shares by SITC sections (%)								
		0 + 1	2 + 4	3	5	6	7	8	9	Total
World	41.5	69.9	2.2	0.5	0.5	12.7	10.3	3.9	...	100
Saint Lucia	8.6	90.2	0.0	0.1	0.3	0.9	6.4	2.0	...	100
Trinidad and Tobago	6.7	88.7	0.8	1.0	0.7	4.0	1.7	3.1	...	100
Barbados	4.7	75.1	0.1	3.0	0.3	10.5	8.6	2.3	...	100
United Kingdom	4.5	71.6	0.0	...	...	0.1	27.1	1.3	...	100
Antigua and Barbuda	3.1	82.3	3.5	0.0	0.4	11.1	1.6	1.1	...	100
Saint Kitts and Nevis	2.8	61.9	0.2	0.0	0.3	31.2	0.8	5.7	...	100
Dominica	2.7	49.7	0.0	...	1.4	35.2	11.3	2.5	...	100
USA	1.7	30.9	14.2	0.0	0.8	3.8	44.7	5.7	...	100
Grenada	1.4	56.5	0.0	...	2.4	26.3	10.3	4.5	...	100
Guyana	0.9	0.2	31.2	...	0.1	39.6	27.1	1.9	...	100

Imports Profile:

In 2010, imports were composed of 21.9 percent of mineral fuels, lubricants and related materials (SITC section 3), 21.6 percent of food, live animals, beverages and tobacco (SITC sections 0+1) and 20.2 percent of machinery and transport equipment (SITC section 7) (see table 2). From 2008 to 2010, top imported products included oils petroleum, bituminous, distillates, except crude (HS code 2710), meat, edible offal of domestic poultry (HS code 0207) and wheat and meslin (HS code 1001) (see table 5).

Table 5: Top 10 import commodities 2008 to 2010

(Value in million US$)

HS code	4-digit heading of Harmonized System 1996	Value (million US$)			Unit value				SITC code
		2008	2009	2010	2008	2009	2010	Unit	
	All Commodities	373.2	333.5	379.5					
2710	Oils petroleum, bituminous, distillates, except crude	46.7	53.1	78.1	0.8	0.6	0.6	US$/kg	334
0207	Meat, edible offal of domestic poultry	9.9	9.7	10.0	1.5	1.5	1.5	US$/kg	012
1001	Wheat and meslin	10.1	8.5	8.4	*0.3*	0.4	0.4	US$/kg	041
2523	Cement (portland, aluminous, slag or hydraulic)	9.4	8.8	7.2	0.1	0.1	0.1	US$/kg	661
2711	Petroleum gases and other gaseous hydrocarbons	7.9	7.1	4.9	3.0	1.1	1.2	US$/kg	343
8703	Motor vehicles for transport of persons (except buses)	6.4	5.9	7.5		*15.8*	*14.0*	thsd US$/unit	781
9403	Other furniture and parts thereof	6.2	4.9	8.0					821
1006	Rice	9.0	5.4	4.3	2.7	0.8	0.8	US$/kg	042
3004	Medicaments, therapeutic, prophylactic use, in dosage	6.2	4.2	5.0	24.4	17.8	25.3	US$/kg	542
8429	Self-propelled earth moving, road making, etc machines	11.1	1.9	2.3	*62.1*	*80.0*	*63.2*	thsd US$/unit	723

Imports: CIF, by origin | **Exports: FOB, by last known destination** | **Trade System: General**

Overview:

From 2007 to 2011, Samoa's exports decreased on average by 13.6 percent each year despite an increase of 29.4 percent in 2010 and amounted to 54.4 mln US$ (see table 1 and graph 1). During the same period, imports increased on average by 6.8 percent each year to 345.9 mln US$ (see table 2 and graph 1). This resulted in a trade deficit of 291.5 mln US$ in 2011 (see graph 1). This deficit came largely from trade with Developed Asia-Pacific (-119.6 mln US$) (see graph 2). Other significant deficits were recorded with South-eastern Asia (-84.7 mln US$), Developed North America (-37.4 mln US$), and Eastern Asia (-30.0 mln US$) (see graph 2). Trade, especially exports, was highly concentrated among a few partners: Australia, the top partner for exports accounted for 61.0 percent of exported goods in 2011 (see table 4) and 6 major partners accounted for 80 percent of imports (see graph 3).

Graph 1: Total imports, exports and trade balance

(Mln US$ by year)

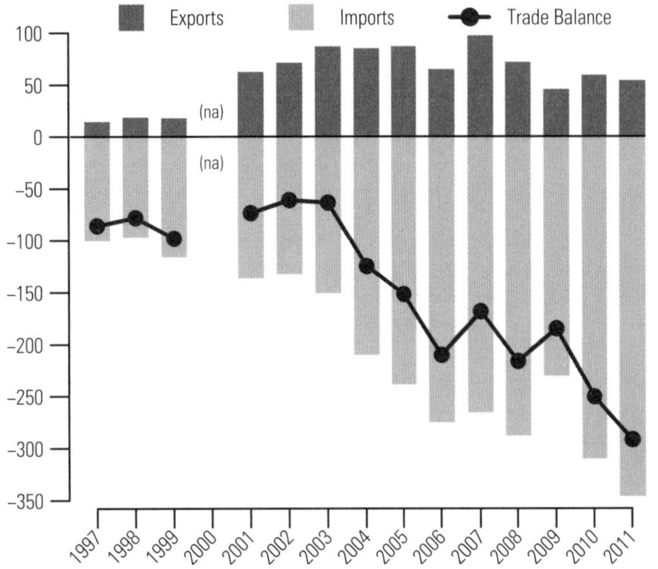

Table 1: Exports by SITC sections

(Value in million US$, growth and shares in percentage)

SITC	2011	Avg. Growth rates (%) 2007-2011	2010-2011	2011 share
Total	54.4	-13.6	-8.6	100.0
0+1	13.5	-0.4	32.8	24.9
2+4	4.2	26.3	51.4	7.7
3	0.0	-71.5	0.5	0.0
5	0.2	9.4	310.6	0.3
6	0.4	-38.3	35.1	0.8
7	33.9	-18.4	-25.4	62.4
8	1.0	10.7	39.4	1.9
9	1.1	-4.8	13378.7	2.1

Table 2: Imports by SITC sections

(Value in million US$, growth and shares in percentage)

SITC	2011	Avg. Growth rates (%) 2007-2011	2010-2011	2011 share
Total	345.9	6.8	11.6	100.0
0+1	87.8	7.9	18.3	25.4
2+4	12.4	11.8	18.6	3.6
3	73.5	10.4	35.0	21.2
5	18.7	9.0	6.6	5.4
6	52.1	12.2	3.5	15.1
7	74.6	30.0	0.3	21.6
8	24.9	9.9	-3.8	7.2
9	1.8	-57.4	-29.9	0.5

Exports Profile:

Machinery and transport equipment (SITC section 7) accounted for 62.4 percent of Samoa's exports in 2011 (see table 1). Other major commodity groups included food, live animals, beverages and tobacco (SITC sections 0+1): they represented 24.9 percent of exports. In addition to Australia, other major partners for exported goods included New Zealand and American Samoa (see table 4). Top exported products over the last 3 years were insulated wire and cable, optical fibre cable (HS code 8544), fish, frozen, whole (HS code 0303) and coconut, palm kernel, babassu oil, fractions, refined (HS code 1513) (see table 3).

Table 3: Top 10 export commodities 2009 to 2011

(Value in million US$)

HS code	4-digit heading of Harmonized System 2007	Value (million US$) 2009	2010	2011	Unit value 2009	2010	2011	Unit	SITC code
	All Commodities	46.0	59.5	54.4					
8544	Insulated (including enamelled or anodised) wire, cable	31.3	45.0	32.2					773
0303	Fish, frozen, excluding fish fillets and other fish meat of heading 03.04	6.2	4.8	6.3	2.3	*3.8*	6.4	US$/kg	034
1513	Coconut (copra), palm kernel or babassu oil	1.1	2.3	3.7	*1.5*	*1.0*	*1.1*	US$/kg	422
9999	Commodities not specified according to kind	3.8	0.0	1.1					931
2203	Beer made from malt	0.7	0.8	1.9	1.9	2.0	1.2	US$/litre	112
2009	Fruit juices (including grape must) and vegetable juices	0.4	0.9	1.4	*3.8*	*1.7*	*2.3*	US$/kg	059
0304	Fish fillets and other fish meat (whether or not minced)	0.1	1.2	1.3	*2.3*	*2.2*	3.6	US$/kg	034
0801	Coconuts, Brazil nuts and cashew nuts, fresh or dried	0.4	0.4	0.6	0.3	0.2	0.5	US$/kg	057
0714	Manioc, arrowroot, sweet potatoes and similar roots	0.4	0.5	0.4	4.5	6.1	4.9	US$/kg	054
8523	Prepared unrecorded media for sound recording	0.1	0.5	0.3	2.4	5.8	5.9	US$/unit	898

Graph 2: Trade Balance by MDG Regions in 2011

(Mln US$)

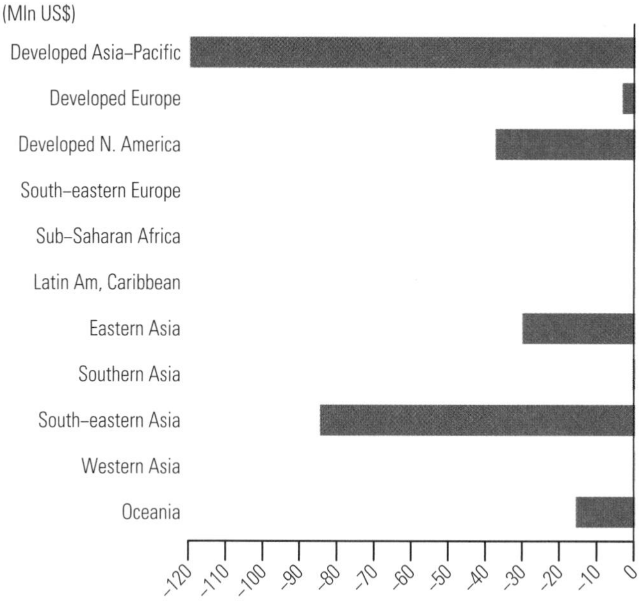

Graph 3: Partner concentration of trade in 2011

(Cumulative share by ranked partners)

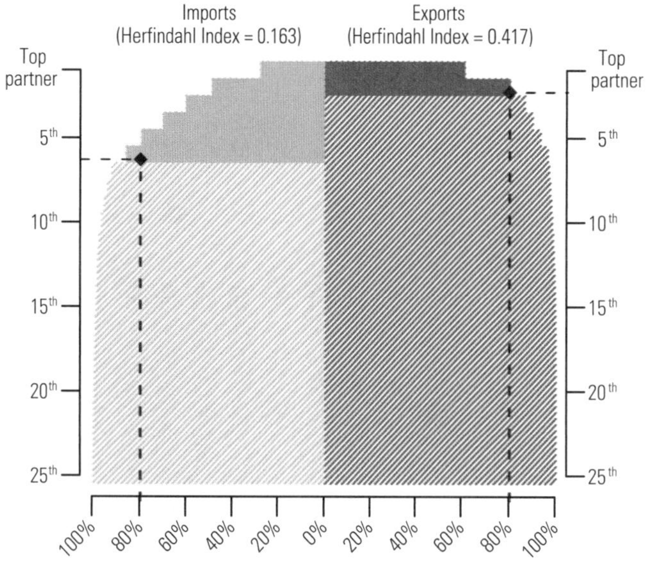

Table 4: Exports by principal countries and SITC sections in 2011

(Value in million US$, percentages of country total)

Country	Total	Shares by SITC sections (%) 0+1	2+4	3	5	6	7	8	9	Total
World	54.4	24.9	7.7	0.0	0.3	0.8	62.4	1.9	2.1	100
Australia	33.2	1.1	2.2	0.0	0.0	0.0	96.6	0.0	0.0	100
New Zealand	10.3	69.7	8.9	0.0	...	3.3	14.7	3.4	0.0	100
American Samoa	3.5	86.0	1.5	0.0	0.6	2.1	1.2	8.4	0.1	100
Tonga	1.9	22.6	0.9	...	0.0	0.8	1.8	14.6	59.2	100
Singapore	1.8	0.0	100.0	...	...	...	...	...	...	100
USA	1.7	99.1	0.8	...	...	0.0	0.0	0.0	...	100
Tokelau	0.3	62.0	0.0	...	5.0	1.7	5.1	26.2	...	100
Japan	0.3	99.8	0.0	...	...	...	0.1	0.0	...	100
Fiji	0.3	10.2	0.2	0.2	46.0	3.2	40.2	0.0	...	100
Malaysia	0.2	0.0	100.0	...	...	...	...	...	...	100

Imports Profile:

In 2011, the top commodity groups for imports were food, live animals, beverages and tobacco (SITC sections 0+1) and machinery and transport equipment (SITC section 7) with 25.4 and 21.6 percent of imported goods, respectively (see table 2). Other major commodities were mineral fuels, lubricants and related materials (SITC section 3) with 21.2 percent and manufactured goods classified chiefly by material (SITC section 6) with 15.1 percent. Over the last three years, top imported products included oils petroleum, bituminous, distillates, except crude (HS code 2710), meat, edible offal of domestic poultry (HS code 0207) and electric motors and generators (excluding generating sets) (HS code 8501) (see table 5).

Table 5: Top 10 import commodities 2009 to 2011

(Value in million US$)

HS code	4-digit heading of Harmonized System 2007	Value (million US$) 2009	2010	2011	Unit value 2009	2010	2011	Unit	SITC code
	All Commodities	230.5	309.8	345.9					
2710	Petroleum oils, other than crude	41.7	52.8	71.4	*1.0*	*0.6*	*0.8*	US$/kg	334
9999	Commodities not specified according to kind	38.3	2.3	1.8					931
0207	Meat and edible offal, of the poultry of heading 01.05	10.9	13.6	17.5	1.1	0.8	1.3	US$/kg	012
8501	Electric motors and generators (excluding generating sets)	0.0	0.4	21.1	0.4	1.9	131.9	thsd US$/unit	716
1701	Cane or beet sugar and chemically pure sucrose, in solid form	5.4	5.9	7.9	*0.7*	*0.6*	*0.7*	US$/kg	061
8703	Motor cars and other motor vehicles principally designed for the transport	1.9	8.2	5.9	7.2	4.4	11.9	thsd US$/unit	781
0204	Meat of sheep or goats, fresh, chilled or frozen	5.8	4.9	3.7	2.5	3.2	3.8	US$/kg	012
1101	Wheat or meslin flour	4.6	4.2	5.5	*0.0*	*0.0*	*0.0*	US$/kg	046
8901	Cruise ships, excursion boats, ferry-boats, cargo ships, barges	...	14.2	...		14.2		mln US$/unit	793
1604	Prepared or preserved fish; caviar	3.8	4.5	5.4	1.5	1.3	1.5	US$/kg	037

Sao Tome and Principe

Imports: CIF, by origin | **Exports: FOB, by last known destination** | **Trade System: Special**

Overview:

After three years of continuous growth marked by a peak of 10.6 mln US$ in 2008, the value of the exports of Sao Tome and Principe significantly dropped by 23.7 percent in 2009 and dropped again by 21.4 percent to 6.4 mln US$ in 2010 (see table 1 and graph 1). During the same period, imports showed an average annual growth of 12.1 percent (see table 2 and graph 1). In 2010, it increased by 8.6 percent to 112.2 mln US$ (see table 2 and graph 1), resulting in a trade deficit of 105.8 mln US$ (see graph 1). Trade deficit with Developed Europe amounted to 69.4 mln US$ (see graph 2). Other major trade deficits were recorded with Sub-Saharan Africa (-25.4 mln US$) and Eastern Asia (-4.2 mln US$). Both exports and imports were highly concentrated among a few partners: 4 (respectively 3) major partners accounted for more than 80 percent of exports (respectively imports) in 2010 (see graph 3).

Graph 1: Total imports, exports and trade balance

(Mln US$ by year)

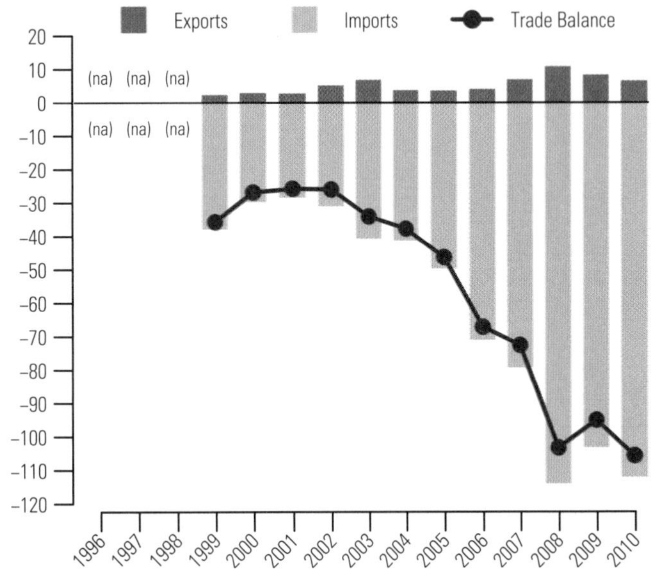

Table 1: Exports by SITC sections

(Value in million US$, growth and shares in percentage)

SITC	2010	Avg. Growth rates (%) 2006-2010	2009-2010	2010 share
Total	6.4	13.3	-21.4	100.0
0+1	5.8	12.3	0.7	90.8
2+4	0.3	69.0	348.7	4.5
6	0.0	-8.3	-40.5	0.5
7	0.2	9.8	85.6	3.3
8	0.1	136.7	35.2	0.9
9	0.0	...	-99.1	0.0

Table 2: Imports by SITC sections

(Value in million US$, growth and shares in percentage)

SITC	2010	Avg. Growth rates (%) 2006-2010	2009-2010	2010 share
Total	112.2	12.1	8.6	100.0
0+1	30.8	10.8	-3.7	27.5
2+4	4.1	16.8	-37.0	3.7
3	18.0	5.9	13.3	16.1
5	5.7	16.3	-5.9	5.1
6	13.4	4.0	1.6	11.9
7	30.5	20.7	30.8	27.2
8	9.3	16.1	53.5	8.3
9	0.3	31.1	46.6	0.2

Exports Profile:

In 2010, food, live animals, beverages and tobacco (SITC sections 0+1), inedible crude materials (except fuels), animal and vegetable oils, fats and waxes (SITC sections 2+4) and machinery and transport equipment (SITC section 7) accounted for nearly all the exports (see table 1). Exports of food, live animals, beverages and tobacco (SITC sections 0+1) represented 90.8 percent of total exports. Portugal, Belgium and the Netherlands were the three major markets for exports in 2010 (see table 4). Exports to Portugal were largely food, live animals, beverages and tobacco (SITC sections 0+1) while exports to Belgium and Netherlands were exclusively commodities specified in SITC sections 0+1. From 2008 to 2010, top exported products were cocoa beans, whole or broken, raw or roasted (HS code 1801), oils petroleum, bituminous, distillates, except crude (HS code 2710) and chocolate and other foods containing cocoa (HS code 1806).

Table 3: Top 10 export commodities 2008 to 2010

(Value in million US$)

HS code	4-digit heading of Harmonized System 1996	Value (million US$) 2008	2009	2010	Unit value 2008	2009	2010	Unit	SITC code
	All Commodities	10.6	8.1	6.4					
1801	Cocoa beans, whole or broken, raw or roasted	5.0	5.5	5.4	2.3	2.0	2.2	US$/kg	072
2710	Oils petroleum, bituminous, distillates, except crude	4.9	1.9	...	1.0	0.6		US$/kg	334
1806	Chocolate and other foods containing cocoa	0.1	0.1	0.2	21.6	20.9	20.6	US$/kg	073
8703	Motor vehicles for transport of persons (except buses)	0.1	0.0	0.1		*13.0*	*14.5*	thsd US$/unit	781
9999	Commodities not elsewhere specified	...	0.2	0.0					931
1507	Soya-bean oil, fractions, not chemically modified	0.0	...	0.2	6.8		1.5	US$/kg	421
0801	Coconuts, Brazil nuts and cashew nuts, fresh or dried	0.0	0.1	0.1	0.1	0.2	0.2	US$/kg	057
9403	Other furniture and parts thereof	0.0	0.0	0.0					821
0603	Cut flowers, dried flowers for bouquets, etc	0.0	0.0	0.0	0.9	1.1	1.2	US$/kg	292
7326	Articles of iron or steel nes	0.0	0.0	0.0	*5.2*	0.4	1.4	US$/kg	699

Graph 2: Trade Balance by MDG Regions in 2010

(Mln US$)

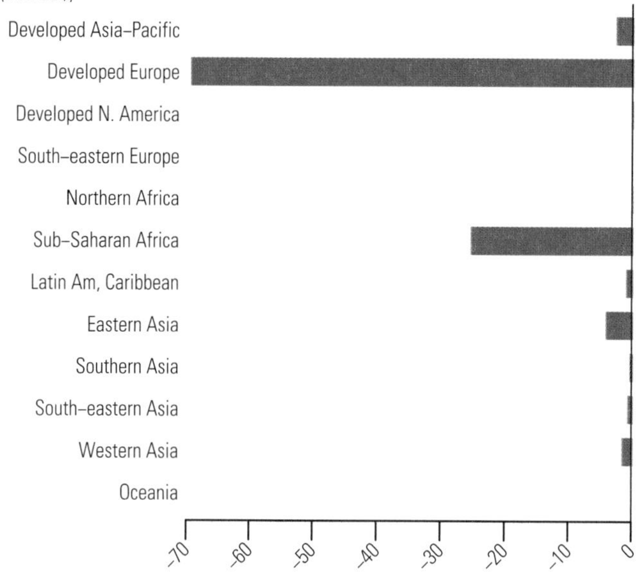

Graph 3: Partner concentration of trade in 2010

(Cumulative share by ranked partners)

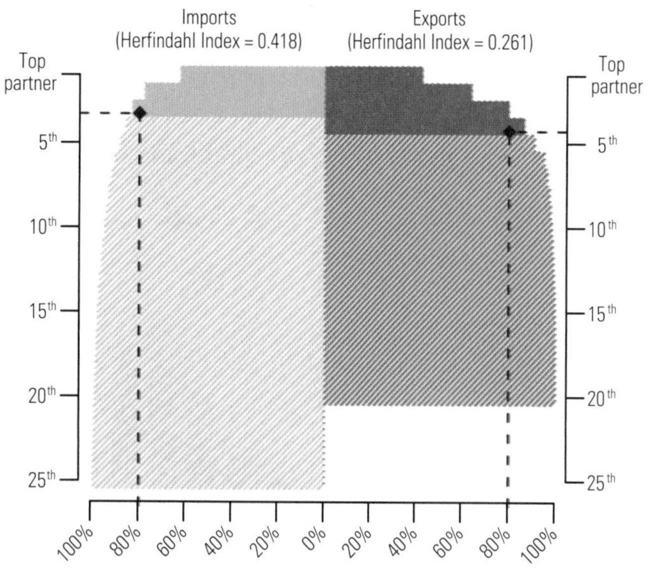

Table 4: Exports by principal countries and SITC sections in 2010

(Value in million US$, percentages of country total)

Country	Total	Shares by SITC sections (%) 0+1	2+4	3	5	6	7	8	9	Total
World	6.4	90.8	4.5	...	...	0.5	3.3	0.9	0.0	100
Portugal	2.7	91.4	1.9	...	...	0.8	4.6	1.2	...	100
Belgium	1.4	100.0	0.0	...	...	...	...	...	...	100
Netherlands	1.0	100.0	0.0	...	...	...	...	...	...	100
Areas, nes	0.4	100.0	0.0	...	...	0.0	...	...	...	100
Norway	0.3	100.0	0.0	...	...	...	...	...	...	100
Nigeria	0.3	6.1	88.9	...	...	0.5	3.7	0.2	0.5	100
Angola	0.1	69.5	4.4	...	...	3.2	21.6	0.2	1.0	100
Italy	0.1	100.0	0.0	...	...	...	...	...	...	100
USA	0.0	79.6	0.0	...	...	0.4	20.0	...	...	100
United Rep. of Tanzania	0.0	0.0	0.0	...	...	...	100.0	...	...	100

Imports Profile:

In 2010, imports of food, live animals, beverages and tobacco (SITC sections 0+1) decreased by 3.7 percent and represented 27.5 percent of total imports while imports of mineral fuels, lubricants and related materials (SITC section 3) increased by 13.3 percent to represent 16.1 percent of imports (see table 2). Machinery and transport equipment (SITC section 7) was another major commodity groups for imports: it accounted for 27.2 percent of imports in 2010. From 2008 to 2010, top imported products were oils petroleum, bituminous, distillates, except crude (HS code 2710), motor vehicles for transport of persons (except buses) (HS code 8703) and rice (HS code 1006) (see table 5).

Table 5: Top 10 import commodities 2008 to 2010

(Value in million US$)

HS code	4-digit heading of Harmonized System 1996	Value (million US$) 2008	2009	2010	Unit value 2008	2009	2010	Unit	SITC code
	All Commodities	114.0	103.3	112.2					
2710	Oils petroleum, bituminous, distillates, except crude	26.1	15.3	17.7	1.2	0.6	0.7	US$/kg	334
8703	Motor vehicles for transport of persons (except buses)	5.9	5.7	7.1		*16.4*	*15.4*	thsd US$/unit	781
1006	Rice	4.3	4.5	4.5	0.9	1.0	1.2	US$/kg	042
2204	Grape wines(including fortified), alcoholic grape must	3.9	3.5	4.7	*1.4*	*1.3*	*1.2*	US$/litre	112
2523	Cement (portland, aluminous, slag or hydraulic)	3.6	3.0	4.2	0.3	0.2	0.2	US$/kg	661
1507	Soya-bean oil, fractions, not chemically modified	3.5	4.9	2.2	1.3	1.6	1.0	US$/kg	421
1101	Wheat or meslin flour	3.5	2.9	3.5	0.7	0.5	0.5	US$/kg	046
8711	Motorcycles, bicycles etc with auxiliary motor	0.9	2.2	3.5					785
2202	Waters, non-alcoholic sweetened or flavoured beverages	1.5	2.1	2.6	*0.8*	*0.9*	*1.0*	US$/litre	111
1701	Solid cane or beet sugar and chemically pure sucrose	1.1	3.2	0.9	0.6	0.6	0.6	US$/kg	061

Saudi Arabia

Imports: CIF, by origin | **Exports: FOB, by sale** | **Trade System: General**

Overview:

After several years of continuous growth marked by a peak of 313.5 bln US$ in 2008, the value of the exports of Saudi Arabia dropped by 38.6 percent in 2009 but increased again in 2010 by 30.6 percent to amount to 251.1 bln US$, still well below its 2008 level (see table 1 and graph 1). Imports showed a less pronounced development with an increase of 11.8 percent to 106.9 bln US$ in 2010 (see table 2 and graph 1). Trade balance recorded a surplus of 144.3 bln US$ in 2010 (see graph 1). This surplus was accounted for largely by trade with Eastern Asia at 140.6 bln US$ (see graph 2). Trade recorded large deficits with Developed Asia-Pacific (-10.1 bln US$), Western Asia (-9.7 bln US$) and Developed Europe (-6.2 bln US$). Imports were diversified: in 2010, 21 major partners accounted for 80 percent of imports (see graph 3). See footnote*.

Graph 1: Total imports, exports and trade balance

(Bln US$ by year)

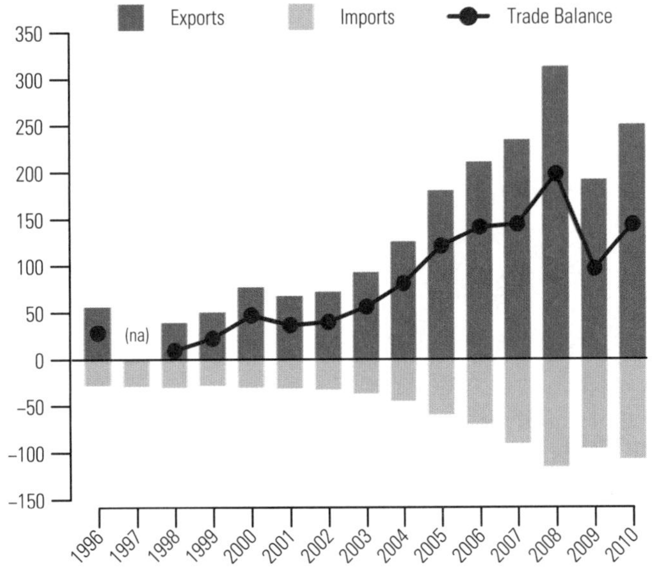

Exports Profile:

Saudi Arabia's exports in 2010 were largely mineral fuels, lubricants and related materials (SITC section 3): they accounted for 85.7 percent of exported goods (see table 1). They also accounted for the majority of exports to all major partners (see table 4). Petroleum oils and oils obtained from bituminous minerals, crude (HS code 2709), the top exported commodity, accounted for 75.4 percent of exports in 2010 (see table 3). From 2008 to 2010, other major commodities for exports were petroleum oils, other than crude (HS code 2710) and petroleum gases and other gaseous hydrocarbons (HS code 2711).

Table 1: Exports by SITC sections

(Value in million US$, growth and shares in percentage)

SITC	2010	Avg. Growth rates (%) 2006-2010	2009-2010	2010 share
Total	251 143.0	4.4	30.6	100.0
0+1	2 901.1	19.0	8.4	1.2
2+4	518.4	-1.8	6.9	0.2
3	215 248.7	3.4	32.0	85.7
5	21 851.8	16.1	55.9	8.7
6	4 317.0	6.8	6.6	1.7
7	4 736.7	3.4	-24.5	1.9
8	1 192.8	6.9	4.2	0.5
9	376.6	-7.0	-36.9	0.1

Table 2: Imports by SITC sections

(Value in million US$, growth and shares in percentage)

SITC	2010	Avg. Growth rates (%) 2006-2010	2009-2010	2010 share
Total	106 863.0	11.2	11.8	100.0
0+1	15 735.8	15.2	18.8	14.7
2+4	3 682.3	21.4	50.5	3.4
3	243.8	11.2	15.4	0.2
5	10 804.8	13.1	13.9	10.1
6	19 720.3	7.6	21.1	18.5
7	45 344.5	9.6	4.0	42.4
8	8 852.7	10.9	-6.2	8.3
9	2 478.8	54.8	200.3	2.3

Table 3: Top 10 export commodities 2008 to 2010

(Value in million US$)

HS code	4-digit heading of Harmonized System 2007	Value (million US$) 2008	2009	2010	Unit value 2008	2009	2010	Unit	SITC code
	All Commodities	313 462.2	192 313.8	251 143.0					
2709	Petroleum oils and oils obtained from bituminous minerals, crude	247 097.2	142 194.2	189 433.6	0.7	0.5	0.6	US$/kg	333
2710	Petroleum oils, other than crude	21 534.4	15 175.3	17 955.3	*0.7*	*0.5*	*0.6*	US$/kg	334
2711	Petroleum gases and other gaseous hydrocarbons	10 286.3	5 252.1	7 050.6	0.8	0.5	0.7	US$/kg	343
3901	Polymers of ethylene, in primary forms	4 120.1	3 431.2	6 256.9	1.1	0.8	1.0	US$/kg	571
9999	Commodities not specified according to kind	9 984.5	124.9	190.9					931
2905	Acyclic alcohols and their derivatives	2 839.6	2 361.5	3 333.7	0.3	*0.2*	0.3	US$/kg	512
3902	Polymers of propylene or of other olefins, in primary forms	1 506.7	1 714.2	3 429.2	*1.4*	1.0	1.2	US$/kg	575
2902	Cyclic hydrocarbons	1 372.1	1 184.0	1 812.4	1.0	0.7	*0.9*	US$/kg	511
3102	Mineral or chemical fertilisers, nitrogenous	1 690.0	1 054.5	1 233.0	0.4	0.3	0.3	US$/kg	562
8703	Motor cars and other motor vehicles principally designed for the transport	893.4	839.6	706.7		*15.6*	*14.6*	thsd US$/unit	781

*Export partners are defined as regions only, resulting in the high export concentration shown in graph 3

Graph 2: Trade Balance by MDG Regions in 2010

(Bln US$)

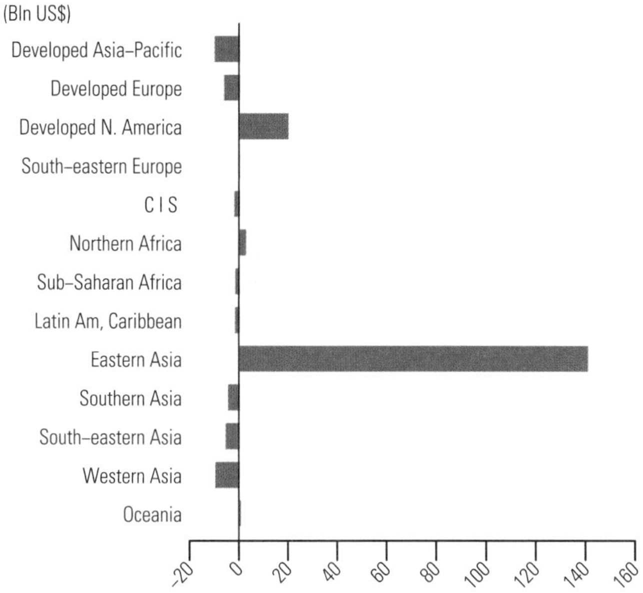

Graph 3: Partner concentration of trade in 2010

(Cumulative share by ranked partners)

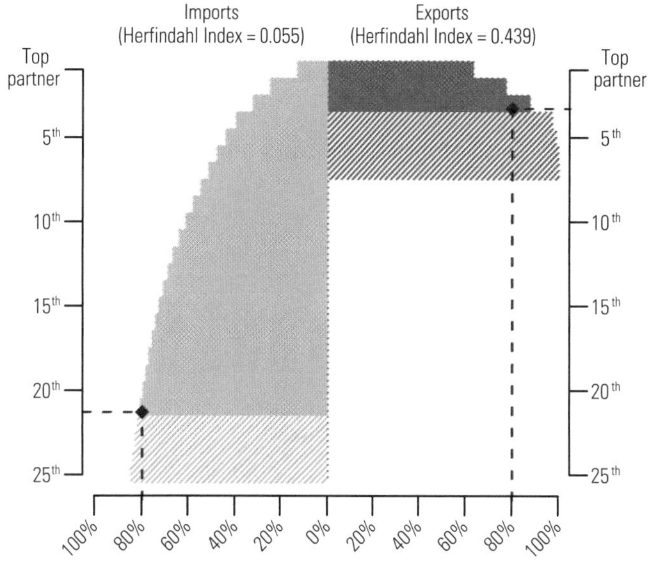

Table 4: Exports by principal countries and SITC sections in 2010

(Value in million US$, percentages of country total)

Country	Total	Shares by SITC sections (%)								
		0 + 1	2 + 4	3	5	6	7	8	9	Total
World	251 143.0	1.2	0.2	85.7	8.7	1.7	1.9	0.5	0.1	100
Other Asia, nes	158 727.9	1.1	0.2	88.1	7.2	1.5	1.5	0.3	0.0	100
North America and Central America, nes	35 187.7	0.0	0.0	96.9	1.8	0.2	0.8	0.1	0.0	100
Areas, nes	25 640.2	4.1	0.6	60.2	21.3	6.3	4.9	1.9	0.7	100
Other Europe, nes	24 085.4	0.1	0.1	82.3	12.9	0.7	3.0	0.3	0.6	100
Other Africa, nes	4 277.7	1.5	0.1	79.0	17.2	1.2	0.5	0.4	0.2	100
South America, nes	2 723.6	0.0	0.0	92.5	6.6	0.3	0.6	0.0	...	100
Oceania, nes	500.5	0.2	0.2	23.9	69.8	3.4	0.5	2.0	0.1	100

Imports Profile:

In 2010, imports were composed of 42.4 percent of machinery and transport equipment (SITC section 7), 18.5 percent of manufactured goods classified chiefly by material (SITC section 6) and 14.7 percent of food, live animals, beverages and tobacco (SITC sections 0+1). From 2008 to 2010, top three products for imports were motor cars and other motor vehicles principally designed for the transport of persons (HS code 8703), electrical apparatus for line telephony or line telegraphy (HS code 8517) and motor vehicles for the transport of goods (HS code 8704) (see table 5).

Table 5: Top 10 import commodities 2008 to 2010

(Value in million US$)

HS code	4-digit heading of Harmonized System 2007	Value (million US$)			Unit value				SITC code
		2008	2009	2010	2008	2009	2010	Unit	
	All Commodities	115 133.9	95 552.2	106 863.0					
9999	Commodities not specified according to kind	55 403.6	169.0	1 503.3					931
8703	Motor cars and other motor vehicles principally designed for the transport	9 016.9	8 259.9	10 639.9		*19.2*	*21.2*	thsd US$/unit	781
8517	Electrical apparatus for line telephony or line telegraphy	2 564.0	3 115.8	3 355.4					764
8704	Motor vehicles for the transport of goods	2 280.7	2 058.3	2 123.3	*20.7*			thsd US$/unit	782
1003	Barley	2 919.5	1 283.9	1 917.2	0.4	0.2	0.3	US$/kg	043
8803	Parts of goods of heading 88.01 or 88.02	1 834.3	1 876.0	1 778.4	804.5	*620.6*	*542.1*	US$/kg	792
8471	Automatic data processing machines and units thereof	977.0	1 550.9	1 708.1					752
1006	Rice	1 494.6	1 385.6	1 310.5	1.2	1.0	1.0	US$/kg	042
3003	Medicaments (excluding goods of heading 30.02, 30.05 or 30.06)	1 168.6	1 570.2	1 316.0	*128.6*	*132.4*		US$/kg	542
3004	Medicaments (excluding goods of heading 30.02, 30.05 or 30.06)	547.0	1 313.2	1 704.9	*49.0*		*74.8*	US$/kg	542

Senegal

Imports: CIF, by origin | Exports: FOB, by last known destination | Trade System: General

Overview:

Since 2007, the value of the exports of Senegal increased on average by 13.2 percent each year and amounted to 2.5 bln US$ in 2011 (see table 1 and graph 1). Similarly, imports increased on average by 4.9 percent each year to reach 5.9 bln US$ (see table 2 and graph 1). The trade balance registered a deficit of 3.4 bln US$ in 2011 (see graph 1). Most of this deficit came from trade with Developed Europe: deficit with this region amounted to 1.9 bln US$ in 2011 (see graph 2). Trade recorded significant deficits with Eastern Asia (-409.2 mln US$) and Latin America and the Caribbean (-372.5 mln US$) but a surplus with Sub-Saharan Africa and Southern Asia (+182.4 mln US$ and +160.3 mln US$ respectively). Senegal's trade was diversified across partners: in 2011, 15 (respectively 18) major partners accounted for 80 percent of exports (respectively imports) (see graph 3).

Graph 1: Total imports, exports and trade balance

(Bln US$ by year)

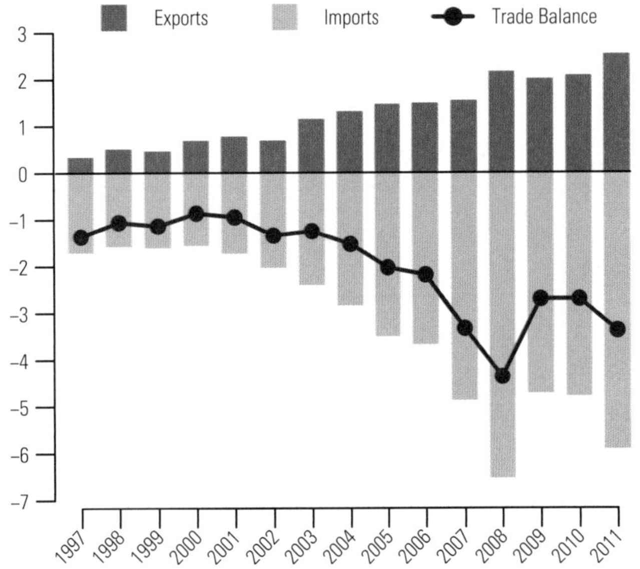

Exports Profile:

In 2011, exports of food, live animals, beverages and tobacco (SITC sections 0+1) increased by 38.5 percent to account for 26.4 percent of total exports (see table 1). Other major commodity groups included chemicals and related products, n.e.s. (SITC section 5) and manufactured goods classified chiefly by material (SITC section 6) which accounted respectively for 18.7 and 16.5 percent of exports. Mali, India and Switzerland were the three major partners in 2011 (see table 4). A large share of exported goods, (largely mineral fuels, lubricants and related materials (SITC section 3)) was reported as supplied to foreign vessels and aircrafts and the partner was unknown. Top exported products over the last three years were petroleum oils, other than crude (HS code 2710), diphosphorus pentaoxide; phosphoric acid; (HS code 2809) and gold (including gold plated with platinum) (HS code 7108) (see table 3).

Table 1: Exports by SITC sections

(Value in million US$, growth and shares in percentage)

SITC	2011	Avg. Growth rates (%) 2007-2011	2010-2011	2011 share
Total	2541.7	13.2	21.7	100.0
0+1	670.9	7.9	38.5	26.4
2+4	224.6	7.0	32.9	8.8
3	374.4	5.9	-14.2	14.7
5	475.8	18.2	47.0	18.7
6	419.0	21.6	27.0	16.5
7	95.1	2.7	-1.9	3.7
8	34.0	-8.0	-20.7	1.3
9	247.9	111.0	20.9	9.8

Table 2: Imports by SITC sections

(Value in million US$, growth and shares in percentage)

SITC	2011	Avg. Growth rates (%) 2007-2011	2010-2011	2011 share
Total	5908.9	4.9	23.6	100.0
0+1	1197.6	2.9	26.4	20.3
2+4	270.5	1.1	4.2	4.6
3	1876.8	9.7	31.3	31.8
5	502.3	4.4	31.1	8.5
6	632.5	-0.8	11.9	10.7
7	1206.2	6.5	20.3	20.4
8	218.8	-1.2	14.0	3.7
9	4.2	21.5	70.3	0.1

Table 3: Top 10 export commodities 2009 to 2011

(Value in million US$)

HS code	4-digit heading of Harmonized System 2007	Value (million US$) 2009	2010	2011	Unit value 2009	2010	2011	Unit	SITC code
	All Commodities	2017.4	2088.1	2541.7					
2710	Petroleum oils, other than crude	434.9	430.4	364.9	0.7	0.7	1.0	US$/kg	334
2809	Diphosphorus pentaoxide; phosphoric acid	148.1	199.0	340.8	0.6	0.7	0.9	US$/kg	522
7108	Gold (including gold plated with platinum)	181.2	205.0	247.7	21.8	24.6	32.3	thsd US$/kg	971
2523	Portland cement, aluminous cement, slag cement	149.8	201.5	238.0	0.1	0.1	0.1	US$/kg	661
0302	Fish, fresh or chilled, excluding fish fillets	86.9	78.0	82.0	5.5	9.9	9.9	US$/kg	034
0303	Fish, frozen, excluding fish fillets and other fish meat of heading 03.04	63.1	71.6	99.1	1.2	1.1	1.3	US$/kg	034
1508	Ground-nut oil and its fractions	38.5	57.8	79.4	1.2	1.2	1.4	US$/kg	421
0307	Molluscs, whether in shell or not	49.9	42.6	81.8	4.0	4.4	5.8	US$/kg	036
2104	Soups and broths and preparations therefor	39.8	44.6	69.3	2.6	2.4	2.6	US$/kg	098
2402	Cigars, cheroots, cigarillos and cigarettes	41.4	45.4	52.6	11.7	16.3	17.7	US$/kg	122

Graph 2: Trade Balance by MDG Regions in 2011

(Bln US$)

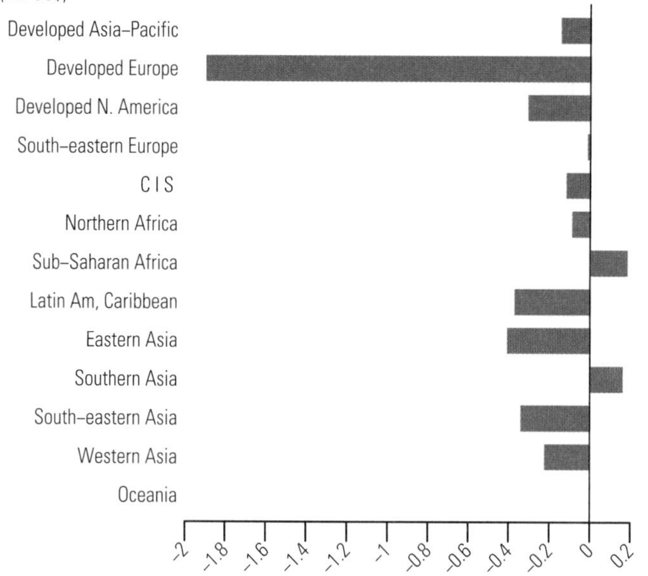

Graph 3: Partner concentration of trade in 2011

(Cumulative share by ranked partners)

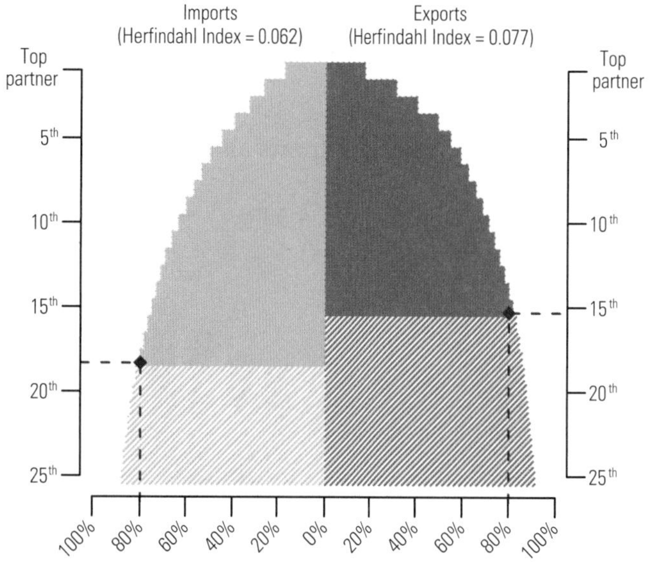

Table 4: Exports by principal countries and SITC sections in 2011

(Value in million US$, percentages of country total)

Country	Total	Shares by SITC sections (%)								
		0 + 1	2 + 4	3	5	6	7	8	9	Total
World	2 541.7	26.4	8.8	14.7	18.7	16.5	3.7	1.3	9.8	100
Mali	439.6	16.9	2.2	16.8	7.8	51.6	2.7	1.9	...	100
India	356.6	0.0	4.1	...	95.6	0.2	0.1	0.0	...	100
Bunkers	227.2	0.5	0.0	98.3	1.1	0.0	0.0	0.1	0.0	100
Switzerland	221.5	0.8	4.8	...	...	0.2	0.0	0.0	94.1	100
Guinea	135.9	32.8	2.1	3.2	18.3	37.5	4.4	1.7	0.1	100
France	112.6	53.6	26.7	...	6.9	2.3	5.6	3.3	1.6	100
Gambia	85.4	30.4	4.9	2.9	11.5	40.0	4.1	6.2	...	100
Mauritania	85.2	12.0	0.2	6.1	16.2	46.8	16.0	2.7	0.0	100
Spain	74.2	90.9	4.2	0.1	0.2	1.1	2.8	0.4	0.3	100
Italy	69.1	88.1	4.9	0.0	0.0	2.8	2.6	0.3	1.3	100

Imports Profile:

In 2011, imported goods were composed of 31.8 percent of mineral fuels, lubricants and related materials (SITC section 3), 20.4 percent of machinery and transport equipment (SITC section 7) and 20.3 percent of food, live animals, beverages and tobacco (SITC sections 0+1) (see table 2). The top three imported products over the last three years were petroleum oils, other than crude (HS code 2710), petroleum oils, crude (HS code 2709) and rice (HS code 1006) (see table 5).

Table 5: Top 10 import commodities 2009 to 2011

(Value in million US$)

HS code	4-digit heading of Harmonized System 2007	Value (million US$)			Unit value				SITC code
		2009	2010	2011	2009	2010	2011	Unit	
	All Commodities	4712.9	4782.2	5908.9					
2710	Petroleum oils, other than crude	560.0	829.4	1131.4	0.5	0.7	0.9	US$/kg	334
2709	Petroleum oils and oils obtained from bituminous minerals, crude	391.8	451.2	539.3	0.5	0.7	0.9	US$/kg	333
1006	Rice	326.9	289.5	376.4	0.4	0.4	0.5	US$/kg	042
8703	Motor cars and other motor vehicles principally designed for the transport	143.2	145.0	155.8	*20.5*	*21.5*		thsd US$/unit	781
1001	Wheat and meslin	110.9	127.3	170.6	0.3	0.3	0.4	US$/kg	041
3004	Medicaments (excluding goods of heading 30.02, 30.05 or 30.06)	122.8	125.8	157.4	21.3	19.9	23.9	US$/kg	542
0402	Milk and cream, concentrated or containing added sugar	115.3	104.0	87.4	2.5	3.2	3.9	US$/kg	022
8517	Electrical apparatus for line telephony or line telegraphy	118.6	85.5	84.0					764
7213	Bars and rods, hot-rolled, in irregularly wound coils	70.8	86.4	120.8	0.5	0.6	0.8	US$/kg	676
2711	Petroleum gases and other gaseous hydrocarbons	70.8	88.9	103.9	0.6	0.8	1.0	US$/kg	343

Serbia

Imports: CIF, by origin | **Exports: FOB, by last known destination** | **Trade System: General**

Overview:

In 2011, the value of the exports of Serbia increased by 20.2 percent to reach 11.8 bln US$. Similarly, imports increased by 20.3 percent to 20.1 bln US$ in 2011. This resulted in a trade deficit of 8.4 bln US$ in 2011 (see graph 1). This deficit came largely from trade with Developed Europe (-4.4 bln US$), Commonwealth of Independent States (-2.3 bln US$) and Eastern Asia (-1.7 bln US$) (see graph 2). Trade, however, recorded a surplus with South-eastern Europe (+1.3 bln US$). In 2011, Serbia's trade was diversified across partners: 15 (respectively 20) major partners accounted for 80 percent of exports (respectively imports) (see graph 3). See footnote*.

Graph 1: Total imports, exports and trade balance

(Bln US$ by year)

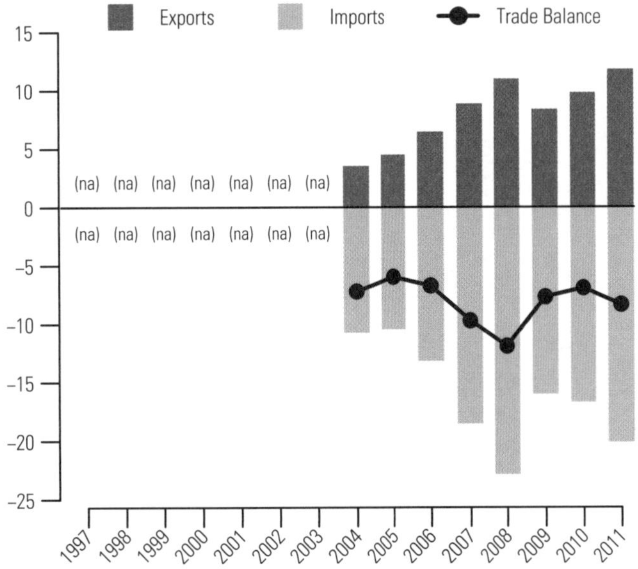

Exports Profile:

Manufactured goods classified chiefly by material (SITC section 6) accounted for 29.6 percent of exported goods in 2011 (see table 1). Other major commodity groups included food, live animals, beverages and tobacco (SITC sections 0+1), machinery and transport equipment (SITC section 7) and miscellaneous manufactured articles (SITC section 8). They accounted respectively for 20.1, 16.7 and 12.8 percent of exports. Germany, Italy and Bosnia Herzegovina were the three largest markets for exports in 2011 (see table 4). Main exported commodities over the last three years included flat-rolled products of iron or non-alloy steel (HS code 7208), maize (corn) (HS code 1005) and fruit and nuts (HS code 0811) (see table 3).

Table 1: Exports by SITC sections

(Value in million US$, growth and shares in percentage)

SITC	2011	Avg. Growth rates (%) 2007-2011	2010-2011	2011 share
Total	11775.4	7.5	20.2	100.0
0+1	2365.3	11.5	18.3	20.1
2+4	859.9	14.1	40.7	7.3
3	496.0	21.0	-0.9	4.2
5	998.3	2.2	14.1	8.5
6	3480.9	3.1	22.5	29.6
7	1961.7	11.6	23.1	16.7
8	1507.1	4.8	22.5	12.8
9	106.2	24.6	-25.6	0.9

Table 2: Imports by SITC sections

(Value in million US$, growth and shares in percentage)

SITC	2011	Avg. Growth rates (%) 2007-2011	2010-2011	2011 share
Total	20139.4	2.1	20.3	100.0
0+1	1240.0	5.5	39.2	6.2
2+4	835.4	3.7	21.3	4.1
3	3970.8	5.6	33.2	19.7
5	2950.7	3.2	41.4	14.7
6	3852.4	-1.2	26.9	19.1
7	4617.2	-3.6	54.2	22.9
8	1547.6	-1.4	27.0	7.7
9	1125.4	263.5	-60.4	5.6

Table 3: Top 10 export commodities 2009 to 2011

(Value in million US$)

HS code	4-digit heading of Harmonized System 2007	Value (million US$) 2009	2010	2011	Unit value 2009	2010	2011	Unit	SITC code
	All Commodities	8345.1	9794.5	11775.4					
7208	Flat-rolled products of iron or non-alloy steel	357.5	607.8	542.2	0.5	0.7	0.8	US$/kg	673
1005	Maize (corn)	288.1	334.9	455.5	0.2	0.2	0.3	US$/kg	044
0811	Fruit and nuts	252.1	251.9	299.9	2.0	1.7	1.9	US$/kg	058
4011	New pneumatic tyres, of rubber	198.2	239.8	316.8					625
8544	Insulated (including enamelled or anodised) wire, cable	129.7	209.8	321.8	*9.6*	*9.3*	*11.3*	US$/kg	773
2716	Electrical energy	200.5	237.8	180.2	*79.0*	*54.8*	*60.9*	US$/MWh	351
6115	Panty hose, tights, stockings, socks and other hosiery	187.0	189.9	210.3	*16.2*	*16.1*	*18.8*	US$/kg	846
3004	Medicaments (excluding goods of heading 30.02, 30.05 or 30.06)	173.7	190.7	207.1	*13.6*	*11.2*	*13.6*	US$/kg	542
7210	Flat-rolled products of iron or non-alloy steel	157.9	181.4	183.4	1.0	1.0	1.2	US$/kg	674
2710	Petroleum oils, other than crude	150.6	175.1	195.7	0.5	0.6	0.9	US$/kg	334

*Special trade system up to 2008

Graph 2: Trade Balance by MDG Regions in 2011

(Bln US$)

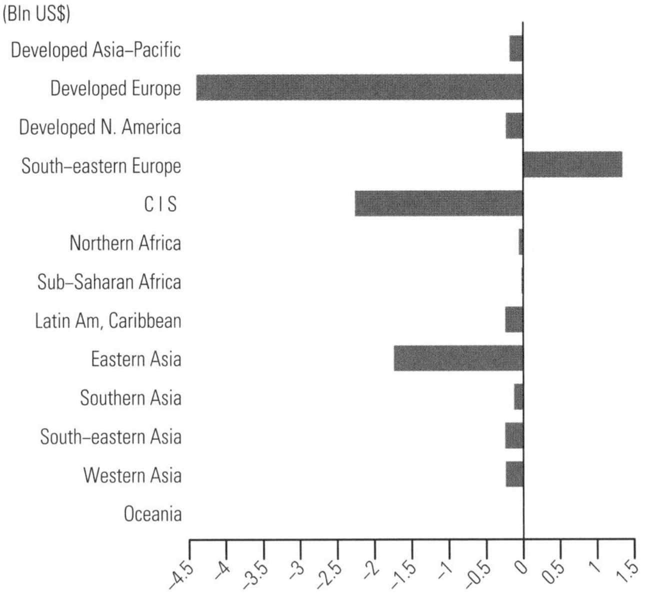

Graph 3: Partner concentration of trade in 2011

(Cumulative share by ranked partners)

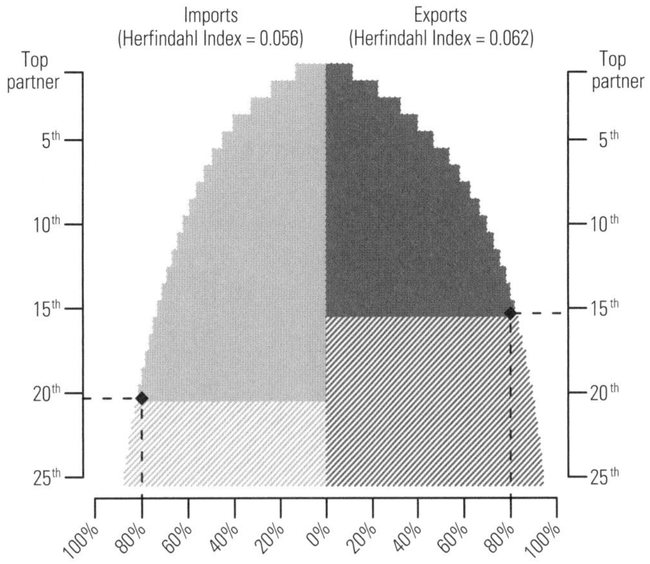

Table 4: Exports by principal countries and SITC sections in 2011

(Value in million US$, percentages of country total)

Country	Total	Shares by SITC sections (%)								
		0 + 1	2 + 4	3	5	6	7	8	9	Total
World	11775.4	20.1	7.3	4.2	8.5	29.6	16.7	12.8	0.9	100
Germany	1329.7	13.4	6.0	0.7	4.9	25.6	35.1	14.4	0.0	100
Italy	1306.1	9.0	5.2	0.2	7.3	43.0	6.2	29.0	0.1	100
Bosnia Herzegovina	1191.2	35.1	4.9	4.7	14.2	19.3	11.1	10.7	0.0	100
Montenegro	890.7	34.9	4.9	8.7	11.0	13.6	12.3	14.6	0.0	100
Romania	812.5	43.4	1.3	6.0	11.2	29.7	3.4	4.9	0.1	100
Russian Federation	792.2	20.0	0.8	0.2	8.5	34.2	25.6	10.8	0.0	100
Slovenia	526.1	6.2	17.9	1.1	6.0	30.5	25.4	12.5	0.4	100
TFYR of Macedonia	524.6	29.3	11.5	7.8	13.2	20.8	9.3	8.1	0.0	100
Croatia	468.0	18.3	9.3	2.1	9.4	36.9	11.5	12.6	0.0	100
Austria	371.3	14.5	12.0	0.2	2.6	35.4	27.7	7.2	0.3	100

Imports Profile:

In 2011, major commodity groups for imports included machinery and transport equipment (SITC section 7), mineral fuels, lubricants and related materials (SITC section 3) and manufactured goods classified chiefly by material (SITC section 6) (see table 2). They accounted respectively for 22.9, 19.7 and 19.1 percent of imports. Over the last three years, petroleum oils and oils obtained from bituminous minerals, crude (HS code 2709), petroleum gases and other gaseous hydrocarbons (HS code 2711) and petroleum oils, other than crude (HS code 2710) were the top three products for imports (see table 5).

Table 5: Top 10 import commodities 2009 to 2011

(Value in million US$)

HS code	4-digit heading of Harmonized System 2007	Value (million US$)			Unit value				SITC code
		2009	2010	2011	2009	2010	2011	Unit	
	All Commodities	16047.4	16734.5	20139.4					
9999	Commodities not specified according to kind	3063.0	2838.9	1125.2					931
2709	Petroleum oils and oils obtained from bituminous minerals, crude	1001.3	1088.2	1193.0	0.4	0.6	0.8	US$/kg	333
2711	Petroleum gases and other gaseous hydrocarbons	765.7	948.0	1185.8	0.6	0.6	0.7	US$/kg	343
2710	Petroleum oils, other than crude	215.6	377.8	1028.7	*0.6*	*0.8*	*1.0*	US$/kg	334
8703	Motor cars and other motor vehicles principally designed for the transport	452.2	302.0	596.0		*16.4*		thsd US$/unit	781
3004	Medicaments (excluding goods of heading 30.02, 30.05 or 30.06)	280.2	283.1	608.6	*37.4*	*42.6*	*64.0*	US$/kg	542
8517	Electrical apparatus for line telephony or line telegraphy	236.3	270.2	346.1					764
2704	Coke and semi-coke of coal, of lignite or of peat	193.7	285.0	275.0	0.3	0.4	0.4	US$/kg	325
7403	Refined copper and copper alloys, unwrought	110.5	277.2	246.6	5.3	*7.5*	*9.2*	US$/kg	682
2601	Iron ores and concentrates, including roasted iron pyrites	108.1	222.8	242.3	0.1	0.1	0.1	US$/kg	281

Seychelles

Imports: CIF, by origin | **Exports: FOB, by last known destination** | **Trade System: General**

Overview:

From 2004 to 2008, Seychelles' exports increased on average by 4.0 percent each year and amounted to 340.6 mln US$ (see table 1 and graph 1). During the same period, imports increased nearly twofold, on average by 19.8 percent to reach 1.0 bln US$ (see table 2 and graph 1). The trade balance recorded a deficit of 681.3 mln US$ (see graph 1). Trade was in deficit with nearly all MDG regions except a surplus of 0.3 mln US$ with Commonwealth of Independent States (see graph 2). Large deficits were recorded with Western Asia (-236.4 mln US$), Developed Europe (-165.2 mln US$) and South-eastern Asia (-134.9 mln US$) (see graph 2). Trade, especially exports, was concentrated among a few partners: in 2008, 4 partners accounted for 80 percent of exports (compared to 12 major partners for imports) (see graph 3).

Graph 1: Total imports, exports and trade balance

(Bln US$ by year)

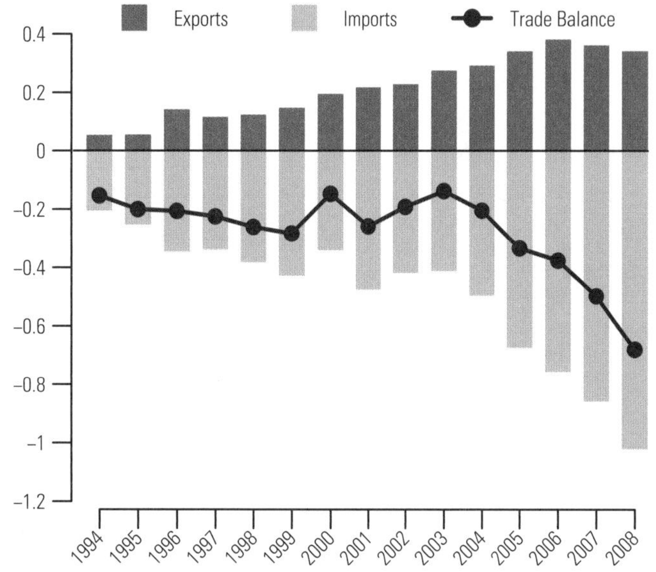

Exports Profile:

Two commodity groups accounted for most of Seychelles' exports in 2008: commodities and transactions not classified elsewhere (SITC section 9) and food, live animals, beverages and tobacco (SITC sections 0+1) respectively with 54.9 and 41.2 percent (see table 1). Top partners for exports were Saudi Arabia, France and United Kingdom (see table 4). In 2008, exports to United Kingdom and France were almost exclusively food, live animals, beverages and tobacco (SITC sections 0+1). From 2006 to 2008, top exported commodities included prepared or preserved fish, fish eggs, caviar (HS code 1604), oils petroleum, bituminous, distillates, except crude (HS code 2710) and fish, cured, smoked, fish meal for human consumption (HS code 0305) (see table 3).

Table 1: Exports by SITC sections

(Value in million US$, growth and shares in percentage)

SITC	2008	Avg. Growth rates (%) 2004-2008	2007-2008	2008 share
Total	340.6	4.0	-5.4	100.0
0+1	140.2	-6.6	-28.6	41.2
2+4	3.2	226.8	113.5	0.9
3	0.0	-89.2	-100.0	0.0
5	0.2	-64.6	-63.9	0.1
6	1.3	6.0	370.9	0.4
7	4.5	80.2	364.8	1.3
8	4.0	22.4	-15.1	1.2
9	187.2	272.7	82898.9	54.9

Table 2: Imports by SITC sections

(Value in million US$, growth and shares in percentage)

SITC	2008	Avg. Growth rates (%) 2004-2008	2007-2008	2008 share
Total	1 021.9	19.8	18.9	100.0
0+1	159.5	6.9	-10.4	15.6
2+4	39.7	23.7	63.1	3.9
3	126.5	-0.8	-41.7	12.4
5	35.7	10.8	-0.8	3.5
6	145.2	17.1	31.5	14.2
7	240.3	35.9	12.1	23.5
8	71.3	15.5	27.2	7.0
9	203.8	90.5	780.3	19.9

Table 3: Top 10 export commodities 2006 to 2008

(Value in million US$)

HS code	4-digit heading of Harmonized System 1992	Value (million US$) 2006	2007	2008	Unit value 2006	2007	2008	Unit	SITC code
	All Commodities	379.9	360.1	340.6					
1604	Prepared or preserved fish, fish eggs, caviar	187.1	183.2	90.9	4.9	5.6	*6.7*	US$/kg	037
2710	Oils petroleum, bituminous, distillates, except crude	161.1	155.5	0.0			1.0	US$/kg	334
9999	Commodities not specified according to kind	0.2	0.2	187.2					931
0305	Fish,cured, smoked, fish meal for human consumption	0.1	0.1	43.7	11.5	*9.4*	*0.7*	US$/kg	035
9018	Instruments etc for medical, surgical, dental, etc use	10.6	1.1	1.5					774
2301	Flour etc of meat, fish or offal for animal feed	4.5	4.4	0.7	0.6	0.6	0.6	US$/kg	081
0306	Crustaceans	4.6	2.6	0.5	7.4	*7.0*	*17.4*	US$/kg	036
9020	Breathing appliances and gas masks	3.0	3.3	0.8	144.3	106.1	144.3	US$/kg	872
0302	Fish, fresh or chilled, whole	2.7	2.0	1.2	7.1	7.3	4.5	US$/kg	034
1504	Fish, marine mammal fat or oil not chemically modified	0.2	1.5	3.1	1.8	2.0	5.7	US$/kg	411

Graph 2: Trade Balance by MDG Regions in 2008

(Mln US$)

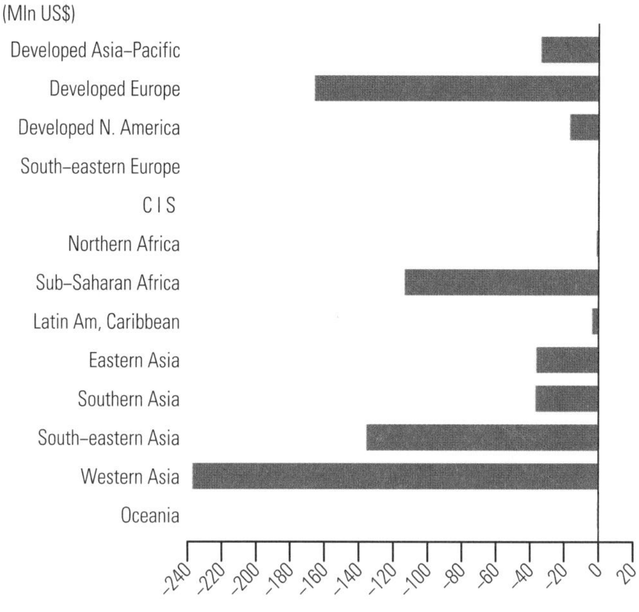

Graph 3: Partner concentration of trade in 2008

(Cumulative share by ranked partners)

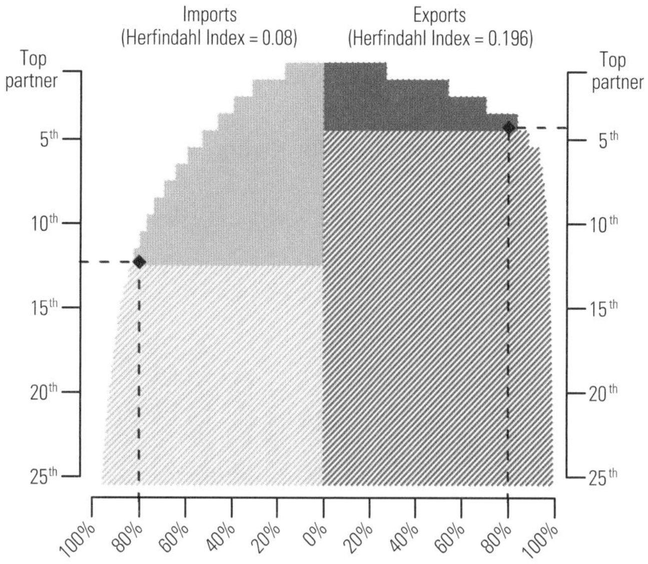

Table 4: Exports by principal countries and SITC sections in 2008

(Value in million US$, percentages of country total)

Country	Total	Shares by SITC sections (%) 0+1	2+4	3	5	6	7	8	9	Total
World	340.6	41.2	0.9	0.0	0.1	0.4	1.3	1.2	54.9	100
Areas, nes	93.1	0.0	0.0	...	...	...	...	...	100.0	100
Saudi Arabia	91.5	0.0	0.0	...	...	...	0.0	0.0	100.0	100
France	55.2	94.9	0.0	...	0.0	0.6	1.0	2.8	0.8	100
United Kingdom	45.7	95.8	0.0	...	0.0	0.1	3.4	0.3	0.4	100
Italy	16.3	99.6	0.0	...	...	0.3	0.1	0.0	0.0	100
Germany	15.9	98.2	0.1	0.0	0.3	0.1	0.4	0.5	0.4	100
Netherlands	3.9	62.7	0.0	...	...	...	0.2	37.0	0.0	100
Switzerland	2.7	1.2	98.6	...	...	0.0	...	0.0	0.1	100
Sri Lanka	2.4	99.6	0.0	...	...	...	0.0	0.0	0.3	100
USA	1.8	0.4	0.0	...	4.3	0.1	70.5	24.4	0.3	100

Imports Profile:

In 2008, imports of machinery and transport equipment (SITC section 7) increased by 12.1 percent and accounted for 23.5 percent of imported goods (see table 2). Other major commodity groups included commodities and transactions not classified elsewhere (SITC section 9) and food, live animals, beverages and tobacco (SITC sections 0+1) respectively with 19.9 and 15.6 percent of imports. From 2006 to 2008, top imported products were oils petroleum, bituminous, distillates, except crude (HS code 2710), fish, frozen, whole (HS code 0303) and passenger and goods transport ships, boats (HS code 8901) (see table 5).

Table 5: Top 10 import commodities 2006 to 2008

(Value in million US$)

HS code	4-digit heading of Harmonized System 1992	Value (million US$) 2006	2007	2008	Unit value 2006	2007	2008	Unit	SITC code
	All Commodities	757.4	859.2	1021.9					
2710	Oils petroleum, bituminous, distillates, except crude	199.5	213.2	125.1			2.3	US$/kg	334
9999	Commodities not specified according to kind	53.8	22.9	203.5					931
0303	Fish, frozen, whole	93.8	78.9	59.9	1.0	0.7	*1.7*	US$/kg	034
8901	Passenger and goods transport ships, boats	1.8	80.9	63.6	0.4	8.1		mln US$/unit	793
8703	Motor vehicles for transport of persons (except buses)	11.4	15.8	20.1	11.7	11.7		thsd US$/unit	781
8903	Yachts, pleasure, sports vessels, rowing boats, canoes	20.4	8.4	14.0	*7.1*	85.2		thsd US$/unit	793
4407	Wood sawn, chipped lengthwise, sliced or peeled	8.1	7.8	18.0	121.0	35.8	*337.4*	US$/m^3	248
8309	Stoppers, caps, lids, crown corks, etc off base metal	9.5	9.0	11.7	3.8	3.1	*3.2*	US$/kg	699
9403	Other furniture and parts thereof	6.2	6.2	17.0					821
7310	Tank, cask, box, container, iron/steel, capacity <300	13.8	8.4	4.9	2.2	2.6	*2.9*	US$/kg	692

Singapore

Imports: CIF, by origin | **Exports: FOB, by last known destination** | **Trade System: General**

Overview:

From 2007 to 2011, the value of Singapore's exports increased on average by 8.2 percent each year to reach it's peak of 409.5 bln US$ in 2011 and overcoming the sharp decline of 20.2 percent in 2009 (see table 1 and graph 1). Imports showed a similar development with an average increase of 8.6 percent each year and amounted to 365.8 bln US$ in 2011 (see table 2 and graph 1). This resulted in a trade surplus of 43.7 bln US$ in 2011 (see graph 1). Large surpluses were recorded with South-eastern Asia (+49.5 bln US$) and Eastern Asia (+28.6 bln US$) (see graph 2). However, trade was in deficit with Western Asia (-35.7 bln US$), Developed North America (-16.7 bln US$) and Developed Europe (-10.0 bln US$). Singapore's trade was diversified across partners: in 2011, 15 major partners accounted for 80 percent of exports as well as imports (see graph 3).

Graph 1: Total imports, exports and trade balance

(Bln US$ by year)

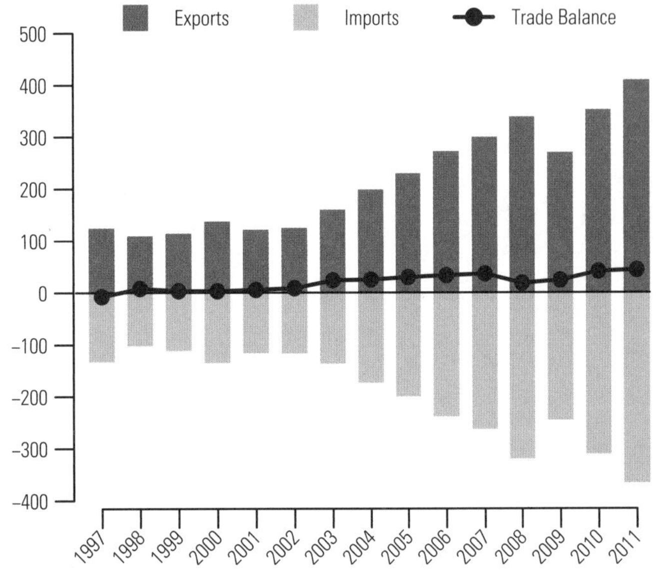

Exports Profile:

Machinery and transport equipment (SITC section 7) accounted for nearly half of Singapore's exports in 2011: 45.8 percent (see table 1). Other major commodity groups were mineral fuels, lubricants and related materials (SITC section 3) and chemicals and related products, n.e.s. (SITC section 5) respectively with 19.8 and 12.6 percent. In 2011, Malaysia, China, Hong Kong SAR and Indonesia were the three largest markets for exports (see table 4). From 2009 to 2011, main exported products included electronic integrated circuits (HS code 8542), petroleum oils, other than crude (HS code 2710) and parts and accessories for use with machines of heading 84.69 to 84.72 (HS code 8473) (see table 3).

Table 1: Exports by SITC sections

(Value in million US$, growth and shares in percentage)

SITC	2011	Avg. Growth rates (%) 2007-2011	2010-2011	2011 share
Total	409503.6	8.2	16.4	100.0
0+1	8315.8	15.2	30.0	2.0
2+4	3064.4	7.7	21.8	0.7
3	80978.6	18.3	42.8	19.8
5	51510.3	11.2	29.7	12.6
6	15733.6	2.9	17.1	3.8
7	187532.9	3.4	4.4	45.8
8	28493.9	10.1	16.0	7.0
9	33874.1	14.3	17.2	8.3

Table 2: Imports by SITC sections

(Value in million US$, growth and shares in percentage)

SITC	2011	Avg. Growth rates (%) 2007-2011	2010-2011	2011 share
Total	365770.5	8.6	17.7	100.0
0+1	11021.7	12.3	21.5	3.0
2+4	4210.5	15.7	46.7	1.2
3	119319.1	22.7	47.0	32.6
5	25277.8	12.6	21.9	6.9
6	24382.8	5.4	28.4	6.7
7	149858.7	2.1	4.1	41.0
8	25473.7	7.0	17.0	7.0
9	6226.2	-6.9	-49.3	1.7

Table 3: Top 10 export commodities 2009 to 2011

(Value in million US$)

HS code	4-digit heading of Harmonized System 2007	Value (million US$) 2009	2010	2011	Unit value 2009	2010	2011	Unit	SITC code
	All Commodities	269832.5	351867.2	409503.6					
8542	Electronic integrated circuits	54906.2	77027.2	75633.3					776
2710	Petroleum oils, other than crude	39960.4	55199.8	79210.7	*0.5*		*0.9*	US$/kg	334
9999	Commodities not specified according to kind	18292.6	24935.5	32103.6					931
8473	Parts and accessories for use with machines of heading 84.69 to 84.72	8890.1	11306.2	10548.7					759
8471	Automatic data processing machines and units thereof	7572.2	9008.2	8450.9	*90.2*	*98.9*	*72.1*	US$/unit	752
8443	Printing machinery used for printing by means of the printing type, blocks	7977.5	8761.7	8168.1					726
8541	Diodes, transistors and similar semiconductor devices	6617.1	9037.1	7471.0					776
8517	Electrical apparatus for line telephony or line telegraphy	5425.6	6197.8	8164.7					764
8431	Parts suitable for use principally with the machinery of headings 84.25	5289.1	4438.0	5024.2	*16.0*		*15.9*	US$/kg	723
8523	Prepared unrecorded media for sound recording	4103.6	4988.5	5625.0	3.2	3.8	4.3	US$/unit	898

Graph 2: Trade Balance by MDG Regions in 2011

(Bln US$)

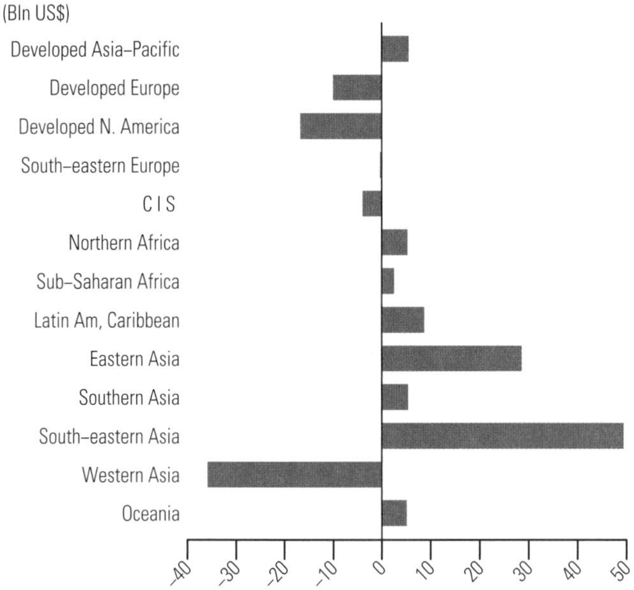

Graph 3: Partner concentration of trade in 2011

(Cumulative share by ranked partners)

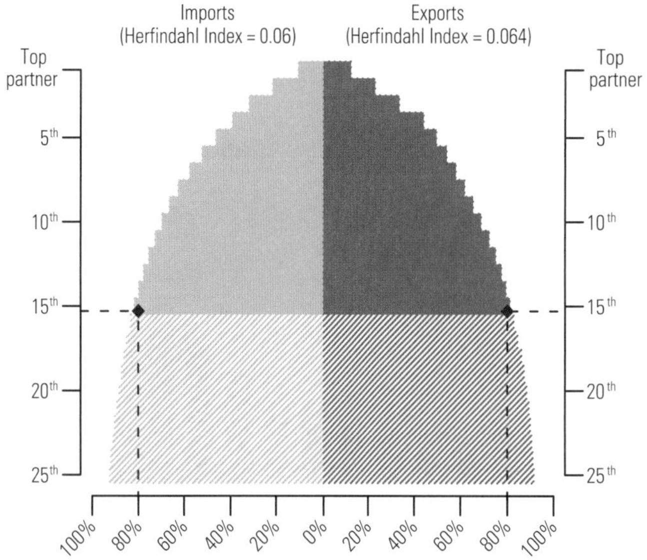

Table 4: Exports by principal countries and SITC sections in 2011

(Value in million US$, percentages of country total)

Country	Total	Shares by SITC sections (%)								
		0 + 1	2 + 4	3	5	6	7	8	9	Total
World	409503.6	2.0	0.7	19.8	12.6	3.8	45.8	7.0	8.3	100
Malaysia	49988.3	2.2	0.7	35.4	7.5	5.7	40.9	5.3	2.3	100
China, Hong Kong SAR	45168.7	0.8	0.3	18.7	2.9	1.7	63.5	4.8	7.3	100
Indonesia	42782.1	2.2	0.9	35.2	9.4	7.2	37.6	5.8	1.7	100
China	42682.0	1.8	1.0	18.0	17.8	3.8	48.9	7.1	1.5	100
USA	22359.5	0.9	0.4	2.1	13.7	1.6	64.6	14.8	1.9	100
Japan	18393.6	4.5	1.1	5.1	14.0	2.9	54.2	14.0	4.2	100
Australia	16026.9	2.8	0.4	52.5	8.5	3.4	22.1	6.6	3.8	100
Rep. of Korea	15480.4	1.1	0.7	5.5	14.2	2.6	66.6	6.1	3.2	100
Other Asia, nes	15034.8	2.3	0.3	4.9	10.4	3.3	71.6	4.8	2.4	100
India	14044.7	2.0	1.3	21.1	15.4	5.0	41.9	10.7	2.5	100

Imports Profile:

In 2011, machinery and transport equipment (SITC section 7) accounted for the largest share of imported products: 41.0 percent (see table 2). Mineral fuels, lubricants and related materials (SITC section 3), largely non crude petroleum oils, accounted for 32.6 percent of imports. From 2009 to 2011, top imported products were petroleum oils, other than crude (HS code 2710), electronic integrated circuits (HS code 8542), and petroleum oils and oils obtained from bituminous minerals, crude (HS code 2709) (see table 5).

Table 5: Top 10 import commodities 2009 to 2011

(Value in million US$)

HS code	4-digit heading of Harmonized System 2007	Value (million US$)			Unit value				SITC code
		2009	2010	2011	2009	2010	2011	Unit	
	All Commodities	245784.7	310791.1	365770.5					
2710	Petroleum oils, other than crude	38639.5	56950.2	80335.8	*0.4*		*0.8*	US$/kg	334
8542	Electronic integrated circuits	38014.3	52564.0	50716.7					776
2709	Petroleum oils and oils obtained from bituminous minerals, crude	20099.4	24067.4	33584.4	*0.5*	*0.6*	0.8	US$/kg	333
8517	Electrical apparatus for line telephony or line telegraphy	6433.7	7988.3	9882.3					764
8473	Parts and accessories for use with machines of heading 84.69 to 84.72	6879.8	7767.3	6805.0					759
9999	Commodities not specified according to kind	7231.9	8454.1	4255.9					931
8471	Automatic data processing machines and units thereof	4466.4	5808.5	6465.0	*64.6*	*80.2*	*84.2*	US$/unit	752
8431	Parts suitable for use principally with the machinery of headings 84.25	5049.8	5404.5	5179.0	*17.4*		*18.0*	US$/kg	723
8541	Diodes, transistors and similar semiconductor devices	3801.6	4984.4	5022.7					776
8411	Turbo-jets, turbo-propellers and other gas turbines	3565.5	4586.2	5378.5					714

Slovakia

Imports: CIF, by origin | **Exports: FOB, by last known destination** | **Trade System: Special**

Overview:

From 2007 to 2011, Slovakia's exports increased on average by 7.8 percent each year to 78.5 bln US$ (see table 1 and graph 1). During the same period, imports increased on average by 6.7 percent each year to reach 76.7 bln US$ (see table 2 and graph 1). The trade balance recorded a surplus of 1.8 bln US$ in 2011 (see graph 1). By MDG regions, trade recorded a surplus of 15.9 bln US$ with Developed Europe (see graph 1). However, large deficits were recorded with Eastern Asia (-8.5 bln US$) and the Commonwealth of Independent States (-5.8 bln US$). Both imports and exports were diversified across partners: in 2011, 12 (respectively 11) major partners accounted for 80 percent of exports (respectively imports) (see graph 3).

Graph 1: Total imports, exports and trade balance

(Bln US$ by year)

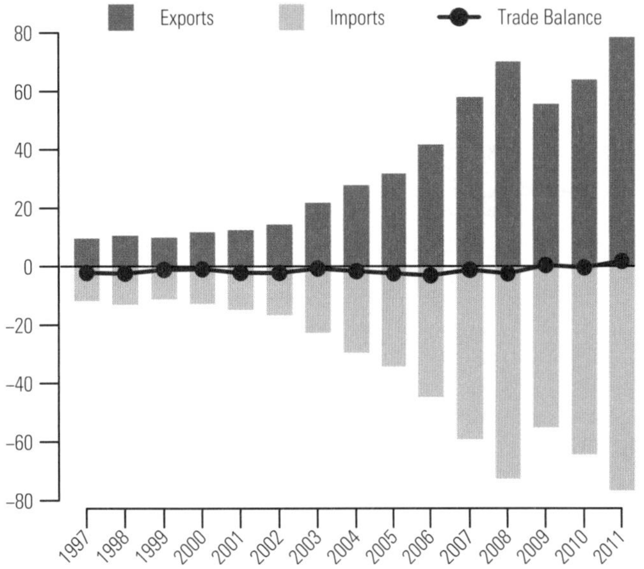

Exports Profile:

In 2011, machinery and transport equipment (SITC section 7) accounted for the majority of exported goods (53.2 percent) (see table 1). Other major commodity groups were manufactured goods classified chiefly by material (SITC section 6) and miscellaneous manufactured articles (SITC section 8) respectively with 18.6 and 9.8 percent of exports. Germany, Czech Republic and Poland were the top three markets for exports in 2011. From 2009 to 2011, main exported products were motor cars and other motor vehicles principally designed for the transport of persons (HS code 8703), reception apparatus for television (HS code 8528) and petroleum oils, other than crude (HS code 2710) (see table 3).

Table 1: Exports by SITC sections

(Value in million US$, growth and shares in percentage)

SITC	2011	Avg. Growth rates (%) 2007-2011	2010-2011	2011 share
Total	78 487.2	7.8	22.6	100.0
0+1	3 174.2	10.9	33.0	4.0
2+4	2 259.7	14.0	21.6	2.9
3	5 033.7	18.1	63.0	6.4
5	3 865.8	10.0	29.4	4.9
6	14 633.4	5.1	19.9	18.6
7	41 730.0	8.0	19.3	53.2
8	7 654.3	8.6	20.9	9.8
9	136.1	-41.6	-21.2	0.2

Table 2: Imports by SITC sections

(Value in million US$, growth and shares in percentage)

SITC	2011	Avg. Growth rates (%) 2007-2011	2010-2011	2011 share
Total	76 690.3	6.7	19.1	100.0
0+1	4 455.2	10.2	18.3	5.8
2+4	3 029.4	14.4	17.7	4.0
3	11 293.9	15.3	38.0	14.7
5	6 753.9	6.8	24.0	8.8
6	11 903.0	3.8	21.5	15.5
7	30 605.1	4.2	10.7	39.9
8	8 405.0	7.5	25.0	11.0
9	244.8	-4.6	-0.1	0.3

Table 3: Top 10 export commodities 2009 to 2011

(Value in million US$)

HS code	4-digit heading of Harmonized System 2007	Value (million US$) 2009	2010	2011	Unit value 2009	2010	2011	Unit	SITC code
	All Commodities	55 553.0	63 998.6	78 487.2					
8703	Motor cars and other motor vehicles principally designed for the transport	7 617.4	9 103.9	11 750.9		*18.4*		thsd US$/unit	781
8528	Reception apparatus for television	7 898.4	7 623.1	7 594.7	*360.8*			US$/unit	761
2710	Petroleum oils, other than crude	2 220.1	2 412.3	3 914.1	*0.6*	*0.7*	*1.0*	US$/kg	334
8708	Parts and accessories of the motor vehicles of headings 87.01 to 87.05	1 787.3	2 322.1	2 999.9	*8.3*	*8.0*	*8.9*	US$/kg	784
8544	Insulated (including enamelled or anodised) wire, cable	1 084.7	1 274.4	1 620.9		*3.1*	*7.8*	US$/kg	773
8707	Bodies (including cabs), for the motor vehicles of headings 87.01 to 87.05	1 116.7	1 131.3	1 483.1	*21.7*		*24.8*	thsd US$/unit	784
8517	Electrical apparatus for line telephony or line telegraphy	436.3	1 013.7	1 757.1					764
8529	Parts suitable for use with the apparatus of headings 85.25 to 85.28	1 093.9	1 207.7	897.1	*26.3*	*39.8*	*5.4*	US$/kg	764
7210	Flat-rolled products of iron or non-alloy steel	926.5	1 054.8	1 136.9	*1.0*	*1.0*	*1.2*	US$/kg	674
4011	New pneumatic tyres, of rubber	667.6	990.5	1 338.6	*87.7*		*90.7*	US$/unit	625

Graph 2: Trade Balance by MDG Regions in 2011

(Bln US$)

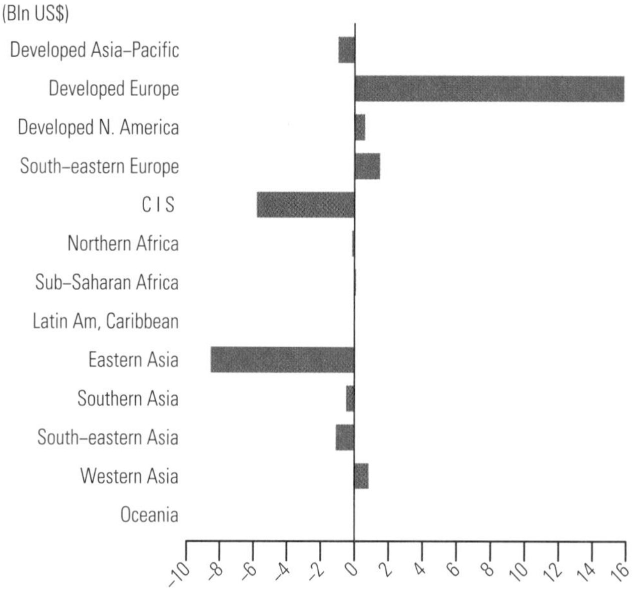

Graph 3: Partner concentration of trade in 2011

(Cumulative share by ranked partners)

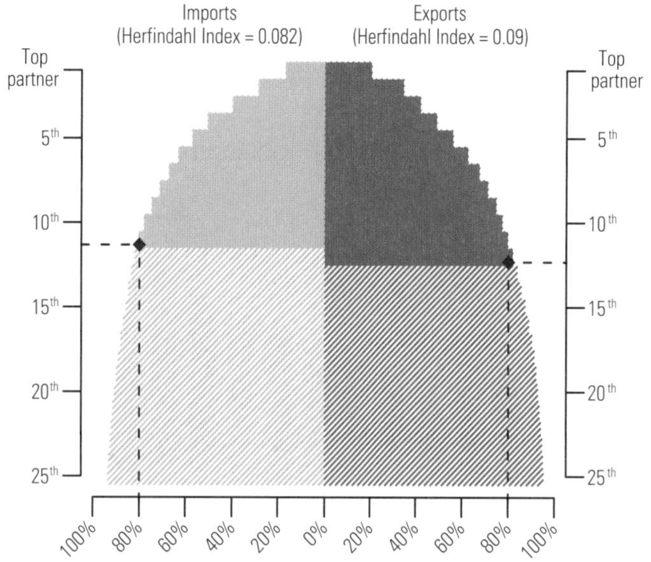

Table 4: Exports by principal countries and SITC sections in 2011

(Value in million US$, percentages of country total)

Country	Total	0 + 1	2 + 4	3	5	6	7	8	9	Total
		Shares by SITC sections (%)								
World	78487.2	4.0	2.9	6.4	4.9	18.6	53.2	9.8	0.2	100
Germany	15995.2	0.8	1.1	1.7	3.3	17.7	63.0	12.2	0.1	100
Czech Rep.	11127.2	6.7	4.5	13.4	8.1	27.0	30.0	9.6	0.6	100
Poland	5710.9	5.5	4.4	10.6	8.1	28.9	32.0	10.3	0.3	100
Hungary	5547.5	18.1	9.6	11.4	6.5	19.1	25.0	10.1	0.2	100
Austria	5504.7	4.6	4.5	25.2	3.0	22.0	32.3	8.1	0.1	100
France	5053.0	0.4	0.2	4.8	3.7	12.5	69.1	9.3	0.0	100
Italy	3893.5	4.1	4.3	3.3	6.8	22.4	49.7	9.2	0.1	100
Russian Federation	2881.5	0.9	0.5	0.0	4.3	6.6	80.6	7.0	0.0	100
United Kingdom	2838.4	1.9	0.7	2.2	1.3	8.5	73.6	11.6	0.1	100
China	2075.2	0.0	0.4	0.0	1.0	1.1	95.4	2.2	0.0	100

Imports Profile:

Slovakia's imports were composed of 39.9 percent of machinery and transport equipment (SITC section 7), 15.5 percent of manufactured goods classified chiefly by material (SITC section 6) and 14.7 percent of mineral fuels, lubricants and related materials (SITC section 3) (see table 2). Main imported products from 2009 to 2011 were parts and accessories of the motor vehicles of headings 87.01 to 87.05 (HS code 8708), parts suitable for use with the apparatus of headings 85.25 to 85.28 (HS code 8529) and petroleum oils and oils obtained from bituminous minerals, crude (HS code 2709) (see table 5).

Table 5: Top 10 import commodities 2009 to 2011

(Value in million US$)

HS code	4-digit heading of Harmonized System 2007	Value (million US$) 2009	2010	2011	Unit value 2009	2010	2011	Unit	SITC code
	All Commodities	55159.9	64382.0	76690.3					
8708	Parts and accessories of the motor vehicles of headings 87.01 to 87.05	3759.6	4791.3	6426.8	*3.8*	*4.6*	*5.8*	US$/kg	784
8529	Parts suitable for use with the apparatus of headings 85.25 to 85.28	3902.4	4364.6	2324.4	*26.8*	*44.2*	*17.1*	US$/kg	764
2709	Petroleum oils and oils obtained from bituminous minerals, crude	2397.8	3040.2	4652.7	*0.4*	*0.5*	*0.8*	US$/kg	333
2711	Petroleum gases and other gaseous hydrocarbons	2273.2	2793.0	3599.4	*0.5*	*0.5*	*0.6*	US$/kg	343
8703	Motor cars and other motor vehicles principally designed for the transport	1765.5	1677.9	1629.1		*17.2*		thsd US$/unit	781
3004	Medicaments (excluding goods of heading 30.02, 30.05 or 30.06)	1549.3	1430.0	1752.3	*3.6*	68.7	*120.3*	US$/kg	542
8528	Reception apparatus for television	1354.4	1548.0	1458.8	*221.9*			US$/unit	761
2710	Petroleum oils, other than crude	850.7	1208.5	1599.1	*0.9*	*1.1*	*1.5*	US$/kg	334
8544	Insulated (including enamelled or anodised) wire, cable	818.5	1071.4	1284.6		*8.8*	*10.5*	US$/kg	773
8517	Electrical apparatus for line telephony or line telegraphy	590.4	782.5	1184.3					764

Imports: CIF, by origin/consignment for intra-eu | **Exports: FOB, by last known destination** | **Trade System: Special**

Overview:

In 2011, the value of the exports of Slovenia increased by 17.9 percent to amount to 28.5 bln US$ (see table 1 and graph 1). Imports showed a similar development with an increase by 16.9 percent to 30.8 bln US$ in 2011 (see table 2 and graph 1). This resulted in a trade deficit of 2.3 bln US$ in 2011, slightly higher than the 2010 deficit of 2.2 bln US$ (see graph 1). This deficit came largely from trade with Eastern Asia (-1.7 bln US$) (see graph 2). Trade recorded surpluses with South-eastern Europe (+1.1 bln US$) and Commonwealth of Independent States (+0.6 bln US$). In 2011, Slovenia's trade was diversified across partners: 15 (respectively 18) major partners accounted for 80 percent of exports (respectively imports) (see graph 3).

Graph 1: Total imports, exports and trade balance

(Bln US$ by year)

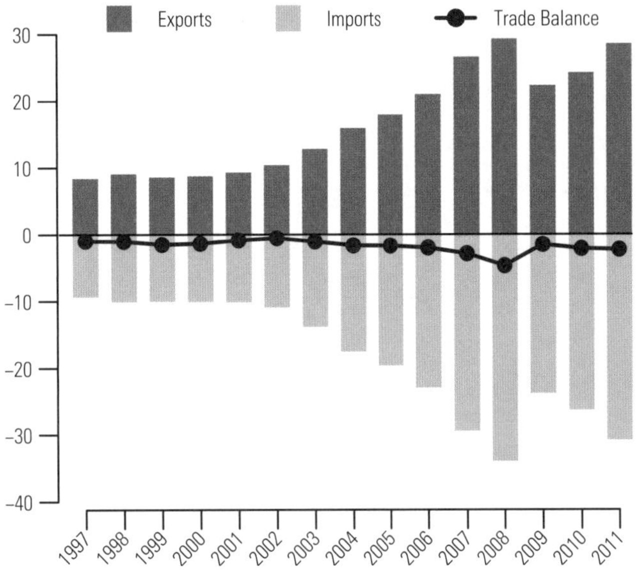

Table 1: Exports by SITC sections

(Value in million US$, growth and shares in percentage)

SITC	2011	Avg. Growth rates (%) 2007-2011	Avg. Growth rates (%) 2010-2011	2011 share
Total	28516.3	1.8	17.9	100.0
0+1	1038.8	5.5	17.3	3.6
2+4	1115.3	7.7	17.7	3.9
3	1782.1	36.5	72.9	6.2
5	4525.1	5.7	16.0	15.9
6	6503.4	-0.5	21.2	22.8
7	10512.9	-0.6	11.7	36.9
8	2961.3	-2.7	13.9	10.4
9	77.4	14.0	61.9	0.3

Table 2: Imports by SITC sections

(Value in million US$, growth and shares in percentage)

SITC	2011	Avg. Growth rates (%) 2007-2011	Avg. Growth rates (%) 2010-2011	2011 share
Total	30827.0	1.1	16.9	100.0
0+1	2252.8	5.3	17.3	7.3
2+4	1862.2	1.8	7.1	6.0
3	4854.7	15.0	42.2	15.7
5	4119.1	3.8	14.6	13.4
6	5904.8	-2.9	16.3	19.2
7	8735.8	-3.7	10.2	28.3
8	2911.5	1.5	12.8	9.4
9	186.1	25.8	68.2	0.6

Exports Profile:

In 2011, exports of machinery and transport equipment (SITC section 7) increased by 11.7 percent and accounted for 36.9 percent of Slovenia's exports (see table 1). Other major commodity groups for exports were manufactured goods classified chiefly by material (SITC section 6) and chemicals and related products, n.e.s. (SITC section 5), respectively with 22.8 and 15.9 percent of exports. Germany, Italy and Austria were the top three markets for exported goods (see table 4). Nearly half (49.0 percent) of exports to Germany and a majority of exports to France (75.0 percent) were machinery and transport equipment (SITC section 7). Over the last three years, motor cars and other motor vehicles principally designed for the transport of persons (HS code 8703), medicaments (excluding goods of heading 30.02, 30.05 or 30.06) (HS code 3004) and parts and accessories of the motor vehicles of headings 87.01 to 87.05 (HS code 8708) were the top commodities for exports (see table 3).

Table 3: Top 10 export commodities 2009 to 2011

(Value in million US$)

HS code	4-digit heading of Harmonized System 2007	Value (million US$) 2009	Value (million US$) 2010	Value (million US$) 2011	Unit value 2009	Unit value 2010	Unit value 2011	Unit	SITC code
	All Commodities	22294.0	24188.0	28516.3					
8703	Motor cars and other motor vehicles principally designed for the transport	2634.1	2514.0	2498.4	9.7	9.8	10.7	thsd US$/unit	781
3004	Medicaments (excluding goods of heading 30.02, 30.05 or 30.06)	1927.1	1953.9	2208.0	27.8	80.2	96.7	US$/kg	542
8708	Parts and accessories of the motor vehicles of headings 87.01 to 87.05	524.3	596.9	723.8	7.6	7.2	7.9	US$/kg	784
2716	Electrical energy	387.7	530.1	892.2	60.1	60.8	72.7	US$/MWh	351
2710	Petroleum oils, other than crude	314.0	487.6	873.9	0.7	0.8	1.1	US$/kg	334
8516	Electric instantaneous or storage water heaters and immersion heaters	440.0	466.1	491.8					775
8414	Air or vacuum pumps, air or other gas compressors and fans	402.2	477.1	476.0					743
4011	New pneumatic tyres, of rubber	369.3	423.7	471.8	43.4	45.1	57.5	US$/unit	625
9401	Seats (other than those of heading 94.02)	381.7	382.8	453.8					821
8512	Electrical lighting or signalling equipment	283.4	400.5	523.8					778

Graph 2: Trade Balance by MDG Regions in 2011

(Bln US$)

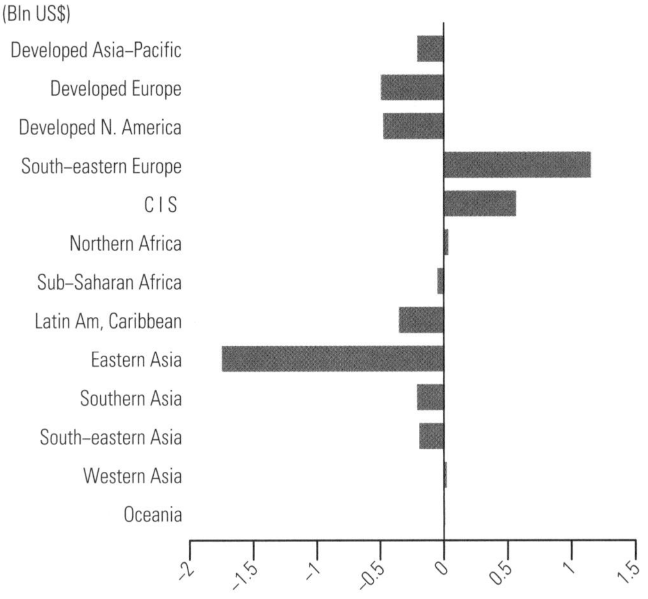

Graph 3: Partner concentration of trade in 2011

(Cumulative share by ranked partners)

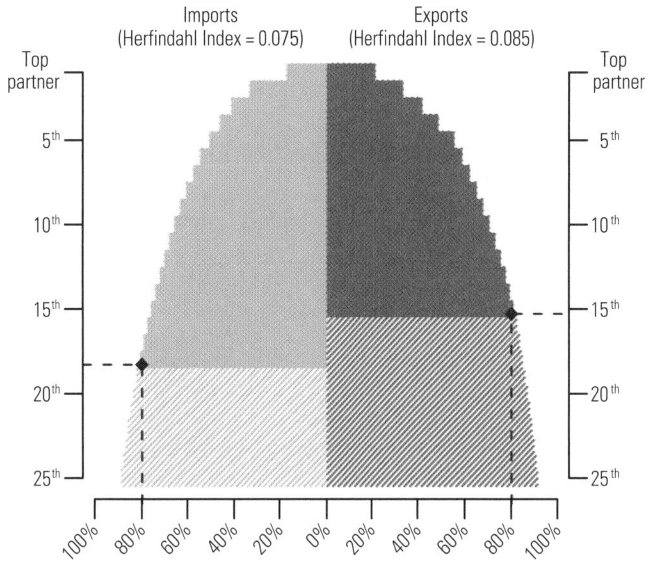

Table 4: Exports by principal countries and SITC sections in 2011

(Value in million US$, percentages of country total)

Country	Total	Shares by SITC sections (%)								
		0 + 1	2 + 4	3	5	6	7	8	9	Total
World	28516.3	3.6	3.9	6.2	15.9	22.8	36.9	10.4	0.3	100
Germany	6110.4	0.6	1.7	1.4	7.5	28.4	49.0	11.2	0.1	100
Italy	3444.3	7.6	14.9	10.0	9.7	27.8	20.5	8.9	0.5	100
Austria	2371.1	4.8	6.8	16.6	8.8	21.8	27.2	13.8	0.2	100
France	1946.6	0.8	0.2	0.1	6.1	13.9	75.0	4.0	...	100
Croatia	1917.8	4.8	1.7	27.0	17.6	18.5	17.6	12.7	0.0	100
Serbia	952.1	7.1	1.2	2.2	27.9	22.6	27.6	11.0	0.4	100
Poland	899.3	0.9	1.1	0.2	35.8	25.4	28.7	7.8	0.1	100
Hungary	863.0	11.4	2.5	5.5	20.7	19.7	33.2	7.0	0.1	100
Bosnia Herzegovina	783.4	11.3	2.0	10.2	19.1	23.6	25.0	8.8	0.0	100
Russian Federation	755.8	3.8	0.4	0.0	46.9	13.7	29.7	5.1	0.3	100

Imports Profile:

Similar to exports, machinery and transport equipment (SITC section 7), manufactured goods classified chiefly by material (SITC section 6) and mineral fuels, lubricants and related materials (SITC section 3) were the three largest commodity groups for imports in 2011 (see table 2). They accounted respectively for 28.3, 19.2 and 15.7 percent of imports. Over the last three years, petroleum oils, other than crude (HS code 2710), motor cars and other motor vehicles principally designed for the transport of persons (HS code 8703) and parts and accessories of the motor vehicles of headings 87.01 to 87.05 (HS code 8708) were the main products for imports (see table 5).

Table 5: Top 10 import commodities 2009 to 2011

(Value in million US$)

HS code	4-digit heading of Harmonized System 2007	Value (million US$)			Unit value				SITC code
		2009	2010	2011	2009	2010	2011	Unit	
	All Commodities	23844.3	26360.4	30827.0					
2710	Petroleum oils, other than crude	1815.1	2325.1	3424.7	0.6	0.7	*1.0*	US$/kg	334
8703	Motor cars and other motor vehicles principally designed for the transport	1160.7	1281.2	1463.6	13.5	13.2	15.3	thsd US$/unit	781
8708	Parts and accessories of the motor vehicles of headings 87.01 to 87.05	890.3	905.2	868.9	7.3	7.2	7.8	US$/kg	784
3004	Medicaments (excluding goods of heading 30.02, 30.05 or 30.06)	743.0	755.7	812.5	77.8	75.3	84.5	US$/kg	542
2711	Petroleum gases and other gaseous hydrocarbons	425.2	517.6	575.7	0.5	0.6	0.7	US$/kg	343
2716	Electrical energy	282.8	408.7	663.5	76.7	67.1	72.8	US$/MWh	351
8544	Insulated (including enamelled or anodised) wire, cable	250.4	313.1	365.9	7.1	8.0	*9.3*	US$/kg	773
7601	Unwrought aluminium	178.5	338.5	337.4	1.9	2.4	2.7	US$/kg	684
7204	Ferrous waste and scrap; remelting scrap ingots of iron or steel	140.9	308.4	385.0	0.5	0.6	0.7	US$/kg	282
8517	Electrical apparatus for line telephony or line telegraphy	223.8	251.6	326.4					764

Solomon Islands

Imports: CIF, by origin **Exports: FOB, by last known destination** **Trade System: Special**

Overview:

From 2003 to 2007, exports of Solomon Islands increased on average by 24.2 percent each year and amounted to 158.5 mln US$ in 2007(see table 1 and graph 1). During the same period, imports increased on average by 32.0 percent each year to reach 285.0 mln US$ (see table 2 and graph 1). The trade balance recorded a deficit of 126.5 mln US$ compared to 27.2 mln US$ in 2003. Large deficits were recorded with Developed Asia-Pacific (-115.1 mln US$), South-eastern Asia (-71.3 mln US$) and Oceania (-18.0 mln US$) (see graph 2). However, trade recorded a surplus amounting to 64.1 mln US$ with Eastern Asia. Trade was concentrated among a few partners: in 2007, 7 (respectively 6) major partners accounted for 80 percent of exports (respectively imports) (see graph 3).

Graph 1: Total imports, exports and trade balance

(Mln US$ by year)

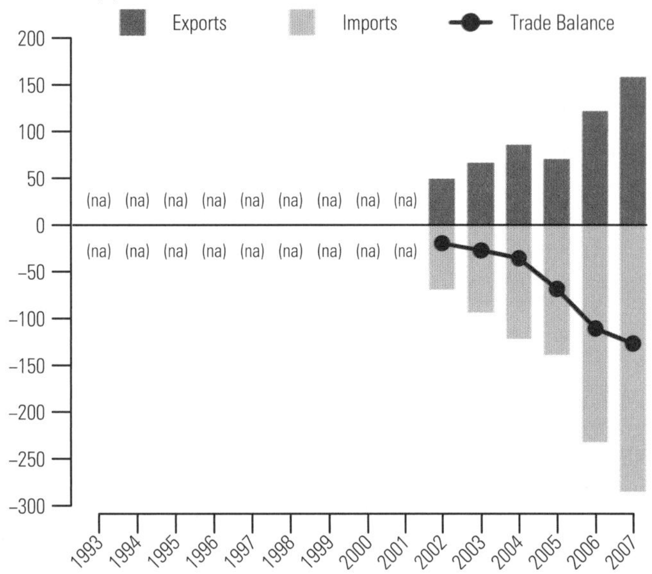

Table 1: Exports by SITC sections

(Value in million US$, growth and shares in percentage)

SITC	2007	Avg. Growth rates (%) 2003-2007	Avg. Growth rates (%) 2006-2007	2007 share
Total	158.5	24.2	30.3	100.0
0+1	29.1	39.7	62.3	18.3
2+4	127.4	37.5	44.7	80.4
5	0.0	9.3	5192.9	0.0
6	0.2	35.3	334.1	0.1
7	0.2	-19.7	-85.1	0.1
8	0.0	-7.8	96.8	0.0
9	1.5	-49.4	-89.4	0.9

Table 2: Imports by SITC sections

(Value in million US$, growth and shares in percentage)

SITC	2007	Avg. Growth rates (%) 2003-2007	Avg. Growth rates (%) 2006-2007	2007 share
Total	285.0	32.0	22.7	100.0
0+1	55.8	26.3	5.3	19.6
2+4	3.1	28.4	-13.2	1.1
3	71.7	45.5	169.4	25.2
5	16.4	32.0	-1.9	5.8
6	37.2	35.6	16.8	13.0
7	81.3	46.1	9.0	28.5
8	19.3	36.5	-23.3	6.8
9	0.2	-64.4	-70.1	0.1

Exports Profile:

In 2007, exports of inedible crude materials (except fuels), animal and vegetable oils, fats and waxes (SITC sections 2+4) and food, live animals, beverages and tobacco (SITC sections 0+1) increased respectively by 44.7 and 62.3 percent accounting largely for the increase in total exports by 30.3 percent (see table 1). They accounted respectively for 80.4 and 18.3 percent of exported goods. China, Thailand and Philippines were the three major partners for exports (see table 4). Top exported products from 2005 to 2007 included wood in the rough, whether or not stripped of bark or sapwood (HS code 4403), fish,dried,salted or in brine (HS code 0305) and palm oil and its fractions (HS code 1511) (see table 3).

Table 3: Top 10 export commodities 2005 to 2007

(Value in million US$)

HS code	4-digit heading of Harmonized System 2002	Value (million US$) 2005	2006	2007	Unit value 2005	2006	2007	Unit	SITC code
	All Commodities	70.4	121.6	158.5					
4403	Wood in the rough, whether or not stripped of bark or sapwood	55.5	78.9	100.3					247
0305	Fish, dried, salted or in brine	0.1	8.3	8.2					035
1511	Palm oil and its fractions	...	2.0	14.0					422
0302	Fish, fresh or chilled, excluding fish fillets	0.5	4.3	10.8					034
1801	Cocoa beans, whole or broken, raw or roasted	4.8	4.1	6.0					072
9999	Commodities not specified according to kind	0.0	13.4	0.0					931
1203	Copra	3.2	2.6	6.5					223
4407	Wood sawn or chipped lengthwise, sliced or peeled	1.8	3.2	5.3					248
1604	Prepared or preserved fish; caviar	0.8	0.8	1.6					037
7108	Gold (including gold plated with platinum)	0.8	0.7	1.5					971

Graph 2: Trade Balance by MDG Regions in 2007

(Mln US$)

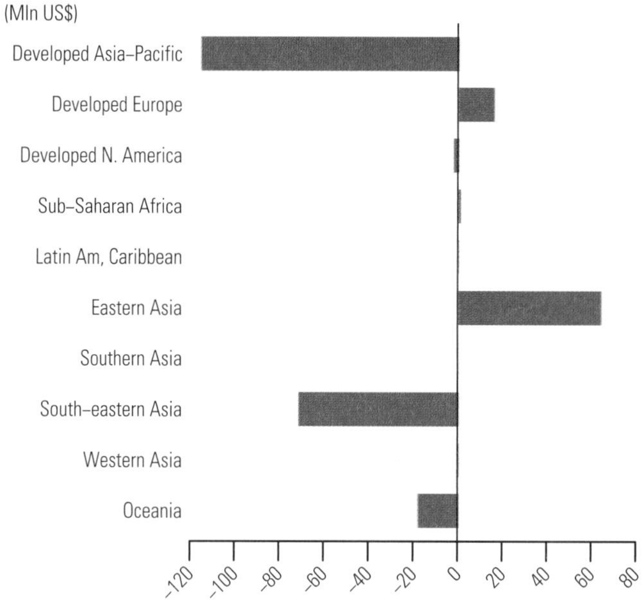

Graph 3: Partner concentration of trade in 2007

(Cumulative share by ranked partners)

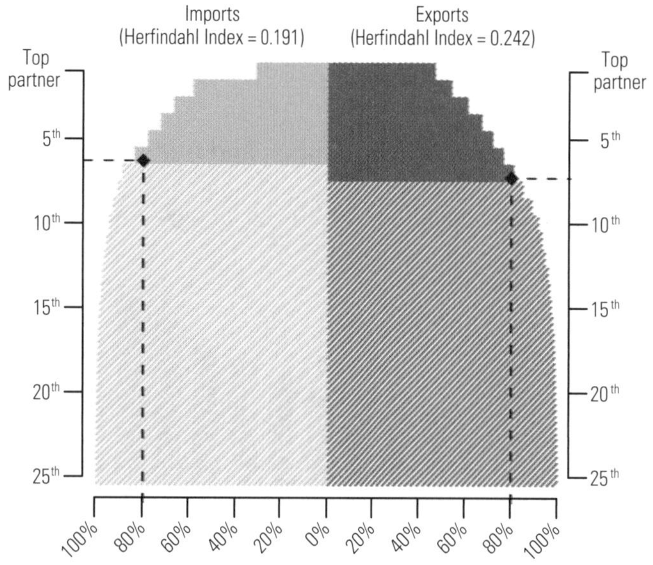

Table 4: Exports by principal countries and SITC sections in 2007

(Value in million US$, percentages of country total)

Country	Total	Shares by SITC sections (%)								
		0 + 1	2 + 4	3	5	6	7	8	9	Total
World	158.5	18.3	80.4	...	0.0	0.1	0.1	0.0	0.9	100
China	73.8	0.0	99.9	...	...	0.0	0.0	...	...	100
Thailand	11.4	83.3	16.7	...	...	...	...	...	...	100
Philippines	11.2	0.0	99.8	...	...	0.2	...	...	...	100
Dem. People's Rep. of Korea	9.6	0.6	99.4	...	...	...	0.0	...	...	100
Japan	7.6	10.6	89.4	...	...	...	0.0	...	...	100
Italy	7.4	99.7	0.3	...	...	...	...	...	...	100
Singapore	6.9	77.8	22.2	...	...	...	...	...	...	100
Spain	6.4	0.0	100.0	...	...	...	...	...	...	100
United Kingdom	6.1	0.0	100.0	...	...	...	...	...	...	100
Australia	4.6	10.0	57.4	...	...	0.1	1.8	0.3	30.5	100

Imports Profile:

In 2007, imports were composed of 28.5 percent of machinery and transport equipment (SITC section 7), 25.2 percent of mineral fuels, lubricants and related materials (SITC section 3) and 19.6 percent of food, live animals, beverages and tobacco (SITC sections 0+1) (see table 2). From 2005 to 2007, top imported products were petroleum oils, other than crude (HS code 2710), rice (HS code 1006) and self-propelled bulldozers, angledozers, graders, levellers, scrapers (HS code 8429) (see table 5).

Table 5: Top 10 import commodities 2005 to 2007

(Value in million US$)

HS code	4-digit heading of Harmonized System 2002	Value (million US$)			Unit value				SITC code
		2005	2006	2007	2005	2006	2007	Unit	
	All Commodities	138.8	232.3	285.0					
2710	Petroleum oils, other than crude	3.6	24.9	70.0					334
1006	Rice	17.8	19.8	22.0					042
8429	Self-propelled bulldozers, angledozers, graders, levellers, scrapers	5.3	6.0	8.6					723
8704	Motor vehicles for the transport of goods	1.3	6.5	7.2					782
8431	Parts suitable for use principally with the machinery of headings 84.25	3.0	5.4	4.4					723
8703	Motor cars and other motor vehicles principally designed for the transport	2.4	3.8	5.3					781
4901	Printed books, brochures, leaflets and similar printed matter	1.2	7.9	2.0					892
1001	Wheat and meslin	2.2	3.1	3.8					041
1701	Cane or beet sugar and pure sucrose, in solid form	2.0	2.9	2.5					061
1902	Pasta, whether or not cooked or stuffed	1.9	2.8	2.6					048

South Africa

Imports: FOB, by origin | **Exports: FOB, by last known destination** | **Trade System: General**

Overview:

From 2007 to 2011, South Africa's exports increased on average by 9.8 percent each year and amounted to 93.0 bln US$ in 2011 (see table 1 and graph 1). Imports increased on average by 5.7 percent each year and reached 99.7 bln US$ (see table 2 and graph 1). This resulted in a trade deficit of 6.8 bln US$ in 2011 (see graph 1). The trade balance recorded deficits with MDG regions such as Developed Europe (-8.1 bln US$), Western Asia (-5.0 bln US$), Southern Asia (-4.3 bln US$) and South-eastern Asia (-3.5 bln US$) (see graph 2). Large surpluses were recorded with Sub-Saharan Africa (+6.7 bln US$), Developed Asia-Pacific (+2.1 bln US$) and Northern Africa (+0.4 bln US$). South Africa's trade was diversified across partners: in 2011, 22 major partners accounted for 80 percent of both exports and imports (see graph 3).

Graph 1: Total imports, exports and trade balance

(Bln US$ by year)

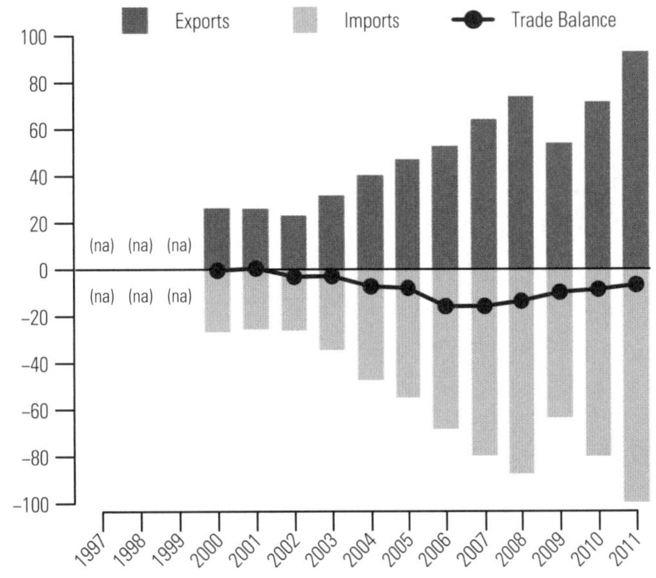

Exports Profile:

In 2011, manufactured goods classified chiefly by material (SITC section 6) and inedible crude materials (except fuels), animal and vegetable oils, fats and waxes (SITC sections 2+4) accounted for respectively 29.0 and 20.0 percent of total exports (see table 1). Machinery and transport equipment (SITC section 7) accounted for 17.1 percent of exports. Major markets for exports were China, USA and Japan (see table 4). More than two-thirds (72.3 percent) of exports to China were inedible crude materials (except fuels), animal and vegetable oils, fats and waxes (SITC sections 2+4). Over the last three years, South Africa's main commodities for exports were platinum, unwrought or in semi-manufactured forms, or in powder form (HS code 7110), iron ores and concentrates, including roasted iron pyrites (HS code 2601), and coal; briquettes, ovoids and similar solid fuels manufactured from coal (HS code 2701) (see table 3).

Table 1: Exports by SITC sections

(Value in million US$, growth and shares in percentage)

SITC	2011	Avg. Growth rates (%) 2007-2011	Avg. Growth rates (%) 2010-2011	2011 share
Total	92975.6	9.8	30.1	100.0
0+1	6578.1	12.1	10.1	7.1
2+4	18548.8	26.8	40.2	20.0
3	9705.6	9.5	34.8	10.4
5	6145.2	9.1	21.0	6.6
6	26936.3	0.8	9.6	29.0
7	15931.0	4.4	18.4	17.1
8	1791.7	2.4	5.4	1.9
9	7339.0	101.8	2650.1	7.9

Table 2: Imports by SITC sections

(Value in million US$, growth and shares in percentage)

SITC	2011	Avg. Growth rates (%) 2007-2011	Avg. Growth rates (%) 2010-2011	2011 share
Total	99726.0	5.7	24.4	100.0
0+1	4917.8	9.9	29.9	4.9
2+4	3372.4	1.2	34.4	3.4
3	21237.9	9.4	35.1	21.3
5	10260.7	9.4	18.4	10.3
6	10485.1	3.2	20.7	10.5
7	35108.5	4.2	23.6	35.2
8	8252.8	6.5	15.9	8.3
9	6090.7	1.1	16.0	6.1

Table 3: Top 10 export commodities 2009 to 2011

(Value in million US$)

HS code	4-digit heading of Harmonized System 2007	Value (million US$) 2009	Value (million US$) 2010	Value (million US$) 2011	Unit value 2009	Unit value 2010	Unit value 2011	Unit	SITC code
	All Commodities	53863.9	71484.3	92975.6					
7110	Platinum, unwrought or in semi-manufactured forms, or in powder form	6766.6	9377.1	10990.5	*16.6*	*25.5*	37.1	thsd US$/kg	681
2601	Iron ores and concentrates, including roasted iron pyrites	3135.3	5408.4	9001.8	0.1	0.1	0.2	US$/kg	281
2701	Coal; briquettes, ovoids and similar solid fuels manufactured from coal	4204.2	5468.6	7523.8	0.1	*0.1*	0.1	US$/kg	321
7202	Ferro-alloys	2657.2	4670.8	4652.5	0.8	*1.1*	1.1	US$/kg	671
8703	Motor cars and other motor vehicles principally designed for the transport	3062.5	4116.9	4284.6	19.7	19.9	20.5	thsd US$/unit	781
7108	Gold (including gold plated with platinum)	...	...	6936.8			96.4	thsd US$/kg	971
8421	Centrifuges, including centrifugal dryers	1639.1	2185.1	2846.1					743
7102	Diamonds, whether or not worked, but not mounted or set	1304.2	1952.1	2249.1	123.6	186.5	286.3	US$/carat	667
2710	Petroleum oils, other than crude	1115.4	1209.2	1430.7	*0.5*	*0.6*	0.7	US$/kg	334
8704	Motor vehicles for the transport of goods	853.6	1169.2	1701.1	6.2	10.2	9.4	thsd US$/unit	782

Graph 2: Trade Balance by MDG Regions in 2011

(Bln US$)

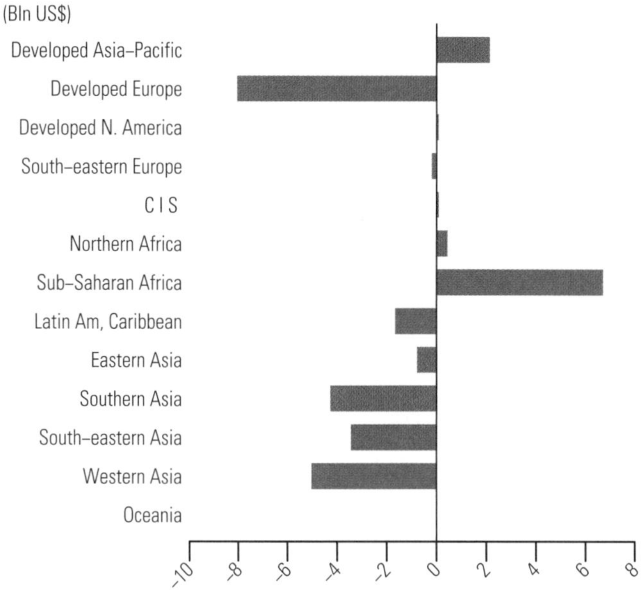

Graph 3: Partner concentration of trade in 2011

(Cumulative share by ranked partners)

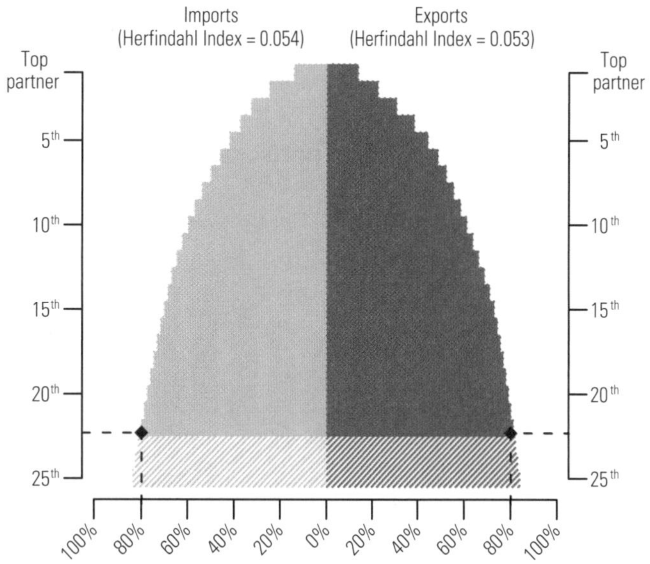

Table 4: Exports by principal countries and SITC sections in 2011

(Value in million US$, percentages of country total)

Country	Total	Shares by SITC sections (%)								
		0 + 1	2 + 4	3	5	6	7	8	9	Total
World	92975.6	7.1	20.0	10.4	6.6	29.0	17.1	1.9	7.9	100
China	12425.3	0.8	72.3	10.6	2.1	13.5	0.7	0.1	...	100
USA	8356.6	2.3	5.4	2.7	12.0	39.9	35.8	1.7	0.1	100
Japan	7663.0	2.4	19.9	1.0	3.0	67.0	6.6	0.0	0.0	100
Areas, nes	7133.6	0.0	0.0	2.8	0.0	0.0	0.0	0.0	97.2	100
Germany	5488.0	4.5	9.9	3.1	2.5	26.0	48.2	5.7	0.2	100
United Kingdom	3990.6	14.5	8.5	2.2	2.8	53.7	15.1	2.2	0.9	100
India	3372.8	0.2	19.5	54.6	10.9	9.2	5.1	0.3	0.1	100
Netherlands	2943.3	23.0	29.1	11.7	6.2	19.5	9.9	0.5	0.1	100
Switzerland	2777.9	1.1	0.4	0.0	0.1	97.0	1.0	0.3	0.0	100
Zimbabwe	2448.1	15.5	7.7	7.3	18.5	18.1	26.8	5.9	0.1	100

Imports Profile:

In 2011, imports of machinery and transport equipment (SITC section 7) went up by 23.6 percent and accounted for 35.2 percent of imported goods (see table 2). Imports of mineral fuels, lubricants and related materials (SITC section 3) increased by 35.1 percent and represented 21.3 percent of imports. Over the last three years, top products for imports were petroleum oils and oils obtained from bituminous minerals, crude (HS code 2709), petroleum oils, other than crude (HS code 2710) and motor cars and other motor vehicles principally designed for the transport (HS code 8703) (see table 5).

Table 5: Top 10 import commodities 2009 to 2011

(Value in million US$)

HS code	4-digit heading of Harmonized System 2007	Value (million US$)			Unit value				SITC code
		2009	2010	2011	2009	2010	2011	Unit	
	All Commodities	63766.1	80139.3	99726.0					
2709	Petroleum oils and oils obtained from bituminous minerals, crude	10294.4	11199.5	14085.6	0.4	0.6	0.8	US$/kg	333
9999	Commodities not specified according to kind	3512.5	5241.6	6078.7					931
2710	Petroleum oils, other than crude	2462.6	3364.0	5737.8	0.6	0.8	1.0	US$/kg	334
8703	Motor cars and other motor vehicles principally designed for the transport	2335.8	4067.2	5078.5	14.2	15.3	16.3	thsd US$/unit	781
8517	Electrical apparatus for line telephony or line telegraphy	2159.9	3000.9	3377.3					764
8471	Automatic data processing machines and units thereof	1197.2	1623.9	1941.8	*152.0*	*173.5*	189.8	US$/unit	752
3004	Medicaments (excluding goods of heading 30.02, 30.05 or 30.06)	1221.9	1588.1	1726.7	*54.6*	*58.1*	51.4	US$/kg	542
8708	Parts and accessories of the motor vehicles of headings 87.01 to 87.05	951.1	1192.6	1375.1	*4.0*	*9.3*	9.7	US$/kg	784
8443	Printing machinery used for printing by means of the printing type, blocks	746.1	977.4	1079.0					726
8802	Other aircraft (for example, helicopters, aeroplanes); spacecraft	627.4	702.2	1308.4	0.0	1.5	3.7	mln US$/unit	792

Source: UN Comtrade

Spain

Imports: CIF, by origin/consignment for intra-eu | Exports: FOB, by last known destination | Trade System: Special

Overview:

From 2006 to 2010, the value of exports of Spain increased on average by 3.6 percent each year despite a drop of 20.1 percent in 2009 and amounted to 246.3 bln US$ (see table 1 and graph 1). Imports, on the other hand, decreased on average by 1.1 percent each year and amounted to 315.5 bln US$ (see table 2 and graph 1). The trade balance in 2010 recorded a deficits of 69.3 bln US$ (see graph 1). By MDG regions, large deficits were recorded with Eastern Asia (-23.5 bln US$), Sub-Saharan Africa (-8.1 bln US$) and Southern Asia (-6.9 bln US$) (see graph 2). Spain's trade was well diversified across partners: in 2010, 21 (respectively 25) major partners accounted for 80 percent of exports (respectively imports) (see graph 3).

Graph 1: Total imports, exports and trade balance

(Bln US$ by year)

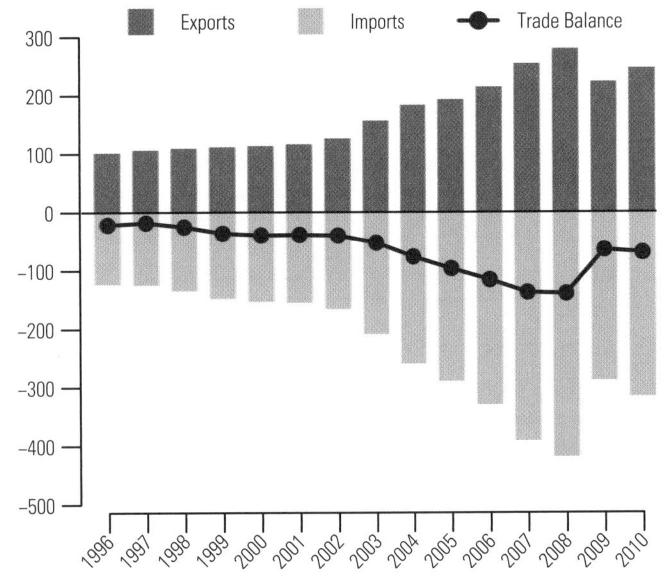

Exports Profile:

In 2010, Spain's exports were composed of 33.8 percent of machinery and transport equipment (SITC section 7), 17.1 percent of manufactured goods classified chiefly by material (SITC section 6) and 14.4 percent of chemicals and related products, n.e.s. (SITC section 5) (see table 1). The three largest markets for exported products were France, Germany and Portugal (see table 4). From 2008 to 2010, main exported products were motor cars and other motor vehicles principally designed for the transport (HS code 8703), petroleum oils, other than crude (HS code 2710) and parts and accessories of the motor vehicles of headings 87.01 to 87.05 (HS code 8708) (see table 3).

Table 1: Exports by SITC sections

(Value in million US$, growth and shares in percentage)

SITC	2010	Avg. Growth rates (%) 2006-2010	2009-2010	2010 share
Total	246 265.3	3.6	10.4	100.0
0+1	33 656.6	6.4	2.8	13.7
2+4	9 429.6	7.1	25.8	3.8
3	12 507.7	6.1	23.4	5.1
5	35 457.6	8.5	18.0	14.4
6	42 083.2	2.6	16.0	17.1
7	83 165.2	-0.5	5.8	33.8
8	21 741.9	4.0	0.9	8.8
9	8 223.5	20.4	30.6	3.3

Table 2: Imports by SITC sections

(Value in million US$, growth and shares in percentage)

SITC	2010	Avg. Growth rates (%) 2006-2010	2009-2010	2010 share
Total	315 547.2	-1.1	9.8	100.0
0+1	29 679.4	3.7	1.6	9.4
2+4	15 752.4	1.8	30.5	5.0
3	58 231.6	3.0	23.0	18.5
5	44 485.6	5.1	3.9	14.1
6	35 192.8	-5.0	10.1	11.2
7	91 079.2	-6.9	6.2	28.9
8	39 551.7	2.8	6.1	12.5
9	1 574.5	-3.7	51.7	0.5

Table 3: Top 10 export commodities 2008 to 2010

(Value in million US$)

HS code	4-digit heading of Harmonized System 2007	Value (million US$) 2008	2009	2010	Unit value 2008	2009	2010	Unit	SITC code
	All Commodities	279 231.5	223 132.2	246 265.3					
8703	Motor cars and other motor vehicles principally designed for the transport	30 146.6	26 087.2	26 011.2	13.4	13.5	*13.3*	thsd US$/unit	781
2710	Petroleum oils, other than crude	14 901.9	8 134.1	10 119.0	0.9	0.6	0.7	US$/kg	334
8708	Parts and accessories of the motor vehicles of headings 87.01 to 87.05	12 500.3	9 015.6	10 260.3	*7.1*	6.5	5.8	US$/kg	784
3004	Medicaments (excluding goods of heading 30.02, 30.05 or 30.06)	9 163.6	8 817.4	9 506.6	*69.7*	64.8	63.2	US$/kg	542
9999	Commodities not specified according to kind	6 396.7	5 774.4	6 763.6					931
8704	Motor vehicles for the transport of goods	7 455.8	3 475.0	4 798.5	13.7	16.7	*18.2*	thsd US$/unit	782
0805	Citrus fruit, fresh or dried	3 571.8	3 449.7	3 386.7	1.1	1.0	1.0	US$/kg	057
2204	Wine of fresh grapes, including fortified wines	2 886.8	2 645.7	2 495.2	*1.2*	1.8		US$/litre	112
6908	Glazed ceramic flags and paving, hearth or wall tiles	3 108.9	2 225.5	2 202.2	*10.4*	*8.6*	*8.8*	US$/m^2	662
1509	Olive oil and its fractions	2 706.2	2 152.2	2 466.0	*4.1*	3.3	2.9	US$/kg	421

Graph 2: Trade Balance by MDG Regions in 2010

(Bln US$)

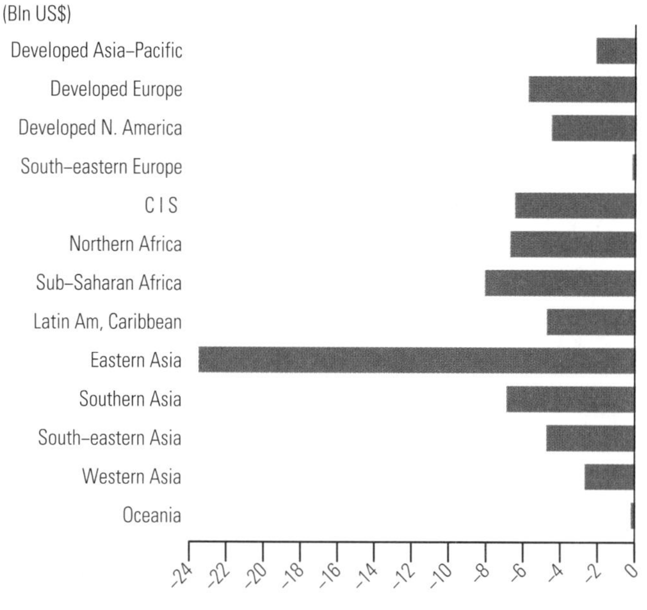

Graph 3: Partner concentration of trade in 2010

(Cumulative share by ranked partners)

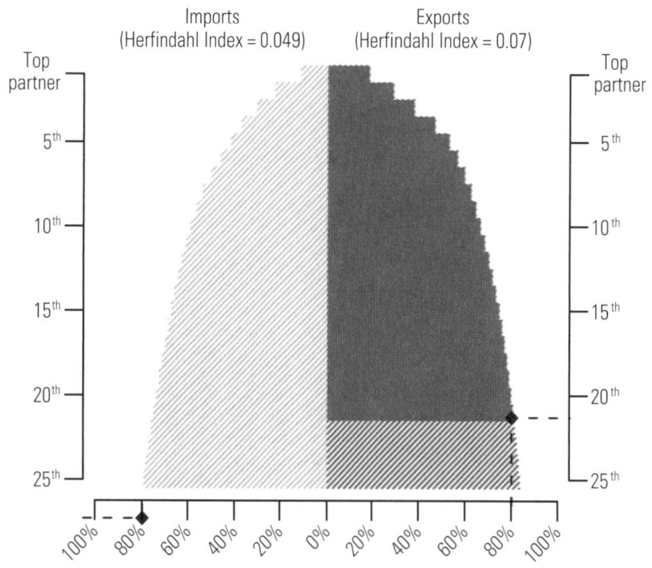

Table 4: Exports by principal countries and SITC sections in 2010

(Value in million US$, percentages of country total)

Country	Total	Shares by SITC sections (%) 0 + 1	2 + 4	3	5	6	7	8	9	Total
World	246265.3	13.7	3.8	5.1	14.4	17.1	33.8	8.8	3.3	100
France	45008.1	14.7	2.2	1.8	10.4	17.1	44.0	9.1	0.7	100
Germany	25784.5	17.0	2.1	0.8	13.7	17.1	42.7	6.0	0.5	100
Portugal	21973.5	17.6	4.1	4.5	11.8	22.6	23.1	14.5	1.8	100
Italy	21600.3	14.6	8.0	1.5	17.1	16.6	31.3	8.8	2.2	100
United Kingdom	15238.3	19.5	2.1	1.9	13.7	14.1	39.4	7.0	2.3	100
USA	8665.4	11.2	4.0	15.1	18.3	16.6	25.6	8.0	1.2	100
Netherlands	7698.0	21.3	5.6	10.3	21.8	11.6	22.7	5.9	1.0	100
Belgium	6921.5	13.9	2.4	4.6	17.3	14.6	35.2	9.8	2.2	100
Bunkers	5160.5	0.2	0.0	24.8	0.2	0.5	0.8	0.2	73.3	100
Turkey	4974.2	1.4	2.1	2.8	17.5	19.4	46.3	7.1	3.4	100

Imports Profile:

Machinery and transport equipment (SITC section 7) also accounted for a large share of imported goods (28.9 percent) (see table 1). Other major commodity groups for imports included mineral fuels, lubricants and related materials (SITC section 3) and chemicals and related products, n.e.s. (SITC section 5) respectively with 18.5 and 14.1 percent of imports. From 2008 to 2010, main imported goods included petroleum oils and oils obtained from bituminous minerals, crude (HS code 2709), motor cars and other motor vehicles principally designed for the transport (HS code 8703) and parts and accessories of the motor vehicles of headings 87.01 to 87.05 (HS code 8708) (see table 5).

Table 5: Top 10 import commodities 2008 to 2010

(Value in million US$)

HS code	4-digit heading of Harmonized System 2007	Value (million US$) 2008	2009	2010	Unit value 2008	2009	2010	Unit	SITC code
	All Commodities	418728.3	287501.6	315547.2					
2709	Petroleum oils and oils obtained from bituminous minerals, crude	41099.0	22831.4	30132.8	0.7	0.4	0.6	US$/kg	333
8703	Motor cars and other motor vehicles principally designed for the transport	22187.4	12921.7	11608.9	*18.9*	17.5	*16.2*	thsd US$/unit	781
8708	Parts and accessories of the motor vehicles of headings 87.01 to 87.05	17520.9	13499.9	14786.4	*8.0*	8.3	5.0	US$/kg	784
2710	Petroleum oils, other than crude	18474.8	11065.2	14522.3	*0.9*	0.5	0.6	US$/kg	334
2711	Petroleum gases and other gaseous hydrocarbons	16947.0	10781.4	11160.6	*0.5*	0.4	0.4	US$/kg	343
3004	Medicaments (excluding goods of heading 30.02, 30.05 or 30.06)	11173.8	12569.6	11567.3	*70.9*	94.0	78.0	US$/kg	542
8517	Electrical apparatus for line telephony or line telegraphy	5943.1	4635.3	5054.2					764
8471	Automatic data processing machines and units thereof	5031.3	3911.2	4504.5	132.9	33.8	*153.4*	US$/unit	752
8541	Diodes, transistors and similar semiconductor devices	8857.6	1429.4	2401.5					776
8528	Reception apparatus for television	3025.0	2664.5	3284.4	191.1	103.4		US$/unit	761

Sri Lanka

Imports: CIF, by origin | **Exports: FOB, by last known destination** | **Trade System: General**

Overview:

In 2011, the value of the exports of Sri Lanka increased by 20.6 percent to amount to 10.0 bln US$ (see table 1 and graph 1). Imports recorded an increase of 59.4 percent to amount to 19.7 bln US$ in 2011. This resulted in a trade deficit of 9.7 bln US$ in 2011, more than double the 2010 deficit of 4.0 bln US$ (see graph 1). Large deficits were recorded with Southern Asia (-5.3 bln US$), Eastern Asia (-3.3 bln US$) and South-eastern Asia (-2.5 bln US$) (see graph 2). Trade recorded a surplus of 1.7 bln US$ with Developed North America. Sri Lanka's trade was diversified across partners: in 2011, 20 (respectively 15) major partners accounted for 80 percent of exports (respectively imports) (see graph 3).

Graph 1: Total imports, exports and trade balance

(Bln US$ by year)

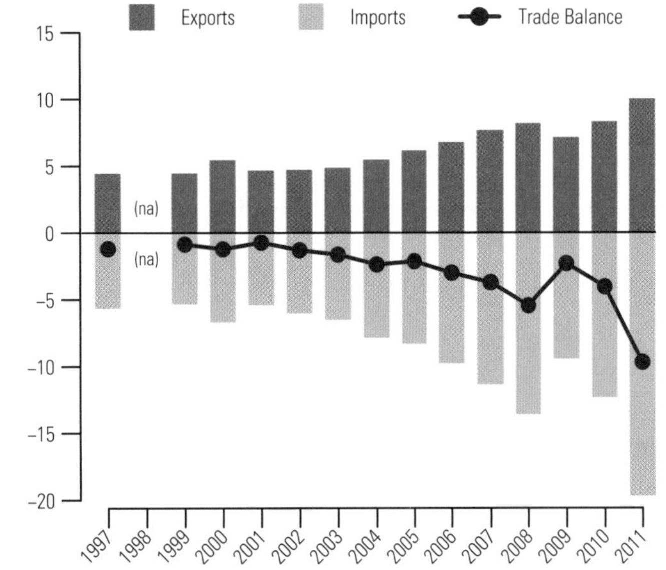

Table 1: Exports by SITC sections

(Value in million US$, growth and shares in percentage)

SITC	2011	Avg. Growth rates (%) 2007-2011	Avg. Growth rates (%) 2010-2011	2011 share
Total	10011.3	6.9	20.6	100.0
0+1	2562.1	11.4	15.8	25.6
2+4	452.6	-0.2	17.0	4.5
3	44.1	112.3	236.3	0.4
5	139.6	14.4	42.7	1.4
6	1560.0	8.7	29.1	15.6
7	530.1	0.7	20.2	5.3
8	4722.7	7.4	23.9	47.2
9	0.0	-92.5	-100.0	0.0

Table 2: Imports by SITC sections

(Value in million US$, growth and shares in percentage)

SITC	2011	Avg. Growth rates (%) 2007-2011	Avg. Growth rates (%) 2010-2011	2011 share
Total	19696.5	14.7	59.4	100.0
0+1	2302.6	18.3	30.8	11.7
2+4	639.2	12.6	73.2	3.2
3	3985.2	10.4	93.1	20.2
5	1956.0	15.3	41.6	9.9
6	4818.9	10.5	37.1	24.5
7	4664.8	22.5	76.2	23.7
8	721.3	10.3	36.7	3.7
9	608.6	27.3	587.9	3.1

Exports Profile:

In 2011, exports were composed of 47.2 percent of miscellaneous manufactured articles (SITC section 8), 25.6 percent of food, live animals, beverages and tobacco (SITC sections 0+1) and 15.6 percent of manufactured goods classified chiefly by material (SITC section 6). USA, United Kingdom and Italy were the three largest markets for exports (see table 4). The majority of exports to USA, United Kingdom and Italy were composed respectively of 78.9, 83.5 and 81.7 percent of miscellaneous manufactured articles (SITC section 8). From 2009 to 2011, top exported products were tea, whether or not flavoured (HS code 0902), women's or girls' suits, ensembles, jackets, blazers, dresses, skirts (HS code 6204) and women's or girls' slips, petticoats, briefs, panties, nightdresses (HS code 6108) (see table 3).

Table 3: Top 10 export commodities 2009 to 2011

(Value in million US$)

HS code	4-digit heading of Harmonized System 2007	Value (million US$) 2009	2010	2011	Unit value 2009	2010	2011	Unit	SITC code
	All Commodities	7121.5	8304.1	10011.3					
0902	Tea, whether or not flavoured	1175.7	1366.8	1475.0	*4.1*	*4.4*	*4.6*	US$/kg	074
6204	Women's or girls' suits, ensembles, jackets, blazers, dresses, skirts	564.6	584.2	630.4	*6.9*	*7.0*	*7.6*	US$/unit	842
6108	Women's or girls' slips, petticoats, briefs, panties, knitted or crocheted	359.3	407.0	481.2	*1.5*	1.5	*1.6*	US$/unit	844
6203	Men's or boys' suits, ensembles, jackets, blazers, trousers	324.9	368.9	433.4	*7.4*	*7.5*	*8.7*	US$/unit	841
6109	T-shirts, singlets and other vests, knitted or crocheted	338.2	345.6	409.1	*3.1*	*3.2*	*3.5*	US$/unit	845
6212	Brassieres, girdles, corsets, braces, suspenders, garters	310.0	326.7	397.2	*68.1*	*59.6*	*51.0*	US$/kg	845
7102	Diamonds, whether or not worked, but not mounted or set	296.7	310.6	380.9	*520.4*	*579.3*		US$/carat	667
6104	Women's or girls' suits, ensembles, jackets, blazers, dresses, skirts	238.3	239.7	334.3	*5.7*	*5.7*	*6.6*	US$/unit	844
4012	Retreaded or used pneumatic tyres of rubber	116.1	200.7	353.1					625
4001	Natural rubber, balata, gutta-percha, guayule, chicle	98.6	170.5	206.2	*1.8*	3.3	4.8	US$/kg	231

Graph 2: Trade Balance by MDG Regions in 2011

(Bln US$)

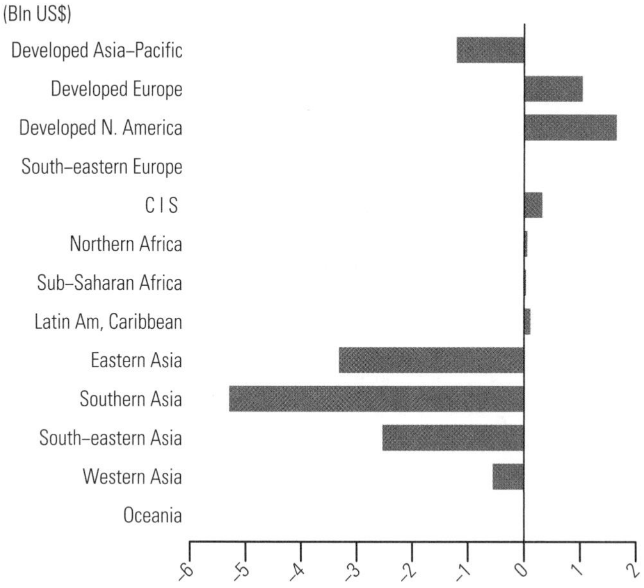

Graph 3: Partner concentration of trade in 2011

(Cumulative share by ranked partners)

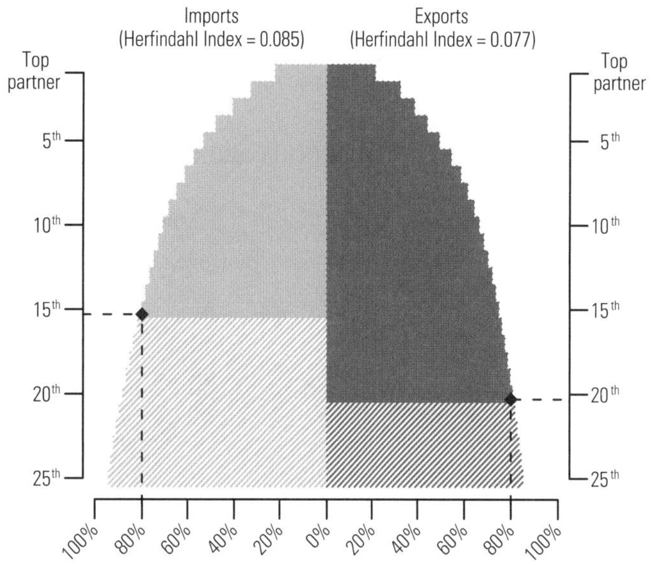

Table 4: Exports by principal countries and SITC sections in 2011

(Value in million US$, percentages of country total)

Country	Total	Shares by SITC sections (%) 0+1	2+4	3	5	6	7	8	9	Total
World	10011.3	25.6	4.5	0.4	1.4	15.6	5.3	47.2	0.0	100
USA	2143.9	3.5	1.7	...	1.7	12.8	1.4	78.9	...	100
United Kingdom	1110.3	5.3	0.6	0.0	0.4	4.0	3.3	86.5	...	100
Italy	609.6	7.4	1.9	...	0.7	7.6	0.8	81.7	...	100
Belgium	545.8	8.0	0.6	...	0.1	64.6	0.2	26.5	...	100
India	521.3	28.2	10.5	2.3	2.2	25.9	18.0	12.9	...	100
Germany	508.3	14.1	4.1	...	1.0	18.7	6.5	55.5	...	100
Singapore	406.4	8.5	2.0	2.8	1.6	2.8	34.0	48.3	...	100
United Arab Emirates	297.0	61.4	2.4	0.1	1.6	13.2	3.4	17.8	...	100
Russian Federation	281.2	89.7	0.6	...	1.6	0.7	0.8	6.7	...	100
Japan	223.5	43.3	16.7	...	2.5	10.7	5.1	21.7	...	100

Imports Profile:

Imports in 2011 were composed of 24.5 percent of manufactured goods classified chiefly by material (SITC section 6), 23.7 percent of machinery and transport equipment (SITC section 7) and 20.2 percent of mineral fuels, lubricants and related materials (SITC section 3). From 2009 to 2011, top products for imports were petroleum oils, other than crude (HS code 2710), petroleum oils and oils obtained from bituminous minerals, crude (HS code 2709) and motor cars and other motor vehicles principally designed for the transport (HS code 8703) (see table 5).

Table 5: Top 10 import commodities 2009 to 2011

(Value in million US$)

HS code	4-digit heading of Harmonized System 2007	Value (million US$) 2009	2010	2011	Unit value 2009	2010	2011	Unit	SITC code
	All Commodities	9431.9	12353.7	19696.5					
2710	Petroleum oils, other than crude	869.6	1128.6	2268.3	*0.5*	*0.7*	*0.9*	US$/kg	334
2709	Petroleum oils and oils obtained from bituminous minerals, crude	844.7	751.6	1354.1	0.4	*0.6*	*0.8*	US$/kg	333
8703	Motor cars and other motor vehicles principally designed for the transport	64.2	445.8	919.7	*2.0*	*3.7*	*4.7*	thsd US$/unit	781
6006	Other knitted or crocheted fabrics	308.0	372.3	510.2	*7.6*	*8.4*	*9.3*	US$/kg	655
1701	Cane or beet sugar and chemically pure sucrose, in solid form	214.8	359.1	419.7	*0.5*	*0.7*	*0.7*	US$/kg	061
7102	Diamonds, whether or not worked, but not mounted or set	260.6	274.1	449.3	*469.7*	496.5		US$/carat	667
1001	Wheat and meslin	268.7	236.5	448.9	0.3	*0.3*	0.3	US$/kg	041
5209	Woven fabrics of cotton, containing 85 % or more by weight of cotton	272.7	297.5	383.9	*5.4*	*6.4*	*8.1*	US$/kg	652
8704	Motor vehicles for the transport of goods	62.5	215.4	543.1	*11.0*	*7.5*	*9.7*	thsd US$/unit	782
0402	Milk and cream, concentrated or containing added sugar	157.1	247.4	329.9	2.5	*3.4*	*3.9*	US$/kg	022

Sudan

Imports: CIF, by consignment | **Exports: FOB, by last known destination** | **Trade System: General**

Overview:

From 2005 to 2009, Sudan's exports increased on average by 19.1 percent each year and amounted to 9.1 bln US$ (see table 1 and graph 1). Imports increased on average by 3.9 percent and amounted to 8.6 bln US$ (see table 2). The trade balance recorded a surplus of 0.5 bln US$ in 2009 ending the large deficits that existed in the earlier years. By MDG regions, trade was in deficit with most of the MDG regions (see graph 2). Large deficits were recorded with Developed Europe (-1.2 bln US$), Developed Asia-Pacific (-0.9 bln US$) and Western Asia (-0.7 bln US$). By partners, Imports were relatively more diversified among partners: in 2009, 3 major partners accounted for 80 percent of exports compared to 18 major partners for imports (see graph 3).

Graph 1: Total imports, exports and trade balance

(Bln US$ by year)

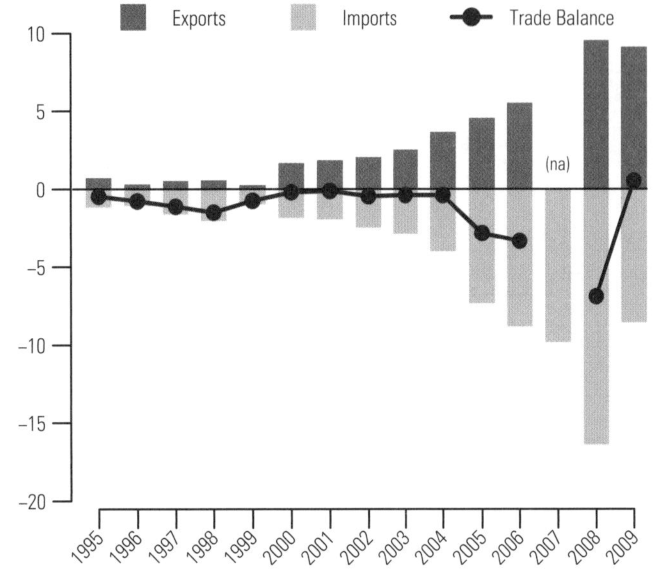

Table 1: Exports by SITC sections

(Value in million US$, growth and shares in percentage)

SITC	2009	Avg. Growth rates (%) 2005-2009	2008-2009	2009 share
Total	9079.5	19.1	-4.4	100.0
0+1	298.5	12.4	136.6	3.3
2+4	281.3	-4.5	-24.2	3.1
3	7151.8	17.6	-20.0	78.8
5	0.1	-50.0	-87.3	0.0
6	20.4	72.3	-26.7	0.2
7	46.3	-17.4	40.1	0.5
8	1.7	-15.7	-45.3	0.0
9	1279.5	77.6	39629.4	14.1

Exports Profile:

In 2009, Sudan's exports were composed of 78.8 percent of mineral fuels, lubricants and related materials (SITC section 3), almost exclusively crude petroleum oils (see tables 1 and 3). Other major commodity groups include commodities and transactions not classified elsewhere (SITC section 9) and food, live animals, beverages and tobacco (SITC sections 0+1), respectively with 14.1 and 3.3 percent of exports. China, the major market for exports, accounted for 65.3 percent of exports in 2009 (see table 4). Other major markets for exports were United Arab Emirates and Canada. From 2007 to 2009, petroleum oils and oils obtained from bituminous minerals, crude (HS code 2709), gold (including gold plated with platinum) (HS code 7108) and petroleum oils, other than crude (HS code 2710) were the three main products for exports (see table 3).

Table 2: Imports by SITC sections

(Value in million US$, growth and shares in percentage)

SITC	2009	Avg. Growth rates (%) 2005-2009	2008-2009	2009 share
Total	8589.9	3.9	-47.7	100.0
0+1	1221.0	9.8	2.6	14.2
2+4	182.2	2.4	125.3	2.1
3	346.9	-1.2	2324.2	4.0
5	920.6	9.1	132.8	10.7
6	1807.3	4.0	33.7	21.0
7	3254.6	-0.1	-62.9	37.9
8	817.5	13.5	25.4	9.5
9	39.7	0.1	-99.0	0.5

Table 3: Top 10 export commodities 2007 to 2009

(Value in million US$)

HS code	4-digit heading of Harmonized System 2007	Value (million US$) 2007	2008	2009	Unit value 2007	2008	2009	Unit	SITC code
	All Commodities	...	9500.9	9079.5					
2709	Petroleum oils and oils obtained from bituminous minerals, crude	...	8685.1	6951.5		0.3	*0.2*	US$/kg	333
7108	Gold (including gold plated with platinum)	...	...	1278.5			11.2	thsd US$/kg	971
2710	Petroleum oils, other than crude	...	248.6	200.3		0.6	*0.4*	US$/kg	334
1207	Other oil seeds and oleaginous fruits, whether or not broken	...	171.6	153.8		1.5	1.1	US$/kg	222
0104	Live sheep and goats	...	50.0	224.2					001
1301	Lac; natural gums, resins, gum-resins and oleoresins (for example, balsams)	...	69.0	61.3		1.8	1.6	US$/kg	292
5201	Cotton, not carded or combed	...	58.3	40.2		2.0	1.4	US$/kg	263
0106	Other live animals	...	20.7	20.2					001
7204	Ferrous waste and scrap; remelting scrap ingots of iron or steel	...	33.1	5.8		0.2	0.1	US$/kg	282
1212	Locust beans, seaweeds and other algae	...	19.1	18.0		1.1	1.5	US$/kg	292

Graph 2: Trade Balance by MDG Regions in 2009

(Bln US$)

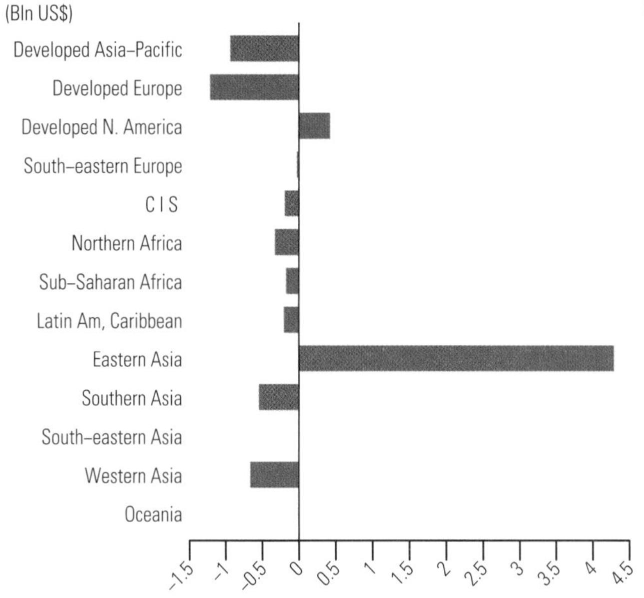

Graph 3: Partner concentration of trade in 2009

(Cumulative share by ranked partners)

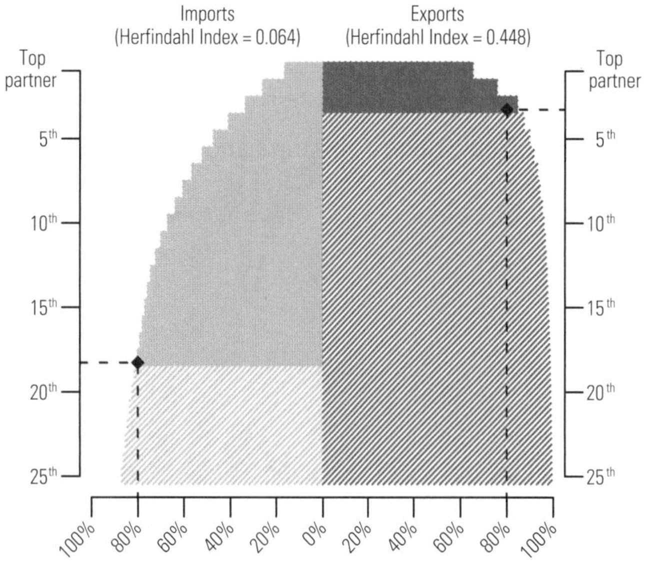

Table 4: Exports by principal countries and SITC sections in 2009

(Value in million US$, percentages of country total)

Country	Total	Shares by SITC sections (%)								
		0 + 1	2 + 4	3	5	6	7	8	9	Total
World	9079.5	3.3	3.1	78.8	0.0	0.2	0.5	0.0	14.1	100
China	5932.2	0.0	0.6	99.3	0.0	0.0	0.0	0.0	0.0	100
United Arab Emirates	951.1	0.4	0.4	48.2	0.0	0.4	0.6	0.0	50.1	100
Canada	802.1	0.0	0.0	...	...	...	0.0	0.0	100.0	100
Saudi Arabia	254.4	90.9	7.5	...	0.0	1.5	0.1	0.0	0.0	100
Japan	213.1	0.0	2.3	97.7	...	0.0	0.0	0.0	0.0	100
India	164.6	0.1	8.8	84.3	0.0	0.3	5.9	0.5	0.0	100
Indonesia	143.3	0.0	0.0	99.9	...	0.0	0.1	0.0	0.0	100
Singapore	94.5	0.0	3.9	96.1	...	0.1	0.0	0.0	0.0	100
Egypt	93.5	27.8	69.7	0.0	0.0	0.3	0.8	0.4	1.0	100
Ethiopia	67.6	0.0	0.0	99.8	0.0	...	0.2	0.0	0.0	100

Imports Profile:

In 2009, imports of machinery and transport equipment (SITC section 7) decreased by 62.9 percent and accounted for 37.9 percent of imported goods (see table 2). Other major commodity groups included manufactured goods classified chiefly by material (SITC section 6) and food, live animals, beverages and tobacco (SITC sections 0+1), respectively with 21.0 and 14.2 percent of imports. From 2007 to 2009, top imported goods included other aircraft (for example, helicopters, aeroplanes); spacecraft (HS code 8802), parts of goods of heading 88.01 or 88.02 (HS code 8803) and electrical apparatus for line telephony or line telegraphy (HS code 8517) (see table 5).

Table 5: Top 10 import commodities 2007 to 2009

(Value in million US$)

HS code	4-digit heading of Harmonized System 2007	Value (million US$)			Unit value				SITC code
		2007	2008	2009	2007	2008	2009	Unit	
	All Commodities	9853.6	16416.7	8589.9					
8802	Other aircraft (for example, helicopters, aeroplanes); spacecraft	482.2	4572.1	26.6	234.3			thsd US$/unit	792
9999	Commodities not specified according to kind	64.4	3956.7	39.7					931
8803	Parts of goods of heading 88.01 or 88.02	120.5	1466.6	26.3	460.0	*328.1*	82.4	US$/kg	792
8517	Electrical apparatus for line telephony or line telegraphy	1094.5	101.0	118.0					764
8704	Motor vehicles for the transport of goods	473.9	281.8	532.7	25.4			thsd US$/unit	782
8703	Motor cars and other motor vehicles principally designed for the transport	301.3	401.9	405.0	7.9		*18.5*	thsd US$/unit	781
1001	Wheat and meslin	161.3	493.1	389.5	0.2	0.7	0.5	US$/kg	041
8431	Parts suitable for use principally with the machinery of headings 84.25	636.4	100.7	145.1	88.4	24.8	16.3	US$/kg	723
3003	Medicaments (excluding goods of heading 30.02, 30.05 or 30.06)	568.0	132.2	163.5	143.3	28.1	29.0	US$/kg	542
8443	Printing machinery used for printing by means of the printing type, blocks	645.1	193.4	19.4					726

Imports: CIF, by origin | **Exports: FOB, by last known destination** | **Trade System: General**

Overview:

From 2006 to 2010, Suriname's exports increased on average by 14.6 percent each year and reached its peak of 2.0 bln US$ in 2010 (see table 1 and graph 1). Imports showed a less pronounced development with an average increase of 8.4 percent to 1.4 bln US$ (see table 2 and graph 1). The trade balance recorded a trade surplus 0.6 bln US$ in 2010. By MDG regions, trade with Developed North America recorded a surplus amounting to 375.0 mln US$ (see graph 2). Large surpluses were also recorded with Developed Europe (+353.3 mln US$) and Western Asia (+274.4 mln US$). The trade balance recorded significant deficits with Latin America and the Caribbean (-208.5 mln US$) and Eastern Asia (-104.7 mln US$). Both imports and exports were highly concentrated among a few partners: in 2010, 8 (respectively 6) major partners accounted for 80 percent of exports (respectively imports) (see graph 3).

Graph 1: Total imports, exports and trade balance

(Bln US$ by year)

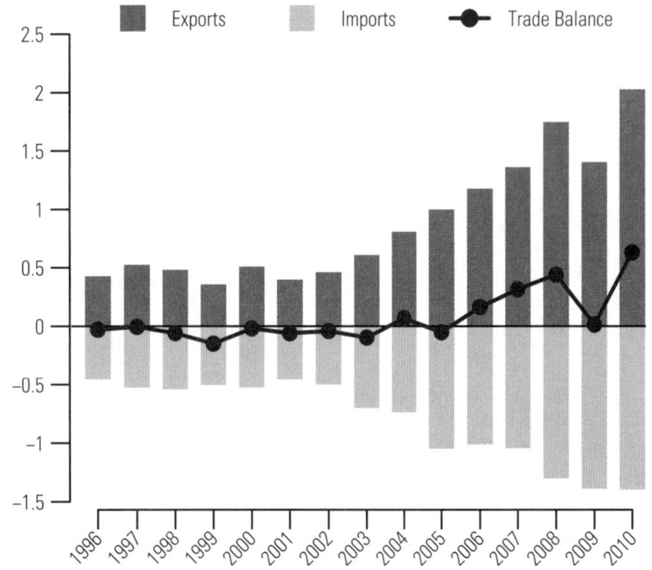

Exports Profile:

Suriname's exports were composed largely of commodities and transactions not classified elsewhere (SITC section 9): they represented 81.9 percent of exported goods in 2010 (see table 1). Exports of mineral fuels, lubricants and related materials (SITC section 3) increased by 305.8 percent in 2010 and represented 13.0 percent of exports. In 2010, top partners for exports were Canada, United Arab Emirates and Belgium (see table 4). From 2008 to 2010, top exported products were oils petroleum, bituminous, distillates, except crude (HS code 2710), rice (HS code 1006) and liqueur, spirits and undenatured ethyl alcohol <80% (HS code 2208) (see table 3).

Table 1: Exports by SITC sections

(Value in million US$, growth and shares in percentage)

SITC	2010	Avg. Growth rates (%) 2006-2010	2009-2010	2010 share
Total	2025.6	14.6	44.5	100.0
0+1	48.6	6.7	-13.1	2.4
2+4	14.8	17.5	-11.3	0.7
3	263.6	49.1	305.8	13.0
5	3.7	0.5	-39.3	0.2
6	5.1	-11.0	-1.1	0.3
7	21.3	0.7	9.4	1.1
8	9.1	31.5	-14.5	0.4
9	1659.3	12.4	35.7	81.9

Table 2: Imports by SITC sections

(Value in million US$, growth and shares in percentage)

SITC	2010	Avg. Growth rates (%) 2006-2010	2009-2010	2010 share
Total	1397.5	8.4	0.5	100.0
0+1	194.4	22.4	10.9	13.9
2+4	36.8	27.1	29.6	2.6
3	264.1	8.1	21.8	18.9
5	162.5	39.4	-18.9	11.6
6	219.8	27.9	2.2	15.7
7	390.9	16.7	-11.0	28.0
8	122.3	21.6	13.1	8.7
9	6.8	-62.1	1.6	0.5

Table 3: Top 10 export commodities 2008 to 2010

(Value in million US$)

HS code	4-digit heading of Harmonized System 1992	Value (million US$) 2008	2009	2010	Unit value 2008	2009	2010	Unit	SITC code
	All Commodities	1743.4	1401.8	2025.6					
9999	Commodities not specified according to kind	1435.7	1222.8	1659.3					931
2710	Oils petroleum, bituminous, distillates, except crude	187.7	64.4	263.0	0.6	0.3	0.5	US$/kg	334
1006	Rice	32.3	21.2	37.8	0.6	0.4	0.4	US$/kg	042
2208	Liqueur, spirits and undenatured ethyl alcohol <80%	11.5	8.6	0.1		*4.1*	*2.8*	US$/litre	112
2202	Waters, non-alcoholic sweetened or flavoured beverages	3.9	5.4	4.6	*0.6*	*0.6*	*0.4*	US$/litre	111
1507	Soya-bean oil, fractions, not chemically modified	6.5	5.1	0.0	1.4	1.2	0.9	US$/kg	421
9406	Prefabricated buildings	5.3	1.9	1.0	2.2	3.1		US$/kg	811
3402	Organic surface active agent, preparation, except soap	2.6	2.7	2.7	1.0	1.1	1.1	US$/kg	554
8431	Parts for use with lifting, moving machinery	0.2	2.3	5.5	2.9	5.5	10.7	US$/kg	723
7204	Ferrous waste or scrap, ingots or iron or steel	2.1	2.0	1.9	0.2	0.1	0.1	US$/kg	282

Graph 2: Trade Balance by MDG Regions in 2010

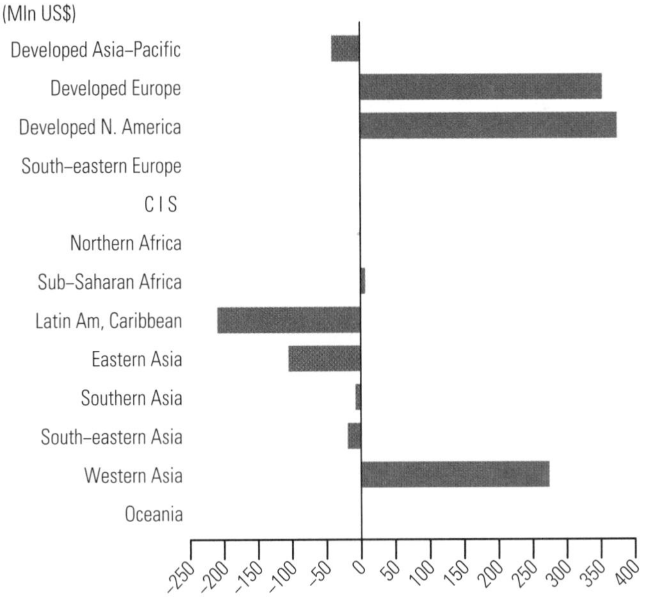

Graph 3: Partner concentration of trade in 2010

(Cumulative share by ranked partners)

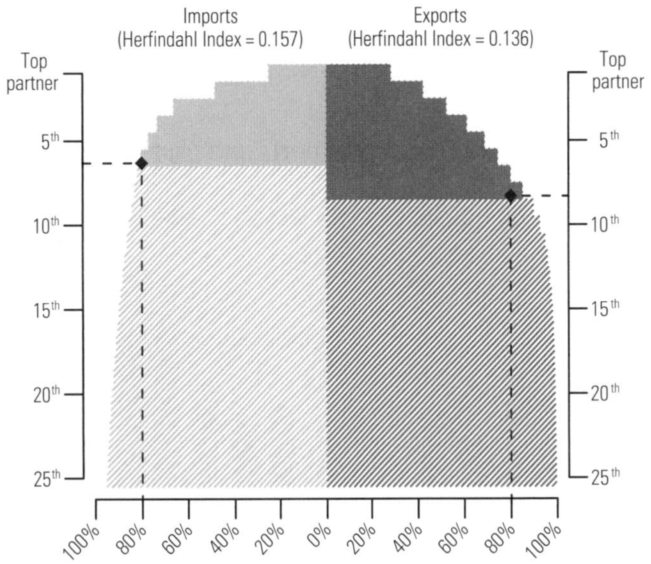

Table 4: Exports by principal countries and SITC sections in 2010

(Value in million US$, percentages of country total)

Country	Total	Shares by SITC sections (%)								
		0 + 1	2 + 4	3	5	6	7	8	9	Total
World	2025.6	2.4	0.7	13.0	0.2	0.3	1.1	0.4	81.9	100
Canada	577.4	0.0	0.0	...	...	0.1	0.0	0.0	99.9	100
United Arab Emirates	278.3	0.0	0.0	...	...	...	...	0.0	100.0	100
Belgium	204.2	0.1	0.4	...	...	0.0	0.0	0.0	99.5	100
Switzerland	179.0	0.0	0.0	...	0.0	...	0.0	0.0	100.0	100
USA	153.6	0.1	0.5	0.0	0.1	0.7	6.0	1.4	91.2	100
Guyana	113.7	6.1	0.1	90.6	0.3	0.8	0.6	1.5	0.0	100
Barbados	111.2	0.1	0.0	99.4	0.2	0.0	0.1	0.1	0.1	100
Netherlands	104.5	12.6	3.2	0.4	0.2	0.8	5.1	0.6	77.0	100
Norway	95.4	0.0	0.0	...	...	...	...	...	100.0	100
France	55.6	4.0	0.5	0.6	0.2	0.4	1.6	2.6	90.2	100

Imports Profile:

In 2010, Suriname's imports were composed of 28.0 percent of machinery and transport equipment (SITC section 7), 18.9 percent of mineral fuels, lubricants and related materials (SITC section 3) and 15.7 percent of manufactured goods classified chiefly by material (SITC section 6) (see table 2). From 2008 to 2010, top imported products were oils petroleum, bituminous, distillates, except crude (HS code 2710), motor vehicles for transport of persons (except buses) (HS code 8703) and motor vehicles for the transport of goods (HS code 8704) (see table 5).

Table 5: Top 10 import commodities 2008 to 2010

(Value in million US$)

HS code	4-digit heading of Harmonized System 1992	Value (million US$)			Unit value				SITC code
		2008	2009	2010	2008	2009	2010	Unit	
	All Commodities	1304.3	1390.1	1397.5					
2710	Oils petroleum, bituminous, distillates, except crude	190.4	208.4	255.5	0.8	0.7	0.7	US$/kg	334
9999	Commodities not specified according to kind	323.0	6.6	6.5					931
8703	Motor vehicles for transport of persons (except buses)	51.6	44.0	46.2			*17.0*	thsd US$/unit	781
8704	Motor vehicles for the transport of goods	60.5	41.3	29.8					782
8429	Self-propelled earth moving, road making, etc machine	30.2	31.9	27.1	*66.9*		*62.3*	thsd US$/unit	723
2815	Hydroxides and peroxides of sodium and potassium	3.4	56.9	23.4	*0.7*	0.2	0.1	US$/kg	522
8431	Parts for use with lifting, moving machinery	8.7	51.2	19.9	6.0	23.7	8.3	US$/kg	723
2523	Cement (portland, aluminous, slag or hydraulic)	5.9	27.5	23.5	0.1	0.1	0.1	US$/kg	661
2402	Cigars, cigarettes etc, tobacco or tobacco substitute	15.3	18.3	21.6	16.6	19.0	25.7	US$/kg	122
0207	Meat, edible offal of domestic poultry	16.9	16.1	17.4	1.2	1.0	1.0	US$/kg	012

Swaziland

Imports: CIF, by origin | **Exports: FOB, by last known destination** | **Trade System: General**

Overview:

From 2003 to 2007, Swaziland's exports dropped on average by 9.4 percent each year and amounted to 1.1 bln US$ in 2007 (see table 1 and graph 1). During the same period, imports dropped on average by 3.4 percent each year and amounted to 1.3 bln US$ resulting in a trade deficit of 156.8 mln US$ (see table 2 and graph 1). This deficit compares with a surplus of 368.5 mln US$ in 2004. Deficit with Sub-Saharan Africa alone amounted to 136.9 mln US$ (see graph 2). However, trade recorded surplus with Developed Europe (+122.0 mln US$). Both imports and exports were concentrated among a few partners. In 2007, imported goods were almost exclusively from the top partner, and 2 major partners accounted for 80 percent of exports (see graph 3).

Graph 1: Total imports, exports and trade balance

(Bln US$ by year)

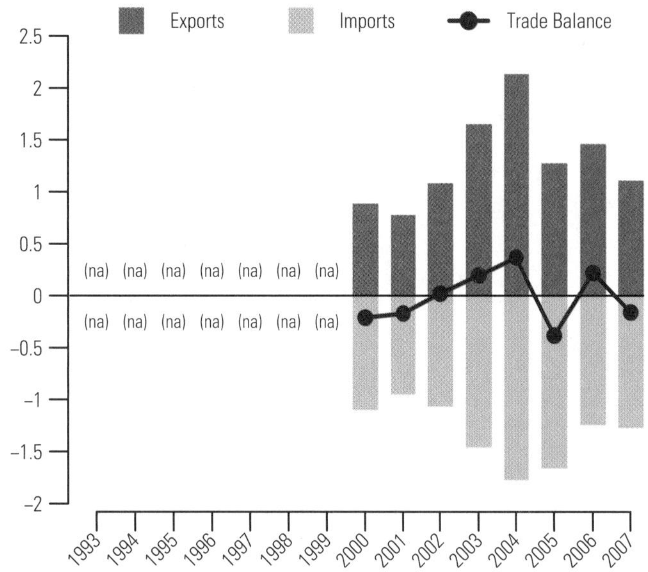

Table 1: Exports by SITC sections

(Value in million US$, growth and shares in percentage)

SITC	2007	Avg. Growth rates (%) 2003-2007	2006-2007	2007 share
Total	1 113.3	-9.4	-23.9	100.0
0+1	235.0	-0.7	-38.5	21.1
2+4	85.8	-12.9	-37.3	7.7
3	14.0	6.9	-7.3	1.3
5	600.9	0.5	-5.9	54.0
6	31.8	-10.9	-12.4	2.9
7	44.8	-6.4	-15.0	4.0
8	99.2	-34.8	-50.1	8.9
9	1.8	-23.7	-3.6	0.2

Exports Profile:

In 2007, exports were composed of 54.0 percent of chemicals and related products, n.e.s. (SITC section 5), 21.1 percent of food, live animals, beverages and tobacco (SITC sections 0+1) and 8.9 percent of miscellaneous manufactured articles (SITC section 8). Top markets for exports were South Africa, Italy and Namibia (see table 4). From 2005 to 2007, top exported products were mixed odoriferous substances for industrial use (HS code 3302), solid cane or beet sugar and chemically pure sucrose (HS code 1701) and prepr binder for foundry (HS code 3824) (see table 3).

Table 2: Imports by SITC sections

(Value in million US$, growth and shares in percentage)

SITC	2007	Avg. Growth rates (%) 2003-2007	2006-2007	2007 share
Total	1 270.1	-3.4	2.2	100.0
0+1	248.3	2.9	38.4	19.5
2+4	33.8	-9.5	9.0	2.7
3	178.5	10.0	-1.0	14.1
5	166.8	-9.5	5.2	13.1
6	243.4	-2.0	-2.8	19.2
7	240.6	-10.6	-14.0	18.9
8	146.8	-0.4	9.3	11.6
9	11.9	-18.2	-58.2	0.9

Table 3: Top 10 export commodities 2005 to 2007

(Value in million US$)

HS code	4-digit heading of Harmonized System 1996	Value (million US$) 2005	2006	2007	Unit value 2005	2006	2007	Unit	SITC code
	All Commodities	1 277.8	1 462.8	1 113.3					
3302	Mixted odoriferous substances for industrial use	435.5	356.0	319.1	7.8	12.5	44.3	US$/kg	551
1701	Solid cane or beet sugar and chemically pure sucrose	145.7	262.0	165.7	0.5	0.4	0.2	US$/kg	061
3824	Prepr binder for foundry	100.0	184.9	215.5	2.8	*9.3*	42.1	US$/kg	598
4703	Chemical wood pulp, soda or sulphate, not dissolving	58.3	87.8	28.5	0.1	0.5	0.3	US$/kg	251
6109	T-shirts, singlets and other vests, knitted or crocheted	59.4	45.8	14.7	2.2	*1.9*	5.4	US$/unit	845
6204	Women's or girls' suits, jacket, dress, skirt, etc.	35.4	34.5	14.3	4.6	*4.6*		US$/unit	842
2916	Unsaturated acyclic, cyclic monocarboxylc acid, derivatives	15.0	31.1	25.0	6.0	7.4	14.4	US$/kg	513
4911	Printed matter nes, catalogues, pictures and photos	21.2	19.5	24.1	11.6	15.7	15.8	US$/kg	892
8418	Refrigerators, freezers and heat pumps nes	18.4	21.4	24.2					741
6203	Men's or boys' suits, jackets, trousers etc.	28.9	28.7	4.4	4.4	*7.8*		US$/unit	841

Graph 2: Trade Balance by MDG Regions in 2007

(Mln US$)

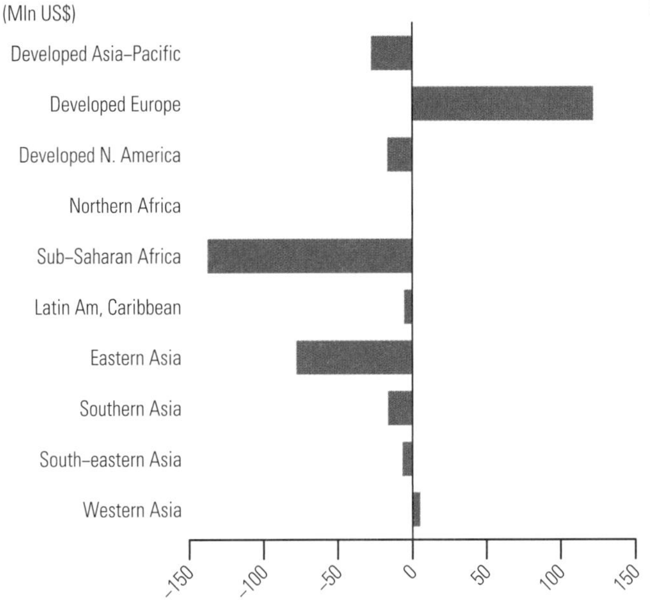

Graph 3: Partner concentration of trade in 2007

(Cumulative share by ranked partners)

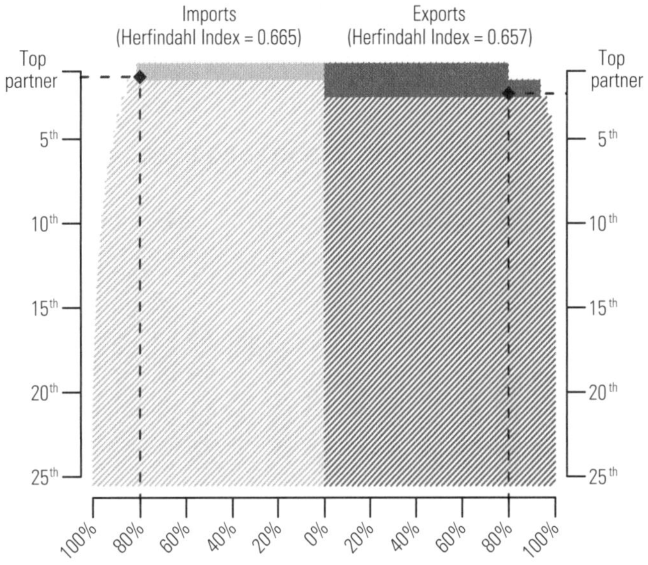

Table 4: Exports by principal countries and SITC sections in 2007

(Value in million US$, percentages of country total)

Country	Total	Shares by SITC sections (%)								
		0 + 1	2 + 4	3	5	6	7	8	9	Total
World	1 113.3	21.1	7.7	1.3	54.0	2.9	4.0	8.9	0.2	100
South Africa	888.5	8.0	8.0	1.6	67.0	3.4	4.7	7.3	0.1	100
Italy	153.5	100.0	0.0	...	...	...	...	...	...	100
Namibia	31.1	3.9	0.0	...	14.8	...	0.0	81.3	...	100
Mozambique	20.2	21.2	68.8	0.7	1.2	3.0	3.7	1.4	...	100
United Arab Emirates	5.6	0.0	0.0	...	...	...	1.6	98.4	...	100
Botswana	3.3	0.0	0.0	...	0.1	0.2	32.5	35.9	31.3	100
Australia	2.2	99.9	0.0	...	0.1	...	...	...	...	100
Zambia	1.5	20.9	0.0	...	0.6	...	51.0	27.5	...	100
Lesotho	1.3	0.0	53.5	...	...	30.9	0.2	6.3	9.1	100
United Kingdom	1.3	94.5	0.0	...	...	4.7	0.9	...	...	100

Imports Profile:

In 2007, imports were composed of 19.5 percent of food, live animals, beverages and tobacco (SITC sections 0+1), 19.2 percent of manufactured goods classified chiefly by material (SITC section 6) and 18.9 percent of machinery and transport equipment (SITC section 7). From 2005 to 2007, top imported products were oils petroleum, bituminous, distillates, except crude (HS code 2710), mixted odoriferous substances for industrial use (HS code 3302) and motor vehicles for transport of persons (except buses) (HS code 8703) (see table 5).

Table 5: Top 10 import commodities 2005 to 2007

(Value in million US$)

HS code	4-digit heading of Harmonized System 1996	Value (million US$)			Unit value				SITC code
		2005	2006	2007	2005	2006	2007	Unit	
	All Commodities	1 656.1	1 242.4	1 270.1					
2710	Oils petroleum, bituminous, distillates, except crude	157.8	145.5	147.8	*0.5*	*0.6*		US$/kg	334
3302	Mixted odoriferous substances for industrial use	137.4	26.7	14.9	5.6	13.1	11.9	US$/kg	551
8703	Motor vehicles for transport of persons (except buses)	46.0	38.3	31.9	2.6	*0.3*	0.1	thsd US$/unit	781
1005	Maize (corn)	18.2	14.7	48.4	0.2	0.2	0.0	US$/kg	044
8704	Motor vehicles for the transport of goods	26.7	26.6	23.7	484.1	381.7	112.2	US$/unit	782
9999	Commodities not elsewhere specified	25.5	28.4	11.7					931
2523	Cement (portland, aluminous, slag or hydraulic)	27.7	15.5	15.4	0.6	0.5	0.2	US$/kg	661
8708	Parts and accessories for motor vehicles	22.4	16.7	16.8	2.9	4.4	2.0	US$/kg	784
6002	Other knitted or crocheted fabrics	15.6	16.9	21.2	6.6			US$/kg	655
3004	Medicaments, therapeutic, prophylactic use, in dosage	18.5	14.7	18.3	2.7	3.7	5.7	US$/kg	542

Sweden

Imports: CIF, by origin/consignment for intra-eu | **Exports: FOB, by last known destination** | **Trade System: Special**

Overview:

After several years of continuous growth marked by a peak of 183.9 bln US$ in 2008, the value of Sweden's exports dropped by 28.7 percent in 2009 but bounced back in 2010 by 20.6 percent to amount to 158.1 bln US$ (see table 1 and graph 1). Imports increased by 23.7 percent and amounted to 148.4 bln US$ (see table 2 and graph 1). The trade surplus decreased from 11.2 bln US$ in 2009 to 9.7 bln US$ in 2010 (see graph 1). By MDG regions, top trade surpluses were recorded with Developed North America (+8.1 bln US$), Western Asia (+3.8 bln US$) and Sub-Saharan Africa (+2.4 bln US$) among others (see graph 2). Major trade deficits were recorded with Developed Europe (-7.6 bln US$), the Commonwealth of Independent States (-3.7 bln US$) and Eastern Asia (-3.0 bln US$). In 2010, exports were more diversified across partners than imports: 20 major partners accounted for 80 percent of exports compared to 14 major partners for imports (see graph 3).

Graph 1: Total imports, exports and trade balance

(Bln US$ by year)

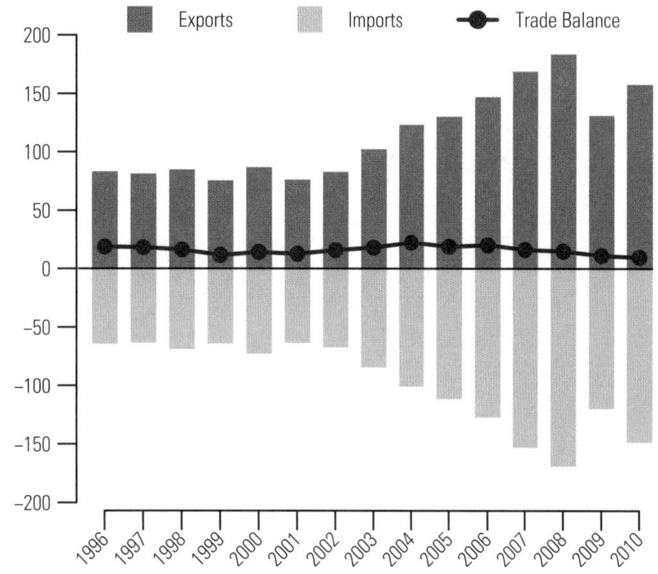

Table 1: Exports by SITC sections

(Value in million US$, growth and shares in percentage)

SITC	2010	Avg. Growth rates (%) 2006-2010	2009-2010	2010 share
Total	158079.2	1.8	20.6	100.0
0+1	7119.6	9.5	15.9	4.5
2+4	10874.7	5.7	33.4	6.9
3	11054.6	7.7	37.2	7.0
5	17956.5	2.9	8.0	11.4
6	29356.5	0.8	21.2	18.6
7	58246.9	-0.9	21.8	36.8
8	13691.1	3.6	7.1	8.7
9	9779.3	3.2	34.1	6.2

Table 2: Imports by SITC sections

(Value in million US$, growth and shares in percentage)

SITC	2010	Avg. Growth rates (%) 2006-2010	2009-2010	2010 share
Total	148421.2	4.0	23.7	100.0
0+1	12211.8	8.1	9.6	8.2
2+4	5355.2	4.2	31.2	3.6
3	19908.0	6.1	43.3	13.4
5	16080.6	5.8	10.3	10.8
6	20023.3	1.7	30.1	13.5
7	53126.1	2.4	29.5	35.8
8	16147.8	3.3	11.3	10.9
9	5568.5	9.7	4.4	3.8

Exports Profile:

In 2010, exports of machinery and transport equipment (SITC section 7), the largest commodity group for exports, increased by 21.8 percent and represented 36.8 percent of exported goods (see table 1). Other major commodity groups included manufactured goods classified chiefly by material (SITC section 6) and chemicals and related products, n.e.s. (SITC section 5) respectively with 18.6 and 11.4 percent of exports. In addition to Norway, other major markets for exports in 2010 were Germany and United Kingdom (see table 4). Sweden's main exported products over the last three years were petroleum oils, other than crude (HS code 2710), electrical apparatus for line telephony or line telegraphy (HS code 8517) and medicaments (excluding goods of heading 30.02, 30.05 or 30.06) (HS code 3004) (see table 3).

Table 3: Top 10 export commodities 2008 to 2010

(Value in million US$)

HS code	4-digit heading of Harmonized System 2007	Value (million US$) 2008	2009	2010	Unit value 2008	2009	2010	Unit	SITC code
	All Commodities	183880.6	131116.2	158079.2					
2710	Petroleum oils, other than crude	11621.7	6871.1	9354.2	*0.8*	*0.5*	*0.6*	US$/kg	334
9999	Commodities not specified according to kind	10927.0	6718.4	9052.8					931
8517	Electrical apparatus for line telephony or line telegraphy	9695.7	6513.1	9360.0					764
3004	Medicaments (excluding goods of heading 30.02, 30.05 or 30.06)	7438.2	7347.7	7539.2	*147.1*	*141.3*	*148.3*	US$/kg	542
8703	Motor cars and other motor vehicles principally designed for the transport	8445.2	4369.1	5318.7	29.9	26.0	*18.2*	thsd US$/unit	781
8708	Parts and accessories of the motor vehicles of headings 87.01 to 87.05	5108.5	3028.5	4409.5	*8.5*	*8.8*	*9.1*	US$/kg	784
4407	Wood sawn or chipped lengthwise, sliced or peeled	3439.7	2983.4	3317.1	*286.6*			US$/m³	248
4810	Paper and paperboard, coated on one or both sides with kaolin	3367.5	2752.6	2969.1	*1.1*	*1.0*	*1.0*	US$/kg	641
4802	Uncoated paper and paperboard, of a kind used for writing	2283.4	1989.7	2109.0	*1.0*	*0.9*	*0.9*	US$/kg	641
4804	Uncoated kraft paper and paperboard, in rolls or sheets	2315.7	1828.6	2086.0	*0.9*	*0.7*	*0.8*	US$/kg	641

Graph 2: Trade Balance by MDG Regions in 2010

(Bln US$)

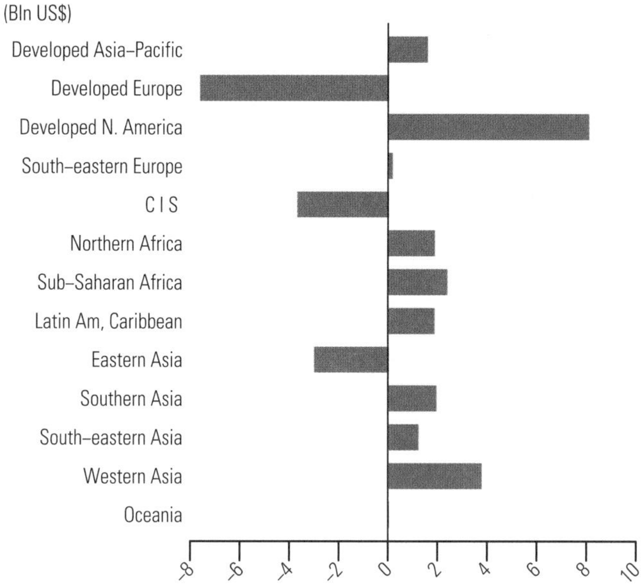

Graph 3: Partner concentration of trade in 2010

(Cumulative share by ranked partners)

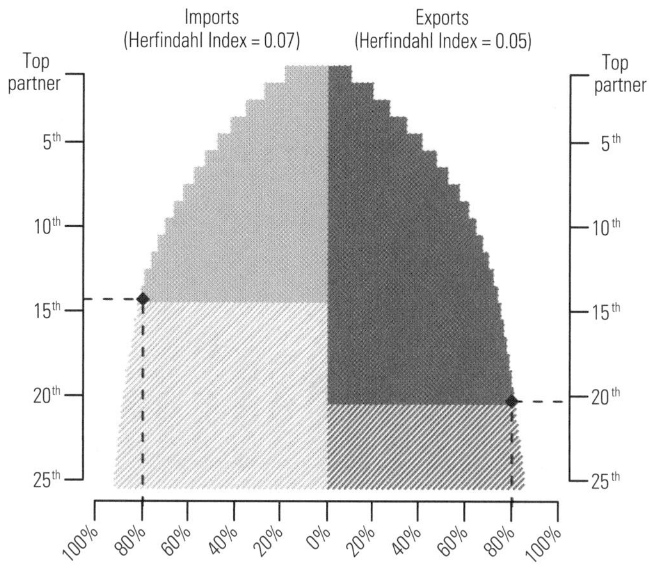

Table 4: Exports by principal countries and SITC sections in 2010

(Value in million US$, percentages of country total)

Country	Total	Shares by SITC sections (%)								
		0 + 1	2 + 4	3	5	6	7	8	9	Total
World	158079.2	4.5	6.9	7.0	11.4	18.6	36.8	8.7	6.2	100
Norway	15754.2	4.6	4.3	11.0	9.3	18.6	32.9	16.4	2.9	100
Germany	15751.9	3.5	10.5	3.2	12.3	31.5	25.0	7.3	6.7	100
United Kingdom	11690.5	3.5	9.7	19.9	13.1	19.8	21.0	5.9	7.1	100
USA	11598.7	4.0	0.8	6.2	14.0	10.7	51.5	8.3	4.6	100
Denmark	10338.5	7.8	5.1	10.9	8.7	16.8	31.6	14.2	4.9	100
Finland	9778.6	7.2	7.6	4.5	9.7	16.8	31.8	15.0	7.3	100
Netherlands	7805.3	2.2	16.3	12.8	5.1	22.7	29.8	5.8	5.4	100
France	7748.8	8.1	4.0	8.2	17.7	14.9	35.9	7.3	3.8	100
Belgium	6392.3	1.9	3.3	7.2	15.5	11.7	50.1	5.8	4.6	100
China	4945.0	0.6	9.9	0.1	12.7	16.9	51.5	5.0	3.4	100

Imports Profile:

Similar to exports, machinery and transport equipment (SITC section 7) also accounted for a large share of imports in 2010 (see table 2). It represented 35.8 percent of total imports. Other major commodity groups for imports included manufactured goods classified chiefly by material (SITC section 6) and mineral fuels, lubricants and related materials (SITC section 3) respectively with 13.5 and 13.4 percent of imported goods. Petroleum oils and oils obtained from bituminous minerals, crude (HS code 2709), petroleum oils, other than crude (HS code 2710) and motor cars and other motor vehicles principally designed for the transport (HS code 8703) were the top imported goods over the last three years (see table 5).

Table 5: Top 10 import commodities 2008 to 2010

(Value in million US$)

HS code	4-digit heading of Harmonized System 2007	Value (million US$)			Unit value				SITC code
		2008	2009	2010	2008	2009	2010	Unit	
	All Commodities	168981.7	119948.7	148421.2					
2709	Petroleum oils and oils obtained from bituminous minerals, crude	13310.8	7324.2	10424.7	*0.7*	*0.4*	*0.6*	US$/kg	333
2710	Petroleum oils, other than crude	7519.4	4464.3	5993.6	*0.8*	*0.5*	*0.7*	US$/kg	334
8703	Motor cars and other motor vehicles principally designed for the transport	6146.4	4528.9	6643.9	20.6	*18.9*	*17.9*	thsd US$/unit	781
9999	Commodities not specified according to kind	5772.9	5252.1	5491.0					931
8708	Parts and accessories of the motor vehicles of headings 87.01 to 87.05	6503.7	3596.9	5039.3	*8.9*	*9.4*	*8.5*	US$/kg	784
8517	Electrical apparatus for line telephony or line telegraphy	4381.8	3281.2	4286.4					764
8471	Automatic data processing machines and units thereof	3641.7	2799.7	3407.2	182.6	188.8		US$/unit	752
3004	Medicaments (excluding goods of heading 30.02, 30.05 or 30.06)	3187.5	2964.6	2798.7	*78.3*	*74.0*	*67.0*	US$/kg	542
8542	Electronic integrated circuits	1341.1	1517.8	3412.0					776
8528	Reception apparatus for television	1837.0	1626.3	1795.6	318.7	312.8		US$/unit	761

Imports: CIF, by origin | Exports: FOB, by last known destination | Trade System: Special

Overview:

From 2007 to 2011, the value of the exports of Switzerland-Liechtenstein increased on average by 8.0 percent each year despite a drop of 14.0 percent in 2009 and reached its peak of 234.4 bln US$ (see table 1 and graph 1). During the same period, imports increased on average by 6.5 percent each year to reach 207.3 bln US$ in 2011 (see table 2 and graph 1). This resulted in a trade surplus of 27.2 bln US$ in 2011 (see graph 1). Switzerland-Liechtenstein's trade recorded surpluses with several MDG regions. The top trade surpluses were with Developed North America (+16.3 bln US$), Eastern Asia (+13.3 bln US$) and Western Asia (+8.4 bln US$) (see graph 2). A major trade deficit was recorded with Developed Europe (-28.7 bln US$). In 2011, exports were more diversified across partners than imports: 18 major partners accounted for 80 percent of exports compared to 11 major partners for imports (see graph 3).

Graph 1: Total imports, exports and trade balance

(Bln US$ by year)

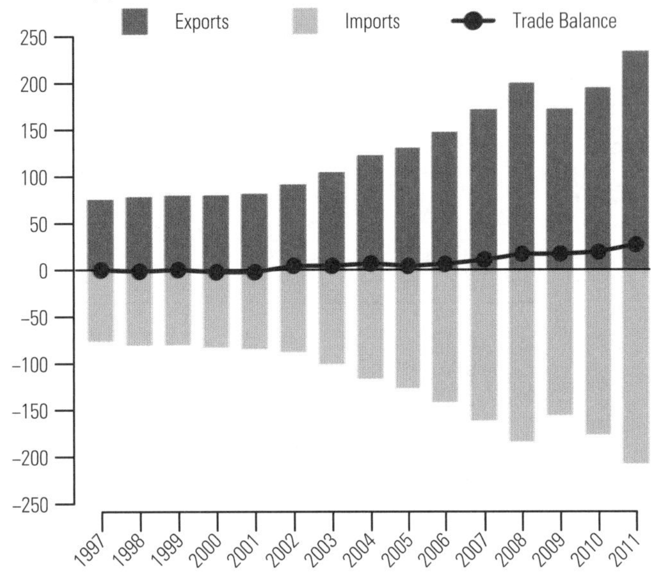

Table 1: Exports by SITC sections

(Value in million US$, growth and shares in percentage)

SITC	2011	Avg. Growth rates (%) 2007-2011	2010-2011	2011 share
Total	234426.3	8.0	19.8	100.0
0+1	8572.5	13.0	17.8	3.7
2+4	2509.9	6.3	16.7	1.1
3	7161.5	15.0	29.9	3.1
5	83564.2	8.9	11.9	35.6
6	22122.9	2.5	8.0	9.4
7	48812.1	3.4	19.4	20.8
8	54975.9	9.4	26.4	23.5
9	6707.4	139.8	493.7	2.9

Table 2: Imports by SITC sections

(Value in million US$, growth and shares in percentage)

SITC	2011	Avg. Growth rates (%) 2007-2011	2010-2011	2011 share
Total	207263.2	6.5	17.6	100.0
0+1	11467.8	8.2	16.5	5.5
2+4	3226.6	3.4	4.1	1.6
3	17437.0	12.3	33.3	8.4
5	44258.1	5.2	16.1	21.4
6	31882.6	4.3	21.4	15.4
7	55071.1	5.3	16.6	26.6
8	41643.2	8.2	12.5	20.1
9	2276.7	27.9	38.5	1.1

Exports Profile:

Chemicals and related products, n.e.s. (SITC section 5), the largest commodity group for exports in 2011, increased by 11.9 percent and represented 35.6 percent of total exports (see table 1). Other major commodity groups for exports were miscellaneous manufactured articles (SITC section 8) and machinery and transport equipment (SITC section 7), respectively with 23.5 and 20.8 percent of exports. Germany, USA and Italy were the three largest markets for exports in 2011 (see table 4). Over the last three years, main exported goods were medicaments (excluding goods of heading 30.02, 30.05 or 30.06) (HS code 3004), human blood; animal blood prepared for therapeutic uses (HS code 3002) and wrist-watches, pocket-watches and other watches, including stop-watches (HS code 9102) (see table 3).

Table 3: Top 10 export commodities 2009 to 2011

(Value in million US$)

HS code	4-digit heading of Harmonized System 2007	Value (million US$) 2009	2010	2011	Unit value 2009	2010	2011	Unit	SITC code
	All Commodities	172474.1	195609.3	234426.3					
3004	Medicaments (excluding goods of heading 30.02, 30.05 or 30.06)	25733.7	27614.9	31634.1	*284.9*	*301.2*	*337.6*	US$/kg	542
3002	Human blood; animal blood prepared for therapeutic uses	14309.5	16575.6	20294.6	*4.0*	*4.3*	*4.3*	thsd US$/kg	541
9102	Wrist-watches, pocket-watches and other watches, including stop-watches	7214.0	9468.2	12987.8	338.5	367.6		US$/unit	885
9021	Orthopaedic appliances, including crutches, surgical belts and trusses	5713.6	5772.1	6170.9					899
9101	Wrist-watches, pocket-watches and other watches, including stop-watches	4184.5	5133.5	7448.6	10.5	11.1		thsd US$/unit	885
2933	Heterocyclic compounds with nitrogen hetero-atom(s) only	4813.9	5082.8	5867.6	*266.7*			US$/kg	515
7113	Articles of jewellery and parts thereof, of precious metal	3919.2	4799.5	6878.8	*101.4*	*119.2*	*142.3*	thsd US$/kg	897
2716	Electrical energy	4183.6	4863.7	6262.7	80.1	73.6	*60.9*	US$/MWh	351
7110	Platinum, unwrought or in semi-manufactured forms, or in powder form	2786.3	4717.0	4945.9		*33.0*	*39.5*	thsd US$/kg	681
2924	Carboxyamide-function compounds; amide-function compounds of carbonic acid	2393.7	2329.9	2581.9	*95.9*	*53.2*	*45.3*	US$/kg	514

Graph 2: Trade Balance by MDG Regions in 2011

(Bln US$)

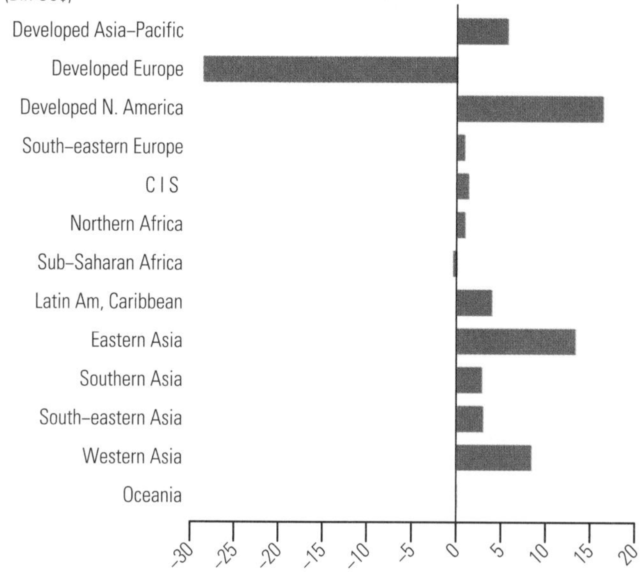

Graph 3: Partner concentration of trade in 2011

(Cumulative share by ranked partners)

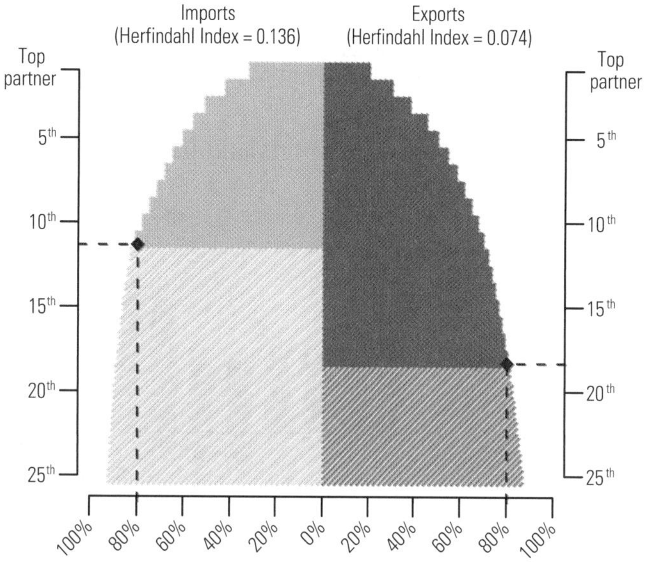

Table 4: Exports by principal countries and SITC sections in 2011

(Value in million US$, percentages of country total)

Country	Total	Shares by SITC sections (%)								
		0 + 1	2 + 4	3	5	6	7	8	9	Total
World	234 426.3	3.7	1.1	3.1	35.6	9.4	20.8	23.5	2.9	100
Germany	47 297.9	2.9	2.5	7.8	27.4	12.9	25.7	16.9	3.9	100
USA	24 037.2	3.1	0.1	0.5	42.3	7.5	17.4	26.8	2.3	100
Italy	18 175.3	3.0	3.2	12.2	42.1	8.1	11.4	17.7	2.3	100
France	16 795.9	5.3	0.9	3.1	36.2	10.0	17.9	24.4	2.3	100
United Kingdom	11 218.3	4.6	0.4	0.3	36.8	19.1	15.7	21.9	1.1	100
China	9 959.6	0.6	0.2	0.1	14.2	7.9	44.0	30.1	3.0	100
China, Hong Kong SAR	8 912.1	1.4	0.1	0.0	5.3	20.9	5.0	67.0	0.3	100
Japan	7 501.4	4.3	0.1	0.0	48.9	5.8	10.3	29.1	1.4	100
Austria	7 469.3	4.5	2.9	0.8	35.8	12.4	21.1	13.2	9.3	100
Spain	6 548.9	6.4	0.2	0.2	60.5	3.8	13.7	13.8	1.4	100

Imports Profile:

In 2011, Switzerland-Liechtenstein's imports were composed of 26.6 percent of machinery and transport equipment (SITC section 7), 21.4 percent of chemicals and related products, n.e.s. (SITC section 5) and 20.1 percent of miscellaneous manufactured articles (SITC section 8) (see table 2). Over the last three years, main products for imports were medicaments (excluding goods of heading 30.02, 30.05 or 30.06) (HS code 3004), motor cars and other motor vehicles principally designed for the transport (HS code 8703) and articles of jewellery and parts thereof, of precious metal (HS code 7113) (see table 5).

Table 5: Top 10 import commodities 2009 to 2011

(Value in million US$)

HS code	4-digit heading of Harmonized System 2007	Value (million US$)			Unit value				SITC code
		2009	2010	2011	2009	2010	2011	Unit	
	All Commodities	155 378.1	176 280.6	207 263.2					
3004	Medicaments (excluding goods of heading 30.02, 30.05 or 30.06)	12 324.1	12 536.4	14 735.2	*209.5*	*218.8*	*256.8*	US$/kg	542
8703	Motor cars and other motor vehicles principally designed for the transport	7 175.8	8 965.3	11 550.7	*25.9*	*26.9*		thsd US$/unit	781
7113	Articles of jewellery and parts thereof, of precious metal	4 001.3	6 829.9	8 675.4	*38.1*	*41.5*	*59.3*	thsd US$/kg	897
2710	Petroleum oils, other than crude	4 522.0	5 132.0	6 816.2	*0.6*	0.7	1.0	US$/kg	334
2933	Heterocyclic compounds with nitrogen hetero-atom(s) only	3 594.7	4 759.4	5 481.5	*53.8*			US$/kg	515
3002	Human blood; animal blood prepared for therapeutic uses	3 570.5	4 200.5	5 380.2	*0.9*	*0.9*	*1.0*	thsd US$/kg	541
2716	Electrical energy	2 800.6	3 590.6	5 040.4	56.1	53.9	*60.4*	US$/MWh	351
7110	Platinum, unwrought or in semi-manufactured forms, or in powder form	3 812.9	3 197.4	3 898.1		*34.2*	*41.1*	thsd US$/kg	681
8471	Automatic data processing machines and units thereof	2 598.8	3 116.3	3 511.6	279.9	300.7		US$/unit	752
2709	Petroleum oils and oils obtained from bituminous minerals, crude	2 126.1	2 748.2	3 621.8	0.4	0.6	0.8	US$/kg	333

Syrian Arab Republic

Imports: CIF, by consignment | Exports: FOB, by last known destination | Trade System: Special

Overview:

After reaching a peak of 14.4 bln US$ in 2008, the value of the exports of Syrian Arab Republic dropped in 2009 by 32.6 percent but bounced back in 2010 by 17.1 percent to reach 11.4 bln US$ (see table 1 and graph 1). Imports also increased in 2010 by 13.7 percent and amounted to 17.6 bln US$ (see table 2 and graph 1). The trade balance recorded a deficit of 6.2 bln US$ in 2010 (see graph 1). By MDG regions, trade recorded large deficits with Eastern Asia (-2.3 bln US$) and the Commonwealth of Independent States (-2.2 bln US$) (see graph 2). Large surplus was recorded with Western Asia at 1.5 bln US$. Trade, especially imports, was diversified across partners: in 2010, 23 major partners accounted for 80 percent of imports compared to 13 major partners for exports (see graph 3).

Graph 1: Total imports, exports and trade balance

(Bln US$ by year)

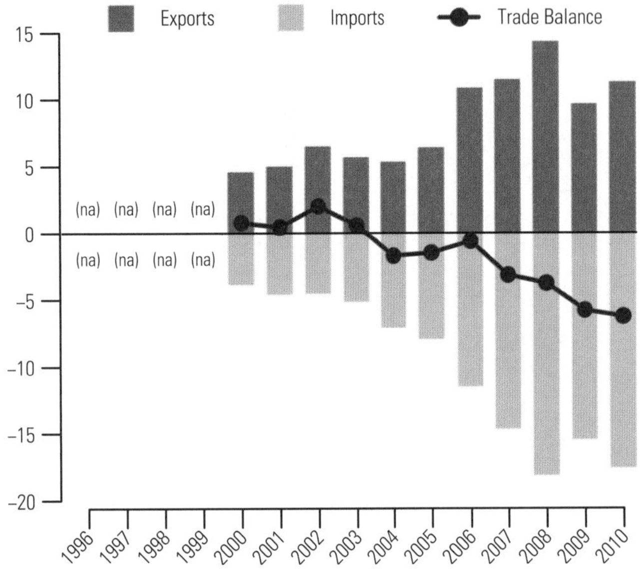

Exports Profile:

In 2010, mineral fuels, lubricants and related materials (SITC section 3) accounted for the majority of exported goods (49.9 percent) (see table 1). Other major commodity groups were food, live animals, beverages and tobacco (SITC sections 0+1) and manufactured goods classified chiefly by material (SITC section 6) respectively with 19.9 percent and 10.0 percent . Iraq, Italy and Germany were the top three markets in 2010 (see table 4). From 2008 to 2010, top exported products included petroleum oils, crude (HS code 2709), petroleum oils, other than crude (HS code 2710) and waters with added sugar (HS code 2202) (see table 3).

Table 1: Exports by SITC sections

(Value in million US$, growth and shares in percentage)

SITC	2010	Avg. Growth rates (%) 2006-2010	2009-2010	2010 share
Total	11352.9	1.0	17.1	100.0
0+1	2263.4	7.4	-10.9	19.9
2+4	527.7	0.0	35.9	4.6
3	5663.5	6.5	54.5	49.9
5	703.1	7.0	2.3	6.2
6	1140.0	-1.6	-3.9	10.0
7	243.4	-17.0	-37.7	2.1
8	808.3	-10.6	-0.2	7.1
9	3.5	-73.9	-85.5	0.0

Table 2: Imports by SITC sections

(Value in million US$, growth and shares in percentage)

SITC	2010	Avg. Growth rates (%) 2006-2010	2009-2010	2010 share
Total	17561.6	11.2	13.7	100.0
0+1	3205.7	24.6	11.5	18.3
2+4	994.4	16.3	-15.2	5.7
3	3451.1	2.6	74.4	19.7
5	2290.1	16.8	7.1	13.0
6	3686.3	11.2	-14.8	21.0
7	3611.7	10.4	39.4	20.6
8	317.6	12.2	23.2	1.8
9	4.7	-62.0	-95.3	0.0

Table 3: Top 10 export commodities 2008 to 2010

(Value in million US$)

HS code	4-digit heading of Harmonized System 2007	Value (million US$) 2008	2009	2010	Unit value 2008	2009	2010	Unit	SITC code
	All Commodities	14380.0	9693.8	11352.9					
2709	Petroleum oils and oils obtained from bituminous minerals, crude	4708.8	2865.5	4325.8	0.6	0.4	0.5	US$/kg	333
2710	Petroleum oils, other than crude	836.7	715.8	1160.8	0.7	0.5	0.7	US$/kg	334
2202	Waters with added sugar	843.5	159.0	105.5	*0.5*	*0.3*	*0.2*	US$/litre	111
5205	Cotton yarn (other than sewing thread), containing 85 % or more	608.2	137.6	191.2	3.2	2.1	2.9	US$/kg	651
5407	Woven fabrics of synthetic filament yarn	447.8	206.4	169.1	2.9	3.2	3.3	US$/kg	653
3402	Organic surface-active agents (other than soap)	292.7	188.6	328.0	1.2	0.8	0.9	US$/kg	554
2510	Natural calcium phosphates	388.9	139.7	202.5	0.2	0.1	0.1	US$/kg	272
8544	Insulated (including enamelled or anodised) wire, cable	350.0	232.3	37.6	5.6	5.6	4.4	US$/kg	773
0104	Live sheep and goats	236.2	137.4	216.1					001
0407	Birds' eggs, in shell, fresh, preserved or cooked	72.2	316.3	131.7	1.5	3.4	1.7	US$/kg	025

Graph 2: Trade Balance by MDG Regions in 2010

(Bln US$)

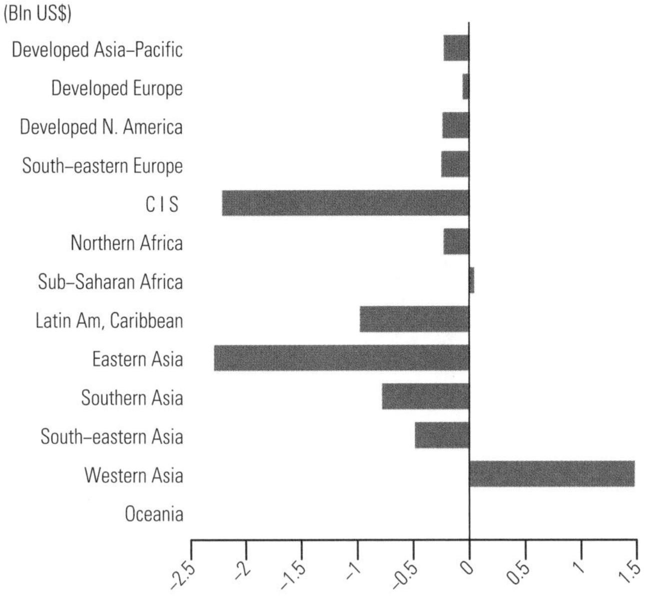

Graph 3: Partner concentration of trade in 2010

(Cumulative share by ranked partners)

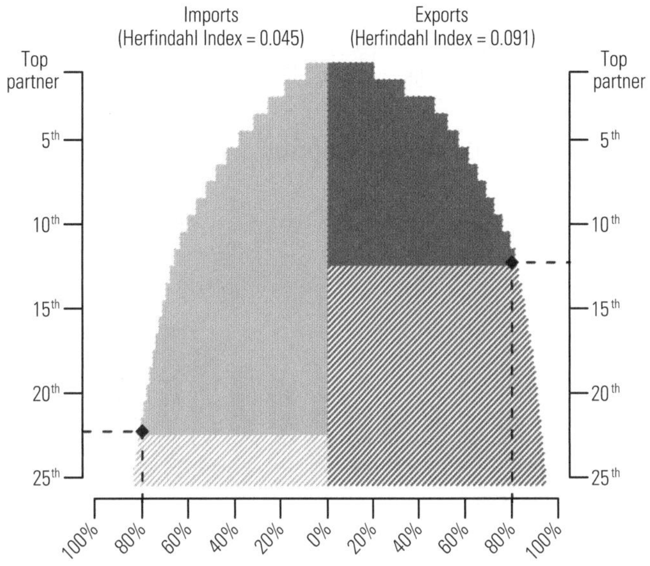

Table 4: Exports by principal countries and SITC sections in 2010

(Value in million US$, percentages of country total)

Country	Total	0 + 1	2 + 4	3	5	6	7	8	9	Total
		Shares by SITC sections (%)								
World	11352.9	19.9	4.6	49.9	6.2	10.0	2.1	7.1	0.0	100
Iraq	2294.5	50.7	0.6	0.0	19.0	11.2	3.2	15.2	0.0	100
Italy	1520.2	0.1	0.7	95.5	0.2	3.2	0.3	0.2	...	100
Germany	1477.1	0.5	0.4	95.1	0.1	2.0	0.1	1.9	0.0	100
Turkey	629.2	2.8	17.0	47.0	5.3	23.2	0.9	3.8	...	100
Saudi Arabia	542.6	52.5	4.3	0.0	6.1	19.1	2.9	14.7	0.3	100
France	484.9	0.4	0.9	95.3	0.6	0.6	0.1	2.0	...	100
Lebanon	436.2	25.7	14.7	30.6	8.2	14.2	2.5	3.8	0.2	100
Jordan	405.9	57.6	5.3	7.1	6.7	15.6	3.5	4.1	0.1	100
USA	399.6	1.0	0.5	97.7	0.1	0.2	0.0	0.6	0.0	100
Netherlands	397.2	0.7	0.2	98.8	0.0	0.2	0.0	0.0	...	100

Imports Profile:

In 2010, imports of the Syrian Arab Republic were composed of 21.0 percent of manufactured goods classified chiefly by material (SITC section 6), 20.6 percent of machinery and transport equipment (SITC section 7) and 19.7 percent of mineral fuels, lubricants and related materials (SITC section 3) (see table 2). From 2008 to 2010, top imported products included petroleum oils, other than crude (HS code 2710), semi-finished products of iron or non-alloy steel (HS code 7207) and motor cars and other motor vehicles principally designed for the transport (HS code 8703) (see table 5).

Table 5: Top 10 import commodities 2008 to 2010

(Value in million US$)

HS code	4-digit heading of Harmonized System 2007	Value (million US$) 2008	2009	2010	Unit value 2008	2009	2010	Unit	SITC code
	All Commodities	18104.7	15442.8	17561.6					
2710	Petroleum oils, other than crude	5363.2	1638.5	3002.9	0.8	0.5	0.7	US$/kg	334
7207	Semi-finished products of iron or non-alloy steel	1128.3	855.3	552.2	0.6	0.4	0.5	US$/kg	672
8703	Motor cars and other motor vehicles principally designed for the transport	541.5	516.1	718.0	*13.6*		*15.6*	thsd US$/unit	781
1701	Cane or beet sugar and chemically pure sucrose, in solid form	314.6	530.0	740.6	0.4	0.4	0.6	US$/kg	061
1005	Maize (corn)	258.2	360.1	420.8	0.3	0.2	0.2	US$/kg	044
3901	Polymers of ethylene, in primary forms	343.1	323.0	353.6	1.6	1.1	1.3	US$/kg	571
7208	Flat-rolled products of iron or non-alloy steel	325.3	408.8	249.6	0.7	0.5	0.6	US$/kg	673
2711	Petroleum gases and other gaseous hydrocarbons	322.6	265.9	339.5	*0.8*	0.6	0.8	US$/kg	343
7210	Flat-rolled products of iron or non-alloy steel	246.0	348.8	188.7	0.9	0.7	0.8	US$/kg	674
1201	Soya beans, whether or not broken	166.9	340.0	222.5	0.3	0.4	0.4	US$/kg	222

Thailand

Imports: CIF, by origin | **Exports: FOB, by last known destination** | **Trade System: Special**

Overview:

From 2007 to 2011, Thailand's exports increased on average by 10.5 percent each year despite a decline of 13.3 percent in 2009 and amounted to 228.8 bln US$ in 2011 (see table 1 and graph 1). Similarly, imports increased on average by 12.3 percent each year and reached 228.5 bln US$ (see table 2 and graph 1). The trade balance recorded a surplus of 340.7 mln US$, well below the 2010 surplus of 12.9 bln US$ (see graph 1). Trade with South-eastern Asia, Developed North America and Southern Asia recorded surpluses amounting respectively to 15.1 bln US$, 9.1 bln US$ and 5.7 bln US$ (see graph 2). Trade recorded significant deficits with Western Asia (-20.5 bln US$) and Developed Asia-Pacific (-17.8 bln US$) among others. Compared to imports, exports were diversified across partners in 2011: 21 major partners accounted for 80 percent of exports compared to 16 major partners for imports (see graph 3).

Graph 1: Total imports, exports and trade balance

(Bln US$ by year)

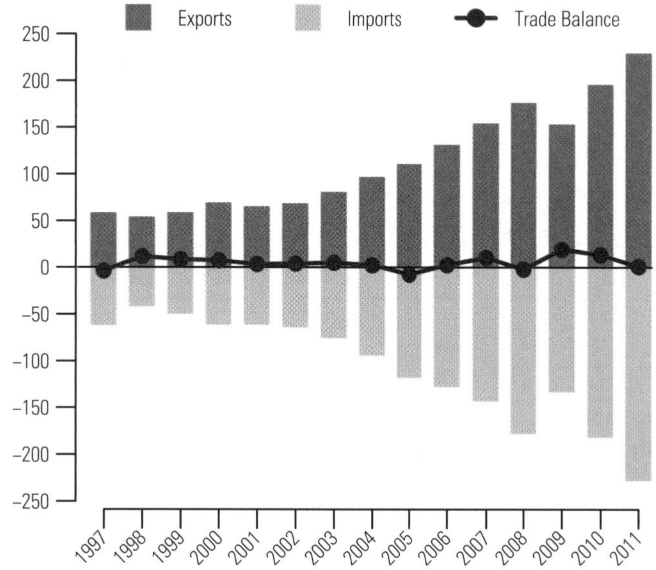

Table 1: Exports by SITC sections

(Value in million US$, growth and shares in percentage)

SITC	2011	Avg. Growth rates (%) 2007-2011	Avg. Growth rates (%) 2010-2011	2011 share
Total	228824.0	10.5	17.2	100.0
0+1	30671.1	15.4	24.6	13.4
2+4	18220.9	20.0	57.9	8.0
3	12871.2	17.1	33.5	5.6
5	22787.6	17.0	34.6	10.0
6	28837.5	8.3	21.2	12.6
7	85847.6	5.7	4.2	37.5
8	23660.0	10.0	19.1	10.3
9	5928.1	23.3	-9.0	2.6

Exports Profile:

In 2011, exports of Thailand were composed of 37.5 percent of machinery and transport equipment (SITC section 7), 13.4 percent of food, live animals, beverages and tobacco (SITC sections 0+1) and 12.6 percent of manufactured goods classified chiefly by material (SITC section 6) (see table 1). Top markets for exports were China, Japan and USA all having large shares of exports of machinery and transport equipment (SITC section 7) (see table 4). From 2009 to 2011, Thailand's main exported products were automatic data processing machines and units thereof (HS code 8471), natural rubber, balata, gutta-percha, guayule, chicle (HS code 4001) and petroleum oils, other than crude (HS code 2710) (see table 3).

Table 2: Imports by SITC sections

(Value in million US$, growth and shares in percentage)

SITC	2011	Avg. Growth rates (%) 2007-2011	Avg. Growth rates (%) 2010-2011	2011 share
Total	228483.3	12.3	25.3	100.0
0+1	9218.1	15.4	23.4	4.0
2+4	7823.7	12.9	32.7	3.4
3	43495.8	13.8	37.4	19.0
5	23762.2	11.5	19.4	10.4
6	39168.0	7.0	18.2	17.1
7	74631.0	10.1	16.1	32.7
8	13900.8	10.7	14.2	6.1
9	16483.6	58.0	110.0	7.2

Table 3: Top 10 export commodities 2009 to 2011

(Value in million US$)

HS code	4-digit heading of Harmonized System 2007	Value (million US$) 2009	2010	2011	Unit value 2009	2010	2011	Unit	SITC code
	All Commodities	152497.2	195311.5	228824.0					
8471	Automatic data processing machines and units thereof	11175.6	12852.1	11189.6	*29.0*			US$/unit	752
4001	Natural rubber, balata, gutta-percha, guayule, chicle	4308.0	7896.0	13176.4	1.6	*2.9*	*4.4*	US$/kg	231
2710	Petroleum oils, other than crude	6302.5	7797.9	10093.2	*1.3*	*1.0*	*1.1*	US$/kg	334
8542	Electronic integrated circuits	6444.6	8066.2	7910.4					776
7108	Gold (including gold plated with platinum)	5667.8	6493.8	5897.3	7.9	*2.5*	*40.7*	thsd US$/kg	971
8703	Motor cars and other motor vehicles principally designed for the transport	4090.8	7027.6	6264.7	*3.1*	*16.5*		thsd US$/unit	781
1006	Rice	5046.5	5341.1	6507.5	0.6	*0.6*	*0.6*	US$/kg	042
8704	Motor vehicles for the transport of goods	3538.7	5844.0	5360.8					782
8708	Parts and accessories of the motor vehicles of headings 87.01 to 87.05	3003.4	4156.0	4581.9	7.7	*7.8*	*8.4*	US$/kg	784
8473	Parts and accessories for use with machines of heading 84.69 to 84.72	3042.7	3634.0	4001.2	170.5	*152.8*	*161.6*	US$/kg	759

Graph 2: Trade Balance by MDG Regions in 2011

(Bln US$)

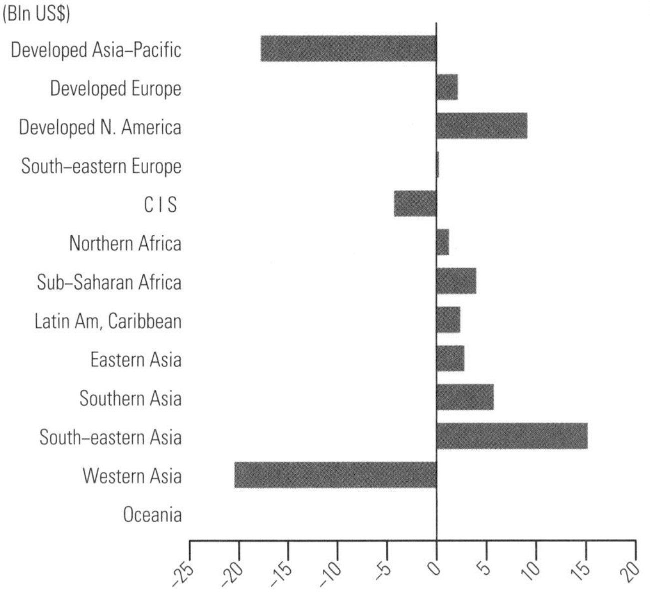

Graph 3: Partner concentration of trade in 2011

(Cumulative share by ranked partners)

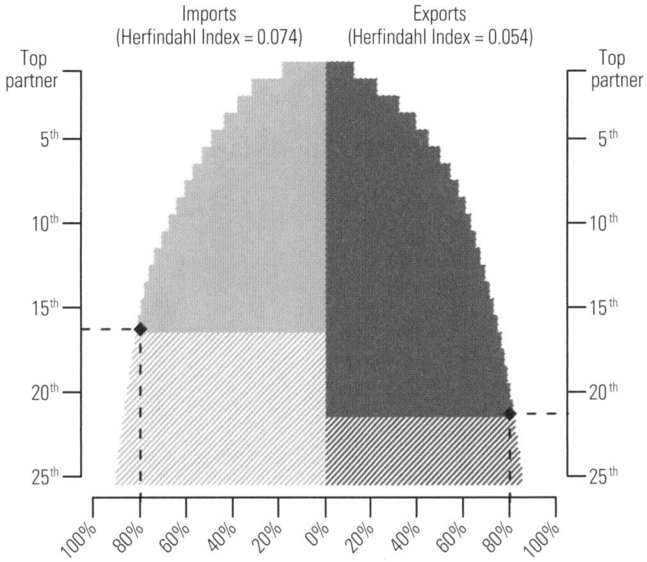

Table 4: Exports by principal countries and SITC sections in 2011

(Value in million US$, percentages of country total)

Country	Total	Shares by SITC sections (%) 0 + 1	2 + 4	3	5	6	7	8	9	Total
World	228824.0	13.4	8.0	5.6	10.0	12.6	37.5	10.3	2.6	100
China	27402.4	7.7	23.7	4.1	20.7	11.9	29.3	2.5	0.0	100
Japan	24070.3	19.0	9.2	1.7	9.2	12.3	36.7	11.4	0.5	100
USA	21893.1	18.6	5.2	3.3	2.1	11.9	38.4	20.5	0.0	100
China, Hong Kong SAR	16479.0	4.2	0.6	1.0	4.0	13.7	39.6	29.9	7.0	100
Malaysia	12398.7	7.4	15.0	9.6	9.6	11.3	43.9	3.0	0.2	100
Singapore	11450.1	4.9	2.0	35.5	6.0	7.4	37.8	5.5	0.7	100
Indonesia	10078.0	14.4	3.5	2.0	19.8	11.1	46.6	2.4	0.3	100
Australia	7997.1	10.0	0.4	3.4	8.7	11.1	50.3	8.9	7.0	100
Viet Nam	7059.2	10.1	5.7	12.7	16.3	22.5	29.3	3.4	0.0	100
India	5181.4	1.5	10.9	1.5	25.8	18.5	34.1	7.2	0.6	100

Imports Profile:

Machinery and transport equipment (SITC section 7) accounted for about one-third (32.7 percent) of imports (see table 2). Other major commodity groups included mineral fuels, lubricants and related materials (SITC section 3) and manufactured goods classified chiefly by material (SITC section 6) respectively with 19.0 and 17.1 percent of imports. From 2009 to 2011, main imported goods were petroleum oils and oils obtained from bituminous minerals, crude (HS code 2709), electronic integrated circuits (HS code 8542) and gold (including gold plated with platinum) (HS code 7108) (see table 5).

Table 5: Top 10 import commodities 2009 to 2011

(Value in million US$)

HS code	4-digit heading of Harmonized System 2007	Value (million US$) 2009	2010	2011	Unit value 2009	2010	2011	Unit	SITC code
	All Commodities	133769.6	182393.4	228483.3					
2709	Petroleum oils and oils obtained from bituminous minerals, crude	19008.3	23893.9	32897.4	*0.5*	*0.6*	*0.8*	US$/kg	333
8542	Electronic integrated circuits	8104.1	10762.0	10105.6					776
7108	Gold (including gold plated with platinum)	3785.0	7848.9	16464.8	30.7	*37.5*	*50.1*	thsd US$/kg	971
8708	Parts and accessories of the motor vehicles of headings 87.01 to 87.05	2857.3	5065.5	5533.0	9.0	*10.2*	*10.8*	US$/kg	784
2711	Petroleum gases and other gaseous hydrocarbons	3029.9	3769.0	4944.0	0.3	*0.4*	*0.4*	US$/kg	343
8473	Parts and accessories for use with machines of heading 84.69 to 84.72	4023.5	4050.7	3586.3	65.1	*51.8*	*48.2*	US$/kg	759
8471	Automatic data processing machines and units thereof	1818.2	2327.2	3252.4	*54.2*			US$/unit	752
8517	Electrical apparatus for line telephony or line telegraphy	1698.0	2248.1	3125.6					764
8523	Prepared unrecorded media for sound recording	1943.1	2303.9	2412.8	2.2	2.4	2.5	US$/unit	898
7326	Other articles of iron or steel	1659.2	2218.8	2307.8	9.0	*8.8*	*8.2*	US$/kg	699

The former Yugoslav Republic of Macedonia

Imports: CIF, by origin | **Exports: FOB, by last known destination** | **Trade System: Special**

Overview:

Since 2007, exports of The Former Yugoslav Republic of Macedonia increased on average by 7.3 percent each year and amounted to 4.5 bln US$ in 2011 (see table 1 and graph 1). Imports increased on average 7.6 percent over the same period to amount to 7.0 bln US$ in 2011 (see table 2 and graph 1). The trade balance recorded a deficit of 2.5 bln US$ in 2011 (see graph 1). By MDG regions, TFYR of Macedonia recorded a trade deficit of 1.0 bln US$ with Developed Europe (see graph 2). Major trade deficits were also recorded with Commonwealth of Independent States (-709.2 mln US$) and Western Asia (-281.1 mln US$). South-eastern Europe is the only region with a trade surplus (+224.9 mln US$). In 2011, imports were more diversified across partners than exports: 16 major partners accounted for 80 percent of imported goods compared to 12 major partners for exports (see graph 3). See footnote*.

Graph 1: Total imports, exports and trade balance

(Bln US$ by year)

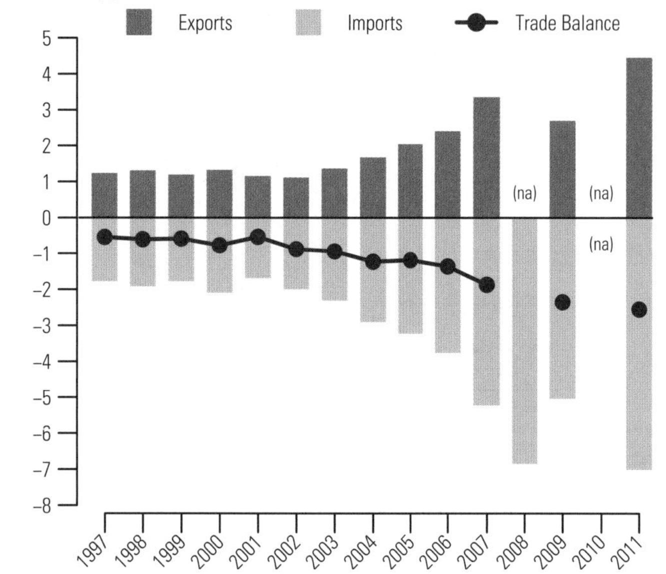

Exports Profile:

In 2011, TFYR of Macedonia's exports were composed of 27.6 percent of manufactured goods classified chiefly by material (SITC section 6), 18.7 percent of miscellaneous manufactured articles (SITC section 8) and 16.7 percent of chemicals and related products, n.e.s. (SITC section 5) (see table 1). Germany, Serbia and Bulgaria were the three main markets for exports (see table 4). Over the last three years, top exported goods included reaction initiators, reaction accelerators and catalytic preparations (HS code 3815), ferro-alloys (HS code 7202) and petroleum oils, other than crude (HS code 2710) (see table 3).

Table 1: Exports by SITC sections

(Value in million US$, growth and shares in percentage)

SITC	2011	Avg. Growth rates (%) 2007-2011	2010-2011	2011 share
Total	4 455.4	7.3	...	100.0
0+1	608.2	7.5	...	13.7
2+4	306.4	15.4	...	6.9
3	372.4	22.5	...	8.4
5	746.1	54.1	...	16.7
6	1 231.5	-4.9	...	27.6
7	352.6	23.9	...	7.9
8	834.5	1.8	...	18.7
9	3.6	16.8	...	0.1

Table 2: Imports by SITC sections

(Value in million US$, growth and shares in percentage)

SITC	2011	Avg. Growth rates (%) 2007-2011	2010-2011	2011 share
Total	7 007.3	7.6	...	100.0
0+1	740.9	7.6	...	10.6
2+4	441.6	6.7	...	6.3
3	1 436.9	10.1	...	20.5
5	824.4	14.3	...	11.8
6	1 950.3	7.1	...	27.8
7	1 182.0	3.3	...	16.9
8	418.9	4.7	...	6.0
9	12.2	26.8	...	0.2

Table 3: Top 10 export commodities 2009 to 2011

(Value in million US$)

HS code	4-digit heading of Harmonized System 2007	Value (million US$) 2009	2010	2011	Unit value 2009	2010	2011	Unit	SITC code
	All Commodities	2 691.5	...	4 455.4					
9999	Commodities not specified according to kind	706.3	...	1.9					931
3815	Reaction initiators, reaction accelerators and catalytic preparations	6.1	...	541.5	99.2		183.2	US$/kg	598
7202	Ferro-alloys	29.6	...	513.2	1.0		2.9	US$/kg	671
2710	Petroleum oils, other than crude	12.5	...	303.6	0.6		1.0	US$/kg	334
6204	Women's or girls' suits, ensembles, jackets, blazers, dresses, skirts	141.7	...	161.2	15.9		18.6	US$/unit	842
7208	Flat-rolled products of iron or non-alloy steel	27.4	...	220.4	0.5		0.7	US$/kg	673
6206	Women's or girls' blouses, shirts and shirt-blouses	112.0	...	96.4	7.8		11.4	US$/unit	842
2401	Unmanufactured tobacco; tobacco refuse	88.1	...	118.1	5.5		5.4	US$/kg	121
6205	Men's or boys' shirts	91.8	...	106.2	*13.1*		13.5	US$/unit	841
6203	Men's or boys' suits, ensembles, jackets, blazers, trousers	92.0	...	103.9	23.4		23.4	US$/unit	841

*2009 data having high number of non-standard commodity codes

Graph 2: Trade Balance by MDG Regions in 2011

(Bln US$)

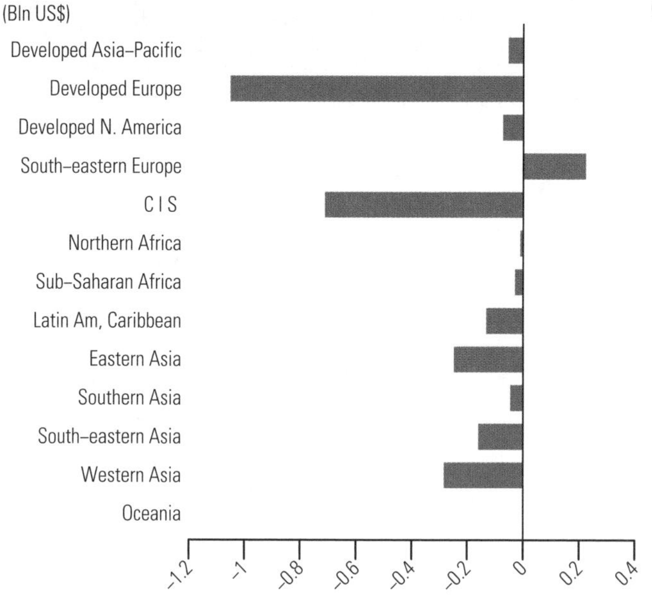

Graph 3: Partner concentration of trade in 2011

(Cumulative share by ranked partners)

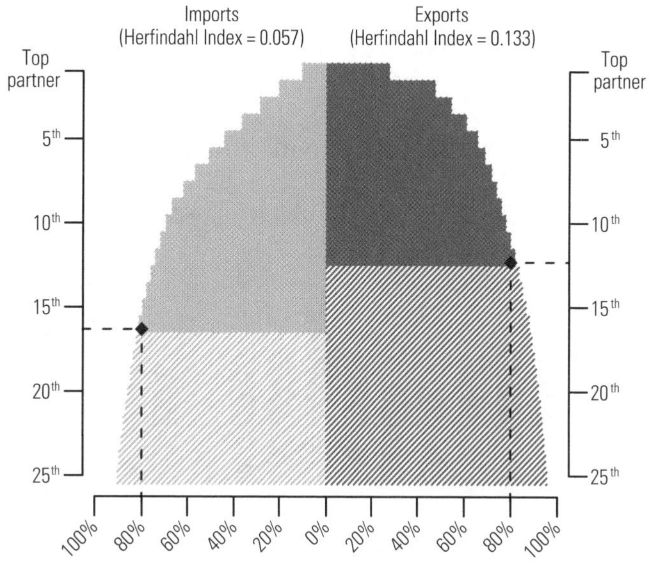

Table 4: Exports by principal countries and SITC sections in 2011

(Value in million US$, percentages of country total)

Country	Total	Shares by SITC sections (%) 0 + 1	2 + 4	3	5	6	7	8	9	Total
World	4455.4	13.7	6.9	8.4	16.7	27.6	7.9	18.7	0.1	100
Germany	1241.9	3.0	0.5	0.1	43.5	6.1	10.8	36.0	0.0	100
Serbia	874.2	20.8	2.0	37.5	9.0	23.0	4.4	3.2	0.0	100
Bulgaria	307.7	8.9	59.6	0.5	7.6	16.9	2.6	3.7	0.3	100
Italy	289.7	8.3	1.9	0.1	3.1	52.8	1.2	32.6	0.1	100
Greece	215.2	21.4	17.8	0.3	1.7	24.4	3.2	31.3	0.0	100
Croatia	139.6	29.5	1.9	0.1	8.8	50.6	3.7	5.4	0.0	100
China	127.5	0.8	1.1	0.0	0.3	95.5	2.4	0.0	0.0	100
Ukraine	95.8	2.9	0.0	...	0.5	83.8	12.8	0.1	0.0	100
Bosnia Herzegovina	93.1	42.5	1.2	0.0	21.8	26.2	6.1	2.3	0.0	100
Slovenia	88.2	12.7	1.6	38.6	3.4	23.8	13.0	6.9	0.0	100

Imports Profile:

In 2011, imports were composed of 27.8 percent of manufactured goods classified chiefly by material (SITC section 6), 20.5 percent of mineral fuels, lubricants and related materials (SITC section 3) and 16.9 percent of machinery and transport equipment (SITC section 7) (see table 2). Over the last three years, top imported products included petroleum oils and oils obtained from bituminous minerals, crude (HS code 2709), petroleum oils, other than crude (HS code 2710) and platinum, unwrought or in semi-manufactured forms, or in powder form (HS code 7110) (see table 5).

Table 5: Top 10 import commodities 2009 to 2011

(Value in million US$)

HS code	4-digit heading of Harmonized System 2007	Value (million US$) 2009	2010	2011	Unit value 2009	2010	2011	Unit	SITC code
	All Commodities	5043.1	...	7007.3					
9999	Commodities not specified according to kind	846.4	...	12.2					931
2709	Petroleum oils and oils obtained from bituminous minerals, crude	...	...	578.1			0.8	US$/kg	333
2710	Petroleum oils, other than crude	49.7	...	429.8	0.8		1.0	US$/kg	334
7110	Platinum, unwrought or in semi-manufactured forms, or in powder form	0.0	...	382.1			50.0	thsd US$/kg	681
8703	Motor cars and other motor vehicles principally designed for the transport	169.0	...	189.0	12.8		4.7	thsd US$/unit	781
2716	Electrical energy	120.9	...	228.0	75.8		70.0	US$/MWh	351
7208	Flat-rolled products of iron or non-alloy steel	111.9	...	216.7	0.5		0.7	US$/kg	673
3004	Medicaments (excluding goods of heading 30.02, 30.05 or 30.06)	109.6	...	128.4	36.8		39.8	US$/kg	542
2711	Petroleum gases and other gaseous hydrocarbons	55.9	...	101.9	0.6		0.8	US$/kg	343
5208	Woven fabrics of cotton, containing 85 % or more by weight of cotton	66.1	...	81.9	20.8		25.3	US$/kg	652

Togo

Imports: CIF, by origin | **Exports: FOB, by last known destination** | **Trade System: Special**

Overview:

In 2011, exports of Togo increased by 29.7 percent and amounted to 865.5 mln US$ (see table 1 and graph 1). Similarly, imports increased by 22.1 percent and amounted to 1.2 bln US$ in 2011 (see table 2 and graph 1). This resulted in a trade deficit of 342.2 mln US$ in 2011 (see graph 1). This deficit came largely from trade with Developed Europe (-381.3 mln US$) , Eastern Asia (-124.5 mln US$) and Western Asia (-51.7 mln US$) (see graph 2). Major surplus was recorded with Sub-Saharan Africa (+321.8 mln US$). Togo's exports were diversified in 2011: 14 major partners accounted for 80 percent of exports compared to 22 major partners for imports (see graph 3).

Graph 1: Total imports, exports and trade balance

(Bln US$ by year)

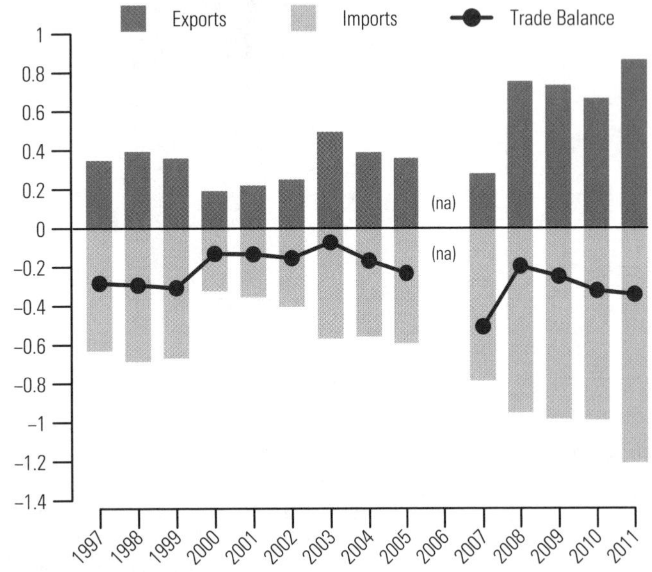

Table 1: Exports by SITC sections

(Value in million US$, growth and shares in percentage)

SITC	2011	Avg. Growth rates (%) 2007-2011	2010-2011	2011 share
Total	865.5	32.6	29.7	100.0
0+1	76.7	17.7	7.6	8.9
2+4	329.3	49.8	67.6	38.0
3	5.7	358.7	499.9	0.7
5	104.4	134.3	31.5	12.1
6	197.5	4.8	10.9	22.8
7	25.2	101.2	-24.5	2.9
8	93.4	100.0	9.3	10.8
9	33.3	...	50.0	3.8

Exports Profile:

In 2011, the majority of the exports of Togo were inedible crude materials (except fuels), animal and vegetable oils, fats and waxes (SITC sections 2+4) and manufactured goods classified chiefly by material (SITC section 6): they accounted respectively for 38.0 and 22.8 percent of exports (see table 1). Major destinations in 2011 were China, Burkina Faso and Benin (see table 4). More than 99.0 percent of exports to China were inedible crude materials (except fuels), animal and vegetable oils, fats and waxes (SITC sections 2+4). The top commodities for exports in 2011 were cotton, not carded or combed (HS code 5201), portland cement, aluminous cement, slag cement (HS code 2523) and natural calcium phosphates (HS code 2510) (see table 3).

Table 2: Imports by SITC sections

(Value in million US$, growth and shares in percentage)

SITC	2011	Avg. Growth rates (%) 2007-2011	2010-2011	2011 share
Total	1 207.7	11.3	22.1	100.0
0+1	186.2	14.7	26.3	15.4
2+4	50.2	16.6	42.8	4.2
3	186.4	-3.3	35.4	15.4
5	117.5	13.2	4.9	9.7
6	309.0	12.9	33.6	25.6
7	267.6	24.6	16.4	22.2
8	90.8	8.0	-5.4	7.5
9	0.0	...	1940.0	0.0

Table 3: Top 10 export commodities 2009 to 2011

(Value in million US$)

HS code	4-digit heading of Harmonized System 2007	Value (million US$) 2009	2010	2011	Unit value 2009	2010	2011	Unit	SITC code
	All Commodities	734.7	667.2	865.5					
5201	Cotton, not carded or combed	136.1	141.7	268.2	1.3	1.4	1.9	US$/kg	263
2523	Portland cement, aluminous cement, slag cement	119.0	117.4	121.7	0.1	0.1	0.1	US$/kg	661
2510	Natural calcium phosphates	151.1	47.2	42.5	0.1	0.1	0.3	US$/kg	272
3923	Articles for the conveyance or packing of goods, of plastics	33.1	30.9	47.8	1.7	1.4	1.7	US$/kg	893
3105	Mineral or chemical fertilisers	24.1	30.1	45.8	0.7	0.5	0.6	US$/kg	562
3304	Beauty or make-up preparations	26.7	27.6	34.4	3.6	3.6	3.5	US$/kg	553
7108	Gold (including gold plated with platinum)	4.3	21.5	33.3	2.1	2.0	2.1	thsd US$/kg	971
4601	Plaits and similar products of plaiting materials	11.6	12.3	17.5	2.1	2.1	2.3	US$/kg	899
2202	Waters with added sugar	11.2	12.7	14.8	*0.6*	*0.7*	*0.7*	US$/litre	111
1801	Cocoa beans, whole or broken, raw or roasted	15.5	10.4	9.3	0.4	0.5	0.4	US$/kg	072

Graph 2: Trade Balance by MDG Regions in 2011

(Mln US$)

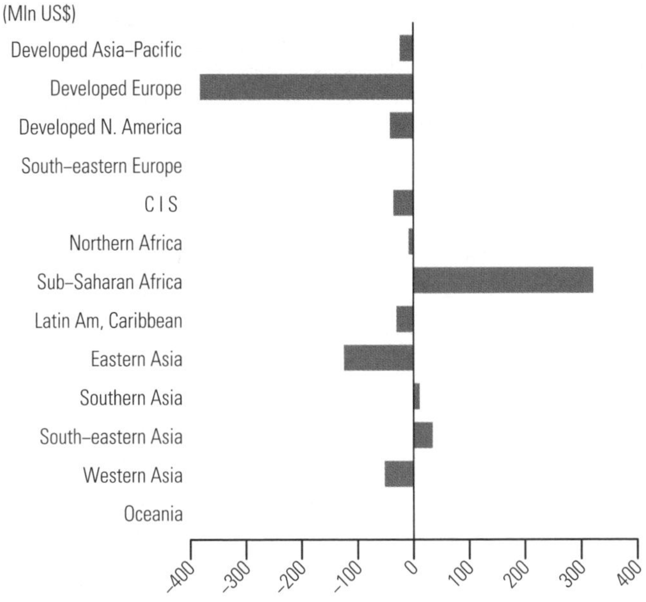

Graph 3: Partner concentration of trade in 2011

(Cumulative share by ranked partners)

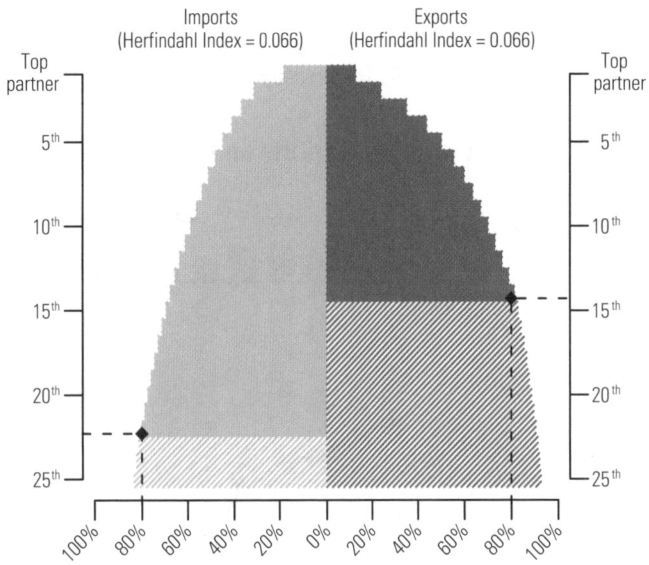

Table 4: Exports by principal countries and SITC sections in 2011

(Value in million US$, percentages of country total)

Country	Total	Shares by SITC sections (%) 0+1	2+4	3	5	6	7	8	9	Total
World	865.5	8.9	38.0	0.7	12.1	22.8	2.9	10.8	3.8	100
China	108.5	0.5	99.2	...	...	0.0	0.3	0.0	...	100
Burkina Faso	99.2	12.8	0.6	0.3	17.1	51.4	5.4	12.5	...	100
Benin	97.0	14.1	1.1	0.7	18.7	42.9	1.2	21.3	...	100
Niger	75.2	8.4	1.1	0.8	10.9	61.5	2.3	15.0	...	100
Ghana	55.4	9.5	2.1	1.9	8.3	64.5	4.0	9.6	...	100
Nigeria	45.7	0.2	0.9	...	70.8	2.3	0.7	25.1	...	100
Indonesia	38.1	0.1	99.9	...	...	...	...	...	...	100
Côte d'Ivoire	31.4	19.7	0.3	3.0	38.1	13.7	10.9	14.3	...	100
Malaysia	29.6	12.7	87.3	...	...	0.1	...	...	...	100
Switzerland	26.9	0.2	0.0	0.7	...	...	0.0	0.0	99.1	100

Imports Profile:

Togo's imports in 2011 were composed of 25.6 percent of manufactured goods classified chiefly by material (SITC section 6), 22.2 percent of machinery and transport equipment (SITC section 7) and 15.4 percent of both mineral fuels, lubricants and related materials (SITC section 3) and food, live animals, beverages and tobacco (SITC sections 0+1) (see table 2). In addition to petroleum oils, other than crude (HS code 2710), other major imported products in 2011 were portland cement, aluminous cement, slag cement (HS code 2523) and medicaments (excluding goods of heading 30.02, 30.05 or 30.06) (HS code 3004) (see table 3).

Table 5: Top 10 import commodities 2009 to 2011

(Value in million US$)

HS code	4-digit heading of Harmonized System 2007	Value (million US$) 2009	2010	2011	Unit value 2009	2010	2011	Unit	SITC code
	All Commodities	983.9	989.5	1 207.7					
2710	Petroleum oils, other than crude	144.0	132.1	174.6	0.6	0.4	0.9	US$/kg	334
2523	Portland cement, aluminous cement, slag cement	78.3	71.1	93.3	0.1	0.1	0.1	US$/kg	661
3004	Medicaments (excluding goods of heading 30.02, 30.05 or 30.06)	56.5	70.6	48.8	16.4	18.0	13.8	US$/kg	542
8703	Motor cars and other motor vehicles principally designed for the transport	35.4	36.5	46.2	*17.2*	*19.1*		thsd US$/unit	781
8517	Electrical apparatus for line telephony or line telegraphy	31.1	33.7	34.2					764
7213	Bars and rods, hot-rolled, in irregularly wound coils	18.7	17.7	32.4	0.6	0.6	0.7	US$/kg	676
1001	Wheat and meslin	20.3	14.4	29.5	0.4	0.3	0.4	US$/kg	041
8504	Electrical transformers, static converters	50.4	6.6	5.9					771
5208	Woven fabrics of cotton, containing 85 % or more by weight of cotton	17.9	16.1	24.2	1.6	1.6	1.6	US$/kg	652
0303	Fish, frozen, excluding fish fillets and other fish meat of heading 03.04	7.0	21.2	28.3	0.7	0.6	0.6	US$/kg	034

Tonga

Imports: CIF, by origin | **Exports: FOB, by last known destination** | **Trade System: General**

Overview:

From 2006 to 2010, Tonga's exports dropped on average by 3.7 percent each year and amounted to 8.3 mln US$ in 2010 (see table 1 and graph 1). During the same period, imports increased on average by 8.0 percent each year to reach 158.8 mln US$ in 2010 (see table 2 and graph 1). This resulted in a trade deficit of 150.5 mln US$, higher than the 136.8 deficit in 2009 (see graph 1). By MDG regions, deficits with Developed Asia-Pacific and South-eastern Asia amounted respectively to 66.4 mln US$ and 37.4 mln US$ (see graph 2). Major deficits were also recorded with Developed North America (-19.6 mln US$) and Oceania (-16.0 mln US$). Both imports and exports were concentrated among a few partners: in 2010, 4 (respectively 5) major partners accounted for 80 percent of exports (respectively imports) (see graph 3).

Graph 1: Total imports, exports and trade balance

(Mln US$ by year)

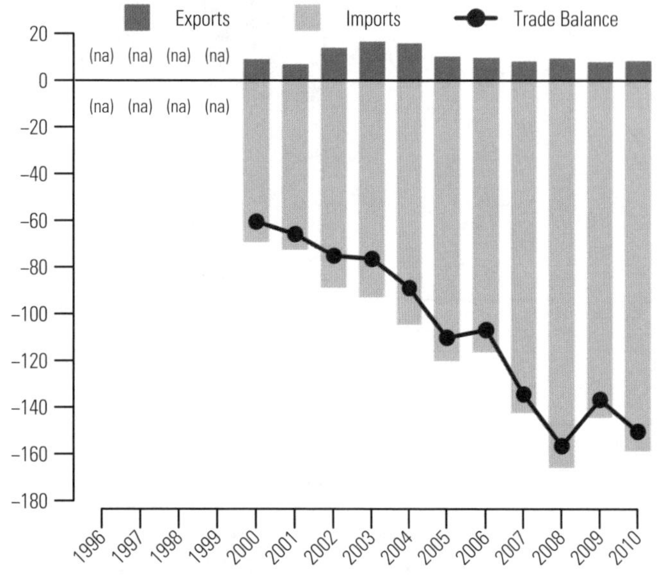

Exports Profile:

Tonga's exports in 2010 were dominated by food, live animals, beverages and tobacco (SITC sections 0+1) with 88.5 percent of total exports (see table 1). Other commodity groups include chemicals and related products, n.e.s. (SITC section 5) and inedible crude materials (except fuels), animal and vegetable oils, fats and waxes (SITC sections 2+4) respectively with 4.4 percent and 3.5 percent. Major markets for exported goods were China, Hong Kong SAR, New Zealand and USA (see table 4). From 2008 to 2010, top products for exports were molluscs, whether in shell or not (HS code 0307), fish, fresh or chilled, excluding fish fillets (HS code 0302) and manioc, arrowroot, sweet potatoes and similar roots (HS code 0714) (see table 3).

Table 1: Exports by SITC sections

(Value in million US$, growth and shares in percentage)

SITC	2010	Avg. Growth rates (%) 2006-2010	2009-2010	2010 share
Total	8.3	-3.7	5.9	100.0
0+1	7.3	14.2	9.1	88.5
2+4	0.3	-14.8	6.4	3.5
5	0.4	6.7	29.7	4.4
6	0.0	-19.0	-41.3	0.4
7	0.0	-19.7	-98.2	0.0
8	0.2	26.2	-33.0	2.8
9	0.0	-71.5	35.6	0.3

Table 2: Imports by SITC sections

(Value in million US$, growth and shares in percentage)

SITC	2010	Avg. Growth rates (%) 2006-2010	2009-2010	2010 share
Total	158.8	8.0	9.8	100.0
0+1	45.7	15.6	-5.2	28.8
2+4	4.6	78.3	34.5	2.9
3	36.2	4.6	22.9	22.8
5	7.4	52.0	8.7	4.7
6	21.0	29.8	39.4	13.2
7	31.0	34.2	14.1	19.5
8	12.0	42.1	37.7	7.6
9	1.0	-60.1	-83.1	0.6

Table 3: Top 10 export commodities 2008 to 2010

(Value in million US$)

HS code	4-digit heading of Harmonized System 2007	Value (million US$) 2008	2009	2010	Unit value 2008	2009	2010	Unit	SITC code
	All Commodities	9.3	7.8	8.3					
0307	Molluscs, whether in shell or not	0.2	2.3	2.5	7.8	9.2	12.0	US$/kg	036
0302	Fish, fresh or chilled, excluding fish fillets	1.6	1.0	1.7	5.2	8.2	8.1	US$/kg	034
0714	Manioc, arrowroot, sweet potatoes and similar roots	1.7	1.1	0.5	0.6	0.5	0.4	US$/kg	054
0305	Fish, dried, salted or in brine	0.0	0.9	0.9	4.2	10.6	8.7	US$/kg	035
7204	Ferrous waste and scrap; remelting scrap ingots of iron or steel	1.7	0.1	0.1	0.2	0.3	0.2	US$/kg	282
0709	Other vegetables, fresh or chilled	0.9	0.2	0.3		0.5	0.4	US$/kg	054
1212	Locust beans, seaweeds and other algae	0.4	0.4	0.5	6.1	10.4	7.5	US$/kg	292
0801	Coconuts, Brazil nuts and cashew nuts, fresh or dried	0.3	0.3	0.4	0.5	0.9	1.2	US$/kg	057
3208	Paints and varnishes	0.4	0.2	0.3	*4.8*	*5.3*	*4.7*	US$/kg	533
0508	Coral and similar materials, unworked or simply prepared	0.3	0.1	0.1					291

Graph 2: Trade Balance by MDG Regions in 2010

(Mln US$)

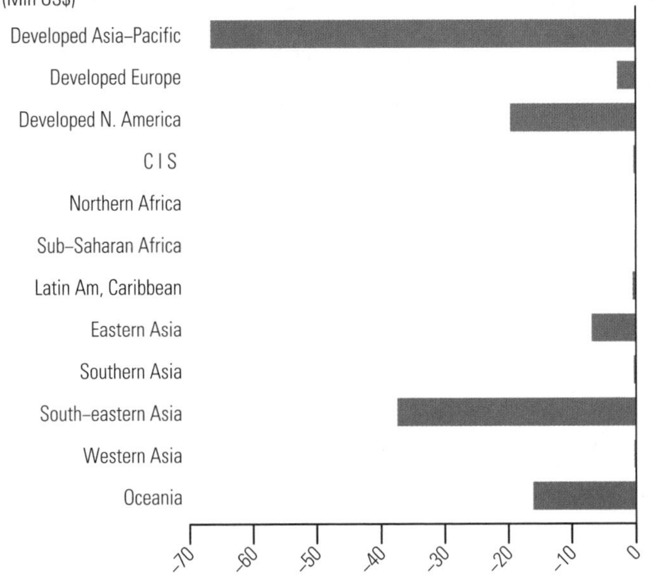

Graph 3: Partner concentration of trade in 2010

(Cumulative share by ranked partners)

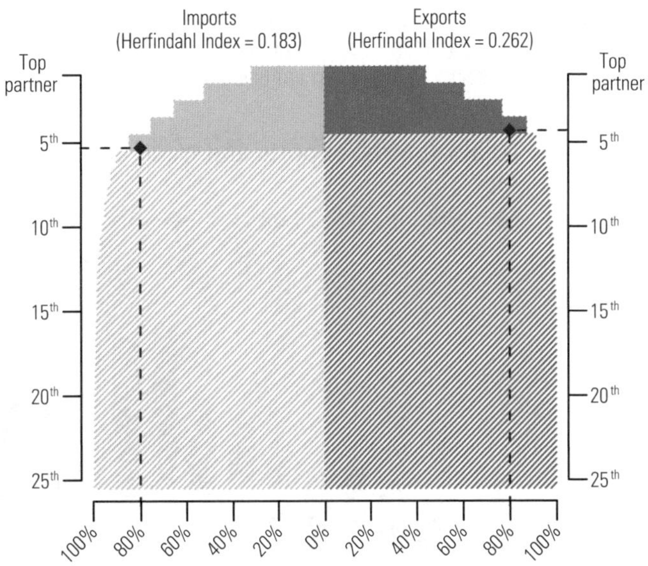

Table 4: Exports by principal countries and SITC sections in 2010

(Value in million US$, percentages of country total)

Country	Total	Shares by SITC sections (%)								
		0 + 1	2 + 4	3	5	6	7	8	9	Total
World	8.3	88.5	3.5	...	4.4	0.4	0.0	2.8	0.3	100
China, Hong Kong SAR	3.6	99.1	0.9	...	...	...	...	...	...	100
New Zealand	1.4	83.7	5.8	...	0.6	1.2	0.1	7.5	1.1	100
USA	1.3	84.2	8.8	...	0.0	0.0	...	7.0	0.0	100
Japan	0.9	99.8	0.2	...	0.0	...	...	...	...	100
Samoa	0.3	4.5	0.0	...	94.8	...	0.2	0.5	...	100
Australia	0.3	88.1	0.1	...	0.0	0.7	0.0	9.3	1.8	100
American Samoa	0.1	44.5	0.1	...	51.4	...	...	4.0	...	100
Other Asia, nes	0.1	1.4	82.4	...	...	16.1	...	0.1	...	100
Rep. of Korea	0.0	94.5	0.0	...	...	5.5	...	...	...	100
China	0.0	99.4	0.3	...	...	0.0	0.1	0.2	...	100

Imports Profile:

In 2010, imports were composed of 28.8 percent of food, live animals, beverages and tobacco (SITC sections 0+1), 22.8 percent of mineral fuels, lubricants and related materials (SITC section 3) and 19.5 percent of machinery and transport equipment (SITC section 7) (see table 2). From 2008 to 2010, top imported products were oils petroleum, bituminous, distillates, except crude (HS code 2710), meat, edible offal of domestic poultry (HS code 0207) and meat of sheep or goats, fresh, chilled or frozen (HS code 0204) (see table 5).

Table 5: Top 10 import commodities 2008 to 2010

(Value in million US$)

HS code	4-digit heading of Harmonized System 2007	Value (million US$)			Unit value				SITC code
		2008	2009	2010	2008	2009	2010	Unit	
	All Commodities	165.9	144.6	158.8					
2710	Petroleum oils, other than crude	41.2	27.5	34.2					334
0207	Meat and edible offal, of the poultry of heading 01.05	6.1	9.5	8.9	1.3	1.1	1.2	US$/kg	012
0204	Meat of sheep or goats, fresh, chilled or frozen	5.8	5.3	3.2	2.1	2.5	3.1	US$/kg	012
9999	Commodities not specified according to kind	6.9	5.9	1.0					931
8517	Electrical apparatus for line telephony or line telegraphy	4.8	3.7	5.0					764
8703	Motor cars and other motor vehicles principally designed for the transport	4.6	5.7	3.1	0.1	0.3	1.3	thsd US$/unit	781
1101	Wheat or meslin flour	3.3	3.0	3.1	0.7	0.6	*0.6*	US$/kg	046
1602	Other prepared or preserved meat, meat offal or blood	3.4	2.5	3.1	2.8	4.5	*3.9*	US$/kg	017
2402	Cigars, cheroots, cigarillos and cigarettes	3.2	2.5	2.3		*21.1*		US$/kg	122
2202	Waters with added sugar	2.4	2.5	2.3	0.8	0.7	0.6	US$/litre	111

Trinidad and Tobago

Imports: CIF, by origin | **Exports: FOB, by last known destination** | **Trade System: Special**

Overview:

After reaching a peak of 18.7 bln US$ in 2008, the value of the exports of Trinidad and Tobago dropped in 2009 by 51.1 percent but increased again in 2010 by 20.3 percent to reach 11.0 bln US$ (see table 1 and graph 1). Imports, on the other hand, decreased in 2010 by 6.8 percent and amounted to 6.5 bln US$ (see table 2 and graph 1). The trade balance recorded a surplus of 4.5 bln US$ in 2010(see graph 1). By MDG regions, trade recorded large surpluses with Developed North America (+3.5 bln US$), Latin America and the Caribbean (+2.1 bln US$) and Developed Europe (+0.4 bln US$) (see graph 2). However, trade with Sub-Saharan Africa recorded a deficit of 0.5 bln US$. By partners, 15 major partners accounted for 80 percent of exports compared to 13 major partners for imports in 2010 (see graph 3)

Graph 1: Total imports, exports and trade balance

(Bln US$ by year)

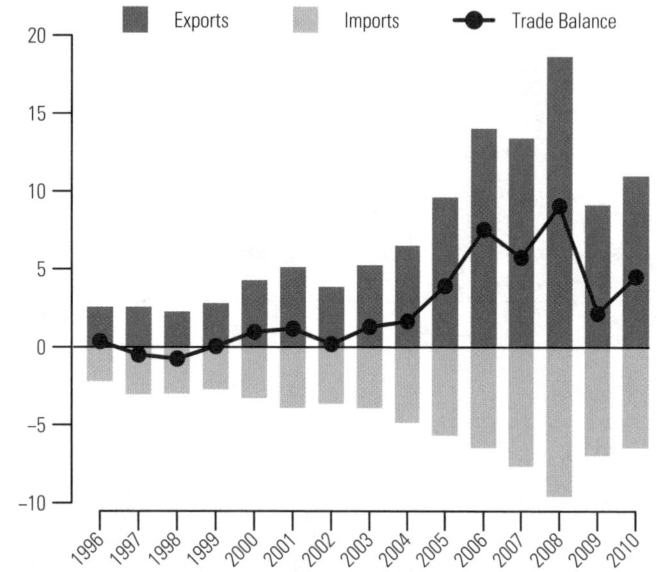

Table 1: Exports by SITC sections

(Value in million US$, growth and shares in percentage)

SITC	2010	Avg. Growth rates (%) 2006-2010	Avg. Growth rates (%) 2009-2010	2010 share
Total	10981.7	-5.9	20.3	100.0
0+1	261.5	-5.1	-10.4	2.4
2+4	577.3	86.9	106.6	5.3
3	6683.7	-11.1	-3.4	60.9
5	2382.1	3.9	171.8	21.7
6	658.1	0.0	54.0	6.0
7	354.3	24.1	34.9	3.2
8	64.2	-5.2	-8.1	0.6
9	0.5	7.2	19.6	0.0

Table 2: Imports by SITC sections

(Value in million US$, growth and shares in percentage)

SITC	2010	Avg. Growth rates (%) 2006-2010	Avg. Growth rates (%) 2009-2010	2010 share
Total	6479.6	0.0	-6.8	100.0
0+1	677.0	9.2	3.0	10.4
2+4	363.4	3.4	47.0	5.6
3	2157.6	-1.3	-5.8	33.3
5	495.0	-1.5	-9.1	7.6
6	743.4	-1.7	-18.3	11.5
7	1680.3	-0.7	-12.5	25.9
8	357.9	0.2	-4.9	5.5
9	5.0	-9.4	-44.3	0.1

Exports Profile:

In 2010, mineral fuels, lubricants and related materials (SITC section 3) was the largest commodity group for exports (see table 1) and accounted for 60.9 percent of exports. Other major commodity groups included chemicals and related products, n.e.s. (SITC section 5) and manufactured goods classified chiefly by material (SITC sections 6) respectively with 21.7 and 6.0 percent of exports. The top three markets for exports were USA, Jamaica and Barbados (see table 4). The majority of exports to these partners were mineral fuels, lubricants and related materials (SITC section 3). From 2008 to 2010, top exported goods were petroleum products: petroleum gases and other gaseous hydrocarbons (HS code 2711), petroleum oils, other than crude (HS code 2710) and petroleum oils and oils obtained from bituminous minerals, crude (HS code 2709) (see table 3).

Table 3: Top 10 export commodities 2008 to 2010

(Value in million US$)

HS code	4-digit heading of Harmonized System 2007	Value (million US$) 2008	2009	2010	Unit value 2008	2009	2010	Unit	SITC code
	All Commodities	18650.4	9126.0	10981.7					
2711	Petroleum gases and other gaseous hydrocarbons	5846.0	3830.0	1885.0	0.5	0.3	*0.4*	US$/kg	343
2710	Petroleum oils, other than crude	5132.9	1985.9	3430.9	0.8	0.5	*0.6*	US$/kg	334
2709	Petroleum oils and oils obtained from bituminous minerals, crude	2067.6	1101.5	1367.5	1.0	0.5	0.6	US$/kg	333
2814	Ammonia, anhydrous or in aqueous solution	1775.2	336.6	1376.7	0.7	0.2	0.3	US$/kg	522
2905	Acyclic alcohols and their derivatives	1058.9	299.8	616.5		0.2	0.2	US$/kg	512
2601	Iron ores and concentrates, including roasted iron pyrites	484.6	236.1	522.0	0.4	0.3	0.4	US$/kg	281
7203	Ferrous products obtained by direct reduction of iron ore	307.7	150.6	303.2	0.3	0.2	0.3	US$/kg	671
3102	Mineral or chemical fertilisers, nitrogenous	364.1	152.9	218.5	0.6	0.3	0.3	US$/kg	562
7213	Bars and rods, hot-rolled, in irregularly wound coils	245.3	81.1	176.0	0.8	0.4	0.2	US$/kg	676
8905	Light-vessels, fire-floats, dredgers, floating cranes and other vessels	61.4	129.4	226.3	15.4	25.9	37.7	mln US$/unit	793

Graph 2: Trade Balance by MDG Regions in 2010

(Bln US$)

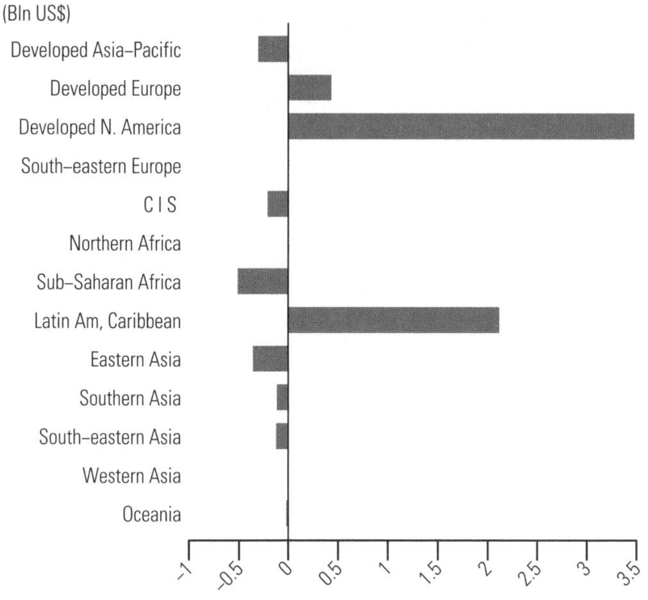

Graph 3: Partner concentration of trade in 2010

(Cumulative share by ranked partners)

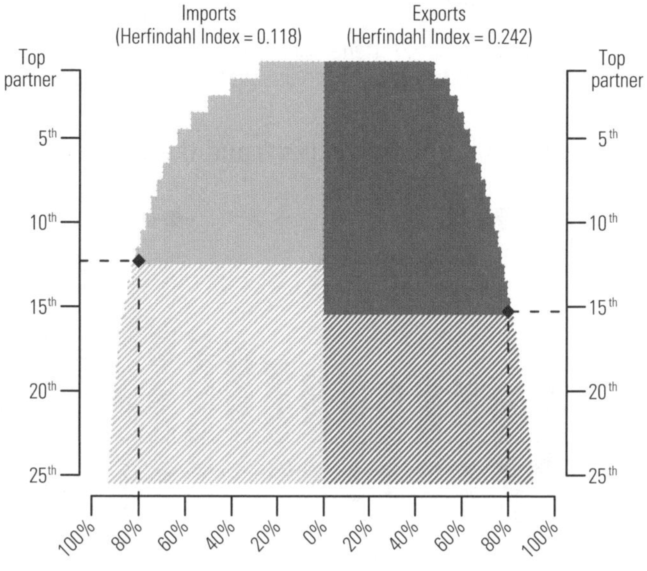

Table 4: Exports by principal countries and SITC sections in 2010

(Value in million US$, percentages of country total)

Country	Total	Shares by SITC sections (%) 0 + 1	2 + 4	3	5	6	7	8	9	Total
World	10981.7	2.4	5.3	60.9	21.7	6.0	3.2	0.6	0.0	100
USA	5278.7	0.4	9.8	55.4	31.9	0.7	1.6	0.2	0.0	100
Jamaica	710.0	9.3	0.2	85.3	1.5	2.3	0.6	0.8	0.0	100
Barbados	373.6	7.4	0.0	84.7	2.2	3.4	0.6	1.7	0.0	100
Suriname	300.3	7.7	0.6	83.6	2.3	3.3	1.0	1.5	0.0	100
Colombia	287.4	1.3	0.3	76.3	17.4	3.1	1.5	0.1	...	100
Guyana	268.5	11.0	0.7	68.5	7.0	8.5	1.7	2.7	0.0	100
France	246.1	1.1	0.0	68.9	24.0	5.6	0.2	0.1	0.0	100
Spain	218.8	0.0	0.0	62.7	11.6	25.5	0.2	...	...	100
United Kingdom	214.4	2.2	0.1	80.7	14.8	0.4	1.0	0.9	0.1	100
Brazil	210.9	0.0	2.7	31.0	51.1	14.0	0.9	0.3	...	100

Imports Profile:

In 2010, imports were composed of 33.3 percent of mineral fuels, lubricants and related materials (SITC section 3), 25.9 percent of machinery and transport equipment (SITC section 7) and 11.5 percent of manufactured goods classified chiefly by material (SITC section 6) (see table 2). Top imported products over the last three years were petroleum oils and oils obtained from bituminous minerals, crude (HS code 2709), iron ores and concentrates, including roasted iron pyrites (HS code 2601) and machinery, plant or laboratory equipment (HS code 8419) (see table 5).

Table 5: Top 10 import commodities 2008 to 2010

(Value in million US$)

HS code	4-digit heading of Harmonized System 2007	Value (million US$) 2008	2009	2010	Unit value 2008	2009	2010	Unit	SITC code
	All Commodities	9591.4	6955.4	6479.6					
2709	Petroleum oils and oils obtained from bituminous minerals, crude	3145.6	2135.6	2035.7	0.7	0.4	0.6	US$/kg	333
2601	Iron ores and concentrates, including roasted iron pyrites	469.0	141.6	254.3	0.2	0.1	0.2	US$/kg	281
8419	Machinery, plant or laboratory equipment	411.1	360.6	34.9					741
8703	Motor cars and other motor vehicles principally designed for the transport	230.5	122.1	152.8	*1.8*	0.6	*1.3*	thsd US$/unit	781
2710	Petroleum oils, other than crude	212.7	150.6	115.6	*0.9*	*0.6*	*1.1*	US$/kg	334
8704	Motor vehicles for the transport of goods	136.8	85.3	105.9	0.6	*0.7*	2.0	thsd US$/unit	782
7304	Tubes, pipes and hollow profiles, seamless, of iron (other than cast iron)	104.1	178.8	38.3	*2.3*	*6.4*	*5.8*	US$/kg	679
3004	Medicaments (excluding goods of heading 30.02, 30.05 or 30.06)	99.4	101.9	90.4	*3.0*	*8.2*	*13.4*	US$/kg	542
7308	Structures (excluding prefabricated buildings of heading 94.06)	195.1	57.3	34.8	*2.8*	*3.0*	*1.1*	US$/kg	691
8517	Electrical apparatus for line telephony or line telegraphy	91.1	84.9	98.6					764

Imports: CIF, by origin | Exports: FOB, by last known destination | Trade System: General

Overview:

From 2006 to 2010, the value of exports of Tunisia increased on average by 8.9 percent each year despite a drop of 25.2 percent in 2009 and amounted to 16.4 bln US$ (see table 1 and graph 1). During the same period, imports increased on average by 10.3 percent each year and amounted to 22.2 bln US$ (see table 2 and graph 1). This resulted in a trade deficit of 5.8 bln US$ in 2010 (see graph 1). By MDG regions, large deficits were recorded with Eastern Asia (-1.8 bln US$), Developed Europe (-1.5 bln US$) and Commonwealth of Independent States (-1.4 bln US$) (see graph 2). Trade, especially imports, was diversified across partners: in 2010, 16 major partners accounted for 80 percent of imports compared to 10 major partners for exports (see graph 3)

Graph 1: Total imports, exports and trade balance

(Bln US$ by year)

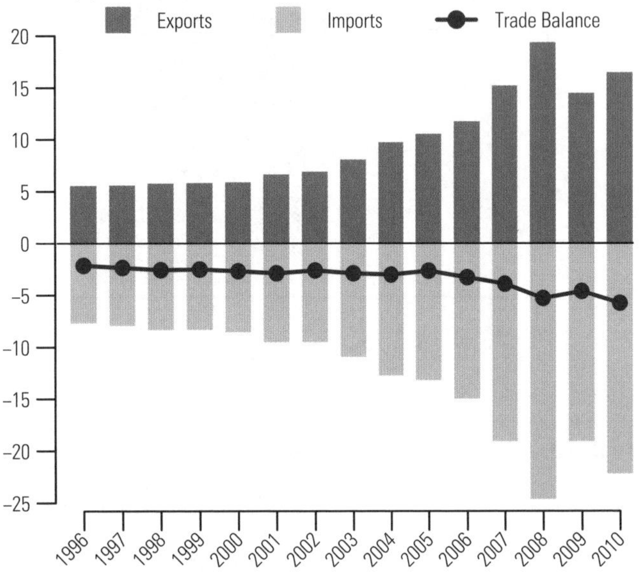

Table 1: Exports by SITC sections

(Value in million US$, growth and shares in percentage)

SITC	2010	Avg. Growth rates (%) 2006-2010	2009-2010	2010 share
Total	16426.6	8.9	13.7	100.0
0+1	841.3	8.4	0.6	5.1
2+4	695.1	-7.6	-0.3	4.2
3	2328.0	11.3	18.2	14.2
5	1790.4	14.2	17.7	10.9
6	1630.6	8.0	10.6	9.9
7	4678.2	18.2	29.1	28.5
8	4461.1	3.0	3.3	27.2
9	1.9	-6.0	-39.4	0.0

Exports Profile:

In 2010, Tunisia's exports were composed of 28.5 percent of machinery and transport equipment (SITC section 7), 27.2 percent of miscellaneous manufactured articles (SITC section 8) and 14.2 percent of mineral fuels, lubricants and related materials (SITC section 3) (see table 1). Top markets for exported goods were France, Italy and Germany (see table 4). From 2008 to 2010, top exported goods included petroleum oils and oils obtained from bituminous minerals, crude (HS code 2709), insulated (including enamelled or anodised) wire, cable (HS code 8544) and men's or boys' suits, ensembles, jackets, blazers, trousers (HS code 6203) (see table 3).

Table 2: Imports by SITC sections

(Value in million US$, growth and shares in percentage)

SITC	2010	Avg. Growth rates (%) 2006-2010	2009-2010	2010 share
Total	22215.4	10.3	16.3	100.0
0+1	1589.4	12.8	25.1	7.2
2+4	1208.4	12.1	26.8	5.4
3	2793.7	5.9	28.3	12.6
5	2301.6	11.5	11.4	10.4
6	4797.3	7.5	10.7	21.6
7	7751.4	14.4	17.4	34.9
8	1764.4	5.7	4.7	7.9
9	9.1	-6.8	39.4	0.0

Table 3: Top 10 export commodities 2008 to 2010

(Value in million US$)

HS code	4-digit heading of Harmonized System 2007	Value (million US$) 2008	2009	2010	Unit value 2008	2009	2010	Unit	SITC code
	All Commodities	19320.0	14445.1	16426.6					
2709	Petroleum oils and oils obtained from bituminous minerals, crude	2630.8	1553.1	2080.8	0.8	0.4	0.6	US$/kg	333
8544	Insulated (including enamelled or anodised) wire, cable	1025.0	1004.2	1292.3	13.8	12.4	12.8	US$/kg	773
6203	Men's or boys' suits, ensembles, jackets, blazers, trousers	867.9	646.4	618.4	*5.4*	9.1		US$/unit	841
6211	Track suits, ski suits and swimwear; other garments	728.2	624.3	690.8					845
3105	Mineral or chemical fertilisers	878.3	372.7	536.4	1.0	0.3	0.5	US$/kg	562
8536	Electrical apparatus for switching or protecting electrical circuits	672.6	548.7	490.3	27.9	22.3	22.9	US$/kg	772
2809	Diphosphorus pentaoxide; phosphoric acid	725.1	310.1	362.1	1.1	0.4	0.5	US$/kg	522
2710	Petroleum oils, other than crude	707.8	411.8	238.7	0.8	0.5	0.7	US$/kg	334
1509	Olive oil and its fractions	620.3	395.7	308.8	3.7	2.8	2.8	US$/kg	421
6204	Women's or girls' suits, ensembles, jackets, blazers, dresses, skirts	488.9	411.0	333.8	17.4	19.2		US$/unit	842

Graph 2: Trade Balance by MDG Regions in 2010

(Bln US$)

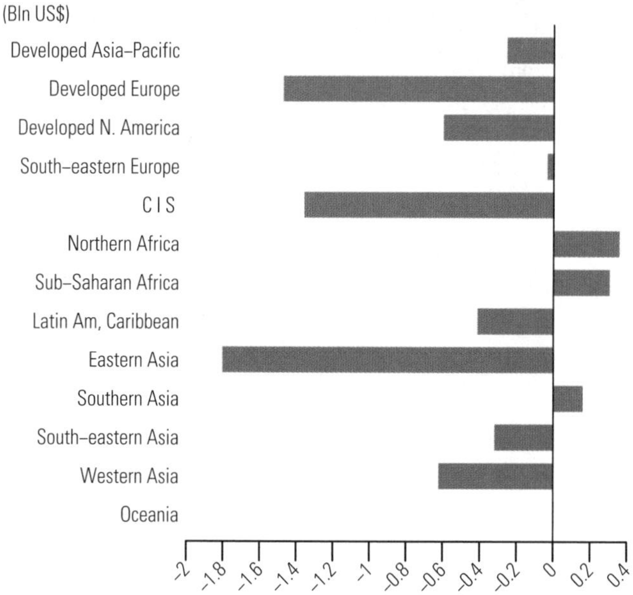

Graph 3: Partner concentration of trade in 2010

(Cumulative share by ranked partners)

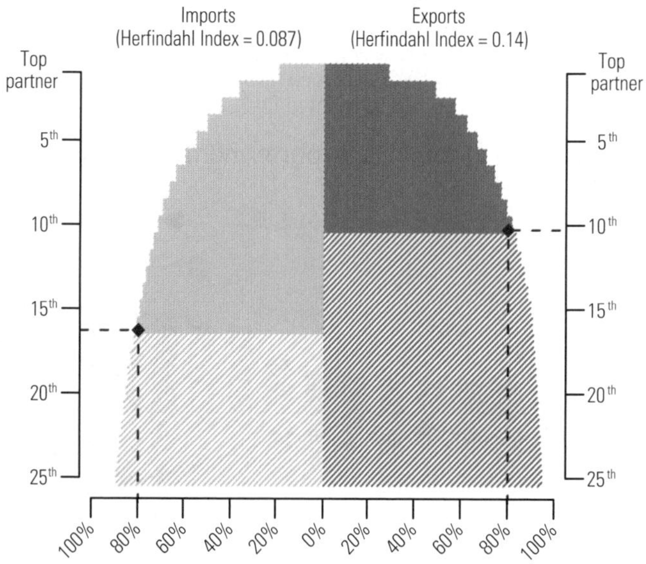

Table 4: Exports by principal countries and SITC sections in 2010

(Value in million US$, percentages of country total)

Country	Total	Shares by SITC sections (%)								
		0 + 1	2 + 4	3	5	6	7	8	9	Total
World	16426.6	5.1	4.2	14.2	10.9	9.9	28.5	27.2	0.0	100
France	4717.3	3.0	0.7	9.3	3.7	8.3	42.6	32.4	0.0	100
Italy	3264.9	3.8	6.3	20.1	3.9	6.8	16.5	42.6	0.0	100
Germany	1388.1	1.6	0.7	1.1	0.1	1.9	58.2	36.4	...	100
United Kingdom	824.8	0.7	0.3	60.9	3.6	6.6	12.3	15.6	...	100
Libya	732.3	19.5	6.5	2.3	16.5	39.1	11.2	4.9	0.0	100
Spain	637.1	6.0	5.6	22.4	4.3	14.8	23.1	23.8	...	100
Areas, nes	578.4	10.5	4.4	2.7	31.2	11.5	23.0	16.8	...	100
Algeria	474.7	5.8	2.1	0.2	16.1	34.0	33.7	8.0	...	100
USA	388.5	1.5	18.8	44.9	5.2	1.3	14.4	13.8	...	100
Netherlands	360.1	1.6	1.8	38.6	0.9	3.8	11.3	42.0	...	100

Imports Profile:

Tunisia's imports in 2010 were composed of machinery and transport equipment (SITC section 7), manufactured goods classified chiefly by material (SITC section 6) and mineral fuels, lubricants and related materials (SITC section 3) respectively with 34.9, 21.6 and 12.6 percent of imports (see table 2). From 2008 to 2010, top imported commodities included petroleum oils, other than crude (HS code 2710), motor cars and other motor vehicles principally designed for the transport (HS code 8703) and petroleum gases and other gaseous hydrocarbons (HS code 2711) (see table 5).

Table 5: Top 10 import commodities 2008 to 2010

(Value in million US$)

HS code	4-digit heading of Harmonized System 2007	Value (million US$)			Unit value				SITC code
		2008	2009	2010	2008	2009	2010	Unit	
	All Commodities	24638.4	19096.2	22215.4					
2710	Petroleum oils, other than crude	2237.5	1106.7	1883.8	0.8	0.5	0.7	US$/kg	334
8703	Motor cars and other motor vehicles principally designed for the transport	662.8	652.2	778.9	14.7	*14.8*	*14.2*	thsd US$/unit	781
2711	Petroleum gases and other gaseous hydrocarbons	844.7	487.0	623.3	0.5	0.3	0.5	US$/kg	343
5209	Woven fabrics of cotton, containing 85 % or more by weight of cotton	641.8	528.0	534.2	13.4	12.4	12.0	US$/kg	652
1001	Wheat and meslin	810.6	322.2	476.2	0.5	0.3	0.2	US$/kg	041
2709	Petroleum oils and oils obtained from bituminous minerals, crude	935.5	502.5	162.4	0.8	0.5	0.5	US$/kg	333
2503	Sulphur of all kinds	936.5	121.8	144.9	0.5	0.1	0.1	US$/kg	274
8536	Electrical apparatus for switching or protecting electrical circuits	432.6	323.9	379.0	24.3	25.1	23.1	US$/kg	772
8544	Insulated (including enamelled or anodised) wire, cable	384.5	294.2	400.8	15.3	14.1	13.2	US$/kg	773
8704	Motor vehicles for the transport of goods	298.0	326.7	339.8	19.6	19.1	18.6	thsd US$/unit	782

Turkey

Imports: CIF, by origin | **Exports: FOB, by last known destination** | **Trade System: Special**

Overview:

After several years of continuous growth marked by a peak of 132.0 bln US$ in 2008, the value of the exports of Turkey contracted sharply in 2009 (by 22.6 percent) but bounced back in 2010 by 11.6 percent to amount to 114.0 bln US$, still well below its 2008 level (see table 1 and graph 1). Imports showed a more pronounced development with an increase by 31.7 percent to 185.5 bln US$ in 2010 (see table 2 and graph 1). The trade deficit increased from 38.7 bln US$ in 2009 to 71.6 bln US$ in 2010 (see graph 1). By MDG regions, large deficits were recorded with the Eastern Asia (-21.0 bln US$), Developed Europe (-19.8 bln US$) and Commonwealth of Independent States (-19.8 bln US$) (see graph 2). Trade with Western Asia recorded a surplus amounting to 11.6 bln US$. Turkey's trade was highly diversified across partners: more than 25 major partners accounted for 80 percent of exports while 25 major partners accounted for 80 percent of imports (see graph 3).

Graph 1: Total imports, exports and trade balance

(Bln US$ by year)

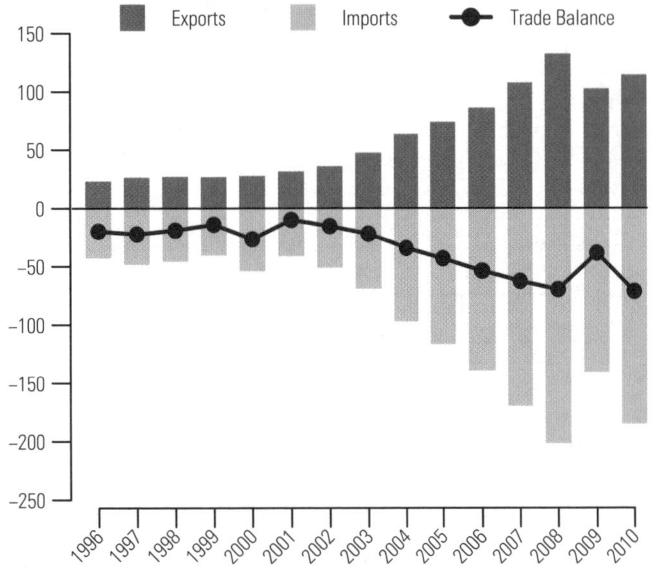

Exports Profile:

In 2010, Turkey's exports were composed of 29.1 percent of manufactured goods classified chiefly by material (SITC section 6), 27.9 percent of machinery and transport equipment (SITC section 7) and 17.2 percent of miscellaneous manufactured articles (SITC section 8) (see table 1). Major partners for exports were Germany, United Kingdom and Italy (see table 4). Over the last three years, top exported products were motor cars and other motor vehicles principally designed for the transport (HS code 8703), other bars and rods of iron or non-alloy steel (HS code 7214) and petroleum oils, other than crude (HS code 2710) (see table 3).

Table 1: Exports by SITC sections

(Value in million US$, growth and shares in percentage)

SITC	2010	Avg. Growth rates (%) 2006-2010	2009-2010	2010 share
Total	113979.5	7.4	11.6	100.0
0+1	11405.5	11.4	13.4	10.0
2+4	3738.8	12.6	41.1	3.3
3	4405.3	5.4	12.9	3.9
5	6100.7	14.2	26.1	5.4
6	33213.8	8.6	16.1	29.1
7	31824.3	4.8	10.5	27.9
8	19618.3	4.1	12.9	17.2
9	3672.7	21.1	-37.8	3.2

Table 2: Imports by SITC sections

(Value in million US$, growth and shares in percentage)

SITC	2010	Avg. Growth rates (%) 2006-2010	2009-2010	2010 share
Total	185541.0	7.4	31.7	100.0
0+1	4955.1	25.1	21.8	2.7
2+4	16439.7	12.9	48.7	8.9
3	26703.9	7.0	34.0	14.4
5	25062.1	8.5	24.9	13.5
6	31801.9	6.3	37.2	17.1
7	53879.2	5.8	31.3	29.0
8	11502.8	10.1	26.3	6.2
9	15196.3	3.4	22.3	8.2

Table 3: Top 10 export commodities 2008 to 2010

(Value in million US$)

HS code	4-digit heading of Harmonized System 2007	Value (million US$) 2008	2009	2010	Unit value 2008	2009	2010	Unit	SITC code
	All Commodities	132002.4	102138.5	113979.5					
8703	Motor cars and other motor vehicles principally designed for the transport	7474.4	6087.5	6210.3	14.0	13.3	12.8	thsd US$/unit	781
7214	Other bars and rods of iron or non-alloy steel	8800.1	3920.0	3422.0	0.9	0.4	0.6	US$/kg	676
2710	Petroleum oils, other than crude	7083.6	3501.6	3984.8	0.8	0.6	0.6	US$/kg	334
8704	Motor vehicles for the transport of goods	5165.6	2302.8	3333.5	15.1	14.2	13.2	thsd US$/unit	782
7108	Gold (including gold plated with platinum)	3624.5	4639.0	2070.6	25.5	28.2	37.0	thsd US$/kg	971
6109	T-shirts, singlets and other vests, knitted or crocheted	2904.7	2398.9	2759.8	4.6	4.0	4.1	US$/unit	845
8708	Parts and accessories of the motor vehicles of headings 87.01 to 87.05	2876.6	1997.3	2673.6	5.0	5.1	4.8	US$/kg	784
6204	Women's or girls' suits, ensembles, jackets, blazers, dresses, skirts	2196.3	1704.7	1855.5	13.7	12.4	12.5	US$/unit	842
8528	Reception apparatus for television	1994.4	1743.4	1751.5	*191.9*	202.8	209.2	US$/unit	761
8544	Insulated (including enamelled or anodised) wire, cable	2087.5	1404.2	1805.7	6.6	4.9	5.8	US$/kg	773

Graph 2: Trade Balance by MDG Regions in 2010

(Bln US$)

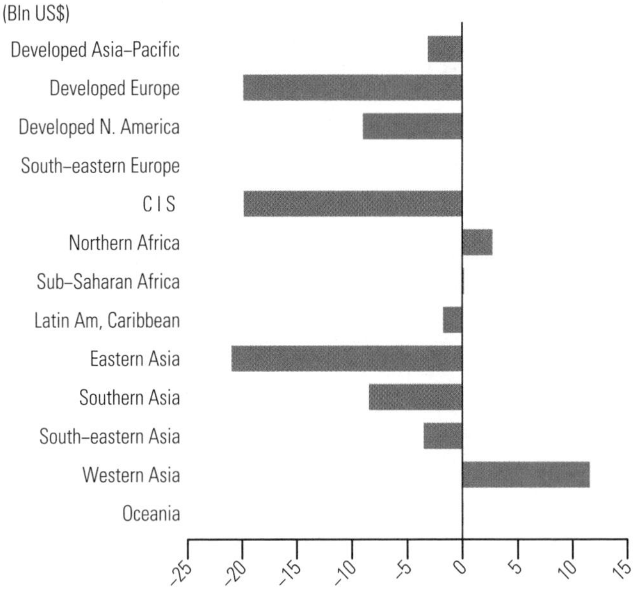

Graph 3: Partner concentration of trade in 2010

(Cumulative share by ranked partners)

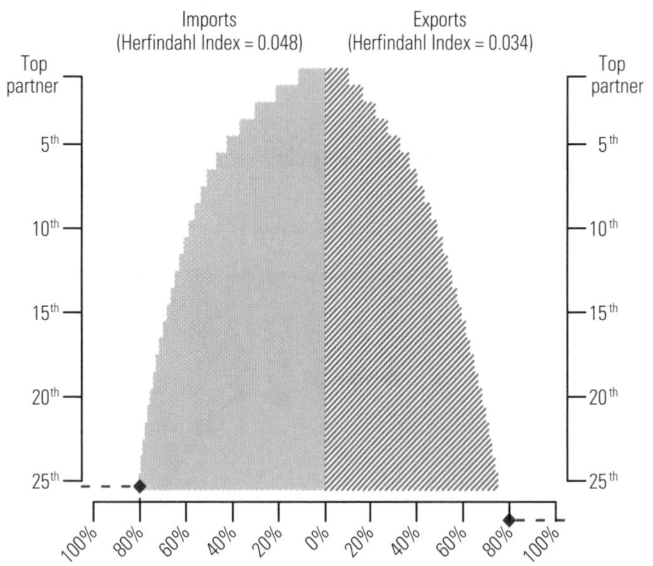

Table 4: Exports by principal countries and SITC sections in 2010

(Value in million US$, percentages of country total)

Country	Total	Shares by SITC sections (%) 0+1	2+4	3	5	6	7	8	9	Total
World	113979.5	10.0	3.3	3.9	5.4	29.1	27.9	17.2	3.2	100
Germany	11486.8	10.0	1.4	0.7	2.9	22.0	31.5	31.1	0.4	100
United Kingdom	7238.4	4.8	1.2	2.8	2.1	15.5	39.2	31.9	2.4	100
Italy	6508.6	8.2	1.9	1.2	4.1	27.3	42.1	13.5	1.7	100
France	6055.1	7.2	0.5	0.3	2.1	14.8	53.8	21.1	0.2	100
Iraq	6041.9	23.7	2.3	3.8	7.0	33.3	17.5	12.3	0.0	100
Russian Federation	4631.5	20.7	2.3	2.9	8.7	28.3	23.4	13.1	0.5	100
USA	3773.9	10.5	0.8	5.2	2.9	35.7	28.4	13.0	3.5	100
Spain	3563.5	3.6	2.3	1.0	3.9	18.8	35.1	33.6	1.8	100
United Arab Emirates	3337.7	3.1	0.4	11.7	1.8	42.1	8.0	20.5	12.4	100
Iran	3043.4	5.5	0.4	5.8	8.7	44.1	24.3	7.2	4.0	100

Imports Profile:

Imported goods in 2010 were composed of 29.0 percent of machinery and transport equipment (SITC section 7), 17.1 percent of manufactured goods classified chiefly by material (SITC section 6) and 14.4 percent of mineral fuels, lubricants and related materials (SITC section 3) (see table 2). Over the last three years, major products for imports included petroleum oils and oils obtained from bituminous minerals, crude (HS code 2709), petroleum oils, other than crude (HS code 2710) and ferrous waste and scrap; remelting scrap ingots of iron or steel (HS code 7204) (see table 5).

Table 5: Top 10 import commodities 2008 to 2010

(Value in million US$)

HS code	4-digit heading of Harmonized System 2007	Value (million US$) 2008	2009	2010	Unit value 2008	2009	2010	Unit	SITC code
	All Commodities	201960.8	140869.0	185541.0					
9999	Commodities not specified according to kind	16443.5	10795.3	12672.8					931
2709	Petroleum oils and oils obtained from bituminous minerals, crude	15638.9	6415.4	9647.0	0.7	0.5	0.6	US$/kg	333
2710	Petroleum oils, other than crude	10994.9	8511.3	10979.1	1.0	0.6	0.7	US$/kg	334
7204	Ferrous waste and scrap; remelting scrap ingots of iron or steel	8961.2	4239.5	7120.5	0.5	0.3	0.4	US$/kg	282
8703	Motor cars and other motor vehicles principally designed for the transport	4554.3	4266.8	6821.8	17.9	16.3	15.8	thsd US$/unit	781
8708	Parts and accessories of the motor vehicles of headings 87.01 to 87.05	5173.8	3401.0	4433.1	10.1	10.0	9.6	US$/kg	784
3004	Medicaments (excluding goods of heading 30.02, 30.05 or 30.06)	3354.2	3125.0	3292.9	115.4	105.1	93.5	US$/kg	542
2701	Coal; briquettes, ovoids and similar solid fuels manufactured from coal	3302.6	3046.8	3211.4	0.2	0.1	0.1	US$/kg	321
7108	Gold (including gold plated with platinum)	4991.0	1632.3	2523.4	27.8	31.0	39.4	thsd US$/kg	971
7208	Flat-rolled products of iron or non-alloy steel	4649.9	1926.6	2443.8	0.9	0.6	0.6	US$/kg	673

Turks and Caicos Islands

Imports: CIF, by origin **Exports: FOB, by last known destination** **Trade System: General**

Overview:

After a peak of 24.8 mln US$ in 2008, the value of the exports of Turks and Caicos Islands dropped by 16.2 percent in 2009 and amounted to 20.8 mln US$ (see table 1 and graph 1). Imports showed a more pronounced development with a drop of 36.5 percent in 2009 to 375.4 mln US$ (see table 2 and graph 1). The trade balance recorded a deficit of 354.6 mln US$ in 2009, compared to 566.5 mln US$ in 2008 (see graph 1). This deficit was accounted for mainly by trade with Developed North America (-348.5 mln US$) (see graph 2). Imports and exports were concentrated with one partner country (see graph 3).

Graph 1: Total imports, exports and trade balance

(Mln US$ by year)

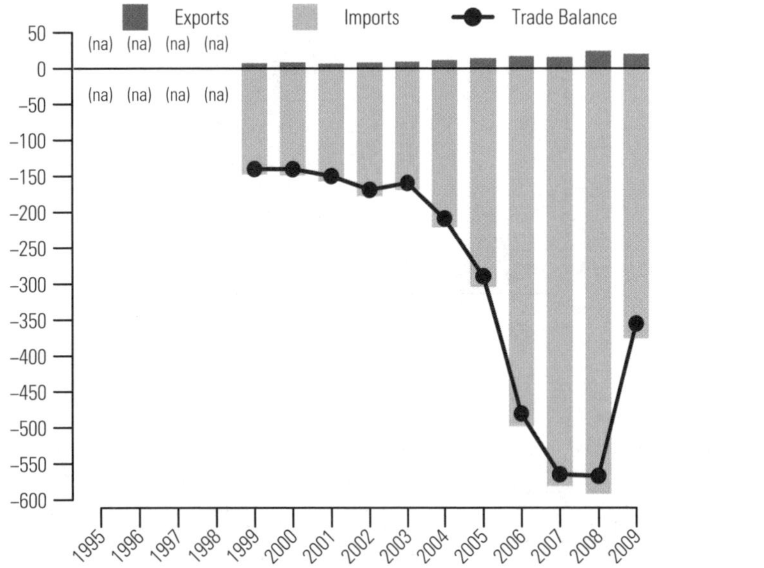

Table 1: Exports by SITC sections

(Value in million US$, growth and shares in percentage)

SITC	2009	Avg. Growth rates (%) 2005-2009	2008-2009	2009 share
Total	20.8	9.0	-16.2	100.0
0+1	4.4	-10.8	-5.3	21.2
2+4	0.2	-43.0	-15.8	0.9
3	0.0	35.5	-92.6	0.2
5	0.1	36.9	-54.4	0.4
6	1.1	3.4	-13.3	5.5
7	12.5	36.8	-13.1	60.3
8	1.0	-4.1	29.0	4.6
9	1.4	51.1	-48.4	6.9

Table 2: Imports by SITC sections

(Value in million US$, growth and shares in percentage)

SITC	2009	Avg. Growth rates (%) 2005-2009	2008-2009	2009 share
Total	375.4	5.4	-36.5	100.0
0+1	77.4	16.3	-4.3	20.6
2+4	10.8	-3.2	-43.3	2.9
3	42.3	7.7	-40.9	11.3
5	20.9	8.1	-42.4	5.6
6	62.0	-1.1	-45.7	16.5
7	77.4	-4.5	-46.1	20.6
8	73.8	19.5	-31.5	19.7
9	10.7	5.6	-40.0	2.8

Exports Profile:

In 2009, 60.3 percent of exports were reported as machinery and transport equipment (SITC section 7) (see table 1). Food, live animals, beverages and tobacco (SITC sections 0+1) and commodities and transactions not classified elsewhere (SITC section 9) accounted respectively for 21.2 and 6.9 percent of exports. USA, the top partner for exports was the destination of over 99.0 percent of exports (see table 4). From 2007 to 2009, top products for exports were crustaceans, molluscs and other aquatic invertebrates (HS code 1605), crustaceans, whether in shell or not (HS code 0306) and self-propelled bulldozers, angledozers, graders, levellers, scrapers (HS code 8429) (see table 3).

Table 3: Top 10 export commodities 2007 to 2009

(Value in million US$)

HS code	4-digit heading of Harmonized System 2002	Value (million US$) 2007	2008	2009	Unit value 2007	2008	2009	Unit	SITC code
	All Commodities	16.3	24.8	20.8					
1605	Crustaceans, molluscs and other aquatic invertebrates	2.7	3.4	3.3					037
0306	Crustaceans, whether in shell or not	2.9	1.1	1.1					036
8429	Self-propelled bulldozers, angledozers, graders, levellers, scrapers	...	2.2	2.3					723
9999	Commodities not specified according to kind	1.2	2.8	0.3					931
8430	Other moving, grading, levelling, scraping, excavating, tamping, compacting	...	3.1	0.2					723
8703	Motor cars and other motor vehicles principally designed for the transport	0.5	0.9	1.3					781
8503	Parts suitable for use principally with the machines of heading 85.01	0.5	0.6	1.7					716
8519	Turntables (record-decks), record-players, cassette-players	0.0	1.6	0.0					763
8502	Electric generating sets and rotary converters	0.3	1.0	0.3					716
8427	Fork-lift trucks; other works trucks	0.5	0.8	0.3					744

Graph 2: Trade Balance by MDG Regions in 2009

(Mln US$)

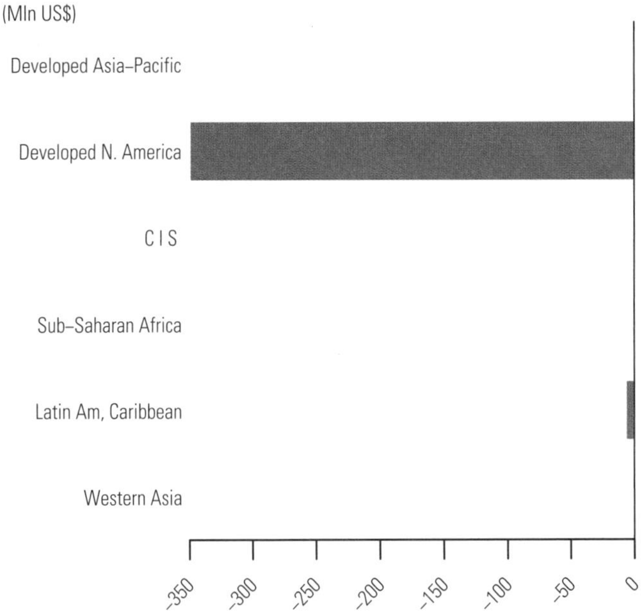

Graph 3: Partner concentration of trade in 2009

(Cumulative share by ranked partners)

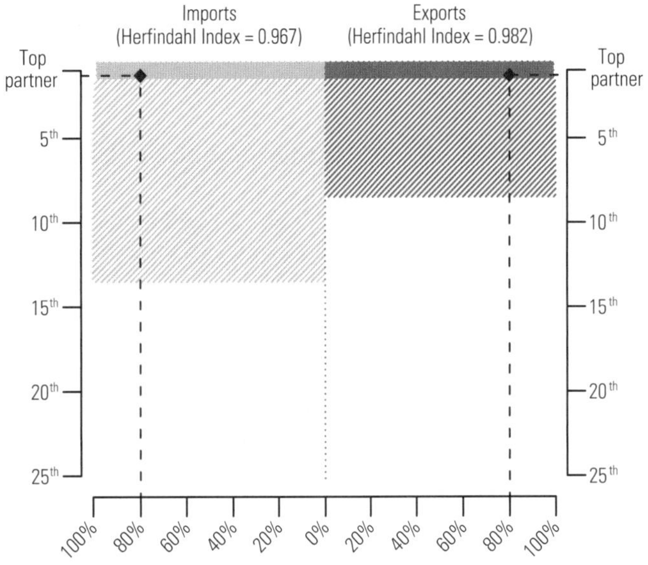

Table 4: Exports by principal countries and SITC sections in 2009

(Value in million US$, percentages of country total)

Country	Total	Shares by SITC sections (%)								
		0+1	2+4	3	5	6	7	8	9	Total
World	20.8	21.2	0.9	0.2	0.4	5.5	60.3	4.6	6.9	100
USA	20.6	21.7	0.9	0.2	0.4	5.6	60.8	4.7	5.8	100
Saint Vincent and the Grenadines	0.2	0.0	0.0	...	...	6.8	93.2	...	...	100
Haiti	0.0	0.0	0.0	...	...	...	100.0	...	...	100
Dominican Rep.	0.0	0.0	0.0	...	...	...	91.2	...	8.8	100
Bahamas	0.0	0.0	0.0	...	...	...	100.0	...	...	100
Jamaica	0.0	0.0	0.0	...	...	...	100.0	...	...	100

Imports Profile:

Imports in 2009 were composed of 20.6 percent each of food, live animals, beverages and tobacco (SITC sections 0+1) and machinery and transport equipment (SITC section 7) (see table 2). Other major commodity groups for imports were miscellaneous manufactured articles (SITC section 8) and manufactured goods classified chiefly by material (SITC section 6), respectively with 19.7 and 16.5 percent of imports. Over the last three years, top imported products were petroleum oils, other than crude (HS code 2710), unused postage, revenue or similar stamps of current or new issue (HS code 4907) and printed books, brochures, leaflets and similar printed matter (HS code 4901) (see table 5).

Table 5: Top 10 import commodities 2007 to 2009

(Value in million US$)

HS code	4-digit heading of Harmonized System 2002	Value (million US$)			Unit value				SITC code
		2007	2008	2009	2007	2008	2009	Unit	
	All Commodities	580.6	591.3	375.4					
2710	Petroleum oils, other than crude	46.2	68.7	40.4					334
4907	Unused postage, revenue or similar stamps of current or new issue	24.8	24.2	18.9					892
4901	Printed books, brochures, leaflets and similar printed matter	35.0	20.9	11.8					892
8703	Motor cars and other motor vehicles principally designed for the transport	27.7	23.4	10.4					781
9999	Commodities not specified according to kind	18.6	17.6	10.5					931
9403	Other furniture and parts thereof	13.0	16.0	9.4					821
8535	Electrical apparatus for switching or protecting electrical circuits	7.8	5.3	4.8					772
8544	Insulated (including enamelled or anodised) wire, cable	6.7	7.3	3.8					773
3917	Tubes, pipes and hoses, and fittings therefor	6.6	6.9	4.2					581
2009	Fruit juices (including grape must) and vegetable juices	5.8	5.6	5.1					059

Uganda

Imports: CIF, by origin | **Exports: FOB, by last known destination** | **Trade System: General**

Overview:

From 2006 to 2010, Uganda's exports increased on average by 13.9 percent each year to reach 1.6 bln US$ in 2010 (see table 1 and graph 1). During the same period, imports also increased on average by 16.2 percent each year to 4.7 bln US$ (see table 2 and graph 1). This resulted in a trade deficit amounting to 3 bln US$ in 2010 (see graph 1). This deficit was largely accounted for by trade with Southern Asia which recorded a deficit of 706.3 mln US$ (see graph 2). Trade also recorded a deficit of 630.2 mln US$ with Western Asia and 495.2 mln US$ with Eastern Asia. Uganda's trade was relatively diversified across partners: 13 (respectively 16) major partners accounted for 80 percent of exports (respectively imports) (see graph 3).

Graph 1: Total imports, exports and trade balance

(Bln US$ by year)

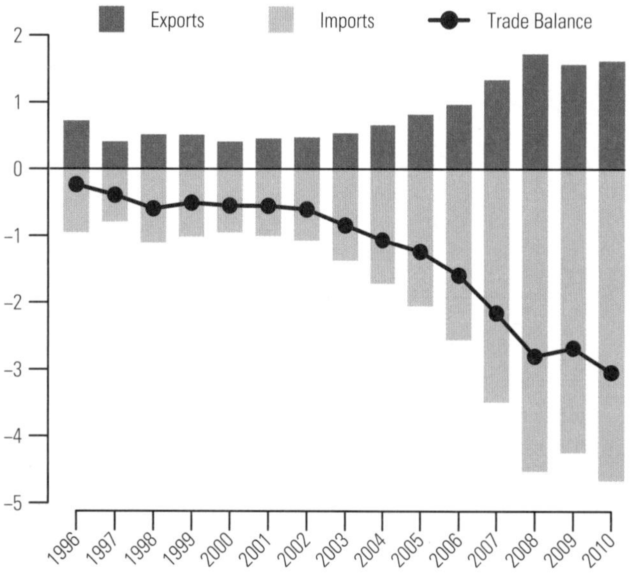

Table 1: Exports by SITC sections

(Value in million US$, growth and shares in percentage)

SITC	2010	Avg. Growth rates (%) 2006-2010	Avg. Growth rates (%) 2009-2010	2010 share
Total	1618.6	13.9	3.3	100.0
0+1	819.2	13.1	11.1	50.6
2+4	163.7	8.7	-1.3	10.1
3	88.3	20.3	-23.8	5.5
5	53.4	35.5	-12.2	3.3
6	223.3	40.2	-0.5	13.8
7	197.4	21.9	-3.8	12.2
8	42.1	27.3	1.2	2.6
9	31.1	-29.0	87.5	1.9

Table 2: Imports by SITC sections

(Value in million US$, growth and shares in percentage)

SITC	2010	Avg. Growth rates (%) 2006-2010	Avg. Growth rates (%) 2009-2010	2010 share
Total	4664.3	16.2	9.8	100.0
0+1	381.4	11.0	-0.9	8.2
2+4	283.4	18.4	31.8	6.1
3	932.4	14.7	25.4	20.0
5	574.5	14.2	2.9	12.3
6	769.8	15.6	1.1	16.5
7	1409.7	20.8	10.7	30.2
8	312.3	13.7	1.3	6.7
9	0.8	-35.8	-29.5	0.0

Exports Profile:

In 2010, food, live animals, beverages and tobacco (SITC sections 0+1) accounted for half of Uganda's exports (50.6 percent) (see table 1). Other major commodity groups included manufactured goods classified chiefly by material (SITC section 6), machinery and transport equipment (SITC section 7) and inedible crude materials (except fuels), animal and vegetable oils, fats and waxes (SITC sections 2+4) respectively with 13.8, 12.2 and 10.1 percent of exports. Major partners for exports in 2010 were Sudan, Kenya and Democratic Republic of the Congo (see table 4). Coffee, whether or not roasted or decaffeinated (HS code 0901), the top commodity for exports over the last three years, accounted for 17.5 percent of exports in 2010 (see table 3). Other top commodities included fish fillets and other fish meat (whether or not minced) (HS code 0304) and portland cement, aluminous cement, slag cement (HS code 2523) (see table 3).

Table 3: Top 10 export commodities 2008 to 2010

(Value in million US$)

HS code	4-digit heading of Harmonized System 2007	Value (million US$) 2008	Value 2009	Value 2010	Unit value 2008	Unit value 2009	Unit value 2010	Unit	SITC code
	All Commodities	1724.3	1567.6	1618.6					
0901	Coffee, whether or not roasted or decaffeinated	403.2	280.2	283.9	2.0	1.5	1.8	US$/kg	071
0304	Fish fillets and other fish meat (whether or not minced)	108.2	87.1	99.6	4.6	4.9	5.6	US$/kg	034
2523	Portland cement, aluminous cement, slag cement	77.9	83.2	72.2	0.1	0.2	0.2	US$/kg	661
2710	Petroleum oils, other than crude	49.0	101.5	74.5	*0.7*	*1.0*	*0.7*	US$/kg	334
8517	Electrical apparatus for line telephony or line telegraphy	70.4	61.5	81.0					764
2401	Unmanufactured tobacco; tobacco refuse	66.2	56.6	61.7	2.5	2.0	2.6	US$/kg	121
0902	Tea, whether or not flavoured	47.2	59.8	68.3	1.0	1.2	1.2	US$/kg	074
1701	Cane or beet sugar and chemically pure sucrose, in solid form	38.0	43.1	58.0	0.4	0.5	0.6	US$/kg	061
0602	Other live plants (including their roots), cuttings and slips; mushroom spawn	42.7	48.3	46.6					292
1516	Animal or vegetable fats and oils	29.2	35.9	35.3	1.2	1.1	0.3	US$/kg	431

Graph 2: Trade Balance by MDG Regions in 2010

(Mln US$)

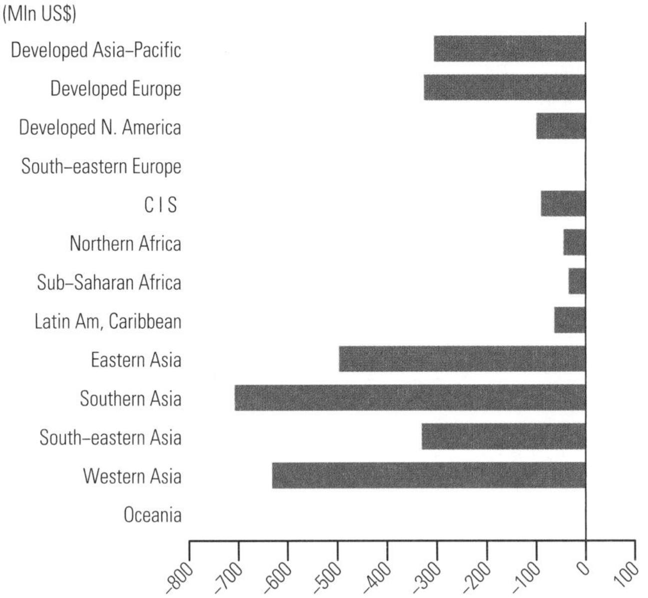

Graph 3: Partner concentration of trade in 2010

(Cumulative share by ranked partners)

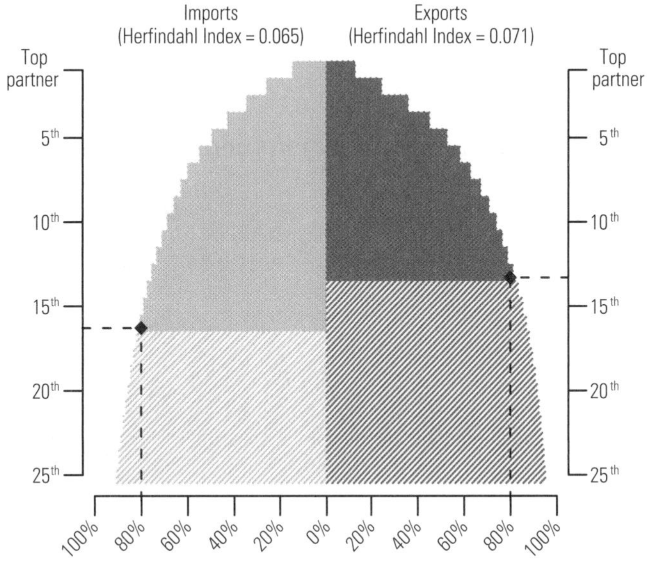

Table 4: Exports by principal countries and SITC sections in 2010

(Value in million US$, percentages of country total)

Country	Total	Shares by SITC sections (%) 0 + 1	2 + 4	3	5	6	7	8	9	Total
World	1618.6	50.6	10.1	5.5	3.3	13.8	12.2	2.6	1.9	100
Sudan	208.6	58.3	5.3	0.5	3.1	14.3	12.1	6.1	0.3	100
Kenya	190.3	72.8	5.3	3.3	0.9	3.9	12.9	0.9	...	100
Dem.Rep. of the Congo	184.0	32.5	6.4	0.5	5.5	34.4	15.2	5.4	0.0	100
Rwanda	149.3	19.7	16.7	0.8	14.5	40.5	5.5	2.2	0.2	100
United Arab Emirates	120.9	4.3	2.5	0.0	0.3	0.8	66.9	0.3	24.9	100
Netherlands	89.9	38.0	46.4	...	0.0	13.5	1.8	0.2	...	100
Germany	73.6	95.9	3.4	0.0	0.0	0.0	0.5	0.2	...	100
Areas, nes	72.2	0.0	0.0	100.0	...	...	...	...	...	100
Switzerland	57.5	90.9	5.4	...	0.3	2.6	0.7	0.1	...	100
Burundi	51.3	26.4	7.4	0.7	7.1	47.1	5.8	5.5	0.1	100

Imports Profile:

Uganda's imports in 2010 were composed of 30.2 percent of machinery and transport equipment (SITC section 7), 20.0 percent of mineral fuels, lubricants and related materials (SITC section 3) and 16.5 percent of manufactured goods classified chiefly by material (SITC section 6) (see table 2). From 2008 to 2010, top commodities for imports were petroleum oils, other than crude (HS code 2710), electrical apparatus for line telephony or line telegraphy (HS code 8517) and palm oil and its fractions (HS code 1511) (see table 5).

Table 5: Top 10 import commodities 2008 to 2010

(Value in million US$)

HS code	4-digit heading of Harmonized System 2007	Value (million US$) 2008	2009	2010	Unit value 2008	2009	2010	Unit	SITC code
	All Commodities	4525.9	4247.4	4664.3					
2710	Petroleum oils, other than crude	821.9	710.7	897.4	0.9	0.6	0.7	US$/kg	334
8517	Electrical apparatus for line telephony or line telegraphy	243.2	191.5	174.6					764
1511	Palm oil and its fractions	188.7	122.2	177.1	1.1	0.7	0.9	US$/kg	422
3004	Medicaments (excluding goods of heading 30.02, 30.05 or 30.06)	174.5	154.5	153.5	*13.7*	12.1	14.5	US$/kg	542
8703	Motor cars and other motor vehicles principally designed for the transport	120.8	138.3	186.0	4.2	4.3	5.8	thsd US$/unit	781
1001	Wheat and meslin	111.3	142.8	129.1	0.4	0.4	0.3	US$/kg	041
2523	Portland cement, aluminous cement, slag cement	99.6	115.2	104.9	0.1	0.1	0.1	US$/kg	661
8704	Motor vehicles for the transport of goods	84.9	90.8	100.3	6.7	4.5	*10.5*	thsd US$/unit	782
7210	Flat-rolled products of iron or non-alloy steel	100.7	70.6	81.1	1.5	1.1	1.2	US$/kg	674
1701	Cane or beet sugar and chemically pure sucrose, in solid form	60.3	63.5	78.1	*0.4*	0.5	0.6	US$/kg	061

Ukraine

Imports: CIF, by origin | **Exports: FOB, by last known destination** | **Trade System: General**

Overview:

In 2011, the value of the exports of Ukraine increased by 33 percent to amount to 68.4 bln US$ (see table 1 and graph 1). Imports showed a similar development with an increase by 36 percent to amount to 82.6 bln US$ in 2011 (see table 2 and graph 1). This resulted in a trade deficit of 14.2 bln US$ in 2011 (see graph 1). This deficit came largely from trade with the Commonwealth of Independent States (-10.5 bln US$), Developed Europe (-9.1 bln US$) and Eastern Asia (-4.9 bln US$) (see graph 2). Trade, however, recorded a large surplus with Western Asia (+7.0 bln US$). Trade, especially exports, was well diversified across partners: more than 25 major partners accounted for 80 percent of exports in 2011; 16 major partners accounted for 80 percent of imports (see graph 3).

Graph 1: Total imports, exports and trade balance

(Bln US$ by year)

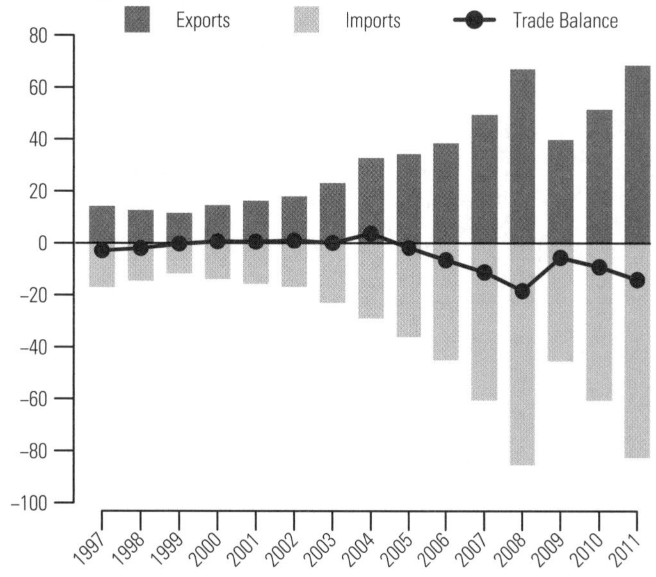

Table 1: Exports by SITC sections

(Value in million US$, growth and shares in percentage)

SITC	2011	Avg. Growth rates (%) 2007-2011	2010-2011	2011 share
Total	68393.0	8.5	33.0	100.0
0+1	8061.2	20.2	28.2	11.8
2+4	10881.5	20.1	37.8	15.9
3	5691.1	21.3	55.4	8.3
5	5412.8	5.8	58.1	7.9
6	24159.0	1.4	26.5	35.3
7	11564.0	8.8	29.9	16.9
8	2198.5	6.2	22.8	3.2
9	424.9	-1.1	16.0	0.6

Table 2: Imports by SITC sections

(Value in million US$, growth and shares in percentage)

SITC	2011	Avg. Growth rates (%) 2007-2011	2010-2011	2011 share
Total	82607.5	8.1	36.0	100.0
0+1	5526.9	11.6	9.2	6.7
2+4	2822.1	5.2	7.9	3.4
3	28605.2	15.8	45.9	34.6
5	10599.6	9.3	22.8	12.8
6	11081.0	5.1	27.0	13.4
7	19033.0	0.2	60.4	23.0
8	3850.8	7.0	6.0	4.7
9	1088.9	20.4	80.9	1.3

Exports Profile:

Manufactured goods classified chiefly by material (SITC section 6), the largest commodity group for exports, accounted for 35.3 percent of exported goods in 2011 (see table 1). Other major commodity groups included machinery and transport equipment (SITC section 7) and inedible crude materials (except fuels), animal and vegetable oils, fats and waxes (SITC sections 2+4), respectively with 16.9 and 15.9 percent of exports. In addition to Russian Federation, other major partners included Turkey and Italy (see table 4). Over the last three years, top exported products included semi-finished products of iron or non-alloy steel (HS code 7207), flat-rolled products of iron or non-alloy steel (HS code 7208) and iron ores and concentrates (HS code 2601) (see table 3).

Table 3: Top 10 export commodities 2009 to 2011

(Value in million US$)

HS code	4-digit heading of Harmonized System 2002	Value (million US$) 2009	2010	2011	Unit value 2009	2010	2011	Unit	SITC code
	All Commodities	39695.6	51430.3	68393.0					
7207	Semi-finished products of iron or non-alloy steel	3919.6	5341.1	6481.2	0.3	0.5	0.6	US$/kg	672
7208	Flat-rolled products of iron or non-alloy steel	2077.5	2997.1	4120.5	0.4	*0.6*	0.7	US$/kg	673
2601	Iron ores and concentrates	1242.7	2456.2	3786.3	0.0	0.1	0.1	US$/kg	281
1512	Sunflower-seed, safflower or cotton-seed oil	1618.4	2370.3	3146.1	*0.7*	*0.9*	1.2	US$/kg	421
2710	Petroleum oils, other than crude	1202.3	2196.0	3338.7	0.4	*0.5*	0.8	US$/kg	334
8606	Railway or tramway goods vans and wagons, not self-propelled	489.5	1913.4	3038.0	39.5	51.7	68.9	thsd US$/unit	791
1005	Maize (corn)	1012.8	785.9	1982.7	0.1	0.2	0.3	US$/kg	044
1001	Wheat and meslin	1778.0	906.4	1070.3	0.1	0.2	0.3	US$/kg	041
7214	Other bars and rods of iron or non-alloy steel	822.5	1249.0	1540.0	0.4	*0.5*	0.7	US$/kg	676
3102	Mineral or chemical fertilisers, nitrogenous	820.8	879.0	1690.1	0.2	0.2	0.3	US$/kg	562

Graph 2: Trade Balance by MDG Regions in 2011

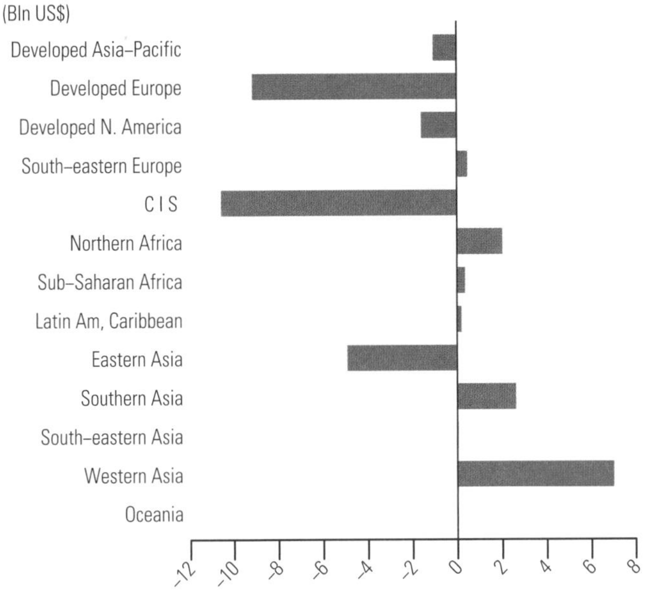

Graph 3: Partner concentration of trade in 2011

(Cumulative share by ranked partners)

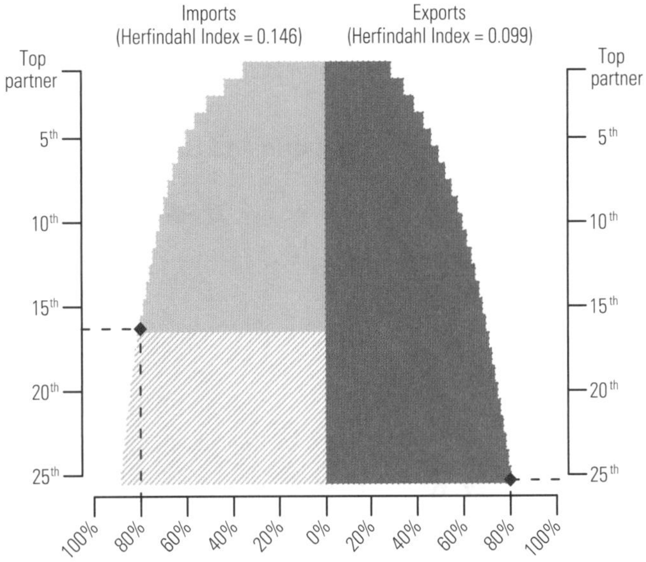

Table 4: Exports by principal countries and SITC sections in 2011

(Value in million US$, percentages of country total)

Country	Total	Shares by SITC sections (%) 0 + 1	2 + 4	3	5	6	7	8	9	Total
World	68393.0	11.8	15.9	8.3	7.9	35.3	16.9	3.2	0.6	100
Russian Federation	19819.7	9.3	5.7	14.1	5.2	26.2	35.6	3.7	0.3	100
Turkey	3748.6	8.3	28.3	6.4	11.4	45.0	0.5	0.1	0.0	100
Italy	3039.5	5.3	12.0	3.5	4.4	71.1	0.7	2.9	0.0	100
Poland	2794.1	7.0	32.5	4.3	7.9	32.9	10.5	4.7	0.1	100
India	2265.3	1.1	42.1	6.2	17.8	23.8	8.1	0.8	0.1	100
China	2180.0	0.4	82.1	0.3	10.3	2.3	2.9	1.2	0.6	100
Belarus	1922.3	14.2	9.4	9.0	10.1	37.2	16.4	3.6	0.2	100
Kazakhstan	1857.5	16.5	3.9	0.1	5.6	27.8	39.5	6.2	0.4	100
Germany	1763.9	3.6	11.7	0.5	8.1	34.5	26.2	15.2	0.3	100
Lebanon	1362.2	5.3	1.8	0.4	0.2	92.1	0.1	0.0	0.0	100

Imports Profile:

In 2011, imports were composed of 34.6 percent of mineral fuels, lubricants and related materials (SITC section 3), 23.0 percent of machinery and transport equipment (SITC section 7) and 13.4 percent of manufactured goods classified chiefly by material (SITC section 6) (see table 2). From 2009 to 2011, petroleum products were the top three products for imports: petroleum gases and other gaseous hydrocarbons (HS code 2711), petroleum oils, other than crude (HS code 2710) and petroleum oils, crude (HS code 2709) (see table 5).

Table 5: Top 10 import commodities 2009 to 2011

(Value in million US$)

HS code	4-digit heading of Harmonized System 2002	Value (million US$) 2009	2010	2011	Unit value 2009	2010	2011	Unit	SITC code
	All Commodities	45412.9	60737.1	82607.5					
2711	Petroleum gases and other gaseous hydrocarbons	8015.9	9521.0	14290.4	0.3	*0.8*	0.5	US$/kg	343
2710	Petroleum oils, other than crude	2688.5	3905.0	6955.3	0.5	*0.7*	1.0	US$/kg	334
2709	Petroleum oils, crude	2989.6	4171.3	4272.4	0.4	0.5	0.8	US$/kg	333
3004	Medicaments (excluding goods of heading 30.02, 30.05 or 30.06)	1873.6	2128.9	2463.5	65.8	*68.6*	72.7	US$/kg	542
8703	Motor cars and other motor vehicles principally designed for the transport	934.7	1743.5	2979.5	15.3	16.3	15.7	thsd US$/unit	781
2701	Coal; briquettes, ovoids and similar solid fuels manufactured from coal	795.1	1781.4	2760.9	0.1	*0.1*	0.2	US$/kg	321
8525	Transmission apparatus for radio-telephony, radio-broadcasting	440.2	895.5	732.4	91.4	72.0	*71.2*	US$/unit	764
8401	Nuclear reactors; fuel elements (cartridges), non-irradiated	488.1	608.1	600.4	1.1	1.3	1.6	thsd US$/kg	718
2602	Manganese ores and concentrates	374.1	649.8	496.9	0.4	0.5	0.4	US$/kg	287
3901	Polymers of ethylene, in primary forms	382.6	500.6	595.3	1.3	1.6	1.8	US$/kg	571

Imports: CIF, by origin | **Exports: FOB, by last known destination** | **Trade System: Special**

Overview:

After reaching a peak of 210.0 bln US$ in 2008, the value of the exports of United Arab Emirates contracted sharply by 16.8 percent in 2009 but increased again in 2010 by 13.5 percent to amount to 198.4 bln US$ (see table 1 and graph 1). Imports increased by 10.0 percent in 2010 to 180.7 bln US$ (see table 2 and graph 1). The trade surplus went up from 10.5 bln US$ in 2009 to 17.6 bln US$ in 2010 (see graph 1). By MDG regions, large surpluses were recorded with Eastern Asia (+51.0 bln US$), Southern Asia (+8.9 bln US$) and Western Asia (+3.9 bln US$). Trade was in deficit with Developed Europe (-22.7 bln US$), Developed North America (-10.0 bln US$) and Developed Asia-Pacific (-9.8 bln US$). Exports were concentrated among few partners but imports were diversified: in 2010, 6 major partners accounted for 80 percent of exports compared to 16 major partners for imports (see graph 3).

Graph 1: Total imports, exports and trade balance

(Bln US$ by year)

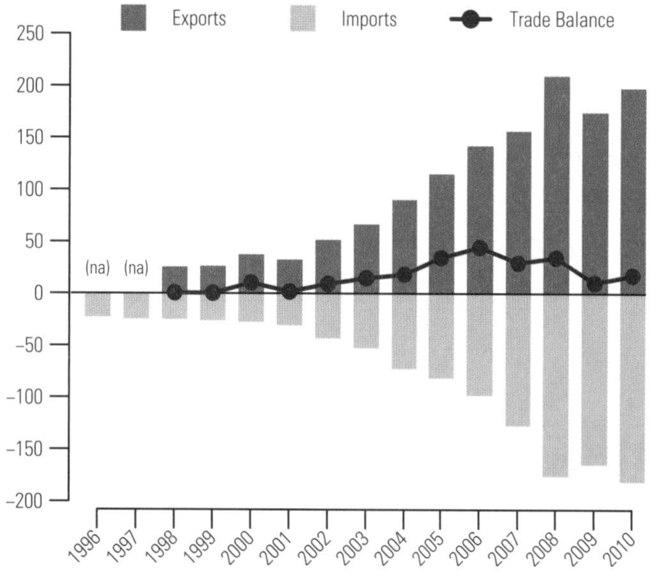

Table 1: Exports by SITC sections

(Value in million US$, growth and shares in percentage)

SITC	2010	Avg. Growth rates (%) 2006-2010	Avg. Growth rates (%) 2009-2010	2010 share
Total	198362.0	8.6	13.5	100.0
0+1	4487.5	18.6	25.1	2.3
2+4	1413.9	-1.0	6.9	0.7
3	74046.6	0.5	14.7	37.3
5	3272.5	14.9	18.7	1.6
6	22744.9	28.9	54.7	11.5
7	20113.7	16.1	21.2	10.1
8	7618.4	20.0	15.7	3.8
9	64664.5	11.8	0.1	32.6

Table 2: Imports by SITC sections

(Value in million US$, growth and shares in percentage)

SITC	2010	Avg. Growth rates (%) 2006-2010	Avg. Growth rates (%) 2009-2010	2010 share
Total	180726.0	16.6	10.0	100.0
0+1	10396.1	15.8	14.7	5.8
2+4	3140.5	10.5	12.9	1.7
3	2028.5	25.1	13.4	1.1
5	8411.6	12.8	11.9	4.7
6	31640.7	14.1	22.5	17.5
7	41922.4	9.8	-6.5	23.2
8	16197.0	11.9	8.3	9.0
9	66989.0	26.6	16.6	37.1

Exports Profile:

In 2010, more than a third of exported goods were mineral fuels, lubricants and related materials (SITC section 3) (see table 1): they represented 37.3 percent. Commodities and transactions not classified elsewhere (SITC section 9) accounted for 32.6 percent of exports. Other major commodity groups for exports included manufactured goods classified chiefly by material (SITC section 6) and machinery and transport equipment (SITC section 7), respectively with 11.5 and 10.1 percent of exports. Other Asia, nes, Asia, nes and India were the three major partners for exported goods (see table 4). From 2008 to 2010, top exported commodities were petroleum oils, crude (HS code 2709), petroleum oils, other than crude (HS code 2710) and gold (including gold plated with platinum) (HS code 7108) (see table 3).

Table 3: Top 10 export commodities 2008 to 2010

(Value in million US$)

HS code	4-digit heading of Harmonized System 2002	Value (million US$) 2008	Value (million US$) 2009	Value (million US$) 2010	Unit value 2008	Unit value 2009	Unit value 2010	Unit	SITC code
	All Commodities	210000.0	174725.0	198362.0					
2709	Petroleum oils, crude	80481.7	43535.4	65482.1					333
9999	Commodities not specified according to kind	46858.4	53154.1	51994.9					931
2710	Petroleum oils, other than crude	22797.1	15852.0	6514.1	*0.8*			US$/kg	334
7108	Gold (including gold plated with platinum)	7960.7	10520.8	11508.4	*27.6*			thsd US$/kg	971
7102	Diamonds, whether or not worked, but not mounted or set	6687.3	7692.7	15193.9	*126.0*			US$/carat	667
7113	Articles of jewellery and parts thereof, of precious metal	3710.0	3046.3	3689.2	*25.4*			thsd US$/kg	897
8703	Motor cars and other motor vehicles principally designed for the transport	3882.6	3283.5	3237.1					781
2711	Petroleum gases and other gaseous hydrocarbons	2.7	5157.5	2030.7	2.0			US$/kg	343
8517	Electrical apparatus for line telephony or line telegraphy	159.7	1791.7	2352.2					764
7110	Platinum, unwrought or in semi-manufactured forms, or in powder form	4032.8	2.8	6.4	59.5			thsd US$/kg	681

Graph 2: Trade Balance by MDG Regions in 2010

(Bln US$)

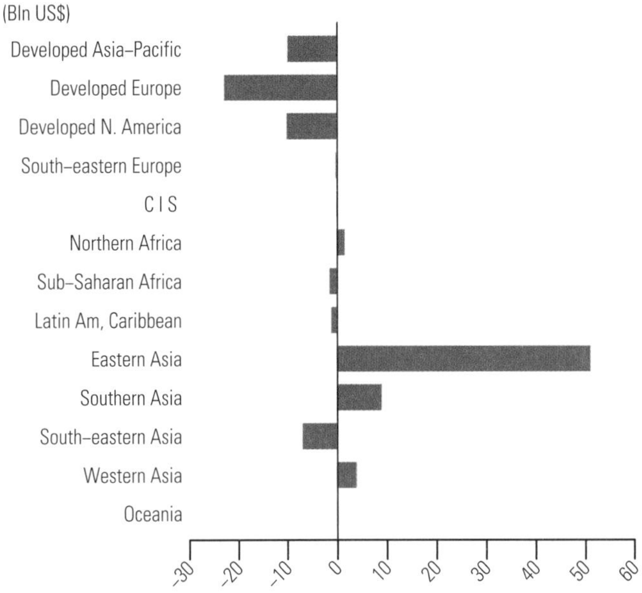

Graph 3: Partner concentration of trade in 2010

(Cumulative share by ranked partners)

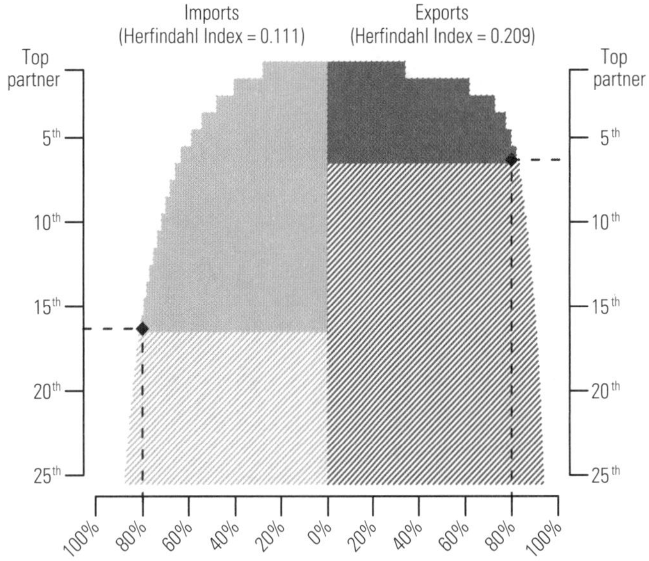

Table 4: Exports by principal countries and SITC sections in 2010

(Value in million US$, percentages of country total)

Country	Total	Shares by SITC sections (%)								
		0 + 1	2 + 4	3	5	6	7	8	9	Total
World	198362.0	2.3	0.7	37.3	1.6	11.5	10.1	3.8	32.6	100
Other Asia, nes	68028.8	0.0	0.0	99.8	0.0	0.1	0.0	0.0	0.0	100
Areas, nes	54475.1	0.1	0.0	3.8	0.0	0.4	0.2	0.0	95.5	100
India	21842.9	1.0	2.1	0.2	0.9	61.7	1.3	1.0	31.9	100
Iran	9320.3	12.3	1.2	0.8	3.8	20.3	43.8	15.1	2.6	100
Iraq	4584.7	12.2	0.4	0.9	1.8	15.9	52.1	16.5	0.1	100
Switzerland	4420.2	0.0	0.0	0.0	0.2	3.7	0.5	5.1	90.5	100
Saudi Arabia	2493.8	13.1	1.4	0.9	10.3	15.4	35.0	10.4	13.4	100
Afghanistan	2238.4	7.8	0.2	0.5	1.5	3.9	82.3	3.8	0.0	100
Bahrain	1851.0	3.4	1.3	0.9	2.1	4.9	44.2	37.7	5.5	100
Qatar	1776.1	7.6	9.3	0.2	4.0	14.5	32.6	26.0	5.7	100

Imports Profile:

In 2010, imports were composed of 37.1 percent of commodities and transactions not classified elsewhere (SITC section 9), 23.2 percent of machinery and transport equipment (SITC section 7) and 17.5 percent of manufactured goods classified chiefly by material (SITC section 6) (see table 2). From 2008 to 2010, top imported products were gold (including gold plated with platinum) (HS code 7108), diamonds, whether or not worked, but not mounted or set (HS code 7102) and motor cars and other motor vehicles principally designed for the transport (HS code 8703) (see table 5).

Table 5: Top 10 import commodities 2008 to 2010

(Value in million US$)

HS code	4-digit heading of Harmonized System 2002	Value (million US$)			Unit value				SITC code
		2008	2009	2010	2008	2009	2010	Unit	
	All Commodities	175485.7	164251.0	180726.0					
9999	Commodities not specified according to kind	21482.5	42663.7	48773.7					931
7108	Gold (including gold plated with platinum)	13225.6	14513.0	18051.1	*25.3*			thsd US$/kg	971
7102	Diamonds, whether or not worked, but not mounted or set	7352.7	7223.5	13108.0	*151.5*			US$/carat	667
8703	Motor cars and other motor vehicles principally designed for the transport	11033.3	5203.5	7324.5					781
7113	Articles of jewellery and parts thereof, of precious metal	6154.3	5172.2	6150.9	*22.8*			thsd US$/kg	897
7214	Other bars and rods of iron or non-alloy steel	6770.1	842.1	698.7	1.0			US$/kg	676
8803	Parts of goods of heading 88.01 or 88.02	1737.9	3462.4	2807.1	416.0			US$/kg	792
8517	Electrical apparatus for line telephony or line telegraphy	451.5	2901.5	2843.5					764
8802	Other aircraft (for example, helicopters, aeroplanes); spacecraft	2340.7	1603.8	2191.6					792
8411	Turbo-jets, turbo-propellers and other gas turbines	1304.1	2166.9	2161.1					714

United Kingdom

Imports: CIF, by origin/consignment for intra-eu **Exports: FOB, by last known destination** **Trade System: General**

Overview:

In 2011, the value of the exports of United Kingdom increased by 16.3 to amount to 472.1 bln US$ (see table 1 and graph 1). Imports showed a similar development with an increase of 12.8 percent to 634.4 bln US$ in 2011 (see table 2 and graph 1). This resulted in a trade deficit of 162.3 bln US$ in 2011, slightly higher than the 2010 deficit of 156.6 bln US$ (see graph 1). This deficit came largely from trade with Developed Europe (-111.5 bln US$) and Eastern Asia (-41.4 bln US$) (see graph 2). Trade, however, recorded surpluses with Developed North America (+9.9 bln US$) and Western Asia (+2.1 bln US$). United Kingdom's trade was well diversified across partners: in 2011, respectively 22 and 21 major partners accounted for 80 percent of exports and imports (see graph 3).

Graph 1: Total imports, exports and trade balance

(Bln US$ by year)

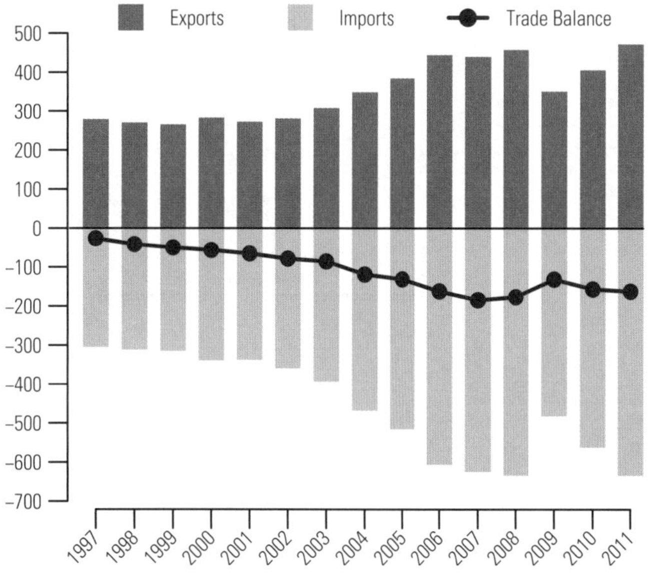

Table 1: Exports by SITC sections

(Value in million US$, growth and shares in percentage)

SITC	2011	Avg. Growth rates (%) 2007-2011	2010-2011	2011 share
Total	472095.6	1.8	16.3	100.0
0+1	28937.2	5.4	16.8	6.1
2+4	13558.4	6.9	27.3	2.9
3	64379.1	8.8	25.9	13.6
5	79189.3	2.4	9.1	16.8
6	55236.8	-1.3	23.4	11.7
7	147869.6	-0.6	15.2	31.3
8	53599.8	0.1	12.1	11.4
9	29325.5	3.9	13.8	6.2

Exports Profile:

In 2011, machinery and transport equipment (SITC section 7), chemicals and related products, n.e.s. (SITC section 5) and mineral fuels, lubricants and related materials (SITC section 3) accounted respectively 31.3, 16.8 and 13.6 percent of exported goods (see table 1). The three major markets for exports were USA, Germany and France (see table 4). Main exported goods over the last three years were medicaments (excluding goods of heading 30.02, 30.05 or 30.06) (HS code 3004), motor cars and other motor vehicles principally designed for the transport (HS code 8703) and petroleum oils and oils obtained from bituminous minerals, crude (HS code 2709) (see table 3).

Table 2: Imports by SITC sections

(Value in million US$, growth and shares in percentage)

SITC	2011	Avg. Growth rates (%) 2007-2011	2010-2011	2011 share
Total	634412.5	0.4	12.8	100.0
0+1	57381.7	2.2	11.0	9.0
2+4	19833.2	-0.5	19.1	3.1
3	90512.1	11.3	43.2	14.3
5	75727.4	2.9	11.4	11.9
6	80151.7	-0.4	16.6	12.6
7	192482.0	-3.1	8.6	30.3
8	94436.2	-0.8	10.4	14.9
9	23888.0	-3.2	-24.1	3.8

Table 3: Top 10 export commodities 2009 to 2011

(Value in million US$)

HS code	4-digit heading of Harmonized System 2007	Value (million US$) 2009	2010	2011	Unit value 2009	2010	2011	Unit	SITC code
	All Commodities	351163.5	405868.9	472095.6					
3004	Medicaments (excluding goods of heading 30.02, 30.05 or 30.06)	25887.6	26845.9	24759.6	*75.6*	*118.0*	*137.0*	US$/kg	542
9999	Commodities not specified according to kind	22378.7	25714.7	29257.8					931
8703	Motor cars and other motor vehicles principally designed for the transport	18494.6	26499.2	32077.0	18.9	*21.5*	*16.0*	thsd US$/unit	781
2709	Petroleum oils and oils obtained from bituminous minerals, crude	19561.5	24491.2	27274.2	0.4	0.6	0.8	US$/kg	333
2710	Petroleum oils, other than crude	15593.2	20213.9	28854.0	*0.5*	*0.7*	0.9	US$/kg	334
8411	Turbo-jets, turbo-propellers and other gas turbines	14916.4	15597.0	18866.9					714
7102	Diamonds, whether or not worked, but not mounted or set	5525.7	7613.1	9114.4	105.1	*124.8*	*184.2*	US$/carat	667
2208	Alcohol of a strength by volume of less than 80 % vol	5900.6	6563.2	8384.9	*15.9*	*17.7*	*19.2*	US$/litre	112
8517	Electrical apparatus for line telephony or line telegraphy	5365.9	5746.4	6386.6					764
8708	Parts and accessories of the motor vehicles of headings 87.01 to 87.05	4911.8	5566.0	6635.0	*8.4*	*8.4*	*9.1*	US$/kg	784

Graph 2: Trade Balance by MDG Regions in 2011

(Bln US$)

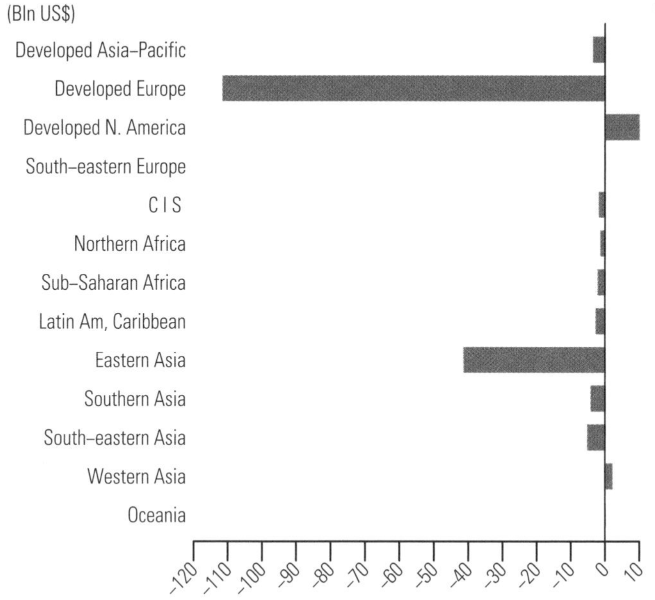

Graph 3: Partner concentration of trade in 2011

(Cumulative share by ranked partners)

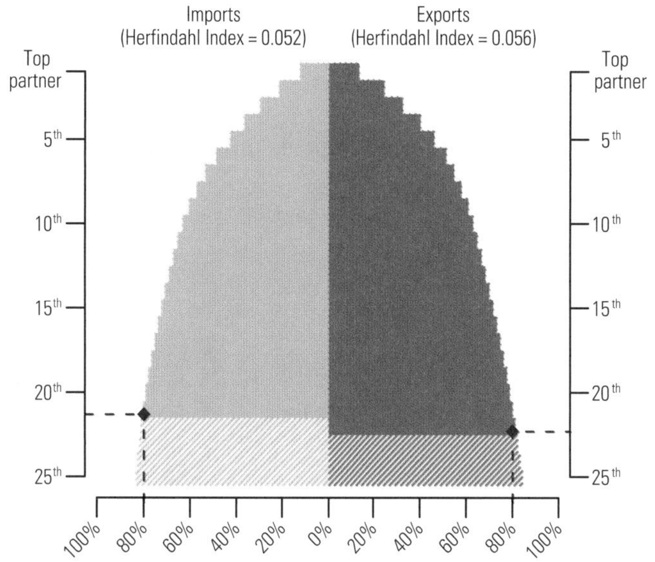

Table 4: Exports by principal countries and SITC sections in 2011

(Value in million US$, percentages of country total)

Country	Total	Shares by SITC sections (%) 0 + 1	2 + 4	3	5	6	7	8	9	Total
World	472095.6	6.1	2.9	13.6	16.8	11.7	31.3	11.4	6.2	100
USA	62570.1	4.3	0.5	13.4	21.9	8.3	30.9	12.8	7.8	100
Germany	52961.8	3.3	2.6	13.0	20.2	12.3	32.0	9.6	7.0	100
France	36960.1	9.3	1.7	18.2	15.5	10.6	23.3	10.5	10.9	100
Netherlands	36342.7	5.2	1.7	45.3	14.0	5.7	18.9	6.7	2.6	100
Ireland	27602.4	18.3	1.7	20.5	13.3	11.4	16.4	16.6	1.7	100
Belgium	24613.4	3.4	2.1	25.5	16.5	22.1	21.6	5.3	3.4	100
Italy	15851.1	5.2	3.1	6.1	20.0	11.3	38.2	12.3	3.8	100
Spain	15147.4	10.2	5.2	6.3	23.2	8.4	29.1	9.8	7.8	100
China	14062.7	2.0	17.6	0.5	12.4	7.7	48.9	7.6	3.3	100
Sweden	9845.0	3.6	1.9	18.8	13.8	16.5	33.6	9.7	2.1	100

Imports Profile:

In 2011, machinery and transport equipment (SITC section 7) accounted for 30.3 percent of imported goods (see table 2). Other major commodity groups included miscellaneous manufactured articles (SITC section 8) and mineral fuels, lubricants and related materials (SITC section 3) respectively with 14.9 and 14.3 percent of imports. Over the last three years, top commodities for imports included petroleum oils and oils obtained from bituminous minerals, crude (HS code 2709), motor cars and other motor vehicles principally designed for the transport (HS code 8703) and petroleum oils, other than crude (HS code 2710) (see table 5).

Table 5: Top 10 import commodities 2009 to 2011

(Value in million US$)

HS code	4-digit heading of Harmonized System 2007	Value (million US$) 2009	2010	2011	Unit value 2009	2010	2011	Unit	SITC code
	All Commodities	482893.4	562501.1	634412.5					
2709	Petroleum oils and oils obtained from bituminous minerals, crude	22642.2	30142.7	44863.3	0.4	0.6	0.8	US$/kg	333
8703	Motor cars and other motor vehicles principally designed for the transport	25842.6	31320.2	34470.2	15.0	*16.5*	*17.8*	thsd US$/unit	781
9999	Commodities not specified according to kind	26708.3	31455.1	23878.1					931
2710	Petroleum oils, other than crude	14136.5	18241.1	24816.0	*0.6*	0.7	1.0	US$/kg	334
3004	Medicaments (excluding goods of heading 30.02, 30.05 or 30.06)	15155.9	16720.4	17061.8	51.5	*71.9*	*64.5*	US$/kg	542
8517	Electrical apparatus for line telephony or line telegraphy	11817.4	14649.6	15627.3					764
8471	Automatic data processing machines and units thereof	11727.2	13250.9	13222.9	96.4	*178.4*	*168.8*	US$/unit	752
8708	Parts and accessories of the motor vehicles of headings 87.01 to 87.05	9555.4	13004.3	15117.8	*8.7*	*8.9*	*9.3*	US$/kg	784
8411	Turbo-jets, turbo-propellers and other gas turbines	10979.0	11832.5	13154.9					714
2711	Petroleum gases and other gaseous hydrocarbons	7699.5	10986.9	15002.3	0.3	0.3	0.4	US$/kg	343

United Republic of Tanzania

Imports: CIF, by origin | Exports: FOB, by last known destination | Trade System: General

Overview:

In 2011, the value of the exports of United Republic of Tanzania increased by 16.9 percent to amount to 4.7 bln US$ (see table 1 and graph 1). Imports showed a similar development with an increase by 39.6 percent to 11.2 bln US$ in 2011. This resulted in a trade deficit of 6.5 bln US$ (see graph 1). Large deficits were recorded with Western Asia (-1.9 bln US$), Southern Asia (-1.5 bln US$) and Developed Europe (-1.3 bln US$) (see graph 2). Trade recorded a surplus of 117.8 mln US$ with Sub-Saharan Africa. By partner, trade was diversified: in 2011, 11 (respectively 17) major partners accounted for 80 percent of exports (respectively imports) (see graph 3).

Graph 1: Total imports, exports and trade balance

(Bln US$ by year)

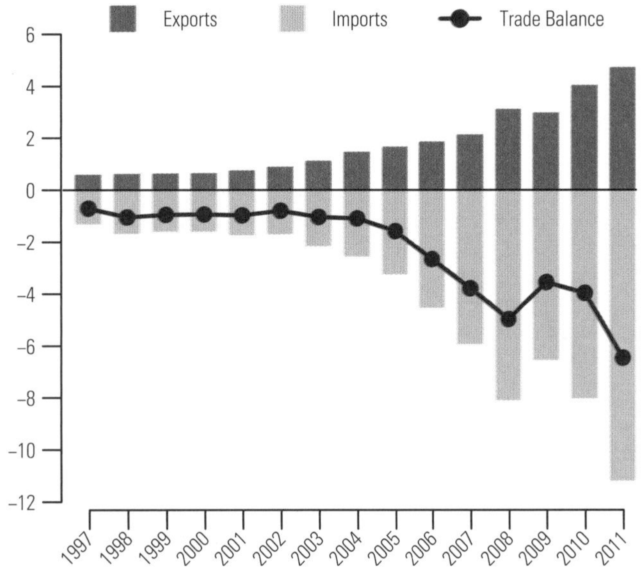

Table 1: Exports by SITC sections

(Value in million US$, growth and shares in percentage)

SITC	2011	Avg. Growth rates (%) 2007-2011	2010-2011	2011 share
Total	4735.0	22.0	16.9	100.0
0+1	834.8	5.6	-0.5	17.6
2+4	1363.3	31.5	3.0	28.8
3	35.9	24.8	-53.5	0.8
5	130.8	21.9	-25.7	2.8
6	354.9	12.7	0.9	7.5
7	187.6	18.4	4.4	4.0
8	97.1	10.4	-22.6	2.0
9	1730.6	32.8	77.1	36.6

Table 2: Imports by SITC sections

(Value in million US$, growth and shares in percentage)

SITC	2011	Avg. Growth rates (%) 2007-2011	2010-2011	2011 share
Total	11184.2	17.2	39.6	100.0
0+1	782.0	17.2	35.1	7.0
2+4	441.7	7.3	42.6	3.9
3	3592.6	19.4	62.5	32.1
5	1291.9	17.3	23.2	11.6
6	1430.3	15.4	24.4	12.8
7	3230.7	18.7	35.7	28.9
8	409.6	14.7	25.1	3.7
9	5.4	-43.1	5.2	0.0

Exports Profile:

In 2011, the majority of United Republic of Tanzania's exports were of commodities and transactions not classified elsewhere (SITC section 9) accounting for 36.6 percent of totals exports. Other major commodity groups were inedible crude materials (except fuels), animal and vegetable oils, fats and waxes (SITC sections 2+4) and food, live animals, beverages and tobacco (SITC sections 0+1), respectively with 28.8 and 17.6 percent of exports. Top markets for exports included Switzerland, South Africa and China (see table 4). Over 96 and 94 percent of exports to Switzerland and South Africa, respectively, were mainly commodities and transactions not classified elsewhere (SITC section 9) while 98.2 percent of exports to China were inedible crude materials (except fuels), animal and vegetable oils, fats and waxes (SITC sections 2+4). In addition to gold (including gold plated with platinum) (HS code 7108), other major products exported from 2009 to 2011 included precious metal ores and concentrates (HS code 2616) and manganese ores and concentrates (HS code 2602) (see table 3).

Table 3: Top 10 export commodities 2009 to 2011

(Value in million US$)

HS code	4-digit heading of Harmonized System 2007	Value (million US$) 2009	2010	2011	Unit value 2009	2010	2011	Unit	SITC code
	All Commodities	2982.4	4050.5	4735.0					
7108	Gold (including gold plated with platinum)	818.6	966.1	1718.2	2.0	3.0	39.7	thsd US$/kg	971
2616	Precious metal ores and concentrates	497.7	461.5	541.0	6.8	8.8	11.7	US$/kg	289
2602	Manganese ores and concentrates	...	356.8	477.7		8.7	12.2	US$/kg	287
0901	Coffee, whether or not roasted or decaffeinated	115.2	117.3	146.6	2.0	2.9	3.6	US$/kg	071
0801	Coconuts, Brazil nuts and cashew nuts, fresh or dried	90.9	126.3	125.4	0.9	0.9	1.1	US$/kg	057
0304	Fish fillets and other fish meat (whether or not minced)	104.5	115.6	119.3	5.1	5.6	5.6	US$/kg	034
2401	Unmanufactured tobacco; tobacco refuse	90.4	129.2	106.6	2.1	1.9	1.4	US$/kg	121
0713	Dried leguminous vegetables, shelled, whether or not skinned or split	58.7	92.2	67.3	0.5	0.6	0.6	US$/kg	054
5201	Cotton, not carded or combed	89.0	72.4	53.6	1.1	1.3	1.8	US$/kg	263
1207	Other oil seeds and oleaginous fruits, whether or not broken	69.5	55.8	77.0	0.8	0.8	1.0	US$/kg	222

Graph 2: Trade Balance by MDG Regions in 2011

(Bln US$)

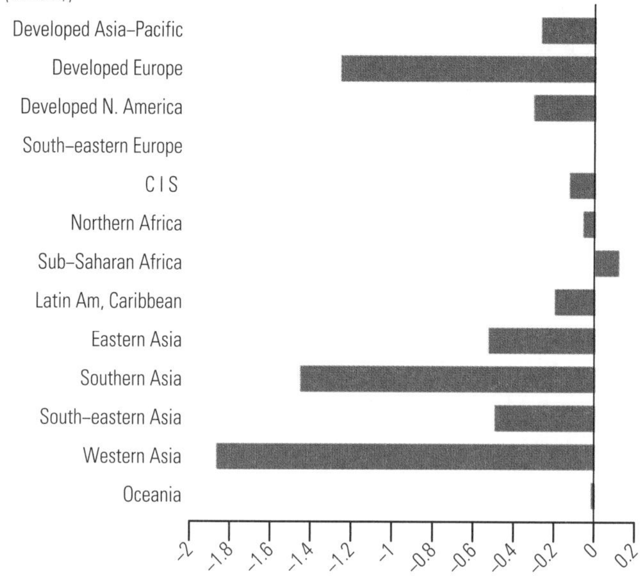

Graph 3: Partner concentration of trade in 2011

(Cumulative share by ranked partners)

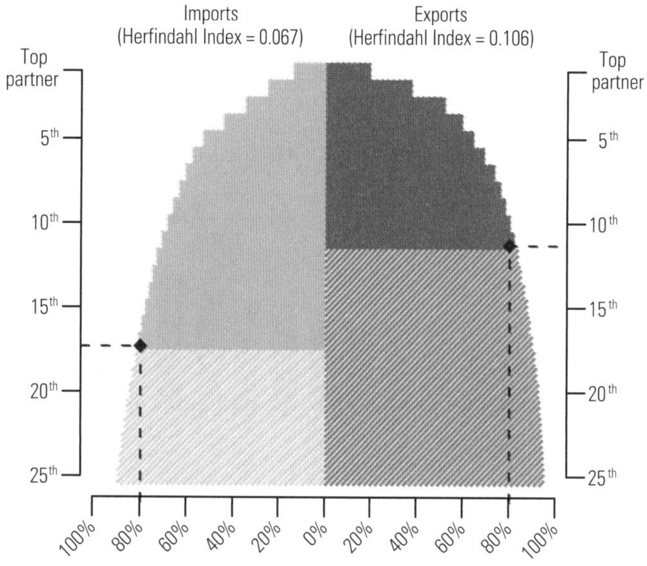

Table 4: Exports by principal countries and SITC sections in 2011

(Value in million US$, percentages of country total)

Country	Total	Shares by SITC sections (%)								
		0 + 1	2 + 4	3	5	6	7	8	9	Total
World	4735.0	17.6	28.8	0.8	2.8	7.5	4.0	2.0	36.6	100
Switzerland	916.3	1.4	1.8	...	0.1	0.4	0.0	0.0	96.3	100
South Africa	857.6	1.3	0.1	0.0	0.2	0.5	2.1	1.2	94.7	100
China	677.4	0.2	98.2	0.0	0.7	0.8	0.1	0.0	...	100
Japan	356.2	14.4	81.2	...	...	0.3	3.9	0.0	0.1	100
Germany	229.3	15.4	81.2	0.0	0.0	0.4	2.6	0.4	0.0	100
Kenya	221.3	24.1	5.1	5.9	3.3	39.8	17.9	3.6	0.4	100
India	210.2	80.5	8.8	0.0	0.5	9.2	0.9	0.0	0.0	100
Dem.Rep. of the Congo	128.1	40.3	8.5	3.7	7.3	29.2	3.2	7.6	0.1	100
Rwanda	95.2	26.7	3.2	5.2	36.8	21.9	3.4	2.8	0.0	100
Netherlands	94.9	31.6	40.7	...	0.1	0.3	6.7	0.3	20.3	100

Imports Profile:

Mineral fuels, lubricants and related materials (SITC section 3), machinery and transport equipment (SITC section 7) and manufactured goods classified chiefly by material (SITC section 6) were the three major commodity groups for imports: they accounted respectively for 32.1, 28.9 and 12.8 percent of imported goods in 2011 (see table 2). From 2009 to 2011, top imported goods were petroleum oils, other than crude (HS code 2710), wheat and meslin (HS code 1001) and motor cars and other motor vehicles principally designed for the transport (HS code 8703) (see table 5).

Table 5: Top 10 import commodities 2009 to 2011

(Value in million US$)

HS code	4-digit heading of Harmonized System 2007	Value (million US$)			Unit value				SITC code
		2009	2010	2011	2009	2010	2011	Unit	
	All Commodities	6530.8	8012.9	11184.2					
2710	Petroleum oils, other than crude	1430.2	2152.9	3517.8	0.4	0.6	1.0	US$/kg	334
1001	Wheat and meslin	209.3	291.9	404.4	0.3	0.3	0.4	US$/kg	041
8703	Motor cars and other motor vehicles principally designed for the transport	239.2	300.6	260.8	*19.8*	*20.0*		thsd US$/unit	781
8704	Motor vehicles for the transport of goods	218.4	221.2	270.0					782
1511	Palm oil and its fractions	106.1	173.3	274.6	0.6	0.8	1.2	US$/kg	422
7208	Flat-rolled products of iron or non-alloy steel	143.6	173.6	232.1	1.0	1.1	1.0	US$/kg	673
8517	Electrical apparatus for line telephony or line telegraphy	155.6	118.0	201.7					764
3901	Polymers of ethylene, in primary forms	92.7	176.3	168.4	1.6	2.3	2.2	US$/kg	571
8431	Parts suitable for use principally with the machinery of headings 84.25	114.6	111.7	208.4	1.2	22.0	5.4	US$/kg	723
4011	New pneumatic tyres, of rubber	106.6	128.2	140.8					625

Source: UN Comtrade

United States of America, including Puerto Rico and U.S.V.I.

Imports: CIF, by origin | **Exports: FOB, by last known destination** | **Trade System: General**

Overview:

From 2007 to 2011, exports of United States of America, including Puerto Rico and U.S.V.I. increased on average by 6.2 percent each year and amounted to 1,479.7 bln US$ in 2011 (see table 1 and graph 1). Imports increased on average by 2.9 percent each year and reached 2,262.6 bln US$ (see table 2 and graph 1). This resulted in a trade deficit of 782.9 bln US$ in 2011, higher than the 2010 deficit of 689.4 bln US$ (see graph 1). Trade was in deficit with nearly all MDG regions (see graph 2). The largest deficit was recorded with Eastern Asia (-312.7 bln US$). Other major deficits were recorded with Developed Europe (-107.4 bln US$), Latin America & the Caribbean (-79.6 bln US$) and Sub-Saharan Africa (-54.6 bln US$). Trade was well diversified across partners: in 2011, respectively 22 and 20 major partners accounted for 80 percent of exports and imports (see graph 3).

Graph 1: Total imports, exports and trade balance

(Bln US$ by year)

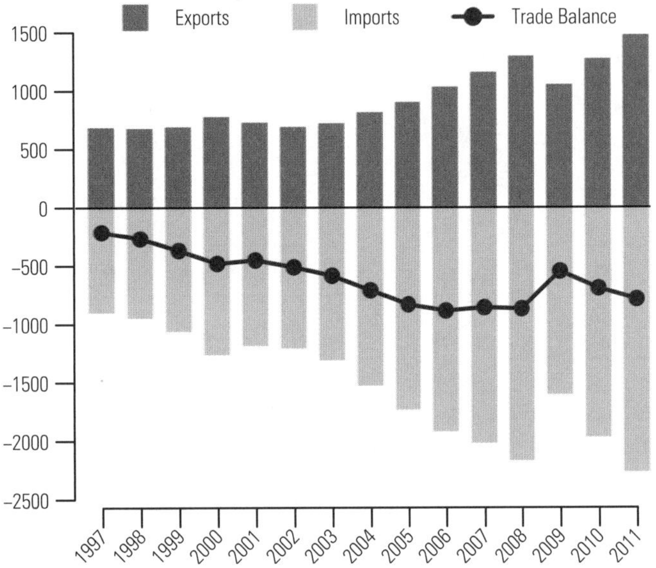

Table 1: Exports by SITC sections

(Value in million US$, growth and shares in percentage)

SITC	2011	Avg. Growth rates (%) 2007-2011	2010-2011	2011 share
Total	1 479 730.2	6.2	15.9	100.0
0+1	107 717.7	10.0	22.2	7.3
2+4	97 215.5	10.4	13.7	6.6
3	129 233.2	32.5	60.1	8.7
5	207 029.9	7.6	9.7	14.0
6	139 413.7	5.5	16.7	9.4
7	500 949.5	-1.7	11.5	33.9
8	143 306.5	3.1	7.1	9.7
9	154 864.3	31.9	17.7	10.5

Table 2: Imports by SITC sections

(Value in million US$, growth and shares in percentage)

SITC	2011	Avg. Growth rates (%) 2007-2011	2010-2011	2011 share
Total	2 262 585.6	2.9	15.1	100.0
0+1	106 101.2	6.2	15.3	4.7
2+4	44 164.1	4.9	26.9	2.0
3	464 214.5	5.7	28.0	20.5
5	202 080.8	6.2	14.2	8.9
6	239 789.2	0.2	18.0	10.6
7	810 310.6	1.8	11.3	35.8
8	320 380.8	1.0	6.8	14.2
9	75 544.5	3.5	10.2	3.3

Exports Profile:

In 2011, machinery and transport equipment (SITC section 7), the largest commodity group, increased by 11.5 percent and accounted for 33.9 percent of exported goods (see table 1). Other major commodity groups of exports were 14.0 percent of chemicals and related products, n.e.s. (SITC section 5) and 10.5 percent of commodities and transactions not classified elsewhere (SITC section 9). Major markets for exports were Canada, Mexico and China (see table 4). From 2009 to 2011, top products for exports included petroleum oils, other than crude (HS code 2710), motor cars and other motor vehicles principally designed for the transport (HS code 8703) and electronic integrated circuits (HS code 8542) (see table 3).

Table 3: Top 10 export commodities 2009 to 2011

(Value in billion US$)

HS code	4-digit heading of Harmonized System 2007	Value (billion US$) 2009	2010	2011	Unit value 2009	2010	2011	Unit	SITC code
	All Commodities	1 056.7	1 277.1	1 479.7					
9999	Commodities not specified according to kind	105.5	113.7	121.6					931
2710	Petroleum oils, other than crude	36.5	53.7	91.0	0.5	0.6	0.8	US$/kg	334
8703	Motor cars and other motor vehicles principally designed for the transport	28.4	39.3	48.4	16.8	18.4	19.5	thsd US$/unit	781
8542	Electronic integrated circuits	30.1	37.6	35.7					776
8708	Parts and accessories of the motor vehicles of headings 87.01 to 87.05	23.7	32.6	37.7			*9.2*	US$/kg	784
8471	Automatic data processing machines and units thereof	20.3	23.9	27.4	441.5	402.8	246.7	US$/unit	752
8517	Electrical apparatus for line telephony or line telegraphy	19.2	23.4	27.4					764
3004	Medicaments (excluding goods of heading 30.02, 30.05 or 30.06)	22.5	23.1	24.3	164.1	167.2	137.9	US$/kg	542
9018	Instruments and appliances used in medical, surgical, dental or veterinary	20.1	22.0	23.6					872
1201	Soya beans, whether or not broken	16.5	18.6	17.6	0.4	0.4	0.5	US$/kg	222

Graph 2: Trade Balance by MDG Regions in 2011

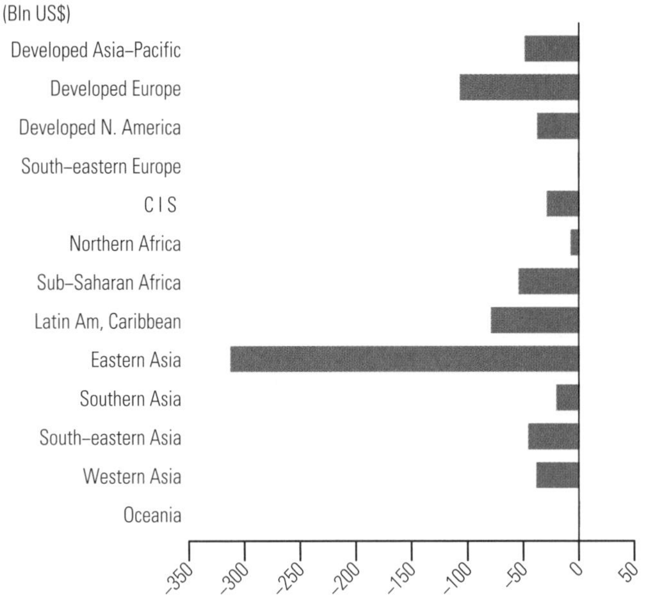

Graph 3: Partner concentration of trade in 2011

(Cumulative share by ranked partners)

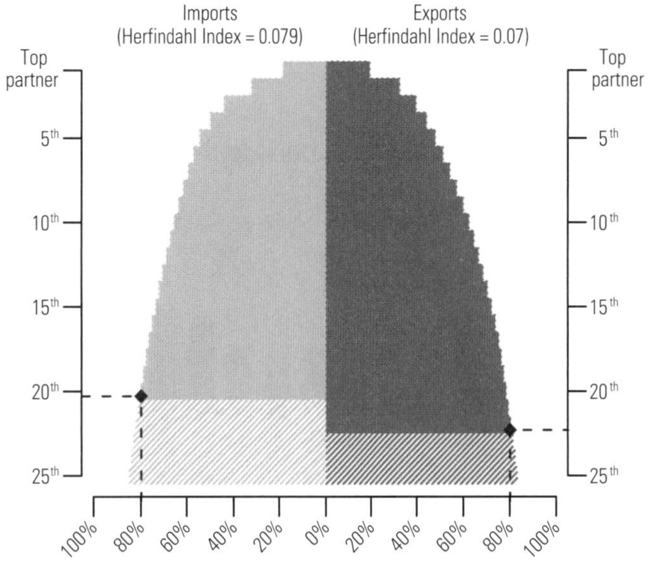

Table 4: Exports by principal countries and SITC sections in 2011

(Value in million US$, percentages of country total)

Country	Total	Shares by SITC sections (%)								
		0 + 1	2 + 4	3	5	6	7	8	9	Total
World	1 479 730.2	7.3	6.6	8.7	14.0	9.4	33.9	9.7	10.5	100
Canada	280 710.2	7.5	3.2	6.4	11.4	13.7	42.2	10.3	5.4	100
Mexico	197 543.6	7.2	4.2	11.8	11.8	12.6	41.5	6.9	3.9	100
China	103 878.4	4.9	31.2	1.9	13.8	5.2	28.9	6.8	7.2	100
Japan	66 160.4	21.0	6.4	3.8	18.7	5.6	20.9	15.5	8.1	100
United Kingdom	55 939.4	2.6	3.4	3.3	16.4	7.1	22.0	13.7	31.4	100
Germany	48 779.2	2.7	4.5	2.8	16.0	8.2	37.7	13.2	14.9	100
Rep. of Korea	43 504.8	13.9	10.5	5.9	15.4	6.5	32.6	9.2	6.0	100
Brazil	42 943.4	0.8	2.8	14.7	22.8	4.6	33.9	6.3	14.1	100
Netherlands	42 825.7	3.9	3.8	27.0	20.4	3.8	21.2	14.1	5.8	100
China, Hong Kong SAR	36 489.2	8.8	2.0	0.1	7.6	13.4	29.6	13.5	25.0	100

Imports Profile:

Imports in 2011 were composed of 35.8 percent of machinery and transport equipment (SITC section 7), 20.5 percent of mineral fuels, lubricants and related materials (SITC section 3) and 14.2 percent of miscellaneous manufactured articles (SITC section 8) (see table 2). Top imported products over the last three years were petroleum oils and oils obtained from bituminous minerals, crude (HS code 2709), motor cars and other motor vehicles principally designed for the transport (HS code 8703) and petroleum oils, other than crude (HS code 2710) (see table 5).

Table 5: Top 10 import commodities 2009 to 2011

(Value in billion US$)

HS code	4-digit heading of Harmonized System 2007	Value (billion US$)			Unit value				SITC code
		2009	2010	2011	2009	2010	2011	Unit	
	All Commodities	1 601.9	1 966.5	2 262.6					
2709	Petroleum oils and oils obtained from bituminous minerals, crude	200.6	266.6	342.9	0.4	0.6	0.7	US$/kg	333
8703	Motor cars and other motor vehicles principally designed for the transport	82.2	116.8	124.6	19.1	*20.4*	21.2	thsd US$/unit	781
2710	Petroleum oils, other than crude	54.6	69.3	94.5	0.5	0.6	0.8	US$/kg	334
8517	Electrical apparatus for line telephony or line telegraphy	59.3	71.9	77.5					764
8471	Automatic data processing machines and units thereof	54.3	71.4	81.2	119.6	131.9	146.7	US$/unit	752
9999	Commodities not specified according to kind	55.3	56.0	59.9					931
3004	Medicaments (excluding goods of heading 30.02, 30.05 or 30.06)	45.4	49.9	49.6	267.6	254.3	228.7	US$/kg	542
8708	Parts and accessories of the motor vehicles of headings 87.01 to 87.05	29.9	43.4	50.2			*10.2*	US$/kg	784
8528	Reception apparatus for television	33.5	35.8	31.5	203.3	213.8	209.0	US$/unit	761
8542	Electronic integrated circuits	16.5	21.9	27.6					776

Imports: CIF, by origin | **Exports: FOB, by last known destination** | **Trade System: Special**

Overview:

After several years of continuous growth marked by a peak of 5.9 bln US$ in 2008, the value of the exports of Uruguay dropped by 9.4 percent in 2009 and amounted to 5.4 bln US$ (see table 1 and graph 1). Imports showed a more pronounced development with a decline of 23.8 percent in 2009 to 6.9 bln US$ (see table 2 and graph 1). The trade deficit dropped by half to 1.5 bln US$ in 2009 (see graph 1). Major deficits were recorded with Latin America and the Caribbean (-1.7 bln US$), Eastern Asia (-0.6 bln US$) and Developed North America (-0.4 bln US$) (see graph 2). Trade with Western Asia recorded a surplus of 0.3 bln US$. Compared to imports, exports were well diversified across partners: 18 major partners accounted for 80 percent of exports compared to 8 major partners for imports (see graph 3).

Graph 1: Total imports, exports and trade balance

(Bln US$ by year)

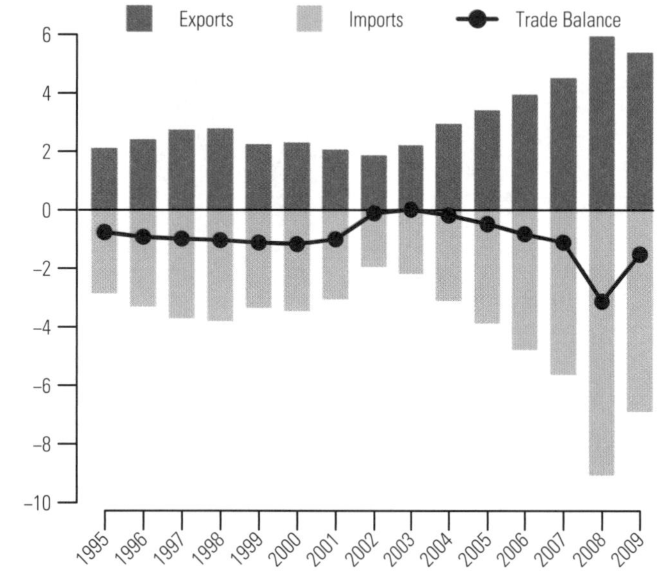

Table 1: Exports by SITC sections

(Value in million US$, growth and shares in percentage)

SITC	2009	Avg. Growth rates (%) 2005-2009	2008-2009	2009 share
Total	5385.5	12.1	-9.4	100.0
0+1	2924.4	14.5	-5.1	54.3
2+4	1037.7	21.5	-0.8	19.3
3	73.5	-18.0	-62.5	1.4
5	347.1	15.0	-13.0	6.4
6	466.6	-1.3	-27.5	8.7
7	181.7	16.5	-16.6	3.4
8	294.8	5.9	1.9	5.5
9	59.7	8.6	-13.4	1.1

Exports Profile:

Exports of food, live animals, beverages and tobacco (SITC sections 0+1), the largest commodity group, decreased by 5.1 percent in 2009 and represented 54.3 percent of exported goods (see table 1). Other major commodity groups included inedible crude materials (except fuels), animal and vegetable oils, fats and waxes (SITC sections 2+4) and manufactured goods classified chiefly by material (SITC section 6). They accounted respectively for 19.3 and 8.7 percent of exports in 2009. Major destinations for exports included Brazil, Argentina and China (see table 4). The majority of exports to Brazil were food, live animals, beverages and tobacco (SITC sections 0+1). Over the last three years, top export commodities were meat of bovine animals, frozen (HS code 0202), rice (HS code 1006) and soya beans, whether or not broken (HS code 1201) (see table 3).

Table 2: Imports by SITC sections

(Value in million US$, growth and shares in percentage)

SITC	2009	Avg. Growth rates (%) 2005-2009	2008-2009	2009 share
Total	6906.7	15.5	-23.8	100.0
0+1	626.1	21.8	-1.7	9.1
2+4	243.7	7.4	-23.4	3.5
3	1683.0	15.6	-39.2	24.4
5	1110.7	10.2	-26.5	16.1
6	750.1	8.7	-19.6	10.9
7	1948.2	21.3	-16.6	28.2
8	545.0	18.0	-3.6	7.9
9	0.0	...	548.9	0.0

Table 3: Top 10 export commodities 2007 to 2009

(Value in million US$)

HS code	4-digit heading of Harmonized System 2007	Value (million US$) 2007	2008	2009	Unit value 2007	2008	2009	Unit	SITC code
	All Commodities	4517.5	5941.9	5385.5					
0202	Meat of bovine animals, frozen	566.7	875.1	739.3	2.7	4.1	3.3	US$/kg	011
1006	Rice	280.0	443.5	461.2	0.4	0.6	0.5	US$/kg	042
1201	Soya beans, whether or not broken	209.1	327.4	455.8	0.3	0.4	0.4	US$/kg	222
0201	Meat of bovine animals, fresh or chilled	229.1	318.3	213.1	5.5	9.1	6.4	US$/kg	011
4403	Wood in the rough, whether or not stripped of bark or sapwood	113.3	173.8	196.4		*5.5*	17.8	US$/m³	247
4107	Leather further prepared after tanning or crusting	206.2	171.2	99.3	24.2	25.0	22.2	US$/kg	611
0402	Milk and cream, concentrated or containing added sugar	125.2	178.6	156.8	2.9	3.7	2.1	US$/kg	022
1107	Malt, whether or not roasted	87.8	170.4	173.4	0.4	0.7	0.6	US$/kg	048
1001	Wheat and meslin	21.2	131.5	260.5	0.2	0.3	0.2	US$/kg	041
0406	Cheese and curd	110.6	149.5	130.2	3.8	5.3	3.7	US$/kg	024

Graph 2: Trade Balance by MDG Regions in 2009

(Bln US$)

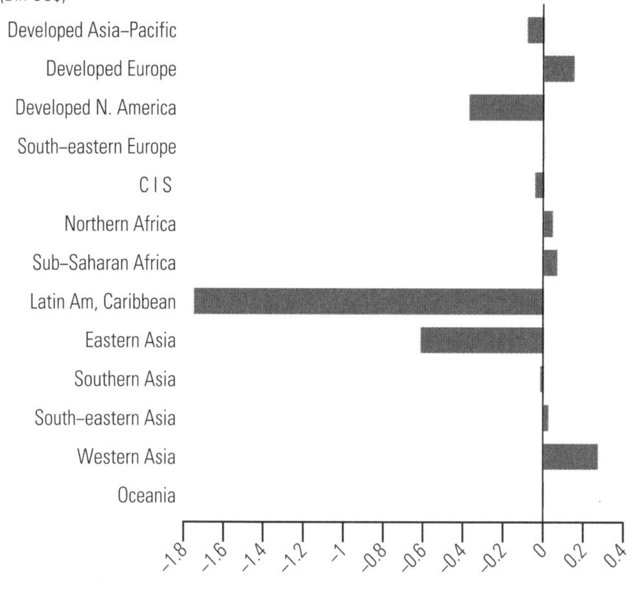

Graph 3: Partner concentration of trade in 2009

(Cumulative share by ranked partners)

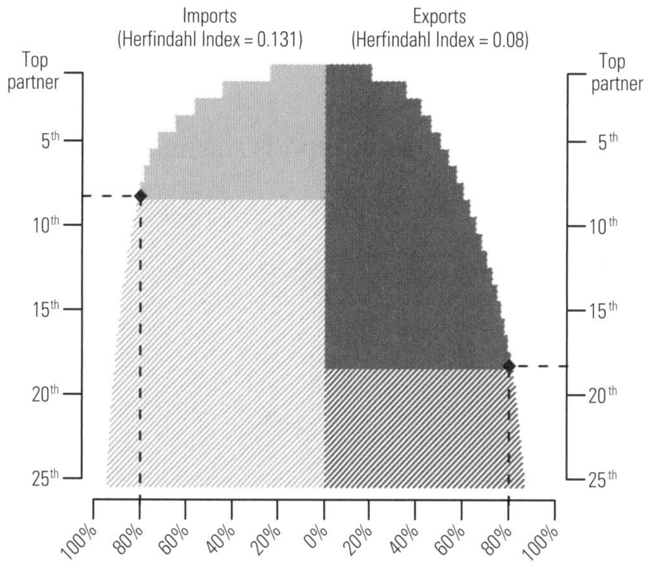

Table 4: Exports by principal countries and SITC sections in 2009

(Value in million US$, percentages of country total)

Country	Total	Shares by SITC sections (%)								
		0 + 1	2 + 4	3	5	6	7	8	9	Total
World	5385.5	54.3	19.3	1.4	6.4	8.7	3.4	5.5	1.1	100
Brazil	1099.1	59.9	2.2	1.3	9.7	11.9	3.3	11.8	...	100
Free Zones	801.4	22.6	71.2	...	4.1	1.2	0.2	0.8	...	100
Argentina	345.6	5.3	2.1	3.4	17.6	24.9	29.7	16.9	...	100
China	234.0	24.9	68.6	...	0.4	5.9	0.2	0.0	...	100
Russian Federation	217.6	99.3	0.1	...	0.3	0.2	...	0.0	...	100
Venezuela	187.5	60.0	1.7	...	8.4	2.1	4.6	23.2	...	100
USA	187.4	63.7	9.7	0.0	2.9	16.2	3.2	4.3	...	100
Germany	158.9	52.9	15.1	...	0.0	20.4	1.1	10.5	...	100
Spain	151.3	63.7	28.5	...	3.3	2.6	0.9	1.1	...	100
United Kingdom	142.6	90.2	3.1	1.1	0.0	4.8	0.4	0.5	...	100

Imports Profile:

In 2009, imports of machinery and transport equipment (SITC section 7), the largest commodity group, decreased by 16.6 percent and accounted for 28.2 percent of imported goods (see table 2). Other major commodity groups included mineral fuels, lubricants and related materials (SITC section 3) and chemicals and related products, n.e.s. (SITC section 5) respectively with 24.4 and 16.1 percent of imports. Over the last three years, top products for imports were petroleum oils and oils obtained from bituminous minerals, crude (HS code 2709), petroleum oils, other than crude (HS code 2710) and electrical apparatus for line telephony or line telegraphy (HS code 8517) (see table 5).

Table 5: Top 10 import commodities 2007 to 2009

(Value in million US$)

HS code	4-digit heading of Harmonized System 2007	Value (million US$) 2007	2008	2009	Unit value 2007	2008	2009	Unit	SITC code
	All Commodities	5627.7	9069.4	6906.7					
2709	Petroleum oils and oils obtained from bituminous minerals, crude	708.8	1638.2	815.7	0.5	0.7	0.4	US$/kg	333
2710	Petroleum oils, other than crude	444.7	896.7	559.7	0.6	0.9	0.5	US$/kg	334
8517	Electrical apparatus for line telephony or line telegraphy	150.0	241.2	153.1					764
2716	Electrical energy	61.3	168.5	263.0	78.0	175.4	179.3	thsd US$/ MWh	351
8703	Motor cars and other motor vehicles principally designed for the transport	120.3	172.3	192.5	9.0	9.6	9.2	thsd US$/unit	781
3808	Insecticides, rodenticides, fungicides, herbicides	99.8	172.6	107.3	3.8	6.6	4.0	US$/kg	591
8708	Parts and accessories of the motor vehicles of headings 87.01 to 87.05	111.8	155.7	107.1	6.0	6.3	6.5	US$/kg	784
3105	Mineral or chemical fertilisers	125.7	166.9	76.2	0.5	1.0	0.4	US$/kg	562
8704	Motor vehicles for the transport of goods	91.1	149.4	126.4	12.2	12.8	13.4	thsd US$/unit	782
3907	Polyacetals, other polyethers and epoxide resins, in primary forms	99.3	125.5	96.7	1.4	1.6	1.1	US$/kg	574

Vanuatu

Imports: CIF, by origin | **Exports: FOB, by last known destination** | **Trade System: General**

Overview:

In 2007, Vanuatu's exports dropped by 18.5 percent to 29.9 mln US$ while imports increased by 26.8 percent and amounted to 201.7 mln US$ (see tables 1, 2 and graph 1). This resulted in a trade deficit of 171.8 mln US$ (see graph 1). Trade was in deficit with nearly all MDG regions (see graph 2). Deficit with Developed Asia-Pacific alone amounted to 102.2 mln US$. Significant deficits were recorded with South-eastern Asia (-29.8 mln US$), Oceania (-20.4 mln US$) and Eastern Asia (-17.8 mln US$). Vanuatu's trade was concentrated among a few partners: in 2007, 9 (respectively 6) major partners accounted for 80 percent of exports (respectively imports) (see graph 3).

Graph 1: Total imports, exports and trade balance

(Mln US$ by year)

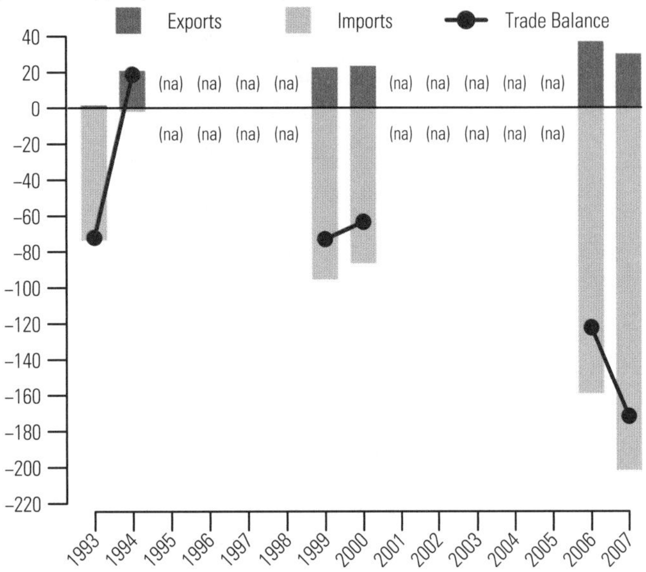

Exports Profile:

In 2007, exports of inedible crude materials (except fuels), animal and vegetable oils, fats and waxes (SITC sections 2+4) increased by 30.8 percent and represented 34.4 percent of exported goods (see table 1). However, exports of food, live animals, beverages and tobacco (SITC sections 0+1) and commodities and transactions not classified elsewhere (SITC section 9) dropped respectively by 29.0 and 38.8 percent accounting for 29.3 and 27.7 percent of exported goods. Major partners for exports were Philippines, New Caledonia and Fiji (see table 4). In 2007, exports to Philippines were exclusively inedible crude materials (except fuels), animal and vegetable oils, fats and waxes (SITC sections 2+4). From 2005 to 2007, top exported products were locust beans, seaweed, sugar beet, cane, for food (HS code 1212), copra (HS code 1203) and coconut, palm kernel, babassu oil, fractions, refined (HS code 1513) (see table 3).

Table 1: Exports by SITC sections

(Value in million US$, growth and shares in percentage)

SITC	2007	Avg. Growth rates (%) 2003-2007	2006-2007	2007 share
Total	29.9	...	-18.5	100.0
0+1	8.7	...	-29.0	29.3
2+4	10.3	...	30.8	34.4
3	0.1	...	20099.0	0.5
5	0.3	...	-29.0	1.1
6	0.5	...	-3.6	1.7
7	0.9	...	76.6	2.9
8	0.8	...	-50.6	2.5
9	8.3	...	-38.8	27.7

Table 2: Imports by SITC sections

(Value in million US$, growth and shares in percentage)

SITC	2007	Avg. Growth rates (%) 2003-2007	2006-2007	2007 share
Total	201.7	...	26.8	100.0
0+1	41.0	...	21.7	20.3
2+4	4.3	...	72.7	2.1
3	36.5	...	93.0	18.1
5	13.7	...	-10.0	6.8
6	32.1	...	25.7	15.9
7	49.4	...	20.1	24.5
8	19.2	...	0.6	9.5
9	5.6	...	79.8	2.8

Table 3: Top 10 export commodities 2005 to 2007

(Value in million US$)

HS code	4-digit heading of Harmonized System 1996	Value (million US$) 2005	2006	2007	Unit value 2005	2006	2007	Unit	SITC code
	All Commodities	...	36.7	29.9					
9999	Commodities not elsewhere specified	...	13.5	8.3					931
1212	Locust beans, seaweed, sugar beet, cane, for food	...	6.3	4.4		11.3	14.2	US$/kg	292
1203	Copra	...	2.9	4.8		0.2	0.5	US$/kg	223
1513	Coconut, palm kernel, babassu oil, fractions, refined	...	1.7	4.8		*0.7*	*0.6*	US$/kg	422
1801	Cocoa beans, whole or broken, raw or roasted	...	2.5	2.2		1.4	1.8	US$/kg	072
0202	Meat of bovine animals, frozen	...	2.1	1.6		2.8	3.5	US$/kg	011
4401	Fuel wood, wood in chips or particles, wood waste	...	1.9	0.1		0.3	2.2	US$/kg	246
9606	Buttons, press and snap fasteners, etc.	...	0.8	0.2		25.1	37.0	US$/kg	899
0201	Meat of bovine animals, fresh or chilled	...	0.9	0.1		2.9	4.6	US$/kg	011
4407	Wood sawn, chipped lengthwise, sliced or peeled	...	0.5	0.3		262.8	106.4	US$/$m^3$	248

Graph 2: Trade Balance by MDG Regions in 2007

(Mln US$)

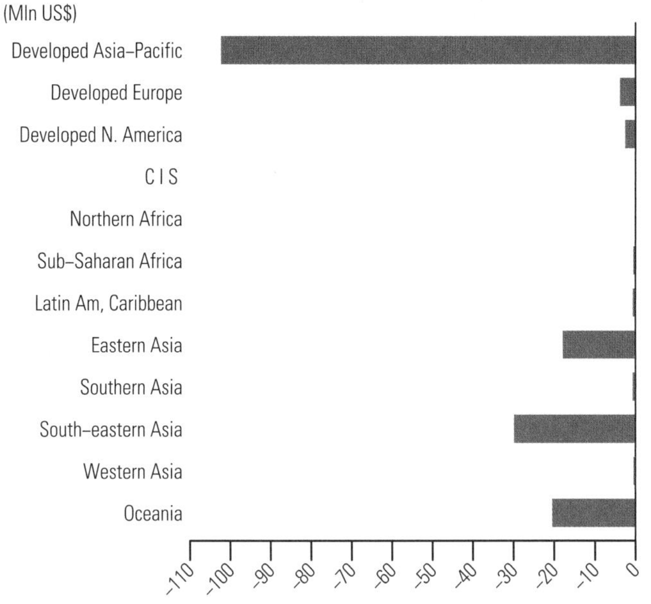

Graph 3: Partner concentration of trade in 2007

(Cumulative share by ranked partners)

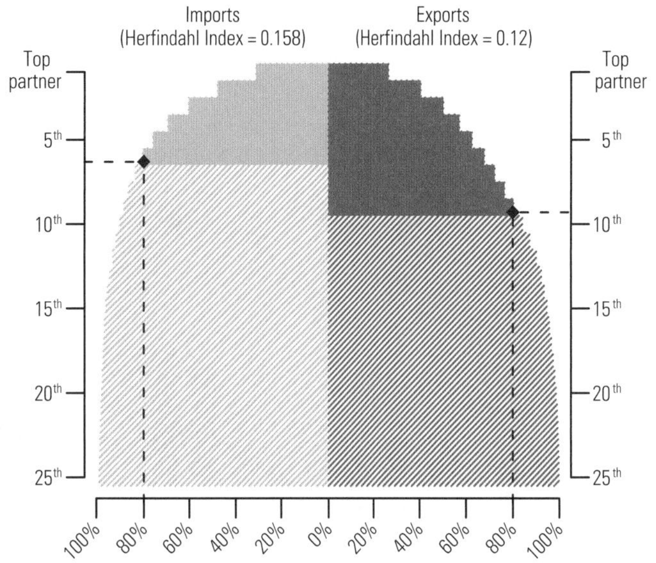

Table 4: Exports by principal countries and SITC sections in 2007

(Value in million US$, percentages of country total)

Country	Total	Shares by SITC sections (%)								
		0 + 1	2 + 4	3	5	6	7	8	9	Total
World	29.9	29.3	34.4	0.5	1.1	1.7	2.9	2.5	27.7	100
Areas, nes	8.0	0.0	0.0	...	...	...	...	...	100.0	100
Philippines	4.2	0.0	100.0	...	...	...	...	...	...	100
New Caledonia	2.9	73.6	10.4	0.0	0.3	1.9	1.3	10.4	2.1	100
Fiji	2.0	95.1	0.0	0.0	...	0.0	4.8	0.0	0.1	100
Japan	1.6	60.5	0.3	...	...	3.9	35.2	...	...	100
Singapore	1.6	97.9	2.1	...	...	0.0	...	0.0	0.0	100
Germany	1.3	0.0	99.9	...	...	...	0.1	...	...	100
France	1.3	49.6	48.5	...	...	0.1	0.8	1.0	0.0	100
Belgium	1.1	0.0	100.0	...	...	...	...	...	...	100
Netherlands	1.1	0.1	99.9	...	...	...	...	...	...	100

Imports Profile:

In 2007, imports were composed of 24.5 percent of machinery and transport equipment (SITC section 7) and 20.3 percent of food, live animals, beverages and tobacco (SITC sections 0+1) (see table 2). Imports of mineral fuels, lubricants and related materials (SITC section 3) increased nearly twofold (93.0 percent) and accounted for 18.1 percent of imported goods. From 2005 to 2007, top imported products were oils petroleum, bituminous, distillates, except crude (HS code 2710), rice (HS code 1006) and motor vehicles for the transport of goods (HS code 8704) (see table 5).

Table 5: Top 10 import commodities 2005 to 2007

(Value in million US$)

HS code	4-digit heading of Harmonized System 1996	Value (million US$)			Unit value				SITC code
		2005	2006	2007	2005	2006	2007	Unit	
	All Commodities	...	159.1	201.7					
2710	Oils petroleum, bituminous, distillates, except crude	...	17.3	34.7		*0.7*	*0.7*	US$/kg	334
1006	Rice	...	7.5	7.6		0.6	0.7	US$/kg	042
8704	Motor vehicles for the transport of goods	...	3.6	8.7		16.4	*15.0*	thsd US$/unit	782
3004	Medicaments, therapeutic, prophylactic use, in dosage	...	7.0	3.5		59.4	49.1	US$/kg	542
9999	Commodities not elsewhere specified	...	3.1	5.6					931
2523	Cement (portland, aluminous, slag or hydraulic)	...	3.3	3.9		0.1	0.1	US$/kg	661
8429	Self-propelled earth moving, road making, etc machines	...	1.6	3.9		34.2	*49.8*	thsd US$/unit	723
8703	Motor vehicles for transport of persons (except buses)	...	1.5	3.3		7.8	7.4	thsd US$/unit	781
9403	Other furniture and parts thereof	...	2.8	2.0					821
1905	Baked bread, pastry, wafers, rice paper, biscuits, etc	...	2.0	2.6		1.8	2.0	US$/kg	048

Venezuela (Bolivarian Republic of)

Imports: CIF, by origin **Exports: FOB, by last known destination** **Trade System: General**

Overview:

After a significant drop in 2009 by 32.2 percent, Venezuela's exports bounced back in 2010 by 18.3 percent to amount to 67.0 bln US$, still well below its 2008 level (see table 1 and graph 1). Imports, on the other hand, continued to dropped by 16.4 percent in 2010 and amounted to 32.3 bln US$ (see table 2 and graph 2). This resulted in a trade surplus of 34.6 bln US$ in 2010 compared to 17.9 bln US$ in 2009 (see graph 1). By MDG regions, trade recorded large surpluses with Eastern Asia (+2.8 bln US$) and Latin America and the Caribbean (+2.4 bln US$) (see graph 2). Significant deficits were recorded with Developed Europe (-2.8 bln US$) and Developed Asia-Pacific (-0.6 bln US$). In 2010, 13 major partners accounted for 80 percent of imported goods (see graph 3). See footnote*.

Graph 1: Total imports, exports and trade balance

(Bln US$ by year)

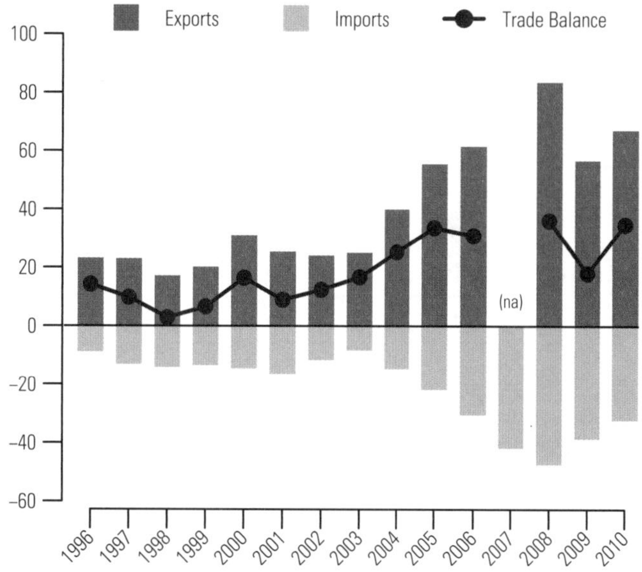

Table 1: Exports by SITC sections

(Value in million US$, growth and shares in percentage)

SITC	2010	Avg. Growth rates (%) 2006-2010	2009-2010	2010 share
Total	66962.7	2.2	18.3	100.0
0+1	124.6	2.2	89.2	0.2
2+4	932.2	41.3	246.7	1.4
3	62541.1	2.4	15.3	93.4
5	799.8	3.7	183.0	1.2
6	1951.0	-10.1	34.9	2.9
7	500.9	1.7	112.4	0.7
8	83.8	9.1	61.1	0.1
9	29.4	15.7	...	0.0

Exports Profile:

Venezuela's exports in 2010 were almost exclusively (93.4 percent) mineral fuels, lubricants and related materials (SITC section 3) (see table 1). Other top commodities were manufactured goods classified chiefly by material (SITC section 6) and inedible crude materials (except fuels), animal and vegetable oils, fats and waxes (SITC sections 2+4) with respectively 2.9 percnet and 1.4 percent. Major partners for exports were USA, China and Colombia (see table 4). From 2008 to 2010, top three exported goods were petroleum oils, crude (HS code 2709), petroleum oils, other than crude (HS code 2710) and ferrous products obtained by direct reduction of iron ore (HS code 7203) (see table 3).

Table 2: Imports by SITC sections

(Value in million US$, growth and shares in percentage)

SITC	2010	Avg. Growth rates (%) 2006-2010	2009-2010	2010 share
Total	32342.9	1.4	-16.4	100.0
0+1	4443.1	22.1	-22.7	13.7
2+4	1073.1	11.5	-2.8	3.3
3	295.4	18.0	-79.5	0.9
5	6577.0	18.4	-0.8	20.3
6	3937.6	5.6	-31.5	12.2
7	12409.8	-0.5	-6.7	38.4
8	3540.1	10.4	-17.6	10.9
9	66.8	-67.7	-83.9	0.2

Table 3: Top 10 export commodities 2008 to 2010

(Value in million US$)

HS code	4-digit heading of Harmonized System 2002	Value (million US$) 2008	2009	2010	Unit value 2008	2009	2010	Unit	SITC code
	All Commodities	83477.8	56583.1	66962.7					
2709	Petroleum oils, crude	61005.6	35844.0	44156.6	1.0	0.4	0.6	US$/kg	333
2710	Petroleum oils, other than crude	16856.4	18357.0	18160.4	*0.8*	*1.0*	*0.7*	US$/kg	334
7203	Ferrous products obtained by direct reduction of iron ore	658.6	293.5	565.9	0.3	0.2	0.3	US$/kg	671
7601	Unwrought aluminium	716.4	339.0	436.7	2.5	1.5	3.1	US$/kg	684
2601	Iron ores and concentrates	509.7	172.4	682.9	0.1	0.0	0.1	US$/kg	281
7202	Ferro-alloys	278.8	129.1	260.2	3.2	2.3	3.6	US$/kg	671
2701	Coal; briquettes, ovoids and similar solid fuels manufactured from coal	296.0	15.2	192.7	0.1	0.1	0.1	US$/kg	321
7208	Flat-rolled products of iron or non-alloy steel	222.7	146.5	105.2	0.9	0.4	1.3	US$/kg	673
2818	Artificial corundum, whether or not chemically defined	163.7	53.8	223.3	0.4	0.2	0.7	US$/kg	285
7209	Flat-rolled products of iron or non-alloy steel	217.5	114.8	32.9	0.9	0.5	1.2	US$/kg	673

*Major export partners are defined as regions only, resulting in high export concentration shown in graph 3.

Graph 2: Trade Balance by MDG Regions in 2010

(Bln US$)

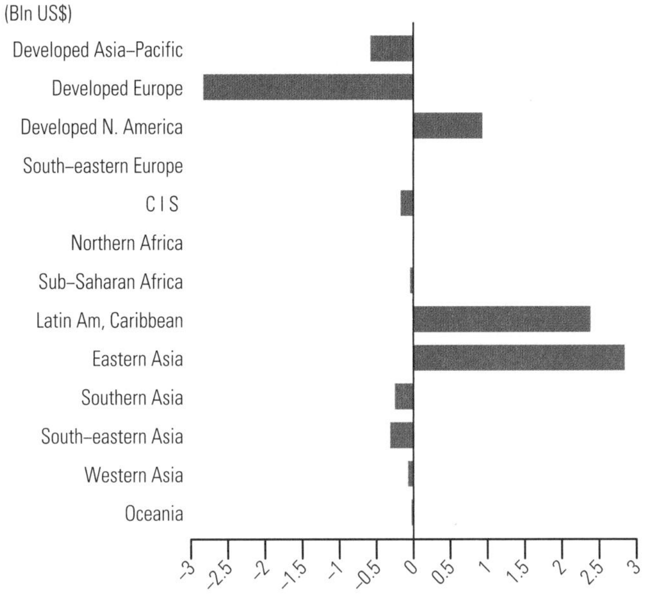

Graph 3: Partner concentration of trade in 2010

(Cumulative share by ranked partners)

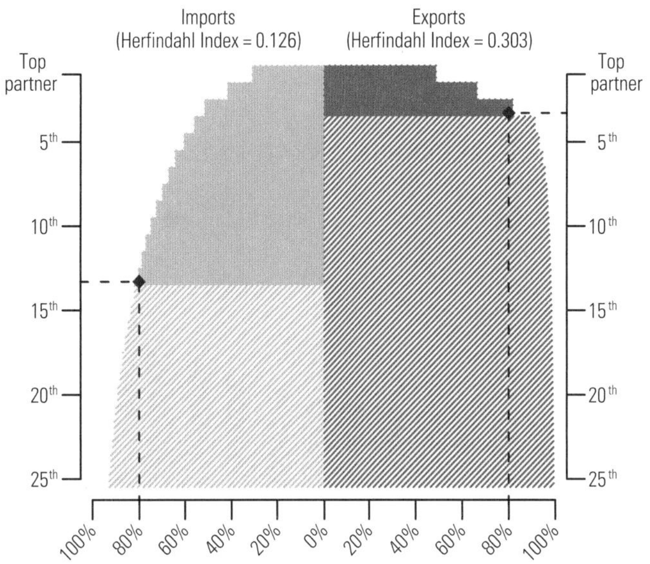

Table 4: Exports by principal countries and SITC sections in 2010

(Value in million US$, percentages of country total)

Country	Total	Shares by SITC sections (%) 0 + 1	2 + 4	3	5	6	7	8	9	Total
World	66 962.7	0.2	1.4	93.4	1.2	2.9	0.7	0.1	0.0	100
Areas, nes	32 690.8	0.0	0.0	100.0	...	...	...	...	...	100
South America, nes	11 788.3	0.0	0.0	100.0	...	...	...	...	...	100
North America and Central America, nes	10 233.5	0.0	0.0	100.0	...	...	...	...	...	100
Other Asia, nes	6 398.5	0.0	0.0	99.8	0.0	0.1	...	0.0	...	100
Other Europe, nes	1 215.6	0.0	0.0	100.0	...	...	...	...	...	100
USA	970.9	2.1	3.1	7.2	18.3	45.9	22.2	1.2	...	100
China	719.4	0.0	60.5	...	0.5	38.7	0.2	0.0	...	100
Colombia	591.4	1.5	0.3	0.5	34.8	34.0	21.2	7.7	...	100
Brazil	272.5	0.0	0.3	25.0	18.4	47.6	6.5	2.2	...	100
Mexico	253.2	0.2	0.4	0.0	33.0	61.2	4.3	0.8	...	100

Imports Profile:

In 2010, imports were composed of 38.4 percent of machinery and transport equipment (SITC section 7), 20.3 percent of chemicals and related products, n.e.s. (SITC section 5) and 13.7 percent food, live animals, beverages and tobacco (SITC sections 0+1) (see table 2). From 2008 to 2010, top imported products were medicaments (excluding goods of heading 30.02, 30.05 or 30.06) (HS code 3004), transmission apparatus for radio-telephony, radio-broadcasting (HS code 8525) and live bovine animals (HS code 0102) (see table 5).

Table 5: Top 10 import commodities 2008 to 2010

(Value in million US$)

HS code	4-digit heading of Harmonized System 2002	Value (million US$) 2008	2009	2010	Unit value 2008	2009	2010	Unit	SITC code
	All Commodities	47 450.1	38 676.6	32 342.9					
3004	Medicaments (excluding goods of heading 30.02, 30.05 or 30.06)	1 389.2	1 818.6	1 986.3	*26.8*	*39.5*	47.2	US$/kg	542
8525	Transmission apparatus for radio-telephony, radio-broadcasting	1 982.6	1 204.6	1 023.8					764
0102	Live bovine animals	468.8	617.1	1 011.3	*814.9*	*934.0*	*814.3*	US$/unit	001
8471	Automatic data processing machines and units thereof	872.8	623.6	424.8					752
8411	Turbo-jets, turbo-propellers and other gas turbines	374.3	500.9	918.0					714
9018	Instruments and appliances used in medical, surgical, dental or veterinary	479.1	493.6	805.7					872
2304	Oil-cake and other solid residues	559.4	468.7	559.3	0.5	0.5	0.5	US$/kg	081
1001	Wheat and meslin	726.5	419.2	407.7	0.5	0.3	0.3	US$/kg	041
8502	Electric generating sets and rotary converters	140.4	228.4	1 153.9					716
8703	Motor cars and other motor vehicles principally designed for the transport	1 139.5	65.5	297.8		*15.9*	*19.8*	thsd US$/unit	781

Imports: CIF, by origin | **Exports: FOB, by last known destination** | **Trade System: General**

Overview:

After several years of continuous growth, the value of the Viet Nam's exports dropped by 8.9 percent in 2009 but bounced back in 2010 by 26.5 percent to amount to 72.2 bln US$ (see table 1 and graph 1). Imports showed a similar development with an increase of 21.3 percent and amounted to 84.8 bln US$ (see table 2 and graph 1). This resulted in a trade deficit of 12.6 bln US$ in 2010 compared to 18.0 bln US$ deficit in 2008 (see graph 1). By MDG regions, large deficits were recorded with Eastern Asia (-24.1 bln US$) and South-eastern Asia (-6.0 bln US$) (see graph 2). However, large surpluses were recorded with Developed North America (+10.9 bln US$), Developed Europe (+6.6 bln US$) and Sub-Saharan Africa (+750.5 mln US$). Trade, especially exports, was diversified across partners: 18 major partners accounted for 80 percent of exports compared to 11 major partners for imports (see graph 3).

Graph 1: Total imports, exports and trade balance

(Bln US$ by year)

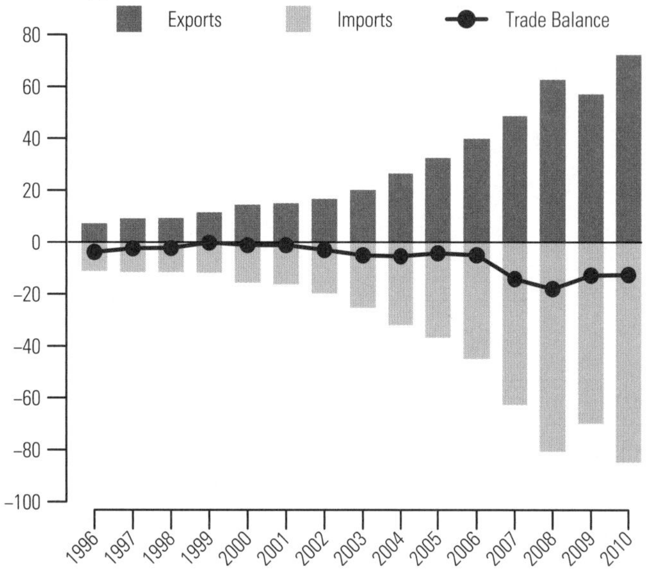

Table 1: Exports by SITC sections

(Value in million US$, growth and shares in percentage)

SITC	2010	Avg. Growth rates (%) 2006-2010	2009-2010	2010 share
Total	72 236.7	16.1	26.5	100.0
0+1	13 729.0	15.8	17.3	19.0
2+4	3 400.0	16.3	72.3	4.7
3	7 979.7	-4.8	-6.2	11.0
5	1 875.8	24.1	48.1	2.6
6	8 395.7	30.2	62.4	11.6
7	11 476.1	28.7	55.1	15.9
8	24 918.1	18.7	25.3	34.5
9	462.2	30.8	-61.2	0.6

Table 2: Imports by SITC sections

(Value in million US$, growth and shares in percentage)

SITC	2010	Avg. Growth rates (%) 2006-2010	2009-2010	2010 share
Total	84 838.6	17.2	21.3	100.0
0+1	6 467.9	27.7	31.4	7.6
2+4	5 176.7	22.1	39.3	6.1
3	8 140.4	5.0	8.6	9.6
5	12 475.0	18.7	22.1	14.7
6	22 389.0	16.6	26.0	26.4
7	24 764.8	23.2	12.9	29.2
8	4 172.5	16.9	27.5	4.9
9	1 252.1	-11.7	98.2	1.5

Exports Profile:

In 2010, exports were composed of 34.5 percent of miscellaneous manufactured articles (SITC section 8), 19.0 percent of food, live animals, beverages and tobacco (SITC sections 0+1) and 15.9 percent of machinery and transport equipment (SITC section 7) (see table 1). Major markets for exported goods were USA, China and Japan (see table 4). A large share of exports to the USA were miscellaneous manufactured articles (SITC section 8) at 68.0 percent. From 2008 to 2010, top exported products included petroleum oils, crude (HS code 2709), rice (HS code 1006) and footwear with outer soles of rubber, plastics, leather (HS code 6403) (see table 3).

Table 3: Top 10 export commodities 2008 to 2010

(Value in million US$)

HS code	4-digit heading of Harmonized System 2007	Value (million US$) 2008	2009	2010	Unit value 2008	2009	2010	Unit	SITC code
	All Commodities	62 685.1	57 096.3	72 236.7					
2709	Petroleum oils and oils obtained from bituminous minerals, crude	10 356.8	6 194.6	5 023.5	0.8	0.5		US$/kg	333
1006	Rice	2 895.9	2 666.1	3 249.5	*0.6*	*0.4*		US$/kg	042
6403	Footwear with outer soles of rubber, plastics, leather	2 332.0	2 054.1	2 444.0	*27.2*	*29.5*	*33.1*	US$/pair	851
9403	Other furniture and parts thereof	1 841.6	1 739.7	2 129.6					821
0901	Coffee, whether or not roasted or decaffeinated	2 113.8	1 730.6	1 851.4			*1.5*	thsd US$/kg	071
0304	Fish fillets and other fish meat (whether or not minced)	1 855.8	1 622.0	1 823.2					034
4001	Natural rubber, balata, gutta-percha, guayule, chicle	1 562.7	1 108.7	2 089.9			3.1	thsd US$/kg	231
8443	Printing machinery used for printing by means of the printing type, blocks	1 354.0	1 314.5	1 761.2					726
6204	Women's or girls' suits, ensembles, jackets, blazers, dresses, skirts	1 485.4	1 365.1	1 565.1					842
0306	Crustaceans, whether in shell or not	1 407.1	1 397.4	1 608.8	*6.8*	*6.9*	*6.2*	US$/kg	036

Graph 2: Trade Balance by MDG Regions in 2010

(Bln US$)

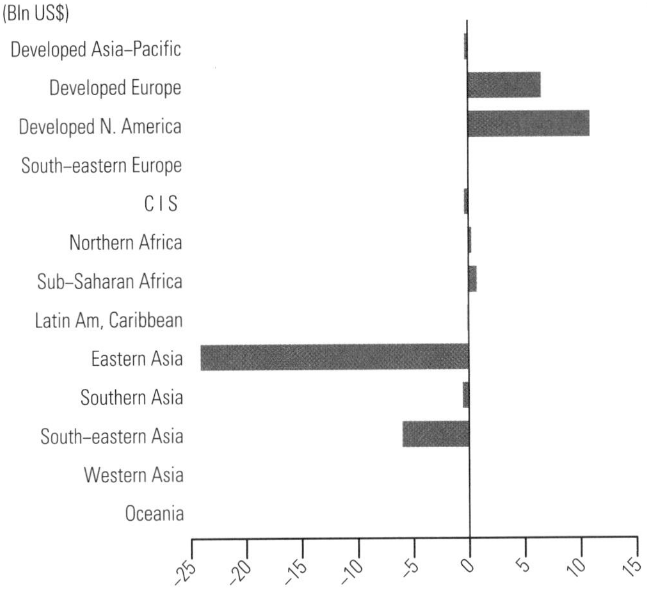

Graph 3: Partner concentration of trade in 2010

(Cumulative share by ranked partners)

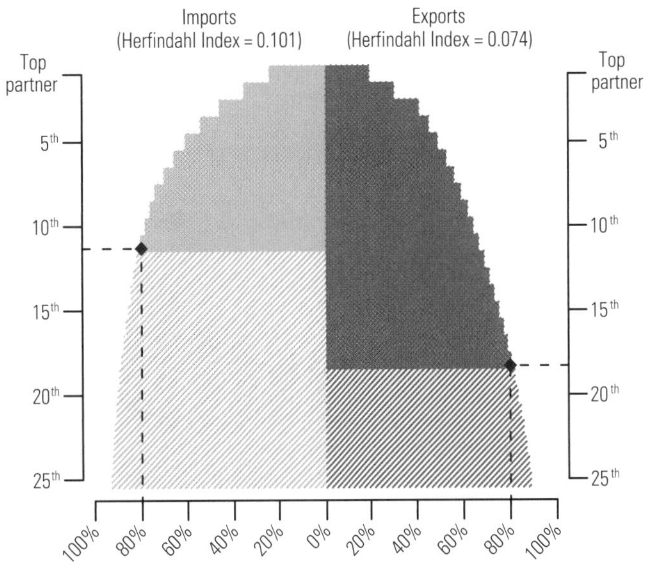

Table 4: Exports by principal countries and SITC sections in 2010

(Value in million US$, percentages of country total)

Country	Total	Shares by SITC sections (%) 0 + 1	2 + 4	3	5	6	7	8	9	Total
World	72236.7	19.0	4.7	11.0	2.6	11.6	15.9	34.5	0.6	100
USA	14250.9	12.5	0.7	2.6	0.3	5.6	10.3	68.0	0.0	100
China	7742.9	12.2	22.5	22.3	6.3	14.1	13.6	4.0	4.9	100
Japan	7727.7	14.2	3.0	6.0	3.5	10.6	32.8	29.9	0.0	100
Rep. of Korea	3092.2	16.3	5.8	24.0	1.9	23.1	9.0	19.9	0.0	100
Australia	2704.0	10.5	0.3	69.3	0.6	4.4	6.3	8.7	0.0	100
Switzerland	2652.0	3.4	0.0	0.6	0.1	0.7	1.0	93.1	1.2	100
Germany	2372.7	22.8	3.8	0.0	0.6	9.7	13.7	49.4	0.0	100
Singapore	2121.3	18.8	1.2	32.3	2.3	18.1	22.9	4.5	0.0	100
Malaysia	2093.1	15.4	8.4	40.7	4.5	18.6	7.6	4.9	0.0	100
Philippines	1706.4	62.0	0.1	2.5	5.1	6.3	19.9	4.1	0.0	100

Imports Profile:

Imports in 2010 were composed of 29.2 percent machinery and transport equipment (SITC section 7), 26.4 percent of manufactured goods classified chiefly by material (SITC section 6) and 14.7 percent of chemicals and related products, n.e.s. (SITC section 5) (see table 2). From 2008 to 2010, top imported products were petroleum oils, other than crude (HS code 2710), flat-rolled products of iron or non-alloy steel (HS code 7208) and electrical apparatus for line telephony and line telegraphy (HS code 8517) (see table 5).

Table 5: Top 10 import commodities 2008 to 2010

(Value in million US$)

HS code	4-digit heading of Harmonized System 2007	Value (million US$) 2008	2009	2010	Unit value 2008	2009	2010	Unit	SITC code
	All Commodities	80713.8	69948.8	84838.6					
2710	Petroleum oils, other than crude	11322.2	6507.6	6454.2	*0.8*			US$/kg	334
7208	Flat-rolled products of iron or non-alloy steel	2497.6	2132.5	2386.4		0.5		US$/kg	673
8517	Electrical apparatus for line telephony or line telegraphy	1909.4	2520.3	2406.9					764
7108	Gold (including gold plated with platinum)	2728.1	382.3	964.6					971
7207	Semi-finished products of iron or non-alloy steel	1647.3	1038.4	1083.0		0.4		US$/kg	672
2304	Oil-cake and other solid residues	1044.5	1028.5	1218.2	*0.3*	*0.5*	*0.5*	US$/kg	081
8542	Electronic integrated circuits	769.9	831.8	1463.1					776
3004	Medicaments (excluding goods of heading 30.02, 30.05 or 30.06)	819.9	1042.9	1164.4					542
3901	Polymers of ethylene, in primary forms	947.0	869.1	1129.2			*1.4*	thsd US$/kg	571
8708	Parts and accessories of the motor vehicles of headings 87.01 to 87.05	1054.3	889.3	934.3					784

Yemen

Imports: CIF, by origin | **Exports: FOB, by last known destination** | **Trade System: Special**

Overview:

After a peak of 7.6 bln US$ in 2008, the value of the exports of Yemen dropped by 17.5 percent in 2009 to 6.3 bln US$ (see table 1 and graph 1). Imports showed a similar development with a decline by 12.9 percent in 2009 to 9.2 bln US$ (see table 2 and graph 1). The trade balance recorded a deficit of 2.9 bln US$ in 2009, slightly below the deficit in 2008 of 3.0 bln US$ (see graph 1). By MDG regions, trade recorded deficits with Developed Europe (-1.7 bln US$), Western Asia (-1.6 bln US$) and Developed North America (-0.6 bln US$) (see graph 2). However, surpluses were recorded with South-eastern Asia (+1.0 bln US$), Southern Asia (+0.8 bln US$) and Eastern Asia (+0.5 bln US$) among others. Compared to exports, imports were more diversified across partners: 6 major partners accounted for 80 percent of exports compared to 19 major partners for imports (see graph 3).

Graph 1: Total imports, exports and trade balance

(Bln US$ by year)

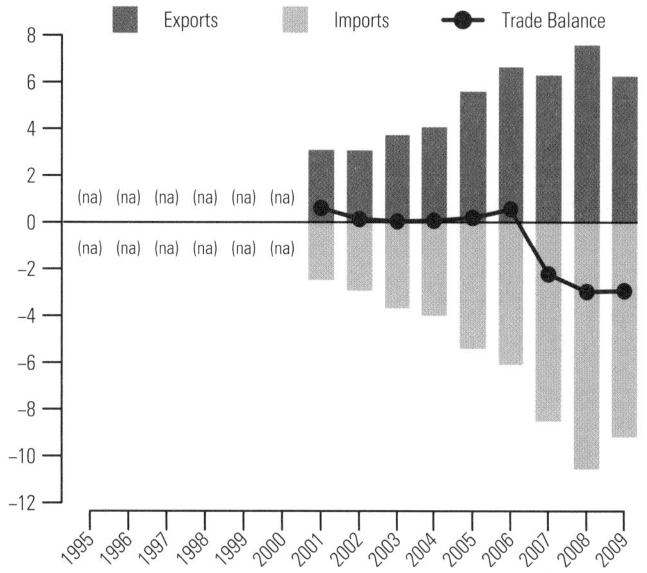

Table 1: Exports by SITC sections

(Value in million US$, growth and shares in percentage)

SITC	2009	Avg. Growth rates (%) 2005-2009	Avg. Growth rates (%) 2008-2009	2009 share
Total	6259.0	2.8	-17.5	100.0
0+1	365.9	10.9	-4.2	5.8
2+4	25.6	8.1	6.1	0.4
3	5599.7	2.0	-16.8	89.5
5	37.6	24.7	13.7	0.6
6	53.5	31.1	56.8	0.9
7	145.0	8.7	-57.9	2.3
8	21.3	14.3	-42.4	0.3
9	10.4	-24.2	7886.8	0.2

Table 2: Imports by SITC sections

(Value in million US$, growth and shares in percentage)

SITC	2009	Avg. Growth rates (%) 2005-2009	Avg. Growth rates (%) 2008-2009	2009 share
Total	9184.8	14.2	-12.9	100.0
0+1	2433.8	15.1	-0.4	26.5
2+4	209.8	2.4	-12.8	2.3
3	1922.3	16.5	-36.7	20.9
5	634.4	7.8	-5.2	6.9
6	1234.6	10.7	-4.1	13.4
7	2147.8	17.2	-12.2	23.4
8	587.1	14.0	55.8	6.4
9	15.1	116.5	-66.8	0.2

Exports Profile:

In 2009, exports of mineral fuels, lubricants and related materials (SITC section 3), which accounted for 89.5 percent of Yemen's exports, dropped by 16.8 percent. Other major commodity groups included food, live animals, beverages and tobacco (SITC sections 0+1) and machinery and transport equipment (SITC section 7), which accounted respectively for 5.8 and 2.3 percent of exports and declined by 4.2 and 57.9 percent in 2009. Top markets for exports in 2009 were China, India and Thailand (see table 4). From 2007 to 2009, major exported products were petroleum oils, crude (HS code 2709), petroleum oils, other than crude (HS code 2710) and oils and other products of high temperature coal tar (HS code 2707) (see table 3).

Table 3: Top 10 export commodities 2007 to 2009

(Value in million US$)

HS code	4-digit heading of Harmonized System 2002	Value (million US$) 2007	Value (million US$) 2008	Value (million US$) 2009	Unit value 2007	Unit value 2008	Unit value 2009	Unit	SITC code
	All Commodities	6298.9	7583.8	6259.0					
2709	Petroleum oils, crude	4972.8	5879.9	5034.5	0.5	0.7	0.4	US$/kg	333
2710	Petroleum oils, other than crude	592.4	755.1	464.0	*0.5*	0.7	0.6	US$/kg	334
2707	Oils and other products of high temperature coal tar	132.7	93.9	34.7	0.7	0.7	0.6	US$/kg	335
0302	Fish, fresh or chilled, excluding fish fillets	72.8	72.3	82.2	1.5	1.0	1.9	US$/kg	034
0303	Fish, frozen, excluding fish fillets	47.7	62.1	47.1	1.4	1.3	1.2	US$/kg	034
8703	Motor cars and other motor vehicles principally designed for the transport	18.2	77.1	35.3	9.3	0.8	18.8	thsd US$/unit	781
0307	Molluscs, whether in shell or not	28.9	44.7	38.7	3.0	2.9	2.2	US$/kg	036
2402	Cigars, cheroots, cigarillos and cigarettes	25.6	18.3	24.4	5.0	5.0	5.0	US$/kg	122
2711	Petroleum gases and other gaseous hydrocarbons	0.1	...	66.2	0.5		0.2	US$/kg	343
8430	Other moving, grading, levelling, scraping, excavating, tamping, compacting	2.8	56.3	5.7	5.4	1.2	127.1	thsd US$/unit	723

Graph 2: Trade Balance by MDG Regions in 2009

(Bln US$)

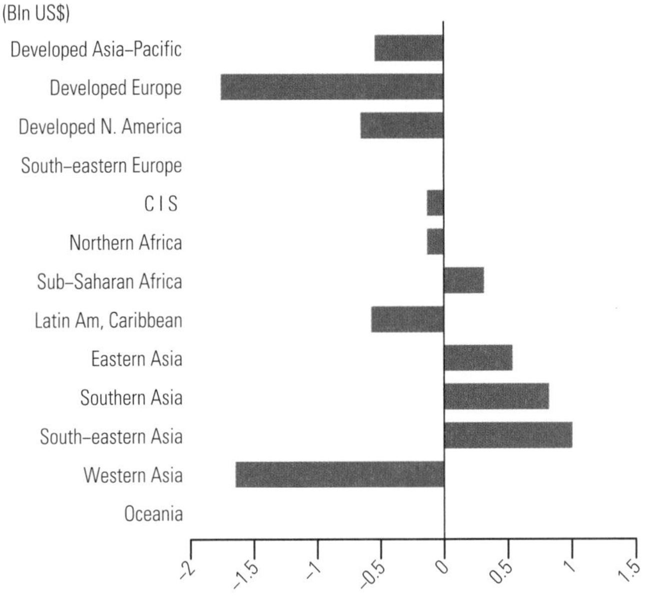

Graph 3: Partner concentration of trade in 2009

(Cumulative share by ranked partners)

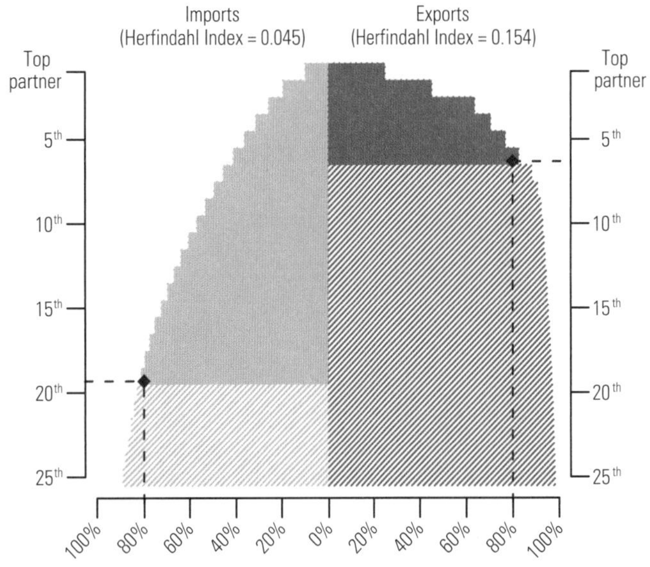

Table 4: Exports by principal countries and SITC sections in 2009

(Value in million US$, percentages of country total)

Country	Total	Shares by SITC sections (%) 0+1	2+4	3	5	6	7	8	9	Total
World	6259.0	5.8	0.4	89.5	0.6	0.9	2.3	0.3	0.2	100
China	1577.8	0.9	0.0	98.0	0.4	0.3	0.2	0.1	0.0	100
India	1259.8	0.2	0.1	99.2	0.0	0.4	0.0	0.0	...	100
Thailand	1148.9	1.0	0.0	98.8	...	0.0	0.2	0.0	...	100
Singapore	432.4	0.1	0.0	96.4	...	0.3	3.1	0.0	0.1	100
South Africa	393.7	0.1	0.0	99.9	0.0	0.0	0.0	0.0	...	100
United Arab Emirates	361.8	2.4	1.5	93.1	0.1	0.3	0.1	0.3	2.3	100
Japan	341.9	0.9	0.0	85.9	0.0	0.0	13.1	0.1	...	100
Saudi Arabia	162.6	90.6	2.7	0.1	0.5	4.2	0.1	1.7	0.0	100
Kuwait	96.7	0.9	0.1	98.3	0.4	0.0	0.1	0.1	...	100
Somalia	41.8	56.8	3.9	0.2	34.5	1.5	0.0	3.1	...	100

Imports Profile:

Yemen's imports of food, live animals, beverages and tobacco (SITC sections 0+1) decreased slightly by 0.4 and accounted for 26.5 percent of imported goods. Other major commodity groups included machinery and transport equipment (SITC section 7) and mineral fuels, lubricants and related materials (SITC section 3): they accounted respectively for 23.4 and 20.9 percent of imports. From 2007 to 2009, top products for imports were petroleum oils, other than crude (HS code 2710), wheat and meslin (HS code 1001) and motor cars and other motor vehicles principally designed for the transport (HS code 8703) (see table 5).

Table 5: Top 10 import commodities 2007 to 2009

(Value in million US$)

HS code	4-digit heading of Harmonized System 2002	Value (million US$) 2007	2008	2009	Unit value 2007	2008	2009	Unit	SITC code
	All Commodities	8510.7	10546.2	9184.8					
2710	Petroleum oils, other than crude	1819.2	3023.2	1911.5	0.6	0.7	0.5	US$/kg	334
1001	Wheat and meslin	671.9	955.7	735.6	0.3	0.4	0.3	US$/kg	041
8703	Motor cars and other motor vehicles principally designed for the transport	370.6	524.0	593.2	10.1	12.1	12.9	thsd US$/unit	781
1006	Rice	155.4	250.3	303.8	0.4	0.8	0.7	US$/kg	042
7214	Other bars and rods of iron or non-alloy steel	197.9	195.4	296.4	0.4	0.5	0.4	US$/kg	676
1701	Cane or beet sugar and pure sucrose, in solid form	201.0	203.2	245.6	0.3	0.3	0.4	US$/kg	061
3004	Medicaments (excluding goods of heading 30.02, 30.05 or 30.06)	198.7	218.7	220.9	*10.7*	12.2	21.4	US$/kg	542
0402	Milk and cream, concentrated or containing added sugar	157.6	169.6	132.2	3.2	4.3	2.6	US$/kg	022
8704	Motor vehicles for the transport of goods	128.9	150.4	174.6	18.8	23.6	34.2	thsd US$/unit	782
0207	Meat and edible offal, of the poultry of heading 01.05	129.2	123.7	172.0	1.4	1.7	1.6	US$/kg	012

Zambia

Imports: CIF, by origin | **Exports: FOB, by last known destination** | **Trade System: General**

Overview:

After several years of continuous growth marked by a peak of 5.1 bln US$ in 2008, the value of the exports of Zambia dropped in 2009 (by 15.4 percent) but increased again in 2010 by 67.0 percent to amount to 7.2 bln US$, well above its 2008 level (see table 1 and graph 1). Imports showed a similar development with an increase by 40.3 percent to 5.3 bln US$ in 2010 (see table 2 and graph 1). This resulted in a trade surplus of 1.9 bln US$ in 2010, much higher than the 2009 surplus of 0.5 bln US$ (see graph 1). By MDG region, trade recorded deficits with Sub-Saharan Africa (-2.0 bln US$), Western Asia (-0.4 bln US$) and Southern Asia (-0.1 bln US$) while Developed Europe and Eastern Asia recorded surpluses, respectively 3.5 bln and 1.1 bln US$ (see graph 2). Zambia's trade was relatively concentrated among a few partners: respectively 3 and 7 major partners accounted for 80 percent of exports and imports (see graph 3).

Graph 1: Total imports, exports and trade balance

(Bln US$ by year)

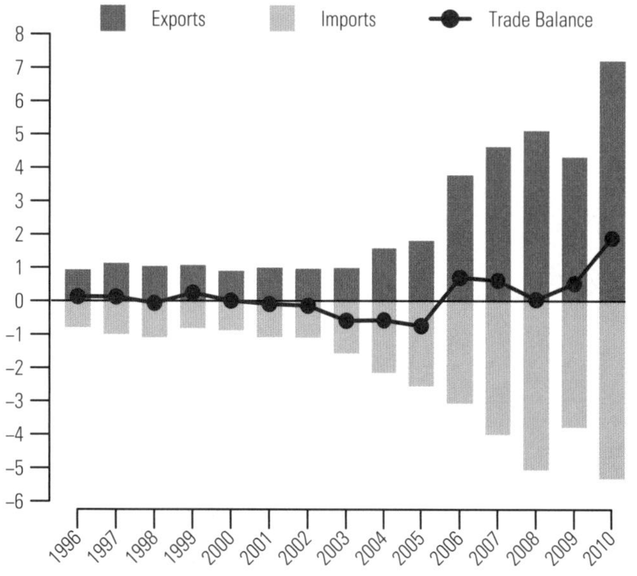

Table 1: Exports by SITC sections

(Value in million US$, growth and shares in percentage)

SITC	2010	Avg. Growth rates (%) 2006-2010	2009-2010	2010 share
Total	7200.3	17.6	67.0	100.0
0+1	407.9	16.9	29.5	5.7
2+4	623.6	3.2	6.4	8.7
3	36.5	12.5	-4.5	0.5
5	138.2	54.9	58.2	1.9
6	5761.3	19.4	87.5	80.0
7	136.9	6.7	-1.4	1.9
8	24.5	23.5	-17.5	0.3
9	71.4	292.5	57.5	1.0

Table 2: Imports by SITC sections

(Value in million US$, growth and shares in percentage)

SITC	2010	Avg. Growth rates (%) 2006-2010	2009-2010	2010 share
Total	5320.8	14.7	40.3	100.0
0+1	166.2	-2.4	-0.1	3.1
2+4	981.8	64.5	107.0	18.5
3	616.9	7.3	16.7	11.6
5	927.0	19.9	30.8	17.4
6	869.6	19.0	40.9	16.3
7	1528.6	5.5	40.8	28.7
8	208.2	4.6	6.2	3.9
9	22.5	298.4	45.1	0.4

Exports Profile:

In 2010, exports of manufactured goods classified chiefly by material (SITC section 6), the largest commodity group for exports, increased by 87.5 percent and represented 80.0 percent of exported goods (see table 1). Exports of inedible crude materials (except fuels), animal and vegetable oils, fats and waxes (SITC sections 2+4), the other major commodity group for exports, also increased by 6.4 percent and represented 8.7 percent of exports in 2010. Switzerland, the top partner for exports, accounted for a large share (51.0 percent) of total exports in 2010 (see table 4). Other major partners for exports included China and South Africa. Over the last three years, copper products were the top commodities for exports (see table 3). These are refined copper and copper alloys, unwrought (HS code 7403), copper plates, sheets and strip, of a thickness exceeding 0.15 mm (HS code 7409) and copper ores and concentrates (HS code 2603). They accounted respectively for 63.5, 9.5 and 3.3 percent of exports in 2010.

Table 3: Top 10 export commodities 2008 to 2010

(Value in million US$)

HS code	4-digit heading of Harmonized System 2007	Value (million US$) 2008	2009	2010	Unit value 2008	2009	2010	Unit	SITC code
	All Commodities	5098.7	4312.1	7200.3					
7403	Refined copper and copper alloys, unwrought	2113.7	2249.9	4575.4	6.9	4.6	6.7	US$/kg	682
7409	Copper plates, sheets and strip, of a thickness exceeding 0.15 mm	996.6	534.6	681.8	7.4	5.5	5.7	US$/kg	682
2603	Copper ores and concentrates	688.6	287.9	238.6	2.0	0.7	1.8	US$/kg	283
8105	Cobalt mattes and other intermediate products of cobalt metallurgy	294.0	75.2	194.4	74.6	10.5	26.1	US$/kg	689
7408	Copper wire	149.4	102.5	151.0	8.6	5.4	7.9	US$/kg	682
1701	Cane or beet sugar and chemically pure sucrose, in solid form	57.9	96.1	141.6	0.6	0.6	0.5	US$/kg	061
2401	Unmanufactured tobacco; tobacco refuse	71.7	84.7	117.7	2.9	3.2	3.4	US$/kg	121
2605	Cobalt ores and concentrates	24.8	101.6	116.1	4.0	2.1	3.3	US$/kg	287
2620	Ash and residues	27.2	59.4	91.2	35.2	30.6	14.1	US$/kg	288
5201	Cotton, not carded or combed	33.6	45.7	47.1	1.5	1.2	1.4	US$/kg	263

Graph 2: Trade Balance by MDG Regions in 2010

(Bln US$)

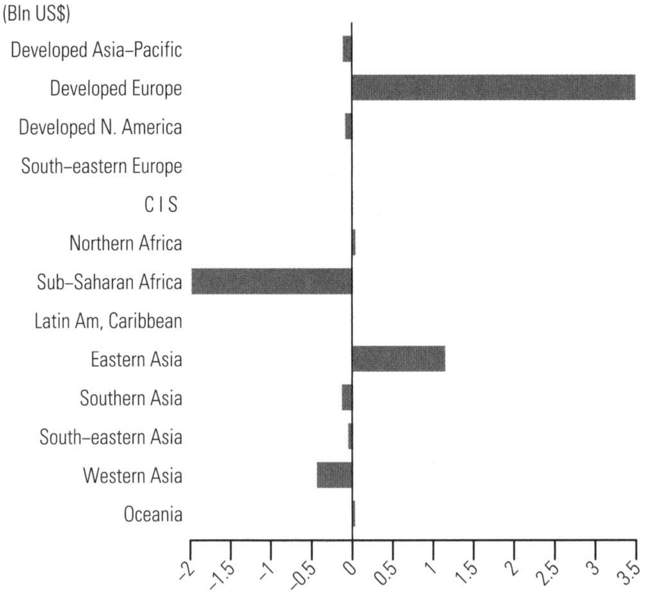

Graph 3: Partner concentration of trade in 2010

(Cumulative share by ranked partners)

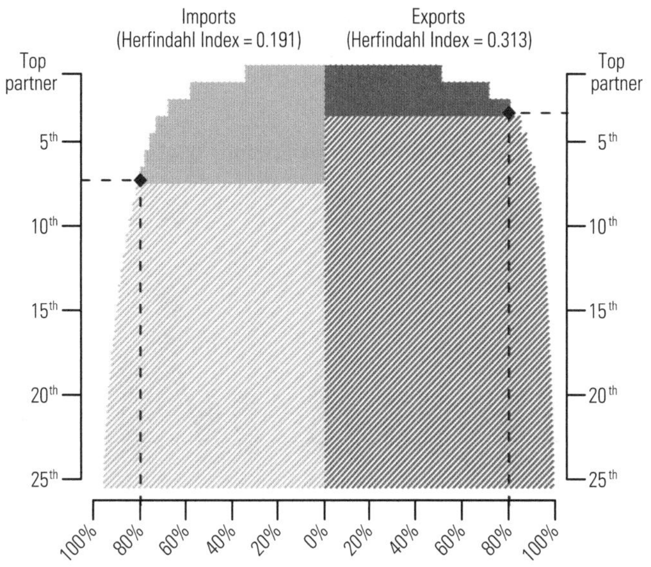

Table 4: Exports by principal countries and SITC sections in 2010

(Value in million US$, percentages of country total)

Country	Total	Shares by SITC sections (%)								
		0 + 1	2 + 4	3	5	6	7	8	9	Total
World	7200.3	5.7	8.7	0.5	1.9	80.0	1.9	0.3	1.0	100
Switzerland	3673.5	0.0	8.2	0.0	0.1	91.7	0.0	0.0	0.0	100
China	1455.4	1.0	3.6	0.0	0.1	95.1	0.2	0.0	...	100
South Africa	657.8	5.4	22.2	0.1	2.8	51.4	9.2	1.7	7.2	100
Dem.Rep. of the Congo	333.5	26.3	5.8	3.2	29.2	20.2	13.0	2.3	0.0	100
United Arab Emirates	176.2	0.1	0.1	...	0.0	99.7	0.0	0.0	0.0	100
United Kingdom	134.8	8.2	4.6	...	0.2	82.7	0.8	0.2	3.4	100
Zimbabwe	120.6	72.9	4.4	4.1	6.2	5.1	5.9	1.2	0.3	100
Malawi	102.7	66.6	1.8	0.3	5.3	20.7	4.3	0.8	0.2	100
Belgium	72.4	3.5	93.7	...	0.0	0.0	2.1	0.0	0.7	100
Egypt	49.2	0.0	0.0	...	...	100.0	...	...	0.0	100

Imports Profile:

In 2010, imports of machinery and transport equipment (SITC section 7) increased by 40.8 percent and accounted for 28.7 percent of imported goods (see table 2). Other major commodity groups for imports included inedible crude materials (except fuels), animal and vegetable oils, fats and waxes (SITC section 2+4) and chemicals and related products, n.e.s. (SITC section 5) respectively with 18.5 and 17.4 percent of imports. From 2008 to 2010, major imported products were petroleum oils and oils obtained from bituminous minerals, crude (HS code 2709), copper ores and concentrates (HS code 2603) and refined copper and copper alloys, unwrought (HS code 7403) (see table 5).

Table 5: Top 10 import commodities 2008 to 2010

(Value in million US$)

HS code	4-digit heading of Harmonized System 2007	Value (million US$)			Unit value				SITC code
		2008	2009	2010	2008	2009	2010	Unit	
	All Commodities	5060.5	3792.6	5320.8					
2709	Petroleum oils and oils obtained from bituminous minerals, crude	481.9	430.8	508.8	0.9	0.3	0.7	US$/kg	333
2603	Copper ores and concentrates	425.8	255.5	620.5	1.6	0.7	2.3	US$/kg	283
7403	Refined copper and copper alloys, unwrought	100.7	124.3	237.6	6.0	4.7	6.2	US$/kg	682
8704	Motor vehicles for the transport of goods	189.1	99.7	149.8					782
2710	Petroleum oils, other than crude	280.0	64.7	68.5	1.6	1.3	1.4	US$/kg	334
8429	Self-propelled bulldozers, angledozers, graders, levellers, scrapers	109.3	60.2	179.9	*63.4*		*70.0*	thsd US$/unit	723
3004	Medicaments (excluding goods of heading 30.02, 30.05 or 30.06)	137.4	97.0	72.5	42.4	33.7	21.4	US$/kg	542
2605	Cobalt ores and concentrates	0.9	83.3	219.7	1.3	2.0	3.1	US$/kg	287
8474	Machinery for sorting, screening, separating, washing, crushing, grinding	109.8	78.3	96.4					728
3102	Mineral or chemical fertilisers, nitrogenous	75.1	92.5	112.0	0.7	0.6	0.6	US$/kg	562

Zimbabwe

Imports: CIF, by origin | **Exports: FOB, by last known destination** | **Trade System: General**

Overview:

Despite reaching a peak of 6.4 bln US$ in 2006, Zimbabwe's exports from 2006 to 2010 dropped on average by 16.0 percent each year and amounted to 3.2 bln US$ in 2010 (see table 1 and graph 1). During the same period, imports went up on average by 36.9 percent each year and amounted to 9.0 bln US$ in 2010 (see table 2 and graph 1). This increase is due to the large rise in imports in 2010 by 156.7 percent. In 2010, trade balance recorded a deficit of 5.9 bln US$ (graph 1). By MDG regions, large deficits were recorded with Sub-Saharan Africa (-3.5 bln US$), Developed North America (-747.5 mln US$) and Western Asia (-486.7 mln US$) among others (see graph 2). Zimbabwe's trade was concentrated among a few partners: in 2010, 6 (respectively 8) major partners accounted for 80 percent of exports (respectively imports) (see graph 3).

Graph 1: Total imports, exports and trade balance

(Bln US$ by year)

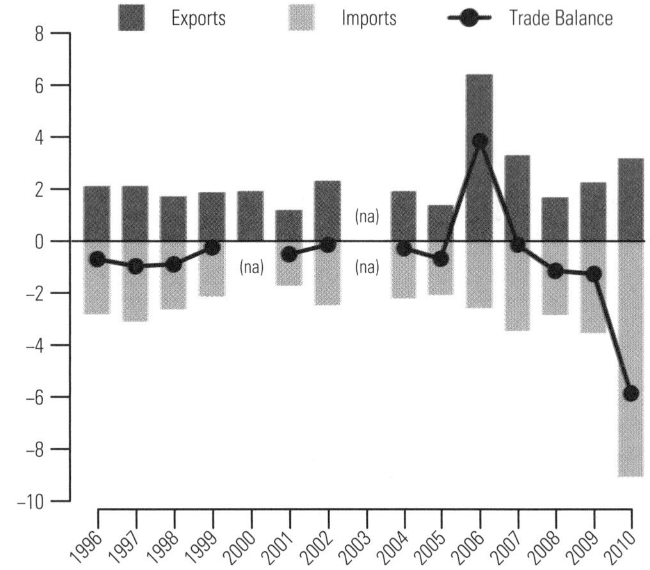

Exports Profile:

In 2010, Zimbabwe's exports were composed of 37.6 percent of inedible crude materials (except fuels), animal and vegetable oils, fats and waxes (SITC sections 2+4), 18.9 percent of miscellaneous manufactured articles (SITC section 8) and 18.1 percent of food, live animals, beverages and tobacco (SITC sections 0+1) (see table 2). Major partners for exports included South Africa, United Arab Emirates and China (see table 4). From 2008 to 2010, top exported products were unused postage, revenue or similar stamps of current or new issue (HS code 4907), nickel mattes, nickel oxide sinters and other intermediate products (HS code 7501) and unmanufactured tobacco: tobacco refuse (HS code 2401) (see table 3).

Table 1: Exports by SITC sections

(Value in million US$, growth and shares in percentage)

SITC	2010	Avg. Growth rates (%) 2006-2010	Avg. Growth rates (%) 2009-2010	2010 share
Total	3 199.2	-16.0	41.0	100.0
0+1	577.9	-11.2	46.4	18.1
2+4	1 203.2	-1.4	24.8	37.6
3	46.7	-62.8	115.9	1.5
5	21.8	-48.0	-0.3	0.7
6	415.9	-10.9	122.4	13.0
7	41.5	-34.6	-51.4	1.3
8	605.0	7.4	23.0	18.9
9	287.2	17.3	181.4	9.0

Table 2: Imports by SITC sections

(Value in million US$, growth and shares in percentage)

SITC	2010	Avg. Growth rates (%) 2006-2010	Avg. Growth rates (%) 2009-2010	2010 share
Total	9 051.5	36.9	156.7	100.0
0+1	1 487.9	56.0	121.1	16.4
2+4	1 551.3	40.2	411.2	17.1
3	984.6	14.5	116.8	10.9
5	687.0	17.5	56.7	7.6
6	1 022.7	36.7	158.7	11.3
7	2 090.0	37.6	90.6	23.1
8	821.3	70.2	616.1	9.1
9	406.8	121.3	694.2	4.5

Table 3: Top 10 export commodities 2008 to 2010

(Value in million US$)

HS code	4-digit heading of Harmonized System 2007	Value (million US$) 2008	2009	2010	Unit value 2008	2009	2010	Unit	SITC code
	All Commodities	1 693.9	2 268.9	3 199.2					
4907	Unused postage, revenue or similar stamps of current or new issue	64.4	435.3	559.1	9.3	17.2	10.3	thsd US$/kg	892
7501	Nickel mattes, nickel oxide sinters and other intermediate products	149.1	251.8	440.7	39.2	34.9	60.8	US$/kg	284
2401	Unmanufactured tobacco; tobacco refuse	99.9	241.8	420.0	*1.6*	4.5	4.7	US$/kg	121
2604	Nickel ores and concentrates	132.7	170.5	269.8	2.2	2.2	3.4	US$/kg	284
0603	Cut flowers and flower buds of a kind suitable for bouquets	185.8	334.1	9.3	*22.4*	87.5	1.9	US$/kg	292
7108	Gold (including gold plated with platinum)	8.1	102.1	287.2	3.6	23.4	1.9	thsd US$/kg	971
7102	Diamonds, whether or not worked, but not mounted or set	14.2	26.0	323.1	75.1	20.9	53.8	US$/carat	667
5201	Cotton, not carded or combed	88.0	102.4	146.1	1.2	1.1	1.7	US$/kg	263
7202	Ferro-alloys	47.5	30.9	194.5	2.6	3.5	1.3	US$/kg	671
1701	Cane or beet sugar and chemically pure sucrose, in solid form	39.3	73.5	48.5	0.5	0.5	0.4	US$/kg	061

Graph 2: Trade Balance by MDG Regions in 2010

(Bln US$)

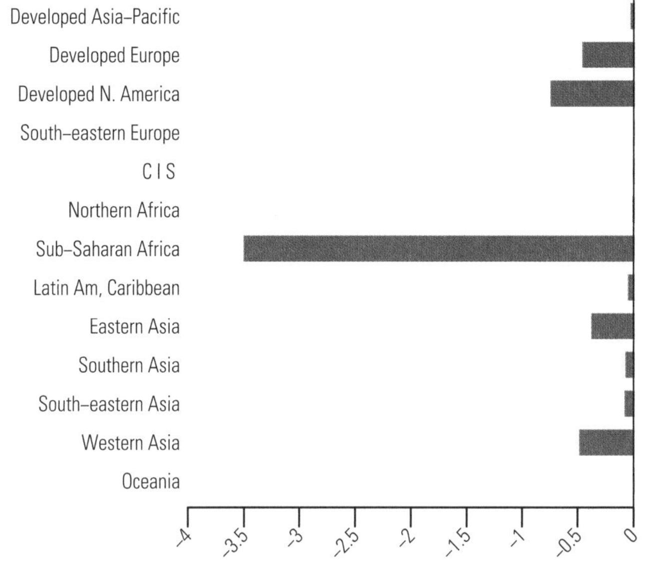

Graph 3: Partner concentration of trade in 2010

(Cumulative share by ranked partners)

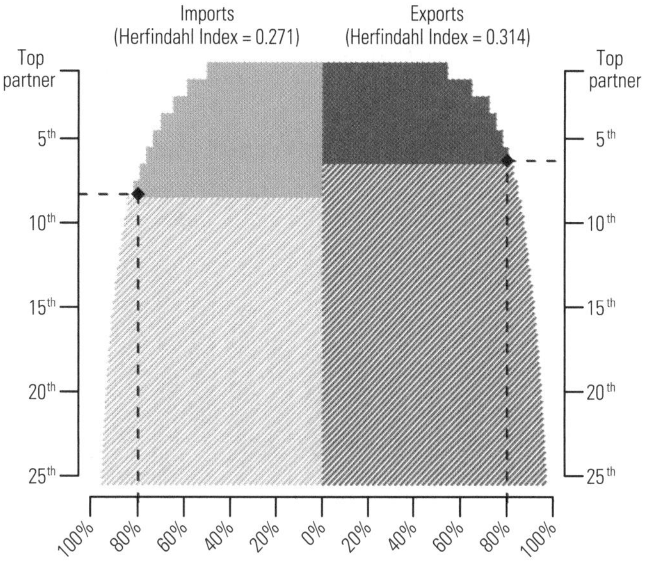

Table 4: Exports by principal countries and SITC sections in 2010

(Value in million US$, percentages of country total)

Country	Total	Shares by SITC sections (%) 0+1	2+4	3	5	6	7	8	9	Total
World	3199.2	18.1	37.6	1.5	0.7	13.0	1.3	18.9	9.0	100
South Africa	1734.5	3.6	43.7	0.3	0.4	1.9	0.5	33.1	16.6	100
United Arab Emirates	329.2	6.6	67.8	...	...	25.3	0.3	0.0	...	100
China	237.3	74.8	13.2	0.0	0.3	11.5	0.1	0.1	...	100
United Kingdom	96.4	72.6	24.9	...	0.0	0.6	0.2	1.7	...	100
Mozambique	91.9	67.0	2.4	0.6	0.8	25.1	2.6	1.4	0.0	100
Italy	76.9	0.2	13.3	...	...	85.1	1.0	0.4	...	100
Zambia	74.2	18.0	4.8	20.2	3.7	21.9	18.4	12.9	...	100
Belgium	60.4	62.0	8.8	...	0.0	28.9	0.1	0.2	...	100
Germany	46.7	42.9	12.8	0.0	0.2	40.5	0.4	3.3	...	100
Malawi	34.6	9.7	15.5	0.5	13.1	42.0	11.7	7.3	...	100

Imports Profile:

In 2010, there was an increase in trade in all of the commodity groups for imports (see table 2). Imports of machinery and transport equipment (SITC section 7) increased by 90.6 percent and accounted for 23.1 percent of imports. Other major commodity groups included inedible crude materials (except fuels), animal and vegetable oils, fats and waxes (SITC sections 2+4) (17.1 percent) and food, live animals, beverages and tobacco (SITC sections 0+1) (16.4 percent): they increased respectively by 411.2 and 121.1 percent in 2010. From 2008 to 2010, top imported products were petroleum oils, other than crude (HS code 2710), motor vehicles for the transport of goods (HS code 8704) and nickel mattes, nickel oxide sinters and other intermediate products (HS code 7501) (see table 5)

Table 5: Top 10 import commodities 2008 to 2010

(Value in million US$)

HS code	4-digit heading of Harmonized System 2007	Value (million US$) 2008	2009	2010	Unit value 2008	2009	2010	Unit	SITC code
	All Commodities	2831.8	3526.8	9051.5					
2710	Petroleum oils, other than crude	266.1	334.8	858.7	0.9	0.3	0.9	US$/kg	334
8704	Motor vehicles for the transport of goods	200.4	269.5	456.6					782
7501	Nickel mattes, nickel oxide sinters and other intermediate products	107.9	138.6	590.9	9.9	11.6	21.0	US$/kg	284
8703	Motor cars and other motor vehicles principally designed for the transport	97.5	139.0	481.5		*7.6*	*15.1*	thsd US$/unit	781
2401	Unmanufactured tobacco; tobacco refuse	33.4	32.9	541.3	3.5	3.9	4.5	US$/kg	121
4907	Unused postage, revenue or similar stamps of current or new issue	1.8	0.1	559.3	0.1	0.1	9.5	thsd US$/kg	892
1005	Maize (corn)	169.9	104.9	57.2	0.3	0.1	0.3	US$/kg	044
8517	Electrical apparatus for line telephony or line telegraphy	23.7	97.6	210.5					764
7102	Diamonds, whether or not worked, but not mounted or set	0.5	0.0	325.4	2.8	1.4	53.9	US$/carat	667
7108	Gold (including gold plated with platinum)	0.0	0.1	287.2	2.7	1.0	1.9	thsd US$/kg	971

European Union (27 member states)

Imports: CIF, by origin | **Exports: FOB, by last known destination** | **Trade System: General**

Overview:

From 2007 to 2011, EU-27's exports increased on average by 3.2 percent each year to reach 1,934.2 bln US$ in 2011, surpassing its previous peak in 2008 and overcoming the sharp decline in 2009 (see table 1 and graph 1). During the same period, imports increased on average by 4.5 percent each year and reached 2,347.3 bln US$ in 2011 (see table 2 and graph 1). This resulted in a trade deficit of 413.1 bln US$, much higher than the deficit of 190.8 bln US$ in 2010 (see graph 1). In 2011, trade with Eastern Asia and Commonwealth of Independent States recorded deficits respectively of 232.3 and 167.7 bln US$ (see graph 2). The trade balance recorded surpluses with Developed North America (+78.8 bln US$) and Western Asia (+43.0 bln US$). By partners, both exports and imports were diversified: in 2011, 24 major partners accounted for 80 percent of exports (compared to 23 major partners for imports) (see graph 3).

Graph 1: Total imports, exports and trade balance

(Bln US$ by year)

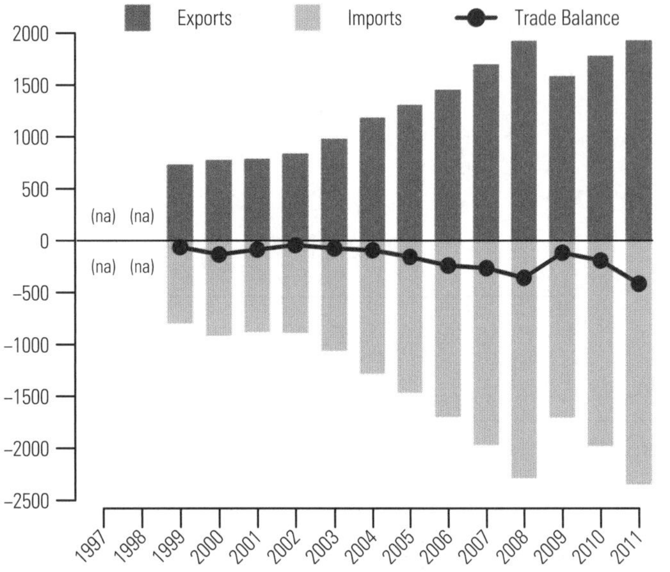

Exports Profile:

Machinery and transport equipment (SITC section 7) accounted for 42.1 percent of EU-27's exports (see table 1). Other major commodity groups for exports included chemicals and related products, n.e.s. (SITC section 5), manufactured goods classified chiefly by material (SITC section 6) and miscellaneous manufactured articles (SITC section 8): they accounted respectively for 15.9, 12.7 and 10.2 percent of exported goods. Main destinations for exports included USA, China and Switzerland (see table 4). Over the last three years, top exported products were motor cars and other motor vehicles principally designed for the transport (HS code 8703), medicaments (excluding goods of heading 30.02, 30.05 or 30.06) (HS code 3004) and petroleum oils, other than crude (HS code 2710) (see table 3).

Table 1: Exports by SITC sections

(Value in million US$, growth and shares in percentage)

SITC	2011	Avg. Growth rates (%) 2007-2011	Avg. Growth rates (%) 2010-2011	2011 share
Total	1 934 205.9	3.2	8.4	100.0
0+1	111 929.4	7.2	11.2	5.8
2+4	54 803.4	8.3	13.1	2.8
3	119 510.2	9.2	27.3	6.2
5	307 453.1	4.5	2.3	15.9
6	245 393.7	0.7	9.8	12.7
7	814 329.6	2.5	8.3	42.1
8	197 893.3	2.2	8.5	10.2
9	82 893.2	0.6	-1.0	4.3

Table 2: Imports by SITC sections

(Value in million US$, growth and shares in percentage)

SITC	2011	Avg. Growth rates (%) 2007-2011	Avg. Growth rates (%) 2010-2011	2011 share
Total	2 347 286.7	4.5	18.8	100.0
0+1	126 575.7	5.1	18.7	5.4
2+4	118 605.0	5.5	27.8	5.1
3	652 905.4	10.4	41.5	27.8
5	208 050.4	6.3	18.5	8.9
6	251 758.3	-0.1	23.0	10.7
7	612 127.8	1.6	4.3	26.1
8	297 932.3	3.1	11.3	12.7
9	79 331.8	1.4	-1.4	3.4

Table 3: Top 10 export commodities 2009 to 2011

(Value in billion US$)

HS code	4-digit heading of Harmonized System 2007	Value (billion US$) 2009	2010	2011	Unit value 2009	2010	2011	Unit	SITC code
	All Commodities	1 588.6	1 784.9	1 934.2					
8703	Motor cars and other motor vehicles principally designed for the transport	66.7	101.2	118.5	*19.4*	*23.6*	22.1	thsd US$/unit	781
9999	Commodities not specified according to kind	119.9	71.2	65.8					931
3004	Medicaments (excluding goods of heading 30.02, 30.05 or 30.06)	82.2	87.4	86.8	*144.3*	*140.1*	*126.2*	US$/kg	542
2710	Petroleum oils, other than crude	61.0	78.5	103.0	*0.5*	*0.7*	*0.8*	US$/kg	334
8802	Other aircraft (for example, helicopters, aeroplanes); spacecraft	35.7	40.3	41.4	13.3	*13.0*	*5.7*	mln US$/unit	792
8708	Parts and accessories of the motor vehicles of headings 87.01 to 87.05	27.2	38.9	43.1	*11.5*	*10.7*	*10.2*	US$/kg	784
8411	Turbo-jets, turbo-propellers and other gas turbines	30.6	32.4	32.3					714
8517	Electrical apparatus for line telephony or line telegraphy	27.1	31.8	34.7					764
3002	Human blood; animal blood prepared for therapeutic uses	16.1	17.5	21.7	*434.6*	*498.9*	*560.6*	US$/kg	541
7102	Diamonds, whether or not worked, but not mounted or set	13.5	19.8	21.7	110.5	*126.4*	*170.7*	US$/carat	667

Graph 2: Trade Balance by MDG Regions in 2011

(Bln US$)

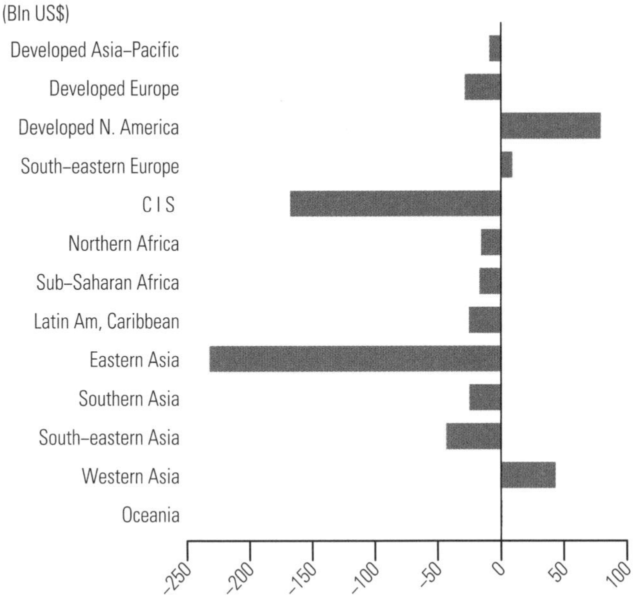

Graph 3: Partner concentration of trade in 2011

(Cumulative share by ranked partners)

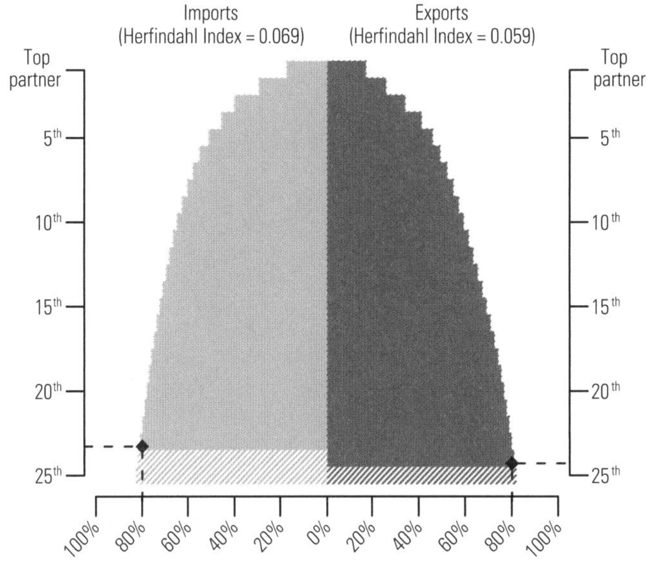

Table 4: Exports by principal countries and SITC sections in 2011

(Value in million US$, percentages of country total)

Country	Total	Shares by SITC sections (%) 0 + 1	2 + 4	3	5	6	7	8	9	Total
World	1934205.9	5.8	2.8	6.2	15.9	12.7	42.1	10.2	4.3	100
USA	329320.3	4.6	1.1	7.2	23.3	10.2	40.4	11.4	1.7	100
China	172032.6	2.5	7.2	1.0	10.3	9.5	60.0	7.0	2.4	100
Switzerland	155112.8	4.8	1.7	5.0	18.9	14.6	26.2	17.8	11.1	100
Russian Federation	136907.3	8.4	1.8	1.0	16.3	10.9	48.2	11.8	1.6	100
Turkey	91764.0	3.2	6.4	5.5	15.9	14.5	45.0	7.2	2.2	100
Japan	61827.9	8.8	3.5	0.5	25.7	8.5	33.7	16.4	2.8	100
Norway	58784.1	6.7	3.4	5.8	9.3	15.6	43.2	14.1	1.7	100
India	51050.4	0.8	6.0	0.8	10.1	34.0	39.3	6.8	2.4	100
Brazil	45118.3	2.8	1.6	3.5	20.4	11.6	50.2	6.3	3.5	100
United Arab Emirates	41182.4	5.3	1.0	4.2	9.5	14.4	51.3	12.3	2.1	100

Imports Profile:

In 2011, mineral fuels, lubricants and related materials (SITC section 3) was the largest commodity group accounting for 27.8 percent of imported goods (see table 2). Other major commodities were machinery and transport equipment (SITC section 7) and miscellaneous manufactured articles (SITC section 8) respectively with 26.1 and 12.7 percent of total imports. Over the last three years, top imported products were petroleum products: petroleum oils and oils obtained from bituminous minerals, crude (HS code 2709), petroleum gases and other gaseous hydrocarbons (HS code 2711) and petroleum oils, other than crude (HS code 2710) (see table 5).

Table 5: Top 10 import commodities 2009 to 2011

(Value in billion US$)

HS code	4-digit heading of Harmonized System 2007	Value (billion US$) 2009	2010	2011	Unit value 2009	2010	2011	Unit	SITC code
	All Commodities	1704.7	1975.7	2347.3					
2709	Petroleum oils and oils obtained from bituminous minerals, crude	225.6	292.7	408.7	*0.4*	*0.6*	*0.8*	US$/kg	333
9999	Commodities not specified according to kind	113.9	69.8	65.7					931
2711	Petroleum gases and other gaseous hydrocarbons	64.4	69.2	105.4	*0.4*	*0.4*	*0.5*	US$/kg	343
2710	Petroleum oils, other than crude	53.9	70.1	101.8	*0.5*	*0.7*	*0.9*	US$/kg	334
8517	Electrical apparatus for line telephony or line telegraphy	43.1	51.5	57.9					764
8471	Automatic data processing machines and units thereof	43.3	52.1	53.5	*100.8*	*115.1*	*118.6*	US$/unit	752
3004	Medicaments (excluding goods of heading 30.02, 30.05 or 30.06)	34.3	33.6	37.0	*220.3*	*211.9*	*194.7*	US$/kg	542
8703	Motor cars and other motor vehicles principally designed for the transport	30.6	29.1	33.7	*13.3*	*13.1*	14.5	thsd US$/unit	781
8541	Diodes, transistors and similar semiconductor devices	17.8	35.0	32.3					776
8411	Turbo-jets, turbo-propellers and other gas turbines	24.5	24.7	27.7					714